CHILTON BOOK COMPANY

REPAIR MANUAL

FORD VANS 1961 to 1988

All U.S. and Canadian models of E-100 • E-150 • E-200 • E-250 • E-300 • E-350 Vans and Club Wagons, including Diesel Engines

President, Chilton Enterprises	David S. Loewith
Senior Vice President	Ronald A. Hoxter
Publisher and Editor-In-Chief	Kerry A. Freeman, S.A.E.
Executive Editors	Dean F. Morgantini, S.A.E., W. Calvin Settle, Jr., S.A.E.
Managing Editor	Nick D'Andrea
Special Products Managers	Eric O. Cole, Ken Grabowski, A.S.E., S.A.E.
Senior Editors	Debra Gaffney, Michael L. Grady
	Kevin M. G. Maher, Richard J. Rivele, S.A.E.
	Richard T. Smith, Jim Taylor
	Ron Webb
Project Managers	Martin J. Gunther, Richard Schwartz
Production Manager	Andrea Steiger
Product Systems Manager	Robert Maxey
Director of Manufacturing	Mike D'Imperio

CHILTON BOOK COMPANY

ONE OF THE DIVERSIFIED PUBLISHING COMPANIES, A PART OF CAPITAL CITIES/ABC, INC.

Manufactured in the United States of America
Thirteenth Printing, July 1995

CONTENTS

SAFETY NOTICE

Proper service and repair procedures are vital to the safe, reliable operation of all motor vehicles, as well as the personal safety of those performing repairs. This book outlines procedures for servicing and repairing vehicles using safe, effective methods. The procedures contain many NOTES, CAUTIONS and WARNINGS which should be followed along with standard safety procedures to eliminate the possibility of personal injury or improper service which could damage the vehicle or compromise its safety.

It is important to note that repair procedures and techniques, tools and parts for servicing motor vehicles, as well as the skill and experience of the individual performing the work vary widely. It is not possible to anticipate all of the conceivable ways or conditions under which vehicles may be serviced, or to provide cautions as to all of the possible hazards that may result. Standard and accepted safety precautions and equipment should be used during cutting, grinding, chiseling, prying, or any other process that can cause material removal or projectiles.

Some procedures require the use of tools specially designed for a specific purpose. Before substituting another tool or procedure, you must be completely satisfied that neither your personal safety, nor the performance of the vehicle will be endangered.

Although the information in this guide is based on industry sources and is as complete as possible at the time of publication, the possibility exists that the manufacturer made later changes which could not be included here. While striving for total accuracy, Chilton Book Company cannot assume responsibility for any errors, changes, or omissions that may occur in the compilation of this data.

PART NUMBERS

Part numbers listed in this reference are not recommendations by Chilton for any product by brand name. They are references that can be used with interchange manuals and aftermarket supplier catalogs to locate each brand supplier's discrete part number.

SPECIAL TOOLS

Special tools are recommended by the vehicle manufacturer to perform their specific job. Use has been kept to a minimum, but where absolutely necessary, they are referred to in the text by the part number of the tool manufacturer. These tools can be purchased, under the appropriate part number, from Owatonna Tool Company, Owatonna, MN 55060 or an equivalent tool can be purchased locally from a tool supplier or parts outlet. Before substituting any tool for the one recommended, read the SAFETY NOTICE at the top of this page.

ACKNOWLEDGMENTS

Chilton Book Company expresses its appreciation to the Ford Motor Company, Dearborn, Michigan for their generous assistance.

Manufactured in the United States of America
        90   765

Chilton's Repair Manual: Ford Vans 1961–88
ISBN 0-8019-7841-6 pbk.
Library of Congress Catalog Card No. 87-47934

General Information and Maintenance

HOW TO USE THIS BOOK

Chilton's Repair Manual for 1961-88 Ford Vans is intended to help you learn more about the inner workings of your vehicle and save you money on its upkeep and operation.

The first two chapters will be the most used, since they contain maintenance and tune-up information and procedures. Studies have shown that a properly tuned and maintained truck can get at least 10% better gas mileage than an out-of-tune truck. The other chapters deal with the more complex systems of your truck. Operating systems from engine through brakes are covered to the extent that the average do-it-yourselfer becomes mechanically involved. This book will not explain such things as rebuilding the differential for the simple reason that the expertise required and the investment in special tools make this task uneconomical. It will give you detailed instructions to help you change your own brake pads and shoes, replace spark plugs, and do many more jobs that will save you money, give you personal satisfaction, and help you avoid expensive problems.

A secondary purpose of this book is a reference for owners who want to understand their truck and/or their mechanics better. In this case, no tools at all are required.

Before removing any bolts, read through the entire procedure. This will give you the overall view of what tools and supplies will be required. There is nothing more frustrating than having to walk to the bus stop on Monday morning because you were short one bolt on Sunday afternoon. So read ahead and plan ahead. Each operation should be approached logically and all procedures thoroughly understood before attempting any work.

All chapters contain adjustments, maintenance, removal and installation procedures, and repair or overhaul procedures. When repair is not considered practical, we tell you how to remove the part and then how to install the new or rebuilt replacement. In this way, you at least save the labor costs. Backyard repair of such components as the alternator is just not practical.

Two basic mechanic's rules should be mentioned here. One, whenever the left side of the truck or engine is referred to, it is meant to specify the driver's side of the truck. Conversely, the right side of the truck means the passenger's side. Secondly, most screws and bolt are removed by turning counterclockwise, and tightened by turning clockwise.

Safety is always the most important rule. Constantly be aware of the dangers involved in working on an automobile and take the proper precautions. (See the section in this chapter Servicing Your Vehicle Safely and the SAFETY NOTICE on the acknowledgement page.)

Pay attention to the instructions provided. There are 3 common mistakes in mechanical work:

1. Incorrect order of assembly, disassembly or adjustment. When taking something apart or putting it together, doing things in the wrong order usually just costs you extra time; however, it CAN break something. Read the entire procedure before beginning disassembly. Do everything in the order in which the instructions say you should do it, even if you can't immediately see a reason for it. When you're taking apart something that is very intricate (for example, a carburetor), you might want to draw a picture of how it looks when assembled at one point in order to make sure you get everything back in its proper position. (We will supply exploded views whenever possible). When making adjustments, especially tune-up adjustments, do them in order; often, one adjustment affects

another, and you cannot expect even satisfactory results unless each adjustment is made only when it cannot be changed by any order.

2. Overtorquing (or undertorquing). While it is more common for over-torquing to cause damage, undertorquing can cause a fastener to vibrate loose causing serious damage. Especially when dealing with aluminum parts, pay attention to torque specifications and utilize a torque wrench in assembly. If a torque figure is not available, remember that if you are using the right tool to do the job, you will probably not have to strain yourself to get a fastener tight enough. The pitch of most threads is so slight that the tension you put on the wrench will be multiplied many, many times in actual force on what you are tightening. A good example of how critical torque is can be seen in the case of spark plug installation, especially where you are putting the plug into an aluminum cylinder head. Too little torque can fail to crush the gasket, causing leakage of combustion gases and consequent overheating of the plug and engine parts. Too much torque can damage the threads, or distort the plug which changes the spark gap.

There are many commercial products available for ensuring that fasteners won't come loose, even if they are not torqued just right (a very common brand is Loctite®). If you're worried about getting something together tight enough to hold, but loose enough to avoid mechanical damage during assembly, one of these products might offer substantial insurance. Read the label on the package and make sure the products is compatible with the materials, fluids, etc. involved before choosing one.

3. Crossthreading. This occurs when a part such as a bolt is screwed into a nut or casting at the wrong angle and forced. Cross threading is more likely to occur if access is difficult. It helps to clean and lubricate fasteners, and to start threading with the part to be installed going straight in. Then, start the bolt, spark plug, etc. with your fingers. If you encounter resistance, unscrew the part and start over again at a different angle until it can be inserted and turned several turns without much effort. Keep in mind that many parts, especially spark plugs, used tapered threads so that gentle turning will automatically bring the part you're treading to the proper angle if you don't force it or resist a change in angle. Don't put a wrench on the part until its's been turned a couple of turns by hand. If you suddenly encounter resistance, and the part has not seated fully, don't force it. Pull it back out and make sure it's clean and threading properly.

Always take your time and be patient; once you have some experience, working on your truck will become an enjoyable hobby.

TOOLS AND EQUIPMENT

Naturally, without the proper tools and equipment it is impossible to properly service you vehicle. It would be impossible to catalog each tool that you would need to perform each or any operation in this book. It would also be unwise for the amateur to rush out and buy an expensive set of tool on the theory that he may need on or more of them at sometime.

The best approach is to proceed slowly gathering together a good quality set of those tools that are used most frequently. Don't be misled by the low cost of bargain tools. It is far better to spend a little more for better quality. Forged wrenches, 10 or 12 point sockets and fine tooth ratchets are by far preferable to their less expensive counterparts. As any good mechanic can tell you, there are few worse experiences than trying to work on a truck with bad tools. Your monetary savings will be far outweighed by frustration and mangled knuckles.

Begin accumulating those tools that are used most frequently; those associated with routine maintenance and tune-up.

In addition to the normal assortment of screwdrivers and pliers you should have the following tools for routine maintenance jobs:

1. SAE (or Metric) or SAE/Metric wrenches-sockets and combination open end-box end wrenches in sizes from ⅛″ (3 mm) to ¾″ (19 mm) and a spark plug socket ($^{13}/_{16}$″ or ⅝″ depending on plug type).

If possible, buy various length socket drive extensions. One break in this department is that the metric sockets available in the U.S. will all fit the ratchet handles and extensions you may already have (¼″, ⅜″, and ½″ drive).

2. Jackstands for support.
3. Oil filter wrench.
4. Oil filler spout for pouring oil.
5. Grease gun for chassis lubrication.
6. Hydrometer for checking the battery.
7. A container for draining oil.
8. Many rags for wiping up the inevitable mess.

In addition to the above items there are several others that are not absolutely necessary, but handy to have around. these include oil dry, a transmission funnel and the usual supply of lubricants, antifreeze and fluids, although these can be purchased as needed. This is a basic list for routine maintenance, but only your personal needs and desire can accurately determine you list of tools.

The second list of tools is for tune-ups. While the tools involved here are slightly more sophisticated, they need not be outrageously expensive. There are several inexpensive tach/dwell meters on the market that are every bit as good for the average mechanic as a $100.00 professional model. Just be sure that it goes to a least 1,200-1,500 rpm on the tach scale and that it works on 4, 6, 8 cylinder engines. (A special tach is needed for diesel engines). A basic list of tune-up equipment could include:

1. Tach/dwell meter.
2. Spark plug wrench.
3. Timing light (a DC light that works from the truck's battery is best, although an AC light that plugs into 110V house current will suffice at some sacrifice in brightness).
4. Wire spark plug gauge/adjusting tools.
5. Set of feeler blades.

Here again, be guided by your own needs. A feeler blade will set the points as easily as a dwell meter will read well, but slightly less accurately. And since you will need a tachometer anyway. . . well, make your own decision.

In addition to these basic tools, there are several other tools and gauges you may find useful. These include:

1. A compression gauge. The screw-in type is slower to use, but eliminates the possibility of a faulty reading due to escaping pressure.
2. A manifold vacuum gauge.
3. A test light.
4. An induction meter. This is used for determining whether or not there is current in a wire. These are handy for use if a wire is broken somewhere in a wiring harness.

As a final not, you will probably find a torque wrench necessary for all but the most basic work. The beam type models are perfectly adequate, although the newer click type are more precise.

Special Tools

Normally, the use of special factory tools is avoided for repair procedures, since these are not readily available for the do-it-yourself mechanic. When it is possible to preform the job with more commonly available tools, it will be pointed out, but occasionally, a special tool was designed to perform a specific function and should be used. Before substituting another tool, you should be convinced that neither your safety nor the performance of the vehicle will be compromised.

Some special tools are available commercially from major tool manufacturers. Others can be purchased from your Ford Dealer or from the Owatonna Tool Company, Owatonna, Minnesota 55060.

SERVICING YOUR VEHICLE SAFELY

It is virtually impossible to anticipate all of the hazards involved with automotive maintenance and service but care and common sense will prevent most accidents.

The rules of safety for mechanics range from "don't smoke around gasoline" to "use the proper tool for the job." The trick to avoiding injuries is to develop safe work habits and take every possible precaution.

Do's

• Do keep a fire extinguisher and first aid kit within easy reach.

• Do wear safety glasses or goggles when cutting, drilling, grinding, or prying, even if you have 20/20 vision. If you wear glasses for the sake of vision, then they should be made of hardened glass that can serve also as safety glasses, or wear safety glasses over your regular glasses.

• Do shield your eyes whenever you work around the battery. Batteries contain sulphuric acid; in case of contact with the eyes or skin, flush the area with water or a mixture of water and baking soda and get medical attention immediately.

• Do use safety stands for any under-truck service. Jacks are for raising vehicles; safety stands are for making sure the vehicle stays raised until you want it to come down. Whenever the vehicle is raised, block the wheels remaining on the ground and set the parking brake.

• Do use adequate ventilation when working with any chemicals. Like carbon monoxide, the asbestos dust resulting from brake lining wear can be poisonous in sufficient quantities.

• Do disconnect the negative battery cable when working on the electrical system. The primary ignition system can contain up to 40,000 volts.

• Do follow manufacturer's directions whenever working with potentially hazardous materials. Both brake fluid and antifreeze are poisonous if taken internally.

• Do properly maintain your tools. Loose hammerheads, mushroomed punches and chisels, frayed or poorly grounded electrical cords, excessively worn screwdrivers, spread wrenches (open end), cracked sockets, slipping ratchets, or faulty droplight sockets can cause accidents.

• Do use the proper size and type of tool for the job being done.

• Do when possible, pull on a wrench handle rather than push on it, and adjust your stance to prevent a fall.

• Do be sure that adjustable wrenches are tightly adjusted on the nut or bolt and pulled so that the face is on the side of the fixed jaw.

• Do select a wrench or socket that fits the nut or bolt. The wrench or socket should sit straight, not cocked.

• Do strike squarely with a hammer. Avoid glancing blows.

• Do set the parking brake and block the drive wheels if the work requires that the engine be running.

Don't's

• Don't run an engine in a garage or anywhere else without proper ventilation — EVER! Carbon monoxide is poisonous; it takes a long time to leave the human body and you can build up a deadly supply of it in your system by simply breathing in a little every day. You may not realize you are slowly poisoning yourself. Always use proper vents, window, fans or open the garage door.

• Don't work around moving parts while wearing a necktie or other loose clothing. Short sleeves are much safer than long, loose sleeves and hard-toed shoes with neoprene soles protect your toes and give a better grip on slippery surfaces. Jewelry such as watches, fancy belt buckles, beads or body adornment of any kind is not safe working around a truck. Long hair should be hidden under a hat or cap.

• Don't use pockets for toolboxes. A fall or bump can drive a screwdriver deep into your body. Even a wiping cloth hanging from the back pocket can wrap around a spinning shaft or fan.

• Don't smoke when working around gasoline, cleaning solvent or other flammable material.

• Don't smoke when working around the battery. When the battery is being charged, it gives off explosive hydrogen gas.

• Don't use gasoline to wash your hands; there are excellent soaps available. Gasoline may contain lead, and lead can enter the body through a cut, accumulating in the body until you are very ill. Gasoline also removes all the natural oils from the skin so that bone dry hands will such up oil and grease.

• Don't service the air conditioning system unless you are equipped with the necessary tools and training. The refrigerant, R-12, is extremely cold and when exposed to the air, will instantly freeze any surface it comes in contact with, including your eyes. Although the refrigerant is normally non-toxic, R-12 becomes a deadly poisonous gas in the presence of an open flame. One good whiff of the vapors from burning refrigerant can be fatal.

• Don't ever use a bumper jack (the jack that comes with the vehicle) for anything other than changing tires! If you are serious about maintaining your truck yourself, invest in a hydraulic floor jack of at least 1½ ton capacity. It will pay for itself many times over through the years.

HISTORY

The Econoline series was introduced in 1961. Ford thus became the first American manufacturer to offer a van series as we now know it.

The Econoline series originally included a pick-up version, a closed van, a window van with or without seats and a Club Wagon series with two trim levels. The Club Wagons were originally given the Falcon designation.

Initial engine availiblity was limited to the 6-144 and 6-170; essentially the same engine.

One point of confusion to clarify here is: whether or not there was a 1968 Econoline. All Ford vans during the years 1961-67 had essentially identical styling. All were mid-engined, with the engine located between and slightly behind the front seats.

The first new-look Econoline was introduced in the 1969 model year. 1967 vans were sold in the interim. Some may have been sold as 1968 models, but they were in fact, 1967 models. **In this book we will not refer to a 1968 model.**

In 1975 the styling was once again changed, putting the engine far forward and making the van considerably larger, both inside and out. This design continues today.

SERIAL NUMBER IDENTIFICATION

Vehicle Identification Number (VIN)

Through 1979

The vehicle identification plate is located on the right side of the cowl top panel under the hood. There are three lines of information on the plate, which consists of arrangements of letters and numbers.

The first line from the top of the warranty number, contains codes that identifies the series of vehicle, the engine, and assembly plant, and the numerical sequence in which the vehicle was built.

The second line of numbers contains codes that identify the wheelbase (inches), color, model code, trim code, body type code, transmission code and the rear axle code.

The third line give the maximum gross vehicle weight (GVW) in lbs., the certified net horsepower @ rpm, and the D.S.O. number, which is the district to which the vehicle was delivered and if applicable, specially ordered, factory installed equipment.

1980

The VIN is located in the lower center of the Safety Certification Label. This number is also the same as the vehicle Serial Number and the

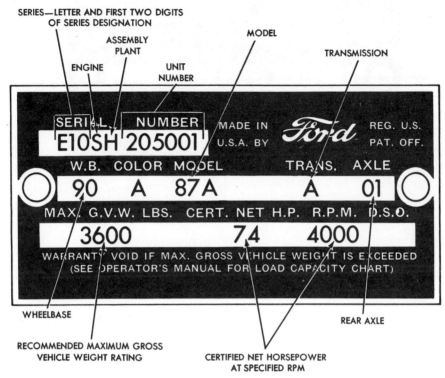

1961–62 Vehicle Identification Plate

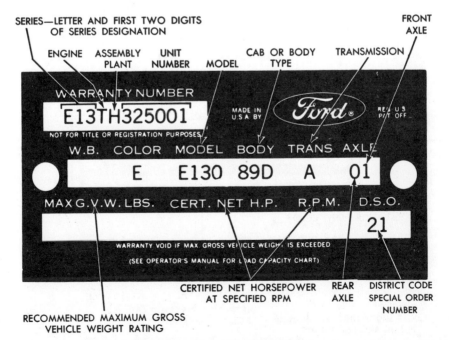

1963–65 Vehicle Identification Plate

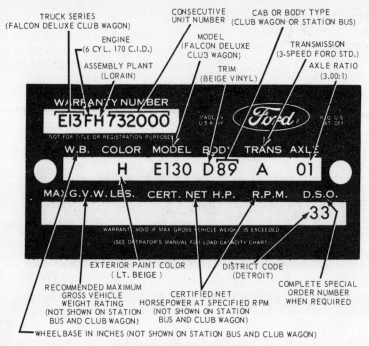

1966 Vehicle Identification Plate

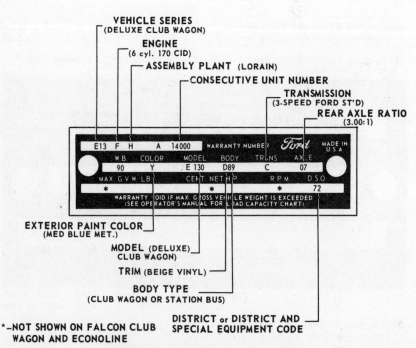

1967–68 Vehicle Identification Plate

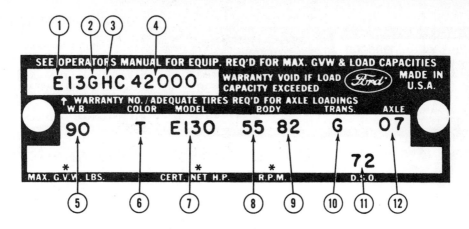

① VEHICLE SERIES CODE

② ENGINE CODE

③ ASSEMBLY PLANT CODE

④ CONSECUTIVE UNIT NUMBER

⑤ WHEELBASE (INCHES)

⑥ EXTERIOR PAINT COLOR CODE

⑦ MODEL CODE

⑧ TRIM CODE

⑨ BODY TYPE CODE

⑩ TRANSMISSION CODE

⑪ DISTRICT/SPEC. ORDER CODES

⑫ AXLE CODE

✳ NOT SHOWN FOR BRONCO OR CLUB WAGON

1969 Vehicle Identification Plate

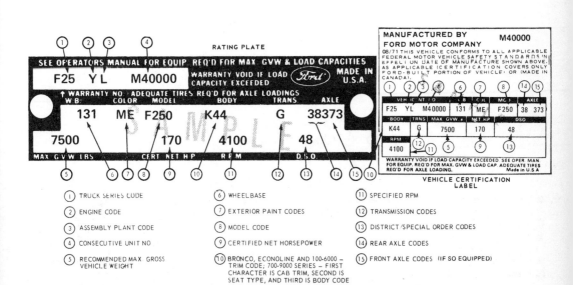

① TRUCK SERIES CODE

② ENGINE CODE

③ ASSEMBLY PLANT CODE

④ CONSECUTIVE UNIT NO

⑤ RECOMMENDED MAX. GROSS VEHICLE WEIGHT

⑥ WHEELBASE

⑦ EXTERIOR PAINT CODES

⑧ MODEL CODE

⑨ CERTIFIED NET HORSEPOWER

⑩ BRONCO, ECONOLINE AND 100-6000 – TRIM CODE; 700-9000 SERIES – FIRST CHARACTER IS CAB TRIM, SECOND IS SEAT TYPE, AND THIRD IS BODY CODE

⑪ SPECIFIED RPM

⑫ TRANSMISSION CODES

⑬ DISTRICT/SPECIAL ORDER CODES

⑭ REAR AXLE CODES

⑮ FRONT AXLE CODES (IF SO EQUIPPED)

1970–72 Vehicle Identification Plate

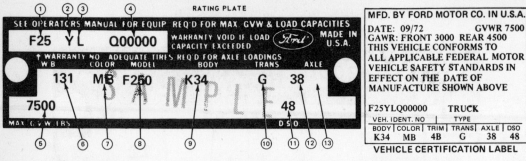

1973–77 Vehicle Identification Plate

1. TRUCK SERIES CODE
2. ENGINE CODE
3. ASSEMBLY PLANT CODE
4. CONSECUTIVE UNIT NO.
5. RECOMMENDED MAX. GROSS VEHICLE WEIGHT
6. WHEELBASE
7. EXTERIOR PAINT CODES
8. MODEL CODE
9. BRONCO, ECONOLINE AND 100-6000 – TRIM CODE; 700-9000 SERIES – FIRST CHARACTER IS CAB TRIM, SECOND IS SEAT TYPE, AND THIRD IS BODY CODE
10. TRANSMISSION CODES
11. DISTRICT/SPECIAL ORDER CODES
12. REAR AXLE CODES
13. FRONT AXLE CODES (IF SO EQUIPPED)

MFD. BY FORD MOTOR CO. IN U.S.A.
DATE: 09/72   GVWR 7500
GAWR: FRONT 3000 REAR 4500
THIS VEHICLE CONFORMS TO ALL APPLICABLE FEDERAL MOTOR VEHICLE SAFETY STANDARDS IN EFFECT ON THE DATE OF MANUFACTURE SHOWN ABOVE

F25YLQ00000	TRUCK				
VEH. IDENT. NO			TYPE		
BODY	COLOR	TRIM	TRANS	AXLE	DSO
K34	MB	4B	G	38	48

VEHICLE CERTIFICATION LABEL

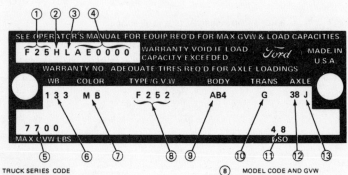

1978–80 Vehicle Identification Plate

1. TRUCK SERIES CODE
2. ENGINE CODE
3. ASSEMBLY PLANT CODE
4. SEQUENTIAL SERIAL AND WARRANTY NUMBER
5. RECOMMENDED MAXIMUM GROSS VEHICLE WEIGHT RATING IN POUNDS
6. WHEEL BASE IN INCHES
7. EXTERIOR PAINT CODES
8. MODEL CODE AND GVW
9. INTERIOR TRIM, SEAT AND BODY/CAB TYPE
10. TRANSMISSION CODE
11. DISTRICT/SPECIAL ORDER CODES
12. REAR AXLE CODES
13. FRONT AXLE CODES (IF SO EQUIPPED)

1 FTBF25G5DLA00001

1. Position 1, 2, and 3 — Manufacturer, Make and Type (World Manufacturer Identifier)
2. Position 4 — Brakes/GVWR Class
3. Position 5, 6, and 7 — Model or Line, Series, Chassis, Cab or Body Type
4. Position 8 — Engine Type
5. Position 9 — Check Digit
6. Position 10 — Model Year
7. Position 11 — Assembly Plant
8. Position 12 — Constant "A" until sequence number of 99,999 is reached, then changes to a constant "B" and so on
9. Position 13 through 17 — Sequence number — begins at 00001

1981–86 Vehicle Identification Number codes

COMPLETE VEHICLES

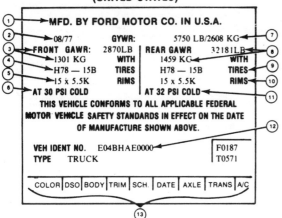

(UNITED STATES)

MFD. BY FORD MOTOR CO. IN U.S.A.

08/77	**GYWR:**	5750 LB/2608 KG
FRONT GAWR:	2870LB	REAR GAWR	32181LB
1301 KG	**WITH**	1459 KG	**WITH**
H78 — 15B	**TIRES**	H78 — 15B	**TIRES**
15 x 5.5K	**RIMS**	15 x 5.5K	**RIMS**
AT 30 PSI COLD		AT 32 PSI COLD

THIS VEHICLE CONFORMS TO ALL APPLICABLE FEDERAL
MOTOR VEHICLE SAFETY STANDARDS IN EFFECT ON THE DATE
OF MANUFACTURE SHOWN ABOVE.

VEH IDENT NO. E04BHAE0000   F0187
TYPE   TRUCK   T0571

| COLOR | DSO | BODY | TRIM | SCH. | DATE | AXLE | TRANS | A/C |

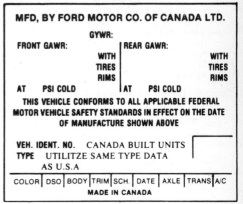

(CANADA)

MFD, BY FORD MOTOR CO. OF CANADA LTD.

GYWR:

FRONT GAWR:		REAR GAWR:	
	WITH		**WITH**
	TIRES		**TIRES**
	RIMS		**RIMS**
AT PSI COLD		AT PSI COLD

THIS VEHICLE CONFORMS TO ALL APPLICABLE FEDERAL
MOTOR VEHICLE SAFETY STANDARDS IN EFFECT ON THE DATE
OF MANUFACTURE SHOWN ABOVE

VEH. IDENT. NO.   CANADA BUILT UNITS
TYPE   UTILITZE SAME TYPE DATA
       AS U.S.A

| COLOR | DSO | BODY | TRIM | SCH. | DATE | AXLE | TRANS | A/C |

MADE IN CANADA

1 Name of Manufacturer
2 Date of Manufacture
3 Front Gross Axle Weight Ratings in Pounds (LB) and Kilograms (KG)
4 Front Tire Size
5 Rim Size
6 Front Tire Cold PSI
7 Gross Vehicle Weight Rating in Pounds (LB) and Kilograms (KG)
8 Rear Gross Axle Weight Rating in Pounds (LB) and Kilograms (KG)
9 Rear Tire Size
10 Rim Size
11 Rear Tire Cold PSI
12 Vehicle Identification Number
13 Vehicle Data

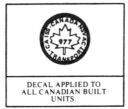

DECAL APPLIED TO
ALL CANADIAN BUILT
UNITS.

INCOMPLETE VEHICLES

THE INCOMPLETE VEHICLE LABEL IS ATTACHED TO A BOOKLET (INCOMPLETE VEHICLE MANUAL) AND SECURED TO A SUITABLE INTERIOR LOCATION FOR INFORMATION USE AT DESTINATION.

(UNITED STATES)

THIS INCOMPLETE VEHICLE MFD. BY
FORD MOTOR COMPANY
THE AMERICAN ROAD
DEARBORN, MICHIGAN 48121 ON: 08/77
VEH. IDENT. NO. E37HHAE0002
GVWR 1000 LB/4335 KG

FRONT GAWR	REAR GAWR	REAR REAR GAWR
4000 LB	6700 LB	LB
1814 KG	3039 KG	KG

	FRONT	REAR
	8.00 — 16.5E	8.00 — 16.5E
	16.5 x 6.0	16.5 x 6.0
	60	55

TIRES
RIMS
PSI COLD

MAY BE
COMPLETED AS: TRUCK BUS (NOT SCHOOL BUS)

(EXPORT)

THIS INCOMPLETE VEHICLE MFD. BY
FORD MOTOR COMPANY
THE AMERICAN ROAD
DEARBORN, MICHIGAN 48121 ON: 08/77
VEH. IDENT. NO.
GVWR

| FRONT GAWR | REAR GAWR | REAR REAR GAWR |
| | | |

| | FRONT | REAR |
| | | |

TIRES
RIMS
PSI COLD

MAY BE   THIS VEHICLE MFD FOR EXPORT
COMPLETED AS: ONLY ON DATE SHOWN ABOVE

NOTE — The same information is on all safety certification decal although the location of the information on the decal may be different.

1978–80 Vehicle Certification Plates

COMPLETE VEHICLES

(UNITED STATES)

```
           MFD. BY FORD MOTOR CO. IN U.S.A.
DATE:  8/79                  GVWR:  7650 LB/3470 KG
FRONT GAWR:  3050 LB         REAR GAWR:  5300 LB
     1383 KG         WITH       2404 KG        WITH
     F78-15B         TIRES      F78-15B        TIRES
     15x5.5 K        RIMS       15x5.5 K       RIMS
AT 32 PSI COLD               AT 32 PSI COLD

THIS VEHICLE CONFORMS TO ALL APPLICABLE FEDERAL MOTOR VEHICLE SAFETY
STANDARDS IN EFFECT ON THE DATE OF MANUFACTURE SHOWN ABOVE

VEHICLE IDENTIFICATION NO.   1FTBF25G BLA00000

TYPE     TRUCK

EXTERIOR PAINT COLORS                             DSO
   WB  | TYPE GVW | BODY | TRANS | AXLE
```

(CANADA)

```
        MFD. BY FORD MOTOR CO. OF CANADA LTD.
DATE:                        GVWR:
FRONT GAWR:                  REAR GAWR:
                     WITH                        WITH
                     TIRES                       TIRES
                     RIMS                        RIMS
AT     PSI COLD              AT     PSI COLD

THIS VEHICLE CONFORMS TO ALL APPLICABLE FEDERAL MOTOR VEHICLE SAFETY
STANDARDS IN EFFECT ON THE DATE OF MANUFACTURE SHOWN ABOVE

VEH. IDENT. NO.    CANADA BUILT UNITS
TYPE     UTILIZE SAME TYPE DATA
         AS U.S.A.

EXTERIOR PAINT COLORS                             DSO
   WB  | TYPE GVW | BODY | TRANS | AXLE
```

(QUEBEC)

```
         FABR. AUX E-U PAR LA FORD MOTOR CO.
DATE:                     PNBV:
PNBE AVANT:               PNBE ARRIERE:
                     AVEC
                    ◄PNEUS►
                    ◄JANTES►
A   LB/PO² A FROID        A   LB/PO² A FROID

CE VEHICULE EST CONFORME A TOUTES LES NORMES FEDERALES DE SECURITE
DES V.A. EN VIGUEUR A LA DATE DE FABR. INIQUEE CI-DESSUS.

N° D'IDENT.
   DU VEHICULE
TYPE
```

FOR VEHICLES MFD IN U.S.A. FOR QUEBEC, CANADA.

```
         FABR. PAR FORD DU CANADA LIMITEE
DATE:                     PNBV:
PNBE AVANT:               PNBE ARRIERE:
                     AVEC
                    ◄PNEUS►
                    ◄JANTES►
A   LB/PO² A FROID        A   LB/PO² A FROID

CE VEHICULE EST CONFORME A TOUTES LES NORMES FEDERALES DE SECURITE
DES V.A. EN VIGUEUR A LA DATE DE FABR. INIQUEE CI-DESSUS.

N° D'IDENT.
   DU VEHICULE
TYPE
COULEUR                          4° COMM SPEC.
 EMPATT | TYPE/PSV | CARR | TRANSM | PONT
                MADE IN CANADA
```

FOR VEHICLES MFD. IN CANADA FOR QUEBEC, CANADA.

INCOMPLETE VEHICLES

THE INCOMPLETE VEHICLE RATING DECAL IS INSTALLED ON THE DRIVER'S DOOR LOCK PILLAR IN PLACE OF THE SAFETY COMPLIANCE CERTIFICATION LABEL.

VEHICLE RATING DECAL

```
         INCOMPLETE VEHICLE MANUFACTURED BY

GVWR: 3050 LB/1383 KG
VEHICLE IDENTIFICATION NUMBER   1FTBF25G BLA00000

EXTERIOR PAINT COLORS   2H                 48  DSO
  WB     TYPE-GVW    BODY    TRANS    AXLE

  133     F27        AB4      G       38      1980
```

DECAL APPLIED TO
ALL CANADIAN BUILT
UNITS.

1981–86 Vehicle Certification Plates

Warranty Number. The first three places indicate the truck series code. The 4th place is the engine code. The fifth place is the assembly plant code. The remaining digits are the consecutive serial number.

1981-88

The VIN is a combination of 17 numbers and letters located on a metal plate riveted to the top left (driver's side) of the instrument panel, visible through the windshield. This number is also found on the Safety Compliance Certification Label. The 8th digit is the engine code; the 10th digit is the model year code.

Engine

The engine identification tag identifies the cubic inch displacement of the engine, the model year, the year and month in which the engine was built, where it was built and the change level number. The change level is usually the number one (1), unless there are parts on the engine that will not be completely interchangeable and will require minor modification.

The engine identification tag is located under the ignition coil attaching bolt on all engines except the 6.9L and 7.3L diesels. The diesel engine I.D. number is stamped on the front of the block in front of the left cylinder head.

Transmission

The transmission identification letter is located on a metal tag or plate attached to the case or it is stamped directly on the transmission case.

Drive Axle

The drive axle code is found stamped on a flat surface on the axle tube, next to the differential housing, or, on a tag secured by one of the differential housing cover bolts.

ROUTINE MAINTENANCE

NOTE: *All maintenance procedures included in this chapter refer to both gasoline and diesel engines except where noted.*

Engine Application Chart

No. of Cylinders and Cu. In. Displacement	Actual Displacement			Type	Built by	Engine Code	Years
	Cu. In.	CC	Liters				
6-144	144.3	2,364.9	2.4	OHV	Ford	S	1961–64
6-170	169.7	2,781.1	2.8	OHV	Ford	T	1961–65
						F	1966–70
6-200	199.8	3,274.4	3.3	OHV	Ford	S	1965
6-240	239.7	3,929.1	3.9	OHV	Ford	A	1965–74
6-300	300.1	4,917.5	4.9	OHV	Ford	B	1973–79
						E	1980–82
						Y	1983–88
						9	1981–82 LPG
						K	1979 HD
8-302	301.5	4,942.2	5.0	OHV	Ford	G	1969–74
						G	1979
						F	1980–85
						N	1985–88
8-351W	351.9	5,765.9	5.8	OHV	Ford	H	1975–79
						G	1980–84
						H	1985–88
8-400	402.1	6,589.6	6.6	OHV	Ford	Z	1980–82
8-420	420.2	6,886.1	6.9	OHV	N.I.	1	1983–87
8-444	443.6	7,270.0	7.3	OHV	N.I.	1	1988
8-460	459.8	7,535.5	7.5	OHV	Ford	A	1975–79
						L	1980–87
						G	1988

N.I.: Navistar International

Manual Transmission Application Chart

Transmission Types	Years	Models
Ford 3.03 3-speed	1961–86	All
Dagenham 4-speed	1964	E-100
Ford 4-speed OD	1978–83 1984–85 1986–87	E-100—350 E-150—350 E-150
Mazda M50D 5-sp Overdrive	1988	E-150 w/6-300
ZF S5-42 5-speed Overdrive	1988	E-150 w/6-300

Automatic Transmission Application Chart

Transmission	Years	Models
Ford C4 3-speed	1964–74 1975–81	All models E-100, 150 w/6-cyl.
Ford C6 3-speed	1975–87 1988	All models All except E-150/250 w/8-302
Ford AOD 4-speed	1983–87 1988	All models with 6-300 or 8-302 E-150 w/6-300 or 8-302 E-250 w/8-302

Drive Axle Application Chart

Axle Type	Models	Years
Ford 7.25 in. integral carrier	E-100, E-200	1961–67
Ford 8.75 in. removable carrier	E-100, E-200, E-300 E-100, E-200	1961–67 1969–74
Ford 8.8 in. integral carrier	E-150	1987–88
	E-250, E-350	1984–86
	E-100 through E-350	1983
Ford 9.0 in. removable carrier	E-150	1984–86
	E-100, E-150, E-200, E-300	1961–83
Ford 10.25 in. integral carrier	E-250	1985
Dana 60-3 integral carrier	E-250 LD E-300	1981–88 1969–74
Dana 61-1 integral carrier	E-250 HD E-350 SRW	1983–88
	E-350 SRW	1981–82
	E-250 E-350 SRW or DRW	1975–80
Dana 61-2 integral carrier	E-250	1979–84
Dana 70 integral carrier	E-250 HD E-350 SRW or DRW	1984–85
	E-350 DRW	1980–83
	E-250 E-350 SRW or DRW	1978–79
Dana 70-4	E-350 DRW	1975–79
Dana 70-1 integral carrier	E-350 DRW	1985–88
Dana 70-2U integral carrier	E-350 DRW	1985–88

Air Cleaner

Oil Bath Type

To service the oil bath type air cleaner:

1. Remove the air cleaner from the engine by unscrewing the wing nut on top of the air cleaner.

2. Remove the oil cup from the body of the air cleaner and remove all of the oil from the oil cup.

3. Remove all of the dirt from the inside of the coil cup with a safe solvent.

4. Wash the filter element in solvent, air dry it, and then fill the oil cup to the indicated level with clean oil.

5. Assemble the air cleaner element to the oil cup, making sure that the gasket is in place between the two pieces.

6. Mount the air cleaner assembly in the carburetor, making sure that the gasket between the air cleaner and the carburetor is in place and making a good seal.

7. Secure the air cleaner to the carburetor with the wing nut.

Paper Element Type

The paper cartridge should be replaced according to the Preventive Maintenance Schedule at the end of this chapter.

NOTE: *Check the air filter more often if the vehicle is operated under severe dusty conditions and replace or clean it as necessary.*

REPLACEMENT

Carbureted Engines

1. Open the engine compartment hood.

2. Remove the wing nut holding the air cleaner assembly to the top of the carburetor.

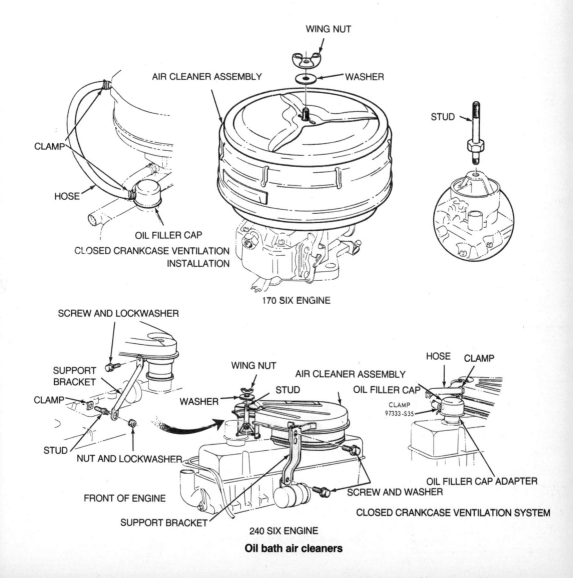

Oil bath air cleaners

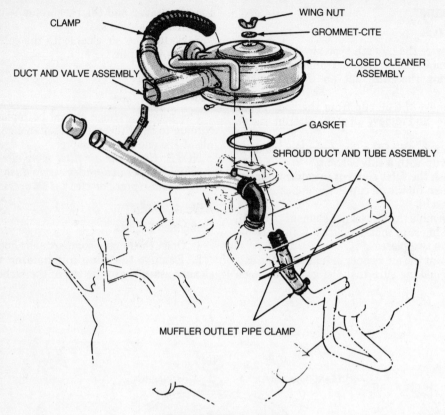

CLAMP

WING NUT

GROMMET-CITE

DUCT AND VALVE ASSEMBLY

CLOSED CLEANER
ASSEMBLY

GASKET

SHROUD DUCT AND TUBE ASSEMBLY

MUFFLER OUTLET PIPE CLAMP

1969–72 8-302 air cleaner

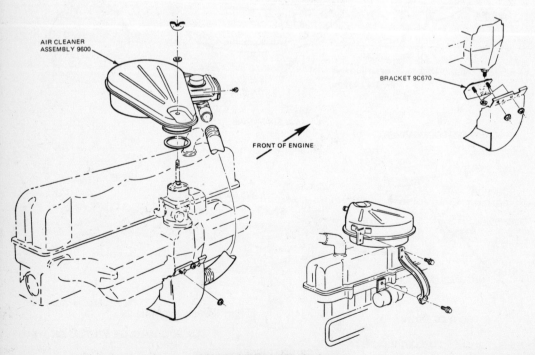

AIR CLEANER
ASSEMBLY 9600

BRACKET 9C670

FRONT OF ENGINE

1969–74 6-240, 6-300 air cleaner

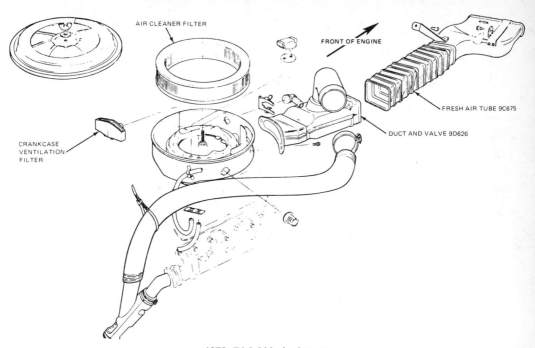

1973–74 8-302 air cleaner

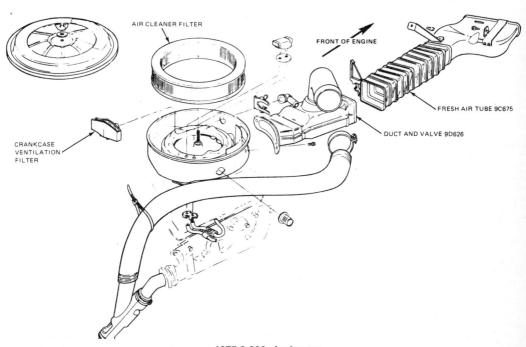

1975 8-302 air cleaner

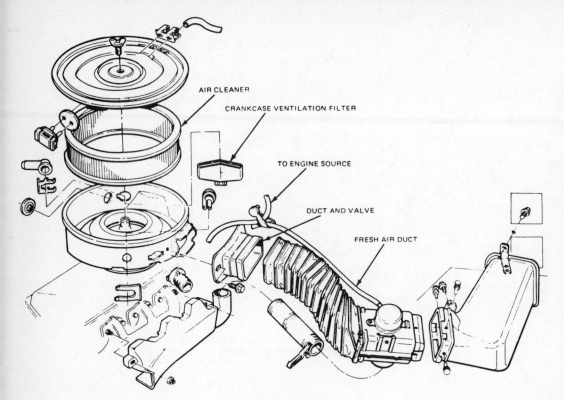

AIR CLEANER

CRANKCASE VENTILATION FILTER

TO ENGINE SOURCE

DUCT AND VALVE

FRESH AIR DUCT

1975 8-460 air cleaner

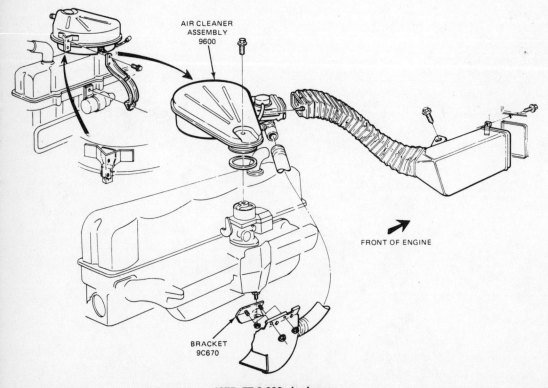

AIR CLEANER ASSEMBLY 9600

FRONT OF ENGINE

BRACKET 9C670

1975–77 6-300 air cleaner

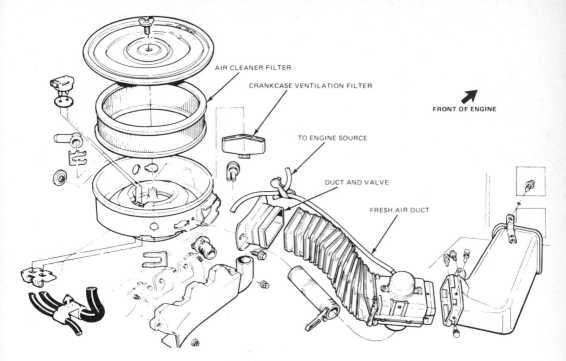

AIR CLEANER FILTER

CRANKCASE VENTILATION FILTER

TO ENGINE SOURCE

FRONT OF ENGINE

DUCT AND VALVE

FRESH AIR DUCT

1976–77 8-460 air cleaner

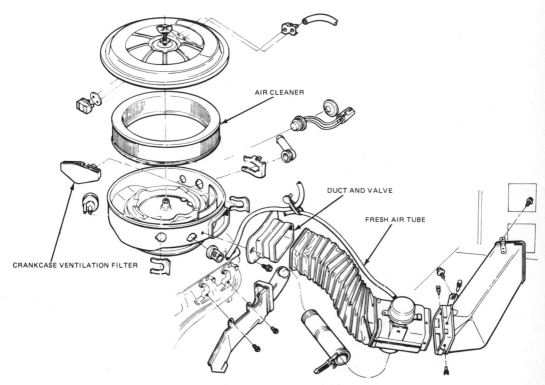

AIR CLEANER

DUCT AND VALVE

FRESH AIR TUBE

CRANKCASE VENTILATION FILTER

1975–77 8-351 air cleaner

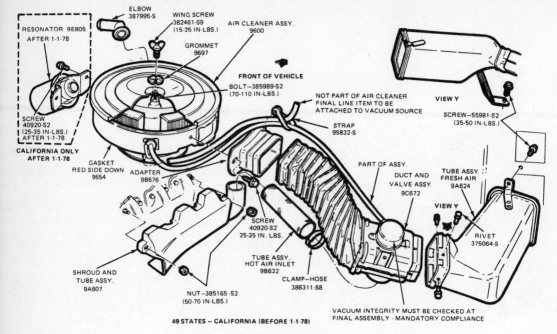

1978 8-460 air cleaner

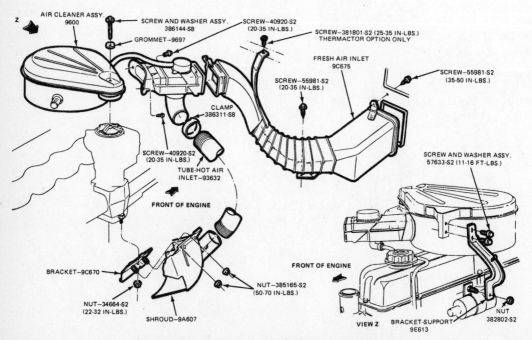

1978 6-300 air cleaner for Canada with heated fuel intake

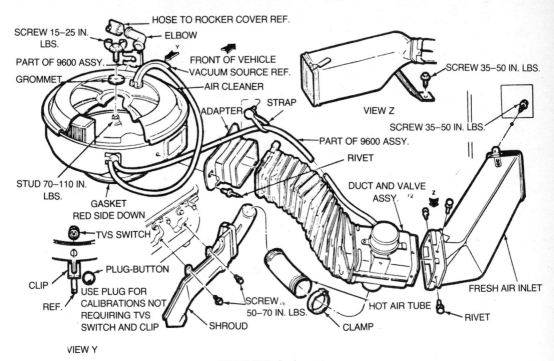

1978 8-351 air cleaner

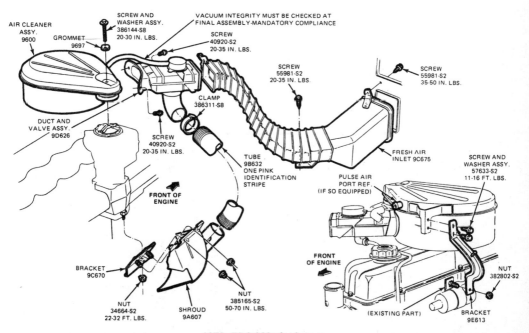

1978–79 6-300 air cleaner

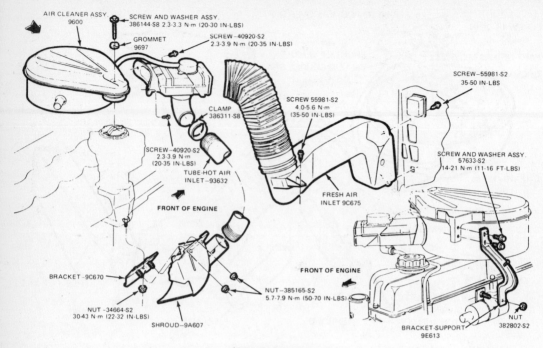

1980 6-300 air cleaner

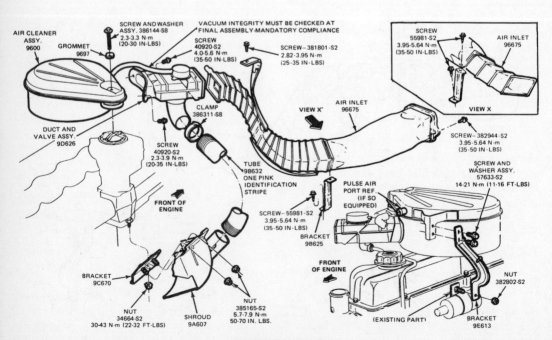

1981 6-300 air cleaner

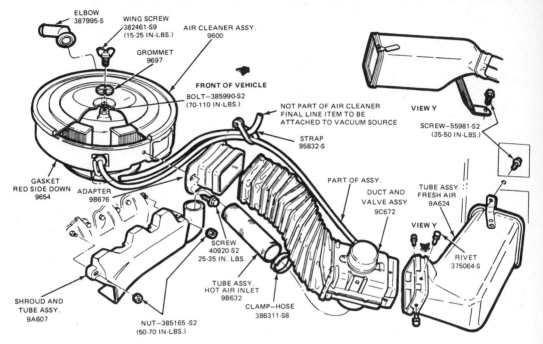

Air cleaner used on the 1979–81 8-302, 8-351, 8-460; 1980–81 8-400

3. Disconnect the crankcase ventilation hose at the air cleaner and remove the entire air cleaner assembly from the carburetor.

4. Remove and discard the old filter element, and inspect the condition of the air cleaner mounting gasket. Replace the gasket as necessary.

NOTE: *A crankcase ventilation filter is located in the side of the air cleaner body. The filter should be replaced rather than cleaned. Simply pull the old filter out of the body every 20,000 miles (or more frequently if the vehicle has been used in extremely dusty conditions) and push a new filter into place.*

5. Install the air cleaner body on the carburetor so that the word **FRONT** faces toward the front of the vehicle.

6. Place the new filter element in the air cleaner body and install the cover and tighten the wing nut. If the word **TOP** appears on the element, make sure that the side that the word appears on is facing up when the element is in place.

7. Connect the crankcase ventilation hose to the air cleaner.

Fuel Injected Engines

1. Loosen the two clamps that secure the hose assembly to the air cleaner.

2. Remove the two screws that attach the air cleaner to the bracket.

3. Disconnect the hose and inlet tube from the air cleaner.

4. Remove the screws attaching the air cleaner cover.

5. Remove the air filter and tubes.

6. Installation is the reverse of removal. Don't overtighten the hose clamps! A torque of 12-15 in.lb. is sufficient.

Diesel Engines

1. Open the engine compartment hood.

2. Remove the wing nut holding the air cleaner assembly.

3. Remove and discard the old filter element, and inspect the condition of the air cleaner mounting gasket. Replace the gasket as necessary.

4. Place the new filter element in the air cleaner body and install the cover and tighten the wing nut.

Carbureted Engine Fuel Filter
REPLACEMENT

CAUTION: *NEVER SMOKE WHEN WORKING AROUND OR NEAR GASOLINE! MAKE SURE THAT THERE IS NO IGNITION SOURCE NEAR YOU WORK AREA!*

Sediment Bowl Type

Early 6-144 engines used, as a fuel filter, a fuel pump-mounted glass bowl sediment trap.

To service this sediment bowl, simply unscrew the bail wire nut, swing the bail wire out

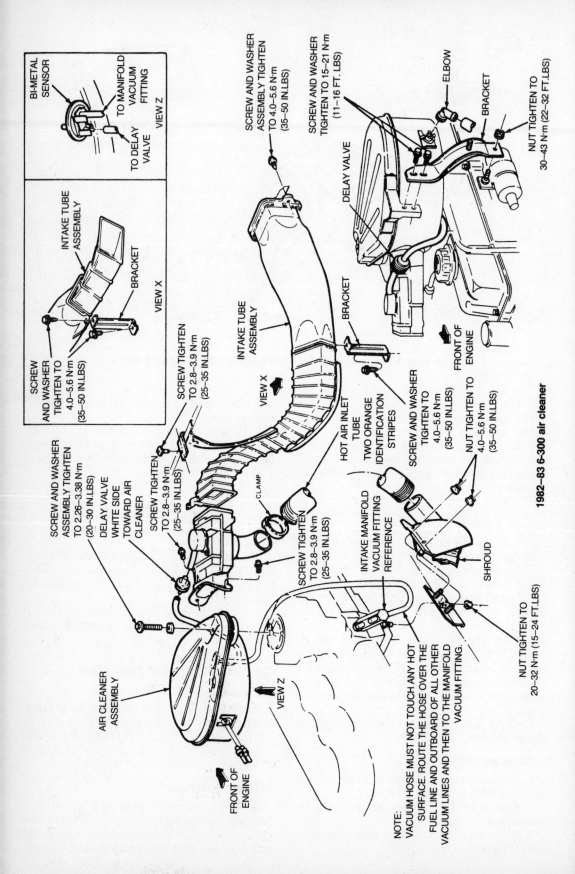

BI-METAL SENSOR

TO MANIFOLD VACUUM FITTING

TO DELAY VALVE

VIEW Z

INTAKE TUBE ASSEMBLY

BRACKET

VIEW X

SCREW AND WASHER ASSEMBLY TIGHTEN TO 4.0–5.6 N·m (35–50 IN.LBS)

SCREW AND WASHER ASSEMBLY TIGHTEN TO 4.0–5.6 N·m (35–50 IN.LBS)

SCREW AND WASHER TIGHTEN TO 15–21 N·m (11–16 FT. LBS)

ELBOW

BRACKET

NUT TIGHTEN TO 30–43 N·m (22–32 FT.LBS)

DELAY VALVE

SCREW AND WASHER ASSEMBLY TIGHTEN TO 2.26–3.38 N·m (20–30 IN.LBS)

DELAY VALVE WHITE SIDE TOWARD AIR CLEANER

SCREW TIGHTEN TO 2.8–3.9 N·m (25–35 IN.LBS)

SCREW TIGHTEN TO 2.8–3.9 N·m (25–35 IN.LBS)

INTAKE TUBE ASSEMBLY

VIEW X

BRACKET

CLAMP

SCREW TIGHTEN TO 2.8–3.9 N·m (25–35 IN.LBS)

HOT AIR INLET TUBE TWO ORANGE IDENTIFICATION STRIPES

SCREW AND WASHER TIGHTEN TO 4.0–5.6 N·m (35–50 IN.LBS)

NUT TIGHTEN TO 4.0–5.6 N·m (35–50 IN.LBS)

INTAKE MANIFOLD VACUUM FITTING REFERENCE

SHROUD

FRONT OF ENGINE

1982–83 6-300 air cleaner

AIR CLEANER ASSEMBLY

VIEW Z

FRONT OF ENGINE

NUT TIGHTEN TO 20–32 N·m (15–24 FT.LBS)

NOTE: VACUUM HOSE MUST NOT TOUCH ANY HOT SURFACE. ROUTE THE HOSE OVER THE FUEL LINE AND OUTBOARD OF ALL OTHER VACUUM LINES AND THEN TO THE MANIFOLD VACUUM FITTING.

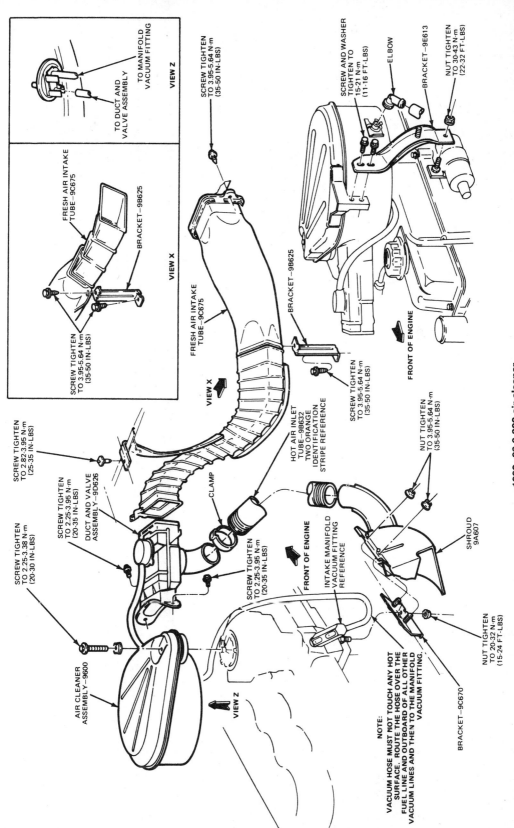

1982–83 6-300 air cleaner

TO MANIFOLD VACUUM FITTING

TO DUCT AND VALVE ASSEMBLY

VIEW Z

SCREW TIGHTEN TO 3.95-5.64 N·m (35-50 IN-LBS)

SCREW AND WASHER TIGHTEN TO 15-21 N·m (11-16 FT-LBS)

ELBOW

BRACKET—9E613

NUT TIGHTEN TO 30-43 N·m (22-32 FT-LBS)

FRESH AIR INTAKE TUBE—9C675

BRACKET—9B625

VIEW X

SCREW TIGHTEN TO 3.95-5.64 N·m (35-50 IN-LBS)

FRESH AIR INTAKE TUBE—9C675

BRACKET—9B625

FRONT OF ENGINE

VIEW X

SCREW TIGHTEN TO 3.95-5.64 N·m (35-50 IN-LBS)

HOT AIR INLET TUBE—9B632 TWO ORANGE IDENTIFICATION STRIPE REFERENCE

NUT TIGHTEN TO 3.95-5.64 N·m (35-50 IN-LBS)

SCREW TIGHTEN TO 2.82-3.95 N·m (25-35 IN-LBS)

SCREW TIGHTEN TO 2.25-3.95 N·m (20-35 IN-LBS)

DUCT AND VALVE ASSEMBLY—9D626

CLAMP

SCREW TIGHTEN TO 2.25-3.95 N·m (20-35 IN-LBS)

FRONT OF ENGINE

INTAKE MANIFOLD VACUUM FITTING REFERENCE

SHROUD 9A607

SCREW TIGHTEN TO 2.25-3.38 N·m (20-30 IN-LBS)

AIR CLEANER ASSEMBLY—9600

NUT TIGHTEN TO 20-32 N·m (15-24 FT-LBS)

BRACKET—9C670

VIEW Z

NOTE:
VACUUM HOSE MUST NOT TOUCH ANY HOT SURFACE. ROUTE THE HOSE OVER THE FUEL LINE AND OUTBOARD OF ALL OTHER VACUUM LINES AND THEN TO THE MANIFOLD VACUUM FITTING.

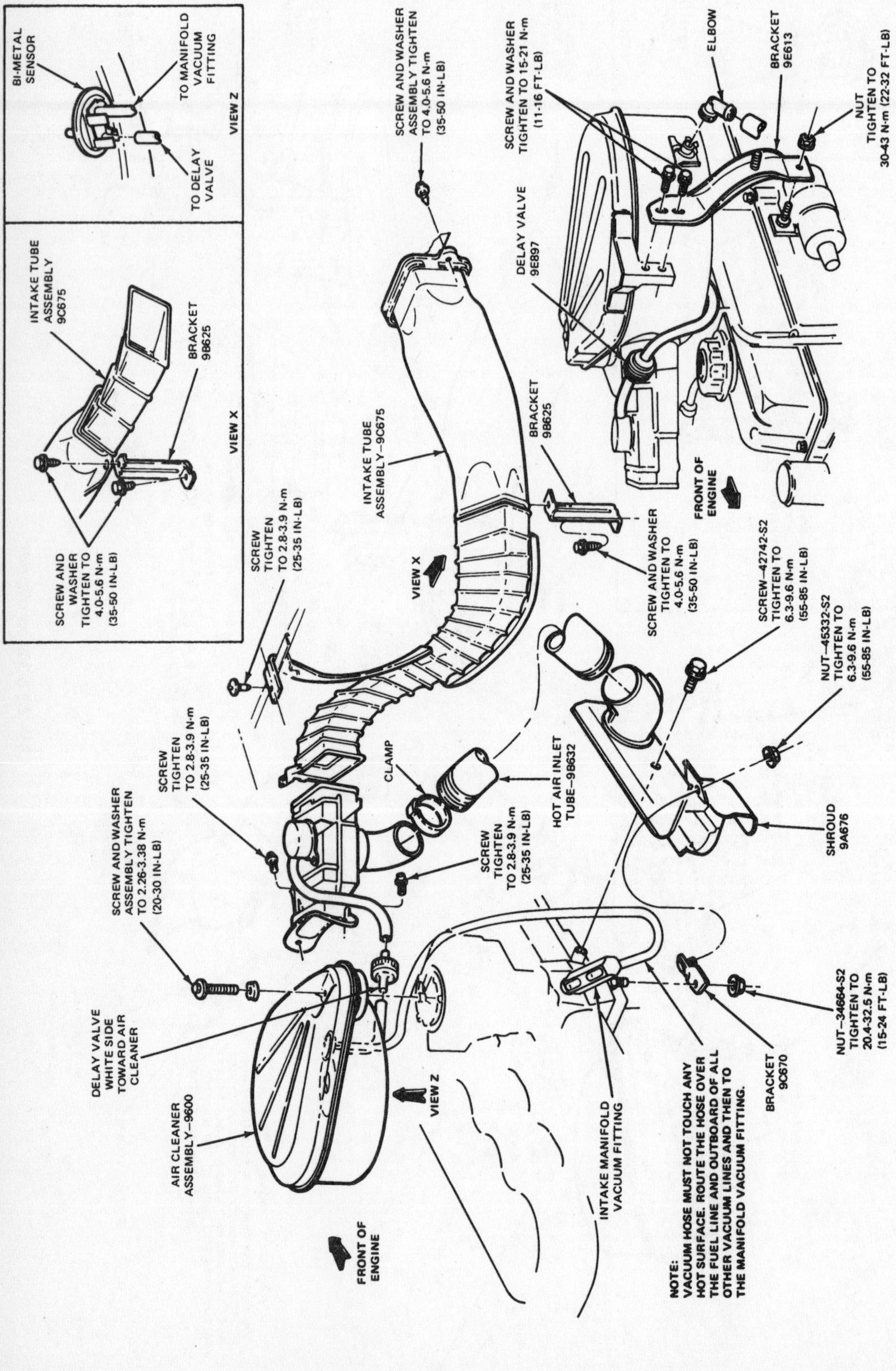

BI-METAL SENSOR

TO MANIFOLD VACUUM FITTING

TO DELAY VALVE

VIEW Z

INTAKE TUBE ASSEMBLY 9C675

BRACKET 9B625

VIEW X

SCREW AND WASHER TIGHTEN TO 4.0-5.6 N·m (35-50 IN·LB)

SCREW TIGHTEN TO 2.8-3.9 N·m (25-35 IN·LB)

SCREW AND WASHER ASSEMBLY TO 4.0-5.6 N·m (35-50 IN·LB)

SCREW AND WASHER TIGHTEN TO 15-21 N·m (11-16 FT·LB)

DELAY VALVE 9E897

ELBOW

BRACKET 9E613

NUT TIGHTEN TO 30-43 N·m (22-32 FT·LB)

INTAKE TUBE ASSEMBLY—9C675

BRACKET 9B625

SCREW AND WASHER TIGHTEN TO 4.0-5.6 N·m (35-50 IN·LB)

SCREW—42742-S2 TIGHTEN TO 6.3-9.6 N·m (55-85 IN·LB)

NUT—45332-S2 TIGHTEN TO 6.3-9.6 N·m (55-85 IN·LB)

FRONT OF ENGINE

SCREW TIGHTEN TO 2.8-3.9 N·m (25-35 IN·LB)

CLAMP

HOT AIR INLET TUBE—9B632

SHROUD 9A676

SCREW AND WASHER ASSEMBLY TIGHTEN TO 2.26-3.38 N·m (20-30 IN·LB)

SCREW TIGHTEN TO 2.8-3.9 N·m (25-35 IN·LB)

SCREW TIGHTEN TO 2.8-3.9 N·m (25-35 IN·LB)

DELAY VALVE WHITE SIDE TOWARD AIR CLEANER

AIR CLEANER ASSEMBLY—9600

VIEW Z

NUT—34664-S2 TIGHTEN TO 20.4-32.5 N·m (15-24 FT·LB)

BRACKET 9C670

INTAKE MANIFOLD VACUUM FITTING

FRONT OF ENGINE

NOTE: VACUUM HOSE MUST NOT TOUCH ANY HOT SURFACE. ROUTE THE HOSE OVER THE FUEL LINE AND OUTBOARD OF ALL OTHER VACUUM LINES AND THEN TO THE MANIFOLD VACUUM FITTING.

1984 6-300 air cleaner

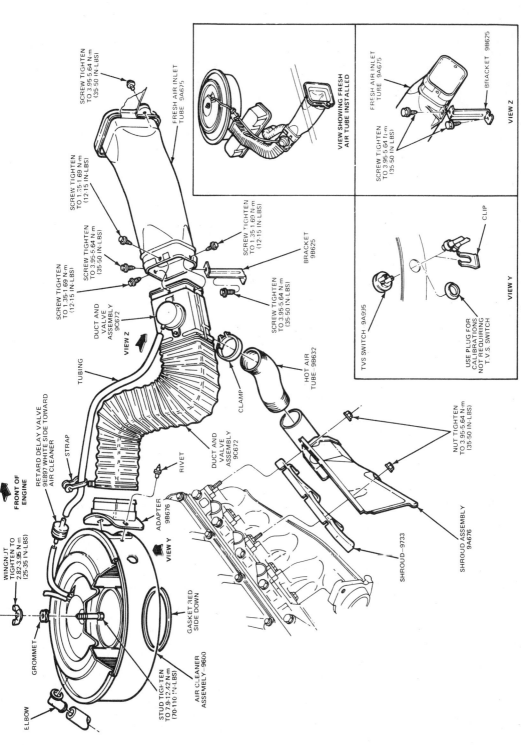

SCREW TIGHTEN TO 3.95-5.64 N·m (35-50 IN-LBS)

FRESH AIR INLET TUBE 9A675

VIEW SHOWING FRESH AIR TUBE INSTALLED

FRESH AIR INLET TUBE 9A675

BRACKET 9B625

VIEW Z

SCREW TIGHTEN TO 3.95-5.64 N·m (35-50 IN-LBS)

SCREW TIGHTEN TO 1.35-1.69 N·m (12-15 IN-LBS)

SCREW TIGHTEN TO 3.95-5.64 N·m (35-50 IN-LBS)

SCREW TIGHTEN TO 1.35-1.69 N·m (12-15 IN-LBS)

BRACKET 9B625

SCREW TIGHTEN TO 3.95-5.64 N·m (35-50 IN-LBS)

CLIP

SCREW TIGHTEN TO 1.35-1.69 N·m (12-15 IN-LBS)

SCREW TIGHTEN TO 3.95-5.64 N·m (35-50 IN-LBS)

DUCT AND VALVE ASSEMBLY 9C672

VIEW Z

TVS SWITCH 9A995

USE PLUG FOR CALIBRATIONS NOT REQUIRING T.V.S. SWITCH

VIEW Y

TUBING

HOT AIR TUBE - 9B632

CLAMP

RETARD DELAY VALVE 9E897 WHITE SIDE TOWARD AIR CLEANER

STRAP

DUCT AND VALVE ASSEMBLY 9C672

NUT TIGHTEN TO 3.95-5.64 N·m (35-50 IN-LBS)

RIVET

SHROUD ASSEMBLY 9A676

ADAPTER 9B676

VIEW Y

SHROUD - 9733

FRONT OF ENGINE

WING NUT TIGHTEN TO 2.82-3.95 N·m (25-35 IN-LBS)

GASKET RED SIDE DOWN

GROMMET

AIR CLEANER ASSEMBLY - 9600

STUD TIGHTEN TO 7.9-12.42 N·m (70-110 IN-LBS)

ELBOW

1982 8-400 air cleaner

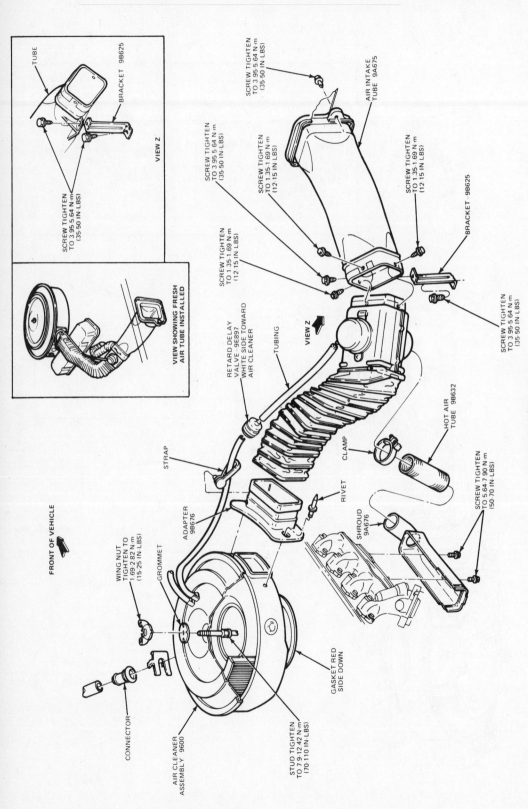

1982–85 8-302 air cleaner

TUBE

BRACKET 9B625

VIEW Z

SCREW TIGHTEN
TO 3.95-5.64 N·m
(35-50 IN-LBS)

VIEW SHOWING FRESH
AIR TUBE INSTALLED

SCREW TIGHTEN
TO 3.95-5.64 N·m
(35-50 IN-LBS)

SCREW TIGHTEN
TO 3.95-5.64 N·m
(35-50 IN-LBS)

AIR INTAKE
TUBE 9A675

SCREW TIGHTEN
TO 3.95-5.64 N·m
(35-50 IN-LBS)

SCREW TIGHTEN
TO 1.35-1.69 N·m
(12-15 IN LBS)

SCREW TIGHTEN
TO 1.35-1.69 N·m
(12-15 IN LBS)

BRACKET - 9B625

SCREW TIGHTEN
TO 1.35-1.69 N·m
(12-15 IN LBS)

SCREW TIGHTEN
TO 3.95-5.64 N·m
(35-50 IN-LBS)

RETARD DELAY
VALVE -9E897
WHITE SIDE TOWARD
AIR CLEANER

TUBING

VIEW Z

HOT AIR
TUBE 9B632

CLAMP

SCREW TIGHTEN
TO 5.64-7.90 N·m
(50-70 IN-LBS)

STRAP

ADAPTER
9B676

RIVET

SHROUD
9A676

FRONT OF VEHICLE

WING NUT
TIGHTEN TO
1.69-2.82 N·m
(15-25 IN-LBS)

GROMMET

CONNECTOR

AIR CLEANER
ASSEMBLY 9600

STUD TIGHTEN
TO 7.9-12.42 N·m
(70-110 IN-LBS)

GASKET RED
SIDE DOWN

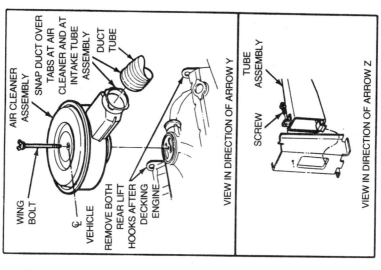

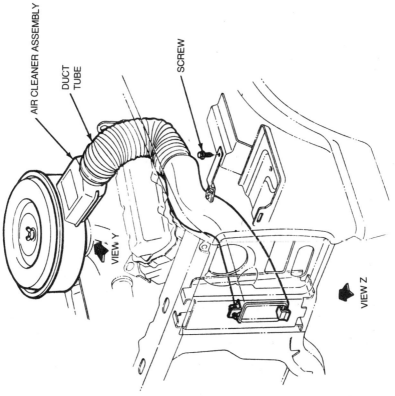

1983—85 diesel air cleaner

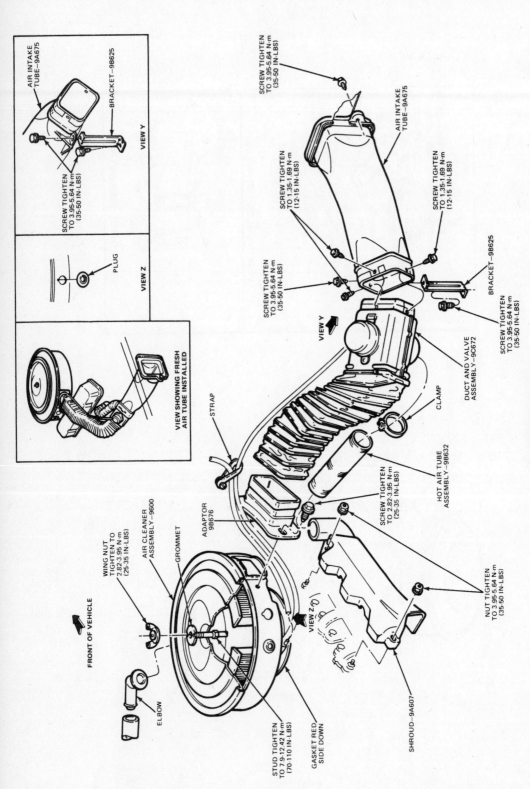

AIR INTAKE TUBE—9A675

BRACKET—9B625

VIEW Y

SCREW TIGHTEN TO 3.95-5.64 N·m (35-50 IN-LBS)

PLUG

VIEW Z

VIEW SHOWING FRESH AIR TUBE INSTALLED

SCREW TIGHTEN TO 3.95-5.64 N·m (35-50 IN-LBS)

SCREW TIGHTEN TO 1.35-1.69 N·m (12-15 IN-LBS)

AIR INTAKE TUBE—9A675

SCREW TIGHTEN TO 1.35-1.69 N·m (12-15 IN-LBS)

SCREW TIGHTEN TO 3.95-5.64 N·m (35-50 IN-LBS)

VIEW Y

BRACKET—9B625

SCREW TIGHTEN TO 3.95-5.64 N·m (35-50 IN-LBS)

DUCT AND VALVE ASSEMBLY—9C672

CLAMP

STRAP

HOT AIR TUBE ASSEMBLY—9B632

SCREW TIGHTEN TO 2.82-3.95 N·m (25-35 IN-LBS)

NUT TIGHTEN TO 3.95-5.64 N·m (35-50 IN-LBS)

ADAPTOR 9B676

AIR CLEANER ASSEMBLY—9600

GROMMET

WING NUT TIGHTEN TO 2.82-3.95 N·m (25-35 IN-LBS)

FRONT OF VEHICLE

ELBOW

VIEW Z

STUD TIGHTEN TO 7.9-12.42 N·m (70-110 IN-LBS)

GASKET RED SIDE DOWN

SHROUD—9A607

1982–85 8-460 air cleaner

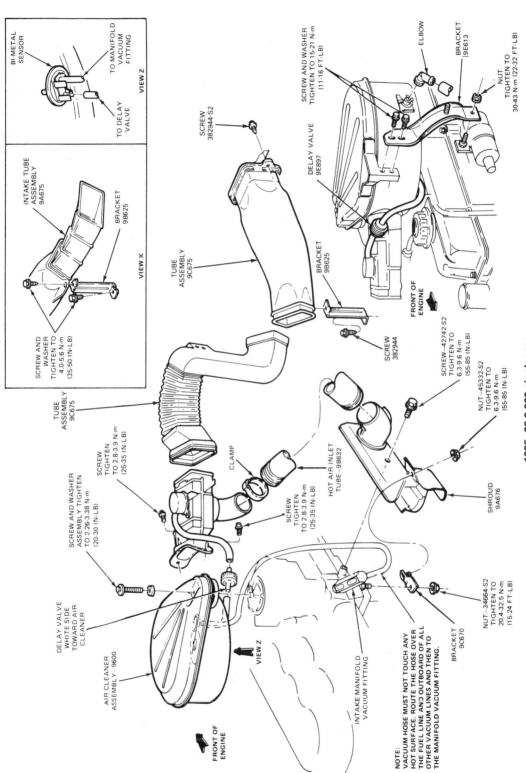

1985–86 6-300 air cleaner

NOTE:
VACUUM HOSE MUST NOT TOUCH ANY
HOT SURFACE. ROUTE THE HOSE OVER
THE FUEL LINE AND OUTBOARD OF ALL
OTHER VACUUM LINES AND THEN TO
THE MANIFOLD VACUUM FITTING.

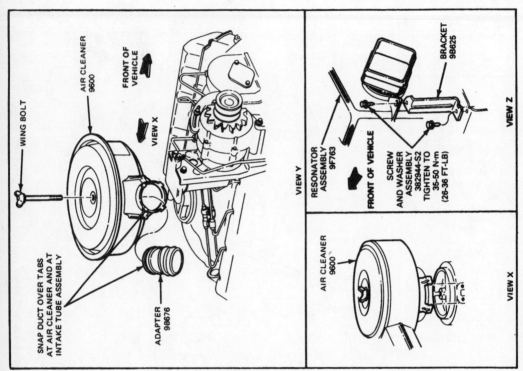

WING BOLT

AIR CLEANER
9600

FRONT OF
VEHICLE

VIEW X

SNAP DUCT OVER TABS
AT AIR CLEANER AND AT
INTAKE TUBE ASSEMBLY

ADAPTER
9B676

VIEW Y

RESONATOR
ASSEMBLY
9F763

FRONT OF VEHICLE

SCREW
AND WASHER
ASSEMBLY
382944-S2
TIGHTEN TO
35-50 N·m
(26-36 FT-LB)

BRACKET
9B625

VIEW Z

AIR CLEANER
9600

VIEW X

1986 diesel air cleaner

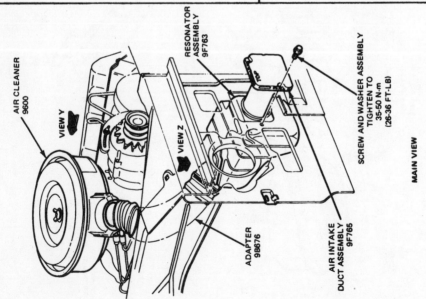

AIR CLEANER
9600

VIEW Y

RESONATOR
ASSEMBLY
9F763

TOP

SCREW AND WASHER ASSEMBLY
TIGHTEN TO
35-50 N·m
(26-36 FT-LB)

VIEW Z

ADAPTER
9B676

AIR INTAKE
DUCT ASSEMBLY
9F765

MAIN VIEW

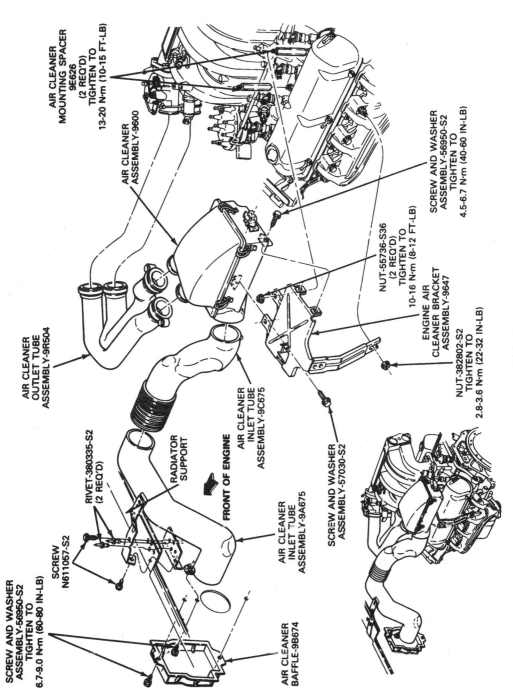

AIR CLEANER MOUNTING SPACER
9E626
(2 REQ'D)
TIGHTEN TO
13-20 N·m (10-15 FT-LB)

AIR CLEANER
ASSEMBLY-9600

AIR CLEANER
OUTLET TUBE
ASSEMBLY-9R504

SCREW AND WASHER
ASSEMBLY-56950-S2
TIGHTEN TO
4.5-6.7 N·m (40-60 IN-LB)

NUT-55736-S36
(2 REQ'D)
TIGHTEN TO
10-16 N·m (8-12 FT-LB)

ENGINE AIR
CLEANER BRACKET
ASSEMBLY-9647

NUT-382802-S2
TIGHTEN TO
2.8-3.6 N·m (22-32 IN-LB)

SCREW AND WASHER
ASSEMBLY-56950-S2
TIGHTEN TO
6.7-9.0 N·m (60-80 IN-LB)

SCREW
N611057-S2

RIVET-380335-S2
(2 REQ'D)

RADIATOR
SUPPORT

FRONT OF ENGINE

AIR CLEANER
INLET TUBE
ASSEMBLY-9C675

AIR CLEANER
INLET TUBE
ASSEMBLY-9A675

SCREW AND WASHER
ASSEMBLY-57030-S2

AIR CLEANER
BAFFLE-9B674

1986 8-302 air cleaner

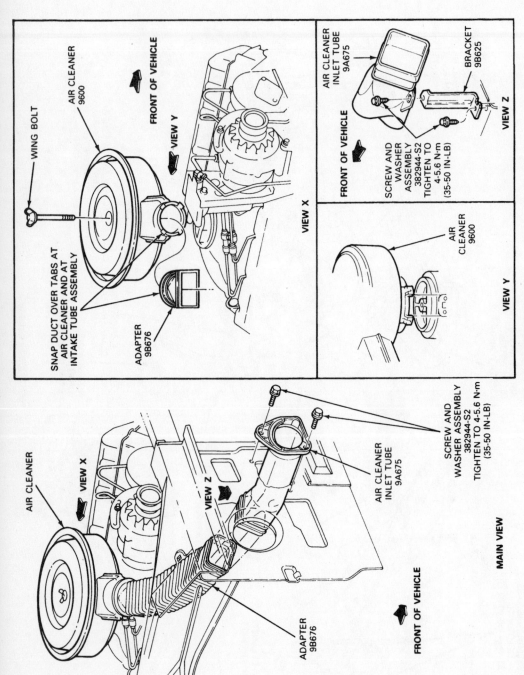

WING BOLT

AIR CLEANER
9600

FRONT OF VEHICLE

VIEW Y

SNAP DUCT OVER TABS AT
AIR CLEANER AND AT
INTAKE TUBE ASSEMBLY

ADAPTER
9B676

VIEW X

AIR CLEANER
INLET TUBE
9A675

BRACKET
9B625

FRONT OF VEHICLE

SCREW AND
WASHER
ASSEMBLY
382944-S2
TIGHTEN TO
4-5.6 N·m
(35-50 IN-LB)

VIEW Z

AIR
CLEANER
9600

VIEW Y

AIR CLEANER

VIEW X

VIEW Z

AIR CLEANER
INLET TUBE
9A675

SCREW AND
WASHER ASSEMBLY
382944-S2
TIGHTEN TO 4-5.6 N·m
(35-50 IN-LB)

ADAPTER
9B676

FRONT OF VEHICLE

MAIN VIEW

1987 diesel air cleaner

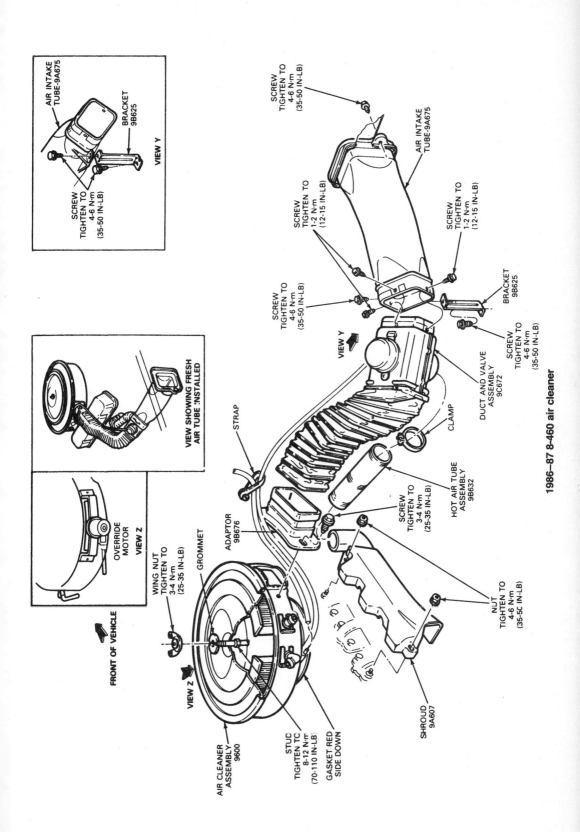

1986—87 8-460 air cleaner

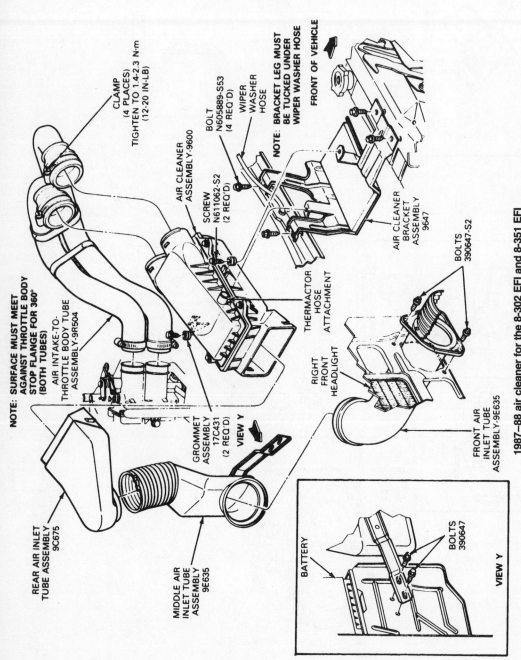

NOTE: SURFACE MUST MEET AGAINST THROTTLE BODY STOP FLANGE FOR 360° (BOTH TUBES)

AIR INTAKE-TO-THROTTLE BODY TUBE ASSEMBLY-9R504

CLAMP (4 PLACES) TIGHTEN TO 1.4-2.3 N·m (12-20 IN-LB)

AIR CLEANER ASSEMBLY-9600

SCREW N611062-S2 (2 REQ'D)

BOLT N605889-S53 (4 REQ'D)

WIPER WASHER HOSE

NOTE: BRACKET LEG MUST BE TUCKED UNDER WIPER WASHER HOSE

FRONT OF VEHICLE

AIR CLEANER BRACKET ASSEMBLY 9647

BOLTS 390647-S2

THERMACTOR HOSE ATTACHMENT

RIGHT FRONT HEADLIGHT

GROMMET ASSEMBLY 17C431 (2 REQ'D)

VIEW Y

REAR AIR INLET TUBE ASSEMBLY 9C675

MIDDLE AIR INLET TUBE ASSEMBLY 9E635

FRONT AIR INLET TUBE ASSEMBLY-9E635

1987–88 air cleaner for the 8-302 EFI and 8-351 EFI

BATTERY

BOLTS 390647

VIEW Y

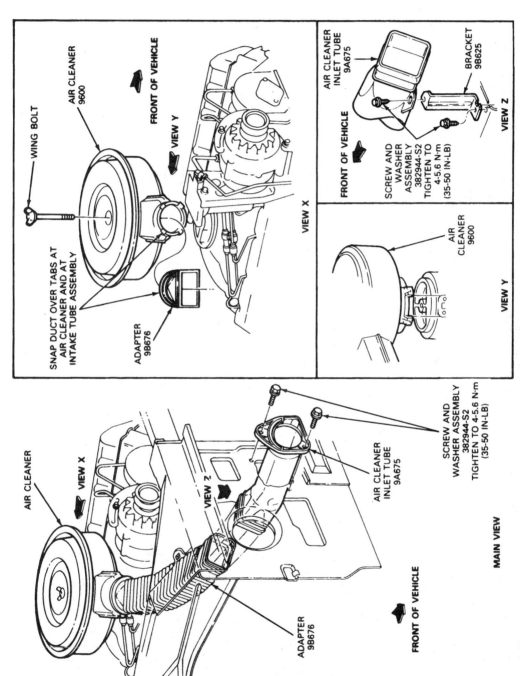

1988 diesel air cleaner

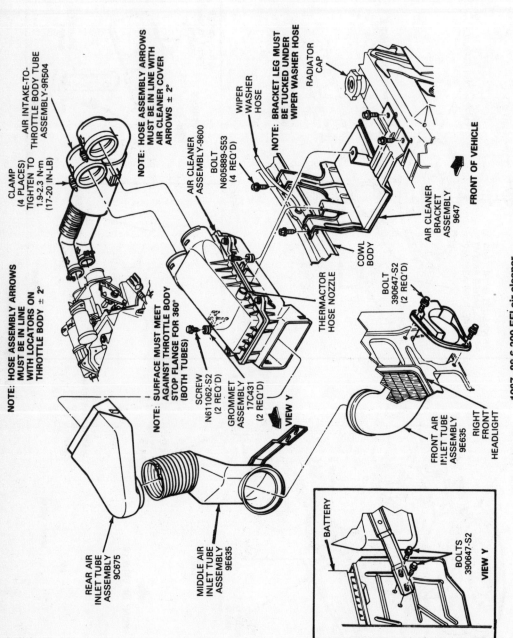

NOTE: HOSE ASSEMBLY ARROWS MUST BE IN LINE WITH LOCATORS ON THROTTLE BODY ± 2°

CLAMP (4 PLACES) TIGHTEN TO 1.9-2.3 N·m (17-20 IN-LB)

AIR INTAKE-TO-THROTTLE BODY TUBE ASSEMBLY-9R504

NOTE: HOSE ASSEMBLY ARROWS MUST BE IN LINE WITH AIR CLEANER COVER ARROWS ± 2°

WIPER WASHER HOSE

AIR CLEANER ASSEMBLY-9600

BOLT N605889-S53 (4 REQ'D)

NOTE: BRACKET LEG MUST BE TUCKED UNDER WIPER WASHER HOSE

RADIATOR CAP

FRONT OF VEHICLE

NOTE: SURFACE MUST MEET AGAINST THROTTLE BODY STOP FLANGE FOR 360° (BOTH TUBES)

SCREW N611062-S2 (2 REQ'D)

GROMMET ASSEMBLY 17C431 (2 REQ'D)

VIEW Y

THERMACTOR HOSE NOZZLE

COWL BODY

BOLT 390647-S2 (2 REQ'D)

AIR CLEANER BRACKET ASSEMBLY 9647

REAR AIR INLET TUBE ASSEMBLY 9C675

MIDDLE AIR INLET TUBE ASSEMBLY 9E635

FRONT AIR INLET TUBE ASSEMBLY 9E635

RIGHT FRONT HEADLIGHT

BATTERY

BOLTS 390647-S2

VIEW Y

1987–88 6-300 EFI air cleaner

of the way and remove the glass bowl. Wash the bowl with carburetor cleaner and wipe it dry. Make sure that the gasket is in good shape before installing the bowl.

It is a good idea, on these older engines, to install an in-line, aftermarket fuel filter somewhere in the fuel line between the pump and the carburetor.

Fuel Pump Mounted Screw-On Types

Some later 6-144 engines and early 6-170 engines came equipped with a cartridge-type screw-on fuel filter which mounted on the fuel pump. These filters look like small oil filters and are serviced in the same manner.

Place a catch pan under the filter and unscrew it from the pump. Screw the new filter in place, securely. Don't overtighten it! Overtightening can distort the gasket, casuing leakage.

Carburetor Mounted Types
Except the 2700VV/7200VV and 4180 4-bbl

A carburetor mounted gas filter is used on all later model engines. These filters screw into the float chamber. To replace one of these filters:

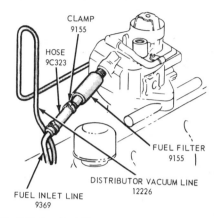

1966–67 inline fuel filter

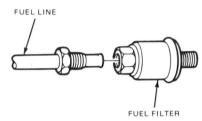

Carburetor mounted screw-in filter

1. Wait until the engine is cold.
2. Remove the air cleaner assembly.
3. Place some absorbant rags under the filter.
4. Remove the hose clamp and slide the rubber hose from the filter.

CAUTION: *It is possible for gasoline to spray in all directions when removing the hose! This rarely happens, but it is possible, so protect your eyes!*

5. Move the fuel line out of the way and unscrew the filter from the carburetor.
6. Coat the threads of the new filter with non-hardening, gasoline-proof sealer and screw it into place by hand. Tighten it snugly with a wrench.

WARNING: *Do not overtighten the filter! The threads in the carburetor bowl are soft metal and are easily stripped! You don't want to damage these threads!!!*

7. Connect the hose to the new filter. Most replacement filters come with a new hose and clamps. Use them.
8. Remove the fuel-soaked rags, wipe up any spilled fuel and start the engine. Check the filter connections for leaks.

2700VV/7200VV and 4180 4-bbl

Model 2700VV and 7200VV carburetors use a replaceable filter located behind the carburetor inlet fitting. To replace these filters:

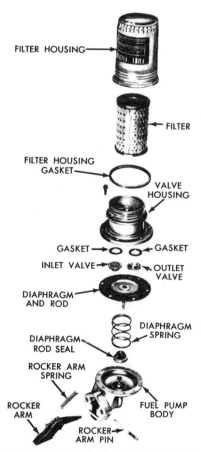

Fuel pump with pump-mounted cartridge filter

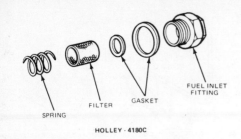

SPRING FILTER GASKET FUEL INLET FITTING

HOLLEY - 4180C

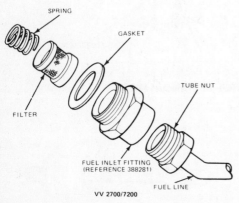

SPRING

GASKET

TUBE NUT

FILTER

FUEL INLET FITTING
(REFERENCE 388281)

FUEL LINE

VV 2700/7200

Fuel filters used on the Holley 4180C and VV2700/7200

1. Wait until the engine is cold.
2. Remove the air cleaner assembly.
3. Place some absorbant rags under the inlet fitting.
4. Using a back-up wrench on the inlet fitting, unscrew the fuel line from the inlet fitting.
CAUTION: *It is possible for gasoline to spray in all directions when unscrewing the line! This rarely happens, but it is possible, so protect your eyes!*
5. Move the fuel line out of the way and unscrew the inlet fiting from the carburetor.
6. Pull out the filter. The spring behind the filter may come with it.
7. Install the new filter. Some new filters come with a new spring. Use it.
8. Coat the threads of the inlet fitting with non-hardening, gasoline-proof sealer and screw it into place by hand. Tighten it snugly with the wrench.
WARNING: *Do not overtighten the inlet fitting! The threads in the carburetor bowl are soft metal and are easily stripped! You don't want to damage these threads!!*
9. Using the back-up wrench on the inlet fitting, screw the fuel line into the fitting and tighten it snugly. Do not overtighten the fuel line!
10. Remove the fuel-soaked rags, wipe up any spilled fuel and start the engine. Check the connections for leaks.

Fuel Injected Gasoline Filters

CAUTION: *Fuel lines on vehicles equipped with EFI can remain pressurized for long periods of time after the engine has been shut off. Before opening any fuel line connection, the system must be depressurized.*

RELIEVING FUEL SYSTEM PRESSURE

1. Disconnect the electrical connection at the fuel pump relay, inertia switch or in-line high pressure fuel pump, whichever is most convenient.
2. Crank the engine for about 10 seconds.
NOTE: *The engine may start and run for a brief time. If this happens, let it run until it shuts off, then crank the engine for an additional 5 seconds.*
3. Reconnect the electrical connector.
4. Disconnect the battery ground cable.

FUEL FILTER REPLACEMENT

The inline filter is mounted on the same bracket as the fuel supply pump on the frame rail under the truck, back by the fuel tank. To replace the filter:
1. Raise and support the rear end on jackstands.
2. With the engine off, depressurize the fuel system.
3. Remove the quick-disconnect fittings at both ends of the filter. See Chapter 5.
4. Remove the filter and retainer from the bracket.
5. Remove the rubber insulator ring from the filter.
6. Remove the filter from the retainer.
7. Install the new filter into the retainer, noting the direction of the flow arrow.
8. Install a new rubber insulator ring.

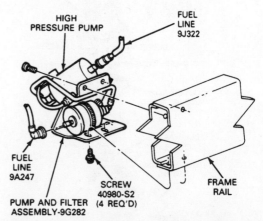

HIGH PRESSURE PUMP

FUEL LINE 9J322

FUEL LINE 9A247

SCREW 40980-S2 (4 REQ'D)

PUMP AND FILTER ASSEMBLY-9G282

FRAME RAIL

Inline fuel filter used on fuel injected gasoline engines

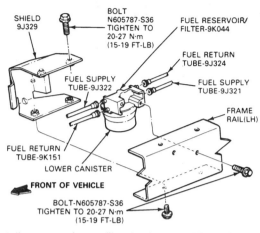

Inline reservoir type filter for the 8-302 EFI engine

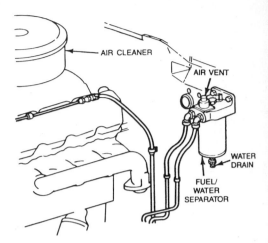

Water drain petcock located on the bottom of the fuel/water separator

9. Install the retainer and filter on the bracket and tighten the screws to 60 in.lb.

10. Install the fuel lines using new retainer clips.

11. Start the engine and check for leaks.

Diesel Engine Fuel Filter

The 6.9L and 7.3L diesel engines use a one-piece spin-on fuel filter.

1. Remove the spin-on filter by unscrewing it counterclockwise with your hands or a strap wrench.

2. Clean the filter mounting surface.

3. Coat the gasket or the replacement filter with clean diesel fuel. This helps ensure a good seal.

NOTE: *Do not add fuel to the new fuel filter. Allow the engine to draw fuel through the filter.*

4. Tighten the filter by hand until the gasket touches the filter mounting surface.

5. Tighten the filter an additional ½ turn.

NOTE: *After changing the fuel filter, the en-*

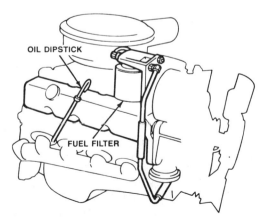

Oil dipstick and fuel filter locations

gine will purge the trapped air as it runs. The engine may run roughly and smoke excessively until the air is cleared from the system.

Fuel/Water Separator

Diesel Engines

The 6.9L and 7.3L diesel engines are equipped with a fuel/water separator in the fuel supply line. A Water in Fuel indicator light is provided on the instrument panel to alert the driver. The light should glow when the ignition switch is in the Start position to indicate proper light and water sensor function. If the light glows continuously while the engine is running, the water must be drained from the separator as soon as possible to prevent damage to the fuel injection system.

1. Shut off the engine. Failure to shut the engine off before draining the separator will cause air to enter the system.

2. Unscrew the vent on the top center of the separator unit 2½ to 3 turns.

3. Unscrew the drain screw on the bottom of the separator 1½ to 2 turns and drain the water into an appropriate container.

4. After the water is completely drained, close the water drain fingertight.

5. Tighten the vent until snug, then turn it an additional ¼ turn.

6. Start the engine and check the Water in Fuel indicator light; it should not be lit. If it is lit and continues to stay so, there is a problem somewhere else in the fuel system.

NOTE: *All but very early production models have a drain hose connected to separator which allows water to drain directly into a container placed underneath the vehicle.*

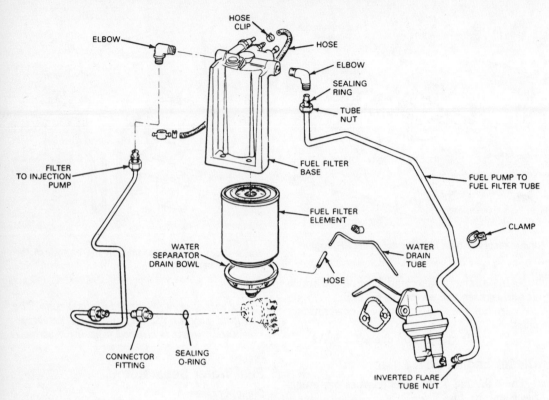

Diesel fuel/water separator

PCV Valve

Gasoline Engines Only

Check the PCV valve according to the Preventive Maintenance Schedule at the end of this chapter to see if it is free and not gummed up, stuck or blocked. To check the valve, remove it from the engine and work the valve by sticking a screwdriver in the crankcase side of the valve. It should move. It is possible to clean the PCV valve by soaking it in a solvent and blowing it out with compressed air. This can re-store the valve to some level of operating order. This should be used only as an emergency measure. Otherwise the valve should be replaced.

Evaporative Canister

Gasoline Engines Only

The fuel evaporative emission control canister should be inspected for damage or leaks at the hose fittings every 24,000 miles. Repair or replace any old or cracked hoses. Replace the canister if it is damaged in any way. The canister is located under the hood, to the right of the engine.

Battery

Loose, dirty, or corroded battery terminals are a major cause of "no-start." Every 3 months or so, remove the battery terminals and clean them, giving them a light coating of petroleum jelly when you are finished. This will help to retard corrosion.

Check the battery cables for signs of wear or chafing and replace any cable or terminal that looks marginal. Battery terminals can be easily cleaned and inexpensive terminal cleaning tools are an excellent investment that will pay for themselves many times over. They can usually be purchased from any well-equipped auto store or parts department. Side terminal bat-

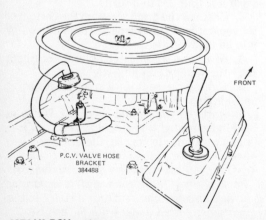

1974 V8 PCV system

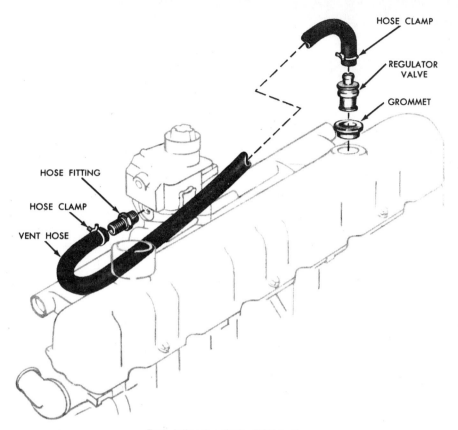

HOSE CLAMP

REGULATOR VALVE

GROMMET

HOSE FITTING

HOSE CLAMP

VENT HOSE

Early inline 6-cylinder PCV system

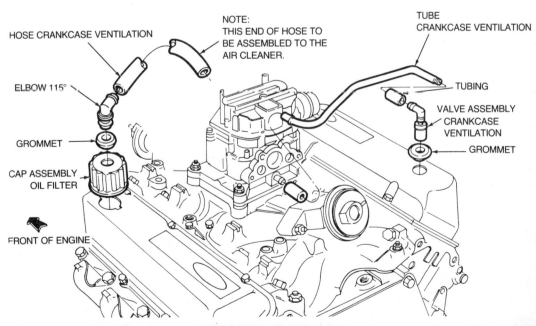

HOSE CRANKCASE VENTILATION

NOTE:
THIS END OF HOSE TO
BE ASSEMBLED TO THE
AIR CLEANER.

TUBE
CRANKCASE VENTILATION

ELBOW 115°

TUBING

VALVE ASSEMBLY
CRANKCASE
VENTILATION

GROMMET

GROMMET

CAP ASSEMBLY
OIL FILTER

FRONT OF ENGINE

1975 and later PCV system

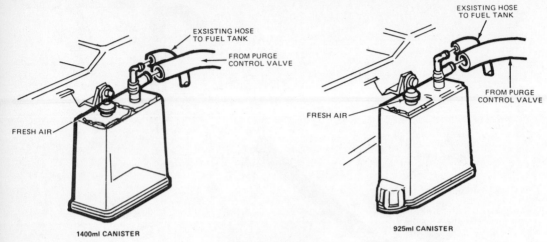

1400ml CANISTER

925ml CANISTER

Evaporative canisters

teries require a different tool to clean the threads in the battery case. The accumulated white powder and corrosion can be cleaned from the top of the battery with an old toothbrush and a solution of baking soda and water.

Unless you have a maintenance-free battery, check the electrolyte level (see Battery under Fluid Level Checks in this chapter) and check the specific gravity of each cell. Be sure that the vent holes in each cell cap are not blocked by grease or dirt. The vent holes allow hydrogen gas, formed by the chemical reaction in the battery, to escape safely.

REPLACEMENT BATTERIES

The cold power rating of a battery measures battery starting performance and provides an approximate relationship between battery size and engine size. The cold power rating of a replacement battery should match or exceed your engine size in cubic inches.

FLUID LEVEL (EXCEPT MAINTENANCE FREE BATTERIES)

Check the battery electrolyte level at least once a month, or more often in hot weather or during periods of extended truck operation. The level can be checked through the case on translucent polypropylene batteries; the cell caps must be removed on other models. The electrolyte level in each cell should be kept filled to the split ring inside, or the line marked on the outside of the case.

If the level is low, add only distilled water, or colorless, odorless drinking water, through the opening until the level is correct. Each cell is completely separate from the others, so each must be checked and filled individually.

If water is added in freezing weather, the truck should be driven several miles to allow the water to mix with the electrolyte. Otherwise, the battery could freeze.

SPECIFIC GRAVITY (@ 80°F.) AND CHARGE	
Specific Gravity Reading (use the minimum figure for testing)	
Minimum	**Battery Charge**
1.260	100% Charged
1.230	75% Charged
1.200	50% Charged
1.170	25% Charged
1.140	Very Little Power Left
1.110	Completely Discharged

Battery specific gravity. Some testers have colored balls which correspond to the numerical values in the left column

SPECIFIC GRAVITY (EXCEPT MAINTENANCE FREE BATTERIES)

At least once a year, check the specific gravity of the battery. It should be between 1.20 in.Hg and 1.26 in.Hg at room temperature.

The specific gravity can be check with the use of an hydrometer, an inexpensive instrument available from many sources, including auto parts stores. The hydrometer has a squeeze bulb at one end and a nozzle at the other. Battery electrolyte is sucked into the hydrometer until the float is lifted from its seat. The specific gravity is then read by noting the position of the float. Generally, if after charging, the specific gravity between any two cells varies more than 50 points (0.50), the battery is bad and should be replaced.

It is not possible to check the specific gravity in this manner on sealed (maintenance free) batteries. Instead, the indicator built into the top of the case must be relied on to display any signs of battery deterioration. If the indicator is dark, the battery can be assumed to be OK. If the indicator is light, the specific gravity is low, and the battery should be charged or replaced.

CABLES AND CLAMPS

Once a year, the battery terminals and the cable clamps should be cleaned. Loosen the clamps and remove the cables, negative cable first. On batteries with posts on top, the use of a puller specially made for the purpose is recom-

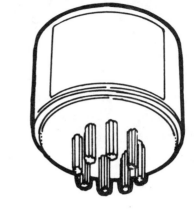

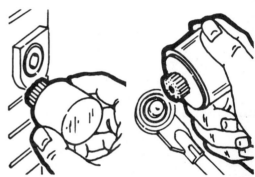

Special tools are available for cleaning the terminals and cable clamps on side terminal batteries

Cleaning the inside of the cable end

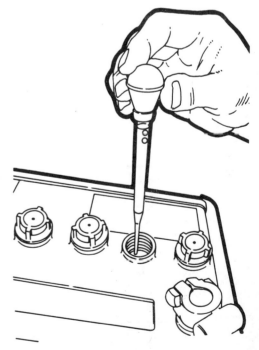

An inexpensive hydrometer will quickly test the battery's state of charge

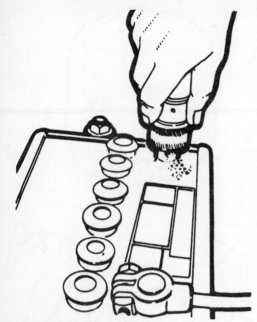

Cleaning the battery terminal

mended. These are inexpensive, and available in auto parts stores. Side terminal battery cables are secured with a bolt.

Clean the cable lamps and the battery terminal with a wire brush, until all corrosion, grease, etc., is removed and the metal is shiny. It is especially important to clean the inside of the clamp thoroughly, since a small deposit of foreign material or oxidation there will prevent a sound electrical connection and inhibit either starting or charging. Special tools are available for cleaning these parts, one type for conventional batteries and another type for side terminal batteries.

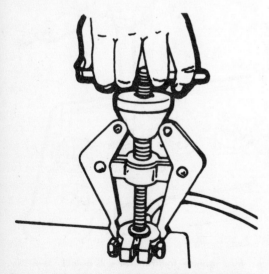

Use a small puller to remove the battery cables

Before installing the cables, loosen the battery holddown clamp or strap, remove the battery and check the battery tray. Clear it of any debris, and check it for soundness. Rust should be wire brushed away, and the metal given a coat of anti-rust paint. Replace the battery and tighten the holddown clamp or strap securely, but be careful not to overtighten, which will crack the battery case.

After the clamps and terminals are clean, re-install the cables, negative cable last; do not hammer on the clamps to install. Tighten the clamps securely, but do not distort them. Give the clamps and terminals a thin external coat of grease after installation, to retard corrosion.

Check the cables at the same time that the terminals are cleaned. If the cable insulation is cracked or broken, or if the ends are frayed, the cable should be replaced with a new cable of the same length and gauge.

CAUTION: *Keep flame or sparks away from the battery; it gives off explosive hydrogen gas. Battery electrolyte contains sulphuric acid. If you should splash any on your skin or in your eyes, flush the affected area with plenty of clear water. If it lands in your eyes, get medical help immediately.*

Belts

Once a year or at 12,000 mile intervals, the tension (and condition) of the alternator, power steering (if so equipped), air conditioning (if so equipped), and Thermactor air pump drive belts should be checked, and, if necessary, adjusted. Loose accessory drive belts can lead to poor engine cooling and diminish alternator, power steering pump, air conditioning compressor or Thermactor air pump output. A belt that is too tight places a severe strain on the water pump, alternator, power steering pump, compressor or air pump bearings.

Replace any belt that is so glazed, worn or stretched that it cannot be tightened sufficiently.

NOTE: *The material used in late model drive belts is such that the belts do not show wear. Replace belts at least every three years.*

On vehicles with matched belts, replace both belts. New ½", ⅜" and $^{15}/_{32}$" wide belts are to be adjusted to a tension of 140 lbs.; ¼" wide belts are adjusted to 80 lbs., measured on a belt tension gauge. Any belt that has been operating for a minimum of 10 minutes is considered a used belt. In the first 10 minutes, the belt should stretch to its maximum extent. After 10 minutes, stop the engine and recheck the belt tension. Belt tension for a used belt should be maintained at 110 lbs. (all except ¼" wide belts) or 60 lbs. (¼" wide belts). If a belt tension gauge

HOW TO SPOT WORN V-BELTS

V-Belts are vital to efficient engine operation—they drive the fan, water pump and other accessories. They require little maintenance (occasional tightening) but they will not last forever. Slipping or failure of the V-belt will lead to overheating. If your V-belt looks like any of these, it should be replaced.

Cracking or weathering

This belt has deep cracks, which cause it to flex. Too much flexing leads to heat build-up and premature failure. These cracks can be caused by using the belt on a pulley that is too small. Notched belts are available for small diameter pulleys.

Softening (grease and oil)

Oil and grease on a belt can cause the belt's rubber compounds to soften and separate from the reinforcing cords that hold the belt together. The belt will first slip, then finally fail altogether.

Glazing

Glazing is caused by a belt that is slipping. A slipping belt can cause a run-down battery, erratic power steering, overheating or poor accessory performance. The more the belt slips, the more glazing will be built up on the surface of the belt. The more the belt is glazed, the more it will slip. If the glazing is light, tighten the belt.

Worn cover

The cover of this belt is worn off and is peeling away. The reinforcing cords will begin to wear and the belt will shortly break. When the belt cover wears in spots or has a rough jagged appearance, check the pulley grooves for roughness.

Separation

This belt is on the verge of breaking and leaving you stranded. The layers of the belt are separating and the reinforcing cords are exposed. It's just a matter of time before it breaks completely.

is not available, the following procedures may be used.

ADJUSTMENTS FOR ALL EXCEPT THE SERPENTINE (SINGLE) BELT

On models equipped with an electric cooling fan, disconnect the negative battery cable or fan motor wiring harness connector before replacing or adjusting drive belts. The fan may come on, under certain circumstances, even though the ignition is off.

Alternator (Fan Drive) Belt

1. Position the ruler perpendicular to the drive belt at its longest straight run. Test the tightness of the belt by pressing it firmly with your thumb. The deflection should not exceed ¼".

2. If the deflection exceeds ¼", loosen the alternator mounting and adjusting arm bolts.

3. Place a 1" open-end or adjustable wrench on the adjusting ridge cast on the body, and pull on the wrench until the proper tension is achieved.

4. Holding the alternator in place to maintain tension, tighten the adjusting arm bolt. Recheck the belt tension. When the belt is properly tensioned, tighten the alternator mounting bolt.

Power Steering Drive Belt

6-CYLINDER

1. Hold a ruler perpendicularly to the drive belt at its longest run, test the tightness of the belt by pressing it firmly with your thumb. The deflection should not exceed ¼".

2. To adjust the belt tension, loosen the adjusting and mounting bolts on the front face of the steering pump cover plate (hub side).

3. Using a pry bar or broom handle on the pump hub, move the power steering pump toward or away from the engine until the proper tension is reached. Do not pry against the reservoir as it is relatively soft and easily deformed.

4. Holding the pump in place, tighten the adjusting arm bolt and then recheck the belt tension. When the belt is properly tensioned tighten the mounting bolts.

V8 MODELS

1. Position a ruler perpendicular to the drive belt at its longest run. Test the tightness of the belt by pressing it firmly with your thumb. The deflection should be about ¼".

2. To adjust the belt tension, loosen the three bolts in the three elongated adjusting slots at the power steering pump attaching bracket.

3. Turn the steering pump drive belt adjusting nut as required until the proper deflection

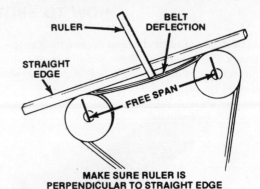

MAKE SURE RULER IS PERPENDICULAR TO STRAIGHT EDGE

Measuring belt deflection

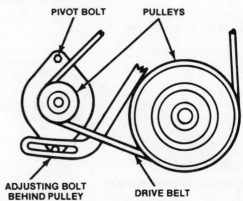

Some accessories can be moved only if the pivot bolt is loosened

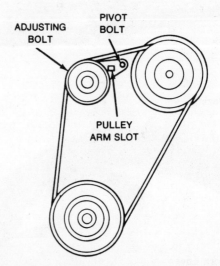

Some pulleys have a rectangular slot to aid in moving the accessory

is obtained. Turning the adjusting nut clockwise will increase tension and decrease deflection; counterclockwise will decrease tension and increase deflection.

4. Without disturbing the pump, tighten the three attaching bolts.

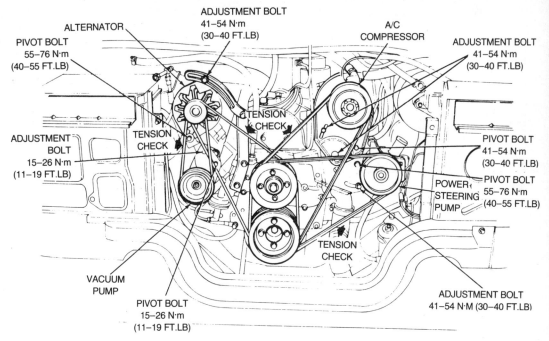

Diesel engine accessory drive belts

Air Conditioning Compressor Drive Belt

1. Position a ruler perpendicular to the drive belt at its longest run. Test the tightness of the belt by pressing it firmly with your thumb. The deflection should not exceed ¼".

2. If the engine is equipped with an idler pulley, loosen the idler pulley adjusting bolt, insert a pry bar between the pulley and the engine (or in the idler pulley adjusting slot), and adjust the tension accordingly. If the engine is not equipped with an idler pulley, the alternator must be moved to accomplish this adjustment, as outlined under Alternator (Fan Drive) Belt.

3. When the proper tension is reached, tighten the idler pulley adjusting bolt (if so equipped) or the alternator adjusting and mounting bolts.

Thermactor Air Pump Drive Belt

1. Position a ruler perpendicular to the drive belt at its longest run. Test the tightness of the belt by pressing it firmly with your thumb. The deflection should be about ¼".

2. To adjust the belt tension, loosen the adjusting arm bolt slightly. If necessary, also loosen the mounting belt slightly.

3. Using a pry bar or broom handle, pry against the pump rear cover to move the pump toward or away from the engine as necessary.
CAUTION: *Do not pry against the pump housing itself, as damage to the housing may result.*

4. Holding the pump in place, tighten the ad-

justing arm bolt and recheck the tension. When the belt is properly tensioned, tighten the mounting bolt.

SERPENTINE (SINGLE) DRIVE BELT MODELS

Most models feature a single, wide, ribbed V-belt that drives the water pump, alternator, and (on some models) the air conditioner compressor. To install a new belt, loosen the bracket lock bolt, retract the belt tensioner with a pry bar and slide the old belt off of the pulleys. Slip on a new belt and release the tensioner and tighten the lock bolt. The spring powered tensioner eliminates the need for periodic adjustments.
WARNING: *Check to make sure that the V-ribbed belt is located properly in all drive pulleys before applying tensioner pressure.*

Hoses

CAUTION: *On models equipped with an electric cooling fan, disconnect the negative battery cable, or fan motor wiring harness connector before replacing any radiator/heater hose. The fan may come on, under certain circumstances, even though the ignition is Off.*

REPLACEMENT

Inspect the condition of the radiator and heater hoses periodically. Early spring and at

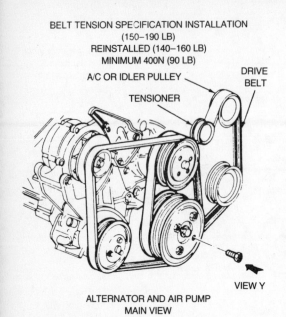

BELT TENSION SPECIFICATION INSTALLATION
(150–190 LB)
REINSTALLED (140–160 LB)
MINIMUM 400N (90 LB)

A/C OR IDLER PULLEY
TENSIONER
DRIVE BELT

VIEW Y

ALTERNATOR AND AIR PUMP
MAIN VIEW

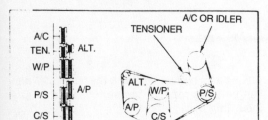

A/C
TEN.
W/P
P/S
C/S

ALT.
A/P

TENSIONER
A/C OR IDLER

ALT.
W/P
A/P
C/S
P/S

VIEW Y

8-460 EFI engine accessory drive belts

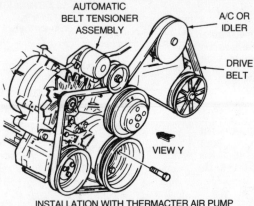

AUTOMATIC
BELT TENSIONER
ASSEMBLY

A/C OR IDLER

DRIVE BELT

VIEW Y

INSTALLATION WITH THERMACTER AIR PUMP

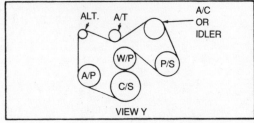

ALT.   A/T
A/C OR IDLER

W/P   P/S
A/P   C/S

VIEW Y

8-302, 8-351 EFI engine accessory drive belts

the beginning of the fall or winter, when you are performing other maintenance, are good times. Make sure the engine and cooling system are cold. Visually inspect for cracking, rotting or collapsed hoses, replace as necessary. Run your hand along the length of the hose. If a

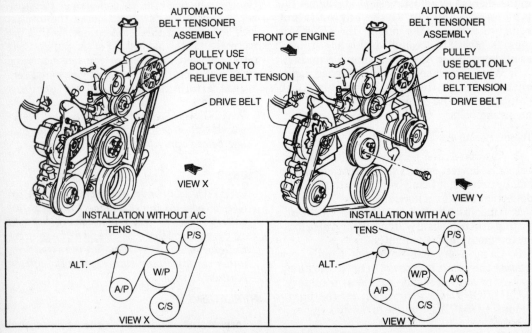

AUTOMATIC
BELT TENSIONER
ASSEMBLY

PULLEY USE
BOLT ONLY TO
RELIEVE BELT TENSION

DRIVE BELT

VIEW X

INSTALLATION WITHOUT A/C

FRONT OF ENGINE

AUTOMATIC
BELT TENSIONER
ASSEMBLY

PULLEY
USE BOLT ONLY
TO RELIEVE
BELT TENSION

DRIVE BELT

VIEW Y

INSTALLATION WITH A/C

TENS
P/S
ALT.
W/P
A/P
C/S

VIEW X

TENS
P/S
ALT.
W/P   A/C
A/P
C/S

VIEW Y

6-300 EFI engine accessory drive belts

HOW TO SPOT BAD HOSES

Both the upper and lower radiator hoses are called upon to perform difficult jobs in an inhospitable environment. They are subject to nearly 18 psi at under hood temperatures often over 280°F., and must circulate nearly 7500 gallons of coolant an hour—3 good reasons to have good hoses.

Swollen hose

A good test for any hose is to feel it for soft or spongy spots. Frequently these will appear as swollen areas of the hose. The most likely cause is oil soaking. This hose could burst at any time, when hot or under pressure.

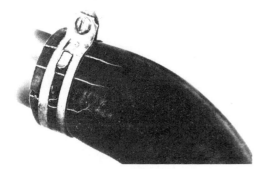

Cracked hose

Cracked hoses can usually be seen but feel the hoses to be sure they have not hardened; a prime cause of cracking. This hose has cracked down to the reinforcing cords and could split at any of the cracks.

Frayed hose end (due to weak clamp)

Weakened clamps frequently are the cause of hose and cooling system failure. The connection between the pipe and hose has deteriorated enough to allow coolant to escape when the engine is hot.

Debris in cooling system

Debris, rust and scale in the cooling system can cause the inside of a hose to weaken. This can usually be felt on the outside of the hose as soft or thinner areas.

weak or swollen spot is noted when squeezing the hose wall, replace the hose.

1. Drain the cooling system into a suitable container (if the coolant is to be reused).

CAUTION: *When draining the coolant, keep in mind that cats and dogs are attracted by the ethylene glycol antifreeze, and are quite likely to drink any that is left in an uncovered container or in puddles on the ground. This will prove fatal in sufficient quantity. Always drain the coolant into a sealable container. Coolant should be reused unless it is contaminated or several years old.*

2. Loosen the hose clamps at each end of the hose that requires replacement.

3. Twist, pull and slide the hose off the radiator, water pump, thermostat or heater connection.

4. Clean the hose mounting connections. Position the hose clamps on the new hose.

5. Coat the connection surfaces with a water resistant sealer and slide the hose into position. Make sure the hose clamps are located beyond the raised bead of the connector (if equipped) and centered in the clamping area of the connection.

6. Tighten the clamps to 20-30 in.lb. Do not overtighten.

7. Fill the cooling system.

8. Start the engine and allow it to reach normal operating temperature. Check for leaks.

Exhaust Manifold Heat Riser Valve

Check the thermostatic spring of the valve to make sure it is hooked up on the stop pin. The spring stop is at the top of the valve housing when the valve is properly installed.

Make sure the spring holds the valve closed. Actuate the counterweight by hand to make sure it moves freely through approximately 90° of rotation without binding.

The valve is closed when the engine is cold. However, a properly operating valve will open when very light finger pressure is applied to the counterweight. Rapidly accelerate the engine to make sure the valve momentarily opens. The valve is designed to open when the engine is at normal operating temperature and is operated at high rpm.

Lubricate and free the value with the non-flammable solvent if the valve is sluggish or stuck.

Cooling System
FLUID RECOMMENDATIONS

When additional coolant is required to maintain the proper level, always add a 50/50 mixture of antifreeze/coolant and water.

LEVEL CHECK

CAUTION: *Exercise extreme care when removing the cap from a hot radiator. Wait a few minutes until the engine has time to cool somewhat, then wrap a thick towel around the radiator cap and slowly turn it counterclockwise to the first stop. Step back and allow the pressure to release from the cooling system. Then, when the steam has stopped venting, press down on the cap, turn it one more stop counterclockwise and remove the cap.*

The coolant level in the radiator should be checked on a monthly basis, preferably when the engine is cold. On a cold engine, the coolant level should be maintained at one inch below the filler neck on vertical flow radiators, and 2½″ below the filler neck at the **COLD FILL** mark on crossflow radiators. On trucks

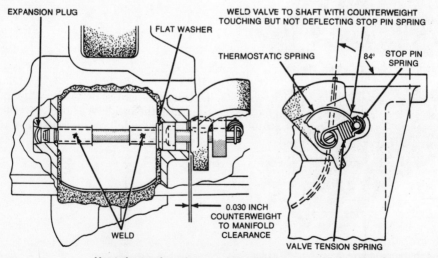

Heat riser valve plate position and counterweight clearance

equipped with the Coolant Recovery System, the level is maintained at the **COLD LEVEL** mark in the translucent plastic expansion bottle. Top up as necessary with a mixture of 50% water and 50% ethylene glycol antifreeze, to ensure proper rust, freezing and boiling protection. If you have to add coolant more often than once a month or if you have to add more than one quart at a time, check the cooling system for leads. Also check for water in the crankcase oil, indicating a blown cylinder head gasket.

DRAIN AND REFILL

CAUTION: *When draining the coolant, keep in mind that cats and dogs are attracted by the ethylene glycol antifreeze, and are quite likely to drink any that is left in an uncovered container or in puddles on the ground. This will prove fatal in sufficient quantity. Always drain the coolant into a sealable container. Coolant should be reused unless it is contaminated or several years old.*

Completely draining and refilling the cooling system every two years at least will remove accumulated rust, scale and other deposits.

NOTE: *Use a good quality antifreeze with water pump lubricants, rust inhibitors and other corrosion inhibitors along with acid neutralizers. Use a permanent type coolant that meets specification ESE-M97B44A or the equivalent.*

1. Drain the existing antifreeze and coolant. Open the radiator and engine drain petcocks (models equipped), or disconnect the bottom radiator hose, at the radiator outlet. Set the heater temperature controls to the full HOT position.

NOTE: *Before opening the radiator petcock, spray it with some penetrating lubricant.*

2. Close the petcock or reconnect the lower hose and fill the system with water.

3. Add a can of quality radiator flush. If equipped with a diesel engine, be sure the flush is safe to use in engines having aluminum components.

4. Idle the engine until the upper radiator hose gets hot.

5. Drain the system again.

6. Repeat this process until the drained water is clear and free of scale.

7. Close all petcocks and connect all the hoses.

8. If equipped with a coolant recovery system, flush the reservoir with water and leave empty.

9. Determine the capacity of your cooling system (see capacities specifications). Add a 50/50 mix of quality antifreeze (ethylene glycol) and water to provide the desired protection.

SYSTEM INSPECTION

Most permanent antifreeze/coolant have a colored dye added which makes the solution an excellent leak detector. When servicing the cooling system, check for leakage at:
- All hoses and hose connections
- Radiator seams, radiator core, and radiator draincock
- All engine block and cylinder head freeze (core) plugs, and drain plugs
- Edges of all cooling system gaskets (head gaskets, thermostat gasket)
- Transmission fluid cooler
- Heating system components, water pump
- Check the engine oil dipstick for signs of coolant in the engine oil
- Check the coolant in the radiator for signs of oil in the coolant

Investigate and correct any indication of coolant leakage.

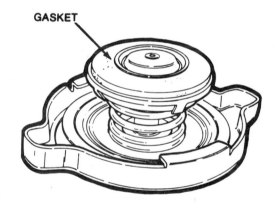

GASKET

Checking the radiator cap gasket for cracks or wear

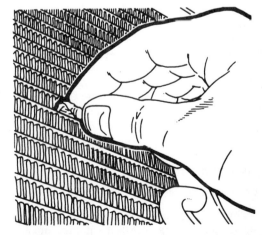

Keep the radiator fins clear of debris for maximum cooling

Testing coolant condition with a tester

Check the Radiator Cap

While you are checking the coolant level, check the radiator cap for a worn or cracked gasket. If the cap doesn't seal properly, fluid will be lost and the engine will overheat.

A worn cap should be replaced with a new one.

Clean Radiator of Debris

Periodically clean any debris such as leaves, paper, insects, etc., from the radiator fins. Pick the large pieces off by hand. The smaller pieces can be washed away with water pressure from a hose.

Carefully straighten any bent radiator fins with a pair of needle nose pliers. Be careful, the fins are very soft. Don't wiggle the fins back and forth too much. Straighten them once and try not to move them again.

CHECKING SYSTEM PROTECTION

A 50/50 mix of coolant concentrate and water will usually provide protection to –35°F (–37°C). Freeze protection may be checked by using a cooling system hydrometer. Inexpensive hydrometers (floating ball types) may be obtained from a local department store (automotive section) or an auto supply store. Follow the directions packaged with the coolant hydrometer when checking protection.

Air Conditioning
GENERAL SERVICING PROCEDURES

The most important aspect of air conditioning service is the maintenance of pure and adequate charge of refrigerant in the system. A refrigeration system cannot function properly if a significant percentage of the charge is lost. Leaks are common because the severe vibration encountered in an automobile can easily cause a sufficient cracking or loosening of the air conditioning fittings. As a result, the extreme operating pressures of the system force refrigerant out.

The problem can be understood by considering what happens to the system as it is operated with a continuous leak. Because the expansion valve regulates the flow of refrigerant to the evaporator, the level of refrigerant there is fairly constant. The receiver/drier stores any excess of refrigerant, and so a loss will first appear there as a reduction in the level of liquid. As this level nears the bottom of the vessel, some refrigerant vapor bubbles will begin to appear in the stream of liquid supplied to the expansion valve. This vapor decreases the capacity of the expansion valve very little as the valve opens to compensate for its presence. As the quantity of liquid in the condenser decreases, the operating pressure will drop there and throughout the high side of the system. As the R-12 continues to be expelled, the pressure available to force the liquid through the expansion valve will continue to decrease, and, even-

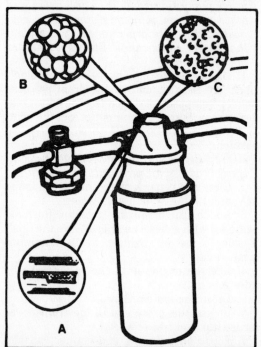

Oil streaks (A), constant bubbles (B) or foam (C) indicate there is not enough refrigerant in the system. Occasional bubbles during initial operation is normal. A clear sight glass indicates a proper charge of refrigerant or no refrigerant at all, which can be determined by the presence of cold air at the outlets in the car. If the glass is clouded with a milky white substance, have the receiver/drier checked professionally

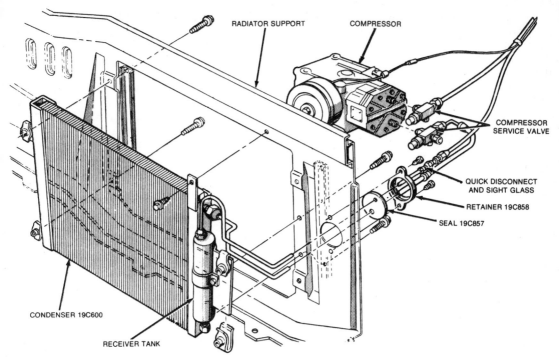

RADIATOR SUPPORT   COMPRESSOR

COMPRESSOR SERVICE VALVE

QUICK DISCONNECT AND SIGHT GLASS

RETAINER 19C858

SEAL 19C857

CONDENSER 19C600

RECEIVER TANK

Typical air conditioning installation

tually, the valve's orifice will prove to be too much of a restriction for adequate flow even with the needle fully withdrawn.

At this point, low side pressure will start to drop, and severe reduction in cooling capacity, marked by freeze-up of the evaporator coil, will result. Eventually, the operating pressure of the evaporator will be lower than the pressure of the atmosphere surrounding it, and air will be drawn into the system wherever there are leaks in the low side.

Because all atmospheric air contains at least some moisture, water will enter the system and mix with the R-12 and the oil. Trace amounts of moisture will cause sludging of the oil, and corrosion of the system. Saturation and clogging of the filter/drier, and freezing of the expansion valve orifice will eventually result. As air fills the system to a greater and greater extend, it will interfere more and more with the normal flows of refrigerant and heat.

A list of general precautions that should be observed while doing this follows:

1. Keep all tools as clean and dry as possible.
2. Thoroughly purge the service gauges and hoses of air and moisture before connecting them to the system. Keep them capped when not in use.
3. Thoroughly clean any refrigerant fitting before disconnecting it, in order to minimize the entrance of dirt into the system.
4. Plan any operation that requires opening the system beforehand in order to minimize the length of time it will be exposed to open air. Cap or seal the open ends to minimize the entrance of foreign material.

5. When adding oil, pour it through an extremely clean and dry tube or funnel. Keep the oil capped whenever possible. Do not use oil that has not been kept tightly sealed.

6. Use only refrigerant 12. Purchase refrigerant intended for use in only automotive air conditioning system. Avoid the use of refrigerant 12 that may be packaged for another use, such as cleaning, or powering a horn, as it is impure.

7. Completely evacuate any system that has been opened to replace a component, other than when isolating the compressor, or that has leaked sufficiently to draw in moisture and air. This requires evacuating air and moisture with a good vacuum pump for at least one hour.

If a system has been open for a considerable length of time it may be advisable to evacuate the system for up to 12 hours (overnight).

8. Use a wrench on both halves of a fitting that is to be disconnected, so as to avoid placing torque on any of the refrigerant lines.

ADDITIONAL PREVENTIVE MAINTENANCE CHECKS

Antifreeze

In order to prevent heater core freeze-up during A/C operation, it is necessary to maintain permanent type antifreeze protection of + 15°F (−9°C) or lower. A reading of −15°F (−26°C) is ideal since this protection also supplies sufficient corrosion inhibitors for the protection of the engine cooling system.

WARNING: *Do not use antifreeze longer than specified by the manufacturer.*

Radiator Cap

For efficient operation of an air conditioned truck's cooling system, the radiator cap should have a holding pressure which meets manufacturer's specifications. A cap which fails to hold these pressure should be replaced.

Condenser

Any obstruction of or damage to the condenser configuration will restrict the air flow which is essential to its efficient operation. It is therefore, a good rule to keep this unit clean and in proper physical shape.

NOTE: *Bug screens are regarded as obstructions.*

Condensation Drain Tube

This single molded drain tube expels the condensation, which accumulates on the bottom of the evaporator housing, into the engine compartment.

If this tube is obstructed, the air conditioning performance can be restricted and condensation buildup can spill over onto the vehicle's floor.

SAFETY PRECAUTIONS

Because of the importance of the necessary safety precautions that must be exercised when working with air conditioning systems and R-12 refrigerant, a recap of the safety precautions are outlined.

1. Avoid contact with a charged refrigeration system, even when working on another part of the air conditioning system or vehicle. If a heavy tool comes into contact with a section of copper tubing or a heat exchanger, it can easily cause the relatively soft material to rupture.

2. When it is necessary to apply force to a fitting which contains refrigerant, as when checking that all system couplings are securely tightened, use a wrench on both parts of the fitting involved, if possible. This will avoid putting torque on the refrigerant tubing. (It is advisable, when possible, to use tube or line wrenches when tightening these flare nut fittings.)

3. Do not attempt to discharge the system by merely loosening a fitting, or removing the service valve caps and cracking these valves. Precise control is possibly only when using the service gauges. Place a rag under the open end of the center charging hose while discharging the system to catch any drops of liquid that might escape. Wear protective gloves when connecting or disconnecting service gauge hoses.

4. Discharge the system only in a well ventilated area, as high concentrations of the gas can exclude oxygen and act as an anesthetic. When leak testing or soldering this is particularly important, as toxic gas is formed when R-12 contacts any flame.

5. Never start a system without first verifying that both service valves are backseated, if equipped, and that all fittings throughout the system are snugly connected.

6. Avoid applying heat to any refrigerant line or storage vessel. Charging may be aided by using water heated to less than 125°F (52°C) to warm the refrigerant container. Never allow a refrigerant storage container to sit out in the sun, or near any other source of heat, such as a radiator.

7. Always wear goggles when working on a system to protect the eyes. If refrigerant contacts the eye, it is advisable in all cases to see a physician as soon as possible.

8. Frostbite from liquid refrigerant should be treated by first gradually warming the area with cool water, and then gently applying petroleum jelly. A physician should be consulted.

9. Always keep refrigerant can fittings capped when not in use. Avoid sudden shock to the can which might occur from dropping it, or from banging a heavy tool against it. Never carry a refrigerant can in the passenger compartment of a truck.

10. Always completely discharge the system before painting the vehicle (if the paint is to be baked on), or before welding anywhere near the refrigerant lines.

TEST GAUGES

Most of the service work performed in air conditioning requires the use of a set of two gauges, one for the high (head) pressure side of the system, the other for the low (suction) side.

The low side gauge records both pressure and vacuum. Vacuum readings are calibrated from 0 to 30 inches Hg and the pressure graduations read from 0 to no less than 60 psi.

The high side gauge measures pressure from 0 to at last 600 psi.

Both gauges are threaded into a manifold that contains two hand shut-off valves. Proper manipulation of these valves and the use of the attached test hoses allow the user to perform the following services:

1. Test high and low side pressures.

2. Remove air, moisture, and contaminated refrigerant.

3. Purge the system (of refrigerant).

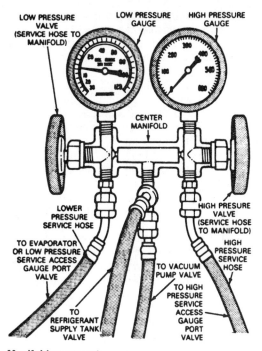

Manifold gauge set

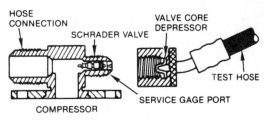

Schrader valve

4. Charge the system (with refrigerant).

The manifold valves are designed so that they have no direct effect on gauge readings, but serve only to provide for, or cut off, flow of refrigerant through the manifold. During all testing and hook-up operations, the valves are kept in a close position to avoid disturbing the refrigeration system. The valves are opened only to purge the system or refrigerant or to charge it.

INSPECTION

CAUTION: *The compressed refrigerant used in the air conditioning system expands into the atmosphere at a temperature of −21.7°F(−*

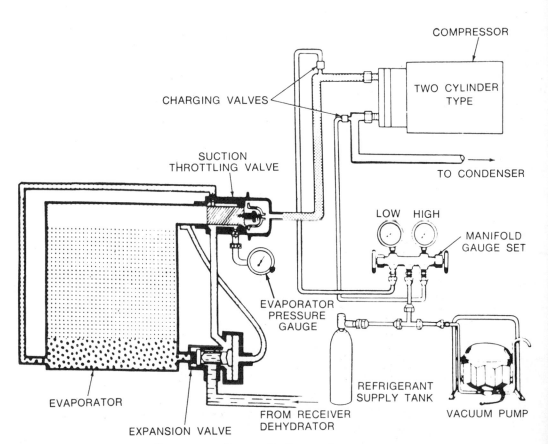

Gauge connections on the Tecumseh compressor

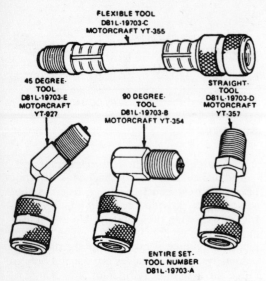

FLEXIBLE TOOL
D81L-19703-C
MOTORCRAFT YT-355

45 DEGREE-
TOOL
D81L-19703-E
MOTORCRAFT
YT-927

90 DEGREE-
TOOL
D81L-19703-B
MOTORCRAFT YT-354

STRAIGHT-
TOOL
D81L-19703-D
MOTORCRAFT
YT-357

ENTIRE SET-
TOOL NUMBER
D81L-19703-A

High pressure service valve and adapter

30°C) or lower. This will freeze any surface, including your eyes, that it contacts. In addition, the refrigerant decomposes into a poisonous gas in the presence of a flame. Do not open or disconnect any part of the air conditioning system._

Sight Glass Check

You can safely make a few simple checks to determine if your air conditioning system needs service. The tests work best if the temperature is warm (about 70°F [21.1°C]).

NOTE: _If your vehicle is equipped with an aftermarket air conditioner, the following system check may not apply. You should con- tact the manufacturer of the unit for instructions on systems checks._

1. Place the automatic transmission in Park or the manual transmission in Neutral. Set the parking brake.

2. Run the engine at a fast idle (about 1,500 rpm) either with the help of a friend or by temporarily readjusting the idle speed screw.

3. Set the controls for maximum cold with the blower on High.

4. Locate the sight glass in one of the system lines. Usually it is on the left alongside the top of the radiator.

5. If you see bubbles, the system must be recharged. Very likely there is a leak at some point.

6. If there are no bubbles, there is either no refrigerant at all or the system is fully charged. Feel the two hoses going to the belt driven compressor. If they are both at the same temperature, the system is empty and must be recharged.

7. If one hose (high pressure) is warm and the other (low pressure) is cold, the system may be all right. However, you are probably making these tests because you think there is something wrong, so proceed to the next step.

8. Have an assistant in the truck turn the fan control on and off to operate the compressor clutch. Watch the sight glass.

9. If bubbles appear when the clutch is disengaged and disappear when it is engaged, the system is properly charged.

10. If the refrigerant takes more than 45 seconds to bubble when the clutch is disengaged, the system is overcharged. This usually causes poor cooling at low speeds.

WARNING: _If it is determined that the system has a leak, it should be corrected as soon_

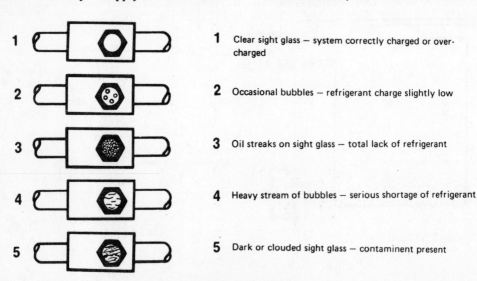

1   Clear sight glass — system correctly charged or over-charged

2   Occasional bubbles — refrigerant charge slightly low

3   Oil streaks on sight glass — total lack of refrigerant

4   Heavy stream of bubbles — serious shortage of refrigerant

5   Dark or clouded sight glass — contaminent present

Sight glass inspection

as possible. Leaks may allow moisture to enter and cause a very expensive rust problem.

Exercise the air conditioner for a few minutes, every two weeks or so, during the cold months. This avoids the possibility of the compressor seals drying out from lack of lubrication.

TESTING THE SYSTEM

1. Connect a gauge set.
2. Close (clockwise) both gauge set valves.
3. Park the truck in the shade, at least 5 feet from any walls. Start the engine, set the parking brake, place the transmission in NEUTRAL and establish an idle of 1,100-1,300 rpm.
4. Run the air conditioning system for full cooling, in the MAX or COLD mode.
5. The low pressure gauge should read 5-20 psi; the high pressure gauge should indicate 120-180 psi.

WARNING: *These pressures are the norm for an ambient temperature of 70-80°F (21-27°F). Higher air temperatures along with high humidity will cause higher syustem pressures. At idle speed and an ambient temperature of 110°F (43°F), the high pressure reading can exceed 300 psi.*

Under these extreme conditions, you can keep the pressures down by directing a large electric floor fan through the condenser.

DISCHARGING THE SYSTEM

1. Remove the caps from the high and low pressure charging valves in the high and low pressure lines.
2. Turn both manifold gauge set hand valves to the fully closed (clockwise) position.
3. Connect the manifold gauge set.
4. If the gauge set hoses do not have the gauge port actuating pins, install fitting adapters T71P-19703-S and R on the manifold gauge set hoses. If the truck does not have a service access gauge port valve, connect the gauge set low pressure hose to the evaporator service access gauge port valve. A special adapter, T77L-19703-A, is required to attach the manifold gauge set to the high pressure service access gauge port valve.
5. Place the end of the center hose away from you and the truck.
6. Open the low pressure gauge valve slightly and allow the system pressure to bleed off.
7. When the system is just about empty, open the high pressure valve very slowly to avoid losing an excessive amount of refrigerant oil. Allow any remaining refrigerant to escape.

EVACUATING THE SYSTEM

NOTE: *This procedure requires the use of a vacuum pump.*

1. Connect the manifold gauge set.
2. Discharge the system.
3. Make sure that the low pressure gauge set hose is connected to the low pressure service gauge port on the top center of the accumulator/drier assembly and the high pressure hose connected to the high pressure service gauge port on the compressor discharge line.
4. Connect the center service hose to the inlet fitting of the vacuum pump.
5. Turn both gauge set valves to the wide open position.
6. Start the pump and note the low side gauge reading.
7. Operate the pump until the low pressure gauge reads 25-30 in.Hg. Continue running the vacuum pump for 10 minutes more. If you've replaced some component in the system, run the pump for an additional 20-30 minutes.
8. Leak test the system. Close both gauge set valves. Turn off the pump. The needle should remain stationary at the point at which the pump was turned off. If the needle drops to zero rapidly, there is a leak in the system which must be repaired.

LEAK TESTING

Some leak tests can be performed with a soapy water solution. There must be at least a ½ lb. charge in the system for a leak to be detected. The most extensive leak tests are performed with either a Halide flame type leak tester or the more preferable electronic leak tester.

In either case, the equipment is expensive, and, the use of a Halide detector can be **extremely** hazardous!

CHARGING THE SYSTEM

CAUTION: *NEVER OPEN THE HIGH PRESSURE SIDE WITH A CAN OF REFRIGERANT CONNECTED TO THE SYSTEM! OPENING THE HIGH PRESSURE SIDE WILL OVERPRESSURIZE THE CAN, CAUSING IT TO EXPLODE!*

Systems With Sight Glass

In this procedure the refrigerant enters the suction side of the system as a vapor while the compressor is running. Before proceeding, the system should be in a partial vacuum after adequate evacuation. Both hand valves on the gauge manifold should be closed.

1. Attach both test hoses to their respective service valve ports. Mid-position manually operated service valves, if present.
2. Install the dispensing valve (closed position) on the refrigerant container. (Single and multiple refrigerant manifolds are available to accommodate one to four 15 oz. cans.)

Pressure Diagnosis

Condition	Possible Cause	Correction
Low side low— High side low	System refrigerant low	Evacuate, leak test, and charge system
Low side high— High side low	Internal leak in compressor— worn	Remove compressor cylinder head and inspect compressor. Replace valve plate assembly if necessary. If compressor pistons, rings, or cylinders are excessively worn or scored, replace compressor.
	Head gasket leaking	Install new cylinder head gasket
	Expansion valve	Replace expansion valve
	Drive belt slipping	Set belt tension
Low side high— High side high	Clogged condenser fins	Clean out condenser fins
	Air in system	Evacuate, leak test, and charge system
	Expansion valve	Replace expansion valve
	Loose or worn fan belts	Adjust or replace belts as necessary
Low side low— High side high	Expansion valve	Replace expansion valve
	Restriction in liquid line	Check line for kinks—replace if necessary
	Restriction in receiver	Replace receiver
	Restriction in condenser	Replace condenser
Low side and high side normal (inadequate cooling)	Air in system	Evacuate, leak test, and charge system
	Moisture in system	Evacuate, leak test, and charge system.

3. Attach the center charging hose to the refrigerant container valve.

4. Open dispensing valve on the refrigerant valve.

5. Loosen the center charging hose coupler where it connect to the gauge manifold to allow the escaping refrigerant to purge the hose of contaminants.

6. Tighten the center charging hose connector.

7. Purge the low pressure test hose at the gauge manifold.

8. Start the truck engine, roll down the truck windows and adjust the air conditioner to maximum cooling. The truck engine should be at normal operating temperature before proceeding. The heated environment helps the liquid vaporize more efficiently.

9. Crack open the low side hand valve on the manifold. Manipulate the valve so that the refrigerant that enters the system does not cause the low side pressure to exceed 40 psi. Too sudden a surge may permit the entrance of unwanted liquid to the compressor. Since liquids cannot be compressed, the compressor will suffer damage if compelled to attempt it. If the suction side of the system remains in a vacuum the system is blocked. Locate and correct the condition before proceeding any further.

NOTE: *Placing the refrigerant can in a container of warm water (no hotter than +125°F [+51.6°C]) will speed the charging process. Slight agitation of the can is helpful too, but be careful not to turn the can upside down.*

Systems Without Sight Glass

1. Connect the gauge set.

2. Close (clockwise) both gauge set valves.

3. Connect the center hose to the refrigerant can opener valve.

4. Make sure the can opener valve is closed, that is, the needle is raised, and connect the valve to the can. Open the valve, puncturing the can with the needle.

5. Loosen the center hose fitting at the pressure gauge, allowing refrigerant to purge the hose of air. When the air is bled, tighten the fitting.

CAUTION: *IF THE LOW PRESSURE GAUGE SET HOSE IS NOT CONNECTED TO THE ACCUMULATOR/DRIER, KEEP THE CAN IN AN UPRIGHT POSITION!*

6. Disconnect the wire harness snap-lock connector from the clutch cycling pressure switch and install a jumper wire across the two terminals of the connector.

7. Open the low side gauge set valve and the can valve.

8. Allow refrigerant to be drawn into the system.

9. When no more refrigerant is drawn into the system, start the engine and run it at about 1,500 rpm. Turn on the system and operate it at the full high position. The compressor will operate and pull refrigerant gas into the system.

NOTE: *To help speed the process, the can may be placed, upright, in a pan of warm water, not exceeding 125°F (52°C).*

10. If more than one can of refrigerant is needed, close the can valve and gauge set low side valve when the can is empty and connect a new can to the opener. Repeat the charging process until no more refirgerant is drawn into the system. The frost line on the outside of the can will indicate what portion of the can has been used.

CAUTION: *NEVER ALLOW THE HIGH PRESSURE SIDE READING TO EXCEED 240 psi.*

11. When the charging process has been completed, close the gauge set valve and can valve. Remove the jumper wire and reconnect the cycling clutch wire. Run the system for at least five minutes to allow it to normalize. Low pressure side reading should be 4-25 psi; high pressure reading should be 120-210 psi at an ambient temperature of 70-90°F (21-32°C).

12. Loosen both service hoses at the gauges to allow any refrigerant to escape. Remove the gauge set and install the dust caps on the service valves.

NOTE: *Multi-can dispensers are available which allow a simultaneous hook-up of up to four 1 lb. cans of R-12.*

CAUTION: *Never exceed the recommended maximum charge for the system. The maximum charge for systems is:*

- Through 1974: 2¼ lb.
- 1975-88 without rear auxiliary system: 3½ lb.
- 1975-88 with rear auxiliary system: 4¼ lb.

Troubleshooting Basic Air Conditioning Problems

Problem	Cause	Solution
There's little or no air coming from the vents (and you're sure it's on)	• The A/C fuse is blown • Broken or loose wires or connections • The on/off switch is defective	• Check and/or replace fuse • Check and/or repair connections • Replace switch
The air coming from the vents is not cool enough	• Windows and air vent wings open • The compressor belt is slipping • Heater is on • Condenser is clogged with debris • Refrigerant has escaped through a leak in the system • Receiver/drier is plugged	• Close windows and vent wings • Tighten or replace compressor belt • Shut heater off • Clean the condenser • Check system • Service system
The air has an odor	• Vacuum system is disrupted • Odor producing substances on the evaporator case • Condensation has collected in the bottom of the evaporator housing	• Have the system checked/repaired • Clean the evaporator case • Clean the evaporator housing drains
System is noisy or vibrating	• Compressor belt or mountings loose • Air in the system	• Tighten or replace belt; tighten mounting bolts • Have the system serviced

Sight glass condition
  Constant bubbles, foam or oil streaks
  Clear sight glass, but no cold air
  Clear sight glass, but air is cold
  Clouded with milky fluid
	• Undercharged system
	• No refrigerant at all
	• System is OK
	• Receiver drier is leaking dessicant
		• Charge the system
		• Check and charge the system
		• Have system checked

Large difference in temperature of lines	• System undercharged	• Charge and leak test the system
Compressor noise	• Broken valves • Overcharged • Incorrect oil level	• Replace the valve plate • Discharge, evacuate and install the correct charge • Isolate the compressor and check the oil level. Correct as necessary.

Troubleshooting Basic Air Conditioning Problems (cont.)

Problem	Cause	Solution
Compressor noise (cont.)	• Piston slap • Broken rings • Drive belt pulley bolts are loose	• Replace the compressor • Replace the compressor • Tighten with the correct torque specification
Excessive vibration	• Incorrect belt tension • Clutch loose • Overcharged • Pulley is misaligned	• Adjust the belt tension • Tighten the clutch • Discharge, evacuate and install the correct charge • Align the pulley
Condensation dripping in the passenger compartment	• Drain hose plugged or improperly positioned • Insulation removed or improperly installed	• Clean the drain hose and check for proper installation • Replace the insulation on the expansion valve and hoses
Frozen evaporator coil	• Faulty thermostat • Thermostat capillary tube improperly installed • Thermostat not adjusted properly	• Replace the thermostat • Install the capillary tube correctly • Adjust the thermostat
Low side low—high side low	• System refrigerant is low • Expansion valve is restricted	• Evacuate, leak test and charge the system • Replace the expansion valve
Low side high—high side low	• Internal leak in the compressor—worn • Cylinder head gasket is leaking • Expansion valve is defective • Drive belt slipping	• Remove the compressor cylinder head and inspect the compressor. Replace the valve plate assembly if necessary. If the compressor pistons, rings or cylinders are excessively worn or scored replace the compressor • Install a replacement cylinder head gasket • Replace the expansion valve • Adjust the belt tension
Low side high—high side high	• Condenser fins obstructed • Air in the system • Expansion valve is defective • Loose or worn fan belts	• Clean the condenser fins • Evacuate, leak test and charge the system • Replace the expansion valve • Adjust or replace the belts as necessary
Low side low—high side high	• Expansion valve is defective • Restriction in the refrigerant hose • Restriction in the receiver/drier • Restriction in the condenser	• Replace the expansion valve • Check the hose for kinks—replace if necessary • Replace the receiver/drier • Replace the condenser
Low side and high side normal (inadequate cooling)	• Air in the system • Moisture in the system	• Evacuate, leak test and charge the system • Evacuate, leak test and charge the system

Windshield Wipers

Intense heat from the sun, snow, and ice, road oils and the chemicals used in windshield washer solvent combine to deteriorate the rubber wiper refills. The refills should be replaced about twice a year or whenever the blades begin to streak or chatter.

WIPER REFILL REPLACEMENT

Normally, if the wipers are not cleaning the windshield properly, only the refill has to be replaced. The blade and arm usually require replacement only in the event of damage. It is not necessary (except on new Tridon® refills) to remove the arm or the blade to replace the refill (rubber part), though you may have to position the arm higher on the glass. You can do this turning the ignition switch on and operating the wipers. When they are positioned where they are accessible, turn the ignition switch to the **off** position.

There are several types of refills and your vehicle could have any kind, since aftermarket

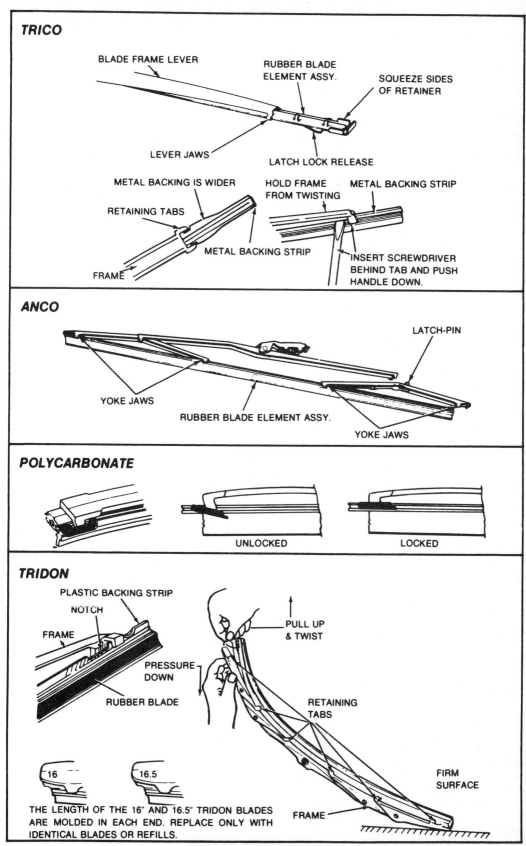

TRICO

BLADE FRAME LEVER

RUBBER BLADE ELEMENT ASSY.

SQUEEZE SIDES OF RETAINER

LEVER JAWS

LATCH LOCK RELEASE

METAL BACKING IS WIDER

RETAINING TABS

FRAME

METAL BACKING STRIP

HOLD FRAME FROM TWISTING

METAL BACKING STRIP

INSERT SCREWDRIVER BEHIND TAB AND PUSH HANDLE DOWN.

ANCO

LATCH-PIN

YOKE JAWS

RUBBER BLADE ELEMENT ASSY.

YOKE JAWS

POLYCARBONATE

UNLOCKED

LOCKED

TRIDON

PLASTIC BACKING STRIP

NOTCH

FRAME

PULL UP & TWIST

PRESSURE DOWN

RUBBER BLADE

RETAINING TABS

16

16.5

THE LENGTH OF THE 16" AND 16.5" TRIDON BLADES ARE MOLDED IN EACH END. REPLACE ONLY WITH IDENTICAL BLADES OR REFILLS.

FRAME

FIRM SURFACE

Popular styles of wiper refills

blades and arms may not use exactly the same type refill as the original equipment.

Most Anco® styles use a release button that is pushed down to allow the refill to slide out of the yoke jaws. The new refill slides in and locks in place.

Some Trico® refills are removed by locating where the metal backing strip or the refill is wider. Insert a small screwdriver blade between the frame and metal backing strip. Press down to release the refill from the retaining tab.

Other Trico® blades are unlocked at one end by squeezing 2 metal tabs, and the refill is slid out of the frame jaws. When the new refill is installed, the tabs will click into place, locking the refill.

The polycarbonate type is held in place by a locking lever that is pushed downward out of the groove in the arm to free the refill. When the new refill is installed, it will lock in place automatically.

The Tridon® refill has a plastic backing strip with a notch about 1″ (25mm) from the end. Hold the blade (frame) on a hard surface so that the frame is tightly bowed. Grip the tip of the backing strip and pull up while twisting counterclockwise. The backing strip will snap out of the retaining tab. Do this for the remaining tabs until the refill is free of the arm. The length of these refills is molded into the end and they should be replaced with identical types.

No matter which type of refill you use, be sure that all of the frame claws engage the refill. Before operating the wipers, be sure that no part of the metal frame is contacting the windshield.

Tires and Wheels

The tires should be rotated as specified in the Maintenance Intervals Chart. Refer to the accompanying illustrations for the recommended rotation patterns.

The tires on your truck should have built-in tread wear indicators, which appear as $\frac{1}{2}$″ (12.7mm) bands when the tread depth gets as low as $\frac{1}{16}$″ (1.6mm). When the indicators appear in 2 or more adjacent grooves, it's time for new tires.

For optimum tire life, you should keep the tires properly inflated, rotate them often and have the wheel alignment checked periodically.

Some late models have the maximum load pressures listed in the V.I.N. plate on the left door frame. In general, pressure of 28–32 psi would be suitable for highway use with moderate loads and passenger truck type tires (load range B, non-flotation) of original equipment size. Pressures should be checked before driving, since pressure can increase as much as 6

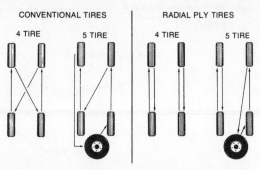

Tire rotation patterns—the radial tire pattern may also be used for bias or bias-belted tires

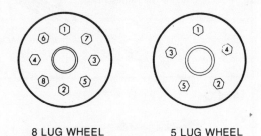

8 LUG WHEEL   5 LUG WHEEL

Lug nut torque sequences

psi due to heat. It is a good idea to have an accurate gauge and to check pressures weekly. Not all gauges on service station air pumps are to be trusted. In general, truck type tires require higher pressures and flotation type tires, lower pressures.

TIRE ROTATION

It is recommended that you have the tires rotated every 6,000 miles. There is no way to give a tire rotation diagram for every combination of tires and vehicles, but the accompanying diagrams are a general rule to follow. Radial tires should not be cross-switched; they last longer if their direction of rotation is not changed. Truck tires sometimes have directional tread, indicated by arrows on the sidewalls; the arrow shows the direction of rotation. They will wear very rapidly if reversed. Studded snow tires will lose

Recommended Lug Nut Torques

1961–86	5 lug		90 ft. lbs.
1968–73	8 lug		135 ft. lbs.
1974–88	8 lug	E-250	90 ft. lbs.
		E-300, 350	135 ft. lbs.
		E-300, 350 dual wheels	210 ft. lbs.

Tread wear indicators are built into all new tires. When they appear, it's time to replace the tires

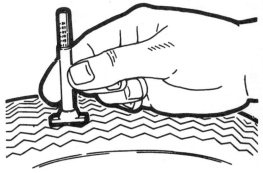

Tread depth can also be checked with an inexpensive gauge made for the purpose

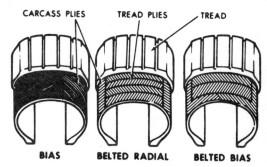

CARCASS PLIES   TREAD PLIES   TREAD

BIAS   BELTED RADIAL   BELTED BIAS

Types of tire construction

Tread depth can be checked with a penny; when the top of Lincoln's head is visible, it's time for new tires

their studs if their direction of rotation is reversed.

NOTE: *Mark the wheel position or direction of rotation on radial tires or studded snow tires before removing them.*

If your truck is equipped with tires having different load ratings on the front and the rear, the tires should not be rotated front to rear. Rotating these tires could affect tire life (the tires with the lower rating will wear faster, and could become overloaded), and upset the handling of the truck.

TIRE USAGE

The tires on your truck were selected to provide the best all around performance for normal operation when inflated as specified. Oversize tires (Load Range D) will not increase the maximum carrying capacity of the vehicle, although they will provide an extra margin of tread life.

Be sure to check overall height before using larger size tires which may cause interference with suspension components or wheel wells. When replacing conventional tire sizes with other tire size designations, be sure to check the manufacturer's recommendations. Interchangeability is not always possible because of differences in load ratings, tire dimensions, wheel well clearances, and rim size. Also due to differences in handling characteristics, 70 Series and 60 Series tires should be used only in pairs on the same axle; radial tires should be used only in sets of four.

The wheels must be the correct width for the tire. Tire dealers have charts of tire and rim compatibility. A mismatch can cause sloppy handling and rapid tread wear. The old rule of thumb is that the tread width should match the rim width (inside bead to inside bead) within an inch. For radial tires, the rim width should be 80% or less of the tire (not tread) width.

The height (mounted diameter) of the new tires can greatly change speedometer accuracy, engine speed at a given road speed, fuel mileage, acceleration, and ground clearance. Tire manufacturers furnish full measurement specifications. Speedometer drive gears are available for correction.

NOTE: *Dimensions of tires marked the same size may vary significantly, even among tires from the same manufacturer.*

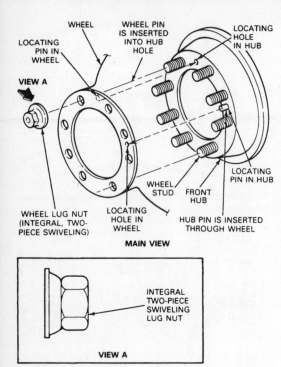

Front wheel installation for E-350 models equipped with dual rear wheels

The spare tire should be usable, at least for low speed operation, with the new tires.

TIRE DESIGN

For maximum satisfaction, tires should be used in sets of five. Mixing or different types (radial, bias-belted, fiberglass belted) should be avoided. Conventional bias tires are constructed so that the cords run bead-to-bead at an angle. Alternate plies run at an opposite angle. This type of construction gives rigidity to both tread and sidewall. Bias-belted tires are similar in construction to conventional bias ply tires. Belts run at an angle and also at a 90° angle to the bead, as in the radial tire. Tread life is improved considerably over the conventional bias tire. The radial tire differs in construction, but instead of the carcass plies running at an angle of 90° to each other, they run at an angle of 90° to the bead. This gives the tread a great deal of rigidity and the sidewall a great deal of flexibility and accounts for the characteristic bulge associated with radial tires.

Radial tire are recommended for use on all Ford trucks. If they are used, tire sizes and wheel diameters should be selected to maintain ground clearance and tire load capacity equivalent to the minimum specified tire. Radial tires should always be used in sets of five, but in an emergency radial tires can be used with caution on the rear axle only. If this is done, both tires on the rear should be of radial design.

NOTE: *Radial tires should never be used on only the front axle.*

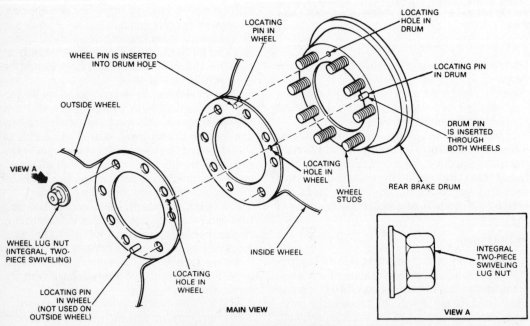

E-350 dual rear wheel installation

Troubleshooting Basic Wheel Problems

Problem	Cause	Solution
The car's front end vibrates at high speed	• The wheels are out of balance • Wheels are out of alignment	• Have wheels balanced • Have wheel alignment checked/adjusted
Car pulls to either side	• Wheels are out of alignment • Unequal tire pressure • Different size tires or wheels	• Have wheel alignment checked/adjusted • Check/adjust tire pressure • Change tires or wheels to same size
The car's wheel(s) wobbles	• Loose wheel lug nuts • Wheels out of balance • Damaged wheel • Wheels are out of alignment • Worn or damaged ball joint • Excessive play in the steering linkage (usually due to worn parts) • Defective shock absorber	• Tighten wheel lug nuts • Have tires balanced • Raise car and spin the wheel. If the wheel is bent, it should be replaced • Have wheel alignment checked/adjusted • Check ball joints • Check steering linkage • Check shock absorbers
Tires wear unevenly or prematurely	• Incorrect wheel size • Wheels are out of balance • Wheels are out of alignment	• Check if wheel and tire size are compatible • Have wheels balanced • Have wheel alignment checked/adjusted

Troubleshooting Basic Tire Problems

Problem	Cause	Solution
The car's front end vibrates at high speeds and the steering wheel shakes	• Wheels out of balance • Front end needs aligning	• Have wheels balanced • Have front end alignment checked
The car pulls to one side while cruising	• Unequal tire pressure (car will usually pull to the low side) • Mismatched tires • Front end needs aligning	• Check/adjust tire pressure • Be sure tires are of the same type and size • Have front end alignment checked
Abnormal, excessive or uneven tire wear See "How to Read Tire Wear"	• Infrequent tire rotation • Improper tire pressure • Sudden stops/starts or high speed on curves	• Rotate tires more frequently to equalize wear • Check/adjust pressure • Correct driving habits
Tire squeals	• Improper tire pressure • Front end needs aligning	• Check/adjust tire pressure • Have front end alignment checked

Tire Size Comparison Chart

"Letter" sizes			Inch Sizes	Metric-inch Sizes		
"60 Series"	"70 Series"	"78 Series"	1965–77	"60 Series"	"70 Series"	"80 Series"
			5.50-12, 5.60-12	165/60-12	165/70-12	155-12
		Y78-12	6.00-12			
		W78-13	5.20-13	165/60-13	145/70-13	135-13
		Y78-13	5.60-13	175/60-13	155/70-13	145-13
			6.15-13	185/60-13	165/70-13	155-13, P155/80-13
A60-13	A70-13	A78-13	6.40-13	195/60-13	175/70-13	165-13

Tire Size Comparison Chart (cont.)

"Letter" sizes			Inch Sizes	Metric-inch Sizes		
"60 Series"	"70 Series"	"78 Series"	1965–77	"60 Series"	"70 Series"	"80 Series"
B60-13	B70-13	B78-13	6.70-13	205/60-13	185/70-13	175-13
			6.90-13			
C60-13	C70-13	C78-13	7.00-13	215/60-13	195/70-13	185-13
D60-13	D70-13	D78-13	7.25-13			
E60-13	E70-13	E78-13	7.75-13			195-13
			5.20-14	165/60-14	145/70-14	135-14
			5.60-14	175/60-14	155/70-14	145-14
			5.90-14			
A60-14	A70-14	A78-14	6.15-14	185/60-14	165/70-14	155-14
	B70-14	B78-14	6.45-14	195/60-14	175/70-14	165-14
	C70-14	C78-14	6.95-14	205/60-14	185/70-14	175-14
D60-14	D70-14	D78-14				
E60-14	E70-14	E78-14	7.35-14	215/60-14	195/70-14	185-14
F60-14	F70-14	F78-14, F83-14	7.75-14	225/60-14	200/70-14	195-14
G60-14	G70-14	G77-14, G78-14	8.25-14	235/60-14	205/70-14	205-14
H60-14	H70-14	H78-14	8.55-14	245/60-14	215/70-14	215-14
J60-14	J70-14	J78-14	8.85-14	255/60-14	225/70-14	225-14
L60-14	L70-14		9.15-14	265/60-14	235/70-14	
	A70-15	A78-15	5.60-15	185/60-15	165/70-15	155-15
B60-15	B70-15	B78-15	6.35-15	195/60-15	175/70-15	165-15
C60-15	C70-15	C78-15	6.85-15	205/60-15	185/70-15	175-15
	D70-15	D78-15				
E60-15	E70-15	E78-15	7.35-15	215/60-15	195/70-15	185-15
F60-15	F70-15	F78-15	7.75-15	225/60-15	205/70-15	195-15
G60-15	G70-15	G78-15	8.15-15/8.25-15	235/60-15	215/70-15	205-15
H60-15	H70-15	H78-15	8.45-15/8.55-15	245/60-15	225/70-15	215-15
J60-15	J70-15	J78-15	8.85-15/8.90-15	255/60-15	235/70-15	225-15
	K70-15		9.00-15	265/60-15	245/70-15	230-15
L60-15	L70-15	L78-15, L84-15	9.15-15			235-15
	M70-15	M78-15				255-15
		N78-15				

Note: Every size tire is not listed and many size comparisons are approximate, based on load ratings. Wider tires than those supplied new with the vehicle, should always be checked for clearance.

FLUIDS AND LUBRICANTS

Oil and Fuel Recommendations

Gasoline Engines

All 1961-74 Ford Vans are designed to run on leaded gasoline. From 1975, any truck originally equipped with a catalyic converter must use unleaded gasoline.

The recommended oil viscosities for sustained temperatures ranging from below 0°F (–18°C) to above 32°F (0°C) are listed in this chapter. They are broken down into multiviscosities and single viscosities. Multiviscosity oils are recommended because of their wider range of acceptable temperatures and driving conditions.

When adding oil to the crankcase or changing the oil or filter, it is important that oil of an equal quality to original equipment be used in your truck. The use of inferior oils may void the warranty, damage your engine, or both.

The SAE (Society of Automotive Engineers) grade number of oil indicates the viscosity of

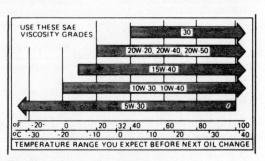

Gasoline engine oil selection chart

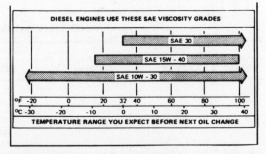

Diesel engine oil selection chart

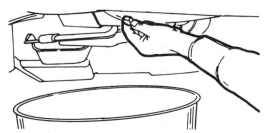

By keeping inward pressure on the plug as you unscrew it, oil won't escape past the threads

Remove the oil filter with a strap wrench

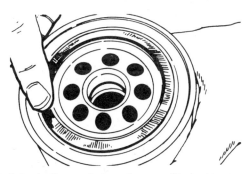

Lubricate the gasket on the new filter with clean engine oil. A dry gasket may not make a good seal and will allow the filter to leak

the oil (its ability to lubricate at a given temperature). The lower the SAE number, the lighter the oil; the lower the viscosity, the easier it is to crank the engine in cold weather but the less the oil will lubricate and protect the engine in high temperatures. This number is marked on every oil container.

Oil viscosities should be chosen from those oils recommended for the lowest anticipated temperatures during the oil change interval. Due to the need for an oil that embodies both good lubrication at high temperatures and easy cranking in cold weather, multigrade oils have been developed. Basically, a multigrade oil is thinner at low temperatures and thicker at high temperatures. For example, a 10W-40 oil (the W stands for winter) exhibits the characteristics of a 10 weight (SAE 10) oil when the truck is first started and the oil is cold. Its lighter weight allows it to travel to the lubricating surfaces quicker and offer less resistance to starter motor cranking than, say, a straight 30 weight (SAE 30) oil. But after the engine reaches operating temperature, the 10W-40 oil begins acting like straight 40 weight (SAE 40) oil, its heavier weight providing greater lubrication with less chance of foaming than a straight 30 weight oil.

The API (American Petroleum Institute) designations, also found on the oil container, indicates the classification of engine oil used under certain given operating conditions. Only oils designated for use Service SF heavy duty detergent should be used in your truck. Oils of the SF type perform may functions inside the engine besides their basic lubrication. Through a balanced system of metallic detergents and polymeric dispersants, the oil prevents high and low temperature deposits and also keeps sludge and dirt particles in suspension. Acids, particularly sulphuric acid, as well as other by-products of engine combustion are neutralized by the oil. If these acids are allowed to concen-

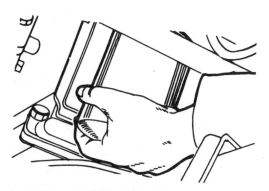

Install the new oil filter by hand

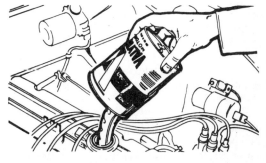

Add oil through the capped opening in the cylinder head cover

trate, they can cause corrosion and rapid wear of the internal engine parts.

WARNING: *Non-detergent motor oils or straight mineral oils should not be used in your Ford gasoline engine.*

Diesel Engines

Diesel engines require different engine oil from those used in gasoline engines. Besides doing the things gasoline engine oil does, diesel oil must also deal with increased engine heat and the diesel blow-by gases, which create sulphuric acid, a high corrosive.

Under the American Petroleum Institute (API) classifications, gasoline engine oil codes begin with an **S**, and diesel engine oil codes begin with a **C**. This first letter designation is followed by a second letter code which explains what type of service (heavy, moderate, light) the oil is meant for. For example, the top of a typical oil can will include: API SERVICES SF, CD. This means the oil in the can is a superior, heavy duty engine oil when used in a diesel engine.

Many diesel manufacturers recommend an oil with both gasoline and diesel engine API classifications.

NOTE: *Ford specifies the use of an engine oil conforming to API service categories of both SF and CD. DO NOT use oils labeled as only SF or only CD as they could cause engine damage.*

Fuel makers produce two grades of diesel fuel, No. 1 and No. 2, for use in automotive diesel engines. Generally speaking, No. 2 fuel is recommended over No. 1 for driving in temperatures above 20°F (–7°C). In fact, in many areas, No. 2 diesel is the only fuel available. By comparison, No. 2 diesel fuel is less volatile than No. 1 fuel, and gives better fuel economy. No. 2 fuel is also a better injection pump lubricant.

Two important characteristics of diesel fuel are its cetane number and its viscosity.

The cetane number of a diesel fuel refers to the ease with which a diesel fuel ignites. High cetane numbers mean that the fuel will ignite with relative ease or that it ignites well at low temperatures. Naturally, the lower the cetane number, the higher the temperature must be to ignite the fuel. Most commercial fuels have cetane numbers that range from 35 to 65. No. 1 diesel fuel generally has a higher cetane rating than No. 2 fuel.

Viscosity is the ability of a liquid, in this case diesel fuel, to flow. Using straight No. 2 diesel fuel below 20°F (–7°C) can cause problems, because this fuel tends to become cloudy, meaning wax crystals begin forming in the fuel. 20°F (–7°C) is often call the cloud point for No. 2 fuel.

In extremely cold weather, No. 2 fuel can stop flowing altogether. In either case, fuel flow is restricted, which can result in no start condition or poor engine performance. Fuel manufacturers often winterize No. 2 diesel fuel by using various fuel additives and blends (no. 1 diesel fuel, kerosene, etc.) to lower its winter time viscosity. Generally speaking, though, No. 1 diesel fuel is more satisfactory in extremely cold weather.

NOTE: *No. 1 and No. 2 diesel fuels will mix and burn with no ill effects, although the engine manufacturer will undoubtedly recommend on or the other. Consult the owner's manual for information.*

Depending on local climate, most fuel manufacturers make winterized No. 2 fuel available seasonally.

Many automobile manufacturers publish pamphlets giving the locations of diesel fuel stations nationwide. Contact the local dealer for information.

Do not substitute home heating oil for automotive diesel fuel. While in some cases, home heating oil refinement levels equal those of diesel fuel, many times they are far below diesel engine requirements. The result of using dirty home heating oil will be a clogged fuel system, in which case the entire system may have to be dismantled and cleaned.

One more word on diesel fuels. Don't thin diesel fuel with gasoline in cold weather. The lighter gasoline, which is more explosive, will cause rough running at the very least, and may cause extensive damage to the fuel system if enough is used.

Engine Oil Level Check

Check the engine oil level every time you fill the gas tank. The oil level should be above the ADD mark and not above the FULL mark on the dipstick. Make sure that the dipstick is inserted into the crankcase as far as possible and that the vehicle is resting on level ground. Also, allow a few minutes after turning off the engine for the oil to drain into the pan or an inaccurate reading will result.

1. Open the hood and remove the engine oil dipstick.

2. Wipe the dipstick with a clean, lint-free rag and reinsert it. Be sure to insert it all the way.

3. Pull out the dipstick and note the oil level. It should be between the **SAFE** (MAX) mark and the **ADD** (MIN) mark.

4. If the level is below the lower mark, replace the dipstick and add fresh oil to bring the level within the proper range. Do not overfill.

5. Recheck the oil level and close the hood.

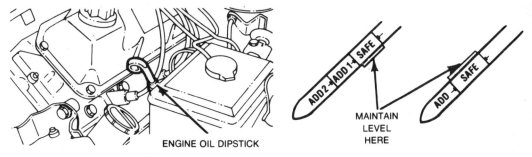

ENGINE OIL DIPSTICK

MAINTAIN
LEVEL
HERE

Checking engine oil level

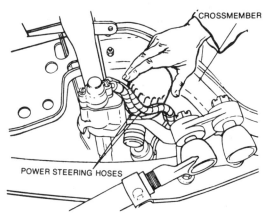

CROSSMEMBER

POWER STEERING HOSES

Removing the oil filter through 1974 with V8 and power steering

NOTE: *Use a multi-grade oil with API classification SF.*

Engine Oil and Filter Change

NOTE: *The engine oil and oil filter should be changed at the same time, at the recommended intervals on the maintenance schedule chart.*

The oil should be changed more frequently if the vehicle is being operated in very dusty areas. Before draining the oil, make sure that the engine is at operating temperature. Hot oil will hold more impurities in suspension and will flow better, allowing the removal of more oil and dirt.

Loosen the drain plug with a wrench, then, unscrew the plug with your fingers, using a rag to shield your fingers from the heat. Push in on the plug as you unscrew it so you can feel when all of the screw threads are out of the hole. You can then remove the plug quickly with the minimum amount of oil running down your arm and you will also have the plug in your hand and not in the bottom of a pan of hot oil. Drain the oil into a suitable receptacle. Be careful of the oil. If it is at operating temperatures it is hot enough to burn you.

The oil filter is located on the left side of all the engines installed in Ford trucks, for longest engine life, it should be changed every time the oil is changed. To remove the filter, you may need an oil filter wrench since the filter may have been fitted too tightly and the heat from the engine may have made it even tighter. A filter wrench can be obtained at an auto parts store and is well worth the investment, since it will save you a lot of grief. Loosen the filter with the filter wrench. With a rag wrapped around the filter, unscrew the filter from the boss on the side of the engine. Be careful of hot oil that will run down the side of the filter. Make sure that you have a pan under the filter before you start to remove it from the engine; should some of the hot oil happen to get on you, you will have a place to dump the filter in a hurry. Wipe the base of the mounting boss with a clean, dry cloth. When you install the new filter, smear a small amount of oil on the gasket with your finger, just enough to coat the entire surface, where it comes in contact with the mounting plate. When you tighten the filter, rotate if only a half turn after it comes in contact with the mounting boss.

Transmission

FLUID RECOMMENDATIONS

Manual Transmissions:
- All models — SAE 85W/90

Automatic Transmissions:
- C4 — Type F
- C6 through 1976 — Type F
- C6 1977 and later — Dexron®II
- AOD — Dexron®II

LEVEL CHECK

Automatic Transmissions

It is very important to maintain the proper fluid level in an automatic transmission. If the level is either too high or too low, poor shifting operation and internal damage are likely to occur. For this reason a regular check of the fluid level is essential.

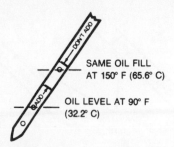

SAME OIL FILL
AT 150° F (65.6° C)

OIL LEVEL AT 90° F
(32.2° C)

Typical fluid level expansion with the rise from room to operating temperature

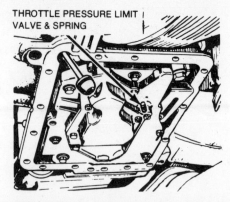

THROTTLE PRESSURE LIMIT
VALVE & SPRING

C4 throttle pressure limit valve and spring. They are held in place by the filter. The valve is installed with the large end toward the valve body; the spring fits over the valve stem

1. Drive the vehicle for 15-20 minutes to allow the transmission to reach operating temperature.

2. Park the truck on a level surface, apply the parking brake and leave the engine idling. Shift the transmission and engage each gear, then place the gear selector in **P** (PARK).

3. Wipe away any dirt in the areas of the transmission dipstick to prevent it from falling into the filler tube. Withdraw the dipstick, wipe it with a clean, lint-free rag and reinsert it until it seats.

4. Withdraw the dipstick and note the fluid level. It should be between the upper (FULL) mark and the lower (ADD) mark.

5. If the level is below the lower mark, use a funnel and add fluid in small quantities through the dipstick filler neck. Keep the engine running while adding fluid and check the level after each small amount. Do not overfill.

Manual Transmission

The fluid level should be checked every 6 months/6,000 miles, whichever comes first.

1. Park the truck on a level surface, turn off the engine, apply the parking brake and block the wheels.

2. Remove the filler plug from the side of the transmission case with a proper size wrench. The fluid level should be even with the bottom of the filler hole.

3. If additional fluid is necessary, add it through the filler hole using a siphon pump or squeeze bottle.

4. Replace the filler plug; do not overtighten.

DRAIN AND REFILL

Automatic Transmission

NOTE: *Some early models may have a drain plug in the transmission pan. If this is the case, simply remove the plug and drain the fluid into a catch pan. Pan removal is not necessary.*

The torque converter on the C4 and C6 transmissions has a drain plug. If the con-

verter is drained, refill the C4 with 5 quarts of fluid and the C6 with 8 quarts of fluid.

1. Raise the vehicle so the transmission oil pan is readily accessible.

2. On the C4 disconnect the fluid filler tube from the pan and allow the fluid to drain into an appropriate container. On the C6 and AOD,

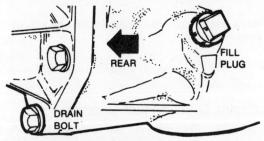

REAR

FILL
PLUG

DRAIN
BOLT

Manual transmission fill and drain plugs, using a tailshaft bolt as the drain plug

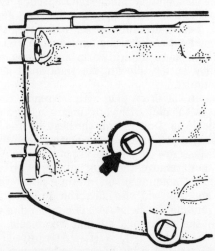

Manual transmission fill and drain plugs with the drain plug at the bottom center

start removing the pan bolts so that the fluid drains from one corner.

NOTE: *It is not recommended that the drained fluid be used over again; refill the transmission with new fluid. However, in an emergency situation, the old fluid can be re-used. The old fluid should be strained through a #100 screen or a fine mesh cloth before being reinstalled.*

3. Remove the transmission oil pan attaching bolts, pan and gasket.

4. Clean the transmission oil pan and transmission mating surfaces.

5. Install the transmission oil pan in the re-

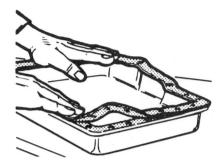

Install a new pan gasket

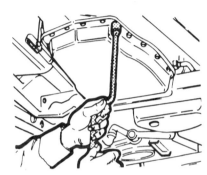

Many late model vehicles have no drain plug. Loosen the pan bolts and allow one corner of the pan to hang, so that the fluid will drain out

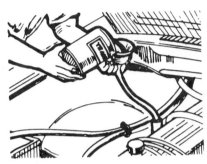

Fill the transmission with the required amount of fluid. Do not overfill. Start the engine and run the selector through all the shift points. Check the fluid and add as necessary

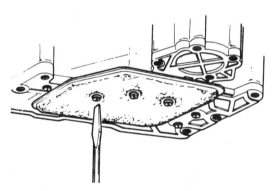

Removing automatic transmission filter

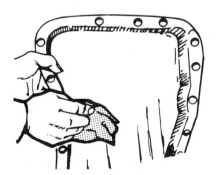

Clean the pan thoroughly with a safe solvent and allow it to air dry

verse order of removal, torquing the attaching bolts to 12-16 ft.lb. and using a new gasket. Fill the transmission with 3 qts. of the correct type fluid, check the operation of the transmission and check for leakage.

NOTE: *The C4 automatic transmission uses Type F automatic transmission fluid only. The C6 through 1976 uses Type F. The 1977 and later C6 and all AOD use type CJ or Dexron®II. When starting the engine after the transmission fluid has been drained, do not race the engine. Move the gear shift selector through all of the ranges before moving the vehicle.*

FILTER SERVICE

1. Remove the transmission oil pan and gasket.

2. Remove the fine mesh oil screen by removing the machine screws holding it to the lower valve body.

WARNING: *When removing the filter on C4 transmissions, be careful not to lose the throttle pressure limit valve and spring when separating the filter from the valve body.*

3. Install the new filter screen and transmission oil pan gasket in the reverse order of removal.

Manual Transmission

1. Place a suitable drain pan under the transmission.
2. Remove the drain plug and allow the gear lube to drain out.
3. Replace the drain plug, remove the filler plug and fill the transmission to the proper level with the required fluid.
4. Reinstall the filler plug.

Drive Axles

FLUID LEVEL CHECK

Clean the area around the fill plug, which is located in the housing cover, before removing the plug. The lubricant level should be maintained to the bottom of the fill hole with the axle in its normal running position. If lubricant does not appear at the hole when the plug is removed, additional lubricant should be added. Use hypoid gear lubricant SAE 80 or 90.

NOTE: *If the differential is of the limited slip type, be sure and use special limited slip differential additive.*

DRAIN AND REFILL

Drain and refill the front and rear axle housing every 24,000 miles, or every day if the vehicle is operated in deep water. Remove the oil with a suction gun. Refill the axle housings with the proper oil. Be sure and clean the area around the drain plug before removing the plug. See the section on level checks.

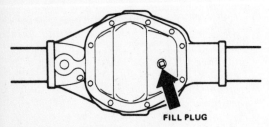

FILL PLUG

Dana/Spicer axle fill plug location

Brake Master Cylinder

On 1961-67 vans, the master cylinder is located beneath a plate on the driver's side floor pan. To check the fluid level, remove the floor pan cover and unscrew the master cylinder lid. The fluid level should be within ¼″ of the top of the reservoir.

On 1969 and later vans, the master cylinder reservoir is located under the hood, on the driver's side firewall. Before removing the master cylinder reservoir cap, make sure the vehicle is

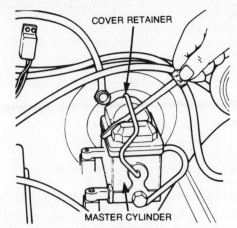

COVER RETAINER

MASTER CYLINDER

1969–85 brake master cylinder

resting on level ground and clean all dirt away from the top of the master cylinder.

To remove the cap on 1961-67 vans by unscrewing the holddown bolt and removing the cap; on 1969-85 vans by prying off the retaining clip; on 1985-88 vans by unscrewing the cap on the plastic reservoir. The brake fluid level should be within ¼″ (6mm) of the top of the reservoir.

If the level of the brake fluid is less than half the volume of the reservoir, it is advised that you check the brake system for leaks. Leaks in the hydraulic brake system most commonly occur at the wheel cylinder.

On 1969 and later vans, there is a rubber diaphragm in the top of the master cylinder cap. As the fluid level lowers in the reservoir due to normal brake shoe wear or leakage, the diaphragm takes up the space. This is to prevent the loss of brake fluid out the vented cap and contamination by dirt. After filling the master cylinder to the proper level with heavy duty brake fluid, but before replacing the cap, fold the rubber diaphragm up into the cap, then replace the cap in the reservoir and tighten the retaining bolt or snap the retaining clip into place.

Hydraulic Clutch Reservoir

The hydraulic fluid reservoirs on these systems are mounted on the firewall. Fluid level checks are performed like those on the brake hydraulic system. The proper fluid level is indicated by a step on the reservoir. Keep the reservoir topped up with Ford Heavy-Duty Brake fluid or equivalent; do not overfill.

CAUTION: *Carefully clean the top and sides of the reservoir before opening, to prevent contamination of the system with dirt, etc. Remove the reservoir diaphragm before adding fluid, and replace after filling.*

See the illustration of the hydraulic clutch assembly in Chapter 7.

Manual Steering Gear

LEVEL CHECK

1961-67

1. Center the steering wheel.
2. Remove the access plate from the driver's side floor pan.
3. Remove the steering gear housing filler plug.
4. If a bubble has formed in the access hole, break it with a clean tool.
5. Slowly turn the steering wheel to the left until the linkage reaches its stop. The lubricant should rise within the cover lower bolt hole. If it does, replace the plug. If not, go on to Step 6.
6. Slowly turn the steering wheel to the right until the linkage reaches its stop.
7. Remove the cover-to-housing top retaining bolt.
8. Fill the gear through the filler plug hole until lubricant comes out the bolt hole.
9. Install the lower cover-to-housing attaching bolt and the filler plug.

1969-74

1. Center the steering wheel.
2. Remove the steering gear housing filler plug.
3. If a bubble has formed in the access hole, break it with a clean tool.
4. Slowly turn the steering wheel to the left, then to the right until the linkage reaches its stops. The lubricant should rise in the filler plug hole.
5. If lubricant does not rise in the fillerhole, turn the steering wheel all the way to the left stop to position the ball nut away from the filler hole. Add steering gear lubricant until the gear is full.

NOTE: *The location of the steering gear does not allow the removal of a cover bolt to act as a vent. To prevent air from being trapped and forming pockets while fluid is being added, it is suggested that you adapt a length of 1/4" hose to the end of the grease gun. This hose is then inserted into the filler hole and down as far as possible. That way, the lower cavity can be filled first and air can be expelled out the hole as the gear is filled*

6. Install the filler plug.

1975-88

These gears are permanantly lubricated. No provision is made for refilling. If lubicant leaks out, the gear must be disassembled and serviced.

Power Steering Reservoir

Position the vehicle on level ground. Run the engine until the fluid is at normal operating temperature. Turn the steering wheel all the way to the left and right several times. Position the wheels in the straight ahead position, then shut off the engine. Check the fluid level on the dipstick which is attached to the reservoir cap. The level should be between the ADD and FULL marks on the dipstick. Add fluid accordingly. Do not overfill. Use power steering fluid.

Chassis Greasing

The lubrication chart indicates where the grease fittings are located. The vehicle should be greased according to the intervals in the Preventive Maintenance Schedule at the end of this chapter.

Front Wheel Bearings

ADJUSTMENT

The front wheels each rotate on a set of opposed, tapered roller bearings as shown in the accompanying illustration. The grease retainer at the inside of the hub prevents lubricant from leaking into the brake drum.

1. Raise and support the front end on jackstands.
2. Remove the grease cap and remove excess grease from the end of the spindle.
3. Remove the cotter pin and nut lock shown in the illustration.
4. Rotate the wheel, hub and drum assembly while tightening the adjusting nut to 17-25 ft.lb. in order to seat the bearings.
5. Back off the adjusting nut 1/2, then retighten the adjusting nut to 10-15 in.lb.
6. Locate the nut lock on the adjusting nut so that the castellations on the lock are lined up with the cotter pin hole in the spindle.
7. Install the new cotter pin, bending the ends of the cotter pin around the castellated flange of the nut lock.
8. Check the wheel for proper rotation, then install the grease cap. If the wheel still does not rotate properly, inspect and clean or replace the wheel bearings and cups.

REMOVAL, REPACKING, AND INSTALLATION

Before handling the bearings, there are a few things that you should remember to do and not to do.

Remember to DO the following:

• Remove all outside dirt from the housing before exposing the bearing.

• Treat a used bearing as gently as you would a new one.

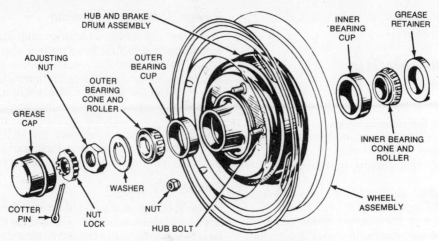

Front hub assembly with drum brakes

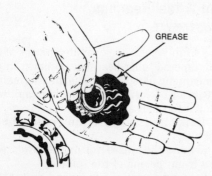

Packing the wheel bearings with grease by hand

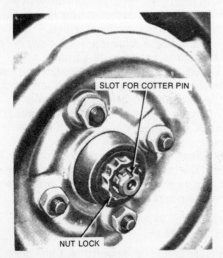

Nut lock installed so that a slot is aligned with cotter pin hole

• Work with clean tools in clean surroundings.

• Use clean, dry canvas gloves, or at least clean, dry hands.

• Clean solvents and flushing fluids are a must.

• Use clean paper when laying out the bearings to dry.

• Protect disassembled bearings from rust and dirt. Cover them up.

• Use clean rags to wipe bearings.

• Keep the bearings in oil-proof paper when they are to be stored or are not in use.

• Clean the inside of the housing before replacing the bearing.

Do NOT do the following:

• Don't work in dirty surroundings.

• Don't use dirty, chipped or damaged tools.

• Try not to work on wooden work benches or use wooden mallets.

• Don't handle bearings with dirty or moist hands.

• Do not use gasoline for cleaning; use a safe solvent.

• Do not spin-dry bearings with compressed air. They will be damaged.

• Do not spin dirty bearings.

• Avoid using cotton waste or dirty cloths to wipe bearings.

• Try not to scratch or nick bearing surfaces.

• Do not allow the bearing to come in contact with dirt or rust at any time.

1. Raise and support the front end on jackstands.

2. Remove the wheel cover. Remove the wheel.

3. Remove the caliper from the disc and wire it to the underbody to prevent damage to the brake hose. See Chapter 9

4. Remove the grease cap from the hub. Then, remove the cotter pin, nut lock, adjusting nut and flat washer from the spindle. Remove the outer bearing assembly from the hub.

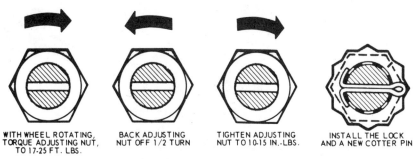

WITH WHEEL ROTATING,   BACK ADJUSTING   TIGHTEN ADJUSTING   INSTALL THE LOCK
TORQUE ADJUSTING NUT,   NUT OFF 1/2 TURN   NUT TO 10-15 IN.-LBS. AND A NEW COTTER PIN
TO 17-25 FT. LBS.

Front wheel bearing adjusting sequence

5. Pull the hub and disc assembly off the wheel spindle.

6. Remove and discard the old grease retainer. Remove the inner bearing cone and roller assembly from the hub.

7. Clean all grease from the inner and outer bearing cups with solvent. Inspect the cups for pits, scratches, or excessive wear. If the cups are damaged, remove them with a drift.

8. Clean the inner and outer cone and roller assemblies with solvent and shake them dry. If the cone and roller assemblies show excessive wear or damage, replace them with the bearing cups as a unit.

9. Clean the spindle and the inside of the hub with solvent to thoroughly remove all old grease.

10. Covering the spindle with a clean cloth, brush all loose dirt and dust from the brake assembly. Remove the cloth carefully so as to not get dirt on the spindle.

11. If the inner and/or outer bearing cups were removed, install the replacement cups on the hub. Be sure that the cups seat properly in the hub.

12. It is imperative that all old grease be removed from the bearings and surrounding surfaces before repacking. The new lithium-based grease is not compatible with the sodium base grease used in the past.

13. Install the hub and disc on the wheel spindle. To prevent damage to the grease retainer and spindle threads, keep the hub centered on the spindle.

14. Install the outer bearing cone and roller assembly and the flat washer on the spindle. Install the adjusting nut.

15. Adjust the wheel bearings by torquing the adjusting nut to 17-25 ft.lb. with the wheel rotating to seat the bearing. Then back off the adjusting nut ½ turn. Retighten the adjusting nut to 10-15 in.lb. Install the locknut so that the castellations are aligned with the cotter pin hole. Install the cotter pin. Bend the ends of the cotter pin around the castellations of the locknut to prevent interference with the radio static

collector in the grease cap. Install the grease cap.

WARNING: *New bolts must be used when servicing floating caliper units. The upper bolt must be tightened first. For floating caliper units, see Caliper Assembly Service in the Brake Chapter. For sliding caliper units, see Shoe and Lining Replacement in the Brake Section.*

11. Install the wheels.

12. Install the wheel cover.

Rear Axle Bearings

The rear wheel bearings on the vans equipped with a Dana 60, 61, 70 or 80 full floating rear axle are packed with wheel bearing grease. Axle lubricant can also flow into the wheel hubs and bearings, however, wheel bearing grease is the primary lubricant. The wheel bearing grease provides lubrication until the axle lubricant reaches the bearings during normal operation.

1. Set the parking brake and loosen the axle shaft bolts.

2. Raise the rear wheels off the floor and place jackstands under the rear axle housing so that the axle is parallel with the floor.

3. Remove the axle shaft bolts.

4. Remove the axle shaft and gaskets.

5. With the axle shaft removed, remove the gasket from the axle shaft flange studs.

6. Bend the lockwasher tab away from the locknut, and then remove the locknut, lockwasher, and the adjusting nut.

7. Remove the outer bearing cone and pull the wheel straight off the axle.

8. With a piece of hardwood or a brass drift which will just clear the outer bearing cup, drive the inner bearing cone and inner seal out of the wheel hub.

9. Wash all the old grease or axle lubricant out of the wheel hub, using a suitable solvent.

10. Wash the bearing cups and rollers and inspect them for pitting, galling, and uneven wear patterns. Inspect the roller for end wear.

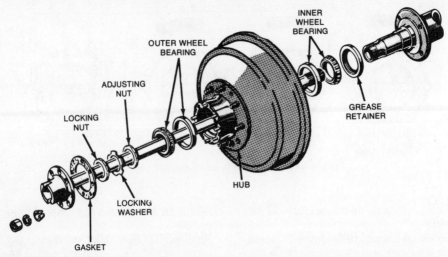

Full-floating rear axle bearings through 1974—this early model retains the axle shaft flange with stud nuts and tapered dowels instead of bolts

11. If the bearing cups are to be replaced, drive them out with a brass drift. Install the new cups with a block of wood and hammer or press them in.

12. if the bearing cups are properly seated, a 0.0015″ (0.038mm) feeler gauge will not fit between the cup and the wheel hub. The gauge should not fit beneath the cup. Check several places to make sure the cups are squarely seated.

13. Pack each bearing cone and roller with a bearing packer or in the manner previously outlined for the front wheel bearings. Use a multipurpose wheel bearing grease.

14. Place the inner bearing cone and roller as-

sembly in the wheel hub. Install a new inner seal in the hub with a seal installation tool.

15. Install the wheel.

16. Install and tighten the bearing adjusting nut to 50-80 ft.lbs. for vans through 1974; 120-140 ft.lb. for 1975 and later models, while rotating the wheel.

17. On models through 1974, back off (loosen) the adjusting nut ⅜ of a turn, install a new locking washer coated with chassis lube, smooth side out. Install the locknut and tighten it to 90-110 ft.lb. Bend 2 locking waher tabs over the locknut.

18. On 1975 and later models, back off the adjusting nut ⅛-¼ turn. The wheel should rotate freely and the endplay should be 0.001-0.010″

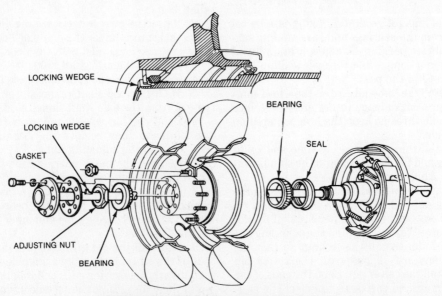

1975 and later full floating rear axle bearings

ROUTINE SERVICE
Engine Compartment Service Points

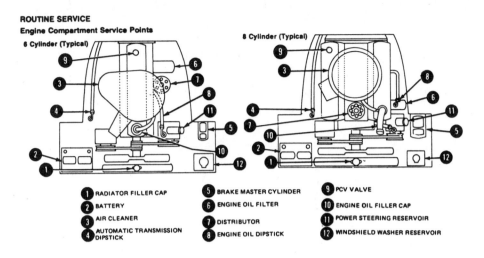

1 RADIATOR FILLER CAP	**5** BRAKE MASTER CYLINDER	**9** PCV VALVE
2 BATTERY	**6** ENGINE OIL FILTER	**10** ENGINE OIL FILLER CAP
3 AIR CLEANER	**7** DISTRIBUTOR	**11** POWER STEERING RESERVOIR
4 AUTOMATIC TRANSMISSION DIPSTICK	**8** ENGINE OIL DIPSTICK	**12** WINDSHIELD WASHER RESERVOIR

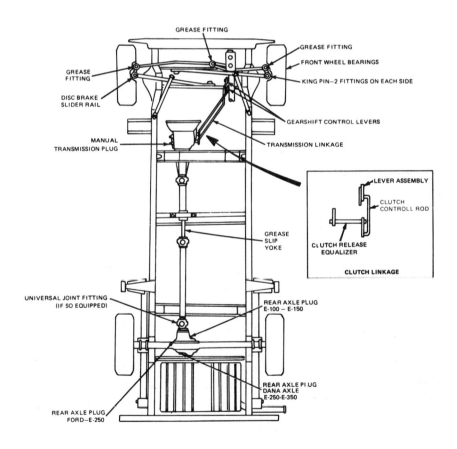

Typical service and lubrication points through 1980

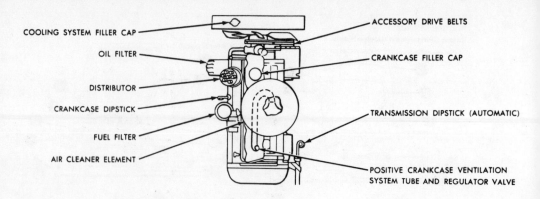

COOLING SYSTEM FILLER CAP

OIL FILTER

DISTRIBUTOR

CRANKCASE DIPSTICK

FUEL FILTER

AIR CLEANER ELEMENT

ACCESSORY DRIVE BELTS

CRANKCASE FILLER CAP

TRANSMISSION DIPSTICK (AUTOMATIC)

POSITIVE CRANKCASE VENTILATION
SYSTEM TUBE AND REGULATOR VALVE

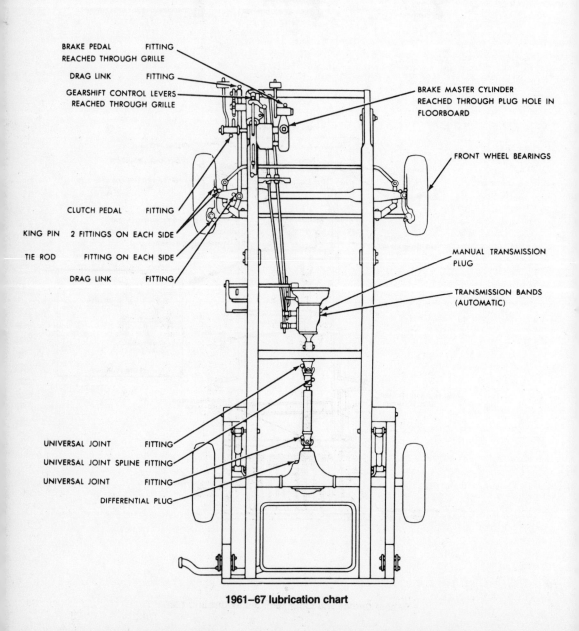

BRAKE PEDAL   FITTING
REACHED THROUGH GRILLE

DRAG LINK   FITTING

GEARSHIFT CONTROL LEVERS
REACHED THROUGH GRILLE

CLUTCH PEDAL   FITTING

KING PIN   2 FITTINGS ON EACH SIDE

TIE ROD   FITTING ON EACH SIDE

DRAG LINK   FITTING

UNIVERSAL JOINT   FITTING

UNIVERSAL JOINT SPLINE FITTING

UNIVERSAL JOINT   FITTING

DIFFERENTIAL PLUG

BRAKE MASTER CYLINDER
REACHED THROUGH PLUG HOLE IN
FLOORBOARD

FRONT WHEEL BEARINGS

MANUAL TRANSMISSION
PLUG

TRANSMISSION BANDS
(AUTOMATIC)

1961–67 lubrication chart

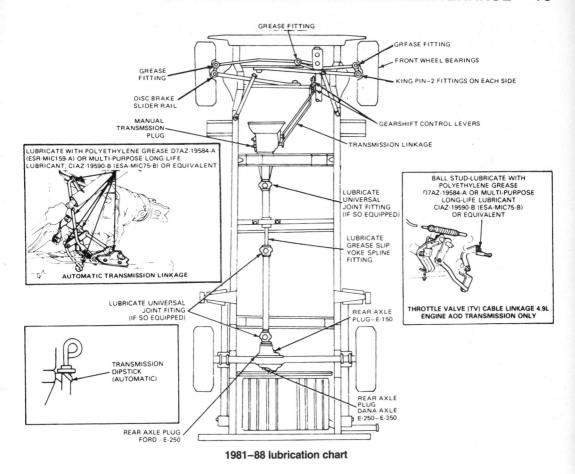

1981–88 lubrication chart

(0.025-0.25mm) measured with a dial indicator. Position the locking wedge in the keyway slot and carefully drive the wedge into position. The wedge must be bottomed against the shoulder of the adjusting nut when fully installed.

NOTE: *The locking wedge and the adjusting nut can be used over again, as long as the locking wedge cut a new groove in the nylon retainer material within the ⅛ to ⅜ turn specified. The wedge must not be pressed into the previously cut groove.*

19. Apply axle lube to a new lockwasher and install it with the smooth side out.

20. Install the locknut and tighten it to 90-110 ft.lb. The wheel must rotate freely after the locknut if tightened. The wheel end-play should be within 0.001-0.010" (0.0254-0.254mm).

21. Bend two lockwasher tabs inward over an adjusting nut flat and two lockwasher tabs outward over the locknut flat.

22. Install the axle shaft, gasket, lockbolts, and washers. Tighten the bolts to 40-50 ft.lb.

23. Adjust the brakes, if necessary.

PUSHING AND TOWING

To push-start your vehicle, (manual transmission only), check to make sure that bumpers of both vehicles are aligned so neither will be damaged. Be sure that all electrical system components are turned off (headlight, heater, blower, etc.). Turn on the ignition switch. Place the shift lever in Third or Fourth and push in the clutch pedal. At about 15 mph, signal the driver of the pushing vehicle to fall back, depress the accelerator pedal, and release the clutch pedal slowly. The engine should start.

When you are doing the pushing, make sure that the two bumpers match so you won't damage the vehicle you are to push. Another good idea is to put an old tire between the two vehicles. Try to keep your truck right up against the other vehicle while you are pushing. If the two vehicles do separate, stop and start over again instead of trying to catch up and ramming the other vehicle. Also try, as much as possible, to avoid riding or slipping the clutch.

If your truck has to be towed by a tow truck, it can be towed forward for any distance with the driveshaft connected as long as it is done fairly slowly. Otherwise disconnect the driveshaft at the rear axle and tie it up. On E-250HD and E-350, the rear axle shafts can be removed and the hub covered to prevent lubricant loss.

JACKING

It is very important to be careful about running the engine, on vehicles equipped with limited slip differentials, while the vehicle is up on the jack. This is because when the drive train is engaged, power is transmitted to the wheel with the best traction and the vehicle will drive off the jack if one drive wheel is in contact with the floor, resulting in possible damage or injury.

Jack a Ford truck from under the axles, radius arms, or spring hangers and the frame. Be sure and block the diagonally opposite wheel. Place jackstands under the vehicle at the points mentioned or directly under the frame when you are going to work under the vehicle.

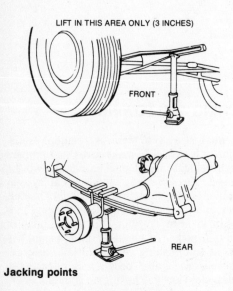

LIFT IN THIS AREA ONLY (3 INCHES)

FRONT

REAR

Jacking points

E-250, 300 front jacking point

JUMP STARTING A DUAL-BATTERY DIESEL

Ford vans equipped with the 420 cid or 444 cid (6.9L and 7.3L) V8 diesel utilize two 12 volt batteries, one on either side of the engine compartment. The batteries are connected in a parallel circuit (positive terminal to positive terminal, negative terminal to negative terminal). Hooking the batteries up in parallel circuit increases battery cranking power without increasing total battery voltage output. Output remains at 12 volts. On the other hand, hooking two 12 volt batteries up in a series circuit (positive terminal to negative terminal, positive terminal to negative terminal) increases total battery output to 24 volts (12 volts plus 12 volts).

CAUTION: *NEVER hook the batteries up in a series circuit or the entire electrical system will go up in smoke, especially the starter.*

In the event that a diesel needs to be jump started, use the following procedure.

1. Turn all lights off.
2. Turn on the heater blower motor to remove transient voltage.
3. Connect one jumper cable to the passenger side battery positive (+) terminal and the other cable clamp to the positive (+) terminal to the booster (good) battery.
4. Connect one end of the other jumper cable to the negative (–) terminal of the booster (good) battery and the other cable clamp to an engine bolt head, alternator bracket or other solid, metallic point on the diesel engine. DO NOT connect this clamp to the negative (–) terminal of the bad battery.

CAUTION: *Be very careful to keep the jumper cables away from moving parts (cooling fan, belts, etc.) on both engines.*

5. Start the engine of the donor truck and run it at moderate speed.
6. Start the engine of the diesel.
7. When the diesel starts, remove the cable from the engine block before disconnecting the positive terminal.

TRAILER TOWING

Factory trailer towing packages are available on most trucks. However, if you are installing a trailer hitch and wiring on your truck, there are a few thing that you ought to know.

Trailer Weight

Trailer weight is the first, and most important, factor in determining whether or not your vehicle is suitable for towing the trailer you have in mind. The horsepower-to-weight ratio

JUMP STARTING A DEAD BATTERY

The chemical reaction in a battery produces explosive hydrogen gas. This is the safe way to jump start a dead battery, reducing the chances of an accidental spark that could cause an explosion.

Jump Starting Precautions

1. Be sure both batteries are of the same voltage.
2. Be sure both batteries are of the same polarity (have the same grounded terminal).
3. Be sure the vehicles are not touching.
4. Be sure the vent cap holes are not obstructed.
5. Do not smoke or allow sparks around the battery.
6. In cold weather, check for frozen electrolyte in the battery. Do not jump start a frozen battery.
7. Do not allow electrolyte on your skin or clothing.
8. Be sure the electrolyte is not frozen.
CAUTION: *Make certain that the ignition key, in the vehicle with the dead battery, is in the OFF position. Connecting cables to vehicles with on-board computers will result in computer destruction if the key is not in the OFF position.*

Jump Starting Procedure

1. Determine voltages of the two batteries; they must be the same.
2. Bring the starting vehicle close (they must not touch) so that the batteries can be reached easily.
3. Turn off all accessories and both engines. Put both cars in Neutral or Park and set the handbrake.
4. Cover the cell caps with a rag—do not cover terminals.
5. If the terminals on the run-down battery are heavily corroded, clean them.
6. Identify the positive and negative posts on both batteries and connect the cables in the order shown.
7. Start the engine of the starting vehicle and run it at fast idle. Try to start the car with the dead battery. Crank it for no more than 10 seconds at a time and let it cool off for 20 seconds in between tries.
8. If it doesn't start in 3 tries, there is something else wrong.
9. Disconnect the cables in the reverse order.
10. Replace the cell covers and dispose of the rags.

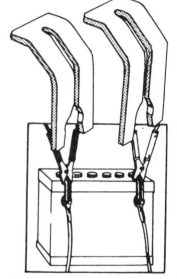

Side terminal batteries occasionally pose a problem when connecting jumper cables. There frequently isn't enough room to clamp the cables without touching sheet metal. Side terminal adaptors are available to alleviate this problem and should be removed after use.

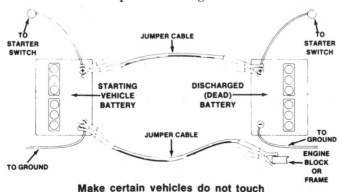

Make certain vehicles do not touch

This hook-up for negative ground cars only

Recommended Equipment Checklist

Equipment	Class I Trailers Under 2,000 pounds	Class II Trailers 2,000-3,500 pounds	Class III Trailers 3,500-6,000 pounds	Class IV Trailers 6,000 pounds and up
Hitch	Frame or Equalizing	Equalizing	Equalizing	Fifth wheel Pick-up truck only
Tongue Load Limit**	Up to 200 pounds	200-350 pounds	350-600 pounds	600 pounds and up
Trailer Brakes	Not Required	Required	Required	Required
Safety Chain	3/16" diameter links	1/4" diameter links	5/16" diameter links	—
Fender Mounted Mirrors	Useful, but not necessary	Recommended	Recommended	Recommended
Turn Signal Flasher	Standard	Constant Rate or heavy duty	Constant Rate or heavy duty	Constant Rate or heavy duty
Coolant Recovery System	Recommended	Required	Required	Required
Transmission Oil Cooler	Recommended	Recommended	Recommended	Recommended
Engine Oil Cooler	Recommended	Recommended	Recommended	Recommended
Air Adjustable Shock Absorbers	Recommended	Recommended	Recommended	Recommended
Flex or Clutch Fan	Recommended	Recommended	Recommended	Recommended
Tires	***	***	***	***

NOTE: The information in this chart is a guide. Check the manufacturer's recommendations for your car if in doubt.

*Local laws may require specific equipment such as trailer brakes or fender mounted mirrors. Check your local laws. Hitch weight is usually 10-15% of trailer gross weight and should be measured with trailer loaded.

**Most manufacturer's do not recommend towing trailers of over 1,000 pounds with compacts. Some intermediates cannot tow Class III trailers.

***Check manufacturer's recommendations for your specific car/trailer combination.

—Does not apply

should be calculated. The basic standard is a ratio of 35:1. That is, 35 pounds of GVW for every horsepower.

To calculate this ratio, multiply you engine's rated horsepower by 35, then subtract the weight of the vehicle, including passengers and luggage. The resulting figure is the ideal maximum trailer weight that you can tow. One point to consider: a numerically higher axle ratio can offset what appears to be a low trailer weight. If the weight of the trailer that you have in mind is somewhat higher than the weight you just calculated, you might consider changing your rear axle ratio to compensate.

Hitch Weight

There are three kinds of hitches: bumper mounted, frame mounted, and load equalizing.

Bumper mounted hitches are those which attach solely to the vehicle's bumper. Many states prohibit towing with this type of hitch, when it attaches to the vehicle's stock bumper, since it subjects the bumper to stresses for which it was not designed. Aftermarket rear step bumpers,

designed for trailer towing, are acceptable for use with bumper mounted hitches.

Frame mounted hitches can be of the type which bolts to two or more points on the frame, plus the bumper, or just to several points on the frame. Frame mounted hitches can also be of the tongue type, for Class I towing, or, of the receiver type, for Classes II and III.

Load equalizing hitches are usually used for large trailers. Most equalizing hitches are welded in place and use equalizing bars and chains to level the vehicle after the trailer is hooked up.

The bolt-on hitches are the most common, since they are relatively easy to install.

Check the gross weight rating of your trailer. Tongue weight is usually figured as 10% of gross trailer weight. Therefore, a trailer with a maximum gross weight of 2,000 lb. will have a maximum tongue weight of 200 lb. Class I trailers fall into this category. Class II trailers are those with a gross weight rating of 2,000-3,500 lb., while Class III trailers fall into the 3,500-6,000 lb. category. Class IV trailers are those over 6,000 lb. and are for use with fifth wheel trucks, only.

When you've determined the hitch that you'll need, follow the manufacturer's installation instructions, exactly, especially when it comes to fastener torques. The hitch will subjected to a lot of stress and good hitches come with hardened bolts. Never substitute an inferior bolt for a hardened bolt.

Wiring

Wiring the truck for towing is fairly easy. There are a number of good wiring kits available and these should be used, rather than trying to design your own. All trailers will need brake lights and turn signals as well as tail lights and side marker lights. Most states require extra marker lights for overly wide trailers. Also, most states have recently required back-up lights for trailers, and most trailer manufacturers have been building trailers with back-up lights for several years.

Additionally, some Class I, most Class II and just about all Class III trailers will have electric brakes.

Add to this number an accessories wire, to operate trailer internal equipment or to charge the trailer's battery, and you can have as many as seven wires in the harness.

Determine the equipment on your trailer and buy the wiring kit necessary. The kit will contain all the wires needed, plus a plug adapter set which included the female plug, mounted on the bumper or hitch, and the male plug, wired into, or plugged into the trailer harness.

When installing the kit, follow the manufacturer's instructions. The color coding of the wires is standard throughout the industry.

One point to note, some domestic vehicles, and most imported vehicles, have separate turn signals. On most domestic vehicles, the brake lights and rear turn signals operate with the same bulb. For those vehicles with separate turn signals, you can purchase an isolation unit so that the brake lights won't blink whenever the turn signals are operated, or, you can go to your local electronics supply house and buy four diodes to wire in series with the brake and turn signal bulbs. Diodes will isolate the brake and turn signals. The choice is yours. The isolation units are simple and quick to install, but far more expensive than the diodes. The diodes, however, require more work to install properly, since they require the cutting of each bulb's wire and soldering in place of the diode.

One final point, the best kits are those with a spring loaded cover on the vehicle mounted socket. This cover prevents dirt and moisture from corroding the terminals. Never let the vehicle socket hang loosely. Always mount it securely to the bumper or hitch.

Cooling
ENGINE

One of the most common, if not THE most common, problem associated with trailer towing is engine overheating.

With factory installed trailer towing packages, a heavy duty cooling system is usually included. Heavy duty cooling systems are available as optional equipment on most trucks, with or without a trailer package. If you have one of these extra-capacity systems, you shouldn't have any overheating problems.

If you have a standard cooling system, without an expansion tank, you'll definitely need to get an aftermarket expansion tank kit, preferably one with at least a 2 quart capacity. These kits are easily installed on the radiator's overflow hose, and come with a pressure cap designed for expansion tanks.

Another helpful accessory is a Flex Fan. These fan are large diameter units are designed to provide more airflow at low speeds, with blades that have deeply cupped surfaces. The blades then flex, or flatten out, at high speed, when less cooling air is needed. These fans are far lighter in weight than stock fans, requiring less horsepower to drive them. Also, they are far quieter than stock fans.

If you do decide to replace your stock fan with a flex fan, note that if your truck has a fan clutch, a spacer between the flex fan and water pump hub will be needed.

Aftermarket engine oil coolers are helpful for prolonging engine oil life and reducing overall engine temperatures. Both of these factors increase engine life.

While not absolutely necessary in towing Class I and some Class II trailers, they are recommended for heavier Class II and all Class III towing.

Engine oil cooler systems consist of an adapter, screwed on in place of the oil filter, a remote filter mounting and a multi-tube, finned heat exchanger, which is mounted in front of the radiator or air conditioning condenser.

TRANSMISSION

An automatic transmission is usually recommended for trailer towing. Modern automatics have proven reliable and, of course, easy to operate, in trailer towing.

The increased load of a trailer, however, causes an increase in the temperature of the automatic transmission fluid. Heat is the worst enemy of an automatic transmission. As the temperature of the fluid increases, the life of the fluid decreases.

It is essential, therefore, that you install an automatic transmission cooler.

The cooler, which consists of a multi-tube, finned heat exchanger, is usually installed in front of the radiator or air conditioning compressor, and hooked inline with the transmission cooler tank inlet line. Follow the cooler manufacturer's installation instructions.

Select a cooler of at least adequate capacity, based upon the combined gross weights of the truck and trailer.

Cooler manufacturers recommend that you use an aftermarket cooler in addition to, and not instead of, the present cooling tank in your truck's radiator. If you do want to use it in place of the radiator cooling tank, get a cooler at least two sizes larger than normally necessary.

NOTE: *A transmission cooler can, sometimes, cause slow or harsh shifting in the transmission during cold weather, until the fluid has a chance to come up to normal operating temperature. Some coolers can be purchased with or retrofitted with a temperature bypass valve which will allow fluid flow through the cooler only when the fluid has reached operating temperature, or above.*

Capacities Chart

Years	Engine	Engine Oil Incl. Filter (qt.)	Transmission (pt.) 3-sp	4-sp	Auto *	Drive Axle (pt.)	Fuel Tank (gal.)	Cooling System (qt.) std.	w/AC	ExtraCool
1961	6-144	4.5	2.5	—	—	2.0	14.0	12.3	—	—
	6-170	4.5	2.5	—	—	2.0	14.0	12.3	—	—
1962	6-144	4.5	2.5	—	—	2.0	14.0	12.3	—	—
	6-170	4.5	2.5	—	—	2.0	14.0	12.3	—	—
1963	6-144	4.5	3.0	—	—	2.0	14.0	10.5	—	—
	6-170	4.5	3.0	—	—	2.0	14.0	12.3	—	—
1964	6-144	4.5	3.0	—	—	2.0	14.0	12.3	—	—
	6-170	4.5	3.0	4.8	15.0	①	14.0	9.5	—	—
1965	6-170	4.5	3.0	—	15.0	①	14.0	9.5	—	—
	6-200	4.5	3.0	—	15.0	①	14.0	9.5	—	—
	6-240	5.0	3.0	—	15.0	①	14.0	9.5	—	—
1966	6-170	4.5	3.0	—	15.6	①	14.0	10.0	—	—
	6-240	5.0	3.0	—	17.8	①	14.0	12.0	—	—
1967–68	6-170	4.5	3.0	—	16.0	①	14.0	10.0	—	—
	6-240	5.0	3.0	—	21.0	①	14.0	12.0	—	—
1969	6-170	4.5	3.5	—	—	②	15.0	10.0	—	—
	6-240	5.0	3.5	—	20.5	②	15.0	12.0	—	16.3
	8-302	5.0	3.5	—	20.5	②	15.0	16.3	—	—
1970	6-170	4.5	3.5	—	20.5	5.0	③	9.0	—	—
	6-240	5.0	3.5	—	20.5	6.0	③	14.4	16.3	14.4
	8-302	5.0	3.5	—	20.5	6.0	③	15.2	17.5	17.5
1971	6-240	5.0	3.5	—	20.5	②	21.0	14.4	16.7	16.7
	8-302	5.0	3.5	—	20.5	②	21.0	15.2	17.5	17.5
1972	6-240	5.0	3.5	—	20.5	②	21.0	14.4	16.7	16.7
	8-302	5.0	3.5	—	20.5	②	21.0	15.2	17.5	17.5
1973	6-240	5.0	3.5	—	20.5	②	④	14.4	16.7	16.7
	6-300	5.0	3.5	—	20.5	②	④	14.5	16.3	16.3
	8-302	5.0	3.5	—	20.5	②	④	15.2	17.5	17.5

Capacities Chart (cont.)

Years	Engine	Engine Oil Incl. Filter (qt.)	Transmission (pt.)			Drive Axle (pt.)	Fuel Tank (gal.)	Cooling System (qt.)		
			3-sp	4-sp	Auto*			std.	w/AC	ExtraCool
1974	6-240	5.0	3.5	—	20.5	②	④	14.4	16.7	16.7
	6-300	5.0	3.5	—	20.5	②	④	14.5	16.3	16.3
	8-302	6.0	3.5	—	20.5	②	④	15.2	17.5	17.5
1975	6-300	6.0	3.5	—	⑤	②	⑥	14.5	—	—
	8-351W	6.0	3.5	—	24.5	②	⑥	20.0	24.0	24.0
	6-460	6.0	—	—	24.5	②	⑥	28.0	28.0	—
1976	6-300	6.0	3.5	—	20.0	⑧	⑥	⑦	—	—
	8-351W	6.0	3.5	—	24.5	⑧	⑥	20.0	24.0	24.0
	6-460	6.0	—	—	24.5	⑧	⑥	28.0	28.0	—
1977	6-300	6.0	3.5	—	20.0	⑨	⑥	⑦	—	—
	8-351W	6.0	3.5	—	24.5	⑨	⑥	17.0	20.0	20.0
	6-460	6.0	—	—	24.5	⑨	⑥	28.0	28.0	—
1978	6-300	6.0	3.5	5.0	20.5	⑨	⑥	14.5	—	—
	8-351W	6.0	3.5	—	24.5	⑨	⑥	17.0	20.0	20.0
	6-460	6.0	—	—	24.5	⑨	⑥	28.0	28.0	—
1979	6-300	6.0	3.5	5.0	20.5	⑩	⑪	15.0	20.0	—
	8-302	6.0	3.5	4.5	23.5	⑩	⑪	⑫	17.5	18.5
	8-351W	6.0	—	—	24.5	⑩	⑪	20.0	20.0	21.0
	6-460	6.0	—	—	24.5	⑩	⑪	28.0	28.0	—
1980	6-300	6.0	3.5	5.0	20.5	⑩	⑪	15.0	20.0	—
	8-302	6.0	3.5	4.5	23.5	⑩	⑪	⑫	17.5	18.5
	8-351W	6.0	—	—	24.5	⑩	⑪	20.0	20.0	21.0
	8-400	6.0	—	—	24.5	⑩	⑪	22.0	24.0	28.0
	6-460	6.0	—	—	24.5	⑩	⑪	28.0	28.0	—
1981	6-300	6.0	3.5	5.0	20.5	⑩	⑪	15.0	20.0	—
	8-302	6.0	3.5	4.5	23.5	⑩	⑪	⑫	17.5	18.5
	8-351W	6.0	—	—	24.5	⑩	⑪	20.0	20.0	21.0
	8-400	6.0	—	—	24.5	⑩	⑪	22.0	24.0	28.0
	6-460	6.0	—	—	24.5	⑩	⑪	28.0	28.0	—
1982	6-300	6.0	3.5	5.0	20.5	⑩	⑪	15.0	20.0	—
	8-302	6.0	3.5	4.5	23.5	⑩	⑪	⑫	17.5	18.5
	8-351W	6.0	—	—	24.5	⑩	⑪	20.0	20.0	21.0
	8-400	6.0	—	—	24.5	⑩	⑪	22.0	24.0	28.0
	6-460	6.0	—	—	24.5	⑩	⑪	28.0	28.0	—
1983	6-300	6.0	3.5	5.0	20.5	⑩	⑪	15.0	20.0	—
	8-302	6.0	3.5	4.5	23.5	⑩	⑪	⑫	17.5	18.5
	8-351W	6.0	—	—	24.5	⑩	⑪	20.0	20.0	21.0
	8-420	10.0	—	5.0	24.5	⑩	⑪	31.0	31.0	—
	6-460	6.0	—	—	24.5	⑩	⑪	28.0	28.0	—

Capacities Chart (cont.)

Years	Engine	Engine Oil Incl. Filter (qt.)	Transmission (pt.)			Drive Axle (pt.)	Fuel Tank (gal.)	Cooling System (qt.)		
			3-sp	4-sp	Auto*			std.	w/AC	ExtraCool
1984	6-300	6.0	3.5	5.0	20.5	(10)	(11)	15.0	20.0	—
	8-302	6.0	3.5	4.5	23.5	(10)	(11)	(12)	17.5	18.5
	8-351W	6.0	—	—	24.5	(10)	(11)	20.0	20.0	21.0
	8-420	10.0	—	5.0	24.5	(10)	(11)	31.0	31.0	—
	6-460	6.0	—	—	24.5	(10)	(11)	28.0	28.0	—
1985	6-300	6.0	3.5	(13)	(14)	(15)	(11)	(16)	(17)	—
	8-302	6.0	—	—	23.5	(15)	(11)	17.5	17.5	18.5
	8-351W	6.0	—	—	24.5	(15)	(11)	20.0	21.0	—
	8-420	10.0	—	5.0	24.5	(15)	(11)	31.0	31.0	—
	6-460	6.0	—	—	24.5	(15)	(11)	28.0	28.0	—
1986	6-300	6.0	3.5	(13)	(14)	(15)	(11)	(16)	(17)	—
	8-302	6.0	—	—	23.5	(15)	(11)	17.5	17.5	18.5
	8-351W	6.0	—	—	24.5	(15)	(11)	20.0	21.0	—
	8-420	10.0	—	5.0	24.5	(15)	(11)	31.0	31.0	—
	6-460	6.0	—	—	24.5	(15)	(11)	28.0	28.0	—
1987	6-300	6.0	3.5	(13)	(14)	(15)	(11)	(16)	(17)	—
	8-302	6.0	—	—	23.5	(15)	(11)	17.5	17.5	18.5
	8-351W	6.0	—	—	24.5	(15)	(11)	20.0	21.0	—
	8-420	10.0	—	5.0	24.5	(15)	(11)	31.0	31.0	—
	6-460	6.0	—	—	24.5	(15)	(11)	28.0	28.0	—
1988	6-300	6.0	—	(18)	(14)	(15)	(11)	(16)	(17)	—
	8-302	6.0	—	—	23.5	(15)	(11)	17.5	17.5	18.5
	8-351W	6.0	—	—	24.5	(15)	(11)	20.0	21.0	—
	8-444	10.0	—	—	24.5	(15)	(11)	31.0	31.0	—
	6-460	6.0	—	—	24.5	(15)	(11)	28.0	28.0	—

*Figure includes torque converter

(1) Std. axle: 4.5
Optional 2,700 lb. axle: 5.0
(2) Ford axles: 5.0
Dana axles: 6.0
(3) With evaporative emission controls: 21.0
Without evaporative emission controls: 24.0
(4) Except E-300 and camper: 20
E-300 and camper: 23.0
(5) C4: 20.5
C6: 24.5
(6) E-100 with evaporative emission controls: 18.0
E-150: 18.0
All others with standard tank: 22.1
Optional auxiliary tank: 18.0
(7) With auto. trans.: 16.6
Without auto. trans.: 14.5
(8) Ford axles: 6.5
Dana axles: 6.0
(9) Ford axles: 6.5
Dana 61-1: 5.0
Dana 70: 5.5

(10) Ford axles: 6.5
Dana 60 & 61-1: 6.0
Dana 70: 5.5
(11) E-100 and 150 with 124 inch wheelbase: 18.0
All others: 22.1 standard
Optional auxiliary tank, except E-350 cutaway: 18.0
Optional tank on E-350 cutaway: 40.0
(12) With auto. trans.: 17.5
Without auto. trans.: 15.0
(13) Except E-350: 4.5
E-350: 3.25
(14) AOD: 24.0
C6: 23.8
(15) Ford axles: 5.5
Dana 60: 6.0
Dana 70: 6.5
(16) Without auxiliary heater: 16.0
With auxiliary heater: 17.8
(17) Without auxiliary heater: 17.5
With auxiliary heater: 19.3
(18) E-150 w/Mazda M50D 5-speed: 7.6
E-350 w/ZF S5-42 5-speed: 6.8

Preventive Maintenance Schedule

Interval	Item	Service
	1961–71	
Every 6 months or 6,000 miles	Chassis fittings	lubricate
	Crankcase	change oil & filter
	Differential	check level
	Tires	rotate
	Transmission, automatic	adjust bands, check level
	Transmission, manual	check level
	Air cleaner, oil bath	clean & fill SAE 30
	Brake master cylinder	check level
	Cooling system	change coolant, inspect
	Drive belts	inspect & adjust
	Manifold heat riser	check
	Oil filler cap	clean
	Power steering	check level
	Spark plugs	change
	Points, condenser, rotor	change
	Fuel mixture	check & adjust
	Ignition wiring	inspect
Every 12 months or 12,000 miles	Free-running hubs	clean and repack
	Intake manifold, 8 cylinder	torque bolts
	Thermactor	inspect hoses & belts
	PCV system	replace valve
	Choke linkage	inspect & adjust
Every 24 months or 24,000 miles	Brakes, drum type	inspect
	Front wheel bearings	clean & repack
	Rear wheel bearings, E-250, 350	clean and repack
	Transmission, manual	change lubricant
	Air cleaner paper element	change
	Distributor shaft or wick	oil with 10W
	Fuel filter	replace
	PCV filter, 1971	replace
	Speedometer and parking brake cables	lubricate
	Steering gear, manual	check level
	Transmission and clutch linkage	lubricate
	1972–73	
Every 4 months or 4,000 miles	Brakes	inspect
	Crankcase	change oil & filter
	Differential	check level
	Chassis fittings	lubricate
	Tires	rotate
	Transmission, automatic	adjust bands, check level
	Transmission, manual	check level
	Air cleaner, oil bath	clean and reflll
	Brake master cylinder	check level
	Cooling system	inspect, change coolant
	Manifold heat riser	inspect
	Oil filler cap, 1972	clean
	PCV filter	replace
	Power steering reservoir	check level
	Spark plugs, leaded fuel	replace
	TRS or throttle solenoid fuse	check
Every 12 months or 12,000 miles	Air cleaner paper element	replace
	Breather cap, 1973	clean
	Distributor points, condenser, rotor	replace
	Drive belts	check and adjust
	EGR system, 1973	clean and inspect
	Fuel filter	replace
	Fuel vapor system	inspect
	Idle speed and mixture	check and adjust
	Ignition coil, 1972 E-100	check for corrosion
	Ignition timing & dwell	check and adjust

Preventive Maintenance Schedule (cont.)

Interval	Item	Service
1972–73		
Every 12 months or 12,000 miles	Intake manifold, 8 cylinder	torque
	Spark control system, E-100	inspect
	Spark delay valve	replace
	Spark plugs, unleaded fuel	replace
	Thermostatic air cleaner	inspect
	Throttle and choke linkage	inspect
Every 24 months or 24,000 miles	Differential, E-250, 350	change lubricant
	Front wheel bearings	clean and repack
	Rear wheel bearings, E-250, 350	clean and repack
	Transmission, manual	change lubricant
	Distributor cap	replace
	Distributor shaft or wick	oil with 10W
1974		
Every 4 months or 4,000 miles	Crankcase	change oil & filter
	Air cleaner oil bath	clean and refill
	Idle speed	adjust
	Manifold heat riser	inspect
Every 6 months or 6,000 miles	Brakes	inspect
	Differential	check level
	Chassis fittings	lubricate
	Transmission, automatic	adjust bands, check level
	Transmission, manual	check level
	Cooling system	change coolant
	Drive belts	check and adjust
	Fuel filter	replace
	Idle speed and mixture	adjust
	PCV filter	replace
	Power steering	check level
	Throttle and choke linkage	inspect
	Ignition timing	adjust
Every 12 months or 12,000 miles	Air cleaner paper element	replace
	Breather cap	clean
	Brake master cylinder	check level
	Distributor points, condenser, rotor	replace
	EGR system	clean and inspect
	Intake manifold, 8 cylinder	torque
	PCV valve	replace
	Spark plugs, leaded fuel	replace
	Thermactor system	inspect
	Thermostatic air cleaner	inspect
Every 18 months or 18,000 miles	Distributor cap	replace
	Spark plugs, unleaded fuel	replace
Every 24 months or 24,000 miles	Front wheel bearings	clean and repack
	Rear wheel bearings, E-250, 350	clean and repack
1975–76		
Every 5 months or 5,000 miles	Brakes	inspect
	Crankcase	change oil & filter
	Differential	check level
	Chassis fittings	lubricate
	Transmission, automatic	adjust bands, check level
	Transmission, manual	check level
	Air cleaner oil bath	clean and refill
	Power steering	check level
	Idle speed	adjust
	Throttle kickdown exc E-100	check
	Throttle solenoid-off speed	check

Preventive Maintenance Schedule (cont.)

Interval	Item	Service
1975–76		
Every 6 months	Cooling system	inspect, change coolant
Every 15 months or 15,000 miles	Brake master cylinder	check level
	Parking brake linkage	oil with 10W
	Air cleaner element	replace
	Air cleaner temperature valve	check
	Choke system	inspect
	Distributor cap and rotor	inspect
	Distributor wick	oil with 10W
	Drive belts	check & adjust
	EGR system	clean and inspect
	Fuel filter	replace
	Ignition timing	adjust
	Intake manifold, 302 V8	torque
	Manifold heat riser	inspect
	PCV system	inspect
	Spark plugs	replace
	Spark plug wires	inspect
	Thermactor system	inspect
Every 20 months or 20,000 miles	Front wheel bearings	clean and repack
	Rear wheel bearings, Dana axle	clean and repack
Every 25 months or 25,000 miles	Differential, Dana	change lubricant
	Transmission, 4-speed	change lubricant
Every 30 months or 30,000 miles	Air cleaner crankcase filter	replace
	EEC canister	inspect
	Fuel vapor system	inspect
	PCV valve	replace
1977–83 E-100 Only		
Every 6 months	Cooling system	change coolant
Every 7 months or 7,500 miles	Crankcase	change oil and filter
	Drive belts	check and adjust
	Idle speed and TSP-off speed	adjust
	Ignition timing	check and adjust
	Chassis fittings	lubricate
	Clutch linkage	inspect and oil
	Transmission, automatic	adjust bands, check level
Every 15 months or 15,000 miles	Exhaust system heat shields	inspect
Every 22 months or 22,500 miles	Spark plugs	replace
	Exhaust control valve, 300cid	inspect
	PCV valve	replace
	Idle mixture	adjust
	Choke system	inspect
	Thermactor delay valve	inspect
Every 30 months or 30,000 miles	Air cleaner element	replace
	Air cleaner crankcase filter	replace
	Air cleaner temperature control valve	check
	Fuel vapor system	inspect
	Front wheel bearings	clean and repack
	Brakes	inspect
	Brake master cylinder	check level
1977–88 E-150, 250, 350 Gasoline Engine		
Every 6 months or 6,000 miles	Crankcase	change oil & filter
	Cooling system	change coolant
	Idle speed and TSP-off speed	adjust

Preventive Maintenance Schedule (cont.)

Interval	Item	Service
1977–88 E-150, 250, 350 Gasoline Engine		
Every 6 months or 6,000 miles	Ignition timing	adjust
	Decel throttle control system	check
	Chassis fittings	lubricate
	Clutch linkage	inspect and oil
	Exhaust system heat shields	inspect
	Transmission, automatic	adjust bands, check level
Every 15 months or 15,000 miles	Spark plugs	replace
	Exhaust control valve	check & lubricate
	Drive belts	check and adjust
	Air cleaner temperature control	check
	Choke system	check
	Thermactor system	check
	Crankcase breather cap	clean
	EGR system	clean and inspect
	PCV system	clean and inspect
1983–88 E250, 350 Diesel Engine		
Every 6 months or 5,000 miles	Crankcase	change oil & filter
	Cooling system	change coolant
	Chassis fittings	lubricate
	U-Joints and slip yokes	lubricate
	Clutch linkage	inspect and oil
	Exhaust system	inspect
	Transmission, automatic	adjust bands, check level
	Fuel water separator	drain water
Every 15 months or 15,000 miles	Drive belts	check and adjust
	Clutch reservoir fluid level	check
	Fan and Fan shroud	inspect
	Crankcase breather cap	clean
	Fuel Filter	replace
Every 30 months or 30,000 miles	Air cleaner element	replace
	Air cleaner crankcase filter	replace
	Fuel vapor system	inspect
	Brake master cylinder	check
	Brakes	inspect
	Front wheel bearings	clean and repack
	Rear wheel bearings, Dana axles	clean and repack
1977–88 E-150, 250, 350		
Every 30 months or 30,000 miles	PCV valve	replace
	Air cleaner element	replace
	Air cleaner crankcase filter	replace
	Fuel vapor system	inspect
	Brake master cylinder	check
	Brakes	inspect
	Front wheel bearings	clean and repack
	Rear wheel bearings, Dana axles	clean and repack

Engine Performance and Tune-Up

2

TUNE-UP PROCEDURES

In order to extract the full measure of performance and economy from your engine it is essential that it be properly tuned at regular intervals. A regular tune-up will keep your vehicle's engine running smoothly and will prevent the annoying minor breakdowns and poor performance associated with an untuned engine.

A complete tune-up should be performed every 12,000 miles or twelve months, whichever comes first. This interval should be halved if the vehicle is operated under severe conditions, such as trailer towing, prolonged idling, continual stop and start driving, or if starting or running problems are noticed. It is assumed that the routine maintenance described in Chapter 1

has been kept up, as this will have a decided effect on the results of a tune-up. All of the applicable steps of a tune-up should be followed in order, as the result is a cumulative one.

If the specifications on the tune-up sticker in the engine compartment disagree with the Tune-Up Specifications chart in this chapter, the figures on the sticker must be used. The sticker often reflects changes made during the production run.

Spark Plugs

A typical spark plug consists of a metal shell surrounding a ceramic insulator. A metal electrode extends downward through the center of the insulator and protrudes a small distance. Located at the end of the plug and attached to

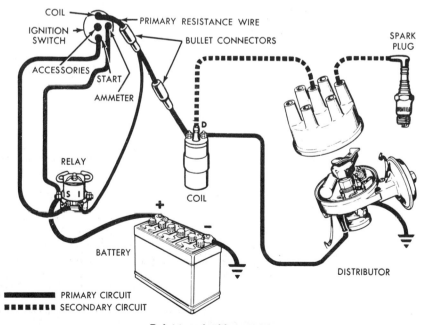

COIL
IGNITION SWITCH
PRIMARY RESISTANCE WIRE
BULLET CONNECTORS
SPARK PLUG
ACCESSORIES
START
AMMETER
D
RELAY
S I
COIL
+
−
BATTERY
DISTRIBUTOR
PRIMARY CIRCUIT
SECONDARY CIRCUIT

Point-type ignition system

Troubleshooting Engine Performance

Problem	Cause	Solution
Hard starting (engine cranks normally)	• Binding linkage, choke valve or choke piston	• Repair as necessary
	• Restricted choke vacuum diaphragm	• Clean passages
	• Improper fuel level	• Adjust float level
	• Dirty, worn or faulty needle valve and seat	• Repair as necessary
	• Float sticking	• Repair as necessary
	• Faulty fuel pump	• Replace fuel pump
	• Incorrect choke cover adjustment	• Adjust choke cover
	• Inadequate choke unloader adjustment	• Adjust choke unloader
	• Faulty ignition coil	• Test and replace as necessary
	• Improper spark plug gap	• Adjust gap
	• Incorrect ignition timing	• Adjust timing
	• Incorrect valve timing	• Check valve timing; repair as necessary
Rough idle or stalling	• Incorrect curb or fast idle speed	• Adjust curb or fast idle speed
	• Incorrect ignition timing	• Adjust timing to specification
	• Improper feedback system operation	• Refer to Chapter 4
	• Improper fast idle cam adjustment	• Adjust fast idle cam
	• Faulty EGR valve operation	• Test EGR system and replace as necessary
	• Faulty PCV valve air flow	• Test PCV valve and replace as necessary
	• Choke binding	• Locate and eliminate binding condition
	• Faulty TAC vacuum motor or valve	• Repair as necessary
	• Air leak into manifold vacuum	• Inspect manifold vacuum connections and repair as necessary
	• Improper fuel level	• Adjust fuel level
	• Faulty distributor rotor or cap	• Replace rotor or cap
	• Improperly seated valves	• Test cylinder compression, repair as necessary
	• Incorrect ignition wiring	• Inspect wiring and correct as necessary
	• Faulty ignition coil	• Test coil and replace as necessary
	• Restricted air vent or idle passages	• Clean passages
	• Restricted air cleaner	• Clean or replace air cleaner filler element
	• Faulty choke vacuum diaphragm	• Repair as necessary
Faulty low-speed operation	• Restricted idle transfer slots	• Clean transfer slots
	• Restricted idle air vents and passages	• Clean air vents and passages
	• Restricted air cleaner	• Clean or replace air cleaner filter element
	• Improper fuel level	• Adjust fuel level
	• Faulty spark plugs	• Clean or replace spark plugs
	• Dirty, corroded, or loose ignition secondary circuit wire connections	• Clean or tighten secondary circuit wire connections
	• Improper feedback system operation	• Refer to Chapter 4
	• Faulty ignition coil high voltage wire	• Replace ignition coil high voltage wire
	• Faulty distributor cap	• Replace cap
Faulty acceleration	• Improper accelerator pump stroke	• Adjust accelerator pump stroke
	• Incorrect ignition timing	• Adjust timing
	• Inoperative pump discharge check ball or needle	• Clean or replace as necessary
	• Worn or damaged pump diaphragm or plston	• Replace diaphragm or piston

Troubleshooting Engine Performance (cont.)

Problem	Cause	Solution
Faulty acceleration (cont.)	· Leaking carburetor main body cover gasket	· Replace gasket
	· Engine cold and choke set too lean	· Adjust choke cover
	· Improper metering rod adjustment (BBD Model carburetor)	· Adjust metering rod
	· Faulty spark plug(s)	· Clean or replace spark plug(s)
	· Improperly seated valves	· Test cylinder compression, repair as necessary
	· Faulty ignition coil	· Test coil and replace as necessary
	· Improper feedback system operation	· Refer to Chapter 4
Faulty high speed operation	· Incorrect ignition timing	· Adjust timing
	· Faulty distributor centrifugal advance mechanism	· Check centrifugal advance mechanism and repair as necessary
	· Faulty distributor vacuum advance mechanism	· Check vacuum advance mechanism and repair as necessary
	· Low fuel pump volume	· Replace fuel pump
	· Wrong spark plug air gap or wrong plug	· Adjust air gap or install correct plug
	· Faulty choke operation	· Adjust choke cover
	· Partially restricted exhaust manifold, exhaust pipe, catalytic converter, muffler, or tailpipe	· Eliminate restriction
	· Restricted vacuum passages	· Clean passages
	· Improper size or restricted main jet	· Clean or replace as necessary
	· Restricted air cleaner	· Clean or replace filter element as necessary
	· Faulty distributor rotor or cap	· Replace rotor or cap
	· Faulty ignition coil	· Test coil and replace as necessary
	· Improperly seated valve(s)	· Test cylinder compression, repair as necessary
	· Faulty valve spring(s)	· Inspect and test valve spring tension, replace as necessary
	· Incorrect valve timing	· Check valve timing and repair as necessary
	· Intake manifold restricted	· Remove restriction or replace manifold
	· Worn distributor shaft	· Replace shaft
	· Improper feedback system operation	· Refer to Chapter 4
Misfire at all speeds	· Faulty spark plug(s)	· Clean or replace spark plug(s)
	· Faulty spark plug wire(s)	· Replace as necessary
	· Faulty distributor cap or rotor	· Replace cap or rotor
	· Faulty ignition coil	· Test coil and replace as necessary
	· Primary ignition circuit shorted or open intermittently	· Troubleshoot primary circuit and repair as necessary
	· Improperly seated valve(s)	· Test cylinder compression, repair as necessary
	· Faulty hydraulic tappet(s)	· Clean or replace tappet(s)
	· Improper feedback system operation	· Refer to Chapter 4
	· Faulty valve spring(s)	· Inspect and test valve spring tension, repair as necessary
	· Worn camshaft lobes	· Replace camshaft
	· Air leak into manifold	· Check manifold vacuum and repair as necessary
	· Improper carburetor adjustment	· Adjust carburetor
	· Fuel pump volume or pressure low	· Replace fuel pump
	· Blown cylinder head gasket	· Replace gasket
	· Intake or exhaust manifold passage(s) restricted	· Pass chain through passage(s) and repair as necessary
	· Incorrect trigger wheel installed in distributor	· Install correct trigger wheel

Troubleshooting Engine Performance (cont.)

Problem	Cause	Solution
Power not up to normal	• Incorrect ignition timing • Faulty distributor rotor • Trigger wheel loose on shaft • Incorrect spark plug gap • Faulty fuel pump • Incorrect valve timing • Faulty ignition coil • Faulty ignition wires • Improperly seated valves • Blown cylinder head gasket • Leaking piston rings • Worn distributor shaft • Improper feedback system operation	• Adjust timing • Replace rotor • Reposition or replace trigger wheel • Adjust gap • Replace fuel pump • Check valve timing and repair as necessary • Test coil and replace as necessary • Test wires and replace as necessary • Test cylinder compression and repair as necessary • Replace gasket • Test compression and repair as necessary • Replace shaft • Refer to Chapter 4
Intake backfire	• Improper ignition timing • Faulty accelerator pump discharge • Defective EGR CTO valve • Defective TAC vacuum motor or valve • Lean air/fuel mixture	• Adjust timing • Repair as necessary • Replace EGR CTO valve • Repair as necessary • Check float level or manifold vacuum for air leak. Remove sediment from bowl
Exhaust backfire	• Air leak into manifold vacuum • Faulty air injection diverter valve • Exhaust leak	• Check manifold vacuum and repair as necessary • Test diverter valve and replace as necessary • Locate and eliminate leak
Ping or spark knock	• Incorrect ignition timing • Distributor centrifugal or vacuum advance malfunction • Excessive combustion chamber deposits • Air leak into manifold vacuum • Excessively high compression • Fuel octane rating excessively low • Sharp edges in combustion chamber • EGR valve not functioning properly	• Adjust timing • Inspect advance mechanism and repair as necessary • Remove with combustion chamber cleaner • Check manifold vacuum and repair as necessary • Test compression and repair as necessary • Try alternate fuel source • Grind smooth • Test EGR system and replace as necessary
Surging (at cruising to top speeds)	• Low carburetor fuel level • Low fuel pump pressure or volume • Metering rod(s) not adjusted properly (BBD Model Carburetor) • Improper PCV valve air flow • Air leak into manifold vacuum • Incorrect spark advance • Restricted main jet(s) • Undersize main jet(s) • Restricted air vents • Restricted fuel filter • Restricted air cleaner • EGR valve not functioning properly • Improper feedback system operation	• Adjust fuel level • Replace fuel pump • Adjust metering rod • Test PCV valve and replace as necessary • Check manifold vacuum and repair as necessary • Test and replace as necessary • Clean main jet(s) • Replace main jet(s) • Clean air vents • Replace fuel filter • Clean or replace air cleaner filter element • Test EGR system and replace as necessary • Refer to Chapter 4

TROUBLESHOOTING BASIC POINT-TYPE IGNITION SYSTEM PROBLEMS

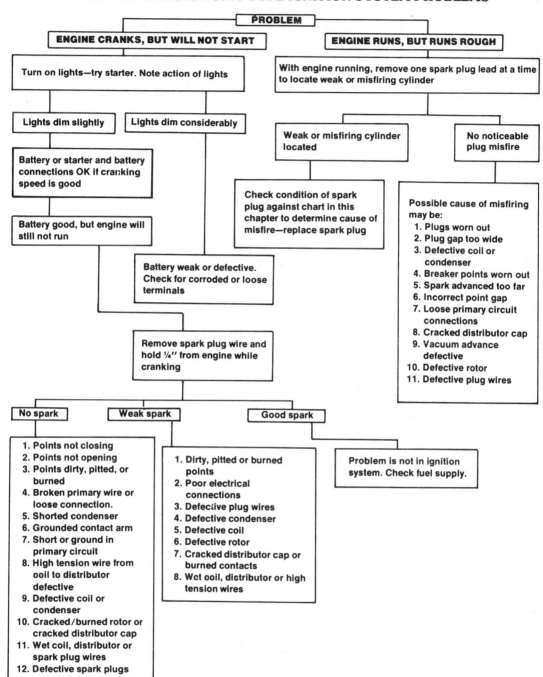

the side of the outer metal shell is the side electrode. The side electrode bends in at a 90° angle so that its tip is even with, and parallel to, the tip of the center electrode. The distance between these two electrodes (measured in thousandths of an inch) is called the spark plug gap. The spark plug in no way produces a spark but merely provides a gap across which the current can arc. The coil produces anywhere from 20,000 to 40,000 volts which travels to the distributor where it is distributed through the spark plug wires to the spark plugs. The current passes along the center electrode and jumps the gap to the side electrode, and, in do doing, ignites the air/fuel mixture in the combustion chamber.

Tune-Up Specifications
Gasoline Engines

| Years | Engine | Spark Plugs | | Distributor | | Ignition Timing (deg.) | | Valve * Clearance | | Idle Speed | |
		Type	Gap (in.)	Point Gap (in.)	Dwell (deg.)	Man. Trans.	Auto. Trans.	In.	Exh.	Man. Trans.	Auto. Trans.
1961	6-144	BF-82	0.034	0.25	35–38	6B	—	0.018	0.018	550	—
	6-170	BF-82	0.034	0.25	35–38	6B	—	0.018	0.018	550	—
1962	6-144	BF-82	0.034	0.25	35–38	6B	—	0.018	0.018	550	—
	6-170	BF-82	0.034	0.25	35–38	6B	—	0.018	0.018	550	—
1963	6-144	BF-82	0.035	0.25	35–38	4B	—	0.018	0.018	550	—
	6-170	BF-82	0.035	0.25	35–38	4B	—	0.018	0.018	550	—
1964	6-144	BF-82	0.035	0.25	35–38	4B	—	0.018	0.018	600	—
	6-170	BF-82	0.035	0.25	35–38	4B	8B	0.018	0.018	600	575
1965	6-170	BF-82	0.035	0.25	35–38	4B	8B	0.018	0.018	600	575
	6-200	BF-82	0.035	0.25	35–38	6B	10B	Hyd.	Hyd.	600	525
	6-240	BF-82	0.035	0.25	35–38	6B	8B	Hyd.	Hyd.	525	525
1966	6-170	BF-82	0.035	0.25	37–42	①	①	0.018	0.018	②	②
	6-240	BTF-42	0.035	0.25	37–42	③	③	Hyd.	Hyd.	④	④
1967–68	6-170	BF-82	0.035	0.25	37–42	③	③	0.018	0.018	⑤	⑤
	6-240	BTF-42	0.035	0.25	37–42	③	③	Hyd.	Hyd.	⑥	⑥
1969	6-170	BF-82	0.034	0.27	35–40	6B	—	0.018	0.018	700	—
	6-240	BTF-42	0.034	0.27	⑦	⑧	⑧	Hyd.	Hyd.	④	④
	8-302	BTF-31	0.030	0.021	⑨	6B	6B	Hyd.	Hyd.	625	550
1970	6-170	BF-82	0.034	0.27	35–40	6B	—	0.018	0.018	775	—
	6-240	BTF-42	0.034	0.27	35–40	6B	6B	Hyd.	Hyd.	⑩	⑩
	8-302	BTF-31	0.030	⑪	⑫	6B	6B	Hyd.	Hyd	⑬	⑬
1971	6-240	⑭	⑮	⑯	⑰	6B	6B	Hyd.	Hyd.	⑱	⑱
	8-302	BTF-31	0.030	⑪	⑫	6B	6B	Hyd.	Hyd.	⑬	⑬
1972	6-240	⑭	⑮	⑯	⑰	6B	6B	Hyd.	Hyd.	⑱	⑱
	8-302	BTF-31	0.030	⑪	⑫	6B	6B	Hyd.	Hyd.	⑬	⑬
1973	6-240	BRF-42	0.034	0.027	33–39	6B	6B	Hyd.	Hyd.	⑱	⑱
	6-300	⑲	0.034	0.027	33–39	6B	6B	Hyd.	Hyd.	⑱	⑱
	8-302	BRF-42	0.034	0.017	24–30	6B	6B	Hyd.	Hyd.	⑬	⑬
1974	6-240	BRF-42	0.034	Electronic		6B	6B	Hyd.	Hyd.	850	650
	6-300	⑲	0.034	Electronic		⑳	6B	Hyd.	Hyd.	㉑	㉑
	8-302	BRF-42	㉒	Electronic		6B	6B	Hyd.	Hyd.	900	650
1975	6-300	BTRF-42	0.044	Electronic		12B	12B	Hyd.	Hyd.	700	550
	8-351W	ARF-42	0.044	Electronic		14B	14B	Hyd.	Hyd.	900	650
	8-460	ARF-42	0.044	Electronic		—	12B	Hyd.	Hyd.	—	650
1976	6-300	BTRF-42	0.044	Electronic		12B	㉓	Hyd.	Hyd.	700	550
	8-351W	㉔	0.044	Electronic		8B	㉕	Hyd.	Hyd.	650	650
	8-460	ARF-42	0.044	Electronic		—	12B	Hyd.	Hyd.	—	650

Tune-Up Specifications (cont.)

Gasoline Engines

| Years | Engine | Spark Plugs | | Distributor | | Ignition Timing (deg.) | | Valve* Clearance | | Idle Speed | |
		Type	Gap (in.)	Point Gap (in.)	Dwell (deg.)	Man. Trans.	Auto. Trans.	In.	Exh.	Man. Trans.	Auto. Trans.
1977	6-300	BSF-42	0.044	Electronic		[26]	[26]	Hyd.	Hyd.	[27]	[27]
	8-351W	[28]	0.044	Electronic		[29]	[29]	Hyd.	Hyd.	[30]	[30]
	8-460	ASF-42	0.044	Electronic		—	12B	Hyd.	Hyd.	—	650
1978	6-300	BSF-42	[31]	Electronic		[32]	[32]	Hyd.	Hyd.	[32]	[32]
	8-351W	ASF-42	0.044	Electronic		—	[32]	Hyd.	Hyd.	—	[32]
	8-460	ASF-42	0.044	Electronic		—	[32]	Hyd.	Hyd.	—	[32]
1979	6-300	BSF-42	0.044	Electronic		[32]	[32]	Hyd.	Hyd.	[32]	[32]
	8-302	ASF-42	0.044	Electronic		[32]	[32]	Hyd.	Hyd.	[32]	[32]
	8-351W	ASF-42	0.044	Electronic		—	[32]	Hyd.	Hyd.	—	[32]
	8-460	ASF-42	0.044	Electronic		—	[32]	Hyd.	Hyd.	—	[32]
1980	6-300	BSF-42	0.044	Electronic		[32]	[32]	Hyd.	Hyd.	[32]	[32]
	8-302	ASF-42	0.044	Electronic		[32]	[32]	Hyd.	Hyd.	[32]	[32]
	8-351W	ASF-42	0.044	Electronic		—	[32]	Hyd.	Hyd.	—	[32]
	8-460	ASF-42	0.044	Electronic		—	[32]	Hyd.	Hyd.	—	[32]
1981	6-300	BSF-42	0.044	Electronic		[32]	[32]	Hyd.	Hyd.	[32]	[32]
	8-302	ASF-42	0.044	Electronic		[32]	[32]	Hyd.	Hyd.	[32]	[32]
	8-351W	ASF-42	0.044	Electronic		—	[32]	Hyd.	Hyd.	—	[32]
	8-460	ASF-32	0.044	Electronic		—	[32]	Hyd.	Hyd.	—	[32]
1982	6-300	BSF-42	0.044	Electronic		[32]	[32]	Hyd.	Hyd.	[32]	[32]
	8-302	ASF-42	0.044	Electronic		[32]	[32]	Hyd.	Hyd.	[32]	[32]
	8-351W	ASF-42	0.044	Electronic		—	[32]	Hyd.	Hyd.	—	[32]
	8-460	ASF-32	0.044	Electronic		—	[32]	Hyd.	Hyd.	—	[32]
1983	6-300	BSF-42	0.044	Electronic		[32]	[32]	Hyd.	Hyd.	[32]	[32]
	8-302	ASF-42	0.044	Electronic		[32]	[32]	Hyd.	Hyd.	[32]	[32]
	8-351W	ASF-42	0.044	Electronic		—	[32]	Hyd.	Hyd.	—	[32]
	8-460	ASF-42	0.044	Electronic		—	[32]	Hyd.	Hyd.	—	[32]
1984	6-300	BSF-42	0.044	Electronic		[32]	[32]	Hyd.	Hyd.	[32]	[32]
	8-302	ASF-42	0.044	Electronic		[32]	[32]	Hyd.	Hyd.	[32]	[32]
	8-351W	ASF-42	0.044	Electronic		—	[32]	Hyd.	Hyd.	—	[32]
	8-460	ASF-42	0.044	Electronic		—	[32]	Hyd.	Hyd.	—	[32]
1985	6-300	BSF-42	0.044	Electronic		[32]	[32]	Hyd.	Hyd.	[32]	[32]
	8-302	ASF-32	0.044	Electronic		[32]	[32]	Hyd.	Hyd.	[32]	[32]
	8-351W	ASF-42	0.044	Electronic		—	[32]	Hyd.	Hyd.	—	[32]
	8-460	ASF-42	0.044	Electronic		—	[32]	Hyd.	Hyd.	—	[32]
1986	6-300	BSF-42	0.044	Electronic		[32]	[32]	Hyd.	Hyd.	[32]	[32]
	8-302	ASF-32	0.044	Electronic		[32]	[32]	Hyd.	Hyd.	[32]	[32]
	8-351W	ASF-32	0.044	Electronic		—	[32]	Hyd.	Hyd.	—	[32]
	8-460	ASF-42	0.044	Electronic		—	[32]	Hyd.	Hyd.	—	[32]

Tune-Up Specifications (cont.)
Gasoline Engines

Years	Engine	Spark Plugs Type	Gap (in.)	Distributor Point Gap (in.)	Dwell (deg.)	Ignition Timing (deg.) Man. Trans.	Auto. Trans.	Valve* Clearance In.	Exh.	Idle Speed Man. Trans.	Auto. Trans.
1987	6-300	BSF-42	0.044	Electronic		③2	③2	Hyd.	Hyd.	③2	③2
	8-302	ASF-42	0.044	Electronic		③2	③2	Hyd.	Hyd.	③2	③2
	8-351W	ASF-32	0.044	Electronic		—	③2	Hyd.	Hyd.	—	③2
	8-460	ASF-42	0.044	Electronic		—	③2	Hyd.	Hyd.	—	③2
1988	6-300	BSF-42	0.044	Electronic		③2	③2	Hyd.	Hyd.	③2	③2
	8-302	ASF-42	0.044	Electronic		—	③2	Hyd.	Hyd.	—	③2
	8-351W	ASF-32	0.044	Electronic		—	③2	Hyd.	Hyd.	—	③2
	8-460	ASF-42	0.044	Electronic		—	③2	Hyd.	Hyd.	—	③2

① With Thermactor: TDC
   Without Thermactor: MT 4B; AT 8B
② With Thermactor: MT 650; AT 575
   Without Thermactor: MT 600; AT 525
③ With Thermactor: TDC
   Without Thermactor: MT 6B; AT 10B
④ With Thermactor: MT 650; AT 575
   Without Thermactor: MT & AT 525
⑤ With Thermactor: MT 700; AT 550
   Without Thermactor: MT 575; AT 500
⑥ With Thermactor: MT 600; AT 500
   Without Thermactor: MT 525; AT 500
⑦ With Thermactor: 35–40
   Without Thermactor: 37–42
⑧ With Thermactor: MT & AT 6B
   Without Thermactor: MT 6B; AT 10B
⑨ With Thermactor: 26–31
   Without Thermactor: 24–29
⑩ E-300 van: MT 600; AT 550
   E-100, E-200, E-300 bus:
      MT 850 solenoid on/500 solenoid off
      AT 575 solenoid on/500 solenoid off
⑪ Except E-300: 0.021
   E-300: 0.017
⑫ Except E-100: 24–29
   E-100: 26–31
⑬ MT: 800 solenoid on/500 solenoid off
   AT: 600 solenoid on/500 solenoid off
⑭ Except E-300 van: BTF-42
   E-300 van: BTF-31
⑮ BTF-42: 0.034
   BTF-31: 0.030
⑯ Except E-300 van: 0.027
   E-300 van: 0.025

⑰ Except E-300 van: 35–40
   E-300 van: 37–42
⑱ E-300 van: MT 600; AT 500
   E-100, E-200, E-300 bus:
      MT 850 solenoid on/500 solenoid off
      AT 600 solenoid on/500 solenoid off
⑲ Except E-300 van: BRF-42
   E-300 van: BRF-31
⑳ Except Calif.: 10B
   Calif.: 6B
㉑ Except E-300 van: MT 700; AT 550
   E-300 van: MT 600; AT 550
㉒ Except Calif.: 0.044
   Calif.: 0.054
㉓ Except Calif.: 12B
   Calif.: 6B
㉔ Except E-100: ARF-32
   E-100: ARF-42
㉕ Except Calif.: 8B
   Calif.: 12B
㉖ Except E-100: 10B
   E-100: 6B
㉗ Except E-100: MT & AT 600
   E-100: MT 700; AT 550
㉘ Except E-100: ASF-34
   E-100: ASF-42
㉙ Except E-100: MT & AT 8B
   E-100 Calif.: MT 8B; AT 14B
   E-100 High Altitude: MT & AT 12B
   All other E-100: see underhood sticker
㉚ Except E-100: MT 650; AT 550
   E-100: MT 700; AT 550
㉛ All except E-100 and California vehicles: 0.54
   E-100 and California vehicles: 0.044
㉜ See underhood sticker

SPARK PLUG HEAT RANGE

Spark plug heat range is the ability of the plug to dissipate heat. The longer the insulator (or the farther it extends into the engine), the hotter the plug will operate; the shorter the insulator the cooler it will operate. A plug that absorbs little heat and remains too cool will quickly accumulate deposits of oil and carbon since it is not hot enough to burn them off. This leads to plug fouling and consequently to misfiring. A plug that absorbs too much heat will have no deposits, but, due to the excessive heat, the electrodes will burn away quickly and in some instances, preignition may result. Preignition takes place when plug tips get so hot that they glow sufficiently to ignite the fuel/air mixture before the actual spark occurs. This early ignition will usually cause a pinging during low speeds and heavy loads.

The general rule of thumb for choosing the correct heat range when picking a spark plug is:

Tune-Up Specifications
Diesel Engines

Years	Engine	Static Timing	Dynamic Timing	Opening Pressure (psi)	Curb Idle Speed (rpm)	Fast Idle Speed (rpm)	Maximum Compression Pressure (psi)
1983–87	8-420	Index	①	1,850	②	850–900	440
1988	8-444	Index	①	1,850	②	850–900	440

Static timing is set by aligning the index mark on the pump mounting flange with the index mark on the pump mounting adapter.

① Cetane rating of 38–42: Up to 3,000 ft.—6°ATDC ± 1°
　　　　　　　　　　　　Over 3,000 ft.—7°ATDC ± 1°
Cetane rating of 43–46: Up to 3,000 ft.—5°ATDC ± 1°
　　　　　　　　　　　　Over 3,000 ft.—6°ATDC ± 1°

Cetane rating of 47–50: Up to 3,000 ft.—4°ATDC ± 1°
　　　　　　　　　　　　Over 3,000 ft.—5°ATDC ± 1°

② 1983–84: 725–775
　　1985–88: 650–700

if most of your driving is long distance, high speed travel, use a colder plug; if most of your driving is stop and go, use a hotter plug. Original equipment plugs are compromise plugs, but most people never have occasion to change their plugs from the factory-recommended heat range.

REPLACING SPARK PLUGS

A set of spark plugs usually requires replacement after about 20,000 to 30,000 miles, depending on your style of driving. In normal operation, plug gap increases about 0.001" for every 1,000-2,500 miles. As the gap increases, the plug's voltage requirement also increases. It re-

quires a greater voltage to jump the wider gap and about two to three times as much voltage to fire a plug at high speeds than at idle.

When you're removing spark plugs, you should work on one at a time. Don't start by removing the plug wires all at once, because unless you number them, they may become mixed up. Take a minute before you begin and number the wires with tape. The best location for numbering is near where the wires come out of the cap.

NOTE: *On models equipped with electronic ignition, apply a small amount of silicone dielectric compound (D7AZ-19A331-A or the equivalent) to the inside of the terminal boots*

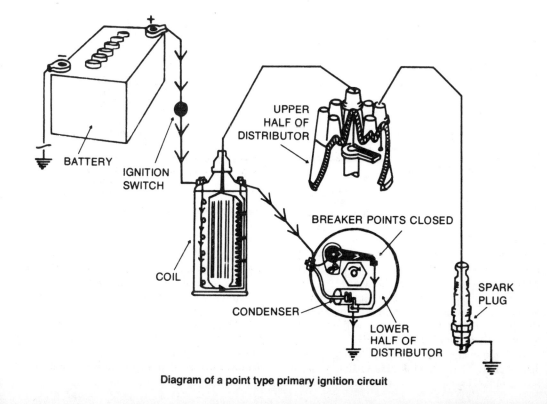

Diagram of a point type primary ignition circuit

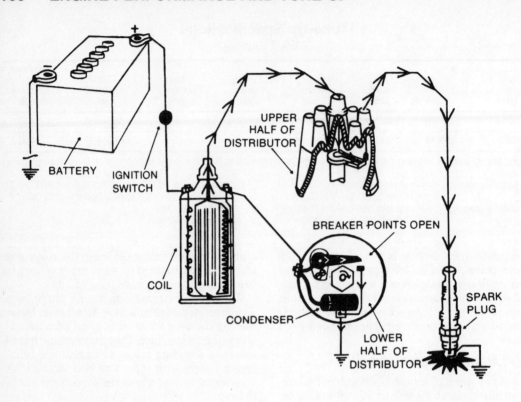

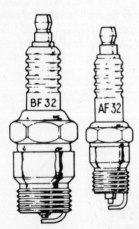

Typical spark plugs—left is $^{13}/_{16}$ in. (18 mm); right is ⅝ in. (14 mm)

Cross section of a spark plug

whenever an ignition wire is disconnected from the plug, or coil/distributor cap connection.

1. Twist the spark plug boot and remove the boot and wire from the plug. Do not pull on the wire itself as this will ruin the wire.

2. If possible, use a brush or gag to clean the area around the spark plug. Make sure that all the dirt is removed so that none will enter the cylinder after the plug is removed.

3. Remove the spark plug using the proper size socket. Truck models use either a ⅝" or

$^{13}/_{16}$" size socket depending on the engine. Turn the socket counterclockwise to remove the plug. Be sure to hold the socket straight on the plug to avoid breaking the plug, or rounding off the hex on the plug.

4. Once the plug is out, check it against the plugs shown in the Color section to determine engine condition. This is crucial since plug readings are vital signs of engine condition.

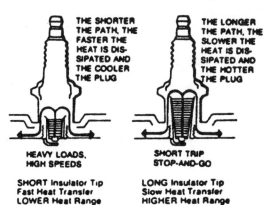

THE SHORTER THE PATH, THE FASTER THE HEAT IS DISSIPATED AND THE COOLER THE PLUG

THE LONGER THE PATH, THE SLOWER THE HEAT IS DISSIPATED AND THE HOTTER THE PLUG

HEAVY LOADS, HIGH SPEEDS

SHORT TRIP STOP-AND-GO

SHORT Insulator Tip
Fast Heat Transfer
LOWER Heat Range
COLD PLUG

LONG Insulator Tip
Slow Heat Transfer
HIGHER Heat Range
HOT PLUG

Spark plug heat range

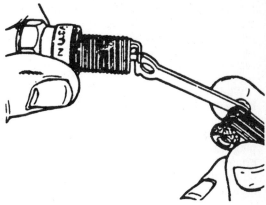

Adjust the electrode gap by bending the side electrode

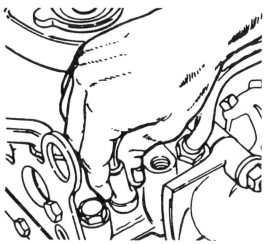

Twist and pull on the rubber boot to remove the spark plug wires; never pull on the wire itself

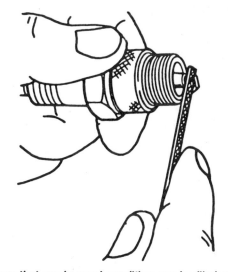

Plugs that are in good condition can be filed and re-used

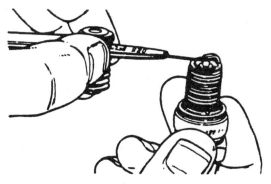

Always use a wire gauge to check the electrode gap

5. Use a round wire feeler gauge to check the plug gap. The correct size gauge should pass through the electrode gap with a slight drag. If you're in doubt, try one size smaller and one larger. The smaller gauge should go through easily while the larger one shouldn't go through at all. If the gap is incorrect, use the electrode bending tool on the end of the gauge to adjust the gap. When adjusting the gap, always bend the side electrode. The center electrode is non-adjustable.

6. Squirt a drop of penetrating oil on the threads of the new plug and install it. Don't oil the threads too heavily. Turn the plug in clockwise by hand until it is snug.

7. When the plug is finger tight, tighten it with a wrench. If you don't have a torque wrench, tighten the plug as shown.

8. Install the plug boot firmly over the plug. Proceed to the next plug.

CHECKING AND REPLACING SPARK PLUG CABLES

Visually inspect the spark plug cables for burns, cuts, or breaks in the insulation. Check the spark plug boots and the nipples on the distributor cap and coil. Replace any damaged wiring. If no physical damage is obvious, the wires can be checked with an ohmmeter for excessive resistance. (See the tune-up and troubleshooting section).

When installing a new set of spark plug cables, replace the cables on at a time so there will be no mixup. Start by replacing the longest cable first. Install the boot firmly over the spark plug. Route the wire exactly the same as the original. Insert the nipple firmly into the tower on the distributor cap. Repeat the process for each cable.

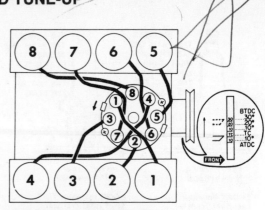

1975–88 8-351; 1980–82 8-400
firing order 1-3-7-2-6-5-4-8
distributor rotation: counterclockwise

FIRING ORDERS

To avoid confusion, replace spark plug wires one at a time.

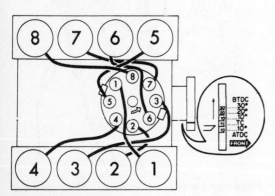

302 V8 through 1974
firing order: 1-5-4-2-6-3-7-8
distributor rotation: counterclockwise

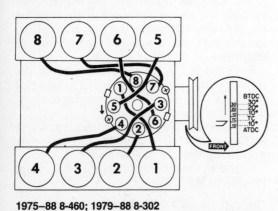

1975–88 8-460; 1979–88 8-302
firing order: 1-5-4-2-6-3-6-7-8
distributor rotation: counterclockwise
NOTE: Squares are the latches on 1975–76 models; circles are the latches on 1977–88 models

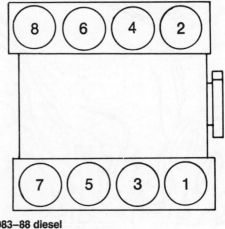

1983–88 diesel
firing order 1-2-7-3-4-5-6-8

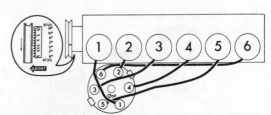

144, 170, 200 6-cylinder
firing order: 1-5-3-6-2-4
distributor rotation: clockwise

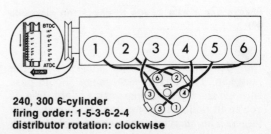

240, 300 6-cylinder
firing order: 1-5-3-6-2-4
distributor rotation: clockwise

POINT TYPE IGNITION

All 1961-73 and some 1974 Ford vans use breaker point type ignition systems.

Breaker Points

The points function as a circuit breaker for the primary circuit of the ignition system. The ignition coil must boost the 12 volts of electrical pressure supplied by the battery to as much as 25,000 volts in order to fire the plugs. To do this, the coil depends on the points and the condenser to make a clean break in the primary circuit.

The coil has both primary and secondary circuits. When the ignition is turned on, the battery supplies voltage through the coil to the

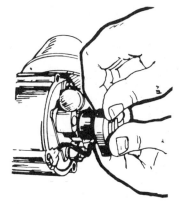

Removing the rotor on the point-type distributor

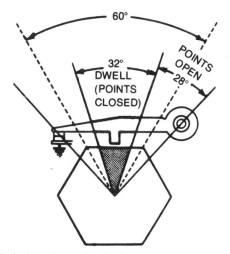

Typical breaker point dwell

Removing the point holddown screws

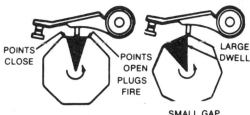

NORMAL DWELL-NORMAL GAP   SMALL GAP EXCESSIVE DWELL

Removing the condenser

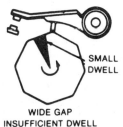

WIDE GAP INSUFFICIENT DWELL

Dwell angle functions

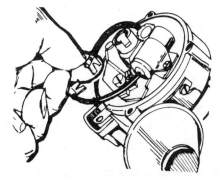

Removing the wires from the points

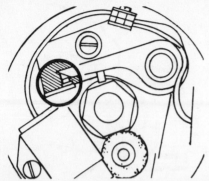

Once the points are installed, make certain that the contact surfaces are properly aligned. If there is misalignment, correct it by bending the STATIONARY arm, NOT THE MOVING ARM! Use a pair of needle-nosed pliers to bend the arm.

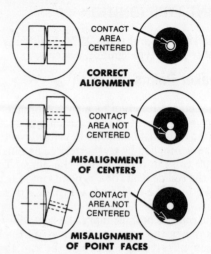

CONTACT AREA CENTERED

CORRECT ALIGNMENT

CONTACT AREA NOT CENTERED

MISALIGNMENT OF CENTERS

CONTACT AREA NOT CENTERED

MISALIGNMENT OF POINT FACES

Alignment of the breaker point contacts

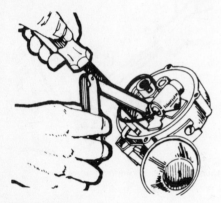

Adjusting the points

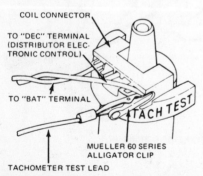

COIL CONNECTOR

TO "DEC" TERMINAL (DISTRIBUTOR ELECTRONIC CONTROL)

TO "BAT" TERMINAL

TACH TEST

MUELLER 60 SERIES ALLIGATOR CLIP

TACHOMETER TEST LEAD

Attaching dwell/tachometer lead to coil connector (electronic ignition)

points. The points are connected to ground, completing the primary circuit. As the current passes through the coil, a magnetic field is created in the iron center core of the oil. As the cam in the distributor turns, the points open and the primary circuit collapses. The magnetic field in the primary circuit of the coil cuts through the secondary circuit winding around the iron core. Because of the scientific phenom-

enon called electromagnetic induction, the battery voltage is increased to a level sufficient to fire the spark plugs.

When the points open, the electrical charge in the primary circuit jumps the gap created between the two open contacts of the points. If this electrical charge were not transferred elsewhere, the metal contacts of the points would melt and the gap between the points would start to change rapidly. If this gap is not maintained, the points will not break the primary circuit. If the primary circuit is not broken, the secondary circuit will not have enough voltage to fire the spark plugs.

Condenser

The function of the condenser is to absorb excessive voltage from the points when they open and thus prevent the points from becoming pitted or burned.

It is interesting to note that the above cycle must be completed by the ignition system every time spark fires. In a V8 engine, all of the spark plugs fire once for every two revolutions of the crankshaft. That means that in one revolution, four spark plugs fire. So when the engine is at an idle speed of 800 rpm, the points are opening and closing 3,200 times a minute.

There are two ways to check the breaker point gap: it can be done with a feeler gauge or a dwell meter. Either way you set the points, you are basically adjusting the amount of time that the points remain open. The time is measured in degrees of distributor rotation. When you measure the gap between the breaker points with a feeler gauge, you are setting the maximum amount the points will open when the rubbing block on the points is on a high point of the distributor cam. When you adjust the points with a dwell mete, you are adjusting the number of degrees that the points will remain closed before they start to open as a high point of the distributor cam approaches the rubbing block of the points.

When you replace a set of points, always replace the condenser at the same time.

When you change the point gap or dwell, you will also have the ignition timing. So, if the point gap or dwell is changed, the ignition timing must be adjusted also.

INSPECTION OF THE POINTS

1. Disconnect the high tension wire from the top of the distributor and the coil.

2. Remove the distributor cap by prying off the spring clips on the sides of the cap.

3. Remove the rotor from the distributor shaft by pulling it straight up. Examine the condition of the rotor. If it is cracked or the metal tip is excessively worn or burned it should be replaced.

4. Pry open the contacts of the points with a screwdriver and check the condition of the contacts. If they are excessively worn, burned or pitted, they should be replaced.

5. If the points are in good condition, adjust them, and replace the rotor and the distributor cap. If the points need to be replaced, follow the replacement procedure given below.

REPLACEMENT OF THE BREAKER POINTS AND CONDENSER

1. Remove the coil high tension wire from the top of the distributor cap. Remove the distributor cap from the distributor and place it out of the way. Remove the rotor from the distributor shaft.

2. Loosen the screw that holds the condenser lead to the body of the breaker points and remove the condenser lead from the points.

3. Remove the screw that holds and grounds the condenser to the distributor body. Remove the condenser from the distributor and discard it.

4. Remove the points assembly attaching screws and adjustment lockscrews. A screwdriver with a holding mechanism will come in handy here so you don't drop a screw into the distributor and have to remove the entire distributor to retrieve it.

5. Remove the points. Wipe off the cam and apply new cam lubricant. Discard the old set of points.

6. Position the new set of points with the locating peg in the hole on the breaker plate, and install the screws that hold the assembly onto the plate. Do not tighten them all the way.

7. Attach the new condenser to the plate to the ground screw.

8. Attach the condenser lead to the points at the proper place.

9. Apply a small amount of cam lubricant to the shaft where the rubbing block of the points touches.

Dwell Angle

ADJUSTMENT OF THE BREAKER POINTS WITH A FEELER GAUGE

1. If the contact points of the assembly are not parallel, bent the stationary contact so they make contact across across the entire surface of the contacts. Bend only the stationary bracket part of the point assembly, not the movable contact.

2. Turn the engine until the rubbing block of the points is on one of the high points of the distributor cam. You can do this by either turning the ignition switch to the start position and releasing it quickly (bumping the engine) or by using a wrench on the bolt that holds the crankshaft pulley to the crankshaft. Be sure to remove the wrench before starting the engine!

3. Place the correct size feeler gauge between the contacts. Make sure it is parallel with the contact surfaces.

4. With your free hand, insert a screw driver into the notch provided for adjustment or into the eccentric adjusting screw, then twist the screw driver to either increase or decrease the gap to the proper setting.

5. Tighten the adjustment lockscrew and recheck the contact gap to make sure that it didn't change when the lockscrew was tightened.

6. Replace the rotor and distributor cap, and the high tension wire that connects the top of the distributor and the coil. Make sure that the rotor is firmly seated all the way onto the distributor shaft. Align the tab in the base of the distributor cap with the notch in the distributor body. Make sure that the cap is firmly seated on the distributor and that the retainer springs are in place. Make sure that the end of the high tension wire is firmly placed in the top of the distributor and the coil.

ADJUSTMENT OF THE BREAKER POINTS WITH A DWELL METER

1. Adjust the points with a feeler gauge as described above.

2. Connect the dwell meter to ignition circuit according to the manufacturer's instructions. One lead of the meter is connected to a ground an the other lead is to be connected to the distributor post on the coil. An adapter is usually provided for this purpose.

3. If the dwell meter has a set line on it, adjust the meter to zero the indicator.

4. Start the engine.

NOTE: *Be careful when working on any vehicle while the engine is running. Make sure that the transmission is in Neutral and that the parking brake is applied. Keep hands, clothing, tools, and the wires of the test instruments clear of the rotating fan blades.*

5. Observe the reading on the dwell meter. If the reading is within the specified range, turn off the engine and remove the dwell meter.

6. If the reading is above the specified range, the breaker point gap is too small. If the reading gets below the specified range, the gap is too large. In either case, the engine must be stopped and the gap adjusted in the manner previously covered. After making the adjustment, start the engine and check the reading on the dwell meter. When the correct reading is obtained, disconnect the dwell meter.

7. Check the adjustment of the ignition timing.

ELECTRONIC IGNITION SYSTEMS

Basically, four electronic ignition systems have been used in Ford Motor Company vehicles from 1974-88:

1. DuraSpark I
2. DuraSpark II
3. DuraSpark III
4. Universal Distributor-TFI (EEC-IV)

In 1974, Ford began the use of breakerless ignition systems. The original system was named simply, Breakerless Ignition System. Later, in 1977, this system was named DuraSpark. DuraSpark I and DuraSpark II systems are nearly identical in operation, and virtually identical in appearance. The DuraSpark I uses a special control module which senses current flow through the ignition coil and adjusts the coil on-time for maximum spark intensity. If the DuraSpark I module senses that the ignition is ON, but the distributor shaft is not turning, the current to the coil is turned OFF by the module. The DuraSpark II system does not have this feature. The coil is energized for the full amount of time that the ignition switch is ON. Keep this in mind when servicing the DuraSpark II system, as the ignition system could inadvertently fire while performing ignition system services (such as distributor cap removal) while the ignition is ON. All DuraSpark II systems are easily identified by having a two-piece, flat topped distributor cap.

DuraSpark I was discontinued after the 1981 model year.

In 1980, the new DuraSpark III system was introduced. This version is based on the previous systems, but the input signal is controlled by the EEC system, rather than as function of engine timing and distributor armature position. The distributor, rotor, cap, and control module are unique to this system; the spark plugs and plug wires are the same as those used with the DuraSpark II system. Although the DuraSpark II and III control modules are similar in appearance, they cannot be interchanged between systems.

Some 1978 and later engines use a special DuraSpark Dual Mode ignition control module. The module is equipped with an altitude sensor, and an economy modulator. This module, when combined with the additional switches and sensor, varies the base engine timing according to altitude and engine load conditions. DuraSpark Dual Mode ignition control modules have three wiring harness from the module.

Some 1981 and later DuraSpark II systems used with some 8-302 cu.in. engines are quipped with a Universal Ignition Module (UIM) which includes a run-retard function. The operation of the module is basically the same as the DuraSpark Dual Mode module.

The Universal Distributor (EEC-IV) has a diecast base which incorporates an externally mounted TFI-IV ignition module, and contains a Hall Effect vane switch stator assembly and provision for fixed octane adjustment. No distributor calibration is required and initial timing adjustment is normally not required. The primary function of the EEC-IV Universal Distributor system is to direct high secondary voltage to the spark plugs. In addition, the distributor supplies crankshaft position and frequency information to a computer using a profile Ignition Pickup. The Hall Effect switch in the distributor consists of a Hall Effect device on one side and a magnet on the other side. A rotary cup which has windows and tabs rotates and passes through the space between the device and the magnet. When a window is between the sides of the switch the magnetic path is not completed and the switch is Off, sending no signal. When a tab passes between the switch the magnetic path is completed and the Hall Effect Device is turned On and a signal is sent. The voltage pulse (signal) is used by is EEC-IV system for sensing crankshaft position and computing the desired spark advance based on engine demand and calibration.

DuraSpark I
OPERATION

With the ignition switch **ON**, the primary circuit is on and the ignition coil is energized. When the armature spokes approach the magnetic pickup coil assembly, they induce the voltage which tells the amplifier to turn the coil pri-

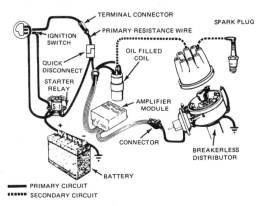

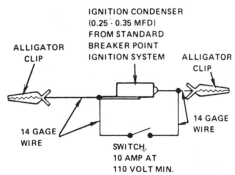

Make a special jumper wire to test the Dura Spark ignition

DuraSpark I components

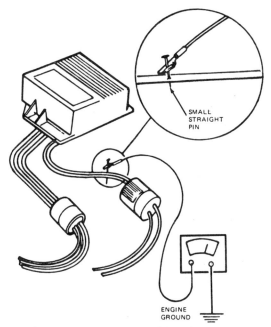

Pierce the wire with a straight pin to connect tester

mary current off. A timing circuit in the amplifier module will turn the current on again after the coil field has collapsed. When the current is on, it flows from the battery through the ignition switch, the primary windings of the ignition coil, and through the amplifier module circuits to ground. When the current is off, the magnetic field built up in the ignition coil is allowed to collapse, inducing a high voltage into the secondary windings of the coil. High voltage is produced each time the field is thus built up and collapsed. When DuraSpark is used in conjunction with the EEC, the EEC computer tells the DuraSpark module when to turn the coil primary current off or on. In this case, the armature position is only a reference signal of engine timing, used by the EEC computer in com-

bination with other reference signals to determine optimum ignition spark timing.

The high voltage flows through the coil high tension lead to the distributor cap where the rotor distributes it to one of the spark plug terminals in the distributor cap. This process is repeated for every power stroke of the engine.

Ignition system troubles are caused by a failure in the primary and/or the secondary circuit; incorrect ignition timing; or incorrect distributor advance. Circuit failures may be caused by shorts, corroded or dirty terminals, loose connections, defective wire insulation, cracked distributor cap or rotor, defective pick-up coil assembly or amplifier module, defective distributor points or fouled spark plugs.

If an engine starting or operating trouble is attributed to the ignition system, start the engine and verify the complaint. On engines that will not start, be sure that there is gasoline in the fuel tank and the fuel is reaching the carburetor. Then locate the ignition system problem using the following procedures.

TROUBLESHOOTING DURASPARK I

The following DuraSpark II troubleshooting procedures may be used on DuraSpark I systems with a few variations. The DuraSpark I module has internal connections which shut off the primary circuit in the run mode when the engine stalls. To perform the above troubleshooting procedures, it is necessary to by-pass these connections. However, with these connections by-passed, the current flow in the primary becomes so great that it will damage both the ignition coil and module unless a ballast resistor is installed in series with the primary circuit at the BAT terminal of the ignition coil. Such a resistor is available from Ford (Motorcraft part number DY-36). A 1.3Ω, 100 watt wire-wound power resistor can also be used.

To install the resistor, proceed as follows.

WARNING: *The resistor will become very hot during testing.*

1975 Test Sequence

	Test Voltage Between	Should Be	If Not, Conduct
Key On	Socket #4 and Engine Ground	Battery Voltage ± 0.1 Volt	Module Bias Test
	Socket #1 and Engine Ground	Battery Voltage ± 0.1 Volt	Battery Source Test
Cranking	Socket #5 and Engine Ground	8 to 12 volts	Cranking Test
	Jumper #1 to #8 Read #6	more than 6 volts	Starting Circuit Test
	Pin #7 and Pin #8	½ volt minimum AC or any DC volt wiggle	Distributor Hardware Test
	Test Voltage Between	*Should Be*	*If Not, Conduct*
Key Off	Socket #7 and #3 Socket #8 and Engine Ground Socket #7 and Engine Ground Socket #3 and Engine Ground	400 to 800 ohms 0 ohms more than 70,000 ohms	Magnetic Pick-up (Stator) Test
	Socket #4 and Coil Tower Socket #1 and Pin #6	7000 to 13000 ohms 1.0 to 2.0 ohms	Coil Test
	Socket #1 and Engine Ground	more than 4.0 ohms	Short Test
	Socket #4 and Pin #6	1.0 to 2.0 ohms	Resistance Wire Test

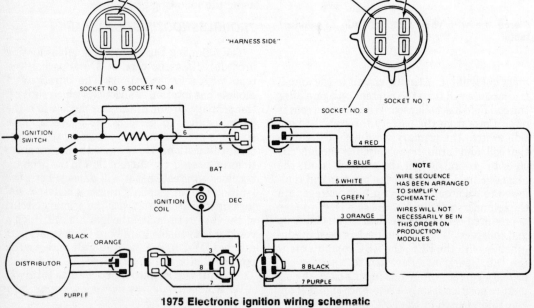

1975 Electronic ignition wiring schematic

1976 Test Sequence

	Test Voltage Between	Should Be	If Not, Conduct
Key On	Socket #4 and Engine Ground	Battery Voltage ± 0.1 Volt	Battery Source Test
	Socket #1 and Engine Ground	Battery Voltage ± 0.1 Volt	Battery Source Test
Cranking	Socket #5 and Engine Ground	8 to 12 volts	Check Supply Circuit (starting) through Ignition Switch
	Jumper #1 to #8 Read #6	more than 6 volts	Starting Circuit Test
	Pin #3 and Pin #8	½ volt minimum AC or any DC volt wiggle	Distributor Hardware Test
	Test Voltage Between	*Should Be*	*If Not, Conduct*
Key Off	Socket #8 and #3 Socket #7 and Engine Ground Socket #8 and Engine Ground Socket #3 and Engine Ground	400 to 800 ohms 0 ohms more than 70,000 ohms more than 70,000 ohms	Magnetic Pick-up (Stator) Test
	Socket #4 and Coil Tower	7000 to 13,000 ohms	Coil Test
	Socket #1 and Engine Ground	more than 4.0 ohms	Short Test

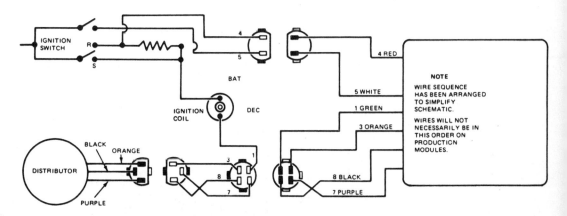

1976 Electronic ignition wiring schematic

1977–82 Test Sequence

	Test Voltage Between	Should Be	If Not, Conduct
Key On	Socket #4 and Engine Ground	Battery Voltage ± 0.1 Volt	Module Bias Test
	Socket #1 and Engine Ground	Battery Voltage ± 0.1 Volt	Battery Source Test
Cranking	Socket #5 and Engine Ground	8 to 12 volts	Cranking Test
	Jumper #1 to #8—Read Coil "Bat" Term & Engine Ground	more than 6 volts	Starting Circuit Test
	Sockets #7 and #3	½ volt minimum wiggle	Distributor Hardware Test
	Test Voltage Between	**Should Be**	**If Not, Conduct**
Key Off	Sockets #7 and #3 Socket #8 and Engine Ground Socket #7 and Engine Ground Socket #3 and Engine Ground	400 to 800 ohms 0 ohms more than 70,000 ohms more than 70,000 ohms	Magnetic Pick-up (Stator) Test
	Socket #4 and Coil Tower	7000 to 13,000 ohms	Coil Test
	Socket #1 and Coil "Bat" Term	1.0 to 2.0 ohms Breakerless & Dura-Spark II	
		0.5 to 1.5 ohms Dura-Spark I	
	Socket #1 and Engine Ground	more than 4.0 ohms	Short Test
	Socket #4 and Coil "Bat" Term (Except Dura-Spark I)	1.0 to 2.0 ohms Breakerless	Resistance Wire Test
		0.7 to 1.7 ohms Dura Spark II	

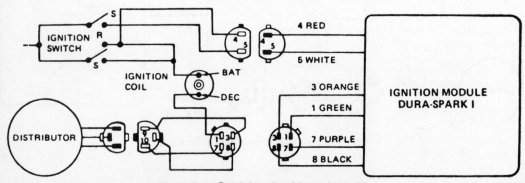

1977–81 Dura-Spark I basic wiring schematic

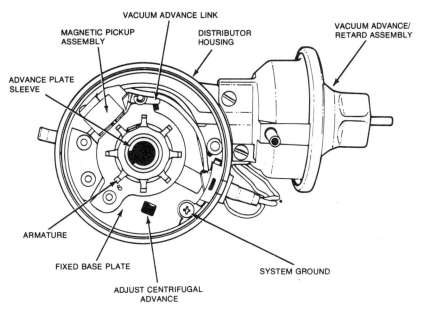

V8 breakerless distributor; cap and rotor removed

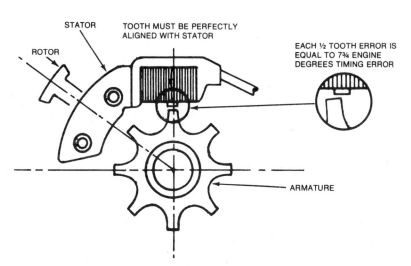

8-cylinder breakerless distributor static timing position

1. Release the BAT terminal lead from the coil by inserting a paper cup through the hole in the rear of the horseshoe coil connector and manipulating it against the locking tab in the connector until the lead comes free.

2. Insert a paper clip in the BAT terminal of the connector of the coil. Using jumper leads, connect the ballast resistor as shown.

3. Using a straight pin, pierce both the red and white leads of the module to short these two together. This will by-pass the internal connections of the module which turn off the ignition circuit when the engine is not running.

CAUTION: *Pierce the wires only AFTER the*

ballast resistor is in place or you could damage the ignition coil and module.

4. With the ballast resistor and by-pass in place, proceed with the DuraSpark II troubleshooting procedures.

Dura Spark II
SYSTEM OPERATION

With the ignition switch **ON**, the primary circuit is on and the ignition coil is energized. When the armature spokes approach the magnetic pickup coil assembly, they induce the voltage which tells the amplifier to turn the coil pri-

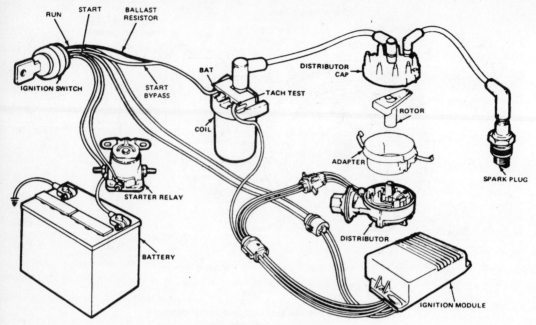

DuraSpark II components

mary current off. A timing circuit in the ampli-fier module will turn the current on again after the coil field has collapsed. When the current is on, it flows from the battery through the igni-tion switch, the primary windings of the igni-tion coil, and through the amplifier module cir-cuits to ground. When the current is off, the magnetic field built up in the ignition coil is al-lowed to collapse, inducing a high voltage into the secondary windings of the coil. High voltage is produced each time the field is thus built up and collapsed. When DuraSpark is used in con-junction with the EEC, the EEC computer tells the DuraSpark module when to turn the coil primary current off or on. In this case, the ar-mature position is only a reference signal of en-gine timing, used by the EEC computer in com-bination with other reference signals to deter-mine optimum ignition spark timing.

The high voltage flows through the coil high tension lead to the distributor cap where the ro-tor distributes it to one of the spark plug termi-nals in the distributor cap. This process is re-peated for every power stroke of the engine.

Ignition system troubles are caused by a fail-ure in the primary and/or the secondary circuit; incorrect ignition timing; or incorrect distribu-tor advance. Circuit failures may be caused by shorts, corroded or dirty terminals, loose con-nections, defective wire insulation, cracked dis-tributor cap or rotor, defective pick-up coil as-sembly or amplifier module, defective distribu-tor points or fouled spark plugs.

If an engine starting or operating trouble is attributed to the ignition system, start the en-gine and verify the complaint. On engines that will not start, be sure that there is gasoline in the fuel tank and the fuel is reaching the carbu-retor. Then locate the ignition system problem using the following procedures.

TROUBLESHOOTING DURASPARK II

The following procedures can be used to de-termine whether the ignition system is working or not. If these procedures fail to correct the problem, a full troubleshooting procedure should be performed.

Preliminary Checks

1. Check the battery's state of charge and connections.
2. Inspect all wires and connections for breaks, cuts, abrasions, or burn spots. Repair as necessary.
3. Unplug all connectors one at a time and inspect for corroded or burned contacts. Repair and plug connectors back together. DO NOT re-move the dielectric compound in the connectors.
4. Check for loose or damaged spark plug or coil wires. A wire resistance check is given at the end of this section. If the boots or nipples are removed on 8mm ignition wires, reline the inside of each with new silicone dielectric com-pound (Motorcraft WA-10).

Special Tools

To perform the following tests, two special tools are needed; the ignition test jumper shown in the illustration and a modified spark plug. Use the illustration to assembly the ignition test jumper. The test jumper must be used when performing the following tests. The modified spark plug is basically a spark plug with the side electrode removed. Ford makes a special tool called a Spark Tester for this purpose, which besides not having a side electrode is equipped with a spring clip so that it can be grounded to engine metal. It is recommended that the Spark Tester be used as there is less change of being shocked.

Run Mode Spark Test

NOTE: *The wire colors given here are the main colors of the wires, not the dots or hashmarks.*

STEP 1

1. Remove the distributor cap and rotor from the distributor.

2. With the ignition off, turn the engine over by hand until one of the teeth on the distributor armature aligns with the magnet in the pickup coil.

3. Remove the coil wire from the distributor cap. Install the modified spark plug (see Special Tools, above) in the coil wire terminal and using heavy gloves and insulated pliers, hold the spark plug shell against the engine block.

4. Turn the ignition to RUN (not START) and tap the distributor body with a screwdriver handle. There should be a spark at the modified spark plug or at the coil wire terminal.

5. If a good spark is evident, the primary circuit is OK: perform the Start Mode Spark Test. If there is no spark, proceed to STEP 2.

STEP 2

1. Unplug the module connector(s) which contain(s) the green and black module leads.

2. In the harness side of the connector(s), connect the special test jumper (see Special Tools, above) between the leads which connect to the green and black leads of the module pig tails. Use paper clips on connector socket holes to make contact. Do not allow clips to ground.

3. Turn the ignition switch to RUN (not START) and close the test jumper switch. Leave closed for about 1 second, then open. Repeat several times. There should be a spark each time the switch is opened.

4. If there is no spark, the problem is probably in the primary circuit through the ignition switch, the coil, the green lead or the black lead, or the ground connection in the distributor; Perform STEP 3. If there is a spark, the primary circuit wiring and coil are probably OK. The problem is probably in the distributor pick-up, the module red wire, or the module: perform STEP 6.

STEP 3

1. Disconnect the test jumper lead from the black lead and connect it to a good ground. Turn the test jumper switch on and off several times as in STEP 2.

2. If there is no spark, the problem is probably in the green lead, the coil, or the coil feed circuit: perform STEP 5.

3. If there is spark, the problem is probably in the black lead or the distributor ground connection: perform STEP 4.

STEP 4

1. Connect an ohmmeter between the black lead and ground. With the meter on its lowest scale, there should be no measurable resistance in the circuit. If there is resistance, check the distributor ground connection and the black lead from the module. Repair as necessary, remove the ohmmeter, plug in all connections and repeat STEP 1.

2. If there is no resistance, the primary ground wiring is OK: perform STEP 6.

STEP 5

1. Disconnect the test jumper from the green lead and ground and connect it between the TACH-TEST terminal of the coil and a good ground to the engine.

2. With the ignition switch in the RUN position, turn the jumper switch on. Hold it on for about 1 second then turn it off as in Step 2. Repeat several times. There should be a spark each time the switch in turned off. If there is no spark, the problem is probably in the primary circuit running through the ignition switch to the coil BAT terminal, or in the coil itself. Check coil resistance (test given later in this section), and check the coil for internal shorts or opens. Check the coil feed circuit for opens, shorts, or high resistance. Repair as necessary, reconnect all connectors and repeat STEP 1. If there is spark, the coil and its feed circuit are OK. The problem could be in the green lead between the coil and the module. Check for an open or short, repair as necessary, reconnect all connectors and repeat STEP 1.

STEP 6

To perform this step, a voltmeter which is not combined with a dwell meter is needed. The slight needle oscillations (½v) you'll be looking for may not be detectable on the combined voltmeter/dwell meter unit.

1. Connect a voltmeter between the orange and purple leads on the harness side of the module connectors.

CAUTION: *On catalytic converter equipped cars, disconnect the air supply line between the Thermactor by-pass valve and the manifold before cranking the engine with the igni-*

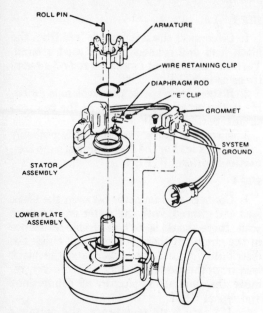

DuraSpark II stator replacement

tion off. *This will prevent damage to the catalytic converter. After testing, run the engine for at least 3 minutes before reconnecting the by-pass valve, to clear excess fuel from the exhaust system.*

2. Set the voltmeter on its lowest scale and crank the engine. The meter needle should oscillate slightly (about ½v). If the meter does not oscillate, check the circuit through the magnetic pick-up in the distributor for open, shorts, shorts to ground and resistance. Resistance between the orange and purple leads should be 400-1,000Ω, and between each lead and ground should be more than 70,000Ω. Repair as necessary, reconnect all connectors and repeat STEP 1.

If the meter oscillates, the problem is probably in the power feed to the module (red wire) or in the module itself: proceed to STEP 7.

STEP 7

1. Remove all meters and jumpers and plug in all connectors.

2. Turn the ignition switch to the RUN position and measure voltage between the battery positive terminal and engine ground. It should be 12 volts.

3. Next, measure voltage between the red lead of the module and engine ground. To mark this measurement, it will be necessary to pierce the red wire with a straight pin and connect the voltmeter to the straight pin and to ground. DO NOT ALLOW THE STRAIGHT PIN TO GROUND ITSELF!

4. The two readings should be within one volt of each other. If not within one volt, the problem is in the power feed to the red lead. Check for shorts, open, or high resistance and correct as necessary. After repairs, repeat Step 1.

If the readings are within one volt, the problem is probably in the module. Replace it with a good module and repeat STEP 1. If this corrects the problem, reconnect the old module and repeat STEP 1. If the problem returns, permanently install the new module.

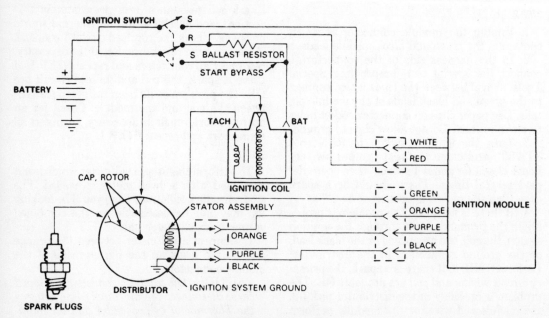

DuraSpark II schematic

Start Mode Spark Test

NOTE: *The wire colors given here are the main colors of the wires, not the dots or hashmarks.*

1. Remove the coil wire from the distributor cap. Install the modified spark plug mentioned under Special Tools, above, in the coil wire and ground it to engine metal either by its spring clip (Spark Tester) or by holding the spark plug shell against the engine block with insulated pliers.

NOTE: *See CAUTION under STEP 6 of Run Mode Spark Test, above.*

2. Have an assistant crank the engine using the ignition switch and check for spark. If there is good spark, the problem is probably in distributor cap, rotor, ignition cables or spark plugs. If there is no spark, proceed to Step 3.

3. Measure the battery voltage. Next, measure the voltage at the white wire of the module while cranking the engine. To mark this measurement, it will be necessary to pierce the white wire with a straight pin and connect the voltmeter to the straight pin and to ground. DO NOT ALLOW THE STRAIGHT PIN TO GROUND ITSELF. The battery voltage and the voltage at the white wire should be within 1 volt of each other. If the readings are not within 1 volt of each other, check and repair the feed through the ignition switch to the white wire. Recheck for spark (Step 1). If the readings are within 1 volt of each other, or if there is still no spark after the power feed to white wire is repaired, proceed to Step 4.

4. Measure the coil BAT terminal voltage while cranking the engine. The reading should be within 1 volt of battery voltage. If the readings are not within 1 volt of each other, check and repair the feed through the ignition switch to the coil. If the readings are within 1 volt of each other, the problem is probably in the ignition module. Substitute another module and repeat the test for spark (Step 1).

TFI-IV System
SYSTEM OPERATION

The TFI-IV ignition system features a universal distributor using no centrifugal or vacuum advance. The distributor has a die cast base which incorporates an integrally mounted TFI (Thick Film Integrated) ignition module, a Hall Effect vane switch stator assembly and provision for fixed octane adjustment. The TFI system uses an E-Core ignition coil in lieu of the DuraSpark coil. No distributor calibration is required and initial timing is not a normal adjustment, since advance etc. is controlled by the EEC-IV system.

GENERAL TESTING

Ignition Coil Test

The ignition coil must be diagnosed separately from the rest of the ignition system.

1. Primary resistance is measured between the two primary (low voltage) coil terminals, with the coil connector disconnected and the ignition switch off. Primary resistance should be 0.3-1.0Ω.

2. On DuraSpark ignitions, the secondary resistance is measured between the BATT and high voltage (secondary) terminals of the ignition coil with the ignition off, and the wiring from the coil disconnected. Secondary resistance must be $8{,}000$-$11{,}500\Omega$.

3. If resistance tests are okay, but the coil is still suspected, test the coil on a coil tester by

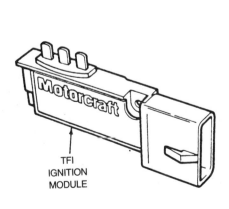

TFI
IGNITION
MODULE

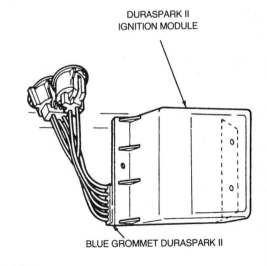

DURASPARK II
IGNITION MODULE

BLUE GROMMET DURASPARK II

Ignition modules

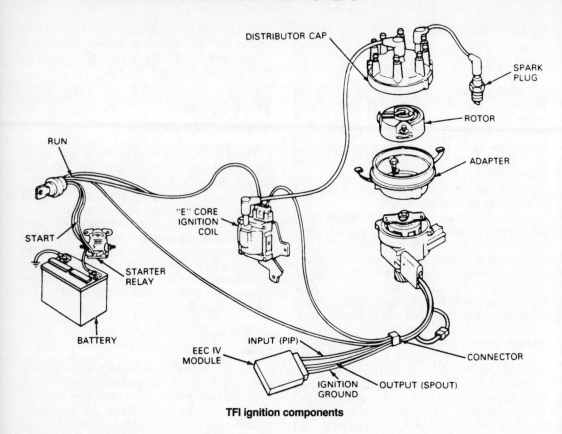

DISTRIBUTOR CAP

SPARK PLUG

ROTOR

ADAPTER

RUN

"E" CORE IGNITION COIL

START

STARTER RELAY

BATTERY

EEC IV MODULE

INPUT (PIP)

IGNITION GROUND

OUTPUT (SPOUT)

CONNECTOR

TFI ignition components

PIP
SPOUT
START
RUN
COIL
IGN GND

BATT

ST
ACC
OFF
RUN

IGN SW

TFI IV MODULE (DIST)

START
RUN
COIL
PIP
SPOUT
IGN GND

CONNECTOR

D4AB-14489-GA

TO EEC IV

E-CORE COIL

TFI schematic

following the test equipment manufacturer's instructions for a standard coil. If the reading differs from the original test, check for a defective harness.

Spark Plug Wire Resistance

Resistance on these wires must not exceed 5,000Ω per foot. To properly measure this, remove the wires from the plugs, and remove the distributor cap. Measure the resistance through the distributor cap at that end. Do not pierce any ignition wire for any reason. Measure only from the two ends.

NOTE: *Silicone grease must be re-applied to the spark plug wires whenever they are removed. When removing the wires from the spark plugs, a special tool should be used. do not pull on the wires. Grasp and twist the boot to remove the wire. Whenever the high tension wires are removed from the plugs, coil, or distributor, silicone grease must be applied to the boot before reconnection. Use a clean small screwdriver blase to coat the entire interior surface with Ford silicone grease D7AZ-19A331-A, Dow Corning #111, or General Electric G-627.*

Adjustments

The air gap between the armature and magnetic pick-up coil in the distributor is not adjustable, nor are there any adjustment for the amplifier module. Inoperative components are simply replaced. Any attempt to connect components outside the vehicle may result in component failure.

TROUBLESHOOTING THE TFI-IV SYSTEM

NOTE: *After performing any test which requires piercing a wire with a straight pin, remove the straight pin and seal the holes in the wire with silicone sealer.*

Ignition Coil Secondary Voltage

1. Disconnect the secondary (high voltage) coil wire from the distributor cap and install a spark tester between the coil wire and ground.
2. Crank the engine. A good, strong spark should be noted at the spark tester. If spark is noted, but the engine will not start, check the spark plugs, spark plug wiring, and fuel system. If there is no spark at the tester: Check the ignition coil secondary wire resistance; it should be no more than 5,000Ω per foot. Inspect the ignition coil for damage and/or carbon tracking. With the distributor cap removed, verify that the distributor shaft turns with the engine; if it does not, repair the engine as required. If the fault was not found proceed to the next test.

Ignition Coil Primary Circuit Switching

1. Insert a small straight pin in the wire which runs from the coil negative (–) terminal to the TFI module, about 1″ from the module.
WARNING: *The pin must not touch ground!*
2. Connect a 12 VDC test lamp between the straight pin and an engine ground.
3. Crank the engine, noting the operation of the test lamp. If the test lamp flashes, proceed to the next test. If the test lamp lights but does not flash, proceed to the Wiring Harness test. If the test lamp does not light at all, proceed to the Primary Circuit Continuity test.

Ignition Coil Resistance

Refer to the General Testing for an explanation of the resistance tests. Replace the ignition coil if the resistance is out of the specification range.

Wiring Harness

1. Disconnect the wiring harness connector from the TFI module; the connector tabs must be PUSHED to disengage the connector. Inspect the connector for damage, dirt, and corrosion.
2. Attach the negative lead of a voltmeter to the base of the distributor. Attach the other voltmeter lead to a small straight pin. With the ignition switch in the RUN position, insert the straight pin into the No. 1 terminal of the TFI module connector. Note the voltage reading. With the ignition switch in the RUN position, move the straight pin to the No. 2 connector terminal. Again, note the voltage reading. Move the straight pin to the No. 3 connector terminal, then turn the ignition switch to the START position. Note the voltage reading then turn the ignition OFF.
3. The voltage readings should all be at least 90% of the available battery voltage. If the readings are okay, proceed to the Stator Assembly and Module test. If any reading is less than 90% of the battery voltage, inspect the wiring, connectors, and/or ignition switch for defects. if the voltage is low only at the No. 1 terminal, proceed to the ignition coil primary voltage test.

Stator Assembly and Module

1. Remove the distributor from the engine.
2. Remove the TFI module from the distributor.
3. Inspect the distributor terminals, ground screw, and stator wiring for damage. Repair as necessary.
4. Measure the resistance of the stator assembly, using an ohmmeter. If the ohmmeter reading is 800-975Ω, the stator is okay, but the TFI module must be replaced. If the ohmmeter

reading is less than 800Ω or more than 975Ω; the TFI module is okay, but the stator module must be replaced.

5. Repair as necessary and install the TFI module and the distributor.

TFI Module

1. Remove the distributor cap from the distributor, and set it aside (spark plug wires intact).

2. Disconnect the TFI harness connector.

3. Remove the distributor.

4. Remove the two TFI module retaining screws.

5. To disengage the modules terminals from the distributor base connector, pull the right side of the module down the distributor mounting flange and then back up. Carefully pull the module toward the flange and away from the distributor.

WARNING: *Step 5 must be followed EXACTLY; failure to do so will result in damage to the distributor module connector pins.*

6. Coat the TFI module baseplate with a thin layer of silicone grease (FD7AZ-19A331-A or its equivalent).

7. Place the TFI module on the distributor base mounting flange. Position the module assembly toward the distributor bowl and carefully engage the distributor connector pins. Install and torque the two TFI module retaining screws to 9-16 in.lb.

8. Install the distributor assembly.

9. Install the distributor cap and check the engine timing.

Primary Circuit Continuity

This test is performed in the same manner as the previous Wiring Harness test, but only the No. 1 terminal conductor is tested (ignition switch in Run position). If the voltage is less than 90% of the available battery voltage, proceed to the coil primary voltage test.

Ignition Coil Primary Voltage

1. Attach the negative lead of a voltmeter to the distributor base.

2. Turn the ignition switch ON and connect the positive voltmeter lead to the negative (–) ignition coil terminal. Note the voltage reading and turn the ignition OFF. If the voltmeter reading is less than 90% of the available battery voltage, inspect the wiring between the ignition module and the negative (–) coil terminal, then proceed to the last test, which follows.

Ignition Coil Supply Voltage

1. Attach the negative lead of a voltmeter to the distributor base.

2. Turn the ignition switch ON and connect the positive voltmeter lead to the positive (+) ignition coil terminal. Note the voltage reading then turn the ignition OFF. If the voltage reading is at least 90% of the battery voltage, yet the engine will still not run; first, check the ignition coil connector and terminals for corrosion, dirt, and/or damage; second, replace the ignition switch if the connectors and terminal are okay.

3. Connect any remaining wiring.

IGNITION TIMING

Ignition timing is the measurement, in degrees of crankshaft rotation, of the point at which the spark plugs fire in each of the cylinders. It is measured in degrees before or after Top Dead Center (TDC) of the compression stroke.

Ideally, the air/fuel mixture in the cylinder will be ignited by the spark plug just as the piston passes TDC of the compression stroke. If this happens, the piston will be beginning the power stroke just as the compressed and ignited air/fuel mixture starts to expand. The expansion of the air/fuel mixture then forces the piston down on the power stroke and turns the crankshaft.

Because it takes a fraction of a second for the spark plug to ignite the mixture in the cylinder,

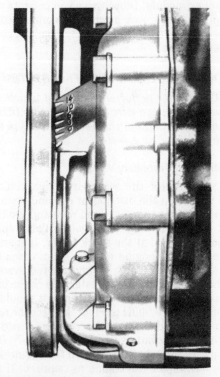

Typical timing marks: 1961–67 6-cylinder

Timing marks for 1968 and later sixes

Timing marks for the 302 V8

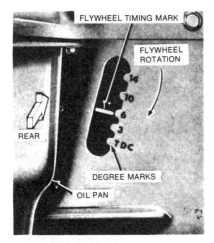

Timing marks for some sixes

Typically pulley-mounted timing marks for V8, except 302

setting for the ignition timing is 5°BTDC, each spark plug must fire 5° before each piston reaches TDC. This only holds true, however, when the engine is at idle speed.

As the engine speed increases, the piston go faster. The spark plugs have to ignite the fuel even sooner if it is to be completely ignited when the piston reaches TDC.

With the both the Point Type and DuraSpark systems, the distributor has a means to advance the timing of the spark as the engine speed increases. This is accomplished by centrifugal weights within the distributor and a vacuum diaphragm mounted on the side of the distributor. It is necessary to disconnect the vacuum lines from the diaphragm when the ignition timing is being set.

With the TFI-IV system, ignition timing is calculated at all phases of vehicle operation by the TFI module.

If the ignition is set too far advanced (BTDC), the ignition and expansion of the fuel in the cylinder will occur too soon and tend to force the piston down while it is still traveling up. This causes engine ping. If the ignition spark is set too far retarded after TDC (ATDC), the piston will have already passed TDC and started on its way down when the fuel is ignited. This will cause the piston to be forced down for only a portion of its travel. This will result in poor engine performance and lack of power.

The timing is best checked with a timing light. This device is connected in series with the No. 1 spark plug. The current that fires the spark plug also causes the timing light to flash.

There is a notch on the crankshaft pulley on all 6-cyl. engines. A scale of degrees of crankshaft rotation is attached to the engine block in

the spark plug must fire a little before the piston reaches TDC. Otherwise, the mixture will not be completely ignited as the piston passes TDC and the full power of the explosion will not be used by the engine.

The timing measurement is given in degrees of crankshaft rotation before the piston reaches TDC (BTDC, or Before Top Dead Center). If the such a position that the notch will pass close by the scale. On the V8 engines, the scale is located on the crankshaft pulley and a pointer is attached to the engine block so that the scale will pass close by. When the engine is running, the timing light is aimed at the mark on the crankshaft pulley and the scale.

IGNITION TIMING ADJUSTMENT

With the DuraSpark system, only an initial timing adjustment is possible. Ignition timing is not considered to be a part of tune-up or routine maintenance.

With the TFI-IV system no ignition timing adjustment is possible and none should be attempted.

Point Type Systems

1. Locate the timing marks on the crankshaft pulley and the front of the engine.
2. Clean off the timing marks so that you can see them.
3. Mark the timing marks with a piece of chalk or white paint. Color the mark on the scale that will indicate the correct timing when it is aligned with the mark on the pulley or the pointer. It is also helpful to mark the notch in the pulley or the tip of the pointer with a small dab of color.
4. Attach a dwell meter/tachometer to the engine.
5. Attach a timing light according to the manufacturer's instructions.
6. Disconnect the distributor vacuum line at the distributor and plug the vacuum line. A small bolt, center punch or similar object is satisfactory for a plug.
7. Check to make sure that all of the wires clear the fan and then start the engine.
8. Adjust the idle to the correct setting.
9. Aim the timing light at the timing marks. If the marks that you put on the pulley and the engine are aligned when the light flashes, the timing is correct. Turn off the engine and remove the tachometer and the timing light. If the marks are not in alignment, proceed with the following steps.
10. Loosen the distributor lockbolt just enough so that the distributor can be turned with a little effort.
11. With the timing light aimed at the pulley and the marks on the engine, turn the distributor in the direction of rotor rotation to regard the spark, and in the opposite direction of rotor rotation to the advance spark. Align the marks on the pulley and the engine with the flashes of the timing light.
12. When the marks are aligned, tighten the distributor lockbolt and recheck the timing with the timing light to make sure that the dis-

tributor did not move when you tightened the lockbolt.
13. Turn off the engine and remove the timing light.

DuraSpark Systems

1. Locate the timing marks on the crankshaft pulley and the front of the engine.
2. Clean the timing marks so that you can see them.
3. Mark the timing marks with a piece of chalk or with paint. Color the mark on the scale that will indicate the correct timing when it is aligned with the mark on the pulley or the pointer. It is also helpful to mark the notch in the pulley or the tip of the pointer with a small dab of color.
4. Attach a tachometer to the engine.
5. Attach a timing light according to the manufacturer's instructions. If the timing light has three wires, one is attached to the No. 1 spark plug with an adapter. The other wires are connected to the battery. The red wire goes to the positive side of the battery and the black wire is connected to the negative terminal of the battery.
6. Disconnect the vacuum line to the distributor at the distributor and plug the vacuum line. A golf tee does a fine job.
7. Check to make sure that all of the wires clear the fan and then start the engine.
8. Adjust the idle to the correct setting.
9. Aim the timing light at the timing marks. if the marks that you put on the flywheel or pulley and the engine are aligned with the light flashes, the timing is correct. Turn off the engine and remove the tachometer and the timing light. If the mark are not in alignment, replace the ignition module.

CARBURETOR ADJUSTMENTS

Idle Speed and Mixture

1961-73

1. With the engine off, turn the idle fuel mixture screw and limiter cap to the full counterclockwise position.
2. Turn the idle speed adjusting screw(s) out until the throttle plate(s) seats in the throttle bore(s).
3. Make certain that the solenoid plunger is not interfering with the throttle lever.
4. Turn the idle speed adjusting screw in until it just contacts the stop on the throttle shaft and lever assembly, then turn the screw inward 1½ turns.
5. Start the engine and warm it up.
6. Check, and if necessary, adjust the ignition timing.

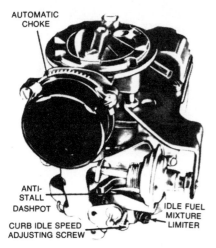

Carter Model YF 1-bbl carburetor adjustments

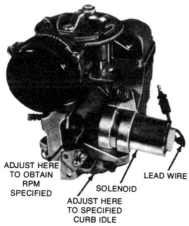

Carter Model YF 1-bbl carburetor equipped with a solenoid

7. Put the transmission in neutral (manual) or drive (automatic). Set the parking brake. Block the wheels.

8. Check that the choke plate is in the full open position; turn the headlights on high beam.

9. Install a tachometer according to the manufacturer's instructions.

10. If possible leave the air cleaner on while making adjustments.

11. Loosen the solenoid locknut and turn the solenoid in or out to obtain the specified idle speed.

12. Disconnect the solenoid lead wire and place the automatic transmission in neutral.

13. Adjust the carburetor throttle stop screw to obtain 500 rpm.

14. Connect the lead wire and open the throttle slightly by hand.

15. Turn the mixture adjusting screw(s) in-

ward to obtain the smoothest possible idle with the air cleaner installed.

Idle Speed Adjustment

1974-76

1. Remove the air cleaner and plug the vacuum lines.

2. Set the parking brake and block the wheels.

3. Connect a tachometer according to the manufacturer's instructions.

4. Run the engine to normalize underhood temperatures.

5. Check, and if necessary, reset the ignition timing.

6. Make certain that the choke plate is fully open.

7. Place the manual transmission in neutral; the automatic in Drive. Block the wheels.

8. Turn the solenoid adjusting screw in or out to obtain the specified idle speed. The idle speed is the higher of the two rpm figures on the underhood specification sticker.

9. Disconnect the solenoid lead wire. Place the automatic transmission in neutral.

10. Turn the solenoid off adjusting screw to obtain the solenoid off rpm. This is the lower of the two rpm figures on the underhood specifications sticker.

11. Connect the solenoid lead wire and open the throttle slightly to allow the solenoid plunger to extend.

12. Stop the engine, replace the air cleaner and connect the vacuum lines. Check the idle speed. Readjust if necessary with the air cleaner installed.

1977-87

1. Remove the air cleaner and disconnect and plug the vacuum lines.

2. Block the wheels, apply the parking brake, turn off all accessories, start the engine and run it to normalize underhood temperatures.

3. Check that the choke plate is fully open and connect a tachometer according to the manufacturer's instructions.

4. Check the throttle stop positioner (TSP)-off speed as follows:

　a. Collapse the plunger by forcing the throttle lever against it.

　b. Place the transmission in neutral and check the engine speed. If necessary, adjust to specified TSP-Off speed with the throttle adjusting screw. See the underhood sticker.

5. Place the manual transmission in neutral; the automatic in Drive and make certain the TSP plunger is extended.

6. Turn the TSP until the specified idle speed is obtained.

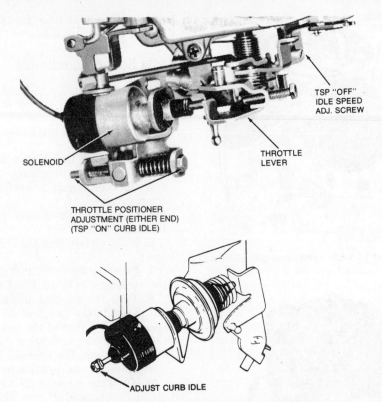

SOLENOID

TSP "OFF"
IDLE SPEED
ADJ. SCREW

THROTTLE
LEVER

THROTTLE POSITIONER
ADJUSTMENT (EITHER END)
(TSP "ON" CURB IDLE)

ADJUST CURB IDLE

Adjustment for two types of throttle solenoids

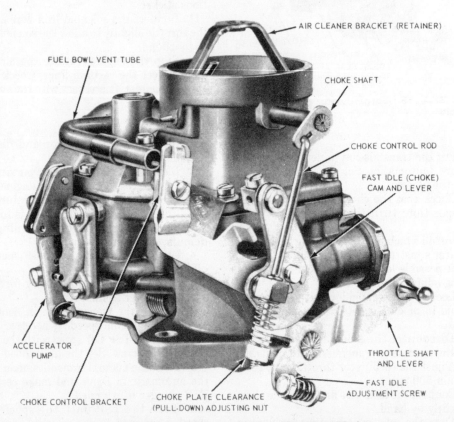

AIR CLEANER BRACKET (RETAINER)

FUEL BOWL VENT TUBE

CHOKE SHAFT

CHOKE CONTROL ROD

FAST IDLE (CHOKE)
CAM AND LEVER

ACCELERATOR
PUMP

THROTTLE SHAFT
AND LEVER

FAST IDLE
ADJUSTMENT SCREW

CHOKE CONTROL BRACKET

CHOKE PLATE CLEARANCE
(PULL-DOWN) ADJUSTING NUT

Ford Model 1100 1-bbl carburetor used on the 170 six

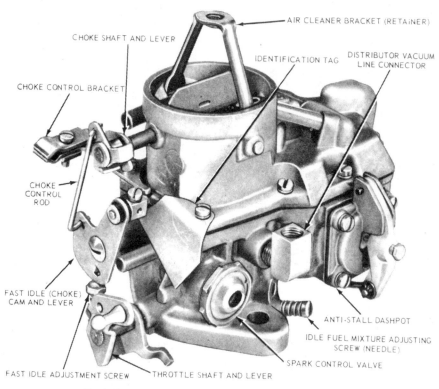

Ford Model 1100 1-bbl carburetor used on the 240 six

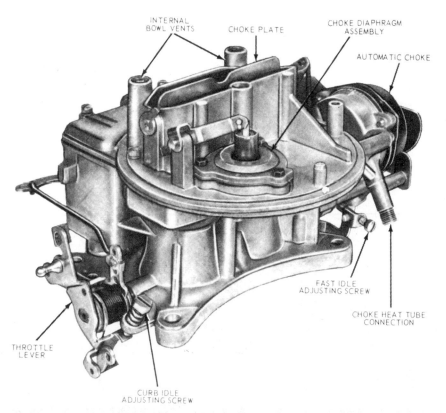

Autolite Model 2100 2-bbl carburetor—view shows the curb idle adjustment screws

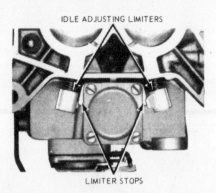

Autolite Model 2100 2-bbl carburetor—bottom view showing the idle mixture screws with limiter caps

7. Install the air cleaner and connect the vacuum lines. Check the idle speed. Adjust, if necessary, with the air cleaner on.

Idle Mixture Adjustment

1974-87

NOTE: *For this procedure, Ford recommends a propane enrichment procedure. This requires special equipment not available to the general public. In lieu of this equipment the following procedure may be followed to obtain satisfactory idle mixture.*

1. Block the wheels, set the parking brake and run the engine to bring it to normal operating temperature.

2. Disconnect the hose between the emission canister and the air cleaner.

3. On engines equipped with the Thermactor® air injection system, the routing of the vacuum lines connected to the dump valve will have to be temporarily changed. Mark them for reconnection before switching them.

4. For valves with one or two vacuum lines at the side, disconnect and plug the lines.

5. For valves with one vacuum line at the top, check the line to see if it is connected to the intake manifold or an intake manifold source such as the carburetor or distributor vacuum line. If not, remove and plug the line at the dump valve and connect a temporary length of vacuum hose from the dump valve fitting to a source of intake manifold vacuum.

6. Remove the limiter caps from the mixture screws by CAREFULLY cutting them with a sharp knife.

7. Place the transmission in neutral and run the engine at 2,500 rpm for 15 seconds.

8. Place the automatic transmission in Drive; the manual in neutral.

9. Adjust the idle speed to the higher of the two figures given on the underhood sticker.

10. Turn the idle mixture screws to obtain the

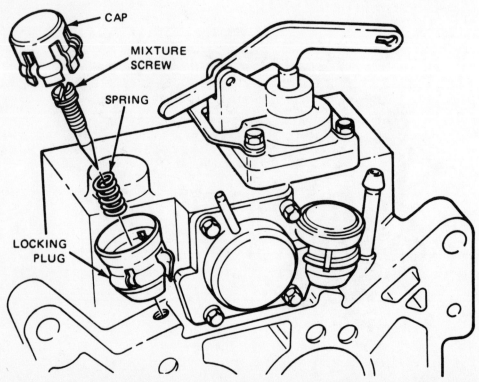

Some 1980 and later 2150 models have 2-piece metal plugs and caps in place of plastic limiter caps on the idle mixture adjusting screws. They should be carefully removed before attempting any adjustments.

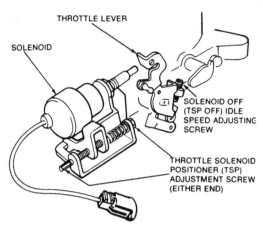

Throttle solenoid positioner adjustment—Motorcraft 2100, 2150, 4300, 4350

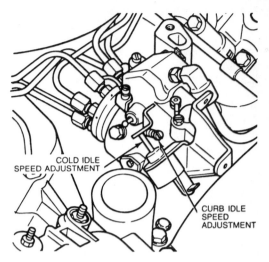

Idle speed adjustment locations

highest possible rpm, leaving the screws in the leanest position that will maintain this rpm.

11. Repeat steps 7 thru 10 until further adjustment of the mixture screws does not increase the rpm.

12. Turn the screws in until the lower of the two idle speed figures is reached. Turn the screws in ¼ turn increments each to insure a balance.

13. Turn the engine off and remove the tachometer. Reinstall all equipment.

NOTE: *Rough idle, that cannot be corrected by normal service procedures on 1977 and later models, may be cause by leakage between the EGR valve body and diaphragm. To determine if this is the cause:*

1. Tighten the EGR bolts to 15 ft.lb. Connect a vacuum gauge to the intake manifold.

2. Lift to exert a sideways pressure on the diaphragm housing. If the idle changes or the reading on the vacuum gauge varies, replace the EGR valve.

GASOLINE FUEL INJECTION ADJUSTMENTS

These engines have idle speed controlled by the TFI-IV/EEC-IV system and no adjustment is possible.

DIESEL FUEL SYSTEM ADJUSTMENTS

Curb Idle Adjustment

1. Place the transmission in neutral or park.
2. Bring the engine up to normal operating temperature.
3. Idle speed is measured with manual transmission in neutral and automatic transmission

in Drive with the wheels blocked and parking brake ON.

4. Check the curb idle speed, using a magnetic pickup tachometer suitable for diesel engines. The part number of the Ford tachometer is Rotunda 99-0001. Adjust the idle speed to 600-700 rpm.

NOTE: *Always check the underhood emissions control information sticker for the latest idle and adjustment specifications.*

5. Place the transmission in neutral or park and momentarily speed up the engine. Allow the rpm to drop to idle and recheck the idle speed. Readjust if necessary.

Fast Idle Adjustment

1. Place the transmission in neutral or park.
2. Start the engine and bring up to normal operating temperatures.
3. Disconnect the wire from the fast idle solenoid.
4. Apply battery voltage to activate the solenoid plunger.
5. Speed up the engine momentarily to set the plunger.
6. The fast idle should be between 850-900 rpm. Adjust the fast idle by turning the solenoid plunger in or out.
7. Speed up the engine momentarily and recheck the fast idle. Readjust if necessary.
8. Remove the battery voltage from the solenoid and reconnect the solenoid wire.

VALVE LASH

Valve adjustment determines how far the valves enter the cylinder and how long they stay open and closed.

If the valve clearance is too large, part of the lift of the camshaft will be used in removing the excessive clearance. Consequently, the valve will not be opening as far as it should. This condition has two effects: the valve train components will emit a tapping sound as they take up the excessive clearance and the engine will perform poorly because the valves don't open fully and allow the proper amount of gases to flow into and out of the engine.

If the valve clearance is too small, the intake valve and the exhaust valves will open too far and they will not fully seal on the cylinder head when they close. When a valve seats itself on the cylinder head, it does two things: it seals the combustion chamber so that none of the gases in the cylinder escape and it cools itself by transferring some of the heat it absorbs from the combustion in the cylinder to the cylinder head and to the engine's cooling system. If the valve clearance is too small, the engine will run poorly because of the gases escaping from the combustion chamber. The valves will also become overheated and will warp, since they cannot transfer heat unless they are touching the valve seat in the cylinder head.

NOTE: *While all valve adjustments must be made as accurately as possible, it is better to have the valve adjustment slightly loose than slightly tight as a burned valve may result from overly tight adjustments.*

ADJUSTMENT

6-144, 6-170 w/Solid Lifters

1. Start the engine and let it run until it has reached operating temperature.
2. Remove the valve cover and gasket.
3. With the engine idling, adjust the valve lash using a step-type feeler gauge. This type of feeler gauge is sometimes more commonly

Adjusting valve clearance on 144,170 6 Cyl. with solid lifters using step-type feeler gauge

known as a "go, no-go" type feeler gauge. The proper clearance is reached when the smaller step on the gauge blade will pass through the gap while the larger step on the the same blade will not pass through the gap.

Pass the proper size gauge blade between the valve stem and the rocker arm. If the clearance is correct, move on to the next valve. If the clearance is in need of adjustment, turn the adjusting screw on the opposite end of the rocker arm with a wrench until the proper clearance is reached. Turn the screw clockwise to decrease the clearance and counterclockwise to increase the clearance. Use this procedure for all of the valves.

4. After all of the valves have been adjusted, replace the valve cover gasket and cover. If the gasket is made of rubber, and it is not torn, squashed or otherwise damaged it can be used again. If the gasket is cork, it is advised that the gasket be replaced.

5. Tighten the valve cover retaining bolts to 3-5 ft.lb. (36-60 in.lb.).

6-240, 6-300

1. Crank the engine until the TDC mark on the crankshaft damper is aligned with timing pointer on the cylinder front cover.
2. Scribe a mark on the damper at this point.
3. Scribe two more marks on the damper, each equally spaced from the first mark (see illustration).
4. With the engine on TDC of the compression stroke, (mark A aligned with the pointer) back off the rocker arm adjusting nut until there is end-play in the pushrod. Tighten the adjusting nut until all clearance is removed, then tighten the adjusting nut one additional turn. To determine when all clearance is removed from the rocker arm, turn the pushrod with the fingers. When the pushrod can no longer be turned, all clearance has been removed.
5. Repeat this procedure for each valve, turning the crankshaft ⅓ turn to the next mark each time and following the engine firing order of 1-5-3-6-2-4.

1969 8-302

Some early models are equipped with adjustable rockers whereas the later models are equipped with positive stop type rocker mounting studs. Positive stop equipped rockers are adjusted by turning the adjusting nut down until it stops. You can identify a positive stop mounting stud by determining whether or not the shank portion of the stud that is exposed just above the cylinder head is the same diameter as the threaded portion at the top of the stud, to which the rocker arm retaining nut at-

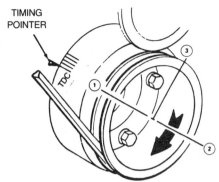

With No. 1 at TDC at end of compression stroke make a chalk mark at points 2 and 3 approximately 90 degrees apart

TIMING POINTER

POSITION 1—NO. 1 AT TDC AT END OF COMPRESSION STROKE.
POSITION 2—ROTATE THE CRANKSHAFT 180 DEGREES (ONE HALF REVOLUTION) CLOCKWISE FROM POSITION 1.
POSITION 3—ROTATE THE CRANKSHAFT 270 DEGREES (THREE QUARTER REVOLUTION CLOCKWISE FROM POSITION 2.

Position of the crankshaft for checking and adjusting valve clearance

taches. If the shank portion is larger than the threaded area, it is a positive stop mounting stud. Use the procedure given below for adjusting the valve lash on positive stop type mounting stud equipped vehicles.

There are two different procedures for adjusting the valves on the V8 engines. One is a preferred procedure and one is an alternate procedure. The preferred procedure is recommended, but the alternate procedure may be used.

NOTE: *These procedures are not tune-up procedures, but rebuild procedures to be performed only after valve train reassembly.*

PREFERRED PROCEDURE THROUGH 1969

1. Position the piston(s) on TDC of the compression stroke, using the timing mark on the crankshaft pulley as a reference for starting with the No.1 cylinder. You can tell if a piston is coming up on its compression stroke by removing the spark plug of the cylinder you are working on and placing your thumb over the hole while the engine is cranked over. Air will try to force its way past you thumb when the piston comes upon the compression stroke. Make sure

Inspect the rocker arms, balls, studs, and nuts:

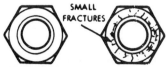

SMALL FRACTURES

Stress cracks in the rocker nuts

that the high tension coil wire leading to the distributor is removed before cranking the engine. Remove the valve covers.

2. Starting with No.1 cylinder, and the piston in the position as mentioned above, apply pressure to slowly bleed down the valve lifter until the plunger is completely bottomed.

3. While holding the valve lifter in the fully collapsed position, check the available clearance between the rocker arm and the valve stem tip. Use a feeler gauge.

4. If the clearance is not within the specified amount, rotate the rocker arm stud nut clockwise to decrease the clearance and counterclockwise to increase the clearance. Normally, one turn of the rocker arm stud nut will vary the clearance by 0.066″. Check the breakaway torque of each stud nut with a torque wrench, turning it counterclockwise. It should be anywhere from 4.5 to 15 ft.lb. Replace the nut and/or the stud as necessary.

5. When both valves for the No.1 cylinder have been adjusted, proceed on to the other valves, following the firing order sequence 1-5-4-2-6-3-7-8.

6. Replace the valve covers and gaskets.

ALTERNATE PROCEDURE THROUGH 1969

Follow Step 1 of the preferred procedure given above, but instead of collapsing the lifter as in Step 2, loosen the rocker retaining nut until there is endplay present in the pushrod; then tighten the nut to remove all pushrod-to-rocker arm clearance has been eliminated, tighten the stud nut an additional ¾ turn to place the lifter plunger in the desired operating range.

Repeat this procedure for all of the cylinders, using the firing order sequence as a guide. It takes ¼ turn of the crankshaft to bring the next piston in the firing order sequence up to TDC at the end of its compression stroke.

Collapsed Tappet Gap Clearance:
Allowable: 0.071-0.193″
Desired: 0.096-0.165″

1970 and Later 8-302
8-351
8-460

1. Crank the engine until the No. 1 cylinder is at TDC of the compression stroke and the timing pointer is aligned with the mark on the crankshaft damper.

2. Scribe a mark on the damper at this point.

3. Scribe two additional marks on the damper (see illustration).

4. With the timing pointer aligned with mark 1 on the damper, tighten the following valves on the specified torque:

● 8-302 and 8-460: Nos. 1, 7 and 8 Intake; Nos. 1, 5 and 4 Exhaust

● 8-351: Nos. 1, 4 and 8 Intake; Nos. 1,3 and 7 Exhaust

5. Rotate the crankshaft 180° to point 2 and tighten the following valves:

● 8-302 and 8-460: Nos. 5 and 4 Intake; Nos. 2 and 6 Exhaust

● 8-351: Nos. 3 and 7 Intake; Nos. 6 and 6 Exhaust

6. Rotate the crankshaft 270° to point 3 and tighten the following valves:

● 8-302 and 8-460: Nos. 2, 3 and 6 Intake; Nos. 7, 3 and 8 Exhaust

● 8-351: Nos. 2, 5 and 6 Intake; Nos. 4, 5 and 8 Exhaust

7. Rocker arm tightening specifications are:

● 8-302 and 8-351: tighten the nut until it contacts the rocker shoulder, then torque to 18-20 ft.lb.

● 8-460: tighten the nut until it contacts the rocker shoulder, then torque to 18-22 ft.lb.

Engine and Engine Overhaul

3

ENGINE ELECTRICAL

Understanding the Engine Electrical System

The engine electrical system can be broken down into three separate and distinct systems:

1. The starting system.
2. The charging system.
3. The ignition system.

BATTERY AND STARTING SYSTEM

Basic Operating Principles

The battery is the first link in the chain of mechanisms which work together to provide cranking of the automobile engine. In most modern cars, the battery is a lead/acid electrochemical device consisting of six 2v subsections connected in series so the unit is capable of producing approximately 12v of electrical pressure. Each subsection, or cell, consists of a series of positive and negative plates held a short distance apart in a solution of sulfuric acid and water. The two types of plates are of dissimilar metals. This causes a chemical reaction to be set up, and it is this reaction which produces current flow from the battery when its positive and negative terminals are connected to an electrical appliance such as a lamp or motor. The continued transfer of electrons would eventually convert the sulfuric acid in the electrolyte to water, and make the two plates identical in chemical composition. As electrical energy is removed from the battery, its voltage output tends to drop. Thus, measuring battery voltage and battery electrolyte composition are two ways of checking the ability of the unit to supply power. During the starting of the engi000897ectrical energy is removed from the battery. However, if the charging circuit is in good condition and the operating conditions are normal, the power removed from the battery will be replaced by the generator (or alternator) which will force electrons back through the battery, reversing the normal flow, and restoring the battery to its original chemical state.

The battery and starting motor are linked by very heavy electrical cables designed to minimize resistance to the flow of current. Generally, the major power supply cable that leaves the battery goes directly to the starter, while other electrical system needs are supplied by a smaller cable. During starter operation, power flows from the battery to the starter and is grounded through the car's frame and the battery's negative ground strap.

The starting motor is a specially designed, direct current electric motor capable of producing a very great amount of power for its size. One thing that allows the motor to produce a great deal of power is its tremendous rotating speed. It drives the engine through a tiny pinion gear (attached to the starter's armature), which drives the very large flywheel ring gear at a greatly reduced speed. Another factor allowing it to produce so much power is that only intermittent operation is required of it. This, little allowance for air circulation is required, and the windings can be built into a very small space.

The starter solenoid is a magnetic device which employs the small current supplied by the starting switch circuit of the ignition switch. This magnetic action moves a plunger which mechanically engages the starter and electrically closes the heavy switch which connects it to the battery. The starting switch circuit consists of the starting switch contained within the ignition switch, a transmission neutral safety switch or clutch pedal switch, and the wiring necessary to connect these in series with the starter solenoid or relay.

A pinion, which is a small gear, is mounted to a one-way drive clutch. This clutch is splined to the starter armature shaft. When the ignition switch is moved to the **start** position, the solenoid plunger slides the pinion toward the flywheel ring gear via a collar and spring. If the teeth on the pinion and flywheel match properly, the pinion will engage the flywheel immediately. If the gear teeth butt one another, the spring will be compressed and will force the gears to mesh as soon as the starter turns far enough to allow them to do so. As the solenoid plunger reaches the end of its travel, it closes the contacts that connect the battery and starter and then the engine is cranked.

As soon as the engine starts, the flywheel ring gear begins turning fast enough to drive the pinion at an extremely high rate of speed. At this point, the one-way clutch begins allowing the pinion to spin faster than the starter shaft so that the starter will not operate at excessive speed. When the ignition switch is released from the starter position, the solenoid is de-energized, and a spring contained within the solenoid assembly pulls the gear out of mesh and interrupts the current flow to the starter.

Some starter employ a separate relay, mounted away from the starter, to switch the motor and solenoid current on and off. The relay thus replaces the solenoid electrical switch, buy does not eliminate the need for a solenoid mounted on the starter used to mechanically engage the starter drive gears. The relay is used to reduce the amount of current the starting switch must carry.

THE CHARGING SYSTEM

Basic Operating Principles

The automobile charging system provides electrical power for operation of the vehicle's ignition and starting systems and all the electrical accessories. The battery services as an electrical surge or storage tank, storing (in chemical form) the energy originally produced by the engine driven generator. The system also provides a means of regulating generator output to protect the battery from being overcharged and to avoid excessive voltage to the accessories.

The storage battery is a chemical device incorporating parallel lead plates in a tank containing a sulfuric acid/water solution. Adjacent plates are slightly dissimilar, and the chemical reaction of the two dissimilar plates produces electrical energy when the battery is connected to a load such as the starter motor. The chemical reaction is reversible, so that when the generator is producing a voltage (electrical pressure) greater than that produced by the battery, electricity is forced into the battery, and the battery is returned to its fully charged state.

The vehicle's generator is driven mechanically, through V-belts, by the engine crankshaft. It consists of two coils of fine wire, one stationary (the stator), and one movable (the rotor). The rotor may also be known as the armature, and consists of fine wire wrapped around an iron core which is mounted on a shaft. The electricity which flows through the two coils of wire (provided initially by the battery in some cases) creates an intense magnetic field around both rotor and stator, and the interaction between the two fields creates voltage, allowing the generator to power the accessories and charge the battery.

There are two types of generators: the earlier is the direct current (DC) type. The current produced by the DC generator is generated in the armature and carried off the spinning armature by stationary brushes contacting the commutator. The commutator is a series of smooth metal contact plates on the end of the armature. The commutator is a series of smooth metal contact plates on the end of the armature. The commutator plates, which are separated from one another by a very short gap, are connected to the armature circuits so that current will flow in one directions only in the wires carrying the generator output. The generator stator consists of two stationary coils of wire which draw some of the output current of the generator to form a powerful magnetic field and create the interaction of fields which generates the voltage. The generator field is wired in series with the regulator.

Newer automobiles use alternating current generators or alternators, because they are more efficient, can be rotated at higher speeds, and have fewer brush problems. In an alternator, the field rotates while all the current produced passes only through the stator winding. The brushes bear against continuous slip rings rather than a commutator. This causes the current produced to periodically reverse the direction of its flow. Diodes (electrical one-way switches) block the flow of current from traveling in the wrong direction. A series of diodes is wired together to permit the alternating flow of the stator to be converted to a pulsating, but unidirectional flow at the alternator output. The alternator's field is wired in series with the voltage regulator.

The regulator consists of several circuits. Each circuit has a core, or magnetic coil of wire, which operates a switch. Each switch is connected to ground through one or more resistors. The coil of wire responds directly to system voltage. When the voltage reaches the required level, the magnetic field created by the winding of wire closes the switch and inserts a resistance into the generator field circuit, thus reducing the output. The contacts of the switch cycle open and close many times each second to precisely control voltage.

While alternators are self-limiting as far as maximum current is concerned, DC generators employ a current regulating circuit which responds directly to the total amount of current flowing through the generator circuit rather than to the output voltage. The current regulator is similar to the voltage regulator except that all system current must flow through the energizing coil on its way to the various accessories.

Ignition Coil
REMOVAL AND INSTALLATION

1. Disconnect the battery ground.
2. Disconnect the two small and one large wires from the coil.
3. Disconnect the condenser connector from the coil, if equipped.
4. Unbolt and remove the coil.
5. Installation is the reverse of removal.

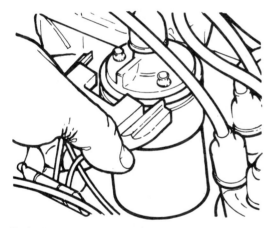

Typical coil connector removal

Ignition Module
REMOVAL AND INSTALLATION

Removing the module, on all models, is a matter of simply removing the fasteners that attach it to the fender or firewall and pulling apart the connectors. When unplugging the connectors, pull them apart with a firm, straight pull. NEVER PRY THEM APART! To pry them will cause damage. When reconnecting them, coat the mating ends with silicone dielectric grease to waterproof the connection. Press the connectors together firmly to overcome any vacuum lock caused by the grease.
NOTE: *If the locking tabs weaken or break, don't replace the unit. Just secure the connection with electrical tape or tie straps.*

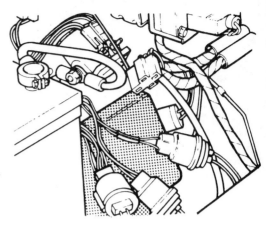

Typical control module

Point-Type Distributors
REMOVAL AND INSTALLATION

NOTE: *Some 8-351 and 8-400 distributors will be VERY hard to remove! Have patience and use lots of penetrating lubricant. Be careful to avoid damaging the distributor body!*
1. Remove the air cleaner assembly, taking note of the hose locations.
2. Disconnect the primary wire at the coil.
3. Noting the position of the vacuum line(s) on the distributor diaphragm, disconnect the lines at the diaphragm. Unsnap the two distributor cap retaining clamps and remove the cap. Position the cap and ignition wires to one side.
NOTE: *If it is necessary to disconnect the ignition wires from the cap to get enough room to remove the distributor, make sure to label every wire and the cap for accurate reinstallation.*
4. Using a chalk or paint, carefully mark the position of the distributor rotor in relation to the distributor housing and mark the position of the distributor housing. This is very important because the distributor must be reinstalled in the exact same location from which it was removed, if correct ignition timing is to be maintained.
5. Remove the distributor holddown bolt and clamp. Remove the distributor from the engine. Make sure that the oil pump (intermediate) driveshaft does not come out with the distributor. If it does, remove it from the distributor shaft, coat its lower end with heavy grease, and reinsert it, making sure that it fully engages the oil pump drive.
NOTE: *Do not disturb the engine while the distributor is removed. If you turn the engine over with the distributor removed, you will have to retime the engine.*
    a. If the engine was cranked (disturbed) with the distributor removed, it will now be

necessary to retime the engine. If the distributor has been installed incorrectly and the engine will not start, remove the distributor from the engine and start over again. Hold the distributor close to the engine and install the cap on the distributor in its normal position. Locate the No. 1 spark plug tower on the distributor cap. Scribe a mark on the body of the distributor directly below the No.1 spark plug wire tower on the distributor cap. Remove the distributor cap from the distributor and move the distributor and cap to one side. Remove the No. 1 spark plug and crank the engine over until the No. 1 cylinder is on its compression stroke. To accomplish this, place a wrench on the lower engine pulley and turn the engine slowly in a clockwise (6-cyl.) or counterclockwise (V8) direction until the TDC mark on the crankshaft damper aligns with the timing pointer. If you place your finger in the No. 1 spark plug hole, you will feel air escaping as the piston rises in the combustion chamber. The rotor must be at the No. 1 firing position to install the distributor. Make sure that the oil pump intermediate shaft properly engages the distributor shaft. It may be necessary to crank the engine with the starter, after the distributor drive gear is partially engaged, in order to engage the oil pump intermediate shaft. Install, but do not tighten the retaining clamp and bolt. Rotate the distributor to advance the timing to a point where the points are just starting to open. Tighten the clamp.

b. If the engine was not cranked (disturbed) when the distributor was removed, position the distributor in the block with the rotor aligned with the mark previously scribed on the distributor body and the marks on the distributor body and cylinder block in alignment. Install the distributor holddown bolt and clamp fingertight.

6. Install the distributor cap and wires.

7. Connect the primary wire at the coil.

8. Install the Thermactor air pump mounting bolt, if removed, and adjust the air pump drive belt tension, if necessary, as outlined in Chapter 1.

9. Install the air cleaner, if removed.

10. Check the ignition timing as outlined in Chapter 2.

Electronic Distributor
REMOVAL

NOTE: *Some 8-351 and 8-400 distributors will be VERY hard to remove! Have patience and use lots of penetrating lubricant. Be careful to avoid damaging the distributor body!*

Carbureted Engines (DuraSpark)

1. Remove the air cleaner assembly, taking note of the hose locations.

2. Disconnect the distributor wiring connector from the vehicle wiring harness.

3. Noting the position of the vacuum line(s) on the distributor diaphragm, disconnect the lines at the diaphragm. Unsnap the two distributor cap retaining clamps and remove the cap, rotor and adapter.

NOTE: *If it is necessary to disconnect ignition wires from the cap to get enough room to remove the distributor, make sure to label every wire and the cap for easy and accurate reinstallation.*

4. Rotate the engine to align any pole on the armature with the pole on the stator.

5. Install the rotor. Using chalk or paint, carefully mark the position of the distributor rotor in relation to the distributor housing and mark the position of the distributor housing in relation to the engine block. When this is done, you should have a line on the distributor housing directly in line with the tip of the rotor and another line on the engine block directly in line with the mark on the distributor housing. This is very important because the distributor must be installed in the exact same location from which it was removed, if correct ignition timing is to be maintained.

6. Remove the distributor holddown bolt and clamp. Remove the distributor from the engine. Make sure that the oil pump (intermediate) driveshaft does not come out with the distributor. If it does, remove it from the distributor shaft, coat its lower end with heavy grease, and reinsert it, making sure that it fully engages the oil pump drive.

NOTE: *Do not disturb the engine while the distributor is removed. If you turn the engine over with the distributor removed, you will have to retime the engine.*

INSTALLATION
ENGINE NOT ROTATED

Carbureted Engines (DuraSpark)

1. If the engine was not cranked (disturbed) when the distributor was removed, position the distributor in the block with the armature and stator poles aligned, the rotor aligned with the mark previously scribed on the distributor body and the marks on the distributor body and cylinder block in alignment. Install the distributor holddown bolt and clamp finger tight.

2. If the stator and armature poles cannot be aligned by rotating the distributor, pull the distributor out just far enough to disengage the drive gear and rotate the ditributor shaft to engage a different gear tooth.

3. Install the distributor cap and wires.

4. Connect the distributor wring connector to the wiring harness. Tighten the holddown bolt.

5. Install the air cleaner, if removed.

6. Check the ignition timing as outlined in Chapter 2.

INSTALLATION
CRANKSHAFT OR CAMSHAFT ROTATED

Carbureted Engines (DuraSpark)

If the engine is cranked (disturbed) with the distributor removed, it will now be necessary to retime the engine.

1. Rotate the engine so that No.1 piston is at TDC of the compression stroke.

2. Align the timing marks to the correct initial timing shown on the underhood decal.

3. Install the distributor with the rotor in the No.1 firing position and any armature pole aligned with the stator pole.

NOTE: *Make sure that the oil pump intermediate shaft properly engages the distributor shaft. It may be necessary to crank the engine after the distributor gear is partially engaged in order to engage the oil pump intermediate shaft and fully seat the distributor in the block.*

4. If it was necessary to rotate the engine to align the oil pump, repeat Steps 1, 2 and 3.

5. Install the holddown bolt finger tight.

6. Install the distributor cap and wires.

7. Connect the distributor wring connector to the wiring harness. Tighten the holddown bolt.

8. Install the air cleaner, if removed.

9. Check the ignition timing as outlined in Chapter 2.

10. When everything is set, tighten the holddown bolt to 25 ft.lb.

REMOVAL

Fuel Injected Engines (TFI-IV Systems)

1. Disconect the primary wiring connector from the distributor.

2. Mark the position of the cap's No.1 terminal on the distributor base.

3. Unclip and remove the cap. Remove the adapter.

4. Remove the rotor.

5. Remove the TFI connector.

6. Matchmark the distributor base and engine for installation reference.

7. Remove the holddown bolt and lift out the distributor.

INSTALLATION

Fuel Injected Engines (TFI-IV System)

1. Rotate the engine so that the No.1 piston is at TDC of the compression stroke.

2. Align the timing marks so that the engine is set at the initial timing shown on the underhood sticker.

3. Install the rotor on the shaft and rotate the shaft so that the rotor tip points to the No.1 mark made on the distributor base.

4. Continue rotating the shaft so that the leading edge of the vane is centered on the vane switch assembly.

5. Position the distributor in the block and rotate the distributor body to align the leading edge of the vane and vane switch. Verify that the rotor tip points to the No.1 mark on the body.

NOTE: *If the vane and vane switch cannot be aligned by rotating the distributor body in the engine, pull the distributor out just far enough to disengage the gears and rotate the shaft to engage a different gear tooth. Repeat Steps 3, 4 and 5.*

6. Install and finger tighten the holddown bolt.

7. Connect the TFI and primary wiring.

8. Install the rotor, if not already done.

NOTE: *Coat the brass portions of the rotor with a $\frac{1}{32}$" (0.8mm) thick coating of silicone dielectric compound.*

9. Install the cap and adapter (as necessary). Install the wires and start the engine.

10. Check and set the initial timing.

11. Tighten the holddown bolt to 25 ft.lb.

Alternators and Generators

All 1961-63 and some 1964 vans had generators. Beginning in 1964, all vans are equipped with alternators.

An alternator differs from a DC shunt generator in that the armature is stationary, and is called the stator, while the field rotates and is called the rotor. The higher current values in the alternator's stator are conducted to the external circuit through fixed leads and connections, rather than through a rotating commutator and brushes as in a DC generator. This eliminates a major point of maintenance.

The alternator charging system is a negative (–) ground system which consists of an alternator, a regulator, a charge indicator, a storage battery and wiring connecting the components, and fuse link wire.

The alternator is belt-driven from the engine. Energy is supplied from the alternator/regulator system to the rotating field through two brushes to two slip-rings. The slip-rings are mounted on the rotor shaft and are connected to the field coil. This energy supplied to the rotating field from the battery is called excitation current and is used to initially energize the field to begin the generation of

Alternator and Regulator Specifications

Year	Alternator Part No. or Manufacturer (color code)	Alternator Field Current @ 12 v	Alternator Output (amps)	Regulator Part No. or Manufacturer	Field Relay Air Gap (in.)	Field Relay Point Gap (in.)	Field Relay Volts to Close	Regulator Air Gap (in.)	Regulator Point Gap (in.)	Regulator Volts @ 75°
1961–63	C2DF-10000-B*	1.2–1.8	25	Ford	NA	NA	12.4–13.2	NA	NA	14.6–15.4
1964	Ford Gen.*	1.0–1.5	30	Ford	NA	NA	12.4–13.2	NA	NA	14.6–15.4
	Ford Alt.	2.4–2.6	42	Ford	0.025	.018	2.5	0.048	0.012	13.6–14.2
1965	Autolite	2.8–3.3	45	Autolite	0.017	—	2.5	0.052	0.020	14.1–14.7
1966–67	Autolite (purple)	2.5	38	Autolite	0.014	—	2.5–4	0.052	0.020	14.1–14.9
	Autolite (orange)	2.9	45	Autolite	0.014	—	2.5–4	0.052	0.020	14.1–14.9
	Autolite (red)	2.9	55	Autolite	0.014	—	2.5–4	0.052	0.020	14.1–14.9
1969–75	Autolite (purple)	2.4	38	Autolite	—	—	2.0–4.2	—	—	13.5–15.3
	Autolite (orange)	2.9	42	Autolite	—	—	2.0–4.2	—	—	13.5–15.3
	Autolite (red)	2.9	55	Autolite	—	—	2.0–4.2	—	—	13.5–15.3
1976–80	Autolite (orange)	2.9	40	Autolite	—	—	—	—	—	—
	Autolite (green)	2.9	60	Autolite	—	—	—	—	—	—
1981–88	Autolite (orange)	4.3	40	Autolite	—	—	—	—	—	—
	Autolite (green)	4.3	60	Autolite	—	—	—	—	—	—
	Autolite (black)	4.0	70	Autolite	—	—	—	—	—	—
	Autolite (red)	4.0	100	Autolite	—	—	—	—	—	—

*Generator
NA: Not applicable

electricity. Once the alternator starts to generate electricity, the excitation current comes from its own output rather than the battery.

The alternator produces power in the form of alternating current. The alternating current is rectified by 6 diodes into direct current. The direct current is used to charge the battery and power the rest of the electrical system.

When the ignition key is turned on, current flows from the battery, through the charging system indicator light on the instrument panel, to the voltage regulator, and to the alternator. Since the alternator is not producing any current, the alternator warning light comes on. When the engine is started, the alternator begins to produce current and turns the alternator light off. As the alternator turns and produces current, the current is divided in two ways: part to the battery to charge the battery and power the electrical components of the vehicle, and part is returned to the alternator to enable it to increase its output. In this situation, the alternator is receiving current from the battery and from itself. A voltage regulator is wired into the current supply to the alternator to prevent it from receiving too much current which would cause it to put out too much current. Conversely, if the voltage regulator does not allow the alternator to receive enough current, the battery will not be fully charged and will eventually go dead.

The battery is connected to the alternator at all times, whether the ignition key is turned on or not. If the battery were shorted to ground, the alternator would also be shorted. This would damage the alternator. To prevent this, a fuse link is installed in the wiring between the battery and the alternator. If the battery is shorted, the fuse link is melted, protecting the alternator.

An alternator is better that a conventional, DC shunt generator because it is lighter and more compact, because it is designed to supply the battery and accessory circuits through a wide range of engine speeds, and because it eliminates the necessary maintenance of replacing brushes and servicing commutators.

ALTERNATOR PRECAUTIONS

To prevent damage to the alternator and regulator, the following precautions should be taken when working with the electrical system.

1. Never reverse the battery connections.

2. Booster batteries for starting must be connected properly: positive-to-positive and negative-to-ground.

3. Disconnect the battery cables before using a fast charger; the charger has a tendency to force current through the diodes in the opposite direction for which they were designed. This burns out the diodes.

4. Never use a fast charger as a booster for starting the vehicle.

5. Never disconnect the voltage regulator while the engine is running.

6. Avoid long soldering times when replacing diodes or transistors. Prolonged heat is damaging to AC generators.

7. Do not use test lamps of more than 12 volts (V) for checking diode continuity.

8. Do not short across or ground any of the terminals on the AC generator.

9. The polarity of the battery, generator, and regulator must be matched and considered before making any electrical connections within the system.

10. Never operate the alternator on an open circuit. make sure that all connections within the circuit are clean and tight.

11. Disconnect the battery terminals when performing any service on the electrical system. This will eliminate the possibility of accidental reversal of polarity.

12. Disconnect the battery ground cable if arc welding is to be done on any part of the car.

CHARGING SYSTEM TROUBLESHOOTING

There are many possible ways in which the charging system can malfunction. Often the source of a problem is difficult to diagnose, requiring special equipment and a good deal of experience. This is usually not the case, however, where the charging system fails completely and causes the dash board warning light to come on or the battery to become dead. To troubleshoot a complete system failure only two pieces of equipment are needed: a test light, to determine that current is reaching a certain point; and a current indicator (ammeter), to determine the direction of the current flow and its measurement in amps.

This test works under three assumptions:

1. The battery is known to be good and fully charged.

2. The alternator belt is in good condition and adjusted to the proper tension.

3. All connections in the system are clean and tight.

NOTE: *In order for the current indicator to give a valid reading, the car must be equipped with battery cables which are of the same gauge size and quality as original equipment battery cables.*

1. Turn off all electrical components on the car. Make sure the doors of the car are closed. If the car is equipped with a clock, disconnect the clock by removing the lead wire from the rear of the clock. Disconnect the positive battery cable from the battery and connect the ground wire on a test light to the disconnected positive battery cable. Touch the probe end of the test light to the positive battery post. The test light should not light. If the test light does light, there is a short or open circuit on the car.

2. Disconnect the voltage regulator wiring harness connector at the voltage regulator. Turn on the ignition key. Connect the wire on a test light to a good ground (engine bolt). Touch the probe end of a test light to the ignition wire connector into the voltage regulator wiring connector. This wire corresponds to the I terminal on the regulator. If the test light goes on, the charging system warning light circuit is complete. If the test light does not come on and the warning light on the instrument panel is on, either the resistor wire, which is parallel with the warning light, or the wiring to the voltage regulator, is defective. If the test light does not come on and the warning light is not on, either the bulb is defective or the power supply wire form the battery through the ignition switch to the bulb has an open circuit. Connect the wiring harness to the regulator.

3. Examine the fuse link wire in the wiring harness from the starter relay to the alternator.

If the insulation on the wire is cracked or split, the fuse link may be melted. Connect a test light to the fuse link by attaching the ground wire on the test light to an engine bolt and touching the probe end of the light to the bottom of the fuse link wire where it splices into the alternator output wire. If the bulb in the test light does not light, the fuse link is melted.

4. Start the engine and place a current indicator on the positive battery cable. Turn off all electrical accessories and make sure the doors are closed. If the charging system is working properly, the gauge will show a draw of less than 5 amps. If the system is not working properly, the gauge will show a draw of more than 5 amps. A charge moves the needle toward the battery, a draw moves the needle away from the battery. Turn the engine off.

5. Disconnect the wiring harness from the voltage regulator at the regulator at the regulator connector. Connect a male spade terminal (solderless connector) to each end of a jumper wire. Insert one end of the wire into the wiring harness connector which corresponds to the **A** terminal on the regulator. Insert the other end of the wire into the wiring harness connector which corresponds to the **F** terminal on the regulator. Position the connector with the jumper wire installed so that it cannot contact any metal surface under the hood. Position a current indicator gauge on the positive battery cable. Have an assistant start the engine. Observe the reading on the current indicator. Have your assistant slowly raise the speed of the engine to about 2,000 rpm or until the current indicator needle stops moving, whichever comes first. Do not run the engine for more than a short period of time in this condition. If the wiring harness connector or jumper wire becomes excessively hot during this test, turn off the engine and check for a grounded wire in the regulator wiring harness. If the current indicator shows a charge of about three amps less than the output of the alternator, the alternator is working properly. If the previous tests showed a draw, the voltage regulator is defective. If the gauge does not show the proper charging rate, the alternator is defective.

REMOVAL AND INSTALLATION

While internal alternator repairs are possible, they require specialized tools and training. Therefore, it is advisable to replace a defective alternator, or have it repaired by a qualified shop.

1. Open the hood and disconnect the battery ground cable.

2. Remove the adjusting arm bolt.

3. Remove the alternator or generator through-bolt. Remove the drive belt from the alternator or generator pulley and lower the alternator or generator.

NOTE: *Some engines are equipped with a ribbed, K-section belt and automatic tensioner. A special tool must be made to remove the tension from the tensioner arm. Loosen the idler pulley pivot and adjuster bolts before using the tool. See the accompanying illustration for tool details.*

4. Label all of the leads to the alternator or generator so that you can install them correctly and disconnect the leads from the alternator or generator.

5. Remove the alternator or generator from the vehicle.

6. To install, reverse the above procedure. Torque the pivot bolt to 58 ft.lb.; the adjusting bolt to 25 ft.lb.; the wire terminal nuts to 60-90 in.lb.

BELT TENSION ADJUSTMENT

The fan belt drives the alternator and water pump. if the belt is too loose, it will slip and the alternator will not be able to produce it rated current. Also, the water pump will not operate efficiently and the engine could overheat.

Check the tension of the belt by pushing your thumb down on the longest span of the belt, midway between the pulleys. Belt deflection should be approximately ½" (13mm).

To adjust the belt tension, proceed as follows:

1. Loosen the alternator mounting bolt and the adjusting arm bolts.

2. Apply pressure on the alternator front housing only, moving the alternator away from the engine to tighten the belt. Do not apply pressure to the rear of the cast aluminum housing of an alternator; damage to the housing could result.

3. Tighten the alternator mounting bolt and the adjusting arm bolts when the correct tension is reached.

1961-64 Generator Regulator

The voltage regulators that are used with shunt type generators are serviceable and can be adjusted. These regulators have three units: the circuit breaker, the voltage regulator and the current limiting regulator. Each has a separate function.

VOLTAGE REGULATOR

The function of the voltage regulator unit is to hold the generated voltage at a predetermined value as long as the circuit values allow the voltage to build to the operating load.

The electromagnet of the voltage regulator unit has a winding of many turns of fine wire and is connected across the charging circuit so that the system voltage controls the amount of magnetism. The contacts of the voltage regulator unit are connected in the generator field circuit so that the field circuit is completed through the contacts when they are closed and through a resistor when the contacts are opened.

When the voltage rises to a predetermined amount, there is sufficient magnetism created by the regulator winding to pull the armature down. This opens the contacts and inserts resistance in the field circuit of the generator, thus reducing the field current. The generated voltage immediately drops, reducing the pull on the armature to the point where the spring closes the contacts. The output again rises and the cycle is repeated.

These cycles occur at sufficiently high frequencies to hold the generated voltage at a constant level and they will continue as long as the voltage of the circuit is high enough to keep the voltage regulator unit in operation. When there is a current load that is great enough to lower the battery voltage below the operating voltage of the voltage regulating unit, the contacts will remain closed and the generator will maintain a charging rate that is limited by its speed and capacity output.

CURRENT LIMITING REGULATOR

The function of the current limiting regulator is to limit the output of the generator to its maximum safe output.

The electromagnet of the current regulator unit consists of a winding of heavy wire connected in a series with the generator output. When the generator output reaches a predetermined level, the current in the winding produces enough magnetism to overcome spring tension and pull the armature down. This opens the contacts and inserts resistance in the field circuit of the generator. With the field current reduced by the resistance, the generator output falls and there is no longer sufficient magnetism to hold the contacts open. As soon as the spring closes the contacts, the output and the cycle is repeated. These cycles occur at a high enough frequency to limit the output to a minimum fluctuation.

VOLTAGE TESTS AND ADJUSTMENTS

Circuit Breaker

The circuit breaker is the unit with the heavy wire windings and is located on the end of the unit.

1. Connect an ammeter in series with the regulator **B** (battery) terminal and the lead that is removed from that terminal. Connect a voltmeter from the regulator **A** (armature) terminal to the regulator base.

2. Disconnect the field lead from the regulator **F** terminal and insert a variable resistance between the lead and the regulator terminal.

3. Run the generator at about 1,000 generator rpm. Insert all of the resistance in the field circuit. Slowly reduce the resistance, noting the voltage reading just before the change caused by the closing of the circuit breaker. Increase the charging rate to the figure specified for the regulator being tested, then reduce the charging rate by inserting resistance into the field circuit. Note the charging rate just before the circuit breaker opens and the ammeter reading drops to zero. The closing voltage and the opening voltage or current should be within the limits specified.

4. To adjust the closing voltage, change the armature spring tension by bending the hanger at the lower end of the spring. Increase the spring tension to raise the closing voltage or decrease the tension to lower the voltage. To adjust the opening voltage, raise or lower the stationary contact, keeping the contacts perfectly aligned. Increasing the contact gap lowers the opening voltage. Change the contact gap by expanding or contracting the contact gap by expanding or contracting the stationary contact bracket, keeping the contacts aligned. Do not adjust the gap between the contacts to less than the specified minimum.

Voltage Regulator

The voltage regulator unit is the one with the fine wire winding.

1. Connect the ammeter as noted above and connect the voltmeter from the regulator **B** terminal to the regulator base. Remove the variable resistance from the field circuit.

2. Run the generator at one half maximum output for 15 minutes to make sure the regulator is at normal temperature. Have the cover on the unit during this warmup period and also when taking the readings.

3. Stop the engine, then bring it to approximately 2,500 generator rpm. Adjust the amperage to one half of the maximum output by turning on lights or accessories and then note the voltmeter reading. This reading should be within the limits specified for the voltage regulator.

4. To adjust the operating voltage, change the armature spring tension by bending the hanger at the lower end of the armature spring. After each adjustment, stop the engine and then restart it. Bring it up to speed and adjust the current before taking a reading. The clicks of the opening and closing of the contacts should be regular and clear without irregularities. If the tone is not clear and regular, remove the regulator cover and inspect the contacts. The contacts should be flat and not burned ex-

cessively, and should be aligned to make full face contact. Refer to the section on cleaning the contacts if necessary.

Current Regulator

The current regulator is the unit in the middle of the unit with the heavy wire winding.

1. Connect the regulator and instruments as described above for the voltage regulator and run the generator at approximately 3,000 generator rpm. Turn on the lights and accessories so the generator must charge at its maximum rate. The ammeter should show a reading within the specified limits.

2. To adjust the opening amperage, change the armature spring tension by bending the hanger at the lower end of the armature spring. Stop the engine after each adjustment and then restart it. Bring the engine to speed and take an ammeter reading. Keep the cover on the unit when taking the readings. The clocks of the points closing and opening should be clear in tone and regular in frequency without irregularities or misses. If this is not the case, the contacts will have to be serviced.

Contacts

The contacts should be inspected on all three of the units inside the cover of the voltage regulator. The contacts will become grayed and slightly worn during normal use. If the contacts are burned or dirty, or if they are not smooth or aligned properly, they should be adjusted and cleaned. File the contacts smooth. Just file enough so that there is a smooth surface presented to each contact. It is not necessary to file out every trace of pitting. After filing, dampen a clean cloth with a non-oily cleaning compound and pull the cloth between the contacts of each of the three units. Repeat with a clean dry cloth.

NOTE: *Keep in mind that after filing the points, the gap might have been changed enough to affect the performance of the three units. Check the three units and perform the adjustments. It might be a good idea to examine the contacts before making any adjustments. If the contacts need to be serviced, do it before adjusting spring tensions, etc.*

REMOVAL AND INSTALLATION

If the voltage regulator still does not function properly, after all of the checks and adjustments, replace the entire unit. Follow the procedure below.

1. Remove all of the electrical connections. Label them as you remove them so you can replace them in the correct order on the replacement unit.

2. Remove all of the holddown screws and then remove the unit from the vehicle.

3. Install the new voltage regulator using the holddown screws from the old one, or new ones if they are provided with the replacement regulator. Tighten down the holddown screws.

4. Connect the armature lead to the armature terminal of the voltage regulator.

5. Connect the battery lead to the battery terminal of the voltage regulator.

6. Momentarily touch the field lead to the battery terminal of the voltage regulator. This polarizes the generator and voltage regulator so they have the same polarization as the rest of the electrical system. This has to be done every time all of the leads are disconnected from the generator voltage regulator.

7. Connect the field lead to the field terminal of the voltage regulator.

1964-67 Autolite Alternator Regulator
MECHANICAL REGULATOR ADJUSTMENTS

Erratic operation of the regulator, indicated by erratic movement of the voltmeter pointer during a voltage limiter test, may be caused by dirty or pitted regulator contacts. Vehicle ammeter pointer waver at certain critical engine speeds and electrical loads, is normal. Use a very fine abrasive paper such as silicon carbide, 400 grade, to clean the field relay and the voltage limiter contacts. Wear off the sharp edges of the abrasive by rubbing it against another piece of abrasive paper. Fold the abrasive paper over and pull the paper through the contacts to clean them. Keep all oil or grease from contacting the points. Do not use compressed air to clean the regulator. When adjusting the gap spacing use only hospital-clean feeler gauges.

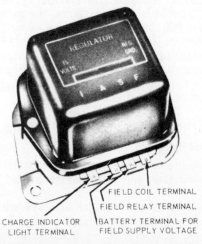

CHARGE INDICATOR LIGHT TERMINAL

FIELD COIL TERMINAL
FIELD RELAY TERMINAL
BATTERY TERMINAL FOR FIELD SUPPLY VOLTAGE

Autolite (Motorcraft) sealed electro-mechanical voltage regulator for 1969 and later models

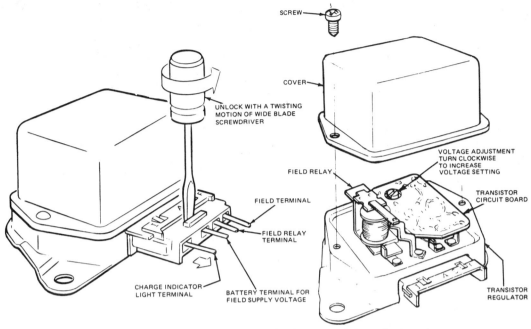

Autolite (Motorcraft) transistorized voltage regulator adjustment

Regulator Gap Adjustments

VOLTAGE LIMITER

The difference between the upper stage and lower stage regulation (0.3 V), is determined by the voltage limiter contact and core gaps. Make the gap adjustment with the regulator removed from the van.

Bend the lower contact bracket to obtain a 0.017-0.022″ (0.43-0.56mm) gap at the lower contacts with the upper contacts closed. Maintain the contacts in alignment.

Adjust the core gap with the upper contacts closed. Loosen the center lockscrew ¼ turn. Use a screwdriver blade in the adjustment slot under the lockscrew. Adjust the core gap for a 0.049-0.056″ (1.24-1.42mm) clearance between the armature and the core at the edge of the core closest to the contact points. Tighten the lockscrew and recheck the core gap.

FIELD RELAY

Place a 0.010-0.018″ (0.25-0.46mm) feeler gauge on top of the core closest to the contact points. Hold the armature down on the gauge. Do not push down on the contact spring arm. Bend the contact post arm until the bottom contact just touches the upper contact.

Regulator Voltage Limiter Adjustments

Final adjustment of the regulator must be made with the regulator at normal operating temperature.

The field relay closing voltage is adjusted by bending the relay frame. To increase the closing voltage, bend the armature frame down. To decrease the closing voltage, bend the frame up.

The voltage limiter is adjusted by bending the voltage limiter spring arm. To increase the voltage setting, bend the adjusting arm downward.

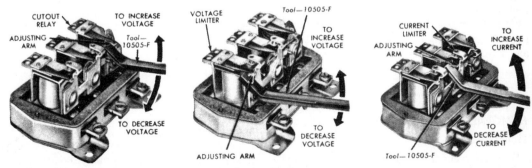

DC generator regulator mechanical adjustments

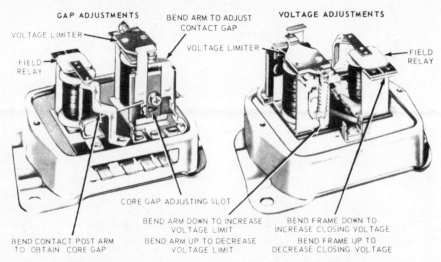

1963–67 Autolite alternator regulator mechanical adjustments

To decrease the voltage setting, bend the adjusting arm upward.

Before setting the voltage and before making a final voltage test, the alternator speed must be reduced to zero and the ignition switch opened momentarily, to cycle the regulator.

Leece-Neville Alternator Regulator

ADJUSTMENTS

1. Run the engine for 10-15 minutes to allow the regulator to reach operating temperature. Connect a voltmeter across the battery posts. Turn off all electrical equipment. Check the voltage at the battery. It should be 13.9-14.1 volts.

2. The voltage control adjustment (voltage limiter) is adjusted at the component closest to the **F** terminal. Remove the regulator cover. Voltage may be increased by raising the spring tension and decreased by lowering the spring tension. To adjust the spring tension, move the lower spring mounting tab.

NOTE: *Voltage will drop about ½ volt when the regulator cover is installed and should be compensated for in the adjustment.*

3. After making the adjustment, cycle the regulator by stopping and starting the engine. This will indicate if the adjustment is stable. If the voltage reading has changed, follow Steps 1 and 2 until the correct voltage is obtained.

Starter Motor

REMOVAL AND INSTALLATION

Except Diesel

1. Disconnect the negative battery cable.
2. Raise the front of the truck and install

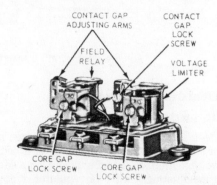

Leece-Neville alternator regulator gap adjustments

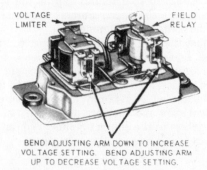

Leece-Neville alternator regulator voltage adjustments

jackstands beneath the frame. Firmly apply the parking brake and place blocks in back of the rear wheels.

3. Tag and disconnect the wiring at the starter.

4. Turn the front wheels fully to the right. On some later models it will be necessary to remove the frame brace. On many models, it will be necessary to remove the two bolts retaining

Troubleshooting Basic Charging System Problems

Problem	Cause	Solution
Noisy alternator	• Loose mountings • Loose drive pulley • Worn bearings • Brush noise • Internal circuits shorted (High pitched whine)	• Tighten mounting bolts • Tighten pulley • Replace alternator • Replace alternator • Replace alternator
Squeal when starting engine or accelerating	• Glazed or loose belt	• Replace or adjust belt
Indicator light remains on or ammeter indicates discharge (engine running)	• Broken fan belt • Broken or disconnected wires • Internal alternator problems • Defective voltage regulator	• Install belt • Repair or connect wiring • Replace alternator • Replace voltage regulator
Car light bulbs continually burn out—battery needs water continually	• Alternator/regulator overcharging	• Replace voltage regulator/alternator
Car lights flare on acceleration	• Battery low • Internal alternator/regulator problems	• Charge or replace battery • Replace alternator/regulator
Low voltage output (alternator light flickers continually or ammeter needle wanders)	• Loose or worn belt • Dirty or corroded connections • Internal alternator/regulator problems	• Replace or adjust belt • Clean or replace connections • Replace alternator or regulator

Battery and Starter Specifications

Year	Engine	Battery Ampere/Hour Capacity	Volts	Ground	Lock Test Amps	Lock Test Volts	Lock Test Torque (ft. lbs.)	No Load Test Amps	No Load Test Volts	No Load Test RPM	Brush Spring Tension (oz)
1961–65	All	45	12	Neg	450	5	8	70	12	9500	45
		55	12	Neg	500	5	9	70	12	9500	45
1966–77	All	45	12	Neg	670	5	15.5	70	12	9500	40
		55	12	Neg	670	5	15.5	70	12	9500	40
		70	12	Neg	670	5	15.5	70	12	9500	40
		80	12	Neg	670	5	15.5	70	12	9500	40
1978	All	41	12	Neg	460	5	9.0	70	12	9500	40
		68	12	Neg	670	5	15.5	80	12	9500	80
					525*	5	17.2	80	11	10,000	50
1979	All	41	12	Neg	460	5	9.0	70	12	9500	40
		53	12	Neg	670	5	15.5	80	12	9500	80
		68	12	Neg							
1980–88	All	36	12	Neg	460	5	9.0	70	12	9500	40
		45	12	Neg	670	5	15.5	80	12	9500	80
		68	12	Neg							
		81	12	Neg							

*Prestolite model with 400 cid engine

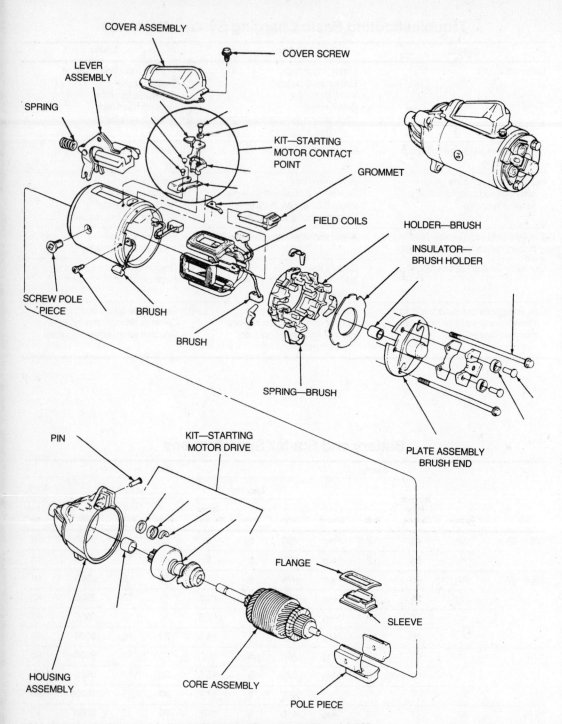

Starter used on the 8-351 and 8-460

the steering idler arm to the frame to gain access to the starter.

5. Remove the starter mounting bolts and remove the starter.

6. Reverse the above procedure to install. Torque the mounting bolts to 12-15 ft.lb. on starters with 3 mounting bolts and 15-20 ft.lb. on starters with 2 mounting bolts. Torque the idler arm retaining bolts to 28-35 ft.lb. (if removed). Make sure that the nut securing the heavy cable to the starter is snugged down tightly.

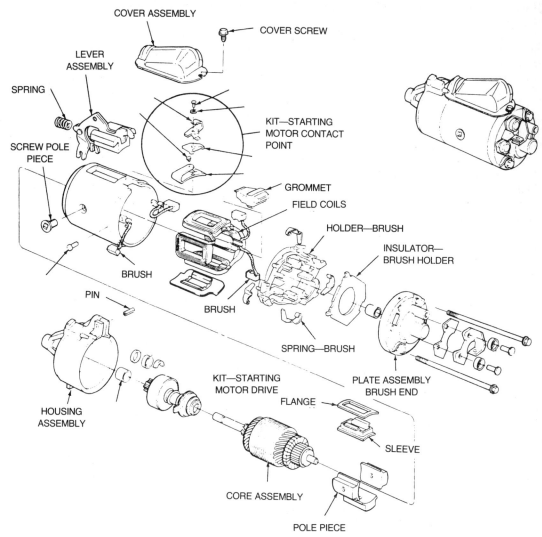

COVER ASSEMBLY

COVER SCREW

LEVER ASSEMBLY

SPRING

KIT—STARTING MOTOR CONTACT POINT

SCREW POLE PIECE

GROMMET

FIELD COILS

HOLDER—BRUSH

INSULATOR— BRUSH HOLDER

BRUSH

PIN

BRUSH

SPRING—BRUSH

PLATE ASSEMBLY BRUSH END

KIT—STARTING MOTOR DRIVE

FLANGE

HOUSING ASSEMBLY

SLEEVE

CORE ASSEMBLY

POLE PIECE

Starter used on the 6-300 and 8-302

8-420 (6.9L) and 8-444 (7.3L) Diesel

1. Disconnect the battery ground cable.
2. Raise the vehicle and disconnect the cables and wires at the starter solenoid.
3. Turn the front wheels to the right and remove the two bolts attaching the steering idler arm to the frame.
4. Remove the starter mounting bolts and remove the starter.
5. Installation is the reverse of removal. Torque the mounting bolts to 20 ft.lb.

OVERHAUL – EXCEPT DIESEL

Brush Replacement

1. Remove the starter from the engine as previously outlined.
2. Remove the starter drive plunger lever cover and gasket.

3. Loosen and remove the brush cover band and remove the brushes from their holder.
4. Remove the two through-bolts from the starter frame.
5. Separate the drive end housing, starter frame and brush end plate assemblies.
6. Remove the starter drive plunger lever and pivot pin, and remove the armature.
7. Remove the ground brush retaining screws from the frame and remove the brushes.
8. Cut the insulated brush leads from the field coils, as close to the field connection point as possible.
9. Clean and inspect the starter motor.
10. Replace the brush end plate if the insulator between the field brush holder and the end plate is cracked or broken.
11. Position the new insulated field brushes

lead on the field coil connection. Position and crimp the clip provided with the brushes to hold the brush lead to the connection. Solder the lead, clip, and connection together using resin core solder. Use a 300 watt soldering iron.

12. Install the ground brush leads to the frame with the retaining screws.

13. Install the starter drive plunger lever and pivot pin, and install the armature.

14. Assemble the drive end housing, starter frame and brush end plate assemblies.

15. Install the two through-bolts in the starter frame. Torque the through-bolts to 55-75 in.lb.

16. Install the brushes in their holders and install the brush cover band.

17. Install the starter drive plunger lever cover and gasket.

18. Install the starter on the engine as previously outlined.

Drive Replacement

1. Remove the starter as outlined previously.

2. Remove the starter drive plunger lever and gasket and the brush cover band.

3. Remove the two through-bolts from the starter frame.

4. Separate the drive end housing from the starter frame.

5. The starter drive plunger lever return spring may fall out after detaching the drive end housing. If not, remove it.

6. Remove the pivot pin which attaches the starter drive plunger lever to the starter frame and remove the lever.

7. Remove the stop ring retainer and stop ring from the armature shaft.

8. Slide the starter drive off the armature shaft.

9. Examine the wear pattern on the starter drive teeth. There should be evidence of full contact between the starter drive teeth and the flywheel ring gear teeth. If there is evidence of irregular wear, examine the flywheel ring gear for damage and replace if necessary.

10. Apply a thin coat of white grease to the armature shaft before installing the drive gear. Place a small amount of grease in the drive end housing bearing. Slide the starter drive on the armature shaft.

11. Install the stop ring retainer and stop ring on the armature shaft.

12. Install the starter drive plunger lever on the starter frame and install the pin.

13. Assemble the drive end housing on the starter frame.

14. install the two through-bolts in the starter frame. Tighten the starter through bolts to 55-75 in.lb.

15. Install the starter drive plunger lever and gasket and the brush cover band.

16. Install the starter as outlined previously.

OVERHAUL – DIESEL

1. Disconnect the field coil connection from the solenoid motor terminal.

2. Remove the solenoid attaching screws, solenoid and plunger return spring. Rotate the solenoid 90° to remove it.

3. Remove the through-bolts and brush end plate.

4. Rempove the brush springs and brushes from the plastic brush holder and remove the brush holder. Keep track of the location of the brush holder with regard to the brush terminals.

5. Remove the frame assembly.

6. Remove the armature assembly.

7. Remove the screw from the gear housing and remove the gear housing.

8. Remove the plunger and lever pivot screw and remove the plunger and lever.

9. Remove the gear, output shaft and drive assembly.

10. Remove the thrust washer, retainer, drive stop ring and slide the drive assembly off of the output shaft.

WARNING: *Don't wash the drive because the solvent will wash out the lubricant, causing the drive to slip. Use a brush or compressed air to clean the drive, field coils, armature, gear and housing.*

11. Inspect the armature windings for broken or burned insulation, and open connections at the commutator. Check for any signs of grounding.

12. Check the commutator for excessive run-out. If the commutator is rough or more than 0.127mm out-of-round, replace it or correct the problem as necessary.

13. Check the plastic brush holder for cracks or broken pads. Replace the brushes if worn to a length less than ¼" (6mm) in length. Inspect the field coils and plastic bobbins for burned or damaged areas. Check the continuity of the coil and brush connections. A brush replacement kit is available. Any other worn or damaged parts should be replaced.

14. Apply a thin coating of Lubriplate 777®, or equivalent on the output shaft splines. Slide the drive assembly onto the shaft and install a new stopring, retainer and thrust washer. Install the shaft and drive assembly into the drive end housing.

15. Install the plunger and lever assembly making sure that the lever notches engage the flange ears of the starter drive. Attach the lever pin screw and tighten it to 10 ft.lb.

Troubleshooting Basic Starting System Problems

Problem	Cause	Solution
Starter motor rotates engine slowly	• Battery charge low or battery defective	• Charge or replace battery
	• Defective circuit between battery and starter motor	• Clean and tighten, or replace cables
	• Low load current	• Bench-test starter motor. Inspect for worn brushes and weak brush springs.
	• High load current	• Bench-test starter motor. Check engine for friction, drag or coolant in cylinders. Check ring gear-to-pinion gear clearance.
Starter motor will not rotate engine	• Battery charge low or battery defective	• Charge or replace battery
	• Faulty solenoid	• Check solenoid ground. Repair or replace as necessary.
	• Damage drive pinion gear or ring gear	• Replace damaged gear(s)
	• Starter motor engagement weak	• Bench-test starter motor
	• Starter motor rotates slowly with high load current	• Inspect drive yoke pull-down and point gap, check for worn end bushings, check ring gear clearance
	• Engine seized	• Repair engine
Starter motor drive will not engage (solenoid known to be good)	• Defective contact point assembly	• Repair or replace contact point assembly
	• Inadequate contact point assembly ground	• Repair connection at ground screw
	• Defective hold-in coil	• Replace field winding assembly
Starter motor drive will not disengage	• Starter motor loose on flywheel housing	• Tighten mounting bolts
	• Worn drive end busing	• Replace bushing
	• Damaged ring gear teeth	• Replace ring gear or driveplate
	• Drive yoke return spring broken or missing	• Replace spring
Starter motor drive disengages prematurely	• Weak drive assembly thrust spring	• Replace drive mechanism
	• Hold-in coil defective	• Replace field winding assembly
Low load current	• Worn brushes	• Replace brushes
	• Weak brush springs	• Replace springs

16. Lubricate the gear and washer. Install the gear and washer on the end of the output shaft.

17. Install the gear housing and tighten the mounting screw to 84 in.lb.

18. After lubricating the pinion, install the armature and washer on the end of the shaft.

19. Position the grommet around the field lead and press it into the starter frame notch. Install the frame assembly on the gear housing, making sure that the grommet is positioned in the notch in the housing.

20. Install the brush holder on the end of the frame, lining up the notches in the brush holder with the ground brush terminals. The brush holder is symmetrical and can be installed with either notch and brush terminal.

21. Install the brush springs and brushes. The positive brush leads must be placed in their respective slots to prevent grounding.

22. Install the brush endplate, making sure that the insulator is properly positioned. Install and tighten the through-bolts to 84 in.lb.

NOTE: *The brush endplate has a threaded hole in the protruding ear which must be oriented properly so the starter-to-vacuum pump support bracket can be installed.*

23. Install the return spring on the solenoid plunger and install the solenoid. Attach the 2 solenoid attaching screws and tighten them to 84 in.lb. Apply a sealing compound to the junction of the solenoid case flange, gear and drive end housings.

24. Attach the motor field terminal to the **M** terminal of the solenoid, and tighten the fasteners to 30 in.lb.

25. Check the starter no-load current draw. Maximum draw should be 190 amps.

Starter Relay

REMOVAL AND INSTALLATION

Gasoline Engines

1. Disconnect the positive battery cable from the battery terminal. With dual batteries, disconnect the connecting cable at both ends.
2. Remove the nut securing the positive battery cable to the relay.
3. Remove the positive cable and any other wiring under that cable.
4. Tag and remove the push-on wires from the front of the relay.
5. Remove the nut and disconnect the cable from the starter side of the relay.
6. Remove the relay attaching bolts and remove the relay.
7. Installation is the reverse of removal.

Battery

REMOVAL AND INSTALLATION

1. Loosen the nuts which secure the cable ends to the battery terminals. Lift the negative battery cables from the terminals first with a twisting motion, then the positive cables.

If there is a battery cable puller available, make use of it.

WARNING: *On vehicles with dual batteries, take great care to avoid ground the disconnected end of the positive cable linking the two batteries, before the other end is disconnected.*

2. Remove the holddown nuts from the battery holddown bracket and remove the bracket and the battery. Lift the battery straight up and out of the vehicle, being sure to keep the battery level to avoid spilling the battery acid.
3. Before installing the battery in the vehicle, make sure that the battery terminals are clean and free from corrosion. Use a battery terminal cleaner on the terminals and on the inside of the battery cable ends. If a cleaner is not available, use coarse grade sandpaper to remove the corrosion. A mixture of baking soda and water poured over the terminals and cable ends will help remove and neutralize any acid buildup.

WARNING: *Take great care to avoid getting any of the baking soda solution inside the battery. If any solution gets inside the battery a violent reaction will take place and/or the battery will be damaged.*

4. Before installing the cables onto the terminals, cut a piece of felt cloth, or something similar into a circle about 3″ (76mm) across.

Cut a hole in the middle about the size of the battery terminals at their base. Push the cloth pieces over the terminals so that they lay flat on the top of the battery. Soak the pieces of cloth with oil. This will keep oxidation to a minimum.

5. Place the battery in the vehicle. Install the cables onto the terminals.

WARNING: *On vehicles with dual batteries, take great care to avoid grounding the disconnected end of the positive cable linking the two batteries, after the other end is connected.*

6. Tighten the nuts on the cable ends.

NOTE: *See Chapter 1 for battery maintenance illustrations.*

7. Smear a light coating of grease on the cable ends and tops of the terminals. This will further prevent the buildup of oxidation on the terminals and the cable ends.

8. Install and tighten the nuts of the battery holddown bracket.

ENGINE MECHANICAL

Engine Overhaul Tips

Most engine overhaul procedures are fairly standard. In addition to specific parts replacement procedures and complete specifications for your individual engine, this section also is a guide to accept rebuilding procedures. Examples of standard rebuilding practice are shown and should be used along with specific details concerning your particular engine.

Competent and accurate machine shop services will ensure maximum performance, reliability and engine life.

In most instances it is more profitable for the do-it-yourself mechanic to remove, clean and inspect the component, buy the necessary parts and deliver these to a shop for actual machine work.

On the other hand, much of the rebuilding work (crankshaft, block, bearings, piston rods, and other components) is well within the scope of the do-it-yourself mechanic.

TOOLS

The tools required for an engine overhaul or parts replacement will depend on the depth of your involvement. With a few exceptions, they will be the tools found in a mechanic's tool kit. More in-depth work will require any or all of the following:

● a dial indicator (reading in thousandths) mounted on a universal base
   ● micrometers and telescope gauges
   ● jaw and screw-type pullers
   ● scraper
   ● valve spring compressor

General Engine Specifications

Engine	Years	Fuel System Type	SAE Net Horsepower @ rpm	SAE Net Torque ft. lb. @ rpm	Bore x Stroke (in.)	Comp. Ratio	Oil Press. (psi.) @ 2000 rpm
6-144	1961	1-bbl	85 @ 4,200	134 @ 2,000	3.50 x 2.50	8.7:1	35–55
	1962	1-bbl	85 @ 4,200	134 @ 2,000	3.50 x 2.50	8.7:1	35–55
	1963	1-bbl	85 @ 4,200	134 @ 2,000	3.50 x 2.50	8.7:1	35–55
	1964	1-bbl	85 @ 4,200	134 @ 2,000	3.50 x 2.50	8.4:1	35–55
6-170	1961	1-bbl	101 @ 4,400	156 @ 2,400	3.50 x 2.94	8.7:1	35–55
	1962	1-bbl	101 @ 4,400	156 @ 2,400	3.50 x 2.94	8.7:1	35–55
	1963	1-bbl	101 @ 4,400	156 @ 2,400	3.50 x 2.94	8.7:1	35–55
	1964	1-bbl	101 @ 4,400	156 @ 2,400	3.50 x 2.94	8.4:1	35–55
	1965	1-bbl	105 @ 4,400	158 @ 2,400	3.50 x 2.94	9.1:1	35–55
	1966	1-bbl	105 @ 4,400	158 @ 2,400	3.50 x 2.94	9.1:1	35–55
	1967	1-bbl	105 @ 4,400	158 @ 2,400	3.50 x 2.94	9.1:1	35–55
	1969	1-bbl	100 @ 4,400	156 @ 2,400	3.50 x 2.94	8.7:1	35–55
	1970	1-bbl	100 @ 4,000	156 @ 2,200	3.50 x 2.94	8.7:1	35–55
6-200	1965	1-bbl	120 @ 4,400	190 @ 2,400	3.68 x 3.13	9.2:1	35–55
6-240	1965	1-bbl	150 @ 4,000	234 @ 2,200	4.00 x 3.18	9.2:1	35–60
	1966	1-bbl	150 @ 4,000	234 @ 2,200	4.00 x 3.18	9.2:1	35–60
	1967	1-bbl	150 @ 4,000	234 @ 2,200	4.00 x 3.18	9.2:1	35–60
	1969	1-bbl	150 @ 4,000	234 @ 2,200	4.00 x 3.18	9.2:1	35–60
	1970	1-bbl	150 @ 4,000	234 @ 2,200	4.00 x 3.18	9.2:1	35–60
	1971	1-bbl	140 @ 4,000	230 @ 2,200	4.00 x 3.18	8.9:1	35–60
	1972	1-bbl	140 @ 4,000	230 @ 2,200	4.00 x 3.18	8.5:1	35–60
	1973	1-bbl	140 @ 4,000	230 @ 2,200	4.00 x 3.18	8.5:1	35–60
	1974	1-bbl	140 @ 4,000	230 @ 2,200	4.00 x 3.18	8.5:1	35–60
6-300	1973	1-bbl	168 @ 3,800	250 @ 1,600	4.00 x 3.98	8.4:1	40–60
	1974	1-bbl	168 @ 3,800	250 @ 1,600	4.00 x 3.98	8.4:1	40–60
	1975	1-bbl	120 @ 3,400	229 @ 1,400	4.00 x 3.98	8.0:1	40–60
	1976	1-bbl	①	②	4.00 x 3.98	③	40–60
	1977	1-bbl	①	②	4.00 x 3.98	8.0:1	40–60
	1978	1-bbl	132 @ 3,600	241 @ 1,800	4.00 x 3.98	③	40–60
	1979	1-bbl	④	⑤	4.00 x 3.98	⑥	40–60
	1980	1-bbl	115 @ 3,200	241 @ 1,200	4.00 x 3.98	⑥	40–60
	1981	1-bbl	115 @ 3,200	241 @ 1,200	4.00 x 3.98	⑥	40–60
	1982	1-bbl	115 @ 3,200	241 @ 1,200	4.00 x 3.98	⑥	40–60
	1983	1-bbl	120 @ 3,200	251 @ 1,600	4.00 x 3.98	8.4:1	40–60
	1984	1-bbl	120 @ 3,200	245 @ 1,600	4.00 x 3.98	8.4:1	40–60
	1985	1-bbl	120 @ 3,200	245 @ 1,600	4.00 x 3.98	8.4:1	40–60
	1986	1-bbl	120 @ 3,200	245 @ 1,600	4.00 x 3.98	8.4:1	40–60
	1987	EFI	120 @ 3,200	245 @ 1,600	4.00 x 3.98	8.4:1	40–60
	1988	EFI	120 @ 3,200	245 @ 1,600	4.00 x 3.98	8.4:1	40–60
8-302	1969	2-bbl	205 @ 4,600	300 @ 2,600	4.00 x 3.00	8.6:1	35–60

General Engine Specifications (cont.)

Engine	Years	Fuel System Type	SAE Net Horsepower @ rpm	SAE Net Torque ft. lb. @ rpm	Bore x Stroke (in.)	Comp. Ratio	Oil Press. (psi.) @ 2000 rpm
8-302 (cont.)	1970	2-bbl	205 @ 4,600	300 @ 2,600	4.00 x 3.00	8.6:1	35–60
	1971	2-bbl	205 @ 4,600	300 @ 2,600	4.00 x 3.00	8.6:1	35–60
	1972	2-bbl	200 @ 4,600	285 @ 2,600	4.00 x 3.00	8.2:1	35–60
	1973	2-bbl	200 @ 4,600	285 @ 2,600	4.00 x 3.00	8.2:1	40–60
	1974	2-bbl	200 @ 4,600	285 @ 2,600	4.00 x 3.00	8.2:1	40–60
	1979	2-bbl	⑦	⑧	4.00 x 3.00	8.4:1	40–60
	1980	2-bbl	138 @ 3,600	242 @ 1,800	4.00 x 3.00	8.4:1	40–60
	1981	2-bbl	138 @ 3,600	242 @ 1,800	4.00 x 3.00	8.4:1	40–60
	1982	2-bbl	138 @ 3,600	242 @ 1,800	4.00 x 3.00	8.4:1	40–60
	1983	2-bbl	139 @ 3,400	250 @ 2,000	4.00 x 3.00	8.4:1	40–60
	1984	2-bbl	150 @ 3,600	250 @ 2,600	4.00 x 3.00	8.4:1	40–60
	1985	2-bbl	150 @ 3,600	250 @ 2,600	4.00 x 3.00	8.4:1	40–60
	1986	EFI	170 @ 3,800	275 @ 2,800	4.00 x 3.00	8.9:1	40–60
	1987	EFI	170 @ 3,800	275 @ 2,800	4.00 x 3.00	8.9:1	40–60
		4-bbl	225 @ 3,600	280 @ 2,800	4.00 x 3.00	9.0:1	40–60
	1988	EFI	170 @ 3,800	275 @ 2,800	4.00 x 3.00	8.9:1	40–60
8-351W	1975	2-bbl	150 @ 3,400	290 @ 1,800	4.00 x 3.50	8.3:1	40–60
	1976	2-bbl	⑨	⑩	4.00 x 3.50	8.3:1	40–60
	1977	2-bbl	⑨	⑩	4.00 x 3.50	8.3:1	40–60
	1978	2-bbl	⑨	⑩	4.00 x 3.50	8.3:1	40–60
	1979	2-bbl	⑪	⑫	4.00 x 3.50	8.3:1	40–60
	1980	2-bbl	142 @ 3,200	251 @ 2,400	4.00 x 3.50	8.3:1	40–60
	1981	2-bbl	142 @ 3,200	251 @ 2,400	4.00 x 3.50	8.3:1	40–60
	1982	2-bbl	142 @ 3,200	251 @ 2,400	4.00 x 3.50	8.3:1	40–60
	1983	2-bbl	145 @ 3,200	270 @ 1,400	4.00 x 3.50	8.3:1	40–60
	1984	2-bbl	160 @ 3,200	280 @ 2,000	4.00 x 3.50	8.3:1	40–60
		4-bbl	210 @ 4,000	305 @ 2,800	4.00 x 3.50	8.3:1	40–60
	1985	2-bbl	160 @ 3,200	280 @ 2,000	4.00 x 3.50	8.3:1	40–60
		4-bbl	210 @ 4,000	305 @ 2,800	4.00 x 3.50	8.3:1	40–60
	1986	4-bbl	210 @ 4,000	305 @ 2,800	4.00 x 3.50	8.3:1	40–60
	1987	4-bbl	210 @ 4,000	305 @ 2,800	4.00 x 3.50	8.3:1	40–60
	1988	EFI	210 @ 3,800	315 @ 2,800	4.00 x 3.50	8.8:1	40–60
8-400	1980	2-bbl	153 @ 3,500	296 @ 1,600	4.00 x 4.00	8.0:1	55–75
	1981	2-bbl	153 @ 3,500	296 @ 1,600	4.00 x 4.00	8.0:1	55–75
	1982	2-bbl	153 @ 3,500	296 @ 1,600	4.00 x 4.00	8.0:1	55–75
8-420	1983	Diesel	161 @ 3,300	307 @ 1,800	4.00 x 4.18	19.7:1	40–60
	1984	Diesel	170 @ 3,300	315 @ 1,400	4.00 x 4.18	20.7:1	40–60
	1986	Diesel	170 @ 3,300	315 @ 1,400	4.00 x 4.18	20.7:1	40–60
	1987	Diesel	170 @ 3,300	315 @ 1,400	4.00 x 4.18	21.5:1	40–60
8-444	1988	Diesel	180 @ 3,300	345 @ 1,400	4.11 x 4.18	21.5:1	40–70

General Engine Specifications (cont.)

Engine	Years	Fuel System Type	SAE Net Horsepower @ rpm	SAE Net Torque ft. lb. @ rpm	Bore x Stroke (in.)	Comp. Ratio	Oil Press. (psi.) @ 2000 rpm
8-460	1975	4-bbl	245 @ 4,000	380 @ 2,600	4.36 x 3.85	8.0:1	40–60
	1976	4-bbl	⑬	⑭	4.36 x 3.85	8.0:1	40–60
	1977	4-bbl	⑬	⑭	4.36 x 3.85	8.0:1	40–60
	1978	4-bbl	⑬	⑭	4.36 x 3.85	8.0:1	40–60
	1979	4-bbl	⑮	⑯	4.36 x 3.85	8.0:1	40–60
	1980	4-bbl	212 @ 4,000	339 @ 2,400	4.36 x 3.85	8.0:1	55–75
	1981	4-bbl	212 @ 4,000	339 @ 2,400	4.36 x 3.85	8.0:1	55–75
	1982	4-bbl	212 @ 4,000	339 @ 2,400	4.36 x 3.85	8.0:1	55–75
	1983	4-bbl	202 @ 4,000	331 @ 2,200	4.36 x 3.85	8.0:1	40–65
	1984	4-bbl	225 @ 4,000	365 @ 2,800	4.36 x 3.85	8.0:1	40–65
	1985	4-bbl	225 @ 4,000	365 @ 2,800	4.36 x 3.85	8.0:1	40–65
	1986	4-bbl	225 @ 4,000	365 @ 2,800	4.36 x 3.85	8.0:1	40–65
	1987	4-bbl	225 @ 4.000	365 @ 2,800	4.36 x 3.85	8.0:1	40–65
	1988	EFI	245 @ 4,000	380 @ 2,800	4.36 x 3.85	8.5:1	40–65

EFI: Electronic fuel injection
① E-100, except Calif.: 122 @ 3,200
E-100 in Calif.: 123 @ 3,200
All others: 120 @ 3,400
② E-100, except Calif.: 252 @ 1,600
E-100 in Calif.: 253 @ 1,600
All others: 229 @ 1,400
③ E-100: 8.9:1
All others: 8.0:1
④ E-100, except Calif., and all E-150: 117 @ 3,000
E-250 with MT: 114 @ 3,000
E-250 with AT: 116 @ 3,200
E-350: 114 @ 3,000
⑤ E-100 and E-150: 243 @ 1,600
E-250 with MT: 234 @ 1,600
E-250 with AT: 247 @ 1,000
E-350: 247 @ 1,000
⑥ Except E-350: 8.9:1
E-350: 8.0:1
⑦ E-100 and E-150, except Calif.: 135 @ 3,400
E-100 in Calif.: 129 @ 3,200
E-150 in Calif.: 137 @ 3,400
E-250: 136 @ 3,400
⑧ E-100 and E-150, except Calif.: 243 @ 2,000
E-100 in Calif.: 238 @ 2,400
E-150 in Calif.: 245 @ 2,000
E-250: 235 @ 2,400
⑨ E-100, except Calif.: 141 @ 3,200

E-100 in Calif.: Man. Tran.—152 @ 3,200
Auto. Tran.—143 @ 3,200
All others: 147 @ 3,400
⑩ Engines subject to noise legislation: 275 @ 1,800
E-100, except Calif.: Man. Tran.—286 @ 2,000
Auto. Tran.—287 @ 1,600
⑪ E-100: 135 @ 2,800
E-150 w/Man. Tran.: 130 @ 3,000
E-150 w/Auto. Tran., except Calif.: 135 @ 2,800
E-150 w/Auto. Tran. in Calif.: 139 @ 3,200
E-250 w/Man. Tran.: 130 @ 3,000
E-250 w/Auto. Tran.: 126 @ 2,800
E-350: 143 @ 3,200
⑫ E-100: 274 @ 1,400
E-150 w/Man. Tran.: 267 @ 1,800
E-150 w/Auto. Tran., except Calif.: 274 @ 1,400
E-150 w/Auto. Tran. in Calif.: 269 @ 1,200
E-250 w/Man. Tran.: 267 @ 1,800
E-250 w/Auto. Tran.: 270 @ 1,400
E-350: 272 @ 2,000
⑬ Engines subject to noise legislation: 230 @ 4,000
All others: 237 @ 4,000
⑭ Engines subject to noise legislation: 359 @ 2,600
All others: 365 @ 2,600
⑮ E-250: 214 @ 3,600
E-350: 217 @ 4,000
⑯ E-250: 362 @ 1,800
E-350: 358 @ 2,600

- ring groove cleaner
- piston ring expander and compressor
- ridge reamer
- cylinder hone or glaze breaker
- Plastigage®
- engine stand

The use of most of these tools is illustrated in this section. Many can be rented for a one-time use from a local parts jobber or tool supply house specializing in automotive work.

Occasionally, the use of special tools is called for. See the information on Special Tools and Safety Notice in the front of this book before substituting another tool.

INSPECTION TECHNIQUES

Procedures and specifications are given in this section for inspecting, cleaning and assessing the wear limits of most major components. Other procedures such as Magnaflux® and

Valve Specifications

Engines	Years	Seat Angle (deg)	Face Angle (deg)	Spring Test Pressure (lbs. @ in.)	Spring Installed Height (in.)	Stem to Guide Clearance (in.)		Stem Diameter (in.)	
						Intake	Exhaust	Intake	Exhaust
6-144	1961–64	45	44	117 @ 1.222	1.585	0.0017	0.0025	0.3104	0.3094
6-170	1961–70	45	44	117 @ 1.222	1.585	0.0017	0.0025	0.3104	0.3094
6-200	1965	45	44	150 @ 1.222	1.590	0.0017	0.0025	0.3104	0.3094
6-240	1965–66	45	44	①	1.700	0.0019	0.0019	0.3420	0.3420
	1967–72	45	44	197 @ 1.300	1.700	0.0019	0.0019	0.3420	0.3420
	1973–74	45	44	②	③	0.0019	0.0019	0.3420	0.3420
6-300	1973–81	45	44	②	③	0.0019	0.0019	0.3420	0.3420
	1982–84	45	44	④	⑤	0.0019	0.0019	0.3420	0.3420
	1985	45	44	⑥	⑤	0.0019	0.0019	0.3420	0.3420
	1986–88	45	44	⑦	⑧	0.0019	0.0019	0.3420	0.3420
8-302	1969–71	45	44	180 @ 1.230	1.660	0.0019	0.0019	0.3420	0.3420
	1972	45	44	180 @ 1.230	1.660	0.0019	0.0024	0.3420	0.3415
	1973–74	45	44	200 @ 1.310	1.690	0.0019	0.0024	0.3420	0.3415
	1979–85	45	44	⑨	⑩	0.0019	0.0024	0.3420	0.3415
	1986–87	45	44	⑨	⑪	0.0019	0.0024	0.3420	0.3415
	1988	45	44	⑱	⑲	0.0010–0.0027	0.0015–0.0032	0.3416–0.3423	0.3411–0.3418
8-351W	1975–76	45	44	200 @ 1.340	1.790	0.0019	0.0024	0.3420	0.3415
	1977–85	45	44	⑫	⑬	0.0019	0.0024	0.3420	0.3415
	1986–87	45	44	⑭	⑮	0.0019	0.0024	0.3420	0.3415
	1988	45	44	200 @ 1.20	⑮	0.0010–0.0027	0.0015–0.0032	0.3416–0.3423	0.3411–0.3428
8-400	1980–82	45	44	226 @ 1.390	⑯	0.0019	0.0024	0.3420	0.3415
8-420	1983–87	⑰	⑰	60 @ 1.798	2.040	0.0021	0.0021	0.3720	0.3720
8-444	1988	⑰	⑰	80 @ 1.833	⑳	0.0055	0.0055	0.3717–0.3724	0.3717–0.3724
8-460	1975–76	45	44	252 @ 1.330	1.810	0.0019	0.0019	0.3420	0.3420
	1977–85	45	44	229 @ 1.330	1.810	0.0019	0.0019	0.3420	0.3420
	1986–88	45	44	229 @ 1.330	1.813	0.0019	0.0019	0.3420	0.3420

① Intake: 190 @ 1.325
  Exhaust: 197 @ 1.300
② Intake: 190 @ 1.300
  Exhaust: 192 @ 1.180
③ Intake: 1.700
  Exhaust: 1.690
④ Intake: 197 @ 1.300
  Exhaust: 192 @ 1.180
⑤ Intake: 1.700
  Exhaust: 1.580
⑥ Intake: 197 @ 1.300
  Exhaust: 180 @ 1.180
⑦ Intake: 175 @ 1.240
  Exhaust: 175 @ 1.070

⑧ Intake: 1.640
  Exhaust: 1.470
⑨ Intake: 202 @ 1.360
  Exhaust: 200 @ 1.200
⑩ Intake: 1.780
  Exhaust: 1.600
⑪ Intake: 1.6885
  Exhaust: 1.594
⑫ Intake: 200 @ 1.340
  Exhaust: 200 @ 1.200
⑬ Intake: 1.790
  Exhaust: 1.800
⑭ Intake: 200 @ 1.360
  Exhaust: 200 @ 1.200

⑮ Intake: 1.782
  Exhaust: 1.594
⑯ Intake: 1.828
  Exhaust: 1.703
⑰ Intake: 30
  Exhaust: 37.5
⑱ Intake: 196–212 @ 1.360
  Exhaust: 190–210 @ 1.200
⑲ Intake: 1.78
  Exhaust: 1.60
⑳ Intake: 1.767
  Exhaust: 1.833

Camshaft Specifications
(All specifications in inches)

Engine	Journal Diameter					Bearing Clearance	Lobe Lift		End Play
	1	2	3	4	5		Int.	Exh.	
6-144	1.8100	1.8100	1.8100	1.8100	—	0.0020	0.2405	0.2395	0.004
6-170	1.8100	1.8100	1.8100	1.8100	—	0.0020	0.2405	0.2395	0.004
6-200	1.8100	1.8100	1.8100	1.8100	1.8100	0.0020	0.2530	0.2320	0.004
6-240	2.0175	2.0175	2.0175	2.0175	—	0.0020	0.2490	0.2490	0.004
6-300	2.0175	2.0175	2.0175	2.0175	—	0.0020	0.2490	0.2490	0.004
8-302	2.0810	2.0660	2.0510	2.0360	2.0210	0.0020	①	②	③
8-351W	2.0810	2.0660	2.0510	2.0360	2.0210	0.0020	0.2600	0.2600	0.004
8-400	2.1243	2.0660	2.0510	2.0360	2.0210	0.0020	0.2474	0.2500	0.004
8-420	2.0995	2.0995	2.0995	2.0995	2.0995	0.0030	0.2535	0.2530	0.005
8-444	2.0995	2.0995	2.0995	2.0995	2.0995	0.0025	0.2535	0.2530	0.005
8-460	2.1243	2.1243	2.1243	2.1243	2.1243	0.0020	0.2530	0.2780	0.004

① 1969–76: 0.2303
   1977 & 1980–85: 0.2375
② 1969–76: 0.2375
   1977 & 1980–85: 0.2470
③ 1969–74: 0.002
   1979–88: 0.004

Crankshaft and Connecting Rod Specifications
(All specifications in inches)

Engines	Years	Crankshaft				Connecting Rod		
		Main Bearing Journal Dia.	Main Bearing Oil Clearance	Shaft End Play	Thrust on No.	Journal Dia.	Oil Clearance	Side Clearance
6-144	1961–63	①	0.0007–0.0025	0.004–0.008	3	②	0.0008–0.0023	0.0040–0.0080
	1964	①	0.0007–0.0026	0.004–0.008	3	②	0.0006–0.0026	0.0040–0.0080
6-170	1961–63	①	0.0007–0.0025	0.004–0.008	3	②	0.0008–0.0023	0.0040–0.0080
	1964–65	①	0.0007–0.0026	0.004–0.008	3	②	0.0006–0.0026	0.0040–0.0080
	1966–69	2.2482–2.2490	0.0005–0.0015	0.004–0.008	3	2.1232–2.1240	0.0008–0.0015	0.0035–0.0105
	1970	2.2482–2.2490	0.0010–0.0015	0.004–0.008	3	2.1232–2.1240	0.0010–0.0015	0.0035–0.0105
6-200	1965	2.2482–2.2490	0.0007–0.0026	0.004–0.008	5	2.1232–2.1240	0.0006–0.0026	0.0035–0.0105
6-240	1965	③	0.0006–0.0024	0.004–0.008	5	④	0.0006–0.0022	0.0060–0.0130
	1966–69	2.3982–2.3990	0.0005–0.0015	0.004–0.008	5	2.1228–2.1236	0.0008–0.0015	0.0060–0.0130
	1970–72	2.3982–2.3990	0.0010–0.0015	0.004–0.008	5	2.1228–2.1236	0.0010–0.0015	0.0060–0.0130
	1973–74	2.3982–2.3990	0.0005–0.0015	0.004–0.008	5	2.1228–2.1236	0.0008–0.0015	0.0060–0.0130

Crankshaft and Connecting Rod Specifications (cont.)
(All specifications in inches)

| Engines | Years | Crankshaft | | | | Connecting Rod | | |
		Main Bearing Journal Dia.	Main Bearing Oil Clearance	Shaft End Play	Thrust on No.	Journal Dia.	Oil Clearance	Side Clearance
6-300	1973	2.3982–2.3990	0.0009–0.0015	0.004–0.008	5	2.1228–2.1236	⑤	0.0060–0.0130
	1974	2.3982–2.3990	0.0009–0.0015	0.004–0.008	5	2.1228–2.1236	⑥	0.0060–0.0130
	1975–88	2.3982–2.3990	0.0008–0.0015	0.004–0.008	5	2.1228–2.1236	0.0008–0.0015	0.0060–0.0130
8-302	1969	2.2482–2.2490	0.0005–0.0015	0.004–0.008	3	2.1228–2.1236	0.0008–0.0015	0.0100–0.0200
	1970–72	2.2482–2.2490	0.0010–0.0015	0.004–0.008	3	2.1228–2.1236	0.0010–0.0015	0.0100–0.0200
	1973–74	2.2482–2.2490	⑦	0.004–0.008	3	2.1228–2.1236	0.0008–0.0015	0.0100–0.0200
	1979–88	2.2482–2.2490	⑦	0.004–0.008	3	2.1228–2.1236	0.0008–0.0015	0.0100–0.0200
8-351W	1975–76	2.9994–3.0002	⑧	0.004–0.008	3	2.3103–2.3111	0.0008–0.0015	0.0100–0.0200
	1977–78	2.9994–3.0002	0.0008–0.0015	0.004–0.008	3	2.3103–2.3111	0.0008–0.0015	0.0100–0.0200
8-400	1980–82	2.9994–3.0002	0.0008–0.0015	0.004–0.008	3	2.3103–2.3111	0.0008–0.0015	0.0100–0.0200
8-420	1983–85	3.1228–3.1236	0.0018–0.0036	0.0020–0.0090	3	2.4980–2.4990	0.0011–0.0026	0.0080–0.0200
	1986	3.1228–3.1236	0.0018–0.0036	0.0020–0.0090	3	2.4980–2.4990	0.0011–0.0026	0.0100–0.0200
	1987	3.1228–3.1236	0.0018–0.0036	0.0020–0.0090	3	2.4980–2.4990	0.0011–0.0026	0.0120–0.0240
8-444	1988	3.1228–3.1236	0.0018–0.0036	0.0020–0.0090	3	2.4980–2.4990	0.0011–0.0026	0.0120–0.0240
8-460	1975–76	2.9994–3.0002	⑨	0.004–0.008	3	2.4992–2.5000	0.0008–0.0015	0.0100–0.0200
	1977–88	2.9994–3.0002	0.0008–0.0015	0.004–0.008	3	2.4992–2.5000	0.0008–0.0015	0.0100–0.0200

① Coded red: 2.2486–2.2490
   Coded blue: 2.2482–2.2486
② Coded red: 2.1236–2.1240
   Coded blue: 2.1232–2.1236
③ Coded red: 2.3986–2.3990
   Coded blue: 2.3982–2.3986
④ Coded red: 2.1232–2.1236
   Coded blue: 2.1228–2.1232
⑤ Light duty: 0.0008–0.0015
   Heavy duty: 0.0009–0.0027

⑥ Light duty: 0.0008–0.0015
   Heavy duty: 0.0009–0.0015
⑦ #1: 0.0001–0.0015
   All others: 0.0005–0.0015
⑧ #1: 0.0005–0.0015
   All others: 0.0008–0.0015
⑨ #1: 0.0008–0.0015
   All others: 0.0008–0.0026

Zyglo® can be used to locate material flaws and stress cracks. Magnaflux® is a magnetic process applicable only to ferrous materials. The Zyglo® process coats the material with a fluorescent dye penetrant and can be used on any material

Check for suspected surface cracks can be more readily made using spot check dye. The dye is sprayed onto the suspected area, wiped off and the area sprayed with a developer. Cracks will show up brightly.

Piston and Ring Specifications

(All specifications in inches)

Engines	Years	Ring Gap			Ring Side Clearance			Piston to Bore Clearance
		#1 Compr.	#2 Compr.	Oil Control	#1 Compr.	#2 Compr.	Oil Control	
6-144	1961–63	0.0100–0.0200	0.0100–0.0200	0.015–0.055	0.0019–0.0036	0.0024–0.0040	snug	0.0018–0.0036
	1964	0.0100–0.0310	0.0100–0.0310	0.015–0.066	0.0019–0.0036	0.0024–0.0040	snug	0.0018–0.0036
6-170	1961–63	0.0100–0.0200	0.0100–0.0200	0.015–0.055	0.0019–0.0036	0.0024–0.0040	snug	0.0018–0.0036
	1964	0.0100–0.0200	0.0100–0.0200	0.015–0.055	0.0019–0.0036	0.0024–0.0040	snug	0.0018–0.0036
	1965	0.0100–0.0200	0.0100–0.0200	0.015–0.055	0.0009–0.0026	0.0020–0.0040	snug	0.0021–0.0027
	1966	0.0100–0.0200	0.0100–0.0200	0.015–0.055	0.0009–0.0026	0.0020–0.0040	snug	0.0014–0.0020
	1967–70	0.0100–0.0200	0.0100–0.0200	0.015–0.055	0.0019–0.0036	0.0020–0.0040	snug	0.0014–0.0020
6-200	1965	0.0100–0.0200	0.0100–0.0200	0.015–0.055	0.0019–0.0036	0.0020–0.0040	snug	0.0020–0.0026
6-240	1965–71	0.0100–0.0200	0.0100–0.0200	0.015–0.055	0.0019–0.0036	0.0020–0.0040	snug	0.0014–0.0022
	1972–74	0.0100–0.0200	0.0100–0.0200	0.015–0.055	0.0024–0.0041	0.0025–0.0045	snug	0.0014–0.0022
6-300	1973–76	0.0100–0.0200	0.0100–0.0200	0.015–0.055	0.0024–0.0041	0.0025–0.0045	snug	0.0014–0.0022
	1977	0.0100–0.0200	0.0100–0.0200	0.015–0.035	0.0019–0.0036	0.0020–0.0040	snug	0.0014–0.0022
	1978	0.0100–0.0200	0.0100–0.0200	0.015–0.055	0.0019–0.0036	0.0020–0.0040	snug	①
	1979–84	0.0100–0.0200	0.0100–0.0200	0.015–0.055	0.0019–0.0036	0.0020–0.0040	snug	0.0014–0.0022
	1985–88	0.0100–0.0200	0.0100–0.0200	0.010–0.055	0.0019–0.0036	0.0020–0.0040	snug	0.0010–0.0018
8-302	1969–72	0.0100–0.0200	0.0100–0.0200	0.015–0.069	0.0019–0.0036	0.0020–0.0040	snug	0.0018–0.0026
	1973–74	0.0100–0.0200	0.0100–0.0200	0.015–0.055	0.0020–0.0040	0.0020–0.0040	snug	0.0018–0.0026
	1979–84	0.0100–0.0200	0.0100–0.0200	0.015–0.035	0.0020–0.0040	0.0020–0.0040	snug	0.0018–0.0026
	1985	0.0100–0.0200	0.0100–0.0200	0.015–0.055	0.0020–0.0040	0.0020–0.0040	snug	0.0018–0.0026
	1986	0.0100–0.0200	0.0100–0.0200	0.015–0.055	0.0020–0.0040	0.0020–0.0040	snug	0.0002–0.0004
	1987–88	0.0100–0.0200	0.0100–0.0200	0.015–0.055	0.0013–0.0033	0.0020–0.0040	snug	0.0013–0.0030
8-351W	1975–76	0.0100–0.0200	0.0100–0.0200	0.015–0.055	0.0020–0.0040	0.0020–0.0040	snug	0.0018–0.0026
	1977	0.0100–0.0200	0.0100–0.0200	0.015–0.035	0.0019–0.0036	0.0020–0.0040	snug	0.0022–0.0030
	1978	0.0100–0.0200	0.0100–0.0200	0.015–0.055	0.0019–0.0036	0.0020–0.0040	snug	0.0022–0.0030

Piston and Ring Specifications (cont.)

(All specifications in inches)

Engines	Years	Ring Gap			Ring Side Clearance			Piston to Bore Clearance
		#1 Compr.	#2 Compr.	Oil Control	#1 Compr.	#2 Compr.	Oil Control	
8-351W (cont).	1979–84	0.0100–0.0200	0.0100–0.0200	0.015–0.035	0.0020–0.0040	0.0020–0.0040	snug	0.0018–0.0026
	1985–86	0.0100–0.0200	0.0100–0.0200	0.015–0.055	0.0020–0.0040	0.0020–0.0040	snug	0.0003–0.0005
	1987–88	0.0100–0.0200	0.0100–0.0200	0.015–0.055	0.0013–0.0033	0.0020–0.0040	snug	0.0013–0.0030
8-400	1980–81	0.0100–0.0200	0.0100–0.0200	0.015–0.035	0.0019–0.0036	0.0025–0.0045	snug	0.0014–0.0022
	1982	0.0100–0.0200	0.0100–0.0200	0.015–0.035	0.0030–0.0040	0.0030–0.0040	snug	0.0014–0.0022
8-420	1983–84	0.0140–0.0240	0.0600–0.0700	0.0100–0.0240	0.0020–0.0040	0.0020–0.0040	0.0010–0.0030	0.0055–0.0075
	1985–87	0.0140–0.0240	0.0600–0.0700	0.0100–0.0240	0.0020–0.0040	0.0020–0.0040	0.0010–0.0030	0.0055–0.0065
8-444	1988	0.0140–0.0240	0.0600–0.0700	0.0100–0.0240	0.0020–0.0040	0.0020–0.0040	0.0010–0.0030	0.0055–0.0065
8-460	1975–76	0.0100–0.0200	0.0100–0.0200	0.015–0.055	0.0020–0.0040	0.0020–0.0040	snug	0.0022–0.0030
	1977	0.0100–0.0200	0.0100–0.0200	0.010–0.030	0.0025–0.0045	0.0025–0.0045	snug	0.0014–0.0022
	1978	0.0100–0.0200	0.0100–0.0200	0.010–0.030	0.0025–0.0045	0.0025–0.0045	snug	0.0022–0.0030
	1979–81	0.0100–0.0200	0.0100–0.0200	0.010–0.035	0.0019–0.0036	0.0020–0.0040	snug	0.0022–0.0030
	1982–88	0.0100–0.0200	0.0100–0.0200	0.010–0.035	0.0025–0.0045	0.0025–0.0045	snug	0.0022–0.0030

① Under 6,000 lb. GVW: 0.0002–0.0004
6,000 lb. GVW and over: 0.0003–0.0005

Torque Specifications

(All specifications in ft. lb.)

Engines	Years	Cyl. Head	Conn. Rod	Main Bearing	Crankshaft Damper	Flywheel	Manifold	
							Intake	Exhaust
6-144	1961–64	65–70	19–24	60–70	45–55	75–85	—	13–18
6-170	1961–64	65–70	19–24	60–70	45–55	75–85	—	13–18
	1965–70	70–75	19–24	60–70	85–100	75–85	—	13–18
6-200	1965	70–75	19–24	60–70	85–100	75–85	—	13–18
6-240	1965–66	70–75	40–45	60–70	130–145	75–85	20–25	20–25
	1967–74	70–75	40–45	60–70	130–150	75–85	23–28	23–28
6-300	1973–76	③	40–45	60–70	130–150	75–85	23–28	23–28
	1977–81	③	40–45	60–70	130–150	75–85	22–32	28–33
	1982–88	③	40–45	60–70	130–150	75–85	22–32	22–32
8-302	1969	④	19–24	60–70	70–90	75–85	20–22	15–20
	1970	④	19–24	60–70	70–90	75–85	23–25	12–16

Torque Specifications (cont.)

(All specifications in ft. lb.)

Engines	Years	Cyl. Head	Conn. Rod	Main Bearing	Crankshaft Damper	Flywheel	Manifold Intake	Manifold Exhaust
8-302 (cont.)	1971–74	④	19–24	60–70	100–130	75–85	23–25	12–16
	1979–88	④	19–24	60–70	70–90	75–85	23–25	18–24
8-351W	1975–76	⑥	19–24	60–70	70–90	75–85	23–25	18–24
	1977–88	⑤	40–45	95–105	70–90	75–85	23–25	18–24
8-400	1980–82	95–105	40–45	35–45	70–90	75–85	①	18–24
8-420	1983–87	②	46–51	95	90	44–50	24	30
8-444	1988	⑦	⑧	⑨	90	44–50	⑩	⑪
8-460	1975–81	⑫	40–45	95–105	70–90	75–85	⑬	28–33
	1982–88	⑫	45–50	95–105	70–90	75–85	⑬	⑭

① ⅜ in. bolts: 22–32
 5⁄32 in. bolts: 17–25
② Three stages: 40; 65; 75
③ Step 1: 50–55 ft. lb.
 Step 2: 60–65 ft. lb.
 Step 3: 70–85 ft. lb.
④ Step 1: 55–65 ft. lb.
 Step 2: 65–72 ft. lb.
⑤ Step 1: 85 ft. lb.
 Step 2: 95 ft. lb.
 Step 3: 105–112 ft. lb.
⑥ Step 1: 30–40 ft. lb.
 Step 2: 45–55 ft. lb.
 Step 3: 65–70 ft. lb.
⑦ Step 1: 65 ft. lb.
 Step 2: 90 ft. lb.
 Step 3: 100 ft. lb.
⑧ Step 1: 38 ft. lb.
 Step 2: 48–53 ft. lb.

⑨ Step 1: 75 ft. lb.
 Step 2: 95 ft. lb.
⑩ Step 1: Tighten to 24 ft. lb.
 Step 2: Run engine to normal operating temperature
 Step 3: Retorque to 24 ft. lb. hot
⑪ Step 1: Tighten to 35 ft. lb.
 Step 2: Run engine to normal operating temperature
 Step 3: Retorque to 35 ft. lb. hot
⑫ Step 1: 70–80 ft. lb.
 Step 2: 100–110 ft. lb.
 Step 3: 130–140 ft. lb.
⑬ Step 1: 8–12 ft. lb.
 Step 2: 12–22 ft. lb.
 Step 3: 22–35 ft. lb.
⑭ 1982–87: 28–33
 1988: 22–30

OVERHAUL TIPS

Aluminum has become extremely popular for use in engines, due to its low weight. Observe the following precautions when handling aluminum parts:

- Never hot tank aluminum parts (the caustic hot tank solution will eat the aluminum.
- Remove all aluminum parts (identification tag, etc.) from engine parts prior to the tanking.
- Always coat threads lightly with engine oil or anti-seize compounds before installation, to prevent seizure.
- Never overtorque bolts or spark plugs especially in aluminum threads.

Stripped threads in any component can be repaired using any of several commercial repair kits (Heli-Coil®, Microdot®, Keenserts®, etc.).

When assembling the engine, any parts that will be frictional contact must be prelubed to provide lubrication at initial start-up. Any product specifically formulated for this purpose can be used, but engine oil is not recommended as a prelube.

When semi-permanent (locked, but removable) installation of bolts or nuts is desired, threads should be cleaned and coated with Loctite® or other similar, commercial non-hardening sealant.

REPAIRING DAMAGED THREADS

Several methods of repairing damaged threads are available. Heli-Coil® (shown here), Keenserts® and Microdot® are among the most widely used. All involve basically the same principle – drilling out stripped threads, tapping the hole and installing a prewound insert – making welding, plugging and oversize fasteners unnecessary.

Two types of thread repair inserts are usually supplied: a standard type for most Inch Coarse, Inch Fine, Metric Course and Metric Fine thread sizes and a spark lug type to fit most spark plug port sizes. Consult the individual manufacturer's catalog to determine exact applications. Typical thread repair kits will contain a selection of prewound threaded inserts, a

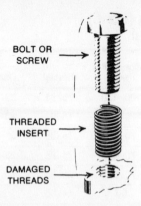

BOLT OR SCREW

THREADED INSERT

DAMAGED THREADS

Damaged bolt holes can be repaired with thread repair inserts

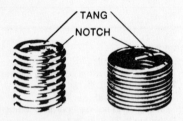

TANG

NOTCH

Standard thread repair insert (left) and spark plug thread insert (right)

Drill out the damaged threads with specified drill. Drill completely through the hole or to the bottom of a blind hole

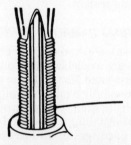

With the tap supplied, tap the hole to receive the thread insert. Keep the tap well oiled and back it out frequently to avoid clogging the threads

tap (corresponding to the outside diameter threads of the insert) and an installation tool. Spark plug inserts usually differ because they require a tap equipped with pilot threads and a combined reamer/tap section. Most manufac-

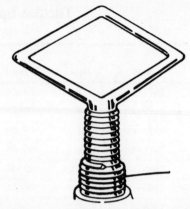

Screw the threaded insert onto the installation tool until the tang engages the slot. Screw the insert into the tapped hole until it is 1/4-1/2 turn below the top surface. After installation break off the tang with a hammer and punch

turers also supply blister-packed thread repair inserts separately in addition to a master kit containing a variety of taps and inserts plus installation tools.

Before effecting a repair to a threaded hole, remove any snapped, broken or damaged bolts or studs. Penetrating oil can be used to free frozen threads. The offending item can be removed with locking pliers or with a screw or stud extractor. After the hole is clear, the thread can be repaired, as shown in the series of accompanying illustrations.

Checking Engine Compression

A noticeable lack of engine power, excessive oil consumption and/or poor fuel mileage measured over an extended period are all indicators of internal engine war. Worn piston rings, scored or worn cylinder bores, blown head gaskets, sticking or burnt valves and worn valve seats are all possible culprits here. A check of each cylinder's compression will help you locate the problems.

The screw-in type compression gauge is more accurate

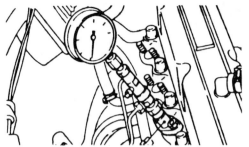
Diesel engines require a special compression gauge adaptor

As mentioned earlier, a screw-in type compression gauge is more accurate that the type you simply hold against the spark plug hole, although it takes slightly longer to use. It's worth it to obtain a more accurate reading. Follow the procedures below.

Gasoline Engines

1. Warm up the engine to normal operating temperature.
2. Remove all the spark plugs.
3. Disconnect the high tension lead from the ignition coil.
4. On fully open the throttle either by operating the carburetor throttle linkage by hand or by having an assistant floor the accelerator pedal.
5. Screw the compression gauge into the no.1 spark plug hole until the fitting is snug.

WARNING: *Be careful not to crossthread the plug hole. On aluminum cylinder heads use extra care, as the threads in these heads are easily ruined.*

6. Ask an assistant to depress the accelerator pedal fully on both carbureted and fuel injected vehicles. Then, while you read the compression gauge, ask the assistant to crank the engine two or three times in short bursts using the ignition switch.
7. Read the compression gauge at the end of each series of cranks, and record the highest of these readings. Repeat this procedure for each of the engine's cylinders. Compare the highest reading of each cylinder to the compression pressure specification in the Tune-Up Specifications chart. The specs in this chart are maximum values.

A cylinder's compression pressure is usually acceptable if it is not less than 80% of maximum. The difference between any two cylinders should be no more than 12-14 pounds.

8. If a cylinder is unusually low, pour a tablespoon of clean engine oil into the cylinder through the spark plug hole and repeat the

U.S. Bolts

SAE Grade Number	1 or 2			5			6 or 7		
Number of lines always 2 less than the grade number.									
Bolt Size (Inches)—(Thread)	Maximum Torque			Maximum Torque			Maximum Torque		
	Ft./Lbs.	Kgm	Nm	Ft./Lbs.	Kgm	Nm	Ft./Lbs.	Kgm	Nm
¼ — 20	5	0.7	6.8	8	1.1	10.8	10	1.4	13.5
— 28	6	0.8	8.1	10	1.4	13.6			
⁵/₁₆ — 18	11	1.5	14.9	17	2.3	23.0	19	2.6	25.8
— 24	13	1.8	17.6	19	2.6	25.7			
³⁄₈ — 16	18	2.5	24.4	31	4.3	42.0	34	4.7	46.0
— 24	20	2.75	27.1	35	4.8	47.5			
⁷/₁₆ — 14	28	3.8	37.0	49	6.8	66.4	55	7.6	74.5
— 20	30	4.2	40.7	55	7.6	74.5			
½ — 13	39	5.4	52.8	75	10.4	101.7	85	11.75	115.2
— 20	41	5.7	55.6	85	11.7	115.2			
⁹/₁₆ — 12	51	7.0	69.2	110	15.2	149.1	120	16.6	162.7
— 18	55	7.6	74.5	120	16.6	162.7			
⁵⁄₈ — 11	83	11.5	112.5	150	20.7	203.3	167	23.0	226.5
— 18	95	13.1	128.8	170	23.5	230.5			
¾ — 10	105	14.5	142.3	270	37.3	366.0	280	38.7	379.6
— 16	115	15.9	155.9	295	40.8	400.0			
⅞ — 9	160	22.1	216.9	395	54.6	535.5	440	60.9	596.5
— 14	175	24.2	237.2	435	60.1	589.7			
1 — 8	236	32.5	318.6	590	81.6	799.9	660	91.3	894.8
— 14	250	34.6	338.9	660	91.3	849.8			

Metric Bolts

Relative Strength Marking	4.6, 4.8			8.8		
Bolt Markings						
Bolt Size Thread Size x Pitch (mm)	Maximum Torque			Maximum Torque		
	Ft./Lbs.	Kgm	Nm	Ft./Lbs.	Kgm	Nm
6 x 1.0	2–3	.2–.4	3–4	3–6	.4–.8	5–8
8 x 1.25	6–8	.8–1	8–12	9–14	1.2–1.9	13–19
10 x 1.25	12–17	1.5–2.3	16–23	20–29	2.7–4.0	27–39
12 x 1.25	21–32	2.9–4.4	29–43	35–-53	4.8–7.3	47–72
14 x 1.5	35–52	4.8–7.1	48–70	57–85	7.8–11.7	77–110
16 x 1.5	51–77	7.0–10.6	67–100	90–120	12.4–16.5	130–160
18 x 1.5	74–110	10.2–15.1	100–150	130–170	17.9–23.4	180–230
20 x 1.5	110–140	15.1–19.3	150–190	190–240	26.2–46.9	160–320
22 x 1.5	150–190	22.0–26.2	200–260	250–320	34.5–44.1	340–430
24 x 1.5	190–240	26.2–46.9	260–320	310–410	42.7–56.5	420–550

compression test. If the compression comes up after adding the oil, it appears that the cylinder's piston rings or bore are damaged or worn. If the pressure remains low, the valves may not be seating properly (a valve job is needed), or the head gasket may be blown near that cylinder. If compression in any two adjacent cylinders is low, and if the addition of oil doesn't help the compression, there is leakage past the head gasket. Oil and coolant water in the combustion chamber can result from this problem. There may be evidence of water droplets on the engine dipstick when a head gasket has blown.

Diesel Engines

Checking cylinder compression on diesel engines is basically the same procedure as on gasoline engines except for the following:

1. A special compression gauge adaptor suitable for diesel engines (because these engines have much greater compression pressures) must be used.

2. Remove the injector tubes and remove the injectors from each cylinder.

WARNING: *Don't forget to remove the washer underneath each injector. Otherwise, it may get lost when the engine is cranked.*

3. When fitting the compression gauge adaptor to the cylinder head, make sure the bleeder of the gauge (if equipped) is closed.

4. When reinstalling the injector assemblies, install new washers underneath each injector.

Design

6-144, 6-170, 6-200

These engines are built on the same design, with the 6-144 being the first of the series. Essentially they are the same engine. The 6-170 is a 6-144 with a longer stroke and an improved oiling system. The 6-200 is a 6-170 with increased bore and stroke, and hydraulic lifters.

All are overhead valve, cast iron block and head design with a sprocket and chain timing drive.

The distributor is gear driven via the camshaft which also drives the oil pump through an intermediate shaft.

The crankshaft in the 6-144 and 6-170 is mounted on 4 main bearings with thrust taken by number 3 bearing.

The crankshaft in the 6-200 is mounted in 7 main bearings with thrust taken by number 3.

The camshaft in the 6-144 and 6-170 rides in 4 bearings; on the 6-200, 5 bearing are used.

6-240, 6-300

These engines are built on the same design, with the 6-240 being the first of the series. Essentially they are the same engine. The 6-300 is a 6-240 with a longer stroke.

Both are overhead valve, cast iron block and head design with gear-to-gear timing drive.

The distributor is gear driven via the camshaft which also drives the oil pump through an intermediate shaft.

The crankshaft in both is mounted on 7 main bearings with thrust taken by number 5 bearing.

The camshaft rides in 4 bearings.

Gasoline V8

All V8s are of a standard overhead valve V design with cast iron heads and block.

On all engines, the crankshaft is supported by 5 main bearings with thrust takcb by the number 3 bearing.

The camshaft rides in 5 bearings and is driven by the crankshaft via a chain.

All engines have hydraulic lifters.

Diesel V8

The engine is a standard overhead valve V design with cast iron heads and block.

The crankshaft is supported by 5 4-bolt main bearings.

Block mounted, internal cooling jets direct oil to the underside of each piston.

The cylinder heads employ replaceable valve seats and guides, and are equipped with precombustion chambers.

Positive rotating valve mechanisms are located at the bottom of each valve spring.

The camshaft rides in 5 bearings and is driven by the crankshaft via a chain.

Engine

REMOVAL AND INSTALLATION

WARNING: *Disconnect the negative battery cable(s) before beginning any work. Always label all disconnected hoses, vacuum lines and wires, to prevent incorrect reassembly. Do not disconnect any air conditioning lines unless you are thoroughly familiar with A/C systems and the hazards involved; escaping refrigerant (Freon®) will freeze any surface it contacts, including skin and eyes. Have the system discharged professionally before required repairs are started.*

6-144 (2.4L)
6-170 (2.8L)
6-200 (3.3L)

1. Drain the cooling system.

CAUTION: *When draining the coolant, keep in mind that cats and dogs are attracted by the ethylene glycol antifreeze, and are quite likely to drink any that is left in an uncovered container or in puddles on the ground. This will prove fatal in sufficient quantity. Always drain the coolant into a sealable container. Coolant should be reused unless it is contaminated or several years old.*

2. Remove the engine cover.
3. Remove the right hand seat.
4. Raise and support the van on jackstands.
5. Disconnect the driveshaft at the transmission flange.
6. Remove the midship bearing support-to-chassis and position the driveshaft out of the way.
7. Disconnect the speedometer cable and housing at the transmission.
8. Disconnect the transmission shift rods at the transmission shift levers.
9. Disconnect the clutch retracting spring.
10. Remove the equalizer bracket at the chassis side rail and remove the clutch equalizer arm and clutch linkage from the cylinder block. Position the assembly out of the way.
11. Position an engine support bar to the chassis and the engine to support the rear of the engine.
12. Remove the bolt and nut attaching the rear engine support to the crossmember to the chassis and remove the crossmember.

FRONT SUPPORT INSULATOR

200 SIX REAR SUPPORT INSULATOR
(MANUAL TRANSMISSION)

170 SIX REAR SUPPORT INSULATOR
(MANUAL TRANSMISSION)

170 SIX REAR SUPPORT INSULATOR
(AUTOMATIC TRANSMISSION)

1961−67 6-144, 6-170 engine supports

Troubleshooting Engine Mechanical Problems

Problem	Cause	Solution
External oil leaks	• Fuel pump gasket broken or improperly seated	• Replace gasket
	• Cylinder head cover RTV sealant broken or improperly seated	• Replace sealant; inspect cylinder head cover sealant flange and cylinder head sealant surface for distortion and cracks
	• Oil filler cap leaking or missing	• Replace cap
	• Oil filter gasket broken or improperly seated	• Replace oil filter
	• Oil pan side gasket broken, improperly seated or opening in RTV sealant	• Replace gasket or repair opening in sealant; inspect oil pan gasket flange for distortion
	• Oil pan front oil seal broken or improperly seated	• Replace seal; inspect timing case cover and oil pan seal flange for distortion
	• Oil pan rear oil seal broken or improperly seated	• Replace seal; inspect oil pan rear oil seal flange; inspect rear main bearing cap for cracks, plugged oil return channels, or distortion in seal groove
	• Timing case cover oil seal broken or improperly seated	• Replace seal
	• Excess oil pressure because of restricted PCV valve	• Replace PCV valve
	• Oil pan drain plug loose or has stripped threads	• Repair as necessary and tighten
	• Rear oil gallery plug loose	• Use appropriate sealant on gallery plug and tighten
	• Rear camshaft plug loose or improperly seated	• Seat camshaft plug or replace and seal, as necessary
	• Distributor base gasket damaged	• Replace gasket
Excessive oil consumption	• Oil level too high	• Drain oil to specified level
	• Oil with wrong viscosity being used	• Replace with specified oil
	• PCV valve stuck closed	• Replace PCV valve
	• Valve stem oil deflectors (or seals) are damaged, missing, or incorrect type	• Replace valve stem oil deflectors
	• Valve stems or valve guides worn	• Measure stem-to-guide clearance and repair as necessary
	• Poorly fitted or missing valve cover baffles	• Replace valve cover
	• Piston rings broken or missing	• Replace broken or missing rings
	• Scuffed piston	• Replace piston
	• Incorrect piston ring gap	• Measure ring gap, repair as necessary
	• Piston rings sticking or excessively loose in grooves	• Measure ring side clearance, repair as necessary
	• Compression rings installed upside down	• Repair as necessary
	• Cylinder walls worn, scored, or glazed	• Repair as necessary
	• Piston ring gaps not properly staggered	• Repair as necessary
	• Excessive main or connecting rod bearing clearance	• Measure bearing clearance, repair as necessary
No oil pressure	• Low oil level	• Add oil to correct level
	• Oil pressure gauge, warning lamp or sending unit inaccurate	• Replace oil pressure gauge or warning lamp
	• Oil pump malfunction	• Replace oil pump
	• Oil pressure relief valve sticking	• Remove and inspect oil pressure relief valve assembly
	• Oil passages on pressure side of pump obstructed	• Inspect oil passages for obstruction

Troubleshooting Engine Mechanical Problems (cont.)

Problem	Cause	Solution
No oil pressure (cont.)	• Oil pickup screen or tube obstructed	• Inspect oil pickup for obstruction
	• Loose oil inlet tube	• Tighten or seal inlet tube
Low oil pressure	• Low oil level	• Add oil to correct level
	• Inaccurate gauge, warning lamp or sending unit	• Replace oil pressure gauge or warning lamp
	• Oil excessively thin because of dilution, poor quality, or improper grade	• Drain and refill crankcase with recommended oil
	• Excessive oil temperature	• Correct cause of overheating engine
	• Oil pressure relief spring weak or sticking	• Remove and inspect oil pressure relief valve assembly
	• Oil inlet tube and screen assembly has restriction or air leak	• Remove and inspect oil inlet tube and screen assembly. (Fill inlet tube with lacquer thinner to locate leaks.)
	• Excessive oil pump clearance	• Measure clearances
	• Excessive main, rod, or camshaft bearing clearance	• Measure bearing clearances, repair as necessary
High oil pressure	• Improper oil viscosity	• Drain and refill crankcase with correct viscosity oil
	• Oil pressure gauge or sending unit inaccurate	• Replace oil pressure gauge
	• Oil pressure relief valve sticking closed	• Remove and inspect oil pressure relief valve assembly
Main bearing noise	• Insufficient oil supply	• Inspect for low oil level and low oil pressure
	• Main bearing clearance excessive	• Measure main bearing clearance, repair as necessary
	• Bearing insert missing	• Replace missing insert
	• Crankshaft end play excessive	• Measure end play, repair as necessary
	• Improperly tightened main bearing cap bolts	• Tighten bolts with specified torque
	• Loose flywheel or drive plate	• Tighten flywheel or drive plate attaching bolts
	• Loose or damaged vibration damper	• Repair as necessary
Connecting rod bearing noise	• Insufficient oil supply	• Inspect for low oil level and low oil pressure
	• Carbon build-up on piston	• Remove carbon from piston crown
	• Bearing clearance excessive or bearing missing	• Measure clearance, repair as necessary
	• Crankshaft connecting rod journal out-of-round	• Measure journal dimensions, repair or replace as necessary
	• Misaligned connecting rod or cap	• Repair as necessary
	• Connecting rod bolts tightened improperly	• Tighten bolts with specified torque
Piston noise	• Piston-to-cylinder wall clearance excessive (scuffed piston)	• Measure clearance and examine piston
	• Cylinder walls excessively tapered or out-of-round	• Measure cylinder wall dimensions, rebore cylinder
	• Piston ring broken	• Replace all rings on piston
	• Loose or seized piston pin	• Measure piston-to-pin clearance, repair as necessary
	• Connecting rods misaligned	• Measure rod alignment, straighten or replace
	• Piston ring side clearance excessively loose or tight	• Measure ring side clearance, repair as necessary
	• Carbon build-up on piston is excessive	• Remove carbon from piston

Troubleshooting Engine Mechanical Problems (cont.)

Problem	Cause	Solution
Valve actuating component noise	• Insufficient oil supply	• Check for: (a) Low oil level (b) Low oil pressure (c) Plugged push rods (d) Wrong hydraulic tappets (e) Restricted oil gallery (f) Excessive tappet to bore clearance
	• Push rods worn or bent • Rocker arms or pivots worn	• Replace worn or bent push rods • Replace worn rocker arms or pivots
	• Foreign objects or chips in hydraulic tappets • Excessive tappet leak-down • Tappet face worn	• Clean tappets • Replace valve tappet • Replace tappet; inspect corresponding cam lobe for wear
	• Broken or cocked valve springs	• Properly seat cocked springs; replace broken springs
	• Stem-to-guide clearance excessive	• Measure stem-to-guide clearance, repair as required
	• Valve bent • Loose rocker arms • Valve seat runout excessive • Missing valve lock • Push rod rubbing or contacting cylinder head • Excessive engine oil (four-cylinder engine)	• Replace valve • Tighten bolts with specified torque • Regrind valve seat/valves • Install valve lock • Remove cylinder head and remove obstruction in head • Correct oil level

Troubleshooting the Cooling System

Problem	Cause	Solution
High temperature gauge indication—overheating	• Coolant level low • Fan belt loose • Radiator hose(s) collapsed • Radiator airflow blocked	• Replenish coolant • Adjust fan belt tension • Replace hose(s) • Remove restriction (bug screen, fog lamps, etc.)
	• Faulty radiator cap • Ignition timing incorrect • Idle speed low • Air trapped in cooling system • Heavy traffic driving	• Replace radiator cap • Adjust ignition timing • Adjust idle speed • Purge air • Operate at fast idle in neutral intermittently to cool engine
	• Incorrect cooling system component(s) installed • Faulty thermostat • Water pump shaft broken or impeller loose • Radiator tubes clogged • Cooling system clogged • Casting flash in cooling passages	• Install proper component(s) • Replace thermostat • Replace water pump • Flush radiator • Flush system • Repair or replace as necessary. Flash may be visible by removing cooling system components or removing core plugs.
	• Brakes dragging • Excessive engine friction • Antifreeze concentration over 68%	• Repair brakes • Repair engine • Lower antifreeze concentration percentage
	• Missing air seals • Faulty gauge or sending unit	• Replace air seals • Repair or replace faulty component

Troubleshooting the Cooling System (cont.)

Problem	Cause	Solution
High temperature gauge indication— overheating (cont.)	• Loss of coolant flow caused by leakage or foaming • Viscous fan drive failed	• Repair or replace leaking component, replace coolant • Replace unit
Low temperature indication— undercooling	• Thermostat stuck open • Faulty gauge or sending unit	• Replace thermostat • Repair or replace faulty component
Coolant loss—boilover	• Overfilled cooling system • Quick shutdown after hard (hot) run • Air in system resulting in occasional "burping" of coolant • Insufficient antifreeze allowing coolant boiling point to be too low • Antifreeze deteriorated because of age or contamination • Leaks due to loose hose clamps, loose nuts, bolts, drain plugs, faulty hoses, or defective radiator • Faulty head gasket • Cracked head, manifold, or block • Faulty radiator cap	• Reduce coolant level to proper specification • Allow engine to run at fast idle prior to shutdown • Purge system • Add antifreeze to raise boiling point • Replace coolant • Pressure test system to locate source of leak(s) then repair as necessary • Replace head gasket • Replace as necessary • Replace cap
Coolant entry into crankcase or cylinder(s)	• Faulty head gasket • Crack in head, manifold or block	• Replace head gasket • Replace as necessary
Coolant recovery system inoperative	• Coolant level low • Leak in system • Pressure cap not tight or seal missing, or leaking • Pressure cap defective • Overflow tube clogged or leaking • Recovery bottle vent restricted	• Replenish coolant to FULL mark • Pressure test to isolate leak and repair as necessary • Repair as necessary • Replace cap • Repair as necessary • Remove restriction
Noise	• Fan contacting shroud • Loose water pump impeller • Glazed fan belt • Loose fan belt • Rough surface on drive pulley • Water pump bearing worn • Belt alignment	• Reposition shroud and inspect engine mounts • Replace pump • Apply silicone or replace belt • Adjust fan belt tension • Replace pulley • Remove belt to isolate. Replace pump. • Check pulley alignment. Repair as necessary.
No coolant flow through heater core	• Restricted return inlet in water pump • Heater hose collapsed or restricted • Restricted heater core • Restricted outlet in thermostat housing • Intake manifold bypass hole in cylinder head restricted • Faulty heater control valve • Intake manifold coolant passage restricted	• Remove restriction • Remove restriction or replace hose • Remove restriction or replace core • Remove flash or restriction • Remove restriction • Replace valve • Remove restriction or replace intake manifold

NOTE: *Immediately after shutdown, the engine enters a condition known as heat soak. This is caused by the cooling system being inoperative while engine temperature is still high. If coolant temperature rises above boiling point, expansion and pressure may push some coolant out of the radiator overflow tube. If this does not occur frequently it is considered normal.*

Troubleshooting the Serpentine Drive Belt

Problem	Cause	Solution
Tension sheeting fabric failure (woven fabric on outside circumference of belt has cracked or separated from body of belt)	• Grooved or backside idler pulley diameters are less than minimum recommended • Tension sheeting contacting (rubbing) stationary object • Excessive heat causing woven fabric to age • Tension sheeting splice has fractured	• Replace pulley(s) not conforming to specification • Correct rubbing condition • Replace belt • Replace belt
Noise (objectional squeal, squeak, or rumble is heard or felt while drive belt is in operation)	• Belt slippage • Bearing noise • Belt misalignment • Belt-to-pulley mismatch • Driven component inducing vibration • System resonant frequency inducing vibration	• Adjust belt • Locate and repair • Align belt/pulley(s) • Install correct belt • Locate defective driven component and repair • Vary belt tension within specifications. Replace belt.
Rib chunking (one or more ribs has separated from belt body)	• Foreign objects imbedded in pulley grooves • Installation damage • Drive loads in excess of design specifications • Insufficient internal belt adhesion	• Remove foreign objects from pulley grooves • Replace belt • Adjust belt tension • Replace belt
Rib or belt wear (belt ribs contact bottom of pulley grooves)	• Pulley(s) misaligned • Mismatch of belt and pulley groove widths • Abrasive environment • Rusted pulley(s) • Sharp or jagged pulley groove tips • Rubber deteriorated	• Align pulley(s) • Replace belt • Replace belt • Clean rust from pulley(s) • Replace pulley • Replace belt
Longitudinal belt cracking (cracks between two ribs)	• Belt has mistracked from pulley groove • Pulley groove tip has worn away rubber-to-tensile member	• Replace belt • Replace belt
Belt slips	• Belt slipping because of insufficient tension • Belt or pulley subjected to substance (belt dressing, oil, ethylene glycol) that has reduced friction • Driven component bearing failure • Belt glazed and hardened from heat and excessive slippage	• Adjust tension • Replace belt and clean pulleys • Replace faulty component bearing • Replace belt
"Groove jumping" (belt does not maintain correct position on pulley, or turns over and/or runs off pulleys)	• Insufficient belt tension • Pulley(s) not within design tolerance • Foreign object(s) in grooves • Excessive belt speed • Pulley misalignment • Belt-to-pulley profile mismatched • Belt cordline is distorted	• Adjust belt tension • Replace pulley(s) • Remove foreign objects from grooves • Avoid excessive engine acceleration • Align pulley(s) • Install correct belt • Replace belt
Belt broken (Note: identify and correct problem before replacement belt is installed)	• Excessive tension • Tensile members damaged during belt installation • Belt turnover • Severe pulley misalignment • Bracket, pulley, or bearing failure	• Replace belt and adjust tension to specification • Replace belt • Replace belt • Align pulley(s) • Replace defective component and belt

Troubleshooting the Serpentine Drive Belt (cont.)

Problem	Cause	Solution
Cord edge failure (tensile member exposed at edges of belt or separated from belt body)	• Excessive tension • Drive pulley misalignment • Belt contacting stationary object • Pulley irregularities • Improper pulley construction • Insufficient adhesion between tensile member and rubber matrix	• Adjust belt tension • Align pulley • Correct as necessary • Replace pulley • Replace pulley • Replace belt and adjust tension to specifications
Sporadic rib cracking (multiple cracks in belt ribs at random intervals)	• Ribbed pulley(s) diameter less than minimum specification • Backside bend flat pulley(s) diameter less than minimum • Excessive heat condition causing rubber to harden • Excessive belt thickness • Belt overcured • Excessive tension	• Replace pulley(s) • Replace pulley(s) • Correct heat condition as necessary • Replace belt • Replace belt • Adjust belt tension

13. Position a transmission jack under the transmission and secure it.

14. Remove the bolts attaching the transmission to the clutch housing and remove the transmission.

15. Disconnect the muffler inlet pipe at the exhaust manifold.

16. Disconnect the ground wire at the cylinder block.

17. Disconnect the ground wire at the starter retaining bolt.

18. Drain the crankcase.

19. Remove the oil filter.

20. Remove the nuts attaching the engine supports to the chassis.

21. Lower the vehicle.

22. Disconnect the battery.

23. Disconnect the radiator upper hose at the radiator.

24. Disconnect the radiator lower hose at the radiator.

25. Remove the radiator.

26. Remove the fan assembly and the spacer.

27. Disconnect the heater hose at the water pump.

28. Remove the air cleaner assembly.

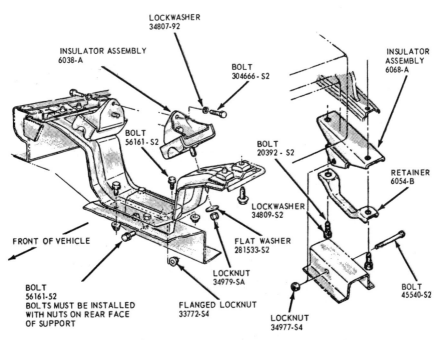

FRONT SUPPORTS   REAR SUPPORT

1969 6-170 engine supports

29. Disconnect the tank-to-pump fuel line at the fuel pump and plug the line.

30. Disconnect the accelerator cable at the carburetor.

31. Disconnect the choke cable, remove it from the mounting bracket and position it out of the way.

32. Remove the accelerator cable mounting bracket from the carburetor and the cylinder head.

33. Disconnect the heater hose at the cylinder head.

34. Disconnect the oil filler pipe at the rocker arm cover and remove the oil filler pipe.

35. Remove the oil dipstick and tube from the cylinder block.

36. Disconnect the engine wire loom and position it out of the way (temp., oil, coil).

37. Disconnect the starter cable at the starter.

38. Remove the alternator from the mounting and adjusting brackets and position the alternator out of the way.

39. Position an engine lifting device to the engine and attach it to a crane boom and lift the engine out of the vehicle through the right front door.

To install the engine:

40. Install the engine into the engine compartment through the right front door and al-low it to rest on the front engine supports and the engine support bar at the rear.

41. Raise and support the van on jackstands.

42. Install the engine support insulator attaching nuts to the chassis mounts. Torque the bolts to 60 ft.lb.

43. Position the transmission to the clutch housing and install the attaching bolts. Torque the bolts to 50 ft.lb.

44. Raise the transmission and position the crossmember to the chassis and the rear engine support.

45. Install the bolts and nut attaching the crossmember to the transmission and chassis. Torque the bolts to 60 ft.lb.

46. Remove the transmission jack and the engine support bar.

47. Position the equalizer arm to the cylinder block mount, position the linkage to the bearing fork, install the equalizer arm mounting bracket retracting spring.

48. Connect the shift rods at the transmission.

49. Connect the speedometer cable at the transmission.

50. Position the driveshaft to the transmission flange and install the U-bolts and nuts. Torque the nuts to 17 ft.lb.

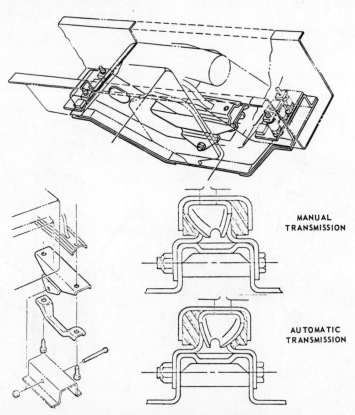

1969–74 8-302 engine rear supports

51. Position the midship bearing support to the chassis and install the attaching bolts.

52. Connect the muffler inlet pipe at the exhaust manifold and tighten the retaining clamp at the cylinder block. Torque the nuts to 30 ft.lb.

53. Connect the ground wire to the starter.

54. Lower the vehicle.

55. Unplug and connect the fuel line from the tank to the fuel pump at the pump.

56. Connect the fuel line from the fuel pump to the carburetor at the filter.

57. Position the engine wire loom in the retainers and connect at the respective locations (i.e., coil, oil, temp.).

58. Position the alternator to the mounting brackets and install the attaching bolts.

59. Connect the starter cable at the starter.

60. Install the dipstick and tube to the cylinder block and support bracket.

61. Connect the heater hose at the cylinder head.

62. Install the accelerator cable mounting bracket to the cylinder head.

63. Connect the accelerator cable to the carburetor, if applicable.

64. Connect the oil filler pipe to the rocker arm cover.

65. Connect the heater hose at the water pump.

66. Connect the heater hose at the engine.

67. Position the alternator drive belt to the pulley and the water pump pulley to the water pump shaft.

68. Install the fan and spacer to the water pump shaft.

69. Adjust the alternator drive belt tension and tighten the attaching bolts.

70. Connect the radiator upper and lower hoses.

71. Clean the oil filter mating surface and install the oil filter.

72. Fill the crankcase with oil.

73. Fill the cooling system.

74. Connect the battery.

75. Start the engine and check for leaks.

76. Adjust the carburetor idle speed and mixture as necessary.

77. Install the air cleaner assembly.

78. Install the right hand seat and the engine cover.

If the torque for a particular fastener was not mentioned above, use the following torque values as a guide:

- $\frac{1}{4}$"-20: 6-9 ft.lb.
- $\frac{5}{16}$"-18: 12-18 ft.lb.
- $\frac{3}{8}$"-16: 22-32 ft.lb.
- $\frac{7}{16}$"-14: 45-57 ft.lb.
- $\frac{1}{2}$"-13: 55-80 ft.lb.
- $\frac{9}{16}$": 85-120 ft.lb.

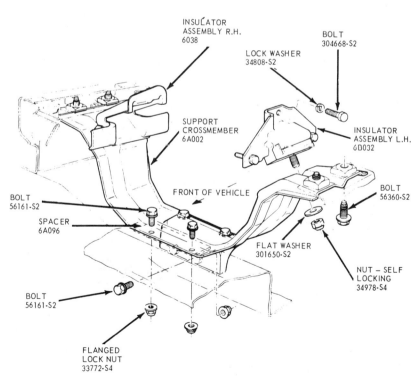

1969–74 6-240; 1973–74 6-300 front engine supports

6-240 (3.9L)
6-300 (4.9L)
Through 1972

1. Remove the engine cover.
2. Remove the air cleaner assembly.
3. Drain the cooling system.

CAUTION: *When draining the coolant, keep in mind that cats and dogs are attracted by the ethylene glycol antifreeze, and are quite likely to drink any that is left in an uncovered container or in puddles on the ground. This will prove fatal in sufficient quantity. Always drain the coolant into a sealable container. Coolant should be reused unless it is contaminated or several years old.*

4. Drain the crankcase.
5. Disconnect the battery positive cable.
6. Disconnect the heater hose from the water pump and the coolant outlet housing.
7. Disconnect the flexible fuel line from the fuel pump.
8. Remove the radiator.
9. Remove the cooling fan, water pump pulley and the fan drive belt.
10. Disconnect the accelerator cable and the choke cable at the carburetor.
11. Remove the carburetor retracting spring.
12. On a vehicle with power brakes, disconnect the vacuum line at the intake manifold.
13. On a vehicle with an automatic transmission, disconnect the transmission kickdown rod at the bellcrank assembly.
14. Disconnect the exhaust manifold from the muffler inlet pipe.

15. Disconnect the body ground strap and the battery ground cable at the engine.
16. Disconnect the engine wiring harness at the ignition coil, coolant temperature sending unit and the oil pressure sending unit. Position the harness out of the way.
17. Remove the alternator mounting bolts and position the alternator out of the way, leaving the wires attached.
18. On a vehicle with power steering, remove the power steering pump from the mounting brackets and position it right-side up and to one side, leaving the lines attached.
19. Raise and support the van on jackstands.
20. Remove the starter.
21. Remove the automatic transmission filler tube bracket, if applicable.
22. Remove the engine rear plate upper right bolt.
23. On a vehicle with manual transmission, remove all the flywheel housing lower attaching bolts.
24. Disconnect the clutch retracting spring.
25. On a vehicle with an automatic transmission:

   a. Remove the converter housing access cover assembly.

   b. Remove the flywheel-to-converter nuts.

   c. Secure the converter assembly in the housing.

   d. Remove the transmission oil cooler lines from the retaining clip at the engine.

   e. Remove the converter housing-to-engine lower attaching bolts.

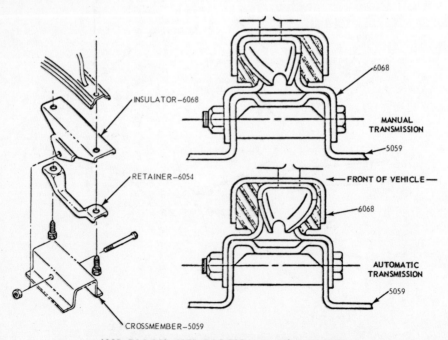

INSULATOR –6068
RETAINER –6054
CROSSMEMBER –5059
6068
MANUAL TRANSMISSION
5059
FRONT OF VEHICLE
6068
AUTOMATIC TRANSMISSION
5059

1969–74 6-240; 1973–74 6-300 rear engine supports

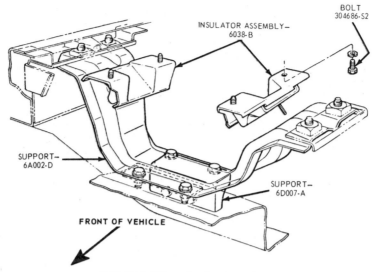

1969–74 8-302 engine front supports

26. Remove the engine from the support insulator bolt.

27. Lower the vehicle and position a transmission jack under the transmission to support it.

28. Remove the remaining flywheel or converter housing-to-engine bolts.

29. Attach the engine lifting device and raise the engine slightly.

30. Carefully pull the engine from the transmission. Lift the engine out of the vehicle.

NOTE: *The 6-240 and 6-300 are removed from the vehicle in the same manner as the 6-170, through the right-side door; consequently, the seat will have to be removed from the right-side if it hasn't already been done. The driver's seat should also be removed to afford the maximum amount of room for working.*

To install the engine:

31. Place a new gasket on the muffler inlet pipe.

32. Lower the engine carefully into the vehicle. Make sure that the studs on the exhaust manifold are aligned with the holes in the muffler inlet pipe and the dowels in the block engage the holes in the flywheel or converter housing.

33. On a vehicle with an automatic transmission, start the converter pilot into the crankshaft. Remove the retainer securing the converter in the housing.

34. On a vehicle with a manual transmission,

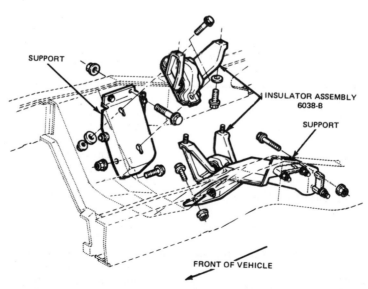

Front engine supports for the 1979–88 8-302; 1975–88 8-351; 1980 8-400

guide the transmission input shaft into the clutch disc. It may be necessary to adjust the position of the transmission with relation to the engine if the transmission input shaft will not enter the clutch disc. If the engine hangs up after the shaft enters, turn the crankshaft slowly with the transmission in gear until the shaft splines mesh with the clutch disc.

35. Install the converter or flywheel housing upper attaching bolts. Torque the bolts to 50 ft.lb.

36. Remove the jack supporting the transmission.

37. Lower the engine until it rests on the engine support and remove the lifting device.

38. Install the front support bolt and nut. Torque the nuts to 60 ft.lb.

39. Install the bracket for the automatic transmission oil cooler lines.

40. Install the remaining converter or flywheel housing attaching bolts. Torque the bolts to 50 ft.lb.

41. Install the converter-to-flex plate bolts. Torque them to 30 ft.lb.

42. Connect the clutch return spring.

43. Install the starter and connect the starter cable.

44. Attach the automatic transmission oil cooler lines in the bracket at the engine block.

45. Install the exhaust manifold to the muffler inlet pipe lockwashers and nuts. Torque the nuts to 30 ft.lb.

46. Connect the engine ground strap and the battery ground cable.

47. On a vehicle with an automatic transmission, connect the kickdown rod to the bellcrank assembly on the intake manifold.

48. Connect the accelerator linkage to the carburetor and install the retracting spring.

49. Connect the choke cable to the carburetor and hand throttle, if equipped.

50. On a vehicle with power brakes, connect the brake vacuum line to the intake manifold.

51. Connect the coil primary wire.

52. Connect the oil pressure and coolant temperature sending unit wires.

53. Connect the flexible fuel line.

54. Connect the heater hoses.

55. Connect the battery positive cable.

56. Install the alternator on the mounting bracket.

57. On a vehicle with power steering, install the power steering pump on the mounting bracket.

58. Install the water pump pulley, spacer, cooling fan and drive belt.

59. Adjust all the belt tensions and tighten the accessories' mounting bolts.

60. Install the radiator.

61. Connect the radiator lower hose to the water pump.

62. Connect the radiator upper hose to the coolant outlet housing.

63. On a vehicle with an automatic transmission, connect the oil cooler lines to the radiator.

64. Install and adjust the hood, if it was removed.

65. Fill the cooling system.

66. Fill the crankcase.

67. Operate the engine at a fast idle and check for leaks.

68. Adjust the carburetor idle speed and mixture.

69. On a vehicle with manual transmission, adjust the clutch pedal free-play.

70. On a vehicle with an automatic transmission, adjust the transmission control linkage. Check the fluid level in the automatic transmission and add as necessary.

71. Install the carburetor air cleaner.

If the torque for a particular fastener was not mentioned above, use the following torque values as a guide:

- $1/4$"-20: 6-9 ft.lb.
- $5/16$"-18: 12-18 ft.lb.
- $3/8$"-16: 22-32 ft.lb.
- $7/16$"-14: 45-57 ft.lb.
- $1/2$"-13: 55-80 ft.lb.
- $9/16$": 85-120 ft.lb.

1974-75 6-240 (3.9L) and 6-300 (4.9L)

1. Disconnect the battery.

2. Drain the cooling system.

CAUTION: *When draining the coolant, keep in mind that cats and dogs are attracted by the ethylene glycol antifreeze, and are quite likely to drink any that is left in an uncovered container or in puddles on the ground. This will prove fatal in sufficient quantity. Always drain the coolant into a sealable container. Coolant should be reused unless it is contaminated or several years old.*

3. Remove the engine cover.

4. Remove the right hand seat.

5. Remove the grille and bumper.

6. Remove the hood lock support bracket.

7. Remove the right and left headlight doors and headlight grilles.

8. Disconnect all hoses and lines at the radiator.

9. Remove the battery deflector.

10. Discharge the air conditioning system. See Chapter 1.

11. Disconnect the refrigerant lines at the condenser. Cap all openings at once!

12. Remove the condenser.

13. Remove the radiator.

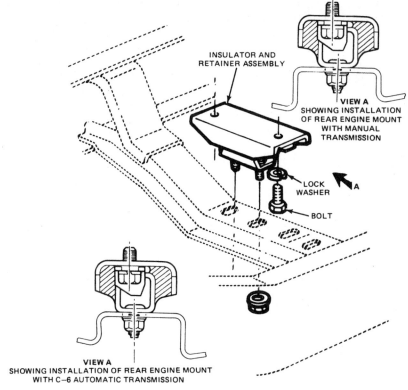

INSULATOR AND
RETAINER ASSEMBLY

VIEW A
SHOWING INSTALLATION
OF REAR ENGINE MOUNT
WITH MANUAL
TRANSMISSION

LOCK
WASHER

A

BOLT

VIEW A
SHOWING INSTALLATION OF REAR ENGINE MOUNT
WITH C–6 AUTOMATIC TRANSMISSION

Rear engine supports for the 1979–88 8-302; 1975–88 8-351; 1980 8-400

14. Disconnect the heater hoses at the engine.

15. Disconnect the temperature sending unit.

16. Disconnect the oil pressure sending unit.

17. Disconnect the ignition wires.

18. Disconnect the starter solenoid.

19. Disconnect the neutral safety switch.

20. Disconnect the back-up light wiring.

21. Remove the engine oil dipstick and oil filler tube.

22. Remove the hoses connecting the rocker cover and air cleaner.

23. Remove the air cleaner and brackets.

24. Disconnect the choke and accelerator cables at the carburetor.

25. Disconnect the auxiliary heater hose at the front heater.

26. Disconnect the hoses at the right front of the engine, and position them out of the way.

27. Disconnect the fuel pump discharge line at the pump.

28. Disconnect the alternator, and remove it from the brackets.

29. Disconnect the refrigerant lines at the compressor. Cap all openings at once!

30. Remove the compressor.

31. Disconnect the ground wires at the block.

32. Disconnect the muffler inlet pipe at the manifold.

33. Disconnect the modulator line at the intake manifold.

34. Raise and support the van on jackstands.

35. Drain the crankcase.

36. Remove the oil filter.

37. Disconnect the starter wiring, and remove the starter.

38. Position an engine support bar on the chassis and engine, and adjust it to take up the slack.

39. On manual transmission vehicles:

a. Disconnect the driveshaft, and remove it. Install a plug in the transmission extension housing.

b. Disconnect the speedometer cable and housing, and secure the assembly out of the way.

c. Remove the nut and bolt holding the rear support to the crossmember.

d. Raise the transmission, remove the mounting bolts, and remove the crossmember.

e. Remove the clutch equalizer arm bolts from the engine. Disconnect the retracting spring, and move the assembly away.

f. Remove the bolts connecting transmission and clutch, and remove the transmission.

40. On automatic transmission vehicles:

a. Remove the bolts connecting the adapter plate and inspection cover to the torque converter.

b. Unbolt and remove the transmission dipstick tube. Drain the transmission.

c. Remove the nuts attaching the converter to the flex plate. Disconnect the fluid cooler and modulator lines at the transmission.

d. Disconnect the driveshaft at the companion flange.

e. Disconnect the speedometer cable and housing from the transmission.

f. Disconnect the shift rod at the lever on the transmission. Jack the transmission up slightly.

g. Remove the nuts and bolts attaching the rear engine mount bracket to the crossmember. Remove the side support bolts, and remove the crossmember.

h. Secure the transmission to the jack with a safety chain, remove the remaining bolts attaching the transmission to the cylinder block, and remove the transmission from the vehicle.

41. Remove the nuts which attach the engine front support insulator.

42. Remove the bellcrank from the block, and position it out of the way.

43. Lower the vehicle.

44. Remove the fan spacer, and water pump pulley.

45. Lift the engine from the vehicle with a lifting hook.

46. Remove the clutch housing on vehicles with manual transmission.

To install:

47. Install the clutch housing on manual transmission vehicles.

48. Hoist the engine into the vehicle, and allow it to rest on the front supports and support tool.

49. Raise and support the van on jackstands.

50. On manual transmission:

a. Raise the transmission and position it behind the clutch housing. Install the mounting bolts.

b. Raise the transmission slightly further, position the crossmember to the chassis and rear support, and install the attaching bolts. Torque crossmember-to-boss bolts to 20-30 ft.lb.

c. Remove the jack and engine support tool. Connect the shift linkage and the speedometer cable housing.

d. Install and connect the driveshaft.

51. Install the engine front support insulator bolts, and torque to 45-55 ft.lb.

52. Install the transmission bellcrank.

53. On automatic transmission equipped vehicles:

a. Position the transmission against the block and install the mounting bolts. Torque to 23-33 ft.lb.

b. Position the crossmember to the rear mount bracket and frame side members. Install the attaching nuts and bolts, and torque to 20-30 ft.lb.

c. Remove the transmission safety chain, and remove the jack. Remove the engine support bar.

d. Install the converter to the flex plate. Connect the vacuum and oil cooler lines to the transmission.

e. Install the dipstick and tube into the transmission oil pan. Install the tube and vacuum line bracket attaching bolt to the block.

f. Connect the driveshaft to the transmission companion flange. Connect the speedometer cable and housing to the transmission. Connect the shift rods to the transmission levers.

g. Install the adapter plate and inspection cover.

54. Install the starter. Torque the nuts to 20 ft.lb.

55. Connect the muffler inlet pipe at the manifold. Torque the nuts to 30 ft.lb.

56. Install the clutch equalizer arm bracket (on manual transmission models). Install the attaching bolts, and connect the retractor spring.

57. Lower the vehicle to the floor.

58. Install the remaining automatic transmission mounting bolts.

59. Install the starter ground wire and remaining starter attaching bolt.

60. Connect the starter cable at the starter.

61. Install the compressor and connect the refrigerant lines.

62. Install the water pump pulley, spacer, and fan assembly.

63. Install the alternator onto its mounting brackets.

64. Install and tension the V-belt.

65. Connect the alternator wiring.

66. Connect the backup light wiring.

67. Connect the neutral safety switch.

68. Connect the alternator and battery ground wires to the block.

69. Connect the transmission modulator line to the manifold.

70. Connect the fuel line from the tank to the fuel pump.

71. Connect the choke and accelerator cables to the carburetor.

72. Install the dipstick tube, and bolt it to the cylinder head.

73. Position the wiring harness, and connect the coil, oil, and temperature leads.

74. Connect the auxiliary heater hoses.

75. Connect the oil filler tube to the rocker arm cover and install the retaining clamp.

76. Install the filler tube bracket to the firewall panel.

77. Install the radiator.

78. Install the condenser and connect the refrigerant lines.

79. Install the battery deflector.

80. Connect the upper radiator hose.

81. Connect the lower radiator hose.

82. Connect the oil cooler lines.

83. Install the headlights.

84. Install the headlight grilles.

85. Install the hood lock bracket.

86. Fill the crankcase.

87. Fill the cooling system.

88. Charge the air conditioning system. See Chapter 1.

89. Fill the automatic transmission.

90. Connect the positive battery cable.

91. Start the engine and allow it to run to normal operating temperature.

92. Adjust idle speed and mixture.

93. Check and, if necessary, adjust the ignition timing.

94. Adjust the throttle and choke linkages.

95. Adjust the automatic transmission linkage.

96. Operate the engine to check for leaks.

97. Install the air cleaner and brackets.

98. Install the engine front cover.

99. Install the right front seat.

100. Install the grille.

101. Install the bumper.

If the torque for a particular fastener was not mentioned above, use the following torque values as a guide:

- $\frac{1}{4}$"-20: 6-9 ft.lb.
- $\frac{5}{16}$"-18: 12-18 ft.lb.
- $\frac{3}{8}$"-16: 22-32 ft.lb.
- $\frac{7}{16}$"-14: 45-57 ft.lb.
- $\frac{1}{2}$"-13: 55-80 ft.lb.
- $\frac{9}{16}$": 85-120 ft.lb.

1975-88 6-300 (4.9L)

WARNING: *When working on fuel injected engines, discharge the fuel system pressure before starting any work that involves disconnecting the fuel system lines. See Fuel Supply Manifold Removal and Installation procedures in Chapter 5.*

1. Take off the engine cover.

2. Drain the coolant.

CAUTION: *When draining the coolant, keep in mind that cats and dogs are attracted by the ethylene glycol antifreeze, and are quite likely to drink any that is left in an uncovered container or in puddles on the ground. This will prove fatal in sufficient quantity. Always drain the coolant into a sealable container. Coolant should be reused unless it is contaminated or several years old.*

3. Remove the air cleaner.

4. On fuel injected engines, remove the throttle body inlet tubes.

5. Discharge the air conditioning system. See Chapter 1.

6. Disconnect the refrigerant lines at the compressor. Cap all openings at once.

7. Remove the compressor.

8. Disconnect the battery.

9. Remove the bumper.

10. Remove the grille.

11. Remove the gravel deflector.

12. Diconnect the refrigerant lines at the condenser. Cap all openings at once.

13. Remove the condenser.

14. Detach the upper radiator hose at the engine.

15. Remove the alternator splash shield.

16. Detach the lower hose at the radiator.

17. Remove the radiator and shroud, if any.

18. Disconnect the engine heater hoses.

19. Disconnect the alternator wires.

20. Remove the power steering pump and support.

21. Disconnect and plug the fuel line at the pump.

22. Disconnect the distributor wires.

23. Disconnect the gauge sending unit wires.

24. On engines with Electronic Engine Controls, disconnect the (EEC) harness from all the sensors.

25. Disconnect the brake booster hose.

26. Disconnect the accelerator cable and bracket.

27. Disconnect the automatic transmission kickdown linkage at the bellcrank.

28. Remove the exhaust manifold heat deflector.

29. Unbolt the exhaust pipe from the manifold.

30. Disconnect the automatic transmission vacuum line from the intake manifold and from the junction.

31. Remove the transmission dipstick tube support bolt at the intake manifold.

32. Remove the upper engine-to-transmission bolts.

33. Remove the starter.

34. Remove the flywheel inspection cover.

35. Remove the four automatic transmission torque converter nuts, then remove the front engine support nuts.

36. Take off the oil filter.

37. Remove the rest of the transmission to en-

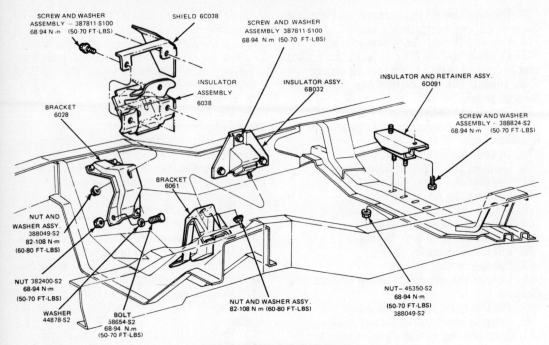

1981—84 6-300 engine supports

gine fasteners, then lift the engine out from the engine compartment with a floor crane.

To install:

38. Lower the engine into the engine compartment and install the lower transmission-to-engine fasteners. Torque the bolts to 50 ft.lb.

39. Install the oil filter.

40. Install the front engine support nuts and tighten them to 70 ft.lb.

41. On trucks with automatic transmissions, install the torque converter-to-flywheel attaching bolts. Torque the bolts to 30 ft.lb.

42. Install the flywheel inspection cover.

43. Install the starter.

44. Install the upper engine-to-transmission bolts. Torque the bolts to 50 ft.lb.

45. Install the transmission dipstick tube support bolt at the intake manifold.

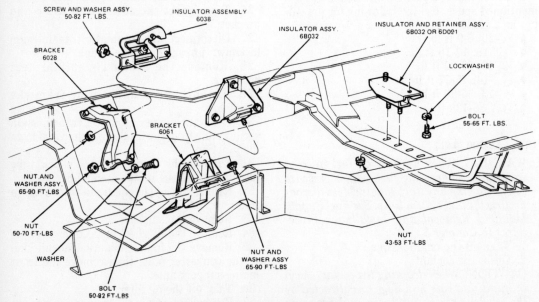

1975—80 6-300 engine supports

46. Connect the automatic transmission vacuum line at the intake manifold and the junction.

47. Connect the exhaust pipe at the manifold. Tighten the nuts to 25-35 ft.lb.

48. Install the exhaust manifold heat deflector.

49. Connect the automatic transmission kickdown linkage at the bellcrank.

50. Connect the accelerator cable and bracket.

51. Connect the brake booster hose.

52. Connect the gauge sending unit wires.

53. Connect the EEC sensors.

54. Connect the distributor wires.

55. Connect the fuel line at the pump.

56. Install the power steering pump and support.

57. Connect the alternator wires.

58. Install the air conditioning compressor. Connect the refrigerant lines.

59. Connect the engine heater hoses.

60. Install the radiator and shroud, if any.

61. Connect the lower hose at the radiator.

62. Install the condenser and connect the refrigerant lines.

63. Charge the refrigerant system. See Chapter 1.

64. Install the alternator splash shield.

65. Connect the upper radiator hose at the engine.

66. Install the gravel deflector.

67. Install the grille.

68. Install the bumper.

69. Connect the battery.

70. Install the air cleaner.

71. Fill the cooling system.

72. Fill the crankcase.

73. Install off the engine cover.

74. Run the engine and check for leaks.

If the torque for a particular fastener was not mentioned above, use the following torque values as a guide:

- ¼"-20: 6-9 ft.lb.
- ⁵⁄₁₆"-18: 12-18 ft.lb.
- ⅜"-16: 22-32 ft.lb.
- ⁷⁄₁₆"-14: 45-57 ft.lb.
- ½"-13: 55-80 ft.lb.
- ⁹⁄₁₆": 85-120 ft.lb.

1969-72 8-302 (5.0L)

1. Remove the engine cover.

2. Remove the right front seat. Also remove the driver's seat if more room to work is desired.

3. Drain the cooling system.

CAUTION: *When draining the coolant, keep in mind that cats and dogs are attracted by the ethylene glycol antifreeze, and are quite likely to drink any that is left in an uncovered container or in puddles on the ground. This will prove fatal in sufficient quantity. Always drain the coolant into a sealable container. Coolant should be reused unless it is contaminated or several years old.*

4. Remove the air cleaner and intake duct assembly, including the crankcase ventilation hose.

5. Disconnect the battery and alternator ground cables at the cylinder block.

6. Remove the oil filler tube at the dash panel and disconnect it at the rocker arm cover.

7. Discharge the air conditioning system. See Chapter 1.

8. Disconnect the refrigerant lines at the compressor. Cap all openings immediately.

9. Disconnect the air conditioning compressor clutch wire.

10. Disconnect the radiator upper hose at the radiator.

11. Disconnect the radiator hose at the radiator.

12. Disconnect the automatic transmission oil cooler lines, if so equipped.

13. Disconnect the refrigerant lines at the condenser. Cap all openings at once.

14. Remove the condenser attaching bolts and lift it out.

15. Disconnect the radiator attaching bolts and remove the radiator.

16. Disconnect the heater hoses at the engine and position them out of the way.

17. Remove the fan, spacer, pulley, and the drive belt.

18. Disconnect the accelerator linkage at the accelerator shaft on the left cylinder head.

19. Disconnect the automatic transmission kickdown rod at the carburetor and the vacuum line at the intake manifold, if so equipped.

20. Disconnect the engine wire harness from the left rocker arm cover and position it out of the way.

21. Remove the upper nut attaching the right exhaust manifold to the muffler inlet pipe.

22. Raise and support the van on jackstands.

23. Drain the crankcase and remove the oil filter.

24. Disconnect the fuel link (tank-to-pump) at the fuel pump.

25. Disconnect the oil dipstick tube bracket from the exhaust manifold and oil pan.

26. On manual transmissions, remove the bolts attaching the equalizer arm bracket to the cylinder block and the clutch housing. This includes the clutch linkage connection and the retracting springs. Remove the bracket.

27. Disconnect the starter cable at the starter and remove the starter.

28. On a vehicle with manual transmission, disconnect the driveshaft at the rear axle and

remove the driveshaft. Install a plug in the end of the transmission.

29. On vehicles with automatic transmissions, disconnect the driveshaft at the companion flange.

30. Disconnect the speedometer cable and the transmission linkage at the transmission.

31. Position a transmission jack under the transmission.

32. Raise the transmission and remove the bolts attaching the crossmember to the chassis.

33. Lower the transmission slightly and remove the bolt and nut attaching the engine rear support to the crossmember. Remove the crossmember.

34. Remove the bolts attaching the manual transmission to the clutch housing and remove the transmission.

35. On a vehicle with an automatic transmission:

    a. Remove the lower front cover from the converter housing.

    b. Remove the transmission dipstick tube and drain the transmission.

    c. Install a plug in the transmission oil pan.

    d. Remove the nuts attaching the transmission converter to the flywheel.

    e. Disconnect the oil cooler lines at the transmission.

    f. Remove the remaining bolts fastening the transmission to the engine and remove the transmission.

36. Position an engine support bar under the engine to steady it.

37. Disconnect the muffler inlet pipes at the exhaust manifolds.

38. Remove the engine front support attaching nuts and washers.

39. Remove the bellcrank bolt from the side of the cylinder block and position the bellcrank assembly out of the way.

40. Lower the vehicle.

41. Remove the bolts attaching the alternator to the cylinder block and the water pump and position it out of the way.

42. Remove the carburetor air horn stud.

43. Disconnect the fuel line (pump-to-carburetor) at the fuel pump.

44. Install an engine lifting device and remove the engine through the right-side door.

To install:

45. Lift the engine into place through the right-side door.

46. Install the engine front support attaching nuts and washers. Torque the nuts to 80 ft.lb.

47. On a vehicle with automatic transmission, position the bellcrank assembly to the cylinder block and install the attaching bolt. Position

the transmission to the engine and install the attaching bolts. Torque the bolts to 50 ft.lb.

48. On a vehicle with manual transmission, position the transmission to the clutch housing and install the attaching bolts. Torque the bolts to 50 ft.lb.

49. Remove the engine support bar.

50. Position the engine rear support crossmember to the chassis and install the attaching bolts.

51. Position the transmission with the engine rear support attached to the crossmember. Install and tighten the bolt and nut. Remove the jack.

52. On a vehicle with an automatic transmission:

    a. Install and tighten the converter-to-flywheel attaching nuts. Torque the bolts to 30 ft.lb.

    b. Connect the oil cooler and vacuum lines at the transmission.

    c. Install the transmission dipstick tube in the pan.

    d. Install the dipstick tube and vacuum line retaining bracket bolt to the cylinder block.

53. Connect the transmission shift linkages and the speedometer cable.

54. On a vehicle with an automatic transmission, connect the driveshaft to the transmission companion flange.

55. On a vehicle with a manual transmission, remove the plug from the transmission and install the driveshaft into the transmission. Connect the rear end of the driveshaft at the rear axle.

56. Install the starter and connect the cable to the starter. Torque the mounting bolts to 20 ft.lb.

57. Install the muffler inlet pipe attaching bolts and nuts (except the upper nut on the right-side exhaust manifold).

58. On a manual transmission, install the bolts connecting the equalizer arm bracket to the cylinder block and clutch housing. This includes connecting the clutch linkage and retracting spring.

59. Connect the fuel line (pump-to-carburetor) at the fuel pump.

60. Position the alternator and adjusting arm to the cylinder block and water pump housing. Install and tighten the attaching bolts.

61. Install the oil filter.

62. Install the oil dipstick tube bracket to the oil pan and the exhaust manifold.

63. Connect the fuel line (tank-to-pump) at the fuel pump.

64. Lower the vehicle.

65. Install the upper nut attaching the right exhaust manifold to the muffler inlet pipe.

66. Connect the engine wire harness at the left rocker arm cover. Connect the battery and the alternator ground cables at the cylinder block.

67. Connect the automatic transmission vacuum line at the intake manifold and the transmission kickdown rod at the carburetor, if so equipped. Connect the accelerator linkage to accelerator shaft on the left side cylinder head.

68. Install the drive belt, pulley, spacer and fan, then tighten the belt tension.

69. Connect the heater hoses at the engine.

70. Install the condenser and connect the refrigerant lines.

71. Position the radiator and install the attaching bolts.

72. Connect the radiator upper and lower hoses and the automatic transmission cooler lines, if so equipped.

73. Install the air conditioning compressor. Connect the refrigerant lines.

74. Charge the refrigerant system. See Chapter 1.

75. Install the oil filler tube.

76. Install the air cleaner and intake duct assembly, including the crankcase ventilation hose.

77. Fill and bleed the cooling system.

78. Fill the crankcase and the automatic transmission, if so equipped.

79. Install the engine cover and the right front seat.

80. Operate the engine at a fast idle and check for leaks.

If the torque for a particular fastener was not mentioned above, use the following torque values as a guide:

- $1/4''$-20: 6-9 ft.lb.
- $5/16''$-18: 12-18 ft.lb.
- $3/8''$-16: 22-32 ft.lb.
- $7/16''$-14: 45-57 ft.lb.
- $1/2''$-13: 55-80 ft.lb.
- $9/16''$: 85-120 ft.lb.

8-351 (5.7L)
8-400 (6.6L)
8-460 (7.5L) through 1987
1979-88 8-302 (5.0L)

WARNING: *When working on fuel injected engines, discharge the fuel system pressure before starting any work that involves disconnecting the fuel system lines. See Fuel Supply Manifold Removal and Installation procedures in Chapter 5.*

1. Take off the engine cover.

2. Drain the coolant.

CAUTION: *When draining the coolant, keep in mind that cats and dogs are attracted by the ethylene glycol antifreeze, and are quite likely to drink any that is left in an uncovered container or in puddles on the ground. This will prove fatal in sufficient quantity. Always drain the coolant into a sealable container. Coolant should be reused unless it is contaminated or several years old.*

3. On carbureted engines, remove the air cleaner and intake duct assembly, plus the crankcase ventilation hose.

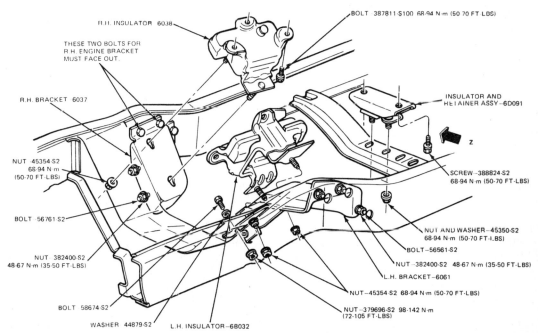

1981–82 8-400 engine supports

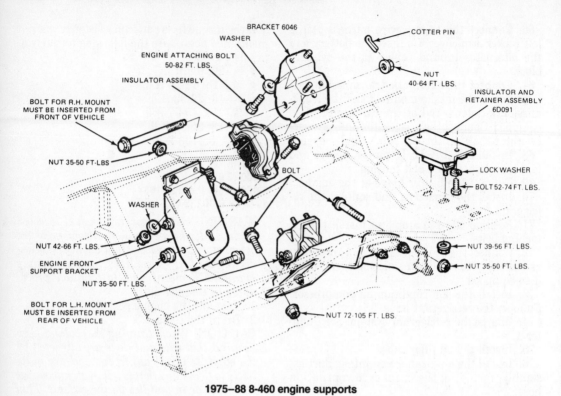

BRACKET 6046
WASHER
ENGINE ATTACHING BOLT
50-82 FT. LBS.
INSULATOR ASSEMBLY
BOLT FOR R.H. MOUNT
MUST BE INSERTED FROM
FRONT OF VEHICLE
NUT 35-50 FT-LBS
WASHER
NUT 42-66 FT. LBS.
ENGINE FRONT
SUPPORT BRACKET
NUT 35-50 FT. LBS.
BOLT FOR L.H. MOUNT
MUST BE INSERTED FROM
REAR OF VEHICLE

COTTER PIN
NUT
40-64 FT. LBS.
INSULATOR AND
RETAINER ASSEMBLY
6D091
LOCK WASHER
BOLT 52-74 FT. LBS.
BOLT
NUT 39-56 FT. LBS.
NUT 35-50 FT. LBS.
NUT 72-105 FT. LBS.

1975–88 8-460 engine supports

4. On fuel injected engines, remove the air intake hoses, PCV tube and carbon canister hose.

5. Disconnect the battery.

6. Remove the bumper.

7. Remove the grille, and gravel deflector.

8. Remove the upper grille support bracket.

9. Remove the hood lock support.

10. Discharge the air conditioning system. See Chapter 1.

11. Remove the air conditioning condenser upper mounting brackets.

12. Remove the condenser. Cap all openings at once!

13. Disconnect the lines at the compressor. Cap all openings at once!

14. On trucks with EFI, disconnect the chassis fuel line at the fuel rails.

15. Disconnect the accelerator linkage and speed control linkage at the carburetor or throttle body.

16. On EFI models, disconnect the throttle bracket from the upper intake manifold and swing it out of the way with the cables still attached.

17. Detach the radiator hoses and the automatic transmission cooler lines, if any.

18. Remove the fan shroud.

19. Remove the fan.

20. Remove the radiator.

21. Pivot the alternator in and detach the wires.

22. Remove the air cleaner, duct and valve.

23. Remove the exhaust manifold shroud and flex tube.

24. Disconnect the automatic transmission shift rod.

25. Disconnect the fuel and choke lines and detach the vacuum lines at the carburetor.

26. Remove the carburetor and spacer.

27. Remove the oil filter.

28. Detach the exhaust pipe from the manifold.

29. Unbolt the automatic transmission tube bracket from the cylinder head.

30. Remove the starter.

31. Remove the engine mount bolts.

32. With automatic transmission, remove the converter inspection cover and unbolt the converter from the flex plate.

33. Unbolt the engine ground cable and support the transmission.

34. Remove the power steering front bracket.

35. Detach only one vacuum line at the rear of the intake manifold.

36. Disconnect the engine wiring loom.

37. Remove the speed control servo from the manifold.

38. Detach the compressor clutch wire.

39. Install a lifting bracket to the intake manifold and attach a floor crane.

40. Remove the transmission to engine bolts, making sure the transmission is supported.

41. Remove the engine.

To install the engine:

42. Lower the engine into the van.

43. Align the converter to the flex plate and the engine dowels to the transmission.

44. With manual transmission, start the transmission shaft into the clutch disc. You may have to turn the crankshaft slowly with the transmission in gear.

45. Install the transmission-to-engine bolts. Torque the bolts to 50 ft.lb.

46. Install the mounting bolts. Torque the nuts to 80 ft.lb.

47. Remove the lifting bracket and floor crane.

48. Connect the compressor clutch wire.

49. Install the speed control servo on the manifold.

50. Connect the engine wiring loom.

51. Attach the vacuum line at the rear of the intake manifold.

52. Install the power steering front bracket.

53. Connect the engine ground cable.

54. With automatic transmission, bolt the converter to the flex plate. Torque the bolts to 30 ft.lb.

55. Install the converter inspection cover. Torque the bolts to 60 in.lb.

56. Install the starter. Torque the mounting bolts to 20 ft.lb.

57. Connect the automatic transmission tube bracket at the cylinder head.

58. Attach the exhaust pipe to the manifold. Tighten the exhaust pipe-to-exhaust manifold nuts to 25-35 ft.lb.

59. Install the oil filter.

60. Install the carburetor and spacer.

61. Connect the fuel and choke lines and attach the vacuum lines at the carburetor.

62. Connect the automatic transmission shift rod.

63. Install the exhaust manifold shroud and flex tube.

64. Install the air cleaner, duct and valve.

65. Pivot the alternator in and connect the wires.

66. Install the radiator.

67. Install the fan.

68. Install the fan shroud.

69. Connect the radiator hoses and the automatic transmission cooler lines, if any.

70. Install the accelerator cable bracket and the heater hoses.

71. On EFI models, connect the throttle bracket to the upper intake manifold.

72. Connect the fuel tank-to-pump fuel line at the fuel pump. On trucks with EFI, disconnect the chassis fuel line at the fuel rails.

73. Connect the lines at the compressor.

74. Install the condenser.

75. Install the air conditioning condenser upper mounting brackets.

76. Install the hood lock support.

77. Install the upper grille support bracket.

78. Install the grille, and gravel deflector.

79. Install the bumper.

80. Connect the battery.

81. On carbureted engines, install the air cleaner and intake duct assembly, plus the crankcase ventilation hose.

82. On fuel injected engines, install the air intake hoses, PCV tube and carbon canister hose.

83. Fill the cooling system.

84. Charge the air conditioning system. See Chapter 1.

85. Run the engine and check for leaks.

86. Install the engine cover.

If the torque for a particular fastener was not mentioned above, use the following torque values as a guide:

- ¼"-20: 6-9 ft.lb.
- $^5/_{16}$"-18: 12-18 ft.lb.
- ⅜"-16: 22-32 ft.lb.
- $^7/_{16}$"-14: 45-57 ft.lb.
- ½"-13: 55-80 ft.lb.
- $^9/_{16}$": 85-120 ft.lb.

1988 8-460 (7.5L)

WARNING: *When working on fuel injected engines, discharge the fuel system pressure before starting any work that involves disconnecting the fuel system lines. See Fuel Supply Manifold Removal and Installation procedures in Chapter 5.*

1. Remove the hood and engine cover.

2. Drain the cooling system.

CAUTION: *When draining the coolant, keep in mind that cats and dogs are attracted by the ethylene glycol antifreeze, and are quite likely to drink any that is left in an uncovered container or in puddles on the ground. This will prove fatal in sufficient quantity. Always drain the coolant into a sealable container. Coolant should be reused unless it is contaminated or several years old.*

3. Disconnect the negative battery cable from the block.

4. Remove the air cleaner assembly.

5. Remove the crankcase ventilation hose.

6. Remove the canister hose.

7. Disconnect the upper and lower radiator hoses.

8. Disconnect the transmission oil cooler lines from the radiator.

9. Disconnect the engine oil cooler lines at the oil filter adapter.

WARNING: *Don't disconnect the lines at the quick-connect fittings behind or at the oil cooler. Disconnecting them may permanently damage them.*

10. Discharge the air conditioning system. See Chapter 1.

11. Disconnect the refrigerant lines at the compressor. Cap the openings at once!

12. Disconnect the refrigerant lines at the condenser. Cap the openings at once!

13. Remove the condenser.

14. Remove the fan shroud from the radiator and position it up, over the fan.

15. Remove the radiator.

16. Remove the fan shroud.

17. Remove the fan, belts and pulley from the water pump.

18. Remove the compressor.

19. Remove the power steering pump from the engine, if so equipped, and position it to one side. Do not disconnect the fluid lines.

20. Disconnect the fuel pump inlet line from the pump and plug the line.

21. Disconnect the oil pressure sending unit wire at the sending unit.

22. Remove the alternator drive belts and disconnect the alternator from the engine, positioning it aside.

23. Disconnect the ground cable from the right front corner of the engine.

24. Disconnect the heater hoses.

25. Remove the transmission fluid filler tube attaching bolt from the right side valve cover and position the tube out of the way.

26. Disconnect all vacuum lines at the rear of the intake manifold.

27. Disconnect the speed control cable at the carburetor, if so equipped.

28. Disconnect the accelerator rod and the transmission kickdown rod and secure them out of the way.

29. Disconnect the engine wiring harness at the connector on the fire wall. Disconnect the primary wire at the coil.

30. Remove the upper flywheel housing-to-engine bolts.

31. Raise the vehicle and disconnect the exhaust pipes at the exhaust manifolds.

32. Disconnect the starter cable and remove the starter. Bring the starter forward and rotate the solenoid outward to remove the assembly.

33. Remove the access cover from the converter housing and remove the flywheel-to-converter attaching nuts.

34. Remove the lower the converter housing-to-engine attaching bolts.

35. Remove the engine mount through bolts attaching the rubber insulator to the frame brackets.

36. Lower the vehicle and place a jack under the transmission to support it.

37. Remove the converter housing-to-engine block attaching bolts (left side).

38. Remove the coil and bracket assembly from the intake manifold.

39. Attach an engine lifting device and carefully take up the weight of the engine.

40. Move the engine forward to disengage it from the transmission and slowly lift it from the truck.

To install the engine:

41. Lower the engine slowly into the truck.

42. Slide the engine rearward to engage it with the transmission and slowly lower it onto the supports.

43. Install the engine support nuts and torque them to 74 ft.lb.

44. Remove the engine lifting device.

45. Install the converter housing-to-engine block upper and left side attaching bolts. Torque the bolts to 50 ft.lb.

46. Install the coil and bracket assembly on the intake manifold.

47. Remove the jack from under the transmission.

48. Lower the truck.

49. Install the upper converter housing-to-engine attaching bolts. Torque the bolts to 50 ft.lb.

50. Install the flywheel-to-converter attaching nuts. Torque the nuts to 34 ft.lb.

51. Install the access cover on the converter housing. Torque the bolts to 60-90 in.lb.

52. Install the starter.

53. Connect the starter cable.

54. Raise the vehicle and connect the exhaust pipes at the exhaust manifolds.

55. Connect the engine wiring harness at the connector on the fire wall.

56. Connect the primary wire at the coil.

57. Connect the accelerator rod and the transmission kickdown rod.

58. Connect the speed control cable.

59. Connect all vacuum lines at the rear of the intake manifold.

60. Install the transmission fluid filler tube attaching bolt from the right side valve cover and position the tube out of the way.

61. Connect the heater hoses.

62. Connect the ground cable at the right front corner of the engine.

63. Install the alternator and drive belts.

64. Connect the oil pressure sending unit wire at the sending unit.

65. Connect the fuel pump inlet line at the pump and plug the line.

66. Install the power steering pump and belt.

67. Install air conditioning compressor. Connect the refrigerant lines.

68. Install the fan, belts and pulley on the water pump.

69. Position the fan shroud over the fan.

70. Install the radiator.

71. Attach the fan shroud.

72. Install the condenser.

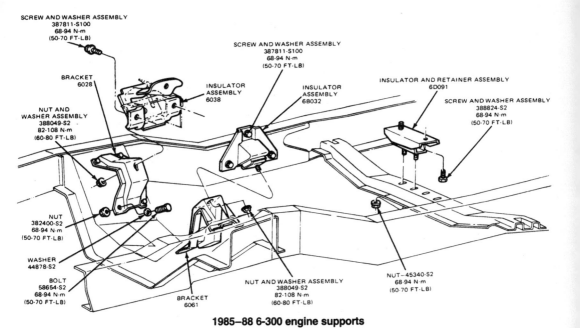

SCREW AND WASHER ASSEMBLY
387811-S100
68-94 N·m
(50-70 FT-LB)

BRACKET
6028

NUT AND
WASHER ASSEMBLY
388049-S2
82-108 N·m
(60-80 FT-LB)

SCREW AND WASHER ASSEMBLY
387811-S100
68-94 N·m
(50-70 FT-LB)

INSULATOR
ASSEMBLY
6038

INSULATOR
ASSEMBLY
68032

INSULATOR AND RETAINER ASSEMBLY
6D091

SCREW AND WASHER ASSEMBLY
388824-S2
68-94 N·m
(50-70 FT-LB)

NUT
382400-S2
68-94 N·m
(50-70 FT-LB)

WASHER
44878-S2

BOLT
58654-S2
68-94 N·m
(50-70 FT-LB)

BRACKET
6061

NUT AND WASHER ASSEMBLY
388049-S2
82-108 N·m
(60-80 FT-LB)

NUT—45340-S2
68-94 N·m
(50-70 FT-LB)

1985–88 6-300 engine supports

73. Connect the refrigerant lines at the condenser.

74. Charge the air conditioning system. See Chapter 1.

75. Connect the engine oil cooler lines at the oil filter adapter.

76. Connect the transmission oil cooler lines at the radiator.

77. Connect the upper and lower radiator hoses.

78. Connect the canister hose.

79. Connect the crankcase ventilation hose.

80. Connect the negative battery cable from the block.

81. Fill the cooling system.

82. Install the air cleaner assembly.

83. Install the hood.

If the torque for a particular fastener was not mentioned above, use the following torque values as a guide:

- 1/4"-20: 6-9 ft.lb.
- 5/16"-18: 12-18 ft.lb.
- 3/8"-16: 22-32 ft.lb.
- 7/16"-14: 45-57 ft.lb.
- 1/2"-13: 55-80 ft.lb.
- 9/16": 85-120 ft.lb.

8-420 (6.9L), 8-444 (7.3L) Diesel Engine.

1. Take off the hood and engine cover.

2. Drain the coolant.

CAUTION: *When draining the coolant, keep in mind that cats and dogs are attracted by the ethylene glycol antifreeze, and are quite likely to drink any that is left in an uncovered container or in puddles on the ground. This*

will prove fatal in sufficient quantity. Always drain the coolant into a sealable container. Coolant should be reused unless it is contaminated or several years old.

3. Remove the air cleaner and intake duct assembly and cover the air intake opening with a clean rag to keep out dirt.

4. Remove the upper grille support bracket.

5. Remove the upper air condenser mounting brackets.

WARNING: *On vehicles equipped with air conditioning, the system must be discharged to remove the condenser. See Chapter 1.*

6. Disconnect the lines at the compressor.

7. Remove the radiator fan shroud halves.

8. Remove the fan and clutch assembly as described under water pump removal in this chapter.

NOTE: *The fan clutch uses left hand threaded bolts. Remove it by turning them clockwise.*

9. Detach the radiator hoses and the transmission cooler lines, if so equipped.

10. Remove the radiator assembly.

11. Remove the power steering pump and position it out of the way.

12. Disconnect the fuel supply line heater.

13. Disconnect the alternator wires at the alternator.

14. Disconnect the oil pressure sending unit wire at the sending unit, remove the sender from the dash panel and lay it on the engine.

15. Disconnect the accelerator cable and the speed control cable, if so equipped, from the injection pump. Remove the cable bracket with

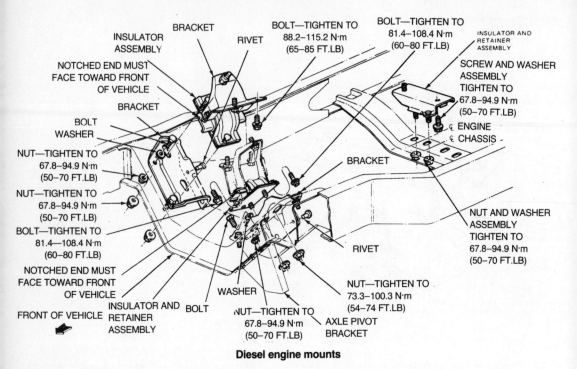

Diesel engine mounts

cables attached, from the intake manifold and position it out of the way.

16. Disconnect the transmission kickdown rod from the injection pump, if so equipped.

17. Disconnect the main wiring harness connector from the right side of the engine and the ground strap from the rear of the engine.

18. Remove the fuel return hose from the left rear of the engine.

19. Remove the two upper transmission-to-engine attaching bolts.

20. Disconnect the heater hoses from the engine.

21. Disconnect the water temperature sender wire.

22. Disconnect the overheat light switch wire and position the wires out of the way.

23. Raise the truck and support on jackstands.

24. Disconnect the battery ground cables from the front of the engine.

25. Disconnect the starter cables from the starter.

26. Remove and plug the fuel line at the fuel pump.

27. Detach the exhaust pipe at the exhaust manifold.

28. Disconnect the engine insulators from the no. 1 crossmember.

29. Remove the flywheel inspection plate and the four converter-to-flywheel attaching nuts, if so equipped.

30. Remove the jackstands and lower the truck.

31. While supporting the transmission, remove the four lower transmission attaching bolts.

32. Attach an engine lifting sling and remove the engine from the truck.

To install the engine:

33. Lower the engine into the truck.

34. Align the converter with the flex plate and the engine dowels with the transmission.

35. While supporting the transmission, install the four lower transmission attaching bolts.

36. Install the four converter-to-flywheel attaching nuts, if so equipped, and the flywheel inspection plate.

37. Connect the engine insulators to the no. 1 crossmember.

38. Connect the exhaust pipe at the exhaust manifold.

39. Install the fuel line at the fuel pump.

40. Connect the starter cables at the starter.

41. Connect the battery ground cables at the front of the engine.

42. Lower the truck.

43. Connect the overheat light switch wire.

44. Connect the water temperature sender wire.

45. Connect the heater hoses at the engine.

46. Install the two upper transmission-to-engine attaching bolts.

47. Install the fuel return hose at the left rear of the engine.

48. Connect the main wiring harness connector at the right side of the engine and the ground strap at the rear of the engine.

49. Connect the transmission kickdown rod at the injection pump, if so equipped.

50. Connect the accelerator cable and the speed control cable, if so equipped, to the injection pump. Install the cable bracket with cables attached, to the intake manifold.

51. Install the oil pressure sender on the dash panel and connect the oil pressure sending unit wire at the sending unit.

52. Connect the alternator wires at the alternator.

53. Connect the fuel supply line heater.

54. Install the power steering pump.

55. Install the radiator assembly.

56. Connect the radiator hoses and the transmission cooler lines, if so equipped.

57. Install the fan and clutch assembly as described under water pump removal in this chapter.

NOTE: *The fan clutch uses left hand threaded bolts. Install it by turning them counterclockwise.*

58. Install the radiator fan shroud halves.

59. Connect the lines at the compressor.

60. Install the upper air condenser mounting brackets.

61. Install the upper grille support bracket.

62. Install the air cleaner and intake duct assembly.

63. Fill the cooling system.

64. Fill the crankcase.

65. Charge the air conditioning system. See Chapter 1.

66. Run the engine and check for leaks.

67. Install the hood and engine cover.

If the torque for a particular fastener was not mentioned above, use the following torque values as a guide:

- $\frac{1}{4}$"-20: 6-9 ft.lb.
- $\frac{5}{16}$"-18: 12-18 ft.lb.
- $\frac{3}{8}$"-16: 22-32 ft.lb.

- $\frac{7}{16}$"-14: 45-57 ft.lb.
- $\frac{1}{2}$"-13: 55-80 ft.lb.
- $\frac{9}{16}$": 85-120 ft.lb.

Rocker Arm Cover

REMOVAL AND INSTALLATION

6-144 (2.4L)
6-170 (2.8L)
6-200 (3.3L)

1. Remove the air cleaner. Pull the PCV hose and valve out of the rubber grommet in the rocker arm cover and place the hose to the side, out of the way.

2. Disconnect the carburetor air vent tube; then remove the rocker arm cover, discarding the gasket.

3. Clean the valve rocker arm cover and cylinder head gasket surfaces.

4. Coat a new gasket with non-hardening gasket sealer and install the gasket in the cover mating surface, making sure that all of the tangs of the gasket are engaged in the notches provided in the cover.

5. Position the cover and gasket on the head.

6. Install the attaching bolts and torque them to 36-60 in.lb.

7. Connect all vacuum lines and components to their proper connection.

8. Retorque the cover bolts to the same specifications.

9. Install the crankcase ventilation system and the air cleaner.

6-240 (3.9L)
6-300 (4.9L)

WARNING: *When working on fuel injected engines, discharge the fuel system pressure before starting any work that involves disconnecting the fuel system lines. See Fuel Supply Manifold Removal and Installation procedures in Chapter 5.*

1. Disconnect the inlet air hose at the oil fill cap. Remove the air cleaner.

2. Disconnect the accelerator cable at the carburetor or throttle body. Remove the cable

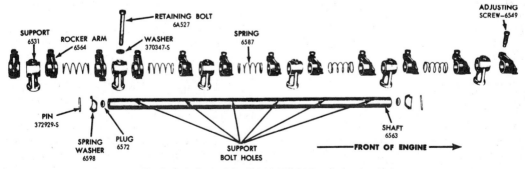

Exploded view of the 6-144,170,200 rocker arm shaft

retracting spring. Remove the accelerator cable bracket from the cylinder head and position the cable and bracket assembly out of the way.

3. Remove the PCV valve from the valve rocker arm cover. Remove the cover bolts and remove the valve rocker arm cover.

4. Clean the valve rocker arm cover and the cylinder head gasket surface.

5. Place the new gasket in the cover making sure that the tabs of the gasket engage in the notches provided in the cover.

6. Install the cover on the cylinder head. Make sure the gasket seats evenly all around the head. Partially tighten the cover bolts in sequence, starting at the middle bolts. Then tighten the bolts to 36-60 in.lb.

7. Install the PCV valve in the rocker arm cover.

8. Install the accelerator cable bracket on the cylinder head and connect the cable to the carburetor.

9. Connect the inlet air hose to the oil fill cap.

10. Install the air cleaner.

1969-77 8-302 (5.0L)

1. Remove the air cleaner and intake duct assembly.

2. Remove the PCV valve and hose from the rocker cover. If the engine is equipped with the Thermactor exhaust emission control system, disconnect the air hose and remove the check valve from the right air manifold.

3. Disconnect the spark plug wires from the spark plugs. Remove the wires from the bracket on top of the rocker cover and position them out of the way.

4. If the engine is equipped with the Thermactor exhaust emission control system, disconnect the air hose at the left air manifold.

5. Remove the rocker cover(s).

6. Clean the valve rocker arm cover and the cylinder head gasket surface.

7. Place the new gasket in the cover making sure that the tabs of the gasket engage in the notches provided in the cover.

8. Install the cover on the cylinder head. Make sure the gasket seats evenly all around the head. Partially tighten the cover bolts in sequence, starting at the middle bolts. Then tighten the bolts to 36-60 in.lb.

9. Install all other parts in reverse order of removal.

1978-88 8-302 (5.0L)
1980-88 8-351W (5.7L)
1984-86 8-351HO (5.7L)

WARNING: *When working on fuel injected engines, discharge the fuel system pressure before starting any work that involves disconnecting the fuel system lines. See Fuel Supply*

Manifold Removal and Installation procedures in Chapter 5.

1. Remove air cleaner and intake duct assembly, including the closed crankcase ventilation hoses. On 8-302 Canadian vans remove vacuum lines and electric solenoid. Remove vacuum solenoid left hand cover only.

2. Remove the PCV valve from the right rocker arm cover.

3. Disconnect the spark plug wires from the spark plugs by grasping, twisting and pulling the molded cap using Tool No. T68P-6666-A or equivalent. Remove the wires and bracket assemblies from the rocker arm cover attaching studs and position out of the way.

4. Remove low voltage wiring clips. Remove rocker arm cover(s).

5. Clean and inspect gasket surfaces. Inspect the gasket sealing surface for damages and distortion due to overtightening of the bolt. Repair and straighten as required.

6. Place the new gaskets in the covers making sure that the tabs of the gasket engage in the notches provided in the cover. Position the cover(s) on the cylinder head(s). Install the bolts and tighten to 36-60 in.lb. Two minutes later tighten the bolts to the same specifications.

7. Install the low voltage wiring clips. Insert the spark plug wires and bracket assembly on the attaching stud on the rocker arm cover(s) and connect the wires to the spark plugs.

8. Install the PCV valve into the oil filler cap in the rocker arm cover. Install the vacuum solenoid, connect the vacuum harness and electric connectors.

9. Install the air cleaner and intake duct assembly, including the crankcase ventilation hoses.

8-400 (6.6L)
8-460 (7.5L)

WARNING: *When working on fuel injected engines, discharge the fuel system pressure before starting any work that involves disconnecting the fuel system lines. See Fuel Supply Manifold Removal and Installation procedures in Chapter 5.*

1. Remove the air cleaner and intake duct assembly. Remove the appropriate crankcase ventilation hose(s) at the valve rocker arm cover(s).

2. Disconnect the spark plug wires form the spark plugs by grasping, twisting, and pulling the molded cap with Tool T74P-6666-A or equivalent. Remove the wires from the bracket on the valve rocker arm cover(s) and position the wire out of the way.

3. Remove the valve rocker arm cover(s).

4. Clean the valve rocker arm cover(s) and the cylinder head gasket surface(s). Apply oil resistant sealer to one side of new cover gas-

ket(s). Lay the cemented side of the gasket(s) in place in the cover(s).

5. Position the cover(s) on the cylinder head(s). Make sure the gasket seats evenly all around the head. Install the bolts. The cover is tightened in two steps. Tighten the bolts to 36-60 in.lb. Two minutes later, tighten the bolts to the same specification.

6. Reconnect the crankcase ventilation hose(s).

7. Install the air cleaner and intake duct assembly.

8. Install the spark plug wires in the bracket on the valve rocker arm cover(s). Connect the spark plug wires.

9. Start the engine and check for leaks.

8-420 (6.9L) and 8-444 (7.3L) Diesel

1. Disconnect the ground cables from both batteries.

2. Remove the valve cover attaching screws and remove both valve covers.

3. Clean the cover and head gasket mating surfaces thoroughly.

4. Coat new valve cover gaskets with non-hardening gasket sealer and install them on the heads.

5. Install the valve covers. Torque the bolts to 36-60 in.lb.

6. Install the battery cables, start the engine and check for leaks.

Rocker Arms and/or Shafts
REMOVAL AND INSTALLATION
6-144 (2.4L)
6-170 (2.8L)
6-200 (3.3L)

1. Remove the air cleaner. Pull the PCV hose and valve out of the rubber grommet in the rocker arm cover and place the hose to the side, out of the way.

2. Disconnect the carburetor air vent tube; then remove the rocker arm cover, discarding the gasket.

3. Remove the rocker arm shaft support bolts by loosening the bolts two turns at a time in sequence.

4. Remove the rocker arm shaft assembly.
NOTE: *If the pushrods are removed, they must be replaced in the same position from which they were removed.*

5. Remove the pin and spring washer from each end of the valve rocker arm shaft.

6. Slide the valve rocker arms, springs and supports off the shaft. Be sure to identify the parts.

7. If it is necessary to remove the plugs from each end of the shaft, drill or pierce the plug on

one end. Working from the open end, knock out the remaining plug.

8. On reassembly all valves, valve stems and valve guides are to be lubricated with SAE 10W-40 SF engine oil. The valve tips are to have Lubriplate® or equivalent applied. The Lubriplate® is to be applied before installation. All rocker arm shafts are to be lubricated with 10W/40 SF engine oil before installation.

9. If the plugs were removed from the ends of the shaft, use a blunt tool or large diameter pin punch and install a plug, cup side out, in each end of the shaft.

10. Install the spring washer and pin on one end of the shaft.

11. Apply Lubriplate® or equivalent to both ends of the pushrods and to the valve stem tip.

12. Install the valve pushrods. Position the valve rocker arm shaft assembly on the cylinder head.

13. Install and tighten all valve rocker arm support bolts, two turns at a time in sequence, until the supports fully contact the cylinder head. Torque the bolts to 30-35 ft.lb.

14. Check the valve clearance and adjust if necessary.

15. If any part which could affect the valve clearance has been changed, check the valve clearance.

16. Clean the valve rocker arm cover and cylinder head gasket surfaces.

17. Install the gasket in the cover making sure that all of the tangs of the gasket are engaged in the notches provided in the cover.

18. Tighten the cover attaching bolts in two steps. First, torque the bolts to 36-60 in.lb.; then, retorque to the same specifications two minutes after initial tightening.

19. Connect all vacuum lines and components to their proper connection.

20. Install the crankcase ventilation system and the air cleaner.

6-240 (3.9L)
6-300 (4.9L)

WARNING: *When working on fuel injected engines, discharge the fuel system pressure before starting any work that involves disconnecting the fuel system lines. See Fuel Supply Manifold Removal and Installation procedures in Chapter 5.*

1. Disconnect the inlet air hose at the oil fill cap. Remove the air cleaner.

2. Disconnect the accelerator cable at the carburetor or throttle body. Remove the cable retracting spring. Remove the accelerator cable bracket from the cylinder head and position the cable and bracket assembly out of the way.

3. Remove the PCV valve from the valve

rocker arm cover. Remove the cover bolts and remove the valve rocker arm cover.

4. Remove the valve rocker arm stud nut, fulcrum seat and rocker arm. Inspect the rocker arm cover bolts for worn or damaged seals under the bolt heads and replace as necessary. If it is necessary to remove a rocker arm stud, see the procedures below.

5. Apply Lubriplate® or equivalent to the top of the valve stem and at the pushrod guide in the cylinder head.

6. Apply Lubriplate® or equivalent to the rocker arm fulcrum seat and the fulcrum seat socket in the rocker arm. Install the valve rocker arm, fulcrum seat and stud nut. Adjust the valve clearance.

7. Clean the valve rocker arm cover and the cylinder head gasket surface. Place the new gasket in the cover making sure that the tabs of the gasket engage in the notches provided in the cover.

8. Install the cover on the cylinder head. Make sure the gasket seats evenly all around the head. Partially tighten the cover bolts in sequence, starting at the middle bolts. Then tighten the bolts to 36-60 in.lb.

9. Install the PCV valve in the rocker arm cover. Install the accelerator cable bracket on the cylinder head and connect the cable to the carburetor.

10. Connect the inlet air hose to the oil fill cap.

11. Install air cleaner.

1969-77 8-302 (5.0L)

1. Remove the air cleaner and intake duct assembly.

2. Remove the PCV valve and hose from the rocker cover. If the engine is equipped with the Thermactor exhaust emission control system, disconnect the air hose and remove the check valve from the right air manifold.

3. Disconnect the spark plug wires from the spark plugs. Remove the wires from the bracket on top of the rocker cover and position them out of the way.

4. If the engine is equipped with the Thermactor exhaust emission control system, disconnect the air hose at the left air manifold.

5. Remove the rocker cover(s).

6. Before removing any of the valve rocker arms, check the torque required to turn the adjusting nut counterclockwise. It should be between 4.5-15 ft.lb. If it is below these specifications replace the stud and/or the nut.

7. Remove the valve rocker arm stud nut, fulcrum seat and rocker arm. If you have to remove or replace a rocker stud, see the procedures below.

8. Assemble the engine in the reverse order

of disassemble. Adjust the valve lash as outlined in Chapter 2.

1978-88 8-302 (5.0L)
1980-88 8-351W (5.7L)
1984-86 8-351HO (5.7L)

WARNING: *When working on fuel injected engines, discharge the fuel system pressure before starting any work that involves disconnecting the fuel system lines. See Fuel Supply Manifold Removal and Installation procedures in Chapter 5.*

1. Remove the air cleaner and intake duct assembly, including the closed crankcase ventilation hoses. On 8-302 Canadian models, remove the vacuum lines and electric solenoid. Remove the vacuum solenoid left hand cover only.

2. Remove the PCV valve from the right rocker arm cover.

3. Disconnect the spark plug wires from the spark plugs by grasping, twisting and pulling the molded cap using Tool No. T68P-6666-A or equivalent. Remove the wires and bracket assemblies from the rocker arm cover attaching studs and position out of the way.

4. Remove low voltage wiring clips. Remove the rocker arm cover(s).

5. Remove the valve rocker arm fulcrum bolt, fulcrum arm and fulcrum guide.

6. Apply Lubriplate® or equivalent to the top of the valve stem, the fulcrum and socket.

7. Install the fulcrum guide, valve rocker arm, fulcrum and fulcrum bolt. Tighten to 18-24 ft.lb.

8. Clean and inspect the gasket surfaces. Inspect the gasket sealing surface for damages and distortion due to overtightening of the bolts. Repair and straighten as required.

9. Place the new gaskets in the covers making sure that the tabs of the gasket engage the notches provided in the cover. Position the cover(s) on the cylinder head(s). Install the bolts and tighten to 3-5 ft.lb. Two minutes later tighten the bolts to the same specifications.

10. Install the low voltage wiring clips. Insert the spark plug wires and bracket assembly on the attaching stud on the rocker arm cover(s) and connect the wires to the spark plugs.

11. Install the PCV valve into the oil filler cap in the rocker arm cover. Install the vacuum solenoid, connect the vacuum harness and electric connectors.

12. Install the air cleaner and intake duct assembly, including the crankcase ventilation hoses.

8-400 (6.6L)
8-460 (7.5L)

WARNING: *When working on fuel injected engines, discharge the fuel system pressure before starting any work that involves discon-necting the fuel system lines. See Fuel Supply Manifold Removal and Installation proce-dures in Chapter 5.*

1. Remove the air cleaner and intake duct assembly. Remove the appropriate crankcase ventilation hose(s) at the valve rocker arm cover(s).

2. Disconnect the spark plug wires form the spark plugs by grasping, twisting, and pulling the molded cap with Tool T74P-6666-A or equivalent. Remove the wires from the bracket on the valve rocker arm cover(s) and position the wire out of the way.

3. Remove the valve rocker arm cover(s).

4. Remove the valve rocker arm bolt, oil deflector, fulcrum seat and rocker arm.

All rocker arms and fulcrum seats are to be lubricated with heavy engine oil SE before installation.

5. Apply Lubriplate® or equivalent to the top of the valve stem. Lubricate the rocker arm and fulcrum seat with 10W/40 SF engine oil.

6. Position the No. 1 piston on TDC at the end of the compression stroke and install the rocker arm, fulcrum seat, on deflector, and fulcrum bolts on the following valves:

- No. 1 Intake No. 1 Exhaust
- No. 4 Intake No. 3 Exhaust
- No. 8 Intake No. 7 Exhaust

Turn the crankshaft 180° and install the rocker arm, fulcrum seat, oil deflector and fulcrum bolts on the following valves:

- No. 3 Intake No. 2 Exhaust
- No. 7 Intake No. 6 Exhaust

Turn the crankshaft 270° and install the rocker arm, fulcrum seat, oil deflector and fulcrum bolts on the following valves:

- No. 2 Intake No. 4 Exhaust
- No. 5 Intake No. 5 Exhaust
- No. 6 Intake No. 8 Exhaust

Be sure that the fulcrum seat base is seated in its slot on the cylinder head before tightening the fulcrum bolts. Tighten the fulcrum bolt to 18-24 ft.lb. Check the valve clearance.

7. Clean the valve rocker arm cover(s) and the cylinder head gasket surface(s). Apply oil resistant sealer to one side of new cover gasket(s). Lay the cemented side of the gasket(s) in place in the cover(s).

8. Position the cover(s) on the cylinder head(s). Make sure the gasket seats evenly all around the head. Install the bolts. The cover is tightened in two steps. Tighten the bolts to 3-5 lb. Two minutes later, tighten the bolts to the same specification.

9. Reconnect the crankcase ventilation hose(s).

10. Install the air cleaner and intake duct assembly.

11. Install the spark plug wires in the bracket on the valve rocker arm cover(s). Connect the spark plug wires.

12. Start the engine and check for leaks.

8-420 (6.9L) and 8-444 (7.3L) Diesel V8

1. Disconnect the ground cables from both batteries.

2. Remove the valve cover attaching screws and remove both valve cover.

3. Remove the valve rocker arm post mounting bolts. Remove the rocker arms and posts in order and mark them with tape so they can be installed in their original positions.

4. If the cylinder heads are to be removed, then the pushrods can now be removed. Make a holder for the pushrods out of a piece of wood or cardboard, and remove the pushrods in order. It is very important that the pushrods be re-installed in their original order. The pushrods can remain in position if no further disassembly is required.

5. If the pushrods were removed, install them in their original locations. make sure they are fully seated in the tappet seats.

NOTE: *The copper colored end of the push-rod goes toward the rocker arm.*

6. Apply a polyethylene grease to the valve stem tips. Install the rocker arms and posts in their original positions.

7. Turn the engine over by hand until the valve timing mark is at the 11:00 position, as viewed from the front of the engine. Install all of the rocker arm post attaching bolts and torque to 27 ft.lb.

8. Install new valve cover gaskets and install the valve cover. Install the battery cables, start the engine and check for leaks.

Rocker Studs
REMOVAL AND INSTALLATION

6-240 (3.9L)
6-300 (4.9L)

1. If it is necessary to remove a rocker arm stud, Tool T79T-6527-A is available. A 0.006" (0.15mm) oversize reamer T62F-6527-B3 or equivalent and a 0.015" (0.38mm) oversize reamer T62F-6527-B5 or equivalent are available. For 0.010" (0.254mm) oversize studs, use reamer T66P-6527-B or equivalent. To press in replacement studs, or use stud replacer T79T-6527-B or equivalent for 6-300.

Rocker arm studs that are broken or have damaged threads may be replaced with standard studs. Loose studs in the head may be replaced with 0.006" (0.152mm), 0.010" (0.254mm) or 0.015" (0.38mm) oversize studs which are available for service.

Standard and oversize studs can be identified by measuring the stud diameter within 1⅛"

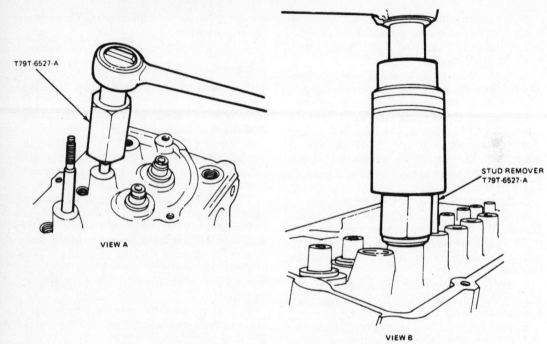

Removing the rocker arm stud on the 6-240,300

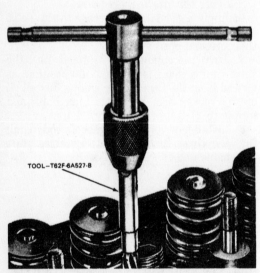

Reaming the rocker arm stud hole on the 6-240,300

2. Position the sleeve of the rocker arm stud remover over the stud with the bearing end down. Thread the puller into the sleeve and over the stud until it is fully bottomed. Hold the sleeve with a wrench; then, rotate the puller clockwise to remove the stud.

If the rocker arm stud was broken off flush with the stud boss, use an easy-out to remove the broken stud following the instructions of the tool manufacturer.

3. If a loose rocker arm stud is being replaced, ream the stud bore using the proper reamer (or reamers in sequence) for the selected oversize stud. Make sure the metal particles do not enter the valve area.

4. Coat the end of the stud with Lubriplate®

(28.6mm) from the pilot end of the stud. The stud diameters are:

- 0.006" (0.152mm) oversize: 0.3774-0.3781" (9.586-9.603mm)
- 0.010" (0.254mm) oversize: 0.3814-0.3821" (9.688-9.705mm)
- 0.015" (0.381mm) oversize: 0.3864-0.3871" (9.814-9.832mm)

When going from a standard size rocker arm stud to a 0.010" (0.254mm) or 0.015" (0.38mm) oversize stud, always use the 0.006" (0.152mm) oversize reamer before finish reaming with the 0.010" (0.254mm) or 0.015" (0.381mm) oversize reamer.

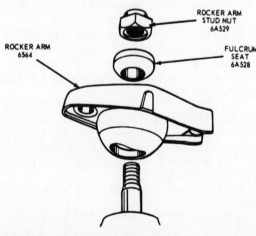

6-240,300 valve rocker arm assembly

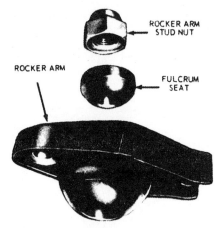

1969–78 V8 rocker arm assembly

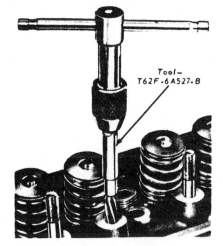

Reaming the rocker arm stud bore on V8 engines

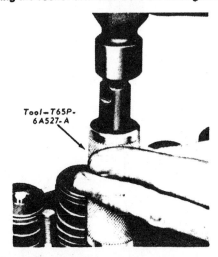

Installing a new rocker arm stud

or it's equivalent. Align the stud with the stud bore; then, tap the sliding driver until it bottoms. When the driver contacts the stud boss, the stud is installed to its correct height.

Gasoline V8

1. To remove the rocker arm stud, which is pressed into the cylinder head, put spaces over the stud until just enough threads are left showing at the top so a nut can be screwed onto the top of the rocker arm stud and get a full bite. Turn the nut clockwise until the stud is re-

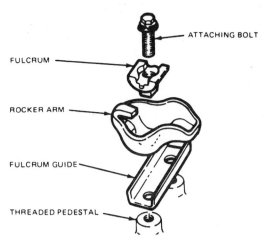

Valve rocker arm assembly for the 8-302,351W 1979 and later

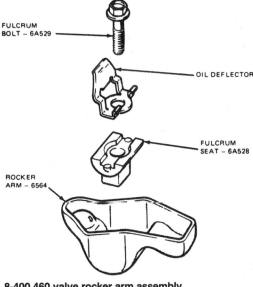

8-400,460 valve rocker arm assembly

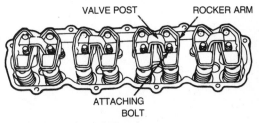

Diesel rocker arm assembly

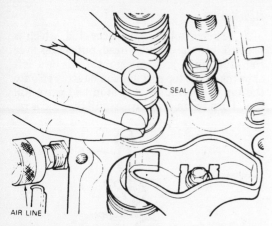

Replacing the valve stem seal

stud mounting hole with a 0.006″ (0.152mm) oversize reamer first, before using the 0.010″ (0.254mm) or 0.015″ (0.381mm) oversize studs. Do not allow metal chips to get down around the valves.

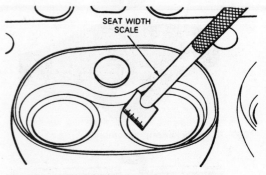

Checking valve seat width

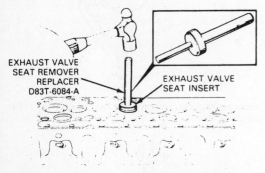

Installing the exhaust seat inserts on the diesel

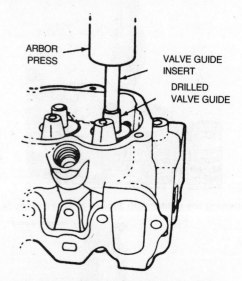

Installing the valve guide inserts on the diesel

moved, adding spacers under the nut as necessary.

Rocker arm studs that are being replaced because of damaged threads or are broken off, may be replaced with standard size replacement studs. If the stud is being replaced because it is loose in the head, it may be replaced with 0.006″ (0.152mm), 0.010″ (0.254mm) or 0.015″ (0.381mm) oversize studs. Ream the

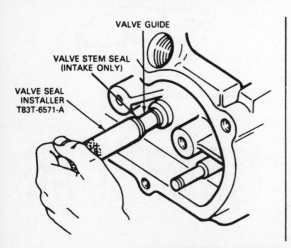

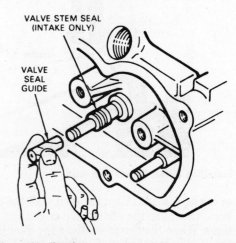

Installing the valve stem seals on the diesel

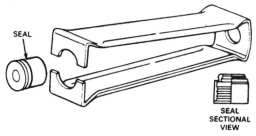

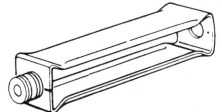

Valve stem seal installation tool for the 8-460

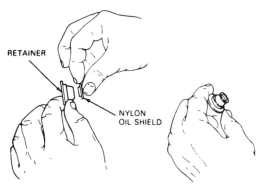

Installing the nylon oil shield

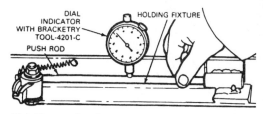

Checking pushrod runout

STEP 1 - SET NO. 1 PISTON ON T.D.C. AT END OF COMPRESSION STROKE ADJUST NO. 1 INTAKE AND EXHAUST

STEP 4 - CHECK NO. 6 INTAKE AND EXHAUST

STEP 2 - CHECK NO. 5 INTAKE AND EXHAUST

STEP 5 - CHECK NO. 2 INTAKE AND EXHAUST

STEP 3 - CHECK NO. 3 INTAKE AND EXHAUST

STEP 6 - CHECK NO. 4 INTAKE AND EXHAUST

6-300 valve clearance checking

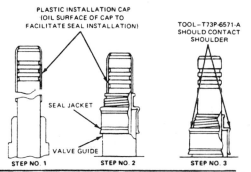

STEP NO. 1– WITH VALVES IN HEAD PLACE PLASTIC INSTALLATION CAP OVER END OF VALVE STEM.

STEP NO. 2– START VALVE STEM SEAL CAREFULLY OVER CAP. PUSH SEAL DOWN UNTIL JACKET TOUCHES TOP OF GUIDE.

STEP NO. 3– REMOVE PLASTIC INSTALLATION CAP. USE INSTALLATION TOOL–T73P-6571-A OR SCREWDRIVERS TO BOTTOM SEAL ON VALVE GUIDE.

Valve stem seal installation

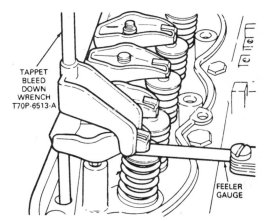

Valve clearance check

To install the rocker arm studs, it is necessary to have a rocker arm stud installer tool, which is readily available in automotive parts and supply stores. The Ford tool number is shown in the accompanying pictures.

2. Screw the new stud into the installer tool and coat the end of the stud with Lubriplate®. Align the stud and installer with the stud bore and tap the tool until it bottoms against the cylinder head. At this point, the stud is installed to the correct height.

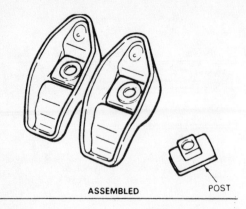

ASSEMBLED   POST

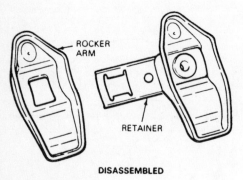

ROCKER ARM

RETAINER

DISASSEMBLED

Diesel rocker arms

HYDRAULIC VALVE LIFTER INSPECTION

NOTE: *The lifters used on diesel engines require a special test fluid, kerosene is not satisfactory.*

Remove the lifters from their bores and remove any gum and varnish with safe solvent. Check the lifters for concave wear. If the bottom of the lifter is worn concave or flat, replace the lifter. Lifters are built with a convex bottom, flatness indicates wear. If a worn lifter is detected, carefully check the camshaft for wear.

To test lifter leak down, submerge the lifter in a container of kerosene. Chuck a used pushrod or its equivalent into a drill press. Position the container of kerosene so the pushrod acts on the lifter plunger. Pump the lifter with the drill press until resistance increases. Pump several more times to bleed any air from the lifter. Apply very firm, constant pressure to the lifter and observe the rate which fluid bleeds out of the lifter. If the lifter bleeds down very quickly (less than 15 seconds), the lifter should be replaced. If the time exceeds 60 seconds, the lifter is sticking and should be cleaned or replaced. If the lifter is operating properly (leak down time 15-60 seconds) and not worn, lubricate and reinstall in engine.

NOTE: *Always inspect the valve pushrods for wear, straightness and oil blockage. Dam-*

aged pushrods will cause erratic valve operation.

Thermostat

NOTE: *It is a good practice to check the operation of a new thermostat before it is installed in an engine. Place the thermostat in a pan of boiling water. If it does not open more than ¼" (6mm), do not install it in the engine.*

REMOVAL AND INSTALLATION

6-144 (2.4L)
6-170 (2.8L)
6-200 (3.3L)
6-240 (3.9L)
6-300 (4.9L)

1. Drain the cooling system below the level of the coolant outlet housing. Use the petcock valve at the bottom of the radiator to drain the system. It is not necessary to remove any of the hoses.

CAUTION: *When draining the coolant, keep in mind that cats and dogs are attracted by the ethylene glycol antifreeze, and are quite likely to drink any that is left in an uncovered container or in puddles on the ground. This will prove fatal in sufficient quantity. Always drain the coolant into a sealable container. Coolant should be reused unless it is contaminated or several years old.*

2. Remove the coolant outlet housing retaining bolts and slide the housing with the hose attached to one side.

3. Remove the thermostat and gasket from the cylinder head and clean both mating surfaces.

4. To install the thermostat, coat a new gasket with water resistant sealer and position it

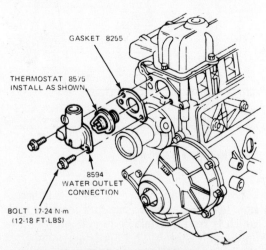

GASKET 8255

THERMOSTAT 8575
INSTALL AS SHOWN

8594
WATER OUTLET
CONNECTION

BOLT 17-24 N·m
(12-18 FT·LBS)

Inline 6-cylinder thermostat installation

on the outlet of the engine. The gasket must be in place before the thermostat is installed.

5. Install the thermostat with the bridge (opposite end of the spring) inside the elbow connection.

6. Position the elbow connection onto the mounting surface of the outlet, so that the thermostat flange is resting on the gasket and install the retaining bolts. Torque the bolts to 15 ft.lb.

7. Fill the radiator and operate the engine until it reaches operating temperature. Check the coolant level and adjust if necessary.

8-302 (5.0L)
8-351 (5.7L)
8-400 (6.6L)
8-460 (7.5L)

1. Drain the cooling system below the level of the coolant outlet housing. Use the petcock valve at the bottom of the radiator to drain the system. It is not necessary to remove any of the hoses.

> CAUTION: *When draining the coolant, keep in mind that cats and dogs are attracted by the ethylene glycol antifreeze, and are quite likely to drink any that is left in an uncovered container or in puddles on the ground. This will prove fatal in sufficient quantity. Always drain the coolant into a sealable container. Coolant should be reused unless it is contaminated or several years old.*

2. Disconnect the bypass hoses at the water pump and intake manifold.

3. Remove the bypass tube.

4. Remove the coolant outlet housing retaining bolts, bend the hose and lift the housing with the hose attached to one side.

5. Remove the thermostat and gasket from the intake manifold and clean both mating surfaces.

6. To install the thermostat, coat a new gasket with water resistant sealer and position it on the outlet of the engine. The gasket must be in place before the thermostat is installed.

7. Install the thermostat with the bridge (opposite end of the spring) inside the elbow connection and the thermostat flange positioned in the recess in the manifold.

8. Position the elbow connection onto the mounting surface of the outlet. Torque the bolts to 18 ft.lb. on the 8-302 and 351; 28 ft.lb. on the 8-460.

9. Install the bypass tube and hoses.

10. Fill the radiator and operate the engine until it reaches operating temperature. Check the coolant level and adjust if necessary.

8-420 (6.9L) and 8-444 (7.3L) Diesel

WARNING: *The factory specified thermostat does not contain an internal bypass. On these engines, an internal bypass is located in the*

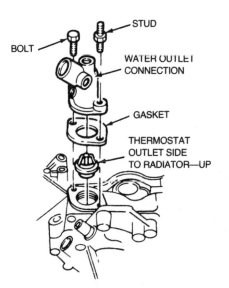

Thermostat installation for the V8

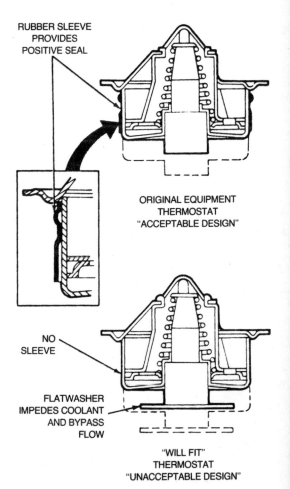

Thermostat positioning

block. *The use of any replacement thermostat other than that meeting the manufacturer's specifications will result in engine overheating! Use only thermostats meeting the specifications of Ford part number E5TZ-8575-C or Navistar International part number 1807945-C1.*

1. Disconnect both battery ground cables.
2. Drain the coolant to a point below the thermostat housing.

CAUTION: *When draining the coolant, keep in mind that cats and dogs are attracted by the ethylene glycol antifreeze, and are quite likely to drink any that is left in an uncovered container or in puddles on the ground. This will prove fatal in sufficient quantity. Always drain the coolant into a sealable container. Coolant should be reused unless it is contaminated or several years old.*

3. Remove the alternator and vacuum pump belts
4. Remove the alternator.
5. Remove the vacuum pump and bracket.
6. Remove all but the lowest vacuum pump/alternator mounting casting bolt.
7. Loosen that lowest bolt and pivot the casting outboard of the engine.

8. Remove the thermostat housing attaching bolts, bend the hose and lift the housing up and to one side.
9. Remove the thermostat and gasket.
10. Clean the thermostat housing and block surfaces thoroughly.
11. Coat a new gasket with waterproof sealer and position the gasket on the manifold outlet opening.
12. Install the thermostat in the manifold opening with the spring element end downward and the flange positioned in the recess in the manifold.
13. Place the outlet housing into position and install the bolts. Torque the bolts to 20 ft.lb.
14. Reposition the casting.
15. Install the vacuum pump and bracket.
16. Install the alternator.
17. Adjust the drive belts.
18. Fill and bleed the cooling system.
19. Connect both battery cables.
20. Run the engine and check for leaks.

Radiator

REMOVAL AND INSTALLATION

1. Drain the cooling system.

CAUTION: *When draining the coolant, keep*

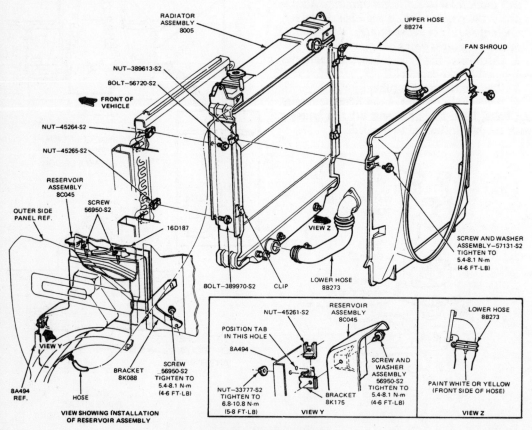

Diesel radiator installation

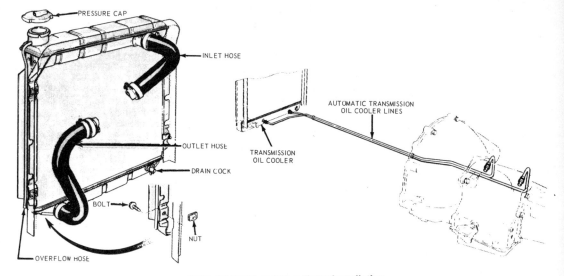

1961–67 6-144, 6-170 radiator installation

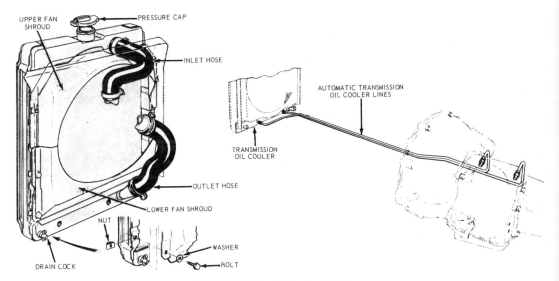

1965–67 6-240 radiator installation

in mind that cats and dogs are attracted by the ethylene glycol antifreeze, and are quite likely to drink any that is left in an uncovered container or in puddles on the ground. This will prove fatal in sufficient quantity. Always drain the coolant into a sealable container. Coolant should be reused unless it is contaminated or several years old.

2. Disconnect the transmission cooling lines from the bottom of the radiator, if so equipped.

3. Remove the retaining bolts at each of the 4 corners of the shroud, if so equipped, and position the shroud over the fan, clear of the radiator.

4. Disconnect the upper and lower hoses from the radiator.

5. Remove the radiator retaining bolts or the upper supports and lift the radiator from the vehicle. On some 6-240 engines, remove the right hood lock bracket and bolts from the radiator grille before removing the radiator.

6. Install the radiator in the reverse order of removal. Fill the cooling system and check for leaks.

Air Conditioning Condenser

REMOVAL AND INSTALLATION

Through 1978

1. Discharge the system. See Chapter 1.

2. Disconnect the refrigerant lines at the condenser and cap all openings immediately!

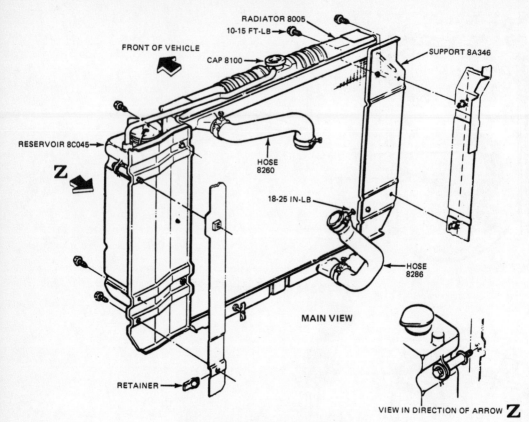

1969–74 6-cylinder radiator installation

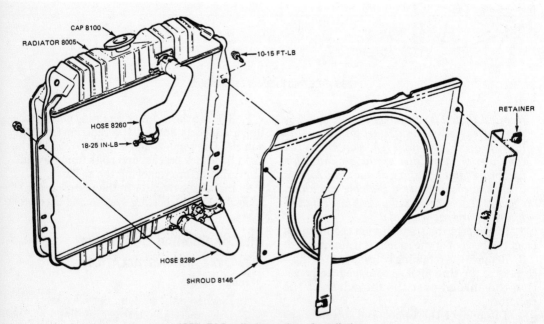

1969–74 8-cylinder radiator installation

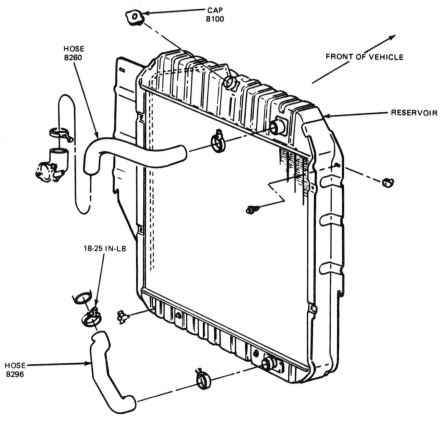

1975–80 6-cylinder radiator installation

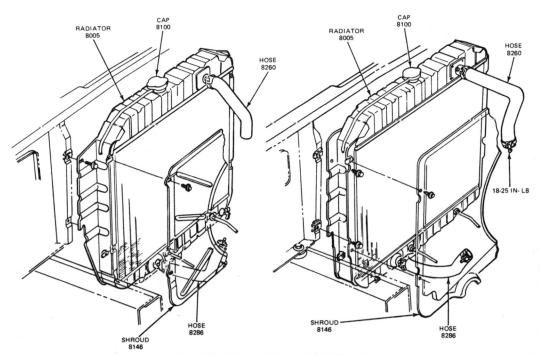

1975–80 8-cylinder radiator installation

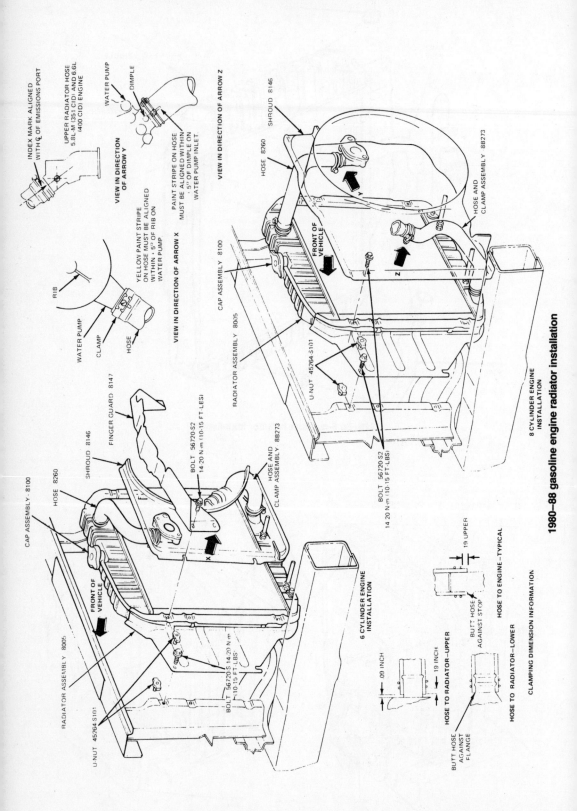

INDEX MARK ALIGNED
WITH ℄ OF EMISSIONS PORT

UPPER RADIATOR HOSE
5.8L-M (351 CID) AND 6.6L
(400 CID) ENGINE

WATER PUMP

DIMPLE

**VIEW IN DIRECTION
OF ARROW Y**

PAINT STRIPE ON HOSE
MUST BE ALIGNED WITHIN
5° OF DIMPLE ON
WATER PUMP INLET

VIEW IN DIRECTION OF ARROW Z

RIB

WATER PUMP

CLAMP

HOSE

YELLOW PAINT STRIPE
ON HOSE MUST BE ALIGNED
WITHIN ± 5° OF RIB ON
WATER PUMP

VIEW IN DIRECTION OF ARROW X

CAP ASSEMBLY · 8100

RADIATOR ASSEMBLY · 8005

U-NUT 45264-S101

BOLT 56720-S2
14 20 N·m (10·15 FT·LBS)

HOSE 8260

SHROUD 8146

HOSE AND
CLAMP ASSEMBLY 8B273

**FRONT OF
VEHICLE**

Z

**8 CYLINDER ENGINE
INSTALLATION**

CAP ASSEMBLY · 8100

HOSE 8260

SHROUD 8146

FINGER GUARD 8147

HOSE AND
CLAMP ASSEMBLY 8B273

BOLT 56720-S2
14 20 N·m (10·15 FT·LBS)

RADIATOR ASSEMBLY · 8005

U-NUT · 45264-S101

BOLT 56720-S 14 20 N·m
(10·15 FT·LBS)

**FRONT OF
VEHICLE**

X

**6 CYLINDER ENGINE
INSTALLATION**

HOSE TO ENGINE—TYPICAL

19 UPPER

BUTT HOSE
AGAINST STOP

HOSE TO RADIATOR—UPPER

.09 INCH

.19 INCH

HOSE TO RADIATOR—LOWER

BUTT HOSE
AGAINST
FLANGE

CLAMPING DIMENSION INFORMATION

1980—88 gasoline engine radiator installation

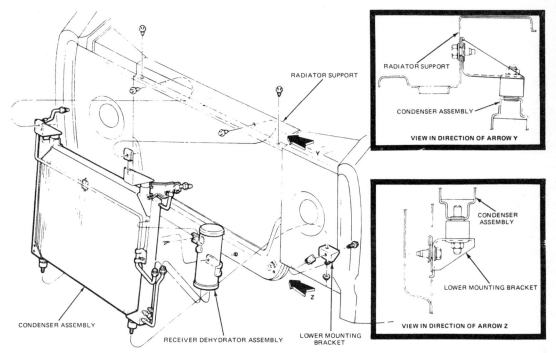

RADIATOR SUPPORT

RADIATOR SUPPORT

CONDENSER ASSEMBLY

VIEW IN DIRECTION OF ARROW Y

Y

CONDENSER
ASSEMBLY

LOWER MOUNTING BRACKET

VIEW IN DIRECTION OF ARROW Z

Z

CONDENSER ASSEMBLY

RECEIVER DEHYDRATOR ASSEMBLY

LOWER MOUNTING
BRACKET

Air conditioning condenser installation

3. Remove the upper radiator mounts and tilt the radiator rearward.

4. Remove the four condenser mounting screws and lift out the condenser.

5. Installation is the reverse of removal. Always use new O-rings coated with clean refrigerant oil at the pipe fittings. Evacuate, charge and leak test the system. See Chapter 1.

1979-85

1. Discharge the system. See Chapter 1.

2. Disconnect the refrigerant lines at the condenser and cap all openings immediately! Always use a back-up wrench when loosening the fittings.

NOTE: *On the diesel, the fittings are spring-lock couplings and a special tool, T81P-19623-G, should be used. The larger opening end of the tool is for ½" discharge lines; the smaller end for ⅜" liquid lines.*

To operate the tool, close the tool and push the tool into the open side of the cage to expand the garter spring and release the female fitting. If the tool is not inserted straight, the garter spring will cock and not release.

After the garter spring is released, pull the fittings apart.

3. Remove the 2 hood latch-to-radiator support screws and position the hood latch out of the way.

4. Remove the 9 screws retaining the top edge of the grille to the radiator support.

5. Remove the screw retaining the center of the grille to the center support.

6. Remove the screw retaining the grille center support to the radiator support.

7. From under the van, reposition the splash shield and remove the two lower condenser retaining nuts.

8. Remove the two bolts securing the top of the condenser to the radiator upper support.

9. Remove the 4 bolts retaining the ends of the radiator upper support to the side supports.

10. Carefully pull the top edge of the grille forward and remove the radiator upper support.

11. Lift out the condenser.

12. If a new condenser is being installed, add 1 fl.oz. of new refrigerant oil to the new condenser. Installation is the reverse of removal. Always us a back-up wrench when tightening the fittings. Torque the fittings to 25-35 ft.lb. Always use new O-rings coated with clean refrigerant oil on the line fittings. Evacuate, charge and leak test the system.

1986-88

1. Discharge the refrigerant system. See Chapter 1.

2. Disconnect the refrigerant lines from the condenser using the proper spring lock tool shown in the accompanying illustration. Cap all opening immediatley!

NOTE: *The fittings are spring-lock cou-*

plings and a special tool, T81P-19623-G, should be used. The larger opening end of the tool is for ½" discharge lines; the smaller end for ⅜" liquid lines.

To operate the tool, close the tool and push the tool into the open side of the cage to expand the garter spring and release the female fitting. If the tool is not inserted straight, the garter spring will cock and not release.

After the garter spring is released, pull the fittings apart.

3. Remove the 2 hood latch-to-radiator support screws and position the hood latch out of the way.

4. Remove the 9 screws retaining the top edge of the grille to the radiator support.

5. Remove the screw retaining the center of the grille to the center support.

6. Remove the screw retaining the grille center support to the radiator support.

7. From under the van, reposition the splash shield and remove the two lower condenser retaining nuts.

8. Remove the two bolts securing the top of the condenser to the radiator upper support.

9. Remove the 4 bolts retaining the ends of the radiator upper support to the side supports.

10. Carefully pull the top edge of the grille forward and remove the radiator upper support.

11. Lift out the condenser.

12. If a new condesner is being installed, add 1 fl.oz. of new refrigerant oil to the new condenser. Installation is the reverse of removal. Always use new O-rings coated with clean refrigerant oil on the line fittings. Evacuate, charge and leak test the system.

Water Pump

REMOVAL AND INSTALLATION

6-144 (2.4L)
6-170 (2.8L)
6-200 (3.3L)

1. Drain the cooling system.
CAUTION: *When draining the coolant, keep in mind that cats and dogs are attracted by the ethylene glycol antifreeze, and are quite likely to drink any that is left in an uncovered container or in puddles on the ground. This will prove fatal in sufficient quantity. Always drain the coolant into a sealable container. Coolant should be reused unless it is contaminated or several years old.*

2. Disconnect the lower radiator hose from the water pump.

3. Remove the drive belt, fan and water pump pulley.

4. Disconnect the heater hose at the water pump.

5. Remove the water pump.

6. Before installing the old water pump, clean the gasket mounting surfaces on the pump and on the cylinder block. If a new water pump is being installed, remove the heater hose fitting from the old pump and install it on the new one. Coat the new gaskets with sealer on both sides and install the water pump in the reverse order of removal.

6-240 (3.9L)
6-300 (4.9L)

1. Drain the cooling system.
CAUTION: *When draining the coolant, keep in mind that cats and dogs are attracted by the ethylene glycol antifreeze, and are quite likely to drink any that is left in an uncovered container or in puddles on the ground. This will prove fatal in sufficient quantity. Always drain the coolant into a sealable container. Coolant should be reused unless it is contaminated or several years old.*

2. Disconnect the lower radiator hose from the water pump.

3. Remove the drive belt, fan, fan spacer, fan shroud, if so equipped, and water pump pulley.

4. Remove the alternator pivot arm from the pump.

5. Disconnect the heater hose at the water pump.

6. Remove the water pump.

7. Before installing the old water pump, clean the gasket mounting surfaces on the pump and on the cylinder block. If a new water pump is being installed, remove the heater hose fitting from the old pump and install it on the new one. Coat the new gaskets with sealer on both sides and install the water pump in the reverse order of removal. Torque the mounting bolts to 18 ft.lb.

8-302 (5.0L)
8-351 (5.7L)
8-400 (6.6L)
8-460 (7.5L)

1. Drain the cooling system.
CAUTION: *When draining the coolant, keep in mind that cats and dogs are attracted by the ethylene glycol antifreeze, and are quite likely to drink any that is left in an uncovered container or in puddles on the ground. This will prove fatal in sufficient quantity. Always drain the coolant into a sealable container. Coolant should be reused unless it is contaminated or several years old.*

2. Remove the bolts securing the fan shroud to the radiator, if so equipped, and position the shroud over the fan.

3. Disconnect the lower radiator hose, heater hose and by-pass hose at the water pump. Re-

move the drive belts, fan, fan spacer and pulley. Remove the fan shroud, if so equipped.

4. Loosen the alternator pivot bolt and the bolt attaching the alternator adjusting arm to the water pump. Remove the power steering pump bracket from the water pump and position it out of the way.

5. Remove the bolts securing the water pump to the timing chain cover and remove the water pump.

6. Install the water pump in the reverse order of removal, using a new gasket. Torque the bolts to 18 ft.lb.

8-420 (6.9L) and 8-444 (7.3L) Diesels

1. Disconnect both battery ground cables.
2. Drain the cooling system.
CAUTION: *When draining the coolant, keep in mind that cats and dogs are attracted by the ethylene glycol antifreeze, and are quite likely to drink any that is left in an uncovered container or in puddles on the ground. This will prove fatal in sufficient quantity. Always drain the coolant into a sealable container. Coolant should be reused unless it is contaminated or several years old.*
3. Remove the radiator shroud halves.
4. Remove the fan clutch and fan.
NOTE: *The fan clutch bolts are left hand thread. Remove them by turning them clockwise.*
5. Remove the power steering pump belt.
6. Remove the air conditioning compressor belt.
7. Remove the vacuum pump drive belt.
8. Remove the alternator drive belt.
9. Remove the water pump pulley.
10. Disconnect the heater hose at the water pump.
11. If you're installing a new pump, remove the heater hose fitting from the old pump at this time.
12. Remove the alternator adjusting arm and bracket.
13. Unbolt the air conditioning compressor and position it out of the way. DO NOT DISCONNECT THE REFRIGERANT LINES!
14. Remove the air conditioning compressor brackets.
15. Unbolt the power steering pump and bracket and position it out of the way. DO NOT DISCONNECT THE POWER STEERING FLUID LINES!
16. Remove the bolts attaching the water pump to the front cover and lift off the pump.
17. Thoroughly clean the mating surfaces of the pump and front cover.
18. Get ahold of two dowel pins - anything that will fit into 2 mounting bolt holes in the front cover. You'll need these to ensure proper

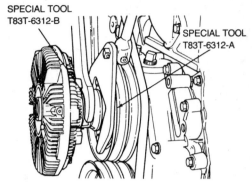

Diesel fan clutch removal

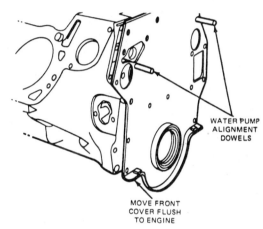

Diesel front cover alignment

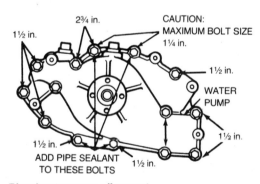

Diesel water pump alignment

bolt hole alignment when you're installing the water pump.
19. Using a new gasket, position the water pump over the dowel pins and into place on the front cover.
20. Install the attaching bolts. The 2 top center and 2 bottom center bolts must be coated with RTV silicone sealant prior to installation. See the illustration. Also, the 4 bolts marked No.1 in the illustration are a different length than the other bolts. Torque the bolts to 14 ft.lb.

21. Install the water pump pulley.

22. Wrap the heater hose fitting threads with Teflon® tape and screw it into the water pump. Torque it to 18 ft.lb.

23. Connect the heater hose to the pump.

24. Install the power steering pump and bracket. Install the belt.

25. Install the air conditioning compressor bracket.

26. Install the air conditioning compressor. Install the belt.

27. Install the alternator adjusting arm and install the belt.

28. Install the vacuum pump drive belt.

29. Adjust all the drive belts.

30. Install the fan and clutch. Remember that the bolts are left hand thread. Turn them counterclockwise to tighten them. Torque them to 45 ft.lb.

31. Install the fan shroud halves.

32. Fill and bleed the cooling system.

33. Connect the battery ground cables.

34. Start the engine and check for leaks.

Intake Manifold

REMOVAL AND INSTALLATION

6-144 (2.4L)
6-170 (2.8L)
6-200 (3.3L)

The intake manifold on these engines is cast as an integral part of the cylinder head.

CAUTION: *Before opening any fuel system connection on fuel injected engines, relieve the fuel system pressure. See Chapter 5.*

6-240 (3.9L)
6-300 (4.9L) with Carburetor

The intake and exhaust manifolds on these engines are known as combination manifolds and are serviced as a unit.

1. Remove the air cleaner. Disconnect the choke cable at the carburetor. Disconnect the accelerator cable or rod at the carburetor. Remove the accelerator retracting spring.

2. On a vehicle with automatic transmission, remove the kick-down rod-retracting spring. Remove the accelerator rod bellcrank assembly.

3. Disconnect the fuel inlet line and the distributor vacuum line from the carburetor.

4. Disconnect the muffler inlet pipe from the exhaust manifold.

5. Disconnect the power brake vacuum line, if so equipped.

6. Remove the bolts and nuts attaching the manifolds to the cylinder head. Lift the manifold assemblies from the engine. Remove and discard the gaskets.

7. To separate the manifold, remove the nuts joining the intake and exhaust manifolds.

8. Clean the mating surfaces of the cylinder head and the manifolds.

9. If the intake and exhaust manifolds have been separated, coat the mating surfaces lightly with graphite grease and place the exhaust manifold over the studs on the intake manifold. Install the lockwashers and nuts. Tighten them finger tight.

10. Install a new intake manifold gasket.

11. Coat the mating surfaces lightly with graphite grease. Place the manifold assemblies in position against the cylinder head. Make sure that the gaskets have not become dislodged. Install the attaching nuts and bolts in the proper sequence to 26 ft.lb. If the intake and exhaust manifolds were separated, tighten the nuts joining them.

12. Position a new gasket on the muffler inlet pipe and connect the inlet pipe to the exhaust manifold.

13. Connect the crankcase vent hose to the intake manifold inlet tube and position the hose clamp.

14. Connect the fuel inlet line and the distributor vacuum line to the carburetor.

15. Connect the accelerator cable to the carburetor and install the retracting spring. Connect the choke cable on the carburetor.

16. On a vehicle with an automatic transmission, install the bellcrank assembly and the kickdown rod retracting spring. Adjust the transmission control linkage.

17. Install the air cleaner.

6-300 with Fuel Injection

1. Relieve the fuel system pressure. See Chapter 5.

2. Disconnect the battery ground cable and drain the cooling system.

CAUTION: *When draining the coolant, keep in mind that cats and dogs are attracted by the ethylene glycol antifreeze, and are quite likely to drink any that is left in an uncovered container or in puddles on the ground. This will prove fatal in sufficient quantity. Always drain the coolant into a sealable container. Coolant should be reused unless it is contaminated or several years old.*

3. Label and disconnect the wiring at the:
- Throttle position sensor
- Air bypass valve
- EVP sensor at the EGR valve
- Injection wiring harness
- Engine coolant temperature sensor

4. Label and disconnect the following vaccum connectors:
- EGR valve
- Thermactor air bypass valve
- Throttle body
- Fuel pressure regulator

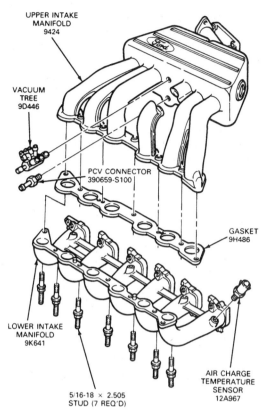

UPPER INTAKE
MANIFOLD
9424

VACUUM
TREE
9D446

PCV CONNECTOR
390659-S100

GASKET
9H486

LOWER INTAKE
MANIFOLD
9K641

5/16-18 × 2.505
STUD (7 REQ'D)

AIR CHARGE
TEMPERATURE
SENSOR
12A967

6-300 EFI upper and lower intake manifolds

- Upper intake manifold vacuum tree

5. Disconnect the PCV hose at the upper intake manifold.

6. Remove the throttle linkage shield.

7. Disconnect the throttle linkage and speed control cables.

8. Unbolt the accelerator cable from its bracket and position it out of the way.

9. Disconnect the air inlet hoses from the throttle body.

10. Remove the EGR tube.

11. Remove the Thermactor tube from the lower intake manifold.

12. Remove the nut attaching the Thermactor bypass valve bracket to the lower intake manifold.

13. Remove the injector heat shield (2 clips).

14. Remove the 7 studs which retain the upper intake manifold.

15. Remove the screw and washer which retains the upper intake manifold support bracket to the upper intake manifold.

16. Remove the upper intake manifold assembly from the lower intake manifold.

17. Move the vacuum harness away from the lower intake manifold.

18. Remove the injector cooling manifold from the lifting eye attachment.

19. Disconnect the fuel supply and return lines at the quick disconnect couplings using tools T81P-19623-G or T81P-19623-G1.

20. Remove the 16 attaching bolts that the lower intake manifold and exhaust manifolds have in common. DON'T REMOVE THE BOLTS THAT ATTACH ONLY THE EXHAUST MANIFOLDS!

21. Remove the lower intake manifold from the head.

22. Clean and inspect all mating surfaces. All surfaces MUST be flat and free from debris or damage!

23. Clean and oil all fastener threads.

24. Position the lower manifold on the head using a new gasket. Tighten the bolts to 30 ft.lb.

25. Reconnect the vacuum lines at the fuel pressure regulator.

26. Position the upper manifold and new gasket on the lower manifold. Install the fasteners finger tight.

27. Install the upper intake manifold support on the manifold and tighten the retaing screw to 30 ft.lb.

28. Torque the upper-to-lower manifold fasteners to 18 ft.lb.

29. Install the injector heat shield.

30. Install the EGR tube. The tube should be routed between the no. 4 and 5 lower intake runners. Torque the fittings to 35 ft.lb.

31. Install the injector cooling manifold and torque the fasteners to 12 ft.lb.

32. Connect the PCV hose.

33. Install the Thermactor tube and tighten the nuts to 12 ft.lb.

34. Install the accelerator cable and throttle linkages.

35. Connect the air inlet hoses to the throttle body.

36. Connect the vacuum hoses.

37. Connect the electrical wiring.

38. Connect the air intake hose, air bypas hose and crankcase vent hose.

39. Connect the battery ground.

40. Refill the cooling system.

41. Install the fuel pressure relief cap. Turn the ignition switch from **OFF** to **ON** at least half a dozen times, **WITHOUT STARTING THE ENGINE**, leaving it in the ON position for about 5 seconds each time. This will build up fuel pressure in the system.

42. Start the engine and allow it to run at idle until normal operating temperature is reached. Check for leaks.

Carbureted V8 Except 8-460 (7.5L)

1. Drain the cooling system, remove the air cleaner and the intake duct assembly.

CAUTION: *When draining the coolant, keep in mind that cats and dogs are attracted by the ethylene glycol antifreeze, and are quite likely to drink any that is left in an uncovered container or in puddles on the ground. This will prove fatal in sufficient quantity. Always drain the coolant into a sealable container. Coolant should be reused unless it is contaminated or several years old.*

2. Disconnect the accelerator rod from the carburetor and remove the accelerator retracting spring. Disconnect the automatic transmission kick-down rod at the carburetor, if so equipped.

3. Disconnect the high tension lead and all other wires from the ignition coil.

4. Disconnect the spark plug wires from the spark plugs by grasping the rubber boots and twisting and pulling at the same time. Remove the wires from the brackets on the rocker covers. Remove the distributor cap and spark plug wire assembly.

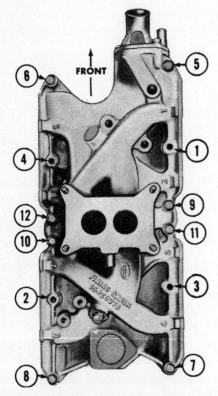

302 and 351W intake manifold tightening sequence

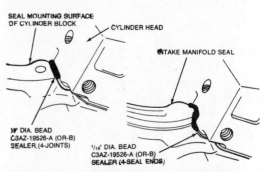

RTV sealer installation, 400 intake manifold

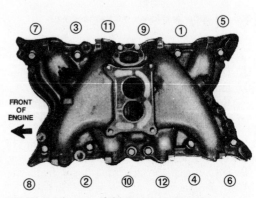

400 V8 intake manifold torque sequence

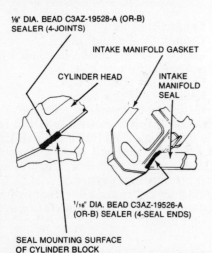

RTV sealer installation, 302, 351W, 460 intake manifold

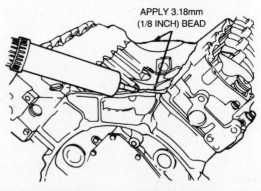

Applying RTV sealer to the intake manifold

5. Remove the carburetor fuel inlet line and the distributor vacuum line from the carburetor.

6. Remove the distributor lockbolt and remove the distributor and vacuum line. See Distributor Removal and Installation.

7. Disconnect the upper radiator hose from the coolant outlet housing and the temperature sending unit wire at the sending unit. Remove the heater hose from the intake manifold.

8. Loosen the clamp on the water pump bypass hose at the coolant outlet housing and slide the hose off the outlet housing.

9. Disconnect the PCV hose at the rocker cover.

10. If the engine is equipped with the Thermactor® exhaust emission control system, remove the air pump to cylinder head air hose at the air pump and position it out of the way. Also remove the air hose at the backfire suppressor valve. Remove the air hose bracket from the valve rocker arm cover and position the air hose out of the way.

11. Remove the intake manifold and carburetor as an assembly. It may be necessary to pry the intake manifold from the cylinder head. Remove all traces of the intake manifold-to-cylinder head gaskets and the two end seals from both the manifold and the other mating surfaces of the engine.

Installation is as follows:

1. Clean the mating surfaces of the intake manifold, cylinder heads, and block with lacquer thinner or similar solvent. Apply a ⅛" (3mm) bead of silicone-rubber RTV sealant at the points shown in the accompanying diagram.

WARNING: *Do not apply sealer to the waffle portions of the seals as the sealer will rupture the end seal material.*

2. Position new seals on the block and press the seal locating extensions into the holes in the mating surfaces.

3. Apply a ¹⁄₁₆" (1.6mm) bead of sealer to the outer end of each manifold seal for the full length of the seal (4 places). As before, do not apply sealer to the waffle portion of the end seals.

NOTE: *This sealer sets in about 15 minutes, depending on brand, so work quickly but carefully. DO NOT DROP ANY SEALER INTO THE MANIFOLD CAVITY. IT WILL FORM AND SET AND PLUG THE OIL GALLERY.*

4. Position the manifold gasket onto the block and heads with the alignment notches under the dowels in the heads. Be sure gasket holes align with head holes.

5. Install the manifold and related equipment in reverse order of removal.

8-302, 8-351 with Fuel Injection

1. Relieve the fuel system pressure. See Chapter 5.

2. Disconnect the battery ground cable and drain the cooling system.

CAUTION: *When draining the coolant, keep in mind that cats and dogs are attracted by the ethylene glycol antifreeze, and are quite likely to drink any that is left in an uncovered container or in puddles on the ground. This will prove fatal in sufficient quantity. Always drain the coolant into a sealable container. Coolant should be reused unless it is contaminated or several years old.*

3. Label and disconnect the wiring at the:
- Throttle position sensor
- Air bypass valve
- EGR sensor

4. Label and disconnect the following vaccum connectors:
- EGR valve
- Fuel pressure regulator
- Upper intake manifold vacuum tree

5. Disconnect the PCV hose at the upper intake manifold.

6. Remove the throttle linkage at the throttle ball and AOD transmission linkage at the throttle body.

7. Unbolt the cable bracket from the manifold and position the cables and bracket away from the engine.

8. Disconnect the 2 canister purge lines at the throttle body.

9. Disconnect the water heater lines from the throttle body.

10. Remove the EGR tube.

11. Remove the screw and washer which retains the upper intake manifold support bracket to the upper intake manifold.

12. Remove the 6 bolts which retain the upper intake manifold.

13. Remove the upper intake manifold assembly from the lower intake manifold.

14. Remove the distributor. (See Chapter 3).

15. Disconnect the wiring at the:
- Engine coolant temperature sensor.
- Engine temperature sending unit.
- Air charge temperature sensor.
- Knock sensor.
- Electrical vacuum regulator.
- Thermactor solenoids.

16. Disconnect the injector wiring harness at the main harness.

17. Remove the EGO ground wire at its intake manifold stud. Note the position of the stud and bround wire for installation.

18. Disconnect the fuel supply and return lines from the fuel rails using tool T81P-19623-G or G1.

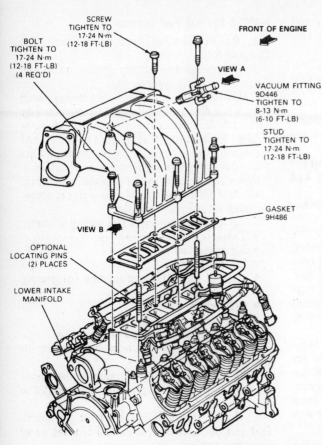

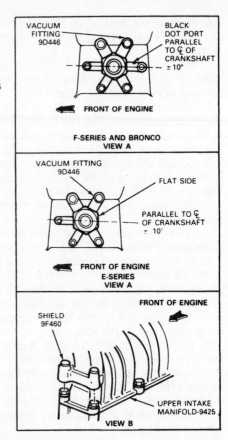

8-302 EFI/8-351 EFI upper intake manifold installation

19. Remove the upper radiator hose.

20. Remove the coolant bypass hose.

21. Disconnect the heater outlet hose at the manifold.

22. Remove the air cleaner bracket.

23. Remove the coil.

24. Noting the location of each bolt, remove the intkae manifold retaining bolts.

25. Remove the lower intake manifold from the head.

26. Clean and inspect all mating surfaces. All surfaces MUST be flat and free from debris or damage!

27. Clean and oil all fastener threads.

28. Place a $\frac{1}{16}''$ bead of RTV silicone sealant to the end seals' junctions.

29. Position the end seals on the block.

30. Install 2 locator pins at opposite corners of the block.

31. Position the lower manifold on the head using new gaskets. Install the bolts and remove the locating pins.

32. Tighten the bolts to 25 ft.lb. in sequence. Wait ten minutes and retorque the bolts in sequence.

33. Install the coil.

34. Connect the cooling system hoses.

35. Connect the fuel supply and return lines.

36. Connect the wiring at the:
- Engine coolant temperature sensor.
- Engine temperature sending unit.
- Air charge temperature sensor.
- Knock sensor.
- Electrical vacuum regulator.
- Thermactor solenoids.

37. Install the distributor.

38. Position the upper manifold and new gasket on the lower manifold. Install the fasteners finger tight.

39. Install the upper intake manifold support on the manifold and tighten the retaing screw to 30 ft.lb.

40. Torque the upper-to-lower manifold fasteners to 18 ft.lb.

41. Install the EGR tube. Torque the fittings to 35 ft.lb.

42. Install the canister purge lines at the throttle body.

43. Connect the water heater lines at the throttle body.

44. Connect the PCV hose.

45. Install the accelerator cable and throttle linkages.

46. Connect the vacuum hoses.

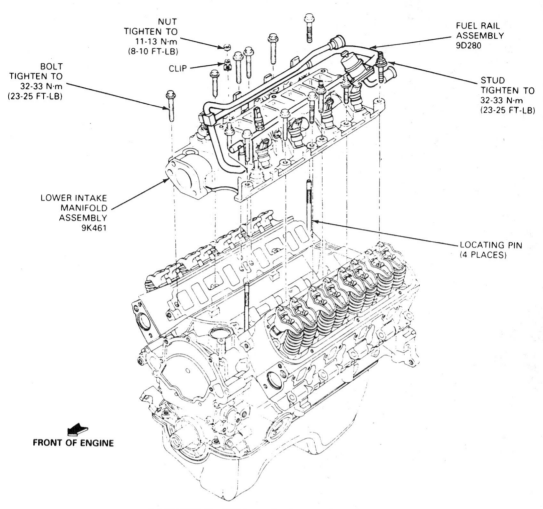

FRONT OF ENGINE

8-302 EFI/8-351 EFI lower intake manifold installation

47. Connect the electrical wiring.

48. Connect the air intake hose, air bypass hose and crankcase vent hose.

49. Connect the battery ground.

50. Refill the cooling system.

51. Install the fuel pressure relief cap. Turn the ignition switch from **OFF** to **ON** at least half a dozen times, **WITHOUT STARTING THE ENGINE,** leaving it in the ON position for about 5 seconds each time. This will build up fuel pressure in the system.

52. Start the engine and allow it to run at idle until normal operating temperature is reached. Check for leaks.

8-460 (7.5L) w/Carburetor

1. Drain the cooling system and remove the air cleaner assembly.

CAUTION: *When draining the coolant, keep in mind that cats and dogs are attracted by the ethylene glycol antifreeze, and are quite likely to drink any that is left in an uncovered container or in puddles on the ground. This will prove fatal in sufficient quantity. Always drain the coolant into a sealable container. Coolant should be reused unless it is contaminated or several years old.*

2. Disconnect the upper radiator hose at the engine.

3. Disconnect the heater hoses at the intake manifold and the water pump. Position them out of the way. Loosen the water pump by-pass hose clamp at the intake manifold.

4. Disconnect the PCV valve and hose at the right valve cover. Disconnect all of the vacuum lines at the rear of the intake manifold and tag them for proper reinstallation.

5. Disconnect the wires at the spark plugs, and remove the wires from the brackets on the valve cover. Disconnect the high tension wire from the coil and remove the distributor cap and wires as an assembly.

6. Disconnect all of the distributor vacuum lines at the carburetor and vacuum control

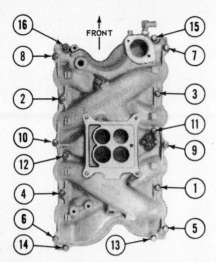

460 V8 intake manifold bolt torque sequence

valve and tag them for proper installation. Remove the distributor and vacuum lines as an assembly.

7. Disconnect the accelerator linkage at the carburetor. Remove the speed control linkage bracket, if so equipped, from the manifold and carburetor.

8. Remove the bolts holding the accelerator linkage bellcrank and position the linkage and return springs out of the way.

9. Disconnect the fuel line at the carburetor.

10. Disconnect the wiring harness at the coil battery terminal, engine temperature sending unit, oil pressure sending until, and other connections as necessary. Disconnect the wiring harness from the clips at the left valve cover and position the harness out of the way.

11. Remove the coil and bracket assembly.

12. Remove the intake manifold attaching bolts and lift the manifold and carburetor from the engine as an assembly. It may be necessary to pry the manifold away from the cylinder heads. Do not damage the gasket sealing surfaces.

Installation is as follows:

1. Clean the mating surfaces of the intake manifold, cylinder heads and block with lacquer thinner or similar solvent. Apply a 1/8″ (3mm) bead of silicone-rubber RTV sealant at the points shown in the accompanying diagram.

WARNING: Do not apply sealer to the waffle portions of the seals as the sealer will rupture the end seal material.

2. Position the new seals on the block and press the seal locating extensions into the holes in the mating surfaces.

3. Apply a 1/16″ (1.6mm) bead of sealer to the outer end of each manifold seal for the full length of the seal (4 places). As before, do not

apply sealer to the waffle portion of the end seals.

NOTE: *This sealer sets in about 15 minutes, depending on brand, so work quickly but carefully. DO NOT DROP ANY SEALER INTO THE MANIFOLD CAVITY. IT WILL FORM AND SET AND PLUG THE OIL GALLERY.*

4. Position the manifold gasket onto the block and heads with the alignment notches under the dowels in the heads. Be sure gasket holes align with head holes.

5. Install the manifold and related equipment in reverse order of removal.

8-460 with Fuel Injection

UPPER INTAKE MANIFOLD

1. Disconnect the throttle and transmission linkages at the throttle body.

2. Remove the two canister purge lines from the throttle body.

3. Tag and disconnect the:
- throttle bypass valve wire
- throttle position sensor wire
- EGR position sensor wire

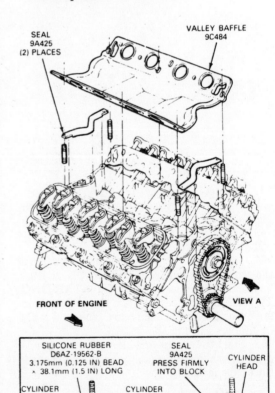

8-460 EFI lower intake manifold installation

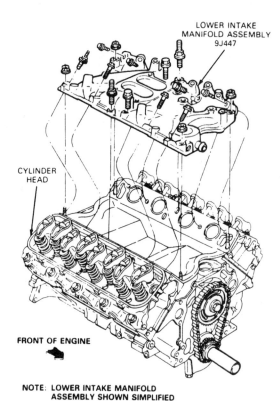

NOTE: LOWER INTAKE MANIFOLD
ASSEMBLY SHOWN SIMPLIFIED
TO CLARIFY INSTALLATION

8-460 EFI intake manifold torque sequence

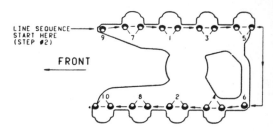

STEP 1.   TORQUE BOLTS TO 33 N·m (24 lbf-ft), IN NUMBERED
SEQUENCE SHOWN ABOVE.
STEP 2.   TORQUE BOLTS TO 33 N·m (24 lbf-ft), IN LINE
SEQUENCE SHOWN ABOVE.

420 V8 diesel intake manifold torque sequence

- MAP sensor vacuum line
- EGR vacuum line
- fuel pressure regulator vacuum line
- EGR valve flange nut
- PCV hose

4. Disconnect the water lines at the throttle body.

5. Remove the 4 upper intake manifold bolts and lift off the manifold.

6. Installation is the reverse of removal. Always use new gaskets. Torque the manifold bolts to 18 ft.lb.

8-420 (6.9L) and 8-444 (7.3L) Diesel

1. Open the hood and remove both battery ground cables.

2. Remove the air cleaner and install clean rags into the air intake of the intake manifold. It is important that no dirt or foreign objects get into the diesel intake.

3. Remove the injection pump as described in Chapter 5 under Diesel Fuel Systems.

4. Remove the fuel return hose from No. 7 and No. 8 rear nozzles and remove the return hose to the fuel tank.

5. Label the positions of the wires and remove the engine wiring harness from the engine.

NOTE: *The engine harness ground cables*

must be removed from the back of the left cylinder head.

6. Remove the bolts attaching the intake manifold to the cylinder heads and remove the manifold.

7. Remove the CDR tube grommet from the valley pan.

8. Remove the bolts attaching the valley pan strap to the front of the engine block, and remove the strap.

9. Remove the valley pan drain plug and remove the valley pan.

10. Apply a ⅛″ (3mm) bead of RTV sealer to each end of the cylinder block as shown in the accompanying illustration.

NOTE: *The RTV sealer should be applied immediately prior to the valley pan installation.*

11. Install the valley pan drain plug, CDR tube and new grommet into the valley pan.

12. Install a new O-ring and new back-up ring on the CDR valve.

13. Install the valley pan strap on the front of the valley pan.

14. Install the intake manifold and torque the bolts to 24 ft.lb. using the sequence shown in the illustration.

15. Reconnect the engine wiring harness and the engine ground wire located to the rear of the left cylinder head.

16. Install the injection pump using the procedure shown in Chapter 5 under Diesel fuel Systems.

17. Install the no. 7 and no. 8 fuel return hoses and the fuel tank return hose.

18. Remove the rag from the intake manifold and replace the air cleaner. Reconnect the battery ground cables to both batteries.

19. Run the engine and check for oil and fuel leaks.

NOTE: *If necessary, purge the nozzle high pressure lines of air by loosening the connector one half to one turn and cranking the engine until solid stream of fuel, devoid of any bubbles, flows from the connection.*

CAUTION: *Keep eyes and hands away from the nozzle spray. Fuel spraying from the nozzle under high pressure can penetrate the skin.*

20. Check and adjust the injection pump timing, as described in Chapter 5 under Diesel Fuel Systems.

Exhaust Manifold
REMOVAL AND INSTALLATION
6-144 (2.4L)
6-170 (2.8L)
6-200 (3.3L)

1. Raise and support the van on jackstands and remove the air cleaner hot air duct.
2. Disconnect the muffler inlet pipe from the exhaust manifold.
3. Remove the attaching bolts and the exhaust manifold.
4. Clean the mating surfaces of the exhaust manifold and the cylinder head.
5. Apply graphite grease to the mating surface of the exhaust manifold.
6. Position the exhaust manifold on the cylinder head and install the attaching bolts and tab washers. Working from the center to the ends, torque the bolts to 18 ft.lb. Lock the bolts by bending one tab of the washer over a flat on the bolt.
7. Place a new gasket on the muffler inlet pipe and install the pipe to the exhaust manifold. Install the air cleaner hot air duct and lower the vehicle.

6-240 (3.9L)
6-300 (4.9L)

The intake and exhaust manifolds on these engines are known as combination manifolds and are serviced as a unit. See Intake Manifold Removal and Installation.

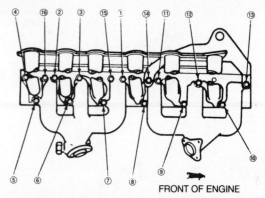

6-300 EFI intake and exhaust manifold bolt torque sequence

Gasoline V8

1. Remove the air cleaner if the manifold being removed has the carburetor heat stove attached to it.
2. On the 8-302, remove the dipstick bracket.
3. Disconnect the exhaust pipe or catalytic converter from the exhaust manifold. Remove and discard the doughnut gasket.
4. Remove the exhaust manifold attaching screws and remove the manifold from the cylinder head.
5. Install the exhaust manifold in the reverse order of removal. Apply a light coat of graphite grease to the mating surface of the manifold. Install and tighten the attaching bolts, starting from the center and working to both ends alternately. Tighten to the proper specifications.

8-420 (6.9L) and 8-444 (7.3L) Diesel

1. Disconnect the ground cables from both batteries.
2. Jack up the truck and safely support it with jackstands.
3. Disconnect the muffler inlet pipe from the exhaust manifolds.

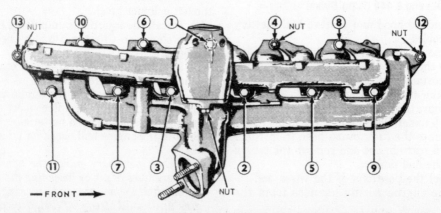

The 240, 300 six-cylinder intake and exhaust manifold torque sequence for the attaching bolts

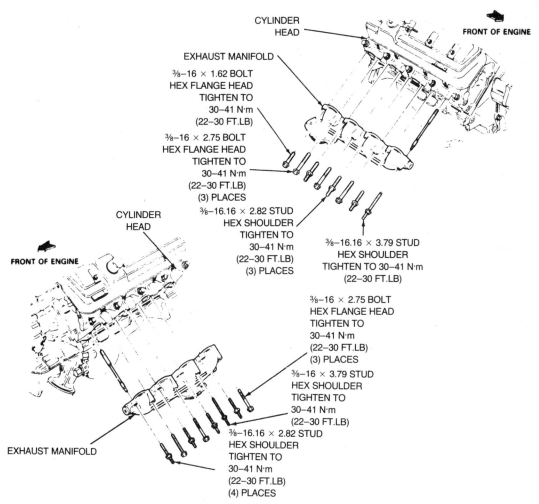

CYLINDER HEAD

FRONT OF ENGINE

EXHAUST MANIFOLD

⅜–16 × 1.62 BOLT
HEX FLANGE HEAD
TIGHTEN TO
30–41 N·m
(22–30 FT.LB)

⅜–16 × 2.75 BOLT
HEX FLANGE HEAD
TIGHTEN TO
30–41 N·m
(22–30 FT.LB)
(3) PLACES

CYLINDER HEAD

⅜–16.16 × 2.82 STUD
HEX SHOULDER
TIGHTEN TO
30–41 N·m
(22–30 FT.LB)
(3) PLACES

FRONT OF ENGINE

⅜–16.16 × 3.79 STUD
HEX SHOULDER
TIGHTEN TO 30–41 N·m
(22–30 FT.LB)

⅜–16 × 2.75 BOLT
HEX FLANGE HEAD
TIGHTEN TO
30–41 N·m
(22–30 FT.LB)
(3) PLACES

⅜–16 × 3.79 STUD
HEX SHOULDER
TIGHTEN TO
30–41 N·m
(22–30 FT.LB)

⅜–16.16 × 2.82 STUD
HEX SHOULDER
TIGHTEN TO
30–41 N·m
(22–30 FT.LB)
(4) PLACES

EXHAUST MANIFOLD

8-460 EFI exhaust manifold installation

4. Lower the truck to remove the right manifold. When removing the left manifold, jack the tuck up. Bend the tabs on the manifold attaching bolts, then remove the bolts and manifold.

5. Before installing, clean all mounting surfaces on the cylinder heads and the manifold. Apply an anti-seize compound on the manifold both threads and install the left manifold, using a new gasket and new locking tabs.

6. Torque the bolts to specifications and bend the tabs over the flats on the bolt heads to prevent the bolts from loosening.

7. Jack up the truck to install the right manifold. Install the right manifold following procedures 5 and 6 above.

8. Connect the inlet pipes to the manifold and tighten. Lower the truck, connect the batteries and run the engine to check for exhaust leaks.

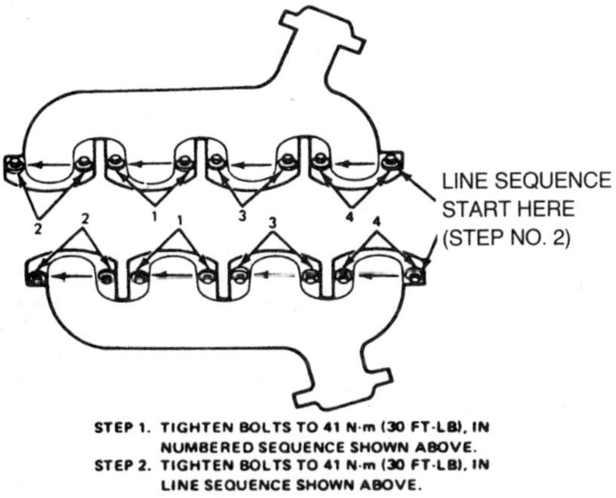

LINE SEQUENCE
START HERE
(STEP NO. 2)

STEP 1. TIGHTEN BOLTS TO 41 N·m (30 FT·LB), IN
NUMBERED SEQUENCE SHOWN ABOVE.
STEP 2. TIGHTEN BOLTS TO 41 N·m (30 FT·LB), IN
LINE SEQUENCE SHOWN ABOVE.

420 V8 diesel exhaust manifold torque sequence

Air Conditioning Compressor
REMOVAL AND INSTALLATION

2-Cylinder York or Tecumseh Compressor

1. Discharge the system and disconnect the two hoses from the compressor. Cap the openings immediately!

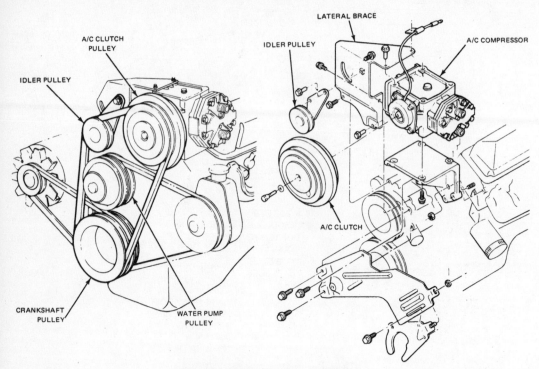

1974–79 8-460 compressor installation

2. Energize the clutch and remove the clutch mounting bolt.

3. Install a ⅝-11 bolt in the clutch driveshaft hole. With the cltuch still energized, tighten the bolt to remove the clutch from the shaft.

4. Disconnect the clutch wire at the connector.

5. Loosen the idler pulley or alternator and

remove the drive belt and clutch, then remove the mounting bolts and compressor.

6. Installation is the reverse of removal. Prior to installation, if a new compressor is being installed, drain the oil from the old compressor into a calibrated container, then drain the oil from the new compressor into a clean container and refill the new compressor with the same

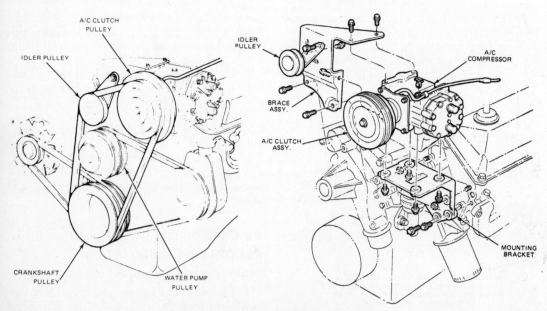

1980–81 8-400/8-460 compressor installation

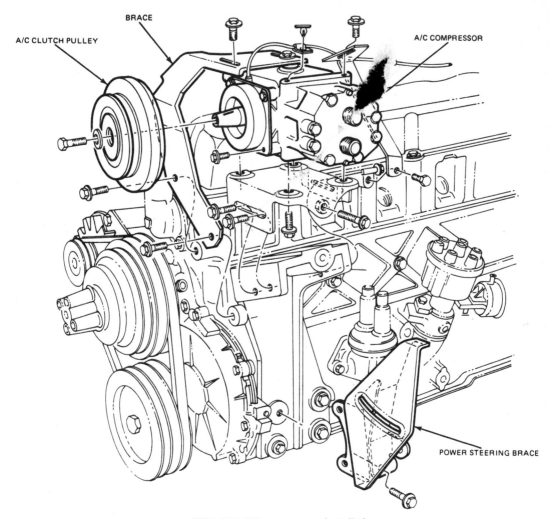

1978–82 6-300 compressor installation

amount of oil that was in the old one. Install the clutch and bolt finger-tight, install the compressor on the mounting bracket and install those bolts finger-tight. Connect the clutch wire and energize the clutch. Tighten the clutch bolt to 23 ft.lb. Tighten the compressor mounting bolts to 30 ft.lb. Make all other connections and evacuate, charge and leak test the system. See Chapter 1.

FS-6 6-Cylinder Axial Compressor

1. Discharge the refrigerant system. See Chapter 1 for the proper procedure.
2. Disconnect the two refrigerant lines from the compressor. Cap the openings immediately!
3. Remove tension from the drive belt. Remove the belt
4. Disconnect the clutch wire at the connector.
5. Remove the bolt attaching the support brace to the front brace and the nut attaching

the support brace to the intake manifold. Remove the support brace.
6. Remove the two bolts attaching the rear support to the bracket.
7. Remove the bolt attaching the compressor tab to the front brace and the two bolts attaching the compressor front legs to the bracket.
8. Remove the compressor.
9. Installation is the reverse of removal. Use new O-rings coated with clean refrigerant oil at all fittings. New, replacement compressors contain 10 oz. of refrigerant oil. Prior to installation, pour off 4 oz. of oil. This will maintain the oil charge in the system. Evacuate, charge and leak test the system.

HR-980 Radial Compressor

1. Discharge the refrigerant system. See Chapter 1 for the proper procedure.
2. Disconnect the two refrigerant lines from the compressor. Cap the openings immediately!

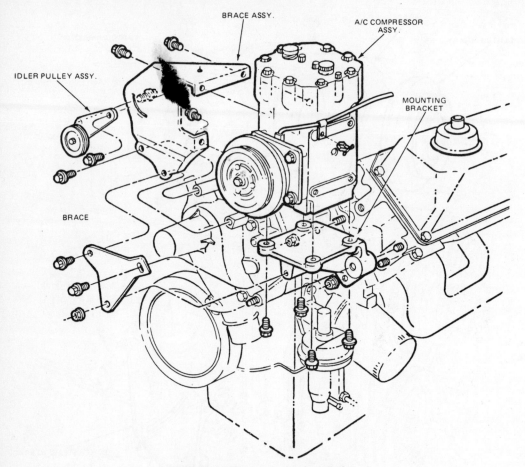

1980—82 8-302 compressor installation

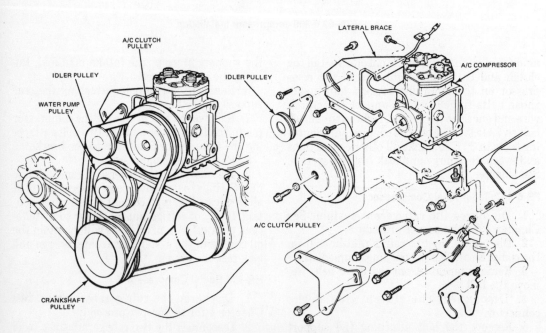

1974—80 8-351 compressor installation

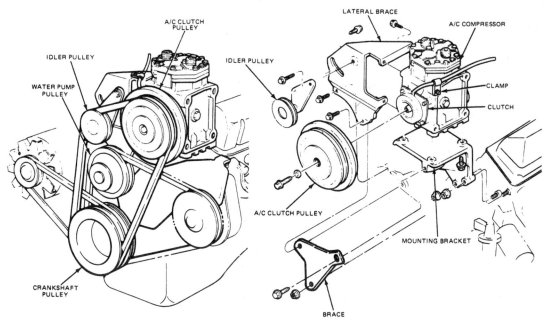

1981–82 8-351 compressor installation

3. Remove the bolt and washer from the adjusting bracket and remove the drive belts.

4. Remove the bolt attaching the compressor bracket to the compressor lower mounting lug.

5. Remove the compressor.

6. Installation is the reverse of removal. If a new compressor is being installed, it contains 8 fl.oz. of refrigerant oil. Prior to installing the compressor, drain 4 oz. of the oil from the compressor. This will maintain the oil charge in the system. Evacuate, charge and leak test the system.

6P148 3-Cylinder Axial Compressor

1. Discharge the refrigerant system. See Chapter 1 for the proper procedure.

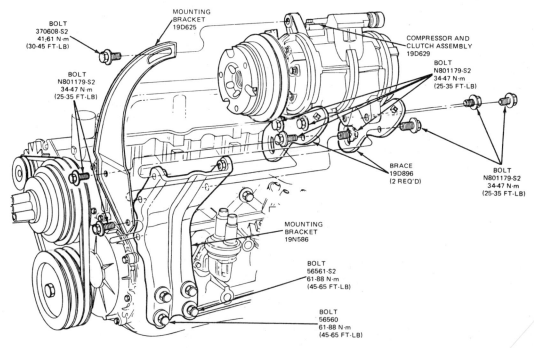

1983–86 6-300 compressor installation

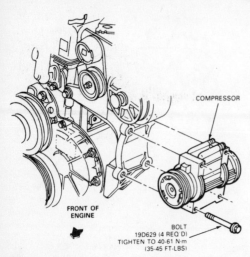

1987–88 6-300 compressor installation

2. Disconnect the two refrigerant lines from the compressor. Cap the openings immediately!

3. Remove tension from the drive belt. Remove the belt.

4. Disconnect the clutch wire at the connector.

5. Unbolt and remove the compressor.

6. Installation is the reverse of removal. Evacuate, charge and leak test the system.

Cylinder Head

REMOVAL AND INSTALLATION

6-144 (2.4L)
6-170 (2.8L)
6-200 (3.3L)

1. Drain the cooling system.

2. Remove the air cleaner.

3. Disconnect the negative battery cable at the cylinder head.

CAUTION: *When draining the coolant, keep in mind that cats and dogs are attracted by the ethylene glycol antifreeze, and are quite likely to drink any that is left in an uncovered container or in puddles on the ground. This will prove fatal in sufficient quantity. Always drain the coolant into a sealable container. Coolant should be reused unless it is contaminated or several years old.*

4. Disconnect the exhaust pipe at the exhaust manifold, pull it away from the manifold and remove the gasket.

5. Disconnect the accelerator linkage and the choke linkage at the gasket.

6. Disconnect the accelerator linkage and the choke linkage at the carburetor.

7. Disconnect the fuel inlet line at the fuel filter hose.

8. Disconnect the distributor vacuum line at the carburetor.

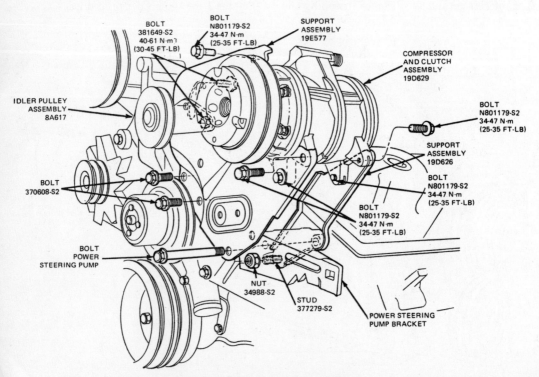

1983–86 8-302 compressor installation

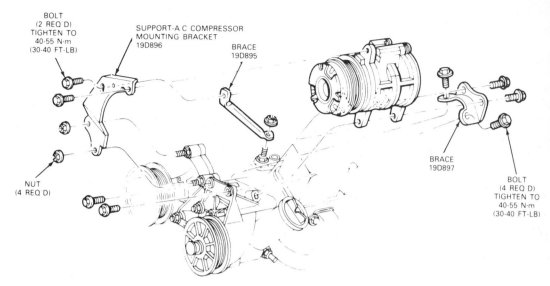

1987 8-302 compressor installation

9. Disconnect the fuel pump vacuum line at the manifold.

10. Disconnect the coolant lines at the carburetor spacer.

11. Disconnect the distributor vacuum line at the distributor.

12. Disconnect the carburetor fuel inlet line at the fuel pump. Remove the lines as a unit.

13. Disconnect the spark plug wires at the spark plugs.

14. Disconnect the temperature sending unit wire at the sending unit.

15. Pull the PCV hose and valve from the rubber grommet in the valve cover, disconnect it from the intake manifold spacer and remove it from the engine.

16. Disconnect the carburetor air vent tube.

17. Remove the valve cover.

18. Remove the valve rocker arm assembly. Remove the rocker arm shaft support bolts by

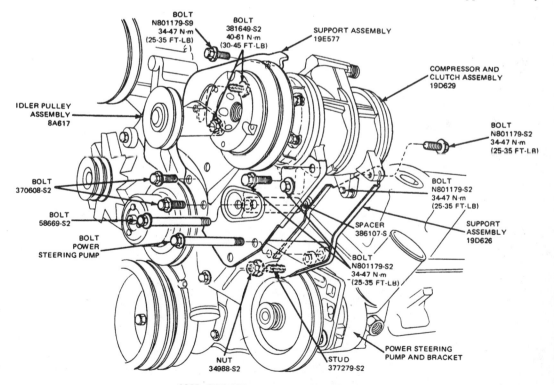

1983–87 8-351 compressor installation

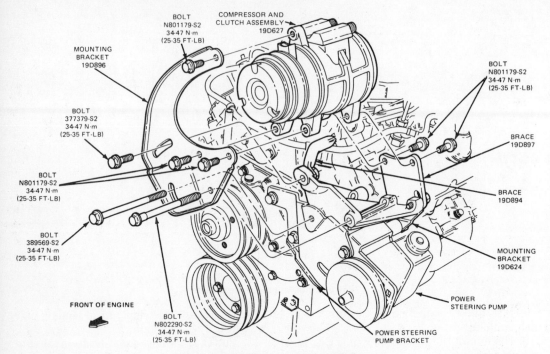

1983–88 diesel compressor installation

loosening the bolts two turns at a time in sequence.

19. Remove the valve pushrods, identifying them so they can be reinstalled in the same positions from which they were removed.

20. Remove the cylinder head bolts and re-move the cylinder head. Do not pry between the cylinder head and the cylinder block because of the possibility of damaging the gasket mating surfaces.

21. Installation is the reverse of removal, noting the following:

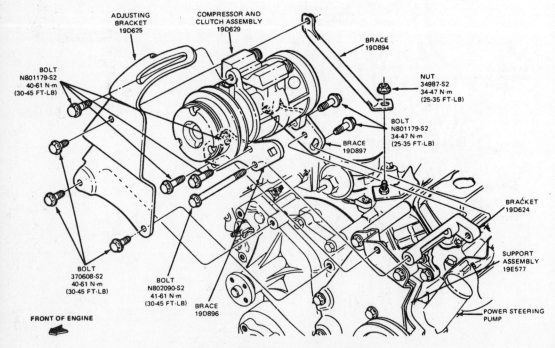

1983–88 8-460 compressor installation

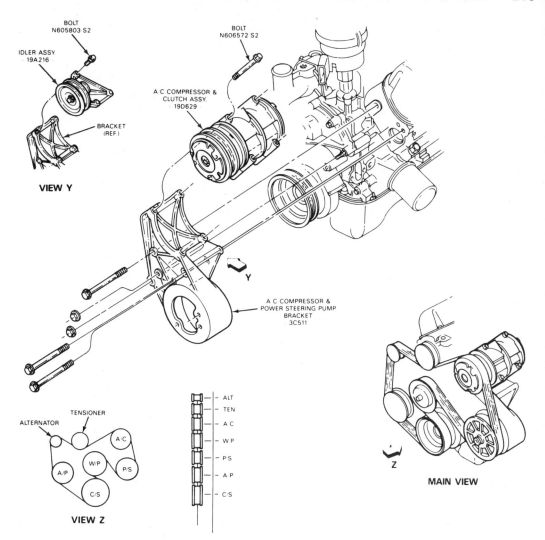

1988 8-302/8-351 compressor installation

a. Clean the head and block surfaces, removing all traces of old gasket material and sealer.

b. If the head was removed because of a gasket failure, check the mating surface of the head and cylinder block for flatness.

c. Apply cylinder head gasket sealer to both sides of the new head gasket.

d. Tighten the cylinder head bolts in the proper sequence, to the correct torque in three progressive steps: 55 ft.lb., 65 ft.lb., and then to specifications.

e. Install the valve pushrods in the same positions from which they were removed.

f. Coat the ends of the pushrods with Lubriplate® or equivalent.

g. Check the pushrods for straightness. Discard bent pushrods.

h. Use a new valve cover gasket.

6-240 (3.9L)
6-300 (4.9L)

WARNING: *When working on fuel injected engines, discharge the fuel system pressure before starting any work that involves disconnecting the fuel system lines. See Fuel Supply Manifold Removal and Installation procedures in Chapter 5.*

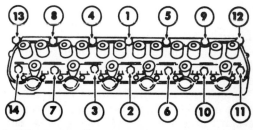

Cylinder head bolt torque sequence, 6-144,170,200

1. Drain the cooling system.
2. Remove the air cleaner.
3. Remove the oil filler tube.
4. Disconnect the battery cable at the cylinder head.

CAUTION: *When draining the coolant, keep in mind that cats and dogs are attracted by the ethylene glycol antifreeze, and are quite likely to drink any that is left in an uncovered container or in puddles on the ground. This will prove fatal in sufficient quantity. Always drain the coolant into a sealable container. Coolant should be reused unless it is contaminated or several years old.*

5. Disconnect the muffler inlet pipe at the exhaust manifold. Pull the muffler inlet pipe down. Remove the gasket.
6. Disconnect the accelerator rod and cable retracting spring.
7. Disconnect the choke control cable if applicable and the accelerator rod at the carburetor or throttle body.
8. Disconnect the transmission kickdown rod.
9. Disconnect the accelerator linkage at the bellcrank assembly.
10. Disconnect the fuel inlet line at the fuel filter hose.
11. Disconnect the distributor vacuum line at the carburetor or throttle body.
12. Disconnect other vacuum lines as necessary for accessibility and identify them for proper connection.
13. Remove the radiator upper hose at the coolant outlet housing.
14. Disconnect the distributor vacuum line at the distributor.
15. Disconnect the fuel outlet line at the fuel pump. Remove the lines as an assembly.
16. Disconnect the spark plug wires at the spark plugs.
17. Disconnect the temperature sending unit wire at the sending unit.
18. Grasp the PCV vent hose near the PCV valve and pull the valve out of the grommet in the valve rocker arm cover.
19. Disconnect the PCV vent hose at the hose fitting in the intake manifold spacer and remove the vent hose and PCV valve.
20. Disconnect the carburetor air vent tube.
21. Remove the valve rocker arm cover.
22. Remove the valve rocker arm shaft assembly.
23. Remove the pushrods in sequence so that they can be identified and reinstalled in their original positions.
24. Remove the cylinder head bolts and remove the cylinder head. Do not pry between the cylinder head and the block as the gasket surfaces maybe damaged.

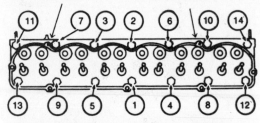

LOCATION FOR ⁵⁄₁₆″–18 LIFTING EYES

Cylinder head bolt torque sequence, 6-240,300

To install the cylinder head:

25. Clean the head and block gasket surfaces. If the cylinder head was removed for a gasket change, check the flatness of the cylinder head and block.
26. Apply sealer to both sides of the new cylinder head gasket. Position the gasket on the cylinder block.
27. Install a new gasket on the flange of the muffler inlet pipe.
28. Lift the cylinder head above the cylinder block and lower it into position using two head bolts installed through the head as guides.
29. Coat the threads of the no. 1 and 6 bolts for the right side of the cylinder head with a small amount of water-resistant sealer. Oil the threads of the remaining bolts. Install, but do not tighten, the two bolts at the opposite ends of the head to hold the head and gasket in position.
30. The cylinder head bolts are tightened in 3 progressive steps. Torque them (in the proper sequence) to 55 ft.lb., then 65 ft.lb. and finally to 75 ft.lb.
31. Apply Lubriplate® to both ends of the pushrods and install them in their original positions.
32. Install the valve rocker arm shaft assembly.
33. Adjust the valves, as necessary.
34. Install the muffler inlet pipe lockwasher and attaching nuts.
35. Connect the radiator upper hose at the coolant outlet housing.
36. Position the distributor vacuum line and the fuel inlet line on the engine.
37. Connect the fuel line at the fuel filter hose and install a new clamp.
38. Install the distributor vacuum line at the carburetor.
39. Connect the accelerator linkage at the bellcrank assembly.
40. Connect the transmission kickdown rod.
41. Connect the accelerator rod retracting spring.
42. Connect the choke control cable (if applicable) and the accelerator rod at the carburetor or throttle body.

43. Connect the distributor vacuum line at the distributor.

44. Connect the carburetor fuel inlet line at the fuel pump.

45. Connect all the vacuum lines using their previous identification for proper connection.

46. Connect the temperature sending unit wire at the sending unit.

47. Connect the spark plug wires.

48. Connect the battery cable at the cylinder head.

49. Fill the cooling system.

50. Install the valve rocker cover.

51. Connect the carburetor air vent tube.

52. Connect the PCV vent hose at the carburetor spacer fitting. Insert the PCV valve with the vent hose attached, into the valve rocker arm cover grommet.

53. Install the air cleaner, start the engine and check for leaks.

Gasoline V8 Except 8-460 (7.5L)

WARNING: *When working on fuel injected engines, discharge the fuel system pressure before starting any work that involves disconnecting the fuel system lines. See Fuel Supply Manifold Removal and Installation procedures in Chapter 5.*

1. Remove the intake manifold, carburetor or EFI.

2. Remove the rocker arm cover(s).

3. If the right cylinder head is to be removed, loosen the alternator adjusting arm bolt and remove the alternator mounting bracket bolt and spacer. Swing the alternator down and out of the way. Remove the air cleaner inlet duct from the right cylinder head assembly.

If the left cylinder head is being removed, remove the bolts fastening the accelerator shaft assembly at the front of the cylinder head. On vehicles equipped with air conditioning, the system must be discharged and the compressor removed. See Chapter 1.

4. Disconnect the exhaust manifold(s) from the muffler inlet pipe(s).

5. Loosen the rocker arm stud nuts so that the rocker arms can be rotated to the side. Remove the pushrods and identify them so that they can be reinstalled in their original positions.

6. Remove the cylinder head bolts and lift the cylinder head from the block.

To install the cylinder head(s):

1. Clean the cylinder head, intake manifold, the valve cover and the head gasket surfaces.

2. A specially treated composition head gasket is used. Do not apply sealer to a composition gasket. Position the new gasket over the locating dowels on the cylinder block. Then, position

the cylinder head on the block and install the attaching bolts.

3. The cylinder head bolts are tightened in 3 progressive steps. Tighten all the bolts in the proper sequence to 50 ft.lb., 60 ft.lb., and then to the final figure. On the 8-351, to 70 ft.lb., 80 ft.lb., and then to the final; figure.

4. Clean the pushrods. Blow out the oil passage in the rods with compressed air. Check the pushrods for straightness by rolling them on a piece of glass. Never try to straighten a pushrod; always replace it.

5. Apply Lubriplate® to the ends of the pushrods and install them in their original positions.

6. Apply Lubriplate® to the rocker arms and their fulcrum seats and install the rocker arms. Adjust the valves.

7. Position a new gasket(s) on the muffler inlet pipe(s) as necessary. Connect the exhaust manifold(s) at the muffler inlet pipe(s).

8. If the right cylinder head was removed, install the alternator, ignition coil and air cleaner duct on the right cylinder head. Adjust the drive belt.

If the left cylinder head was removed, install the accelerator shaft assembly at the front of the cylinder head.

9. Clean the valve rocker arm cover and the cylinder head gasket surfaces. Place the new gaskets in the covers, making sure that the tabs of the gasket engage the notches provided in the cover. Install the compressor, evacuate, charge and leak test the system. See Chapter 1.

10. Install the intake manifold and related parts.

8-460 (7.5L)

WARNING: *When working on fuel injected engines, discharge the fuel system pressure before starting any work that involves disconnecting the fuel system lines. See Fuel Supply Manifold Removal and Installation procedures in Chapter 5.*

1. Remove the intake manifold and carburetor or throttle body as an assembly.

2. Disconnect the exhaust pipe from the exhaust manifold.

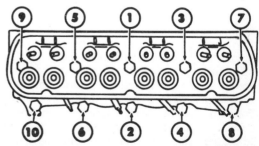

Cylinder head bolt torque sequence, all gasoline V8's

3. Loosen the air conditioning compressor drive belt, if so equipped.

4. Loosen the alternator attaching bolts and remove the bolt attaching the alternator bracket to the right cylinder head.

5. Disconnect the air conditioning compressor from the engine and move it aside, out of the way. DO NOT DISCHARGE THE AIR CONDITIONING SYSTEM.

6. Remove the bolts securing the power steering reservoir bracket to the left cylinder head. Position the reservoir and bracket out of the way.

7. Remove the valve rocker arm covers. Remove the rocker arm bolts, rocker arms, oil deflectors, fulcrums and pushrods in sequence so that they can be reinstalled in their original positions.

8. Remove the cylinder head bolts and lift the head and exhaust manifold off the engine. If necessary, pry at the forward corners of the cylinder head against the casting bosses provided on the cylinder block. Do not damage the gasket mating surfaces of the cylinder head and block by prying against them.

9. Remove all gasket material from the cylinder head and block. Clean all gasket material from the mating surfaces of the intake manifold. If the exhaust manifold was removed, clean the mating surfaces of the cylinder head and exhaust manifold. Apply a thin coat of graphite grease to the cylinder head exhaust port areas and install the exhaust manifold.

10. Position two long cylinder head bolts in the two rear lower bolt holes of the left cylinder head. Place a long cylinder head bolt in the rear lower bolt hole of the right cylinder head. Use rubber bands to keep the bolts in position until the cylinder heads are installed on the cylinder block.

11. Position new cylinder head gaskets on the cylinder block dowels. Do not apply sealer to the gaskets, heads, or block.

12. Place the cylinder heads on the block, guiding the exhaust manifold studs into the exhaust pipe connections. Install the remaining cylinder head bolts. The longer bolts go in the lower row of holes.

13. Tighten all the cylinder head attaching bolts in the proper sequence in three stages: 75 ft.lb., 105 ft.lbs., and finally to 135 ft.lb. When this procedure is used, it is not necessary to retorque the heads after extended use.

14. Make sure that the oil holes in the pushrods are open and install the pushrods in their original positions. Place a dab of Lubriplate to the ends of the pushrods before installing them.

15. Lubricate and install the valve rockers. Make sure that the pushrods remain seated in their lifters.

16. Connect the exhaust pipes to the exhaust manifolds.

17. Install the intake manifold and carburetor assembly. Tighten the intake manifold attaching bolts in the proper sequence to 25-30 ft.lb.

18. Install the air conditioning compressor to the engine.

19. Install the power steering reservoir to the engine.

20. Apply oil-resistant sealer to one side of the new valve cover gaskets and lay the cemented side in place in the valve cover. Install the covers.

21. Install the alternator to the right cylinder head and adjust the alternator drive belt tension.

22. Adjust the air conditioning compressor drive belt tension.

23. Fill the radiator with coolant.

24. Start the engine and check for leaks.

8-420 (6.9L) and 8-444 (7.3L) Diesel

1. Open the hood and disconnect the negative cables from both batteries.

2. Drain the cooling system and remove the radiator fan shroud halves.

CAUTION: *When draining the coolant, keep in mind that cats and dogs are attracted by the ethylene glycol antifreeze, and are quite likely to drink any that is left in an uncovered container or in puddles on the ground. This will prove fatal in sufficient quantity. Always drain the coolant into a sealable container. Coolant should be reused unless it is contaminated or several years old.*

3. Remove the radiator fan and clutch assembly using special tool T83T-6312-A and B. This tool is available through the Owatonna Tool Co. whose address is listed in the front of this boot, or through Ford Dealers. It is also available through many tool rental shops.

NOTE: *The fan clutch uses a left hand thread and must be removed by turning the nut clockwise.*

4. Label and disconnect the wiring from the alternator.

5. Remove the adjusting bolts and pivot bolts from the alternator and the vacuum pump and remove both units.

6. Remove the fuel filter lines and cap to prevent fuel leakage.

7. Remove the alternator, vacuum pump, and fuel filter brackets with the fuel filter attached.

8. Remove the heater hose from the cylinder head.

9. Remove the fuel injection pump as described in Chapter 5 under Diesel Fuel Systems.

10. Remove the intake manifold and valley cover.

11. Jack up the truck and safely support it with jackstands.

12. Disconnect the exhaust pipes from the exhaust manifolds.

13. Remove the clamp holding the engine oil dipstick tube in place and the bolt attaching the transmission oil dipstick to the cylinder head.

14. Lower the truck.

15. Remove the engine oil dipstick tube.

16. Remove the valve covers, rocker arms and pushrods. Keep the pushrods in order so they can be returned to their original positions.

17. Remove the nozzles and glow plugs as described in Chapter 5 under Diesel Fuel Systems.

18. Remove the cylinder head bolts and attach lifting eyes, using special tool T70P-6000 or equivalent, to each end of the cylinder heads.

19. Carefully lift the cylinder heads out of the engine compartment and remove the head gaskets.

NOTE: *The cylinder head prechambers may fall out of the heads upon removal.*

To install:

20. Position the cylinder head gasket on the engine block and carefully lower the cylinder head in place.

NOTE: *Use care in installing the cylinder heads to prevent the prechambers from falling out into the cylinder bores.*

21. Install the cylinder head bolt and torque in 4 steps using the sequence shown in the illustration.

NOTE: *Lubricate the threads and the mating surfaces of the bolt heads and washers with engine oil.*

22. Dip the pushrod ends in clean engine oil

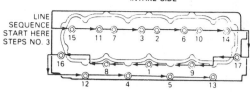

INTAKE SIDE

LINE SEQUENCE START HERE STEPS NO. 3

EXHAUST SIDE

STEP 1. TIGHTEN BOLTS TO 88 N·m (65 FT·LB) IN NUMBERED SEQUENCE SHOWN ABOVE.
STEP 2. TIGHTEN BOLTS TO 115 N·m (85 FT·LB) IN NUMBERED SEQUENCE SHOWN ABOVE.
STEP 3. TIGHTEN BOLTS TO 136 N·m (100 FT·LB) IN LINE SEQUENCE SHOWN ABOVE.
STEP 4. REPEAT STEP NO. 3.

7.3L diesel head bolt torque sequence

and install the pushrods with the copper colored ends toward the rocker arms, making sure the pushrods are fully seated in the tappet pushrod seats.

23. Install the rocker arms and posts in their original positions. Apply Lubriplate® grease to the valve stem tips. Turn the engine over by hand until the timing mark is at the 11 o'clock position as viewed from the front. Install the rocker arm posts, bolts, and torque to 27 ft.lb. Install the valve covers.

24. Install the valley pan and the intake manifold.

25. Install the fuel injection pump as described in Chapter 5 under Diesel Fuel Systems.

26. Connect the heater hose to the cylinder head.

27. Install the fuel filter, alternator, vacuum pump, and their drive belts.

28. Install the engine oil and transmission dip stick.

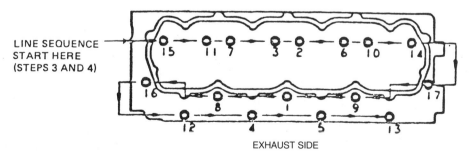

INTAKE SIDE

LINE SEQUENCE START HERE (STEPS 3 AND 4)

EXHAUST SIDE

CYLINDER HEAD BOLTS
STEP 1. TORQUE BOLTS TO 40 FT.-LBS. IN NUMBERED SEQUENCE SHOWN ABOVE.
STEP 2. TORQUE BOLTS TO 65 FT.-LBS. IN NUMBERED SEQUENCE SHOWN ABOVE.
STEP 3. TORQUE BOLTS TO 75 FT.-LBS. IN LINE SEQUENCE SHOWN ABOVE.
STEP 4. REPEAT STEP 3.

420 V8 diesel—cylinder head bolt torque sequence

29. Connect the exhaust pipe the the exhaust manifolds.

30. Reconnect the alternator wiring harness and replace the air cleaner. Connect both battery ground cables.

31. Refill and bleed the cooling system.

32. Run the engine and check for fuel, coolant and exhaust leaks.

NOTE: *If necessary, purge the high pressure fuel lines of air by loosening the connector one half to one turn and cranking the engine until a solid stream of fuel, free from any bubbles, flows from the connections.*

33. Check the injection pump timing. Refer to Chapter 5 for these procedures.

34. Install the radiator fan and clutch assembly using special tools T83T-6312A and B or equivalent.

NOTE: *The fan clutch uses a left hand thread. Tighten by turning the nut counterclockwise. Install the radiator fan shroud halves.*

CLEANING AND INSPECTION

1. With the valves installed to protect the valve seats, remove deposits from the combustion chambers and valve heads with a scraper and a wire brush. Be careful not to damage the cylinder head gasket surface. After the valves are removed, clean the valve guide bores with a valve guide cleaning tool. Using cleaning solvent to remove dirt, grease and other deposits, clean all bolts holes; be sure the oil passage is clean (V8 engines).

2. Remove all deposits from the valves with a fine wire brush or buffing wheel.

3. Inspect the cylinder heads for cracks or excessively burned areas in the exhaust outlet ports.

4. Check the cylinder head for cracks and inspect the gasket surface for burrs and nicks. Replace the head if it is cracked.

5. On cylinder heads that incorporate valve seat inserts, check the inserts for excessive wear, cracks, or looseness.

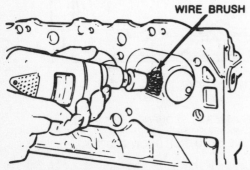

Remove the carbon from the cylinder head with a wire brush and electric drill

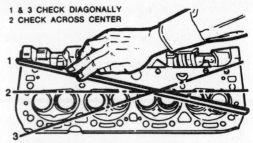

1 & 3 CHECK DIAGONALLY
2 CHECK ACROSS CENTER

Check the cylinder head for warpage

RESURFACING

Cylinder Head Flatness

When the cylinder head is removed, check the flatness of the cylinder head gasket surfaces.

1. Place a straightedge across the gasket surface of the cylinder head. Using feeler gauges, determine the clearance at the center of the straightedge.

2. If warpage exceeds 0.003″ (0.076mm) in a 6″ (152mm) span, or 0.006″ (0.152mm) over the total length, the cylinder head must be resurfaced.

3. If it is necessary to refinish the cylinder head gasket surface, do not plane or grind off more than 0.254mm (0.010″) from the original gasket surface.

NOTE: *When milling the cylinder heads of V8 engines, the intake manifold mounting position is altered, and must be corrected by milling the manifold flange a proportionate amount. Consult an experienced machinist about this.*

Valves and Springs

REMOVAL AND INSTALLATION

1. Block the head on its side, or install a pair of head-holding brackets made especially for valve removal.

2. Use a socket slightly larger than the valve stem and keepers, place the socket over the valve stem and gently hit the socket with a plastic hammer to break loose any varnish buildup.

3. Remove the valve keepers, retainer, spring shield and valve spring using a valve spring compressor (the locking C-clamp type is the easiest kind to use).

4. Put the parts in a separate container numbered for the cylinder being worked on; do not mix them with other parts removed.

5. Remove and discard the valve stem oil seals. A new seal will be used at assembly time.

6. Remove the valves from the cylinder head and place them, in order, through numbered holes punched in a stiff piece of cardboard or wood valve holding stick.

NOTE: *The exhaust valve stems, on some en-*

gines, are equipped with small metal caps. Take care not to lose the caps. Make sure to re-install them at assembly time. Replace any caps that are worn.

7. Use an electric drill and rotary wire brush to clean the intake and exhaust valve ports, combustion chamber and valve seats. In some cases, the carbon will need to be chipped away. Use a blunt pointed drift for carbon chipping. Be careful around the valve seat areas.

8. Use a wire valve guide cleaning brush and safe solvent to clean the valve guides.

9. Clean the valves with a revolving wires brush. Heavy carbon deposits may be removed with the blunt drift.

NOTE: *When using a wire brush to clean carbon on the valve ports, valves etc., be sure that the deposits are actually removed, rather than burnished.*

10. Wash and clean all valve springs, keepers, retaining caps etc., in safe solvent.

11. Clean the head with a brush and some safe solvent and wipe dry.

12. Check the head for cracks. Cracks in the cylinder head usually start around an exhaust valve seat because it is the hottest part of the combustion chamber. If a crack is suspected but cannot be detected visually have the area checked with dye penetrant or other method by the machine shop.

13. After all cylinder head parts are reasonably clean, check the valve stem-to-guide clearance. If a dial indicator is not on hand, a visual inspection can give you a fairly good idea if the guide, valve stem or both are worn.

14. Insert the valve into the guide until slight away from the valve seat. Wiggle the valve sideways. A small amount of wobble is normal, excessive wobble means a worn guide or valve stem. If a dial indicator is on hand, mount the

STEP 1—SET NO. 1 PISTON ON T.D.C. AT END OF COMPRESSION STROKE ADJUST NO. 1 INTAKE AND EXHAUST

STEP 4—ADJUST NO. 6 INTAKE AND EXHAUST

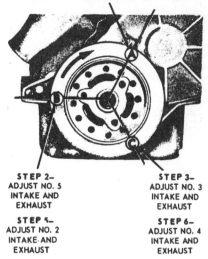

STEP 2—
ADJUST NO. 5 INTAKE AND EXHAUST

STEP 3—
ADJUST NO. 3 INTAKE AND EXHAUST

STEP 5—
ADJUST NO. 2 INTAKE AND EXHAUST

STEP 6—
ADJUST NO. 4 INTAKE AND EXHAUST

Position of crankshaft for valve adjustment, 6-200,240,300

indicator so that the stem of the valve is at 90° to the valve stem, as close to the valve guide as possible. Move the valve off the seat, and measure the valve guide-to-stem clearance by rocking the stem back and forth to actuate the dial indicator. Measure the valve stem using a micrometer and compare to specifications to determine whether stem or guide wear is causing excessive clearance.

15. The valve guide, if worn, must be repaired

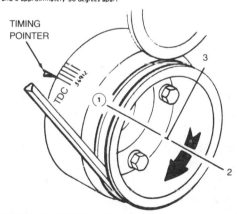

With No. 1 at TDC at end of compression stroke make a chalk mark at points 2 and 3 approximately 90 degrees apart

TIMING POINTER

POSITION 1 – No. 1 at TDC at end of compression stroke.
POSITION 2 – Rotate the crankshaft 180 degrees (one half revolution) clockwise from POSITION 1
POSITION 3 – Rotate the crankshaft 270 degrees (three quarter revolution clockwise from POSITION 2.

Position of the crankshaft for checking and adjusting valve clearance

Adjusting valve clearance on 144,170 6 Cyl. with solid lifters using step-type feeler gauge

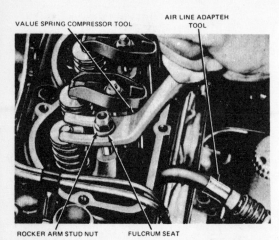

VALUE SPRING COMPRESSOR TOOL   AIR LINE ADAPTER TOOL

ROCKER ARM STUD NUT   FULCRUM SEAT

Compressing valve spring with cylinder head on the engine

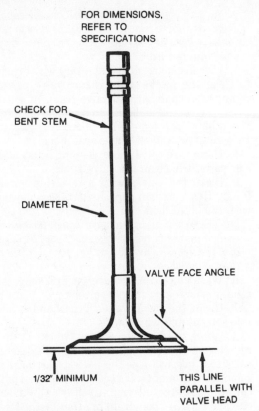

FOR DIMENSIONS, REFER TO SPECIFICATIONS

CHECK FOR BENT STEM

DIAMETER

VALVE FACE ANGLE

1/32" MINIMUM

THIS LINE PARALLEL WITH VALVE HEAD

Critical valve dimensions

before the valve seats can be resurfaced. Ford supplies valves with oversize stems to fit valve guides that are reamed to oversize for repair. The machine shop will be able to handle the guide reaming for you. In some cases, if the guide is not too badly worn, knurling may be all that is required.

16. Reface, or have the valves and valve seats refaced. The valve seats should be a true 45° angle. Remove only enough material to clean up any pits or grooves. Be sure the valve seat is not too wide or narrow. Use a 60° grinding wheel to remove material from the bottom of the seat for raising and a 30° grinding wheel to remove material from the top of the seat to narrow.

17. After the valves are refaced by machine, hand lap them to the valve seat. Clean the grinding compound off and check the position of face-to-seat contact. Contact should be close to the center of the valve face. If contact is close to the top edge of the valve, narrow the seat; if too close to the bottom edge, raise the seat.

18. Valves should be refaced to a true angle of

44°. Remove only enough metal to clean up the valve face or to correct runout. If the edge of a valve head, after machining, is $\frac{1}{32}$" (0.8mm) or less replace the valve. The tip of the valve stem should also be dressed on the valve grinding machine, however, do not remove more than 0.010" (0.254mm).

19. After all valve and valve seats have been machined, check the remaining valve train parts (springs, retainers, keepers, etc.) for wear. Check the valve springs for straightness and tension.

AIR LINE ADAPTER TOOL

OIL SEAL

Removing or installing valve stem seals

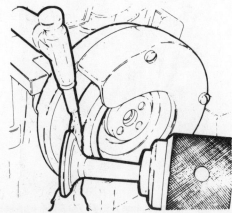

Valve grinding by machine

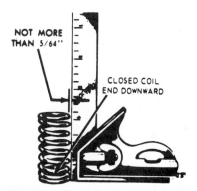

NOT MORE THAN 5/64"

CLOSED COIL END DOWNWARD

Check the valve spring free length and squareness

Check the valve spring test pressure

VALVE STEM OIL SEALS

When installing valve stem oil seals, ensure that a small amount of oil is able to pass the seal to lubricate the valve stems and guide walls, otherwise, excessive wear will occur.

VALVE SEATS

If the valve seat is damaged or burnt and cannot be serviced by refacing, it may be possible to have the seat machined and an insert installed. Consult an automotive machine shop for their advice.

VALVE GUIDES

Worn valve guides can, in most cases, be reamed to accept a valve with an oversized

20. Install the valves in the cylinder head and metal caps.

21. Install new valve stem oil seals.

22. Install the valve keepers, retainer, spring shield and valve spring using a valve spring compressor (the locking C-clamp type is the easiest kind to use).

23. Check the valve spring installed height, shim or replace as necessary.

CHECKING VALVE SPRINGS

Place the valve spring on a flat surface next to a carpenter's square. Measure the height of the spring, and rotate the spring against the edge of the square to measure distortion. If the spring height varies (by comparison) by more than $\frac{1}{16}''$ (1.6mm) or if the distortion exceeds $\frac{1}{16}''$ (1.6mm), replace the spring.

Have the valve springs tested for spring pressure at the installed and compressed (installed height minus valve lift) height using a valve spring tester. Springs should be within one pound, plus or minus each other. Replace springs as necessary.

VALVE SPRING INSTALLED HEIGHT

After installing the valve spring, measure the distance between the spring mounting pad and the lower edge of the spring retainer. Compare the measurement to specifications. If the installed height is incorrect, add shim washers between the spring mounting pad and the spring. Use only washers designed for valve springs, available at most parts houses.

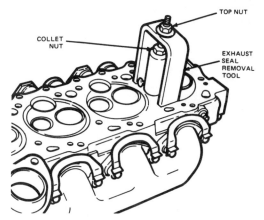

TOP NUT

COLLET NUT

EXHAUST SEAL REMOVAL TOOL

Removing the diesel exhaust valve seats

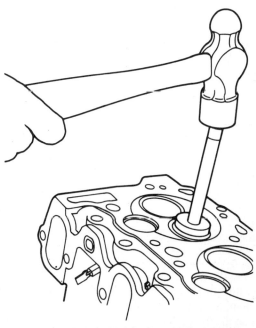

Installing the 420 V8 diesel exhaust valve seats

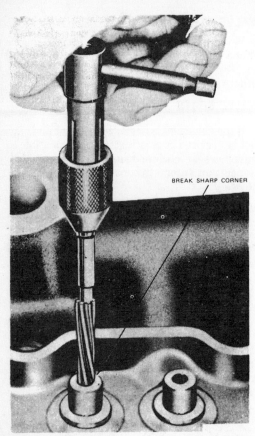

BREAK SHARP CORNER

Reaming valve guides

stem. Valve guides that are not excessively worn or distorted may, in some cases, be knurled rather than reamed. However, if the valve stem is worn reaming for an oversized valve stem is the answer since a new valve would be required.

Knurling is a process in which metal is displaced and raised, thereby reducing clearance. Knurling also produces excellent oil control. The possibility of knurling instead of reaming the valve guides should be discussed with a machinist.

HYDRAULIC VALVE CLEARANCE

Hydraulic valve lifters operate with zero clearance in the valve train, and because of this the rocker arms are nonadjustable. The only means by which valve system clearances can be altered is by installing over or undersize pushrods; but, because of the hydraulic lifter's natural ability to compensate for slack in the valve train, all components of all the valve system should be checked for wear if there is excessive play in the system.

When a valve in the engine is in the closed position, the valve lifter is resting on the base circle of the camshaft lobe and the pushrod is in its lowest position. To remove this additional clearance from the valve train, the valve lifter expands to maintain zero clearance in the valve system. When a rocker arm is loosened or removed from the engine, the lifter expands to it fullest travel. When the rocker arm is reinstalled on the engine, the proper valve setting is obtained by tightening the rocker arm to a specified limit. But with the lifter fully expanded, if the camshaft lobe is on a high point it will require excessive torque to compress the lifter and obtain the proper setting. Because of this, when any component of the valve system has been removed, a preliminary valve adjustment procedure must be followed to ensure that when the rocker arm is reinstalled on the engine and tightened, the camshaft lobe for that cylinder is in the low position.

To determine whether a shorter or loner push rod is necessary, make the following check:

Mark the crankshaft pulley as described under Preliminary Valve Adjustment procedure. Follow each step in the procedure. As each valve is positioned, mount a suitable hydraulic lifter compressor tool on the rocker arm. Slowly apply pressure to bleed down the lifter until the plunger is completely bottomed. Take care to avoid excessive pressure that might bend the pushrod. Hold the lifter in bottom position and check the available clearance between the rocker arm and the valve stem tip with a feeler gauge. If the clearance is less than specified, install an undersized pushrod. If the clearance is greater than specified, install an oversized pushrod. When compressing the valve spring to remove the pushrods, be sure the piston in the individual cylinder is below TDC to avoid contact between the valve and the piston. To replace a pushrod, it will be necessary to remove the valve rocker arm shaft assembly on inline engines. Upon replacement of a valve pushrod, valve rocker arm shaft assembly or hydraulic valve lifter, the engine should not be cranked or rotated until the hydraulic lifters have had an opportunity to leak down to their normal operation position. The leak down rate can be accelerated by using the tool shown on the valve rocker arm and applying pressure in a direction to collapse the lifter.

Collapsed tappet gap

V8 Engines
- 8-302 and 8-351
  Allowable: 0.089-0.193″ (2.260-4.902mm)
  Desired: 0.096-0.163″ (2.438-4.140mm)

Valve Seats

REMOVAL AND INSTALLATION

8-420 (6.9L) and 8-444 (7.3L) Diesel

NOTE: *The diesel is the only engine covered in this guide which has removable valve seats.*

1. Using Ford Rotunda tool 14-0309 the exhaust valve seats may be removed. Position the remover collet into the insert and rotate the collet nut clockwise to expand the collet jaws under the lip of the seat insert.

2. Rotate the top nut clockwise to remove the insert.

NOTE: *If an oversize seat insert is required, the cylinder head should be sent out to a qualified machine shop.*

3. To install a new exhaust valve seat, drive the seat in place using Rotunda tool 14-0309 and a hammer.

Valve seat inserts are supplied for service in standard size, 0.015" (0.381mm) oversize and 0.030" (0.762mm) oversize.

Valve Guides

REAMING VALVE GUIDES

If it becomes necessary to ream a valve guide to install with an oversize stem, a reaming kit is available which contains a oversize reamers and pilot tools.

When replacing a standard size valve with an oversize valve always use the reamer in sequence (smallest oversize first, then next smallest, etc.) so as not to overload the reamers. Always reface the valve seat after the valve guide has been reamed, and use a suitable scraper to brake the sharp corner at the top of the valve guide.

KNURLING

Valve guides which are not excessively worn or distorted may, in some cases, be knurled rather than reamed. Knurling is a process in which metal inside the valve guide bore is displaced and raised (forming a very fine cross-hatch pattern), thereby reducing clearance. Knurling also provides for excellent oil control. The possibility of knurling rather than reaming the guides should be discussed with a machinist.

STEM-TO-GUIDE CLEARANCE

Valve stem-to-guide clearance should be checked upon assembling the cylinder head, and is especially necessary if the valve guides have been reamed or knurled, or if oversize valve have been installed. Excessive oil consumption often is a result of too much clearance between the valve guide and valve stem.

1. Clean the valve stem with lacquer thinner or a similar solvent to remove all gum and varnish. Clean the valve guides using solvent and an expanding wire-type valve guide cleaner (a rifle cleaning brush works well here).

2. Mount a dial indicator so that the stem is 90° to the valve stem and as close to the valve guide as possible.

3. Move the valve off its seat, and measure the valve guide-to-stem clearance by rocking the stem back and forth to actuate the dial indicator. Measure the valve stems using a micrometer and compare to specifications, to determine whether stem or guide wear is responsible for excessive clearance.

VALVE LAPPING

The valve must be lapped into their seats after resurfacing, to ensure proper sealing. Even if the valve have not been refaced, they should be lapped into the head before reassembly.

Set the cylinder head on the workbench, combustion chamber side up. Rest the head on wooden blocks on either end, so there are 2-3" (51-76mm) between the tops of the valve guides and the bench.

1. Lightly lube the valve stem with clean engine oil. Coat the valve seat completely with valve grinding compound. Use just enough compound so that the full width and circumference of the seat are covered.

2. Install the valve in its proper location in the head. Attach the suction cup end of the valve lapping tool to the valve head. It usually helps to put a small amount of saliva into the suction cup to aid it sticking to the valve.

3. Rotate the tool between the palms, changing position and lifting the tool often to prevent grooving. Lap the valve in until a smooth, evenly polished seat and valve face are evident.

4. Remove the valve from the head. Wipe away all traces of grinding compound from the valve face and seat. Wipe out the port with a solvent soaked rag, and swab out the valve guide with a piece of solvent soaked rag to make sure there are no traces of compound grit inside the guide. This cleaning is very important, as the engine will ingest any grit remaining when started.

5. Proceed through the remaining valves, one at a time. Make sure the valve faces, sets, cylinder ports and valve guides are clean before reassembling the valve train.

Diesel Prechambers

REMOVAL AND INSTALLATION

1. Clean and inspect the prechambers and ports for cracks.

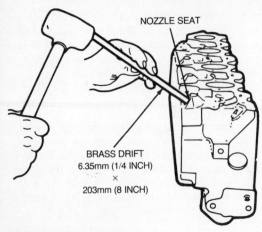

NOZZLE SEAT

BRASS DRIFT
6.35mm (1/4 INCH)
×
203mm (8 INCH)

Diesel prechamber removal

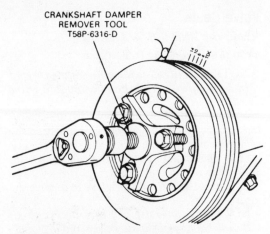

CRANKSHAFT DAMPER
REMOVER TOOL
T58P-6316-D

Removing the 6-300 crankshaft damper

2. If necessary, remove the prechambers by driving them out with a brass drift.

3. To install a new prechamber, coat the mounting edge of the prechamber with a light coating of heavy grease.

4. Position the prechamber in the head and tap it into place with a plastic hammer.

Crankshaft Pulley (Vibration Damper)

REMOVAL AND INSTALLATION

1. Remove the fan shroud, as required. If necessary, drain the cooling system and remove the radiator. Remove drive belts from pulley.

CAUTION: *When draining the coolant, keep in mind that cats and dogs are attracted by*

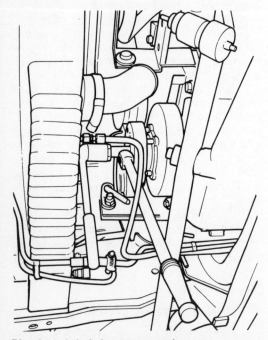

Diesel crankshaft damper removal

the ethylene glycol antifreeze, and are quite likely to drink any that is left in an uncovered container or in puddles on the ground. This will prove fatal in sufficient quantity. Always drain the coolant into a sealable container. Coolant should be reused unless it is contaminated or several years old.

2. On those engines with a separate pulley, remove the retaining bolts and separate the pulley from the vibration damper.

3. Remove the vibration damper/pulley retaining bolt from the crankshaft end.

4. Using a puller, remove the damper/pulley from the crankshaft.

5. Upon installation, align the key slot of the pulley hub to the crankshaft key. Complete the assembly in the reverse order of removal. Torque the retaining bolts to the specifications found in the Torque Specifications Chart.

Oil Pan

REMOVAL AND INSTALLATION

6-144 (2.4L)
6-170 (2.8L)
6-200 (3.3L)
6-240 (3.9L)
6-300 (4.9L)

1. Drain the crankcase and also drain the cooling system.

CAUTION: *When draining the coolant, keep in mind that cats and dogs are attracted by the ethylene glycol antifreeze, and are quite likely to drink any that is left in an uncovered container or in puddles on the ground. This will prove fatal in sufficient quantity. Always drain the coolant into a sealable container. Coolant should be reused unless it is contaminated or several years old.*

2. Remove the oil dipstick.

3. Disconnect the upper radiator hose at the thermostat housing.

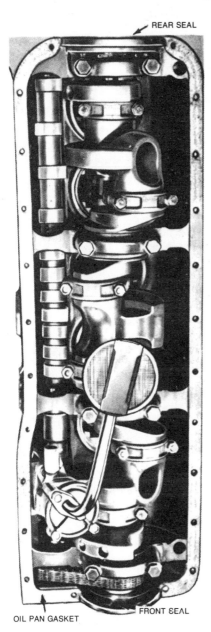

Positioning of the oil pan gaskets and seals on the 144, 170, and 200 six-cylinder

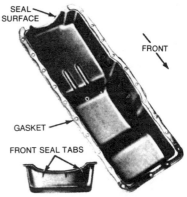

Positioning of the oil pan gaskets and seals on the 240 and 300 six-cylinder

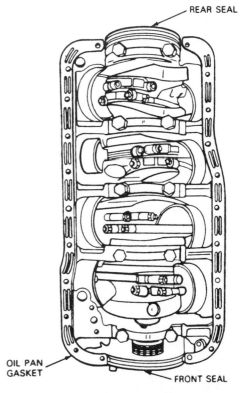

8-302, 351 oil pan gaskets and seals

4. Disconnect the flexible fuel line at the fuel pump.

5. Raise and support the van on jackstands.

6. Remove the air deflector from under the radiator.

7. Disconnect the lower radiator hose at the radiator.

8. Disconnect the starter wires at the starter.

9. Remove the starter.

10. On 1975 and later vans, remove the air cleaner and carburetor.

11. Remove the engine front support insulator-to-support bracket nuts and washers on both supports. Raise the front of the engine with a transmission jack and wood block and place 1″ (25mm) thick wood blocks between the front support insulators and support brackets. Lower the engine and remove the transmission jack.

12. Remove the oil pan attaching bolts and lower the pan to the crossmember.

13. Remove the 2 oil pump inlet tube and screw assembly bolts and drop the assembly in the pan.

14. Remove the oil pan.

15. Remove the oil pump inlet tube attaching bolts.

16. Remove the inlet tube and screen assembly from the oil pump and leave it in the bottom of the oil pan.

17. Remove the oil pan gaskets.

18. Remove the inlet tube and screen from the oil pan.

19. Clean the gasket surfaces of the oil pump, oil pan and cylinder block.

20. Remove the rear main bearing cap-to-oil pan seal and cylinder front cover to oil pan seal. Clean the seal grooves.

21. Apply oil-resistant sealer in the cavities between the bearing cap and cylinder block.

22. Install a new seal in the rear main bearing cap and apply a bead of oil-resistant sealer to the tapered ends of the seal.

23. Install new side gaskets on the oil pan with oil-resistant sealer.

24. Position a new oil pan to cylinder front cover seal on the oil pan.

25. Clean the inlet tube and screen assembly and place it in the oil pan.

26. Position the oil pan under the engine.

27. Install the inlet tube and screen assembly on the oil pump with a new gasket.

28. Tighten the screws to 5-7 ft.lb.

29. Position the oil pan against the cylinder block and install the attaching bolts. Tighten the bolts in sequence to 10-12 ft.lb.

30. Raise the engine with a transmission jack and remove the wood blocks from the engine front supports.

31. Lower the engine until the front support insulators are positioned on the support brackets.

32. Install the washers and nuts on the insulator studs and tighten the nuts.

33. Install the starter and connect the starter cable.

34. Lower the vehicle.

35. Install the radiator.

36. Fill the crankcase and cooling system.

37. Start the engine and check for coolant and oil leaks.

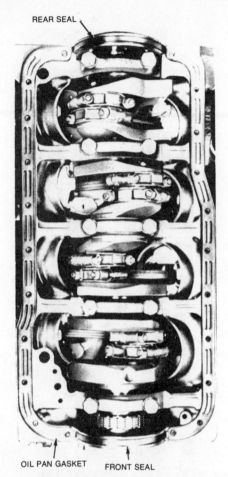

REAR SEAL

OIL PAN GASKET   FRONT SEAL

Positioning of the oil pan gaskets and seals on the 302 V8

8-302 (5.0L)
8-351W (5.7L)

1. Remove the oil dipstick (on pan entry models only).

2. Remove the bolts attaching the fan shroud to the radiator and position the shroud over the fan.

3. Remove the nuts and lockwashers attaching the engine support insulators to the chassis bracket.

4. If equipped with an automatic transmission, disconnect the oil cooler line at the left side of the radiator.

5. Raise the engine and place wood blocks under the engine supports.

6. Drain the crankcase.

7. Remove the oil pan attaching bolts and lower the oil pan onto the crossmember.

8. Remove the two bolts attaching the oil pump pick-up tube to the oil pump. Remove the nut attaching oil pump pick-up tube to the number 3 main bearing cap stud. Lower the pick-up tube and screen into the oil pan.

9. Remove the oil pan from the vehicle.

10. Clean the oil pan, inlet tube and gasket surfaces. Inspect the gasket sealing surface for damage and distortion due to overtightening of the bolts. Repair and straighten as required.

11. Position a new oil pan gasket and seal to the cylinder block.

12. Position the oil pick-up tube and screen to the oil pump, and install the lower attaching bolt and gasket loosely. Install the nut attaching the number 3 main bearing cap stud.

13. Place the oil pan on the crossmember. Install the upper pick-up tube bolt. Tighten the pick-up tube bolts.

14. Position the oil pan on the cylinder block and install the attaching bolts. Tighten the bolts to 10-12 ft.lb.

8-400 (6.6L)
8-460 (7.5L)

1. Raise and support the truck on jackstands.

2. Remove the oil dipstick.

3. Remove the bolts attaching the fan shroud and position it over the fan.

4. Remove the engine support insulators-to-chassis bracket attaching nuts and washers.

5. Disconnect the exhaust pipe at the manifolds.

6. If the vehicle is equipped with an automatic transmission, disconnect the oil cooler line at the left side of the radiator.

7. Raise the engine with a jack placed under the crankshaft damper and a block of wood to act as a cushion. Place wood blocks under the engine supports.

8. Drain the crankcase.

9. Remove the oil filter.

10. Remove the oil pan attaching screws and lower the oil pan onto the crossmember.

11. Remove the two bolts attaching the oil pump pick-up tube to the oil pump. Lower the assembly from the oil pump. Leave it on the bottom of the oil pan.

12. Remove the oil pan and gaskets.

13. Remove the inlet tube and screen from the oil pan.

14. In preparation for installation, clean the gasket surfaces of the oil pump, oil pan and cylinder block.

15. Remove the rear main bearing cap-to-oil pan seal and engine front cover-to-oil pan seal. Clean the seal grooves.

16. Position the oil pan front and rear seal on the engine front cover and the rear main bearing cap, respectively. Be sure that the tabs on the seals are over the oil pan gasket.

17. Clean the inlet tube and screen assembly and place it in the oil pan.

18. Position the oil pan under the engine and install the inlet tube and screen assembly on the oil pump with a new gasket.

19. Position the oil pan against the cylinder block and install the retaining bolts.

20. Assemble the rest of the engine in the reverse order of disassembly, starting with Step 7.

21. Fill the crankcase with oil. Start the engine and check for leaks.

8-420 (6.9L), 8-444 (7.3L) Diesel

1. Disconnect both battery ground cables.

2. Remove the engine oil dipstick.

3. Remove the transmission oil dipstick.

4. Remove the air cleaner and cover the intake opening.

5. Remove the fan and fan clutch.

NOTE: *The fan uses left hand threads. Remove them by turning them clockwise.*

6. Drain the cooling system.

CAUTION: *When draining the coolant, keep in mind that cats and dogs are attracted by the ethylene glycol antifreeze, and are quite likely to drink any that is left in an uncovered container or in puddles on the ground. This will prove fatal in sufficient quantity. Always drain the coolant into a sealable container. Coolant should be reused unless it is contaminated or several years old.*

7. Disconnect the lower radiator hose.

8. Disconnect the power steering return hose and plug the line and pump.

9. Disconnect the alternator wiring harness.

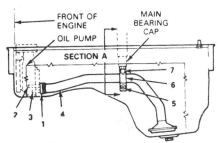

1. OIL PICK-UP TUBE MOUNTING GASKET
2. 5/16"-18 × 2" BOLT AND 5/16" HARDENED WASHER
3. 5/16"-18 × 1-1/2" BOLT AND 5/16" HARDENED WASHER
4. OIL PICK-UP TUBE ASSEMBLY
5. 5/16"-18 × 0.930 BOLT W WASHER
6. OIL TUBE BRACKET
7. 5/16"-18 NUT AND 5/16" LOCK AND HARDENED WASHERS

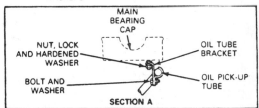

Diesel oil pick-up tube installation

10. Disconnect the fuel line heater connector from the alternator.

11. Raise and support the front end on jackstands.

12. On vans with automatic transmission, disconnect the transmission cooler lines at the radiator and plug them.

13. Disconnect and plug the fuel pump inlet line.

14. Drain the crankcase and remove the oil filter.

15. Remove the engine oil filler tube.

16. Disconnect the exhaust pipes at the manifolds.

17. Disconnect the muffler inlet pipe from the muffler and remove the pipe.

18. Remove the upper inlet mounting stud from the right exhaust manifold.

19. Unbolt the engine from the No.1 crossmember.

20. Lower the vehicle.

21. Install lifting brackets on the front of the engine.

22. Raise the engine until the transmission contact the body.

23. Install wood blocks (2¾" on the left side; 2" on the right side) between the engine insulators and crossmember.

24. Lower the engine onto the blocks.

25. Raise and support the front end on jackstands.

26. Remove the flywheel inspection plate.

27. Position fuel pump inlet line No.1 rearward of the crossmember and position the oil cooler lines out of the way.

28. Remove the oil pan bolts.

29. Lower the oil pan.

NOTE: *The oil pan is sealed to the crankcase with RTV silicone sealant in place of a gasket. It may be necessary to separate the pan from the crankcase with a utility knife.*

CHILTON TIP: *The crankshaft may have to be turned to allow the pan to clear the crankshaft throws.*

30. Clean the pan and crankcase mating surfaces thoroughly.

To install:

31. Apply a ⅛" bead of RTV silicone sealant to the pan mating surfaces, and a ¼" bead on the front and rear covers and in the corners. You have 15 minutes within which to install the pan!

32. Install locating dowels (which you supply) into position as shown.

33. Position the pan on the engine and install the pan bolts loosely.

34. Remove the dowels.

35. Torque the pan bolts to 7 ft.lb. for ¼"-20 bolts; 14 ft.lb. for ⁵⁄₁₆"-18 bolts; 24 ft.lb for ⅜"-16 bolts.

36. Install the flywheel inspection cover.

37. Lower the van.

38. Raise the engine and remove the wood blocks.

39. Lower the engine onto the crossmember and remove the lifting brackets.

40. Raise and support the front end on jackstands.

41. Torque the engine-to-crossmember nuts to 70 ft.lb.

42. Install the upper inlet pipe mounting stud.

43. Install the inlet pipe, using a new gasket.

44. Install the transmission oil filler tube, using a new gasket.

45. Install the oil pan drain plug.

46. Install a new oil filter.

47. Connect the fuel pump inlet line. Make sure that the clip is installed on the crossmember.

48. Connect the transmission cooler lines.

49. Lower the van.

50. Connect all wiring.

51. Connect the power steering return line.

52. Connect the lower radiator hose.

53. Install the fan and fan clutch.

NOTE: *The fan uses left hand threads. Install them by turning them counterclockwise.*

54. Remove the cover and install the air cleaner.

55. Install the dipsticks.

56. Fill the crankcase.

57. Fill and bleed the cooling system.

58. Fill the power steering reservoir.

59. Connect the batteries.

60. Run the engine and check for leaks.

Oil Pump

REMOVAL AND INSTALLATION

Gasoline Engines

1. Remove the oil pan.

2. Remove the oil pump inlet tube and screen assembly.

3. Remove the oil pump attaching bolts and remove the oil pump gasket and intermediate driveshaft.

4. Before installing the oil pump, prime it by filling the inlet and outlet port with engine oil and rotating the shaft of the pump to distribute it.

5. Position the intermediate driveshaft into the distributor socket.

6. Position the new gasket on the pump body and insert the intermediate driveshaft into the pump body.

7. Install the pump and intermediate drive-

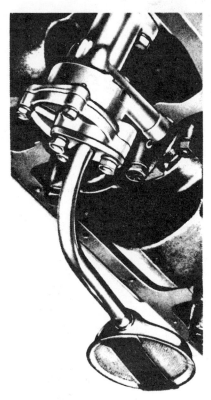

Oil pump with the inlet tube attached—6-144,170,200 engines

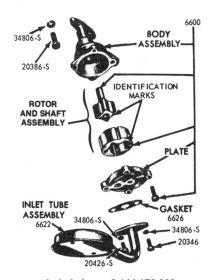

Oil pump exploded view—6-144,170,200

shaft as an assembly. Do not force the pump if it does not seal readily. The driveshaft may be misaligned with the distributor shaft. To align it, rotate the intermediate driveshaft into a new position.

8. Install the oil pump attaching bolts and

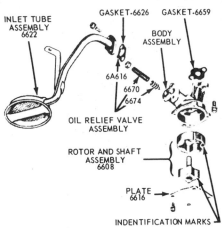

Typical V8 oil pump

torque them to 12-15 ft.lb. on the inline sixes and to 20-25 ft.lb. on the V8s.

Diesel Engines

1. Remove the oil pan.
2. Remove the oil pick-up tube from the pump.
3. Unbolt and remove the oil pump.
4. Assemble the pick-up tube and pump. Use a new gasket.
5. Install the oil pump and torque the bolts to 14 ft.lb.

OVERHAUL

1. Wash all parts in solvent and dry them thoroughly with compressed air. Use a brush to clean the inside of the pump housing and the pressure relief valve chamber. Be sure all dirt and metal particles are removed.
2. Check the inside of the pump housing and the outer race and rotor for damage or excessive wear or scoring.
3. Check the mating surface of the pump cover for wear. If the cover mating surface is worn, scored, or grooved, replace the pump.
4. Measure the inner rotor tip clearance.
5. With the rotor assembly installed in the housing, place a straightedge over the rotor assembly and the housing. Measure the clearance (rotor end play) between the straightedge and the rotor and the outer race.
6. Check the drive shaft to housing bearing clearance by measuring the OD of the shaft and the ID of the housing bearing.
7. Components of the oil pump are not serviced. If any part of the pump requires replacement, replace the complete pump assembly.
8. Inspect the relief valve spring to see if it is collapsed or worn.
9. Check the relief valve piston for scores and free operation in the bore.

NOTE: INNER TO OUTER ROTOR
TIP CLEARANCE MUST
NOT EXCEED .012 WITH
FEELER GAUGE INSERTED
1/2" MINIMUM AND ROTORS
REMOVED FROM PUMP
HOUSING.

Checking inner rotor tip clearance

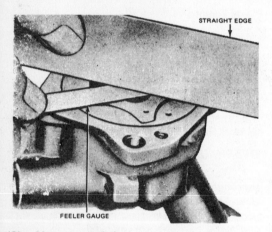

STRAIGHT EDGE

FEELER GAUGE

Checking rotor end play

Engine Oil Cooler

REMOVAL AND INSTALLATION

8-420 (6.9L) and 8-444 (7.3L) Diesel

The diesel oil cooler should be disassembled if the cooler O-rings begin to leak.

1. Disconnect the batteries' ground cables.
2. Remove the radiator fan shroud halves.
3. Remove the fan and clutch assembly using tool T83T-6312-A and B, or equivalent.

NOTE: *The mounting bolts have left hand threads.*

4. Raise and support the front end on jackstands.
5. Drain the engine oil and remove the oil filter. Do not install the drain plug.
6. Remove the nut attaching the left side engine mount insulator to the frame.
7. Slight raise the left side of the engine with a floor jack and place a 1" (25mm) wood block

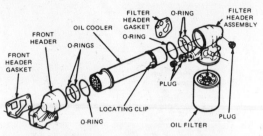

Oil cooler assembly—420 V8 diesel engine

between the insulator and the frame. Allow the engine to rest on the block.

8. Remove the oil cooler-to-block bolts and lower the cooler from the van.
9. Gently rap the front and oil cooler headers to loosen the O-rings. Carefully twist the oil cooler apart.
10. Using a suitable solvent, thoroughly clean the oil cooler and the front and filter headers.
11. Always use new O-rings when reassembling. Lubricate the new rings and all O-ring mating surfaces with clean engine oil. Install the two narrow O-rings into their respective grooves inside the front and filter headers.
12. Place the large O-ring over the oil cooler shell.
13. Press the assembly together, making sure the locating clips align with the slots.
14. Using new gaskets, install the engine oil cooler.
15. Raise the engine, remove the wood block and lower the engine back onto its mount.
16. Install the mount washer and nut. Torque the nut to 80 ft.lb.
17. Install a new oil filter.
18. Install the oil pan drain plug.
19. Refill the crankcase and prime the system to fill the cooler.

WARNING: *Priming the system is strongly recommended to avoid any chance of scuffing or heat build-up during initial engine operation!*

20. Install all other parts in reverse order of removal.

Timing Gear or Chain Front Cover and Oil Seal

REMOVAL AND INSTALLATION

6-144 (2.4L)
6-170 (2.8L)
6-200 (3.3L)

1. Drain the cooling system and disconnect the radiator upper hose at the coolant outlet elbow and remove the two upper radiator retaining bolts.

CAUTION: *When draining the coolant, keep in mind that cats and dogs are attracted by*

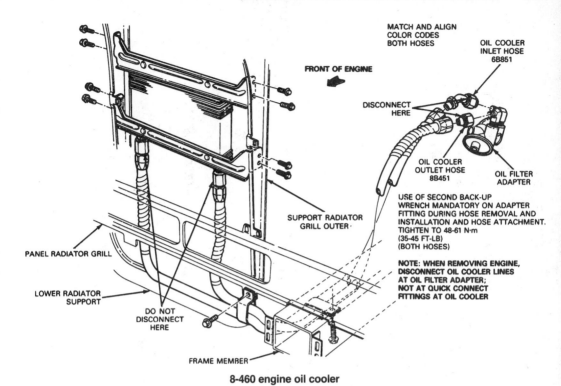

MATCH AND ALIGN COLOR CODES BOTH HOSES

FRONT OF ENGINE

OIL COOLER INLET HOSE 6B851

DISCONNECT HERE

OIL COOLER OUTLET HOSE 8B451

OIL FILTER ADAPTER

SUPPORT RADIATOR GRILL OUTER

USE OF SECOND BACK-UP WRENCH MANDATORY ON ADAPTER FITTING DURING HOSE REMOVAL AND INSTALLATION AND HOSE ATTACHMENT. TIGHTEN TO 48-61 N·m (35-45 FT-LB) (BOTH HOSES)

NOTE: WHEN REMOVING ENGINE, DISCONNECT OIL COOLER LINES AT OIL FILTER ADAPTER; NOT AT QUICK CONNECT FITTINGS AT OIL COOLER

PANEL RADIATOR GRILL

LOWER RADIATOR SUPPORT

DO NOT DISCONNECT HERE

FRAME MEMBER

8-460 engine oil cooler

the ethylene glycol antifreeze, and are quite likely to drink any that is left in an uncovered container or in puddles on the ground. This will prove fatal in sufficient quantity. Always drain the coolant into a sealable container. Coolant should be reused unless it is contaminated or several years old.

2. Raise the vehicle and drain the crankcase.

3. Remove the splash shield and the automatic transmission oil cooling lines, if so equipped, then remove the radiator.

4. Loosen and remove the fan belt, fan and pulley.

5. Use a gear puller to remove the crankshaft pulley damper.

6. Remove the cylinder front cover retaining bolts and gently pry the cover away from the block. Remove the gasket.

7. Drive out the old seal with a pin punch from the rear of the cover. Clean out the recess in the cover.

8. Coat the new seal with grease and drive it into the cover until it is fully seated. Check the seal to make sure that the spring around the seal is in the proper position.

9. Clean the cylinder front cover and the gasket surface of the cylinder block. Apply an oil-resistant sealer to the new front cover gasket and install the gasket onto the cover.

10. Install the cylinder front cover onto the engine.

NOTE: Trim away the exposed portion of the old oil pan gasket flush with the front of the engine block. Cut and position the required portion of a new gasket to the oil pan and apply sealer to both sides.

11. Lubricate the hub of the crankshaft damper pulley with Lubriplate® to prevent damage to the seal during installation or on initial starting of the engine.

12. Install and assemble the remaining components in the reverse order of removal, starting from Step 4. Start the engine and check for leaks.

6-240 (3.9L)
6-300 (4.9L)

1. Drain the cooling system and disconnect the radiator upper hose at the coolant outlet elbow and remove the two upper radiator retaining bolts.

CAUTION: When draining the coolant, keep in mind that cats and dogs are attracted by the ethylene glycol antifreeze, and are quite likely to drink any that is left in an uncovered container or in puddles on the ground. This will prove fatal in sufficient quantity. Always drain the coolant into a sealable container. Coolant should be reused unless it is contaminated or several years old.

2. Raise the vehicle and drain the crankcase.

3. Remove the splash shield and the automatic transmission oil cooling lines, if so equipped, then remove the radiator.

4. Loosen and remove the fan belt, fan and pulley.

5. Use a gear puller to remove the crankshaft pulley damper.

6. Remove the cylinder front cover retaining bolts and gently pry the cover away from the block. Remove the gasket.

7. Drive out the old seal with a pin punch from the rear of the cover. Clean out the recess in the cover.

8. Coat the new seal with grease and drive it into the cover until it is fully seated. Check the seal to make sure that the spring around the seal is in the proper position.

9. Clean the cylinder front cover and the gasket surface of the cylinder block. Apply an oil-resistant sealer to the new front cover gasket and install the gasket onto the cover.

10. Position the front cover assembly over the end of the crankshaft and against the cylinder block. Start, but do not tighten, the cover and pan attaching screws. Slide a front cover alignment tool (Ford part no. T68P-6019-A or equivalent) over the crank stub and into the seal bore of the cover. Tighten all front cover and oil pan attaching screws to 12-18 ft.lb. front cover; 10-15 ft.lb. oil pan, tightening the oil pan screws first.

NOTE: *Trim away the exposed portion of the old oil pan gasket flush with the front of the engine block. Cut and position the required portion of a new gasket to the oil pan and apply sealer to both sides.*

11. Lubricate the hub of the crankshaft damper pulley with Lubriplate® to prevent damage to the seal during installation or on initial starting of the engine.

12. Install and assemble the remaining components in the reverse order of removal, starting from Step 4. Start the engine and check for leaks.

Gasoline V8 Except 8-460 (7.5L)

WARNING: *When working on fuel injected engines, discharge the fuel system pressure before starting any work that involves disconnecting the fuel system lines. See Fuel Supply Manifold Removal and Installation procedures in Chapter 5.*

1. Drain the cooling system and the crankcase.

CAUTION: *When draining the coolant, keep in mind that cats and dogs are attracted by the ethylene glycol antifreeze, and are quite likely to drink any that is left in an uncovered container or in puddles on the ground. This will prove fatal in sufficient quantity. Always drain the coolant into a sealable container. Coolant should be reused unless it is contaminated or several years old.*

2. Disconnect the upper and lower radiator hoses from the water pump, transmission oil cooler lines from the radiator, and remove the radiator.

Alignment of the timing marks on the crankshaft and camshaft timing chain sprockets of the 144, 170, 200 6-cylinder

Alignment of the timing marks on the crankshaft and camshaft timing chain sprockets on the V8

Alignment of the timing marks on the crankshaft and camshaft timing gears on the 240, 300 six-cylinder

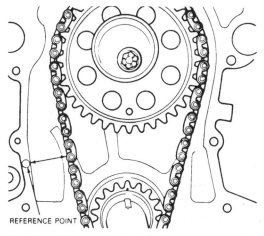

Checking V8 timing chain deflection

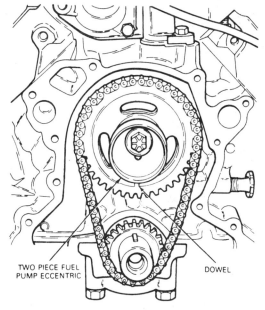

Fuel pump eccentric installed on the 8-302 and 8-351

3. Disconnect the heater hose from the water pump. Slide the water pump by-pass hose clamp toward the water pump.

4. Loosen the alternator pivot bolt and the bolt which secures the alternator adjusting arm to the water pump. Position the alternator out of the way.

5. Remove the power steering pump and air conditioning compressor from their mounting brackets, if so equipped.

6. Remove the bolts holding the fan shroud to the radiator, if so equipped. Remove the fan, spacer, pulley and drive belts.

7. Remove the crankshaft pulley from the crankshaft damper. Remove the damper attaching bolt and washer and remove the damper with a puller.

8. Disconnect the fuel pump outlet line at the fuel pump. Disconnect the vacuum inlet and outlet lines from the fuel pump. Remove the fuel pump attaching bolts and lay the pump to one side with the fuel inlet line still attached.

9. Remove the oil level dipstick and the bolt holding the dipstick tube to the exhaust manifold on the 8-302.

10. Remove the oil pan-to-cylinder front cover attaching bolts. Use a sharp, thin cutting blade to cut the oil pan gasket flush with the cylinder block. Remove the front cover and water pump as an assembly.

11. Discard the front cover gasket.

12. Place the front seal removing tool (Ford part no. T70P-6B070-A or equivalent) into the front cover plate and over the front of the seal as shown in the illustration. Tighten the two through bolts to force the seal puller under the seal flange, then alternately tighten the four puller bolts a half turn at a time to pull the oil seal from the cover.

13. Coat a new front cover oil seal with Lubriplate® or equivalent and place it onto the front oil seal alignment and installation tool (Ford part no. T70P-6B070-A or equivalent) as shown in the illustration. Place the tool and the seal onto the end of the crankshaft and push it toward the engine until the seal starts into the front cover.

14. Place the installation screw, washer, and nut onto the end of the crankshaft, then thread the screw into the crankshaft. Tighten the nut against the washer and tool to force the seal into the front cover plate. Remove the tool.

15. Apply Lubriplate® or equivalent to the oil seal rubbing surface of the vibration damper inner hub to prevent damage to the seal. Coat the front of the crankshaft with engine oil for damper installation.

16. To install the damper, line up the damper keyway with the key on the crankshaft, then install the damper onto the crankshaft. Install the cap screw and washer, and tighten the screw to 80 ft.lb. Install the crankshaft pulley.

17. Assemble the rest of the engine in the reverse order of disassembly.

8-460 (7.5L)

WARNING: *When working on fuel injected engines, discharge the fuel system pressure before starting any work that involves disconnecting the fuel system lines. See Fuel Supply Manifold Removal and Installation procedures in Chapter 5.*

1. Drain the cooling system and crankcase.

CAUTION: *When draining the coolant, keep in mind that cats and dogs are attracted by the ethylene glycol antifreeze, and are quite likely to drink any that is left in an uncovered container or in puddles on the ground. This will prove fatal in sufficient quantity. Always drain the coolant into a sealable container. Coolant should be reused unless it is contaminated or several years old.*

2. Remove the radiator shroud and fan.

3. Disconnect the upper and lower radiator hoses, and the automatic transmission oil cooler lines from the radiator.

4. Remove the radiator upper support and remove the radiator.

5. Loosen the alternator attaching bolts and air conditioning compressor idler pulley and remove the drive belts with the water pump pulley. Remove the bolts attaching the compressor support to the water pump and remove the bracket (support), if so equipped.

6. Remove the crankshaft pulley from the vibration damper. Remove the bolt and washer attaching the crankshaft damper and remove the damper with a puller. Remove the woodruff key from the crankshaft.

7. Loosen the by-pass hose at the water pump, and disconnect the heater return tube at the water pump.

8. Disconnect and plug the fuel inlet and outlet lines at the fuel pump, and remove the fuel pump.

9. Remove the bolts attaching the front cover to the cylinder block. Cut the oil pan seal flush with the cylinder block face with a thin knife blade prior to separating the cover from the cylinder block. Remove the cover and water pump as an assembly. Discard the front cover gasket and oil pan seal.

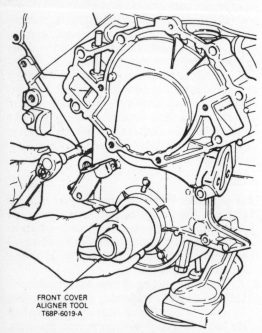

FRONT COVER
ALIGNER TOOL
T68P-6019-A

Aligning the front cover on the 8-460

10. Transfer the water pump if a new cover is going to be installed. Clean all of the gasket sealing surfaces on both the front cover and the cylinder block.

11. Coat the gasket surface of the oil pan with sealer. Cut and position the required sections of a new seal on the oil pan. Apply sealer to the corners.

12. Drive out the old front cover oil seal with a pin punch. Clean out the seal recess in the cover. coat a new seal with Lubriplate® or equivalent grease. Install the seal, making sure the seal spring remains in the proper position. A front cover seal tool, Ford part no. T72J-117 or equivalent, makes installation easier.

13. Coat the gasket surfaces of the cylinder block and cover with sealer and position the new gasket on the block.

14. Position the front cover on the cylinder block. Use care not to damage the seal and gasket or mislocate them.

15. Coat the front cover attaching screws with sealer and install them.

NOTE: *It may be necessary to force the front cover downward to compress the oil pan seal in order to install the front cover attaching bolts. Use a screwdriver or drift to engage the cover screw holes through the cover and pry downward.*

16. Assemble and install the remaining components in the reverse order of removal. Tighten the front cover bolts to 15-20 ft.lb., the water pump attaching screws to 12-15 ft.lb., the crankshaft damper to 70-90 ft.lb., the crankshaft pulley to 35-50 ft.lb., fuel pump to 19-27 ft.lb., the oil pan bolts to 9-11 ft.lb. for the $\frac{5}{16}$" screws and to 7-9 ft.lb. for the ¼" screws, and the alternator pivot bolt to 45-57 ft.lb.

8-420 (6.9L) and 8-444 (7.3L) Diesel

1. Disconnect both battery ground cables. Drain the cooling system.

CAUTION: *When draining the coolant, keep in mind that cats and dogs are attracted by the ethylene glycol antifreeze, and are quite likely to drink any that is left in an uncovered container or in puddles on the ground. This will prove fatal in sufficient quantity. Always drain the coolant into a sealable container. Coolant should be reused unless it is contaminated or several years old.*

2. Remove the air cleaner and cover the air intake on the manifold with clean rags. Do not allow any foreign material to enter the intake.

3. Remove the radiator fan shroud halves.

4. Remove the fan and fan clutch assembly. You will need a puller or ford tool No. T83T-6312-A for this.

NOTE: *The nut is a left hand thread; remove by turning the nut clockwise.*

5. Remove the injection pump as described in Chapter 5 under Diesel Fuel Systems.

6. Remove the water pump.

7. Jack up the truck and safely support it with jackstands.

8. Remove the crankshaft pulley and vibration damper as described in this chapter.

9. Remove the engine ground cables at the front of the engine.

10. Remove the five bolts attaching the engine front cover to the engine block and oil pan.

11. Lower the truck.

12. Remove the front cover.

NOTE: *The front cover oil seal on the diesel must be driven out with an arbor press and a 3¼″ (82.5mm) spacer. Take the cover to a qualified machinist or engine specialist for this procedure. See also steps 14 and 15.*

13. Remove all old gasket material from the front cover, engine block, oil pan sealing surfaces and water pump surfaces.

14. Coat the new front oil seal with Lubriplate® or equivalent grease.

15. The new seal must be installed using a

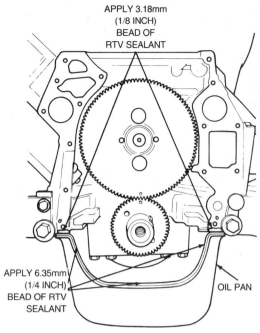

APPLY 3.18mm (1/8 INCH) BEAD OF RTV SEALANT

APPLY 6.35mm (1/4 INCH) BEAD OF RTV SEALANT

OIL PAN

Diesel front cover RTV application

seal installation tool, Ford part no. T83T-6700-A or an arbor press. A qualified machinist or engine specialist can handle seal installation as well as removal. When the seal bottoms out on the front cover surface, it is installed at the proper depth.

16. Install alignment dowels into the engine block to align the front cover and gaskets. These can be made out of round stock. Apply a gasket sealer to the engine block sealing surfaces, then install the gaskets on the block.

17. Apply a ⅛″ (3mm) bead of RTV sealer on the front of the engine block as shown in the illustration. Apply a ¼″ (6mm) bead of RTV sealer on the oil pan as shown.

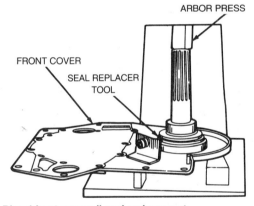

ARBOR PRESS

FRONT COVER

SEAL REPLACER TOOL

Diesel front cover oil seal replacement

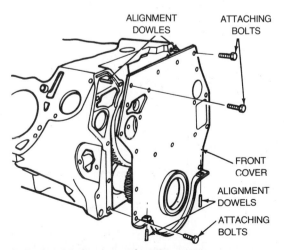

ALIGNMENT DOWLES

ATTACHING BOLTS

FRONT COVER

ALIGNMENT DOWELS

ATTACHING BOLTS

6.9L diesel front cover dowel alignment

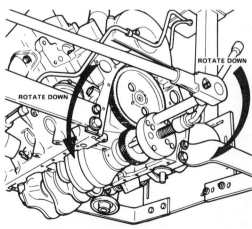

ROTATE DOWN

ROTATE DOWN

Removing the diesel crankshaft drive gear

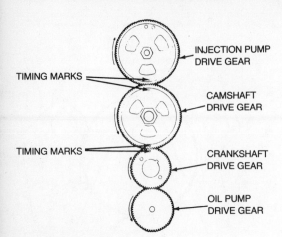

Diesel timing mark alignment

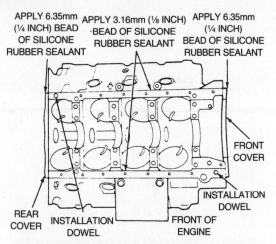

RTV sealant and dowel location for the diesel oil pan

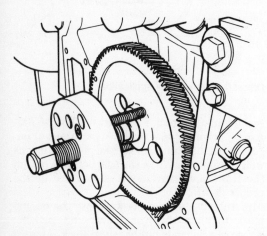

Diesel camshaft gear removal

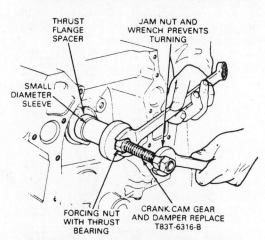

Installing the thrust flange spacer on the diesel

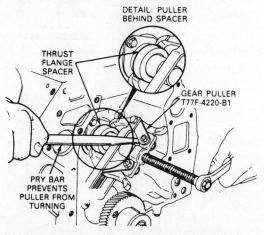

Removing the thrust flange spacer on the diesel

18. Install the front cover immediately after applying RTV sealer. The sealer will begin to cure and lose its effectiveness unless the cover is installed quickly.

19. Install the water pump gasket on the engine front cover. Apply RTV sealer to the four water pump bolts illustrated. Install the water pump and hand tighten all bolts.

WARNING: *The two top water pump bolts must be no more than 1¼" (31.75mm) long bolts any longer will interfere with (hit) the engine drive gears.*

20. Torque the water pump bolts to 19 ft.lb. Torque the front cover bolts to specifications according to bolt size (see Torque Specifications chart).

21. Install the injection pump adaptor and injection pump as described in Chapter 5 under Diesel Fuel System.

22. Install the heater hose fitting in the pump using pipe sealant, and connect the heater hose to the water pump.

23. Jack up the truck and safely support it with jackstands.

24. Lubricate the front of the crankshaft with clean engine oil. Apply RTV sealant to the en-

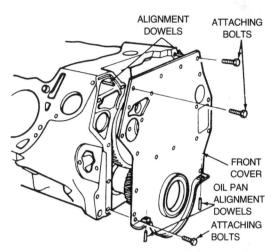

7.3L diesel front cover alignment dowels

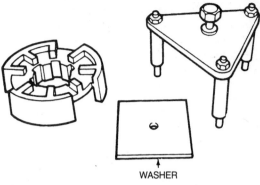

Tools for replacing the diesel front seal

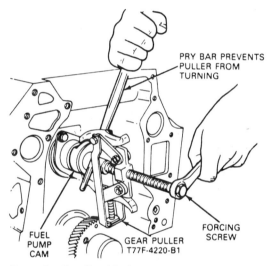

Removing the diesel fuel pump cam

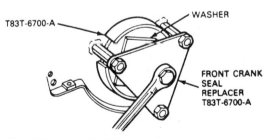

Diesel front seal installation

gine side of the retaining bolt washer to prevent oil seepage past the keyway. Install the crankshaft vibration damper using Ford Special tools T83T-6316B. Torque the damper-to-crankshaft bolt to 90 ft.lb.

25. Install the remaining engine components in the reverse order of removal.

CRANKSHAFT DRIVE GEAR

1. Complete the front cover removal procedures.

2. Install the crankshaft drive gear remover Tool T83T-6316-A, and using a breaker bar to prevent crankshaft rotation, or flywheel holding Tool T74R-6375-A, remove the crankshaft gear.

3. Install the crankshaft gear using Tool T83T-6316-B aligning the crankshaft drive gear timing mark with the camshaft drive gear timing mark.

NOTE: *The gear may be heated to 300-350°F for ease of installation. Heat it in an oven. Do not use a torch.*

4. Complete the front cover installation procedures.

INJECTION PUMP DRIVE GEAR AND ADAPTER

1. Disconnect the battery ground cables from both batteries. Remove the air cleaner and install an intake opening cover.

2. Remove the injection pump. Remove the bolts attaching the injection pump adapter to the engine block, and remove the adapter.

3. Remove the engine front cover. Remove the drive gear.

4. Clean all gasket and sealant surfaces of the components removed with a suitable solvent and dry them thoroughly.

5. Install the drive gear in position, aligning all the drive gear timing marks.

NOTE: *To determine that the No. 1 piston is at TDC of the compression stroke, position the injection pump drive gear dowel at the 4 o'clock position. The scribe line on the vibration damper should be at TDC.*

Use extreme care to avoid disturbing the injection pump drive gear, once it is in position.

6. Install the engine front cover. Apply a 1/8" (3mm) bead of RTV Sealant along the bottom surface of the injection pump adapter.

NOTE: *RTV should be applied immediately prior to adapter installation.*

7. Install the injection pump adaptor. Apply sealer to the bolt threads before assembly.

NOTE: *With the injection pump adapter installed, the injection pump drive gear cannot jump timing.*

8. Install all removed components. Run the engine and check for leaks.

NOTE: *If necessary, purge the high pressure fuel lines of air by loosening the connector one half to one turn and crank the engine until a solid flow of fuel, free of air bubbles, flows from the connection.*

CAMSHAFT DRIVE GEAR, FUEL PUMP CAM, SPACER AND THRUST PLATE

1. Complete the front cover removal procedures.

2. Remove the camshaft allen screw.

3. Install a gear puller, Tool T83T-6316-A and remove the gear. Remove the fuel supply pump, if necessary.

4. Install a gear puller, Tool T77E-4220-B and shaft protector T83T-6316-A and remove the fuel pump cam and spacer, if necessary.

5. Remove the bolts attaching the thrust plate, and remove the thrust plate, if necessary.

6. Install a new thrust plate, if removed.

7. Install the spacer and fuel pump cam against the camshaft thrust flange, using installation sleeve and replacer Tool T83T-6316-B, if removed.

8. Install the camshaft drive gear against the fuel pump cam, aligning the timing mark with the timing mark on the crankshaft drive gear, using installation sleeve and replacer Tool T83T-6316-B.

9. Install the camshaft allen screw and tighten to 18 ft.lb.

10. Install the fuel pump, if removed.

11. Install the front cover, following the previous procedure.

CHECKING TIMING CHAIN DEFLECTION

All Engines Except the 6-240 (3.9L) and 6-300 (4.9L)

To measure timing chain deflection, rotate the crankshaft clockwise to take up slack on the left side of chain. Choose a reference point and measure the distance from this point and the chain. Rotate the crankshaft in the opposite direction to take up slack on the right side of the chain. Force the left (slack) side of the chain out and measure the distance to the reference point chosen earlier. The difference between the two measurements is the deflection.

The timing chain should be replaced if the deflection measurement exceeded the specified limit. The deflection measurement should not exceed ½″ (13mm).

CAMSHAFT ENDPLAY MEASUREMENT

The camshaft gears used on some engines are easily damaged if pried upon while the valve train load is on the camshaft. Loosen the rocker arm nuts or rocker arm shaft support bolts before checking the camshaft endplay.

Push the camshaft toward the rear of engine, install and zero a dial indicator, then pry between the camshaft gear and the block to pull the camshaft forward. If the endplay is exces-

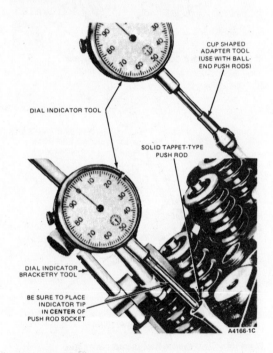

Checking camshaft lobe lift

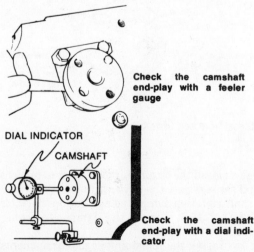

Check the camshaft end-play with a feeler gauge

Check the camshaft end-play with a dial indicator

Checking crankshaft end-play

sive, check for correct installation of the spacer. If the spacer is installed correctly, replace the thrust plate.

MEASURING TIMING GEAR BACKLASH

Use a dial indicator installed on block to measure timing gear backlash. Hold the gear firmly against the block while making the measurement. If excessive backlash exists, replace both gears.

Timing Chain
REMOVAL AND INSTALLATION
All Except the 6-240 (3.9L) and 6-300 (4.9L)

1. Remove the front cover.
2. Rotate the crankshaft counterclockwise to take up the slack on the left side of the chain.
3. Establish a reference point on the cylinder block and measure from this point to the chain.
4. Rotate the crankshaft in the opposite direction to take up the slack on the right side of the chain.
5. Force the left side of the chain out with your fingers and measure the distance between the reference point and the chain. The timing chain deflection is the difference between the two measurements. If the deflection exceeds ½" (13mm), replace the timing chain and sprockets.

To replace the timing chain and sprockets:

6. Turn the crankshaft until the timing marks on the sprockets are aligned vertically.
7. Remove the camshaft sprocket retaining screw and remove the fuel pump eccentric and washers.
8. Alternately slide both of the sprockets and timing chain off the crankshaft and camshaft until free of the engine.
9. Position the timing chain on the sprockets so that the timing marks on the sprockets are aligned vertically. Alternately slide the sprockets and chain onto the crankshaft and camshaft sprockets.
10. Install the fuel pump eccentric washers and attaching bolt on the camshaft sprocket. Tighten to 40-45 ft.lb.
11. Install the front cover.

Timing Gears
REMOVAL AND INSTALLATION
6-240 (3.9L)
6-300 (4.9L)

1. Drain the cooling system and remove the front cover.
   CAUTION: *When draining the coolant, keep in mind that cats and dogs are attracted by the ethylene glycol antifreeze, and are quite*

likely to drink any that is left in an uncovered container or in puddles on the ground. This will prove fatal in sufficient quantity. Always drain the coolant into a sealable container. Coolant should be reused unless it is contaminated or several years old.

2. Crank the engine until the timing marks on the camshaft and crankshaft gears are aligned.
3. Use a gear puller to removal both of the timing gears.
4. Before installing the timing gears, be sure that the key and spacer are properly installed. Align the gear key way with the key and install the gear on the camshaft. Be sure that the timing marks line up on the camshaft and the crankshaft gears and install the crankshaft gear.
5. Install the front cover, and assemble the rest of the engine in the reverse order of disassembly. Fill the cooling system.

8-420 (6.9L) and 8-444 (7.3L) Diesel

1. Follow the procedures for timing gear cover removal and installation, and remove the front cover.
2. To remove the crankshaft gear, install gear puller (Ford part) no. T83T-6316-A or equivalent, and using a breaker bar to prevent the crankshaft from rotating, remove the crankshaft gear. To install the crankshaft gear use tool (Ford part) no. T83T-6316-B or equivalent while aligning the timing marks as shown in the illustration, and press the gear into place.
3. The camshaft gear may be removed by taking out the Allen screw and installing a gear puller, Ford part no. T83T-6316-A or equivalent and removing the gear. The gear may be replaced by using tool (Ford part) no. T83T-6316-B or equivalent. Torque the Allen screw to 12-18 ft.lb.

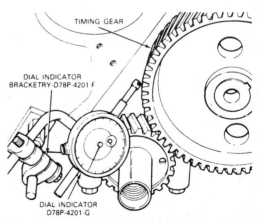

Checking drive gear backlash on the diesel

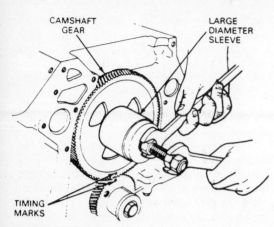

CAMSHAFT GEAR   LARGE DIAMETER SLEEVE

TIMING MARKS

Installing the diesel camshaft gear

Camshaft

REMOVAL AND INSTALLATION

NOTE: *This procedure will probably require removal of the engine for 1961-67 models.*

6-144 (2.4L)
6-170 (2.8L)
6-200 (3.3L)

1. Remove the front cover, align the timing marks, and remove the timing chain and related parts as stated before.
2. Remove the cylinder head as previously outlined.
3. Disconnect the distributor primary wire at the ignition coil. Loosen the distributor lockbolt and remove the distributor.
4. Disconnect and plug the fuel inlet line at the fuel pump. Remove the fuel pump and gasket.
5. Remove the valve tappets with a magnet. Note that the tappets must be replaced in the same positions from which they are removed.
6. Remove the oil level dipstick.
7. Remove the headlight doors and disconnect the light ground wires and the screws. Disconnect the headlights and parking lights.
8. Remove the grille and hood lock as an assembly.
9. Carefully withdraw the camshaft from the engine.
10. In preparation for installing the camshaft, clean the passage that feeds the rocker arm shaft by blowing compressed air into the opening in the block. Oil the camshaft journals and apply Lubriplate® to all of the camshaft lobes. If a new camshaft is being installed, the spacer and dowel from the old camshaft must be used. Carefully slide the camshaft through the bearings.
11. Assemble the engine in the reverse order of disassembly.

6-240 (3.9L)
6-300 (4.9L)

WARNING: *When working on fuel injected engines, discharge the fuel system pressure before starting any work that involves disconnecting the fuel system lines. See Fuel Supply Manifold Removal and Installation procedures in Chapter 5.*

1. Remove the grille, radiator, and timing cover.
2. Remove the distributor, fuel pump, oil pan and oil pump.
3. Align the timing marks. Unbolt the camshaft thrust plate, working through the holes in the camshaft gear.
4. Loosen the rocker arms, remove the pushrods, take off the side cover and remove the valve lifter with a magnet.
5. Remove the camshaft very carefully to prevent nicking the bearings.
6. Oil the camshaft bearing journals and use Lubriplate® or something similar on the lobes. Install the camshaft, gear, and thrust plate, aligning the gear marks. Tighten down the thrust plate. Make sure that the camshaft endplay is not excessive.
7. The last item to be replaced is the distributor. The rotor should be at the firing position for no. 1 cylinder, with the timing gear marks aligned.

V8 Including Diesel

NOTE: *Ford recommends removing the diesel engine for camshaft removal.*

WARNING: *When working on fuel injected engines, discharge the fuel system pressure before starting any work that involves disconnecting the fuel system lines. See Fuel Supply Manifold Removal and Installation procedures in Chapter 5.*

1. Remove the intake manifold and valley pan, if so equipped.
2. Remove the rocker covers, and either remove the rocker arm shafts or loosen the rockers on their pivots and remove the pushrods. The pushrods must be reinstalled in their original positions.
3. Remove the valve lifters in sequence with a magnet. They must be replaced in their original positions.
4. Remove the timing gear cover and timing chain (timing gear on V8 diesel) and sprockets.
5. In addition to the radiator and air conditioning condenser, if so equipped, it may be necessary to remove the front grille assembly and the hook lock assembly to gain the necessary clearance to code the camshaft out of the front of the engine.

NOTE: *A camshaft removal tool, Ford part no. T65L-6250-A and adaptor 14-0314 are needed to remove the diesel camshaft.*

6. Coat the camshaft with engine oil liberally before installing it. Slide the camshaft into the engine very carefully so as not to scratch the bearing bores with the camshaft lobes. Install the camshaft thrust plate and tighten the attaching screws to 9-12 ft.lb. Measure the camshaft end-play. If the end-play is more than 0.009″ (0.228mm), replace the thrust plate. Assemble the remaining components in the reverse order of removal.

CAMSHAFT INSPECTION

Camshaft Lobe Lift

Check the lift of each lobe in consecutive order and make a note of the reading.

1. Remove the fresh air inlet tube and the air cleaner. Remove the heater hose and crankcase ventilation hoses. Remove valve rocker arm cover(s).

2. Remove the rocker arm stud nut or fulcrum bolts, fulcrum seat and rocker arm.

3. Make sure the pushrod is in the valve tappet socket. Install a dial indicator D78P-4201-B or equivalent. so that the actuating point of the indicator is in the push rod socket (or the indicator ball socket adaptor tool 6565-AB is on the end of the push rod) and in the same plane as the push rod movement.

4. Disconnect the I terminal and the S terminal at the starter relay. Install an auxiliary starter switch between the battery and S terminals of the start relay. Crank the engine with the ignition switch off. Turn the crankshaft over until the tappet is on the base circle of the camshaft lobe. At this position, the push rod will be in its lowest position.

5. Zero the dial indicator. Continue to rotate the crankshaft slowly until the push rod is in the fully raised position.

6. Compare the total lift recorded on the dial indicator with the specification shown on the Camshaft Specification chart.

To check the accuracy of the original indicator reading, continue to rotate the crankshaft until the indicator reads zero. If the left on any lobe is below specified wear limits listed, the camshaft and the valve tappet operating on the worn lobe(s) must be replaced.

7. Install the dial indicator and auxiliary starter switch.

8. Install the rocker arm, fulcrum seat and stud nut or fulcrum bolts. Check the valve clearance. Adjust if required (refer to procedure in this chapter).

9. Install the valve rocker arm cover(s) and the air cleaner.

Camshaft End Play

NOTE: *On all gasoline V8 engines, prying against the aluminum-nylon camshaft sprocket, with the valve train load on the camshaft, can break or damage the sprocket. Therefore, the rocker arm adjusting nuts must be backed off, or the rocker arm and shaft assembly must be loosened sufficiently to free the camshaft. After checking the camshaft end play, check the valve clearance. Ad-*

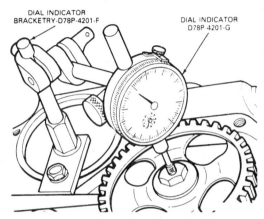

Checking camshaft endplay on gasoline V8s

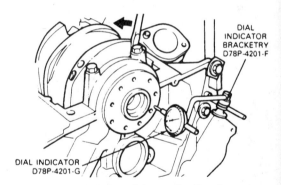

Checking crankshaft endplay on the diesel

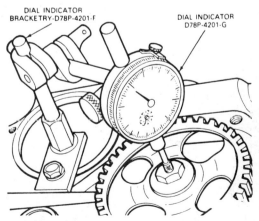

Checking camshaft endplay on the diesel

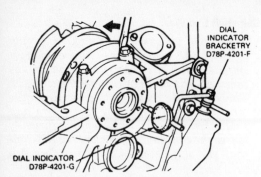

Checking crankshaft endplay on the diesel

just if required (refer to procedure in this chapter).

1. Push the camshaft toward the rear of the engine. Install a dial indicator (Tool D78P-4201-F, -G or equivalent so that the indicator point is on the camshaft sprocket attaching screw.

2. Zero the dial indicator. Position a prybar between the camshaft gear and the block. Pull the camshaft forward and release it. Compare the dial indicator reading with the specifications.

3. If the end play is excessive, check the spacer for correct installation before it is removed. If the spacer is correctly installed, replace the thrust plate.

4. Remove the dial indicator.

CAMSHAFT BEARING REPLACEMENT

1. Remove the engine following the procedures in this chapter and install it on a work stand.

2. Remove the camshaft, flywheel and crankshaft, following the appropriate procedures. Push the pistons to the top of the cylinder.

3. Remove the camshaft rear bearing bore plug. Remove the camshaft bearings with Tool T65L-6250-A or equivalent.

4. Select the proper size expanding collet and back-up nut and assemble on the mandrel. With the expanding collet collapsed, install the

collet assembly in the camshaft bearing and tighten the back-up nut on the expanding mandrel until the collet fits the camshaft bearing.

5. Assemble the puller screw and extension (if necessary) and install on the expanding man-

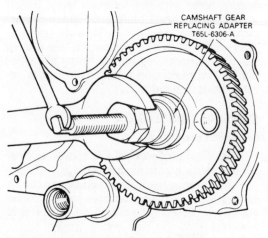

Installing the camshaft gear on the 6-300

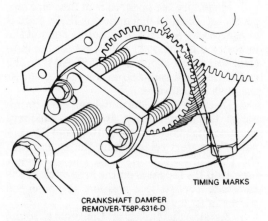

Removing the crankshaft gear from the 6-300

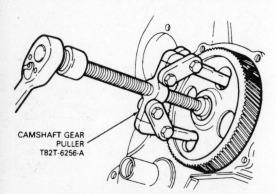

Removing the 6-300 camshaft gear

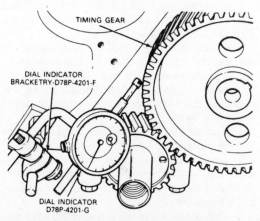

Checking timing gear backlash on the diesel

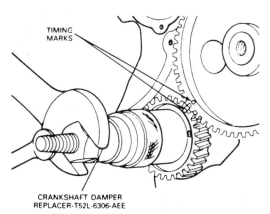

TIMING MARKS

CRANKSHAFT DAMPER
REPLACER-T52L-6306-AEE

Installing the crankshaft gear on the 6-300

drel. Wrap a cloth around the threads of the puller screw to protect the front bearing or journal. Tighten the pulling nut against the thrust bearing and pulling plate to remove the camshaft bearing. Be sure to hold a wrench on the end of the puller screw to prevent it from turning.

6. To remove the front bearing, install the puller from the rear of the cylinder block.

7. Position the new bearings at the bearing bores, and press them in place with tool T65L-6250-A or equivalent. Be sure to center the pulling plate and puller screw to avoid damage to the bearing. Failure to use the correct expanding collet can cause severe bearing damage. Align the oil holes in the bearings with the oil holes in the cylinder block before pressing bearings into place.

NOTE: *Be sure the front bearing is installed 0.020-0.035" (0.508-0.889mm) for the inline six cylinder engines, 0.005-0.020" (0.127-0.508mm) for the gasoline V8, 0.040-0.060" (1.016-1.524mm) for the diesel V8, below the front face of the cylinder block.*

8. Install the camshaft rear bearing bore plug.

9. Install the camshaft, crankshaft, flywheel and related parts, following the appropriate procedures.

10. Install the engine in the truck, following procedures described earlier in this chapter.

Pistons and Connecting Rods
REMOVAL AND INSTALLATION
6-144 (2.4L)
6-170 (2.8L)
6-200 (3.3L)
6-240 (3.9L)
6-300 (4.9L)

1. Drain the cooling system and the crankcase.

CAUTION: *When draining the coolant, keep in mind that cats and dogs are attracted by the ethylene glycol antifreeze, and are quite likely to drink any that is left in an uncovered container or in puddles on the ground. This will prove fatal in sufficient quantity. Always drain the coolant into a sealable container. Coolant should be reused unless it is contaminated or several years old.*

2. Remove the cylinder head.

WARNING: *When working on fuel injected engines, discharge the fuel system pressure before starting any work that involves disconnecting the fuel system lines. See Fuel Supply Manifold Removal and Installation procedures in Chapter 5.*

3. Remove the oil pan, the oil pump inlet tube and the oil pump.

4. Turn the crankshaft until the piston to be removed is at the bottom of its travel and place a cloth on the piston head to collect filings. Using a ridge reaming tool, remove any ridge of carbon or any other deposit from the upper cylinder walls where piston travel ends. Do not cut into the piston ring travel area more than $\frac{1}{32}$" (0.8mm) while removing the ridge.

5. Mark all of the connecting rod caps so that they can be reinstalled in the original positions from which they are removed and remove the connecting rod bearing cap. Also identify the piston assemblies as they, too, must be reinstalled in the same cylinder from which removed.

6. With the bearing caps removed, the connecting rod bearing bolts are potentially damaging to the cylinder walls during removal. To guard against cylinder wall damage, install 4" (101.6mm) or 5" (127mm) lengths of ⅜"

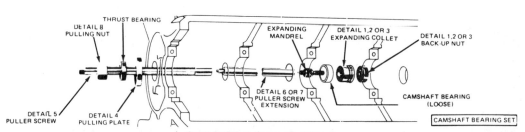

DETAIL 8
PULLING NUT

THRUST BEARING

DETAIL 1,2 OR 3
PULLING NUT

EXPANDING MANDREL

DETAIL 1,2 OR 3
EXPANDING COLLET

DETAIL 1,2 OR 3
BACK-UP NUT

DETAIL 6 OR 7
PULLER SCREW EXTENSION

CAMSHAFT BEARING (LOOSE)

DETAIL 5
PULLER SCREW

DETAIL 4
PULLING PLATE

CAMSHAFT BEARING SET

Camshaft bearing replacement

(9.5mm) rubber tubing onto the connecting rod bolts. These will also protect the crankshaft journal from scratches when the connecting rod is installed, and will serve as a guide for the rod.

7. Squirt some clean engine oil into each cylinder before removing the pistons. Using a wooden hammer handle, push the connecting rod and piston assembly out of the top of the cylinder (pushing from the bottom of the rod). Be careful to avoid damaging both the crank journal and the cylinder wall when removing the rod and piston assembly.

8. Before installing the piston/connecting rod assembly, be sure to clean all gasket mating surfaces, oil the pistons, piston rings and the cylinder walls with light engine oil.

9. Be sure to install the pistons in the cylinders from which they were removed. The connecting rod and bearing caps are numbered from 1 to 6 beginning at the front of the engine. The numbers on the connecting rod and bearing cap must be on the same side when installed in the cylinder bore. If a connecting rod is ever transposed from one engine or cylinder to another, new bearings should be fitted and the connecting rod should be numbered to correspond with the new cylinder number. The notch on the piston head goes toward the front of the engine.

10. Make sure the ring gaps are properly spaced around the circumference of the piston. Make sure rubber hose lengths are fitted to the rod bolts. Fit a piston ring compressor around the piston and slide the piston and connecting rod assembly down into the cylinder bore, pushing it in with the wooden hammer handle. Push the piston down until it is only slightly below the top of the cylinder bore. Guide the connecting rods onto the crankshaft bearing journals carefully, using the rubber hose lengths, to avoid damaging the crankshaft.

11. Check the bearing clearance of all the rod bearings, fitting them to the crankshaft bearing journals.

12. After the bearings have been fitted, apply a light coating of engine oil to the journals and bearings.

13. Turn the crankshaft until the appropriate bearing journal is at the bottom of its stroke, then push the piston assembly all the way down until the connecting rod bearing seats on the crankshaft journal. Be careful not to allow the bearing cap screws to strike the crankshaft bearing journals and damage them.

14. After the piston and connecting rod assemblies have been installed, check the connecting rod side clearance on each crankshaft journal.

15. Prime and install the oil pump and the oil pump intake tube, then install the oil pan.

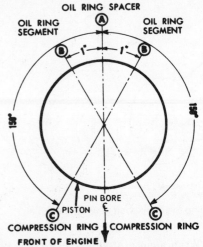

Proper spacing of the piston ring gaps around the circumference of the piston

Installing the piston and connecting rod assembly into the block on the 6-144,170,200 engine

Checking the connecting rod side clearance on the crankshaft journal on the 6-144,170 engine

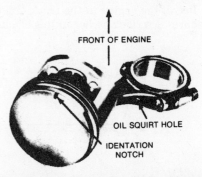

The proper positioning of the pistons and connecting rods in the 144, 170, and 200 six-cylinder

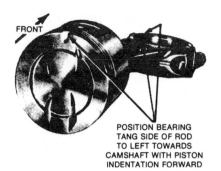

POSITION BEARING
TANG SIDE OF ROD
TO LEFT TOWARDS
CAMSHAFT WITH PISTON
INDENTATION FORWARD

The proper positioning of the pistons and connecting rods in the 240 and 300 six-cylinder

16. Reassemble the rest of the engine in the reverse order of disassembly.

V8 Engines Including Diesel

1. Drain the cooling system and the crankcase.

CAUTION: *When draining the coolant, keep in mind that cats and dogs are attracted by the ethylene glycol antifreeze, and are quite likely to drink any that is left in an uncovered container or in puddles on the ground. This will prove fatal in sufficient quantity. Always drain the coolant into a sealable container. Coolant should be reused unless it is contaminated or several years old.*

2. Remove the intake manifold.
3. Remove the cylinder heads.

WARNING: *When working on fuel injected engines, discharge the fuel system pressure before starting any work that involves disconnecting the fuel system lines. See Fuel Supply Manifold Removal and Installation procedures in Chapter 5.*

4. Remove the oil pan.
5. Remove the oil pump.
6. Turn the crankshaft until the piston to be removed is at the bottom of its travel, then place a cloth on the piston head to collect filings.
7. Remove any ridge of deposits at the end of the piston travel from the upper cylinder bore, using a ridge reaming tool. Do not cut into the

Checking piston ring gap

piston ring travel area more than $\frac{1}{32}$" (0.8mm) when removing the ridge.

8. Make sure that all of the connecting rod bearing caps can be identified, so they will be reinstalled in their original positions.
9. Turn the crankshaft until the connecting rod that is to be removed is at the bottom of its stroke and remove the connecting rod nuts and bearing cap.
10. With the bearing caps removed, the connecting rod bearing bolts are potentially damaging to the cylinder walls during removal. To guard against cylinder wall damage, install four or five inch lengths of $\frac{3}{8}$" (0.8mm) rubber tubing onto the connecting rod bolts. These will also protect the crankshaft journal from scratches when the connecting rod is installed, and will serve as a guide for the rod.
11. Squirt some clean engine oil into each cylinder before removing the piston assemblies. Using a wooden hammer handle, push the connecting rod and piston assembly out of the top of the cylinder (pushing from the bottom of the rod). Be careful to avoid damaging both the crank journal and the cylinder wall when removing the rod and piston assembly.
12. Remove the bearing inserts from the connecting rod and cap if the bearings are to be re-

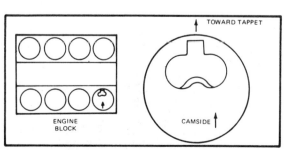

Diesel engine piston positioning

Checking piston ring side clearance

place, and place the cap onto the piston/rod assembly from which it was removed.

13. Install the piston/rod assemblies in the same manner as that for the 6-cylinder engines. See the procedure given for 6-cylinder engines.

NOTE: *The connecting rod and bearing caps are numbered from 1 to 4 in the right bank and from 5 to 8 in in the left bank, beginning at the front of the engine. The numbers on the rod and cap must be on the same side when they are installed in the cylinder bore. Also, the largest chamfer at the bearing end of the rod should be positioned toward the crank pin thrust face of the crankshaft and the notch in the head of the piston faces toward the front of the engine.*

14. See the appropriate component procedures to assemble the engine.

Piston Ring and Wrist Pin

REMOVAL

All of the Ford gasoline engines covered in this guide utilize pressed-in wrist pins, which can only be removed by an arbor press. The diesel pistons are removed in the same way, only the pistons are heated before the wrist pins are pressed out. On both gasoline and diesel engines, the piston/connecting rod assemblies should be taken to an engine specialist or qualified machinist for piston removal and installation.

A piston ring expander is necessary for removing the piston rings without damaging them; any other method (screwdriver blades, pliers, etc.) usually results in the rings being bent, scratched or distorted, or the piston itself being damaged. When the rings are removed, clean the ring grooves using an appropriate ring groove cleaning tool, using care not to cut too deeply. Thoroughly clean all carbon and varnish from the piston with solvent.

WARNING: *Do not use a wire brush or caustic solvent (acids, etc.) on pistons.*
Inspect the pistons for scuffing, scoring, cracks, pitting, or excessive ring groove wear.

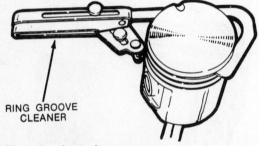

RING GROOVE
CLEANER

Clean the piston ring grooves

If these are evident, the piston must be replaced.

The piston should also be checked in relation to the cylinder diameter. Using a telescoping gauge and micrometer, or a dial gauge, measure the cylinder bore diameter perpendicular (90%) to the piston pin, 2½" (64mm) below the cylinder block deck (surface where the block mates with the heads). Then, with the micrometer, measure the piston, perpendicular to its wrist pin on the skirt. the difference between the two measurements is the piston clearance. If the clearance is within specifications or slightly below (after the cylinders have been bored or hones), finish honing is all that is necessary. If the clearance is excessive, try to obtain a slightly larger piston to bring clearance to within specifications. If this is not possible, obtain the first oversize piston and hone (or if necessary, bore) the cylinder to size. Generally, if the cylinder bore is tapered 0.005" (0.127mm) or more or is out-of-round 0.003" (0.076mm) or more, it is advisable to rebore for the smallest possible oversize piston and rings.

After measuring, mark pistons with a felt tip pen for reference and for assembly.

NOTE: *Cylinder honing and/or boring should be performed by a reputable, professional mechanic with the proper equipment. In some cases, clean-up honing can be done with the cylinder block in the car, but most excessive honing and all cylinder boring must be done with the block stripped and removed from the car.*

Before honing the diesel cylinders, the piston oil cooling jets must be removed. this procedure should be handled by a diesel specialist, as special tools are needed. Jets cannot be reused; new jets should be fitted.

MEASURING THE OLD PISTONS

Check used piston-to-cylinder bore clearance as follows:

1. Measure the cylinder bore diameter with a telescope gauge.

2. Measure the piston diameter. When measuring the pistons for size or taper, measurements must be made with the piston pin removed.

3. Subtract the piston diameter from the cylinder bore diameter to determine piston-to-bore clearance.

4. Compare the piston-to-bore clearances obtained with those clearances recommended. Determine if the piston-to-bore clearance is in the acceptable range.

5. When measuring taper, the largest reading must be at the bottom of the skirt.

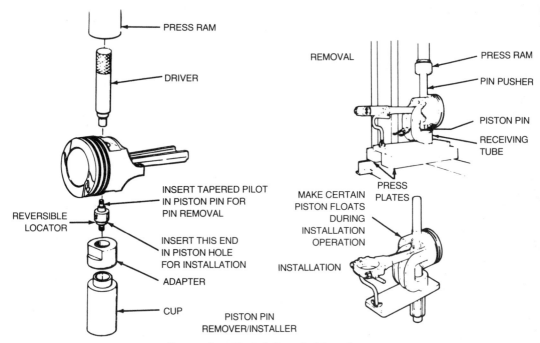

Removal and installation of piston pins

SELECTING NEW PISTONS

1. If the used piston is not acceptable, check the service piston size and determine if a new piston can be selected. (Service pistons are available in standard, high limit and standard oversize.

2. If the cylinder bore must be reconditioned, measure the new piston diameter, then hone the cylinder bore to obtain the preferred clearance.

3. Select a new piston and mark the piston to identify the cylinder for which it was fitted. (On some vehicles, oversize pistons may be found. These pistons will be 0.254mm [0.010"] oversize).

CYLINDER HONING

WARNING: *On diesel engines, the piston cooling jets must be removed prior to honing!*

1. When cylinders are being honed, follow the manufacturer's recommendations for the use of the hone.

2. Occasionally, during the honing operation, the cylinder bore should be thoroughly cleaned and the selected piston checked for correct fit.

3. When finish-honing a cylinder bore, the hone should be moved up and down at a sufficient speed to obtain a very fine uniform surface finish in a cross-hatch pattern of approximately 45-65° included angle. The finish marks

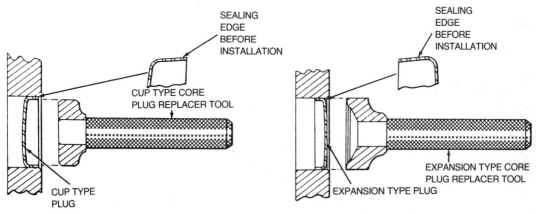

Core plugs and installation tools

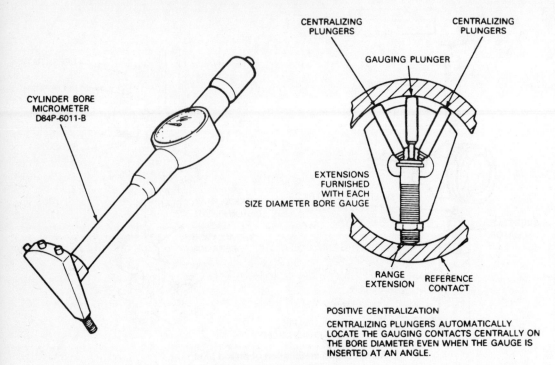

Cylinder bore micrometer

should be clean but not sharp, free from imbedded particles and torn or folded metal.

4. Permanently mark the piston for the cylinder to which it has been fitted and proceed to hone the remaining cylinders.

WARNING: *Handle the pistons with care. Do not attempt to force the pistons through the cylinders until the cylinders have been honed to the correct size. Pistons can be distorted through careless handling.*

5. Thoroughly clean the bores with hot water and detergent. Scrub well with a stiff bristle brush and rinse thoroughly with hot water. It is extremely essential that a good cleaning operation be performed. If any of the abrasive material is allowed to remain in the cylinder bores, it will rapidly wear the new rings and cylinder bores. The bores should be swabbed several times with light engine oil and a clean cloth and then wiped with a clean dry cloth. CYLINDERS SHOULD NOT BE CLEANED WITH KEROSENE OR GASOLINE! Clean the remainder of the cylinder block to remove the excess material spread during the honing operation.

PISTON RING END GAP

Piston ring end gap should be checked while the rings are removed from the pistons. Incorrect end gap indicates that the wrong size rings are being used; ring breakage could occur.

Compress the piston rings to be used in a cylinder, one at a time, into that cylinder. Squirt

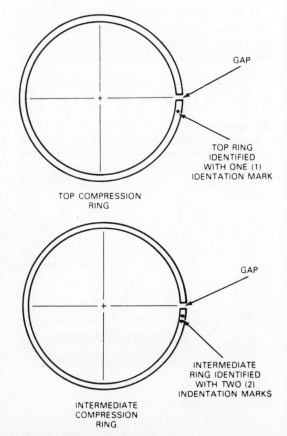

Diesel piston ring identification

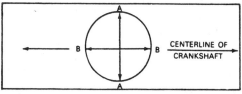

A - At Right angle to center line of engine
B - Parallel to center line of engine

Top Measurement: Make 12.70mm (1/2 inch) below top of block deck

Bottom Measurement: Make within 12.70mm (1/2 inch) above top of piston - when piston is at its lowest travel (B.D.C)

Bore Service Limit: Equals the average of "A" and "B" when measured at the center of the piston travel.

Taper: Equals difference between "A" top and "A" bottom.

Out-of-Round: Equals difference between "A" and "B" when measured at the center of piston travel.

Refer to Specification tables at end of each engine section.

Cylinder bore measurement

clean oil into the cylinder, so that the rings and the top 2" (51mm) of cylinder wall are coated. Using an inverted piston, press the rings approximately 1" (25mm) below the deck of the block (on diesels, measure ring gap clearance with the ring positioned at the bottom of ring travel in the bore). Measure the ring end gap with the feeler gauge, and compare to the Ring Gap chart in this chapter. Carefully pull the ring out of the cylinder and file the ends squarely with a fine file to obtain the proper clearance.

PISTON RING SIDE CLEARANCE CHECK AND INSTALLATION

Check the pistons to see that the ring grooves and oil return holes have been properly cleaned. Slide a piston ring into its groove, and check the side clearance with a feeler gauge. On gasoline engines, make sure you insert the gauge between the ring and its lower land (lower edge of the groove), because any wear that occurs forms a step at the inner portion of the lower land. On diesels, insert the gauge between the ring and the upper land. If the piston grooves have worn to the extend that relatively high steps exist on the lower land, the piston grooves have worn to the extent that relatively high steps exist on the lower land, the piston should be replaced, because these will interfere with the operation of the new rings and ring clearance will be excessive. Piston rings are not furnished in oversize widths to compensate for ring groove wear.

Install the rings on the piston, lowest ring first, using a piston ring expander. There is a high risk of breaking or distorting the rings, or scratching the piston, if the rings are installed by hand or other means.

Position the rings on the piston as illustrated; spacing of the various piston ring gaps is crucial to proper oil retention and even cylinder wear. When installing new rings, refer to the in-

stallation diagram furnished with the new parts.

Connecting Rod Bearings
INSPECTION

Connecting rod bearings for the engines covered in this guide consist of two halves or shells which are interchangeable in the rod and cap. when the shells are placed in position, the ends extend slightly beyond the rod and cap surfaces so that when the rod bolts are torqued the shells will be clamped tightly in place to insure positive seating and to prevent turning. A tang holds the shells in place.

NOTE: *The ends of the bearing shells must never be filed flush with the mating surfaces of the rod and cap.*

If a rod bearing becomes noisy or is worn so that its clearance on the crank journal is sloppy, a new bearing of the correct undersize must be selected and installed since there is a provision for adjustment.

WARNING: *Under no circumstances should the rod end or cap be filed to adjust the bearing clearance, nor should shims of any kind be used.*

Inspect the rod bearings while the rod assemblies are out of the engine. If the shells are scored or show flaking, they should be replaced. If they are in good shape, check for proper clearance on the crank journal (see below). Any scoring or ridges on the crank journal means the crankshaft must be reground and fitted with undersized bearings, or replaced.

CHECKING BEARING CLEARANCE AND REPLACING BEARINGS

NOTE: *Make sure connecting rods and their caps are kept together, and that the caps are installed in the proper direction.*

Replacement bearings are available in standard size, and in undersizes for reground crankshaft. Connecting rod-to-crankshaft bearing clearance is checked using Plastigage® at either the top or bottom of each crank journal. the Plastigage® has a range of 0 to 0.003" (0.076mm).

1. Remove the rod cap with the bearing shell. Completely clean the bearing shell and the crank journal, and blow any oil from the oil hole in the crankshaft.

NOTE: *The journal surfaces and bearing shells must be completely free of oil, because Plastigage® is soluble in oil.*

2. Place a strip of Plastigage® lengthwise along the bottom center of the lower bearing shell, then install the cap with shell and torque the bolt or nuts to specification. DO NOT

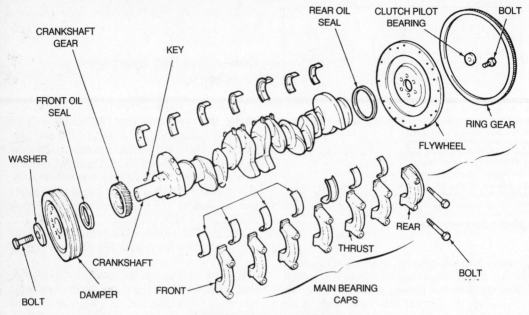

6-300 crankshaft and bearings

TURN the crankshaft with the Plastigage® installed in the bearing.

3. Remove the bearing cap with the shell. The flattened Plastigage® will be found sticking to either the bearing shell or crank journal. Do not remove it yet.

4. Use the printed scale on the Plastigage® envelope to measure the flattened material at

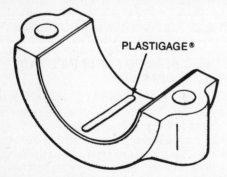

PLASTIGAGE®

Plastigage® installed on the lower bearing shell

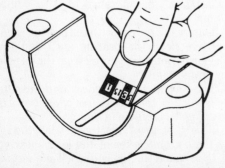

Measure Plastigage® to determine bearing clearance

its widest point. The number within the scale which most closely corresponds to the width of the Plastigage® indicated bearing clearance in thousandths of an inch.

5. Check the specifications chart in this chapter for the desired clearance. It is advisable to install a new bearing if clearance exceeds 0.003″ (0.076mm); however, if the bearing is in good condition and is not being checked because of bearing noise, bearing replacement is not necessary.

6. If you are installing new bearings, try a standard size, then each undersize in order until one is found that is within the specified limits when checked for clearance with Plastigage®. Each under size has its size stamped on it.

7. When the proper size shell is found, clean off the Plastigage® material from the shell, oil the bearing thoroughly, reinstall the cap with its shell and torque the rod bolt nuts to specification.

NOTE: *With the proper bearing selected and the nuts torqued, it should be possible to move the connecting rod back and forth freely on the crank journal as allowed by the specified connecting rod end clearance. If the rod cannot be moved, either the rod bearing is too far undersize or the rod is misaligned.*

Diesel Piston Cooling Jets
REMOVAL AND INSTALLATION

1. Carefully clamp locking pliers on the cooling jet, place a prybar under the pliers to act as a pivot, and pry the jet out of the cylinder.

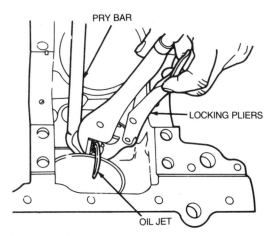

Removing the diesel piston cooling jet

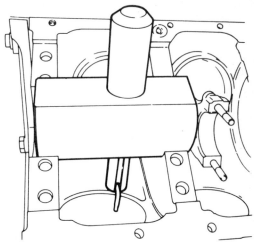

Installing the diesel piston cooling jet

2. Position tool 14-0307 over the main bearing saddles. Place a new cooling jet in the tool, align the tool over the hole and start the jet into the hole.

3. Drive the jet into place by hitting the tool with a hammer until the tool drive bottoms in the body of the tool.

4. Use tool 14-0311 to verify the correct jet alignment. The pointer of the tool must index with the center of the target hole in the tool template. If not, carefully bend the jet tube until the pointer is centered.

Piston and Connecting Rod

ASSEMBLY AND INSTALLATION

Install the connecting rod to the piston making sure piston installation notches and any marks on the rod are in proper relation to one another. Lubricate the wrist pin with clean engine oil and install the pin into the rod and piston assembly by using an arbor press as required. Install the wrist pin snaprings if equipped, and rotate them in their grooves to make sure they are seated. To install the piston and rod assemblies:

1. Make sure the connecting rod big bearings (including end cap) are of the correct size and properly installed.

2. Fit rubber hoses over the connecting rod bolt to protect the crankshaft journals, as in the Piston Removal procedure. Coat the rod bearings with clean oil.

3. Using the proper ring compressor, insert the piston assembly into the cylinder so that the notch in the top of the piston faces the front of the engine (this assumes that the dimple(s) or other markings on the connecting rods are in correct relation to the piston notch(s) .

4. From beneath the engine, coat each crank journal with clean oil. Pull the connecting rod,

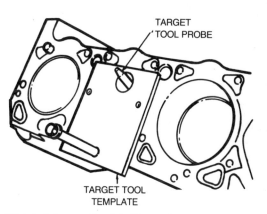

Diesel piston cooling jet alignment

with the bearing shell in place, into position against the crank journal.

5. Remove the rubber hoses. Install the bearing cap and cap nuts and torque to specification.

NOTE: *When more than one rod and piston assembly is being installed, the connecting rod cap attaching nuts should only be tightened enough to keep each rod in position until all have been installed. This will ease the installation of the remaining piston assemblies.*

6. Check the clearance between the sides of the connecting rods and the crankshaft using a feeler gauge. Spread the rods slightly with a screwdriver to insert the gauge. If clearance is below the minimum tolerance, the rod may be machined to provide adequate clearance. If clearance is excessive, substitute an unworn rod, and recheck. If clearance is still outside specifications, the crankshaft must be welded and reground, or replaced.

7. Replace the oil pump if removed, and the oil pan.

8. Install the cylinder head(s) and intake manifold.

Crankshaft and Main Bearings.

REMOVAL AND INSTALLATION

Engine Removed

1. With the engine removed from the vehicle and placed in a work stand, disconnect the spark plug wires from the spark plugs and remove the wires and bracket assembly from the attaching stud on the valve rocker arm cover(s) if so equipped.

2. Disconnect the coil to distributor high tension lead at the coil.

3. Remove the distributor cap and spark plug wires as an assembly.

4. Remove the spark plugs to allow easy rotation of the crankshaft.

5. Remove the fuel pump and oil filter.

6. Slide the water pump by-pass hose clamp (if so equipped) toward the water pump.

7. Remove the alternator and mounting brackets.

8. Remove the crankshaft pulley from the crankshaft vibration damper.

9. Remove the capscrew and washer from the end of the crankshaft. Install a universal puller, Tool T58P-6316-D or equivalent on the crankshaft vibration damper and remove the damper.

10. Remove the cylinder front cover and crankshaft gear, refer to Cylinder Front Cover and Timing Chain in this chapter.

11. Invert the engine on the work stand.

12. Remove the clutch pressure plate and disc (manual shift transmission).

13. Remove the flywheel and engine rear cover plate.

14. Remove the oil pan and gasket.

15. Remove the oil pump.

16. Make sure all bearing caps (main and connecting rod) are marked so that they can be installed in their original locations.

17. Turn the crankshaft until the connecting rod from which the cap is being removed is down, and remove the bearing cap. Push the connecting rod and piston assembly up into the cylinder. Repeat this procedure until all the connecting rod bearing caps are removed.

18. Remove the main bearings caps.

19. Carefully lift the crankshaft out of the block so that the thrust bearing surfaces are not damaged. Handle the crankshaft with care to avoid possible fracture to the finished surfaces.

20. Remove the rear journal seal from the block and rear main bearing cap.

21. Remove the main bearing inserts from the block and bearing caps.

22. Remove the connecting rod bearing inserts from the connecting rods and caps.

23. If the crankshaft main bearing journals have been refinished to a definite undersize, install the correct undersize bearings. Be sure the bearing inserts and bearing bores are clean. Foreign material under the inserts will distort the bearing and cause a failure.

24. Place the upper main bearing inserts in position in the bores with the tang fitting in the slot. Be sure the oil holes in the bearing inserts are aligned with the oil holes in the cylinder block.

25. Install the lower main bearing inserts in the bearing caps.

26. Clean the rear journal oil seal groove and the mating surfaces of the block and rear main bearing cap.

27. Dip the lip-type seal halves in clean engine oil. Install the seals in the bearing cap and block with the undercut side of the seal toward the front of the engine.

NOTE: *This procedure applies only to engines with two piece rear main bearing oil seals. those having one piece seals (6-300 engines) will be installed after the crankshaft is in place.*

28. Carefully lower the crankshaft into place. Be careful not to damage the bearing surfaces.

CHECKING MAIN BEARING CLEARANCES

29. Check the clearance of each main bearing by using the following procedure:

a. Place a piece of Plastigage® or its equivalent, on bearing surface across full width of bearing cap and about ¼" (6mm) off center.

b. Install cap and tighten bolts to specifications. Do not turn crankshaft while Plastigage® is in place.

c. Remove the cap. Using Plastigage® scale, check width of Plastigage® at widest point to get the minimum clearance. Check at narrowest point to get maximum clearance. Difference between readings is taper of journal.

d. If clearance exceeds specified limits, try a 0.001" (0.0254mm) or 0.002" (0.051mm) undersize bearing in combination with the standard bearing. Bearing clearance must be within specified limits. If standard and 0.002" (0.051mm) undersize bearing does not bring clearance within desired limits, refinish crankshaft journal, then install undersize bearings.

NOTE: *Refer to Rear Main Oil Seal removal and installation, for special instructions in applying RTV sealer to rear main bearing cup.*

30. Install all the bearing caps except the thrust bearing cap (no. 3 bearing on all except

the 6-300 which use the no. 5 as the thrust bearing). Be sure the main bearing caps are installed in their original locations. Tighten the bearing cap bolts to specifications.

31. Install the thrust bearing cap with the bolts finger tight.

32. Pry the crankshaft forward against the thrust surface of the upper half of the bearing.

33. Hold the crankshaft forward and pry the thrust bearing cap to the rear. This will align the thrust surfaces of both halves of the bearing.

34. Retain the forward pressure on the crankshaft. Tighten the cap bolts to specifications.

35. Check the crankshaft end play using the following procedures:

   a. Force the crankshaft toward the rear of the engine.

   b. Install a dial indicator (tools D78P-4201-F, -G or equivalent) so that the contact point rests against the crankshaft flange and the indicator axis is parallel to the crankshaft axis.

   c. Zero the dial indicator. Push the crankshaft forward and note the reading on the dial.

   d. If the end play exceeds the wear limit listed in the Crankshaft and Connecting Rod Specifications chart, replace the thrust bearing. If the end play is less than the minimum limit, inspect the thrust bearing faces for scratches, burrs, nicks, or dirt. If the thrust faces are not damaged or dirty, then they probably were not aligned properly. Lubricate and install the new thrust bearing and align the faces following procedures 30 through 34.

36. On 6-300 engines with one piece rear main bearing oil seal, coat a new crankshaft rear oil seal with oil and install using Tool T65P-6701-A or equivalent. Inspect the seal to be sure it was not damaged during installation.

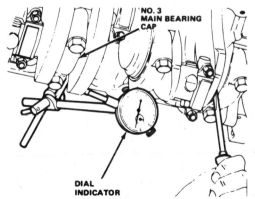

Check the crankshaft end-play with a dial indicator

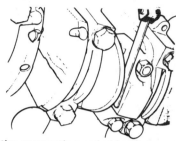

Check the connecting rod side clearance with a feeler gauge

37. Install new bearing inserts in the connecting rods and caps. Check the clearance of each bearing, following the procedure (18a through 18d).

38. After the connecting rod bearings have been fitted, apply a light coat of engine oil to the journals and bearings.

39. Turn the crankshaft throw to the bottom of its stroke. Push the piston all the way down until the rod bearing seats on the crankshaft journal.

40. Install the connecting rod cap. Tighten the nuts to specification.

41. After the piston and connecting rod assemblies have been installed, check the side clearance with a feeler gauge between the connecting rods on each connecting rod crankshaft journal. Refer to Crankshaft and Connecting Rod specifications chart in this chapter.

42. Install the timing chain and sprockets or gears, cylinder front cover and crankshaft pulley and adapter, following steps under Cylinder Front Cover and Timing Chain Installation in this chapter.

Engine in the Truck

1. With the oil pan, oil pump and spark plugs removed, remove the cap from the main bearing needing replacement and remove the bearing from the cap.

2. Make a bearing roll-out pin, using a bent cotter pin as shown in the illustration. Install the end of the pin in the oil hole in the crankshaft journal.

3. Rotate the crankshaft clockwise as viewed from the front of the engine. This will roll the upper bearing out of the block.

4. Lube the new upper bearing with clean engine oil and insert the plain (unnotch) end between the crankshaft and the indented or notched side of the block. Roll the bearing into place, making sure that the oil holes are aligned. Remove the roll pin from the oil hole.

5. Lube the new lower bearing and install it in the main bearing cap. Install the main bearing cap onto the block, making sure it is posi-

tioned in proper direction with the matchmarks in alignment.

6. Torque the main bearing cap to specification.

NOTE: *See Crankshaft Installation for thrust bearing alignment.*

CRANKSHAFT CLEANING AND INSPECTION

NOTE: *Handle the crankshaft carefully to avoid damage to the finish surfaces.*

1. Clean the crankshaft with solvent, and blow out all oil passages with compressed air. On the 6-240 and 6-300 engine, clean the oil seal contact surface at the rear of the crankshaft with solvent to remove any corrosion, sludge or varnish deposits.

2. Use crocus cloth to remove any sharp edges, burrs or other imperfections which might damage the oil seal during installation or cause premature seal wear.

NOTE: *Do not use crocus cloth to polish the seal surfaces. A finely polished surface may produce poor sealing or cause premature seal wear.*

3. Inspect the main and connecting rod journals for cracks, scratches, grooves or scores.

4. Measure the diameter of each journal at least four places to determine out-of-round, taper or undersize condition.

5. On an engine with a manual transmission, check the fit of the clutch pilot bearing in the bore of the crankshaft. A needle roller bearing and adapter assembly is used as a clutch pilot bearing. It is inserted directly into the engine crank shaft. The bearing and adapter assembly cannot be serviced separately. A new bearing must be installed whenever a bearing is removed.

6. Inspect the pilot bearing, when used, for roughness, evidence of overheating or loss of lubricant. Replace if any of these conditions are found.

7. On the 6-240 and 6-300 engine, inspect the rear oil seal surface of the crankshaft for deep grooves, nicks, burrs, porosity, or scratches which could damage the oil seal lip during installation. Remove all nicks and burrs with crocus cloth.

Main Bearings

1. Clean the bearing inserts and caps thoroughly in solvent, and dry them with compressed air.

NOTE: *Do not scrape varnish or gum deposits from the bearing shells.*

2. Inspect each bearing carefully. Bearings that have a scored, chipped, or worn surface should be replaced.

3. The copper-lead bearing base may be visible through the bearing overlay in small localized areas. This may not mean that the bearing is excessively worn. It is not necessary to replace the bearing if the bearing clearance is within recommended specifications.

4. Check the clearance of bearings that appear to be satisfactory with Plastigage® or its equivalent. Fit the new bearings following the procedure Crankshaft and Main Bearings removal and installation, they should be reground to size for the next undersize bearing.

5. Regrind the journals to give the proper clearance with the next undersize bearing. If the journal will not clean up to maximum undersize bearing available, replace the crankshaft.

6. Always reproduce the same journal shoulder radius that existed originally. Too small a radius will result in fatigue failure of the crankshaft. Too large a radius will result in bearing failure due to radius ride of the bearing.

7. After regrinding the journals, chamfer the oil holes, then polish the journals with a #320 grit polishing cloth and engine oil. Crocus cloth may also be used as a polishing agent.

COMPLETING THE REBUILDING PROCESS

Fill the oil pump with oil, to prevent cavitating (sucking air) on initial engine start up. Install the oil pump and the pick-up tube on the engine. Coat the oil pan gasket as necessary, and install the gasket and the oil pan. Mount the flywheel and the crankshaft vibration damper or pulley on the crankshaft.

NOTE: *Always use new bolts when installing the flywheel. Inspect the clutch shaft pilot bushing in the crankshaft. If the bushing is excessively worn, remove it with an expanding puller and a slide hammer, and tap a new bushing into place.*

Position the engine, cylinder head side up. Lubricate the lifters, and install them into their bores. Install the cylinder head, and torque it as specified. Insert the pushrods (where applicable), and install the rocker shaft(s) (if so equipped) or position the rocker.

Install the intake and exhaust manifolds, the carburetor(s), the distributor and spark plugs. Mount all accessories and install the engine in the car. Fill the radiator with coolant, and the crankcase with high quality engine oil.

BREAK-IN PROCEDURE

Start the engine, and allow it to run at low speed for a few minutes, while checking for leaks. Stop the engine, check the oil level, and fill as necessary. Restart the engine, and fill the cooling system to capacity. Check and adjust the ignition timing. Run the engine at low to medium speed (800-2,500 rpm) for approximately ½ hour, and retorque the cylinder head bolts. Road test the car, and check again for leaks.

NOTE: *Some gasket manufacturers recommend not retorquing the cylinder head(s) due to the composition of the head gasket. Follow the directions in the gasket set.*

Flywheel/Flex Plate and Ring Gear

NOTE: *Flex plate is the term for a flywheel mated with an automatic transmission.*

REMOVAL AND INSTALLATION

All Engines

NOTE: *The ring gear is replaceable only on engines mated with a manual transmission. Engines with automatic transmissions have ring gears which are welded to the flex plate.*

1. Remove the transmission and transfer case.

2. Remove the clutch, if equipped, or torque converter from the flywheel. The flywheel bolts should be loosened a little at a time in a cross pattern to avoid warping the flywheel. On cars with manual transmissions, replace the pilot bearing in the end of the crankshaft if removing the flywheel.

3. The flywheel should be checked for cracks and glazing. It can be resurfaced by a machine shop.

4. If the ring gear is to be replaced, drill a hole in the gear between two teeth, being careful not to contact the flywheel surface. Using a cold chisel at this point, crack the ring gear and remove it.

5. Polish the inner surface of the new ring gear and heat it in an oven to about 600°F (316°C). Quickly place the ring gear on the flywheel and tap it into place, making sure that it is fully seated.

WARNING: *Never heat the ring gear past 800°F (426°C), or the tempering will be destroyed.*

6. Position the flywheel on the end of the crankshaft. Torque the bolts a little at a time, in a cross pattern, to the torque figure shown in the Torque Specifications Chart.

7. Install the clutch or torque converter.

8. Install the transmission and transfer case.

Rear Main Oil Seal

REPLACEMENT — TWO PIECE SEAL

6-144 (2.4L)
6-170 (2.8L)
6-200 (3.3L)

1. Drain the crankcase and remove the oil pan, and as necessary, the oil pump.

2. Remove the lower half of the rear main bearing cap and, after removing the oil seal from the cap, drive out the pin in the bottom of the seal groove with a punch.

3. Loosen all the main bearing caps and allow the crankshaft to lower slightly.

NOTE: *Do not allow the crankshaft to drop more than $\frac{1}{32}$" (0.8mm).*

4. With a 6" (152mm) length of $\frac{3}{16}$" (4.8mm) brazing rod, drive up on either exposed end of the top half of the oil seal. When the opposite end of the seal starts to protrude, grasp it with a pair of pliers and gently pull, while the driven end is being tapped.

5. After removing both halves of the old original rope seal and the retaining pin from the

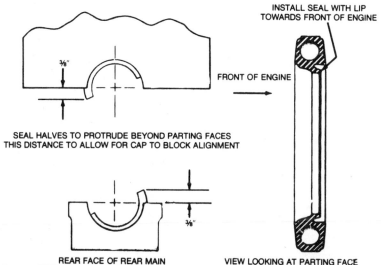

SEAL HALVES TO PROTRUDE BEYOND PARTING FACES THIS DISTANCE TO ALLOW FOR CAP TO BLOCK ALIGNMENT

INSTALL SEAL WITH LIP TOWARDS FRONT OF ENGINE

FRONT OF ENGINE

REAR FACE OF REAR MAIN BEARING CAP AND CYLINDER BLOCK

VIEW LOOKING AT PARTING FACE OF SPLIT, LIP-TYPE CRANKSHAFT SEAL

Proper positioning of the replacement rear main oil seal for all engines except the 6-240 & 300

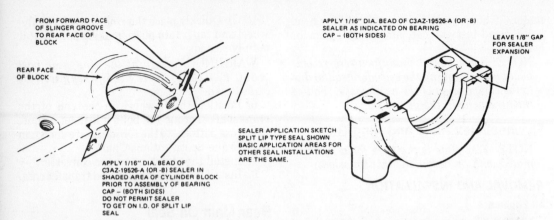

FROM FORWARD FACE OF SLINGER GROOVE TO REAR FACE OF BLOCK

REAR FACE OF BLOCK

APPLY 1/16" DIA. BEAD OF C3AZ-19526-A (OR -B) SEALER AS INDICATED ON BEARING CAP – (BOTH SIDES)

LEAVE 1/8" GAP FOR SEALER EXPANSION

SEALER APPLICATION SKETCH SPLIT LIP TYPE SEAL SHOWN BASIC APPLICATION AREAS FOR OTHER SEAL INSTALLATIONS ARE THE SAME.

APPLY 1/16" DIA. BEAD OF C3AZ-19526-A (OR -B) SEALER IN SHADED AREA OF CYLINDER BLOCK PRIOR TO ASSEMBLY OF BEARING CAP – (BOTH SIDES) DO NOT PERMIT SEALER TO GET ON I.D. OF SPLIT LIP SEAL

Applying RTV sealant to the main bearing cap and block on all 1974–84 engines except the 6-240 & 300

lower half of the bearing cap, carefully clean the seal grooves in the cap and block with solvent.

6. Soak the new rubber replacement seals in clean engine oil.

7. Install the upper half in the block with the undercut side of the seal toward the front of the engine. Slide the seal around the crankshaft journal until ⅜" (9.5mm) protrudes beyond the base of the block.

8. Repeat the above procedure for the lower seal, allowing an equal amount of the seal to protrude beyond the opposite end of the bearing cap.

9. Install the rear bearing cap and torque all the main bearings to the proper specification. Apply sealer only to the rear of the seals.

10. Dip the bearing cap side seals in oil, then immediately install them. Do not use any sealer on the side seals. Tap the seals into place and do not clip the protruding ends.

11. Install the oil pump and oil pan. Fill the crankcase with oil, start the engine and check for leaks.

6-240 (3.9L)
6-300 (4.9L)

If the crankshaft rear oil seal replacement is the only operation being performed, it can be done in the vehicle as detailed in the following procedure. If the oil seal is being replaced in conjunction with a rear main bearing replacement, the engine must be removed from the vehicle and install on a work stand.

1. Remove the starter.

2. Remove the transmission from the vehicle, following procedures in Chapter 7.

3. On manual shift transmission, remove the pressure plate and cover assembly and the clutch disc following the procedure in Chapter 7.

4. Remove the flywheel attaching bolts and remove the flywheel and engine rear cover plate.

5. Use an awl to punch two holes in the crankshaft rear oil seal. Punch the holes on opposite sides of the crankshaft and just above the bearing cap to cylinder block split line. Install a sheet metal screw in each hole. Use two large screwdrivers or small pry bars and pry against both screws at the same time to remove the crankshaft rear oil seal. It may be necessary to place small blocks of wood against the cylinder block to provide a fulcrum point for the pry bars. Use caution throughout this procedure to avoid scratching or otherwise damaging the crankshaft oil seal surface.

6. Clean the oil seal recess in the cylinder block and main bearing cap.

7. Clean, inspect and polish the rear oil seal rubbing surface on the crankshaft. Coat the new oil seal and the crankshaft with a light film of engine oil. Start the seal in the recess with the seal lip facing forward and install it with a seal driver. Keep the tool straight with the centerline of the crankshaft and install the seal until the tool contacts the cylinder block surface. Remove the tool and inspect the seal to be sure it was not damaged during installation.

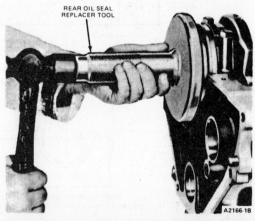

REAR OIL SEAL REPLACER TOOL

A2166-18

Installing rear main oil seal on the 6-240,300 engines

8. Install the engine rear cover plate. Position the flywheel on the crankshaft flange. Coat the threads of the flywheel attaching bolts with oil-resistant sealer and install the bolts. Tighten the bolts in sequence across from each other to the specifications listed in the Torque chart at the beginning of this Chapter.

9. On a manual shift transmission, install the clutch disc and the pressure plate assembly following the procedure in Chapter 7.

10. Install the transmission, following the procedure in Chapter 7.

Gasoline V8

1. Remove the oil pan and the oil pump (if required).

2. Loosen all the main bearing cap bolts, thereby lowering the crankshaft slightly but not to exceed $\frac{1}{32}$" (0.8mm).

3. Remove the rear main bearing cap, and remove the oil seal from the bearing cap and cylinder block. On the block half of the seal use a seal removal tool, or install a small metal screw in one end of the seal, and pull on the screw to remove the seal. Exercise caution to prevent scratching or damaging the crankshaft seal surfaces.

4. Remove the oil seal retaining pin from the bearing cap if so equipped. The pin is not used with the split-lip seal.

5. Carefully clean the seal groove in the cap and block with a brush and solvent such as lacquer thinner, spot remover, or equivalent, or trichlorethylene. Also, clean the area thoroughly, so that no solvent touches the seal.

6. Dip the split lip-type seal halves in clean engine oil.

7. Carefully install the upper seal (cylinder block) into its groove with undercut side of the seal toward the FRONT of the engine, by rotating it on the seal journal of the crankshaft until approximately $\frac{3}{8}$" (9.5mm) protrudes below the parting surface.

Be sure no rubber has been shaved from the outside diameter of the seal by the bottom edge of the groove. Do not allow oil to get on the sealer area.

8. Tighten the remaining bearing cap bolts to the specifications listed in the Torque chart at the beginning of this chapter.

9. Install the lower seal in the rear main bearing cap under undercut side of seal toward the FRONT of the engine, allow the seal to protrude approximately $\frac{3}{8}$" (9.5mm) above the parting surface to mate with the upper seal when the cap is installed.

10. Apply an even $\frac{1}{16}$" (1.6mm) bead of RTV silicone rubber sealer, to the areas shown, following the procedure given in the illustration.

NOTE: *This sealer sets up in 15 minutes.*

11. Install the rear main bearing cap. Tighten the cap bolts to specifications.

12. Install the oil pump and oil pan. Fill the crankcase with the proper amount and type of oil.

13. Operate the engine and check for oil leaks.

8-420 (6.9L) and 8-444 (7.3L) Diesel

1. Remove the transmission, clutch and flywheel assemblies.

2. Remove the engine rear cover.

3. Using an arbor press and a $4\frac{1}{8}$" (104.775mm) diameter spacer, press out the rear oil seal from the cover.

4. To install, clean the rear cover and engine block surfaces. Remove all traces of old RTV sealant from the oil pan and rear cover sealing surface by cleaning with a suitable solvent and drying thoroughly.

5. Coat the new rear oil seal with Lubriplate® or equivalent. Using an arbor press and spacer, install the new seal into the cover.

NOTE: *The seal must be installed from the engine block side of the rear cover, flush with the seal bore inner surface.*

6. Install a seal pilot, ford part no. T83T-6701B or equivalent onto the crankshaft.

7. Apply gasket sealant to the engine block gasket surfaces, and install the rear cover gasket to the engine.

8. Apply a $\frac{1}{4}$" (6mm) bead of RTV sealant onto the oil pan sealing surface, immediately after rear cover installation.

9. Push the rear cover into position on the engine and install the cover bolts. Torque to specification.

10. Position the flywheel on the crankshaft flange. Coat the threads of the flywheel attaching bolts with sealant and install the bolts and flexplate, if equipped. Torque the bolts to specification, alternating across from each bolt.

11. Install the clutch and transmission. Run the engine and check for oil leaks.

One Piece Seal

1. Remove the transmission, clutch assembly or converter and flywheel.

2. (See Step 7 for diesel engines). Lower the oil pan if necessary for working room.

3. On gasoline engines, use an awl to punch two small holes on opposite sides of the seal just above the split between the main bearing cap and engine block. Install a sheet metal screw in each hole. Use two small pry bars and pry evenly on both screws using two small blocks of wood as a fulcrum point for the pry bars. Use caution throughout to avoid scratching or damage to the oil seal mounting surfaces.

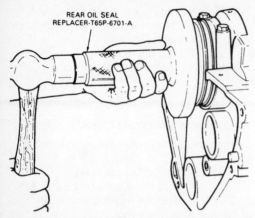

REAR OIL SEAL
REPLACER-T65P-6701-A

Installing the 1-piece rear main seal on gasoline engines

4. When the seal has been removed, clean the mounting recess.

5. Coat the seal and block mounting surfaces with oil. Apply white lube to the contact surface of the seal and crankshaft. Start the seal into the mounting recess and install with seal mounting tool Ford number T82L-6701-A or equivalent.

6. Install the remaining components in the reverse.

7. On the diesel engines, the oil seal is one piece but mounted on a retaining plate. Remove the mounting plate from the rear of the engine and replace the seal. Reinstall in reverse order of removal.

EXHAUST SYSTEM

Safety Precautions

For a number of reasons, exhaust system work can be the most dangerous type of work you can do on your car. Always observe the following precautions:

• Support the car extra securely. Not only will you often be working directly under it, but you'll frequently be using a lot of force, say, heavy hammer blows, to dislodge rusted parts. This can cause a car that's improperly supported to shift and possibly fall.

• Wear goggles. Exhaust system parts are always rusty. Metal chips can be dislodged, even when you're only turning rusted bolts. Attempting to pry pipes apart with a chisel makes the chips fly even more frequently.

• If you're using a cutting torch, keep it a great distance from either the fuel tank or lines. Stop what you're doing and feel the temperature of the fuel bearing pipes on the tank frequently. Even slight heat can expand and/or va-

porize fuel, resulting in accumulated vapor, or even a liquid leak, near your torch.

• Watch where your hammer blows fall and make sure you hit squarely. You could easily tap a brake or fuel line when you hit an exhaust system part with a glancing blow. Inspect all lines and hoses in the area where you've been working.

Special Tools

A number of special exhaust system tools can be rented from auto supply houses or local stores that rent special equipment. A common one is a tail pipe expander, designed to enable you to join pipes of identical diameter.

It may also be quite helpful to use solvents designed to loosen rusted bolts or flanges. Soaking rusted parts the night before you do the job can speed the work of freeing rusted parts considerably. Remember that these solvents are often flammable. Apply only to parts after they are cool!

Muffler, Catalytic Converter, Inlet and Outlet Pipes

REMOVAL AND INSTALLATION

NOTE: *The following applies to exhaust systems using clamped joints. Some models, use welded joints at the muffler. These joints will, of course, have to be cut.*

1. Raise and support the truck on jackstands.

2. Remove the U-clamps securing the muffler and outlet pipe.

3. Disconnect the muffler and outlet pipe bracket and insulator assemblies.

4. Remove the muffler and outlet pipe assembly. It may be necessary to heat the joints to get the parts to come off. Special tools are available to aid in breaking loose the joints.

5. On extended body models, remove the extension pipe.

6. Disconnect the catalytic converter bracket and insulator assembly.

NOTE: *For rod and insulator type hangers, apply a soap solution to the insulator surface and rod ends to allow easier removal of the insulator from the rod end. Don't use oil-based or silicone-based solutions since they will allow the insulator to slip back off once it's installed.*

7. Remove the catalytic converter.

8. On models with Managed Thermactor Air, disconnect the MTA tube assembly.

9. Remove the inlet pipe assembly.

10. Install the components making sure that all the components in the system are properly

aligned before tightening any fasteners. Make sure all tabs are indexed and all parts are clear of surrounding body panels. See the accompanying illustrations for proper clearances and alignment.

Observe the following torque specifications:
- Inlet pipe-to-manifold: 35 ft.lb.

- MTA U-bolt: 60-96 in.lb.
- Inlet pipe or converter-to-muffler or extension: 45 ft.lb.
- Hanger bracket and insulator-to-frame: 24 ft.lb.
- Bracket and insulator-to-exhaust: 15 ft.lb.
- Flat flange bolts (8-460 and diesel) 30 ft.lb.

Emission Controls

EMISSION CONTROLS APPLICATIONS

6-144:
Positive Crankcase Ventilation system (PCV) — later models only

6-170:
Positive Crankcase Ventilation system (PCV) — later models only
Evaporative Emission system (canister) — 1970 California only
Thermactor Emission Control system — 1968-70 models
Ported Exhaust Gas Recirculation system (EGR) — later models only
Improved Combustion System (IMCO) — 1968 w/AT and all 1969-70 models
Deceleration Valve — some 1969-70 models

6-200:
Positive Crankcase Ventilation system (PCV)

6-240:
Positive Crankcase Ventilation system (PCV)
Evaporative Emission system (canister) — 1970 California only; all 1971 and later models
Thermactor Emission Control system — 1968-74 models
Ported Exhaust Gas Recirculation system (EGR)
EGR/Coolant Spark Control (EGR/CSC) — 1974 only
Improved Combustion System (IMCO) — 1968 w/AT and all 1969-74 models
Deceleration Valve — some 1969-74 models
Distributor Modulator (Dist-O-Vac) 1970-71 w/AT
Transmission Regulated Spark system (TRS) — 1972 w/AT

6-300:
Positive Crankcase Ventilation system (PCV)
Evaporative Emission system (canister)

Three-way Catalyst (TWC)
Conventional Oxidation Catalyst (COC)
Electronic Fuel Injection Fuel System (EFI)
Electronic Engine Control IV system (EEC-IV)
EGR/Coolant Spark Control (EGR/CSC) — 1974 and later w/carburetor
Ported Exhaust Gas Recirculation (EGR) — carbureted engines
Electronic (Sonic) Exhaust Gas Recirculation (EEGR) — Fuel injected engines
Thermactor System — 1974-84
Managed Thermactor Air system (MTA) 1985-88
Air Management 1 system (AM1)
Air Management 2 system (AM2)
Thick Film Ignition system (TFI-IV)
Bypass Air idle speed control (BPA)

8-302, 8-351 w/Fuel Injection:
Positive Crankcase Ventilation system (PCV)
Evaporative Emission system (canister)
Three-way Catalyst (TWC)
Conventional Oxidation Catalyst (COC)
Electronic Fuel Injection Fuel System (EFI)
Electronic Engine Control IV system (EEC-IV)
Electronic (Sonic) Exhaust Gas Recirculation (EEGR)
Managed Thermactor Air system (MTA)
Air Management 1 system (AM1)
Air Management 2 system (AM2)
Thick Film Ignition system (TFI-IV)
Bypass Air idle speed control (BPA)

8-302, 8-351 w/Carburetor:
Positive Crankcase Ventilation system (PCV)
Evaporative Emission system (canister)
Three-way Catalyst (TWC)
Conventional Oxidation Catalyst (COC)
EGR/Coolant Spark Control (EGR/CSC) — 1974 and later
Integral backpressure EGR valve (IBP)
Thermactor System — 1974-84

Managed Thermactor Air system (MTA) 1985-87
DuraSpark II Ignition System (DS-II)

8-460 w/4-bbl Carburetor:
Positive Crankcase Ventilation system (PCV)
Evaporative Emission system (canister)
EGR/Coolant Spark Control (EGR/CSC)
Ported Exhaust Gas Recirculation system (EGR)
Thermactor System – 1975-84
Managed Thermactor Air system (MTA) 1985-88
DuraSpark II Ignition System (DS-II)
Cold Start Spark Advance System (CSSA) – 1975-78 only

8-460 w/Fuel Injection:
Positive Crankcase Ventilation system (PCV)
Evaporative Emission system (canister)
4 Reduction-Oxidation Catalysts (REDOX)
Electronic Fuel Injection fuel system (EFI)
Electronic Engine Control IV system (EEC-IV)
Electronic (Sonic) Exhaust Gas Recirculation (EEGR)
Managed Thermactor Air system (MTA)
Thick Film Ignition ignition system (TFI-IV)
Bypass Air idle speed control (BPA)

Positive Crankcase Ventilation System

The crankcase emission control equipment consists of a positive crankcase ventilation (PCV) valve, a closed oil filler cap and the hoses that connect this equipment.

When the engine is running, a small portion of the gases which are formed in the combustion chamber leak by the piston rings and enter the crankcase. Since these gases are under pressure they tend to escape from the crankcase and enter into the atmosphere. If these gases are allowed to remain in the crankcase for any length of time, they would contaminate the engine oil and cause sludge to build up. If the gases are allowed to escape into the atmosphere, they would pollute the air, as they contain unburned hydrocarbons. The crankcase emission control equipment recycles these gases back into the engine combustion chamber, where they are burned.

Crankcase gases are recycled in the following manner. While the engine is running, clean filtered air is drawn into the crankcase through the intake air filter and then through a hose leading to the oil filler cap. As the air passes through the crankcase it picks up the combustion gases and carries them out of the crankcase, up through the PCV valve and into the in-

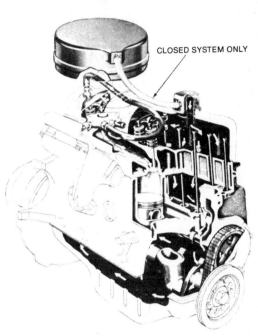

A cutaway view of the typical 6-cylinder positive crankcase ventilation system

take manifold. After they enter the intake manifold they are drawn into the combustion chamber and are burned.

The most critical component of the system is the PCV valve. This vacuum-controlled valve regulates the amount of gases which are recycled into the combustion chamber. At low engine speeds the valve is partially closed, limiting the flow of gases into the intake manifold. As engine speed increases, the valve opens to admit greater quantities of the gases into the intake manifold. If the valve should become blocked or plugged, the gases will be prevented from escaping the crankcase by the normal route. Since these gases are under pressure, they will find their own way out of the crankcase. This alternate route is usually a weak oil seal or gasket in the engine. As the gas escapes by the gasket, it also creates an oil leak. Besides causing oil leaks, a clogged PCV valve also allows these gases to remain in the crankcase for an extended period of time, promoting the formation of sludge in the engine.

The above explanation and the troubleshooting procedure which follows applies to all of the gasoline engines installed in Ford trucks, since all are equipped with PCV systems.

TROUBLESHOOTING

With the engine running, pull the PCV valve and hose from the valve rocker cover rubber grommet.

A hissing noise should be heard as air passes through the valve and a strong vacuum should

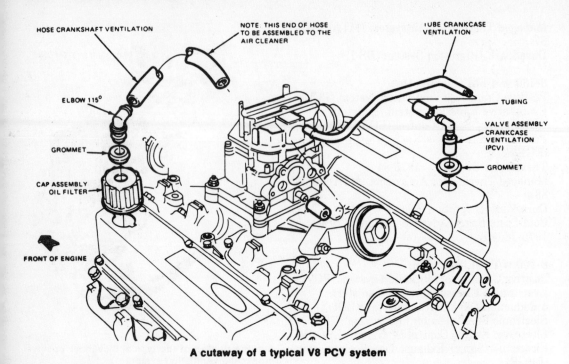

A cutaway of a typical V8 PCV system

be felt when you place a finger over the valve inlet if the valve is working properly. While you have your finger over the PCV valve inlet, check for vacuum leaks in the hose and at the connections.

When the PCV valve is removed from the engine, a metallic licking noise should be heard when it is shaken. This indicates that the metal check ball inside the valve is still free and is not gummed up.

REPLACEMENT

1. Pull the PCV valve and hose from the rubber grommet in the rocker cover.

2. Remove the PCV valve from the hose. Inspect the inside of the PCV valve. If it is dirty,

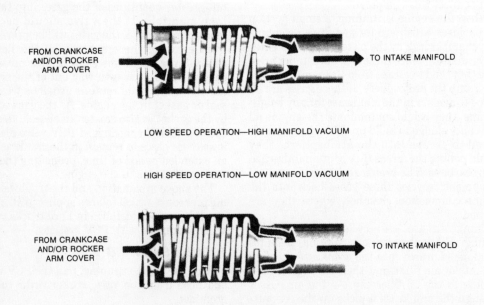

A cutaway view of a PCV valve showing its operation

disconnect it from the intake manifold and clean it in a suitable, safe solvent.

To install, proceed as follows:

1. If the PCV valve hose was removed, connect it to the intake manifold.

2. Connect the PCV valve to its hose.

3. Install the PCV valve into the rubber grommet in the valve rocker cover.

Evaporative Emission Controls

Changes in atmospheric temperature cause fuel tanks to breathe; that is, the air within the tank expands and contracts with outside temperature changes. As the temperature rises, air escapes through the tank vent tube or the vent in the tank cap. The air which escapes contains gasoline vapors. In a similar manner on carbureted engines, the gasoline which fills the carburetor float bowl expands when the engine is stopped. Engine heat causes this expansion. The vapors escape through the air cleaner.

The Evaporative Emission Control System provides a sealed fuel system with the capability to store and condense fuel vapors. The system has three parts: a fill control vent system; a vapor vent and storage system; and a pressure and vacuum relief system (special fill cap).

The fill control vent system is a modification to the fuel tank. It uses a dome air space within the tank which is 10-12% of the tank's volume. The air space is is sufficient to provide for the thermal expansion of the fuel. The space also serves as part of the in-tank vapor vent system.

The in-tank vent system consists of the domed air space previously described and a vapor separator assembly. The separator assembly is mounted to the top of the fuel tank and is secured by a cam-lockring, similar to the one which secures the fuel sending unit. Foam material fills the vapor separator assembly. The foam material separates raw fuel and vapors, thus retarding the entrance of fuel into the vapor line.

The vapor separator is an orifice valve located in the dome of the tank. The restricted size of the orifice, 0.050″ (1.27mm) tends to allow only vapor to pass out of the tank. The orifice valve is connected to the vent line which runs forward to the carbon filled canister in the engine compartment.

The sealed filler cap has a pressure-vacuum relief valve. Under normal operating conditions, the filler cap operates as a check valve, allowing air to enter the tank to replace the fuel consumed. At the same time, it prevents vapors from escaping through the cap. In case of excessive pressure within the tank, the filler cap valve opens to relieve the pressure.

Because the filler cap is sealed, fuel vapors have only one place through which they may escape: the vapor separator assembly at the top of the fuel tank. The vapors pass through the foam material and continue through a single vapor line which leads to a canister in the engine compartment. The canister is filled with activated charcoal.

Another vapor line runs from the top of the carburetor float chamber or the intake manifold, or the throttle body, to the charcoal canister.

As the fuel vapors (hydrocarbons), enter the charcoal canister, they are absorbed by the charcoal. The air is dispelled through the open bottom of the charcoal canister, leaving the hydrocarbons trapped within the charcoal. When

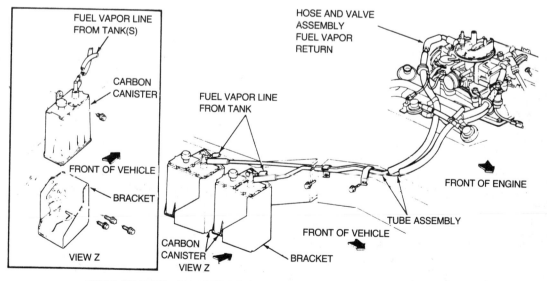

1987 8-460 California and Canada heavy duty carbureted evaporative system

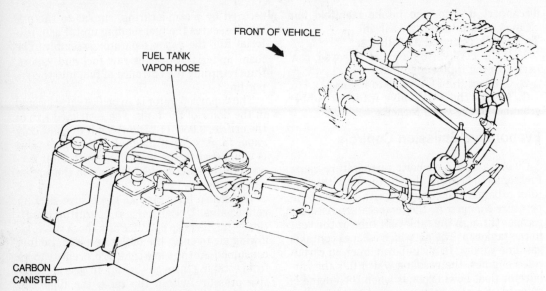

8-351 49 States and Canada heavy duty carbureted evaporative system

the engine is started, vacuum causes fresh air to be drawn into the canister from its open bottom. The fresh air passes through the charcoal picking up the hydrocarbons which are trapped there and feeding them into the engine for burning with the fuel mixture.

DIAGNOSIS AND TESTING

Canister Purge Regulator Valve

1. Disconnect the hoses at the purge regulator valve. Disconnect the electrical lead.
2. Connect a vacuum pump to the vacuum source port.
3. Apply 5 in.Hg to the port. The valve should hold the vacuum. If not, replace it.

Canister Purge Valve

1. Apply vacuum to port **A**. The valve should hold vacuum. If not, replace it.
2. Apply vacuum to port **B**. Valves E5VE-AA, E4VE-AA and E77E-AA should show a slight vacuum leak-down. All other valves should hold vacuum. If the valve doesn't operate properly, replace it.
3. Apply 16 in.Hg to port **A** and apply vacuum to port **B**. Air should pass. On valves E5VE-AA, E4VE-AA and E77E-AA, the flow should be greater than that noted in Step 2.
NOTE: *Never apply vacuum to port C. Doing so will damage the valve.*
4. If the valve fails to perform properly in any of these tests, replace it.

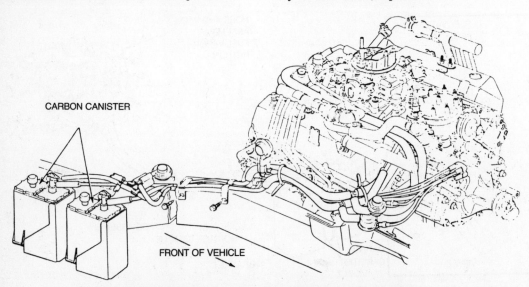

8-460 49 States heavy duty carbureted evaporative system

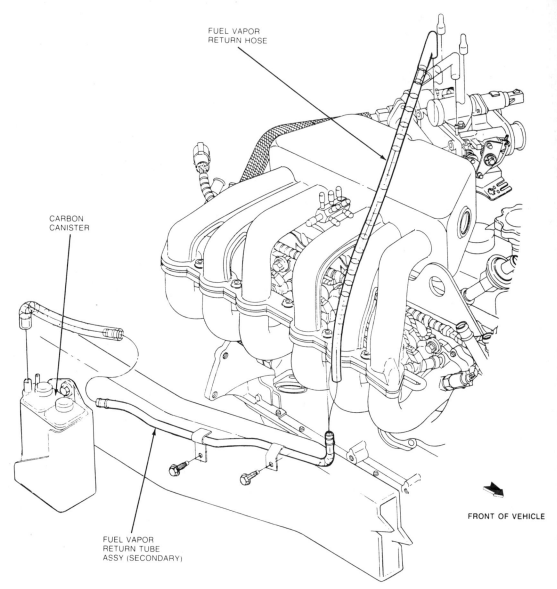

FUEL VAPOR
RETURN HOSE

CARBON
CANISTER

FUEL VAPOR
RETURN TUBE
ASSY (SECONDARY)

FRONT OF VEHICLE

6-300 EFI evaporative system

Catalytic Converters

The catalytic converter, mounted in the trucks exhaust system is a muffler-shaped device containing a ceramic honeycomb shaped material coated with alumina and impregnated with catalytically active precious metals such as platinum, palladium and rhodium.

The catalyst's job is to reduce air pullutants by oxidizing hydrocarbons (HC) and carbon monoxide (CO). Catalysts containing palladium and rhodium also oxidize nitrous oxides (NOx).

On some trucks, the catalyst is also fed by the secondary air system, via a small supply tube in the side of the catalyst.

No maintenance is possible on the converter, other than keeping the heat shield clear of flammable debris, such as leaves and twigs.

Other than external damage, the only significant damage possible to a converter is through the use of leaded gasoline, or by way of a too rich fuel/air mixture. Both of these problems will ruin the converter through contamination of the catalyst and will eventually plug the converter causing loss of power and engine performance.

When this occurs, the cataylst must be replaced. For catalyst replacement, see the Exhaust System section in Chapter 3.

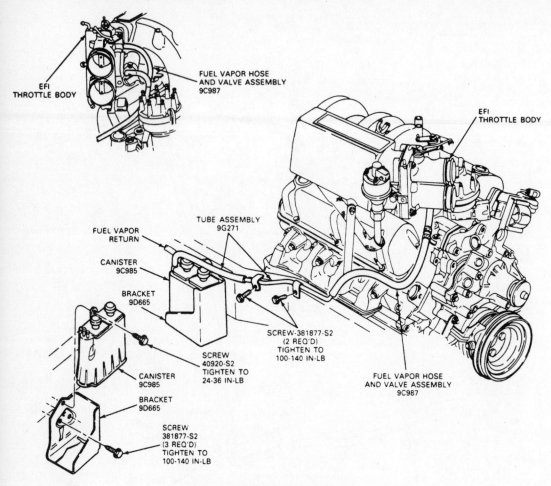

1987—88 8-302 EFI evaporative system

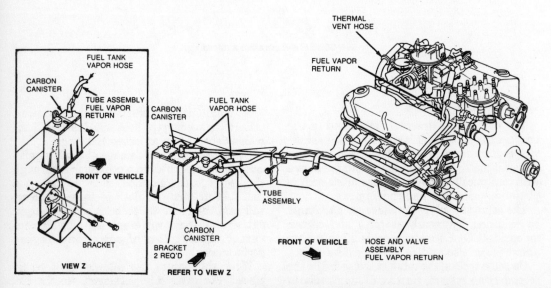

8-351 4-bbl 49 States and High Altitude light duty carbureted evaporative system

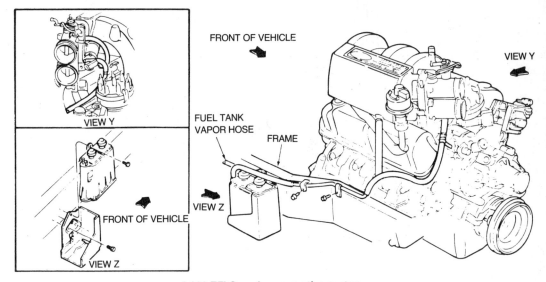

8-302 EFI Canada evaporative system

Electronic Fuel Injection

For a description of and maintenance to the EFI systems, see Chapter 5.

Carbureted Fuel System

For a description of and maintenance to the carburetor, see Chapter 5.

Electronic Engine Controls
EEC-I

Designed to precisely control ignition timing, EGR and Thermactor (air pump) flow, the system consists of Electronic Control Assembly (ECA), seven monitoring sensors, a DuraSpark®II ignition module and coil, a spe-

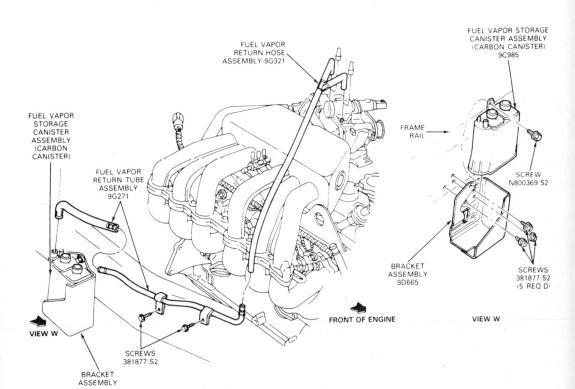

6-300 EFI evaporative system under 8,500 lb. GVW

cial distributor assembly, and an EGR system designed to operate on air pressure.

The ECA is a solid state micro computer, consisting of a processor assembly and a calibration assembly. The processor continuously receives inputs from the seven sensors, which it converts to usable information for the calculating section of the computer. It also performs ignition timing, Thermactor® and EGR flow calculations, processes the information and sends out signals to the ignition module and control solenoids to adjust the timing and flow of the system accordingly. The calibration assembly contains the memory and programming for the processor.

Processor inputs come from sensors monitoring manifold pressure, barometric pressure, engine coolant temperature, inlet air temperature, crankshaft position, throttle position, and EGR valve position.

The manifold absolute pressure sensor determines changes in intake manifold pressure (barometric pressure minus manifold vacuum) which result from changes in engine load and speed, or in atmospheric pressure. It signal is used by the ECA to set part throttle spark advance and EGR flow rate.

Barometric pressure is monitored by a sensor mounted on the firewall. Measurements taken are converted into a usable electrical signal. The ECA uses this reference for altitude-dependent EGR flow requirements.

Engine coolant temperature is measured at the rear of the intake manifold by a sensor consisting of a brass housing containing a thermistor (resistance decreases as temperature rises). When reference voltage (about 9 volts, supplied by the processor to all sensors) is applied to the sensor, the resistance can be measured by the resulting voltage drop. Resistance is then interpreted as coolant temperature by the ECA. This sensor replaces both the PVS and EGR PVS in conventional systems. EGR flow is cut off by the ECA when a predetermined temperature value is reached. The ECA will also advance initial ignition timing to increase idle speed if the coolant overheats due to prolonged idle. A faster idle speed increases coolant and radiator air flow.

Inlet air temperature is measured by a sensor mounted in the air cleaner. It functions in the same way as the coolant sensor. The ECA uses its signal for proper spark advance and Thermactor® flow. At high inlet temperatures (above 90°F [32°C]) the ECA modifies timing advance to prevent spark knock.

The crankshaft is fitted with a 4-lobed powdered metal pulse ring, positioned 10°BTDC. Its position is constantly monitored by the crankshaft position sensor. Signals are sent to the ECA describing both the position of the crankshaft at any given moment, and the frequency of the pulses (engine rpm). These signals are used to determine optimum ignition timing advance. If either the sensor or wiring is broken, the ECA will not receive a signal, and thus be unable to send any signal to the ignition module. This will prevent the engine from starting.

The throttle position sensor is a rheostat connected to the throttle plate shaft. Changes in throttle plate angle change the resistance valve of the reference voltage supplied by the processor. Signals are interpreted in one of three ways by the ECA.

- Closed throttle (idle or deceleration)
- Part throttle (cruise)
- Full throttle (maximum acceleration)

A position sensor is built into the EGR valve. The ECA uses its signal to determine EGR valve position. The valve and position sensor are replaced as a unit, should either fail.

CAUTION: *Because of the complicated nature of this system, special diagnostic tools are necessary for troubleshooting. Any troubleshooting without these tools must be limited to mechanical checks of connectors and wiring.*

The distributor is locked in place during engine manufacture; no rotational adjustment is possible for initial ignition timing, since all timing is controlled by the ECA. There are no mechanical advance mechanisms or adjustments under the rotor, thus there is no need to remove it except for replacement.

EEC-II

The second generation EEC-II system was introduced in 1979. It is based on the EEC-I system, but some changes have been made to reduce complexity and cost, increase the number of controlled functions, and improve reliability and performance.

In general, the EEC-II system operates in the same manner as EEC-I. An Electronic Control Assembly (ECA) monitors reports from six sensors, and adjusts the EGR flow, ignition timing, Thermactor® (air pump) air flow, and carburetor air/fuel mixture in response to the incoming signals. Although there are only six sensors, seven conditions are monitored. The sensors are: (1) Engine Coolant Temperature, (2) Throttle Position, (3) Crankshaft Position, (4) Exhaust Gas Oxygen, (5) Barometric and Manifold Absolute Pressure, and (6) EGR Valve Position. These sensors function in the same manner as the EEC-I sensors, and are described in the EEC-I section. Note that inlet air temperature is not monitored in the EEC-II system, and that the barometric and manifold pressure sensors have been combined into one unit. One more change from the previous system is in the location of the crankshaft sensor: it is mounted on the front of the engine, behind the vibration damper and crankshaft pulley.

The biggest difference between EEC-I and EEC-II is that the newer system is capable of continually monitoring and adjusting the carburetor air/fuel ratio. Monitoring is performed by the oxygen sensor installed in the right exhaust manifold. Adjustment is made via an electric stepper motor installed on the model 7200 VV carburetor.

The stepper motor has four separate armature windings, which can be sequentially energized by the ECA. As the motor varies the position of the carburetor metering valve, the amount of control vacuum exposed to the fuel bowl in correspondingly altered. Increased vacuum reduces pressure in the fuel bowl, causing a leaner air/fuel mixture, and vice-versa. During engine starting and immediately after, the ECA sets the motor at a point dependent on its initial position. Thereafter, the motor position is changed in response to the ECA calculations of the six input signals.

EEC-II is also capable of controlling purging of vapors from the evaporative emission control storage canister. A canister purge solenoid, a combination solenoid and valve, is located in the line between the intake manifold purge fitting and the carbon canister. It controls the flow of vapors from the canister to the intake manifold, opening and closing in response to signals from the ECA.

CAUTION: *As in the case with EEC-I, diagnosis and repair of the system requires special tools and equipment.*

The distributor is locked in place during engine manufacture; no rotational adjustment is possible for initial ignition timing, since all timing is controlled by the ECA. There are no mechanical advance mechanisms or adjustments under the ignition rotor, and thus there is no need to remove it except for replacement.

Air/fuel mixture is entirely controlled by the ECA; no adjustments are possible.

EEC-III

EEC-III was introduced in 1980. It is a third generation system developed entirely from EEC-II. The only real differences between EEC-II and III are contained within the Electronic Control Assembly (ECA) and the DuraSpark® ignition module. The EEC-III system uses a separate program module which plugs into the main ECA module. This change allows various programming calibrations for specific applications to be made to the program module, while allowing the main ECA module

to be standardized. Additionally, EEC-III uses a DuraSpark®III ignition module, which contains fewer electronic functions than the DuraSpark®II module. The functions have been incorporated into the main ECA module. There is no interchangeability between the DuraSpark®II and III models.

NOTE: *Since late 1979 emission controls and air/fuel mixtures have been controlled by various electronic methods. An electronically controlled feedback carburetor is used to precisely calibrate fuel metering, many vacuum check valves, solenoids and regulators have been added and the electronic control boxes (ECU and MCU) can be calibrated and programmed in order to be used by different engines and under different conditions.*

EEC-IV

All fuel injected engines use the EEC-IV system. The Universal Distributor (EEC-IV) has a diecast base which incorporates an externally mounted TFI-IV ignition module, and contains a Hall Effect vane switch stator assembly and provision for fixed octane adjustment. No distributor calibration is required and initial timing adjustment is normally not required. The primary function of the EEC-IV Universal Distributor system is to direct high secondary voltage to the spark plugs. In addition, the distributor supplies crankshaft position and frequency information to a computer using a profile Ignition Pickup. The Hall Effect switch in the distributor consists of a Hall Effect device on one side and a magnet on the other side. A rotary cup which has windows and tabs rotates and passes through the space between the device and the magnet. When a window is between the sides of the switch the magnetic path is not completed and the switch is Off, sending no signal. When a tab passes between the switch the magnetic path is completed and the Hall Effect Device is turned On and a signal is sent. The voltage pulse (signal) is used by is EEC-IV system for sensing crankshaft position and computing the desired spark advance based on engine demand and calibration.

The heart of the EEC-IV system is a microprocessor called the Electronic Control Assembly (ECA). The ECA receives data from a number of sensors, switches and relays. The ECA contains a specific calibration for peak fuel economy, drivability and emissions control. Based on information stored in its memory, the ECA generates signals to control the various engine functions.

The ECA calibration module is located inside the ECA assembly. The calibration module is called a PROM.

On all vans, the ECA is located inside the

truck on the left of the firewall, behind the kick panel.

A potentiometer senses the position of the vane airflow meter in the engine's air induction system and generates a voltage signal that varies with the amount of air drawn into the engine. A sensor in the area of the vane airflow meter measures the temperature of the incoming air and transmits a corresponding electrical signal. Another temperature sensor inserted in the engine coolant tells if the engine is cold or warmed up. And a switch that senses throttle plate position produces electrical signals that tell the control unit when the throttle is closed or wide open.

A special probe (oxygen sensor) in the exhaust manifold measures the amount of oxygen in the exhaust gas, which is in indication of combustion efficiency, and sends a signal to the control unit. The sixth signal, crankshaft position information, is transmitted by a sensor integral with the new-design distributor.

The EEC-IV microcomputer circuit processes the input signals and produces output control signals to the fuel injectors to regulate fuel discharged to the injectors. It also adjusts ignition spark timing to provide the best balance between driveability and economy.

NOTE: *Because of the complicated nature of the Ford system, special tools and procedures are necessary for testing and troubleshooting.*

Exhaust Gas Recirculation (EGR)

On V8 engines, exhaust gases travel through the exhaust gas crossover passage in the intake manifold. On 6-200 engines, an external tube carries exhaust manifold gases to a carburetor spacer. On spacer entry equipped engines, a portion of these gases are diverted into a spacer which is mounted under the carburetor. On floor entry models, a regulated portion of exhaust gases enters the intake manifold through a pair of small holes drilled in the floor of the intake manifold riser. The EGR control valve, which is attached to the rear of the spacer or intake manifold, consists of a vacuum diaphragm with an attached plunger which normally

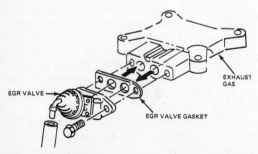

Spacer entry EGR system

EGR VALVE

EGR VALVE GASKET

EXHAUST GAS

blocks exhaust gases from entering the intake manifold.

On all models, the EGR valve is controlled by a vacuum line from the carburetor which passes through a ported vacuum switch. The EGR ported vacuum switch provides vacuum to the EGR valve at coolant temperatures above 125°F (52°C). The vacuum diaphragm then opens the EGR valve permitting exhaust gases to flow through the carburetor spacer and enter the combustion chambers. The exhaust gases are relatively oxygen-free, and tend to dilute the combustion charge. This lowers peak combustion temperature thereby reducing oxides of nitrogen.

On models equipped with an 8-400, an EGR subsystem, consisting of a speed sensor and control amplifier, prevents exhaust gases from entering the combustion mixture when the car is traveling 65 mph or faster.

EGR SYSTEM TEST

1. Allow the engine to warm up, so that the coolant temperature has reached at least 125°F (52°C).

2. Disconnect the vacuum hose which runs from the temperature cut-in valve to the EGR valve at the EGR valve end. Connect a vacuum gauge to this hose with a T-fitting.

3. Increase engine speed. The gauge should indicate a vacuum. If no vacuum is present, check the following:

a. The carburetor — look for a clogged vacuum port.

b. The vacuum hoses — including the vacuum hoses to the transmission modulator.

c. The temperature cut-in valve — if no vacuum is present at its outlet with the engine temperature above 125°F (52°C) and vacuum available from the carburetor, the valve is defective.

4. If all the above tests are positive, check the EGR valve itself.

5. Connect an outside vacuum source and a vacuum gauge to the valve.

6. Apply vacuum to the EGR valve. The valve should open at 3-10 in.Hg, the engine idle speed should slow down and the idle quality should become more rough.

7. If this does not happen, i.e., the EGR valve remains closed, the EGR valve is defective and must be replaced.

8. If the valve stem moves but the idle remains the same, the valve orifice is clogged and must be cleaned.

NOTE: *If an outside vacuum source is not available, disconnect the hose which runs between the EGR valve and the temperature cut-in valve and plug the hose connections on the cut-in valve. Connect the EGR valve hose*

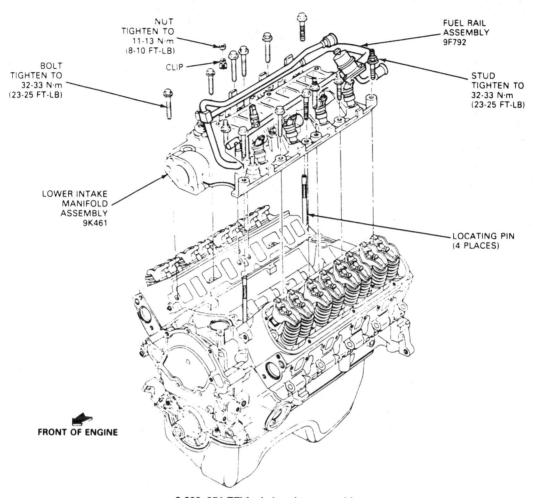

NUT
TIGHTEN TO
11-13 N·m
(8-10 FT-LB)

CLIP

FUEL RAIL
ASSEMBLY
9F792

BOLT
TIGHTEN TO
32-33 N·m
(23-25 FT-LB)

STUD
TIGHTEN TO
32-33 N·m
(23-25 FT-LB)

LOWER INTAKE
MANIFOLD
ASSEMBLY
9K461

LOCATING PIN
(4 PLACES)

FRONT OF ENGINE

8-302, 351 EFI fuel charging assembly

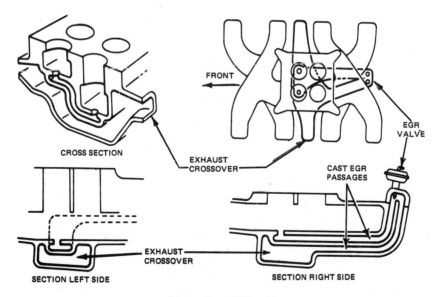

CROSS SECTION

FRONT

EGR
VALVE

EXHAUST
CROSSOVER

CAST EGR
PASSAGES

SECTION LEFT SIDE

EXHAUST
CROSSOVER

SECTION RIGHT SIDE

Floor entry EGR system

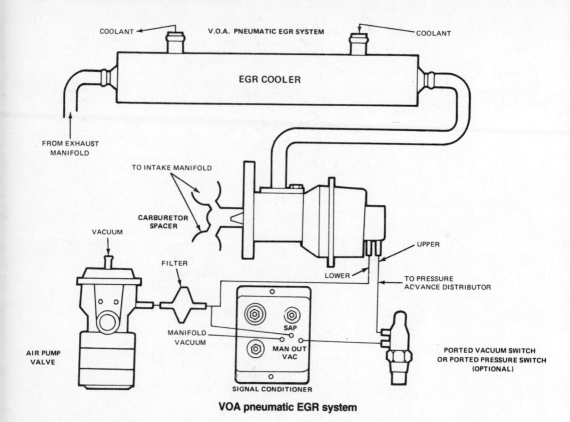

VOA pneumatic EGR system

to a source of intake manifold vacuum and watch the idle. The results should be the same as in steps 6-7, above.

EGR SYSTEM SERVICE

Since the EGR system channels exhaust gases through quite narrow passages, deposits are likely to build up and eventually block the flow of gases. this necessitates servicing of the system at the interval specified in the maintenance chart (see Chapter 1). EGR system service consists of cleaning or replacing the EGR valve and cleaning all the exhaust gas channels.

EGR VALVE CLEANING

Remove the EGR valve for cleaning. Do not strike or pry on the valve diaphragm housing or supports, as this may damage the valve operating mechanism and/or change the valve calibration. Check orifice hole in the EGR valve body for deposits. A small hand drill of no more than 0.060″ (1.5mm) diameter may be used to clean the hole if plugged. Extreme care must be taken to avoid enlarging the hole or damaging the surface of the orifice plate.

NOTE: *The remainder of this procedure refers only to EGR valves which can be disas-*

sembled. *Valves which are riveted or otherwise permanently assembled cannot be cleaned and should be replaced if highly contaminated.*

Separate the diaphragm section from the main mounting body. Clean the valve plates, stem, and the mounting plate, using a small power-driven rotary type wire brush. Take care not to damage the parts. Remove deposits between stem and valve disc by using a steel blade or shim approximately 0.028″ (0.7mm) thick in a sawing motion around the stem shoulder at both sides of the disc. The poppet must wobble and move axially before assembly.

Clean the cavity and passages in the main body of the valve with a power-driven rotary wire brush. If the orifice plate has a hole less than 0.050″ (1.27mm) it must be removed for cleaning. Remove all loosened debris using shop compressed air. Reassemble the diaphragm section on the main body using a new gasket between them. Torque the attaching screws to specification. Clean the orifice plate and the counterbore in the valve body. Reinstall the orifice plate using a small amount of contact cement to retain the plate in place during assembly of the valve to the carburetor spacer. Apply cement only to outer edges of the orifice plate to avoid restriction of the orifice.

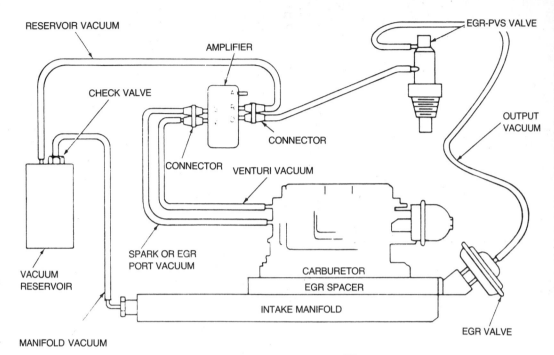

EGR system with vaccum amplifier

EGR Supply Passages and Carburetor Space Cleaning

Remove the carburetor and carburetor spacer on engines so equipped. Clean the supply tube with a small power-driven rotary type wire brush or blast cleaning equipment. Clean the exhaust gas passages in the spacer using a suitable wire brush and/or scraper. The machined holes in the spacer can be cleaned by using a suitable round wire brush. hard encrusted material should be probed loose first, then brushed out.

EGR Exhaust Gas Channel Cleaning

Clean the exhaust gas channel, where applicable, in the intake manifold, using a suitable carbon scraper. Clean the exhaust gas entry port in the intake manifold by hand passing a suitable drill bit through the holes to auger out the deposits. do not use a wire brush. The manifold riser bore(s) should be suitably plugged during the above action to prevent any of the residue from entering the induction system.

Electronic Exhaust Gas Recirculation (EEGR)

The Electronic EGR system (EEGR) is found in all systems in which EGR flow is controlled according to computer commands by means of an EGR valve position sensor (EVP) attached to the valve.

The EEGR valve is operated by a vacuum signal from the dual EGR Solenoid Valves, or the elctronic vacuum regulator which actuates the valve diaphragm.

As supply vacuum overcomes the spring load, the diaphragm is actuated lifting the pintle off of its seat allowing the exhaust gas to flow. The amount of flow is directly proportional to the pintle position. The EVP sensor sends an electrical signal notify the EEC of its position.

The EEGR valve is not servicable. The EVP sensor must be serviced separately.

IBP EGR

The Integral Backpressure (IBP) EGR system combines inputs of EGR port vacuum and

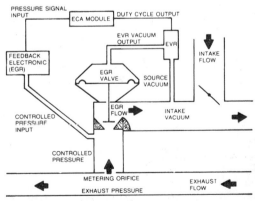

Pressure feedback electronic EGR system vacuum schematic

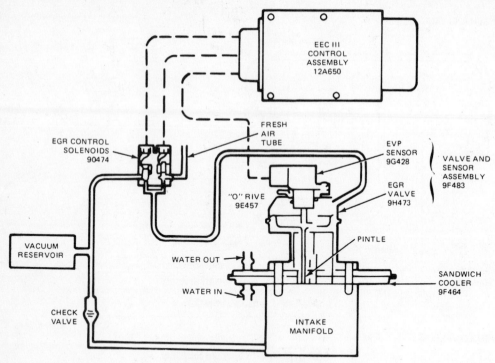

EEC-III EGR vacuum schematic

backpressure into one unit. The valve requires both inputs for proper operation. The valve won't operate on vacuum alone.

There are two types of backpressure valves: the poppet type and the tapered pintle type.

Ported EGR

The ported EGR valve is operated by engine vacuum alone. A vacuum signal from the carburetor activates the EGR valve diaphragm. As the vacuum signal increase it gradually opens the valve pintle allowing exhaust gases to flow. The amount of flow is directly proportional to the pintle position.

Thermactor® System

All 1967 models equipped with manual transmission, all 1974 models manufactured for sale in California, and most 1975–86 models are equipped with a Thermactor emission control system.

The Thermactor emission control system makes use of a belt driven air pump to inject fresh air into the hot exhaust stream through the engine exhaust ports. The result is the extended burning of those fumes which were not completely ignited in the combustion chamber, and the subsequent reduction of some of the

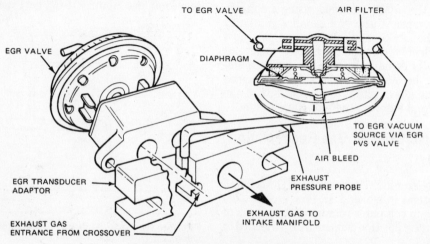

EGR valve backpressure transducer

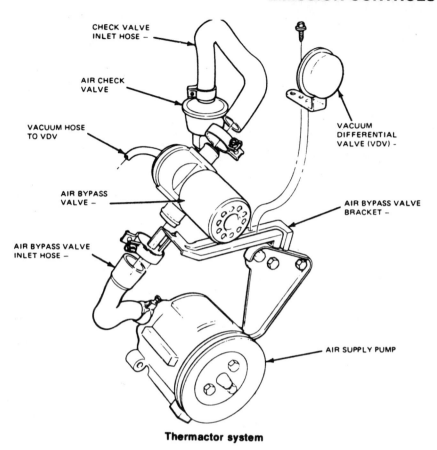

Thermactor system

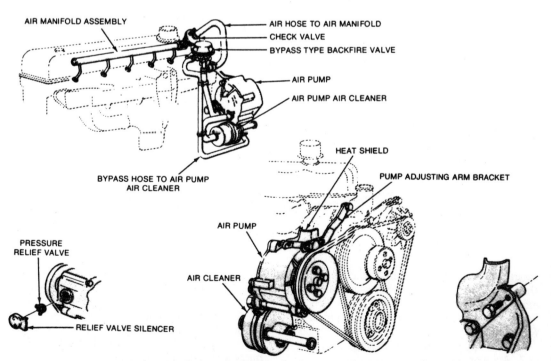

The Thermactor exhaust emission control system installed on a 240 six

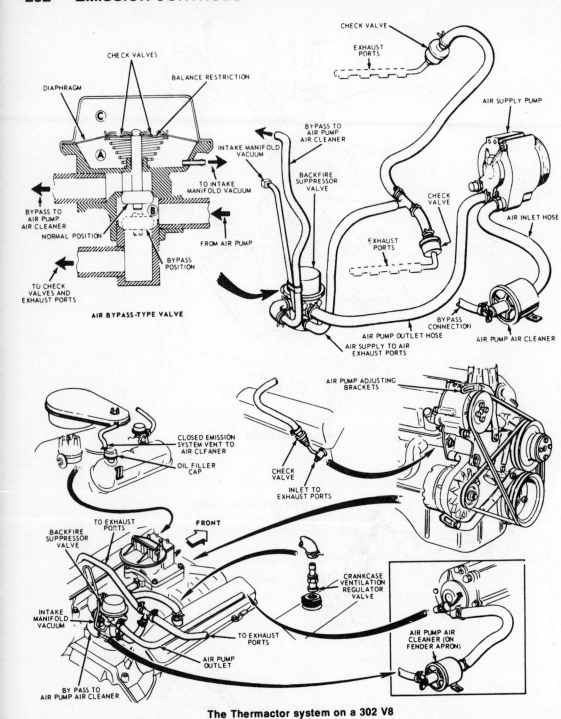

The Thermactor system on a 302 V8

hydrocarbon and carbon monoxide content of the exhaust emissions into harmless carbon dioxide and water.

The Thermactor system is composed of the following components:

1. Air supply pump (belt driven)
2. Air by-pass valve.
3. Check valves
4. Air manifolds (internal or external)
5. Air supply tubes (on external manifolds only).

Air for the Thermactor system is cleaned by means of a centrifugal filter fan mounted on the air pump driveshaft. The air filter does not require a replaceable element.

To prevent excessive pressure, the air pump

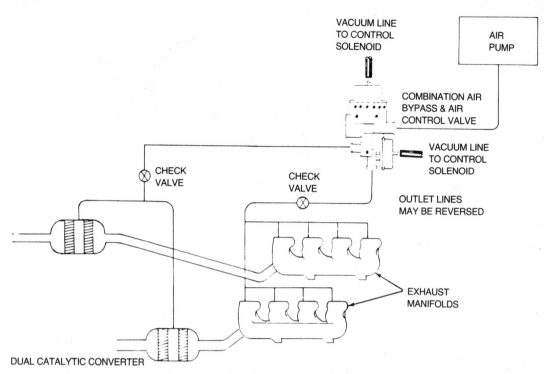

Managed Thermactor system with combined bypass/control valve—electronically controlled

is equipped with a pressure relief valve which uses a replaceable plastic plug to control the pressure setting.

The Thermactor air pump has sealed bearings which are lubricated for the life of the unit, and preset rotor vane and bearing clearances, which do not require any periodic adjustments.

The air supply from the pump is controlled by the air by-pass valve, sometimes called a dump valve. During deceleration, the air bypass valve

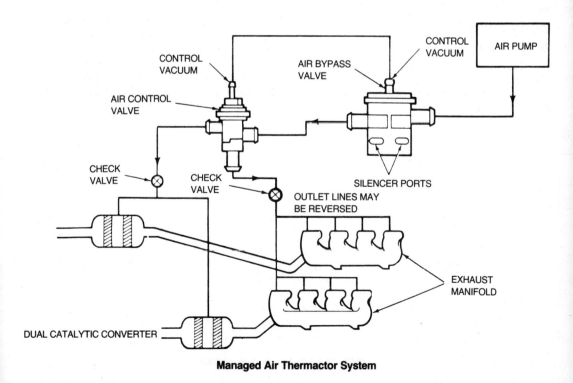

Managed Air Thermactor System

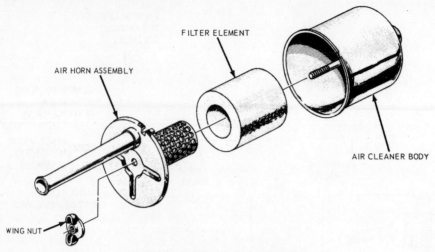

AIR HORN ASSEMBLY

FILTER ELEMENT

AIR CLEANER BODY

WING NUT

Early model Thermactor air cleaner

opens, momentarily diverting the air supply through a silencer and into the atmosphere, thus preventing backfires within the exhaust system.

A check valve is incorporated in the air inlet side of the air manifolds. Its purpose is to prevent exhaust gases from backing up into the Thermactor system. This valve is especially important in the event of drive belt failure, and during deceleration, when the air by-pass valve is dumping the air supply.

The air manifolds and air supply tubes channel the air from the Thermactor air pump into the exhaust ports of each cylinder, thus completing the cycle of the Thermactor system.

REPLACEMENT

Air By-Pass Valve

1. Disconnect the air and vacuum hoses at the air by-pass valve body.

2. Position the air by-pass valve and connect the respective hoses.

Check Valve

1. Disconnect the air supply hose at the valve. Use a 1¼" crowfoot wrench. The valve has a standard, right hand pipe thread.

2. Clean the threads on the air manifold adapter (air supply tube on the V8 engines) with a wire brush. Do not blow compressed air through the check valve in either direction.

3. Install the check valve and tighten.

4. Connect the air supply hose.

Air Manifold

6-CYLINDER ENGINES ONLY

1. Disconnect the air supply hose at the check valve, position the hose out of the way and remove the valve.

2. Loosen all of the air manifold-to-cylinder head tube coupling nuts (compression fittings). Inspect the air manifold for damaged threads and fittings and for leaking connections. Repair

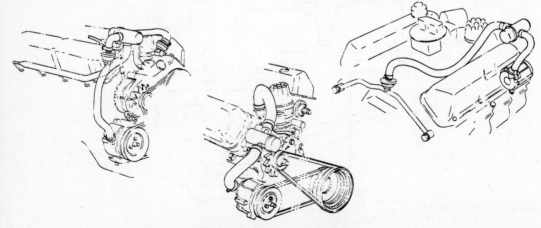

1969–74 8-302 Thermactor system

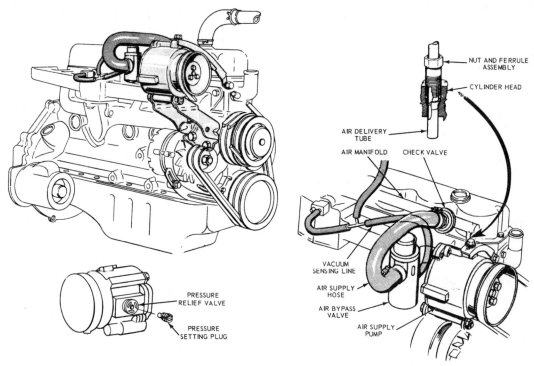

1969 6-240 Thermactor system

or replace as required. Clean the manifold and associated parts with kerosene. Do not dry the parts with compressed air.

3. Position the air manifold on the cylinder head. Be sure that all of the tube coupling nuts are aligned with the cylinder head.

4. Screw each coupling nut into the cylinder head, one or two threads. Tighten the tube coupling nuts.

5. Install the check valve and tighten it.

6. Connect the air supply hose to the check valve.

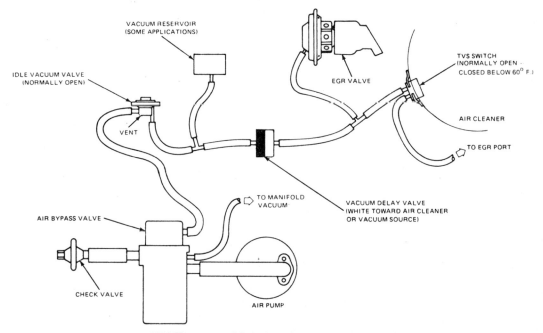

1978 Thermactor idle valve with vacuum delay valve

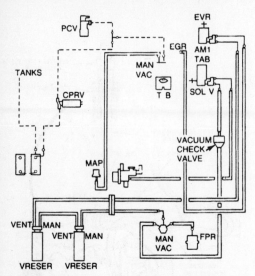

8-460 EFI Managed Thermactor vacuum schematic

Air Supply Tube

V8 ENGINE ONLY

1. Disconnect the air supply hose at the check valve and position the hose out of the way.

2. Remove the check valve.

3. Remove the air supply tube bolt and seal washer.

4. Carefully remove the air supply tube and seal washer from the cylinder head. Inspect the air supply tube for evidence of leaking threads or seal surfaces. Examine the attaching bolt

head, seal washers, and supply tube surface for leaks. Inspect the attaching bolt and cylinder head threads for damage. Clean the air supply tube, seal washers, and bolt with kerosene. Do not dry the parts with compressed air.

5. Install the seal washer and air supply tube on the cylinder head. Be sure that it is positioned in the same manner as before removal.

6. Install the seal washer and mounting bolt. Tighten the bolt.

7. Install the check valve and tighten it.

8. Connect the air supply hose to the check valve.

Air Nozzle

6-CYLINDER ENGINES ONLY

Normally, air nozzles should be replaced during cylinder head reconditioning. A nozzle may be replaced, however, without removing the cylinder head, by removing the air manifold and using a hooked tool.

Clean the nozzle with kerosene and a stiff brush. Inspect the air nozzles for eroded tips.

Air Pump and Filter Fan

1. Loosen the air pump attaching bolts.

2. Remove the drive pulley attaching bolts and pull the pulley off the air pump shaft.

3. Pry the outer disc loose, then remove the centrifugal filter fan. Care must be used to prevent foreign matter from entering the air intake hole, especially if the fan breaks during removal. Do not attempt to remove the metal drive hub.

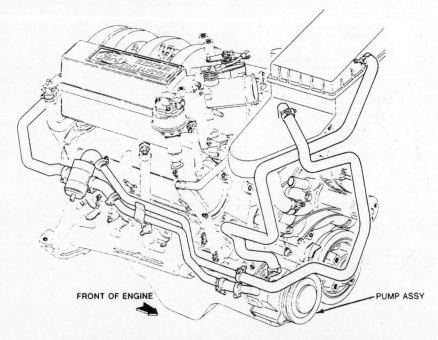

FRONT OF ENGINE   PUMP ASSY

8-351 EFI Managed Thermactor vacuum schematic under 8,500 lb. GVW

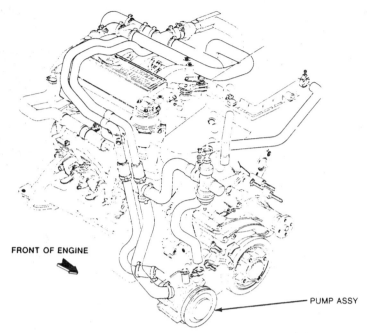

FRONT OF ENGINE

PUMP ASSY

8-351 EFI Managed Thermactor vacuum schematic over 8,500 lb. GVW

4. Install the new filter fan by drawing it into position with the pulley bolts.

NOTE: *Some 1966-67 air pumps have air filters with replaceable, non-cleanable elements.*

Air Pump

1. Disconnect the air outlet hose at the air pump.

2. Loosen the pump belt tension adjuster.

3. Disengage the drive belt.

4. Remove the mounting bolt and air pump.

5. Position the air pump on the mounting bracket and install the mounting bolt.

6. Place the drive belt in the pulley and attach the adjusting arm to the air pump.

7. Adjust the drive belt tension and tighten the adjusting arm and mounting bolts.

8. Connect the air outlet hose to the air pump.

Relief Valve

Do not disassemble the air pump on the truck to replace the relief valve, but remove the pump from the engine.

1. Remove the relief valve on the pump housing and hold it in position with a block of wood.

2. Use a hammer to lightly tap the wood block until the relief valve is seated.

Relief Valve Pressure Setting Plug

1. Compress the locking tabs inward (together) and remove the plastic pressure setting plug.

2. Before installing the new plug, be sure that the plug is the correct one. The plugs are color coded.

3. Insert the plug in the relief valve hole and push in until it snaps into place.

Managed Thermactor Air System

The MTA system is used to inject fresh air into the exhaust manifolds or catalytic converters via an air control valve. Under some operating conditions, the air can be dumped back into the atmosphere via an air bypass valve. On some applications the two valves are combined into one unit. The air bypass valve can be either the normally closed type, when the valves are separate, or the normally open type, when the valves are combined.

Normally Closed Air Bypass Valve Functional Test

1. Disconnect the air supply hose at the valve.

2. Run the engine to normal operating temperature.

3. Disconnect the vacuum line and make sure vacuum is present. If no vacuum is present, remove or bypass any restrictors or delay valves in the vacuum line.

4. Run the engine at 1,500 rpm with the vacuum line connected. Air pump supply air should be heard and felt at the valve outlet.

5. With the engine still at 1,500 rpm, disconnect the vacuum line. Air at the outlet should shut off or dramatically decrease. Air pump

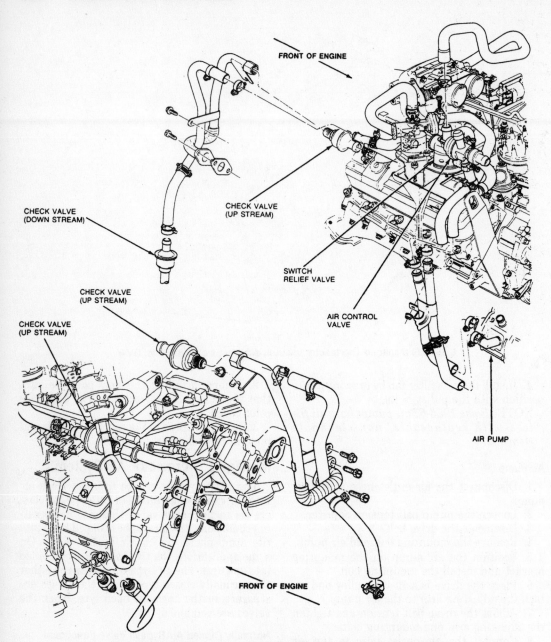

FRONT OF ENGINE

CHECK VALVE
(UP STREAM)

CHECK VALVE
(DOWN STREAM)

CHECK VALVE
(UP STREAM)

CHECK VALVE
(UP STREAM)

SWITCH
RELIEF VALVE

AIR CONTROL
VALVE

AIR PUMP

FRONT OF ENGINE

Dual outlet air pump system for 8-460 EFI engines, over 8,500 lb.GVW

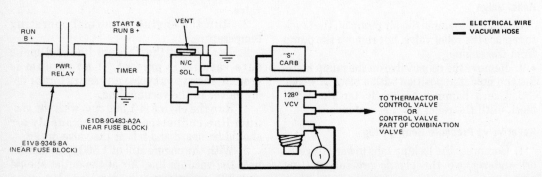

RUN
B +

START &
RUN B +

VENT

PWR.
RELAY

TIMER

N/C
SOL.

"S"
CARB

128°
VCV

ELECTRICAL WIRE
VACUUM HOSE

E1DB-9G483-A2A
(NEAR FUSE BLOCK)

E1VB-9345-BA
(NEAR FUSE BLOCK)

TO THERMACTOR
CONTROL VALVE
OR
CONTROL VALVE
PART OF COMBINATION
VALVE

①

Thermactor air timer system vacuum schematic

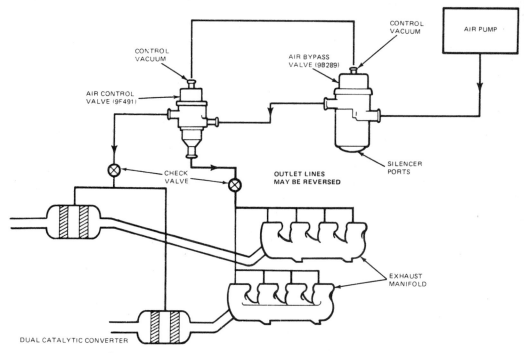

General vacuum schematic for the Managed Thermactor system

supply air should now be felt or heard at the silencer ports.

6. If the valve doesn't pass each of these tests, replace it.

Normally Open Air Bypass Valve Functional Test

1. Disconnect the air supply hose at the valve.

2. Run the engine to normal operating temperature.

3. Disconnect the vacuum lines from the valve.

4. Run the engine at 1,500 rpm with the vacuum lines disconnected. Air pump supply air should be heard and felt at the valve outlet.

5. Shut off the engine. Using a spare length

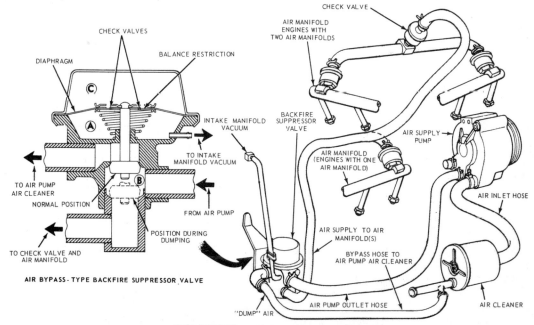

1967 6-240 Thermactor vacuum components

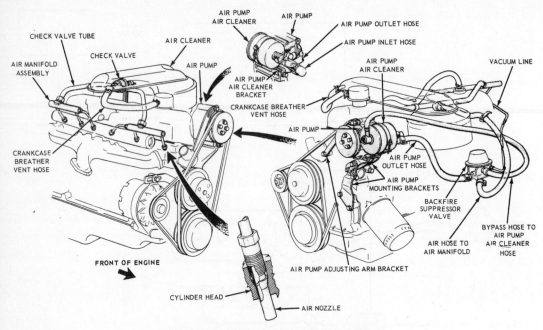

1967–70 6-170 Thermactor exhaust system

of vacuum hose, connect the vacuum nipple of the valve to direct manifold vacuum.

6. Run the engine at 1,500 rpm. Air at the outlet should shut off or dramatically decrease. Air pump supply air should now be felt or heard at the silencer ports.

7. With the engine still in this mode, cap the vacuum vent. Accelerate the engine to 2,000 rpm and suddenly release the throttle. A momentary interruption of air pump supply air should be felt at the valve outlet.

8. If the valve doesn't pass each of these tests, replace it. Reconnect all lines.

Air Control Valve Functional Test

1. Run the engine to normal operating temperature, then increase the speed to 1,500 rpm.

2. Disconnect the air supply hose at the valve inlet and verify that there is airflow present.

3. Reconnect the air supply hose.

4. Disconnect both air supply hoses.

5. Disconnect the vacuum hose from the valve.

6. With the engine running at 1,500 rpm, airflow should be felt and heard at the outlet on the side of the valve, with no airflow heard or felt at the outlet opposite the vacuum nipple.

7. Shut off the engine.

8. Using a spare piece of vacuum hose, connect direct manifold vacuum to the valve's vacuum fitting. Airflow should be heard and felt at the outlet opposite the vacuum nipple, and no airflow should be present at the other outlet.

9. If the valve is not functioning properly, replace it.

Air Supply Pump Functional Check

1. Check and, if necessary, adjust the belt tension. Press at the mid-point of the belt's longest straight run. You should be able to depress the belt about ½″ at most.

2. Run the engine to normal operating temperature and let it idle.

3. Disconnect the air supply hose from the bypass control valve. If the pump is operating properly, airflow should be felt at the pump outlet. The flow should increase as you increase the engine speed. The pump is not servicable and should be replaced if it is not functioning properly.

Thick Film Ignition System

For complete testing and operation of the TFI-IV system, see Chapter 2.

DuraSpark II Ignition System

For complete testing and operation of the DuraSpark II system, see Chapter 2.

Bypass Air Idle Speed Control

The air bypass solenoid is used to control the engine idle speed and is operated by the EEC module.

The valve allows air to pass around the throttle plates to control:
- Cold engine fast idle
- Cold starting
- Dashpot operation
- Over-temperature idle boost
- Engine load correction

The valve is not servicable and correction is by replacement only.

Emissions Maintenance Warning Light (EMW)

DESCRIPTION

All gasoline engined light trucks built for sale outside of California employ this device.

The EMW consists of an instrument panel mounted amber light imprinted with the word EGR, EMISS, or EMISSIONS. The light is connected to a sensor module located under the instrument panel. The purpose is the warn the driver that the 60,000 mile emission system maintenance is required on the vehicle. Specific emission system maintenance requirements are listed in the truck's owner's manual maintenance schedule.

RESETTING THE LIGHT

1. Turn the key to the OFF position.
2. Lightly push a phillips screwdriver through the 0.2″ diameter hole labeled RESET, and lightly press down and hold it.
3. While maintaining pressure with the screwdriver, turn the key to the RUN position. The EMW lamp will light and stay lit as long as you keep pressure on the screwdriver. Hold the screwdriver down for about 5 seconds.
4. Remove the screwdriver. The lamp should go out with 2-5 seconds. If not, repeat steps 1-3.
5. Turn the key OFF.
6. Turn the key to the RUN position. The lamp will light for 2-5 seconds and then go out. If not, repeat the rest procedure.

NOTE: *If the light comes on between 15,000 and 45,000 miles or between 75,000 and 105,000 miles, you'll have to replace the 1,000 hour pre-timed module.*

Improved Combustion System

All 1968 models equipped with automatic transmission, all 1969 models and all 1970 and later models (regardless of other exhaust emission control equipment) are equipped with the Improved Combustion (IMCO) system. The IMCO system controls emissions arising from the incomplete combustion of the air/fuel mixture in the cylinders. The IMCO system incorporates a number of modifications to the distributor spark control system, the fuel system, and the internal design of the engine.

Internal engine modifications include the following: elimination of surface irregularities and crevices as well as a low surface area-to-volume ratio in the combustion chambers, a high velocity intake manifold combined with short exhaust ports, selective valve timing and a higher temperature and capacity cooling system.

Modifications to the fuel system include the following: recalibrated carburetors to achieve a leaner air/fuel mixture, more precise calibration of the choke mechanism, the installation of idle mixture limiter caps and a heated air intake system.

Modifications to the distributor spark control system include the following: a modified centrifugal advance curve, the use of dual diaphragm distributors in most applications, a ported vacuum switch, a deceleration valve and a spark delay valve.

TESTING IMCO® SYSTEM COMPONENTS

Heated Air Intake System

DUCT AND VALVE ASSEMBLY TEST

1. Either start with a cold engine or remove the air cleaner from the engine for at least half an hour. While cooling the air cleaner, leave the engine compartment hood open.
2. Tape a thermometer, of known accuracy, to the inside of the air cleaner so that is is near the temperature sensor unit. Install the air cleaner on the engine but do not fasten its securing nut.
3. Start the engine. With the engine cold and the outside temperature less than 90°F (32°C), the door should in the **HEAT ON position (closed to outside air).**
4. Operate the throttle lever rapidly to ½-¾ of its opening and release it. The air door should open to allow outside air to enter and then close again.
5. Allow the engine to warm up to normal temperature. Watch the door. When it opens to the outside air, remove the cover from the air cleaner. The temperature should be over 90°F (32°C) and no more than 130°F (54°C); 105°F (41°C) is about normal. If the door does not work within these temperature ranges, or fails to work at all, check for linkage or door binding.

If binding is not present and the air door is not working, proceed with the vacuum tests given below. If these indicate no faults in the vacuum motor and the door is not working, the temperature sensor is defective and must be replaced.

VACUUM MOTOR TEST

NOTE: *Be sure that the vacuum hose that runs between the temperature switch and the vacuum motor is not pinched by the retaining clip under the air cleaner. This could prevent the air door from closing.*

1. Check all the vacuum lines and fittings for leaks. Correct any leaks. If none are found, proceed with the test.
2. Remove the hose which runs from the sensor to the vacuum motor. Run a hose directly

from the manifold vacuum source to the vacuum motor.

3. If the motor closes the air door, it is functioning properly and the temperature sensor is defective.

4. If the motor does not close the door and no binding is present in its operation, the vacuum motor is defective and must be replaced.

NOTE: *If an alternator vacuum source is applied to the motor, insert a vacuum gauge in the line by using a T-fitting. Apply at least 9 in.Hg of vacuum in order to operate the motor.*

Dual Diaphragm Distributor Advance and Retard Mechanisms Test

1. Connect a timing light to the engine. Check the ignition timing.

WARNING: *Before proceeding with the tests, disconnect any spark control devices, distributor vacuum valves, etc. If these are left connected, inaccurate results may be obtained.*

2. Remove the retard hose from the distributor and plug it. Increase the engine speed. The timing should advance. If it fails to do so, then the vacuum unit if faulty and must be replaced.

3. Check the timing with the engine at normal idle speed. Unplug the retard hose and connect it to the vacuum unit. The timing should instantly be retarded 4-10°. If this does not occur, the retard diaphragm has a leak and the vacuum unit must be replaced.

Ported Vacuum Switch (Distributor Vacuum Control Valve) Test

1. Check the routing and connection of all vacuum hoses.

2. Attach a tachometer to the engine.

3. Bring the engine up to normal operating temperature. The engine must not be overheated.

4. Note the engine rpm, with the transmission in neutral, and the throttle in the curb idle position.

5. Disconnect the vacuum hose from the intake manifold at the temperature sensing valve. Plug or clamp the hose.

6. Note the idle rpm with the hose disconnected. If there is no change in rpm, the valve is good. If there is a drop of 100 or more rpm, the valve should be replaced. Replace the vacuum line.

7. Check to make sure that the all-season cooling mixture meets specifications, and that the correct radiator cap is in place and functioning.

8. Block the radiator air flow to induce a higher-than-normal temperature condition.

9. Continue to operate until the engine temperature or heat indicator shows above normal.

If engine speed by this time has increased 100 or more rpm, the temperature sensing valve is satisfactory. If not, it should be replaced.

Spark Delay Valve Test

NOTE: *If the distributor vacuum line contains a cut-off solenoid, it must be open during this test.*

1. Detach the vacuum line from the distributor at the spark delay valve end. Connect a vacuum gauge to the valve, in its place.

2. Connect a tachometer to the engine. Start the engine and rapidly increase its speed to 2,000 rpm with the transmission in neutral.

3. As soon as the engine speed is increased, the vacuum gauge reading should drop to zero.

4. Hold the engine speed at a steady 2,000 rpm. It should take longer than two seconds for the gauge to register 6 in.Hg. If it takes lass than two seconds, the valve is defective and must be replaced.

5. If it takes longer than the number of seconds specified in the application chart for the gauge to reach 6 in.Hg, disconnect the vacuum gauge from the spark delay valve. Disconnect the hose which runs from the spark delay valve to the carburetor at the valve end. Connect the vacuum gauge to this hose.

6. Start the engine and increase its speed to 2,000 rpm. The gauge should indicate 10-16 in.Hg. If it does not, there is a blockage in the carburetor vacuum port or else the hose itself is plugged or broken. If the gauge reading is within specification, the valve is defective.

7. Reconnect all vacuum lines and remove the tachometer, once testing is completed.

REMOVAL AND INSTALLATION OF IMCO® SYSTEM COMPONENTS

Temperature Operated Duct and Valve Assembly (Heated Air Intake System)

1. Remove the hex-head cap screws which secure the air intake duct and valve assembly to the air cleaner.

2. Remove the air intake duct and valve assembly from the engine.

3. If inspection reveals that the valve plate is sticking or the thermostat is malfunctioning, remove the thermostat and valve plates as follows:

a. Detach the valve plate tension spring from the valve plate using long-nose pliers.

b. Loosen the thermostat locknut and unscrew the thermostat from the mounting bracket.

c. Grasp the valve plate and withdraw it from the cut.

4. Install the air intake duct and valve assembly on the shroud tube.

5. Connect the air intake duct and valve as-

sembly the air cleaner and tighten the hex-head retaining cap screws.

6. If it was necessary to disassemble the thermostat and air duct and valve, assembly the unit as follows: Install the locknut on the thermostat, and screw the thermostat into the mounting bracket. Install the valve plate tension spring on the valve plate and duct.

7. Install the vacuum override motor (if applicable) and check for proper operation.

Vacuum Operated Duct and Valve Assembly (Heated Air Intake System)

1. Disconnect the vacuum hose at the vacuum motor.

2. Remove the hex-head cap screws which secure the air intake duct and valve assembly to the air cleaner.

3. Remove the duct and valve assembly from the engine.

4. Position the duct and valve assembly to the air cleaner and heat stove tube. Install the attaching cap screws.

5. Connect the vacuum line at the vacuum motor.

Ported Vacuum Switch (Distributor Vacuum Control Valve)

1. Drain about one gallon of coolant out of the radiator.

CAUTION: *When draining the coolant, keep in mind that cats and dogs are attracted by the ethylene glycol antifreeze, and are quite likely to drink any that is left in an uncovered container or in puddles on the ground. This will prove fatal in sufficient quantity. Always drain the coolant into a sealable container. Coolant should be reused unless it is contaminated or several years old.*

2. Tag the vacuum hoses that attach to the control valve and disconnect them.

3. Unscrew and remove the control valve.

4. Install the new control valve.

5. Connect the vacuum hoses.

6. Fill the cooling system.

Spark Delay Valve

1. Locate the spark delay valve in the distributor vacuum line and disconnect it from the line.

2. Install a new spark delay valve in line, making sure that the black end of the valve is connected to the line from the carburetor and the color coded end is connected to the line from the spark delay valve to the distributor.

Spark Delay Valve

The spark delay valve is a plastic spring loaded, color coded valve in the vacuum line to the distributor vacuum advance chamber on some 1972 models. Under heavy throttle application, the valve will close, blocking carburetor vacuum to the distributor vacuum advance mechanism. After the designated period of time, the valve opens, restoring normal carburetor vacuum to the distributor.

Dual Diaphragm Distributor

The dual diaphragm distributor has two diaphragms which operate independently. The outer (primary) diaphragm makes use of carburetor vacuum to advance the ignition timing. The inner (secondary) diaphragm uses intake manifold vacuum to provide additional retardation of ignition timing during closed throttle deceleration and idle, resulting in the reduction of hydrocarbon emissions.

DUAL DIAPHRAGM VACUUM ADVANCE AND VACUUM RETARD FUNCTIONAL CHECK

1. To check vacuum advance, disconnect the vacuum lines from both the advance (outer) and retard (inner) diaphragms. Plug the line removed from the retard diaphragm.

Connect a tachometer and timing light to the engine. Increase the idle speed by setting the screw on the first step of the fast idle cam. Note the ignition timing setting, using a timing light.

Connect the carburetor vacuum line to the advance diaphragm. If the timing advances immediately, the advance unit is functioning properly. Adjust the idle speed to 550-600 rpm.

2. Check the vacuum retardation as follows: using a timing light, note the ignition timing. Remove the plug from the manifold vacuum line and connect the line to the inner diaphragm. Timing should retard immediately.

3. If vacuum retardation is not to specifications, replace the dual diaphragm advance unit. If the advance (vacuum) does not function properly, calibrate the unit on a distributor test stand. If the advance part of the unit cannot be calibrated, or if either diaphragm is leaking, replace the dual diaphragm vacuum advance unit.

Deceleration Valve

Beginning in 1969, some engines were equipped with a distributor vacuum advance control valve (deceleration valve) which is used with dual diaphragm distributors to further aid in controlling ignition timing. The deceleration valve is in the vacuum line which runs from the outer (advance) diaphragm to the carburetor, the normal vacuum supply for the distributor. During deceleration, the intake manifold vacuum rises causing the deceleration valve to close off the carburetor vacuum source and connect the intake manifold vacuum source to the distributor advance diaphragm. The increase in vacuum provides maximum ignition timing advance, thus providing more complete fuel combustion and decreasing exhaust system backfiring.

DISTRIBUTOR DECELERATION VACUUM CONTROL VALVE TEST

1. Connect a tachometer to the engine and bring the engine to the normal operating temperature.

2. Check the idle speed and set it to specifications with the headlights on high beam, as necessary.

3. Turn off the headlights and note the idle rpm.

4. Remove the plastic cover from the valve. Slowly turn the adjusting screw counterclockwise without pressing in. After 5, and no more than 6 turns, the idle speed should suddenly increase to about 1,000 rpm. If the speed does not increase after six turns, push inward on the valve spring retainer and release. Speed should now increase.

5. Slowly turn the adjusting screw clockwise until the idle speed drops to the speed noted in Step 3. Make one more turn clockwise.

6. Increase the engine speed to 2,000 rpm, hold for 5 seconds, and release the throttle. The engine speed should return to idle speed within 4 seconds. If idle is not resumed in 4 seconds, back off the dashpot adjustment and repeat the check. If the idle is not resumed in 3 seconds with the dashpot back off, turn the deceleration valve adjustment screw an additional quarter turn clockwise and repeat the check. Repeat the quarter turn adjustment and idle return checks until the engine returns to idle within the required time.

7. If it takes more than one complete turn from Step 5 to meet the idle return time specification, replace the valve.

Vacuum Operated Heat Control Valve (VOHV)

To further aid cold start driveability during engine warmup, most 1975 and later engines use a VOHV located between the exhaust manifold and the exhaust inlet (header) pipe.

When the engine is first started, the valve is closed, blocking exhaust gases from exiting from one bank of cylinders. These gases are then diverted back through the intake manifold crossover passage under the carburetor. The result is quick heat to the carburetor and choke.

The VOHV is controlled by a ported vacuum switch which uses manifold vacuum to keep the vacuum motor on the valve closed until the coolant reaches a predetermined warm-up valve. When the engine is warmed up, the PVS shuts off vacuum to the VOHV, and a strong return spring opens the VOHV butterfly.

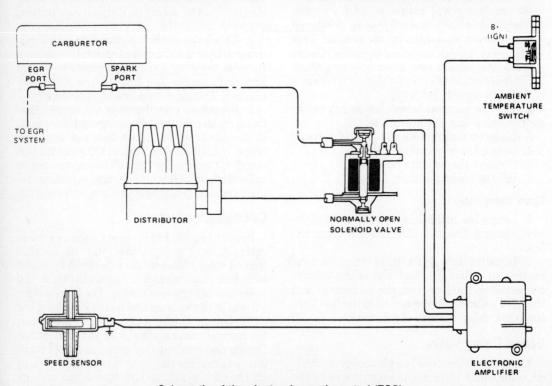

Schematic of the electronic spark control (ESC)

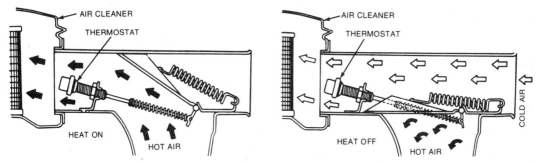

Operation of the thermostatically controlled air cleaner

Thermostatically Controlled Air Cleaner System (TAC)

This system consists of a heat shroud which is integral with the right side exhaust manifold, a hot air hose and a special air cleaner assembly equipped with a thermal sensor and vacuum motor and air valve assembly.

The temperature of the carburetor intake air is thermostatically controlled by means of a valve plate and a vacuum override built into a duct assembly attached to the air cleaner. The exhaust manifold shroud tube is attached to the shroud over the exhaust manifold for the source of heated air.

The thermal sensor is attached to the air valve actuating lever, along with the vacuum motor lever, both of which control the position of the air valve to supply either heated air from the exhaust manifold or cooler air from the engine compartment.

During the warm-up period, when the under-the-hood temperatures are low, the thermal sensor doesn't exert enough tension on the air valve actuating lever to close (heat off) the air valve. Thus, the carburetor receives heated air from around the exhaust manifold.

As the temperature of the air entering the air cleaner approaches approximately 110°F (43°C), the thermal sensor begins to push on the air valve actuating lever and overcome the spring tension which holds the air valve in the open (heat on) position. The air valve begins to move to the closed (heat off) position, allowing only under-the-hood air to enter the air cleaner.

The air valve in the air cleaner will also open, regardless of the air temperature, during heavy acceleration to obtain maximum airflow through the air cleaner. The extreme decrease in intake manifold vacuum during heavy acceleration permits the vacuum motor to override the thermostatic control. This opens the system to both heated air and air from the engine compartment.

HEATED AIR INTAKE TEST

1. With the engine completely cold, look inside the cold air duct and make sure that the valve plate is fully in the up position (closing the cold air duct).
2. Start the engine and bring it to operating temperature.
3. Stop the engine and look inside the cold air duct again. The valve plate should be down, allowing an opening from the cold air duct into the air cleaner.
4. If the unit appears to be malfunctioning, remove it and examine it to make sure that the springs are not broken or disconnected, and replace the thermostat if all other parts appear intact and properly connected.

EGR/Coolant Spark Control (CSC) System

The EGR/CSC system is used on most 1974 and later models. It regulates both distributor spark advance and the EGR valve operation according to coolant temperature by sequentially switching vacuum signals.

The major EGR/CSC system components are:
1. 95°F (35°C) EGR/PVS valve;
2. Spark Delay Valve (SDV);
3. Vacuum check valve.

When the engine coolant temperature is below 82°F (28°C), the EGR/PVS valve admits carburetor EGR port vacuum (occurring at about 2,500 rpm) directly to the distributor advance diaphragm, through the one-way check valve.

At the same time, the EGR/PVS valve shuts off carburetor EGR vacuum to the EGR valve and transmission diaphragm.

When engine coolant temperature is 95°F (35°C) and above, the EGR/PVS valve is actuated and directs carburetor EGR vacuum to the EGR valve and transmission instead of the distributor. At temperatures between 82-95°F (28-

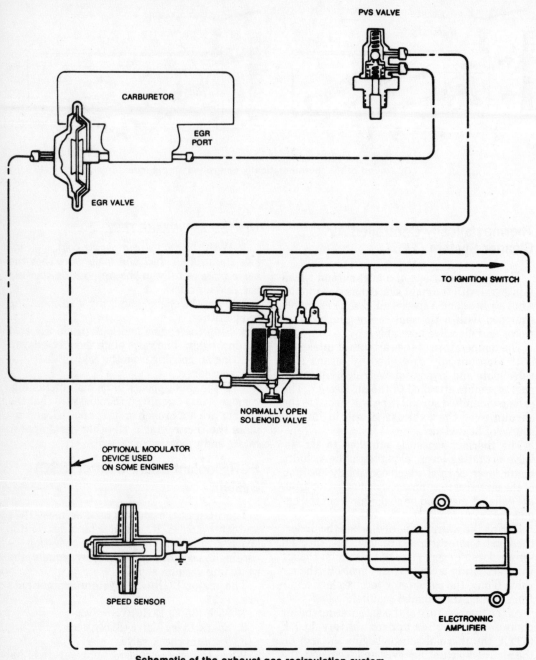

Schematic of the exhaust gas recirculation system

35°C), the EGR/PVS valve may be open, closed, or in mid-position.

The SDV valve delay carburetor spark vacuum to the distributor advance diaphragm by restricting the vacuum signal through the SDV valve for a predetermined time. During normal acceleration, little or not vacuum is admitted to the distributor advance diaphragm until acceleration is completed, because of (1) the time delay of the SDV valve and (2) the rerouting of

EGR port vacuum if the engine coolant temperature is 95°F (35°C) or higher.

The check valve blocks off vacuum signal from the SDV to the EGR/PVS so that carburetor spark vacuum will not be dissipated when the EGR/PVS is actuated above 95°F (35°C).

The 235°F (113°C) PVS is not part of the EGR/CSC system, but is connected to the distributor vacuum advance to prevent engine overheating while idling (as on previous mod-

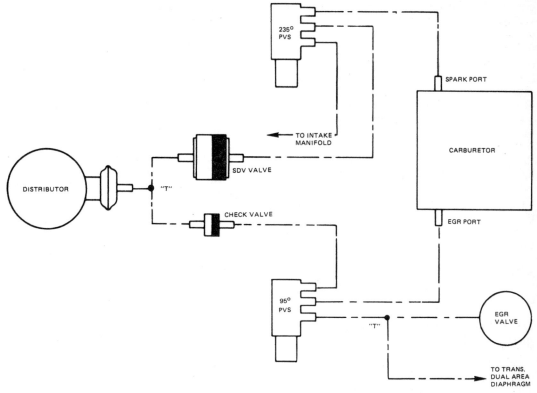

EGR/CSC vacuum schematic

els). At idle speed, no vacuum is generated at either the carburetor spark port or EGR port and engine timing is fully retarded. When engine coolant temperature reaches 235°F (113°C), however, the valve is actuated to admit intake manifold vacuum to the distributor advance diaphragm. This advances the engine timing and speeds up the engine. The increase in coolant flow and fan speed lowers engine temperature.

Distributor Modulator System (Dist-O-Vac)

1970-71 models equipped with the 6-240 and automatic transmission use this system.

The system is used in conjunction with the IMCO system components with the exception of the deceleration valve.

The three components of the system are: the speed sensor; the thermal switch; the electronic control module.

The control module consists of two sub-assemblies: the elctronic control amplifier and the 3-way solenoid valve.

The speed sensor, a small unit mounted in the speedometer cable contains a rotating magnet and a stationary winding which is insulated from ground. The magnet, which rotates with the speedometer cable, generates a small volt-

age which increases as the speed increases. The voltage is directed to the electronic control amplifier.

The thermal switch consists of a bi-metallic element switch which is mounted in the right door pillar and senses the outside air temperature. The switch is closed at 58°F or lower. The switch feeds the electronic control amplifier.

Within the electronic control module case is a printed circuit board and electronic amplifier. The speed sensor and thermal switch is the dominant circuit. When the temperature of the outside air is 58°F or lower, the circuit is closed, so that regardless of speed, the electronic amplifier will not trigger the 3-way solenoid valve. Above 58°F, however, the thermal switch circuit is open, allowing the circuit from the speed sensor to take over and control the action of the solenoid valve.

The 3-way solenoid valve is located within the electronic control module and below the printed circuit board of the amplifier. It is vented to the atmosphere at the top and connected at the bottom to the carburetor spark port (small hose) and primary side of the distributor (large hose). The large hose is channeled through the temperature sensing valve. The small hose is equipped with an air bleed to provide a positive airflow in the direction of the carburetor. The air bleed purges the hose of vacuum, thus assuring that raw gasoline will not be drawn through the hose and into the distributor.

When the thermal switch is closed, or when it is open and the speed sensor is not sending a strong enough voltage signal (road speed below 35 mph), the amplifier will not activate the solenoid valve and the valve is in the closed position, blocking the passage of air from the small tube through the large tube. With the valve in this position, the large hose is vented to the atmosphere through the top opening in the 3-way valve. Consequently, no vacuum is being supplied to the primary diaphragm on the distributor, and therefore, no vacuum advance.

When the air temperature is above 58°F and.or the road speed is sufficient to generate the required voltage (35 mph or greater), the valve opens, blocking the vent and opening the vacuum line from the carburetor spark port to the distribtor primary port.

Transmission Regulated Spark System (TRS)

1972 vans equipped with the 6-240 and automatic transmission use this system.

The TRS system differs from the Dist-O-Vac and ESC systems in that the speed sensor and amplifier are replaced by a switch on the transmission. The switch is operated by mechanical linkage that opens the switch when the transmission enters DRIVE.

The switch, when opened, triggers the opening of the vacuum lines to the distributor, thus providing vacuum advance.

The switch is also rendered inoperative when the outside air temperature is below 65°F.

So, in short, when the air temperature is below 65°F and/or the transmission is in 1st or 2nd gear, there is no vacuum to the distributor.

Ported Vacuum Switch Valve (PVS)

The PVS valve is a temperature sensing valve found on the distributor vacuum advance line, and is installed in the coolant outlet elbow. During prolonged periods of idle, or any other situation which causes engine operating temperatures to be higher than normal, the valve, which under normal conditions simply connects the vacuum advance diaphragm to its vacuum source within the carburetor, closes the normal source vacuum port and engages an alternate source vacuum port. This alternate source is from the intake manifold which, under idle conditions, maintains a high vacuum. This increase in vacuum supply to the distributor diaphragm advances the timing, increasing the idle speed. The increase in idle speed causes

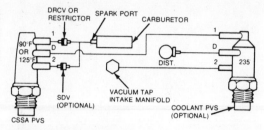

Typical CSSA system

a directly proportional increase in the operation of the cooling system. When the engine has cooled sufficiently, the vacuum supply is returned to its normal source, the carburetor.

DISTRIBUTOR TEMPERATURE SENSING VACUUM CONTROL VALVE TEST

1. Check the routing and connection of all the vacuum hoses.

2. Attach a tachometer to the engine.

3. Bring the engine up to the normal operating temperature. The engine must not be overheated.

4. Note the engine rpm, with the transmission in Neutral, and the throttle at curb idle.

5. Disconnect the vacuum hose from the intake manifold at the temperature sensing valve. Plug or clamp the hose.

6. Note the idle rpm with the hose disconnected. If there is no change in rpm, the valve is good. If there is a drop of 100 or more rpm, the valve should be replaced. Replace the vacuum line.

7. Check to make sure that the all season coolant mixture meets specifications and that the correct radiator cap is in place and functioning.

8. Block the radiator airflow to induce a higher-than-normal temperature condition.

9. Continue to operate the engine until the temperature or heat indicator shows above normal.

If the engine speed, by this time, has increased 100 or more rpm, the temperature

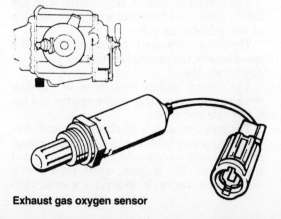

Exhaust gas oxygen sensor

sensing valve is satisfactory. If not, it should be replaced.

Cold Start Spark Advance System (CSSA)

All 1975-78 8-460 engines are equipped with this system. It is a modification of the existing spark control system to aid in cold start driveability. The system uses a coolant temperature sensing vacuum switch located in the thermostat housing. When the engine temperature is below 125°F, it permits full manifold vacuum to

the distributor diaphragm. After the engine warms up, normal spark control resumes.

Oxygen Sensor
REMOVAL AND INSTALLATION

The oxygen sensor is located in the exhaust headpipe. To replace it, unplug the connector and unscrew the sensor.

Replacement senors will be packaged with anti-sieze compound for the threads. If not, or if you are reinstalling the old unit, the threads MUST be coated with anti-sieze compound! Torque the sensor to 12 ft.lb.

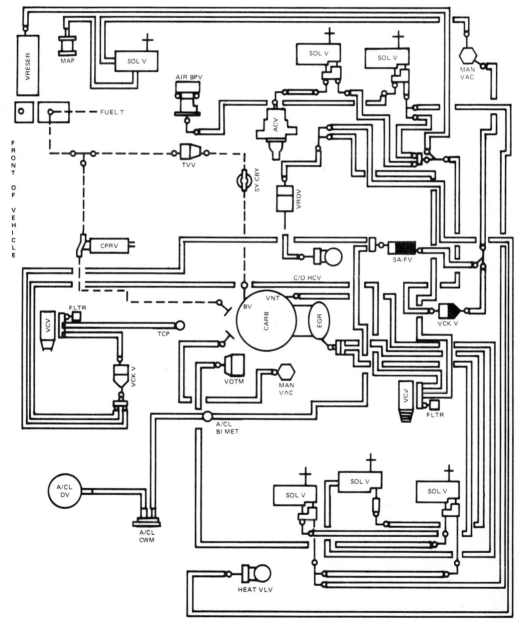

EEC-III, FBC vacuum schematic for the 8-302

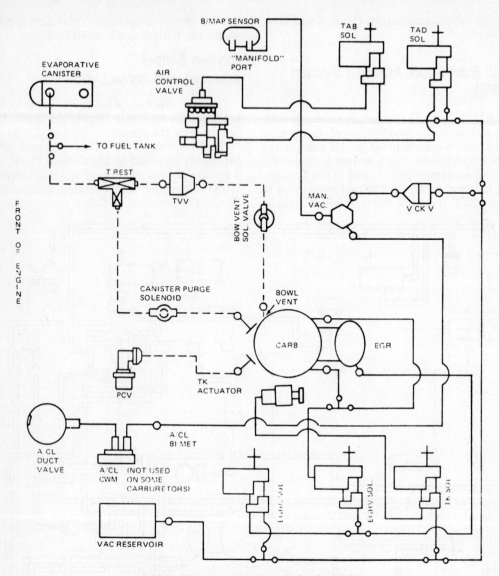

EEC-III, FBC vacuum schematic for the 8-351

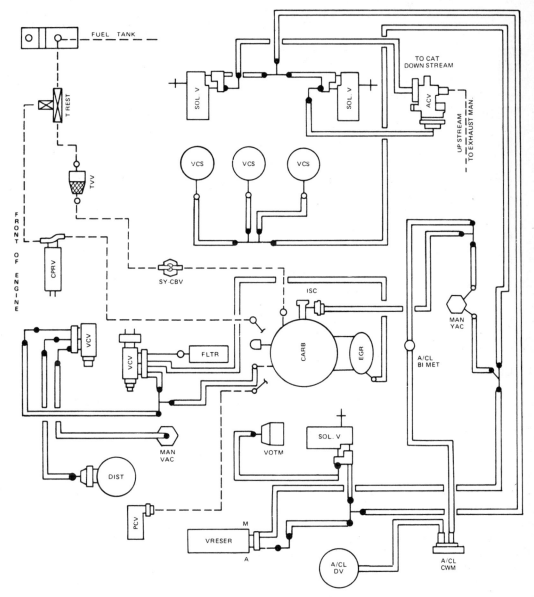

V8 MCU vacuum schematic

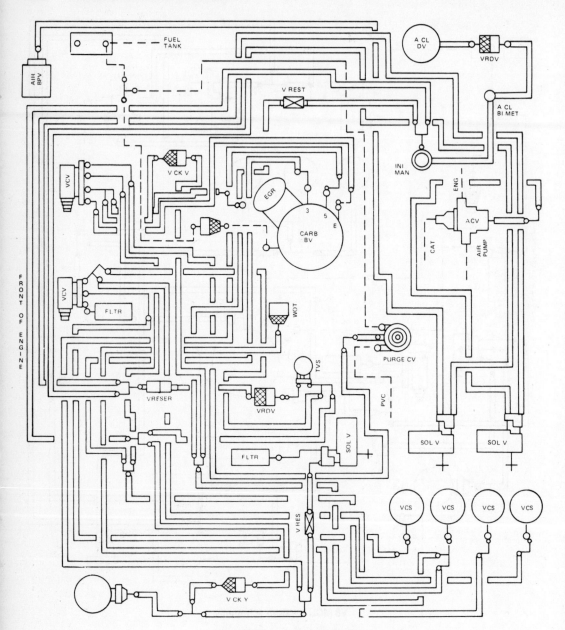

6-300 MCU vacuum schematic

Fuel System

5

GENERAL FUEL SYSTEM COMPONENTS

CAUTION: *Never smoke when working around gasoline! Avoid all sources of sparks or ignition. Gasoline vapors are EXTREMELY volatile!*

Mechanical Fuel Pump

A mechanical pump is used on all carbureted engines, except the 8-460. The mechanical fuel pump is camshaft eccentric-actuated and located on the left side of the engine.

REMOVAL

1. Disconnect the fuel inlet and outlet lines at the fuel pump. Discard the fuel inlet retaining clamp.
2. Remove the pump retaining bolts then remove the pump assembly and gasket from the engine. Discard the gasket.

INSTALLATION

1. If a new pump is to be installed, remove the fuel line connector fitting from the old pump and install it in the new pump.
2. Remove all gasket material from the

Troubleshooting Basic Fuel System Problems

Problem	Cause	Solution
Engine cranks, but won't start (or is hard to start) when cold	• Empty fuel tank • Incorrect starting procedure • Defective fuel pump • No fuel in carburetor • Clogged fuel filter • Engine flooded • Defective choke	• Check for fuel in tank • Follow correct procedure • Check pump output • Check for fuel in the carburetor • Replace fuel filter • Wait 15 minutes; try again • Check choke plate
Engine cranks, but is hard to start (or does not start) when hot— (presence of fuel is assumed)	• Defective choke	• Check choke plate
Rough idle or engine runs rough	• Dirt or moisture in fuel • Clogged air filter • Faulty fuel pump	• Replace fuel filter • Replace air filter • Check fuel pump output
Engine stalls or hesitates on acceleration	• Dirt or moisture in the fuel • Dirty carburetor • Defective fuel pump • Incorrect float level, defective accelerator pump	• Replace fuel filter • Clean the carburetor • Check fuel pump output • Check carburetor
Poor gas mileage	• Clogged air filter • Dirty carburetor • Defective choke, faulty carburetor adjustment	• Replace air filter • Clean carburetor • Check carburetor
Engine is flooded (won't start accompanied by smell of raw fuel)	• Improperly adjusted choke or carburetor	• Wait 15 minutes and try again, without pumping gas pedal • If it won't start, check carburetor

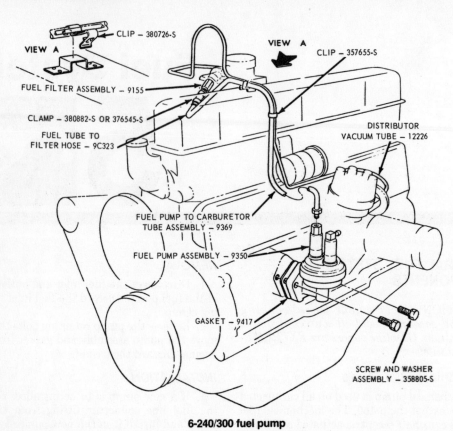

CLIP – 380726-S

VIEW A

VIEW A

CLIP – 357655-S

FUEL FILTER ASSEMBLY – 9155

CLAMP – 380882-S OR 376545-S

FUEL TUBE TO
FILTER HOSE – 9C323

DISTRIBUTOR
VACUUM TUBE – 12226

FUEL PUMP TO CARBURETOR
TUBE ASSEMBLY – 9369

FUEL PUMP ASSEMBLY – 9350

GASKET – 9417

SCREW AND WASHER
ASSEMBLY – 358805-S

6-240/300 fuel pump

mounting pad and pump flange. Apply oil resistant sealer to both sides of a new gasket.

3. Position the new gasket on the pump flange and hold the pump in position against the mounting pad. make sure that the rocker arm is riding on the camshaft eccentric.

4. Press the pump tight against the pad, install the retaining bolts and alternately torque them to 12-15 ft.lb. on all 6-cylinder engines; 20-24 ft.lb. on the 8-302; 14-20 on the 8-351; 19-27 ft.lb. on the 8-400 and 8-460. Connect the fuel lines. Use new clamp on the fuel lines.

5. Operate the engine and check for leaks.

TESTING

Incorrect fuel pump pressure and low volume (flow rate) are the two most likely fuel pump troubles that will affect engine performance. Low pressure will cause a lean mixture and fuel starvation at high speeds and excessive pressure will cause high fuel consumption and carburetor flooding.

To determine that the fuel pump is in satisfactory operating condition, tests for both fuel pump pressure and volume should be performed.

The test are performed with the fuel pump installed on the engine and the engine at normal operating temperature and at idle speed.

Before the test, make sure that the replaceable fuel filter has been changed at the proper mileage interval. If in doubt, install a new filter.

Pressure Test

1. Remove the air cleaner assembly. Disconnect the fuel inlet line of the fuel filter at the carburetor. Use care to prevent fire, due to fuel spillage. Place an absorbent cloth under the connection before removing the line to catch any fuel that might flow out of the line.

2. Connect a pressure gauge, a restrictor and a flexible hose between the fuel filter and the carburetor.

3. Position the flexible hose and the restrictor so that the fuel can be discharged into a suitable, graduated container.

4. Before taking a pressure reading, operate the engine at the specified idle rpm and vent the system into the container by opening the hose restrictor momentarily.

5. Close the hose restrictor, allow the pressure to stabilize and note the reading. The pressure should be 5 psi.

If the pump pressure is not within 4-6 psi and the fuel lines and filter are in satisfactory condition, the pump is defective and should be replaced.

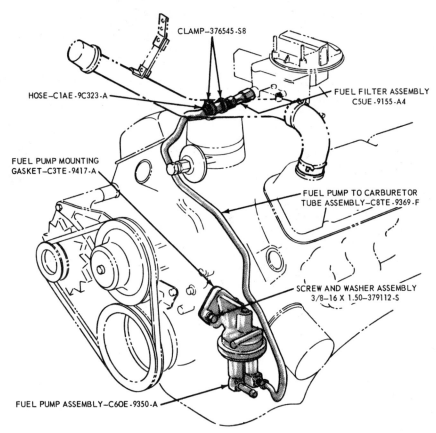

CLAMP—376545-S8

HOSE—C1AE-9C323-A

FUEL FILTER ASSEMBLY
C5UE-9155-A4

FUEL PUMP MOUNTING
GASKET—C3TE-9417-A

FUEL PUMP TO CARBURETOR
TUBE ASSEMBLY—C8TE-9369-F

SCREW AND WASHER ASSEMBLY
3/8—16 X 1.50—379112-S

FUEL PUMP ASSEMBLY—C6OE-9350-A

Carbureted V8 fuel pump, except 8-460

If the pump pressure is within the proper range, perform the test for fuel volume.

Volume Test

1. Operate the engine at the specified idle rpm.

2. Open the hose restrictor and catch the fuel in the container while observing the time it takes to pump 1 pint. On engines through 1973, it should take 30 seconds to pump 1 pint of fuel. On 1974 and later engines, 1 pint should be pumped in 20 seconds.

If the pump does not operate to specifications, check for proper fuel tank venting or a restriction in the fuel line leading from the fuel tank to the carburetor before replacing the fuel pump.

Electric Fuel Pump

Two electric pumps are used on fuel injected models; a low pressure boost pump mounted in the fuel tank and a high pressure pump mounted on the vehicle frame.

Models equipped with the 8-460 (7.5L) carbureted engines use a single low pressure pump mounted in the fuel tank.

On injected models the low pressure pump is used to provide pressurized fuel to the inlet of the high pressure pump and helps prevent noise and heating problems. The externally mounted high pressure pump is capable of supplying 15.9 gallons of fuel an hour. System pressure is controlled by a pressure regulator mounted on the engine.

On internal fuel tank mounted pumps tank removal is required. Frame mounted models can be accessed from under the vehicle. Prior to servicing release system pressure (see Fuel Supply Manifold details). Disconnect the negative battery cable prior to pump removal.

Vans with dual fuel tanks have a pump in each tank, which feed the high pressure pump mounted on the frame.

REMOVAL AND INSTALLATION

In-Tank Pump

MID-SHIP FUEL TANK(S)

1. Disconnect the negative battery cable.

2. Depressurize the system and drain as much fuel as possible from the tank.

3. Raise the truck and safely support it on jackstands.

4. On trucks with dual tanks, disconnect the

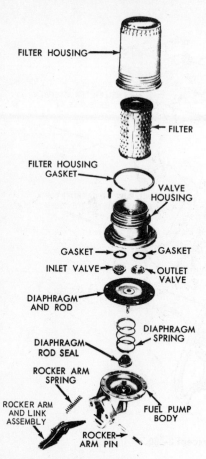

FILTER HOUSING

FILTER

FILTER HOUSING GASKET

VALVE HOUSING

GASKET — GASKET

INLET VALVE — OUTLET VALVE

DIAPHRAGM AND ROD

DIAPHRAGM SPRING

DIAPHRAGM ROD SEAL

ROCKER ARM SPRING

ROCKER ARM AND LINK ASSEMBLY

FUEL PUMP BODY

ROCKER ARM PIN

Fuel pump w/cartridge-type filter

ground wire at each tank after draining the tanks.

5. Disconnect the fuel supply, return and vent lines at the tank(s).

6. Disconnect the wiring harness to the fuel pump.

7. Support the fuel tank(s), loosen and remove the mounting straps. Remove the fuel tank(s).

8. Disconnect the lines and harness at the pump flange.

9. Clean the outside of the mounting flange and retaining ring. Turn the fuel pump lock ring counterclockwise and remove.

10. Remove the fuel pump.

11. Clean the mounting surfaces. Put a light coat of grease on the mounting surfaces and on the new sealing ring. Install the new fuel pump.

12. Installation is in the reverse order of removal. Torque the strap bolts to 25-30 ft.lb. Fill the tank with a least 13 gals. of fuel. Turn the ignition key ON for three seconds. Repeat 6 or 7 times until the fuel system is pressurized. check for any fitting leaks. Start the engine and check for leaks.

AFT-OF-AXLE TANK

1. Disconnect the negative battery cable.

2. Depressurize the system and drain as much fuel as possible from the tank.

3. Raise the rear of the truck and safely support it on jackstands.

4. Disconnect the fuel supply, return and vent lines at the tank(s).

5. On trucks with dual tanks, disconnect the ground wire at each tank after draining the tanks.

6. Disconnect the wiring harness to the fuel pump.

7. If you have a metal tank: Support the fuel tank(s), loosen and remove the mounting straps. Remove the fuel tank(s).

If you have a plastic tank: Support the tank and remove the bolts attaching the combination skid plate and tank support. Lower the tank and finish removing any hard-to-get-at hoses.

8. Disconnect the lines and harness at the pump flange.

9. Clean the outside of the mounting flange and retaining ring. Turn the fuel pump lock ring counterclockwise and remove.

10. Remove the fuel pump.

11. Clean the mounting surfaces. Put a light coat of grease on the mounting surfaces and on the new sealing ring. Install the new fuel pump.

12. Installation is in the reverse order of removal. Torque the metal tank's strap bolts to 27-37 ft.lb., using thread locking compound. Torque the plastic tank's attaching bolts to 25-35 ft.lb., without using thread locking compound. Fill the tank with a least 10 gals. of fuel. Turn the ignition key ON for three seconds. Repeat 6 or 7 times until the fuel system is pressurized. check for any fitting leaks. Start the engine and check for leaks.

External Pump

1. Disconnect the negative battery cable.

2. Depressurize the fuel system.

3. Raise and support the rear of the vehicle on jackstands.

4. Disconnect the inlet and outlet fuel lines.

5. Remove the pump from the mounting bracket.

6. Install in reverse order, make sure the pump is indexed correctly in the mounting bracket Insulator.

7. Disconnect the fuel inlet line of the fuel filter at the carburetor. Use care to prevent fire, due to fuel spillage. Place an absorbent cloth under the connection before removing the line to catch any fuel that might flow out of the line.

8. Connect a pressure gauge, a restrictor and flexible hose between the fuel filter and the carburetor.

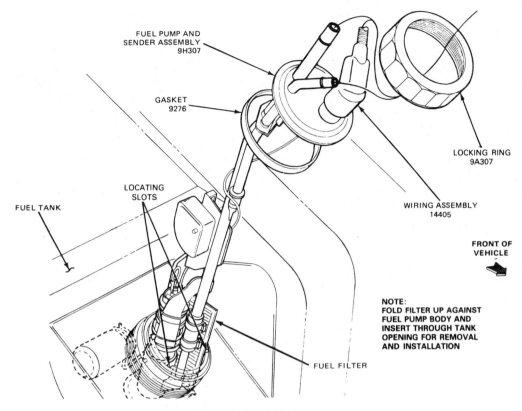

FUEL PUMP AND
SENDER ASSEMBLY
9H307

GASKET
9276

LOCATING
SLOTS

FUEL TANK

LOCKING RING
9A307

WIRING ASSEMBLY
14405

FRONT OF
VEHICLE

NOTE:
FOLD FILTER UP AGAINST
FUEL PUMP BODY AND
INSERT THROUGH TANK
OPENING FOR REMOVAL
AND INSTALLATION

FUEL FILTER

In-tank electric fuel pump

9. Position the flexible hose and the restrictor so that the fuel can be discharged into a suitable, graduated container.

10. Before taking a pressure reading, operate the Engine at the specified idle rpm and vent the system into the container by opening the hose restrictor momentarily.

11. Close the hose restrictor, allow the pressure to stabilize and note the reading. The pressure should be 5 psi. If the pump pressure is not within 4-6 psi and the fuel lines and filter are in satisfactory condition, the pump is defective and should be replaced. If the pump pressure is within the proper range, perform the test for fuel volume.

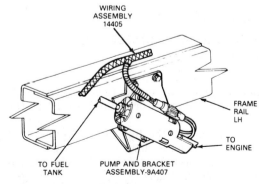

WIRING
ASSEMBLY
14405

FRAME
RAIL
LH

TO
ENGINE

TO FUEL
TANK

PUMP AND BRACKET
ASSEMBLY-9A407

8-460 frame mounted fuel pump

VOLUME TEST

1. Operate the engine at the specified idle rpm.

2. Open the hose restrictor and catch the fuel in the container while observing the time it takes to pump 1 pint. 1 pint should be pumped in 20 seconds. If the pump does not pump to specifications, check for proper fuel tank venting or a restriction in the fuel line leading from the fuel tank to the carburetor before replacing the fuel pump.

Quick-Connect Line Fittings
REMOVAL AND INSTALLATION

NOTE: *Quick-Connect (push) type fittings must be disconnected using proper procedures or the fitting may be damaged. Two types of retainers are used on the push connect fittings. Line sizes of 3/8" and 5/16" use a hairpin clip retainer. 1/4" line connectors use a Duck bill clip retainer.*

Hairpin Clip

1. Clean all dirt and/or grease from the fittings. Spread the two clip legs about an 1/8" each to disengage from the fitting and pull the clip outward from the fitting. Use finger pressure only, do not use any tools.

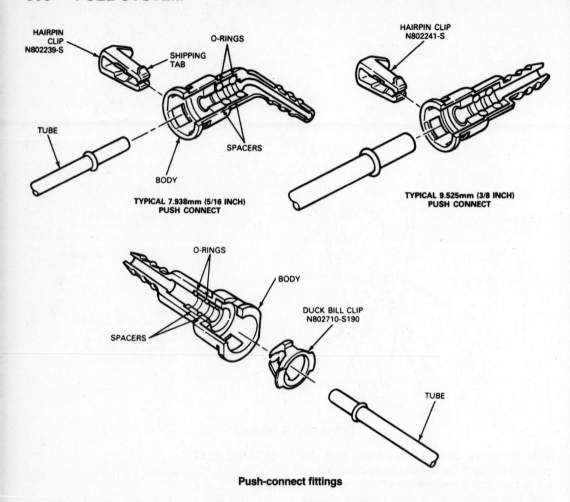

Push-connect fittings

2. Grasp the fittings and hose assembly and pull away from the steel line. Twist the fitting and hose assembly slightly while pulling, if necessary, when a sticking condition exists.

3. Inspect the hairpin clip for damage, replace the clip if necessary. Reinstall the clip in position on the fitting.

4. Inspect the fitting and inside of the connector to insure freedom Of dirt or obstruction. Install fitting into the connector and push together. A click will be heard when the hairpin snaps into proper connection. Pull on the line to insure full engagement.

Duck Bill Clip

1. A special tool is available for Ford for removing the retaining clip (Ford Tool No. T82L-9500-AH). If the tool is not on hand see Step 2. Align the slot on the push connector disconnect tool with either tab on the retaining clip. Pull the line from the connector.

2. If the special clip tool is not available, use a pair of narrow 6" locking pliers with a jaw width of 0.2" or less. Align the jaws of the pliers with the openings of the fitting case and com-

press the part of the retaining clip that engages the case. Compressing the retaining clip will release the fitting which may be pulled from the connector. Both sides of the clip must be compressed at the same time to disengage.

3. Inspect the retaining clip, fitting end and connector. Replace the clip if any damage is apparent.

4. Push the line into the steel connector until a click is heard, indicating the clip is in place. Pull on the line to check engagement.

Fuel Tank

REMOVAL AND INSTALLATION

Mid-Ships Fuel Tank

1. Drain the fuel from the tank into a suitable container by either removing the drain plug, if so equipped, or siphoning through the filler cap opening.

2. Disconnect the fuel gauge sending unit wire and fuel outlet line.

3. Disconnect the air relief tube from the filler neck and fuel tank.

4. Loosen the filler neck hose clamp at the

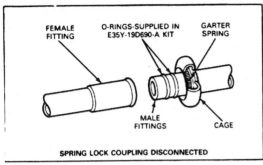

SPRING LOCK COUPLING DISCONNECTED

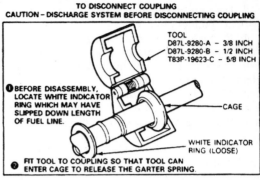

TO DISCONNECT COUPLING
CAUTION – DISCHARGE SYSTEM BEFORE DISCONNECTING COUPLING

TOOL
D87L-9280-A – 3/8 INCH
D87L-9280-B – 1/2 INCH
T83P-19623-C – 5/8 INCH

❶ BEFORE DISASSEMBLY, LOCATE WHITE INDICATOR RING WHICH MAY HAVE SLIPPED DOWN LENGTH OF FUEL LINE.

❷ FIT TOOL TO COUPLING SO THAT TOOL CAN ENTER CAGE TO RELEASE THE GARTER SPRING.

TO CONNECT COUPLING

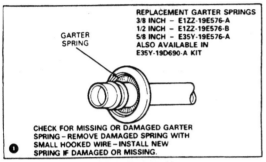

REPLACEMENT GARTER SPRINGS
3/8 INCH – E1ZZ-19E576-A
1/2 INCH – E1ZZ-19E576-B
5/8 INCH – E35Y-19E576-A
ALSO AVAILABLE IN E35Y-19D690-A KIT

❶ CHECK FOR MISSING OR DAMAGED GARTER SPRING – REMOVE DAMAGED SPRING WITH SMALL HOOKED WIRE – INSTALL NEW SPRING IF DAMAGED OR MISSING.

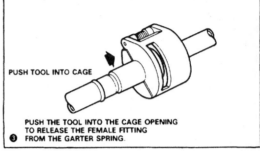

PUSH TOOL INTO CAGE

❸ PUSH THE TOOL INTO THE CAGE OPENING TO RELEASE THE FEMALE FITTING FROM THE GARTER SPRING.

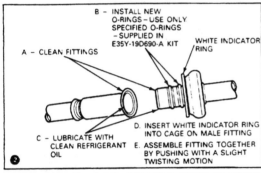

B – INSTALL NEW O-RINGS – USE ONLY SPECIFIED O-RINGS – SUPPLIED IN E35Y-19D690-A KIT

A – CLEAN FITTINGS

C – LUBRICATE WITH CLEAN REFRIGERANT OIL

D. INSERT WHITE INDICATOR RING INTO CAGE ON MALE FITTING

E. ASSEMBLE FITTING TOGETHER BY PUSHING WITH A SLIGHT TWISTING MOTION

❷

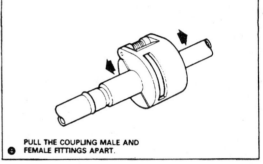

❹ PULL THE COUPLING MALE AND FEMALE FITTINGS APART.

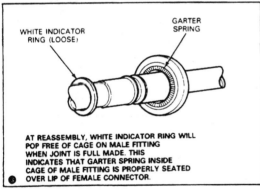

AT REASSEMBLY, WHITE INDICATOR RING WILL POP FREE OF CAGE ON MALE FITTING WHEN JOINT IS FULL MADE. THIS INDICATES THAT GARTER SPRING INSIDE CAGE OF MALE FITTING IS PROPERLY SEATED OVER LIP OF FEMALE CONNECTOR.

❸

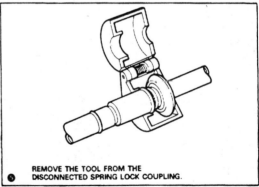

❺ REMOVE THE TOOL FROM THE DISCONNECTED SPRING LOCK COUPLING.

Metal spring-lock connectors

fuel tank and pull the filler neck away from the tank.

5. Remove the retaining strap mounting nuts and bolts and lower the tank to the floor.

6. If a new tank is being installed, change over the fuel gauge sending unit to the new tank.

7. Install the fuel tank in the reverse order of removal. Torque the strap nuts to 30 ft.lb.

Behind-The-Axle Fuel Tank

1. Raise the rear of the truck.
2. Disconnect the negative battery cable.

3. Disconnect the fuel gauge sending unit wire at the fuel tank.

4. Remove the fuel drain plug or siphon the fuel from the tank into a suitable container.

5. Loosen the fuel line hose clamps, slide the clamps forward and disconnect the fuel one at the fuel gauge sending unit.

6. Loosen the clamps on the fuel filler pipe and vent hose as necessary and disconnect the filler pipe hose and vent hose from the tank.

7. If the tank is the metal type, support the tank and remove the bolts attaching the tank support or skid plate to the frame. Carefully lower the tank or tank/skid plate assembly and disconnect the vent tube from the vapor emission control valve in the top of the tank. Finish removing the filler pipe and filler pipe vent hose if not possible previously. Remove the tank from under the vehicle.

9. If the tank is the plastic type, support the tank and remove the bolts attaching the combination skid plate and tank support to the frame. Carefully lower the tank and disconnect the vent tube from the vapor emission control valve in the top of the tank. Finish removing the filler pipe and filler pipe vent hose if it was not possible previously. Remove the skid plate and tank from under the vehicle. Remove the skid plate from the tank.

10. If the sending unit is to be removed, turn the unit retaining ring counterclockwise and remove the sending unit, retaining ring and gasket. Discard the gasket.

11. Install the tank in the reverse order of removal.

With metal tanks, use thread adhesive such as Locktite® on the bolt threads. Torque these bolts to 27-37 ft.lb.

With plastic tanks, DO NOT use thread adhesive. Torque the bolts to 25-35 ft.lb.

CARBURETED FUEL SYSTEM EXCEPT 2700/7200VV

CAUTION: *Never smoke when working around gasoline! Avoid all sources of sparks or ignition. Gasoline vapors are EXTREMELY volatile!*

Carburetor

REMOVAL AND INSTALLATION

1. Remove the air cleaner.

2. Remove the throttle cable or rod from the throttle lever. Disconnect the distributor vacuum line, EGR vacuum line, if so equipped, the

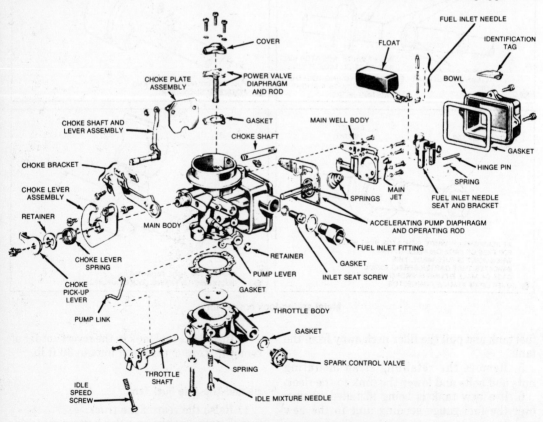

Holley 1904 carburetor assembly, exploded view

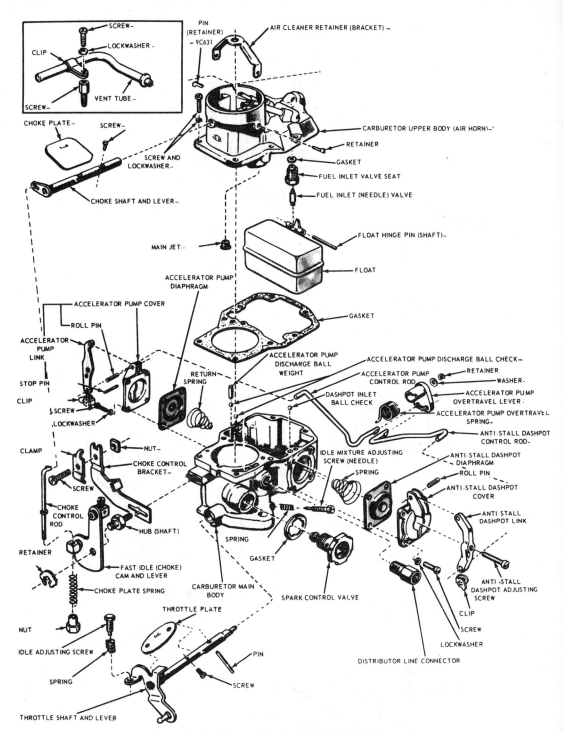

An exploded view of the Ford 1100 1-bb1 carburetor

inline fuel filter and the choke heat tube at the carburetor.

3. Disconnect the choke clean air tube from the air horn. Disconnect the choke actuating cable, if so equipped.

4. Remove the carburetor retaining nuts then remove the carburetor. Remove the carburetor mounting gasket, spacer (if so equipped), and the lower gasket from the intake manifold.

5. Before installing the carburetor, clean the gasket mounting surfaces of the spacer and carburetor. Place the spacer between two new gas-

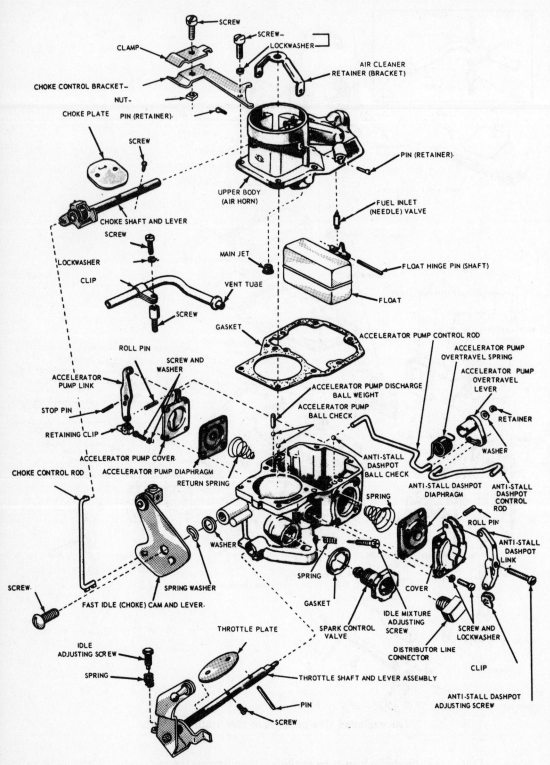

An exploded view of the Ford 1101 1-bbl carburetor

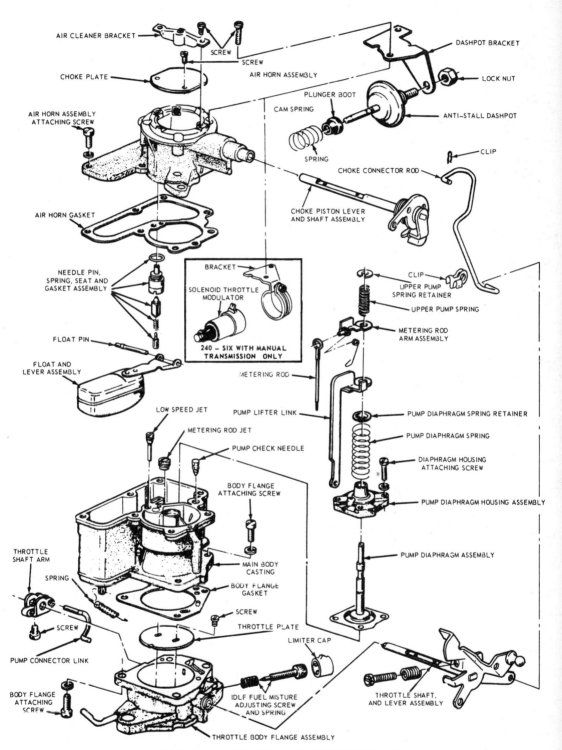

An exploded view of the Carter Model YF 1-bbl carburetor

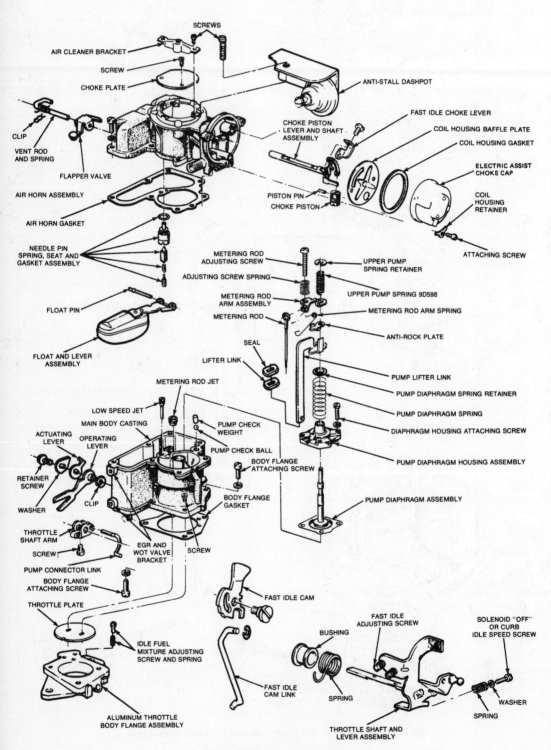

SCREWS

AIR CLEANER BRACKET

SCREW

CHOKE PLATE

CLIP

VENT ROD
AND SPRING

FLAPPER VALVE

AIR HORN ASSEMBLY

AIR HORN GASKET

NEEDLE PIN
SPRING, SEAT AND
GASKET ASSEMBLY

FLOAT PIN

FLOAT AND LEVER
ASSEMBLY

METERING ROD JET

LOW SPEED JET

MAIN BODY CASTING

ACTUATING
LEVER

OPERATING
LEVER

RETAINER
SCREW

WASHER

CLIP

THROTTLE
SHAFT ARM

SCREW

PUMP CONNECTOR LINK

BODY FLANGE
ATTACHING SCREW

THROTTLE PLATE

IDLE FUEL
MIXTURE ADJUSTING
SCREW AND SPRING

ALUMINUM THROTTLE
BODY FLANGE ASSEMBLY

ANTI-STALL DASHPOT

FAST IDLE CHOKE LEVER

CHOKE PISTON
LEVER AND SHAFT
ASSEMBLY

COIL HOUSING BAFFLE PLATE

COIL HOUSING GASKET

ELECTRIC ASSIST
CHOKE CAP

PISTON PIN

CHOKE PISTON

COIL
HOUSING
RETAINER

ATTACHING SCREW

METERING ROD
ADJUSTING SCREW

ADJUSTING SCREW SPRING

METERING ROD
ARM ASSEMBLY

METERING ROD

SEAL

LIFTER LINK

PUMP CHECK
WEIGHT

PUMP CHECK BALL

BODY FLANGE
ATTACHING SCREW

BODY FLANGE
GASKET

EGR AND
WOT VALVE
BRACKET

SCREW

UPPER PUMP
SPRING RETAINER

UPPER PUMP SPRING 9D598

METERING ROD ARM SPRING

ANTI-ROCK PLATE

PUMP LIFTER LINK

PUMP DIAPHRAGM SPRING RETAINER

PUMP DIAPHRAGM SPRING

DIAPHRAGM HOUSING ATTACHING SCREW

PUMP DIAPHRAGM HOUSING ASSEMBLY

PUMP DIAPHRAGM ASSEMBLY

FAST IDLE CAM

FAST IDLE
ADJUSTING SCREW

BUSHING

FAST IDLE
CAM LINK

SPRING

THROTTLE SHAFT AND
LEVER ASSEMBLY

SOLENOID "OFF"
OR CURB
IDLE SPEED SCREW

WASHER

SPRING

Carter YFA-1 exploded view

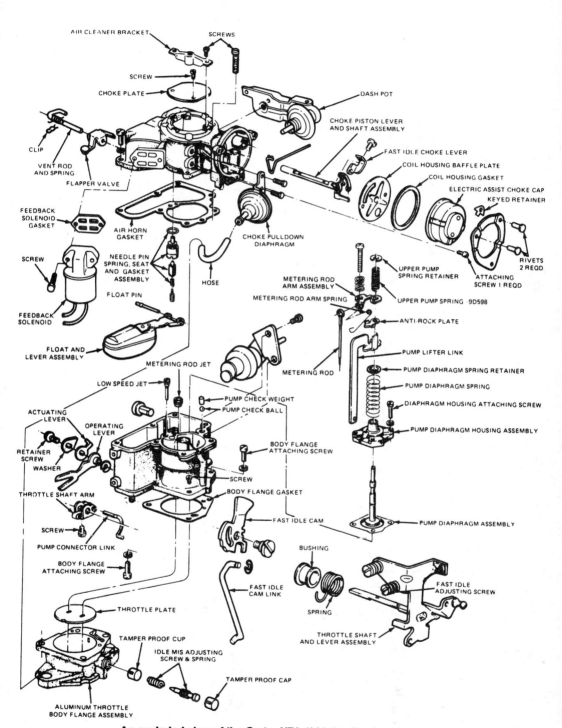

An exploded view of the Carter YFA 1bbl. feedback carburetor

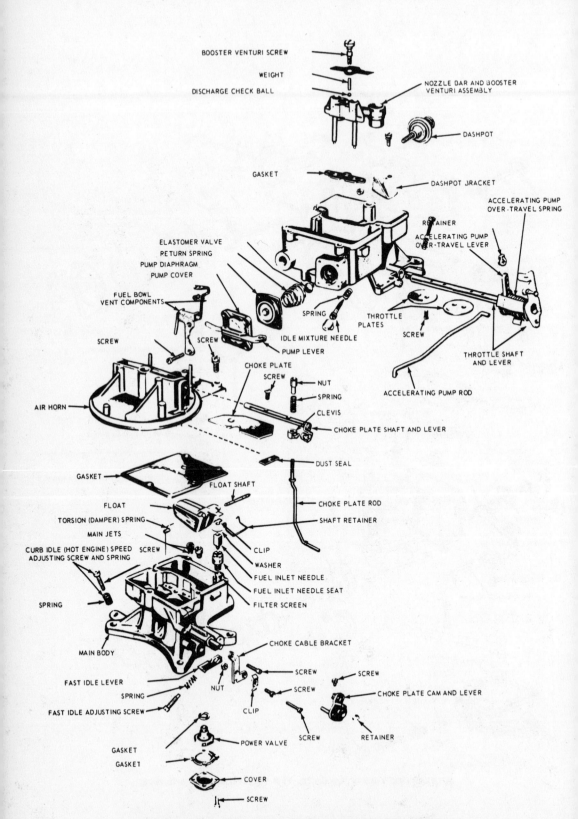

BOOSTER VENTURI SCREW

WEIGHT

DISCHARGE CHECK BALL

NOZZLE BAR AND BOOSTER VENTURI ASSEMBLY

DASHPOT

GASKET

DASHPOT BRACKET

ACCELERATING PUMP OVER-TRAVEL SPRING

RETAINER

ACCELERATING PUMP OVER-TRAVEL LEVER

ELASTOMER VALVE
RETURN SPRING
PUMP DIAPHRAGM
PUMP COVER

FUEL BOWL VENT COMPONENTS

SPRING

THROTTLE PLATES

SCREW

THROTTLE SHAFT AND LEVER

SCREW

SCREW

IDLE MIXTURE NEEDLE

PUMP LEVER

ACCELERATING PUMP ROD

CHOKE PLATE

SCREW

NUT

SPRING

AIR HORN

CLEVIS

CHOKE PLATE SHAFT AND LEVER

DUST SEAL

GASKET

FLOAT SHAFT

FLOAT

CHOKE PLATE ROD

TORSION (DAMPER) SPRING

SHAFT RETAINER

MAIN JETS

CURB IDLE (HOT ENGINE) SPEED ADJUSTING SCREW AND SPRING

SCREW

CLIP

WASHER

FUEL INLET NEEDLE

SPRING

FUEL INLET NEEDLE SEAT

FILTER SCREEN

MAIN BODY

CHOKE CABLE BRACKET

FAST IDLE LEVER

SCREW

SCREW

SPRING

NUT

SCREW

CHOKE PLATE CAM AND LEVER

FAST IDLE ADJUSTING SCREW

CLIP

SCREW

RETAINER

GASKET

POWER VALVE

GASKET

COVER

SCREW

An exploded view of the Autolite Model 2100 2-bbl carburetor

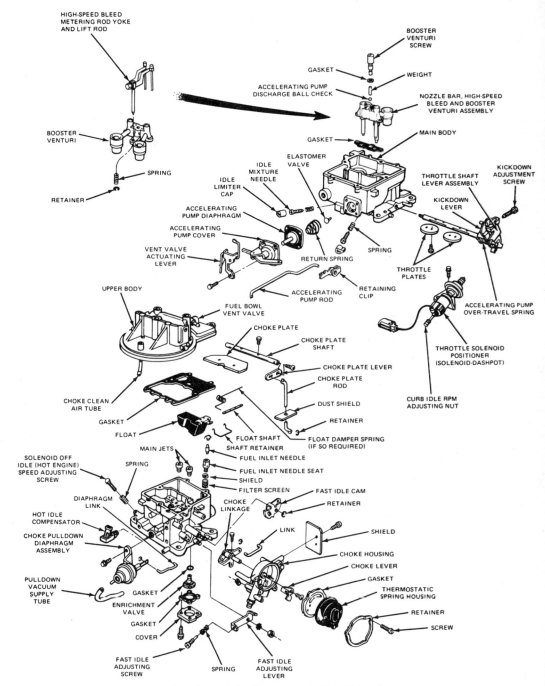

An exploded view of the Motorcraft 2150 2-bbl carburetor

kets and position the spacer and gaskets on the intake manifold. Position the carburetor body flange, snug the nuts, then alternately tighten each nut in a criss-cross pattern.

6. Connect the inline fuel filter, throttle cable, choke heat tube, distributor vacuum line, EGR vacuum line, and choke cable.

7. Connect the choke clean air line to the air horn.

8. Adjust the engine idle speed, the idle fuel mixture and anti-stall dashpot (if so equipped). Install the air cleaner.

FLOAT AND FUEL LEVEL ADJUSTMENT
Holley 1904

1. Remove the carburetor.
2. Remove the float bowl cover.

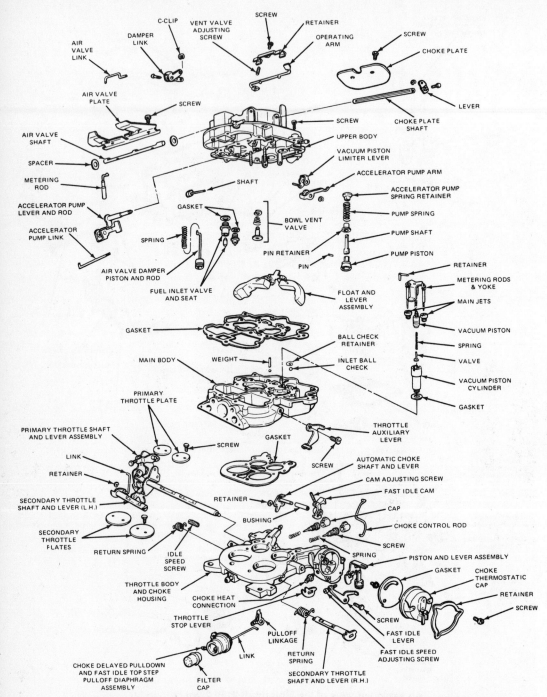

An exploded view of the Motorcraft 4350 4-bbl carburetor used on the 460 V8

3. Place a $23/32''$ feeler gauge between the float arm and inlet needle and invert the carburetor.

4. Tighten the seat screw to set the fuel level.

5. Remove the feeler gauge.

6. With the carburetor inverted, place an $11/64''$ gauge between the top of the float and the

inside surface of the float chamber. The gauge should pass lightly between the float and the chamber. If not, bend the tab on the float arm to adjust it.

7. Upright the carburetor. Slide a $3/16''$ gauge between the bottom of the float and float cham-

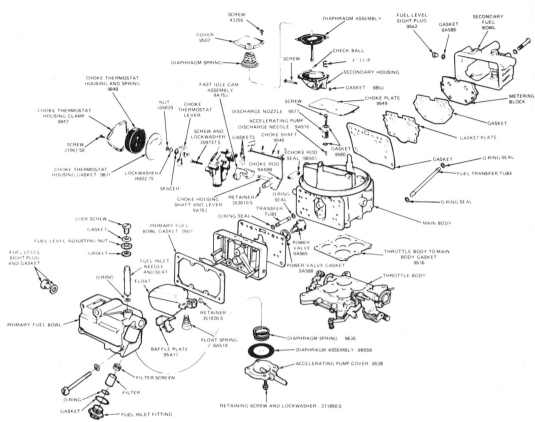

Motorcraft 4180 4-bbl. carburetor used on 1981–86 460 V8

ber. The gauge should pass lightly between the float and chamber. If not, adjust the float by bending the upright tang on the float lever.

8. Install the float bowl cover using a new gasket.

9. Install the carburetor using a new mounting gasket.

10. Run the engine and check for leaks.

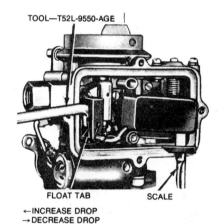

Holley 1904 float drop setting

←INCREASE DROP
→DECREASE DROP

FLOAT TAB   SCALE

TOOL—T52L-9550-AGE

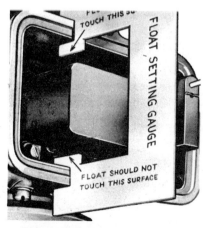

Holley 1904 bench float setting

Ford Model 1100, 1101 1-bbl and Carter Model YF, YFA and YFA Feedback 1-bbl

1. Remove the carburetor air horn and gasket from the carburetor.

2. Invert the air horn assembly, and check the clearance from the top of the float to the bottom of the air horn. Hold the air horn at eye level when gauging the float level. The float

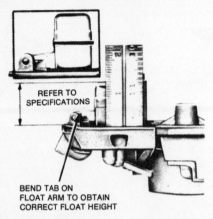

Float level adjustment for the Autolite (Ford) Model 1100 1-bbl carburetor

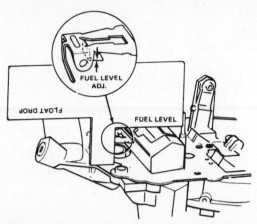

Float level adjustment for the Motorcraft 7200 VV 2-bbl. carburetor

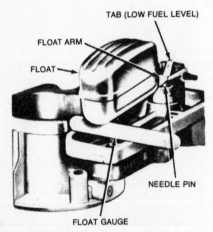

Float level adjustment for the Carter Model YF 1-bbl carburetor

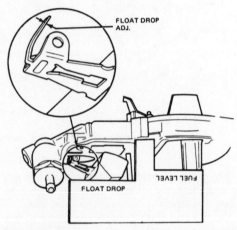

Float drop adjustment for the Motorcraft 7200 VV 2-bbl. carburetor

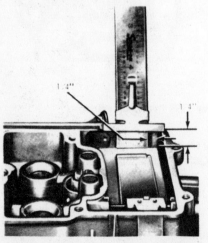

Float level adjustment for the Autolite Model 2100 and 2150 2-bbl carburetor

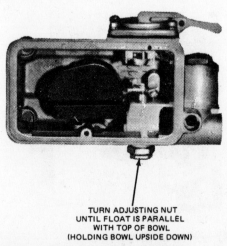

Dry float adjustment, Motorcraft 4180

arm (lever) should be resting on the needle pin. Do not load the needle when adjusting the float. Bend the float arm as necessary to adjust the float level (clearance). Do not bend the tab at the end of the float arm, because it prevents the float from striking the bottom of the fuel bowl when empty.

3. Turn the air horn over and hold it upright and let the float hang free. Measure the maximum clearance from the top of the float to the bottom of the air horn with the float gauge. Hold the air horn at eye level when gauging the dimension. To adjust the float drop, bend the tab at the end of the float arm.

4. Install the carburetor air horn with a new gasket.

Autolite (Motorcraft) Model 2100, 2150 2-bbl (Wet Adjustment)

1. Operate the engine until it reaches normal operating temperature. Place the vehicle on a level surface and stop the engine.

2. Remove the carburetor air cleaner assembly.

3. Remove the air horn attaching screws and the carburetor identification tag. Temporarily, leave the air horn and gasket in position on the carburetor main body and start the engine. Let the engine idle for a few minutes, then rotate the air horn out of the way and remove the air horn gasket to provide access to the float assembly.

4. While the engine is idling, use a scale to measure the vertical distance from the top machined surface of the carburetor main body to the level of the fuel in the fuel bowl. The measurement must be made at least ¼" (6mm) away from any vertical surface to assure an accurate reading, because the surface of the fuel is concave, being higher at the edges than in the center. Care must be exercised to measure the fuel level at the point of contact with the float.

5. If any adjustment is required, stop the engine to minimize the hazard of fire due to spilled gasoline. To adjust the fuel level, bend the float tab contacting the fuel inlet valve upward in relation to the original position to raise the fuel level, and downward to lower it. Each time the float is adjusted, the engine must be started and permitted to idle for a few minutes to stabilize the fuel level. Check the fuel level after each adjustment, until the specified level is obtained.

6. Assemble the carburetor in the reverse order of disassembly, using a new gasket between the air horn and the main carburetor body.

Holley 4180C

To perform a preliminary dry float adjustment on both the primary and secondary fuel bowl float assemblies, remove the fuel bowls and invert them allowing the float to rest on the fuel inlet valve and set assembly. the fuel inlet valve and seat can be rotated until the float is parallel with the fuel bowl floor (actually the top of the fuel bowl chamber inverted). Note that this is an initial dry float setting which must be rechecked with the carburetor assembled and on the engine to obtain the proper wet fuel level.

This carburetor has an externally adjustable needle and seat assembly which allows the fuel level to be checked and adjust without removing the carburetor from the engine.

1. Run the engine with the vehicle resting on a level surface until the engine temperature has normalized.

2. Remove the air cleaner assembly.

3. Place a suitable container or an absorbent cloth below the fuel level sight plug in the fuel bowl.

4. Stop the engine and remove the sight plug and gasket on the primary float bowl. The fuel level in the bowl should be at the lower edge of the sight plug hole, plus or minus ¹⁄₁₆".

CAUTION: *Never loosen the lockscrew or nut, or attempt to adjust the fuel level with the sight plug removed or the engine running, since fuel will spray out creating a fire hazard!*

5. To adjust the fuel level, install the sight plug and gasket, loosen one on the lower fuel bowl retaining screws and drain the fuel from the bowl only if the level is too high. Loosen the lockscrew on top of the fuel bowl just enough to allow the adjusting nut to be turned. Turn the adjusting nut about ½ of a turn in to lower the

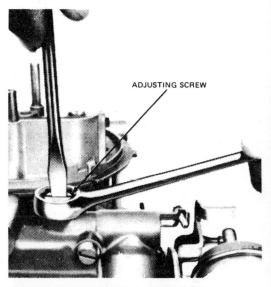

ADJUSTING SCREW

Wet float adjustment, Motorcraft 4180

fuel level and out to raise the fuel level. By turning the adjusting nut $5/32$ of a turn, the fuel level will change $1/32''$ at the sight plug.

6. Start the engine and allow the fuel level to stabilize. Check the fuel level as outlined in Step 4.

7. Repeat the procedure for the secondary float bowl adjustment.

8. Install the air cleaner assembly if no further adjustments are necessary.

Motorcraft 4350

1. Remove the carburetor.

2. Remove the air horn assembly and remove the gasket.

3. Invert the air horn.

4. Use a T-scale, made for 4300 series carburetors, to measure the distance bewteen the flat surface of the free end of each float pontoon and the air horn casting surface.

NOTE: *Don't allow the vertical scale to contact any gasket sealing ridge on the casting surface.*

5. The float pontoons should just touch the T-scale. If one float is lower than the other, twist the float and lever assembly slightly to correct the condition.

6. To adjust the float level, bend the tab which contacts the needle and seat assembly.

If a T-scale is not available, you can make your own adjusting tool. The accompanying illustrations show you exactly what to do. The fabrication illustration also shows you how to

make a tab bending tool. To use the bending tool:

a. To raise the float: insert the open end of the tool to the right side of the float lever tab and between the needle and float hinge. Raise the float lever off of the needle and bend the tab downward.

b. To lower the float: insert the bending tool to the left of the float lever tab, between the needle and float hinge. Support the float lever and bend the tab upward.

SECONDARY THROTTLE PLATE ADJUSTMENT

Holley 4180C

1. Remove the carburetor.

2. Hold the secondary throttle plates closed.

3. Turn the secondary throttle shaft lever stop screw out until the secondary throttle plates seat in the throttle bores.

4. Turn the screw back in until the screw just touches the lever, then $3/8$ turn more.

FAST IDLE ADJUSTMENT

Holley 1904 1-bbl
Ford Model 1100, 1101 1-bbl

The fast idle is controlled by the idle adjusting screw bearing against the bottom of the choke cam and lever during idle or closed throttle conditions. The choke cam and lever opens the throttle slightly, through contact of the idle adjusting screw with the cam, as the manual choke position is selected. Higher engine idle

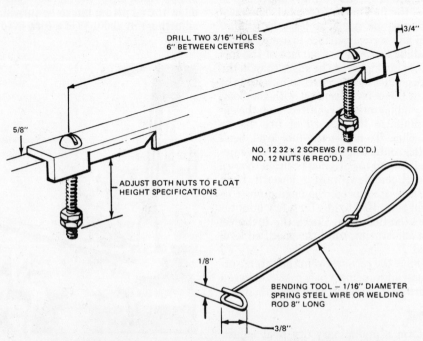

DRILL TWO 3/16" HOLES
6" BETWEEN CENTERS

3/4"

5/8"

NO. 12 32 x 2 SCREWS (2 REQ'D.)
NO. 12 NUTS (6 REQ'D.)

ADJUST BOTH NUTS TO FLOAT
HEIGHT SPECIFICATIONS

1/8"

BENDING TOOL — 1/16" DIAMETER
SPRING STEEL WIRE OR WELDING
ROD 8" LONG

3/8"

Motorcraft 4350 float gauge and bending tool fabrication details

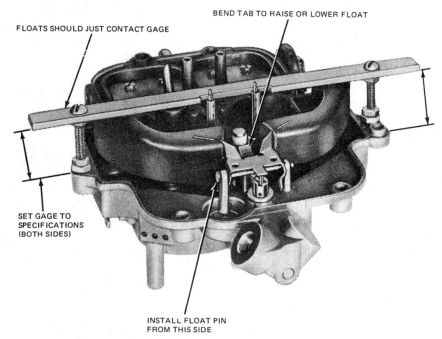

FLOATS SHOULD JUST CONTACT GAGE

BEND TAB TO RAISE OR LOWER FLOAT

SET GAGE TO
SPECIFICATIONS
(BOTH SIDES)

INSTALL FLOAT PIN
FROM THIS SIDE

Using the fabricated float level gauge on the Motorcraft 4350

speeds are automatically provided through contact of the idle adjusting screw with the cam. The curb idle must be adjusted correctly for the fast idle to be proper during application of the choke.

Carter Model YF 1-bbl

1963–74

1. Position the fast idle screw on the kickdown step of the fast idle cam against the shoulder of the high step.

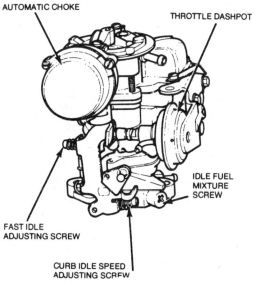

AUTOMATIC CHOKE

THROTTLE DASHPOT

IDLE FUEL
MIXTURE
SCREW

FAST IDLE
ADJUSTING SCREW

CURB IDLE SPEED
ADJUSTING SCREW

Carburetor speed adjustments for the Carter YF 1-bbl carburetor

2. Adjust by bending the choke plat connecting rod to obtain the specified clearance between the lower edge of the choke plate and the carburetor air horn. Use a drill bit inserted between the lower edge of the choke plate and the carburetor air horn.

3. With the engine at operating temperature, air cleaner removed and a tachometer attached according to the manufacturer's instructions, manually rotate the fast idle cam to the top or second step as specified while holding the choke plate fully open. Turn the fast idle adjustment screw inward or outward as required to obtain the specified speed.

4. When setting the fast idle speed, all distributor vacuum and EGR controls must be disconnected and plugged to insure proper speeds during cold operation.

Carter YF, and YFA 1-bbl

1975–86

1. Run the engine to normal operating temperature.

2. Remove the air cleaner and attach a tachometer to the engine according to the manufacturer's instructions.

3. Manually rotate the fast idle to the top step while holding the choke plate fully opened.

4. Rotate the cam until the fast idle adjusting screw rests on the cam step specified on the underhood emissions sticker.

5. Turn the fast idle speed adjusting screw to obtain the speed specified in the Tune-Up Charts.

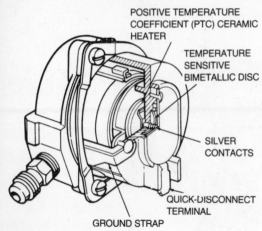

POSITIVE TEMPERATURE COEFFICIENT (PTC) CERAMIC HEATER

TEMPERATURE SENSITIVE BIMETALLIC DISC

SILVER CONTACTS

QUICK-DISCONNECT TERMINAL

GROUND STRAP

Electric choke components

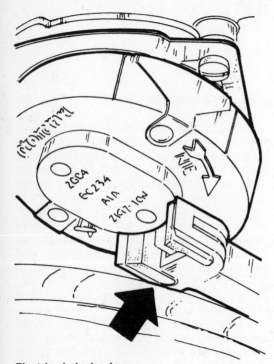

Electric choke hookup

NOTE: *When this operation is performed outdoors in cold weather, all vacuum controls to the distributor and EGR valve must be bypassed. This can be done by connecting a jumper hose from the DIST port on the carburetor to the vacuum advance port of the distributor and by disconnecting and plugging the EGR vacuum source hose.*

Autolite (Motorcraft) Model 2100, 2150 2-bbl

The fast idle speed adjustment is made in the same manner as for the Model YF carburetor, starting at Step 3.

To adjust the model 2100 fast idle cam clearance, follow the procedure given below:

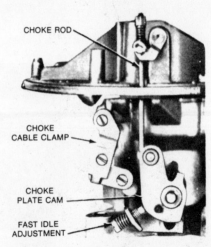

CHOKE ROD

CHOKE CABLE CLAMP

CHOKE PLATE CAM

FAST IDLE ADJUSTMENT

Fast idle speed adjustment on the Autolite/Motorcraft 2100, 2150 2-bbl carburetor

1. Rotate the choke thermostatic spring housing 90° in the rich direction.
2. Position the idle speed screw on the high step of the cam.
3. Depress the choke pulldown diaphragm against the diaphragm stop screw to place the choke in the pulldown position.
4. While holding the choke pulldown diaphragm depressed, open the throttle slightly and allow the fast idle cam to fall.
5. Close the throttle and check the position of the fast idle cam. The screw should contact the cam at the V mark on the cam.
6. Adjust the fast idle cam adjusting screw to obtain the proper setting.

Holley 4180C 4-bbl
Motorcraft 4350 4-bbl

1. Remove the spark delay valve, if so equipped, from the Distributor vacuum advance line, and route the vacuum line directly to the advance side of the distributor.

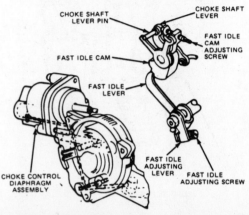

CHOKE SHAFT LEVER PIN

CHOKE SHAFT LEVER

FAST IDLE CAM ADJUSTING SCREW

FAST IDLE CAM

FAST IDLE LEVER

CHOKE CONTROL DIAPHRAGM ASSEMBLY

FAST IDLE ADJUSTING LEVER

FAST IDLE ADJUSTING SCREW

Fast idle speed adjustment for the Motorcraft 7200 VV 2-bbl. carburetor

2. Trace the EGR signal vacuum line from the EGR valve to the carburetor and if there is EGR/PVS valve or temperature vacuum switch located in the vacuum line routing, disconnect the EGR vacuum line at the EGR valve and plug the line.

3. If not equipped with an EGR/PVS valve or temperature vacuum switch do not detach the EGR vacuum line.

4. Trace the purge valve vacuum line from the purge valve located on the canister, to the first point where the vacuum line can be detached from the underhood hose routing. Disconnect the vacuum line at that point, cap the open port, and plug the vacuum line.

WARNING: *To prevent damage to the purge valve do not disconnect the vacuum line at the purge valve.*

5. With the engine running at normal operating temperature, the choke plate fully opened and the manual transmission in Neutral and the automatic transmission in Park, place the fast idle level on the 2nd or kickdown step of the fast idle cam.

6. Adjust the fast idle screw to within 100 rpm of the specified speed given on the Vehicle Emission Control Decal.

7. Reconnect all vacuum lines.

VACUUM OPERATED THROTTLE MODULATOR ADJUSTMENT

Holley 4180C

1. Set the parking brake, put the transmission in Park or Neutral and run the engine up to operating temperature.

2. Turn off the air conditioning and heater controls.

3. Disconnect and plug the vacuum hoses at the air control valve and EGR valve and purge control valve.

4. Place the transmission in the position specified on the underhood decal.

5. If necessary, check and adjust the curb idle rpm.

6. Place the transmission in Neutral or Park and rev the engine. Place the transmission in the specified position according to the underhood decal and recheck the curb idle rpm. Readjust if necessary.

7. Connect an external vacuum source which provides a minimum of 10″ of vacuum to the VOTM (Vacuum Operated Throttle Modulator) kicker.

8. Place the transmission in the specified position.

9. Adjust the VOTM (throttle kicker) locknut if necessary to obtain the proper idle rpm.

10. Reconnect all vacuum hoses.

DASHPOT ADJUSTMENT

1. Remove the air cleaner.

2. Loosen the anti-stall dashpot locknut.

3. With the choke plate open, hold the throttle plate closed (idle position), and check the clearance between the throttle lever and the dashpot plunger tip with a feeler gauge.

NOTE: *On the Ford Model 1100 1-bbl carburetor, turn the adjusting screw 3 turns in after the screw contacts the diaphragm assembly.*

CHOKE PLATE PULL-DOWN CLEARANCE ADJUSTMENT

Ford 1100

1. Insert a drill or gauge of the specified size between the choke plate and the inside of the air horn, and place the choke linkage in the full choke position.

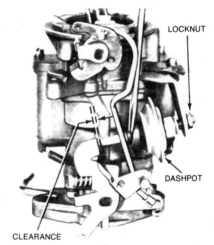

Anti-stall dashpot adjustment on the Carter Model YF 1-bbl carburetor

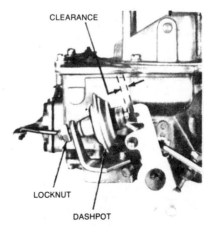

Anti-stall dashpot adjustment on the Autolite Model 2100 2-bbl carburetor

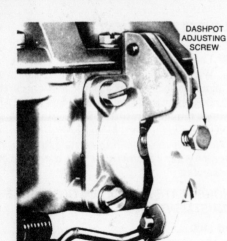

DASHPOT
ADJUSTING
SCREW

ADJUST THROTTLE
TO HOT IDLE POSITION
PRIOR TO ADJUSTING DASHPOT

Anti-stall dashpot adjustment on the Autolite (Ford) Model 1100 1-bbl carburetor

2. While maintaining the full choke position, adjust the nut on the choke connector (pulldown) rod to just contact the swivel on the cam lever.

Carter YF, YFA

1. Remove the air cleaner. Remove the choke thermostatic spring housing from the carburetor.

2. Bend a 0.026″ (0.66mm) diameter wire gauge at a 90° angle approximately ⅛″ (3mm) from one end. Insert the bent end of the gauge between the choke piston slot and the right hand slot in the choke housing. Rotate the choke piston lever counterclockwise until the gauge is snug in the piston slot.

3. Exert a light pressure on the choke piston lever to hold the gauge in place, then use a drill gauge with a diameter equal to the specified clearance between the lower edge of the choke plate and the carburetor bore to check clearance.

4. To adjust the choke plate pulldown clearance, bend the choke piston lever as required to obtain the specified setting. Remove the choke piston lever for bending to prevent distorting the piston link, causing erratic choke operation.

5. Install the choke thermostatic spring housing and gasket. Set the housing to specifications.

Autolite 2100

1. Remove the air cleaner.

2. With the engine at normal operating temperature, loosen the choke thermostatic spring housing retainer screws and set the housing 90° in the rich direction.

3. Disconnect and remove the choke heat tube from the choke housing.

4. Turn the fast idle adjusting screw outward one full turn.

5. Start the engine, then check for the specified clearance between the lower edge of the choke plate and the air horn wall.

6. If the clearance is not within specification the diaphragm stop screw (located on the underside of the choke diaphragm housing) clockwise to decrease or counterclockwise to increase the clearance.

7. Connect the choke heat tube and set the choke thermostatic spring housing to specifications. Adjust the fast idle speed to specifications.

Motorcraft 2150

1. Set throttle on fast idle cam top step.

2. Note index position of choke bimetallic cap. Loosen retaining screws and rotate cap 90° in the rich (closing) direction.

3. Activate pulldown motor by manually forcing pulldown control diaphragm link in the direction of applied vacuum or by applying vacuum to external vacuum tube.

4. Measure vertical hard gauge clearance between choke plate and center of carburetor air horn wall nearest fuel bowl.

Pulldown setting should be within specifications for minimum choke plate opening.

If choke plate pulldown is found to be out of specification, reset by adjusting diaphragm stop on end of choke pulldown diaphragm.

If pulldown is reset, cam clearance should be checked and reset if required.

After pulldown check is completed, reset choke bimetallic cap to recommend index position as specified in the Carburetor Specifications Chart. Check and reset fast idle speed to specifications if necessary.

Holley 4180C

1. Remove the choke thermostat housing, gasket and retainer.

2. Insert a piece of wire into the choke piston bore to move the piston down against the stop screw.

3. Measure the gap between the lower edge of the choke plate and the air horn wall.

4. Turn the adjustment screw to specifications.

5. Reinstall the choke thermostat housing, gasket and retainer.

AUTOMATIC CHOKE HOUSING ADJUSTMENT

All Except the 4180C

Loosen the choke cap retaing screws just enough to trun the cap. Turn the cap until the notch in the cap aligns with the specified index line on the choke housing. See the charts in this chapter or your underhood specifications sticker.

Holley 4180C

This adjustment is present and should not be changed.

ACCELERATOR PUMP LEVER ADJUSTMENT

Ford 1100

1. Insert the roll pin in the lower hole (HI position in the lever stop hold).
2. Position the throttle and choke linkage so that the throttle plate will seat in the throttle bore. Hold the throttle plates in the closed position. Position a gauge or drill of the specified thickness between the roll pin and the cover surface. Bend the accelerating pump actuating rod to obtain the specified gauge or drill clearance between the pump cover and the roll pin in the pump lever.

Holley 4180C

1. Hold the primary throttle plates in the wide open position.
2. Using a feeler gauge, check the clearance accelerator pump operating lever adjustment screw head and the pump arm while depressing the pump arm with your finger. The clearance should be $\frac{1}{64}$" (0.015"; 0.381mm).
3. To make an adjustment, hold the adjusting screw locknut and turn the adjusting screw

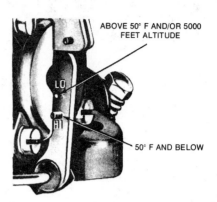

ABOVE 50° F AND/OR 5000 FEET ALTITUDE

LO

HI

50° F AND BELOW

Accelerating pump lever adjustment, Ford 1100

inward to increase, or outward to decrease, the adjustment. $\frac{1}{2}$ turn will change the clearance by $\frac{1}{64}$".

ACCELERATOR PUMP STROKE ADJUSTMENT

Ford 1100

Acceleration requirements in various climates are satisfied by controlling the amount of fuel discharged by the accelerating pump. The pump stroke is controlled by changing the location of the roll pin in the lever stop hole.

For operation in ambient temperatures 50°F (10°C) and below, place the roll pin in the hole of the pump operating lever marked HI (lower hole). For best performance and economy at normal ambient temperatures and high altitude, (above 50°F [10°C] and/or above 5,000' [1,524m] altitude), place the roll pin in the LO (upper hole) of the lever.

Motorcraft 2150

The accelerating pump stroke has been factory set for a particular engine application and should not be readjusted. If the stroke has been

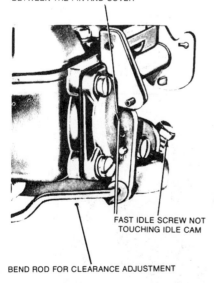

WITH THROTTLE PLATE CLOSED, INSERT A *GAUGE* THAT EQUALS THE SPECIFIED CLEARANCE BETWEEN THE PIN AND COVER

FAST IDLE SCREW NOT TOUCHING IDLE CAM

BEND ROD FOR CLEARANCE ADJUSTMENT

Accelerating pump clearance adjustment, Ford 1100

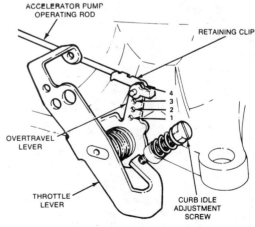

ACCELERATOR PUMP OPERATING ROD

RETAINING CLIP

4
3
2
1

OVERTRAVEL LEVER

THROTTLE LEVER

CURB IDLE ADJUSTMENT SCREW

Motorcraft 2150 accelerating pump stroke adjustment

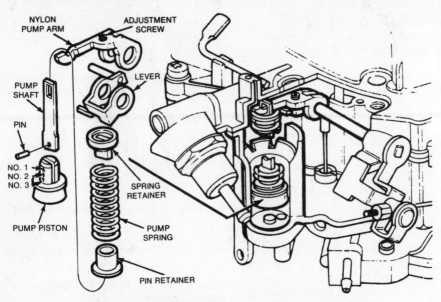

Motorcraft 4180, 4350 accelerating pump stroke adjustment

changed from the specified hole reset to specifications by following these procedures.

1. To release the rod from the retaining clip, lift upward on the portion of the clip that snaps over the shaft and then disengage the rod.

2. Position the clip over the specified hole in the overtravel lever and insert the operating rod through the clip and the overtravel lever. Snap the end of the clip over the rod to secure.

Holley 4180C

This adjustment is preset and should not be changed.

DECHOKE ADJUSTMENT

All Except Holley 4180C and Motorcraft 4350

1. Remove the air cleaner.

2. Hold the throttle plate fully open and close the choke plate as far as possible without forcing it. Use a drill of the proper diameter to check the clearance between the choke plate and air horn.

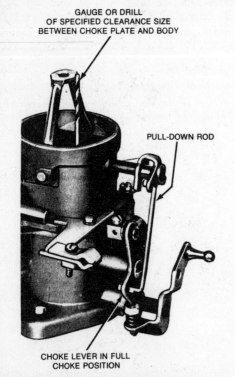

Ford 1100 choke pull-down adjustment

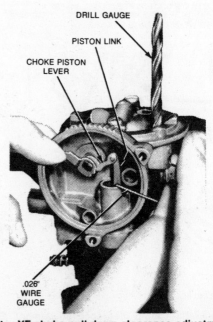

Carter YF choke pull-down clearance adjustment

3. If the clearance is not within specification, adjust by bending the arm on the choke trip lever. Bending the arm downward will increase the clearance, and bending it upward will decrease the clearance. Always recheck the clearance after making any adjustment.

4. If the choke plate clearance and fast idle cam linkage adjustment was performed with the carburetor on the engine, adjust the engine idle speed and fuel mixture. Adjust the dashpot (if so equipped).

Holley 4180C
Motorcraft 4350

1. Hold the throttle plates in the wide open position.

2. Rotate the choke plate downward towards the closed position until the pawl on the fast idle speed lever contacts the fast idle cam.

3. Check the clearance between the lower edge of the choke plate and the air horn wall.

4. Adjust the clearance as specified in the charts in this chapter, by bending the pawl on the fast idle speed lever forward to increase or backward to decrease the clearance.

CARBURETOR TROUBLESHOOTING

The best way to diagnose a bad carburetor is to eliminate all other possible sources of the problem. If the carburetor is suspected to be the problem, first perform all of the adjustments given in this Section. If this doesn't correct the difficulty, then check the following. Check the ignition system to make sure that the spark plugs, breaker points, and condenser are in good condition and adjusted to the proper specifications. Examine the emission control equipment to make sure that all the vacuum lines are connected and none are blocked or clogged. See the first half of this Chapter. Check the ignition timing adjustment. Check all of the vacuum lines on the engine for loose connections, slips or breaks. Torque the carburetor and intake manifold attaching bolts to the proper specifications. If, after performing all of these checks and adjustments, the problem is still not solved, then you can safely assume that the carburetor is the source of the problem.

OVERHAUL

Efficient carburetion depends greatly on careful cleaning and inspection during overhaul since dirt, gum, water or varnish in or on the carburetor parts are often responsible for poor performance.

Overhaul the carburetor in a clean, dust free area. Carefully disassembly the carburetor, referring often to the exploded views. Keep all similar and look-alike parts segregated during disassembly and cleaning to avoid accidental interchange during assembly. Make a note of all jet sizes.

When the carburetor is disassembled, wash all parts (except diaphragms, electric choke units, pump plunger and any other plastic, leather, fiber, or rubber parts) in clean carburetor solvent. Do not leave the parts in the solvent any longer than is necessary to sufficiently loosen the dirt and deposits. Excessive cleaning may remove the special finish from the float bowl and choke valve bodies, leaving these parts unfit for service. Rinse all parts in clean solvent and blow them dry with compressed air or allow them to air dry, while resting on clean, lintless paper. Wipe clean all cork, plastic, leather and fiber parts with clean, lint free cloth.

Blow out all passages and jets with compressed air and be sure that there are no restrictions or blockages. Never use wire or similar tools to clean jets, fuel passages or air bleeds. Clean all jets and valves separately to avoid accidental interchange.

Examine all parts for wear or damage. If wear or damage is found, replace the defective parts. Especially, inspect the following:

1. Check the float needle and seat for wear. If wear is found, replace the complete assembly.

2. Check the float hinge pin for wear and the float(s) for dents or distortion. replace the float if fuel has leaked into it.

3. Check the throttle and choke shaft bores for wear or an out-of-round condition. Damage or wear to the throttle arm, shaft or shaft bore will often require replacement of the throttle body. These parts require a close tolerance of fit; wear may allow air leakage, which could affect starting and idling.

NOTE: *Throttle shaft and bushings are not normally included in overhaul kits. They can be purchased separately.*

4. Inspect the idle mixture adjusting needles for burrs and grooves. Any such condition requires replacement of the needle, since you will not be able to obtain a satisfactory idle.

5. Test the accelerator pump check valves. They should pass air one way, but not the other. Test for proper seating by blowing and sucking on the valve. Replace the valve as necessary. If the valve is satisfactory, wash the valve again to remove moisture.

6. Check the bowl cover for warped surfaces with a straightedge.

7. Closely inspect the valves and seats for wear and damage, replacing as necessary.

8. After the carburetor is assembled, check the choke valve for freedom of operation.

Carburetor overhaul kits are recommended for each overhaul. these kits contain all gaskets and new parts to replace those which deteriorate most rapidly. Failure to replace all of the parts supplied with the kit (especially gaskets) can result in poor performance later.

Most carburetor manufacturers supply overhaul kits of three basic types: minor repair; major repair; and gasket kits.

After cleaning and checking all components, reassemble the carburetor, using new parts and referring to the exploded view. When reassembling, make sure that all screws and jets are right in their seat, but do not overtighten, as the tip will be distorted. Tighten all screws gradually, in rotation. Do not tighten needle valves into their seats; uneven jetting will result. Always use new gaskets. Be sure to adjust the float level.

NOTE: *Most carburetor rebuilding kits contain a sheet of specific instructions pertaining to the carburetor the kit is for.*

CARBURETED FUEL SYSTEM MOTORCRAFT 2700VV/7200VV

Design

Since the design of the 2700VV (variable venturi) carburetor differs considerably from the other carburetors in the Ford lineup, an explanation in the theory and operation is presented here.

In exterior appearance, the variable venturi carburetor is similar to conventional carburetor and, like a conventional carburetor, it uses a normal float and fuel bowl system. However, the similarity end there. In place of the normal choke plate and fixed area venturis, the 2700VV carburetor has a pair of small oblong castings in the top of the upper carburetor body where you would normally expect to see the choke plate. These castings slide back and forth across the top of the carburetor in response to fuel-air demands. Their movement is controlled by a spring-loaded diaphragm valve regulated by a vacuum signal taken below the venturis in the throttle bores. As the throttle is opened, the strength of the vacuum signal increases, opening the venturis and allowing more air to enter the carburetor.

Fuel is admitted into the venturi area by means of tapered metering rods that fit into the main jets. These rods are attached to the venturis, and, as the venturis open or close in response to air demand, the fuel needed to maintain the proper mixture increase or decreases as the metering rods slide in the jets. In comparison to a conventional carburetor with fixed venturis and a variable air supply, this system provides much more precise control of the fuel-air supply during all modes of operation. Because

of the variable venturi principle, there are fewer fuel metering systems and fuel passages. The only auxiliary fuel metering systems required are an idle trim, accelerator pump (similar to a conventional carburetor), starting enrichment, and cold running enrichment.

NOTE: *Adjustment, assembly and disassembly of this carburetor require special tools for some of the operations. These tools are available (see the Tools and Equipment Section). Do not attempt any operations on this carburetor without first checking to see if you need the special tools for that particular operation. The adjustment and repair procedures given here mention when and if you will need the special tools.*

The Motorcraft model 7200 variable venturi (VV) carburetor shares most of its design features with the model 2700VV. The major difference between the two is that the 7200VV is designed to work with Ford's EEC (electronic engine control) feedback system. The feedback system precisely controls the air/fuel ration by varying signals to the feedback control monitor located on the carburetor, which opens or closes the metering valve in response. This expands or reduces the amount of control vacuum above the fuel bowl, leaning or richening the mixture accordingly.

FLOAT LEVEL ADJUSTMENT

1. Remove and invert the upper part of the carburetor, with the gasket in place.
2. Measure the vertical distance between the carburetor body, outside the gasket, and the bottom of the float.
3. To adjust, bend the float operating lever that contacts the needle valve. Make sure that the float remains parallel to the gasket surface.

FLOAT DROP ADJUSTMENT

1. Remove and hold upright the upper part of the carburetor.
2. Measure the vertical distance between the carburetor body, outside the gasket, and the bottom of the float.
3. Adjust by bending the stop tab on the float lever that contacts the hinge pin.

FAST IDLE SPEED ADJUSTMENT

1. With the engine warmed up and idling, place the fast idle lever on the step of the fast idle cam specified on the engine compartment sticker or in the specifications chart. Disconnect and plug the EGR vacuum line.
2. Make sure the high speed cam positioner lever is disengaged.

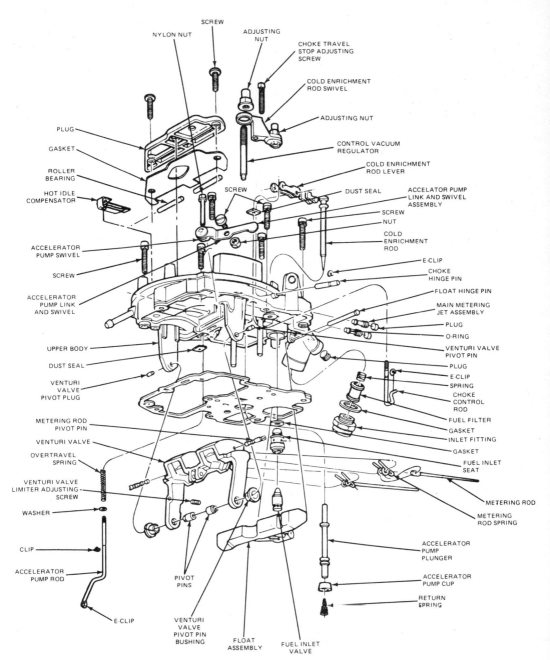

An exploded view of the Motorcraft 7200 VV (variable venturi) 2-bbl. carburetor upper body

3. Turn the fast idle speed screw to adjust to the specified speed.

FAST IDLE CAM ADJUSTMENT

You will need a special tool for this job: Ford calls it a stator cap (#T77L-9848-A). It fits over the choke thermostatic lever when the choke cap is removed.

1. Remove the choke coil cap. On 1980 and later California models, the choke cap is riveted in place. The top rivets will have to be drilled out. The bottom rivet will have to be driven out from the rear. New rivets must be used upon installation.

2. Place the fast idle lever in the corner of the specified step of the fast idle cam (the highest step is first) with the high speed cam positioner retracted.

3. If the adjustment is being made with the carburetor removed, hold the throttle lightly close with a rubber band.

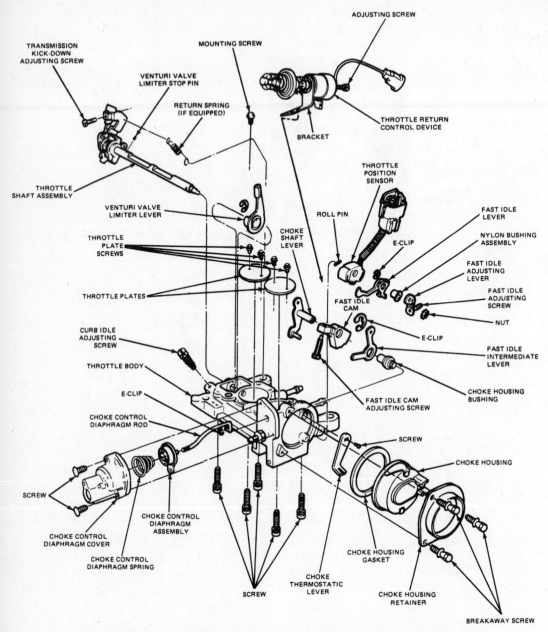

An exploded view of the Motorcraft VV (variable venturi) 2-bbl. carburetor throttle body

4. Turn the stator cap clockwise until the lever contacts the fast idle cam adjusting screw.

5. Turn the fast idle cam adjusting screw until the index mark on the cap lines up with the specified mark on the casting.

6. Remove the stator cap. Install the choke coil cap and set it to the specified housing mark.

COLD ENRICHMENT METERING ROD ADJUSTMENT

A dial indicator and the stator cap are required for this adjustment.

1. Remove the choke coil cap. See Step 1 of the Fast idle Cam Adjustment.

2. Attach a weight to the choke coil mechanism to seat the cold enrichment rod.

3. Install and zero a dial indicator with the tip of top of the enrichment rod. Raise and release the weight to verify zero on the dial indicator.

4. With the stator cap at the index position, the dial indicator should read the specified dimension. Turn the adjusting nut to correct it.

5. Install the choke cap at the correct setting.

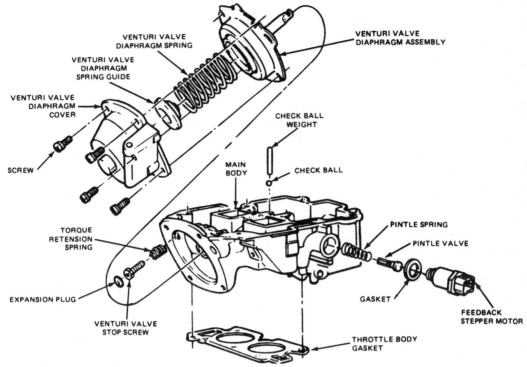

An exploded view of the Motorcraft 7200 VV (variable venturi) 2-bbl. carburetor main body

CONTROL VACUUM ADJUSTMENT

1977 Only

1. Make sure the idle speed is correct.
2. Using a $\frac{5}{32}$" Allen wrench, turn the venturi valve diaphragm adjusting screw clockwise until the valve is firmly closed.
3. Connect a vacuum gauge to the vacuum tap on the venturi valve cover.
4. Idle the engine and use a $\frac{1}{8}$" Allen wrench to turn the venturi by-pass adjusting screw to the specified vacuum setting. You may have to correct the idle speed.
5. Turn the venturi valve diaphragm adjusting screw counterclockwise until the vacuum drops to the specified setting. You will have to work the throttle to get the vacuum to drop.
6. Reset the idle speed.

1980-82

This adjustment is necessary only on non-feedback systems.

1. Remove the carburetor. Remove the venturi valve diaphragm plug with a center-punch.
2. If the carburetor has a venturi valve by-pass, remove it be removing the two cover retaining screw; invert and remove the by-pass screw plug from the cover with a drift. Install the cover.
3. Install the carburetor. Start the engine and allow it to reach normal operating tempera-

ture. Connect a vacuum gauge to the venturi valve cover. Set the idle speed to 500 rpm with the transmission in Drive.

4. Push and hold the venturi valve closed. Adjust the bypass screw to obtain a reading of 8 in. H_2O on the vacuum gauge. Make sure the idle speed remains constant. Open and close the throttle and check the idle speed.
5. With the engine idling, adjust the venturi valve diaphragm screw to obtain a reading of 6 in. H_2O. Set the curb idle to specification. Install new venturi valve bypass and diaphragm plugs.

INTERNAL VENT ADJUSTMENT

1977-78 Only

This adjustment is required whenever the idle speed adjustment is changed.

1. Make sure the idle speed is correct.
2. Place a 0.010" (0.254mm) feeler gauge between the accelerator pump stem and the operating link.
3. Turn the nylon adjusting nut until there is a slight drag on the gauge.

VENTURI VALVE LIMITER ADJUSTMENT

1. Remove the carburetor. Take off the venturi valve cover and the two rollers.
2. Use a center punch to loosen the expansion plug at the rear of the carburetor main body on the throttle side. Remove it.

3. Use an Allen wrench to remove the venturi valve wide open stop screw.

4. Hold the throttle wide open.

5. Apply a light closing pressure on the venturi valve and check the gap between the valve and the air horn wall. To adjust, move the venturi valve to the wide open position and insert an Allen wrench into the stop screw hole. Turn clockwise to increase the gap. Remove the wrench and check the gap again.

6. Replace the wide open stop screw and turn it clockwise until it contact the valve.

7. Push the venturi valve wide open and check the gap. Turn the stop screw to bring the gap to specifications.

8. Reassemble the carburetor with a new expansion plug.

CONTROL VACUUM REGULATOR ADJUSTMENT

There are two systems used. The earlier system's C.V.R. rod threads directly through the arm. The revised system, introduced in late 1977, has a ⅜" nylon hex adjusting nut on the C.V.R. rod and a flange on the rod.

Early System

1. Make sure that the cold enrichment metering rod adjustment is correct.

2. Rotate the choke coil cap half a turn clockwise from the index mark. Work the throttle to set the fast idle cam.

3. Press down lightly on the regulator rod. If there is no down travel, turn the adjusting screw counterclockwise until some travel is felt.

4. Turn the regulator rod clockwise with an Allen wrench until the adjusting nut just begins to rise.

5. Press lightly on the regulator rod. If there is any down travel, turn the adjusting screw clockwise in ¼ turn increments until it is eliminated.

6. Return the choke coil cap to the specified setting.

Revised System

The cold enrichment metering rod adjustment must be checked and set before making this adjustment.

1. After adjusting the cold enrichment metering rod, leave the dial indicator in place but remove the stator cap. Do not re-zero the dial indicator.

2. Press down on the C.V.R. rod until it bottoms on its seat. Measure this amount of travel with the dial indicator.

3. If the adjustment is incorrect, hold the ⅜" C.V.R. adjusting nut with a box wrench to prevent it from turning. Use a ³⁄₃₂" Allen wrench to turn the C.V.R. rod; turning counterclockwise will increase the travel, and vice-versa.

HIGH SPEED CAM POSITIONER ADJUSTMENT
1977-1979 Only

1. Place the high speed cam positioner in the corner of the specified cam step, counting the highest step as the first.

2. Place the fast idle lever in the corner of the positioner.

3. Hold the throttle firmly closed.

4. Remove the diaphragm cover. Adjust the diaphragm assembly clockwise until it lightly bottoms. Turn it counterclockwise ½-1½ turns until the vacuum port and diaphragm hole line up.

5. Replace the cover.

IDLE MIXTURE ADJUSTMENT
1977 Only

The results of this adjustment should be checked with an emissions tester, to make sure that emission limits are not exceeded. Idle mixture (idle trim) is not adjustable 1978 and later models.

1. Remove the air cleaner only.

2. Use a ³⁄₃₂" Allen wrench to adjust the mixture for each barrel by turning the air adjusting screw. Turn it clockwise to richen.

DISASSEMBLY

WARNING: *Special tools are required. If you have any doubts about your ability to successfully complete this procedure, leave it to a professional service person.*

Upper Body

1. Remove the fuel inlet fitting, fuel filter, gasket and spring.

2. Remove the screws retaining the upper body assembly and remove the upper body.

3. Remove the float hinge pin and float assembly.

4. Remove the fuel inlet valve, seat and gasket.

5. Remove the accelerator pump rod and the choke control rod.

6. Remove the accelerator pump link retaining pin and the link.

7. Remove the accelerator pump swivel and the retaining nut.

8. Remove the E-ring on the choke hinge pin and slide the pin out of the casting.

9. Remove the cold enrichment rod adjusting nut, lever and swivel; remove the control vacuum nut and regulator as an assembly.

10. Remove the cold enrichment rod.

11. Remove the venturi valve cover plate and

roller bearings. Remove the venturi valve cover plate and roller bearings. Remove the venturi air bypass screw.

12. Using special tool T77P-9928-A, press the tapered plugs out of the venturi valve pivot pins.

13. Remove the venturi valve pivot pins, bushings and the venturi valve.

14. Remove the metering rod pivot pins, springs and metering rods. Be sure to mark the rods so that you know on which side they belong. Also, keep the venturi valve blocked open when working on the jets.

15. Using tool T77L-9533-B, remove the cup plugs.

16. Using tool T77L-9533-A, turn each main metering jet clockwise, counting the number of turns until they bottom in the casting. You will need to know the number of turns when you reassemble the carburetor. Remove the jets and mark them so that you know on which side they belong. Don't lose the O-rings.

17. Remove the accelerator pump plunger assembly.

18. Remove the idle trim screws. Remove the venturi valve limiter adjusting screw.

19. Assembly is the reverse of disassembly.

Main Body

1. Remove the cranking enrichment solenoid and the O-ring seal.

2. Remove the venturi valve cover, spring guide, and spring. Remove the venturi valve.

3. Remove the throttle body.

4. Remove the choke heat shield.

5. Assembly is in the reverse order.

GASOLINE FUEL INJECTION SYSTEM
6-300 (4.9L) ENGINE

CAUTION: *Never smoke when working around gasoline! Avoid all sources of sparks or ignition. Gasoline vapors are EXTREMELY volatile!*

Relieving Fuel System Pressure

1. Disconnect the electrical connection at the fuel pump relay, inertia switch or in-line high pressure fuel pump, whichever is most convenient.

2. Crank the engine for about 10 seconds. NOTE: *The engine may start and run for a brief time. If this happens, let it run until it shuts off, then crank the engine for an additional 5 seconds.*

3. Reconnect the electrical connector.

4. Disconnect the battery ground cable.

Fuel Charging Assembly
REMOVAL AND INSTALLATION

1. Relieve the fuel system pressure.

2. Disconnect the battery ground cable and drain the cooling system.

CAUTION: *When draining the coolant, keep in mind that cats and dogs are attracted by the ethylene glycol antifreeze, and are quite likely to drink any that is left in an uncovered container or in puddles on the ground. This will prove fatal in sufficient quantity. Always drain the coolant into a sealable container. Coolant should be reused unless it is contaminated or several years old.*

3. Label and disconnect the wiring at the:
- Throttle position sensor
- Air bypass valve
- EVP sensor at the EGR valve
- Injection wiring harness
- Engine coolant temperature sensor

4. Label and disconnect the following vaccum connectors:
- EGR valve
- Thermactor air bypass valve
- Throttle body
- Fuel pressure regulator
- Upper intake manifold vacuum tree

5. Disconnect the PCV hose at the upper intake manifold.

6. Remove the throttle linkage shield.

7. Disconnect the throttle linkage and speed control cables.

8. Unbolt the accelerator cable from its bracket and position it out of the way.

9. Disconnect the air inlet hoses from the throttle body.

10. Remove the EGR tube.

11. Remove the Thermactor tube from the lower intake manifold.

12. Remove the nut attaching the

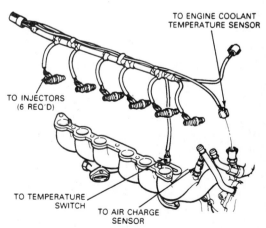

6-300 EFI injectors and fuel rail

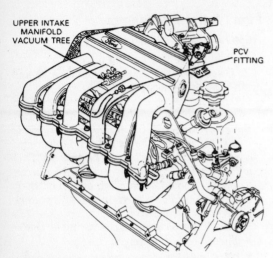

6-300 EFI PCV and vacuum tree fittings

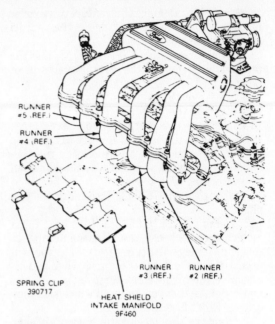

6-300 EFI lower intake manifold heat shield

Thermactor bypass valve bracket to the lower intake manifold.

13. Remove the injector heat shield (2 clips).

14. Remove the 7 studs which retain the upper intake manifold.

15. Remove the screw and washer which retains the upper intake manifold support bracket to the upper intake manifold.

16. Remove the upper intake manifold assembly from the lower intake manifold.

17. Move the vacuum harness away from the lower intake manifold.

18. Remove the injector cooling manifold from the lifting eye attachment.

19. Disconnect the fuel supply and return lines at the quick disconnect couplings using tools T81P-19623-G or T81P-19623-G1.

20. Remove the 16 attaching bolts that the lower intake manifold and exhaust manifolds have in common. DON'T REMOVE THE BOLTS THAT ATTACH ONLY THE EXHAUST MANIFOLDS!

21. Remove the lower intake manifold from the head.

22. Clean and inspect all mating surfaces. All surfaces MUST be flat and free from debris or damage!

23. Clean and oil all fastener threads.

24. Position the lower manifold on the head using a new gasket. Tighten the bolts to 30 ft.lb.

25. Reconnect the vacuum lines at the fuel pressure regulator.

26. Position the upper manifold and new gasket on the lower manifold. Install the fasteners finger tight.

27. Install the upper intake manifold support on the manifold and tighten the retaing screw to 30 ft.lb.

28. Torque the upper-to-lower manifold fasteners to 18 ft.lb.

29. Install the injector heat shield.

30. Install the EGR tube. The tube should be routed between the no. 4 and 5 lower intake runners. Torque the fittings to 35 ft.lb.

31. Install the injector cooling manifold and torque the fasteners to 12 ft.lb.

32. Connect the PCV hose.

33. Install the Thermactor tube and tighten the nuts to 12 ft.lb.

34. Install the accelerator cable and throttle linkages.

35. Connect the air inlet hoses to the throttle body.

36. Connect the vacuum hoses.

37. Connect the electrical wiring.

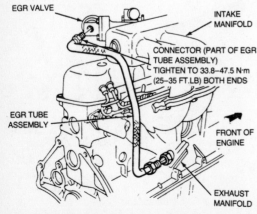

6-300 EFI EGR connections

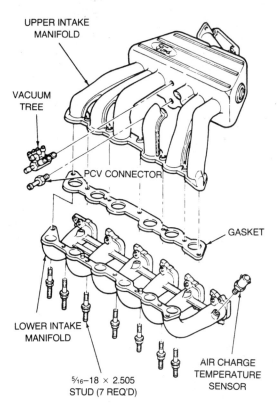

UPPER INTAKE MANIFOLD

VACUUM TREE

PCV CONNECTOR

GASKET

LOWER INTAKE MANIFOLD

⁵⁄₁₆–18 × 2.505 STUD (7 REQ'D)

AIR CHARGE TEMPERATURE SENSOR

6-300 EFI upper and lower intake manifolds

38. Connect the air intake hose, air bypass hose and crankcase vent hose.

39. Connect the battery ground.

40. Refill the cooling system.

41. Install the fuel pressure relief cap. Turn the ignition switch from **OFF** to **ON** at least half a dozen times, **WITHOUT STARTING THE ENGINE**, leaving it in the ON position for about 5 seconds each time. This will build up fuel pressure in the system.

42. Start the engine and allow it to run at idle until normal operating temperature is reached. Check for leaks.

Fuel Injector

REMOVAL AND INSTALLATION

1. Relieve the fuel system pressure.

2. Remove the upper intake manifold assembly.

3. Remove the fuel supply manifold.

4. Disconcct the wiring at each injector.

5. Pull upward on the injector body while gently rocking it from side-to-side.

6. Inspect the O-rings on the injector for any sign of leakage or damage. Replace any suspected O-rings.

7. Inspect the plastic cap at the top of each injector and replace it if any sign of deterioration is noticed.

8. Lubricate the O-rings with clean engine oil ONLY!.

9. Install the injectors by pushing them in with a gentle rocking motion.

10. Install the fuel supply manifold.

11. Connect the electrical wiring.

12. Install the upper intake manifold.

Fuel Pressure Regulator

REMOVAL AND INSTALLATION

1. Relieve the fuel system pressure.

2. Disconnect the vacuum line at the regulator.

3. Remove the 3 allen screws from the regulator housing.

4. Remove the regulator.

5. Inspect the regulator O-ring for signs of deterioration or damage. Discard the gasket.

6. Lubricate the O-ring with clean engine oil ONLY!

7. Make sure that the mounting surfaces are clean.

8. Using a new gasket, install the regulator. Tighten the retaining screws to 40 in.lb.

9. Connect the vacuum line.

Pressure Relief Valve

REMOVAL AND INSTALLATION

1. Relieve the fuel system pressure.

2. Unscrew the valve from the fuel line.

3. When installing the valve, tighten it to 80 in.lb.

4. Tighten the cap to 5 in.lb.

Throttle Position Sensor

REMOVAL AND INSTALLATION

1. Disconnect the wiring harness from the TPS.

2. Matchmark the sensor and throttle body for installation reference.

3. Remove the 2 retaining screws and remove the TPS.

4. Install the TPS so that the wiring harness is parallel with the venturi bores, then, rotate the TPS clockwise to align the scribe marks.

CAUTION: *Slide the rotary tanks into position over the throttle shaft blade, then rotate the TPS CLOCKWISE ONLY to the installed position. FAILURE TO INSTALL THE TPS IN THIS MANNER WILL RESULT IN EXCESSIVE IDLE SPEEDS!*

5. Tighten the retaining screws to 16 in.lb.

NOTE: *When correctly installed, the TPS wirning harness should be pointing directly at the air bypass valve.*

6. Connect the wiring.

Upper Intake Manifold

REMOVAL AND INSTALLATION

1. Relieve the fuel system pressure.
2. Disconnect the battery ground cable and drain the cooling system.

CAUTION: *When draining the coolant, keep in mind that cats and dogs are attracted by the ethylene glycol antifreeze, and are quite likely to drink any that is left in an uncovered container or in puddles on the ground. This will prove fatal in sufficient quantity. Always drain the coolant into a sealable container. Coolant should be reused unless it is contaminated or several years old.*

3. Label and disconnect the wiring at the:
- Throttle position sensor
- Air bypass valve
- EVP sensor at the EGR valve
- Injection wiring harness
- Engine coolant temperature sensor
4. Label and disconnect the following vaccum connectors:
- EGR valve
- Thermactor air bypass valve
- Throttle body
- Fuel pressure regulator
- Upper intake manifold vacuum tree
5. Disconnect the PCV hose at the upper intake manifold.
6. Remove the throttle linkage shield.
7. Disconnect the throttle linkage and speed control cables.
8. Unbolt the accelerator cable from its bracket and position it out of the way.
9. Disconnect the air inlet hoses from the throttle body.
10. Remove the EGR tube.
11. Remove the Thermactor tube from the lower intake manifold.
12. Remove the nut attaching the Thermactor bypass valve bracket to the lower intake manifold.
13. Remove the injector heat shield (2 clips).
14. Remove the 7 studs which retain the upper intake manifold.
15. Remove the screw and washer which retains the upper intake manifold support bracket to the upper intake manifold.
16. Remove the upper intake manifold assembly from the lower intake manifold.
17. Clean and inspect all mating surfaces. All surfaces MUST be flat and free from debris or damage!
18. Clean and oil all fastener threads.
19. Position the upper manifold and new gasket on the lower manifold. Install the fasteners finger tight.
20. Install the upper intake manifold support

on the manifold and tighten the retaing screw to 30 ft.lb.
21. Torque the upper-to-lower manifold fasteners to 18 ft.lb.
22. Install the injector heat shield.
23. Install the EGR tube. The tube should be routed between the no. 4 and 5 lower intake runners. Torque the fittings to 35 ft.lb.
24. Install the injector cooling manifold and torque the fasteners to 12 ft.lb.
25. Connect the PCV hose.
26. Install the Thermactor tube and tighten the nuts to 12 ft.lb.
27. Install the accelerator cable and throttle linkages.
28. Connect the air inlet hoses to the throttle body.
29. Connect the vacuum hoses.
30. Connect the electrical wiring.
31. Connect the air intake hose, air bypas hose and crankcase vent hose.
32. Connect the battery ground.
33. Refill the cooling system.
34. Install the fuel pressure relief cap. Turn the ignition switch from **OFF** to **ON** at least half a dozen times, **WITHOUT STARTING THE ENGINE**, leaving it in the ON position for about 5 seconds each time. This will build up fuel pressure in the system.
35. Start the engine and allow it to run at idle until normal operating temperature is reached. Check for leaks.

Air Intake Throttle Body

REMOVAL AND INSTALLATION

1. Disconnect the air intake hose.
2. Disconnect the throttle position sensor and air by-pass valve connectors.
3. Remove the four throttle body mounting nuts and carefully separate the air throttle body from the upper intake manifold.
4. Remove and discard the mounting gasket. Clean all mounting surfaces using care not to damage the gasket surfaces of the throttle body and manifold. Do not allow any material to drop into the intake manifold.
5. Install the throttle body in the reverse order of removal. The mounting nuts are tightened to 12-15 ft.lb.

Fuel Supply Manifold

REMOVAL AND INSTALLATION

1. Relive the fuel system pressure as noted above.
2. Remove the upper intake manifold assembly.

NOTE: *Special tool T81P-19623-G or equiv-*

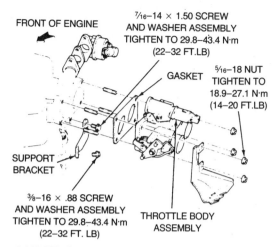

6-300 EFI air throttle body

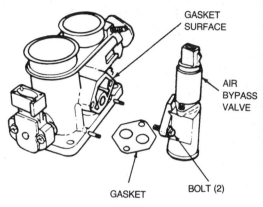

6-300 EFI air bypass valve

alent is necessary to release the garter springs that secure the fuel line/hose connections.

3. Disconnect the fuel crossover hose from the fuel supply manifold. Disconnect the fuel supply and return line connections at the fuel supply manifold.

4. Remove the two fuel supply manifold retaining bolts. Carefully disengage the manifold from the fuel injectors and remove the manifold.

5. When installing: make sure the injector caps are clean and free of contamination. Place the fuel supply manifold over each injector and seat the injectors into the manifold. Make sure the caps are seated firmly.

6. Torque the fuel supply manifold retaining bolts to 15-22 ft.lbs. Install the remaining components in the reverse order of removal.

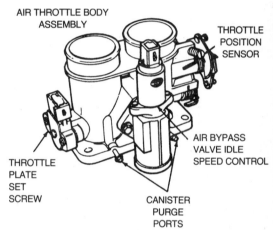

6-300 EFI throttle body

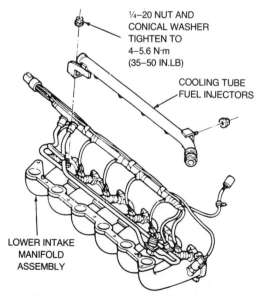

6-300 EFI injector cooling manifold removal

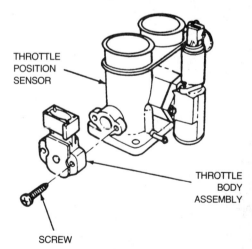

6-300 EFI throttle position sensor

NOTE: *Fuel injectors may be serviced after the fuel supply manifold is removed. Grasp the injector and pull up on it while gently rocking injector from side to side. Inspect the mounting O-rings and replace any that show deterioration.*

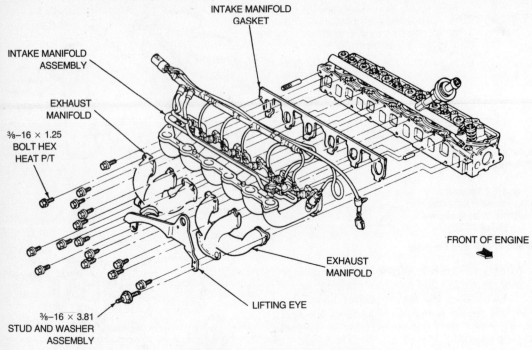

6-300 EFI lower intake manifold removal

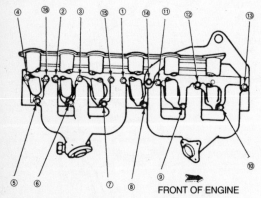

6-300 EFI exhaust manifold torque sequence

GASOLINE FUEL INJECTION
8-302 (5.0L)
8-351 (5.8L)

Relieving Fuel System Pressure

1. Disconnect the electrical connection at the fuel pump relay, inertia switch or in-line high pressure fuel pump, whichever is most convenient.

2. Crank the engine for about 10 seconds.
NOTE: *The engine may start and run for a brief time. If this happens, let it run until it shuts off, then crank the engine for an additional 5 seconds.*

3. Reconnect the electrical connector.
4. Disconnect the battery ground cable.

Air Bypass Valve
REMOVAL AND INSTALLATION

1. Disconnect the wiring at the valve.
2. Remove the 2 retaining screws and lift off the valve.
3. Discard the gasket and clean and inspect the mating surfaces.
4. Install the valve with a new gasket, tightening the screws to 102 in.lb.
5. Connect the wiring.

Air Intake Throttle Body
REMOVAL AND INSTALLATION

1. Disconnect the air intake hose.
2. Disconnect the throttle position sensor and air by-pass valve connectors.
3. Remove the four throttle body mounting nuts and carefully separate the air throttle body from the upper intake manifold.
4. Remove and discard the mounting gasket. Clean all mounting surfaces using care not to damage the gasket surfaces of the throttle body and manifold. Do not allow any material to drop into the intake manifold.
5. Install the throttle body in the reverse order of removal. The mounting nuts are tightened to 12-18 ft.lb.

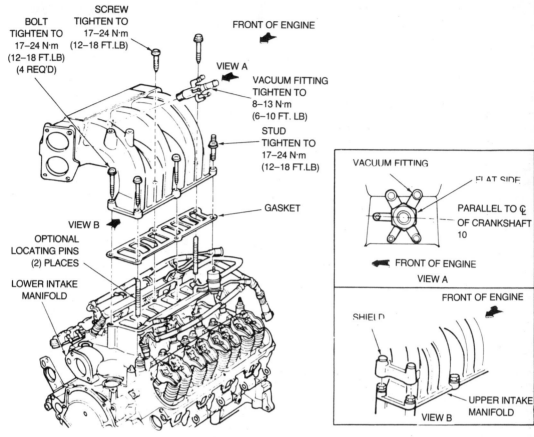

BOLT
TIGHTEN TO
17–24 N·m
(12–18 FT.LB)
(4 REQ'D)

SCREW
TIGHTEN TO
17–24 N·m
(12–18 FT.LB)

FRONT OF ENGINE

VIEW A

VACUUM FITTING
TIGHTEN TO
8–13 N·m
(6–10 FT. LB)

STUD
TIGHTEN TO
17–24 N·m
(12–18 FT.LB)

GASKET

VIEW B

OPTIONAL
LOCATING PINS
(2) PLACES

LOWER INTAKE
MANIFOLD

VACUUM FITTING

FLAT SIDE

PARALLEL TO ₵
OF CRANKSHAFT
10

FRONT OF ENGINE
VIEW A

FRONT OF ENGINE

SHIELD

UPPER INTAKE
MANIFOLD

VIEW B

8-302, 351 EFI upper intake manifold

Fuel Charging Assembly
REMOVAL AND INSTALLATION

1. Relieve the fuel system pressure.
2. Disconnect the battery ground cable and drain the cooling system.

CAUTION: *When draining the coolant, keep in mind that cats and dogs are attracted by the ethylene glycol antifreeze, and are quite likely to drink any that is left in an uncovered container or in puddles on the ground. This will prove fatal in sufficient quantity. Always drain the coolant into a sealable container. Coolant should be reused unless it is contaminated or several years old.*

3. Label and disconnect the wiring at the:
• Throttle position sensor
• Air bypass valve
• EGR sensor
4. Label and disconnect the following vaccum connectors:
• EGR valve
• Fuel pressure regulator
• Upper intake manifold vacuum tree
5. Disconnect the PCV hose at the upper intake manifold.
6. Remove the throttle linkage at the throttle ball and AOD transmission linkage at the throttle body.
7. Unbolt the cable bracket from the manifold and position the cables and bracket away from the engine.
8. Disconnect the 2 canister purge lines at the throttle body.

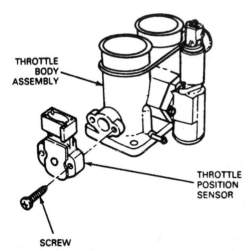

THROTTLE
BODY
ASSEMBLY

THROTTLE
POSITION
SENSOR

SCREW

8-302, 351 throttle position sensor

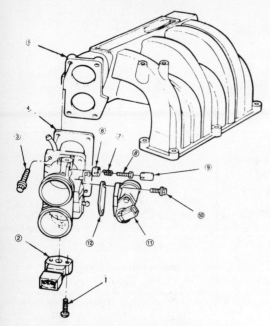

1. Screw and washer assembly—M4 × 22
2. Throttle position sensor
3. Bolt—5 16–18 × 1.25
4. Gasket—air intake charge throttle
5. Manifold—intake upper
6. Plug—throttle plate set screw locking
7. Spring—throttle plate set screw
8. Screw—10.32 × 1 50 hex head slotted
9. Cap—throttle plate set screw
10. Bolt—M6 × 20
11. Air bypass valve assembly
12. Gasket—air bypass

8-302, 351 throttle body removal

9. Disconnect the water heater lines from the throttle body.

10. Remove the EGR tube.

11. Remove the screw and washer which retains the upper intake manifold support bracket to the upper intake manifold.

12. Remove the 6 bolts which retain the upper intake manifold.

13. Remove the upper intake manifold assembly from the lower intake manifold.

14. Remove the distributor. (See Chapter 3).

15. Disconnect the wiring at the:
- Engine coolant temperature sensor.
- Engine temperature sending unit.
- Air charge temperature sensor.
- Knock sensor.
- Electrical vacuum regulator.
- Thermactor solenoids.

16. Disconnect the injector wiring harness at the main harness.

17. Remove the EGO ground wire at its intake manifold stud. Note the position of the stud and bround wire for installation.

18. Disconnect the fuel supply and return lines from the fuel rails using tool T81P-19623-G or G1.

19. Remove the upper radiator hose.

20. Remove the coolant bypass hose.

21. Disconnect the heater outlet hose at the manifold.

22. Remove the air cleaner bracket.

23. Remove the coil.

24. Noting the location of each bolt, remove the intkae manifold retaining bolts.

25. Remove the lower intake manifold from the head.

26. Clean and inspect all mating surfaces. All surfaces MUST be flat and free from debris or damage!

27. Clean and oil all fastener threads.

28. Place a $\frac{1}{16}$" bead of RTV silicone sealant to the end seals' junctions.

29. Position the end seals on the block.

30. Install 2 locator pins at opposite corners of the block.

31. Position the lower manifold on the head using new gaskets. Install the bolts and remove the locating pins.

32. Tighten the bolts to 25 ft.lb. in sequence. Wait ten minutes and retorque the bolts in sequence.

33. Install the coil.

34. Connect the cooling system hoses.

35. Connect the fuel supply and return lines.

36. Connect the wiring at the:
- Engine coolant temperature sensor.
- Engine temperature sending unit.
- Air charge temperature sensor.
- Knock sensor.
- Electrical vacuum regulator.
- Thermactor solenoids.

37. Install the distributor.

38. Position the upper manifold and new gasket on the lower manifold. Install the fasteners finger tight.

39. Install the upper intake manifold support on the manifold and tighten the retaing screw to 30 ft.lb.

40. Torque the upper-to-lower manifold fasteners to 18 ft.lb.

41. Install the EGR tube. Torque the fittings to 35 ft.lb.

42. Install the canister purge lines at the throttle body.

43. Connect the water heater lines at the throttle body.

44. Connect the PCV hose.

45. Install the accelerator cable and throttle linkages.

46. Connect the vacuum hoses.

47. Connect the electrical wiring.

48. Connect the air intake hose, air bypas hose and crankcase vent hose.

49. Connect the battery ground.

50. Refill the cooling system.

51. Install the fuel pressure relief cap. Turn the ignition switch from **OFF** to **ON** at least half a dozen times, **WITHOUT STARTING THE ENGINE,** leaving it in the ON position for about 5 seconds each time. This will build up fuel pressure in the system.

52. Start the engine and allow it to run at idle until normal operating temperature is reached. Check for leaks.

Fuel Injectors

REMOVAL AND INSTALLATION

1. Relieve the fuel system pressure.
2. Disconnect the battery ground.
3. Remove the upper intake manifold.
4. Disconnect the wiring at the injectors.
5. Pull upward on the injector body while gently rocking it from side-to-side.
6. Inspect the O-rings on the injector for any sign of leakage or damage. Replace any suspected O-rings.
7. Inspect the plastic cap at the top of each injector and replace it if any sign of deterioration is noticed.
8. Lubricate the O-rings with clean engine oil ONLY!.
9. Install the injectors by pushing them in with a gentle rocking motion.
10. Install the fuel supply manifold.
11. Connect the electrical wiring.
12. Install the upper intake manifold.

Fuel Pressure Regulator

REMOVAL AND INSTALLATION

1. Relieve the fuel system pressure.
2. Disconnect the vacuum line at the regulator.
3. Remove the 3 allen screws from the regulator housing.
4. Remove the regulator.

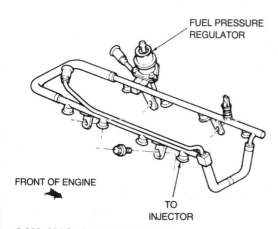

FRONT OF ENGINE

FUEL PRESSURE REGULATOR

TO INJECTOR

8-302, 351 fuel pressure regulator

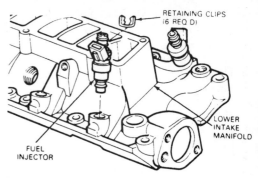

RETAINING CLIPS (6 REQ D)

LOWER INTAKE MANIFOLD

FUEL INJECTOR

8-320, 351 EFI fuel injector

5. Inspect the regulator O-ring for signs of deterioration or damage. Discard the gasket.
6. Lubricate the O-ring with clean engine oil ONLY!
7. Make sure that the mounting surfaces are clean.
8. Using a new gasket, install the regulator. Tighten the retaining screws to 40 in.lb.
9. Connect the vacuum line.

Fuel Supply Manifold

REMOVAL AND INSTALLATION

1. Relieve the fuel system pressure.
2. Remove the upper manifold.
3. Disconnect the chassis fuel inlet and outlet lines at the fuel supply manifold using tool T81P-19623-G or G1.
4. Disconnect the fuel supply and return lines at the fuel supply manifold.
5. Remove the 4 fuel supply manifold retaining bolts.
6. Carefully disengage the manifold from the injectors and lift it off.
7. Inspect all components for signs of damage. Make sure that the injector caps are clean.
8. Place the fuel supply manifold over the injectors and seat the injectors carefully in the manifold.
9. Install the 4 bolts and torque them to 20 ft.lb.
10. Connect the fuel lines.
11. Install the upper manifold.

Lower Intake Manifold

REMOVAL AND INSTALLATION

1. Relieve the fuel system pressure.
2. Disconnect the battery ground cable and drain the cooling system.

CAUTION: *When draining the coolant, keep in mind that cats and dogs are attracted by the ethylene glycol antifreeze, and are quite likely to drink any that is left in an uncovered container or in puddles on the ground. This will prove fatal in sufficient quantity. Always drain the coolant into a sealable container. Coolant should be reused unless it is contaminated or several years old.*

3. Label and disconnect the wiring at the:
- Throttle position sensor
- Air bypass valve
- EGR sensor

4. Label and disconnect the following vaccum connectors:
- EGR valve
- Fuel pressure regulator
- Upper intake manifold vacuum tree

5. Disconnect the PCV hose at the upper intake manifold.

6. Remove the throttle linkage at the throttle ball and AOD transmission linkage at the throttle body.

7. Unbolt the cable bracket from the manifold and position the cables and bracket away from the engine.

8. Disconnect the 2 canister purge lines at the throttle body.

9. Disconnect the water heater lines from the throttle body.

10. Remove the EGR tube.

11. Remove the screw and washer which retains the upper intake manifold support bracket to the upper intake manifold.

12. Remove the 6 bolts which retain the upper intake manifold.

13. Remove the upper intake manifold assembly from the lower intake manifold.

14. Remove the distributor. (See Chapter 3).

15. Disconnect the wiring at the:
- Engine coolant temperature sensor.
- Engine temperature sending unit.
- Air charge temperature sensor.
- Knock sensor.
- Electrical vacuum regulator.
- Thermactor solenoids.

16. Disconnect the injector wiring harness at the main harness.

17. Remove the EGO ground wire at its intake manifold stud. Note the position of the stud and bround wire for installation.

18. Disconnect the fuel supply and return lines from the fuel rails using tool T81P-19623-G or G1.

19. Remove the upper radiator hose.

20. Remove the coolant bypass hose.

21. Disconnect the heater outlet hose at the manifold.

22. Remove the air cleaner bracket.

23. Remove the coil.

24. Noting the location of each bolt, remove the intkae manifold retaining bolts.

25. Remove the lower intake manifold from the head.

26. Clean and inspect all mating surfaces. All surfaces MUST be flat and free from debris or damage!

27. Clean and oil all fastener threads.

28. Place a $1/16''$ bead of RTV silicone sealant to the end seals' junctions.

29. Position the end seals on the block.

30. Install 2 locator pins at opposite corners of the block.

31. Position the lower manifold on the head using new gaskets. Install the bolts and remove the locating pins.

32. Tighten the bolts to 25 ft.lb. in sequence. Wait ten minutes and retorque the bolts in sequence.

33. Install the coil.

34. Connect the cooling system hoses.

35. Connect the fuel supply and return lines.

36. Connect the wiring at the:
- Engine coolant temperature sensor.
- Engine temperature sending unit.
- Air charge temperature sensor.
- Knock sensor.
- Electrical vacuum regulator.
- Thermactor solenoids.

37. Install the distributor.

38. Position the upper manifold and new gasket on the lower manifold. Install the fasteners finger tight.

39. Install the upper intake manifold support on the manifold and tighten the retaing screw to 30 ft.lb.

40. Torque the upper-to-lower manifold fasteners to 18 ft.lb.

41. Install the EGR tube. Torque the fittings to 35 ft.lb.

42. Install the canister purge lines at the throttle body.

43. Connect the water heater lines at the throttle body.

44. Connect the PCV hose.

45. Install the accelerator cable and throttle linkages.

46. Connect the vacuum hoses.

47. Connect the electrical wiring.

48. Connect the air intake hose, air bypass hose and crankcase vent hose.

49. Connect the battery ground.

50. Refill the cooling system.

51. Install the fuel pressure relief cap. Turn the ignition switch from **OFF** to **ON** at least half a dozen times, **WITHOUT STARTING THE ENGINE,** leaving it in the ON position for about 5 seconds each time. This will build up fuel pressure in the system.

52. Start the engine and allow it to run at idle until normal operating temperature is reached. Check for leaks.

Throttle Position Sensor
REMOVAL AND INSTALLATION

1. Disconnect the wiring harness from the TPS.

CHILTON'S
FUEL ECONOMY
& TUNE-UP TIPS

Tune-up • Spark Plug Diagnosis • Emission Controls

Fuel System • Cooling System • Tires and Wheels

General Maintenance

CHILTON'S FUEL ECONOMY & TUNE-UP TIPS

Fuel economy is important to everyone, no matter what kind of vehicle you drive. The maintenance-minded motorist can save both money and fuel using these tips and the periodic maintenance and tune-up procedures in this Repair and Tune-Up Guide.

There are more than 130,000,000 cars and trucks registered for private use in the United States. Each travels an average of 10-12,000 miles per year, and, and in total they consume close to 70 billion gallons of fuel each year. This represents nearly ⅔ of the oil imported by the United States each year. The Federal government's goal is to reduce consumption 10% by 1985. A variety of methods are either already in use or under serious consideration, and they all affect you driving and the cars you will drive. In addition to "down-sizing", the auto industry is using or investigating the use of electronic fuel delivery, electronic engine controls and alternative engines for use in smaller and lighter vehicles, among other alternatives to meet the federally mandated Corporate Average Fuel Economy (CAFE) of 27.5 mpg by 1985. The government, for its part, is considering rationing, mandatory driving curtailments and tax increases on motor vehicle fuel in an effort to reduce consumption. The government's goal of a 10% reduction could be realized — and further government regulation avoided — if every private vehicle could use just 1 less gallon of fuel per week.

How Much Can You Save?

Tests have proven that almost anyone can make at least a 10% reduction in fuel consumption through regular maintenance and tune-ups. When a major manufacturer of spark plugs sur-

TUNE-UP

1. Check the cylinder compression to be sure the engine will really benefit from a tune-up and that it is capable of producing good fuel economy. A tune-up will be wasted on an engine in poor mechanical condition.

2. Replace spark plugs regularly. New spark plugs alone can increase fuel economy 3%.

3. Be sure the spark plugs are the correct type (heat range) for your vehicle. See the Tune-Up Specifications.

Heat range refers to the spark plug's ability to conduct heat away from the firing end. It must conduct the heat away in an even pattern to avoid becoming a source of pre-ignition, yet it must also operate hot enough to burn off conductive deposits that could cause misfiring.

The heat range is usually indicated by a number on the spark plug, part of the manufacturer's designation for each individual spark plug. The numbers in bold-face indicate the heat range in each manufacturer's identification system.

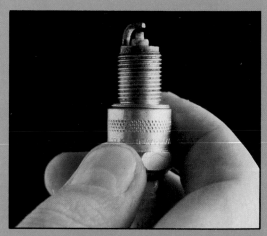

Periodically, check the spark plugs to be sure they are firing efficiently. They are excellent indicators of the internal condition of your engine.

Manufacturer	Typical Designation
AC	R **45** TS
Bosch (old)	WA **145** T30
Bosch (new)	HR **8** Y
Champion	RBL **15** Y
Fram/Autolite	4**15**
Mopar	P-**62** PR
Motorcraft	BRF-**42**
NGK	BP **5** ES-15
Nippondenso	W **16** EP
Prestolite	14GR **5** 2A

On AC, Bosch (new), Champion, Fram/Autolite, Mopar, Motorcraft and Prestolite, a higher number indicates a hotter plug. On Bosch (old), NGK and Nippondenso, a higher number indicates a colder plug.

4. Make sure the spark plugs are properly gapped. See the Tune-Up Specifications in this book.

5. Be sure the spark plugs are firing efficiently. The illustrations on the next 2 pages show you how to "read" the firing end of the spark plug.

6. Check the ignition timing and set it to specifications. Tests show that almost all cars have incorrect ignition timing by more than 2°.

veyed over 6,000 cars nationwide, they found that a tune-up, on cars that needed one, increased fuel economy over 11%. Replacing worn plugs alone, accounted for a 3% increase. The same test also revealed that 8 out of every 10 vehicles will have some maintenance deficiency that will directly affect fuel economy, emissions or performance. Most of this mileage-robbing neglect could be prevented with regular maintenance.

Modern engines require that all of the functioning systems operate properly for maximum efficiency. A malfunction anywhere wastes fuel. You can keep your vehicle running as efficiently and economically as possible, by being aware of your vehicle's operating and performance characteristics. If your vehicle suddenly develops performance or fuel economy problems it could be due to one or more of the following:

PROBLEM	POSSIBLE CAUSE
Engine Idles Rough	Ignition timing, idle mixture, vacuum leak or something amiss in the emission control system.
Hesitates on Acceleration	Dirty carburetor or fuel filter, improper accelerator pump setting, ignition timing or fouled spark plugs.
Starts Hard or Fails to Start	Worn spark plugs, improperly set automatic choke, ice (or water) in fuel system.
Stalls Frequently	Automatic choke improperly adjusted and possible dirty air filter or fuel filter.
Performs Sluggishly	Worn spark plugs, dirty fuel or air filter, ignition timing or automatic choke out of adjustment.

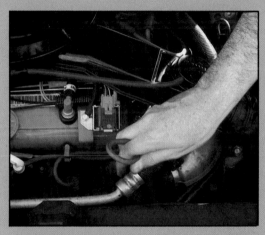

Check spark plug wires on conventional point type ignition for cracks by bending them in a loop around your finger.

Be sure that spark plug wires leading to adjacent cylinders do not run too close together. (Photo courtesy Champion Spark Plug Co.)

7. If your vehicle does not have electronic ignition, check the points, rotor and cap as specified.

8. Check the spark plug wires (used with conventional point-type ignitions) for cracks and burned or broken insulation by bending them in a loop around your finger. Cracked wires decrease fuel efficiency by failing to deliver full voltage to the spark plugs. One misfiring spark plug can cost you as much as 2 mpg.

9. Check the routing of the plug wires. Misfiring can be the result of spark plug leads to adjacent cylinders running parallel to each other and too close together. One wire tends to

pick up voltage from the other causing it to fire "out of time".

10. Check all electrical and ignition circuits for voltage drop and resistance.

11. Check the distributor mechanical and/or vacuum advance mechanisms for proper functioning. The vacuum advance can be checked by twisting the distributor plate in the opposite direction of rotation. It should spring back when released.

12. Check and adjust the valve clearance on engines with mechanical lifters. The clearance should be slightly loose rather than too tight.

SPARK PLUG DIAGNOSIS

Normal

APPEARANCE: This plug is typical of one operating normally. The insulator nose varies from a light tan to grayish color with slight electrode wear. The presence of slight deposits is normal on used plugs and will have no adverse effect on engine performance. The spark plug heat range is correct for the engine and the engine is running normally.

CAUSE: Properly running engine.

RECOMMENDATION: Before reinstalling this plug, the electrodes should be cleaned and filed square. Set the gap to specifications. If the plug has been in service for more than 10-12,000 miles, the entire set should probably be replaced with a fresh set of the same heat range.

Oil Deposits

APPEARANCE: The firing end of the plug is covered with a wet, oily coating.

CAUSE: The problem is poor oil control. On high mileage engines, oil is leaking past the rings or valve guides into the combustion chamber. A common cause is also a plugged PCV valve, and a ruptured fuel pump diaphragm can also cause this condition. Oil fouled plugs such as these are often found in new or recently overhauled engines, before normal oil control is achieved, and can be cleaned and reinstalled.

RECOMMENDATION: A hotter spark plug may temporarily relieve the problem, but the engine is probably in need of work.

Incorrect Heat Range

APPEARANCE: The effects of high temperature on a spark plug are indicated by clean white, often blistered insulator. This can also be accompanied by excessive wear of the electrode, and the absence of deposits.

CAUSE: Check for the correct spark plug heat range. A plug which is too hot for the engine can result in overheating. A car operated mostly at high speeds can require a colder plug. Also check ignition timing, cooling system level, fuel mixture and leaking intake manifold.

RECOMMENDATION: If all ignition and engine adjustments are known to be correct, and no other malfunction exists, install spark plugs one heat range colder.

Photos Courtesy Fram Corporation

Carbon Deposits

APPEARANCE: Carbon fouling is easily identified by the presence of dry, soft, black, sooty deposits.

CAUSE: Changing the heat range can often lead to carbon fouling, as can prolonged slow, stop-and-start driving. If the heat range is correct, carbon fouling can be attributed to a rich fuel mixture, sticking choke, clogged air cleaner, worn breaker points, retarded timing or low compression. If only one or two plugs are carbon fouled, check for corroded or cracked wires on the affected plugs. Also look for cracks in the distributor cap between the towers of affected cylinders.

RECOMMENDATION: After the problem is corrected, these plugs can be cleaned and reinstalled if not worn severely.

MMT Fouled

APPEARANCE: Spark plugs fouled by MMT (Methycyclopentadienyl Maganese Tricarbonyl) have reddish, rusty appearance on the insulator and side electrode.

CAUSE: MMT is an anti-knock additive in gasoline used to replace lead. During the combustion process, the MMT leaves a reddish deposit on the insulator and side electrode.

RECOMMENDATION: No engine malfunction is indicated and the deposits will not affect plug performance any more than lead deposits (see Ash Deposits). MMT fouled plugs can be cleaned, regapped and reinstalled.

High Speed Glazing

APPEARANCE: Glazing appears as shiny coating on the plug, either yellow or tan in color.

CAUSE: During hard, fast acceleration, plug temperatures rise suddenly. Deposits from normal combustion have no chance to fluff-off; instead, they melt on the insulator forming an electrically conductive coating which causes misfiring.

RECOMMENDATION: Glazed plugs are not easily cleaned. They should be replaced with a fresh set of plugs of the correct heat range. If the condition recurs, using plugs with a heat range one step colder may cure the problem.

Ash (Lead) Deposits

APPEARANCE: Ash deposits are characterized by light brown or white colored deposits crusted on the side or center electrodes. In some cases it may give the plug a rusty appearance.

CAUSE: Ash deposits are normally derived from oil or fuel additives burned during normal combustion. Normally they are harmless, though excessive amounts can cause misfiring. If deposits are excessive in short mileage, the valve guides may be worn.

RECOMMENDATION: Ash-fouled plugs can be cleaned, gapped and reinstalled.

Detonation

APPEARANCE: Detonation is usually characterized by a broken plug insulator.

CAUSE: A portion of the fuel charge will begin to burn spontaneously, from the increased heat following ignition. The explosion that results applies extreme pressure to engine components, frequently damaging spark plugs and pistons.

Detonation can result by over-advanced ignition timing, inferior gasoline (low octane) lean air/fuel mixture, poor carburetion, engine lugging or an increase in compression ratio due to combustion chamber deposits or engine modification.

RECOMMENDATION: Replace the plugs after correcting the problem.

Photos Courtesy Champion Spark Plug Co.

EMISSION CONTROLS

13. Be aware of the general condition of the emission control system. It contributes to reduced pollution and should be serviced regularly to maintain efficient engine operation.

14. Check all vacuum lines for dried, cracked or brittle conditions. Something as simple as a leaking vacuum hose can cause poor performance and loss of economy.

15. Avoid tampering with the emission control system. Attempting to improve fuel econ-

FUEL SYSTEM

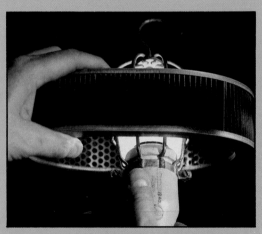

Check the air filter with a light behind it. If you can see light through the filter it can be reused.

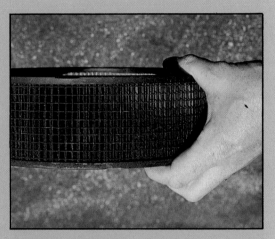

Extremely clogged filters should be discarded and replaced with a new one.

18. Replace the air filter regularly. A dirty air filter richens the air/fuel mixture and can increase fuel consumption as much as 10%. Tests show that 1/3 of all vehicles have air filters in need of replacement.

19. Replace the fuel filter at least as often as recommended.

20. Set the idle speed and carburetor mixture to specifications.

21. Check the automatic choke. A sticking or malfunctioning choke wastes gas.

22. During the summer months, adjust the automatic choke for a leaner mixture which will produce faster engine warm-ups.

COOLING SYSTEM

29. Be sure all accessory drive belts are in good condition. Check for cracks or wear.

30. Adjust all accessory drive belts to proper tension.

31. Check all hoses for swollen areas, worn spots, or loose clamps.

32. Check coolant level in the radiator or ex-pansion tank.

33. Be sure the thermostat is operating properly. A stuck thermostat delays engine warm-up and a cold engine uses nearly twice as much fuel as a warm engine.

34. Drain and replace the engine coolant at least as often as recommended. Rust and scale

TIRES & WHEELS

38. Check the tire pressure often with a pencil type gauge. Tests by a major tire manufacturer show that 90% of all vehicles have at least 1 tire improperly inflated. Better mileage can be achieved by over-inflating tires, but never exceed the maximum inflation pressure on the side of the tire.

39. If possible, install radial tires. Radial tires deliver as much as 1/2 mpg more than bias belted tires.

40. Avoid installing super-wide tires. They only create extra rolling resistance and decrease fuel mileage. Stick to the manufacturer's recommendations.

41. Have the wheels properly balanced.

omy by tampering with emission controls is more likely to worsen fuel economy than improve it. Emission control changes on modern engines are not readily reversible.

16. Clean (or replace) the EGR valve and lines as recommended.

17. Be sure that all vacuum lines and hoses are reconnected properly after working under the hood. An unconnected or misrouted vacuum line can wreak havoc with engine performance.

23. Check for fuel leaks at the carburetor, fuel pump, fuel lines and fuel tank. Be sure all lines and connections are tight.

24. Periodically check the tightness of the carburetor and intake manifold attaching nuts and bolts. These are a common place for vacuum leaks to occur.

25. Clean the carburetor periodically and lubricate the linkage.

26. The condition of the tailpipe can be an excellent indicator of proper engine combustion. After a long drive at highway speeds, the inside of the tailpipe should be a light grey in color. Black or soot on the insides indicates an overly rich mixture.

27. Check the fuel pump pressure. The fuel pump may be supplying more fuel than the engine needs.

28. Use the proper grade of gasoline for your engine. Don't try to compensate for knocking or "pinging" by advancing the ignition timing. This practice will only increase plug temperature and the chances of detonation or pre-ignition with relatively little performance gain.

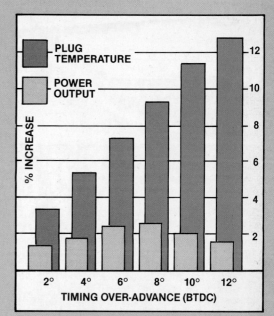

Increasing ignition timing past the specified setting results in a drastic increase in spark plug temperature with increased chance of detonation or preignition. Performance increase is considerably less. (Photo courtesy Champion Spark Plug Co.)

that form in the engine should be flushed out to allow the engine to operate at peak efficiency.

35. Clean the radiator of debris that can decrease cooling efficiency.

36. Install a flex-type or electric cooling fan, if you don't have a clutch type fan. Flex fans use curved plastic blades to push more air at low speeds when more cooling is needed; at high speeds the blades flatten out for less resistance. Electric fans only run when the engine temperature reaches a predetermined level.

37. Check the radiator cap for a worn or cracked gasket. If the cap does not seal properly, the cooling system will not function properly.

42. Be sure the front end is correctly aligned. A misaligned front end actually has wheels going in differed directions. The increased drag can reduce fuel economy by .3 mpg.

43. Correctly adjust the wheel bearings. Wheel bearings that are adjusted too tight increase rolling resistance.

Check tire pressures regularly with a reliable pocket type gauge. Be sure to check the pressure on a cold tire.

GENERAL MAINTENANCE

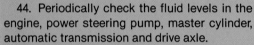

Check the fluid levels (particularly engine oil) on a regular basis. Be sure to check the oil for grit, water or other contamination.

A vacuum gauge is another excellent indicator of internal engine condition and can also be installed in the dash as a mileage indicator.

44. Periodically check the fluid levels in the engine, power steering pump, master cylinder, automatic transmission and drive axle.

45. Change the oil at the recommended interval and change the filter at every oil change. Dirty oil is thick and causes extra friction between moving parts, cutting efficiency and increasing wear. A worn engine requires more frequent tune-ups and gets progressively worse fuel economy. In general, use the lightest viscosity oil for the driving conditions you will encounter.

46. Use the recommended viscosity fluids in the transmission and axle.

47. Be sure the battery is fully charged for fast starts. A slow starting engine wastes fuel.

48. Be sure battery terminals are clean and tight.

49. Check the battery electrolyte level and add distilled water if necessary.

50. Check the exhaust system for crushed pipes, blockages and leaks.

51. Adjust the brakes. Dragging brakes or brakes that are not releasing create increased drag on the engine.

52. Install a vacuum gauge or miles-per-gallon gauge. These gauges visually indicate engine vacuum in the intake manifold. High vacuum = good mileage and low vacuum = poorer mileage. The gauge can also be an excellent indicator of internal engine conditions.

53. Be sure the clutch is properly adjusted. A slipping clutch wastes fuel.

54. Check and periodically lubricate the heat control valve in the exhaust manifold. A sticking or inoperative valve prevents engine warm-up and wastes gas.

55. Keep accurate records to check fuel economy over a period of time. A sudden drop in fuel economy may signal a need for tune-up or other maintenance.

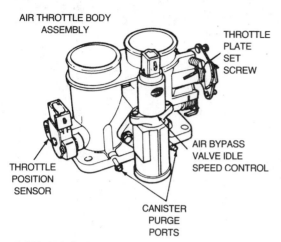

8-302, 351 air throttle body

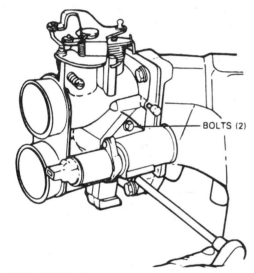

8-302, 351 EFI air bypass valve

2. Matchmark the sensor and throttle body for installation reference.

3. Remove the 2 retaining screws and remove the TPS.

4. Install the TPS so that the wiring harness is parallel with the venturi bores, then, rotate the TPS clockwise to align the scribe marks.

CAUTION: *Slide the rotary tanks into position over the throttle shaft blade, then rotate the TPS CLOCKWISE ONLY to the installed position. FAILURE TO INSTALL THE TPS IN THIS MANNER WILL RESULT IN EXCESSIVE IDLE SPEEDS!*

5. Tighten the retaining screws to 16 in.lb.

NOTE: *When correctly installed, the TPS wirning harness should be pointing directly at the air bypass valve.*

6. Connect the wiring.

GASOLINE FUEL INJECTION 8-460

Relieving Fuel System Pressure

NOTE: *A special tool is necessary for this procedure.*

1. Make sure the ignition switch is in the OFF position.

2. Disconnect the battery ground.

3. Remove the fuel filler cap.

4. Using EFI Pressure Gauge T80L-9974-A, or equivalent, at the fuel pressure relief valve (located in the fuel line in the upper right corner of the engine compartment) relieve the fuel system pressure. A valve cap must first be removed to gain access to the pressure relief valve.

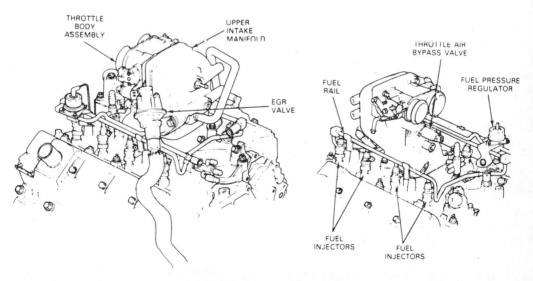

8-460 EFI system components

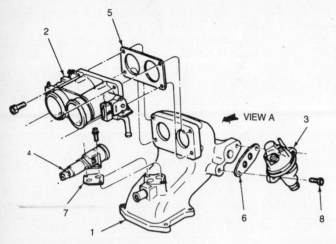

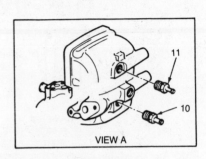

VIEW A

1. Manifold assembly—intake
2. Body assembly—air intake charge throttle
3. Valve assembly—EGR vacuum external
4. Valve assembly—throttle air bypass
5. Gasket—air charge control intake manifold
6. Gasket—EGR valve
7. Gasket—air bypass valve
8. Bolt ⁵⁄₁₆ × 1.5 Hex head ubs (6 reqd)
9. Bolt M6 × 25mm hex head ubs (2 reqd)
10.
11. Connector ³⁄₈ hose × ³⁄₈ external pipe
12. Connector ¼ hose × ³⁄₈ external pipe

8-460 throttle body and upper intake manifold

Upper Intake Manifold
REMOVAL AND INSTALLATION

1. Disconnect the throttle and transmission linkages at the throttle body.
2. Remove the two canister purge lines from the throttle body.
3. Tag and disconnect the:
- throttle bypass valve wire
- throttle position sensor wire
- EGR position sensor wire
- MAP sensor vacuum line
- EGR vacuum line
- fuel pressure regulator vacuum line
- EGR valve flange nut
- PCV hose
4. Disconnect the water lines at the throttle body.
5. Remove the 4 upper intake manifold bolts and lift off the manifold.
6. Installation is the reverse of removal. Always use new gaskets. Torque the manifold bolts to 18 ft.lb.

Throttle Body
REMOVAL AND INSTALLATION

1. Relieve the fuel system pressure.
2. Disconnect the throttle position sensor wire.
3. Disconnect the water lines at the throttle body.
4. Remove the 4 throttle body bolts and carefully lift off the throttle body. Discard the gasket.
5. Installation is the reverse of removal. Torque the bolts to 18 ft.lb.

Throttle Position Sensor
REMOVAL AND INSTALLATION

1. Disconnect the wiring harness from the TPS.
2. Matchmark the sensor and throttle body for installation reference.

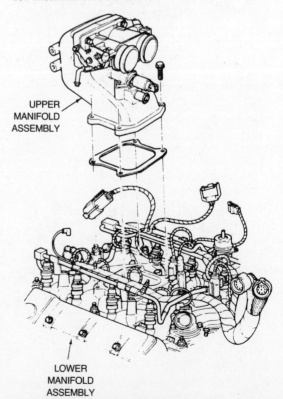

UPPER
MANIFOLD
ASSEMBLY

LOWER
MANIFOLD
ASSEMBLY

8-460 upper intake manifold removal

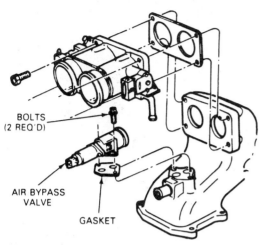

8-460 air bypass valve removal

3. Remove the 2 retaining screws and remove the TPS.

4. Install the TPS so that the wiring harness is parallel with the venturi bores, then, rotate the TPS clockwise to align the scribe marks.

5. Tighten the retaining screws to 16 in.lb. NOTE: *When correctly installed, the TPS wirning harness should be pointing directly at the air bypass valve.*

6. Connect the wiring.

Air Bypass Valve
REMOVAL AND INSTALLATION

1. Disconnect the wiring at the valve.

2. Remove the 2 retaining screws and lift off the valve.

3. Discard the gasket and clean and inspect the mating surfaces.

4. Install the valve with a new gasket, tightening the screws to 102 in.lb.

5. Connect the wiring.

Fuel Supply Manifold
REMOVAL AND INSTALLATION

1. Relieve the fuel system pressure.

2. Remove the upper manifold.

3. Disconnect the chassis fuel inlet and outlet lines at the fuel supply manifold using tool T81P-19623-G or G1.

4. Disconnect the fuel supply and return lines at the fuel supply manifold.

5. Remove the 4 fuel supply manifold retaining bolts.

6. Carefully disengage the manifold from the injectors and lift it off.

7. Inspect all components for signs of damage. Make sure that the injector caps are clean.

8. Place the fuel supply manifold over the injectors and seat the injectors carefully in the manifold.

9. Install the 4 bolts and torque them to 20 ft.lb.

10. Connect the fuel lines.

11. Install the upper manifold.

Fuel Pressure Regulator
REMOVAL AND INSTALLATION

1. Relieve the fuel system pressure.

2. Disconnect the vacuum line at the regulator.

3. Remove the 3 allen screws from the regulator housing.

4. Remove the regulator.

5. Inspect the regulator O-ring for signs of deterioration or damage. Discard the gasket.

6. Lubricate the O-ring with clean engine oil ONLY!

7. Make sure that the mounting surfaces are clean.

8. Using a new gasket, install the regulator. Tighten the retaining screws to 40 in.lb.

9. Connect the vacuum line.

Fuel Injectors
REMOVAL AND INSTALLATION

1. Relieve the fuel system pressure.

2. Disconnect the battery ground.

3. Remove the fuel supply manifold.

4. Disconnect the wiring at the injectors.

5. Pull upward on the injector body while gently rocking it from side-to-side.

6. Inspect the O-rings (2 per injector) on the injector for any sign of leakage or damage. Replace any suspected O-rings.

7. Inspect the plastic cap at the top of each injector and replace it if any sign of deterioration is noticed.

8. Lubricate the O-rings with clean engine oil ONLY!.

9. Install the injectors by pushing them in with a gentle rocking motion.

10. Install the fuel supply manifold.

11. Connect the electrical wiring.

DIESEL ENGINE FUEL SYSTEM
CAUTION: *Never smoke when working around diesel fuel! Avoid all sources of sparks or ignition. Diesel fuel vapors are EXTREMELY volatile!*

Fuel Pump
REMOVAL

1. Loosen the threaded connections with the proper size wrench (a flare nut wrench is preferred) and retighten snugly. Do not remove the lines at this time.

2. Loosen the mounting bolts, one to two turns. Apply force with your hand to loosen the

Carburetor Specifications

HOLLEY 1904

Year	Engine	Float Setting (in.)	Fuel Level Setting (in.)	Float Drop (in.)	Idle Mixture Screw Adjustment	Power Valve Opens (in. Hg)	Spark Control Valve No.
1961–62	144	11/64	23/32	3/16	1–1½ turns out	4–7	728
	170	11/64	23/32	3/16	1–1½ turns out	7–10	35

MOTORCRAFT 4350

Year	Engine	Float Setting (in.)	Supplementary Valve Setting (in.)	Accelerator Pump Rod Location	Initial Choke Pulldown (in.)	Dechoke Minimum (in.)	Choke Cap Setting
1975	460 49s.	15/16	1/16	Inner #2	5/32	1/3	Index
	460 Cal.	31/32	1/16	Inner #2	5/32	1/3	Index
	460 H. Alt.	1	1/32	Inner #2	5/32	1/3	Index
1976	460	1	1/32	Inner #2	5/32	1/3	Index
1977	460	1	1/32	#3	5/32	1/3	Index
1978	460	1	1/32	#3	5/32	1/3	Index

FORD 1100

Year	Engine	Float Setting (in.)	Accelerator Pump Clearance (in.)	Choke Plate Pulldown Clearance (in.)	Dashpot Clearance (in.)	Idle Mixture Adjustment	Spark Control Valve Closes (in. Hg)
1963	144	1	3/16	3/8	—	3/4 turns out	6–8
	170	1	3/16	3/8	3½ turns in	3/4 turns out	6–8
1964	144	1	3/16	3/8	—	1½ turns out	9–10
	170 MT	1	3/16	3/8	—	1½ turns out	8–9
	170 AT	1	3/16	3/8	3½ turns in	1½ turns out	5.5–6.5
1965	170 MT	①	3/16	3/8	—	1½ turns out	8–9
	170 AT	①	3/16	3/8	3½ turns in	1½ turns out	8–9
	200	①	3/16	3/8	—	1½ turns out	8–9
	240	①	7/32	3/8	—	1½ turns out	6.0
1966	170 MT	1 1/32	3/16	3/8	—	1½ turns out	8.5
	170 AT	1 1/32	3/16	3/8	3½ turns in	1½ turns out	8.5
	240 MT	1 1/32	7/32	—	—	1½ turns out	6.0
	240 AT	1 1/32	7/32	—	3½ turns in	1½ turns out	6.0
	240 ②	1 1/50	7/32	—	3½ turns in	1½ turns out	—
1967–68	170 MT	1 3/32	3/16	3/8	—	1½ turns out	—
	170 AT	1 3/32	3/16	3/8	3½ turns in	1½ turns out	—
	170 ②	1 3/32	3/16	3/8	2 turns in	1½ turns out	—
	240 MT	1 3/32 ③	7/32	3/8	—	1½ turns out	—
1969	240 AT	1 3/32	7/32	13/32 ④	3½ turns in ⑤	—	9.0

CARTER YF

Year	Engine	Float Setting (in.)	Dechoke Minimum (in.)	Choke Pulldown (in.)	Dashpot Clearance (in.)	Throttle Plate Fast Idle Clearance (in.)	Fast Idle Speed (rpm)
1969–70	170	7/32	5/64	7/32	7/64	3/64	—
	240 MT	7/32	9/32	7/32	7/64	1/32	—
	240 AT	7/32	9/32	7/32	—	—	850
1971	240 E-300	3/8	9/32	8/32	7/64	—	1750
	240	3/8	9/32	8/32	—	—	1750
1972–73	240	3/8	9/32	8/32	—	—	1750
	300	3/8	9/32	8/32	3/32	—	1750
1974	240	3/8	9/32	8/32	—	6/32	—
	300	3/8	9/32	10/32	3/32	4/32	—
1975	300	3/8	9/32	8/32	—	4/32	—
1976	300	3/8	9/32	10/32	—	4/32	—
	300 Canada	23/32	9/32	10/32	—	4/32	—
	300 Calif.	23/32	9/32	10/32	—	4/32	—
1977	300	25/32	9/32	10/32	—	4/32	—
1978	300	25/32	9/32	8/32	.070	.140	—
	300 E-350	23/32	9/32	8/32	—	4/32	—

For 1979–80 carburetor specifications, see the special section at the end of the carburetor charts.

AUTOLITE 2100

Year	Engine	Float Setting (in.)	Fuel Level (in.)	Fast Idle Cam Clearance (in.)	Choke Pulldown (in.)	Dechoke Minimum (in.)	Choke Cap Setting
1969	302	3/8	3/4	—	1/4	—	—
1970	302 AT	7/16	13/16	.140	3/16	1/16	Index
	302 MT	7/16	13/16	.150	3/16	1/16	2 Rich
1971	302 Bus MT	7/16	13/16	.140	5/32	1/16	Index
	302 Bus AT	7/16	13/16	.140	5/32	1/16	Index
	302 Van ⑥ MT	7/16	13/16	.140	5/32	1/16	Index
	302 Van ⑥ AT	7/16	13/16	.140	5/32	1/16	1 Rich
1972–73	302	7/16	13/16	see text	see text	—	2 Rich
	302 E-300	7/16	13/16	.110	see text	—	2 Rich
1974	302	7/16	13/16	see text	see text	—	2 Rich

MOTORCRAFT 2150

Year	Engine	Float Setting (in.)	Fuel Level (in.)	Fast Idle Cam Clearance (in.)	Choke Pulldown (in.)	Accelerator Pump Rod Location	Choke Cap Setting
1975–76	351W MT	31/64	7/8	see text	5/32	#3	1 NR ⑦
	351W AT	31/64	7/8	see text	5/32	#3	3 NR
	351W AT ⑧	1/2	7/8	see text	5/32	#2	3 NR

MOTORCRAFT 2150 (cont.)

Year	Engine	Float Setting (in.)	Fuel Level (in.)	Fast Idle Cam Clearance (in.)	Choke Pulldown (in.)	Accelerator Pump Rod Location	Choke Cap Setting
1977	351W MT ⑨	7/16	13/16	see text	3/16	#3	3 NR
	351W AT ⑨	7/16	13/16	see text	3/16	#2	3 NR
	351W AT ⑩	31/64	7/8	see text	3/16	#3	1 NR
	351W AT ⑪	31/64	7/8	see text	3/16	#4	2 NR
	351W MT ⑫	31/64	7/8	see text	3/16	#4	1 NR
	351W AT ⑬	31/64	7/8	see text	3/16	#3	2 NR
1978	351W AT ⑨	31/64	7/8	see text	7/32	#2	1 NR
	351W MT ⑨	31/64	7/8	see text	3/16	#3	3 NR
	351W E-350	31/64	7/8	see text	3/16	#3	3 NR

For 1979–80 and 1981–84 carburetor specifications, see the special sections at the end of the carburetor charts.
① rubber float: 1 inch
   metal float: 1 3/32 inch
② with Thermactor
③ with Thermactor: 1 1/32 inch
④ with Imco: 9/32 inch
⑤ with Thermactor or Imco: .10″ clearance between the plunger and lever
⑥ E-300 with GVW over 6,000 lb.
⑦ California: 3 NR
⑧ Canada
⑨ E-100 only
⑩ E-150, 250, 300 California
⑪ E-150, 250, 300 High Altitude
⑫ E-150, 250, 300 49 states
⑬ E-150, 250, 300 49 states before serial #Y0001
49s: 49 states (except California)
MT: Manual transmission
AT: Automatic transmission
NR: Notches rich

1979–80 Carburetor Specifications

Calibration Number●	Choke Plate Pulldown Setting (inches)	Time for Choke Plate to Rotate (Come Off) (Seconds— Maximum)	Air Flow (Pounds Per Minute)	Choke Setting	Fast Idle RPM High Cam	Fast Idle RPM Kick Down	Curb Idle RPM A/C ① Off/On	Curb Idle RPM Non-AC	TSP Off RPM AC	TSP Off RPM Non-AC	Timing RPM
9-51G-RO	.230	80	.06	Index		1600	700	700	500	500	500
9-51J-RO	.230	80	.06	Index		1600	700	700	500	500	500
9-51K-RO	.230	80	.06	Index		1600	700	700	500	500	500
9-51L-RO	.230	80	.06	Index		1600	700	700	500	500	500
9-51M-RO	.230	80	.06	Index		1600	700	700	500	500	500
9-51S-RO	.230	80	.06	Index		1600	700	700	500	500	500
9-51T-RO	.230	80	.06	Index		1600	700	700	500	500	500
9-52G-RO	.230	80	.06	Index		1600	550	550	500	500	500
9-52J-RO	.230	80	.06	Index		1600	550	550	500	500	500
9-52L-RO	.230	80	.06	Index		1600	550	550	500	500	500
9-52M-RO	.230	80	.06	Index		1600	550	550	500	500	500
9-53G-RO	.140	235	.085	3 Rich	2000		700	700			550
9-53H-RO	.140	125	.085	3 Rich	2000		700	700			550

1979–80 Carburetor Specifications (cont.)

Calibration Number●	Choke Plate Pulldown Setting (inches)	Time for Choke Plate to Rotate (Come Off) (Seconds— Maximum)	Air Flow (Pounds Per Minute)	Choke Setting	Fast Idle RPM		Curb Idle RPM		TSP Off RPM		Timing RPM
					High Cam	Kick Down	A/C ① Off/On	Non-AC	AC	Non-AC	
9-54G-RO	.145	150	.079	3 Rich	2000		600	600	550	550	550
9-54H-RO	.145	150	.079	3 Rich	2000		600	600	550	550	550
9-54J-RO	.145	135	.079	2 Rich	2000		600	600	550	550	550
9-54R-RO	.145	135	.079	3 Rich	2000		600	600	550	550	550
9-54S-RO	.136	75	.080	1 Rich	2400		650	650	550	550	550
9-54T-RO	.145	150	.079	3 Rich	2000		600	600	550	550	550
9-54U-RO	.136	75	.080	1 Rich	2400		650	650	550	550	550
9-59H-RO	.135	84	.074	Index	2000		650	650			650
9-59J-RO	.145	84	.074	Index	2000		650	650			650
9-59K-RO	.145	84	.074	Index	2000		650	650			650
9-59S-RO	.135	84	.07	Index	2000		650	650			650
9-59T-RO	.150	84	.07	Index	2000		650	650			650
9-60G-RO	.145	84	.079	Index	2000		550	550			500
9-60H-RO	.150	84	.08	Index	2000		550	550			500
9-60J-RO	.140	84	.079	Index	2000		550	550			500
9-60L-RO	.150	84	.08	Index	2000		550	550			500
9-60M-RO	.150	84	.08	Index	2000		550	550			500
9-60S-RO	.150	84	—	3 Rich	2100		550	550			500
9-61G-RO	.145	84	.074	Index	2000		650	650			650
9-61H-RO	.135	84	.076	Index	2000		650	650			650
9-62J-RO	.145	85	.079	Index	1900		550	550			550
9-62M-RO	.145	85	.079	Index	1900		550	550			500
9-63H-RO	.190	77	.06	Index		1500	800	800	500	500	500
9-64G-RO	.200	67	.06	Index	2200		600	600	500	500	500
9-64H-RO	.200	67	.06	Index	2200		600	600	500	500	500
9-64S-RO	.200	67	.06	Index	2200		600	600	500	500	500
9-66G-RO	.210	130	.09	5 Rich		1600	650 ②	650	800 ③	800	650 TSP Off

① Only for A/C-TSP equipped, A/C compressor electromagnetic clutch de-energized
② Energize A/C electromagnetic clutch
③ De-energize A/C electromagnetic clutch
● Refer to engine calibration code on underhood emissions sticker.

1981 Carburetor Specifications

Check the carburetor part number tag to determine which specifications to use for your vehicle

CARTER YFA

Engine	Part Number	Choke Pulldown Setting	Fast Idle Cam Setting	Dechoke Setting	Choke Plate Come-Off Time	Float Setting (Dry)	Choke Cap Setting	Fast Idle
6-300	D9TE-9510-CA,VA E0TE-9510-AMA,FA	.290	.140	.280	—	.690	Index	1400
	E1TE-9510-UA,ARA, ARB	.230	.140	.280	110 sec.	.780	Index	1400
	E1TE-9510-EA,DA, ANA,TA,EB,ANB	.300	.140	.280	110 sec.	.780	Index	1400

Motorcraft 2150

Engine	Part Number	Choke Pulldown Setting	Fast Idle Cam Setting	Dechoke Setting	Float Level (Wet)	Float Level (Dry)	Accelerator Pump Lever Location	Choke Cap Setting	Fast Idle
8-302	E1TE-9510-CNA,CMA	.125	V-notch	.200	.810	7/16	#2	V-notch	1500
	E1TE-9510-CPA,CRA	.125	V-notch	.200	.810	7/16	#2	V-notch	1500
8-351	E1TE-9510-CCA	.155	V-notch	.250	.875	31/64	#4	V-notch	2000
	E1TE-9510-BHA	.140	V-notch	.200	.875	31/64	#2	3NR	2000
	E1TE-9510-BFA	.140	V-notch	.200	.875	31/64	#2	V-notch	2000
	E1UE-9510-FA	.120	V-notch	.200	.875	31/64	#3	Index	2000
	E1UE-9510-CA, JA	.120	V-notch	.200	.875	31/64	#3	V-notch	2000

Motorcraft 4180

Engine	Part Number	Choke Pulldown Setting	Dechoke Setting	Fuel Level	Choke Cap Setting	Pump Level Location
8-460	All	.195–.225	.295–.335	sight plug	5NR	#1

1982 Carburetor Specifications

Check the carburetor part number tag to determine which specifications to use for your vehicle

CARTER YFA

Engine	Part Number	Choke Pulldown Setting	Fast Idle Cam Setting	Dechoke Setting	Choke Plate Come-Off Time	Float Setting (Dry)	Choke Cap Setting	Fast Idle
6-300	E2TE-9510-BZA, BVA	.270	.140	.280	110 sec.	.780	Index	①
	E2TE-9510-AMA E2UE-9510-EA	.230	.140	.280	110 sec.	.780	Index	①
	E2TE-9510-CEA, JA,KA,DA	.320	.140	.330	110 sec.	.780	2NR	①
	E2TE-9510-YA, AAA,MA,ANA	.300	.140	.280	110 sec.	.780	2NR	①

1982 Carburetor Specifications (cont.)

Check the carburetor part number tag to determine which specifications to use for your vehicle

CARTER YFA

Engine	Part Number	Choke Pulldown Setting	Fast Idle Cam Setting	Dechoke Setting	Choke Plate Come-Off Time	Float Setting (Dry)	Choke Cap Setting	Fast Idle
	D5TE-9510-AGB	.230	.110	.280	110 sec.	.875	1NR	①
	D9TE-9510-CA, CB,VA E2TE-9510-ZA E0TE-9510-AMA, AMB,FA,FB	.290	.140	.280	—	.690	Index	①

① Refer to underhood emission sticker

Motorcraft 2150

Engine	Part Number	Choke Pulldown Setting	Fast Idle Cam Setting	Dechoke Setting	Float Level (Wet)	Float Level (Dry)	Accelerator Pump Lever Location	Choke Cap Setting	Fast Idle
8-302	E2TE-9510-AYA, BEA,CJA	.130	V-notch	.200	.810	7/16	#2	V-notch	①
	E2TE-9510-BFA, BAA,BBA	.125	V-notch	.200	.810	7/16	#2	V-notch	①
	E2TE-9510-CKA	.120	V-notch	.200	.810	7/16	#2	V-notch	①
	E2TE-9510-JA	.130	V-notch	.200	.875	31/64	#2	V-notch	①
	E3TE-9510-BPA, BRA	.130	V-notch	.250	.875	31/64	#3	V-notch	①
8-351	E2UE-9510-FA E1UE-9510-JA	.120	V-notch	.200	.875	31/64	#3	V-notch	①
	E1UE-9510-KA	.120	V-notch	.200	.875	31/64	#2	V-notch	①
	E2UE-9510-AAA, ABA,AKA,ANA,HA, RA,SA	.180	V-notch	.250	.875	31/64	#3	V-notch	①
8-400	E2TE-9510-BGA, BHA	.180	V-notch	.250	.875	31/64	#4	V-notch	①
	E2TE-9510-DCA, DBA	.180	V-notch	.250	.875	31/64	#3	V-notch	①
	E2TE-9510-BJA, BKA	.175	V-notch	.250	.875	31/64	#4	V-notch	①
	E2TE-9510-DDA, DEA	.175	V-notch	.250	.875	31/64	#3	V-notch	①

① Refer to underhood emission sticker

Motorcraft 7200

Engine	Part Number	Fast Idle Cam Setting	Float Drop	Float Level (Dry)	Accelerator Pump Lever Lash	Choke Cap Setting	Fast Idle
8-302	All	.355–.365 ②	1.430–1.490	1.010–1.070	.010 ③	Index	①
8-351	All	.355–.365 ②	1.430–1.490	1.010–1.070	.010 ③	Index	①

① Refer to underhood emission sticker
② 2nd highest step
③ Plus one turn counterclockwise

1982 Carburetor Specifications (cont.)

Motorcraft 4180

Engine	Part Number	Choke Pulldown Setting	Dechoke Setting	Fuel Level	Choke Cap Setting	Pump Level Location
8-460	All	.200–.220	.295–.335	sight plug	2NR	#1

1983 Carburetor Specifications

Check the carburetor part number tag to determine which specifications to use for your vehicle

CARTER YFA

Engine	Part Number	Choke Pulldown Setting	Fast Idle Cam Setting	Dechoke Setting	Choke Plate Come-Off Time	Float Setting (Dry)	Choke Cap Setting	Fast Idle
6-300	E3TE-9510-AMA, APA,YA,ASA,AGA, AHA,AJA,AFA,ANA	.270	.140	.280	90–140 sec.	.780	Red	①
	E3TE-9150-BNA, GA,BDA,ZA,ALA, FA,BKA	.320	.140	.330	90–140 sec.	.780	Red	①
	E3TE-9150-ZA, ABA,BRA,AKA	.300	.140	.280	90–140 sec.	.780	White	①
	E3TE-9510-AAA, ARA	.300	.140	.280	90–140 sec.	.780	Red	①
	D5TE-9510-AGB	.230	.110	.280	—	.375	1NR	①
	E0TE-9510-AMB, FB E2TE-9510-ZA	.290	.140	.280	—	.690	Index	①

① Refer to underhood emission sticker

Motorcraft 2150

Engine	Part Number	Choke Pulldown Setting	Fast Idle Cam Setting	Dechoke Setting	Float Level (Wet)	Float Level (Dry)	Accelerator Pump Lever Location	Choke Cap Setting	Fast Idle
8-302	E3TE-9510-AUA	.142	V-notch	.200	.810	7/16	#3	V-notch	①
	E3TE-9510-BHA	.152	V-notch	.200	.810	7/16	#3	V-notch	①
	E3TE-9510-AYA	.137	V-notch	.250	.810	7/16	#4	V-notch	①
	E3TE-9510-AVA, BEA	.149	V-notch	.250	.810	7/16	#3	V-notch	①
	E3TE-9510-BJA	.157	V-notch	.200	.810	7/16	#4	V-notch	①
	E3TE-9510-BLA, BPA	.157	V-notch	.200	.810	7/16	#3	V-notch	①
	E3TE-9510-BMA	.150	V-notch	.200	.810	7/16	#4	V-notch	①
	E3TE-9510-AZA, BAA E2TE-9510-BPA, BRA	.130	V-notch	.250	.875	31/64	#3	V-notch	①

1983 Carburetor Specifications (cont.)

Motorcraft 2150 (cont.)

Engine	Part Number	Choke Pulldown Setting	Fast Idle Cam Setting	Dechoke Setting	Float Level (Wet)	Float Level (Dry)	Accelerator Pump Lever Location	Choke Cap Setting	Fast Idle
8-351	E3UE-9510-CA E2UE-9510-FA	.120	V-notch	.200	.875	31/64	#3	V-notch	①
	E3UE-9510-BA E2UE-9510-KA	.120	V-notch	.200	.875	31/64	#2	V-notch	①
	E3UE-9510-EA, DA E2UE-9510-ANA, AKA	.180	V-notch	.250	.875	31/64	#3	V-notch	①

① Refer to underhood emission sticker

Motorcraft 7200

Engine	Part Number	Fast Idle Cam Setting	Float Drop	Float Level (Dry)	Accelerator Pump Lever Lash	Choke Cap Setting	Fast Idle
8-351	All	.355–.365 ②	1.43–1.49	1.010–1.070	.010 ③	Index	①

① Refer to underhood emission sticker
② 2nd highest step
③ Plus one turn counterclockwise

Motorcraft 4180

Engine	Part Number	Choke Pulldown Setting	Dechoke Setting	Fuel Level	Choke Cap Setting	Pump Level Location
8-460	All	.210–.230	.300–.330	sight plug	3NR	#1

1984 and Later Carburetor Specifications

Check the carburetor part number tag to determine which specifications to use for your vehicle

Carter YFA

Engine	Part Number	Choke Pulldown Setting	Fast Idle Cam Setting	Dechoke Setting	Choke Plate Come-Off Time	Float Setting (Dry)	Choke Cap Setting	Fast Idle
6-300	E4TE-9510-VA, HA,FA,UA,AAA, GA,EA,ZA	.360	.140	.330	90–141 sec.	.780	Red	①
	D5TE-9510-AGB	.230	1NR	.280	—	.375	—	①
	D5TE-9510-AMB, FB	.290	Index	.280	—	.690	Index	①

① Refer to underhood emission sticker

1984 and Later Carburetor Specifications (cont.)

Motorcraft 2150

Engine	Part Number	Choke Pulldown Setting	Fast Idle Cam Setting	Dechoke Setting	Float Level (Wet)	Float Level (Dry)	Accelerator Pump Lever Location	Choke Cap Setting	Fast Idle
8-302	E4TE-9510-AMA	.140	V-notch	.250	.875	31/64	#3	V-notch	①
	E4TE-9510-AEA	.142	V-notch	.250	.875	31/64	#3	V-notch	①
	E4TE-9510-ALA	.125	V-notch	.250	.875	31/64	#3	V-notch	①
	E4TE-9510-APA	.145	V-notch	.250	.875	31/64	#3	V-notch	①
	E4TE-9510-AKA	.137	V-notch	.250	.875	31/64	#3	V-notch	①
	E4TE-9510-AHA	.150	V-notch	.250	.875	31/64	#4	V-notch	①
	E4TE-9510-AJA	.150	V-notch	.250	.875	31/64	#3	V-notch	①
	E4TE-9510-AFA	.144	V-notch	.250	.875	31/64	#3	V-notch	①
	E3TE-9510-BAA, AZA	.130	V-notch	.250	.875	31/64	#3	V-notch	①
8-351	E4TE-9510-ADA	.152	V-notch	.250	.810	7/16	#4	V-notch	①
	E4TE-9510-ACA	.155	V-notch	.250	.810	7/16	#4	V-notch	①
	E3UE-9510-EA, DA	.180	V-notch	.250	.875	31/64	#3	V-notch	①

① Refer to underhood emission sticker

Motorcraft 4180

Engine	Part Number	Choke Pulldown Setting	Dechoke Setting	Fuel Level	Choke Cap Setting	Pump Level Location
8-460	E3TE-9510-PD,RD	.210–.230	.295–.335	sight plug	3NR	#1
	E3TE-9510-TC,SC	.210–.230	.300–.330	sight plug	3NR	#1

fuel pump if the gasket is stuck. Rotate the engine by nudging the starter, until the fuel pump cam lobe is at the low position. At this position, spring tension against the fuel pump bolts will be greatly reduced.

3. Disconnect the fuel supply pump inlet, outlet and fuel return line.

CAUTION: *Use care to prevent combustion of the spilled fuel.*

4. Remove the fuel pump attaching bolts and remove the pump and gasket. Discard the old gasket.

INSTALLATION

1. Remove the remaining fuel pump gasket material from the engine and from the fuel pump if you are reinstalling the old pump. Make sure both mounting surfaces are clean.

2. Install the attaching bolts into the fuel supply pump and install a new gasket on the bolts. Position the fuel pump onto the mounting pad. Turn the attaching bolts alternately and evenly and tighten the bolts to the specifications according to the size bolts used on the

pump. See the accompanying standard torque chart for reference.

NOTE: *The cam must be at its low position before attempting to install the fuel supply pump. If it is difficult to start the mounting bolts, remove the pump and reinstall with a lever on the bottom side of the cam.*

3. Install the fuel outlet line. Start the fitting by hand to avoid crossthreading.

4. Install the inlet line and the fuel return line.

5. Start the engine and observe all connections for fuel leaks for two minutes.

6. Stop the engine and check all fuel supply pump fuel line connections. Check for oil leaks at the pump mounting pad.

Glow Plug System

The diesel engine utilizes an electric glow plug system to aid in the start of the engine. The function of this stem is to pre-heat the combustion chamber to aid ignition of the fuel.

The system consists of eight glow plugs (one

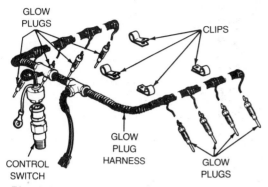

Diesel glow plug wiring harness

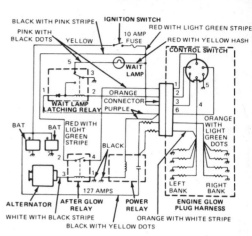

Glow plug electrical schematic—420 V8 diesel engine

for each cylinder), control switch, power relay, after glow relay, wait lamp latching relay, wait lamp and the eight fusible links located between the harness and the glow plug terminal.

On initial start with cold engine, the glow plug system operates as follows: The glow plug control switch energizes the power relay (which is a magnetic switch) and the power relay contacts close. Battery current energizes the glow plugs. Current to the glow plugs and a wait lamp will be shut off when the glow plugs are hot enough. This takes from 2 to 10 second after the key is first turned on. When the wait lamp goes off, the engine is ready to start. After the engine is started the glow plugs begin an on-off cycle for about 40 to 90 seconds. This cycle helps to clear start-up smoke. The control switch (the brain of the operation) is threaded into the left cylinder head coolant jacket. the

control unit senses engine coolant temperature. Since the control unit senses temperature and glow plug operation the glow plug system will not be activated unless needed. On a restart (warm engine) the glow plug system will not be activated unless the coolant temperature drops before 165°F (91°C).

Since the fast start system utilizes 6 volt glow plugs in a 12 volt system to achieve rapid heating of the glow plug, a cycling device is required in the circuit.

CAUTION: *Never bypass the power relay of the glow plug system. Constant battery current (12 volts) to glow plugs will cause them to overheat and fail.*

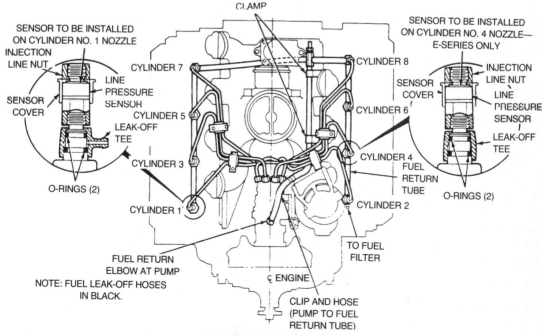

7.3L diesel fuel line routing

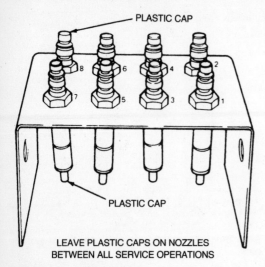

LEAVE PLASTIC CAPS ON NOZZLES
BETWEEN ALL SERVICE OPERATIONS

Diesel nozzle holding fixture

Injection Nozzles

REMOVAL

NOTE: *Before removing the nozzle assemblies, clean the exterior of each nozzle assembly and the surrounding area with clean fuel oil or solvent to prevent entry of dirt into the engine when nozzle assemblies are removed. Also, clean the fuel inlet and fuel leak-off piping connections. Blow dry with compressed air.*

1. Remove the fuel line retaining clamp(s) from the nozzle lines that are to be removed.

2. Disconnect the nozzle fuel inlet (high pressure) and fuel leak-off tees from each nozzle assembly and position out of the way. Cover the open ends of the fuel inlet and outlet or nozzles with protective caps, to prevent dirt from entering.

3. Remove the injection nozzles by turning them counterclockwise. Pull the nozzle assembly with the copper washer attached from the engine. Cover the nozzle fuel opening and spray tip, with plastic caps, to prevent the entry of dirt.

NOTE: *Remove the copper injector nozzle gasket from the nozzle bore with special tool, T71P-19703-C, or equivalent, whenever the gasket does not come out with the nozzle.*

4. Place the nozzle assemblies in a fabricated holder as they are removed from the heads. The holder should be marked with numbers corresponding to the cylinder numbering of the engine. This will allow for reinstallation of the nozzle in the same ports from which they were removed.

INSTALLATION

1. Thoroughly clean the nozzle bore in cylinder head before reinserting the nozzle assembly

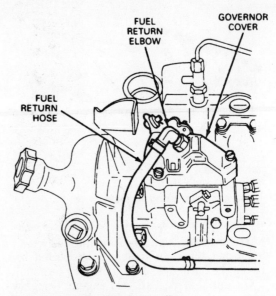

Removing the diesel fuel return line

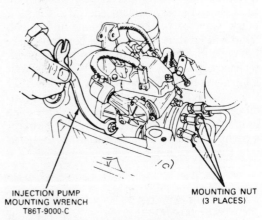

Injection pump mounting nut removal

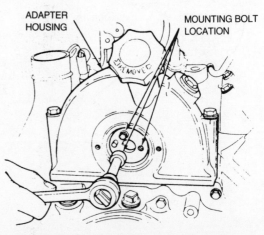

Diesel injection pump drive gear attaching bolts

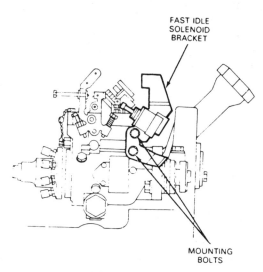

RIGHT SIDE VIEW

Diesel fast idle solenoid bracket

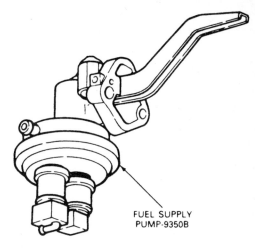

Diesel fuel supply pump

with nozzle seat cleaner, special tool T83T-9527-A or equivalent. Make certain that no small particles of metal or carbon remain on the seating surface. Blow out the particles with compressed air.

2. Remove the protective cap and install a new copper gasket on the nozzle assembly, with a small dab of grease.

NOTE: *Anti-seize compound or equivalent should be used on nozzle threads to aid in installation and future removal.*

3. Install the nozzle assembly into the cylinder head nozzle bore.

4. Tighten the nozzle assembly to 33 ft.lb.

5. Remove the protective caps from nozzle assemblies and fuel lines.

6. Install the leak-off tees to the nozzle assemblies.

NOTE: *Install two new O-ring seals for each fuel return tee.*

7. Connect the high pressure fuel line and tighten, using a flare nut wrench.

8. Install the fuel line retainer clamps.

9. Start the engine and check for leaks.

Injection Pump

WARNING: *Before removing the fuel lines, clean the exterior with clean fuel oil or solvent*

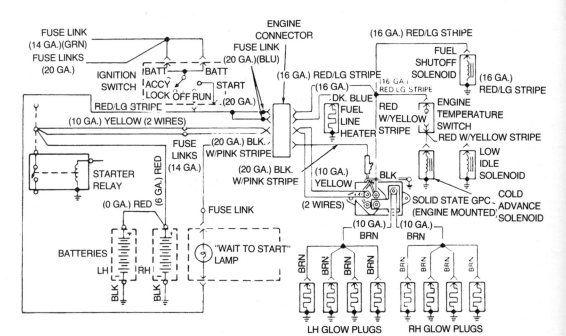

7.3L diesel glow plug schematic

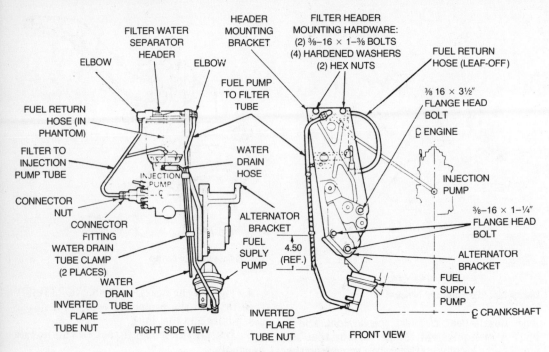

Diesel fuel supply lines

to prevent entry of dirt into the engine when the fuel lines are removed.

Do not wash or steam clean engine while engine is running. Serious damage to injection pump could occur.

REMOVAL

1. Disconnect battery ground cables from both batteries.

2. Remove the engine oil filler neck.

3. Remove the bolts attaching injection pump to drive gear.

4. Disconnect the electrical connectors to injection pump.

5. Disconnect the accelerator cable and speed control cable from throttle lever, if so equipped.

6. Remove the air cleaner and install clean rags to prevent dirt from entering the intake manifold.

7. Remove the accelerator cable bracket, with cables attached, from the intake manifold and position out of the way.

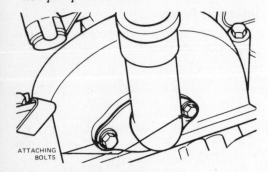

Removing the diesel oil filler neck

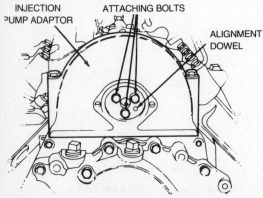

Removing the diesel injection pump drive gear bolts

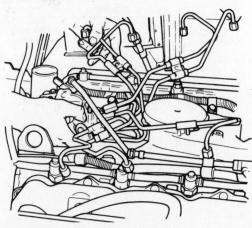

Removing the diesel injection pmp

NOTE: *All fuel lines and fittings must be capped using Fuel System Protective Cap Set T83T-9395-A or equivalent, to prevent fuel contamination.*

8. Remove the fuel filter-to-injection pump fuel line and cap fittings.

9. Remove and cap the injection pump inlet elbow and the injection pump fitting adapter.

10. Remove the fuel return line on injection pump, rotate out of the way, And cap all fittings.

NOTE: *It is not necessary to remove injection lines from injection pump. If lines are to be removed, loosen injection line fittings at injection pump before removing it from engine.*

11. Remove the fuel injection lines from the nozzles and cap lines and nozzles.

12. Remove the three nuts attaching the Injection pump to injection pump adapter using Tool T83T-9000-B.

13. If the injection pump is to be replaced, loosen the injection line retaining clips and the injection nozzle fuel lines with Tool T83T-9396-A and cap all fittings at this time with protective cap set T83T-9395-A or equivalent. Do not install the injection nozzle fuel lines until the new pump is installed in the engine.

14. Lift the Injection pump, with the nozzle lines attached, up and out of the engine compartment.

WARNING: *Do not carry injection pump by Injection nozzle fuel lines as this could cause lines to bend or crimp.*

INSTALLATION

1. Install a new O-ring on the drive gear end of the injection pump.

2. Move the injection pump down and into position.

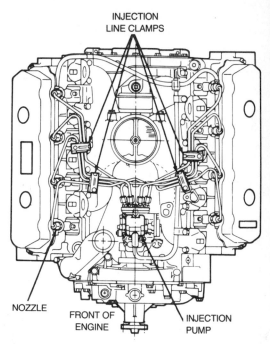

Diesel injection line and clamp installation

3. Position the alignment dowel on injection pump into the alignment hole on Drive gear.

4. Install the bolts attaching the injection pump to drive gear and tighten.

5. Install the nuts attaching injection pump to adapter. Align scribe lines on the injection pump flange and the injection pump adapter and tighten to 14 ft.lbs.

6. If the injection nozzle fuel lines were removed from the injection pump install at this time, refer to Fuel Lines-Installation, in this chapter.

7. Remove the caps from nozzles and the fuel lines and install the fuel line nuts on the nozzles and tighten to 22 ft.lb.

8. Connect the fuel return line to injection pump and tighten the nuts.

9. Install the injection pump fitting adapter with a new O-ring.

10. Clean the old sealant from the injection pump elbow threads, using clean solvent, and dry thoroughly. Apply a light coating of pipe sealant to the elbow threads.

11. Install the elbow in the injection pump adapter and tighten to a minimum of 6 ft.lb. Then tighten further, if necessary, to align the elbow with the injection pump fuel inlet line, but do not exceed 360 degrees of rotation or 10 ft.lb.

12. Remove the caps and connect the fuel filter-to-Injection pump fuel line.

13. Install the accelerator cable bracket to the intake manifold.

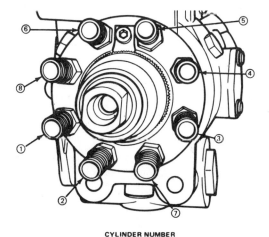

CYLINDER NUMBER

Diesel injection pump numbering sequence

14. Remove the rags from the intake manifold and install the air cleaner.

15. Connect the accelerator and speed control cable, if so equipped, to throttle lever.

16. Install the electrical connectors on injection pump.

17. Clean the injection pump adapter and oil filler neck sealing surfaces.

18. Apply a ⅛″ bead of RTV sealant on the adapter housing.

19. Install the oil filler neck and tighten the bolts.

20. Connect the battery ground cables to both batteries.

21. Run the engine and check for fuel leaks.

22. If necessary, purge high pressure fuel lines of air by loosening connector one half to one turn and cranking engine until solid fuel, free from bubbles flows from connection.

CAUTION: *Keep eyes and hands away from nozzle spray. Fuel spraying from the nozzle under high pressure can penetrate the skin.*

23. Check and adjust injection pump timing as described in this chapter.

Fuel Lines
REMOVAL

NOTE: *Before removing any fuel lines, clean the exterior with clean fuel oil, or solvent to prevent entry of dirt into fuel system when the fuel lines are removed. Blow dry with compressed air.*

1. Disconnect the battery ground cables from both batteries.

2. Remove the air cleaner and cap intake manifold opening with clean rags.

3. Disconnect the accelerator cable and speed control cable, if so equipped, from the injection pump.

4. remove the accelerator cable bracket from the intake manifold and position out of the way with cable(s) attached.

WARNING: *To prevent fuel system contamination, cap all fuel lines and fittings.*

5. Disconnect the fuel line from the fuel filter to injection pump and cap all fittings.

6. Disconnect and cap the nozzle fuel lines at nozzles.

7. Remove the fuel line clamps from the fuel lines to be removed.

8. Remove and cap the injection pump inlet elbow.

9. Remove and cap the inlet fitting adapter.

10. Remove the injection nozzle lines, one at a time, from injection pump using Tool T83T-9396-A.

NOTE: *Fuel lines must be removed following this sequence: 5-6-4-8-3-1-7-2. Install caps on*

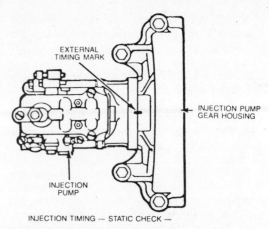

INJECTION TIMING — STATIC CHECK —

Diesel injection timing marks

each end of each fuel line and pump fittings as it is removed and identify each fuel line accordingly.

INSTALLATION

1. Install fuel lines on injection pump, one at a time, and Tighten to 22 ft.lbs.

NOTE: *Fuel lines must be installed in the sequence: 2-7-1-3-8-4-6-5.*

2. Clean the old sealant from the injection pump elbow, using clean solvent, and dry thoroughly.

3. Apply a light coating of pipe sealant on the elbow threads.

Diesel Injection Timing
STATIC TIMING

1. Break the torque of the injection pump mounting nuts (keeping the nuts snug).

2. Rotate the injection pump using Tool T83-9000-C or equivalent to bring the mark on the pump into alignment with the mark on pump mounting adapter.

3. Visually recheck the alignment of the timing marks and tighten injection pump mounting nuts.

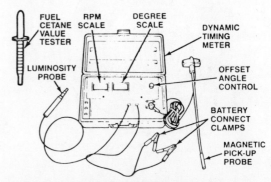

Rotunda 78–0100 dynamic timing meter

Diesel Engine Diagnosis Procedure

Condition	Cause	Correction
Rough idle	Improper adjustment	Adjust idle
	Accelerator control cable binding	Repair or lubricate
	Air or water in the fuel system	Clear air or water from fuel system
	Injection nozzle clogged	Check and clean injector nozzles
	Improper valve clearance	Check valve adjustment
	Injection pump malfunction	Check injection pump
Poor Performance	Air cleaner clogged	Check element
	Accelerator control cable binding	Check control cable for free movement
	Restricted fuel flow (water or air)	Check lines and filter
	Incorrect injection timing	Check injection timing
	Injection pump malfunction	Replace injection pump
Excessive Exhaust Smoke	Restricted air cleaner	Check element
	Air or water in fuel filter	Remove air or water from fuel system
	Improper grade fuel	Check fuel in tank
	Incorrect injection timing	Check injection timing
	Injection pump malfunction	Replace injection pump
	Injector nozzle stuck open	Check injector nozzles
Excessive Fuel Consumption	Restricted air cleaner	Check element
	Leak in fuel lines	Check for leaks
	Incorrect idle speed	Check idle
	Restricted exhaust system	Check exhaust
	Improper grade of fuel	Check fuel in tank
	Injection pump malfunction	Check injection pump operation
Loud Knocking in Engine	Defective fuel injector	Replace fuel injector

Note: If the problem persists after performing these preliminary checks, disassembly and inspection of internal engine components may be necessary for further diagnosis.

DYNAMIC TIMING

1. Bring the engine up to normal operating temperature.

2. Stop the engine and install a dynamic timing meter, Rotunda 78-0100 or equivalent, by placing the magnetic probe pick-up into the probe hole.

3. Remove the no. 1 glow plug wire and remove the glow plug, install the luminosity probe and tighten to 12 ft.lbs. Install the photocell over the probe.

4. Connect the dynamic timing meter to the battery and adjust the offset of the meter.

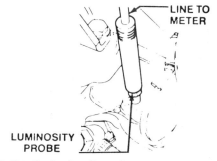

Installing the luminosity probe

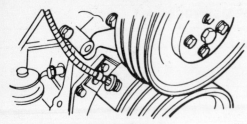

MAGNETIC PICK-UP

Installing the magnetic pick-up

5. Set the transmission in neutral and raise the rear wheels off the ground. Using Rotunda 14-0302, throttle control, set the engine speed to 1,400 rpm with no accessory load. Observe the injection timing on the dynamic timing meter.

NOTE: *Obtain the fuel sample from the vehicle and check the cetane value using the tester supplied with the Ford special tools 78-0100 or equivalent. Refer to the dynamic timing chart to find the correct timing in degrees.*

6. If the dynamic timing is not within plug or minus 2 degrees of specification, then the injection pump timing will require adjustment.

7. Turn the engine off. Note the timing mark alignment. Loosen the injection pump-to-adapter nuts.

8. Rotate the injection pump clockwise (when viewed from the front of the engine) to retard and counterclockwise to advance timing. Two degrees of dynamic timing is approximately 0.030" (75mm) of timing mark movement.

9. Start the engine and recheck the timing. If the timing is not within plus or minus 1 degree of specification, repeat steps 7 through 9.

10. Turn off the engine. Remove the dynamic timing equipment. Lightly coat the glow plug thread with anti-seize compound, install the glow plugs and tighten to 12 ft.lb. Connect the glow plug wires.

Dynamic Timing Specifications

Fuel Cetane Value	Altitude	
	0–3000 Ft ①	Above 3000 Ft ①
38–42	6° ATDC	7° ATDC
43–46	5° ATDC	6° ATDC
47–50	4° ATDC	5° ATDC

① Installation or resetting tolerance for dynamic timing is ± 1°. Service limit is ± 2°.

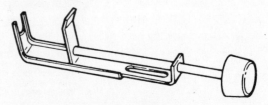

Rotonda 14-0302 Throttle control tool

Chassis Electrical

UNDERSTANDING AND TROUBLESHOOTING ELECTRICAL SYSTEMS

With the rate at which both import and domestic manufacturers are incorporating electronic control systems into their production lines, it won't be long before every new vehicle is equipped with one or more on-board computer, like the EEC-IV unit installed on the truck. These electronic components (with no moving parts) should theoretically last the life of the vehicle, provided nothing external happens to damage the circuits or memory chips.

While it is true that electronic components should never wear out, in the real world malfunctions do occur. It is also true that any computer-based system is extremely sensitive to electrical voltages and cannot tolerate careless or haphazard testing or service procedures. An inexperienced individual can literally do major damage looking for a minor problem by using the wrong kind of test equipment or connecting test leads or connectors with the ignition switch ON. When selecting test equipment, make sure the manufacturers instructions state that the tester is compatible with whatever type of electronic control system is being serviced. Read all instructions carefully and double check all test points before installing probes or making any test connections.

The following section outlines basic diagnosis techniques for dealing with computerized automotive control systems. Along with a general explanation of the various types of test equipment available to aid in servicing modern electronic automotive systems, basic repair techniques for wiring harnesses and connectors is given. Read the basic information before attempting any repairs or testing on any computerized system, to provide the background of information necessary to avoid the most common

and obvious mistakes that can cost both time and money. Although the replacement and testing procedures are simple in themselves, the systems are not, and unless one has a thorough understanding of all components and their function within a particular computerized control system, the logical test sequence these systems demand cannot be followed. Minor malfunctions can make a big difference, so it is important to know how each component affects the operation of the overall electronic system to find the ultimate cause of a problem without replacing good components unnecessarily. It is not enough to use the correct test equipment; the test equipment must be used correctly.

Safety Precautions

CAUTION: *Whenever working on or around any computer based microprocessor control system, always observe these general precautions to prevent the possibility of personal injury or damage to electronic components.*

● Never install or remove battery cables with the key ON or the engine running. Jumper cables should be connected with the key OFF to avoid power surges that can damage electronic control units. Engines equipped with computer controlled systems should avoid both giving and getting jump starts due to the possibility of serious damage to components from arcing in the engine compartment when connections are made with the ignition ON.

● Always remove the battery cables before charging the battery. Never use a high output charger on an installed battery or attempt to use any type of "hot shot" (24 volt) starting aid.

● Exercise care when inserting test probes into connectors to insure good connections without damaging the connector or spreading the pins. Always probe connectors from the rear (wire) side, NOT the pin side, to avoid accidental shorting of terminals during test procedures.

• Never remove or attach wiring harness connectors with the ignition switch ON, especially to an electronic control unit.

• Do not drop any components during service procedures and never apply 12 volts directly to any component (like a solenoid or relay) unless instructed specifically to do so. Some component electrical windings are designed to safely handle only 4 or 5 volts and can be destroyed in seconds if 12 volts are applied directly to the connector.

• Remove the electronic control unit if the vehicle is to be placed in an environment where temperatures exceed approximately 176°F (80°C), such as a paint spray booth or when arc or gas welding near the control unit location in the car.

ORGANIZED TROUBLESHOOTING

When diagnosing a specific problem, organized troubleshooting is a must. The complexity of a modern automobile demands that you approach any problem in a logical, organized manner. There are certain troubleshooting techniques that are standard:

1. Establish when the problem occurs. Does the problem appear only under certain conditions? Were there any noises, odors, or other unusual symptoms?

2. Isolate the problem area. To do this, make some simple tests and observations; then eliminate the systems that are working properly. Check for obvious problems such as broken wires, dirty connections or split or disconnected vacuum hoses. Always check the obvious before assuming something complicated is the cause.

3. Test for problems systematically to determine the cause once the problem area is isolated. Are all the components functioning properly? Is there power going to electrical switches and motors? Is there vacuum at vacuum switches and/or actuators? Is there a mechanical problem such as bent linkage or loose mounting screws? Doing careful, systematic checks will often turn up most causes on the first inspection without wasting time checking components that have little or no relationship to the problem.

4. Test all repairs after the work is done to make sure that the problem is fixed. Some causes can be traced to more than one component, so a careful verification of repair work is important to pick up additional malfunctions that may cause a problem to reappear or a different problem to arise. A blown fuse, for example, is a simple problem that may require more than another fuse to repair. If you don't look for a problem that caused a fuse to blow, for example, a shorted wire may go undetected.

Experience has shown that most problems tend to be the result of a fairly simple and obvious cause, such as loose or corroded connectors or air leaks in the intake system; making careful inspection of components during testing essential to quick and accurate troubleshooting. Special, hand held computerized testers designed specifically for diagnosing the EEC-IV system are available from a variety of aftermarket sources, as well as from the vehicle manufacturer, but care should be taken that any test equipment being used is designed to diagnose that particular computer controlled system accurately without damaging the control unit (ECU) or components being tested.

NOTE: *Pinpointing the exact cause of trouble in an electrical system can sometimes only be accomplished by the use of special test equipment. The following describes commonly used test equipment and explains how to put it to best use in diagnosis. In addition to the information covered below, the manufacturer's instructions booklet provided with the tester should be read and clearly understood before attempting any test procedures.*

TEST EQUIPMENT

Jumper Wires

Jumper wires are simple, yet extremely valuable, pieces of test equipment. Jumper wires are merely wires that are used to bypass sections of a circuit. The simplest type of jumper wire is merely a length of multistrand wire with an alligator clip at each end. Jumper wires are usually fabricated from lengths of standard automotive wire and whatever type of connector (alligator clip, spade connector or pin connector) that is required for the particular vehicle being tested. The well equipped tool box will have several different styles of jumper wires in several different lengths. Some jumper wires are made with three or more terminals coming from a common splice for special purpose testing. In cramped, hard-to-reach areas it is advisable to have insulated boots over the jumper wire terminals in order to prevent accidental grounding, sparks, and possible fire, especially when testing fuel system components.

Jumper wires are used primarily to locate open electrical circuits, on either the ground (-) side of the circuit or on the hot (+) side. If an electrical component fails to operate, connect the jumper wire between the component and a good ground. If the component operates only with the jumper installed, the ground circuit is open. If the ground circuit is good, but the component does not operate, the circuit between the power feed and component is open. You can sometimes connect the jumper wire directly from the battery to the hot terminal of the component, but first make sure the component uses 12 volts in operation. Some electrical components, such as fuel injectors, are designed to operate on about 4 volts and running 12 volts directly to the injector terminals can burn out the wiring. By inserting an inline fuseholder between a set of test leads, a fused jumper wire can be used for bypassing open circuits. Use a 5 amp fuse to provide protection against voltage spikes. When in doubt, use a voltmeter to check the voltage input to the component and measure how much voltage is being applied normally. By moving the jumper wire successively back from the lamp toward the power source, you can isolate the area of the circuit where the open is located. When the component stops functioning, or the power is cut off, the open is in the segment of wire between the jumper and the point previously tested.

CAUTION: *Never use jumpers made from wire that is of lighter gauge than used in the circuit under test. If the jumper wire is of too small gauge, it may overheat and possibly melt. Never use jumpers to bypass high resistance loads (such as motors) in a circuit. Bypassing resistances, in effect, creates a short circuit which may, in turn, cause damage and fire. Never use a jumper for anything other than temporary bypassing of components in a circuit.*

12 Volt Test Light

The 12 volt test light is used to check circuits and components while electrical current is flowing through them. It is used for voltage and ground tests. Twelve volt test lights come in different styles but all have three main parts; a ground clip, a probe, and a light. The most commonly used 12 volt test lights have pick-type probes. To use a 12 volt test light, connect the ground clip to a good ground and probe wherever necessary with the pick. The pick should be sharp so that it can penetrate wire insulation to make contact with the wire, without making a large hole in the insulation. The wrap-around light is handy in hard to reach areas or where it is difficult to support a wire to push a probe pick into it. To use the wrap around light, hook the wire to probed with the hook and pull the trigger. A small pick will be forced through the wire insulation into the wire core.

CAUTION: *Do not use a test light to probe electronic ignition spark plug or coil wires. Never use a pick-type test light to probe wiring on computer controlled systems unless specifically instructed to do so. Any wire insulation that is pierced by the test light probe should be taped and sealed with silicone after testing.*

Like the jumper wire, the 12 volt test light is used to isolate opens in circuits. But, whereas the jumper wire is used to bypass the open to operate the load, the 12 volt test light is used to locate the presence of voltage in a circuit. If the test light glows, you know that there is power up to that point; if the 12 volt test light does not glow when its probe is inserted into the wire or connector, you know that there is an open circuit (no power). Move the test light in successive steps back toward the power source until the light in the handle does glow. When it does glow, the open is between the probe and point previously probed.

NOTE: *The test light does not detect that 12 volts (or any particular amount of voltage) is present; it only detects that some voltage is present. It is advisable before using the test light to touch its terminals across the battery posts to make sure the light is operating properly.*

Self-Powered Test Light

The self-powered test light usually contains a 1.5 volt penlight battery. One type of self-powered test light is similar in design to the 12 volt test light. This type has both the battery and the light in the handle and pick-type probe tip. The second type has the light toward the open tip, so that the light illuminates the contact point. The self-powered test light is dual purpose piece of test equipment. It can be used to test for either open or short circuits when power is isolated from the circuit (continuity test). A powered test light should not be used on any computer controlled system or component unless specifically instructed to do so. Many engine sensors can be destroyed by even this small amount of voltage applied directly to the terminals.

Open Circuit Testing

To use the self-powered test light to check for open circuits, first isolate the circuit from the vehicle's 12 volt power source by disconnecting the battery or wiring harness connector. Connect the test light ground clip to a good ground and probe sections of the circuit sequentially with the test light. (start from either end of the circuit). If the light is out, the open is between the probe and the circuit ground. If the light is on, the open is between the probe and end of the circuit toward the power source.

Short Circuit Testing

By isolating the circuit both from power and from ground, and using a self-powered test light, you can check for shorts to ground in the circuit. Isolate the circuit from power and ground. Connect the test light ground clip to a good ground and probe any easy-to-reach test point in the circuit. If the light comes on, there is a short somewhere in the circuit. To isolate the short, probe a test point at either end of the isolated circuit (the light should be on). Leave the test light probe connected and open connectors, switches, remove parts, etc., sequentially, until the light goes out. When the light goes out, the short is between the last circuit component opened and the previous circuit opened.

NOTE: *The 1.5 volt battery in the test light does not provide much current. A weak battery may not provide enough power to illuminate the test light even when a complete circuit is made (especially if there are high resistances in the circuit). Always make sure that the test battery is strong. To check the battery, briefly touch the ground clip to the probe; if the light glows brightly the battery is strong enough for testing. Never use a self-powered test light to perform checks for opens or shorts when power is applied to the electrical system under test. The 12 volt vehicle power will quickly burn out the 1.5 volt light bulb in the test light.*

Voltmeter

A voltmeter is used to measure voltage at any point in a circuit, or to measure the voltage drop across any part of a circuit. It can also be used to check continuity in a wire or circuit by indicating current flow from one end to the other. Voltmeters usually have various scales on the meter dial and a selector switch to allow the selection of different voltages. The voltmeter has a positive and a negative lead. To avoid damage to the meter, always connect the negative lead to the negative (-) side of circuit (to ground or nearest the ground side of the circuit) and connect the positive lead to the positive (+) side of the circuit (to the power source or the nearest power source). Note that the negative voltmeter lead will always be black and that the positive voltmeter will always be some color other than black (usually red). Depending on how the voltmeter is connected into the circuit, it has several uses.

A voltmeter can be connected either in parallel or in series with a circuit and it has a very high resistance to current flow. When connected in parallel, only a small amount of current will flow through the voltmeter current path; the rest will flow through the normal circuit current path and the circuit will work normally. When the voltmeter is connected in series with a circuit, only a small amount of current can flow through the circuit. The circuit will not work properly, but the voltmeter reading will show if the circuit is complete or not.

Available Voltage Measurement

Set the voltmeter selector switch to the 20V position and connect the meter negative lead to the negative post of the battery. Connect the positive meter lead to the positive post of the battery and turn the ignition switch ON to provide a load. Read the voltage on the meter or digital display. A well charged battery should register over 12 volts. If the meter reads below 11.5 volts, the battery power may be insufficient to operate the electrical system properly. This test determines voltage available from the battery and should be the first step in any electrical trouble diagnosis procedure. Many electrical problems, especially on computer controlled systems, can be caused by a low state of charge in the battery. Excessive corrosion at the battery cable terminals can cause a poor contact that will prevent proper charging and full battery current flow.

Normal battery voltage is 12 volts when fully charged. When the battery is supplying current to one or more circuits it is said to be "under load". When everything is off the electrical system is under a "no-load" condition. A fully charged battery may show about 12.5 volts at no load; will drop to 12 volts under medium load; and will drop even lower under heavy load. If the battery is partially discharged the voltage decrease under heavy load may be excessive, even though the battery shows 12 volts or more at no load. When allowed to discharge further, the battery's available voltage under load will decrease more severely. For this reason, it is important that the battery be fully charged during all testing procedures to avoid errors in diagnosis and incorrect test results.

Voltage Drop

When current flows through a resistance, the voltage beyond the resistance is reduced (the larger the current, the greater the reduction in voltage). When no current is flowing, there is no voltage drop because there is no current flow. All points in the circuit which are connected to the power source are at the same voltage as the power source. The total voltage drop always equals the total source voltage. In a long circuit with many connectors, a series of small, unwanted voltage drops due to corrosion at the connectors can add up to a total loss of voltage which impairs the operation of the normal loads in the circuit.

INDIRECT COMPUTATION OF VOLTAGE DROPS

1. Set the voltmeter selector switch to the 20 volt position.
2. Connect the meter negative lead to a good ground.

3. Probe all resistances in the circuit with the positive meter lead.

4. Operate the circuit in all modes and observe the voltage readings.

DIRECT MEASUREMENT OF VOLTAGE DROPS

1. Set the voltmeter switch to the 20 volt position.

2. Connect the voltmeter negative lead to the ground side of the resistance load to be measured.

3. Connect the positive lead to the positive side of the resistance or load to be measured.

4. Read the voltage drop directly on the 20 volt scale.

Too high a voltage indicates too high a resistance. If, for example, a blower motor runs too slowly, you can determine if there is too high a resistance in the resistor pack. By taking voltage drop readings in all parts of the circuit, you can isolate the problem. Too low a voltage drop indicates too low a resistance. If, for example, a blower motor runs too fast in the MED and/or LOW position, the problem can be isolated in the resistor pack by taking voltage drop readings in all parts of the circuit to locate a possibly shorted resistor. The maximum allowable voltage drop under load is critical, especially if there is more than one high resistance problem in a circuit because all voltage drops are cumulative. A small drop is normal due to the resistance of the conductors.

HIGH RESISTANCE TESTING

1. Set the voltmeter selector switch to the 4 volt position.

2. Connect the voltmeter positive lead to the positive post of the battery.

3. Turn on the headlights and heater blower to provide a load.

4. Probe various points in the circuit with the negative voltmeter lead.

5. Read the voltage drop on the 4 volt scale. Some average maximum allowable voltage drops are:

FUSE PANEL — 7 volts
IGNITION SWITCH — 5 volts
HEADLIGHT SWITCH — 7 volts
IGNITION COIL (+) — 5 volts
ANY OTHER LOAD — 1.3 volts

NOTE: *Voltage drops are all measured while a load is operating; without current flow, there will be no voltage drop.*

Ohmmeter

The ohmmeter is designed to read resistance (ohms) in a circuit or component. Although there are several different styles of ohmmeters, all will usually have a selector switch which permits the measurement of different ranges of resistance (usually the selector switch allows the multiplication of the meter reading by 10, 100, 1000, and 10,000). A calibration knob allows the meter to be set at zero for accurate measurement. Since all ohmmeters are powered by an internal battery (usually 9 volts), the ohmmeter can be used as a self-powered test light. When the ohmmeter is connected, current from the ohmmeter flows through the circuit or component being tested. Since the ohmmeter's internal resistance and voltage are known values, the amount of current flow through the meter depends on the resistance of the circuit or component being tested.

The ohmmeter can be used to perform continuity test for opens or shorts (either by observation of the meter needle or as a self-powered test light), and to read actual resistance in a circuit. It should be noted that the ohmmeter is used to check the resistance of a component or wire while there is no voltage applied to the circuit. Current flow from an outside voltage source (such as the vehicle battery) can damage the ohmmeter, so the circuit or component should be isolated from the vehicle electrical system before any testing is done. Since the ohmmeter uses its own voltage source, either lead can be connected to any test point.

NOTE: *When checking diodes or other solid state components, the ohmmeter leads can only be connected one way in order to measure current flow in a single direction. Make sure the positive (+) and negative (-) terminal connections are as described in the test procedures to verify the one-way diode operation.*

In using the meter for making continuity checks, do not be concerned with the actual resistance readings. Zero resistance, or any resistance readings, indicate continuity in the circuit. Infinite resistance indicates an open in the circuit. A high resistance reading where there should be none indicates a problem in the circuit. Checks for short circuits are made in the same manner as checks for open circuits except that the circuit must be isolated from both power and normal ground. Infinite resistance indicates no continuity to ground, while zero resistance indicates a dead short to ground.

RESISTANCE MEASUREMENT

The batteries in an ohmmeter will weaken with age and temperature, so the ohmmeter must be calibrated or "zeroed" before taking measurements. To zero the meter, place the selector switch in its lowest range and touch the two ohmmeter leads together. Turn the calibration knob until the meter needle is exactly on zero.

NOTE: *All analog (needle) type ohmmeters*

must be zeroed before use, but some digital ohmmeter models are automatically calibrated when the switch is turned on. Self-calibrating digital ohmmeters do not have an adjusting knob, but its a good idea to check for a zero readout before use by touching the leads together. All computer controlled systems require the use of a digital ohmmeter with at least 10 meagohms impedance for testing. Before any test procedures are attempted, make sure the ohmmeter used is compatible with the electrical system or damage to the onboard computer could result.

To measure resistance, first isolate the circuit from the vehicle power source by disconnecting the battery cables or the harness connector. Make sure the key is OFF when disconnecting any components or the battery. Where necessary, also isolate at least one side of the circuit to be checked to avoid reading parallel resistances. Parallel circuit resistances will always give a lower reading than the actual resistance of either of the branches. When measuring the resistance of parallel circuits, the total resistance will always be lower than the smallest resistance in the circuit. Connect the meter leads to both sides of the circuit (wire or component) and read the actual measured ohms on the meter scale. Make sure the selector switch is set to the proper ohm scale for the circuit being tested to avoid misreading the ohmmeter test value.

CAUTION: *Never use an ohmmeter with power applied to the circuit. Like the self-powered test light, the ohmmeter is designed to operate on its own power supply. The normal 12 volt automotive electrical system current could damage the meter.*

Ammeters

An ammeter measures the amount of current flowing through a circuit in units called amperes or amps. Amperes are units of electron flow which indicate how fast the electrons are flowing through the circuit. Since Ohms Law dictates that current flow in a circuit is equal to the circuit voltage divided by the total circuit resistance, increasing voltage also increases the current level (amps). Likewise, any decrease in resistance will increase the amount of amps in a circuit. At normal operating voltage, most circuits have a characteristic amount of amperes, called "current draw" which can be measured using an ammeter. By referring to a specified current draw rating, measuring the amperes, and comparing the two values, one can determine what is happening within the circuit to aid in diagnosis. An open circuit, for example, will not allow any current to flow so the ammeter reading will be zero. More current flows

through a heavily loaded circuit or when the charging system is operating.

An ammeter is always connected in series with the circuit being tested. All of the current that normally flows through the circuit must also flow through the ammeter; if there is any other path for the current to follow, the ammeter reading will not be accurate. The ammeter itself has very little resistance to current flow and therefore will not affect the circuit, but it will measure current draw only when the circuit is closed and electricity is flowing. Excessive current draw can blow fuses and drain the battery, while a reduced current draw can cause motors to run slowly, lights to dim and other components to not operate properly. The ammeter can help diagnose these conditions by locating the cause of the high or low reading.

Multimeters

Different combinations of test meters can be built into a single unit designed for specific tests. Some of the more common combination test devices are known as Volt/Amp testers, Tach/Dwell meters, or Digital Multimeters. The Volt/Amp tester is used for charging system, starting system or battery tests and consists of a voltmeter, an ammeter and a variable resistance carbon pile. The voltmeter will usually have at least two ranges for use with 6, 12 and 24 volt systems. The ammeter also has more than one range for testing various levels of battery loads and starter current draw and the carbon pile can be adjusted to offer different amounts of resistance. The Volt/Amp tester has heavy leads to carry large amounts of current and many later models have an inductive ammeter pickup that clamps around the wire to simplify test connections. On some models, the ammeter also has a zero-center scale to allow testing of charging and starting systems without switching leads or polarity. A digital multimeter is a voltmeter, ammeter and ohmmeter combined in an instrument which gives a digital readout. These are often used when testing solid state circuits because of their high input impedance (usually 10 megohms or more).

The tach/dwell meter combines a tachometer and a dwell (cam angle) meter and is a specialized kind of voltmeter. The tachometer scale is marked to show engine speed in rpm and the dwell scale is marked to show degrees of distributor shaft rotation. In most electronic ignition systems, dwell is determined by the control unit, but the dwell meter can also be used to check the duty cycle (operation) of some electronic engine control systems. Some tach/dwell meters are powered by an internal battery, while others take their power from the car battery in use. The battery powered testers usually require calibration much like an ohmmeter before testing.

Special Test Equipment

A variety of diagnostic tools are available to help troubleshoot and repair computerized engine control systems. The most sophisticated of these devices are the console type engine analyzers that usually occupy a garage service bay, but there are several types of aftermarket electronic testers available that will allow quick circuit tests of the engine control system by plugging directly into a special connector located in the engine compartment or under the dashboard. Several tool and equipment manufacturers offer simple, hand held testers that measure various circuit voltage levels on command to check all system components for proper operation. Although these testers usually cost about $300-$500, consider that the average computer control unit (or ECM) can cost just as much and the money saved by not replacing perfectly good sensors or components in an attempt to correct a problem could justify the purchase price of a special diagnostic tester the first time it's used.

These computerized testers can allow quick and easy test measurements while the engine is operating or while the car is being driven. In addition, the on-board computer memory can be read to access any stored trouble codes; in effect allowing the computer to tell you where it hurts and aid trouble diagnosis by pinpointing exactly which circuit or component is malfunctioning. In the same manner, repairs can be tested to make sure the problem has been corrected. The biggest advantage these special testers have is their relatively easy hookups that minimize or eliminate the chances of making the wrong connections and getting false voltage readings or damaging the computer accidentally.

NOTE: *It should be remembered that these testers check voltage levels in circuits; they don't detect mechanical problems or failed components if the circuit voltage falls within the preprogrammed limits stored in the tester PROM unit. Also, most of the hand held testes are designed to work only on one or two systems made by a specific manufacturer.*

A variety of aftermarket testers are available to help diagnose different computerized control systems. Owatonna Tool Company (OTC), for example, markets a device called the OTC Monitor which plugs directly into the assembly line diagnostic link (ALDL). The OTC tester makes diagnosis a simple matter of pressing the correct buttons and, by changing the internal PROM or inserting a different diagnosis cartridge, it will work on any model from full size to subcompact, over a wide range of years. An adapter is supplied with the tester to allow connection to all types of ALDL links, regardless of the number of pin terminals used. By inserting an updated PROM into the OTC tester, it can be easily updated to diagnose any new modifications of computerized control systems.

Wiring Harnesses

The average automobile contains about ½ mile of wiring, with hundreds of individual connections. To protect the many wires from damage and to keep them from becoming a confusing tangle, they are organized into bundles, enclosed in plastic or taped together and called wire harnesses. Different wiring harnesses serve different parts of the vehicle. Individual wires are color coded to help trace them through a harness where sections are hidden from view.

A loose or corroded connection or a replacement wire that is too small for the circuit will add extra resistance and an additional voltage drop to the circuit. A ten percent voltage drop can result in slow or erratic motor operation, for example, even though the circuit is complete. Automotive wiring or circuit conductors can be in any one of three forms:

1. Single strand wire
2. Multistrand wire
3. Printed circuitry

Single strand wire has a solid metal core and is usually used inside such components as alternators, motors, relays and other devices. Multistrand wire has a core made of many small strands of wire twisted together into a single conductor. Most of the wiring in an automotive electrical system is made up of multistrand wire, either as a single conductor or grouped together in a harness. All wiring is color coded on the insulator, either as a solid color or as a colored wire with an identification stripe. A printed circuit is a thin film of copper or other conductor that is printed on an insulator backing. Occasionally, a printed circuit is sandwiched between two sheets of plastic for more protection and flexibility. A complete printed circuit, consisting of conductors, insulating material and connectors for lamps or other components is called a printed circuit board. Printed circuitry is used in place of individual wires or harnesses in places where space is limited, such as behind instrument panels.

Wire Gauge

Since computer controlled automotive electrical systems are very sensitive to changes in resistance, the selection of properly sized wires is critical when systems are repaired. The wire gauge number is an expression of the cross section area of the conductor. The most common system for expressing wire size is the American Wire Gauge (AWG) system.

Wire cross section area is measured in circular mils. A mil is $\frac{1}{1000}''$ (0.001''); a circular mil is the area of a circle one mil in diameter. For example, a conductor $\frac{1}{4}''$ in diameter is 0.250 in. or 250 mils. The circular mil cross section area of the wire is 250 squared (250^2)or 62,500 circular mils. Imported car models usually use metric wire gauge designations, which is simply the cross section area of the conductor in square millimeters (mm^2).

Gauge numbers are assigned to conductors of various cross section areas. As gauge number increases, area decreases and the conductor becomes smaller. A 5 gauge conductor is smaller than a 1 gauge conductor and a 10 gauge is smaller than a 5 gauge. As the cross section area of a conductor decreases, resistance increases and so does the gauge number. A conductor with a higher gauge number will carry less current than a conductor with a lower gauge number.

NOTE: *Gauge wire size refers to the size of the conductor, not the size of the complete wire. It is possible to have two wires of the same gauge with different diameters because one may have thicker insulation than the other.*

12 volt automotive electrical systems generally use 10, 12, 14, 16 and 18 gauge wire. Main power distribution circuits and larger accessories usually use 10 and 12 gauge wire. Battery cables are usually 4 or 6 gauge, although 1 and 2 gauge wires are occasionally used. Wire length must also be considered when making repairs to a circuit. As conductor length increases, so does resistance. An 18 gauge wire, for example, can carry a 10 amp load for 10 feet without excessive voltage drop; however if a 15 foot wire is required for the same 10 amp load, it must be a 16 gauge wire.

An electrical schematic shows the electrical current paths when a circuit is operating properly. It is essential to understand how a circuit works before trying to figure out why it doesn't. Schematics break the entire electrical system down into individual circuits and show only one particular circuit. In a schematic, no attempt is made to represent wiring and components as they physically appear on the vehicle; switches and other components are shown as simply as possible. Face views of harness connectors show the cavity or terminal locations in all multi-pin connectors to help locate test points.

If you need to backprobe a connector while it is on the component, the order of the terminals must be mentally reversed. The wire color code can help in this situation, as well as a keyway, lock tab or other reference mark.

NOTE: *Wiring diagrams are not included in this book. As trucks have become more complex and available with longer option lists, wiring diagrams have grown in size and complexity. It has become almost impossible to provide a readable reproduction of a wiring diagram in a book this size. Information on ordering wiring diagrams from the vehicle manufacturer can be found in the owner's manual.*

WIRING REPAIR

Soldering is a quick, efficient method of joining metals permanently. Everyone who has the occasion to make wiring repairs should know how to solder. Electrical connections that are soldered are far less likely to come apart and will conduct electricity much better than connections that are only "pig-tailed" together. The most popular (and preferred) method of soldering is with an electrical soldering gun. Soldering irons are available in many sizes and wattage ratings. Irons with higher wattage ratings deliver higher temperatures and recover lost heat faster. A small soldering iron rated for no more than 50 watts is recommended, especially on electrical systems where excess heat can damage the components being soldered.

There are three ingredients necessary for successful soldering; proper flux, good solder and sufficient heat. A soldering flux is necessary to clean the metal of tarnish, prepare it for soldering and to enable the solder to spread into tiny crevices. When soldering, always use a resin flux or resin core solder which is non-corrosive and will not attract moisture once the job is finished. Other types of flux (acid core) will leave a residue that will attract moisture and cause the wires to corrode. Tin is a unique metal with a low melting point. In a molten state, it dissolves and alloys easily with many metals. Solder is made by mixing tin with lead. The most common proportions are 40/60, 50/50 and 60/40, with the percentage of tin listed first. Low priced solders usually contain less tin, making them very difficult for a beginner to use because more heat is required to melt the solder. A common solder is 40/60 which is well suited for all-around general use, but 60/40 melts easier, has more tin for a better joint and is preferred for electrical work.

Soldering Techniques

Successful soldering requires that the metals to be joined be heated to a temperature that will melt the solder – usually 360-460°F (182-238°C). Contrary to popular belief, the purpose of the soldering iron is not to melt the solder itself, but to heat the parts being soldered to a temperature high enough to melt the solder when it is touched to the work. Melting flux-cored solder on the soldering iron will usually destroy the effectiveness of the flux.

NOTE: *Soldering tips are made of copper for good heat conductivity, but must be "tinned" regularly for quick transference of heat to the project and to prevent the solder from sticking to the iron. To "tin" the iron, simply heat it and touch the flux-cored solder to the tip; the solder will flow over the hot tip. Wipe the excess off with a clean rag, but be careful as the iron will be hot.*

After some use, the tip may become pitted. If so, simply dress the tip smooth with a smooth file and "tin" the tip again. An old saying holds that "metals well cleaned are half soldered." Flux-cored solder will remove oxides but rust, bits of insulation and oil or grease must be removed with a wire brush or emery cloth. For maximum strength in soldered parts, the joint must start off clean and tight. Weak joints will result in gaps too wide for the solder to bridge.

If a separate soldering flux is used, it should be brushed or swabbed on only those areas that are to be soldered. Most solders contain a core of flux and separate fluxing is unnecessary. Hold the work to be soldered firmly. It is best to solder on a wooden board, because a metal vise will only rob the piece to be soldered of heat and make it difficult to melt the solder. Hold the soldering tip with the broadest face against the work to be soldered. Apply solder under the tip close to the work, using enough solder to give a heavy film between the iron and the piece being soldered, while moving slowly and making sure the solder melts properly. Keep the work level or the solder will run to the lowest part and favor the thicker parts, because these require more heat to melt the solder. If the soldering tip overheats (the solder coating on the face of the tip burns up), it should be retinned. Once the soldering is completed, let the soldered joint stand until cool. Tape and seal all soldered wire splices after the repair has cooled.

Wire Harness and Connectors

The on-board computer (ECM) wire harness electrically connects the control unit to the various solenoids, switches and sensors used by the control system. Most connectors in the engine compartment or otherwise exposed to the elements are protected against moisture and dirt which could create oxidation and deposits on the terminals. This protection is important because of the very low voltage and current levels used by the computer and sensors. All connectors have a lock which secures the male and female terminals together, with a secondary lock holding the seal and terminal into the connec-

tor. Both terminal locks must be released when disconnecting ECM connectors.

These special connectors are weather-proof and all repairs require the use of a special terminal and the tool required to service it. This tool is used to remove the pin and sleeve terminals. If removal is attempted with an ordinary pick, there is a good chance that the terminal will be bent or deformed. Unlike standard blade type terminals, these terminals cannot be straightened once they are bent. Make certain that the connectors are properly seated and all of the sealing rings in place when connecting leads. On some models, a hinge-type flap provides a backup or secondary locking feature for the terminals. Most secondary locks are used to improve the connector reliability by retaining the terminals if the small terminal lock tangs are not positioned properly.

Molded-on connectors require complete replacement of the connection. This means splicing a new connector assembly into the harness. All splices in on-board computer systems should be soldered to insure proper contact. Use care when probing the connections or replacing terminals in them as it is possible to short between opposite terminals. If this happens to the wrong terminal pair, it is possible to damage certain components. Always use jumper wires between connectors for circuit checking and never probe through weather-proof seals.

Open circuits are often difficult to locate by sight because corrosion or terminal misalignment are hidden by the connectors. Merely wiggling a connector on a sensor or in the wiring harness may correct the open circuit condition. This should always be considered when an open circuit or a failed sensor is indicated. Intermittent problems may also be caused by oxidized or loose connections. When using a circuit tester for diagnosis, always probe connections from the wire side. Be careful not to damage sealed connectors with test probes.

All wiring harnesses should be replaced with identical parts, using the same gauge wire and connectors. When signal wires are spliced into a harness, use wire with high temperature insulation only. With the low voltage and current levels found in the system, it is important that the best possible connection at all wire splices be made by soldering the splices together. It is seldom necessary to replace a complete harness. If replacement is necessary, pay close attention to insure proper harness routing. Secure the harness with suitable plastic wire clamps to prevent vibrations from causing the harness to wear in spots or contact any hot components.

NOTE: *Weatherproof connectors cannot be replaced with standard connectors. Instruc-*

tions are provided with replacement connector and terminal packages. Some wire harnesses have mounting indicators (usually pieces of colored tape) to mark where the harness is to be secured.

In making wiring repairs, it's important that you always replace damaged wires with wires that are the same gauge as the wire being replaced. The heavier the wire, the smaller the gauge number. Wires are color-coded to aid in identification and whenever possible the same color coded wire should be used for replacement. A wire stripping and crimping tool is necessary to install solderless terminal connectors. Test all crimps by pulling on the wires; it should not be possible to pull the wires out of a good crimp.

Wires which are open, exposed or otherwise damaged are repaired by simple splicing. Where possible, if the wiring harness is accessible and the damaged place in the wire can be located, it is best to open the harness and check for all possible damage. In an inaccessible harness, the wire must be bypassed with a new insert, usually taped to the outside of the old harness.

When replacing fusible links, be sure to use fusible link wire, NOT ordinary automotive wire. Make sure the fusible segment is of the same gauge and construction as the one being replaced and double the stripped end when crimping the terminal connector for a good contact. The melted (open) fusible link segment of the wiring harness should be cut off as close to the harness as possible, then a new segment spliced in as described. In the case of a damaged fusible link that feeds two harness wires, the harness connections should be replaced with two fusible link wires so that each circuit will have its own separate protection.

NOTE: *Most of the problems caused in the wiring harness are due to bad ground connections. Always check all vehicle ground connections for corrosion or looseness before performing any power feed checks to eliminate the chance of a bad ground affecting the circuit.*

Repairing Hard Shell Connectors

Unlike molded connectors, the terminal contacts in hard shell connectors can be replaced. Weatherproof hard-shell connectors with the leads molded into the shell have non-replaceable terminal ends. Replacement usually involves the use of a special terminal removal tool that depress the locking tangs (barbs) on the connector terminal and allow the connector to be removed from the rear of the shell. The connector shell should be replaced if it shows any evidence of burning, melting, cracks, or breaks.

Replace individual terminals that are burnt, corroded, distorted or loose.

NOTE: *The insulation crimp must be tight to prevent the insulation from sliding back on the wire when the wire is pulled. The insulation must be visibly compressed under the crimp tabs, and the ends of the crimp should be turned in for a firm grip on the insulation.*

The wire crimp must be made with all wire strands inside the crimp. The terminal must be fully compressed on the wire strands with the ends of the crimp tabs turned in to make a firm grip on the wire. Check all connections with an ohmmeter to insure a good contact. There should be no measurable resistance between the wire and the terminal when connected.

Mechanical Test Equipment

Vacuum Gauge

Most gauges are graduated in inches of mercury (in.Hg), although a device called a manometer reads vacuum in inches of water (in. H_2O). The normal vacuum reading usually varies between 18 and 22 in.Hg at sea level. To test engine vacuum, the vacuum gauge must be connected to a source of manifold vacuum. Many engines have a plug in the intake manifold which can be removed and replaced with an adapter fitting. Connect the vacuum gauge to the fitting with a suitable rubber hose or, if no manifold plug is available, connect the vacuum gauge to any device using manifold vacuum, such as EGR valves, etc. The vacuum gauge can be used to determine if enough vacuum is reaching a component to allow its actuation.

Hand Vacuum Pump

Small, hand-held vacuum pumps come in a variety of designs. Most have a built-in vacuum gauge and allow the component to be tested without removing it from the vehicle. Operate the pump lever or plunger to apply the correct amount of vacuum required for the test specified in the diagnosis routines. The level of vacuum in inches of Mercury (in.Hg) is indicated on the pump gauge. For some testing, an additional vacuum gauge may be necessary.

Intake manifold vacuum is used to operate various systems and devices on late model vehicles. To correctly diagnose and solve problems in vacuum control systems, a vacuum source is necessary for testing. In some cases, vacuum can be taken from the intake manifold when the engine is running, but vacuum is normally provided by a hand vacuum pump. These hand vacuum pumps have a built-in vacuum gauge that allow testing while the device is still attached to the component. For some tests, an additional vacuum gauge may be necessary.

HEATING AND AIR CONDITIONING

Blower Motor and/or Heater Core

REMOVAL AND INSTALLATION

1961-67

The heater blower motor may be removed without removing the heater case, by simply disconnecting the lead-in wires and removing the three attaching bolts.

1. Remove the right side grille-work from around the head light.

2. Working through the opening, remove the six heater case attaching screws.

3. Disconnect the water hoses from the bottom of the heater case.

4. Disconnect the defroster ducts from the case.

5. Remove the remaining attaching screws from inside the van.

6. Lower the heater case to the floor and disconnect the control cables and wiring.

7. Remove the case.

8. Installation is in the reverse of removal. Replace any damaged sealer.

1969-74

1. Open the hood and remove the battery to gain access to the heater mounting bolts.

2. Drain the cooling system.

CAUTION: *When draining the coolant, keep in mind that cats and dogs are attracted by the ethylene glycol antifreeze, and are quite likely to drink any that is left in an uncovered container or in puddles on the ground. This will prove fatal in sufficient quantity. Always drain the coolant into a sealable container. Coolant should be reused unless it is contaminated or several years old.*

3. Disconnect the heater hoses at the heater.

4. Disconnect the heater resistor and the motor leads.

5. From under the hood, remove the 3 heater-to-dash mounting volts. Then, move the heater out of position to gain access to the control cable and disconnect the cable. Remove the heater assembly to a bench.

6. Separate to two halves of the heater case (16 screws and 1 clip).

NOTE: *For heater core replacement, use Steps 7,8 and 14 through 18.*

7. Remove the heater core.

8. Transfer the core pads to the new core, and position the core in the case.

NOTE: *For blower motor replacement, use Steps 9 through 18.*

9. Remove the two screws and lift the motor and wheel from the front half of the heater housing.

10. Remove the blower wheel and motor mounting bracket.

11. Position the new motor in the mounting bracket and install the mounting bolts and nuts.

12. Install the blower wheel.

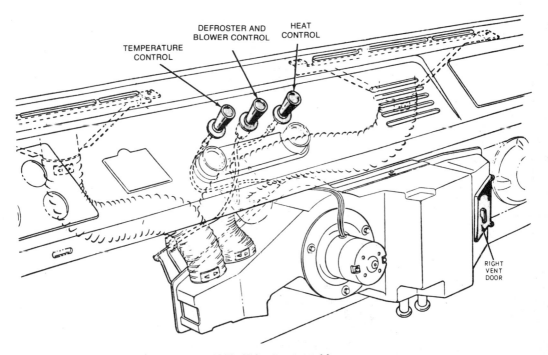

1961–67 heater assembly

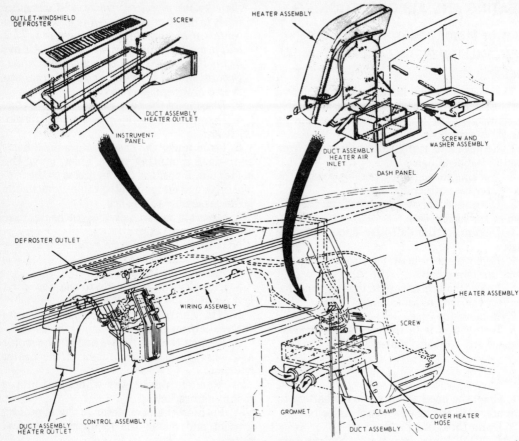

1969–74 heater assembly

13. Position the motor assembly in the housing and install the mounting screws.

14. Position both halves of the case together and install the screws and clip.

15. Place the heater controls in the Off position. Place the heater on the wheel housing as near the installed position as possible. Pull the air door closed (toward the rear of the vehicle) and connect the control cable.

16. Position the heater to the dash, and install the 3 mounting bolts. Use an assistant and make certain that the housing openings line up with the defroster and fresh air openings.

17. Connect the resistor and motor leads.

18. Connect the heater hoses.

19. Install the battery and fill the cooling system. Run the engine and check for leaks.

1975-87 Without Air Conditioning
Except 1978-79 with Deluxe Hi-Lo Heater

HEATER CORE

1. Drain the coolant; remove the battery.
CAUTION: *When draining the coolant, keep in mind that cats and dogs are attracted by the ethylene glycol antifreeze, and are quite likely to drink any that is left in an uncovered container or in puddles on the ground. This will prove fatal in sufficient quantity. Always drain the coolant into a sealable container. Coolant should be reused unless it is contaminated or several years old.*

2. Disconnect the resistor wiring harness and the orange blower motor lead. Remove the ground wire screw from the firewall.

3. Detach the heater hoses and the plastic hose retaining strap.

4. Remove the five mounting screws inside the truck.

5. Remove the heater assembly.

6. Cut the seal at the top and bottom edge of the core retainer. Remove the two screws and the retainer. Slide the core and seal out of the case.

7. Reverse the procedure for installation.

BLOWER MOTOR

1. Disconnect the orange motor leaf wire. Remove the ground wire screw from the firewall.

2. Disconnect the blower motor cooling tube.

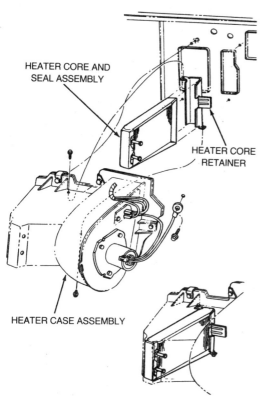

1975–87 heater core wo/air conditioning

3. Remove the four mounting plate screws and the motor assembly.

4. Reverse the procedure for installation.

1978-79 with Deluxe Hi-Lo Heater

HEATER CORE

1. Disconnect the wiring from the resistor on the front face of the blower cover.

2. Disconnect the vacuum line from the outside recirulating door vacuum motor.

3. Remove the 5 blower cover screws and 2 blower scroll cover screws.

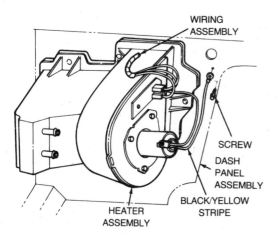

1975–87 blower motor core wo/air conditioning

4. Remove the pushnut and washer from the outside recirc. door shaft.

5. Remove the control cable from the bracket and slide it over the bracket. Remove the wire loop from the door shaft.

6. Remove the 9 blower housing screws.

7. Remove the 3 blend air door housing screws.

8. Drain the cooling system.

CAUTION: *When draining the coolant, keep in mind that cats and dogs are attracted by the ethylene glycol antifreeze, and are quite likely to drink any that is left in an uncovered container or in puddles on the ground. This will prove fatal in sufficient quantity. Always drain the coolant into a sealable container. Coolant should be reused unless it is contaminated or several years old.*

9. Disconnect the heater hoses at the core tubes.

10. Remove the heater core retaining brackets.

11. Remove the heater core and seal.

12. Installation is the reverse of removal.

BLOWER MOTOR

1. Disconnect the wiring from the resistor on the front face of the blower cover.

2. Disconnect the vacuum line from the outside recirculating door vacuum motor.

3. Remove the 5 blower cover screws and 2 blower scroll cover screws.

4. Push the wiring grommet forward and out of the blower motor housing.

5. Remove the 4 screws from the blower motor mounting plate.

6. Remove the blower and wheel.

7. Installation is the reverse of removal.

1975-87 With Air Conditioning

HEATER CORE

1. Disconnect the resistor electrical leads on the front of the blower cover inside the truck. Detach the vacuum line from the vacuum motor. Remove the blower cover.

2. Remove the nut and push washer from the air door shaft. Remove the control cable from the bracket and the air door shaft.

3. Remove the blower motor housing and the air door housing.

4. Drain the coolant and detach the heater hoses.

CAUTION: *When draining the coolant, keep in mind that cats and dogs are attracted by the ethylene glycol antifreeze, and are quite likely to drink any that is left in an uncovered container or in puddles on the ground. This will prove fatal in sufficient quantity. Always drain the coolant into a sealable container.*

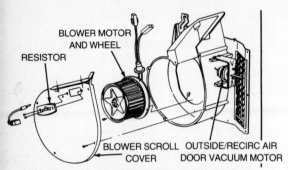

1975–87 blower motor core w/air conditioning

Coolant should be reused unless it is contaminated or several years old.

5. Remove the heater core retaining brackets. Remove the core and seal assembly.

6. Reverse the procedure for installation.

BLOWER MOTOR

1. Disconnect the resistor electrical leads on the front of the blower cover inside the truck.

2. Remove the blower cover.

3. Push the wiring grommet forward out of the housing hole.

4. Remove the blower motor mounting plate. Remove the blower motor.

5. Reverse the procedure for installation.

1988

HEATER CORE

1. Drain the cooling system.

CAUTION: *When draining the coolant, keep in mind that cats and dogs are attracted by the ethylene glycol antifreeze, and are quite likely to drink any that is left in an uncovered container or in puddles on the ground. This will prove fatal in sufficient quantity. Always drain the coolant into a sealable container. Coolant should be reused unless it is contaminated or several years old.*

2. Disconnect the heater hoses at the core tubes in the engine compartment.

3. Remove the instrument panel lower trim panel.

4. Remove the heater core cover from the left side of the heater case (4 screws).

5. Remove the core retaining screw and bracket from the case.

6. Lift out the heater core and seal.

7. Installation is the reverse of removal. If the seal was damaged, replace it.

BLOWER MOTOR

1. Disconnect the wiring at the motor.

2. Remove the 4 mounting screws and lift the blower from the case.

3. Installation is the reverse of removal.

Auxiliary Hot Water Heater

REMOVAL AND INSTALLATION

Heater/Blower Assembly

1964-67

1. Disconnect the battery ground cable.

2. Raise the vehicle on a hoist.

3. Drain the cooling system.

CAUTION: *When draining the coolant, keep in mind that cats and dogs are attracted by the ethylene glycol antifreeze, and are quite likely to drink any that is left in an uncovered container or in puddles on the ground. This will prove fatal in sufficient quantity. Always drain the coolant into a sealable container. Coolant should be reused unless it is contaminated or several years old.*

4. Remove the two hoses from the heater core and plug the hoses.

5. Remove the rubber insulators from the heater assembly retaining studs.

6. Lower the vehicle.

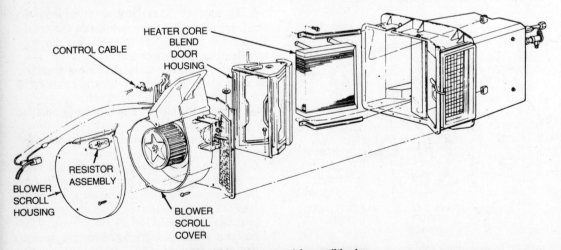

1975–87 heater core w/air conditioning

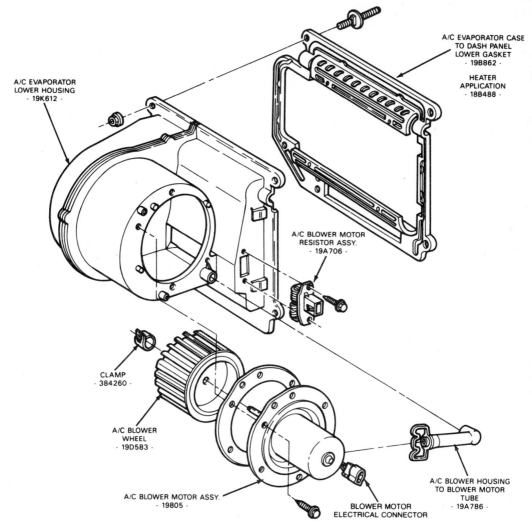

A/C EVAPORATOR CASE
TO DASH PANEL
LOWER GASKET
- 19B862 -

HEATER
APPLICATION
- 18B488 -

A/C EVAPORATOR
LOWER HOUSING
- 19K612 -

A/C BLOWER MOTOR
RESISTOR ASSY.
- 19A706 -

CLAMP
- 384260 -

A/C BLOWER
WHEEL
- 19D583 -

A/C BLOWER MOTOR ASSY.
- 19805 -

BLOWER MOTOR
ELECTRICAL CONNECTOR

A/C BLOWER HOUSING
TO BLOWER MOTOR
TUBE
- 19A786 -

1988 blower motor and wheel

7. Disconnect the two electrical leads at the heater assembly.

8. Remove the heater from the vehicle.

9. Position the heater assembly in the vehicle, inserting the mounting studs through the floor pan.

10. Connect the two electrical leads at the heater assembly.

11. Raise the vehicle on a hoist.

12. Install the four nuts on the heater assembly retaining studs.

13. Install the rubber insulators on the heater core tubes.

14. Remove the plugs from the heater hoses and install the hoses on the heater core tubes securing them with clamps.

15. Lower the vehicle.

16. Add required coolant to the cooling system.

17. Connect the battery ground cable.

Auxiliary Heater Core

1964-67

1. Remove the heater assembly from the vehicle and place on work bench.

2. Remove the heater core from the heater case.

3. Remove the four rubber spacers from the core.

4. Using sealer, install the four rubber spacers to the heater core.

5. Install the core in the heater case and install the four mounting screws.

6. Install the heater assembly in the vehicle.

Auxiliary Heater Blower and/or Core

1969-74

1. Disconnect the battery ground cable.

2. Raise the vehicle on a hoist.

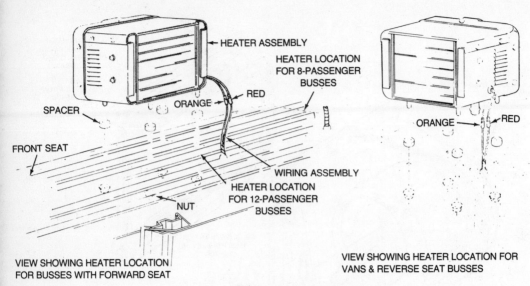

HEATER ASSEMBLY

HEATER LOCATION
FOR 8-PASSENGER
BUSSES

RED

ORANGE

SPACER

FRONT SEAT

ORANGE → RED

WIRING ASSEMBLY

HEATER LOCATION
FOR 12-PASSENGER
BUSSES

NUT

VIEW SHOWING HEATER LOCATION
FOR BUSSES WITH FORWARD SEAT

VIEW SHOWING HEATER LOCATION FOR
VANS & REVERSE SEAT BUSSES

1969–74 auxiliary hot water heater

3. Remove the two hoses from the heater core and plug the hoses.

4. Remove the rubber insulators from the heater core tubes.

5. Remove the four nuts from the heater assembly retaining studs.

6. Lower the vehicle.

7. Disconnect the two electrical leads at the heater assembly.

8. Remove the heater from the vehicle.

9. Position the heater assembly in the vehicle, inserting the mounting studs through the floor pan.

10. Connect the two electrical leads at the heater assembly.

11. Raise the vehicle on a hoist.

12. Install the four nuts on the heater assembly retaining studs.

13. Install the rubber insulators on the heater core tubes.

14. Remove the plugs from the heater hoses and install the hoses on the heater core tubes securing them with clamps.

15. Lower the vehicle.

16. Add required coolant to the cooling system.

17. Connect the battery ground cable.

Auxiliary Heater Case (With or Without Air Conditioning)

1975-88

1. Remove the first bench seat (if so equipped).

2. Discharge the air conditioning system, if so equipped. See Chapter 1.

3. Remove the auxiliary heater and/or air

conditioning cover assembly attaching screws and remove the cover.

4. Drain the cooling system.

CAUTION: *When draining the coolant, keep in mind that cats and dogs are attracted by the ethylene glycol antifreeze, and are quite likely to drink any that is left in an uncovered container or in puddles on the ground. This will prove fatal in sufficient quantity. Always drain the coolant into a sealable container. Coolant should be reused unless it is contaminated or several years old.*

5. Disconnect the heater hoses from the core tubes.

6. On air conditioning systems, disconnect the liquid line from the expansion valve and the suction line from the evaporator core, using a

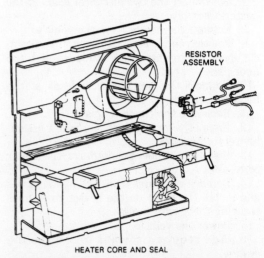

RESISTOR
ASSEMBLY

HEATER CORE AND SEAL

1975–88 auxiliary heater core and resistor

CHASSIS ELECTRICAL **381**

back-up wrench on the fittings. Cap the lines immediately.

7. From under the van, disconnect the blower motor wiring.

8. Remove the case retaining screws. Lift the case, disengaging the wiring harness grommet from the floor seal, and remove the case.

9. Make sure that all seals and grommets are in good condition and in place. Route the wiring harness through the floor seal.

10. Position the case assembly on the floor and install the retaining screws.

11. Connect the heater hoses. Tighten the hose clamps to 12-18 in.lb.

12. If equipped with air conditioning, connect the refrigerant lines, using new O-rings coated with clean refrigerant oil. Tighten the fitting using a back-up wrench.

13. Fill the cooling system.

14. Evacuate, charge and leak test the refrigerant system. See Chapter 1.

15. Run the engine and check for leaks in both the cooling and refrigerant systems.

16. Install the bench seat (if removed) and tighten the retaining bolts 25-45 ft.lb.

Auxiliary Heater Core and Seal Assembly
1975-88

1. Remove the first bench seat (if so equipped).

2. Remove auxiliary heater and/or air conditioning cover attaching screws and remove the cover.

3. Partially drain the engine coolant from the cooling system.

CAUTION: *When draining the coolant, keep in mind that cats and dogs are attracted by the ethylene glycol antifreeze, and are quite likely to drink any that is left in an uncovered container or in puddles on the ground. This will prove fatal in sufficient quantity. Always drain the coolant into a sealable container. Coolant should be reused unless it is contaminated or several years old.*

4. Remove the heater hoses from the auxiliary heater core assembly (2 clamps).

5. Pull the wiring assembly away from the heater core seal.

6. Remove and discard the strap retaining the heater core. Slide the heater core and seal assembly out of the housing slot.

7. Slide the heater core and seal assembly into the housing slot (position the wiring to one side).

8. Install the heater hoses to the heater core assembly (2 clamps).

9. Fill the cooling system to specification.

10. Position the cover assembly to the body side panel and install the attaching screws (15).

11. Install the bench seat (if removed) and tighten the retaining bolts 25-45 ft.lb.

Evaporator Core
REMOVAL AND INSTALLATION
1970-73

1. Remove the engine cover.

2. Remove the rear seat and remove the carpeting or mat.

3. Remove the control housing cover and disconnect the wiring harness.

4. Remove the retaining screws and lift the register from the floor.

5. Carefully position the sensor tube away from the core.

6. Raise a floor jack under the case to just take up the weight of the case.

7. Discharge the refrigerant system. See Chapter 1.

8. Disconnect the refrigerant lines at the core. Plug all openings at once!

9. Remove the rear air duct.

10. Remove the 10 bolts retaining the evaporator to the floor.

11. From under the van, remove the front and rear evaporator retaining nuts. Lower the evaporator on the jack while guiding the wiring through the opening.

12. Remove the cover screws and lift off the cover.

13. Remove the cover seal.

14. Remove the gasket from the top of the case.

15. Remove the top rail retaining screws and lift off the rail.

16. Remove the insulating tape from the expansion valev and remove the valve from the core.

17. Remove the 4 core-to-case screws and lift out the core.

To install:

18. Position the core in the case and install the rail.

19. Install the expansion valve and wrap it with insulating tape.

20. Install the expansion valve cover.

21. Position a new gasket on the case.

22. Raise the case into position, guiding the wiring as you go.

23. Install the retaining nuts and screws.

24. Connect the hoses.

25. Position the sensor tube.

26. Install the air duct and register.

27. Install the carpeting or mat.

28. Connect the wiring and install the cover.

29. Install the engine cover.

30. Evacuate, charge and leak test the system. See Chapter 1.

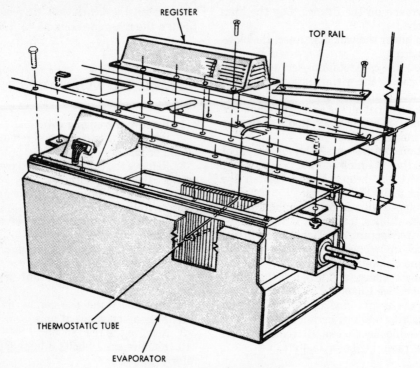

1970–73 evaporator installation

1974-87

1. Disconnect all wiring and vacuum connections at the case.

2. Remove the blower cover.

3. Remove the vacuum motor arm and washer from the outside recirculated door shaft.

4. Remove the control cable from its bracket. Disconnect the cable wire loop from the door shaft.

5. Remove the blower housing.

6. Remove the battery(ies).

7. Drain the cooling system.

CAUTION: *When draining the coolant, keep in mind that cats and dogs are attracted by the ethylene glycol antifreeze, and are quite likely to drink any that is left in an uncovered container or in puddles on the ground. This will prove fatal in sufficient quantity. Always drain the coolant into a sealable container. Coolant should be reused unless it is contaminated or several years old.*

8. Discharge the refrigerant system. See Chapter 1.

9. Disconnect the suction and liquid lines at

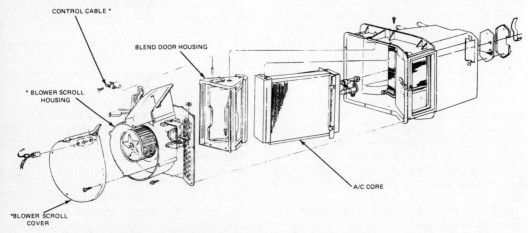

NOTE: REMOVE ALL ASSEMBLIES MARKED   BEFORE
REMOVING HOUSING WITH COMPONENTS FROM
DASH PANEL AND VEHICLE

1976–87 evaporator core replacement

the expansion valve and core. Use a back-up wrench on the fittings. Plug all openings immediately.

10. Disconnect the heater hoses at the core.

11. Remove the drain tube and valve from the barbed end of the drain sump at the bottom of the case.

12. Unbolt and remove the evaporator case from under the instrument panel (5 bolts).

13. Remove the blend door frame assembly.

14. Remove the insulation from the expansion valve bulb.

15. Remove the evaporator tube retainer and seal.

16. Remove the de-icing switch.

17. Installation is the reverse of removal. Use new O-rings coated with clean refrigerant oil and use a back-up wrench on the fittings. Evacuate, charge and leak test the system. See Chapter 1.

1988

1. Disconnect all wiring and vacuum connections at the case.

2. Remove the battery(ies).

3. Disconnect the EEC-IV harness.

4. Drain the cooling system.

CAUTION: *When draining the coolant, keep in mind that cats and dogs are attracted by the ethylene glycol antifreeze, and are quite likely to drink any that is left in an uncovered container or in puddles on the ground. This will prove fatal in sufficient quantity. Always drain the coolant into a sealable container. Coolant should be reused unless it is contaminated or several years old.*

5. Discharge the refrigerant system. See Chapter 1.

6. Disconnect the suction and liquid lines at the receiver/drier and core. Use a back-up wrench on the fittings. Plug all openings immediately.

7. Disconnect the heater hoses at the core.

8. Unbolt and remove the evaporator case from under the instrument panel (5 bolts).

9. Remove the receiver/drier from the case.

10. Remove the accumulator from the case.

11. Pull back the retaining tab and lift the core from the case.

12. Installation is the reverse of removal. Use

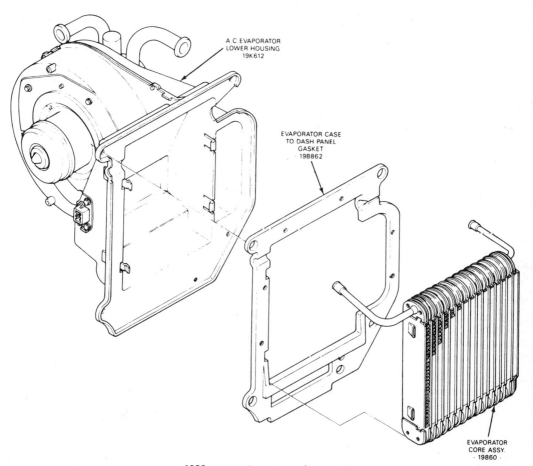

A C EVAPORATOR
LOWER HOUSING
19K612

EVAPORATOR CASE
TO DASH PANEL
GASKET
19B862

EVAPORATOR
CORE ASSY.
· 19860 ·

1988 evaporator core replacement

new O-rings coated with clean refrigerant oil and use a back-up wrench on the fittings. Evacuate, charge and leak test the system. See Chapter 1.

Auxiliary Evaporator Core

REMOVAL AND INSTALLATION

1972-74

1. Remove the rear seat.
2. Raise and support the van on jackstands.
3. From under the van, disconnect the wiring harness at the connector.
4. Discharge the refrigerant system. See Chapter 1.
5. Disconnect the refrigerant lines at the core tubes.
6. Remove the 4 nuts that retain the evaporator to the floor.
7. Lift the evaporator out from inside the van.
8. Remove the 4 retaining screws and lift off the cover.
9. You may now remove either the blower motor or core.
10. Installation is the reverse of removal.

1975-88

1. Remove the first bench seat.
2. Remove the cover assembly retaining screws and lift off the cover.
3. Discharge the refrigerant system. See Chapter 1.
4. Disconnect the liquid and suction lines from the receiver/drier and core. Use a back-up wrench on the fittings. Cap all openings at once.
5. Drain the cooling system.
CAUTION: *When draining the coolant, keep*

in mind that cats and dogs are attracted by the ethylene glycol antifreeze, and are quite likely to drink any that is left in an uncovered container or in puddles on the ground. This will prove fatal in sufficient quantity. Always drain the coolant into a sealable container. Coolant should be reused unless it is contaminated or several years old.

6. Disconnect the hoses from the heater core.
7. Remove the 4 core and bracket retaining bolts and lift the core and expansion valve from the case.
NOTE: *Any time that the core is replaced, a new suction accumulator drier must be installed.*
8. When installing the expansion valve on the core, use new O-rings coated with clean refrigerant oil on the line fittings. Tighten the expansion valve fittings, using a back-up wrench, to 15-20 ft.lb.
9. Clamp the expansion valve capillary bulb to the core outlet tube making sure that the bulb makes good contact with the outlet tube. Make sure that both components are clean. Wrap the bulb and tube with insulating tape such as Motorcraft YZ-1.
10. Wrap the ends of the core with insulating tape.
11. Attach the mounting plate to the expansion valve end of the core.
12. Carefully position the core in the case.
13. Connect the refrigerant lines, using new O-rings coated with clean refrigerant oil. Torque the fittings to 30-35 ft.lb. for the suction line and 10-15 ft.lb for the liquid line. Use a back-up wrench on the fittings.
14. Install the core-to-case screws.
15. Connect the heater hoses. Tighten the

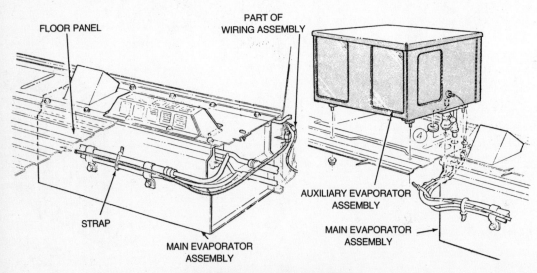

1972–74 dual evaporator installation

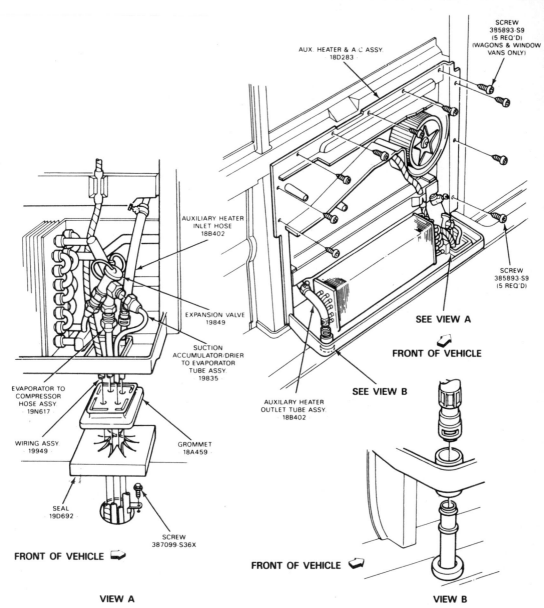

SCREW
385893-S9
(5 REQ'D)
(WAGONS & WINDOW
VANS ONLY)

AUX. HEATER & A.C. ASSY.
18D283

AUXILIARY HEATER
INLET HOSE
18B402

EXPANSION VALVE
19849

SUCTION
ACCUMULATOR/DRIER
TO EVAPORATOR
TUBE ASSY.
19835

EVAPORATOR TO
COMPRESSOR
HOSE ASSY.
19N617

WIRING ASSY.
19949

GROMMET
18A459

SEAL
19D692

SCREW
387099-S36X

FRONT OF VEHICLE

VIEW A

SCREW
385893-S9
(5 REQ'D)

SEE VIEW A

FRONT OF VEHICLE

SEE VIEW B

AUXILARY HEATER
OUTLET TUBE ASSY.
18B402

FRONT OF VEHICLE

VIEW B

1975—80 side mounted auxiliary air conditioner/heater

clamps to 12-18 in.lb. DO NOT
OVERTIGHTEN THE CLAMPS!

16. Fill the cooling system.

17. Evacuate, charge and leak test the
system.

18. Install the cover.

19. Install the bench seat. Torque the bolts to
25-45 ft.lb.

Auxiliary Gasoline Heater
1965-67

IGNITION BASE SERVICE

The breaker points, the breaker cam, and the
condenser are referred to as the ignition base

assembly. The assembly is mounted at one end
of the hot air blower. The breaker points are
protected from water and dirt by a metal snap-
on cover.

To service the breaker points, remove the retaining screws, disconnect the Bowden cable
from the thermostat and lift the cover from the
blower assembly on the left side of the floor
pan. Then, remove the breaker point snap-on
cover and check as follows:

1. Clean and inspect the breaker points.

2. If the breaker points are in good condition,
check the breaker points gap. If the gap on one
lobe of the cam is 0.018", a gap of 0.012" is permissible on the other lobe. Try to bring both

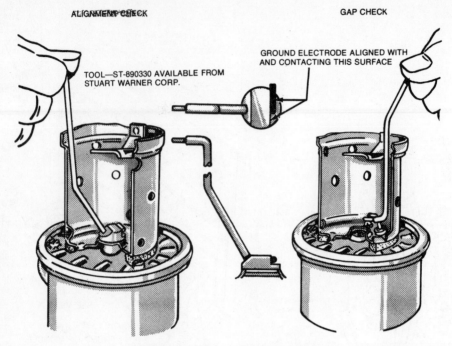

ALIGNMENT CHECK

GAP CHECK

GROUND ELECTRODE ALIGNED WITH
AND CONTACTING THIS SURFACE

TOOL—ST-890330 AVAILABLE FROM
STUART WARNER CORP.

Checking spark plug alignment and gap

gaps within the desired reading by loosening the two ignition unit mounting nuts and shifting the assembly slightly as permitted by bolt hole clearance.

3. If the correct gap limits cannot be obtained by shifting the assembly, the complete ignition unit assembly should be replaced.

Do not attempt to change the gap on used points by turning the threaded stationary point. A cratering action occurs here normally in service.

4. Be sure that the condenser connections are tight. Connections that are loose can result in intermittent and weak sparks. A bright flash can be due to an open circuit at this point.

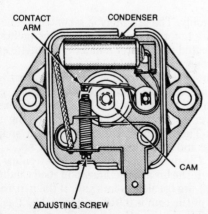

CONTACT
ARM

CONDENSER

CAM

ADJUSTING SCREW

Ignition points adjustment

HEATER HOUSING ASSEMBLY REPAIR

Before performing any service operations, the housing lower cover has to be removed.

Raise the truck on a hoist, remove the retaining screws, the remove the lower cover from the housing. The components are now accessible.

HEAT EXCHANGER AND BURNER ASSEMBLY

Removal and installation

1. Remove the four screws and nuts that join the outer and inner heater shields of the heat exchanger. Remove the overheat switch wire lead from the fuel solenoid, and disconnect the wire connector between the overheat switch and the terminal board. Lift the outer shield half off.

2. Remove the ignition coil high tension cable from the spark plug, and the combustion blower air duct at the burner unit. Also, remove the spark plug ground lead from the terminal board.

3. Disconnect the fuel line from the burner unit.

4. Remove the two screws and nuts that secure the heat exchanger exhaust outlet to the heat exchanger case side. Remove the holding plate, gasket and gasket retainer. Lift out the heat exchanger and burner assembly.

5. Position the heat exchanger and burner assembly in the heater. Position the holding

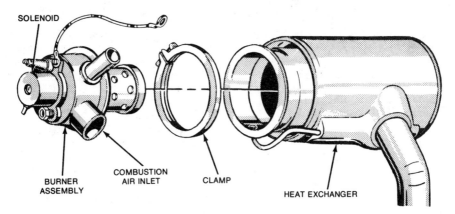

Heat exchanger and burner

plate, gasket retainer, and gasket on the heat exchanger exhaust outlet and install the 2 attaching screws and nuts.

6. Connect the fuel line to the burner unit.

7. Connect the ignition coil high tension cable to the spark plug ground lead to the terminal board.

8. Install the combustion blower air duct to the burner.

9. Position the heat exchanger outer shield half and install the 4 retaining screws and nuts.

10. Connect the overheat switch wire connector between the overheat switch and the terminal board.

IGNITION BASE ASSEMBLY

Removal and Installation

If the ignition base assembly has to be replaced, remove the retaining screws, disconnect the Bowden cable from the thermostat and lift the cover from the blower assembly on the left side of the floor pan.

Remove the two screws securing the assembly to the ventilator blower motor and pull off the unit. Unscrew the cam from the motor shaft.

After a new base has been installed, make adjustment of the breaker points by turning the threaded stationary point until the gap on each lobe of the cam conforms to the procedure outlined in Ignition Base Service, above. After readjustment is complete, lock the stationary point with rosin core solder.

THERMOSTAT AND CONTROL CABLE

Removal and Installation

1. Remove the heater cover retaining screws.

2. Disconnect the Bowden cable from the thermostat and lift the cover from the blower assembly on the left side of the floor pan.

3. Separate the two wires from the connectors on the thermostat microswitch.

4. Disconnect the control cable and remove the thermostat retaining screws.

5. When installing a new thermostat, adjust the control cable for satisfactory operation.

The thermostat is preset at the factory and is not adjustable in service. Any attempt to adjust the switch will almost certainly result in insufficient heater output, or in burned out heat exchanger.

IGNITION COIL

Removal and Installation

1. Disconnect the ignition coil cable from the spark plug at the burner unit.

2. Disconnect the ignition coil two wire leads from the terminal board.

3. Remove the coil mounting bracket two attaching nuts, together with washers and screws, and lift out the bracket and ignition coil and cable. To take the ignition coil from the bracket, remove or loosen the bracket screw.

4. Install the ignition coil in the bracket.

5. Position the coil and bracket in the heater case and install the 2 attaching nuts.

6. Connect the ignition coil terminal wires at the connectors. Connect the high tension lead to the spark and the ignition coil.

SPARK PLUG

Removal and Installation

To service a defective spark plug, the burner assembly should be removed from the heater housing. This can be done without removing the heat exchanger.

1. Disconnect the fuel line, then remove the ignition cable from the spark plug. Remove the spark plug ground wire from the terminal block.

2. Remove the wire terminal to the fuel solenoid.

3. Remove the clamp that secures the heat exchanger to the burner assembly.

4. Disconnect the combustion blower duct at the burner assembly and remove the burner from the housing.

5. After the burner assembly has been removed, take out the screws securing the spark plug retaining plate and remove the spark plug and its sealing copper washers from the burner unit. Give the spark plug a thorough check.

6. When installing the spark plug with the two washers into the burner housing, the spark plug electrode should point away from the large notch in the spark plug porcelain. The large notch indexes with a lug in the burner housing to provide correct electrode alignment. Before installing the spark plug, make certain that the spark plug electrode is in the center of the porcelain insulator.

7. The relationship of the ground electrode to the fuel nozzle is very important. This relationship can be checked by inserting gauge in the center hole of the mixer cup. The ground electrodes should lie flat against the flat surface of the gauge. If necessary, use long nose pliers to bend the ground electrode into the proper position.

8. The other end of the tool gauge can be used to check the gap between the spark plug electrode and the ground electrode. This end is 0.085″ thick. If necessary, bend the ground electrode to adjust the gap. But, after any bending, check once more the alignment of the ground electrode to the fuel nozzle.

9. Assemble the burner to the heat exchanger and connect the combustion blower direct.

10. Connect the wires and the fuel line.

COMBUSTION BLOWER AND FUEL PUMP

Removal and Installation

1. Remove the two clamps and disconnect the blower air hose at the burner and at the blower.

2. Remove the two fuel lines from the burner unit inlet and from the fuel pump inlet.

3. Remove the blower motor ground lead from the terminal block and disconnect the wire connector between the terminal board and the blower motor.

4. Remove the large clamp that holds the blower assembly to the mounting bracket in the case. Lift out the blower assembly.

5. Position the blower to the mounting in the heater case and install the retaining clamp.

6. Connect the motor wire at the connector and the ground wire at the terminal block.

7. Connect the fuel lines to the burner inlet and the fuel pump inlet.

8. Position the air hose to the blower and burner and install the two clamps.

BLOWER AND MOTOR

Removal and Installation

1. Remove the retaining screws, disconnecting the Bowden cable from the thermostat and lift the cover from the blower assembly on the left side of the floor pan.

2. Loosen the clamp and disconnect the hot air duct from the blower housing.

3. Remove the three screws that secure the motor mounting plate to the blower housing.

4. Disconnect the motor ground wire at the passenger compartment deck panel. Also, connect the wire at the breaker points assembly and disconnect the wire connectors to the blower motor.

5. Lift the assembly from the blower housing.

6. Remove the setscrew that holds the blower wheel to the motor shaft and pull off the wheel.

7. Remove the screws that hold the mounting plate to the blower motor and remove the plate and the two spacers.

8. To remove the breaker points assembly, remove the two securing screws and lift off the assembly. Remove the breaker points cam from the motor shaft.

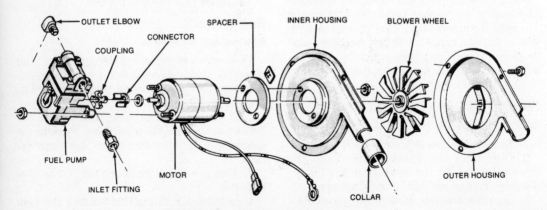

Exploded view of the combustion blower

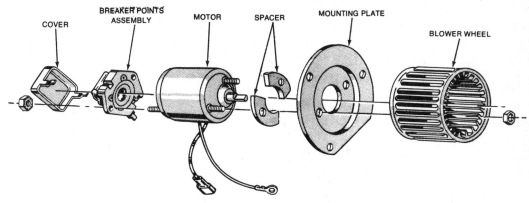

Exploded view of the hot air blower

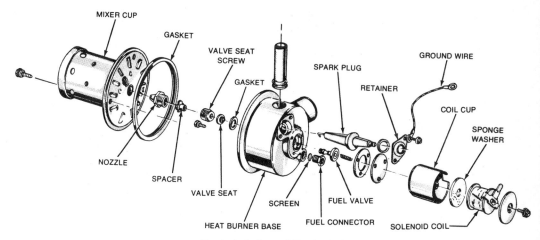

Exploded view of the burner

9. Install the breaker points cam on the motor shaft, then install the breaker points assembly. Check and adjust the points.

10. Place the two spacers on the motor mounting screws and install the mounting plate.

11. Install the blower wheel on the motor shaft.

12. Connect the blower motor and breaker assembly wires and connect the motor ground wire at the passenger compartment deck panel.

13. Mount the motor and blower assembly to the blower housing.

14. Connect the hot air duct to the blower housing.

15. Install the blower assembly cover and connect the thermostat Bowden cable.

Control Unit

REMOVAL AND INSTALLATION

1969-74 Heater Control Unit

1. Remove the knobs from the unit.
2. Remove the glove box.
3. Remove the radio.

4. Remove the control finish panel by removing the clip at the bottom of the panel.

5. Remove the engine cover.

6. Remove the screw retaining the lower edge of the control panel to the instrument panel.

7. Remove the upper retaining screw from the face of the instrument panel and pull the control unit through the glove box opening., disconnecting the cable.

8. Installation is the reverse of removal.

1972-74 Air Conditioning Control Unit

The control unit is separate from the heater controls and is located on the left side panel, directly behind the driver's seat.

1. To replace the thermostatic switch:
   a. Move the carpeting out of the way.
   b. Remove the register from the floor.
   c. Move the sensor tube away from the core.
   d. Remove the control housing cover.
   e. Remove the allen screw that retains the switch lever to the switch and remove the lever.

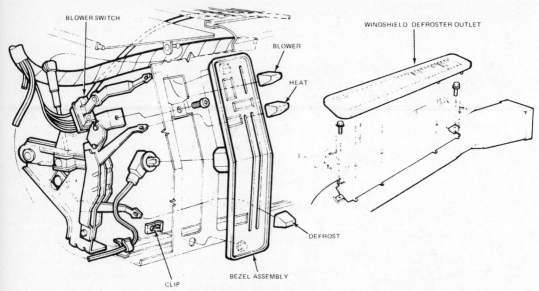

1969–74 heater control unit

f. Disconnect the wiring, remove the retaining screw and remove the switch and capillary tube.

g. Installation is the reverse of removal.

2. To replace the blower switch:

a. Remove the control housing cover.

b. Remove the allen screw retaining the lever to the switch and remove the lever.

c. Disconnect the wiring at the switch.

d. Remove the retaining screw and remove the switch.

e. Installation is the reverse of removal.

1975-88

HEATER AND/OR AIR CONDITIONER

1. Remove the trim applique.

2. Remove the 4 control unit retaining screws.

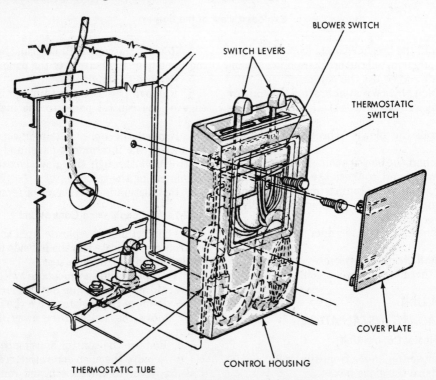

1972–74 air conditioner control housing

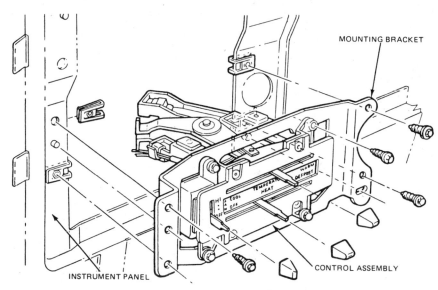

MOUNTING BRACKET

INSTRUMENT PANEL

CONTROL ASSEMBLY

1975–88 control unit

3. Slowly pull the control unit from the instrument panel.

4. Disconnect the electrical connectors, vacuum lines and light bulb. The control cable can be disconnected using needlenosed pliers to depress the tabs. The cable S-bend is removed by rotating the cable wire 90° to the lever.

5. Installation is the reverse of removal. Adjust the cable, if necessary.

RADIO

REMOVAL AND INSTALLATION

1961-67

1. Disconnect the lead wire at the fuse panel.
2. Detach the speaker leads at the radio.
3. Detach the antenna.
4. Pull off the control knobs. Remove the two screws and take off the dial assembly.
5. Remove the shaft nuts and the retaining plate.
6. Remove the right and left support bracket nuts and remove the radio.
7. Reverse the procedure for installation.

1969-74

1. Disconnect the ground cable from the battery.
2. Remove the 8 screws attaching the instrument cluster to the instrument panel. Pull the cluster away from the instrument panel and disconnect the speedometer. Allow the instrument cluster to hang out of the opening.
3. Disconnect the radio power and light wires at the connectors.
4. From under the hood, remove the nut attaching the radio rear mounting bracket to the dash panel.

5. Remove the knobs from the radio control shafts.

6. Remove the 8 screws attaching the radio bezel to the instrument panel. Pull the bezel away from the radio and disconnect the speaker wires at the multiple connector.

7. Remove the radio power wire from the two clips over the instrument cluster opening.

8. Disconnect the antenna lead-in cable from the radio.

9. Remove the 3 screws attaching the radio and mounting bracket to the radio opening, and remove the radio and bracket from the vehicle.

To install the radio:

10. Position the radio and mounting bracket in the instrument panel opening. Route the power wire through the clips over the instrument cluster opening.

11. Install the 3 radio mounting bracket attaching screws.

12. Connect the remaining components and install the instrument cluster in the reverse order of removal.

1975-88

1. Detach the battery ground cable.
2. Remove the heater and air conditioning control knobs. Remove the lighter.
3. Remove the radio knobs and discs.
4. If the van has a lighter, snap out the name plate at the right side to remove the panel attaching screw.
5. Remove the five finish panel screws.
6. Very carefully pry out the cluster panel in two places.

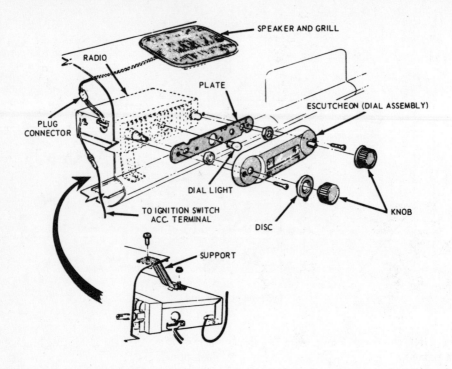

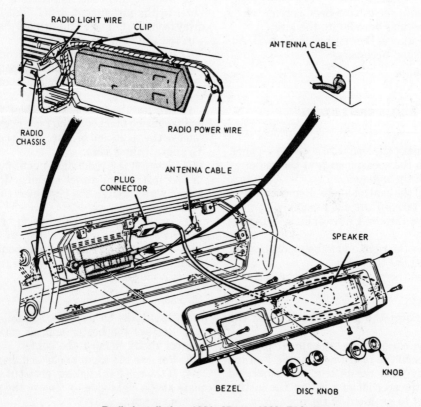

Radio installation: 1961–67 top; 1969–74 bottom

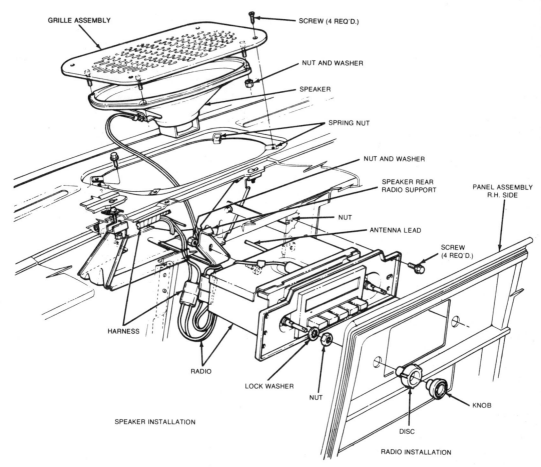

GRILLE ASSEMBLY

SCREW (4 REQ'D.)

NUT AND WASHER

SPEAKER

SPRING NUT

NUT AND WASHER

SPEAKER REAR
RADIO SUPPORT

PANEL ASSEMBLY
R.H. SIDE

NUT

ANTENNA LEAD

SCREW
(4 REQ'D.)

HARNESS

RADIO

LOCK WASHER

NUT

KNOB

SPEAKER INSTALLATION

DISC

RADIO INSTALLATION

1975–88 radio installation

7. Detach the antenna lead and speaker wires.

8. Remove the two nuts and washers and the mounting plate.

9. Remove the four front radio attaching screws. Remove the rear support nut and washer and remove the radio.

10. Reverse the procedure for installation.

WINDSHIELD WIPERS

Wiper Motor

REMOVAL AND INSTALLATION

1961-67

1. Disconnect the switch fed wire from the ignition switch, and the motor control wires at the terminals on the wiper control.

2. Remove the linkage arm retaining clip from the wiper arm lever, and remove the linkage arms.

3. Remove the wiper motor mounting bolts and remove the wiper motor and mounting bracket assembly from the instrument panel.

4. Transfer the mounting bracket from the old motor to the new motor.

5. Position the motor and bracket assembly to the retaining bracket under the instrument panel and install the mounting bolts.

6. Place the linkage arms on the wiper arm levers and install the retaining clips.

7. Connect the wiring and check the motor operation.

1969-74

1. Disconnect the battery ground.

2. Disconnect the motor wiring at the harness connector or junction.

3. Remove the clip and disconnect the motor drive arm from the linkage.

4. Remove the wiper motor bracket bolts and lift the motor and bracket from the van. If a new motor is being installed, transfer the drive arm.

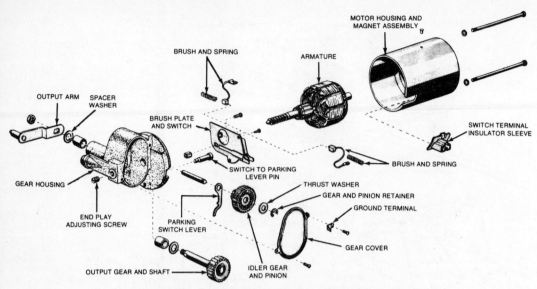

Exploded view of the 1961–64 single speed wiper motor

5. Make sure that the motor is in the PARK position and install the motor and bracket.
6. Connect the linkage.
7. Connect the wiring.
8. Check motor operation.

1975-88

1. Disconnect the battery ground.
2. Remove the fuse panel and bracket.
3. Disconnect the motor wiring.
4. Remove the wiper arms.
5. Remove the outer air intake cowl.

6. Remove the motor linkage clip.
7. Remove the motor mounting bolts and lift out the motor.
8. Transfer the motor drive arm if a new motor is being installed.
9. Make sure the motor is in PARK and install it.
10. Connect the linkage.
11. Connect the wiring.
12. Install the cowl panel.
13. Install the wiper arms.
14. Install the fuse panel and bracket.
15. Check the motor operation.

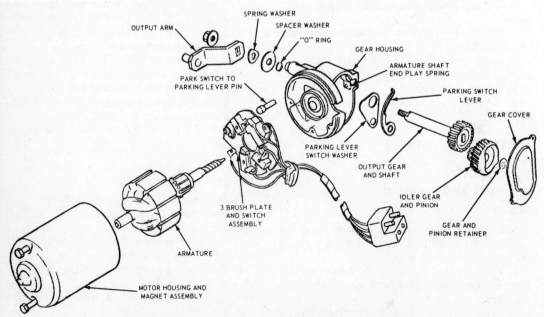

Exploded view of the two-speed windshield wiper motor

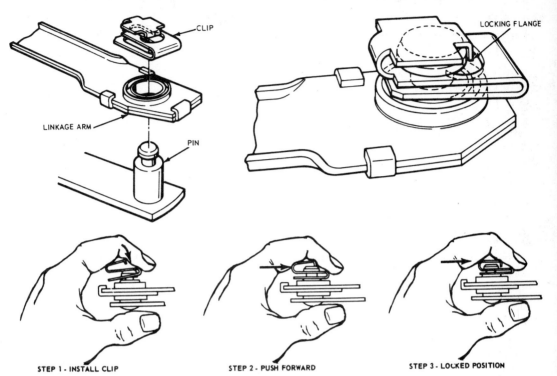

STEP 1 - INSTALL CLIP

STEP 2 - PUSH FORWARD

STEP 3 - LOCKED POSITION

Installation of the wiper arm connecting clip

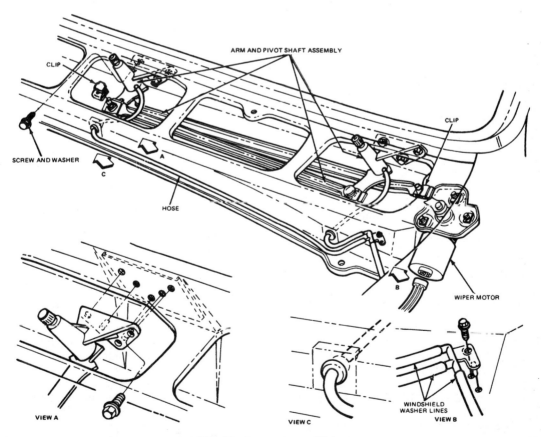

1975–88 wiper motor and linkage

Linkage

REMOVAL AND INSTALLATION

1961-67

1. Remove the wiper arms.
2. Remove the pivot shaft retaining bezels and nuts.
3. From inside the van, remove the retaining clip and washer that secures the linkage to the wiper motor arm, and remove the linkage and pivot shaft from the van.
4. Installation is the reverse of removal.

1969-74

1. Remove the wiper arms.
2. From inside, remove the 6 screws retaining the pivot shafts.
3. Remove the retaining clips securing the linkage to the wiper motor arm and remove the linkage and pivot shafts.
4. Installation is the reverse of removal.

1975-88

1. Diconnect the battery ground.
2. Remove the wiper arms.
3. Detach the washer hoses.
4. Remove the cowl.
5. Remove the linkage clips.
6. Remove the pivot-to-cowl screws and remove the linkage.
7. Installation is the reverse of removal.

INSTRUMENTS AND SWITCHES

Instrument Cluster

REMOVAL AND INSTALLATION

1961-67

1. Disconnect the battery ground cable.
2. Disconnect the speedometer cable at the speedometer head.
3. Remove the screws retaining the instrument cluster assembly to the instrument panel and lift the cluster out at the front of the panel.
4. Disconnect the instrument wires, remove the light sockets and remove the cluster assembly.
5. Position the cluster assembly, connect the instrument wires, and install the light sockets.
6. Install the cluster assembly to the instrument panel. When installing, make sure that all wiring and cables are moved away from the opening in the instrument panel.
7. Connect the speedometer cable and the battery ground cable. Be careful not to link the speedometer cable.
8. Check the operation of all gauges, lights and signals.

1969-70

1. Disconnect the battery ground cable.
2. Remove the screws retaining the instrument cluster assembly to the instrument panel.
3. Carefully lift the cluster away from the instrument panel far enough to gain access to the speedometer cable at the head. The cluster is removed from the front of the panel. Disconnect the speedometer cable at the speedometer head.
4. Disconnect the multiple connector of the cluster wiring loom, and remove the cluster assembly. Individual cluster connections can be disconnected for service as necessary.
5. Connect the speedometer cable and tighten the nut to 18-24 in.lb. Connect the cluster wiring loom multiple connector.
6. Carefully move the instrument cluster into position at the instrument panel, guiding all wiring and cables into position to prevent damage. Be careful not to kink the speedometer cable.
7. Install the screws retaining the instrument cluster to the instrument panel.
8. Connect the battery ground cable and check the operation of all gauges, lights and signals.

1971-74

1. Disconnect the battery ground cable.
2. From the front of the cluster, remove the eight screws that retain the cluster to the instrument panel, and position the cluster part way out of the panel for aces to the back of the cluster.
3. At the back of the cluster, disconnect the speedometer cable from the head and disconnect the multiple (fed) plug from the printed circuit.
4. Disconnect the wire from the flasher unit at the upper left hand corner of the cluster and remove the cluster assembly from the vehicle.
5. Hold the cluster near its opening in the instrument panel and connect: the wire to the flasher unit at the upper left hand corner of the cluster: the multiple feed plug to the printed circuit: and the speedometer cable to the head.
6. Position the cluster to the instrument panel and install the eight retaining screws.

1975-77

1. Disconnect the battery ground cable.
2. Remove seven instrument cluster-to-panel retaining screws.
3. Position cluster part away from the panel for access to the back of the cluster to disconnect the speedometer cable.
   If there is not sufficient access to disengage the speedometer cable form the speedometer, it

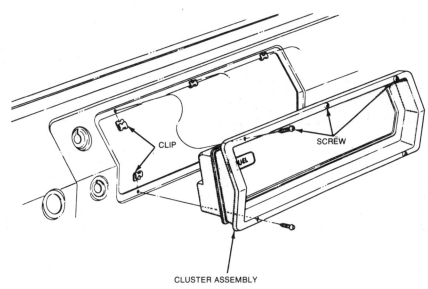

Removal and installation of the 1969–74 instrument cluster

may be necessary to remove the speedometer cable at the transmission and pull cable through cowl, to allow room to reach the speedometer quick disconnect.

4. Disconnect the harness connector plug from the printed circuit board and remove the cluster assembly from the instrument panel.

5. Remove the cluster.

6. Apply approximately $\frac{3}{16}$″ diameter ball of silicone lubricant or equivalent in the drive hole of the speedometer head.

7. Position the cluster near its opening in the instrument panel.

8. Disconnect the harness connector plug to the printed circuit board.

9. Connect the speedometer cable (quick disconnect) to the speedometer head.

10. Connect the speedometer cable and housing assembly to the transmission (if removed).

11. Install the seven instrument cluster-to-panel retaining screws and connect the battery ground cable.

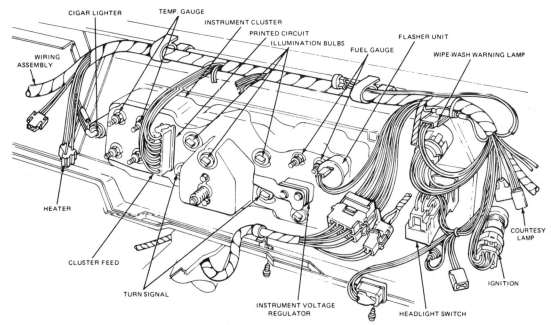

Rear view of a 1974 instrument cluster

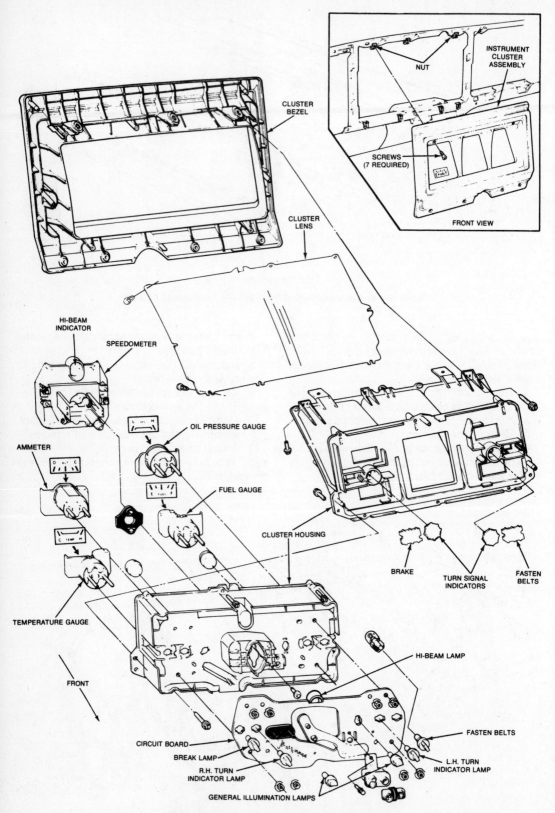

CLUSTER BEZEL

INSTRUMENT CLUSTER ASSEMBLY

NUT

SCREWS (7 REQUIRED)

FRONT VIEW

CLUSTER LENS

HI-BEAM INDICATOR

SPEEDOMETER

OIL PRESSURE GAUGE

AMMETER

FUEL GAUGE

CLUSTER HOUSING

BRAKE

TURN SIGNAL INDICATORS

FASTEN BELTS

TEMPERATURE GAUGE

HI-BEAM LAMP

FRONT

FASTEN BELTS

CIRCUIT BOARD

BREAK LAMP

R.H. TURN INDICATOR LAMP

L.H. TURN INDICATOR LAMP

GENERAL ILLUMINATION LAMPS

Rear view of the 1975–86 instrument cluster

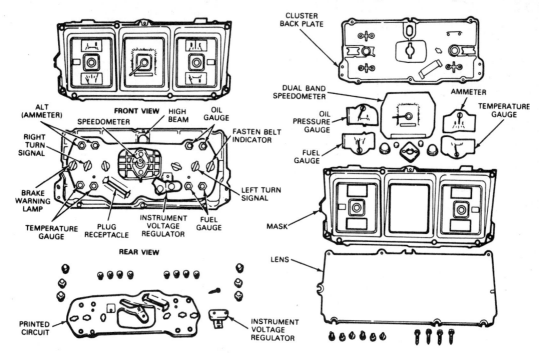

1987—88 instrument cluster

12. Check operation of all gauges, lights, and signals.

1978-88

1. Disconnect the battery ground cable.

2. Remove the two steering column shroud to panel retaining screws and remove the shroud.

3. Loosen the bolts which attach the column to the B and C support to provide sufficient clearance for cluster removal. (Required for tilt steering column vehicles only).

4. Remove the seven instrument cluster to panel retaining screws.

5. Position the cluster slightly away from the panel for access to the back of the cluster to disconnect the speedometer.

If there is not sufficient access to disengage the speedometer cable form the speedometer, it may be necessary to remove the speedometer cable at the transmission and pull the cable through the cowl, to allow room to reach the speedometer quick disconnect.

6. Disconnect the harness connector plug from the printed circuit board and remove the cluster assembly from the instrument panel.

7. Apply an approximately $\frac{3}{16}$" diameter ball of silicone lubricant or equivalent in the drive hole of the speedometer head.

8. Position the cluster near its opening in the instrument panel.

9. Connect the harness connector plug to the printed circuit board.

10. Connect the speedometer cable (quick disconnect) to the speedometer head.

11. Connect the speedometer cable and housing assembly to the transmission (if removed).

12. Install the seven instrument cluster-to-panel retaining screws and connect the battery ground cable.

13. Check the operation of all gauges, lights, and signals.

14. Install the steering column.

15. Position the steering column shroud on the instrument panel and install the two screws.

Speedometer Cable

REMOVAL AND INSTALLATION

1. Reach up behind the cluster and disconnect the cable by depressing the quick disconnect tab and pulling the cable away.

2. Remove the cable from the casing. If the cable is broken, raise the vehicle on a hoist and disconnect the cable from the transmission.

3. Remove the cable from the casing.

4. To remove the casing from the vehicle pull it through the floor pan.

5. To replace the cable, slide the new cable into the casing and connect it at the transmission.

6. Route the cable through the floor pan and position the grommet in its groove in the floor.

7. Push the cable onto the speedometer head.

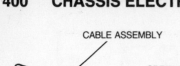

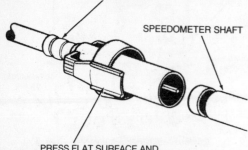

CABLE ASSEMBLY

SPEEDOMETER SHAFT

PRESS FLAT SURFACE AND
PULL CABLE AWAY FROM SPEEDOMETER HEAD

Speedometer cable quick-disconnect

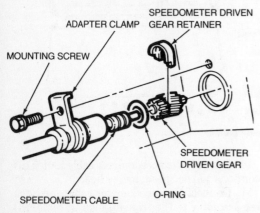

SPEEDOMETER DRIVEN
GEAR RETAINER

ADAPTER CLAMP

MOUNTING SCREW

SPEEDOMETER
DRIVEN GEAR

SPEEDOMETER CABLE   O-RING

Speedometer cable drive gear end

Windshield Wiper Switch
REPLACEMENT
1961-74

1. Disconnect the negative battery cable.
2. Loosen the screw on the wiper control switch knob, and remove the knob.
3. Remove the wiper control switch to instrument panel retaining nut, using Tool T456L-700A or equivalent.
4. Remove the wiper control switch from the instrument panel, and disconnect the feed wire and the motor control wires at the switch.
5. Reverse the procedure for installation.

1975-88

1. Disconnect the negative battery cable.
2. Remove the windshield wiper switch knob.
3. Remove the ignition switch bezel.
4. Remove the headlamp switch knob and shaft by pulling the switch to the headlamp **ON** position then depress the button on top of the switch and pull the knob and shaft out of the headlamp switch.
5. Remove the two screws at the bottom of the finish panel. Then, carefully pry the two up-

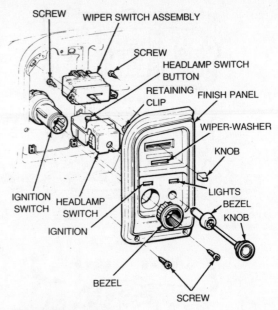

SCREW   WIPER SWITCH ASSEMBLY

SCREW

HEADLAMP SWITCH
BUTTON

RETAINING FINISH PANEL
CLIP

WIPER-WASHER

KNOB

LIGHTS

IGNITION
SWITCH   HEADLAMP
SWITCH

BEZEL

KNOB

IGNITION

BEZEL

SCREW

1975-88 wiper switch

per retainers away from the instrument panel assembly.
6. Disconnect the connector from the wiper switch.
7. Remove the wiper switch attaching screws and remove the switch.
8. Reverse the procedure for installation.

Headlight Switch
REPLACEMENT

1. Remove the headlamp control knob and shaft by pressing the knob release button on the switch housing, with the knob in the full **ON** position.
2. Pull the knob and shaft assembly out of the switch.

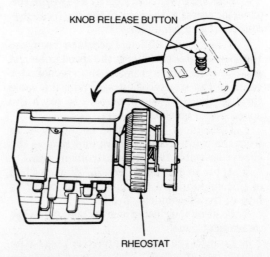

KNOB RELEASE BUTTON

RHEOSTAT

Typical headlight switch

3. Remove the switch, then remove the wiring connector from the switch.

4. To install the switch, connect the wiring connector to the headlamp switch, position the switch in the instrument panel, and install the bezel and mounting nut.

5. Install the knob and shaft assembly by inserting it all the way into the switch until a distinct click is heard. In some instances it may be necessary to rotate the shaft slightly until it engages the switch contact carrier.

6. Connect the battery ground cable.

Ignition Switch and Lock Cylinder

REMOVAL AND INSTALLATION

1961-67

1. Disconnect the negative cable from the battery.

2. Turn the ignition key to the accessory position. Slightly depress the pin in the lock face, turn the key counterclockwise, and pull the key and lock cylinder out of the switch assembly. If only the lock cylinder is to be replaced, proceed to Step 9.

3. Press in on the rear of the switch and rotate the switch 1/8 turn counterclockwise (as viewed from the terminal end). Remove the bezel, switch and spacer.

4. Remove the nut from the back of the ignition switch. Remove the accessory and gauge feed wires from the accessory terminal of the switch. Pull off the insulated plug from the rear of the switch.

5. If a new ignition switch is to be installed, insert a screwdriver into the lock opening of the ignition switch and turn the slot in the switch to a full counterclockwise position.

6. Connect the insulated plug with wires to the back of the ignition switch. Position the accessory and gauge wires onto the ignition switch stud and install the retaining nut.

7. Position the retainer on the switch with the open face away from the switch.

8. Place the switch and spacer to the switch opening and press the switch toward the instrument panel and install the bezel.

9. If a new lock cylinder is to be installed, insert the key in the cylinder and turn the key to the accessory position. Place the lock and key in the ignition switch, depress the pin slightly, and turn the key counterclockwise. Push the new lock cylinder into the switch. Turn the key to check the lock cylinder operation.

10. Connect the battery cable and check the ignition switch operation.

1969-79

1. Disconnect the battery ground cable.

2. Insert the ignition key in the switch. Turn

the key to the accessory position and insert a wire pin in the hole on the ignition switch. Slightly depress the pin while turning the key counterclockwise pat the accessory position; this will release the lock cylinder from the switch assembly. Pull the lock cylinder from the switch with the key. If only the lock cylinder is to be replaced proceed to Step 7.

3. Remove the bezel nut retaining the switch to the instrument panel and lower the switch.

4. Depress the tabs securing the multiple connector to the rear of the ignition switch with a small screwdriver. Pull the multiple connector from the switch and remove the switch.

5. Depress the tabs on the multiple connector and plug the connector into the switch assembly, being sure that thew tabs lock in place.

6. Position the switch to the instrument panel and install the bezel nut.

7. Insert the key in to the lock cylinder and turn the key to the accessory position. Place the cylinder and key in the switch. Push the cylinder into the switch until it is fully seated, then turn the key to the lock position. Turn the key to check the operation of the lock cylinder.

8. Connect the battery ground cable to the battery and check the operation of the switch assembly.

1980-88

These are steering column mounted units. For service procedures, see Chapter 8.

Clock

REMOVAL AND INSTALLATION

1. Disconnect the battery ground.

2. Remove the instrument finish panel covering the clock.

3. Remove the three clock retaining screws.

4. Pull the clock out and disconnect the wiring.

5. Installation is the reverse of removal.

LIGHTING

Headlights

REMOVAL AND INSTALLATION

1. Remove the attaching screws and remove the trim ring, or door. This isn't necessary on 1975 and later models.

2. Loosen or remove the headlight retaining ring by rotating it counterclockwise. Do not disturb the adjusting screw settings.

3. Pull the headlight bulb forward and disconnect the wiring assembly plug from the bulb.

4. Connect the wiring assembly plug to the

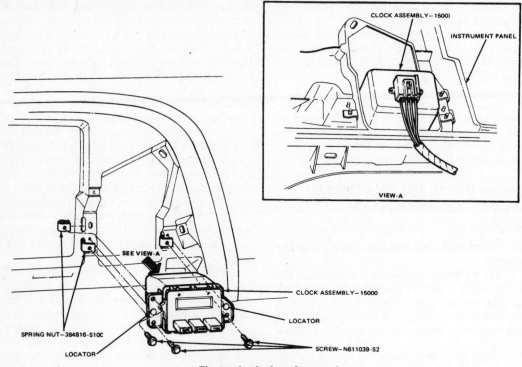

Electronic clock replacement

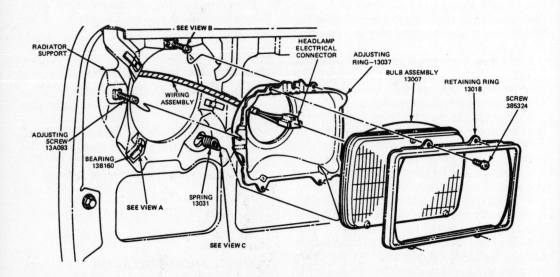

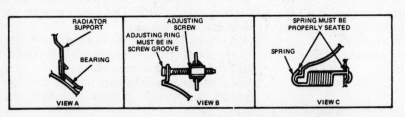

Square headlamp replacement

new bulb. Place the bulb in position, making sure that the locating tabs of the bulb are fitted in the positioning slots.

5. Install the headlight retaining ring.

6. Place the headlight trim ring or door into position, and install the retaining screws.

Parking, Side Marker, and Rear Lamps

REMOVAL AND INSTALLATION

1961-80

Remove the 2 lamp body screws and remove the bulb from the lamp body by turning it counterclockwise. Installation is the reverse of removal.

Front Side Marker Lamps
Rear Lamps
Rear Marker Lamps

REMOVAL AND INSTALLATION

1981-88

Remove the 2 lamp body screws and remove the bulb from the lamp body by turning it counterclockwise. Installation is the reverse of removal.

Parking Lamps

REMOVAL AND INSTALLATION

1981-88

1. Remove the headlamp trim ring and rim.

2. Remove the parking lamp by removing the 2 mounting screws.

3. Pull the lamp body out and turn the bulb socket counterclockwise to remove it.

4. Installation is the reverse of removal.

CIRCUIT PROTECTION

Fuses

The fuse panel is located on the firewall above the driver's left foot.

Circuit Breakers

Two circuit are protected by circuit breakers located in the fuse panel: the power windows (20 amp) and the power door locks (30 amp). The breakers are self-resetting.

Turn Signal and Hazard Flasher Locations

Both the turn signal flasher and the hazard warning flasher are mounted on the fuse panel. The turn signal flasher is mounted on the front

Fuse Link Location Chart
All Models

Circuit	Location	Protective Device
Air Conditioner, Clutch, Blower Relay	Fuse Panel	30 Amp
Air Conditioner	Starter Motor Relay	16 Gauge Fuse Link
Alternator	Starter Motor Relay	16 Gauge* Fuse Link
Alternator	Electric Choke	20 Gauge Fuse Link
Dual Batteries	Starter Motor Relay	14 Gauge Fuse Link

*14 gauge for 70 and 100 amp alternators

of the fuse panel, and the hazard warning flasher is mounted on the rear of the fuse panel.

Fuse Link

The fuse link is a short length of special, Hypalon (high temperature) insulated wire, integral with the engine compartment wiring harness and should not be confused with standard wire. It is several wire gauges smaller than the circuit which it protects. Under no circumstances should a fuse link replacement repair be made using a length of standard wire cut from bulk stock or from another wiring harness.

To repair any blown fuse link use the following procedure:

1. Determine which circuit is damaged, its location and the cause of the open fuse link. If the damaged fuse link is one of three fed by a common No. 10 or 12 gauge feed wire, determine the specific affected circuit.

2. Disconnect the negative battery cable.

3. Cut the damaged fuse link from the wiring harness and discard it. If the fuse link is one of three circuits fed by a single feed wire, cut it out of the harness at each splice end and discard it.

4. Identify and procure the proper fuse link and butt connectors for attaching the fuse link to the harness.

5. To repair any fuse link in a 3-link group with one feed:

   a. After cutting the open link out of the harness, cut each of the remaining undamaged fuse links close to the feed wire weld.

   b. Strip approximately ½" of insulation from the detached ends of the two good fuse links. Then insert two wire ends into one end

REMOVE EXISTING VINYL TUBE SHIELDING
REINSTALL OVER FUSE LINK BEFORE CRIMPING
FUSE LINK TO WIRE ENDS

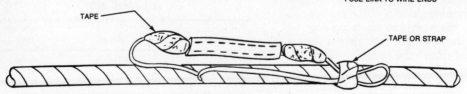

TAPE

TAPE OR STRAP

TYPICAL REPAIR USING THE SPECIAL #17 GA. (9.00" LONG-YELLOW) FUSE LINK REQUIRED FOR THE AIR/COND.
CIRCUITS (2) #687E and #261A LOCATED IN THE ENGINE COMPARTMENT

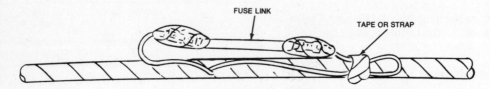

FUSE LINK

TAPE OR STRAP

TYPICAL REPAIR FOR ANY IN-LINE FUSE LINK USING THE SPECIFIED GAUGE FUSE LINK FOR THE SPECIFIC CIRCUIT

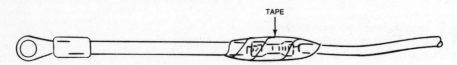

TAPE

TYPICAL REPAIR USING THE EYELET TERMINAL FUSE LINK OF THE SPECIFIED GAUGE FOR ATTACHMENT TO A CIRCUIT WIRE END

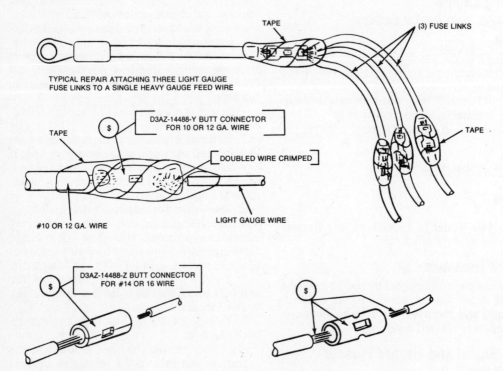

TAPE

(3) FUSE LINKS

TYPICAL REPAIR ATTACHING THREE LIGHT GAUGE
FUSE LINKS TO A SINGLE HEAVY GAUGE FEED WIRE

TAPE

$

D3AZ-14488-Y BUTT CONNECTOR
FOR 10 OR 12 GA. WIRE

DOUBLED WIRE CRIMPED

TAPE

#10 OR 12 GA. WIRE

LIGHT GAUGE WIRE

$

D3AZ-14488-Z BUTT CONNECTOR
FOR #14 OR 16 WIRE

$

FUSIBLE LINK REPAIR PROCEDURE

General fuse link repair procedure

of a butt connector and carefully push one stripped end of the replacement fuse link into the same end of the butt connector and crimp all three firmly together.

NOTE: *Care must be taken when fitting the three fuse links into the butt connector as the internal diameter is a snug it for three wires. Make sure to use a proper crimping tool. Pliers, side cutters, etc. will not apply the proper crimp to retain the wires and withstand a pull test.*

c. After crimping the butt connector to the three fuse links, cut the weld portion from the feed wire and strip approximately ½" of insulation from the cut end. Insert the stripped end into the open end of the butt connector and crimp very firmly.

d. To attach the remaining end of the replacement fuse link, strip approximately ½" of insulation from the wire end of the circuit from which the blown fuse link was removed, and firmly crimp a butt connector or equivalent to the stripped wire. Then, insert the end of the replacement link into the other end of the butt connector and crimp firmly.

e. Using rosin core solder with a consistency of 60 percent tin and 40 percent lead, solder the connectors and the wires at the repairs and insulate with electrical tape.

6. To replace any fuse link on a single circuit in a harness, cut out the damaged portion, strip approximately ½" of insulation from the two wire ends and attach the appropriate replacement fuse link to the stripped wire ends with two proper size butt connectors. Solder the connectors and wires and insulate the tape.

7. To repair any fuse link which has an eyelet terminal on one end such as the charging circuit, cut off the open fuse link behind the weld, strip approximately ½" of insulation from the cut end and attach the appropriate new eyelet fuse link to the cut stripped wire with an appropriate size butt connector. Solder the connectors and wires at the repair and insulate with tape.

8. Connect the negative battery cable to the battery and test the system for proper operation.

NOTE: *Do not mistake a resistor wire for a fuse link. The resistor wire is generally longer and has print stating, "Resistor: don't cut or splice."*

TRAILER WIRING

Wiring the truck for towing is fairly easy. There are a number of good wiring kits available and these should be used, rather than trying to design your own. All trailers will need brake lights and turn signals as well as tail lights and side marker lights. Most states require extra marker lights for overly wide trailers. Also, most states have recently required back-up lights for trailers, and most trailer manufacturers have been building trailers with back-up lights for several years.

Additionally, some Class I, most Class II and just about all Class III trailers will have electric brakes.

Add to this number an accessories wire, to operate trailer internal equipment or to charge the trailer's battery, and you can have as many as seven wires in the harness.

Determine the equipment on your trailer and buy the wiring kit necessary. The kit will contain all the wires needed, plus a plug adapter set which included the female plug, mounted on the bumper or hitch, and the male plug, wired into, or plugged into the trailer harness.

When installing the kit, follow the manufacturer's instructions. The color coding of the wires is standard throughout the industry.

One point to note, some domestic vehicles, and most imported vehicles, have separate turn signals. On most domestic vehicles, the brake lights and rear turn signals operate with the same bulb. For those vehicles with separate turn signals, you can purchase an isolation unit so that the brake lights won't blink whenever the turn signals are operated, or, you can go to your local electronics supply house and buy four diodes to wire in series with the brake and turn signal bulbs. Diodes will isolate the brake and turn signals. The choice is yours. The isolation units are simple and quick to install, but far more expensive than the diodes. The diodes, however, require more work to install properly, since they require the cutting of each bulb's wire and soldering in place of the diode.

One final point, the best kits are those with a spring loaded cover on the vehicle mounted socket. This cover prevents dirt and moisture from corroding the terminals. Never let the vehicle socket hang loosely. Always mount it securely to the bumper or hitch.

Troubleshooting Basic Turn Signal and Flasher Problems

Most problems in the turn signals or flasher system, can be reduced to defective flashers or bulbs, which are easily replaced. Occasionally, problems in the turn signals are traced to the switch in the steering column, which will require professional service.

F = Front   R = Rear   ● = Lights off   ○ = Lights on

Problem		Solution
Turn signals light, but do not flash		• Replace the flasher
No turn signals light on either side		• Check the fuse. Replace if defective. • Check the flasher by substitution • Check for open circuit, short circuit or poor ground
Both turn signals on one side don't work		• Check for bad bulbs • Check for bad ground in both housings
One turn signal light on one side doesn't work		• Check and/or replace bulb • Check for corrosion in socket. Clean contacts. • Check for poor ground at socket
Turn signal flashes too fast or too slow		• Check any bulb on the side flashing too fast. A heavy-duty bulb is probably installed in place of a regular bulb. • Check the bulb flashing too slow. A standard bulb was probably installed in place of a heavy-duty bulb. • Check for loose connections or corrosion at the bulb socket
Indicator lights don't work in either direction		• Check if the turn signals are working • Check the dash indicator lights • Check the flasher by substitution
One indicator light doesn't light		• On systems with 1 dash indicator: See if the lights work on the same side. Often the filaments have been reversed in systems combining stoplights with taillights and turn signals. Check the flasher by substitution • On systems with 2 indicators: Check the bulbs on the same side Check the indicator light bulb Check the flasher by substitution

Troubleshooting Basic Lighting Problems

Problem	Cause	Solution
Lights		
One or more lights don't work, but others do	• Defective bulb(s) • Blown fuse(s) • Dirty fuse clips or light sockets • Poor ground circuit	• Replace bulb(s) • Replace fuse(s) • Clean connections • Run ground wire from light socket housing to car frame
Lights burn out quickly	• Incorrect voltage regulator setting or defective regulator • Poor battery/alternator connections	• Replace voltage regulator • Check battery/alternator connections
Lights go dim	• Low/discharged battery • Alternator not charging • Corroded sockets or connections • Low voltage output	• Check battery • Check drive belt tension; repair or replace alternator • Clean bulb and socket contacts and connections • Replace voltage regulator
Lights flicker	• Loose connection • Poor ground • Circuit breaker operating (short circuit)	• Tighten all connections • Run ground wire from light housing to car frame • Check connections and look for bare wires
Lights "flare"—Some flare is normal on acceleration—if excessive, see "Lights Burn Out Quickly"	• High voltage setting	• Replace voltage regulator
Lights glare—approaching drivers are blinded	• Lights adjusted too high • Rear springs or shocks sagging • Rear tires soft	• Have headlights aimed • Check rear springs/shocks • Check/correct rear tire pressure
Turn Signals		
Turn signals don't work in either direction	• Blown fuse • Defective flasher • Loose connection	• Replace fuse • Replace flasher • Check/tighten all connections
Right (or left) turn signal only won't work	• Bulb burned out • Right (or left) indicator bulb burned out • Short circuit	• Replace bulb • Check/replace indicator bulb • Check/repair wiring
Flasher rate too slow or too fast	• Incorrect wattage bulb • Incorrect flasher	• Flasher bulb • Replace flasher (use a variable load flasher if you pull a trailer)
Indicator lights do not flash (burn steadily)	• Burned out bulb • Defective flasher	• Replace bulb • Replace flasher
Indicator lights do not light at all	• Burned out indicator bulb • Defective flasher	• Replace indicator bulb • Replace flasher

Troubleshooting Basic Dash Gauge Problems

Problem	Cause	Solution
Coolant Temperature Gauge		
Gauge reads erratically or not at all	• Loose or dirty connections • Defective sending unit	• Clean/tighten connections • Bi-metal gauge: remove the wire from the sending unit. Ground the wire for an instant. If the gauge registers, replace the sending unit.

Troubleshooting Basic Dash Gauge Problems (cont.)

Problem	Cause	Solution
Coolant Temperature Gauge		
Gauge reads erratically or not at all (cont.)	· Defective gauge	· Magnetic gauge: disconnect the wire at the sending unit. With ignition ON gauge should register COLD. Ground the wire; gauge should register HOT.
Ammeter Gauge—Turn Headlights ON (do not start engine). Note reaction		
Ammeter shows charge	· Connections reversed on gauge	· Reinstall connections
Ammeter shows discharge	· Ammeter is OK	· Nothing
Ammeter does not move	· Loose connections or faulty wiring	· Check/correct wiring
	· Defective gauge	· Replace gauge
Oil Pressure Gauge		
Gauge does not register or is inaccurate	· On mechanical gauge, Bourdon tube may be bent or kinked	· Check tube for kinks or bends preventing oil from reaching the gauge
	· Low oil pressure	· Remove sending unit. Idle the engine briefly. If no oil flows from sending unit hole, problem is in engine.
	· Defective gauge	· Remove the wire from the sending unit and ground it for an instant with the ignition ON. A good gauge will go to the top of the scale.
	· Defective wiring	· Check the wiring to the gauge. If it's OK and the gauge doesn't register when grounded, replace the gauge.
	· Defective sending unit	· If the wiring is OK and the gauge functions when grounded, replace the sending unit
All Gauges		
All gauges do not operate	· Blown fuse	· Replace fuse
	· Defective instrument regulator	· Replace instrument voltage regulator
All gauges read low or erratically	· Defective or dirty instrument voltage regulator	· Clean contacts or replace
All gauges pegged	· Loss of ground between instrument voltage regulator and car	· Check ground
	· Defective instrument regulator	· Replace regulator
Warning Lights		
Light(s) do not come on when ignition is ON, but engine is not started	· Defective bulb	· Replace bulb
	· Defective wire	· Check wire from light to sending unit
	· Defective sending unit	· Disconnect the wire from the sending unit and ground it. Replace the sending unit if the light comes on with the ignition ON.
Light comes on with engine running	· Problem in individual system	· Check system
	· Defective sending unit	· Check sending unit (see above)

Troubleshooting the Heater

Problem	Cause	Solution
Blower motor will not turn at any speed	• Blown fuse • Loose connection • Defective ground • Faulty switch • Faulty motor • Faulty resistor	• Replace fuse • Inspect and tighten • Clean and tighten • Replace switch • Replace motor • Replace resistor
Blower motor turns at one speed only	• Faulty switch • Faulty resistor	• Replace switch • Replace resistor
Blower motor turns but does not circulate air	• Intake blocked • Fan not secured to the motor shaft	• Clean intake • Tighten security
Heater will not heat	• Coolant does not reach proper temperature • Heater core blocked internally • Heater core air-bound • Blend-air door not in proper position	• Check and replace thermostat if necessary • Flush or replace core if necessary • Purge air from core • Adjust cable
Heater will not defrost	• Control cable adjustment incorrect • Defroster hose damaged	• Adjust control cable • Replace defroster hose

Troubleshooting Basic Windshield Wiper Problems

Problem	Cause	Solution
Electric Wipers		
Wipers do not operate— Wiper motor heats up or hums	• Internal motor defect • Bent or damaged linkage • Arms improperly installed on linking pivots	• Replace motor • Repair or replace linkage • Position linkage in park and reinstall wiper arms
Wipers do not operate— No current to motor	• Fuse or circuit breaker blown • Loose, open or broken wiring • Defective switch • Defective or corroded terminals • No ground circuit for motor or switch	• Replace fuse or circuit breaker • Repair wiring and connections • Replace switch • Replace or clean terminals • Repair ground circuits
Wipers do not operate— Motor runs	• Linkage disconnected or broken	• Connect wiper linkage or replace broken linkage
Vacuum Wipers		
Wipers do not operate	• Control switch or cable inoperative • Loss of engine vacuum to wiper motor (broken hoses, low engine vacuum, defective vacuum/fuel pump) • Linkage broken or disconnected • Defective wiper motor	• Repair or replace switch or cable • Check vacuum lines, engine vacuum and fuel pump • Repair linkage • Replace wiper motor
Wipers stop on engine acceleration	• Leaking vacuum hoses • Dry windshield • Oversize wiper blades • Defective vacuum/fuel pump	• Repair or replace hoses • Wet windshield with washers • Replace with proper size wiper blades • Replace pump

Drive Train

UNDERSTANDING THE MANUAL TRANSMISSION

Because of the way an internal combustion engine breathes, it can produce torque, or twisting force, only within a narrow speed range. Most modern, overhead valve engines must turn at about 2,500 rpm to produce their peak torque. By 4,500 rpm they are producing so little torque that continued increases in engine speed produce no power increases.

The torque peak on overhead camshaft engines is, generally, much higher, but much narrower.

The manual transmission and clutch are employed to vary the relationship between engine speed and the speed of the wheels so that adequate engine power can be produced under all circumstances. The clutch allows engine torque to be applied to the transmission input shaft gradually, due to mechanical slippage. The car can, consequently, be started smoothly from a full stop.

The transmission changes the ratio between the rotating speeds of the engine and the wheels by the use of gears. 4-speed or 5-speed transmissions are most common. The lower gears allow full engine power to be applied to the rear wheels during acceleration at low speeds.

The clutch drive plate is a thin disc, the center of which is splined to the transmission input shaft. Both sides of the disc are covered with a layer of material which is similar to brake lining and which is capable of allowing slippage without roughness or excessive noise.

The clutch cover is bolted to the engine flywheel and incorporates a diaphragm spring which provides the pressure to engage the clutch. The cover also houses the pressure plate. The driven disc is sandwiched between the pressure plate and the smooth surface of the flywheel when the clutch pedal is released,

thus forcing it to turn at the same speed as the engine crankshaft.

The transmission contains a mainshaft which passes all the way through the transmission, from the clutch to the driveshaft. This shaft is separated at one point, so that front and rear portions can turn at different speeds.

Power is transmitted by a countershaft in the lower gears and reverse. The gears of the countershaft mesh with gears on the mainshaft, allowing power to be carried from one to the other. All the countershaft gears are integral with that shaft, while several of the mainshaft gears can either rotate independently of the shaft or be locked to it. Shifting from one gear to the next causes one of the gears to be freed from rotating with the shaft and locks another to it. Gears are locked and unlocked by internal dog clutches which slide between the center of the gear and the shaft. The forward gears usually employ synchronizers; friction members which smoothly bring gear and shaft to the same speed before the toothed dog clutches are engaged.

The clutch is operating properly if:

1. It will stall the engine when released with the vehicle held stationary.

2. The shift lever can be moved freely between first and reverse gears when the vehicle is stationary and the clutch disengaged.

A clutch pedal free-play adjustment is incorporated in the linkage. If there is about 1-2" (25-50mm) of motion before the pedal begins to release the clutch, it is adjusted properly. Inadequate free-play wears all parts of the clutch releasing mechanisms and may cause slippage. Excessive free-play may cause inadequate release and hard shifting of gears.

Some clutches use a hydraulic system in place of mechanical linkage. If the clutch fails to release, fill the clutch master cylinder with flu-

Troubleshooting the Manual Transmission

Problem	Cause	Solution
Transmission shifts hard	• Clutch adjustment incorrect • Clutch linkage or cable binding • Shift rail binding	• Adjust clutch • Lubricate or repair as necessary • Check for mispositioned selector arm roll pin, loose cover bolts, worn shift rail bores, worn shift rail, distorted oil seal, or extension housing not aligned with case. Repair as necessary.
	• Internal bind in transmission caused by shift forks, selector plates, or synchronizer assemblies • Clutch housing misalignment • Incorrect lubricant • Block rings and/or cone seats worn	• Remove, dissemble and inspect transmission. Replace worn or damaged components as necessary. • Check runout at rear face of clutch housing • Drain and refill transmission • Blocking ring to gear clutch tooth face clearance must be 0.030 inch or greater. If clearance is correct it may still be necessary to inspect blocking rings and cone seats for excessive wear. Repair as necessary.
Gear clash when shifting from one gear to another	• Clutch adjustment incorrect • Clutch linkage or cable binding • Clutch housing misalignment • Lubricant level low or incorrect lubricant • Gearshift components, or synchronizer assemblies worn or damaged	• Adjust clutch • Lubricate or repair as necessary • Check runout at rear of clutch housing • Drain and refill transmission and check for lubricant leaks if level was low. Repair as necessary. • Remove, disassemble and inspect transmission. Replace worn or damaged components as necessary.
Transmission noisy	• Lubricant level low or incorrect lubricant • Clutch housing-to-engine, or transmission-to-clutch housing bolts loose • Dirt, chips, foreign material in transmission • Gearshift mechanism, transmission gears, or bearing components worn or damaged • Clutch housing misalignment	• Drain and refill transmission. If lubricant level was low, check for leaks and repair as necessary. • Check and correct bolt torque as necessary • Drain, flush, and refill transmission • Remove, disassemble and inspect transmission. Replace worn or damaged components as necessary. • Check runout at rear face of clutch housing
Jumps out of gear	• Clutch housing misalignment • Gearshift lever loose • Offset lever nylon insert worn or lever attaching nut loose • Gearshift mechanism, shift forks, selector plates, interlock plate, selector arm, shift rail, detent plugs, springs or shift cover worn or damaged • Clutch shaft or roller bearings worn or damaged	• Check runout at rear face of clutch housing • Check lever for worn fork. Tighten loose attaching bolts. • Remove gearshift lever and check for loose offset lever nut or worn insert. Repair or replace as necessary. • Remove, disassemble and inspect transmission cover assembly. Replace worn or damaged components as necessary. • Replace clutch shaft or roller bearings as necessary

Troubleshooting the Manual Transmission (cont.)

Problem	Cause	Solution
Jumps out of gear (cont.)	• Gear teeth worn or tapered, synchronizer assemblies worn or damaged, excessive end play caused by worn thrust washers or output shaft gears	• Remove, disassemble, and inspect transmission. Replace worn or damaged components as necessary.
	• Pilot bushing worn	• Replace pilot bushing
Will not shift into one gear	• Gearshift selector plates, interlock plate, or selector arm, worn, damaged, or incorrectly assembled	• Remove, disassemble, and inspect transmission cover assembly. Repair or replace components as necessary.
	• Shift rail detent plunger worn, spring broken, or plug loose	• Tighten plug or replace worn or damaged components as necessary
	• Gearshift lever worn or damaged	• Replace gearshift lever
	• Synchronizer sleeves or hubs, damaged or worn	• Remove, disassemble and inspect transmission. Replace worn or damaged components.
Locked in one gear—cannot be shifted out	• Shift rail(s) worn or broken, shifter fork bent, setscrew loose, center detent plug missing or worn	• Inspect and replace worn or damaged parts
	• Broken gear teeth on countershaft gear, clutch shaft, or reverse idler gear	• Inspect and replace damaged part
	Gearshift lever broken or worn, shift mechanism in cover incorrectly assembled or broken, worn damaged gear train components	• Disassemble transmission. Replace damaged parts or assemble correctly.
Transfer case difficult to shift or will not shift into desired range	• Vehicle speed too great to permit shifting	• Stop vehicle and shift into desired range. Or reduce speed to 3–4 km/h (2–3 mph) before attempting to shift.
	• If vehicle was operated for extended period in 4H mode on dry paved surface, driveline torque load may cause difficult shifting	• Stop vehicle, shift transmission to neutral, shift transfer case to 2H mode and operate vehicle in 2H on dry paved surfaces
	• Transfer case external shift linkage binding	• Lubricate or repair or replace linkage, or tighten loose components as necessary
	• Insufficient or incorrect lubricant	• Drain and refill to edge of fill hole with SAE 85W-90 gear lubricant only
	• Internal components binding, worn, or damaged	• Disassemble unit and replace worn or damaged components as necessary
Transfer case noisy in all drive modes	• Insufficient or incorrect lubricant	• Drain and refill to edge of fill hole with SAE 85W-90 gear lubricant only. Check for leaks and repair if necessary. Note: If unit is still noisy after drain and refill, disassembly and inspection may be required to locate source of noise.
Noisy in—or jumps out of four wheel drive low range	• Transfer case not completely engaged in 4L position	• Stop vehicle, shift transfer case in Neutral, then shift back into 4L position
	• Shift linkage loose or binding	• Tighten, lubricate, or repair linkage as necessary
	• Shift fork cracked, inserts worn, or fork is binding on shift rail	• Disassemble unit and repair as necessary
Lubricant leaking from output shaft seals or from vent	• Transfer case overfilled	• Drain to correct level
	• Vent closed or restricted	• Clear or replace vent if necessary

Troubleshooting the Manual Transmission (cont.)

Problem	Cause	Solution
Lubricant leaking from output shaft seals or from vent (cont.)	• Output shaft seals damaged or installed incorrectly	• Replace seals. Be sure seal lip faces interior of case when installed. Also be sure yoke seal surfaces are not scored or nicked. Remove scores, nicks with fine sandpaper or replace yoke(s) if necessary.
Abnormal tire wear	• Extended operation on dry hard surface (paved) roads in 4H range	• Operate in 2H on hard surface (paved) roads

id to the proper level and pump the clutch pedal to fill the system with fluid. Bleed the system in the same way as a brake system. If leaks are located, tighten loose connections or overhaul the master or slave cylinder as necessary.

MANUAL TRANSMISSION

LINKAGE ADJUSTMENT

Ford 3.03 3-Speed

1. Place the shift lever in the neutral position.
2. Loosen the adjusting nuts on the transmission levers sufficiently to allow the shift rods to slide freely at the levers.
3. Insert a ¼" diameter rod (1961-75) or ³⁄₁₆" diameter rod (1976 and later) through the pilot hole in the shift tube mounting bracket until it enters the adjustment hole of both levers (1961-75) or through both levers (1976 and later).
4. Place the transmission levers in the neutral position and tighten the adjusting nuts.
5. Remove the rod from the pilot holes and check the operation of the shift levers.

Dagenham 4-Speed

1. Place the shift lever in the neutral position.
2. Loosen the trunnion nuts at the transmis-

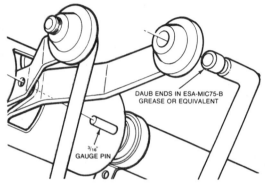

DAUB ENDS IN ESA-MIC75-B GREASE OR EQUIVALENT

³⁄₁₆" GAUGE PIN

1976–84 shift linkage adjustment—3-speed

sion shift levers until the shift rods can slide freely in their trunnions.
3. Insert a ¼" rod through the hole in the lever locating bracket and through the three shift levers.
4. Make sure that the shift levers are in the neutral position and tighten the adjusting nuts.
5. Remove the rod from the pilot holes and check the operation of the shift levers.

SROD 4-Speed

1. Disconnect the 3 shift rods from the shifter.
2. Insert a ¼" diameter rod through the alignment hole in the shifter assembly. Make

Manual Transmission Application Chart

Transmission Types	Years	Models
Ford 3.03 3-speed	1961–86	All
Dagenham 4-speed	1964	E-100
Ford 4-speed OD	1978–83 1984–85 1986–87	E-100—350 E-150—350 E-150
Mazda M50D 5-sp Overdrive	1988	E-150 w/6-300
ZF S5-42 5-speed Overdrive	1988	E-150 w/6-300

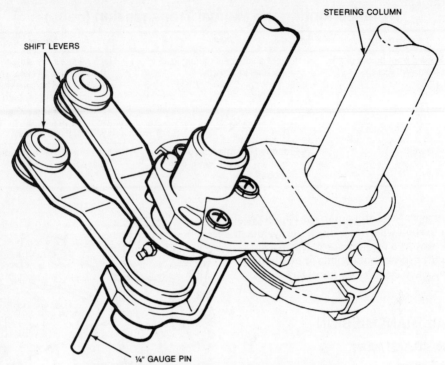

¼" GAUGE PIN

1961–75 shift linkage adjustment—3-speed

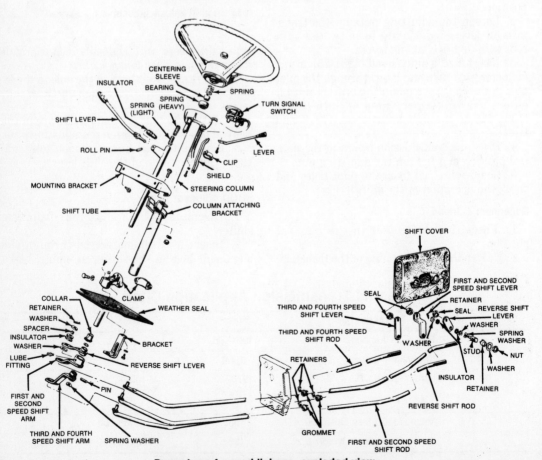

Dagenham 4-speed linkage, exploded view

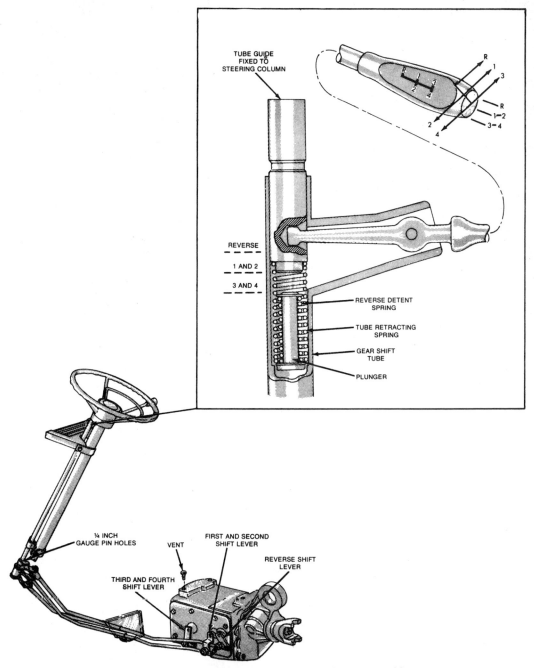

Dagenham 4-speed transmission and linkage assembly

sure that the levers are in the neutral position.

3. Align the three levers as follows:

a. Place the forward (3rd/4th) lever in the mid-position.

b. Place the rearward (1st/2nd) lever in the mid-position.

c. Rotate the middle (reverse) lever counterclockwise to the neutral position.

4. Rotate the output shaft to ensure that the transmission is in neutral.

5. Attach the slotted end of the shift rods over the slots in the shifter assembly.

6. Install and tighten the locknuts to 15-20 ft.lb.

7. Remove the pin and check shifter operation.

Neutral Safety And Back-up Light switch

REMOVAL AND INSTALLATION

1961-74

The switch is located on the steering column tube under the instrument panel. To remove

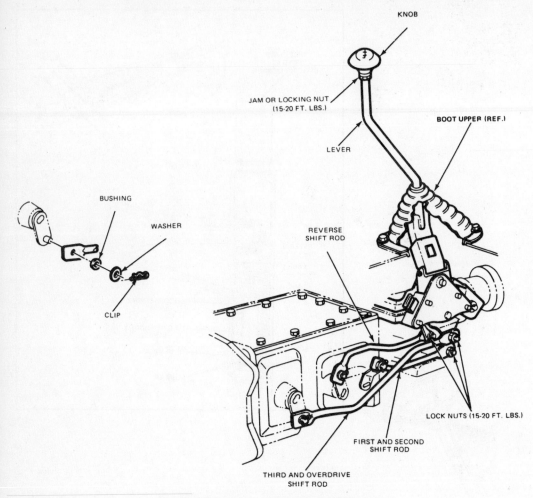

KNOB

JAM OR LOCKING NUT
(15-20 FT. LBS.)

BOOT UPPER (REF.)

LEVER

BUSHING

WASHER

REVERSE
SHIFT ROD

CLIP

LOCK NUTS (15-20 FT. LBS.)

FIRST AND SECOND
SHIFT ROD

THIRD AND OVERDRIVE
SHIFT ROD

4-speed Overdrive shift linkage adjustment

the switch, disconnect the wiring and remove the 2 mounting screws.

If adjustment is needed, loosen the mounting screws, place the selector in Reverse and move the switch so that the actuator depresses the switch plunger.

1975-83 3-Speed

The switch is located on the steering column tube in the engine compartment. To remove the switch, disconnect the wiring and remove the retaining clip.

If adjustment is needed, loosen the clamp screw on the mounting bracket, place the selector in Reverse and move the switch so that the actuator depresses the switch plunger.

1978-87 4-Speed

The switch is located at the floor shift mechanism on the transmission extension housing. It is not adjustable.

To remove the switch, place the selector in

any gear but Reverse, disconnect the wiring and unscrew the switch.

1988

The switch is located on the left side of the transmission case. To remove:

1. Raise and support the front end on jackstands.
2. Disconnect the negative battery cable.
3. Disconnect the back-up switch harness.
4. Remove the back-up switch and the seal.
5. Installation is the reverse of the removal procedure.

Transmission

REMOVAL AND INSTALLATION

CAUTION: *The clutch driven disc contains asbestos, which has been determined to be a cancer causing agent. Never clean clutch surfaces with compressed air! Avoid inhaling any dust from any clutch surface! When*

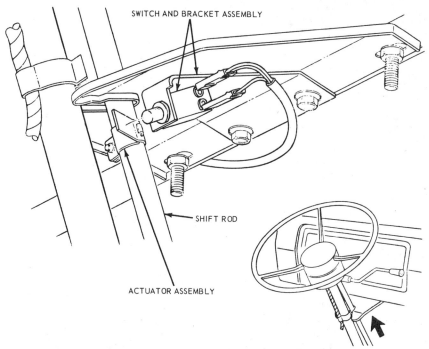

1961–74 back-up light switch

cleaning clutch surfaces, use a commercially available brake cleaning fluid.

Ford 3.03 3-Speed

1. Raise and support the van on jackstands.
2. Drain the lubricant from the transmission by removing the lower extension housing bolt.
3. Matchmark the driveshaft-to-output flange shaft position and disconnect the driveshaft at the transmission. Wire the driveshaft up, out of the way.
4. Disconnect the speedometer cable at the transmission.

5. Disconnect the shift rods at the transmission levers.
6. Disconnect any wiring at the transmission.
7. Support the transmission with a transmission jack. Chain the transmission to the jack.
8. On 1961-67 vans, remove the transmission rear support bolts, lower the engine enough to drop the transmission extension housing from the rear support.
9. On 1969 and later vans, raise the transmission slightly and remove the 4 bolts that retain the transmission support crossmember to the frame side rails. Remove the bolt securing the transmission to the support.

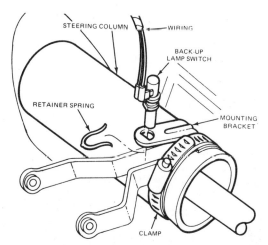

1975–83 back-up light switch w/3-speed manual transmission

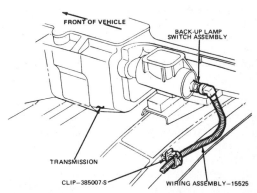

1978–87 back-up light switch w/4-speed manual transmission

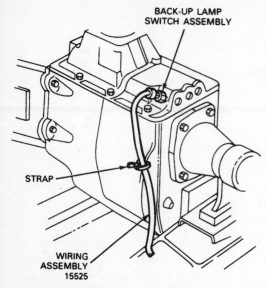

BACK-UP LAMP
SWITCH ASSEMBLY

STRAP

WIRING
ASSEMBLY
15525

1988 back-up light switch

10. Remove the 4 transmission-to-bell housing bolts.

11. On 1969 and later vans, position a jackstand under the rear of the engine to support it.

12. Pull backward on the transmission and roll it back far enough for the input shaft to clear the bell housing.

13. Lower the jack and remove the transmission.

To install:

14. Clean all machined mating surfaces thoroughly.

15. Install a guide pin in each lower bolt hole.

16. Raise the transmission and start the input shaft through the clutch release bearing.

17. Align the input shaft splines with the clutch disc splines. Roll the transmission forward so that the input shaft will enter the clutch disc. If the shaft binds in the release bearing, work the release arm back and forth.

18. Once the transmission is all the way in, install the 2 upper retaining bolts and washers and remove the lower guide pins. Install the lower bolts. Torque the bolts to 50 ft.lb.

19. On 1961-67 vans, raise the engine enough to mount the extension housing on the rear support.

20. On 1969 and later vans, raise the transmission slightly and install the 4 bolts that retain the transmission support crossmember to the frame side rails. Install the bolt securing the transmission to the support.

21. Remove the transmission jack.

22. Connect any wiring at the transmission.

23. Connect the shift rods at the transmission levers. Adjust the shift linkage.

24. Connect the speedometer cable at the transmission.

25. Connect the driveshaft at the transmission, observing the matchmarks.

26. Install the lower extension housing bolt and fill the transmission.

Dagenham 4-Speed

1. Raise and support the van on jackstands. Drain the transmission.

2. Matchmark the driveshaft-to-output flange shaft position and disconnect the driveshaft at the transmission. Wire the driveshaft up, out of the way.

3. Disconnect the speedometer cable at the transmission.

4. Disconnect the shift rods at the transmission levers.

5. Disconnect any wiring at the transmission.

6. Remove the flywheel housing dust cover.

7. Disconnect the battery ground.

8. Remove the starter.

9. Remove the clutch lever return spring.

10. Support the transmission with a transmission jack. Chain the transmission to the jack.

11. Remove the 4 transmission-to-bell housing bolts.

12. Unbolt the extension housing from the crossmember support.

13. Pull backward on the transmission and roll it back far enough for the input shaft to clear the bell housing. Be careful to avoid dropping the spacer plate from between the transmission and flywheel housing.

14. Lower the jack and remove the transmission.

To install:

15. Clean all machined mating surfaces thoroughly.

16. Install a guide pin in each lower bolt hole. Position the spacer plate on the guide pins.

17. Raise the transmission and start the input shaft through the clutch release bearing.

18. Align the input shaft splines with the clutch disc splines. Roll the transmission forward so that the input shaft will enter the clutch disc. If the shaft binds in the release bearing, work the release arm back and forth.

19. Once the transmission is all the way in, install the 2 upper retaining bolts and washers and remove the lower guide pins. Install the lower bolts. Torque the bolts to 35 ft.lb.

20. Raise the engine enough to mount the extension housing on the rear support. Torque the nut to 50 ft.lb.

21. Remove the transmission jack.

22. Install the starter.

23. Connect any wiring at the transmission.

24. Connect the shift rods at the transmission levers. Adjust the shift linkage.

25. Install the dust cover.

26. Install the release lever return spring.

27. Connect the speedometer cable at the transmission.

28. Connect the driveshaft at the transmission, observing the matchmarks.

29. Fill the transmission.

SROD 4-Speed

1. Raise and support the van on jackstands. Prop the clutch pedal in the full up position with a block of wood.

2. Matchmark the driveshaft-to-flange relation.

3. Disconnect the driveshaft at the rear axle and slide it off of the transmission output shaft. Lubricant will leak out of the transmission so be prepared to catch it, or plug the opening with rags or a seal installation tool.

4. Disconnect the speedometer cable at the transmission.

5. Disconnect the shift rods from the shift levers.

6. Remove the shift control from the extension housing and transmission case.

WARNING: *A 6 or and 8 is stamped on the extension housing next to the shift control plate bolt holes. This number refers to the engine — either a 6- or an 8-cylinder. The shift control plate must be installed in the holes corresponding corresponding to your engine type for proper shift linkage operation.*

7. Remove the extension housing-to-rear support bolts.

8. Take up the weight of the transmission with a transmission jack. Chain the transmission to the jack.

9. Raise the transmission just enough to take the weight off of the No.3 crossmember.

10. Unbolt the crossmember from the frame rails and remove it.

11. Place a jackstand under the rear of the engine at the bellhousing.

12. Lower the jack and allow the jackstand to take the weight of the engine. The engine should be angled slightly downward to allow the transmission to roll backward.

13. Remove the transmission-to bellhousing bolts.

14. Roll the jack rearward until the input shaft clears the bellhousing. Lower the jack and remove the transmission.

WARNING: *Do not depress the clutch pedal with the transmission removed.*

To install:

15. Clean all machined mating surfaces thoroughly.

16. Install a guide pin in each lower bolt hole. Position the spacer plate on the guide pins.

17. Raise the transmission and start the input shaft through the clutch release bearing.

18. Align the input shaft splines with the clutch disc splines. Roll the transmission forward so that the input shaft will enter the clutch disc. If the shaft binds in the release bearing, work the release arm back and forth.

19. Once the transmission is all the way in, install the 2 upper retaining bolts and washers and remove the lower guide pins. Install the lower bolts. Torque the bolts to 50 ft.lb.

20. Raise the transmission just enough to allow installation of the No.3 crossmember.

21. Install the crossmember on the frame rails. Torque the bolts to 80 ft.lb.

22. Lower the transmission onto the crossmember and install the nuts. Torque the nuts to 70 ft.lb.

23. Remove the transmission jack.

24. Install the shift control on the extension housing and transmission case.

25. Connect the shift rods at the shift levers.

26. Connect the speedometer cable at the transmission.

27. Slide the driveshaft onto the output shaft and connect the driveshaft at the rear axle, aligning the matchmarks.

Mazda M50D 5-Speed

1. Raise and support the van on jackstands. Prop the clutch pedal in the full up position with a block of wood.

2. Matchmark the driveshaft-to-flange relation.

3. Disconnect the driveshaft at the rear axle and slide it off of the transmission output shaft. Lubricant will leak out of the transmission so be prepared to catch it, or plug the opening with rags or a seal installation tool.

4. Disconnect the speedometer cable at the transmission.

5. Disconnect the shift rods from the shift levers.

6. Remove the shift control from the extension housing and transmission case.

7. Remove the extension housing-to-rear support bolts.

8. Take up the weight of the transmission with a transmission jack. Chain the transmission to the jack.

9. Raise the transmission just enough to take the weight off of the No.3 crossmember.

10. Unbolt the crossmember from the frame rails and remove it.

11. Place a jackstand under the rear of the engine at the bellhousing.

12. Lower the jack and allow the jackstand to take the weight of the engine. The engine

should be angled slightly downward to allow the transmission to roll backward.

13. Remove the transmission-to bellhousing bolts.

14. Roll the jack rearward until the input shaft clears the bellhousing. Lower the jack and remove the transmission.

WARNING: *Do not depress the clutch pedal with the transmission removed.*

To install:

15. Clean all machined mating surfaces thoroughly.

16. Install a guide pin in each lower bolt hole. Position the spacer plate on the guide pins.

17. Raise the transmission and start the input shaft through the clutch release bearing.

18. Align the input shaft splines with the clutch disc splines. Roll the transmission forward so that the input shaft will enter the clutch disc. If the shaft binds in the release bearing, work the release arm back and forth.

19. Once the transmission is all the way in, install the 2 upper retaining bolts and washers and remove the lower guide pins. Install the lower bolts. Torque the bolts to 50 ft.lb.

20. Raise the transmission just enough to allow installation of the No.3 crossmember.

21. Install the crossmember on the frame rails. Torque the bolts to 80 ft.lb.

22. Lower the transmission onto the crossmember and install the nuts. Torque the nuts to 70 ft.lb.

23. Remove the transmission jack.

24. Install the shift control on the extension housing and transmission case.

25. Connect the shift rods at the shift levers.

26. Connect the speedometer cable at the transmission.

27. Slide the driveshaft onto the output shaft and connect the driveshaft at the rear axle, aligning the matchmarks.

S5-42 ZF 5-Speed

1. Place the transmission in neutral.
2. Remove the carpet or floor mat.
3. Remove the ball from the shift lever.
4. Remove the boot and bezel assembly from the floor.
5. Remove the 2 bolts and disengage the upper shift lever from the lower shift lever.
6. Raise and support the van on jackstands.
7. Disconnect the speedometer cable.
8. Disconnect the back-up switch wire.
9. Place a drain pan under the case and drain the case through the drain plug.
10. Position a transmission jack under the case and safety-chain the case to the jack.
11. Remove the driveshaft.
12. Disconnect the clutch linkage.

13. Remove the transmission rear insulator and lower retainer.

14. Unbolt and remove the crossmember.

15. Remove the transmission-to-engine block bolts.

16. Roll the transmission rearward until the input shaft clears, lower the jack and remove the transmission.

17. Install 2 guide studs into the lower bolt holes.

18. Raise the transmission until the input shaft splines are aligned with the clutch disc splines. The clutch release bearing and hub must be properly positioned in the release lever fork.

19. Roll the transmission forward and into position on the front case.

20. Install the bolts and torque them to 50 ft.lb. Remove the guide studs and install and tighten the 2 remaining bolts.

21. Install the crossmember and torque the bolts to 55 ft.lb.

22. Install the transmission rear insulator and lower retainer. Torque the bolts to 60 ft.lb.

23. Connect the clutch linkage.

24. Install the driveshaft.

25. Remove the transmission jack.

26. Fill the transmission.

27. Connect the back-up switch wire.

28. Connect the speedometer cable.

29. Lower the van.

30. Install the boot and bezel assembly.

31. Connect the upper shift to from the lower shift lever. Tighten the bolts to 20 ft.lb.

32. Install the carpet or floor mat.

33. Install the ball from the shift lever.

OVERHAUL

Ford 3.03 3-Speed

The Ford 3.03 is a fully synchronized 3-speed transmission. All gears except reverse are in constant mesh. Forward speed gear changes are accomplished with synchronizer sleeves.

DISASSEMBLY

1. Drain the lubricant by removing the lower extension housing bolt.

2. Remove the case cover and gasket.

3. Remove the long spring that holds the detent plug in the case and remove the detent plug with a small magnet.

4. Remove the extension housing and gasket.

5. Remove the front bearing retainer and gasket.

6. Remove the filler plug on the right side of the transmission case. Working through the plug opening, drive the roll pin out of the case and countershaft with a ¼" (6mm) punch.

7. Hold the countershaft gear with a hook. Install dummy shaft and push the countershaft

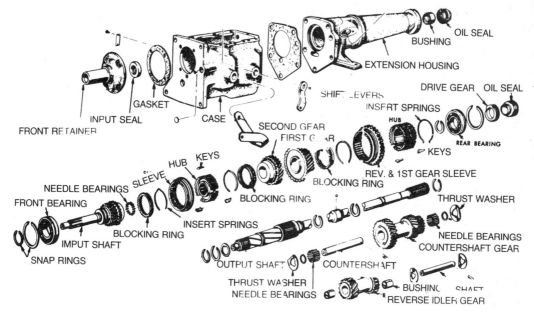

3.03 3-speed exploded view

out of the rear of the case. As the countershaft comes out, lower the gear cluster to the bottom of the case. Remove the countershaft.

8. Remove the snapring that holds the speedometer drive gear on the output shaft. Slip the gear off the shaft and remove the gear lock ball.

9. Remove the snapring that holds the output shaft bearing. Using a special bearing puller, remove the output shaft bearing.

10. Place both shift levers in the neutral (center) position.

11. Remove the set screw that holds the 1st/reverse shift fork to the shift rail. Slip the 1st/reverse shift rail out through the rear of the case.

12. Move the 1st/reverse synchronizer forward as far as possible. Rotate the 1st/reverse shift fork upwards and lift it out of the case.

13. Place the 2nd/3rd shift fork in the 2nd position. Remove the set screw. Rotate the shift rail 90°.

14. Lift the interlock plug out of the case with a magnet.

15. Remove the expansion plug from the 2nd/3rd shift rail by lightly tapping the end of the rail. Remove the 2nd/3rd shift rail.

16. Remove the 2nd/3rd shift rail detent plug and spring from detent bore.

17. Remove the input gear and shaft from the case.

18. Rotate the 2nd/3rd shift fork upwards and remove from case.

19. Using caution, lift the output shaft assembly out through top of case.

20. Lift the reverse idler gear and thrust washers out of case. Remove the countershaft

gear, thrust washer and dummy shaft from case.

21. Remove the snapring from the front of the output shaft. Slip the synchronizer and 2nd gear off shaft.

22. Remove the 2nd snapring from output shaft and remove the thrust washer, 1st gear and blocking ring.

23. Remove the 3rd snapring from the output shaft. The 1st/reverse synchronizer hub is a press fit on the output shaft. Remove the synchronizer hub with an arbor press.

WARNING: *Do not attempt to remove or install the synchronizer hub by prying or hammering.*

Shift Levers & Seals

1. Remove shift levers from the shafts. Slip the levers out of case. Discard shaft sealing O-rings.

2. Lubricate and install new O-rings on shift shafts.

3. Install the shift shafts in the case and secure shift levers.

Input Shaft Bearings

1. Remove the snapring securing the input shaft bearing. Using an arbor press, remove the bearing.

2. Press the input shaft bearing onto shaft using correct tool.

Synchronizers

1. Scribe alignment marks on synchronizer hubs before disassembly. Remove each synchronizer hub from the synchronizer sleeves.

2. Separate the inserts and insert springs from the hubs.

CAUTION: *Do not mix parts from the separate synchronizer assemblies.*

3. Install the insert spring in the hub of the 1st/reverse synchronizer. Be sure that the spring covers all the insert grooves. Start the hub on the sleeve making certain that the scribed marks are properly aligned. Place the 3 inserts in the hub, small ends on the inside. Slide the sleeve and reverse gear onto hub.

4. Install 1 insert spring into a groove on the 2nd/3rd synchronizer hub. Be sure that all 3 insert slots are covered. Align the scribed marks on the hub and sleeve and start the hub into the sleeve. Position the 3 inserts on the top of the retaining spring and push the assembly together. Install the remaining retainer spring so that the spring ends cover the same slots as the 1st spring. Do not stagger the springs. Place a synchronizer blocking ring on the ends of the synchronizer sleeve.

Countershaft Gear Bearings

1. Remove the dummy shaft, needle bearings and bearing retainers from the countershaft gear.

2. Coat the bore in each end of the countershaft gear with grease.

3. Hold the dummy shaft in the gear and install the needle bearings in the case.

4. Place the countershaft gear, dummy shaft, and needle bearings in the case.

5. Place the case in a vertical position. Align the gear bore and the thrust washers with the bores in the case and install the countershaft.

6. Place the case in a horizontal position. Check the countershaft gear end play with a feeler gauge. Clearance should be between 0.004-0.018″ (0.10-0.45mm). If clearance does not come within specifications, replace the thrust washers.

7. Install the dummy shaft in the countershaft gear and leave the gear at the bottom of the transmission case.

ASSEMBLY

1. Cover the reverse idler gear thrust surfaces in the case with a thin film of lubricant, and install the 2 thrust washers in the case.

2. Install the reverse idler gear and shaft in the case. Align the case bore and thrust washers with gear bore and install the reverse idler shaft.

3. Measure the reverse idler gear end play with a feeler gauge. Clearance should be between 0.004-0.018″ (0.10-0.45mm). If end play is not within specifications, replace the thrust washers. If clearance is correct, leave the reverse idler gear in case.

4. Lubricate the output shaft splines and machined surfaces with transmission oil.

5. The 1st/reverse synchronizer hub is a press fit on the output shaft. Hub must be installed in an arbor press. Install the synchronizer hub with the teeth end of the gear facing towards the rear of the shaft.

CAUTION: *Do not attempt to install the 1st/ reverse synchronizer with a hammer.*

6. Place the blocking ring on the tapered surface of the 1st gear.

7. Slide the 1st gear on the output shaft with the blocking ring toward the rear of the shaft. Rotate the gear as necessary to engage the 3 notches in the blocking ring with the synchronizer inserts. Install the thrust washer and snapring.

8. Slide the blocking ring onto the tapered surface of the 2nd gear. Slide the 2nd gear with blocking ring and the 2nd/3rd synchronizer on the mainshaft. Be sure that the tapered surface of 2nd gear is facing the front of the shaft and that the notches in the blocking ring engage the synchronizer inserts. Install the snapring and secure assembly.

9. Cover the core of the input shaft with a thin coat of grease.

WARNING: *A thick film of grease will plug lubricant holes and cause damage to bearings.*

10. Install bearings. Install the input shaft through the front of the case and insert snapring in the bearing groove.

11. Install the output shaft assembly in the case. Position the 2nd/3rd shift fork on the 2nd/ 3rd synchronizer.

12. Place a detent plug spring and a plug in the case. Place the 2nd/3rd synchronizer in the 2nd gear position (toward the rear of the case). Align the fork and install the 2nd/3rd shift rail. It will be necessary to depress the detent plug to install the shift rail in the bore. Move the rail forward until the detent plug enters the forward notch (2nd gear).

13. Secure the fork to the shift rail with a set screw and place the synchronizer in neutral.

14. Install the interlock plug in the case.

15. Place the 1st/reverse synchronizer in the 1st gear position (towards the front of the case). Place the shift fork in the groove of the synchronizer. Rotate the fork into position and install the shift rail. Move the shift rail inward until the center notch (neutral) is aligned with the detent bore. Secure shift fork with set screw.

16. Install a new shift rail expansion plug in the front of the case.

17. Hold the input shaft and blocking ring in position and move the output shaft forward to

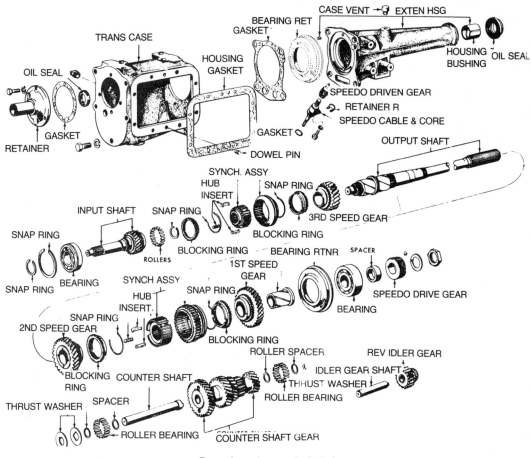

Dagenham 4-sp exploded view

seat the pilot in the roller bearings on the input gear.

18. Tap the input gear bearing into place while holding the output shaft. Install the front bearing retainer and gasket. Torque attaching bolts to 35 ft.lb.

19. Install the large snapring on the rear bearing. Place the bearing on the output shaft with the snapring end toward the rear of the shaft. Press the bearing into place using a special tool. Secure the bearing to the shaft with the snapring.

20. Hold the speedometer drive gear lock ball in the detent and slide the speedometer drive gear into position. Secure with snapring.

21. Place the transmission in the vertical position. Working with a screwdriver through the drain hole in the bottom of the case, align the bore of the countershaft gear and the thrust washer with the bore in the case.

22. Working from the rear of the case, push the dummy shaft out of the countershaft gear with the countershaft. Align the roll pin hole in the countershaft with the matching hole in the case. Drive the shaft into place and install the roll pin.

23. Position the new extension housing gasket on the case with sealer. Install the extension housing and torque to 50 ft.lb.

24. Place the transmission in gear and pour gear oil over entire gear train while rotating the input shaft.

25. Install the remaining detent plug and long spring in case.

26. Position the cover gasket on the case with sealer and install the cover. Torque the cover bolts to 15 ft.lb.

27. Check the operation of the transmission in all gear positions.

Dagenham 4-Speed

1. Remove the shift selector levers from the extension housing.

2. Bend a coat hanger into a hooking-tool and insert it through the clutch release lever opening, unhooking the retainer that holds the clutch release lever to the retainer bracket.

3. Remove the 4 bolts and separate the transmission from the bellhousing.

4. Remove the shift cover from the case (8 bolts).

5. Unbolt and remove the extension housing (4 bolts).

6. Unbolt and remove the input shaft bearing retainer (3 bolts).

7. Working from the front of the case, drive the countershaft rearward with a dummy shaft, until it is clear of the front wall of the case. Continue pushing the countershaft until the dummy shaft and cluster gear drop into the case.

8. Remove the output shaft from the rear of the case.

9. Remove the input gear and bearing from the front of the case.

10. Lift the countershaft gear assembly through the cover opening.

NOTE: *The smallest diameter thrust washer is located bewteen the rear of the countershaft gear and the case. The larger diameter steel and bronze washers are at the front.*

11. Thread a $\frac{5}{16}$"-24 bolt into the rear end of the reverse idler gear shaft and pull the shaft out with a puller.

12. Remove the idler gear.

13. Remove the snapring from the input shaft and pull out the input shaft bearing.

14. Straighten the output shaft locknut tab and remove the nut and lock.

15. Remove the speedometer gear, drive ball and gear spacer.

16. Using a press, remove the output shaft bearing, adapter, 1st gear, 1st and 2nd synchronizer assembly and 2nd gear.

17. Remove the snapring from the front of the 3rd/4th synchronizer.

18. Press the 3rd gear and the 3rd/4th synchronizer from the output shaft.

19. Scribe an alignment mark across the synchronizer's hub and sleeve.

20. Remove the front and rear insert springs from both synchronizer assemblies.

21. Slide the sleeves off the hubs and remove the hub inserts.

22. Remove the snapring from the end of the selector shaft.

23. Remove the flat washer and spring.

24. Remove the 2 bolts, then pull the retainer, selector levers and bracket from the shaft.

25. Drive the short selector lever pin from the shaft.

26. Drive the long trunnion pin from the shaft and remove the trunnion and shaft.

27. Remove the shifter levers from the cam and shafts.

28. Remove the roll pin from the upper fork shaft and remove the shaft and forks.

29. Remove the reverse cam and shafts.

30. Rotate the reverse fork and shaft assembly to disengage the detent ball, then, remove the fork and shaft.

31. Remove the 1st/2nd and 3rd/4th shift cam assemblies.

32. Push the interlock sleeve, spring and remaining ball out of the cover.

33. Remove the 1st/2nd and 3rd/4th-to-reverse interlock pins from the reverse fork and shaft bosses in the cover.

To assemble:

34. Place the 1st/2nd and 3rd/4th-to-reverse interlock pins in the holes in the reverse fork and shaft bosses in the cover.

35. Install the 1st/2nd and 3rd/4th shift cam assemblies.

36. Install the interlock, sleeve, ball, spring and remaining ball in the cover.

37. Hold the 3rd/4th ball in neutral and the 1st/2nd ball depressed while the 1st/2nd cam is installed in the cover.

38. Install the 1st/2nd and 3rd/4th levers, washers and nuts.

39. Check the clearance among the interlock, detent sleeve and the 1st/2nd and 3rd/4th shift cams in and between all shift positions. The sleeve-to-cam clearance must be 0.0005-0.0010" (0.0127-0.0254mm). Various length sleeves are available.

40. With the 1st/2nd and 3rd/4th shift cams in neutral and the 3rd/4th-to-reverse interlock pin resting on the cams, install the reverse shaft detent spring and ball and the reverse fork and shaft.

41. Install the reverse shift cam through the cover and into the aligned fork and shaft.

42. Install the reverse cam operating lever.

43. Position the 1st/2nd and 3rd/4th forks onto the shift cams and install the fork shaft.

44. Align the shaft hole with the one in cover and install the lock pin.

45. Check all positions for freedom of movement.

46. Place the long detent inserts into the slots in the 1st/2nd synchronizer hub and slide the combination sleeve and reverse gear over it, being careful to align the scribed marks. Snap the insert springs into place. The tab on each spring must set into the underside of an insert.

47. Position the short inserts into the slots in the 3rd/4th synchronizer hub and slide the clutch sleeve over it, making sure that the scribe marks are aligned. Install the insert springs in the same way you installed them on the 1st/2nd synchronizer.

48. Place the 2nd gear on the rear of the output shaft with the clutch teeth and tapered synchronizer end toward the rear. Install a blocking ring with the clutch teeth forward.

49. Install the 1st/2nd synchronizer and reverse gear assembly on the rear of the output shaft with the shift fork groove rearward.

50. Install the 1st gear blocking ring with the clutch teeth rearward and the slots engaging the synchronizer inserts.

51. Slide the 1st gear and sleeve onto the output shaft, taper and clutch teeth forward, and the sleeve shoulder rearward.

52. Place the output shaft ball bearing in the recess in the bearing adapter.

53. Position the adapter and bearing on the rear of the output shaft with the adapter forward.

54. Hold the 1st gear and sleeve forward and place the assembly in a press with the tool applied to the bearing inner race. Press the bearing on until it is firmly seated against the 1st gear sleeve.

55. Place the spacer, speedometer gear drive ball, speedometer gear lock and nut on the output shaft. Torque the nut to 80 ft.lb., then loosen it. Retorque it to 20-25 ft.lb. and bend over the flat lockwasher.

56. Place the 3rd gear on the front of the output shaft with the clutch teeth forward. Install a blocking ring.

57. Install the 3rd/4th synchronizer with the wide thrust surface of the hub rearward. Align the blocking ring slots with the synchronizer inserts.

58. Install the snapring into its groove on the front of the output shaft.

59. Place a dummy shaft in the countershaft gear cluster.

60. Starting at either end, drop a steel washer over the shaft and into the gear.

61. Grease each bearing roller and install 22 of them into the gear.

62. Lay another steel washer on the ends of the needles and thrust washers.

63. Repeat Steps 60 through 62 for the other end of the gear.

64. Position the cluster gear in the case with the two thrust washers at the front. Allow the gear assembly to lie in the bottom of the case.

65. Check the gear endplay. It should be 0.004-0.018″ (0.10-0.46mm). Correct it, if necessary, by replacing the thrust washers.

66. Press the input shaft bearing onto the input shaft with the outer race ring groove frontward.

67. Install the snaprings onto the bearing outer race and gear shaft.

68. Grease the roller individually and place 17 of them into the bore of the input gear.

69. Install the input gear assembly.

70. Place the 4th gear blocking ring on the rear of the input gear with the clutch teeth forward.

71. Enter the output shaft assembly through the rear of the case and guide the output shaft front pilot into the input gear bore and bearings. Be certain that the 4th gear synchronizer

blocking ring slots index with the inserts on the 3rd/4th synchronizer assembly.

72. Raise the countershaft gear until the countershaft can be inserted from the rear of the case into the gear and bearings. Push on the shaft until it contacts the front of the case.

73. Position the flat on the rear of the countershaft on a horizontal plane so it will align with the slot in the extension housing. Tap the shaft into place.

74. Install the reverse idler gear with the fork groove toward the rear and the idler shaft flat horizontal and parallel with the countershaft flat.

75. Position a new gasket on the rear of the case, using non-hardening sealer.

76. Install the extension housing. Align the dowel and make sure that the housing is squarely on the case before tightening the attaching bolts. If the bolts are different lengths, install the two longer bolts in the upper right and lower left holes.

77. Using sealer, install the new gasket on the input shaft bearing retainer.

78. With the drain slot facing downward, install the bearing retainer.

79. Apply sealer on the bolt threads and torque the bolts to 12-15 ft.lb.

80. Place the 1st/2nd and 3rd/4th synchronizer in neutral, and the reverse idler gear in reverse.

81. Set the reverse shift lever in the reverse position.

82. Install a new shift cover gasket on the case using non-hardening sealer.

83. Install the shift cover. Coat the bolt threads with sealer and torque the cover bolts to 12-15 ft.lb.

84. Bolt the bellhousing to the transmission. Coat the bolt threads with sealer and torque them to 40-45 ft.lb.

85. Install the clutch release bearing onto the release lever.

86. Position the release lever through the housing from the inside and clip the lever retainer onto its hook.

87. Install the shift selector assembly on the extension housing.

Ford 4-Speed Overdrive

The Ford 4-speed overdrive transmission is fully synchronized in all forward gears. The 4-speed shift control is serviced as a unit and should not be disassembled. The lubricant capacity is 4.5 pints.

Unit Disassembly

1. Remove retaining clips and flat washers from the shift rods at the levers.

2. Remove shift linkage control bracket at-

taching screws and remove shift linkage and control brackets.

3. Remove cover attaching screws. Then lift cover and gasket from the case. Remove the long spring that holds the detent plug in the case. Remove the plug with a magnet.

4. Remove extension housing attaching screws. Then, remove extension housing and gasket.

5. Remove input shaft bearing retainer attaching screws. Then, slide retainer from the input shaft.

6. Working a dummy shaft in from the front of the case, drive the countershaft out the rear of the case. Let the countergear assembly lie in the bottom of the case. Remove the set screw from the 1st/2nd shift fork. Slide the 1st/2nd shift rail out of the rear of the case. Use a magnet to remove the interlock detent from between the 1st/2nd and 3rd/4th shift rails.

7. Locate 1st/2nd speed gear shift lever in neutral. Locate 3rd/4th speed gear shift lever in 3rd speed position.

NOTE: *On overdrive transmissions, locate 3rd/4th speed gear shift lever in the 4th speed position.*

8. Remove the lockbolt that holds the 3rd/4th speed shift rail detent spring and plug in the left side of the case. Remove spring and plug with a magnet.

9. Remove the detent mechanism set screw from top of case. Then, remove the detent spring and plug with a small magnet.

10. Remove attaching screw from the 3rd/4th speed shift fork. Tap lightly on the inner end of the shift rail to remove the expansion plug from front of case. Then, withdraw the 3rd/4th speed shift rail from the front. Do not lose the interlock pin from rail.

11. Remove attaching screw from the 1st and 2nd speed shift fork. Slide the 1st/2nd shift rail from the rear of case.

12. Remove the interlock and detent plugs from the top of the case with a magnet.

13. Remove the snapring or disengage retainer that holds the speedometer drive gear to the output shaft, then remove speedometer gear drive ball.

14. Remove the snapring used to hold the output shaft bearing to the shaft. Pull out the output shaft bearing.

15. Remove the input shaft bearing snaprings. Use a press to remove the input shaft bearing. Remove the input shaft and blocking ring from the front of the case.

16. Move output shaft to the right side of the case. Then, maneuver the forks to permit lifting them from the case.

17. Support the thrust washer and 1st speed gear to prevent sliding from the shaft, then lift output shaft from the case.

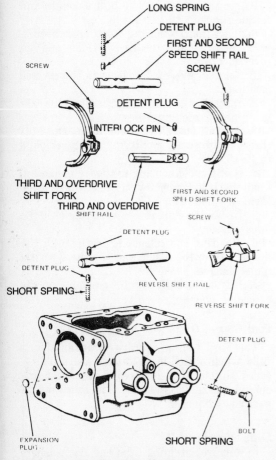

Ford 4-speed shift rails and forks

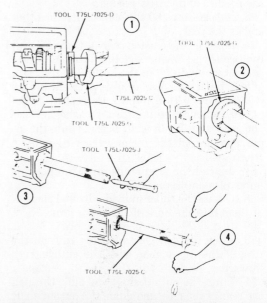

Ford 4-speed output shaft bearing removal

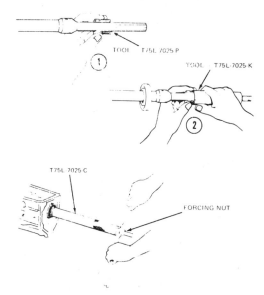

Ford 4-speed output shaft bearing installation

18. Remove reverse gear shift fork attaching screw. Rotate the reverse shift rail 90°, then, slide the shift rail out the rear of the case. Lift out the reverse shift fork.

19. Remove the reverse detent plug and spring from the case with a magnet.

20. Using a dummy shaft, remove the reverse idler shaft from the case.

21. Lift reverse idler gear and thrust washers from the case. Be careful not to drop the bearing rollers or the dummy shaft from the gear.

22. Lift the countergear, thrust washers, rollers and dummy shaft assembly from the case.

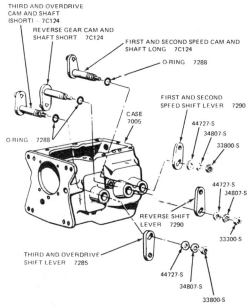

Ford 4-speed shift lever components

23. Remove the next snapring from the front of the output shaft. Then, slide the 3rd/4th synchronizer blocking ring and the 3rd speed gear from the shaft.

24. Remove the next snapring and the 2nd speed gear thrust washer from the shaft. Slide the 2nd speed gear and the blocking ring from the shaft.

25. Remove the snapring, then slide the 1st/2nd synchronizer, blocking ring and the 1st speed gear from the shaft.

26. Remove the thrust washer from rear of the shaft.

Cam & Shaft Seals

1. Remove attaching nut and washers from each shift lever, then remove the 3 levers.

2. Remove the 3 cams and shafts from inside the case.

3. Replace the old O-rings with new ones that have been well lubricated.

4. Slide each cam and shaft into its respective bore in the transmission.

5. Install the levers and secure them with their respective washers and nuts.

Synchronizers

1. Push the synchronizer hub from each synchronizer sleeve.

2. Separate the inserts and springs from the hubs. Do not mix parts of the 1st/2nd with parts of 3rd/4th synchronizers.

3. To assemble, position the hub in the sleeve. Be sure the alignment marks are properly indexed.

4. Place the 3 inserts into place on the hub. Install the insert springs so that the irregular surface (hump) is seated in one of the inserts. Do not stagger the springs.

Countershaft Gear

1. Dismantle the countershaft gear assembly.

2. Assemble the gear by coating each end of the countershaft gear bore with grease.

3. Install dummy shaft in the gear. Then install 21 bearing rollers and a retainer washer in each end of the gear.

Reverse Idler Gear

1. Dismantle reverse idler gear.

2. Assemble reverse idler gear by coating the bore in each end of reverse idler gear with grease.

3. Hold the dummy shaft in the gear and install the 22 bearing rollers and the retainer washer into each end of the gear.

4. Install the reverse idler sliding gear on the splines of the reverse idler gear. Be sure the shift fork groove is toward the front.

Input Shaft Seal

1. Remove the seal from the input shaft bearing retainer.

2. Coat the sealing surface of a new seal with

lubricant, then press the new seal into the input shaft bearing retainer.

Unit Assembly

1. Grease the countershaft gear thrust surfaces in the case. Then, position a thrust washer at each end of the case.

2. Position the countershaft gear, dummy shaft, and roller bearings in the case.

3. Align the gear bore and thrust washers with the bores in the case. Install the countershaft.

4. With the case in a horizontal position, countershaft gear endplay should be from 0.004-0.018″ (0.10-0.45mm). Use thrust washers to obtain play within these limits.

5. After establishing correct endplay, place the dummy shaft in the countershaft gear and allow the gear assembly to remain on the bottom of the case.

6. Grease the reverse idler gear thrust surfaces in the case, and position the 2 thrust washers.

7. Position the reverse idler gear, sliding gear, dummy, etc., in place. Make sure that the shift fork groove in the sliding gear is toward the front.

8. Align the gear bore and thrust washers with the case bores and install the reverse idler shaft.

9. Reverse idler gear endplay should be 0.004-0.018″ (0.10-0.45mm). Use selective thrust washers to obtain play within these limits.

10. Position reverse gear shift rail detent spring and detent plug in the case. Hold the reverse shift fork in place on the reverse idler sliding gear and install the shift rail from the rear of the case. Lock the fork to the rail with the Allen head set screws.

11. Install the 1st/2nd synchronizer onto the output shaft. The 1st and reverse synchronizer hub are a press fit and should be installed with gear teeth facing the rear of the shaft.

NOTE: *On overdrive transmissions, 1st and reverse synchronizer hub is a slip fit.*

12. Place the blocking ring on 2nd gear. Slide 2nd speed gear onto the front of the shaft with the synchronizer coned surface toward the rear.

13. Install the 2nd speed gear thrust washer and snapring.

14. Slide the 4th gear onto the shaft with the synchronizer coned surface front.

15. Place a blocking ring on the 4th gear.

16. Slide the 3rd/4th speed gear synchronizer onto the shaft. Be sure that the inserts in the synchronizer engage the notches in the blocking ring. Install the snapring onto the front of the output shaft.

17. Put the blocking ring on the 1st gear.

18. Slide the 1st gear onto the rear of the output shaft. Be sure that the inserts engage the notches in the blocking ring and that the shift fork groove is toward the rear.

19. Install heavy thrust washer onto the rear of the output shaft.

20. Lower the output shaft assembly into the case.

21. Position the 1st/2nd speed shift fork and the 3rd/4th speed shift fork in place on their respective gears. Rotate them into place.

22. Place a spring and detent plug in the detent bore. Place the reverse shift rail into neutral position.

23. Coat the 3rd/4th speed shift rail interlock pin (tapered ends) with grease, then position it in the shift rail.

24. Align the 3rd/4th speed shift fork with the shift rail bores and slide the shift rail into place. Be sure that the 3 detents are facing the outside of the case. Place the front synchronizer into 4th speed position and install the set screw into the 3rd/4th speed shift fork. Move the synchronizer to neutral position. Install the 3rd/4th speed shift rail detent plug, spring and bolt into the left side of the transmission case. Place the detent plug (tapered ends) in the detent bore.

25. Align 1st/2nd speed shift fork with the case bores and slide the shift rail into place. Lock the fork with the set screw.

26. Coat the input gear bore with a small amount of grease. Then install the 15 bearing rollers.

27. Put the blocking ring in the 3rd/4th synchronizer. Place the input shaft gear in the case. Be sure that the output shaft pilot enters the roller bearing of the input shaft gear.

28. With a new gasket on the input bearing retainer, dip attaching bolts in sealer, install bolts and torque to 30-36 ft.lb.

29. Press on the output shaft bearing, then install the snapring to hold the bearing.

30. Position the speedometer gear drive ball in the output shaft and slide the speedometer drive gear into place. Secure gear with snapring.

31. Align the countershaft gear bore and thrust washers with the bore in the case. Install the countershaft.

32. With a new gasket in place, install and secure the extension housing. Dip the extension housing screws in sealer, then torque screws to 42-50 ft.lb.

33. Install the filler plug and the drain plug.

34. Pour E.P. gear oil over the entire gear train while rotating the input shaft.

35. Place each shift fork in all positions to make sure they function properly. Install the remaining detent plug in the case, followed by the spring.

36. With a new cover gasket in place, install the cover. Dip attaching screws in sealer, then torque screws to 14-19 ft.lb.

37. Coat the 3rd/4th speed shift rail plug bore with sealer. Install a new plug.

38. Secure each shift rod to its respective lever with a spring washer, flat washer and retaining pin.

39. Position the shift linkage control bracket to the extension housing. Install and torque the attaching screws to 12-15 ft.lb.

Mazda 5-Speed

CASE DISASSEMBLY

1. Remove the drain plug.

2. Remove the shift lever from the top cover.

3. Remove the 10 top cover bolts and lift off the cover. Discard the gasket.

4. Remove the 9 extension housing bolts. Pry gently at the indentations provided and separate the extension housing from the case.

NOTE: *If you would like to remove the extension housing seal, remove it with a puller BEFORE separating the extension housing from the case.*

5. Remove the rear oil passage from the extension housing using a 10mm socket.

6. Remove and discard the anti-spill seal from the output shaft.

7. Remove the speedometer drive gear and ball. If you're going to replace the gear, replace it with one of the same color.

8. Lock the transmission into 1st and 3rd gears.

9. Using a hammer and chisel, release the staked areas securing the output shaft and countershaft locknuts.

10. Using a 32mm socket, remove and discard the countershaft rear bearing locknut.

11. Remove the counteshaft bearing and thrust washer.

12. Using Mainshaft Locknut Wrench T88T-7025-A and Remover Tube T75L-7025-B, or equivalents, remove and discard the output shaft locknut.

13. Using a 17mm wrench, remove the reverse idler shaft bolt.

14. Remove the reverse idler gear assembly by pulling it rearward.

15. Remove the output shaft rear bearing from the output shaft using Remover/Replacer Tube T75L-7025-B, Forcing Screw T84T-7025-B, Bearing Puller T77J-7025-H and Puller Ring T77J-7025-J, or equivalents.

16. Using a brass drift, drive the reverse gear from the output shaft.

17. Remove the sleeve from the output shaft.

18. Remove the counter/reverse gear with two needle bearings and the reverse synchronizer ring.

19. Remove the thrust washer and split washer from the countershaft.

20. Using a 12mm wrench, remove the 5th/reverse shift rod fixing bolt.

21. Remove the 5th/reverse hub and sleeve assembly.

22. Remove the 5th/reverse shift fork and rod.

NOTE: *Do not separate the steel ball and spring unless necessary.*

23. Remove the 5th gear synchronizer ring.

24. Remove the 5th/reverse counter lever lockplate retaining bolt and inner circlip.

25. Remove the counter lever assembly from the case.

NOTE: *Do not remove the Torx® nut retaining the counter lever pin at this time.*

26. Remove the 5th gear counter with the needle bearing.

27. Remove the 5th gear from the output shaft using the Bearing Collet Sleeve for the 3½" Bearing Collets T75L-7025-G, Remover/Replacer Tube T85T-7025-A, Forcing Screw T84T-7025-B and Gear Remover Collet T88T-7061-A, or equivalents.

NOTE: *For reference during assembly, observe that the longer of the 2 collars on the 5th gear faces forward.*

28. Remove the 5th gear sleeve and Woodruff key using Forcing Screw T84T-7025-B, Countershaft 5th Gear Sleeve Puller T88T-7025-J, Gear Removal Collets T88T-7025-J1 and Remover/Replacer Tube T77J-7025-B, or equivalents.

29. Remove the 6 center bearing cover retaining bolts and lift off the cover.

NOTE: *There is a reference arrow on the cover which points upward.*

30. Remove the 6 front bearing cover bolts.

31. Remove the front bearing cover by threading 2 of the retaining bolts back into the cover at the service bolt locations (9 and 3 o'clock). Alternately tighten the bolts until the cover pops off. Discard the front bearing oil baffle.

NOTE: *Don't remove the plastic scoop ring from the input shaft at this time.*

32. Remove the oil trough retaining bolt and lift out the oil trough from the upper case.

33. Pull the input shaft forward and remove the input bearing outer race. Pull the output shaft rearward.

34. Pull the input shaft forward and separate it from the output shaft.

35. Incline the output shaft upward and lift it from the case.

36. Remove the input shaft from the case.

37. Remove the countershaft bearing outer races (front and center) by moving the countershaft forward and rearward.

38. Pull the countershaft rearward far enough to permit tool clearance behind the front countershaft bearing. Using Bearing Race Puller T88T-7120-A and Slide Hammer T50T-100-A, or equivalents, remove the front countershaft bearing.

WARNING: *Tap gently during bearing removal. A forceful blow can cause damage to the bearing and/or case.*

39. Remove the countershaft through the upper opening of the case.

40. Input Shaft Disassembly and Assembly:

a. Remove and discard the plastic scoop ring.

b. Press the tapered roller bearing from the input shaft using Bearing Cone Remover T71P-4621-B, or equivalent, and an arbor press.

c. Install the input shaft tapered roller bearing onto the input shaft using a press and Bearing Cone Replacer T88T-7025-B, or equivalent.

d. Install the plastic scoop ring onto the input shaft. Manually rotate the ring clockwise to ensure that the input shaft oil holes properly engage the scoop ring. A click should be heard as the scoop ring notches align with the input shaft holes.

41. Output Shaft Disassembly and Assembly:

a. Remove the pilot bearing needle roller, snapring, needle bearing and spacer from the front (short side) of the output shaft.

b. Position the front (short side) of the shaft upward and lift off the 3rd/4th clutch hub and sleeve assembly, 3rd gear synchronizing ring, 3rd gear, and needle bearing.

c. Turn the shaft so that the long end faces upward.

d. Place the output shaft into a press with the press cradle contacting the lower part of the 2nd gear.

NOTE: *Make sure that the output shaft flange doesn't contact or ride up on the press cradle.*

e. Press off the following as a unit:
- center bearing,
- 1st gear sleeve,
- 1st gear,
- needle bearing,
- 1st/2nd clutch hub and sleeve,
- 1st/2nd synchronizer rings,
- 2nd gear, and
- needle bearing

using Bearing Replacer T53T-4621-B and Bearing Cone Replacer T88T-7025-B, or equivalents. Use T53T-4621-B as a press plate, and Bearing Cone Replacer T88T-7025-B to protect the inner race rollers.

f. Position the output shaft so the rear (long end) faces upward and press on the following parts, in the order listed, using T53T-4621-B and T75L-1165-B, or equivalents:
- 2nd gear needle bearing
- 2nd gear
- 2nd gear synchronizer ring
- 1st/2nd clutch hub and sleeve
- 1st gear synchronizer ring
- 1st gear needle bearing
- 1st gear
- 1st gear sleeve
- center bearing

NOTE: *Make sure that the center bearing race ins installed in the case. When installing the 1st/2nd clutch hub and sleeve make sure that the smaller width sleeve faces the 2nd gear side. Make sure that the reference marks face the rear of the transmission.*

g. Install the center bearing on the output shaft.

h. Position the output shaft so that the front of the shaft flange faces upward. Install the 3rd gear needle bearing, 3rd gear and 3rd gear synchronizer ring.

i. Install the 3rd/4th clutch hub and sleeve:

- Mate the clutch hub synchronizer key groove with the reference mark on the clutch hub sleeve. The mark should face rearward.

- Install the longer flange on the clutch hub sleeve towards the 3rd gear side.

NOTE: *The front and rear sides of the clutch hub are identical, except for the reference mark.*

j. Install the spacer, needle bearing (with rollers upward), retaining ring, and pilot bearing roller.

k. Install the original retaining ring. Using a feeler gauge, check the clutch hub endplay. Endplay should be 0-0.05mm (0-0.0019"). If necessary, adjust the endplay by using a new retaining ring. Retaining ring are available in 0.05mm increments in sizes ranging from 1.5mm to 1.95mm.

42. Countershaft Disassembly and Assembly:

a. Place the countershaft in a press with Bearing Cone Remover T71P-4621-B, or equivalent, and remove the countershaft bearing inner race.

b. Using a press and bearing splitter D84L-1123-A, or equivalent, remove the countershaft front bearing inner race.

c. Assemble the shaft in the press in the reverse order of disassembly.

43. Reverse Idler Gear Shaft Disassembly and Assembly:

a. Remove the following parts:
- Retaining ring
- Spacer
- Idler gear
- Needle bearings

● Thrust washer

b. Install the thrust washer making sure that the tab mates with the groove in the shaft.

c. Install the needle bearings, idler gear and spacer.

d. Install the original retaining ring onto the shaft.

e. Insert a flat feeler gauge between the retaining ring and the reverse idler gear to measure the reverse idler gear endplay. Endplay should be 0.1-0.2mm. If not, use a new retaining ring. Retaining rings are available in 0.5mm increments in thicknesses ranging from 1.5 to 1.9mm.

44. Top Cover Disassembly and Assembly:

a. Remove the dust cover (3 allen screws). Note that the grooves in the bushing align with the slots in the lower shift lever ball and the notch in the lower shift lever faces forward.

b. Remove the back-up lamp switch from the cover.

c. Drive out the spring pins retaining the shift forks to the shift rails. Discard the pins.

d. Place the 5th/reverse shift rail in the fully forward position. Remove the spring pin from the end of the 5th/reverse rail.

e. Remove the 3 rubber plugs from the shift rod service bores.

CAUTION: *Wear safety goggles when performing the shift rail removal procedure! Cover the lock ball bores and friction device and spring seats with a heavy cloth held firmly in place. The ball/friction device and spring can fly out during removal, causing possible personal injury!*

f. Remove the 5th/reverse shift rail from the top cover through the service bore. It may be necessary to rock the shift rail from side-

to-side with a $\frac{5}{16}''$ punch while maintaining rearward pressure.

g. Remove the 1st/2nd shift rail from the cover through the service bore. It may be necessary to rock the shift rail from side-to-side with a $\frac{5}{16}''$ punch while maintaining rearward pressure.

h. Remove the 3rd/4th shift rail from the cover through the service bore. It may be necessary to rock the shift rail from side-to-side with a $\frac{5}{16}''$ punch while maintaining rearward pressure.

i. Remove the 5th/reverse cam lockout plate retaining bolts using a 10mm socket. Remove the plate.

j. Install the 5th/reverse cam lockout plate. Torque the bolts to 72-84 in.lb.

k. Position the 3rd/4th shift rail into the cover through the service bore. It may be necessary to rock the shift rail from side-to-side with a $\frac{5}{16}''$ punch, while maintaining forward pressure.

l. Engage the 3rd/4th shift fork with the shift rail.

m. Position the detent ball and spring into the cover spring seats. Compress the detent ball and spring and push the shift rail into position over the detent ball.

n. Position the friction device and spring into the cover spring seats. Compress the friction device and spring and push the shift rail into position over the friction device.

o. Install the spring pins retaining the shift rail to the cover.

p. Install the spring retaining the 3rd/4th shift fork to the shift rail.

q. Position the 1st/2nd shift rail in the cover through the service bore. It may be necessary to rock the shift rail from side-to-side with a $\frac{5}{16}''$ punch, while maintaining forward pressure.

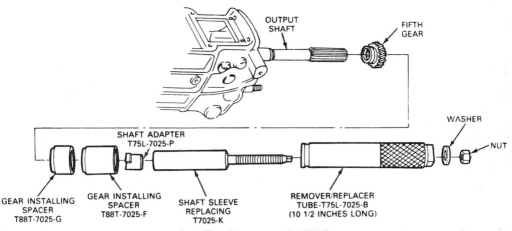

Installing 5th gear on the M50D

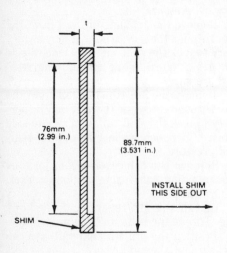

SHIM SELECT CHART — M50D R2

Part Number	Thickness (t)
E8TZ-7029-FA	1.4mm (0.0551 in.)
E8TZ-7029-GA	1.5mm (0.0590 in.)
E8TZ-7029-Ha	1.6mm (0.0629 in.)
E8TZ-7029-Ja	1.7mm (0.0669 in.)
E8TZ-7029-S	1.8mm (0.0708 in.)
E8TZ-7029-T	1.9mm (0.0748 in.)
E8TZ-7029-U	2.0mm (0.0787 in.)
E8TZ-7029-V	2.1mm (0.0826 in.)
E8TZ-7029-W	2.2mm (0.0866 in.)
E8TZ-7029-X	2.3mm (0.0905 in.)
E8TZ-7029-Y	2.4mm (0.0944 in.)
E8TZ-7029-Z	2.5mm (0.0984 in.)
E8TZ-7029-AA	2.6mm (0.1023 in.)
E8TZ-7029-BA	2.7mm (0.1062 in.)
E8TZ-7029-CA	2.8mm (0.1102 in.)
E8TZ-7029-DA	2.9mm (0.1141 in.)
E8TZ-7029-EA	3.0mm (0.1181 in.)

M50D shim selection chart

r. Engage the 1st/2nd shift fork with the shift rail.

s. Position the detent ball and spring into the cover seats.

t. Compress the detent ball and spring and push the shift rail into position over the detent ball.

u. Position the friction device and spring into the cover seats. Compress the friction device and spring and push the shift rail into position over the friction device.

v. Install the spring pins retaining the shift rail to the cover. Install the spring pin retaining the 1st/2nd shift fork to the shift rail.

w. Position the 5th/reverse shift rail in the top cover through the service bore. It may be necessary to rock the shift rail from side-to-side with a $5/16''$ punch, while maintaining forward pressure. Engage the 5th/reverse shift fork with the shift rail. Position the detent ball and spring into the cover seats. Compress the detent ball and spring and push the shift rail into position over the detent ball.

x. Install the spring pins retaining the shift rail to the cover. Install the spring pin retaining the 5th/reverse shift fork to the shift rail. Install the rubber plugs.

y. Install the interlock pins into the 1st/2nd and 3rd/4th shift rails. Note that the pins are different sizes.

WARNING: *Use of the wrong size pins will affect neutral start and/or back-up light switch operation.*

z. Apply non-hardening sealer to the threads of the back-up light switch and install it. Torque the switch to 18-26 ft.lb. Install the dust cover.

GENERAL INSPECTION

Inspect all parts for wear or damage. Replace any part that seems suspect. Output shaft run-out must not exceed 0.05mm. Replace the shaft is it does. Synchronizer-to-gear clearance must not exceed 0.8mm. Replace the synchronizer ring or gear if necessary. Shift fork-to-clutch hub clearance must not exceed 0.8mm.

GENERAL CASE ASSEMBLY

1. Place the countershaft assembly into the case.

2. Place the input shaft in the case. Make

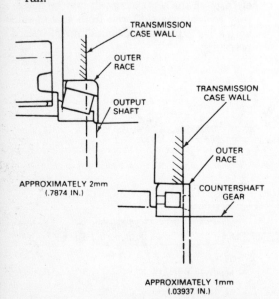

Installing the output shaft center bearing on the M50D

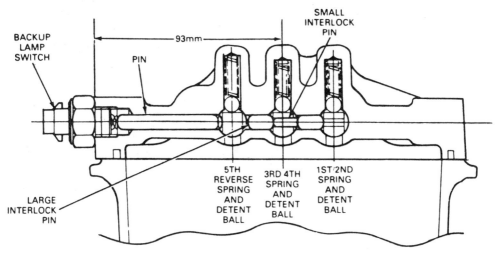

M50D shift rails

sure that the needle roller bearing is on the shaft.

3. Place the output shaft assembly in the case. Mate the input and out shafts. Make sure that the 4th gear synchronizer is installed.

4. Drive the output shaft center bearing into place with a brass drift.

5. Install the countershaft center bearing. Make sure that the center bearing outer races are squarely seated in their bores.

6. Position the center bearing cover on the case with the arrow upwards. Torque the cover bolts to 14-19 ft.lb. Use only bolts marked with a grade **8** on the bolt head.

7. Position the transmission on end with the input end up. Make sure that the input shaft front bearing outer race is squarely positioned in its bore. Install the front cover oil seal with a seal driver.

8. Install the countershaft front bearing.

9. Check and record the following dimensions:

   a. Check and record the height of the input shaft bearing outer race above the transmission front bearing cover mating surface.

   b. Check and record the depth of the front cover outer race bore at the input shaft.

   c. Check and record the depth of the countershaft front bearing race (case-to-cover mating surface).

   d. Check and record the depth of the front cover outer race bore at the output shaft.

10. Select the proper shims using the following formulae:

● Dimension b – (dimension a + the shim thickness) = 0.05-0.15mm

● Dimension c + (dimension d – the shim thickness) = 0.15-0.25mm

Shims are available in 0.1mm increments ranging from 1.4mm to 3.0mm thick.

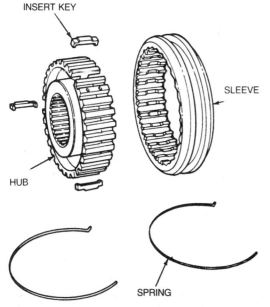

M50D synchronizer exploded view

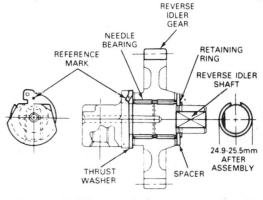

M50D reverse idler gear shaft

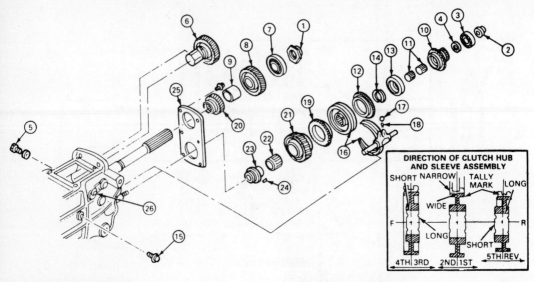

1. Locknut—output shaft
2. Locknut—countershaft
3. Countershaft rear bearing
4. Thurst washer
5. Fixing bolt—reverse idler gear
6. Reverse idle gear assembly
7. Bearing—output shaft rear
8. Reverse gear—output shaft
9. Sleeve—output shaft
10. Countershaft reverse gear
11. Needle bearings
12. Synchronizer ring—reverse
13. Thrust washer
14. Split washer (2 pcs)
15. Fixing bolt—shift rod
16. Shift rail/fork/hub/sleeve assembly
17. Lock ball (steel) shift rail
18. Spring—shift rail
19. Synchronizer ring—5th gear
20. 5th gear—output shaft
21. 5th gear—countershaft
22. Needle bearing—5th gear
23. Sleeve—5th gear
24. Woodruff key
25. Center bearing cover
26. 5th/reverse counter lever lockplate retaining bolt

M50D rear housing components, exploded view

11. Clean the mating surfaces of the transmission and front cover.

12. Wrap the input shaft splines with masking tape.

13. Apply a light coat of oil to the front cover oil seal lip. Position the bearing shim and baffle into the cover. The shim groove should be visible.

14. Install the spacer in the case countershaft front bearing bore. You may want to apply a coating of chassis grease to parts to hold them in place during assembly.

15. Apply a ⅛" wide bead of silicone RTV sealant to the front cover mating surface and the bolt threads. Install the cover and torque the bolts to 9-12 ft.lb. Always us bolts marked grade **6** on the bolt head.

16. Lay the transmission down and install the woodruff key and 5th gear sleeve.

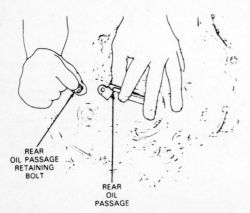

Rear oil passage removal from the M50D 5-speed

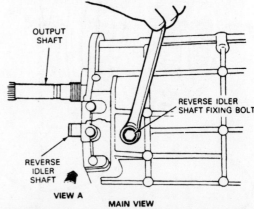

Removing the reverse idler gear shaft retaining bolt on the M50D

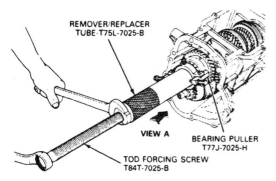

Removing the output shaft rear bearing on the M50D

NOTE: *Install the 5th gear sleeve using the nut, Shaft Adapter T75L-7025-L, Adapter T88T-7025-J2 and Remover/Replacer Tube T75L-7025-B, or equivalents.*

17. Install the 5th gear needle bearing onto the countershaft 5th gear.

18. Install the 5th gear onto the output shaft using Gear Installation Spacers T88T-7025-F, and -G, Shaft Adapter T75L-7025-P, Shaft Adapter Screw T75L-7025-K, Remover/Replacer Tube T75L-7025-B, nut and washer, or equivalents. Make sure that the long flange on the 5th gear faces forward.

19. Install T88T-7025-F. When the tool bot-

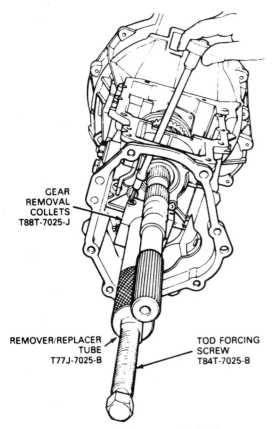

Removing the 5th gear sleeve on the M50D

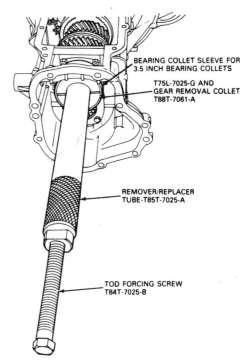

Removing 5th gear from the output shaft on the M50D

toms, add T88T-7025-G and press the 5th gear assembly all the way into position.

20. Position counterlever assembly in the transmission and install the thrust washer and retaining ring. Apply sealant on the counterlever fixing bolt threads. Install the counterlever fixing bolt and torque it to 72-84 in.lb.

21. Position the 5th/reverse shift fork and shift rail in the top cover. Insert the 5th/reverse shift rail through the top cover bore and the 5th/reverse shift fork. Install the spring and detent ball on the lower part of the rod.

22. Assemble the 5th/reverse synchronizer hub, sleeve and 5th gear synchronizer ring on the 5th/reverse shift fork and rod. The longer flange faces front. The reference mark on the synchronizer sleeve faces the reverse gear side.

23. Install the 5th/reverse shift fork and rail assembly on the countershaft. Mate the shift fork gate to the 5th/reverse counterlever end. Install the 5th/reverse fork and shift rail with the threaded fixing bolt bores aligned.

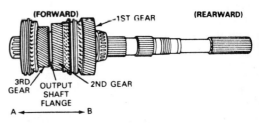

M50D output shaft

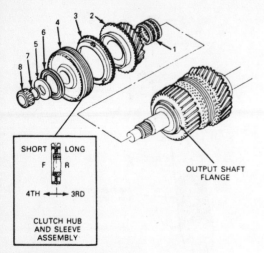

SHORT | LONG
F | R
4TH ← → 3RD

CLUTCH HUB AND SLEEVE ASSEMBLY

OUTPUT SHAFT FLANGE

1. Needle bearing—3rd gear
2. Third gear
3. Synchronizer ring—3rd gear
4. Clutch hub and sleeve assembly—3rd/4th
5. Spacer
6. Needle bearing (plain)
7. Retaining ring
8. Roller bearing—pilot bearing

M50D output shaft exploded view

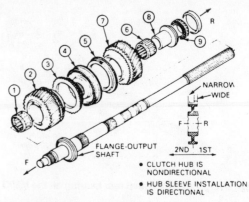

NARROW
WIDE
F | R
2ND | 1ST

FLANGE-OUTPUT SHAFT
F

- CLUTCH HUB IS NONDIRECTIONAL
- HUB SLEEVE INSTALLATION IS DIRECTIONAL

1. Needle bearing—2nd gear
2. 2nd gear
3. Synchronizer ring—2nd gear
4. Clutch hub and sleeve assembly—1st and 2nd
5. Synchronizer ring—1st gear
6. Needle bearing—1st gear
7. 1st gear
8. Sleeve—1st gear
9. Center bearing—inner

M50D output shaft component assembly

NOTE: *It's easier if you place the 5th/reverse shift fork into the rearmost of the three detent positions. Return the shift fork to the neutral position after assembly.*

24. Apply sealant to the 5th/reverse shift rail fixing bolt threads. Install the 5th/reverse shift rail fixing bolt in the case. Torque the 5th/reverse shift rail bolt to 16-22 ft.lb.

25. Apply sealant to the oil passage retaining bolt. Position the oil passage in the case and torque the bolt to 72-84 in.lb.

26. Install the split washer and thrust washer onto the countershaft. If the clutch hub and/or counter reverse gear have been replaced, new split washers must be selected to maintain endplay within specifications. Check the endplay with a flat feeler gauge. Endplay should be 0.2-0.3mm. Split washers are provided in 0.1mm increments ranging from 3.0-3.5mm.

27. Install the reverse synchronizer ring and needle bearings into the counter reverse gear. Install the counter reverse gear and needle bearings onto the countershaft. Install the thrust washer.

28. Push the thrust washer forward by hand against the shoulder on the countershaft. Maintain forward pressure and insert a flat feeler gauge between the thrust washer and the counter reverse gear. Counter reverse endplay should be 0.2-0.3mm. Thrust washers are available in 0.2mm increments ranging from 7.4-7.8mm thicknesses.

29. Temporarily install a spacer, with an inner bore larger than 21mm and an outer diameter smaller than 36mm, 15-20mm overall length, in place of the countershaft bearing. Loosely install the locknut.

30. Install the reverse idler gear assembly. Apply sealant to the threads of the reverse idler gear fixing bolt. Torque the bolt to 58-86 ft.lb.

31. Drive the sleeve and reverse gear assembly into place on the output shaft using Gear Installation Spacer T88T-7025-G, Shaft Adapter T75L-7025-P, Shaft Adapter Screw T75L-7025-P, Shaft Adapter Screw T75L-7025-K, Remover/Replacer Tube T75L-7025-B, nut and washer, or equivalents. Install the reverse gear with the longer flange facing forward.

32. Install the output shaft rear bearing using Gear Installation Spacer T88T-7025-G, Shaft Adapter T75L-7025-P, Shaft Adapter Screw T75L-7025-K, Remover/Replacer Tube T75L-7025-B, nut and washer, or equivalents.

33. Remove the temporary spacer.

34. Install the countershaft rear bearing.

35. Lock the transmission in 1st and 3rd. Install new output shaft and countershaft locknuts. Torque the output shaft locknut to 160-200 ft.lb.; torque the countershaft locknut to 94-144 ft.lb.

WARNING: *Always use new locknuts. Make sure that the bearings are fully seated before torquing the locknuts.*

36. Using a centerpunch, stake the locknuts.

37. Install the speedometer drive gear and steel ball on the output shaft. Install the snapring retaining the speedometer drive gear

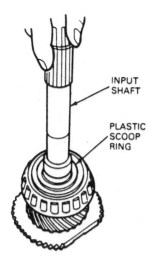

Removing the tapered roller bearing from the M50D input shaft

to the output shaft. The ball can be installed in any of the three detents. Make sure, if you are installing a new speedometer gear, that it is the same color code as the old one.

38. Clean the mating surfaces of the extension housing and case. Apply a ⅛" wide bead of silicone RTV sealant to the case.

NOTE: *If the extension housing bushing is defective, the entire extension housing must be replaced.*

39. Position the extension housing on the case and torque the bolts to 24-34 ft.lb.

40. Place the synchronizers in the neutral position. Make sure that the shift forks in the cover are also in neutral.

41. Using a new gasket, without sealant, place the cover on the case and careful engage the shift forks in the synchronizers. Apply sealant to the two rearmost cover bolts and install them. Install the remaining bolts without sealant. Torque the bolts to 12-16 ft.lb.

42. Install the drain plug. Torque it to 40 ft.lb.

43. Install the rear oil seal into the extension housing. Make sure that the drain hole faces downward.

44. Fill the case with Dexron®II fluid.

ZF S5-42 5-Speed Overdrive

MAIN COMPONENT DISASSEMBLY

1. Place the transmission face downward on a clean work surface.

2. Using a hammer and chisel, bend back the tab on the output shaft flange locknut.

3. Install a holding tool on the flange and loosen, but don't remove, the output shaft locknut.

4. Remove 15 of the 17 bolts holding the rear case cover to the case. Leave 2 bolts at opposite corners.

5. Remove any power take-off (pto) equipment.

6. Remove the shift tower assembly from the case.

7. Remove the interlock plate and compression spring which serves as a reverse gear interlock.

NOTE: *Be careful...these parts tend to fall into the case.*

8. Place a punch against the detent bolt cap, at an angle and slightly off center. Drive the cap inward until spring pressure against its underside forces the cap out of its hole. Repeat this procedure for the other two detent bolt sealing caps in the front case.

CAUTION: *Always wear goggles! The cap is under spring pressure.*

9. Remove the springs from the sealing cap holes.

10. Drive out the sealing caps from the two reverse idler shaft cap screws. Remove the screws.

11. Remove the back-up light switch and switch sealing ring.

12. Using a punch remove the two dowel pins from the two upper corners of the rear case mating surface. Drive them out towards the rear.

13. Remove the two remaining hex bolts from the rear case.

14. Carefully separate the front and rear cases. It may be necessary to push the central shift rail inwards to prevent it from hanging up on the front case. Be careful to ensure that the central shift rail is not lifted off with the front case.

WARNING: *The case mating surfaces are sealed with sealant in place of a gasket. If you experience difficulty in separating the case sections DON'T PRY THEM APART! Tap around the rear case section to break it loose with a rubber or plastic mallet.*

15. Remove the central shift rail and shift finger assembly.

16. Lift the shaft out of the reverse idler gear and remove the gear and two caged roller bearings from the rear case.

17. Remove the three capscrews that retain the shift interlock to the rear case.

18. With the transmission on end, front up, install the Gear Pack Holding Fixture T87T-7025-HH using sling D87L-1000-A on the mainshaft and output shaft assemblies. Pass the sling over the shift rails.

19. Place Shift Rod Support T87T-7025-JH over the ends of the shift rails.

20. Turn the transmission to the horizontal

position with the holding fixture under the gear pack.

21. Remove the output shaft flange retaining nut.

22. Remove the flange. If it's hard to get off, tap it off with a hammer.

23. Carefully pull the gearpack and shift rails, along with their holding fixtures, forward to dislodge them from the rear case.

24. Remove the speedometer drive gear from the mainshaft.

25. Remove the sling from around the shift rails, gearpack and fixture.

26. Turn the shift rails 45° to release them from the shift hubs.

27. Lift the shift rails, forks and interlock, together with the Support Tool from the mainshaft.

28. Using the shift rod support tool as a base, set the shift rail assembly on a work bench with the shift rails in a vertical position. Remove the interlock.

29. Make identifying marks on each shift fork and shift rail and position them in the holding fixture. Lift the shift rails from the support tool.

30. Lift the countershaft off of the workbench stand. Separate the input shaft from the mainshaft. Lift the mainshaft and output shaft from the stand.

31. Remove the rear cover from the holding fixture.

SUBASSEMBLIES

1. Shift Tower:

   a. Remove the lever cover from the shift housing.

   b. Lift the lever, boot, cover and attached parts off the housing.

   c. Slide the two pieces off the cardan joint.

   d. Slide the boot and cover off the top of the gearshift lever.

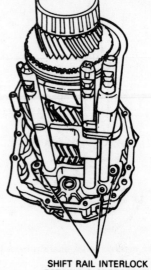

SHIFT RAIL INTERLOCK
RETAINING CAPSCREWS

Removing the shift interlock from the case of the ZF

   e. Invert the cover and remove the boot snapring.

   f. Assemble the parts in reverse order of disassembly.

2. Shift Rails:

   a. Install each shift rail in a soft-jawed vise and drive the roll pins out of the shift forks with a punch.

   b. Assembly is the reverse of disassembly.

3. Rear Case:

   a. Drive the two dowel pins out of the rear case.

   b. Using a slide hammer and internal puller, remove the mainshaft rear bearing outer race from the rear case.

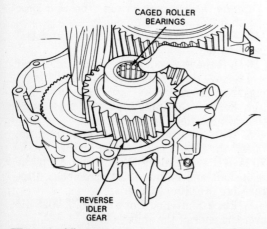

CAGED ROLLER
BEARINGS

REVERSE
IDLER
GEAR

ZF reverse idler gear

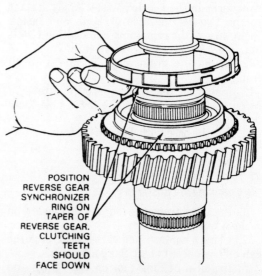

POSITION
REVERSE GEAR
SYNCHRONIZER
RING ON
TAPER OF
REVERSE GEAR.
CLUTCHING
TEETH
SHOULD
FACE DOWN

Installing the reverse gear synchronizer ring on the ZF

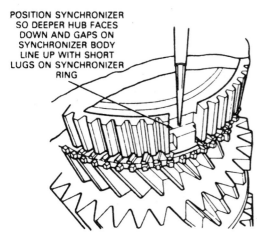

POSITION SYNCHRONIZER
SO DEEPER HUB FACES
DOWN AND GAPS ON
SYNCHRONIZER BODY
LINE UP WITH SHORT
LUGS ON SYNCHRONIZER
RING

Installing the synchronizer body on the ZF mainshaft

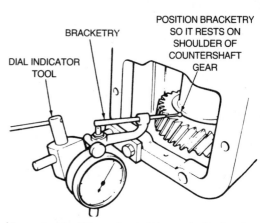

BRACKETRY

POSITION BRACKETRY
SO IT RESTS ON
SHOULDER OF
COUNTERSHAFT
GEAR

DIAL INDICATOR
TOOL

Measuring the ZF countershaft tapered roller bearing preload

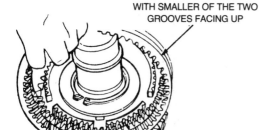

POSITION SLIDING SLEEVE
WITH SMALLER OF THE TWO
GROOVES FACING UP

LINE UP AREAS
WHERE TEETH ARE
CUT AWAY ON SLIDING
SLEEVE WITH GAPS ON
SYNCHRONIZER BODY AND
LUGS ON SYNCHRONIZER
RING

5th/reverse sliding sleeve installation on the ZF

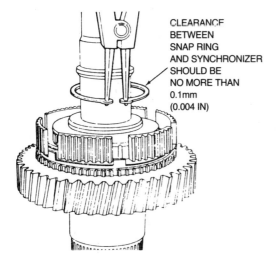

CLEARANCE
BETWEEN
SNAP RING
AND SYNCHRONIZER
SHOULD BE
NO MORE THAN
0.1mm
(0.004 IN)

5th/reverse synchronizer snapring on the ZF

c. Using a drift, drive the mainshaft rear seal out of the rear cover. Discard the seal.

d. Using a slide hammer and bearing cup puller, remove the countershaft rear bearing outer race from the rear case.

e. Remove the central shift rail bearing from the rear cover using Blind Hole Puller D80L-100-Q and Slide Hammer T50T-100-A.

f. To install the central shift rail bearing, heat the rear case bore area to 320°F (160°C) with a heat gun. Insert the ball sleeve and drive the bearing in until it seats against its stop using Needle Bearing Replacer T87T-7025-DH.

g. Heat the rear case in the area around the countershaft rear bearing outer race to 320°F (160°C) with a heat gun. Install the countershaft bearing outer race with a driver until it seats against its stop.

h. Heat the case in the area of the mainshaft outer race to 320°F (160°C) with a heat gun. Drive the bearing cup into its bore with a driver and cup tool, until it seats against its stop.

4. Front Case:

a. Using a slide hammer and cup puller, remove the input shaft bearing outer race from the front case.

b. Remove the baffle and shims. Discard the baffle.

c. Using a punch, drive out the input shaft oil seal from the base of the quill.

d. Remove the O-ring from the quill. Remove the oil seal.

e. Remove the countershaft front bearing outer race using a slide hammer and internal puller.

f. Remove the fluid drain and fill plugs.

g. Remove the sealing caps and three shift rail detents from the case.

h. Remove the roll pins that hold the 5th/

reverse interlock plate from their bores in the case, just below the shift housing.

i. Remove the central shift rail needle bearings from the front case with a slide hammer and blind hole puller.

j. Install the 5th/reverse roll pins into their bores until the bigger one bottoms out. It should stick out about 8mm. The small one sticks out about 4-5mm. Don't allow the small one to bottom out.

k. Heat the front case in the area of the central shift rail bearing bore to 320°F (160°C) with a heat gun. Drive the bearing sleeve in with a driver until it is flush with the surface of the bore.

l. Install the drain and fill plugs. Torque them to 44 ft.lb.

m. Insert the three shift rail detent bolts into their bores. They must seat in the detents and must move freely when installed.

n. Place a new O-ring on the input shaft quill.

o. Position the seal in the front case. Drive it in with a seal driver until it seats against its stop in the quill.

NOTE: *If the countershaft, input shaft, mainshaft or any tapered roller bearing is replaced, it will be necessary to adjust the tapered roller bearings to obtain a preload of 0.02-0.11mm. See the ADJUSTMENTS section below.*

p. Heat the mounting bore in the front case for the tapered roller bearing outer race of the countershaft to 320°F (160°C) with a heat gun. Position the proper thickness shim in the bore. Using a bearing driver, drive the race in until it seats against the stop in the case.

q. Heat the front case in the area of the input shaft tapered roller bearing outer race to 320°F (160°C) with a heat gun.

r. Using the ADJUSTMENT procedures below, position the correct shim pack in the bore for the input shaft bearing outer race. Using a driver, drive the bearing cup into place until it seats against its stop in the bore.

5. Mainshaft:

a. Clamp the output end of the mainshaft in a soft-jawed vise.

b. Remove the 4th gear synchronizer ring from the 3rd/4th synchronizer assembly.

c. Place the bearing collets T87T-7025-FH on either side of the mainshaft front bearing. Position Puller Tube T77J-7025-B in the collets. Pass the Collet Retaining Ring T75L-7025-G over the puller and into the collets so they clamp firmly on the bearing. Pull the bearing from the mainshaft.

d. Remove the 3rd/4th gear sliding sleeve from the mainshaft. Place a cloth around the synchronizer to catch the compression springs, pressure pieces and balls that will be released when the sliding sleeves are removed.

e. Remove the cap ring that retains the 3rd/4th synchronizer body to the mainshaft.

f. Place the Collet Retaining ring T87T-7025-OH over the mainshaft and let it rest on the mainshaft 1st gear.

g. Position the two collet halves T87T-7025-NH on the 3rd/4th synchronizer body and slide the collet retaining ring over the collet halves to hold them in place on the synchronizer body.

h. Place the Shaft Protector D80L-625-4 on the end of the mainshaft. Place a 3-jawed puller on the collet halves and retaining ring, and pull the synchronizer body from the mainshaft.

i. Remove the synchronizer ring from the mainshaft 3rd gear.

j. Remove the 3rd gear from the mainshaft.

k. Remove the 3rd gear caged needle rollers from the mainshaft.

l. Lift the 1st/2nd gear sliding sleeve up as far as it will go. Position Collet Retaining Ring T87T-7025-OH over the mainshaft and let it rest on the 1st gear.

m. Position the two Collet Halves T87T-7025-MH so they seat in the groove in the 1st/2nd sliding sleeve. Pass the retaining ring from below over the two halves and secure them to the sliding sleeve.

n. Position the shaft protector D80L-625-4 on the end of the mainshaft. Position a 3-jawed puller on the collet retaining ring and pull off the 1st/2nd sliding sleeve, 2nd gear, thrust washer, and 3rd gear bearing inner race from the mainshaft.

CAUTION: *Wrap a heavy cloth around the 1st/2nd synchronizer body to catch the springs, pressure pieces and balls.*

5th/reverse interlock plate roll pins on the ZF

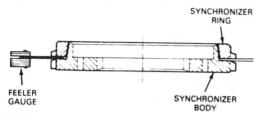

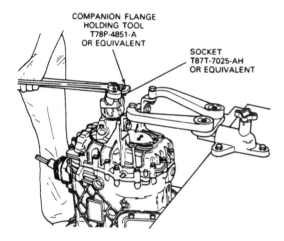

GEARS	CLEARANCE
1	0.6 mm (0.024 inch)
2	0.6 mm (0.024 inch)
3	0.6 mm (0.024 inch)
4	0.6 mm (0.024 inch)
5	. 0.6 mm (0.024 inch)
Reverse	0.2 mm (0.008 inch)

ZF synchronizer ring-to-body wear check

Installing the output flange on the ZF

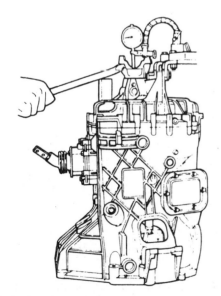

Measuring the preload on the ZF input shaft and mainshaft roller bearings

o. Remove the snapring retaining the 1st/2nd synchronizer to the mainshaft.

p. Reposition the mainshaft in the vise so that the output end is facing upward.

q. Place a bearing gripper on the mainshaft rear tapered roller bearing. The gripper must be used to back the bearing during removal. Place a 3-jawed puller over the mainshaft and onto the gripper. Pull the bearing from the mainshaft.

r. Remove 5th gear from the mainshaft along with its caged needle rollers.

s. Remove the synchronizer ring from the 5th/reverse synchronizer.

t. Remove the snapring from the 5th/reverse synchronizer body. Remove the 5th/reverse sliding sleeve.

CAUTION: *Wrap a heavy cloth around the 1st/2nd synchronizer body to catch the springs, pressure pieces and balls.*

u. Position Collet Retaining Ring T87T-7025-OH over the mainshaft and let it rest on the 1st gear. Position the two Collet Halves T87T-7025-NH so the ridge rests between the synchronizer body and the synchronizer ring. Slide the retaining ring upwards around the collets to secure them in position.

v. Position a 3-jawed puller on the collet retaining ring and pull the 5th/reverse synchronizer body from the mainshaft. Remove the synchronizer ring from the reverse gear. Remove the reverse gear from the mainshaft along with the caged needle bearings.

w. Remove the mainshaft from the vise. Position the mainshaft in a press and press off the 1st gear and 1st/2nd synchronizer body.

x. Remove the 1st gear caged needle rollers.

To assemble the mainshaft:

a. Clamp the input end of the mainshaft in a soft-jawed vise.

b. Place the reverse gear caged needle roller on the mainshaft.

c. Place the reverse gear on the mainshaft over the needle rollers. The clutch teeth must face upwards.

NOTE: *Before installing the original synchronizer ring and body, check them for excessive wear.*

d. Position the reverse gear synchronzier ring on the taper of the first gear.

e. Using a heat gun, heat the 5th/reverse synchronizer body to 320°F (160°C).

WARNING: *Don't heat the synchronizer body for more than 15 minutes.*

f. Position the synchronizer body on the mainshaft splines so that the side with the deeper hub faces downwards and the short lugs on the synchronizer ring engage the gaps in the synchronizer body. Push or lightly tap the synchronizer body down until it stops.

g. Install the snapring on the mainshaft next to the 5th/reverse synchronizer body. The clearance between the snapring and the synchronizer body should be 0-0.1mm, with 0 preferable.

h. Check the reverse gear endplay. Endplay should be 0.15-0.35mm.

i. Position the 5th/reverse sliding sleeve over the synchronizer body with the 2 grooves facing upwards. Align the tooth gaps and lugs. Slide the sleeve down until it rests against the reverse gear clutching teeth.

j. Insert the 3 compression springs and pressure pieces in the recesses of the synchronizer body. If the original springs are being reused, inspect them carefully and replace them if they appear worn or damaged.

k. Push the pressure pieces back with a screwdriver. Push the balls in with a screwdriver and slide the pressure piece against the ball.

l. Place the 5th gear synchronizer ring on the synchronizer body. The short lugs on the synchronizer ring should be located over the gaps in the 5th/reverse synchronizer body.

m. Push the 5th gear synchronizer ring downwards while pulling the sliding sleeve into the center position.

n. Pace the 5th gear caged needle rollers on the mainshaft. Install the 5th gear on the mainshaft over the caged needle rollers.

o. Heat the inner race of the mainshaft rear tapered roller bearing to 320°F (160°C) with a heat gun. Place it on the mainshaft and drive it until it seats against its stop. WARNING: *Don't heat the bearing for more than 15 minutes.*

p. Check the 5th gear endplay. Endplay should be 0.15-0.35mm.

q. Turn the mainshaft over and clamp it on the input end. Place the 1st gear caged needle rollers on the shaft. Place 1st gear over the rollers with the taper facing upward.

r. Place the 1st gear synchronizer ring on the 1st gear taper. Heat the 1st/2nd synchronizer body with a heat gun to 320°F (160°C). Position the synchronzier body on the mainshaft splines so that the short lugs on the synchronizer ring engage the gaps in the synchronizer body. Push the synchronizer body down until it stops against the ring. If the installation was correct, the word ENGINE will appear on the synchronizer body. WARNING: *Don't heat the bearing for more than 15 minutes.*

s. Install a snapring on the mainshaft next to the 1st/2nd synchonizer body. Clearance between the snapring and synchronizer body

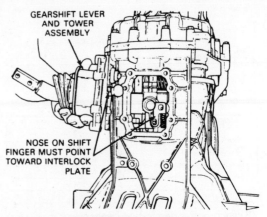

GEARSHIFT LEVER AND TOWER ASSEMBLY

NOSE ON SHIFT FINGER MUST POINT TOWARD INTERLOCK PLATE

Installing the ZF shift tower assembly

should be 0-0.1mm. 1st gear endplay should be 0.15-0.35mm.

t. Position the sliding sleeve over the synchronizer body with its tapered collar facing downward. Align the lugs and tooth gaps, and push the sleeve down until it rests against 1st gear.

u. Insert the three compression springs and pressure pieces in the recesses of the synchronizer body. Push the pressure pieces back with a screwdriver. Push the balls in with a screwdriver and slide the pressure piece against the ball.

v. Place the 2nd gear synchronizer ring on the synchronizer body. The short lugs on the synchronizer ring should be located over the gaps in the 1st/2nd synchronizer body.

w. Push the 2nd gear synchronizer ring downwards while pulling the sliding sleeve into the center position. Pace the 2nd gear caged needle rollers on the mainshaft. Install the 2nd gear on the mainshaft over the caged needle rollers.

x. Heat the thrust washer to 320°F (160°C) with a heat gun. Place it on the mainshaft and drive it until it seats against its stop. WARNING: *Don't heat the washer for more than 15 minutes.*

y. Heat the 3rd gear bearing inner race to 320°F (160°C) with a heat gun. Place the race on the mainshaft and push it down until it seats against its stop. Check the 2nd gear endplay. Endplay should be 0.15-0.45mm. After the 3rd gear has cooled, place the 3rd gear caged needle rollers over it. Place the 3rd gear over the needle rollers with the taper upwards. Place the 3rd gear synchronizer ring on the 3rd gear taper. Heat the 3rd/4th synchronizer body with a heat gun to 320°F (160°C). Position the body on the mainshaft splines so that the short lugs on the synchronizer ring engage the gaps in the body. Push the body down until it stops against the ring. The recess in the body must face upwards.

z. Install a snapring on the mainshaft next to the 1st/2nd synchonizer body. Clearance between the snapring and synchronizer body should be 0-0.1mm. 1st gear endplay should be 0.15-0.35mm. Position the sliding sleeve over the synchronizer body with its tapered collar facing downward. Align the lugs and tooth gaps, and push the sleeve down until it rests against 1st gear. Insert the three compression springs and pressure pieces in the recesses of the synchronizer body. Push the pressure pieces back with a screwdriver. Push the balls in with a screwdriver and slide the pressure piece against the ball. Place the

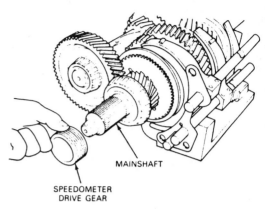

Installing the speedometer gear on the ZF mainshaft

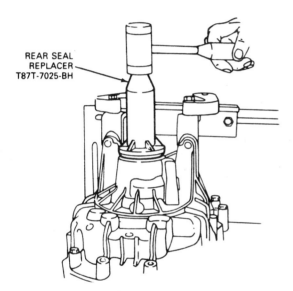

ZF rear oil seal installation

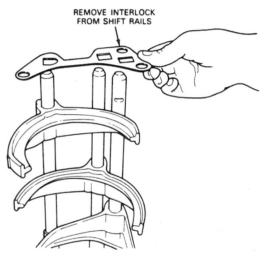

Removing the ZF shift interlock

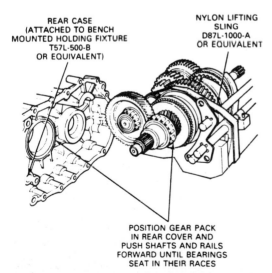

Assembling the ZF rear case to the main case

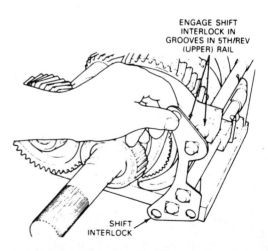

Installing the interlock on the ZF shift rails

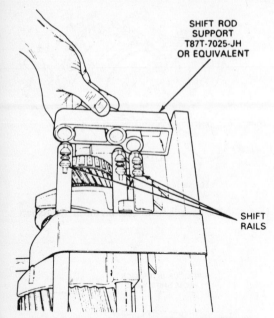

SHIFT ROD
SUPPORT
T87T-7025-JH
OR EQUIVALENT

SHIFT
RAILS

Installing the shift rod support on the ZF shift rails

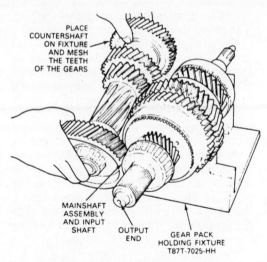

PLACE
COUNTERSHAFT
ON FIXTURE
AND MESH
THE TEETH
OF THE GEARS

MAINSHAFT
ASSEMBLY
AND INPUT
SHAFT

OUTPUT
END

GEAR PACK
HOLDING FIXTURE
T87T-7025-HH

Using the gear pack holding fixture on the ZF

2nd gear synchronizer ring on the synchronizer body. The short lugs on the synchronizer ring should be located over the gaps in the 1st/2nd synchronizer body. Push the 2nd gear synchronizer ring downwards while pulling the sliding sleeve into the center position. Pace the 2nd gear caged needle rollers on the mainshaft. Install the 2nd gear on the mainshaft over the caged needle rollers. Heat the thrust washer to 320°F (160°C) with a heat gun. Place it on the mainshaft and drive it until it seats against its stop.

WARNING: *Don't heat the washer for more than 15 minutes.*

6. Input Shaft Disassembly and Assembly:

a. Position the two Collet Halves (44803 and 44797) of Universal Bearing Remover Set D81L-4220-A around the input shaft bearing cone. Install the pulling tube and pull the bearing from the shaft.

b. Inspect the bearing and shaft thoroughly. Replace any worn or damaged parts.

c. Place the bearing on the shaft.

d. Place the Bearing Cone Replacer T85T-4621-AH over the bearing.

e. Position the shaft, bearing and tool in Press Plate T75L-1165-B.

f. Press the bearing on until it seats against its stop.

INPUT SHAFT AND MAINSHAFT TAPERED ROLLER BEARING PRELOAD MEASUREMENT

This adjustment is necessary whenever a major, related component is replaced.

1. Place the transmission on a holding fixture with the output shaft facing upward.

2. Attach a dial indicator with a magnetic base so that the measurement bar rests on the output end of the mainshaft.

3. Zero the indicator and pry up on the input shaft and mainshaft with a prybar. Note the indicator reading. The shim and shaft seal must have a combined thickness equal to the indicator reading plus 0.02-0.11mm.

COUNTERSHAFT TAPERED ROLLER BEARING PRELOAD MEASUREMENT

1. Using two 10mm hex screws, attach the magnetic mount dial indicator near the pto opening on the front case. Position the dial indicator gauge on the support in such a way that the measurement bar rests against the flat face of the 5th speed helical gear on the countershaft. Zero the gauge.

2. Insert prybars through each of the two pto openings and position them beneath the 5th speed helical gear on the countershaft. Pry upward gently. Preload should be 0.0-0.11mm. Use shims to correct the preload.

MAINSHAFT AND INPUT SHAFT TAPERED ROLLER BEARING PRELOAD ADJUSTMENT

1. Position the transmission with the input shaft facing upwards.

2. Drive the two dowel pins out of their holes in the front and rear cases, and lift the front case off of the rear case.

3. Using a slide hammer and internal puller, remove the countershaft and mainshaft tapered roller bearing outer races from the front case.

4. Fit each race with a shim, or shim and shaft seal, to obtain the required preload determined above. The countershaft preload is set with shims alone. The input shaft and mainshaft preload is set using shims and a baf-

fle. In both cases, parts are installed under the outer race of the tapered roller bearing which seats in the front case.

5. Apply Loctite 574® to the mating surfaces of the front and rear cases.

WARNING: *Do not use silicone type sealer.*

6. Join the case sections and torque the bolts to 16 ft.lb.

SYNCHRONIZER RING AND SYNCHRONIZER BODY WEAR CHECK

1. Install the ring on the body.
2. Insert a feeler gauge and measure the clearance at two opposite positions. If clearance is less than 0.6mm for the forward speed synchronizers and 0.2mm for the reverse synchronizer, replace the ring and/or synchronizer body as required.

SYNCHRONIZER COMPRESSION SPRING TENSION CHECK

The length of all springs should be 14.8mm; the outer diameter should be 5.96mm and the wire diameter should be 0.95mm. Replace any spring that is not to specifications.

MAIN COMPONENT ASSEMBLY

1. Place the input shaft and synchronizer ring assembly over the tapered roller bearing on the input end of the mainshaft.
2. Place the mainshaft and input shaft on Gear Pack Holding Fixture T87T-7025-HH. Place the countershaft on the fixture and mesh the gears of the two shafts.
3. Place the three shift rails and fork assemblies into Shift Rod Support Tool T87T-7025-JH in the same position from which they were removed during disassembly.
4. Position the three shift rail together with the shift rod support tool and interlock, so that the shift forks engage in the correct mainshaft sliding sleeves.
5. Place the shift interlock on the three gearshift rails and engage it in the interlock grooves in the 5th/reverse upper rail.
6. Slide the speedometer worm gear onto the mainshaft until it seats against its stop.
7. Secure the rear cover on the holding fixture T57L-500-B.
8. Position nylon lifting sling D87L-1000-A around the shift rails, holding fixture and mainshaft and countershaft.
9. Position the gear pack into the rear cover and push the shafts and rails forward until the bearings seat in their races and the gearshift rails slide into their retaining holes.
10. Rotate the gear pack and rear case upwards so that the input shaft faces up.
11. Slide the output shaft flange onto the output end of the mainshaft so that it seats against its stop. Screw the hex nut onto the shaft finger-tightly.

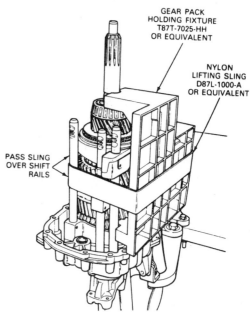

Lifting sling and holding fixture in place on the ZF

NOTE: *Make sure that the mainshaft bearing is not pushed off its race when the flange is installed.*

12. Remove the shift rod support tool from the ends of the shift rails.
13. Remove the strap and gear pack holding fixture.
14. Attach the three capscrews that secure the shift interlock to the rear housing. Torque them to 84 in.lb. Make sure that the interlock still moves freely.
15. Mesh the reverse idler gear and reverse gear. Slide the reverse idler shaft downward through the bearings and into the rear case. Tighten the bolt finger-tightly.
16. Insert the central shift rail and finger assembly into its bore in the rear case.
17. If the tapered roller bearings on the

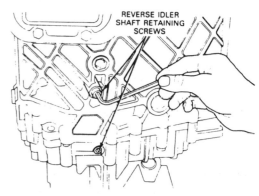

Removing the reverse idler shaft cap screws on the ZF

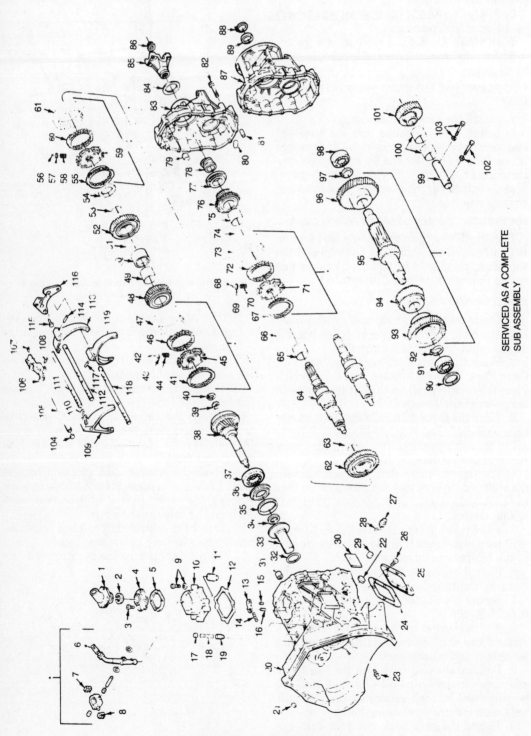

SERVICED AS A COMPLETE
SUB ASSEMBLY

S5-42 ZF 5-speed exploded view

1. Shift lever boot
2. Snap ring
3. Capscrew
4. Shift tower cover
5. Gasket
6. Lower shift lever
7. Guide piece
8. Guide piece
9. Hex bolts
10. Shift housing
11. Shift detent
12. Gasket
13. 5th-reverse interlock
14. Interlock spring
15. Intrelock roll pin
16. Interlock roll pin
17. Sealing cap
18. Spring
19. Shift rail detent
20. Front case
21. Sealing cap
22. Plug—drain
23. Bolt
24. Gasket
25. PTO cover
26. Bolt
27. Backup lamp switch
28. Sealing ring
29. Plug—filler
30. ID plate
31. Central shift rail bearing
32. O-ring
33. Quill
34. Oil seal
35. Shim
36. Baffle
37. Input shaft bearing
38. Input shaft
39. Mainshaft bearing
40. Snap ring
41. 4th gear synchronizer ring
42. Ball
43. Pressure piece
44. Spring
45. 3rd-4th synchronizer body
46. 3rd gear synchronizer ring
47. 3rd-4th sliding sleeve
48. 3rd gear
49. Caged needle rollers
50. Bearing race
51. Thrust washer
52. 2nd gear
53. Caged needle rollers
54. Snap ring
55. 2nd gear synchronizer ring
56. Ball
57. Pressure piece
58. Spring
59. 1st-2nd synchronizer body
60. 1st gear synchronizer ring
61. 1st-2nd sliding sleeve
62. 1st gear
63. Needle rollers
64. Mainshaft
65. Caged needle rollers
66. Reverse gear
67. Reverse gear synchronizer ring
68. Ball
69. Pressure piece
70. Spring
71. 5th-reverse synchronizer body
72. 5th gear synchronizer ring
73. 5th-reverse sliding sleeve
74. Snap ring
75. Caged needle rollers
76. 5th gear
77. Mainshaft bearing
78. Speedometer drive gear (4×2 only)
79. Central shift rail bearing
80. Magnet
81. Dowel
82. Bolt
83. Rear case (4×2)
84. Rear oil seal (4×2)
85. Output yoke (4×2)
86. Locknut (4×2)
87. Rear case (4×4)
88. Snap ring ($r \times 4$)
89. Oil seal (4×4)
90. Shim
91. Front countershaft bearing
92. Snap ring
93. Countershaft drive gear
94. Countershaft 3rd gear
95. Countershaft
96. Countershaft 5th gear
97. Snap ring
98. Countershaft rear bearing
99. Reverse idler shaft
100. Caged needle rollers
101. Reverse idler gear
102. Screw and sealing ring
103. Screw and sealing ring
104. Plug
105. Central shift rail
106. Shift finger
107. Plug
108. Roll pin
109. Roll pin
110. Shift fork
111. Shift rail
112. Shift rail
113. Shift fork
114. Roll pin
115. Bolt
116. Interlock plate
117. Roll pin
118. Shift rail
119. Shift fork

S-42 ZF 5-speed exploded view

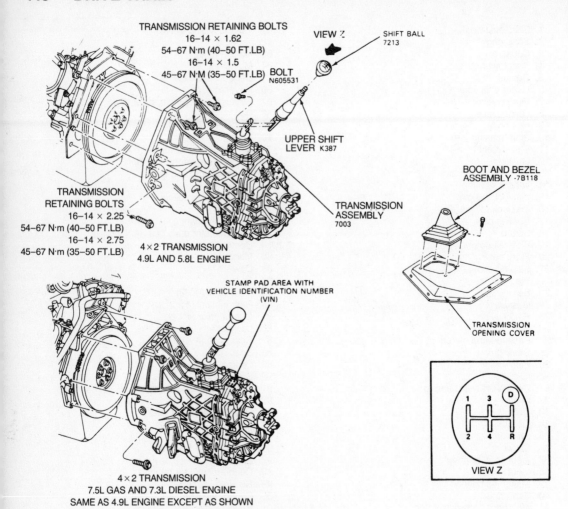

TRANSMISSION RETAINING BOLTS
16–14 × 1.62
54–67 N·m (40–50 FT.LB)
16–14 × 1.5
45–67 N·M (35–50 FT.LB)

BOLT N605531

VIEW Z

SHIFT BALL 7213

UPPER SHIFT LEVER K387

TRANSMISSION RETAINING BOLTS
16–14 × 2.25
54–67 N·m (40–50 FT.LB)
16–14 × 2.75
45–67 N·m (35–50 FT.LB)

4 × 2 TRANSMISSION
4.9L AND 5.8L ENGINE

TRANSMISSION ASSEMBLY 7003

BOOT AND BEZEL ASSEMBLY -7B118

TRANSMISSION OPENING COVER

STAMP PAD AREA WITH VEHICLE IDENTIFICATION NUMBER (VIN)

4 × 2 TRANSMISSION
7.5L GAS AND 7.3L DIESEL ENGINE
SAME AS 4.9L ENGINE EXCEPT AS SHOWN

1 3 D
2 4 R

VIEW Z

S5-42 ZF 5-speed

mainshaft or countershaft do not need adjustment, place a thin coating of Loctite 574® on the rear case mating surface. If the bearings need adjustment, do it at this time, then, apply sealer.

NOTE: *Do not use silicone type sealers.*

18. Push the three shift rail detents back into their holes in the front case.

19. Carefully place the front case half over the shafts and gearshift rails until it rests on the mating surface of the rear case. It may be necessary to push the central shift rail inward to clear the inner surfaces of the front case.

20. Drive in the two dowels that align the rear case and front case. Insert the two hex screws and tighten them finger-tightly.

21. Screw to additional hex screws into the rear case and make them finger tight.

22. If shaft preload adjustment is not necessary, install all the hex screws and torque all of them to 18 ft.lb. If adjustment is necessary, do it at this time, then install and tighten all the hex screws.

23. Insert the reverse idler shaft screws and torque them to 16 ft.lb. Push the sealing cover into the screw heads.

24. Turn the transmission so that the input shaft is facing down.

25. Install the speedometer drive gear on the mainshaft.

26. Remove the hex nut that secures the output shaft flange to the mainshaft. Position the output shaft seal on the Output Shaft Seal Replacer Tool T87T-7025-BH. Position the seal and tool in the opening in the rear case. using a plastic or rubber mallet tap the seal in until it seats in the opening.

27. Install the output shaft flange on the shaft. Hold the flange with a holding fixture and torque the shaft nut to 184 ft.lb.

28. Lock the nut by bending the locktabs.

29. Using new gaskets, install the pto covers and torque the bolts 28 ft.lb.

30. Place the 5th/reverse gear interlock plate into position. Place the gasket over the shift tower mating surface on the front case. Make sure that the stop plate moves freely. Make sure that the plate and spring do not drop into the case.

31. Place the spring above the nose on the interlock plate and move both parts into their proper positions.

WARNING: *Follow this sequence exactly to ensure proper interlock function!*

32. Install the shift tower. The nose on the gearshift finger must point towards the interlock plate. Install the spring washers and torque the screws to 18 ft.lb.

33. Check the interlock operation.

34. Install the compression springs over each detent bolt.

35. Drive the sealing caps over the springs and detent bolts. Each cap should seat $^3/_{64}$″ below the case surface. If you install them any deeper it will cause increased shift effort.

36. Install the back-up lamp switch and new sealing ring. Torque the switch to 15 ft.lb.

CLUTCH

Understanding the Clutch

The purpose of the clutch is to disconnect and connect engine power from the transmission. A car at rest requires a lot of engine torque to get all that weight moving. An internal combustion engine does not develop a high starting torque (unlike steam engines), so it must be allowed to operate without any load until it builds up enough torque to move the car. Torque increases with engine rpm. The clutch allows the engine to build up torque by physically disconnecting the engine from the transmission, relieving the engine of any load or resistance. The transfer of engine power to the transmission (the load) must be smooth and gradual; if it weren't, drive line components would wear out or break quickly. This gradual power transfer is made possible by gradually releasing the clutch pedal. The clutch disc and pressure plate are

Troubleshooting Basic Clutch Problems

Problem	Cause
Excessive clutch noise	Throwout bearing noises are more audible at the lower end of pedal travel. The usual causes are: • Riding the clutch • Too little pedal free-play • Lack of bearing lubrication A bad clutch shaft pilot bearing will make a high pitched squeal, when the clutch is disengaged and the transmission is in gear or within the first 2″ of pedal travel. The bearing must be replaced. Noise from the clutch linkage is a clicking or snapping that can be heard or felt as the pedal is moved completely up or down. This usually requires lubrication. Transmitted engine noises are amplified by the clutch housing and heard in the passenger compartment. They are usually the result of insufficient pedal free-play and can be changed by manipulating the clutch pedal.
Clutch slips (the car does not move as it should when the clutch is engaged)	This is usually most noticeable when pulling away from a standing start. A severe test is to start the engine, apply the brakes, shift into high gear and SLOWLY release the clutch pedal. A healthy clutch will stall the engine. If it slips it may be due to: • A worn pressure plate or clutch plate • Oil soaked clutch plate • Insufficient pedal free-play
Clutch drags or fails to release	The clutch disc and some transmission gears spin briefly after clutch disengagement. Under normal conditions in average temperatures, 3 seconds is maximum spin-time. Failure to release properly can be caused by: • Too light transmission lubricant or low lubricant level • Improperly adjusted clutch linkage
Low clutch life	Low clutch life is usually a result of poor driving habits or heavy duty use. Riding the clutch, pulling heavy loads, holding the car on a grade with the clutch instead of the brakes and rapid clutch engagement all contribute to low clutch life.

the connecting link between the engine and transmission. When the clutch pedal is released, the disc and plate contact each other (clutch engagement), physically joining the engine and transmission. When the pedal is pushed in, the disc and plate separate (the clutch is disengaged), disconnecting the engine from the transmission.

The clutch assembly consists of the flywheel, the clutch disc, the clutch pressure plate, the throwout bearing and fork, the actuating linkage and the pedal. The flywheel and clutch pressure plate (driving members) are connected to the engine crankshaft and rotate with it. The clutch disc is located between the flywheel and pressure plate, and splined to the transmission shaft. A driving member is one that is attached to the engine and transfers engine power to a driven member (clutch disc) on the transmission shaft. A driving member (pressure plate) rotates (drives) a driven member (clutch disc) on contact and, in so doing, turns the transmission shaft. There is a circular diaphragm spring within the pressure plate cover (transmission side). In a relaxed state (when the clutch pedal is fully released), this spring is convex; that is, it is dished outward toward the transmission. Pushing in the clutch pedal actuates an attached linkage rod. Connected to the other end of this rod is the throwout bearing fork. The throwout bearing is attached to the fork. When the clutch pedal is depressed, the clutch linkage pushes the fork and bearing forward to contact the diaphragm spring of the pressure plate. The outer edges of the spring are secured to the pressure plate and are pivoted on rings so that when the center of the spring is compressed by the throwout bearing, the outer edges bow outward and, by so doing, pull the pressure plate in the same direction - away from the clutch disc. This action separates the disc from the plate, disengaging the clutch and allowing the transmission to be shifted into another gear. A coil type clutch return spring attached to the clutch pedal arm permits full release of the pedal. Releasing the pedal pulls the throwout bearing away from the diaphragm spring resulting in a reversal of spring position. As bearing pressure is gradually released from the spring center, the outer edges of the spring bow outward, pushing the pressure plate into closer contact with the clutch disc. As the disc and plate move closer together, friction between the two increases and slippage is reduced until, when full spring pressure is applied (by fully releasing the pedal), The speed of the disc and plate are the same. This stops all slipping, creating a direct connection between the plate and disc which results in the transfer of power from the engine to the transmission. The clutch disc is now rotating

with the pressure plate at engine speed and, because it is splined to the transmission shaft, the shaft now turns at the same engine speed. Understanding clutch operation can be rather difficult at first; if you're still confused after reading this, consider the following analogy. The action of the diaphragm spring can be compared to that of an oil can bottom. The bottom of an oil can is shaped very much like the clutch diaphragm spring and pushing in on the can bottom and then releasing it produces a similar effect. As mentioned earlier, the clutch pedal return spring permits full release of the pedal and reduces linkage slack due to wear. As the linkage wears, clutch free-pedal travel will increase and free-travel will decrease as the clutch wears. Free-travel is actually throwout bearing lash.

The diaphragm spring type clutches used are available in two different designs: flat diaphragm springs or bent spring. The bent fingers are bent back to create a centrifugal boost ensuring quick re-engagement at higher engine speeds. This design enables pressure plate load to increase as the clutch disc wears and makes low pedal effort possible even with a heavy-duty clutch. The throwout bearing used with the bent finger design is 1¼" long and is shorter than the bearing used with the flat finger design. These bearings are not interchangeable. If the longer bearing is used with the bent finger clutch, free-pedal travel will not exist. This results in clutch slippage and rapid wear.

The transmission varies the gear ratio between the engine and rear wheels. It can be shifted to change engine speed as driving conditions and loads change. The transmission allows disengaging and reversing power from the engine to the wheels.

ADJUSTMENTS

Pedal Free-Play

1. Measure the clutch pedal freeplay by depressing the pedal slowly until the freeplay between the release bearing assembly and the pressure plate is removed. Note this measurement. The difference between this measurement and when the pedal is not depressed is the freeplay measurement.

2. If the freeplay measurement is less than
- 1961-67: ⅞-1⅛" (22.2-28.6mm)
- 1969: 1⅛-1⅜" (28.6-34.9mm)
- 1970-72: 1⅛-1½" (28.6-38.1mm)
- 1973-74: 1⅜-1½" (34.9-38.1mm)
- 1975-83: 1¼-1½" (31.8-38.1mm)

the clutch linkage must be adjusted.

3. Loosen the two jam nuts on the release rod under the truck and back off both nuts several turns.

4. Loosen or tighten the first jam nut (nearest the release lever) against the bullet (rod extension) until the proper freeplay is obtained.

5. When the correct freeplay measurement is obtained, hold the first jam nut in position and securely tighten the other nut against the first.

6. Recheck the freeplay adjustment. Total pedal travel is fixed and is not adjustable.

Pedal Height Adjustment

The pedal height is adjustable only on 1969-74 models.

1. Measure the total travel of the pedal. If the total travel is less than 7½" (190½mm) or more than 7¾" (196⅞mm), move the clutch pedal bumper and bracket up or down until the travel is within these limits.

2. To check and adjust the pedal free travel, slowly apply the clutch pedal until the clutch fingers contact the clutch release bearing. The distance the clutch pedal moves is the free travel dimension. If it is not within these limits, loosen the nut at the bullet on the clutch release rod and adjust the bullet until the free travel is within the specified range.

3. Tighten the nut at the turnbuckle.

REMOVAL AND INSTALLATION

CAUTION: *The clutch driven disc contains asbestos, which has been determined to be a cancer causing agent. Never clean clutch surfaces with compressed air! Avoid inhaling any dust from any clutch surface! When cleaning clutch surfaces, use a commercially available brake cleaning fluid.*

With Mechanical Clutch

1. Raise and support the front end on jackstands.

2. Disconnect the clutch linkage and spring.

3. Remove the starter.

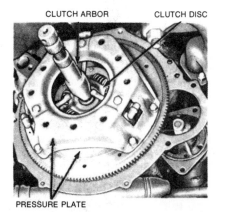

CLUTCH ARBOR   CLUTCH DISC

PRESSURE PLATE

Installing the clutch, using an alignment arbor to align the clutch disc spline

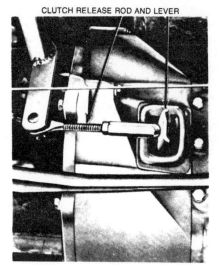

CLUTCH RELEASE ROD AND LEVER

Clutch linkage (pedal travel) adjustment point at the bellhousing

4. Remove the transmission.

5. Remove the throwout bearing and arm.

6. Remove the bellhousing.

7. If you're going to install the same pressure plate, matchmark the pressure plate-to-flywheel relation. Remove the pressure plate bolts, backing them out a little at a time in a criss-cross sequence. This will prevent warping of the pressure plate. When the pressure plate is removed, the driven plate will drop out, so be ready to catch it.

8. Clean the flywheel contact surface with a safe solvent. Inspect the flywheel for cracks, glazing or heat bluing. Minor damage can be taken care of by having the flywheel resurfaced. Excessive damage will mean installing a new flywheel.

9. Position the clutch disc on the flywheel so that an aligning tool or spare transmission mainshaft can enter the clutch pilot bearing and align the disc.

10. When reinstalling the original pressure plate and cover assembly, align the assembly and flywheel according to the marks made during removal. Position the pressure plate and cover assembly on the flywheel, align the pressure plate and disc, and install the retaining bolts. Tighten the bolts in an alternating sequence a few turns at a time until 15-20 ft.lb. is reached.

11. Remove the tool used to align the clutch disc.

12. With the clutch fully released, apply a light coat of grease on the sides of the driving lugs.

13. Position the clutch release bearing and the bearing hub on the release lever. Install the release lever on the fulcrum in the flywheel

housing. Apply a light coating of grease to the release lever fingers and the fulcrum. Fill the groove of the release bearing hub with grease.

14. If the flywheel housing has been removed, position it against the rear engine cover plate and install the attaching bolts and tighten them to 40-50 ft.lb.

15. Install the starter motor.

16. Install the transmission.

17. Connect and adjust the linkage.

With Hydraulic Clutch

1. Raise and support the truck end on jackstands.

2. Remove the clutch slave cylinder.

3. Remove the transmission.

4. If the clutch housing does not have a dust cover, remove the starter. Remove the flywheel housing attaching bolts and remove the housing.

5. If the flywheel housing does have a dust cover, remove the cover and then remove the release lever and bearing from the clutch housing. To remove the release lever:

   a. Remove the dust boot.

   b. Push the release lever forward to compress the slave cylinder.

   c. On all engines except the diesel and the 7.5L gasoline engines, remove the plastic clip that retains the slave cylinder to the bracket. Remove the slave cylidner.

   d. On the diesel and the 7.5L, the steel retaining clip is permanently attached to the slave cylinder. Remove the slave cylinder by prying on the clip to free the tangs while pulling the cylinder clear.

   e. Remove the release lever by pulling it outward.

6. Mark the pressure plate and cover assembly and the flywheel so that they can be reinstalled in the same relative position.

7. Loosen the pressure plate and cover attaching bolts evenly in a staggered sequence a turn at at time until the pressure plate springs are relieved of their tension. Remove the attaching bolts.

8. Remove the pressure plate and cover assembly and the clutch disc from the flywheel.

9. Position the clutch disc on the flywheel so that an aligning tool or spare transmission mainshaft can enter the clutch pilot bearing and align the disc.

10. When reinstalling the original pressure plate and cover assembly, align the assembly and flywheel according to the marks made during removal. Position the pressure plate and cover assembly on the flywheel, align the pressure plate and disc, and install the retaining bolts. Tighten the bolts in an alternating se-

quence a few turns at a time until 15-20 ft.lb. is reached.

11. Remove the tool used to align the clutch disc.

12. With the clutch fully released, apply a light coat of grease on the sides of the driving lugs.

13. Position the clutch release bearing and the bearing hub on the release lever. Install the release lever on the fulcrum in the flywheel housing. Apply a light coating of grease to the release lever fingers and the fulcrum. Fill the groove of the release bearing hub with grease.

14. If the flywheel housing has been removed, position it against the rear engine cover plate and install the attaching bolts and tighten them to 40-50 ft.lb.

15. Install the starter motor.

16. Install the transmission.

17. Install the slave cylinder and bleed the system.

Hydraulic System

The hydraulic clutch system operates much like a hydraulic brake system. When you push down (disengage) the clutch pedal, the mechanical clutch pedal movement is converted into hydraulic fluid movement, which is then converted back into mechanical movement by the slave cylinder to actuate the clutch release lever.

The system consists of a combination clutch fluid reservoir/master cylinder assembly, a slave cylinder mounted on the bellhousing, and connecting tubing.

Fluid level is checked at the master cylinder reservoir. The hydraulic clutch system continually remains in adjustment, like a hydraulic disc brake system, so not clutch linkage or pedal adjustment is necessary.

REMOVAL

The clutch hydraulic system is serviced as a complete assembly and is pre-filled and bled. Individual components are not available.

WARNING: *Prior to any vehicle service that requires removal of the slave cylinder, such as transmission and/or clutch housing removal, the clutch master cylinder pushrod must be disconnected from the clutch pedal. Failure to do this may damage the slave cylinder if the clutch pedal is depressed while the slave cylinder is disconnected.*

1. From inside the truck cab, remove the cotter pin retaining the clutch master cylinder pushrod to the clutch pedal lever. Disconnect the pushrod and remove the bushing.

2. Remove the two nuts retaining the clutch

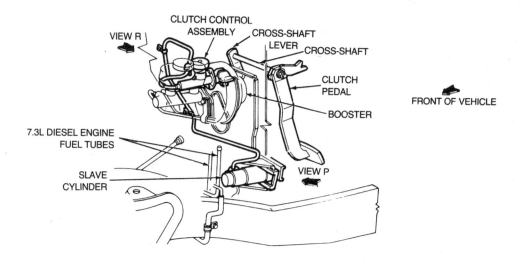

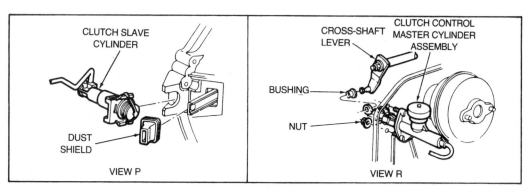

1988 hydraulic clutch system used on the 8-460 and 7.3L diesel

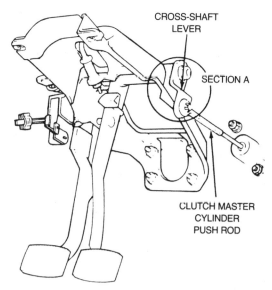

1988 hydraulic clutch system used on the 6-300, 8-302, and 8-351

reservoir and master cylinder assembly to the firewall.

3. From the engine compartment, remove the clutch reservoir and master cylinder assembly from the firewall. Note here how the clutch tubing routes to the slave cylinder.

4. Push the release lever forward to compress the slave cylinder.

5. On all engines except the diesel and the 7.5L gasoline engines, remove the plastic clip that retains the slave cylinder to the bracket. Remove the slave cylinder.

6. On the diesel and the 7.5L, the steel retaining clip is permanently attached to the slave cylinder. Remove the slave cylinder by prying on the clip to free the tangs while pulling the cylinder clear.

7. Remove the release lever by pulling it outward.

8. Remove the clutch hydraulic system from the truck.

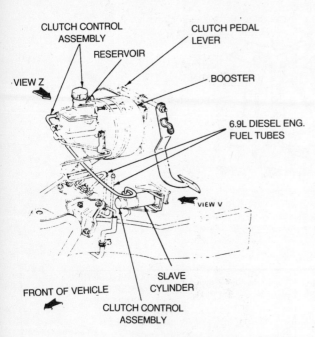
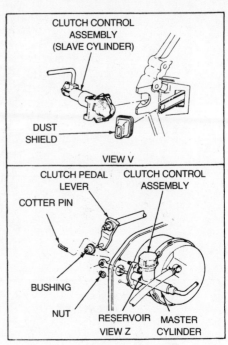

1987 hydraulic clutch system used on the 8-460 and 6.9L diesel

INSTALLATION

1. Position the clutch pedal reservoir and master cylinder assembly into the firewall from inside the cab, and install the two nuts and tighten.

2. Route the clutch tubing and slave cylinder to the bell housing, taking care that the nylon lines are kept away from any hot exhaust system components.

3. Install the slave cylinder by pushing the slave cylinder pushrod into the cylinder. Engage the pushrod into the release lever and slide the slave cylinder into the bell housing lugs. Seat the cylinder into the recess in the lugs.

NOTE: *When installing a new hydraulic system, you'll notice that the slave cylinder contains a shipping strap that propositions the pushrod for installation, and also provides a bearing insert. Following installation of the new slave cylinder, the first actuation of the clutch pedal will break the shipping strap and give normal clutch action.*

4. Clean the master cylinder pushrod bearing and apply a light film of SAE 30 engine oil.

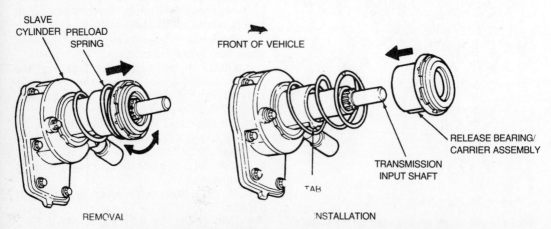

Clutch release bearing removal on systems with a concentric slave cylinder

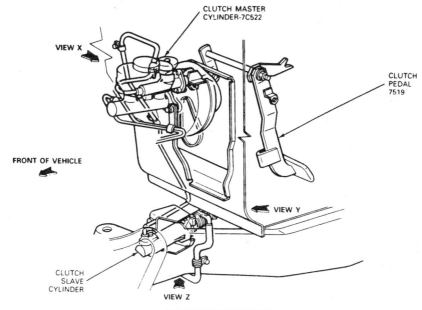

CLUTCH MASTER
CYLINDER-7C522

VIEW X

FRONT OF VEHICLE

CLUTCH
PEDAL
7519

VIEW Y

CLUTCH
SLAVE
CYLINDER

VIEW Z

FOR 4.9, 5.0 AND 5.8 ENGINES
MAIN VIEW

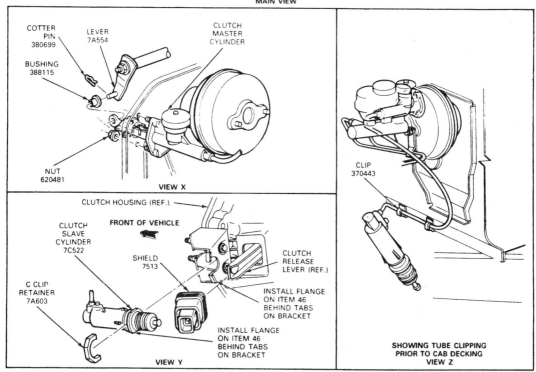

COTTER
PIN
380699

LEVER
7A554

CLUTCH
MASTER
CYLINDER

BUSHING
388115

NUT
620481

VIEW X

CLIP
370443

CLUTCH HOUSING (REF.)

FRONT OF VEHICLE

CLUTCH
SLAVE
CYLINDER
7C522

SHIELD
7513

CLUTCH
RELEASE
LEVER (REF.)

C CLIP
RETAINER
7A603

INSTALL FLANGE
ON ITEM 46
BEHIND TABS
ON BRACKET

INSTALL FLANGE
ON ITEM 46
BEHIND TABS
ON BRACKET

VIEW Y

SHOWING TUBE CLIPPING
PRIOR TO CAB DECKING
VIEW Z

1987 hydraulic clutch system used on the 6-300, 8-302, and 8-351

5. From inside the cab, install the bushing on the clutch pedal lever. Connect the clutch master cylinder pushrod to the clutch pedal lever and install the cotter pin.

6. Check the clutch reservoir and add fluid if required. Depress the clutch pedal at least ten times to verify smooth operation and proper clutch release.

AUTOMATIC TRANSMISSION

Understanding Automatic Transmissions

The automatic transmission allows engine torque and power to be transmitted to the rear wheels within a narrow range of engine operat-

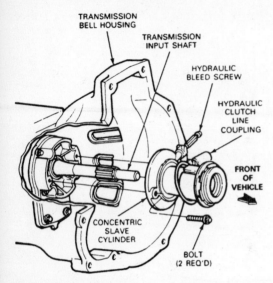

TRANSMISSION
BELL HOUSING
TRANSMISSION
INPUT SHAFT
HYDRAULIC
BLEED SCREW
HYDRAULIC
CLUTCH
LINE
COUPLING
FRONT
OF
VEHICLE
CONCENTRIC
SLAVE
CYLINDER
BOLT
(2 REQ'D)

Slave cylinder removal

ing speeds. The transmission will allow the engine to turn fast enough to produce plenty of power and torque at very low speeds, while keeping it at a sensible rpm at high vehicle speeds. The transmission performs this job entirely without driver assistance. The transmission uses a light fluid as the medium for the transmission of power. This fluid also works in the operation of various hydraulic control circuits and as a lubricant. Because the transmission fluid performs all of these three functions, trouble within the unit can easily travel from one part to another. For this reason, and because of the complexity and unusual operating principles of the transmission, a very sound understanding of the basic principles of operation will simplify troubleshooting.

THE TORQUE CONVERTER

The torque converter replaces the conventional clutch. It has three functions:

1. It allows the engine to idle with the vehicle at a standstill, even with the transmission in gear.

2. It allows the transmission to shift from range to range smoothly, without requiring that the driver close the throttle during the shift.

3. It multiplies engine torque to an increasing extent as vehicle speed drops and throttle opening is increased. This has the effect of making the transmission more responsive and reduces the amount of shifting required.

The torque converter is a metal case which is shaped like a sphere that has been flattened on opposite sides. It is bolted to the rear end of the engine's crankshaft. Generally, the entire met-

al case rotates at engine speed and serves as the engine's flywheel.

The case contains three sets of blades. One set is attached directly to the case. This set forms the torus or pump. Another set is directly connected to the output shaft, and forms the turbine. The third set is mounted on a hub which, in turn, is mounted on a stationary shaft through a one-way clutch. This third set is known as the stator.

A pump, which is driven by the converter hub at engine speed, keeps the torque converter full of transmission fluid at all times. Fluid flows continuously through the unit to provide cooling.

Under low speed acceleration, the torque converter functions as follows:

The torus is turning faster than the turbine. It picks up fluid at the center of the converter and, through centrifugal force, slings it outward. Since the outer edge of the converter moves faster than the portions at the center, the fluid picks up speed.

The fluid then enters the outer edge of the turbine blades. It then travels back toward the center of the converter case along the turbine blades. In impinging upon the turbine blades, the fluid loses the energy picked up in the torus.

If the fluid were now to immediately be returned directly into the torus, both halves of the converter would have to turn at approximately the same speed at all times, and torque input and output would both be the same.

In flowing through the torus and turbine, the fluid picks up two types of flow, or flow in two separate directions. It flows through the turbine blades, and it spins with the engine. The stator, whose blades are stationary when the vehicle is being accelerated at low speeds, converts one type of flow into another. Instead of allowing the fluid to flow straight back into the torus, the stator's curved blades turn the fluid almost 90° toward the direction of rotation of the engine. Thus the fluid does not flow as fast toward the torus, but is already spinning when the torus picks it up. This has the effect of allowing the torus to turn much faster than the turbine. This difference in speed may be compared to the difference in speed between the smaller and larger gears in any gear train. The result is that engine power output is higher, and engine torque is multiplied.

As the speed of the turbine increases, the fluid spins faster and faster in the direction of engine rotation. As a result, the ability of the stator to redirect the fluid flow is reduced. Under cruising conditions, the stator is eventually forced to rotate on its one-way clutch in the direction of engine rotation. Under these conditions, the torque converter begins to behave almost like a solid shaft, with the torus and turbine speeds being almost equal.

THE PLANETARY GEARBOX

The ability of the torque converter to multiply engine torque is limited. Also, the unit tends to be more efficient when the turbine is rotating at relatively high speeds. Therefore, a planetary gearbox is used to carry the power output of the turbine to the driveshaft.

Planetary gears function very similarly to conventional transmission gears. However, their construction is different in that three elements make up one gear system, and, in that all three elements are different from one another. The three elements are: an outer gear that is shaped like a hoop, with teeth cut into the inner surface; a sun gear, mounted on a shaft and located at the very center of the outer gear; and a set of three planet gears, held by pins in a ring-like planet carrier, meshing with both the sun gear and the outer gear. Either the outer gear or the sun gear may be held stationary, providing more than one possible torque multiplica-tion factor for each set of gears. Also, if all three gears are forced to rotate at the same speed, the gearset forms, in effect, a solid shaft.

Most modern automatics use the planetary gears to provide either a single reduction ratio of about 1.8:1, or two reduction gears: a low of about 2.5:1, and an intermediate of about 1.5:1. Bands and clutches are used to hold various portions of the gearsets to the transmission case or to the shaft on which they are mounted. Shifting is accomplished, then, by changing the portion of each planetary gearset which is held to the transmission case or to the shaft.

THE SERVOS AND ACCUMULATORS

The servos are hydraulic pistons and cylinders. They resemble the hydraulic actuators used on many familiar machines, such as bulldozers. Hydraulic fluid enters the cylinder, under pressure, and forces the piston to move to engage the band or clutches.

The accumulators are used to cushion the engagement of the servos. The transmission fluid must pass through the accumulator on the way

Troubleshooting Basic Automatic Transmission Problems

Problem	Cause	Solution
Fluid leakage	• Defective pan gasket	• Replace gasket or tighten pan bolts
	• Loose filler tube	• Tighten tube nut
	• Loose extension housing to transmission case	• Tighten bolts
	• Converter housing area leakage	• Have transmission checked professionally
Fluid flows out the oil filler tube	• High fluid level	• Check and correct fluid level
	• Breather vent clogged	• Open breather vent
	• Clogged oil filter or screen	• Replace filter or clean screen (change fluid also)
	• Internal fluid leakage	• Have transmission checked professionally
Transmission overheats (this is usually accompanied by a strong burned odor to the fluid)	• Low fluid level	• Check and correct fluid level
	• Fluid cooler lines clogged	• Drain and refill transmission. If this doesn't cure the problem, have cooler lines cleared or replaced.
	• Heavy pulling or hauling with insufficient cooling	• Install a transmission oil cooler
	• Faulty oil pump, internal slippage	• Have transmission checked professionally
Buzzing or whining noise	• Low fluid level	• Check and correct fluid level
	• Defective torque converter, scored gears	• Have transmission checked professionally
No forward or reverse gears or slippage in one or more gears	• Low fluid level	• Check and correct fluid level
	• Defective vacuum or linkage controls, internal clutch or band failure	• Have unit checked professionally
Delayed or erratic shift	• Low fluid level	• Check and correct fluid level
	• Broken vacuum lines	• Repair or replace lines
	• Internal malfunction	• Have transmission checked professionally

Lockup Torque Converter Service Diagnosis

Problem	Cause	Solution

No lockup	• Faulty oil pump
	• Sticking governor valve
	• Valve body malfunction
	   (a) Stuck switch valve
	   (b) Stuck lockup valve
	   (c) Stuck fail-safe valve
	• Failed locking clutch
	• Leaking turbine hub seal
	• Faulty input shaft or seal ring
		• Replace oil pump
		• Repair or replace as necessary
		• Repair or replace valve body or its internal components as necessary
		• Replace torque converter
		• Replace torque converter
		• Repair or replace as necessary

Will not unlock	• Sticking governor valve
	• Valve body malfunction
	   (a) Stuck switch valve
	   (b) Stuck lockup valve
	   (c) Stuck fail-safe valve
		• Repair or replace as necessary
		• Repair or replace valve body or its internal components as necessary

Stays locked up at too low a speed in direct	• Sticking governor valve
	• Valve body malfunction
	   (a) Stuck switch valve
	   (b) Stuck lockup valve
	   (c) Stuck fail-safe valve
		• Repair or replace as necessary
		• Repair or replace valve body or its internal components as necessary

Locks up or drags in low or second	• Faulty oil pump
	• Valve body malfunction
	   (a) Stuck switch valve
	   (b) Stuck fail-safe valve
		• Replace oil pump
		• Repair or replace valve body or its internal components as necessary

Sluggish or stalls in reverse	• Faulty oil pump
	• Plugged cooler, cooler lines or fittings
	• Valve body malfunction
	   (a) Stuck switch valve
	   (b) Faulty input shaft or seal ring
		• Replace oil pump as necessary
		• Flush or replace cooler and flush lines and fittings
		• Repair or replace valve body or its internal components as necessary

Loud chatter during lockup engagement (cold)	• Faulty torque converter • Failed locking clutch • Leaking turbine hub seal	• Replace torque converter • Replace torque converter • Replace torque converter
Vibration or shudder during lockup engagement	• Faulty oil pump • Valve body malfunction • Faulty torque converter • Engine needs tune-up	• Repair or replace oil pump as necessary • Repair or replace valve body or its internal components as necessary • Replace torque converter • Tune engine
Vibration after lockup engagement	• Faulty torque converter • Exhaust system strikes underbody • Engine needs tune-up • Throttle linkage misadjusted	• Replace torque converter • Align exhaust system • Tune engine • Adjust throttle linkage
Vibration when revved in neutral Overheating: oil blows out of dip stick tube or pump seal	• Torque converter out of balance • Plugged cooler, cooler lines or fittings • Stuck switch valve	• Replace torque converter • Flush or replace cooler and flush lines and fittings • Repair switch valve in valve body or replace valve body
Shudder after lockup engagement	• Faulty oil pump • Plugged cooler, cooler lines or fittings • Valve body malfunction • Faulty torque converter • Fail locking clutch • Exhaust system strikes underbody • Engine needs tune-up • Throttle linkage misadjusted	• Replace oil pump • Flush or replace cooler and flush lines and fittings • Repair or replace valve body or its internal components as necessary • Replace torque converter • Replace torque converter • Align exhaust system • Tune engine • Adjust throttle linkage

Transmission Fluid Indications

The appearance and odor of the transmission fluid can give valuable clues to the overall condition of the transmission. Always note the appearance of the fluid when you check the fluid level or change the fluid. Rub a small amount of fluid between your fingers to feel for grit and smell the fluid on the dipstick.

If the fluid appears:	It indicates:
Clear and red colored	• Normal operation
Discolored (extremely dark red or brownish) or smells burned	• Band or clutch pack failure, usually caused by an overheated transmission. Hauling very heavy loads with insufficient power or failure to change the fluid, often result in overheating. Do not confuse this appearance with newer fluids that have a darker red color and a strong odor (though not a burned odor).
Foamy or aerated (light in color and full of bubbles)	• The level is too high (gear train is churning oil) • An internal air leak (air is mixing with the fluid). Have the transmission checked professionally.
Solid residue in the fluid	• Defective bands, clutch pack or bearings. Bits of band material or metal abrasives are clinging to the dipstick. Have the transmission checked professionally.
Varnish coating on the dipstick	• The transmission fluid is overheating

to the servo. The accumulator housing contains a thin piston which is sprung away from the discharge passage of the accumulator. When fluid passes through the accumulator on the way to the servo, it must move the piston against spring pressure, and this action smooths out the action of the servo.

THE HYDRAULIC CONTROL SYSTEM

The hydraulic pressure used to operate the servos comes from the main transmission oil pump. This fluid is channeled to the various servos through the shift valves. There is generally a manual shift valve which is operated by the transmission selector lever and an automatic shift valve for each automatic upshift the transmission provides: i.e., 2-speed automatics have a low/high shift valve, while 3-speeds have a 1-2 valve, and a 2-3 valve.

There are two pressures which effect the operation of these valves. One is the governor pressure which is affected by vehicle speed. The other is the modulator pressure which is affected by intake manifold vacuum or throttle position. Governor pressure rises with an increase in vehicle speed, and modulator pressure rises as the throttle is opened wider. By responding to these two pressures, the shift valves cause the upshift points to be delayed with increased throttle opening to make the best use of the engine's power output.

Most transmissions also make use of an auxiliary circuit for downshifting. This circuit may be actuated by the throttle linkage or the vacuum line which actuates the modulator, or by a cable or solenoid. It applies pressure to a special downshift surface on the shift valve or valves.

The transmission modulator also governs the line pressure, used to actuate the servos. In this way, the clutches and bands will be actuated with a force matching the torque output of the engine.

Back-Up Light Switch

The switch is located on the left side of the transmission case. To remove:

Automatic Transmission Application Chart

Transmission	Years	Models
Ford C4 3-speed	1964–74 1975–81	All models E-100, 150 w/6-cyl.
Ford C6 3-speed	1975–87 1988	All models All except E-150/250 w/8-302
Ford AOD 4-speed	1983–87 1988	All models with 6-300 or 8-302 E-150 w/6-300 or 8-302 E-250 w/8-302

1. Raise and support the front end on jackstands.

2. Disconnect the negative battery cable.

3. Disconnect the back-up switch assembly harness.

4. Place the gear selector in neutral.

5. Squeeze the switch tangs together and lift out the switch assembly.

6. Installation is the reverse of the removal procedure.

Transmission

REMOVAL AND INSTALLATION

Through 1967

1. From in the engine compartment, unbolt the throttle linkage bracket from the top of the converter housing

2. Disconnect the neutral switch wire at the in-line connector.

3. Disconnect the back-up light switch wiring.

4. Raise and support the van on jackstands.

5. From in the engine compartment, remove the two upper converter housing-to-engine bolts.

6. Remove the bolt securing the fluid filler tube to the engine cylinder head.

7. Place the drain pan under the transmission fluid pan. If your transmission pan has a drain plug, remove it to drain the fluid and install it when the fluid is drained.

If there is no drain plug, starting at the rear of the pan and working toward the front, loosen the attaching bolts and allow the fluid to drain. Finally remove all of the pan attaching bolts except two at the front, to allow the fluid to further drain. With fluid drained, install two bolts on the rear side of the pan to temporarily hold it in place.

8. Remove the converter drain plug access cover from the lower end of the converter housing.

9. Remove the converter-to-flywheel attaching nuts. Place a wrench on the crankshaft pulley attaching bolt to turn the converter to gain access to the nuts.

10. With the wrench on the crankshaft pulley attaching bolt, turn the converter to gain access to the converter drain plug. Place a drain pan under the converter to catch the fluid and remove the plug. After the fluid has been drained, reinstall the plug.

11. Matchmark the driveshaft-to-rear axle flange position and disconnect the driveshaft from the rear axle. Slide the shaft rearward from the transmission. Install a seal installation tool or rags in the extension housing to prevent fluid leakage.

12. Disconnect the speedometer cable from the extension housing.

13. Disconnect the downshift and manual linkage rods from the levers at the transmission.

14. Disconnect the oil cooler lines from the transmission.

15. Remove the vacuum hose from the vacuum diaphragm unit. Remove the vacuum line retaining clip.

16. Disconnect the cable from the terminal on the starter motor. Remove the three attaching bolts and remove the starter motor.

17. Support the transmission with a transmission jack. Chain the transmission to the jack.

18. Remove the two engine rear support and insulator assembly-to-crossmember attaching bolts.

19. Raise the transmission with a transmission jack and remove the crossmember.

20. Remove the remaining converter housing-to-engine attaching bolts.

21. Move the transmission away from the engine. Lower the jack and remove the converter and transmission assembly from under the vehicle.

To install:

22. Tighten the converter drain plug.

23. Position the converter on the transmission making sure the converter drive flats are fully engaged in the pump gear.

24. With the converter properly installed, place the transmission on the jack. Secure the transmission on the jack with the chain.

25. Raise the transmission into position.

26. Rotate the converter until the studs and drain plug are in alignment with their holes in the flywheel.

27. Move the converter and transmission assembly forward into position, using care not to damage the flywheel and the converter pilot. The converter must rest squarely against the flywheel. The converter hub must enter the end of the crankshaft. This indicates that the converter pilot is not binding in the engine crankshaft.

28. Install the converter housing-to-engine attaching bolts and torque them to 50 ft.lb.

29. Position the crossmember on the frame side rails. Install and tighten the attaching bolts to 60 ft.lb.

30. Remove the transmission jack safety chain from around the transmission.

31. Install the rear support and insulator assembly-to-extension housing mounting bolts and tighten the bolts to 45 ft.lb.

32. Lower the transmission and remove the jack.

33. Secure the engine rear support and insu-

lator assembly to the crossmember with the attaching bolts and tighten them to 80 ft.lb.

34. Connect the vacuum line to the vacuum diaphragm making sure that the line is in the retaining clip.

35. Connect the oil cooler lines to the transmission.

36. Connect the downshift and manual linkage rods to their respective levers on the transmission.

37. Connect the speedometer cable to the extension housing.

38. Secure the starter motor in place with the attaching bolts. Connect the cable to the terminal on the starter.

39. Install a new O-ring on the lower end of the transmission filler tube and insert the tube in the case.

40. Secure the converter-to-flywheel attaching nuts and tighten them to 30 ft.lb.

41. Install the converter housing access cover and secure it with the attaching bolts.

42. Connect the driveshaft.

43. Adjust the shift linkage as required.

44. Lower the vehicle. Then install the two upper converter housing-to-engine bolts and tighten them.

45. Position the transmission fluid filler tube to the cylinder head and secure with the attaching bolts.

46. Make sure the drain pan is securely attached, and fill the transmission to the correct level with Type F fluid.

1969 and Later C4 and C6

1. From in the engine compartment, remove the two upper converter housing-to-engine bolts.

2. Disconnect the neutral switch wire at the in-line connector.

3. Remove the bolt securing the fluid filler tube to the engine cylinder head.

4. Raise and support the truck on jackstands.

5. Place the drain pan under the transmission fluid pan. Starting at the rear of the pan and working toward the front, loosen the attaching bolts and allow the fluid to drain. Finally remove all of the pan attaching bolts except two at the front, to allow the fluid to further drain. With fluid drained, install two bolts on the rear side of the pan to temporarily hold it in place.

6. Remove the converter drain plug access cover from the lower end of the converter housing.

7. Remove the converter-to-flywheel attaching nuts. Place a wrench on the crankshaft pulley attaching bolt to turn the converter to gain access to the nuts.

8. With the wrench on the crankshaft pulley attaching bolt, turn the converter to gain access to the converter drain plug. Place a drain pan under the converter to catch the fluid and remove the plug. After the fluid has been drained, reinstall the plug.

9. Matchmark the driveshaft-to-rear axle flange position and disconnect the driveshaft from the rear axle and slide shaft rearward from the transmission. Install a seal installation tool in the extension housing to prevent fluid leakage.

10. Disconnect the speedometer cable from the extension housing.

11. Disconnect the downshift and manual linkage rods from the levers at the transmission.

12. Disconnect the oil cooler lines from the transmission.

13. Remove the vacuum hose from the vacuum diaphragm unit. Remove the vacuum line retaining clip.

14. Disconnect the cable from the terminal on the starter motor. Remove the three attaching bolts and remove the starter motor.

15. Remove the two engine rear support and insulator assembly-to-attaching bolts.

16. Remove the two engine rear support and insulator assembly-to-extension housing attaching bolts.

17. Remove the six bolts securing the No. 2 crossmember to the frame side rails.

18. Raise the transmission with a transmission jack and remove both crossmembers.

19. Secure the transmission to the jack with the safety chain.

20. Remove the remaining converter housing-to-engine attaching bolts.

21. Move the transmission away from the engine. Lower the jack and remove the converter and transmission assembly from under the vehicle.

To install:

22. Tighten the converter drain plug.

23. Position the converter on the transmission making sure the converter drive flats are fully engaged in the pump gear.

24. With the converter properly installed, place the transmission on the jack. Secure the transmission on the jack with the chain.

25. Rotate the converter until the studs and drain plug are in alignment with their holes in the flywheel.

26. Move the converter and transmission assembly forward into position, using care not to damage the flywheel and the converter pilot. The converter must rest squarely against the flywheel. This indicates that the converter pilot is not binding in the engine crankshaft.

27. Install the converter housing-to-engine

attaching bolts and torque them to 65 ft.lb. for the diesel; 50 ft.lb. for gasoline engines.

28. Remove the transmission jack safety chain from around the transmission.

29. Position the No. 2 crossmember to the frame side rails. Install and tighten the attaching bolts.

30. Position the engine rear support and insulator assembly above the crossmember. Install the rear support and insulator assembly-to-extension housing mounting bolts and tighten the bolts to 45 ft.lb.

31. Lower the transmission and remove the jack.

32. Secure the engine rear support and insulator assembly to the crossmember with the attaching bolts and tighten them to 80 ft.lb.

33. Connect the vacuum line to the vacuum diaphragm making sure that the line is in the retaining clip.

34. Connect the oil cooler lines to the transmission.

35. Connect the downshift and manual linkage rods to their respective levers on the transmission.

36. Connect the speedometer cable to the extension housing.

37. Secure the starter motor in place with the attaching bolts. Connect the cable to the terminal on the starter.

38. Install a new O-ring on the lower end of the transmission filler tube and insert the tube in the case.

39. Secure the converter-to-flywheel attaching nuts and tighten them to 30 ft.lb.

40. Install the converter housing access cover and secure it with the attaching bolts.

41. Connect the driveshaft.

42. Adjust the shift linkage as required.

43. Lower the vehicle. Then install the two upper converter housing-to-engine bolts and tighten them.

44. Position the transmission fluid filler tube to the cylinder head and secure with the attaching bolts.

45. Make sure the drain pan is securely attached, and fill the transmission to the correct level with the Dexron®II fluid.

AOD

1. Raise and support the van on jackstands.

2. Place the drain pan under the transmission fluid pan. Starting at the rear of the pan and working toward the front, loosen the attaching bolts and allow the fluid to drain. Finally remove all of the pan attaching bolts except two at the front, to allow the fluid to further drain. With fluid drained, install two bolts on the rear side of the pan to temporarily hold it in place.

3. Remove the converter drain plug access cover from the lower end of the converter.

4. Remove the converter-to-flywheel attaching nuts. Place a wrench on the crankshaft pulley attaching bolt to turn the converter to gain access to the nuts.

5. Place a drain pan under the converter to catch the fluid. With the wrench on the crankshaft pulley attaching bolt, turn the converter to gain access to the converter drain plug and remove the plug. After the fluid has been drained, reinstall the plug.

6. Matchmark and disconnect the driveshaft from the rear axle and slide shaft rearward from the transmission. Install a seal installation tool in the extension housing to prevent fluid leakage.

7. Disconnect the cable from the terminal on the starter motor. Remove the three attaching bolts and remove the starter motor. Disconnect the neutral start switch wires at the plug connector.

8. Remove the rear mount-to-crossmember attaching bolts and the two crossmember-to-frame attaching bolts.

9. Remove the two engine rear support-to-extension housing attaching bolts.

10. Disconnect the TV linkage rod from the transmission TV lever. Disconnect the manual rod from the transmission manual lever at the transmission.

11. Remove the two bolts securing the bellcrank bracket to the converter housing.

12. Raise the transmission with a transmission jack to provide clearance to remove the crossmember. Remove the rear mount from the crossmember and remove the crossmember from the side supports.

13. Lower the transmission to gain access to the oil cooler lines.

14. Disconnect each oil line from the fittings on the transmission.

15. Disconnect the speedometer cable from the extension housing.

16. Remove the bolt that secures the transmission fluid filler tube to the cylinder block. Lift the filler tube and the dipstick from the transmission.

17. Secure the transmission to the jack with the chain.

18. Remove the converter housing-to-cylinder block attaching bolts.

19. Carefully move the transmission and converter assembly away from the engine and, at the same time, lower the jack to clear the underside of the vehicle.

20. Remove the converter and mount the transmission in a holding fixture.

21. Tighten the converter drain plug.

22. Position the converter on the transmis-

sion, making sure the converter drive flats are fully engaged in the pump gear by rotating the converter.

23. With the converter properly installed, place the transmission on the jack. Secure the transmission to the jack with a chain.

24. Rotate the converter until the studs and drain plug are in alignment with the holes in the flywheel.

25. Move the converter and transmission assembly forward into position, using care not to damage the flywheel and the converter pilot. The converter must rest squarely against the flywheel. This indicates that the converter pilot is not binding in the engine crankshaft.

26. Install and tighten the converter housing-to-engine attaching bolts to 40-50 ft.lb.

27. Remove the safety chain from around the transmission.

28. Install a new O-ring on the lower end of the transmission filler tube. Insert the tube in the transmission case and secure the tube to the engine with the attaching bolt.

29. Connect the speedometer cable to the extension housing.

30. Connect the oil cooler lines to the right side of transmission case.

31. Position the crossmember on the side supports. Torque the bolts to 55 ft.lb. Position the rear mount on the crossmember and install the attaching nuts to 90 ft.lb.

32. Secure the rear support to the extension housing and tighten the bolts to 80 ft.lb.

33. Lower the transmission and remove the jack.

Fluid Pan

REMOVAL AND INSTALLATION

NOTE: *The torque converter on the C4 and C6 transmissions has a drain plug. If the*

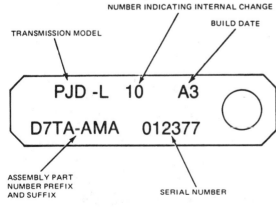

NUMBER INDICATING INTERNAL CHANGE

BUILD DATE

TRANSMISSION MODEL

PJD -L 10 A3

D7TA-AMA 012377

ASSEMBLY PART NUMBER PREFIX AND SUFFIX

SERIAL NUMBER

TAG LOCATED UNDER LOWER FRONT INTERMEDIATE SERVO COVER BOLT

Typical automatic transmission identification tag

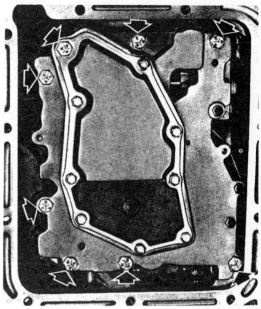

View showing the filter screen, which is attached to the lower valve body. Bolts indicated by arrows are holding the valve body. Do not remove these if the screen only is being serviced

converter is drained, refill the C4 with 5 quarts of fluid and the C6 with 8 quarts of fluid.

1. Raise the vehicle so the transmission oil pan is readily accessible.

2. On the C4 disconnect the fluid filler tube from the pan and allow the fluid to drain into an appropriate container. On the C6 and AOD, start removing the pan bolts so that the fluid drains from one corner.

NOTE: *It is not recommended that the drained fluid be used over again; refill the transmission with new fluid. However, in an emergency situation, the old fluid can be reused. The old fluid should be strained through a #100 screen or a fine mesh cloth before being reinstalled.*

3. Remove the transmission oil pan attaching bolts, pan and gasket.

4. Clean the transmission oil pan and transmission mating surfaces.

5. Install the transmission oil pan in the reverse order of removal, torquing the attaching bolts to 12-16 ft.lb. and using a new gasket. Fill the transmission with 3 qts. of the correct type fluid, check the operation of the transmission and check for leakage.

NOTE: *The C4 automatic transmission uses Type F automatic transmission fluid only. The C6 through 1976 uses Type F. The 1977 and later C6 and all AOD use type CJ or Dexron®II. When starting the engine after the transmission fluid has been drained, do not race the engine. Move the gear shift selector through all of the ranges before moving the vehicle.*

FILTER SERVICE

1. Remove the transmission oil pan and gasket.

2. Remove the fine mesh oil screen by removing the machine screws holding it to the lower valve body.

WARNING: *When removing the filter on C4 transmissions, be careful not to lose the throttle pressure limit valve and spring when separating the filter from the valve body.*

3. Install the new filter screen and transmission oil pan gasket in the reverse order of removal.

Adjustments

INTERMEDIATE BAND ADJUSTMENT

C4 and C6

1. Raise and support the van on jackstands.

2. Clean all dirt away from the band adjusting screw. Remove and discard the locknut.

3. Install a new locknut loosely and tighten the adjusting screw to 10 ft.lb.

4. Back off the adjusting screw EXACTLY 1¾ turns for the C4, or 1½ turns for the C6.

5. Hold the adjusting screw from turning and tighten the locknut to 35-40 ft.lb.

6. Remove the jackstands and lower the vehicle.

REAR BAND (LOW/REVERSE) ADJUSTMENT

C4 Only

1. Clean all dirt from around the band adjusting screw and remove and discard the locknut.

2. Install a new locknut on the adjusting screw. Using a torque wrench, tighten the adjusting screw to 10 ft.lb.

3. Back off the adjusting screw EXACTLY 3 FULL TURNS.

4. Hold the adjusting screw steady and tighten the locknut to 35-45 ft.lb.

SHIFT LINKAGE ADJUSTMENT

1. With the engine stopped, place the transmission selector lever at the steering column in the **N** (neutral) position for models through 1967, or the **D** (drive) for 1969 and C4 and C6 later models. On the later C4 and C6 models, make sure the lever is against the **D** stop. On AOD models, place the lever in the **Overdrive** position.

NOTE: *On 1978 and later models, it will be necessary to hold the lever in the **D** position*

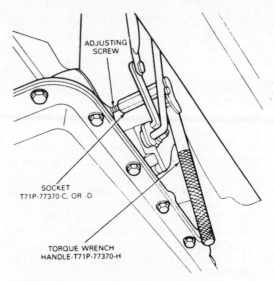

ADJUSTING SCREW

SOCKET
T71P-77370-C, OR -D

TORQUE WRENCH
HANDLE-T71P-77370-H

Adjusting the C6 intermediate band

by suspending an 8 lb. weight from the end of the selector lever.

2. Loosen the shift rod adjusting nut at the transmission lever.

3. On models through 1967, place the transmission lever in the neutral position (4th detent from the rear). On all other models, place the transmission lever in the 2nd detent from the rear.

4. On models through 1967, insert a ¼" gauge pin through the steering column shift rod actuating lever and the steering column shift tube bracket to hold the shift rod linkage in the neutral position.

5. On 1974 and later models: With the selector lever and transmission manual lever in the required position, turn the trunnion so that it slips into the hole in the transmission lever and tighten the adjusting nut to 12-18 ft.lb. Do not allow the rod or shift lever to move while tightening the nut.

6. On models through 1967, turn the trunnion 1 full turn counterclockwise to lengthen

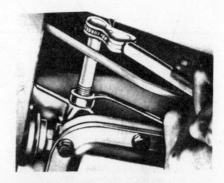

Adjusting the Low-Reverse band

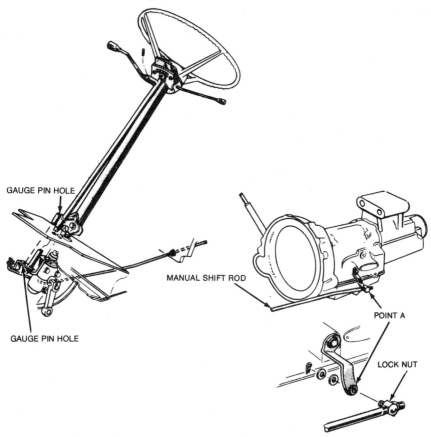

GAUGE PIN HOLE

GAUGE PIN HOLE

MANUAL SHIFT ROD

POINT A

LOCK NUT

Automatic transmission shift control linkage, through 1967

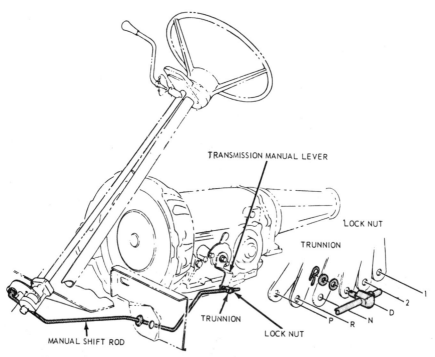

TRANSMISSION MANUAL LEVER

LOCK NUT

TRUNNION

TRUNNION

LOCK NUT

MANUAL SHIFT ROD

P   R   N

D

2   1

Automatic transmission shift control linkage for 1969–73. On the 1972–73 models there are two locknuts on either side of the trunnion

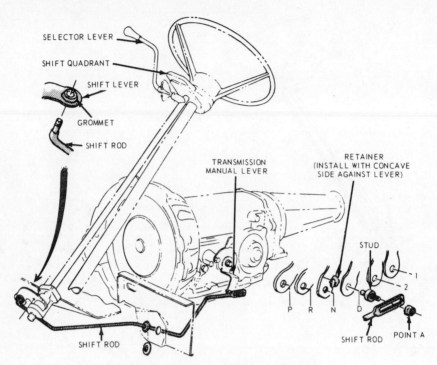

SELECTOR LEVER

SHIFT QUADRANT

SHIFT LEVER

GROMMET

SHIFT ROD

TRANSMISSION MANUAL LEVER

RETAINER (INSTALL WITH CONCAVE SIDE AGAINST LEVER)

STUD

1

2

P R N D

SHIFT ROD

SHIFT ROD

POINT A

1974–85 C4 and C6 shift control linkage

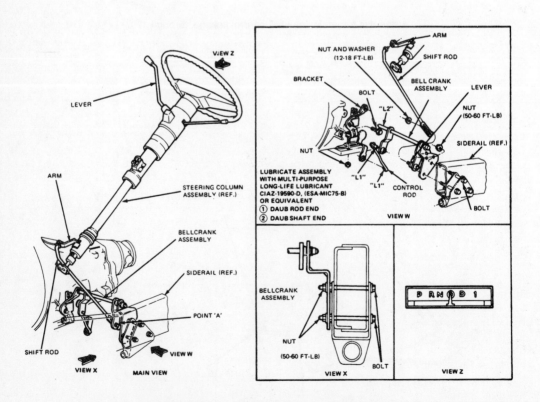

VIEW Z

LEVER

ARM

STEERING COLUMN ASSEMBLY (REF.)

BELLCRANK ASSEMBLY

SIDERAIL (REF.)

POINT 'A'

SHIFT ROD

VIEW X

VIEW W

MAIN VIEW

NUT AND WASHER (12-18 FT-LB)

ARM

SHIFT ROD

BRACKET

BELL CRANK ASSEMBLY

LEVER

BOLT

"L2"

NUT (50-60 FT-LB)

SIDERAIL (REF.)

NUT

"L1"

"L1"

CONTROL ROD

BOLT

LUBRICATE ASSEMBLY WITH MULTI-PURPOSE LONG-LIFE LUBRICANT CIAZ-19590-D, (ESA-MIC75-B) OR EQUIVALENT
1 DAUB ROD END
2 DAUB SHAFT END

VIEW W

BELLCRANK ASSEMBLY

NUT

(50-60 FT-LB)

BOLT

VIEW X

P R N D 1

VIEW Z

AOD shift control linkage on carbureted engines

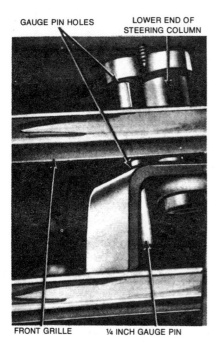

GAUGE PIN HOLES   LOWER END OF
STEERING COLUMN

FRONT GRILLE   ¼ INCH GAUGE PIN

Gauge pin installation, through 1967

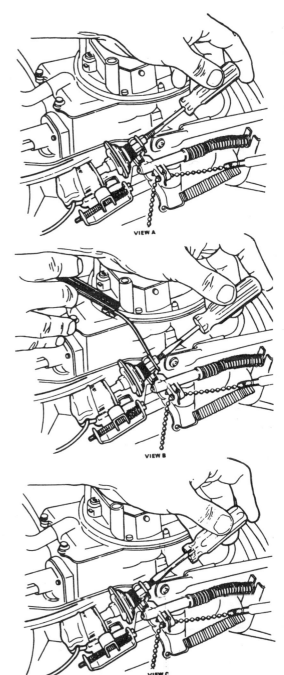

Automatic overdrive throttle linkage adjustment

the rod. Connect the trunnion to the lever. Remove the gauge pin.

7. On 1969-71 models, turn the trunnion 4 full turns counterclockwise to lengthen the rod. Connect the trunnion to the lever.

8. On 1972-73 models, lock the trunnion without turning it. Connect the trunnion to the lever.

9. Check the operation of the shift linkage.

THROTTLE VALVE LINKAGE ADJUSTMENT

Automatic Overdrive

ADJUSTMENT AT THE CARBURETOR

The TV control linkage may be adjusted at the carburetor using the following procedure:

1. Check that the engine idle speed is set to specification. Turn off the engine.

2. De-cam the fast idle cam on the carburetor so that the throttle lever is at its idle stop. Place the shift lever in **N** (neutral), set the parking brake.

3. Back out the linkage lever adjusting screw all the way. The screw end should be flush with the lever face.

4. Turn in the adjusting screw until a thin shim (0.005″ max.) or piece of writing paper fits snugly between the end of the screw and the throttle lever. To eliminate the effects of friction, push the linkage lever forward (tending to close gap) and release it, before checking the clearance between the end of the screw and the throttle lever. Do not apply any load on the levers with tools or hands while checking the gap.

5. Turn in the adjusting screw an additional 4 turns. (Four turns are preferred. Two turns minimum is permissible if the screw travel is limited).

6. If it is not possible to turn in the adjusting screw at least two addition turns or if there was sufficient screw adjusting capacity to obtain an initial gap in Step 2 above, refer to Linkage Adjustment at Transmission.

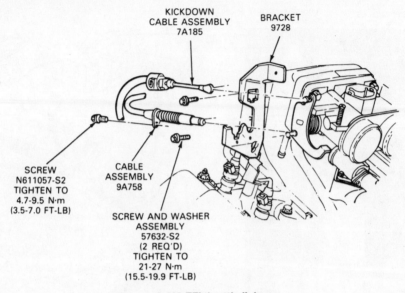

KICKDOWN
CABLE ASSEMBLY
7A185

BRACKET
9728

SCREW
N611057-S2
TIGHTEN TO
4.7-9.5 N·m
(3.5-7.0 FT-LB)

CABLE
ASSEMBLY
9A758

SCREW AND WASHER
ASSEMBLY
57632-S2
(2 REQ'D)
TIGHTEN TO
21-27 N·m
(15.5-19.9 FT-LB)

8-460 EFI throttle linkage

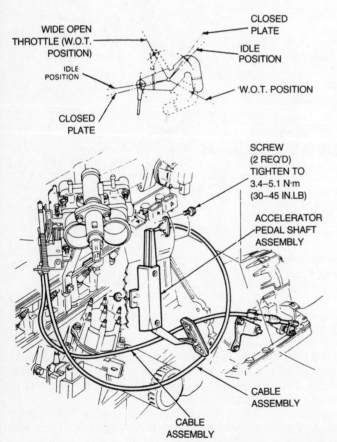

WIDE OPEN
THROTTLE (W.O.T.
POSITION)

IDLE
POSITION

CLOSED
PLATE

CLOSED
PLATE

IDLE
POSITION

W.O.T. POSITION

SCREW
(2 REQ'D)
TIGHTEN TO
3.4–5.1 N·m
(30–45 IN.LB)

ACCELERATOR
PEDAL SHAFT
ASSEMBLY

CABLE
ASSEMBLY

CABLE
ASSEMBLY

6-300 EFI throttle linkage

**C6 AUTOMATIC TRANSMISSION KICKDOWN CABLE
INSTALLATION AND ADJUSTMENT**

1. SELECT KICKDOWN CABLE. INSERT CONDUIT
   FITTING INTO ENGINE BRACKET AND SLIDE CABLE
   END FITTING ONTO NAILHEAD STUD ON
   THROTTLE LEVER. ENSURE THAT THROW-AWAY
   RED SPACER IS SECURED ON CABLE END FITTING.
   IF SPACER IS MISSING, REUSE A DISCARDED ONE.
2. ROUTE CABLE DOWN TO TRANSMISSION AND
   INSERT CONDUIT FITTING INTO BRACKET, THEN
   SNAP CABLE END ONTO BALL STUD ON
   TRANSMISSION LEVER.
3. RATCHET CABLE ADJUSTING MECHANISM TO
   CORRECT SETTING BY ROTATING TO WIDE OPEN
   THROTTLE POSITION, WITH TOOL NO. 52F-23415
   OR BY HAND. REMOVE RED SPACER.

**AOD AUTOMATIC TRANSMISSION TV CABLE
INSTALLATION AND ADJUSTMENT**

1. SELECT TV CABLE. INSERT CONDUIT FITTING INTO
   ENGINE BRACKET. SLIDE CABLE END FITTING OVER
   NAILHEAD STUD ON THROTTLE LEVER.
2. ROUTE CABLE DOWN TO TRANSMISSION. INSERT
   CONDUIT FITTING INTO BRACKET ON
   TRANSMISSION. SNAP CABLE END OVER BALL
   STUD ON TRANSMISSION LEVER. ENSURE SPRING
   IS ON TRANSMISSION TO HOLD TV LEVER IN FULL
   CLOCKWISE POSITION.
3. PUSH DOWN LOCKING TAB AT ENGINE END OF
   CONDUIT FITTING TO LOCK CONDUIT AT CORRECT
   LENGTH. TAB TO BE FLUSH WITH CIRCULAR
   PROFILE OF FITTING.
4. REMOVE SPRING.

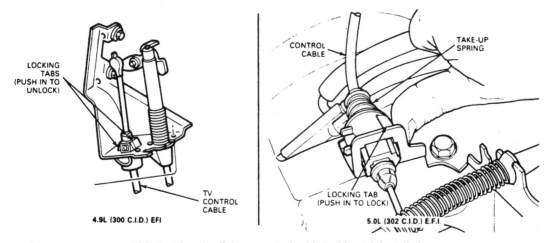

LOCKING
TABS
(PUSH IN TO
UNLOCK)

TV
CONTROL
CABLE

4.9L (300 C.I.D.) EFI

CONTROL
CABLE

TAKE-UP
SPRING

LOCKING TAB
(PUSH IN TO LOCK)

5.0L (302 C.I.D.) E.F.I.

AOD throttle valve linkage control cable locking tab installation

Whenever it is required to adjust the idle speed by more than 50 rpm, the adjustment screw on the linkage lever at the carburetor should also be readjusted as shown.

Idle Speed Change/Turns on Linkage Lever Adjustment Screw

- Less than 50 rpm: No change required
- 50-100 rpm increase: 1½ turns out
- 50-100 rpm decrease: 1½ turns in
- 100-150 rpm increase: 2½ turns out
- 100-150 rpm decrease: 2½ turns in

After making any idle speed adjustments, always verify that the linkage lever and throttle lever are in contact with the throttle lever at its idle stop and the shift lever is in **N** (neutral).

ADJUSTMENT AT THE TRANSMISSION

The linkage lever adjustment screw has limited adjustment capability. If it is not possible to adjust the TV linkage using this screw, the length of the TV control rod assembly must be readjusted using the following procedure. This procedure must also be followed whenever a new TV control rod assembly is installed.

This procedure requires placing the vehicle on jackstands to give access to the linkage components at the transmission TV control lever.

1. Set the engine curb idle speed to specification.

2. With the engine off, de-cam the fast idle cam on the carburetor so that the throttle lever

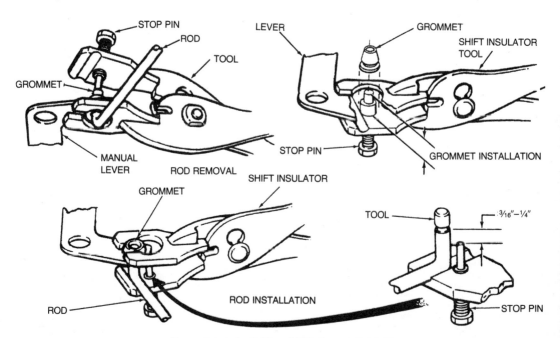

STOP PIN

ROD

TOOL

GROMMET

MANUAL
LEVER

ROD REMOVAL

LEVER

GROMMET

SHIFT INSULATOR
TOOL

STOP PIN

GROMMET INSTALLATION

GROMMET

SHIFT INSULATOR

ROD

ROD INSTALLATION

TOOL

³⁄₁₆″–¼″

STOP PIN

Removing or installing shift linkage grommets

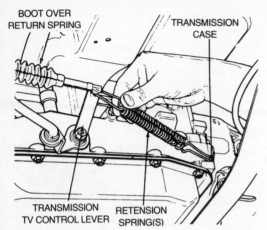

Throttle valve lever retention spring on the 6-300 EFI and 8-302 EFI

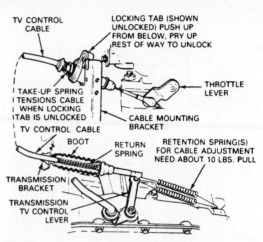

Throttle valve control cable adjustment

is against the idle stop. Place the shift lever in Neutral and set the parking brake.

3. Set the linkage lever adjustment screw at its approximate mid-range.

4. If a new TV control rod assembly is being installed, connect the rod to the linkage lever at the carburetor.

CAUTION: *The following steps involve working in proximity to the exhaust system. Allow the exhaust system to cool before proceeding.*

5. Raise and support the van on jackstands.

6. Using a 13mm box end wrench, loosen the bolt on the sliding trunnion block on the TV control rod assembly. Remove any corrosion

from the control rod and free-up the trunnion block so that it slides freely on the control rod. Insert a pin into the transmission lever grommet.

7. Push up on the lower end of the control rod to insure that the linkage lever at carburetor is firmly against the throttle lever. Release the force on rod. The rod must stay up.

8. Push the TV control lever on the transmission up against its internal stop with a firm force (approximately 5 pounds) and tighten the bolt on the trunnion block. Do not relax the force on the lever until the nut is tightened.

9. Lower the vehicle and verify that the throttle lever is still against the idle stop. If not, repeat steps 2 through 9.

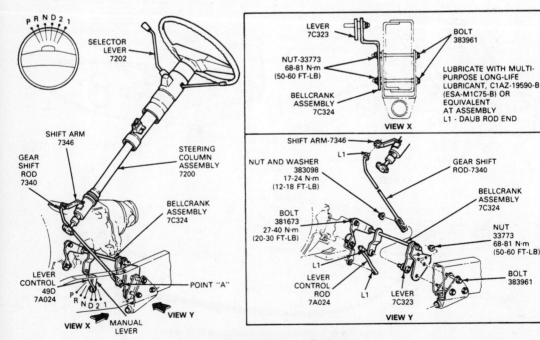

C6 shift linkage adjustment

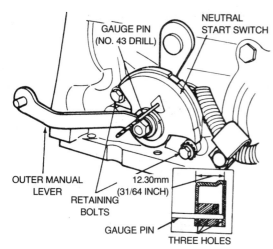

GAUGE PIN (NO. 43 DRILL)

NEUTRAL START SWITCH

OUTER MANUAL LEVER

RETAINING BOLTS

12.30mm (31/64 INCH)

GAUGE PIN

THREE HOLES

C6 neutral start switch adjustment

NEUTRAL SAFETY SWITCH ADJUSTMENT

1. Loosen the two switch adjusting screws.
2. Place the transmission lever in Neutral.
3. Rotate the switch and insert a #43 drill bit, shank end into the gauge pin holes of the switch.
4. The drill bit must be inserted about ½" (12.7mm) into the three holes.
5. Tighten the attaching bolts and remove the drill bit.

THROTTLE KICKDOWN LINKAGE ADJUSTMENT

1. Move the carburetor throttle linkage to the wide open position.
2. Insert a 0.060" thick spacer between the throttle lever and the kickdown adjusting screw.
3. Rotate the transmission kickdown lever until the lever engages the transmission internal stop. Do not use the kickdown rod to turn the transmission lever.
4. Turn the adjusting screw until it contacts the 0.060" spacer.
5. Remove the spacer.

DRIVELINE

Driveshaft

Short wheelbase vans use a single-piece driveshaft; long wheelbase models use a two-piece driveshaft with a support bearing and a sliding spline yoke at the center.

The driveshaft is joined to the transmission output shaft with sliding splines on all manual transmission models; it connects to a fixed yoke on on the output shaft on all long wheelbase manual transmission models and 1964-72 automatic transmission models.

REMOVAL AND INSTALLATION

One-Piece Driveshaft

1. Raise and support the rear end on jackstands.
2. Matchmark the U-joint-to-rear axle flange position.
3. Remove the U-bolts securing the rear U-joint and wrap the bearing caps with masking tape to hold them in place.
4. Pull the U-joint from the flange. It may be necessary to pry it loose.
5. On 1964-72 short wheelbase models with automatic transmission, repeat Steps 2-4 for the front U-joint.

On all other models, slide the driveshaft from the transmission.

6. Plug the extension housing to prevent any fluid loss.
7. Installation is the reverse of removal. Lightly grease the splines before sliding the driveshaft into position. Tighten the bolts to 17-20 ft.lb.

Two-Piece Driveshaft

THROUGH 1977

1. Raise and support the rear end on jackstands.
2. Matchmark the U-joint-to-rear axle and/or transmission flange position. Also, matchmark the relationship of the two driveshaft sections to each other.
3. Remove the U-bolts securing the rear U-joint and wrap the bearing caps with masking tape to hold them in place.
4. Pull the U-joint from the flange. It may be necessary to pry it loose.
5. Slide the front end of the rear driveshaft from the center bearing.
6. Unbolt and remove the center bearing, sliding it off the front driveshaft.
7. On models with a bolted front flange, follow Steps 2-4.

On models with a splined front connection, simply slide the driveshaft from the transmission extension housing.

8. Plug the extension housing to prevent any fluid loss.
7. Installation is the reverse of removal. Lightly grease the splines before sliding the driveshaft into position. Align ALL the matchmarks. Tighten the U-bolts to 17-20 ft.lb. Torque the center bearing mounting bolts to 40-50 ft.lb.

1978-88

1. Raise and support the rear end on jackstands.
2. Matchmark the U-joint-to-rear axle and/or transmission flange position. Also,

Troubleshooting Basic Driveshaft and Rear Axle Problems

When abnormal vibrations or noises are detected in the driveshaft area, this chart can be used to help diagnose possible causes. Remember that other components such as wheels, tires, rear axle and suspension can also produce similar conditions.

BASIC DRIVESHAFT PROBLEMS

Problem	Cause	Solution
Shudder as car accelerates from stop or low speed	• Loose U-joint • Defective center bearing	• Replace U-joint • Replace center bearing
Loud clunk in driveshaft when shifting gears	• Worn U-joints	• Replace U-joints
Roughness or vibration at any speed	• Out-of-balance, bent or dented driveshaft • Worn U-joints • U-joint clamp bolts loose	• Balance or replace driveshaft • Replace U-joints • Tighten U-joint clamp bolts
Squeaking noise at low speeds	• Lack of U-joint lubrication	• Lubricate U-joint; if problem persists, replace U-joint
Knock or clicking noise	• U-joint or driveshaft hitting frame tunnel • Worn CV joint	• Correct overloaded condition • Replace CV joint

BASIC REAR AXLE PROBLEMS

First, determine when the noise is most noticeable.

Drive Noise: Produced under vehicle acceleration.

Coast Noise: Produced while the car coasts with a closed throttle.

Float Noise: Occurs while maintaining constant car speed (just enough to keep speed constant) on a level road.

Road Noise

Brick or rough surfaced concrete roads produce noises that seem to come from the rear axle. Road noise is usually identical in Drive or Coast and driving on a different type of road will tell whether the road is the problem.

Tire Noise

Tire noises are often mistaken for rear axle problems. Snow treads or unevenly worn tires produce vibrations seeming to originate elsewhere. **Temporarily** inflating the tires to 40 lbs will significantly alter tire noise, but will have no effect on rear axle noises (which normally cease below about 30 mph).

Engine/Transmission Noise

Determine at what speed the noise is most pronounced, then stop the car in a quiet place. With the transmission in Neutral, run the engine through speeds corresponding to road speeds where the noise was noticed. Noises produced with the car standing still are coming from the engine or transmission.

Front Wheel Bearings

While holding the car speed steady, lightly apply the footbrake; this will often decease bearing noise, as some of the load is taken from the bearing.

Rear Axle Noises

Eliminating other possible sources can narrow the cause to the rear axle, which normally produces noise from worn gears or bearings. Gear noises tend to peak in a narrow speed range, while bearing noises will usually vary in pitch with engine speeds.

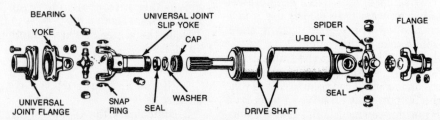

An exploded view of the driveshaft used on 1961–72 short wheelbase and automatic transmission models

NOISE DIAGNOSIS

The Noise Is	Most Probably Produced By
• Identical under Drive or Coast	• Road surface, tires or front wheel bearings
• Different depending on road surface	• Road surface or tires
• Lower as the car speed is lowered	• Tires
• Similar with car standing or moving	• Engine or transmission
• A vibration	• Unbalanced tires, rear wheel bearing, unbalanced driveshaft or worn U-joint
• A knock or click about every 2 tire revolutions	• Rear wheel bearing
• Most pronounced on turns	• Damaged differential gears
• A steady low-pitched whirring or scraping, starting at low speeds	• Damaged or worn pinion bearing
• A chattering vibration on turns	• Wrong differential lubricant or worn clutch plates (limited slip rear axle)
• Noticed only in Drive, Coast or Float conditions	• Worn ring gear and/or pinion gear

matchmark the relationship of the two drive-shaft sections to each other.

3. Remove the U-bolts securing the rear U-joint and wrap the bearing caps with masking tape to hold them in place.

4. Pull the U-joint from the flange. It may be necessary to pry it loose.

5. Disconnect the driveshaft slip yoke from the coupling shaft yoke.

6. Unbolt and remove the center bearing from the frame.

7. Slide the front driveshaft half from the transmission extension housing.

8. Plug the extension housing to prevent any fluid loss.

9. Slide the slip yoke off of the driveshaft.

10. Remove the dust cap, cork seal and spacers from the slip yoke.

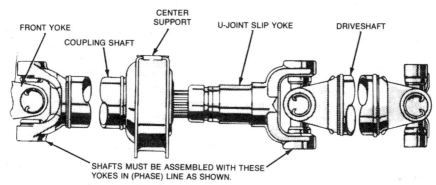

The driveshaft used on all long wheelbase manual transmission and 1961–72 long wheelbase automatic transmission models

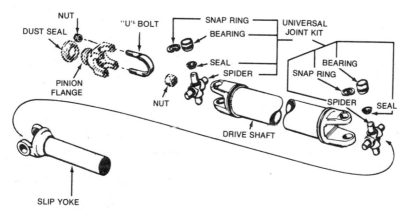

The driveshaft assembly used on all short wheelbase models with manual transmission and 1973–77 short wheelbase automatic transmission models

11. Thoroughly clean and inspect the driveshaft. Look for signs of damage, wear and loose fit among all related parts. Replace any part that appears damaged or excessively worn.

NOTE: *Do not immerse the center bearing in cleaning solution. Wipe it clean with a cloth dampened in cleaner.*

12. Lightly lubricate all splined surfaces with chassis grease.

13. Install the front driveshaft half into the tranmsission.

14. Bolt the center bearing into place. Torque the bolts to 40-50 ft.lb.

15. Slide the dust cap, cork seal and spacers onto the splined end of the driveshaft.

16. Install the driveshaft slip yoke onto the splines of the front driveshaft half. Torque the nut to 60-70 ft.lb.

17. Slide the rear shaft into the slip yoke, align ALL matchmarks. Some models will have stamped alignment arrows.

18. Connect the driveshaft to the rear axle flange. Torque the nuts to 60-70 ft.lb.

19. Lubricate all grease fittings.

U-JOINT OVERHAUL

Except Double Cardan Universal

1. Remove the driveshaft from the vehicle and place it in a vise, being careful not to damage it.

2. Remove the snaprings which retain the bearings in the flange and in the driveshaft.

3. Remove the driveshaft tube from the vise and position the U-joint in the vise with a sock-

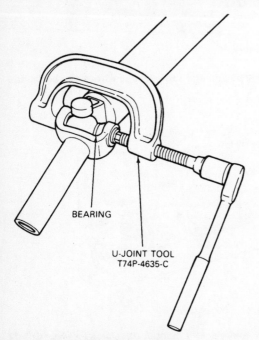

BEARING

U-JOINT TOOL
T74P-4635-C

Removing the single cardan U-joint

et smaller than the bearing cap on one side and a socket larger than the bearing cap on the other side.

4. Slowly tighten the jaws of the vise so that the smaller socket forces the U-joint spider and the opposite bearing into the larger socket.

5. Remove the other side of the spider in the same manner (if applicable) and remove the spider assembly from the driveshaft. Discard the spider assemblies.

6. Clean all foreign matter from the yoke areas at the end of the driveshaft(s).

7. Start the new spider and one of the bearing cap assemblies into a yoke by positioning the yoke in a vise with the spider positioned in place with one of the bearing cap assemblies positioned over one of the holes in the yoke. Slowly close the vise, pressing the bearing cap assembly in the yoke. Press the cap in far enough so that the retaining snapring can be installed. Use the smaller socket to recess the bearing cap.

8. Open the vise and position the opposite bearing cap assembly over the proper hole in the yoke with the socket that is smaller than the diameter of the bearing cap located on the cap. Slowly close the vise, pressing the bearing cap into the hole in the yoke with the socket. Make sure that the spider assembly is in line with the bearing cap as it is pressed in. Press the bearing cap in far enough so that the retaining snapring can be installed.

9. Install all remaining U-joints in the same manner.

10. Install the driveshaft and grease the new U-joints.

Double Cardan Joint

1. Working at the rear axle end of the shaft, mark the position of the spiders, the center yoke, and the centering socket yoke as related to the companion flange. The spiders must be assembled with the bosses in their original position to provide proper clearances.

2. Using a large vise or an arbor press and a socket smaller than the bearing cap on one side and a socket larger than the bearing cap on the other side, drive one of the bearings in toward the center of the universal joint, which will force the opposite bearing out.

3. Remove the driveshaft from the vise.

4. Tighten the bearing in the vise and tap on the yoke to free the bearing from the center yoke. Do not tap on the driveshaft tube.

5. Reposition the sockets on the yoke and force the opposite bearing outward and remove it.

6. Position the sockets on one of the remaining bearings and force it outward approximately 3/8" (9.5mm).

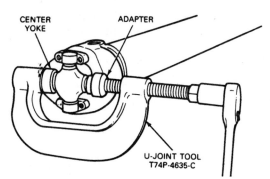

Partially pressing the bearing from the center yoke of the double cardan joint

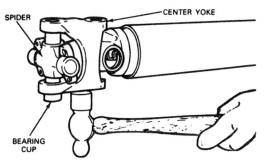

Removing the bearing from the center yoke

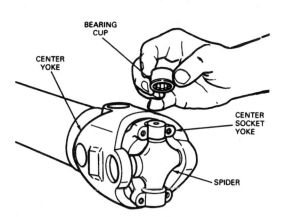

Removing the bearing cup from the center yoke

7. Grip the bearing in the vise and tap on the weld yoke to free the bearing from the center yoke. Do not tap on the driveshaft tube.

8. Reposition the sockets on the yoke to press out the remaining bearing.

9. Remove the spider from the center yoke.

10. Remove the bearings from the driveshaft yoke as outlined above and remove the spider from the yoke.

11. Insert a suitable tool into the centering ball socket located in the companion flange and pry out the rubber seal. Remove the retainer,

three piece ball seat, washer and spring from the ball socket.

12. Inspect the centering ball socket assembly for worn or damaged parts. If any damage is evident replace the entire assembly.

13. Insert the spring, washer, three piece ball seat and retainer into the ball socket.

14. Using a suitable tool, install the centering ball socket seal.

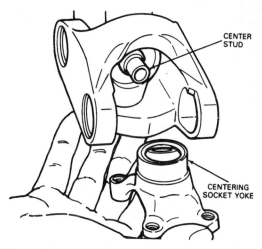

Removing the center yoke socket

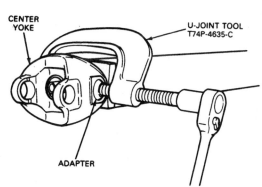

Removing the bearing from the rear of the center yoke

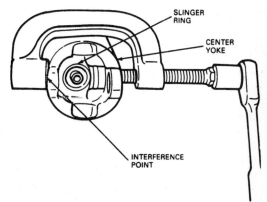

Center yoke interference point

15. Position the spider in the driveshaft yoke. Make sure the spider bosses are in the same position as originally installed. Press in the bearing cups with the sockets and vise. Install the internal snaprings provided in the repair kit.

16. Position the center yoke over the spider ends and press in the bearing cups. Install the snaprings.

17. Install the spider in the companion flange yoke. Make sure the spider bosses are in the position as originally installed. Press on the bearing cups and install the snaprings.

18. Position the center yoke over the spider ends and press on the bearing cups. Install the snaprings.

Center Bearing

REMOVAL AND INSTALLATION

1. Remove the driveshafts.

2. Remove the two center support bearing attaching bolts and remove the assembly from the vehicle.

3. Do not immerse the sealed bearing in any type of cleaning fluid. Wipe the bearing and cushion clean with a cloth dampened with cleaning fluid.

4. Check the bearing for wear or rough action by rotating the inner race while holding the outer race. If wear or roughness is evident, replace the bearing. Examine the rubber cushion for evidence of hardening, cracking, or deterioration. Replace it if it is damaged in any way.

5. Place the bearing in the rubber support and the rubber support in the U-shaped support and install the bearing in the reverse order of removal. Torque the bearing to support bracket fasteners to 50 ft.lb.

REAR AXLE

Understanding Drive Axles

The drive axle is a special type of transmission that reduces the speed of the drive from the engine and transmission and divides the power to the wheels. Power enters the axle from the driveshaft via the companion flange. The flange is mounted on the drive pinion shaft. The drive pinion shaft and gear which carry the power into the differential turn at engine speed. The gear on the end of the pinion shaft drives a large ring gear the axis of rotation of which is 90 degrees away from the of the pinion. The pinion and gear reduce the gear ratio of the axle, and change the direction of rotation to turn the axle shafts which drive both wheels. The axle gear ratio is found by dividing the number of pinion gear teeth into the number of ring gear teeth.

The ring gear drives the differential case. The case provides the two mounting points for the ends of a pinion shaft on which are mounted two pinion gears. The pinion gears drive the two side gears, one of which is located on the inner end of each axle shaft.

By driving the axle shafts through the arrangement, the differential allows the outer drive wheel to turn faster than the inner drive wheel in a turn.

The main drive pinion and the side bearings, which bear the weight of the differential case, are shimmed to provide proper bearing preload, and to position the pinion and ring gears properly.

WARNING: *The proper adjustment of the relationship of the ring and pinion gears is critical. It should be attempted only by those with extensive equipment and/or experience.*

Limited-slip differentials include clutches which tend to link each axle shaft to the differential case. Clutches may be engaged either by spring action or by pressure produced by the torque on the axles during a turn. During turning on a dry pavement, the effects of the clutches are overcome, and each wheel turns at the required speed. When slippage occurs at either wheel, however, the clutches will transmit some of the power to the wheel which has the greater amount of traction. Because of the presence of clutches, limited-slip units require a special lubricant.

Determining Axle Ratio

The drive axle is said to have a certain axle ratio. This number (usually a whole number and a decimal fraction) is actually a comparison of the number of gear teeth on the ring gear and the pinion gear. For example, a 4.11 rear means that theoretically, there are 4.11 teeth on the ring gear and one tooth on the pinion gear or, put another way, the driveshaft must turn 4.11 times to turn the wheels once. Actually, on a 4.11 rear, there might be 37 teeth on the ring gear and 9 teeth on the pinion gear. By dividing the number of teeth on the pinion gear into the number of teeth on the ring gear, the numerical axle ratio (4.11) is obtained. This also provides a good method of ascertaining exactly what axle ratio one is dealing with.

Another method of determining gear ratio is to jack up and support the car so that both rear wheels are off the ground. Make a chalk mark on the rear wheel and the driveshaft. Put the transmission in neutral. Turn the rear wheel one complete turn and count the number of turns that the driveshaft makes. The number of turns that the driveshaft makes in one complete revolution of the rear wheel is an approximation of the rear axle ratio.

Differential Overhaul

A differential overhaul is a complex, highly technical, and time-consuming operation, which requires a great many tools, extensive knowledge of the unit and the way it works, and a high degree of mechanical experience and ability. It is highly advisable that the amateur mechanic not attempt any work on the differential unit.

Improved Traction Differentials

Ford calls their improved traction differential Traction-Lok®. In this assembly, a multiple-disc clutch is employed to control differential action. Repair procedures are the same as for conventional axles (within the scope of this book).

Identification

On a full floating rear axle, the weight of the vehicle is supported by the axle housing. The axle shafts can be removed without disturbing the wheel bearings.

On a semi-floating axle, the outboard end of the axle shaft is supported by the bearing which is mounted in a recess in the end of the axle housing.

The axle shaft on a full-floating rear axle is held in place by a flange and bolts attaching it to the hub on the outboard side. The hub is held to the rear spindle by nuts which are also used to adjust the preload of the rear axle bearings.

The axle shaft on the semi-floating rear axle is held in position by C-locks in the differential housing.

Axle Identification and Ratio are found on an I.D. tag located under one of the bolts on the drifferential housing. Also refer to the Drive Axle Section of the Capacities Chart in Chapter 1 for complete model application.

Axle Shaft, Bearing and Seal

REMOVAL AND INSTALLATION

Ford C-Lock Integral Carrier

1. Raise and safely support the vehicle on jackstands.

Drive Axle Application Chart

Axle Type	Models	Years
Ford 7.25 in. integral carrier	E-100, E-200	1961–67
Ford 8.75 in. removable carrier	E-100, E-200, E-300 E-100, E-200	1961–67 1969–74
Ford 8.8 in. integral carrier	E-150	1987–88
	E-250, E-350	1984–86
	E-100 through E-350	1983
Ford 9.0 in. removable carrier	E-150	1984–86
	E-100, E-150, E-200, E-300	1961–83
Ford 10.25 in. integral carrier	E-250	1985
Dana 60-3 integral carrier	E-250 LD E-300	1981–88 1969–74
Dana 61-1 integral carrier	E-250 HD E-350 SRW	1983–88
	E-350 SRW	1981–82
	E-250 E-350 SRW or DRW	1975–80
Dana 61-2 integral carrier	E-250	1979–84
Dana 70 integral carrier	E-250 HD E-350 SRW or DRW	1984–85
	E-350 DRW	1980–83
	E-250 E-350 SRW or DRW	1978–79
Dana 70-4	E-350 DRW	1975–79
Dana 70-1 integral carrier	E-350 DRW	1985–88
Dana 70-20 integral carrier	E-350 DRW	1985–88

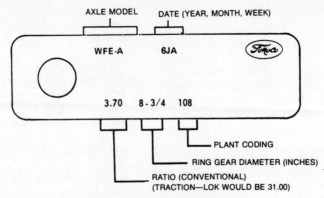

Ford axle identification tag

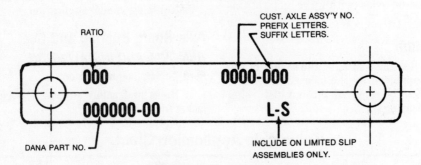

Dana axle identification tag

2. Remove the wheels from the brake drums.

3. Place a drain pan under the housing and drain the lubricant by loosening the housing cover.

4. Remove the locks securing the brake drums to the axle shaft flanges and remove the drums.

5. Remove the housing cover and gasket.

6. Remove the side gear pinion shaft lockbolt and the side gear pinion shaft.

7. Push the axle shafts inward and remove the C-locks from the inner end of the axle shafts. Temporarily replace the shaft and lockbolt to retain the differential gears in position.

8. Remove the axle shafts with a slide hammer. Be sure the seal is not damaged by the splines on the axle shaft.

9. Remove the bearing and oil seal from the housing. Both the seal and bearing can be removed with a slide hammer

10. Two types of bearings are used on some axles, one requiring a press fit and the other a loose fit. A loose fitting bearing does not necessarily indicate excessive wear.

11. Inspect the axle shaft housing and axle shafts for burrs or other irregularities. Replace any work or damaged parts. A light yellow color on the bearing journal of the axle shaft is normal, and does not require replacement of the axle shaft. Slight pitting and wear is also normal.

12. Lightly coat the wheel bearing rollers with axle lubricant. Install the bearings in the axle housing until the bearing seats firmly against the shoulder.

13. Wipe all lubricant from the oil seal bore, before installing the seal.

14. Inspect the original seals for wear. If necessary, these may be replaced with new seals, which are prepacked with lubricant and do not require soaking.

15. Install the oil seal.

16. Remove the lockbolt and pinion shaft. Carefully slide the axle shafts into place. Be careful that you do not damage the seal with the splined end of the axle shaft. Engage the splined end of the shaft with the differential side gears.

17. Install the axle shaft C-locks on the inner end of the axle shafts and seat the C-locks in the counterbore of the differential side gears.

18. Rotate the differential pinion gears until the differential pinion shaft can be installed. Install the differential pinion shaft lockbolt. Tighten to 15-22 ft.lb.

19. Install the brake drum on the axle shaft flange.

20. Install the wheel and tire on the brake drum and tighten the attaching nuts.

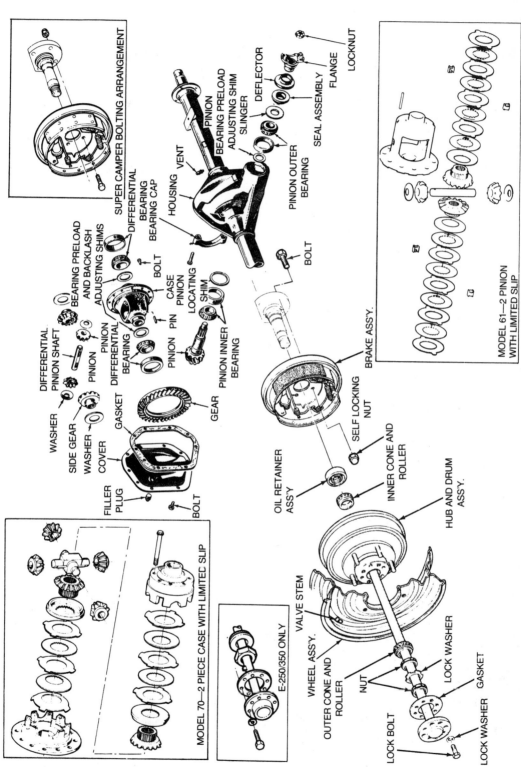

SUPER CAMPER BOLTING ARRANGEMENT

PINION
BEARING PRELOAD
ADJUSTING SHIM
SLINGER
DEFLECTOR
FLANGE
LOCKNUT
SEAL ASSEMBLY
PINION OUTER BEARING

DIFFERENTIAL BEARING
DIFFERENTIAL BEARING CAP
HOUSING VENT
BOLT

BEARING PRELOAD AND BACKLASH ADJUSTING SHIMS
CASE
PINION
LOCATING SHIM
PINION PIN
DIFFERENTIAL BEARING
PINION
PINION INNER BEARING
BOLT
BOLT

DIFFERENTIAL PINION SHAFT
PINION
WASHER
SIDE GEAR
WASHER
COVER
GASKET
GEAR
FILLER PLUG
BOLT

WASHER

BRAKE ASS'Y.

SELF LOCKING NUT

OIL RETAINER ASS'Y.

INNER CONE AND ROLLER

HUB AND DRUM ASS'Y.

MODEL 61—2 PINION WITH LIMITED SLIP

VALVE STEM

WHEEL ASS'Y.
OUTER CONE AND ROLLER
NUT
LOCK WASHER
LOCK BOLT
LOCK WASHER
LOCK WASHER
GASKET

MODEL 70—2 PIECE CASE WITH LIMITEC SLIP

E-250/350 ONLY

1967–80 Dana 60, 61 and 70

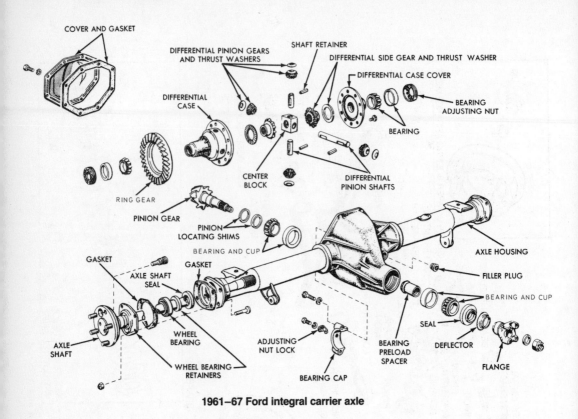

1961–67 Ford integral carrier axle

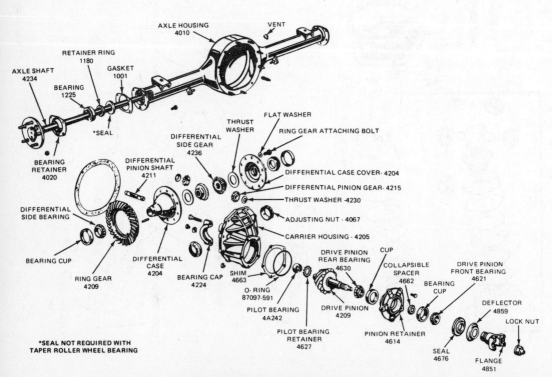

*SEAL NOT REQUIRED WITH
TAPER ROLLER WHEEL BEARING

1961–80 Ford removable carrier axle

21. Clean the gasket surface of the rear housing and install a new cover gasket and the housing cover. Some covers do not use a gasket. On these models, apply a bead of silicone sealer on the gasket surface. The bead should run inside of the bolt holes.

22. Raise the rear axle so that it is in the running position. Add the amount of specified lubricant to bring the lubricant level to ½" (12.7mm) below the filler hole.

Ford 10.25" Ring Gear, Full Floating Integral Carrier

The wheel bearings on the full floating rear axle are packed with wheel bearing grease. Axle lubricant can also flow into the wheel hubs and bearings, however, wheel bearing grease is the primary lubricant. The wheel bearing grease provides lubrication until the axle lubricant reaches the bearings during normal operation.

1. Set the parking brake and loosen the axle shaft bolts.

2. Raise the rear wheels off the floor and place jackstands under the rear axle housing so that the axle is parallel with the floor.

3. Remove the wheels.

4. Remove the brake drums.

5. Remove the axle shaft bolts.

6. Remove the axle shaft and discard the gaskets.

7. With the axle shaft removed, remove the gasket from the axle shaft flange studs.

8. Install Hub Wrench T85T-4252-AH, or equivalent, so that the drive tangs on the tool engage the slots in the hub nut.

NOTE: *The hub nuts are right hand thread on the right hub and left hand thread on the left hub. The hub nuts should be stamped RH and LH.*

Never use power or impact tools on these nuts!

The nuts will ratchet during removal.

9. Remove the hub nut.

10. Install step plate adapter tool D80L-630-7, or equivalent, in the hub.

11. Install puller D80L-1002-L, or equivalent, and loosen the hub to the point of removal. Remove the puller and step plate.

12. Remove the hub, taking care to catch the outer bearing as the hub comes off.

13. Install the hub in a soft-jawed vise and pry out the hub seal.

14. Lift out the inner bearing.

15. Drive out the inner and outer bearing races with a drift.

16. Wash all the old grease or axle lubricant out of the wheel hub, using a suitable solvent.

17. Wash the bearing races and rollers and inspect them for pitting, galling, and uneven wear patterns. Inspect the roller for end wear. Replace any bearing and race that appears in any

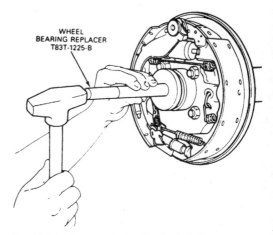

Ford 8.8 inch rear axle bearing installation

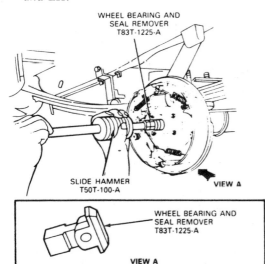

Rear axle bearing and seal removal for the Ford 8.8 inch axle

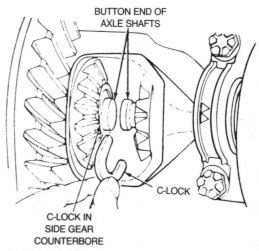

Installing the C-locks

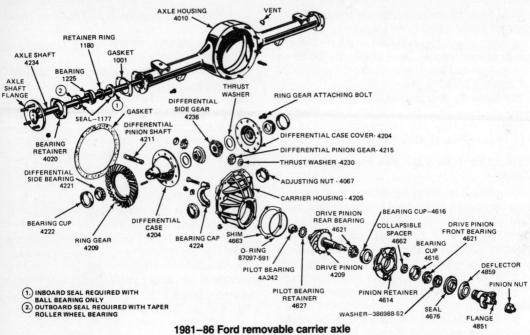

1. INBOARD SEAL REQUIRED WITH BALL BEARING ONLY
2. OUTBOARD SEAL REQUIRED WITH TAPER ROLLER WHEEL BEARING

1981–86 Ford removable carrier axle

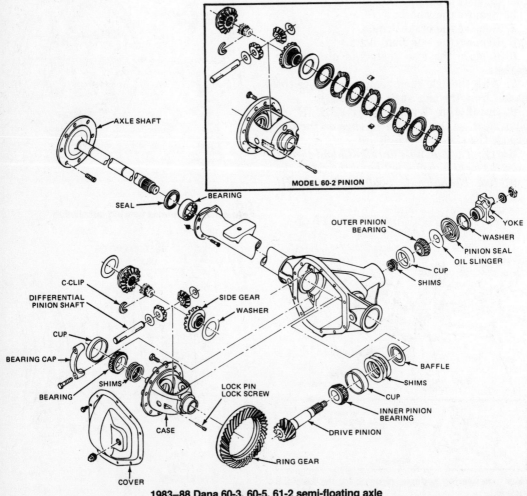

1983–88 Dana 60-3, 60-5, 61-2 semi-floating axle

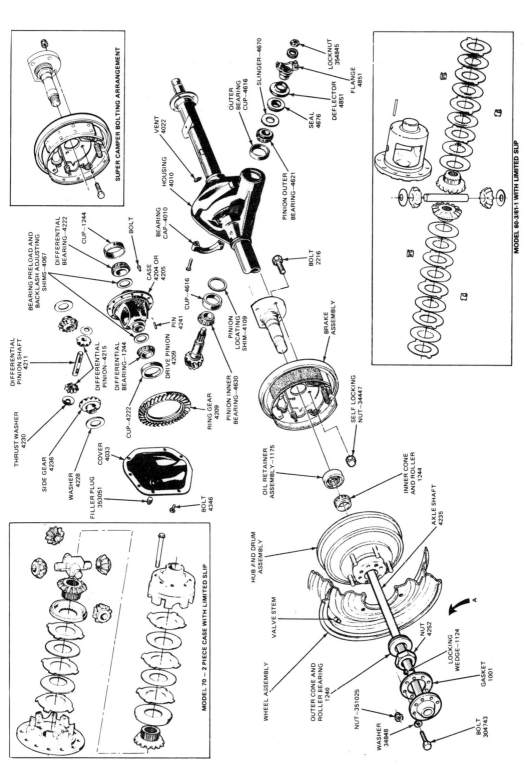

SUPER CAMPER BOLTING ARRANGEMENT

VENT
4022

HOUSING
4010

OUTER
BEARING
CUP—4616

SLINGER—4670

LOCKNUT
354845

FLANGE
4851

SEAL
4676

DEFLECTOR
4851

PINION OUTER
BEARING—4621

BEARING
CAP—4010

BEARING—4222

CUP—1244

BOLT

DIFFERENTIAL
BEARING—4222

CASE
4204 OR
4205

BOLT
2216

BRAKE
ASSEMBLY

CUP—4616

PIN
4241

PINION
LOCATING
SHIM—4109

BEARING PRELOAD AND
BACKLASH ADJUSTING
SHIMS—4067

DIFFERENTIAL
PINION SHAFT
4211

DIFFERENTIAL
PINION—4215

DIFFERENTIAL
BEARING—1244

DRIVE PINION
4209

THRUST WASHER
4230

SIDE GEAR
4236

CUP—4222

PINION INNER
BEARING—4630

RING GEAR
4209

SELF LOCKING
NUT—34447

WASHER
4228

FILLER PLUG
353051

COVER
4033

BOLT
4346

OIL RETAINER
ASSEMBLY—1175

INNER CONE
AND ROLLER
1244

AXLE SHAFT
4235

HUB AND DRUM
ASSEMBLY

VALVE STEM

WHEEL ASSEMBLY

OUTER CONE AND
ROLLER BEARING
1240

NUT—351025

WASHER
34848

NUT
4252

LOCKING
WEDGE—1124

GASKET
1001

BOLT
304743

MODEL 70 – 2 PIECE CASE WITH LIMITED SLIP

MODEL 60-3/61-1 WITH LIMITED SLIP

1981—88 Dana 61-1, 70-2U full-floating axle

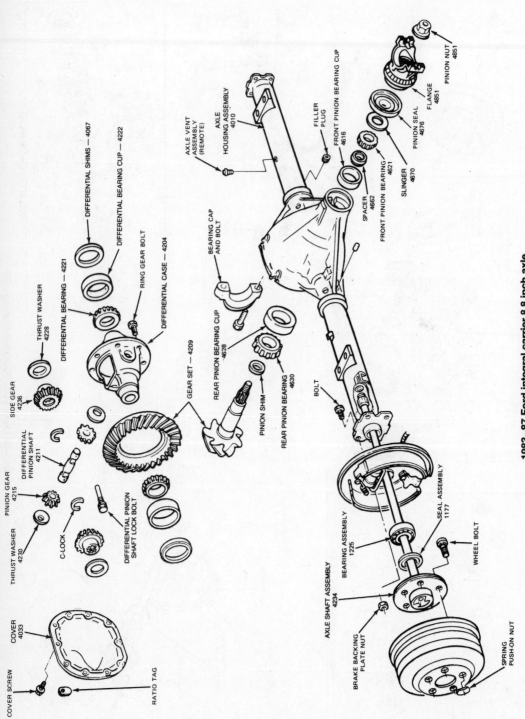

1983–87 Ford integral carrier 8.8 inch axle

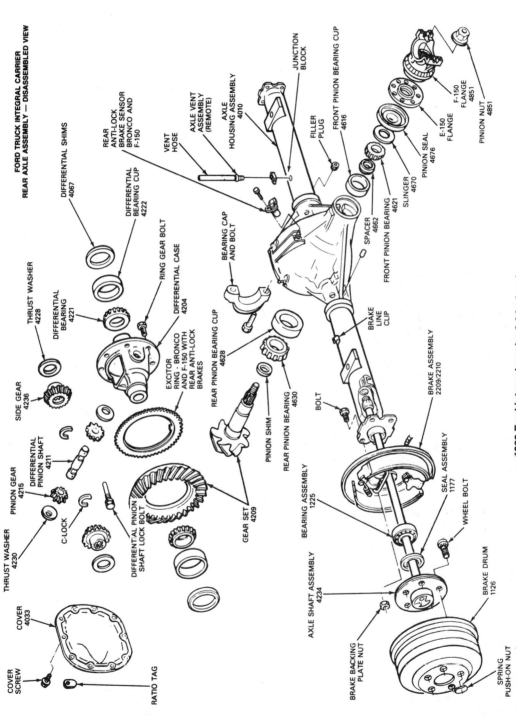

**FORD TRUCK INTEGRAL CARRIER
REAR AXLE ASSEMBLY — DISASSEMBLED VIEW**

DIFFERENTIAL SHIMS
4067

REAR
ANTI-LOCK
BRAKE SENSOR
BRONCO AND
F-150

DIFFERENTIAL
BEARING CUP
4222

THRUST WASHER
4228

DIFFERENTIAL
BEARING
4221

RING GEAR BOLT

DIFFERENTIAL
CASE
4204

SIDE GEAR
4236

EXCITOR
RING - BRONCO
AND F-150 WITH
REAR ANTI-LOCK
BRAKES

THRUST WASHER
4230

PINION GEAR
4215

DIFFERENTIAL
PINION SHAFT
4211

C-LOCK

DIFFERENTIAL PINION
SHAFT LOCK BOLT

GEAR SET
4209

REAR PINION BEARING CUP
4628

PINION SHIM

REAR PINION
BEARING
4630

BOLT

COVER
4033

COVER
SCREW

RATIO TAG

VENT
HOSE

AXLE VENT
ASSEMBLY
(REMOTE)

AXLE
HOUSING ASSEMBLY
4010

JUNCTION
BLOCK

FILLER
PLUG

FRONT PINION BEARING CUP
4616

BEARING CAP
AND BOLT

BRAKE
LINE
CLIP

BEARING ASSEMBLY
1225

AXLE SHAFT ASSEMBLY
4234

BRAKE BACKING
PLATE NUT

SEAL ASSEMBLY
1177

WHEEL BOLT

BRAKE ASSEMBLY
2209/2210

BRAKE DRUM
1126

SPRING
PUSH-ON NUT

FRONT PINION
BEARING
4621

SPACER
4662

SLINGER
4670

PINION SEAL
4676

E-150
FLANGE

F-150
FLANGE
4851

PINION NUT
4851

1988 Ford integral carrier 8.8 inch axle

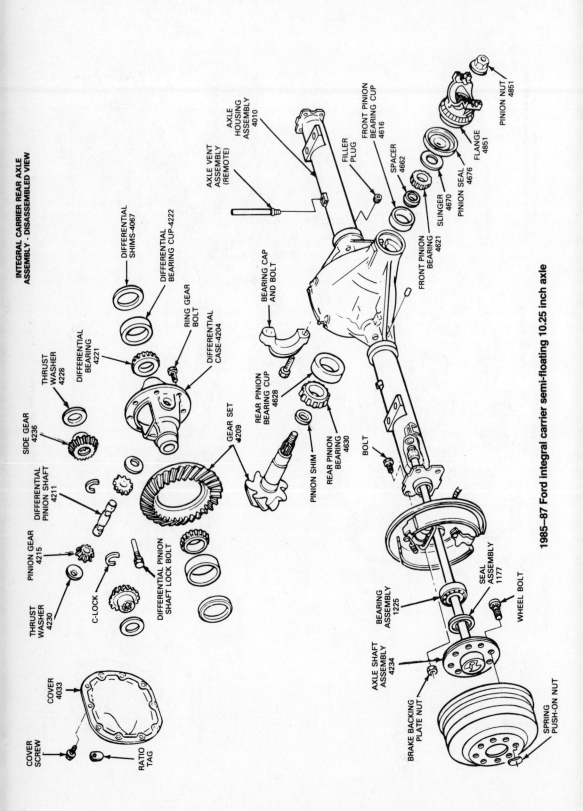

INTEGRAL CARRIER REAR AXLE
ASSEMBLY - DISASSEMBLED VIEW

AXLE HOUSING ASSEMBLY 4010

AXLE VENT ASSEMBLY (REMOTE)

FILLER PLUG

FRONT PINION BEARING CUP 4616

SPACER 4662

SLINGER 4670

PINION SEAL 4676

FLANGE 4851

PINION NUT 4851

FRONT PINION BEARING 4621

DIFFERENTIAL SHIMS-4067

DIFFERENTIAL BEARING CUP-4222

RING GEAR BOLT

BEARING CAP AND BOLT

THRUST WASHER 4228

DIFFERENTIAL BEARING 4221

DIFFERENTIAL CASE-4204

REAR PINION BEARING CUP 4628

REAR PINION BEARING 4630

BOLT

SIDE GEAR 4236

GEAR SET 4209

PINION SHIM

DIFFERENTIAL PINION SHAFT 4211

DIFFERENTIAL PINION SHAFT LOCK BOLT

PINION GEAR 4215

C-LOCK

THRUST WASHER 4230

BEARING ASSEMBLY 1225

SEAL ASSEMBLY 1177

WHEEL BOLT

AXLE SHAFT ASSEMBLY 4234

BRAKE BACKING PLATE NUT

SPRING PUSH-ON NUT

COVER 4033

COVER SCREW

RATIO TAG

1985–87 Ford integral carrier semi-floating 10.25 inch axle

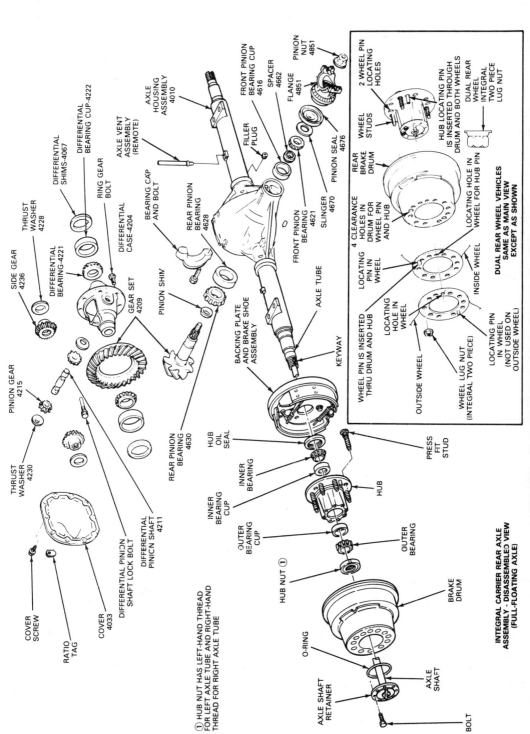

1986–87 Ford integral carrier full-floating 10.25 inch axle

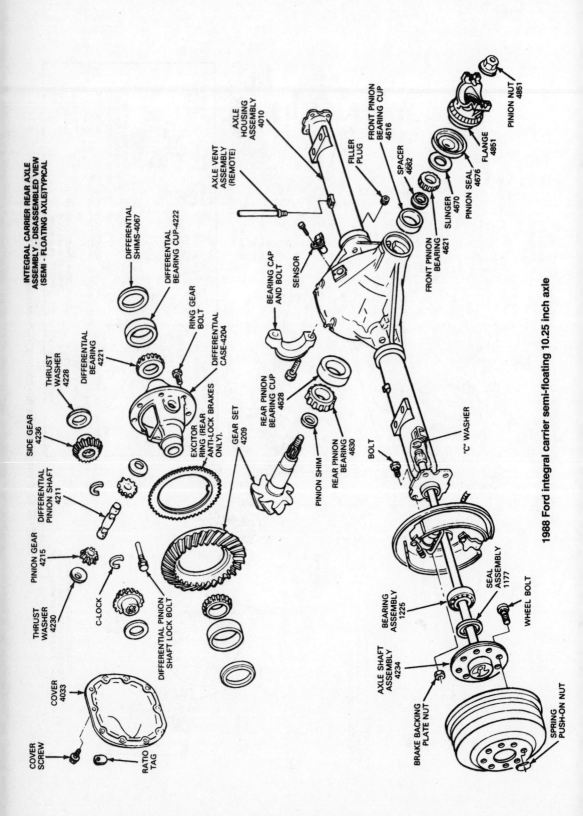

INTEGRAL CARRIER REAR AXLE ASSEMBLY - DISASSEMBLED VIEW (SEMI - FLOATING AXLE)TYPICAL

1988 Ford integral carrier semi-floating 10.25 inch axle

AXLE HOUSING ASSEMBLY 4010

FILLER PLUG

FRONT PINION BEARING CUP 4616

SPACER 4662

SLINGER 4670

PINION SEAL 4676

FLANGE 4851

PINION NUT 4851

AXLE VENT ASSEMBLY (REMOTE)

DIFFERENTIAL SHIMS-4067

DIFFERENTIAL BEARING CUP-4222

RING GEAR BOLT

DIFFERENTIAL CASE-4204

THRUST WASHER 4228

DIFFERENTIAL BEARING 4221

SIDE GEAR 4236

EXCITOR RING (REAR ANTI-LOCK BRAKES ONLY).

FRONT PINION BEARING 4621

BEARING CAP AND BOLT

SENSOR

GEAR SET 4209

REAR PINION BEARING CUP 4628

PINION SHIM

REAR PINION BEARING 4630

BOLT

"C" WASHER

DIFFERENTIAL PINION SHAFT 4211

PINION GEAR 4215

THRUST WASHER 4230

C-LOCK

DIFFERENTIAL PINION SHAFT LOCK BOLT

BEARING ASSEMBLY 1225

SEAL ASSEMBLY 1177

WHEEL BOLT

AXLE SHAFT ASSEMBLY 4234

BRAKE BACKING PLATE NUT

SPRING PUSH-ON NUT

COVER 4033

COVER SCREW

RATIO TAG

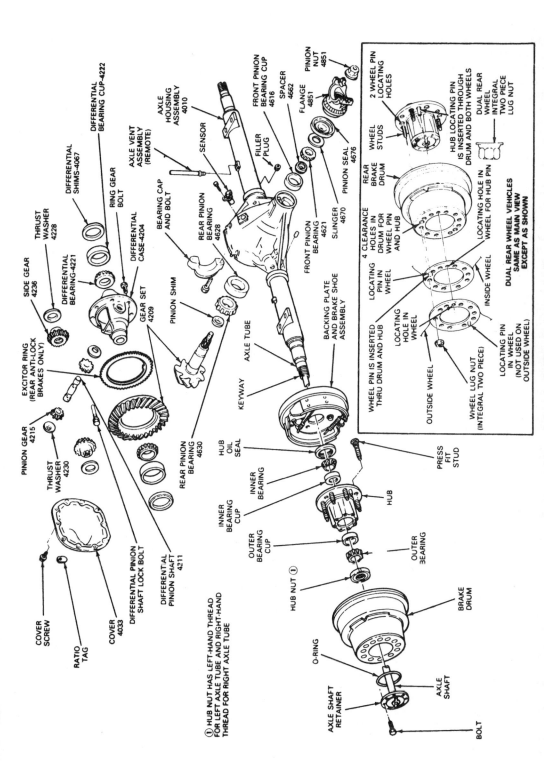

1988 Ford integral carrier full-floating 10.25 inch axle

way damaged. Always repalce the bearings and races as a set.

18. Coat the race bores with a light coat of clean, waterproof wheel bearing grease and drive the races squarely into the bores until they are fully seated. A good indication that the race is seated is when you notice the grease from the bore squishing out under the race when it contact the shoulder. Another indication is a definite change in the metallic tone when you seat the race. Just be very careful to avoid damaging the bearing surface of the race!

19. Pack each bearing cone and roller with a bearing packer or in the manner outlined in Chapter 1 for the front wheel bearings.

20. Place the inner bearing cone and roller assembly in the wheel hub.

NOTE: *Whe installing the new seal, the words OIL SIDE must go inwards towards the bearing!*

21. Place the seal squarely in the hub and drive it into place. The best tool for the job is a seal driver such as T85T-1175-AH, which will stop when the seal is at the proper depth.

NOTE: *If the seal is misaligned or damaged during installation, a new seal must be installed.*

22. Clean the spindle thoroughly. If the spindle is excessively pitted, damaged or has a predominately bluish tint (from overheating), it must be replaced.

23. Coat the spindle with 80W/90 oil.

24. Pack the hub with clean, waterproof wheel bearing grease.

25. Pack the outer bearing with clean, waterproof wheel bearing grease in the same manner as you packed the inner bearing.

26. Place the outer bearing in the hub and install the hub and bearing together on the spindle.

27. Install the hub nut on the spindle. Make sure that the nut tab is located in the keyway prior to thread engagement. Turn the hub nut onto the threads as far as you can by hand, noting the thread direction.

28. Install the hub wrench tool and tighten the nut to 55-65 ft.lb. Rotate the hub occasionally during nut tightening.

29. Ratchet the nut back 5 teeth. **Make sure that you hear 5 clicks!**

30. Inspect the axle shaft O-ring seal and replace it if it looks at all bad.

31. Install the axle shaft.

32. Coat the axle shaft bolt threads with waterproof seal and install them by hand until they seat. **Do not tighten them with a wrench at this time!**

33. Check the diameter across the center of the brake shoes. Check the diameter of the brake drum. Adjust the brake shoes so that

their diameter is 0.030″ less than the drum diameter.

34. Install the brake drum.

35. Install the wheel.

36. Loosen the differential filler plug. If lubricant starts to run out, retighten the plug. If not, remove the plug and fill the housing with 80W/90 gear oil.

37. Lower the truck to the floor.

38. Tighten the wheel lugs to 140 ft.lb.

39. Now tighten the axle shaft bolts. Torque them to 60-80 ft.lb.

Ford Removable Carrier Type

NOTE: *The following procedure requires the use of special tools, including a shop press.*

1. Raise and support the vehicle. Remove the wheel/tire assembly from the brake drum.

2. Remove the clips which secure the brake drum to the axle flange, then remove the drum from the flange.

3. Working through the hole provided in each axle shaft flange, remove the nuts which secure the wheel bearing retainer plate.

4. Pull the axle shaft assembly out of the axle housing. You may need a slide hammer.

NOTE: *The brake backing plate must not be dislodged. Install one nut to hold the plate in place after the axle shaft is removed.*

5. If the axle has ball bearings: Loosen the bearing retainer ring by nicking it in several places with a cold chisel, then slide it off the axle shaft. On models equipped with a thick retaining ring drill a ¼-½″ hole part way through the ring, then break it with a cold chisel. A hydraulic press is needed to press the bearing off and to press the new one on. Press the new bearing and the new retainer ring on separately. Use a slide hammer to pull the old seal out of the axle housing. Carefully drive the new seal evenly into the axle housing, preferably with a seal drive tool.

6. If the axle has tapered roller bearings. Use a slide hammer to remove the bearing cup from the axle housing. Drill a ¼-½″ hole part way through the bearing retainer ring, then break it with a cold chisel. A hydraulic press is needed to press the bearing off and remove the seal. Press on the new seal and bearing, then the new retainer ring. Do not press the bearing and ring on together. Put the cup on the bearing, not in the housing, and lubricate the outer diameter of the cup and seal.

7. With ball bearings: Place a new gasket between the housing flange and backing plate. Carefully slide the axle shaft into place. Turn the shaft to start the splines into the side gear and push it in.

8. With tapered roller bearings: Move the seal out toward the axle shaft flange so there is

at least $\frac{3}{32}$" between the edge of the outer seal and the bearing cup, to prevent snagging on installation. Carefully slide the axle shaft into place. Turn the shaft to start the splines into the side gear and push it in.

9. Install the bearing retainer plate.

10. Replace the brake drum and the wheel and tire.

Dana Models 60, 61, and 70

The wheel bearings on the full floating rear axle are packed with wheel bearing grease. Axle lubricant can also flow into the wheel hubs and bearings, however, wheel bearing grease is the primary lubricant. The wheel bearing grease provides lubrication until the axle lubricant reaches the bearings during normal operation.

1. Set the parking brake and loosen the axle shaft bolts.

2. Raise the rear wheels off the floor and place jackstands under the rear axle housing so that the axle is parallel with the floor.

3. Remove the axle shaft bolts.

4. Remove the axle shaft and gaskets.

5. With the axle shaft removed, remove the gasket from the axle shaft flange studs.

6. Bend the lockwasher tab away from the locknut, and then remove the locknut, lockwasher, and the adjusting nut.

7. Remove the outer bearing cone and pull the wheel straight off the axle.

8. With a piece of hardwood which will just clear the outer bearing cup, drive the inner bearing cone and inner seal out of the wheel hub.

9. Wash all the old grease or axle lubricant out of the wheel hub, using a suitable solvent.

10. Wash the bearing cups and rollers and inspect them for pitting, galling, and uneven wear patterns. Inspect the roller for end wear.

11. If the bearing cups are to be replaced, drive them out with a drift. Install the new cups with a block of wood and hammer or press them in.

12. If the bearing cups are properly seated, a 0.0015" feeler gauge will not fit between the cup and the wheel hub.

13. Pack each bearing cone and roller with a bearing packer or in the manner previously outlined for the front wheel bearings.

14. Place the inner bearing cone and roller assembly in the wheel hub. Install a new inner seal in the hub.

15. Install the wheel.

16. Install and tighten the bearing adjusting nut to 50-80 ft.lb. while rotating the wheel.

17. Back off (loosen) the adjusting nut $\frac{3}{8}$ of a turn.

18. Apply axle lube to a new lockwasher and install it with the smooth side out.

19. Install the locknut and tighten it to 90-110 ft.lb. The wheel must rotate freely after the locknut is tightened. The wheel endplay should be within 0.001-0.010".

20. Bend two lockwasher tabs inward over an adjusting nut flat and two lockwasher tabs outward over the locknut flat.

21. Install the axle shaft, gasket, lockbolts, and washers. Tighten the bolts to 40-50 ft.lb.

22. Adjust the brakes, if necessary.

Differential Carrier

REMOVAL

Removable Type Carrier Only

NOTE: *The C-Lock type carrier is not removable.*

1. Raise the vehicle on a hoist and remove the two rear wheel and tire assemblies.

2. Remove the brake drums from the axle shaft flange studs (back off the brake shoes to make drum removal easier).

3. Working through the access hole provided in each axle shaft flange, remove the nuts that

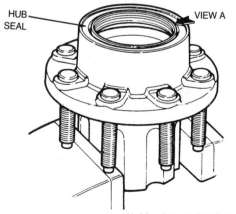
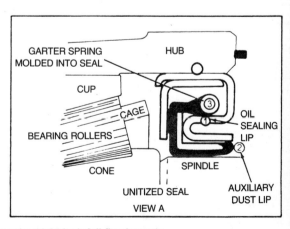

Unitized rear wheel seals on the 10.25 inch full-floating axle

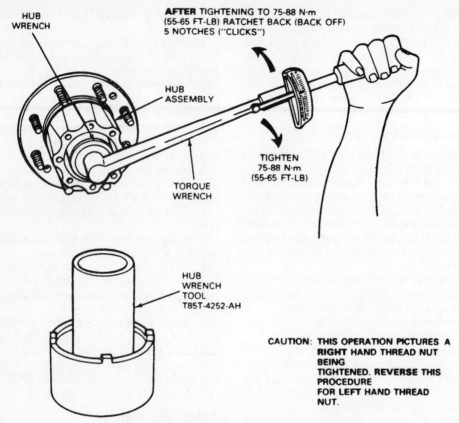

HUB WRENCH

AFTER TIGHTENING TO 75-88 N·m (55-65 FT-LB) RATCHET BACK (BACK OFF) 5 NOTCHES ("CLICKS")

HUB ASSEMBLY

TORQUE WRENCH

TIGHTEN 75-88 N·m (55-65 FT-LB)

HUB WRENCH TOOL T85T-4252-AH

CAUTION: THIS OPERATION PICTURES A RIGHT HAND THREAD NUT BEING TIGHTENED. REVERSE THIS PROCEDURE FOR LEFT HAND THREAD NUT.

Installing the hub nuts for the 10.25 inch full-floating axle

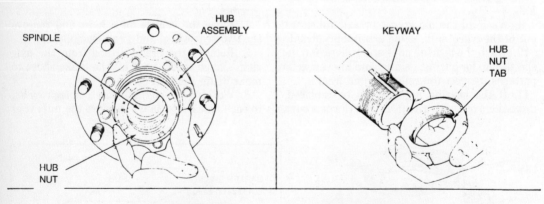

SPINDLE

HUB ASSEMBLY

HUB NUT

KEYWAY

HUB NUT TAB

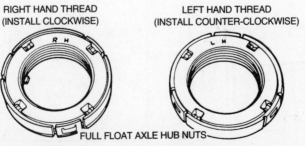

RIGHT HAND THREAD (INSTALL CLOCKWISE)

LEFT HAND THREAD (INSTALL COUNTER-CLOCKWISE)

R H

L H

FULL FLOAT AXLE HUB NUTS

Hub nuts for the 10.25 inch full-floating axle

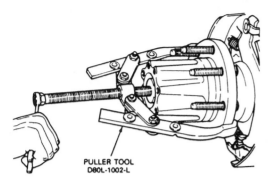

Lossening the hub on the 10.25 inch full-floating axle

secure the rear wheel bearing retainer plate. Pull each axle shaft assembly out of the axle housing using axle shaft puller adapter, Tool T66L-4234-A or equivalent. Wire the brake backing plate to the frame rail. Remove the gasket and discard, if so equipped.

NOTE: *Whenever a rear axle is replaced, The wheel bearing oil seals must be replace. Remove the seals with seal remover, Tool 1175-AC or equivalent (if roller bearing equipped this need not be done).*

4. Make scribe marks on the driveshaft end yoke and the axle companion flange to insure proper position at assembly. Disconnect the driveshaft at the rear axle U-joint. Hold the cups on the spider with tape. Mark the cups so that they will be in their original position rela-

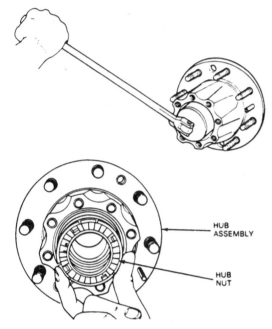

Hub nut removal on the 10.25 inch full-floating axle

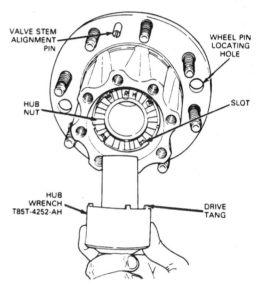

Using a hub wrench to remove the hub nuts on the 10.25 inch full-floating axle

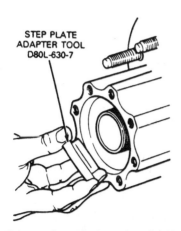

Installing the step plate adapter tool on the 10.25 inch full-floating axle

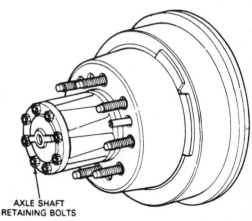

Rear axle shaft retaining bolts on the Ford 10.25 inch full-floating rear axle

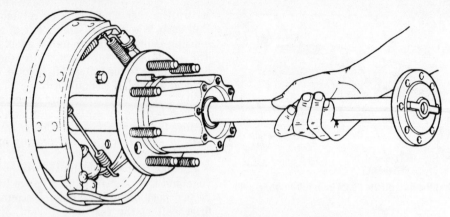

Removing the axle shaft from the Ford 10.25 inch full-floating rear axle

tive to the flange when they are assembled. Remove the driveshaft from the transmission extension housing. Install an oil seal replacer tool in the housing to prevent transmission leakage.

5. Clean area around carrier to housing surfaces with a wire brush and wipe clean, to prevent dirt entry into the housing. Place a drain pan under the carrier and housing, remove the carrier attaching nuts and washers, and drain the axle. Remove the carrier assembly from the axle housing.

NOTE: *Synthetic Type wheel bearing seals must not be cleaned, soaked or washed in cleaning solvent.*

INSTALLATION

1. Clean the axle housing and shaft using kerosene and swabs. To avoid contamination of the of the grease in the sealed ball bearings, do not allow any quantity of solvent directly on the wheel bearings. Clean the mating surfaces of the axle housing and carrier.

2. Position the differential carrier on the studs in the axle housing using a new gasket between the carrier and the housing. To insure a good seal, apply a bead of Silicone Rubber Sealant (D6AZ-19562-A or B). to the gasket. Install the carrier to housing attaching nuts and washers, tighten them to 25-40 ft.lb.

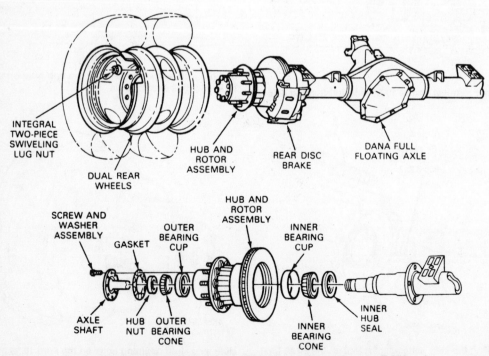

INTEGRAL TWO-PIECE SWIVELING LUG NUT

DUAL REAR WHEELS

HUB AND ROTOR ASSEMBLY

REAR DISC BRAKE

DANA FULL FLOATING AXLE

SCREW AND WASHER ASSEMBLY

GASKET

OUTER BEARING CUP

HUB AND ROTOR ASSEMBLY

INNER BEARING CUP

AXLE SHAFT

HUB NUT

OUTER BEARING CONE

INNER BEARING CONE

INNER HUB SEAL

Rear wheel hub on the Dana full-floating axle used on the E-350

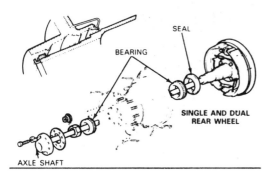

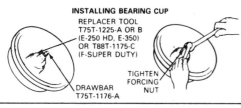

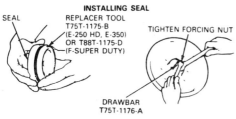

Installation of the rear wheel bearings and seal on the Dana 70 rear axle

3. Remove the oil seal replacer tool from the transmission extension housing. Position the driveshaft so that the U-joint slip yoke splines to the transmission output shaft.

4. Connect the driveshaft to the axle U-joint flange, aligning the scribe marks made on the driveshaft end yoke and the axle U-joint flange during the removal procedure. Install the U-bolts and nuts and tighten them to 20 ft.lb.

5. Install the two axle shaft assemblies in the axle housing. Care must be exercised to prevent damage to the oil seals. Carefully slide the axle shaft into the housing so that the rough forging of the shaft will not damage the oil seal. Timken bearing axle shafts do not require a gasket. Start the axle splines into the differential side gear, and push the shaft in until the bearing bottoms in the housing.

6. Install the bearing retainer plates on the attaching bolts and alternately tighten them to 20-40 ft.lb.

7. Install the two rear brake drums.

8. Install the rear wheel and tire assemblies.

9. If the rear brake shoes were backed off, adjust the brakes.

10. Fill the rear axle with the specified lubricant.

Pinion Seal

REMOVAL AND INSTALLATION

1961-65 Ford Axles

1. Raise and safely support the vehicle with jackstands under the frame rails. Allow the axle to drop to rebound position for working clearance.

2. Remove the rear wheels and brake drums. No drag must be present on the axle.

3. Mark the companion flanges and U-joints for correct reinstallation position.

4. Remove the driveshaft.

5. Make punch matchmarks on the end of the pinion shaft, pinion nut and flange inner surface for reassembly alignment.

6. While holding the flange with a holding tool, remove the integral nut/washer.

7. Place a drain pan under the differential, clean the area around the seal, and mark the yoke-to-pinion relation.

8. Use a 2-jawed puller to remove the pinion flange.

9. Remove the seal with a small prybar.

10. Thoroughly clean the oil seal bore.

NOTE: *If you are not absolutely certain of the proper seal installation depth, the proper seal driver must be used. If the seal is misaligned or damaged during installation, it must be removed and a new seal installed.*

11. Coat the outer edge of the new seal with oil-resistant sealer. Drive the new seal into place with a seal driver such as T55P-4676-A on integral carriers, or T62F-4676-A on removable carriers.

NOTE: *Do not put sealer on the seal lip.*

12. Coat the splines with a small amount of wheel bearing grease and install the flange, aligning the matchmarks. Never hammer the flange onto the pinion!

13. Install a NEW nut on the pinion.

14. Tighten the nut until it contacts the flange surface fully and the matchmarks are aligned.

15. Hold the flange and tighten the nut an addition ¼ turn (90°) beyond the matchmarks.

Pinion seal installation for the Ford 8.8 inch rear axle

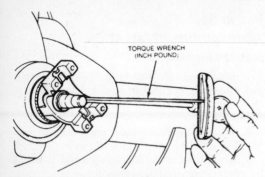

TORQUE WRENCH
(INCH POUND)

Measuring pinion bearing preload

16. Install the driveshaft using the matchmarks. Torque the nuts to 15 ft.lb.

1966 and Later Ford axles, except 10.25" Integral Carrier Axles

NOTE: *A torque wrench capable of at least 225 ft.lb. is required for pinion seal installation.*

1. Raise and safely support the vehicle with jackstands under the frame rails. Allow the axle to drop to rebound position for working clearance.

2. Remove the rear wheels and brake drums. No drag must be present on the axle.

3. Mark the companion flanges and U-joints for correct reinstallation position.

4. Remove the driveshaft.

5. Using an inch pound torque wrench and socket on the pinion yoke nut measure the amount of torque needed to maintain differential rotation through several clockwise revolutions. Record the measurement.

6. Use a suitable tool to hold the companion flange. Remove the pinion nut.

7. Place a drain pan under the differential, clean the area around the seal, and mark the yoke-to-pinion relation.

8. Use a 2-jawed puller to remove the pinion flange.

9. Remove the seal with a small prybar.

10. Thoroughly clean the oil seal bore.

NOTE: *If you are not absolutely certain of the proper seal installation depth, the proper seal driver must be used. If the seal is misaligned or damaged during installation, it must be removed and a new seal installed.*

11. Drive the new seal into place with a seal driver such as T83T-4676-A. Coat the seal lip with clean, waterproof wheelbearing grease.

12. Coat the splines with a small amount of wheel bearing grease and install the yoke, aligning the matchmarks. Never hammer the yoke onto the pinion!

13. Install a NEW nut on the pinion.

14. Hold the yoke with a holding tool. Tighten

the pinion nut to at least 160 ft.lb., taking frequent turning torque readings until the original preload reading is attained.

If the original preload reading, that you noted before disassembly, is lower than the specified reading of 8-14 in.lb. for used bearings; 16-29 in.lb. for new bearings, keep tightening the pinion nut until the specified reading is reached.

If the original preload reading is higher than the specified values, torque the nut just until the original reading is reached.

WARNING: *Under no circumstances should the nut be backed off to reduce the preload reading! If the preload is exceeded, the yoke and bearing must be removed and a new collapsible spacer must be installed. The entire process of preload adjustment must be repeated.*

15. Install the driveshaft using the matchmarks. Torque the nuts to 15 ft.lb.

Ford 10.25" Ring Gear Integral Carrier Axle

NOTE: *A torque wrench capable of at least 225 ft.lb. is required for pinion seal installation.*

1. Raise and safely support the vehicle with jackstands under the frame rails. Allow the axle to drop to the rebound position for working clearance.

2. Remove the rear wheels and brake drums. No drag must be present on the axle.

3. Mark the companion flanges and U-joints for correct reinstallation position.

4. Remove the driveshaft.

5. Using an inch pound torque wrench and socket on the pinion yoke nut measure the amount of torque needed to maintain differential rotation through several clockwise revolutions. Record the measurement.

6. Use a suitable tool to hold the companion flange. Remove the pinion nut.

7. Place a drain pan under the differential, clean the area around the seal, and mark the yoke-to-pinion relation.

8. Use a 2-jawed puller to remove the pinion.

9. Remove the seal with a small prybar.

10. Thoroughly clean the oil seal bore.

NOTE: *If you are not absolutely certain of the proper seal installation depth, the proper seal driver must be used. If the seal is misaligned or damaged during installation, it must be removed and a new seal installed.*

11. Drive the new seal into place with a seal driver such as T83T-4676-A. Coat the seal lip with clean, waterproof wheel bearing grease.

12. Coat the splines with a small amount of wheel bearing grease and install the yoke, aligning the matchmarks. Never hammer the yoke onto the pinion!

13. Install a NEW nut on the pinion.

14. Hold the yoke with a holding tool. Tighten the pinion nut to at least 160 ft.lb., taking frequent turning torque readings until the original preload reading is attained.

If the original preload reading, that you noted before disassembly, is lower than the specified reading of 8-14 in.lb. for used bearings; 16-29 in.lb. for new bearings, keep tightening the pinion nut until the specified reading is reached.

If the original preload reading is higher than the specified values, torque the nut just until the original reading is reached.

WARNING: *Under no circumstances should the nut be backed off to reduce the preload reading! If the preload is exceeded, the yoke and bearing must be removed and a new collapsible spacer must be installed. The entire process of preload adjustment must be repeated.*

15. Install the driveshaft using the matchmarks. Torque the nuts to 15 ft.lb.

Dana Axles

NOTE: *A torque wrench capable of at least 275 ft.lb. is required for pinion seal installation.*

1. Raise and safely support the vehicle with jackstands under the frame rails. Allow the axle to drop to the rebound position for working clearance.

2. Remove the rear wheels and brake drums. No drag must be present on the axle.

3. Mark the companion flanges and U-joints for correct reinstallation position.

4. Remove the driveshaft.

5. Use a suitable tool to hold the companion flange. Remove the pinion nut.

6. Place a drain pan under the differential, clean the area around the seal, and mark the yoke-to-pinion relation.

7. Use a 2-jawed puller to remove the pinion.

8. Remove the seal with a small prybar.

9. Thoroughly clean the oil seal bore.

NOTE: *If you are not absolutely certain of the proper seal installation depth, the proper seal driver must be used. If the seal is misaligned or damaged during installation, it must be removed and a new seal installed.*

10. Coat the new oil seal with wheel bearing grease. Install the seal using oil seal driver T56T-4676-B. After the seal is installed, make sure that the seal garter spring has not become dislodged. If it has, remove and replace the seal.

11. Install the yoke, using flange replacer tool D81T-4858-A if necessary to draw the yoke into place.

12. Install a new pinion nut and washer. Torque the nut to 250-270 ft.lb.

13. Connect the driveshaft. Torque the fasteners to 15-20 ft.lb.

Axle Housing
REMOVAL AND INSTALLATION

Ford Axles, except the 10.25″ Full-Floating Integral Carrier Axle

1. Raise and support the rear end on jackstands under the rear frame members, and support the housing with a floor jack.

2. Matchmark and disconnect the driveshaft at the axle.

3. Remove the wheels and brake drums.

4. Disengage the brake line from the clips that retain the line to the housing.

5. Disconnect the vent tube from the housing.

6. Remove the axle shafts.

7. Remove the brake backing plate from the housing, and support them with wire. Do not disconnect the brake line.

8. Disconnect each rear shock absorber from the mounting bracket stud on the housing.

9. Lower the axle slightly to reduce some of the spring tension. At each rear spring, remove the spring clip (U-bolt) nuts, spring clips, and spring seat caps.

10. Remove the housing from under the vehicle.

To Install:

1. Position the axle housing under the rear springs. Install the spring clips (U-bolts), spring seat clamps and nuts. Tighten the spring clamps evenly to 115 ft.lb.

2. If a new axle housing is being installed, remove the bolts that attach the brake backing plate and bearing retainer from the old housing flanges. Position the bolts in the new housing flanges to hold the brake backing plates in position. Torque the bolts to 40 ft.lb.

3. Install the axle shafts.

4. Connect the vent tube to the housing.

5. Position the brake line to the housing, and secure it with the retaining clips.

6. Raise the axle housing and springs enough to allow connecting the rear shock absorbers to the mounting bracket studs on the housing. Torque the nuts to 60 ft.lb.

7. Connect the driveshaft to the axle. Torque the nuts to 8-15 ft.lb.

8. Install the brake drums and wheels.

Ford 10.25″ Ring Gear Full Floating Integral Carrier

1. Raise and support the rear end on jackstands under the rear frame members, and support the housing with a floor jack.

2. Matchmark and disconnect the driveshaft at the axle.

3. Remove the wheels and brake drums.

4. Disengage the brake line from the clips that retain the line to the housing.

5. Disconnect the vent tube from the housing.

6. Remove the hubs.

7. Remove the brake backing plate from the housing, and support them with wire. Do not disconnect the brake line.

8. Disconnect each rear shock absorber from the mounting bracket stud on the housing.

9. Lower the axle slightly to reduce some of the spring tension. At each rear spring, remove the spring clip (U-bolt) nuts, spring clips, and spring seat caps.

10. Remove the housing from under the vehicle.

To Install:

1. Position the axle housing under the rear springs. Install the spring clips (U-bolts), spring seat clamps and nuts. Tighten the spring clamps evenly to 200 ft.lb.

2. If a new axle housing is being installed, remove the bolts that attach the brake backing plate and bearing retainer from the old housing flanges. Position the bolts in the new housing flanges to hold the brake backing plates in position. Torque the bolts to 40 ft.lb.

3. Connect the vent tube to the housing.

4. Position the brake line to the housing, and secure it with the retaining clips.

5. Raise the axle housing and springs enough to allow connecting the rear shock absorbers to the mounting bracket studs on the housing. Torque the nuts to 60 ft.lb.

6. Connect the driveshaft to the axle. Torque the nuts to 20 ft.lb.

7. Install the brake drums and wheels.

Dana Axles

1. Disconnect the shock absorbers from the rear axle.

2. Loosen the rear axle shaft nuts.

3. Raise and support the rear end on jackstands placed under the frame.

4. Remove the rear wheels.

5. Disconnect the rear stabilizer bar.

6. Disconnect the brake hose at the frame.

7. Disconnect the parking brake cable at the equalizer and remove the cables from the support brackets.

8. Matchmark the driveshaft-to-axle flange position.

9. Disconnect the driveshaft from the rear axle and move it out of the way.

10. Take up the weight of the axle with a floor jack.

11. Remove the nuts from the spring U-bolts and remove the spring seat caps.

12. Lower the axle and roll it from under the van.

13. Installation is the reverse of removal. Torque the spring U-bolt nuts to 160 ft.lb. Bleed the brake system.

Suspension and Steering

8

FRONT SUSPENSION

1961-67 Vans use a solid I-beam front axle suspended with leaf type springs. The front wheel spindles are attached to the ends of the axle with a king pin (spindle bolt).

1969 and later Vans use two I-beam type front axles; one for each wheel. One end of each axle is attached to the spindle and a radius arm, and the other end is attached to a frame pivot bracket on the opposite side of the truck. Coil spring are used.

Leaf Springs

REMOVAL AND INSTALLATION

1. Raise and support the front end on jackstands placed under the frame.
2. Take up the weight of the front axle with a floor jack.
3. Remove the splash shield.

4. Disconnect the shock absorbers at the axle.
5. Remove the U-bolts and spring plate from each end of the axle.
6. Lower the axle and remove the rear shackle nuts and outside plate.
7. Pull the rear shackle assembly and rubber bushings from the bracket and spring.
8. Remove the nut and mounting bolt securing the front end of the spring and remove the spring.

To install:

9. Install new rubber bushings in the rear shackle bracket and rear spring eye.
10. Position the front end of the spring at the shackle and install the bolt and nut. Hand tighten the nut at this point.
11. Connect the rear end of the spring by inserting the upper stud of the rear shackle through the rear shackle bracket and the lower stud through the rear spring eye.

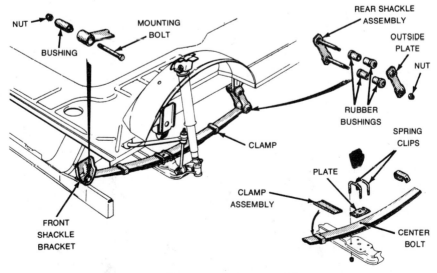

1961–67 front leaf spring assembly

Troubleshooting Basic Steering and Suspension Problems

Problem	Cause	Solution
Hard steering (steering wheel is hard to turn)	• Low or uneven tire pressure • Loose power steering pump drive belt • Low or incorrect power steering fluid • Incorrect front end alignment • Defective power steering pump • Bent or poorly lubricated front end parts	• Inflate tires to correct pressure • Adjust belt • Add fluid as necessary • Have front end alignment checked/adjusted • Check pump • Lubricate and/or replace defective parts
Loose steering (too much play in the steering wheel)	• Loose wheel bearings • Loose or worn steering linkage • Faulty shocks • Worn ball joints	• Adjust wheel bearings • Replace worn parts • Replace shocks • Replace ball joints
Car veers or wanders (car pulls to one side with hands off the steering wheel)	• Incorrect tire pressure • Improper front end alignment • Loose wheel bearings • Loose or bent front end components • Faulty shocks	• Inflate tires to correct pressure • Have front end alignment checked/adjusted • Adjust wheel bearings • Replace worn components • Replace shocks
Wheel oscillation or vibration transmitted through steering wheel	• Improper tire pressures • Tires out of balance • Loose wheel bearings • Improper front end alignment • Worn or bent front end components	• Inflate tires to correct pressure • Have tires balanced • Adjust wheel bearings • Have front end alignment checked/adjusted • Replace worn parts
Uneven tire wear	• Incorrect tire pressure • Front end out of alignment • Tires out of balance	• Inflate tires to correct pressure • Have front end alignment checked/adjusted • Have tires balanced

12. Install the outside plate and hand tighten the nuts.

13. Position the spring center stud on the pilot hole in the axle and install the spring clips and plate. Hand tighten the nuts.

14. Raise the axle with the floor jack until the van is clear of the jackstands and connect the lower end of the shock absorber to the front axle. Torque all fasteners as follows:
- Shock absorber lower nut: 50 ft.lb.
- E-100 Spring-to-axle ½"-13 nut: 45-70 ft.lb.
- E-100 Spring-to-axle 9/16"-12 nut: 85-115 ft.lb.
- E-200/300 Spring-to-axle: 150-200 ft.lb.
- Spring-to-front hanger: 150-200 ft.lb.
- Spring-to-rear hanger: 75-105 ft.lb.

Coil Springs

REMOVAL AND INSTALLATION

1969-74

1. Remove the floor mat to gain access to the shock absorber cover plate.

2. Remove the cover plate.

3. Raise and support the front end on jackstands placed under the frame.

4. Support the front axle with a floor jack.

5. Remove the two upper spring retainer bolts and remove the retainer and clamp.

6. Remove the spring lower retainer bolt and remove the retainer and support.

7. Place a safety chain through the spring to prevent sudden tension release and slowly lower the jack.

8. Remove the spring.

To install:

9. Position the spring on the axle with the pigtails rearward.

10. Loosely install the lower support, retainer and bolt.

11. Install the upper insulator.

12. Raise the axle to position the spring.

13. Make sure that the retainer bolts are approximately flush with the bottom of the clamp bar.

14. Insert the retainer into the hole in the floor with the clamp bar pointed toward the right side.

15. Rotate the retainer assembly 90° clock-

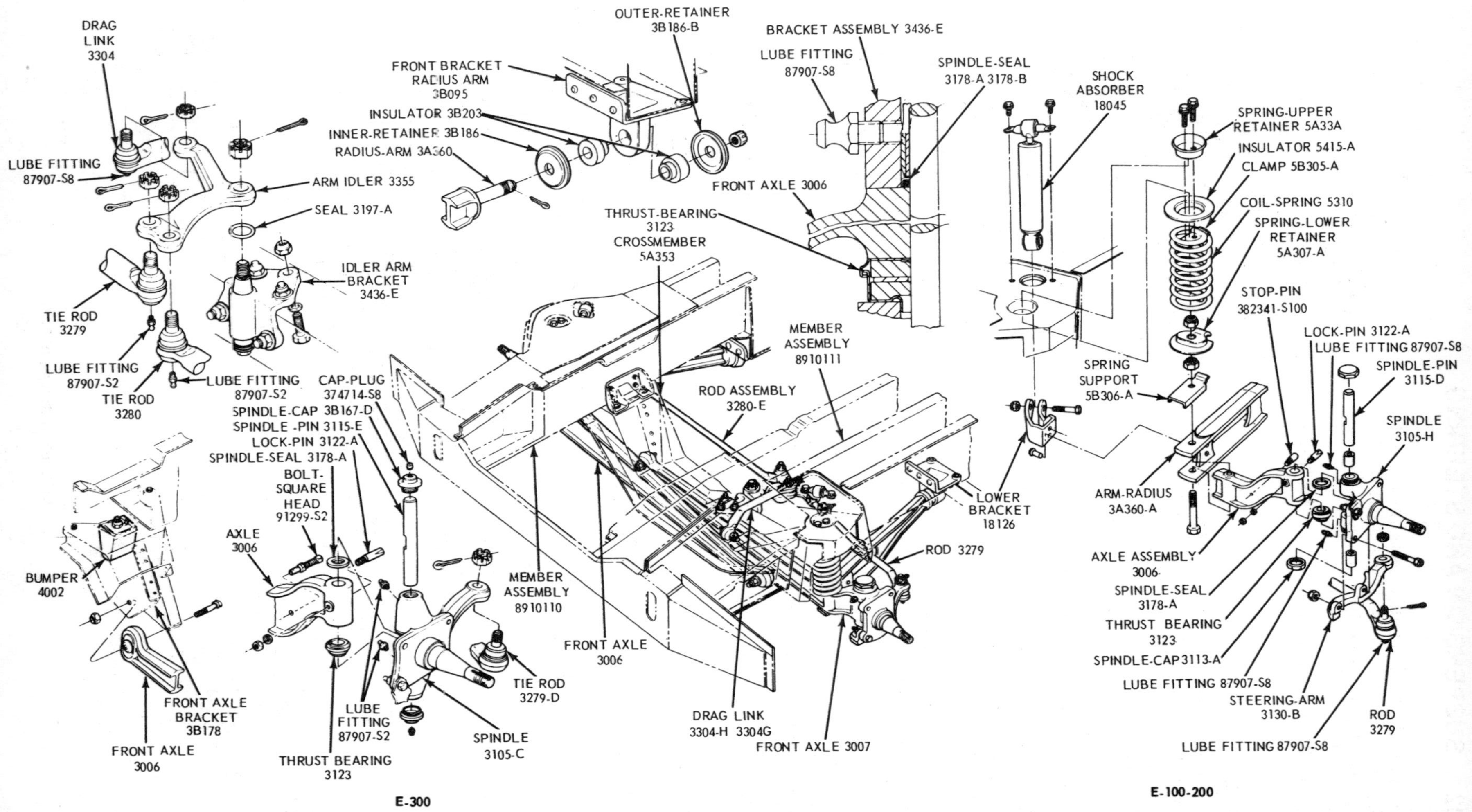

1969—72 front suspension

SPRING-UPPER RETAINER 5A33A
INSULATOR 5415-A
CLAMP 5B305-A
COIL-SPRING 5310
SPRING-LOWER RETAINER 5A307-A
STOP-PIN 382341-S100

LOCK-PIN 3122-A
LUBE FITTING 87907-S8
SPINDLE-PIN 3115-D
SPINDLE 3105-H
ROD 3279

LUBE FITTING 87907-S8
STEERING-ARM 3130-B
LUBE FITTING 87907-S8
SPINDLE-CAP 3113-A
THRUST BEARING 3123
SPINDLE-SEAL 3178-A
AXLE ASSEMBLY 3006-
ARM-RADIUS 3A360-A

SHOCK ABSORBER 18045
SPRING SUPPORT 5B306-A

LUBE FITTING 87907-S8

E.100-200

SPINDLE-SEAL 3178-A 3178-B
BRACKET ASSEMBLY 3436-E
LUBE FITTING 87907-S8
FRONT AXLE 3006

OUTER-RETAINER 3B186-B

FRONT BRACKET RADIUS ARM 3B095
INSULATOR 3B203
INNER-RETAINER 3B186
RADIUS-ARM 3A-60
ARM IDLER 3355
SEAL 3197-A
IDLER ARM BRACKET 3436-E

THRUST-BEARING 3123
CROSSMEMBER 5A353

MEMBER ASSEMBLY 8910111
ROD ASSEMBLY 3280-E

LOWER BRACKET 18126
ROD 3279

FRONT AXLE 3007
DRAG LINK 3304-H 3304G

FRONT AXLE 3006

MEMBER ASSEMBLY 8910110

TIE ROD 3279-D
SPINDLE 3105-C

LUBE FITTING 87907-S2
THRUST BEARING 3123

E-300

LUBE FITTING 87907-S2
CAP-PLUG 374714-S8
SPINDLE-CAP 3B167-D
SPINDLE -PIN 3115-E
LOCK-PIN 3122-A
SPINDLE-SEAL 3178-A
BOLT-SQUARE HEAD 91299-S2
AXLE 3006

LUBE FITTING 87907-S2
TIE ROD 3280

DRAG LINK 3304

LUBE FITTING 87907-S8
LUBE FITTING 87907-S2
TIE ROD 3279

FRONT AXLE BRACKET 3B178
FRONT AXLE 3006

BUMPER 4002

wise until the oval retainer seats in the oval hole. Install the two bolts. Make sure that the clamp bar has trapped the tang on the upper spring end.

16. Tighten the spring retainers to 18-25 ft.lb.

1975-88

1. Raise the front of the vehicle and place jackstands under the frame and a jack under the axle.

2. Remove the wheels.

3. Disconnect the shock absorber from the lower bracket.

4. Remove the two spring upper retainer attaching bolts from the top of the spring upper seat and remove the retainer.

5. Remove the nut attaching the spring lower retainer to the lower seat and axle and remove the retainer.

6. Place a safety chain through the spring to prevent it from suddenly coming loose. Slowly lower the axle and remove the spring.

To install:

7. Place the spring in position and raise the front axle.

8. Position the spring lower retainer over the stud and lower seat, and install the two attaching bolts.

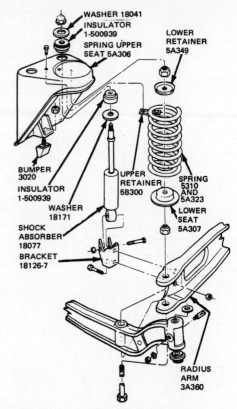

1973–74 front springs and related parts

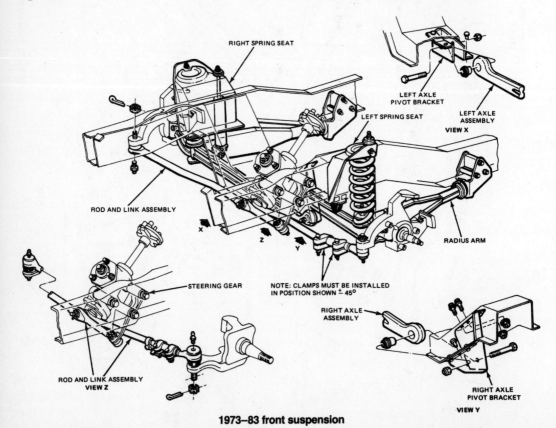

1973–83 front suspension

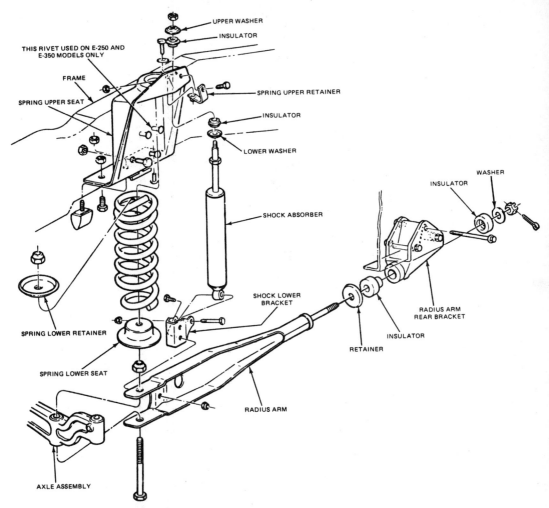

THIS RIVET USED ON E-250 AND E-350 MODELS ONLY

UPPER WASHER

INSULATOR

FRAME

SPRING UPPER SEAT

SPRING UPPER RETAINER

INSULATOR

LOWER WASHER

WASHER

INSULATOR

SHOCK ABSORBER

SHOCK LOWER BRACKET

RADIUS ARM REAR BRACKET

INSULATOR

RETAINER

SPRING LOWER RETAINER

SPRING LOWER SEAT

RADIUS ARM

AXLE ASSEMBLY

Front suspension used on all 1975–76 models and 1977–83 E-100/150

9. Position the upper retainer over the spring coil and against the spring upper seat, and install the two attaching bolts.

10. Observe the following torques:
- 1975-76 Upper retainer bolts: 20-30 ft.lb.
- 1977-78 Upper retainer bolts: 18-25 ft.lb.
- 1979-80 Upper retainer bolts: 30-70 ft.lb.
- 1981-82 Upper retaining bolts: 13-18 ft.lb.
- 1983-88 Upper retaining bolts to 20-30 ft.lb.
- 1976-82 Lower retainer attaching nuts: 30-70 ft.lb.
- 1983-88 Lower retainer attaching nuts: 70-100 ft.lb.
- Shock absorber: 40-60 ft.lb.

Shock Absorbers

TESTING

Bounce Test

Each shock absorber can be tested by bouncing the corner of the truck until maximum up and down movement is obtained. Let go of the truck. It should stop bouncing in 1-2 bounces. If not, the shock should be inspected for damage and possibly replaced.

Inspect the Shock Mounts

Check the shock mountings for worn or defective grommets, loose mounting nuts, interference or missing bump stops. If no apparent defects are noted, continue testing.

Inspecting Shocks for Leaks

Disconnect each shock lower mount and pull down on the shock until it is fully extended. inspect for leaks in the seal area. Shock absorber fluid is very thin and has a characteristic odor and dark brown color. Don't confuse the glossy paint on some shocks with leaking fluid. A slight trace of fluid is a normal condition; they are designed to seep a certain amount of fluid past the seals for lubrication. If you are in doubt as to whether the fluid on the shock is

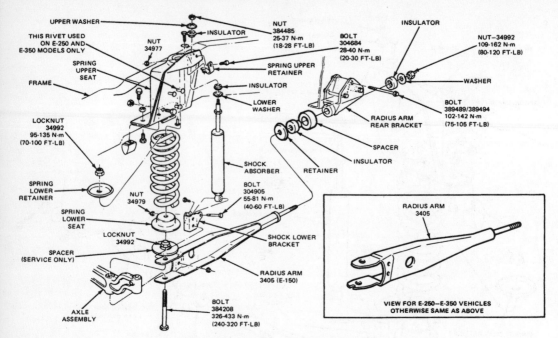

1984–88 front spring and shock absorber

coming from the shock itself or from other source, wipe the seal area clean and manually operate the shock (see the following procedure). Fluid will appear if the unit is leaking.

Manually Operating the Shocks

It may be necessary to fabricate a holding fixture for certain types of shock absorbers. If a suspected problem is in the front shocks, disconnect both front shock lower mountings.

NOTE: *When manually operating air shocks, the air line must be disconnected at the shock.*

Grip the lower end of the shock and pull down (rebound stroke) and then push up (compression stroke). The control arms will limit the movement of front shocks during the compression stroke. Compare the rebound resistance of both shocks and compare the compression resistance. Usually any shock showing a noticeable difference will be the one at fault.

If the shock has internal noises, extend the shock fully then exert an extra pull. If a small additional movement is felt, this usually means a loose piston and the shock should be replaced. Other noises that are cause for replacing shocks are a squeal after a full stroke in both directions, a clicking noise on fast reverse and a lag at reversal near mid-stroke.

REMOVAL AND INSTALLATION

To replace the front shock absorber, remove the self-locking nut, steel washer, and rubber

bushings at the upper end of the shock absorber. Remove the bolt and nut at the lower end and remove the shock absorber.

When installing a new shock absorber, use new rubber bushings. Position the shock absorber on the mounting brackets with the stud end at the top.

Install the rubber bushing, steel washer and self-locking nut at the upper end, and the bolt

1961–67 front shock absorber and stabilizer link lower connections

and nut at the lower end. Observe the following torques:

- Upper end:
  - 1961-67 — 40-55 ft.lb.
  - 1969-1974 — 15-20 ft.lb.
  - 1975 — 18-28 ft.lb.
  - 1976 — 25-35 ft.lb.
  - 1977-82 — 15-25 ft.lb.
  - 1983-88 — 18-28 ft.lb.
- Lower end:
  - 1961-67 — 40-55 ft.lb.
  - 1969-88 — 40-60 ft.lb.

Front Wheel Spindle

REMOVAL AND INSTALLATION

1961-67

1. Raise and support the front end on jackstands.
2. Remove the wheels.
3. Remove the hubs and brake drums.
4. Remove the brake shoes and springs.
5. Remove the wheel cylinders.
6. Unbolt and remove the brake backing plate from the spindle.
7. If a new spindle is being installed, remove the spindle arm-to-spindle retaining nut and cotter pin, then, drive the spindle arm from the spindle with a brass hammer.

If the old spindle is being reused, leave the arm attached to the spindle but disconnect the spindle arm from the connecting rod with a ball joint remover.

On the left spindle, also disconnect the drag link from the spindle arm with the same tool.

8. Drive the spindle bolt locking pin from the spindle bolt and axle.
9. Remove the rubber seals from the grooves in the top and bottom of the spindle bolt.
10. Drive the spindle bolt from the spindle and axle with a drift.
11. Remove the spindle and bearing from the axle. Be aware of any shims.

To install:

12. Position the spindle and bearing on the axle and install the spindle bolt. Torque the bolt to 250 ft.lb.
13. Install shims as necessary to take up the clearance between the upper spindle bore and the axle. Be sure that the notch in the spindle bolt is aligned with the locking pin hole in the axle.
14. Install the locking pin.
15. Install the rubber seals in the grooves in the spindle bolt.
16. If a new spindle is being installed, assemble the spindle arm to the spindle with the retaining nut and cotter pin.

If the original spindle is being installed, connect the spindle arm to the connecting rod end. Torque the nut to 55 ft.lb. On the left spin-

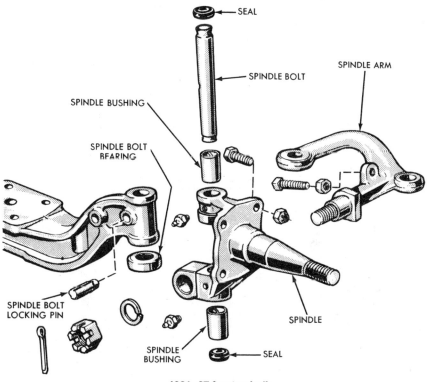

1961–67 front spindle

dle, also connect the steering drag link to the spindle arm. Torque the nut to 55 ft.lb.

17. Install the brake backing plate, wheel cylinder, and brake shoes and springs. Torque the backing plate fasteners to 60 ft.lb.

18. Install the brake drums and hubs, and adjust the wheel bearings.

19. Install the wheels.

20. Bleed the brakes.

1969-74

1. Raise and support the front end on jackstands.

2. Remove the wheels.

3. Remove the hub and drum assembly.

4. On E-100 and 200 models, remove the brake backing plate and spindle-to-spindle arm attaching bolt. Remove the spindle arm and brake backing plate from the spindle. Support the brake backing plate and hose.

5. On E-300 models, disconnect the steering linkage from the spindle and spindle arm.

6. Remove the nut and lockwasher from the locking pin and remove the pin.

7. Remove the upper and lower spindle bolt plugs. Drive the spindle bolt out from the top of the axle and remove the spindle and bearing. Knock out the seal.

8. Make sure that the spindle bolt hole in the axle is free of nicks, burrs or foreign material.

9. Install a new seal and coat the spindle bolt bushings and spindle bolt hole with oil. Place the spindle in position on the axle.

10. Pack the spindle thrust bearing with chassis lube and insert the bearing into the spindle with the open end (lip side) of the bearing seal facing downward into the spindle.

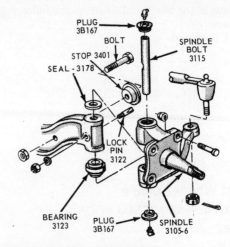

1973–74 E-300 front spindle

11. Install the spindle pin in the spindle with the locking pin notch in the spindle bolt lined up with the locking pin hole in the axle.

12. Drive the spindle bolt through the axle from the top side until the spindle bolt locking pin notch is lined up with the locking pin hole.

13. Make sure that the notch in the spindle pin is lined up with the locking pin hole in the axle and install a new locking pin.

14. Install the locking pin lockwasher and nut. Tighten the nut to 60 ft.lb. and install the spindle bolt plugs. Torque the plugs to 50 ft.lb.

15. On the E-100 and 200, install the backing plate and spindle arm. Torque the backing plate and spindle arm bolts to 30-50 ft.lb. Advance the castellated nut as required to align the cotter pin holes. NEVER BACK OFF THE NUT

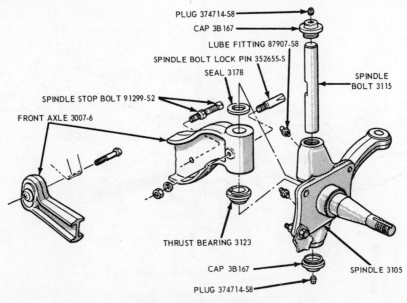

1969–72 E-300 front spindle

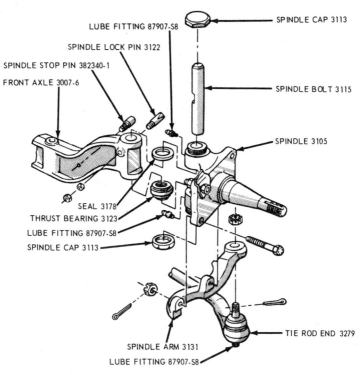

LUBE FITTING 87907-S8

SPINDLE LOCK PIN 3122

SPINDLE STOP PIN 382340-1

FRONT AXLE 3007-6

SPINDLE CAP 3113

SPINDLE BOLT 3115

SPINDLE 3105

SEAL 3178

THRUST BEARING 3123

LUBE FITTING 87907-S8

SPINDLE CAP 3113

TIE ROD END 3279

SPINDLE ARM 3131

LUBE FITTING 87907-S8

1969–72 E-100/200 front spindle

TO ALIGN THE HOLES! Install a new cotter pin.

16. On the E-300, connect the steering linkage to the spindle. Tighten the nut to 50-75 ft.lb. NEVER BACK OFF THE NUT TO ALIGN THE HOLES! Install a new cotter pin.

17. Install the hub and drum. Adjust the wheel bearing.

18. Install the wheels. Lubricate the spindle.

1975-88

1. Jack up the front of the truck and safely support it with jackstands.

2. Remove the wheels.

3. Remove the front brake caliper assembly and hold it out of the way with a piece of wire. Do not disconnect the brake line.

4. Remove the brake rotor from the spindle.

5. Remove the inner bearing cone and seal. discard the seal, as you'll be fitting a new one during installation.

6. Remove the brake dust shield.

7. Disconnect the steering linkage from the spindle arm using a tie rod removal tool.

8. Remove the nut and lockwasher from the lock pin and remove the lock pin.

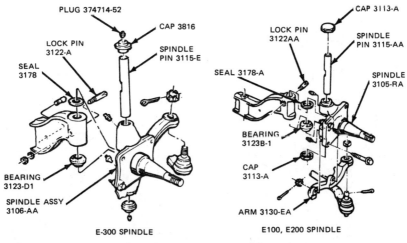

PLUG 374714-52

CAP 3816

LOCK PIN 3122-A

SPINDLE PIN 3115-E

SEAL 3178

BEARING 3123-D1

SPINDLE ASSY 3106-AA

E-300 SPINDLE

CAP 3113-A

LOCK PIN 3122AA

SPINDLE PIN 3115-AA

SEAL 3178-A

SPINDLE 3105-RA

BEARING 3123B-1

CAP 3113-A

ARM 3130-EA

E100, E200 SPINDLE

1973–74 front spindle, under 6,200 lb. GVW

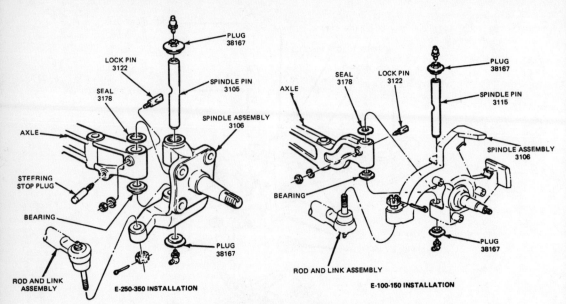

1975–83 front spindles

9. Remove the upper and lower spindle pin plugs.

10. Drive the spindle pin out from the top of the axle and remove the spindle and thrust bearing.

11. Remove the spindle pin seal and thrust bearing.

NOTE: *Always use new cotter pins! When aligning the cotter pin holes, NEVER back-off the nut; always advance the nut to align the holes!*

12. Make sure that the spindle pin holes are clean and free from burrs and nicks. Lightly coat the bore with chassis lube.

13. Install a new spindle pin seal, with the metal backing facing upwards towards the bushing, into the spindle. Gently press the seal into position.

14. Install a new thrust bearing with the lip flange facing down, towards the lower bushing. Press it in until the bearing is firmly seated against the surface of the spindle.

15. Lightly coat the bushing surfaces with chassis lube and place the spindle into position on the axle.

16. Insert the spindle pin, with the **T** stamped on one end, facing the top, and the notch in the pin aligned with the lock pin hole in the axle. Insert the spindle pin through the bushings

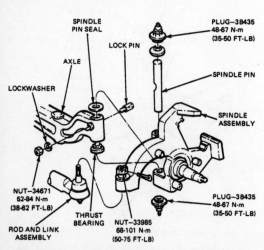

1984–88 E-150 front spindle

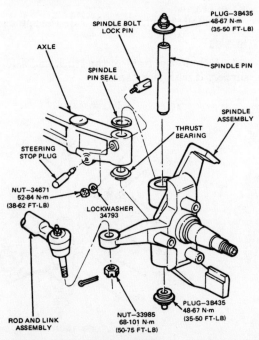

1984–88 E-250/350 front spindle

and the axle from the top, until the spindle pin notch and axle lock pin hole are aligned.

17. Install the lock pin with the threads pointing forward and the wedge groove facing the spindle pin notch. Firmly drive the lock pin into position and install the lockwasher and nut. Tighten the nut to 40-60 ft.lb.

18. Install the spindle pin plugs into the threads at the top and bottom of the spindle. Tighten the plugs to 35-50 ft.lb.

19. Lubricate the spindle pin and bushings with chassis lube through both fittings until grease is visible seeping past the upper seal and the thrust bearing slip joint. If grease does not escape at these top and bottom points, the spindle is installed incorrectly and rapid deterioration of the spindle components will result.

20. Install the brake dust shield.

21. Install the inner bearing cone and seal. Install the hub and rotor on the spindle.

22. Install the outer bearing cone, washer, and nut. Adjust the bearing end-play and install the nut retainer, cotter pin and dust cap.

23. Install the brake caliper. connect the steering linkage to the spindle. Tighten the nut to 70-100 ft.lb. and advance the nut as far necessary to install the cotter pin.

24. Install the wheels. Lower the truck and adjust toe-in if necessary.

Spindle Bushings

REPLACEMENT

1. Remove the spindle.
2. On E-150, use the following tools:
- Reamer T53T-3110-DA
- Remover/Installer/Driver D82T-3110-G
- Driver Handle D82T-3110-C

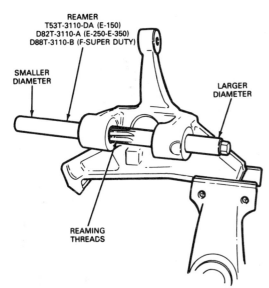

Reaming spindle bushings

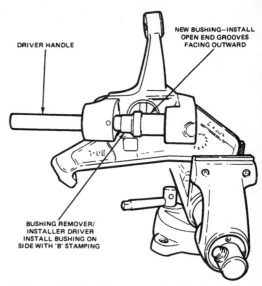

Bottom spindle bushing removal and installation

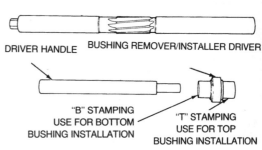

Spindle bushing removal/installation tools

3. On E-250/350, use the following tools
- Reamer D82T-3110-A
- Remover/Installer/Driver D82T-3110-B
- Driver Handle D82T-3110-C

NOTE: *Each side of the Remover/Installer/ Driver is marked with a T or a B. Use the side with the T to install the top spindle bushing; the side with the B to install the bottom spindle bushing.*

4. Remove and discard the seal from the bottom of the upper bushing bore.

5. Remove and install the top spindle bushing first.

a. Install the driver handle through the bottom bore.

b. Position a new bushing on the **T** side stamping of the driver.

c. The bushing must be installed so that the open end grooves will face outward when installed.

d. Position the new bushing and driver over the old bushing, insert the handle into the driver and drive the old bushing out while

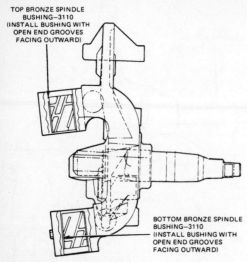

TOP BRONZE SPINDLE
BUSHING—3110
(INSTALL BUSHING WITH
OPEN END GROOVES
FACING OUTWARD)

BOTTOM BRONZE SPINDLE
BUSHING—3110
(INSTALL BUSHING WITH
OPEN END GROOVES
FACING OUTWARD)

Spindle bushing installation

driving the new bushing in. Drive until the tool is seated.

e. The bushing will then be seated to the proper depth of 0.080″ from the bottom of the upper spindle boss.

6. Remove and install the bottom spindle bushing.

a. Insert the driver handle through the top bushing bore.

b. Position a new bushing on the **B** side stamping of the driver. The bushing must be installed so that the open end grooves will face outward when installed.

c. Position the new bushing and driver over the old bushing, insert the handle into the driver and drive the old bushing out while driving the new bushing in. Drive until the tool is seated.

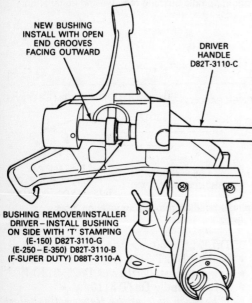

NEW BUSHING
INSTALL WITH OPEN
END GROOVES
FACING OUTWARD

DRIVER
HANDLE
D82T-3110-C

BUSHING REMOVER/INSTALLER
DRIVER – INSTALL BUSHING
ON SIDE WITH 'T' STAMPING
(E-150) D82T-3110-G
(E-250 – E-350) D82T-3110-B
(F-SUPER DUTY) D88T-3110-A

Top spindle bushing removal and installation

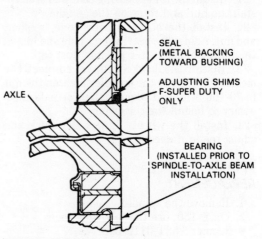

SEAL
(METAL BACKING
TOWARD BUSHING)

ADJUSTING SHIMS
F-SUPER DUTY
ONLY

AXLE

BEARING
(INSTALLED PRIOR TO
SPINDLE-TO-AXLE BEAM
INSTALLATION)

Spindle bearing seal installation

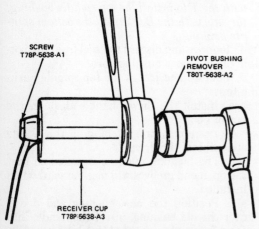

SCREW
T78P-5638-A1

PIVOT BUSHING
REMOVER
T80T-5638-A2

RECEIVER CUP
T78P-5638-A3

Removing axle pivot bushing

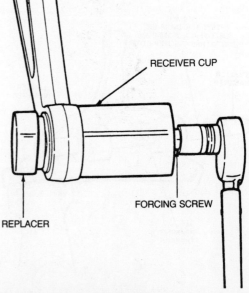

RECEIVER CUP

FORCING SCREW

REPLACER

Installing the axle pivot bushing

d. The bushing will then be seated to the proper depth of 0.130" from the bottom of the upper spindle boss.

7. Ream the new bushings to 0.001-0.003" larger than the diameter of the new spindle pin. Ream the top bushings first. Insert the smaller end of the reamer through the top bore and into the bottom bore until the threads are in position in the top bushing. Turn the tool until the threads exit the top bushing. Ream the bottom bushing. The larger diameter portion of the tool will act as a pilot in the top bushing to properly ream the bottom bushing.

8. Clean all metal shavings from the bushings. Coat the bushings with chassis lube.

9. Install a new seal on the driver on the side with the **T** stamping. Install the handle into the driver and push the seal into position in the bottom of the top bushing bore.

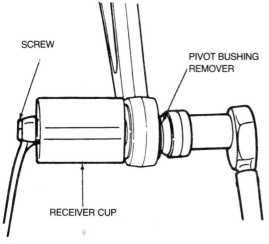

Removing axle pivot bushing

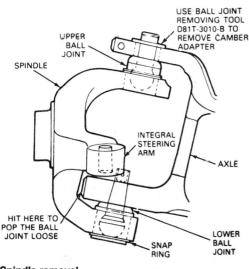

Spindle removal

Radius Arm

REMOVAL AND INSTALLATION

NOTE: *A torque wrench with a capacity of at least 350 ft.lb. is necessary, along with other special tools, for this procedure.*

1. Raise the front of the vehicle and place safety stands under the frame and a jack under the wheel or axle. Remove the wheels.

2. Disconnect the shock absorber from the radius arm bracket.

3. Remove the two spring upper retainer attaching bolts from the top of the spring upper seat and remove the retainer.

4. Remove the nut which attached the spring lower retainer to the lower seat and axle and remove the retainer.

5. Lower the axle and remove the spring.

6. Remove the spring lower seat and shim from the radius arm. The, remove the bolt and nut which attach the radius arm to the axle.

7. Remove the cotter pin, nut and washer from the radius arm rear attachment.

8. Remove the bushing from the radius arm and remove the radius arm from the vehicle.

9. Remove the inner bushing from the radius arm.

10. Position the radius arm to the axle and install the bolt and nut finger-tight.

11. Install the inner bushing on the radius arm and position the arm to the frame bracket.

12. Install the bushing, washer, and attaching nut. Tighten the nut to 120 ft.lb. and install the cotter pin.

13. Tighten the radius arm-to-axle bolt to 269-329 ft.lb.

14. Install the spring seat and insulator on the radius arm so that the hole in the seat fits over the arm-to-axle nut.

15. Install the spring.

16. Connect the shock absorber. Torque the nut and bolt to 40-60 ft.lb.

17. Install the wheels.

Stabilizer Bar

REMOVAL AND INSTALLATION

1. Raise and support the front end on jackstands.

2. Disconnect the right and left stabilizer bar ends from the link assembly.

3. Disconnect the retainer bolts and remove the stabilizer bar.

4. Disconnect the stabilizer link assemblies by loosening the right and left locknuts from their respective brackets. on the I-beams.

To install:

5. Loosely install the entire assembly. The links are marked with an **R** and **L** for identification.

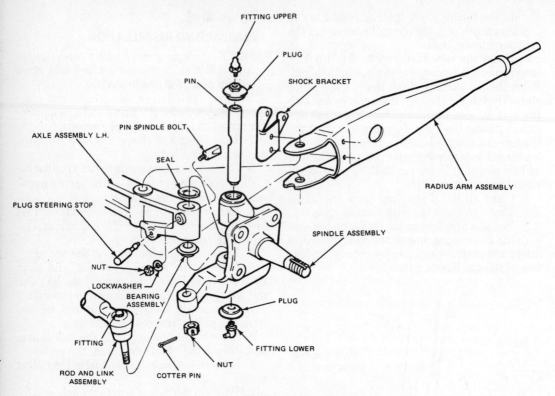

1977–83 E-250/350 radius arm

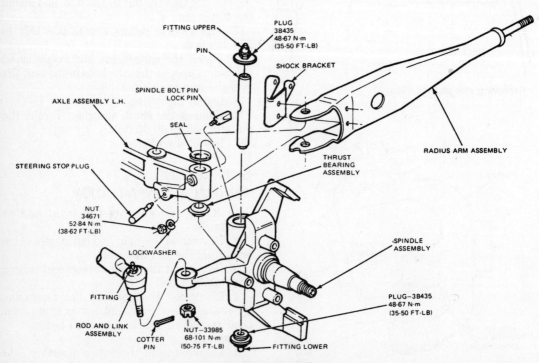

1984–88 E-250/350 radius arm

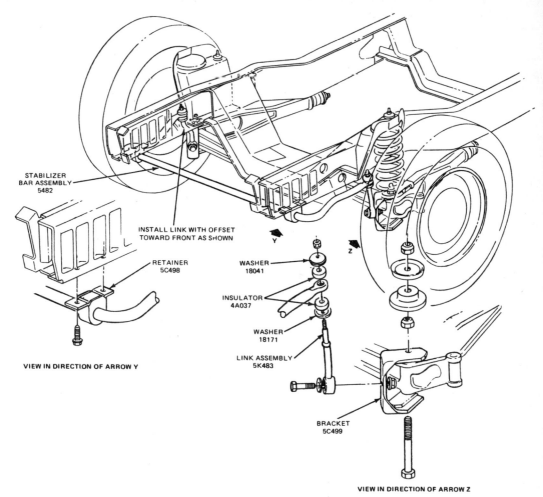

STABILIZER
BAR ASSEMBLY
5482

INSTALL LINK WITH OFFSET
TOWARD FRONT AS SHOWN

RETAINER
5C498

WASHER
18041

INSULATOR
4A037

WASHER
18171

LINK ASSEMBLY
5K483

BRACKET
5C499

VIEW IN DIRECTION OF ARROW Y

VIEW IN DIRECTION OF ARROW Z

1975–84 stabilizer bar

6. Tighten the link-to-stabilizer bar and axle bracket fasteners to 70 ft.lb.

7. Check to make sure that the insulators are properly seated and the stabilizer bar is centered.

8. On the E-150, torque the 6 stabilizer bar to crossmember attaching bolts to 35 ft.lb.

On the E-250 and E-350, torque the stabilizer bar-to-frame retainer bolts to 35 ft.lb.

Torque the frame mounting bracket nuts/bolts to 65 ft.lb.

Solid I-Beam Front Axle

REMOVAL AND INSTALLATION

1. Raise and support the front end on jackstands placed under the frame.

2. Remove the wheels and brake drums.

3. Disconnect the connecting rod from the spindles.

4. Disconnect the drag link from the left spindle arm.

5. At each spindle, do the following:

a. Remove the spindle-to-spindle arm cooter pin and nut, and drive the arm from the spindle with a plastic mallet.

b. Drive the spindle bolt locking pin from the spindle bolt and axle.

c. Remove the threaded caps from the top and bottom of the spindle.

d. Drive the spindle bolt from the spindle and axle.

e. Remove the spindle and brake carrier plate as an assembly from the axle. Tie the assembly up and out of the way.

6. Position a floor jack under the axle.

7. At each end of the axle, remove the nut and washer from the anchor bolt that attaches the lower end of the shock absorber and stabilizer link to the axle. Tap the anchor bolt out.

8. At each front spring, remove the attaching nuts, the two spring U-bolts and plates.

9. Lower the jack and roll the axle from under the van.

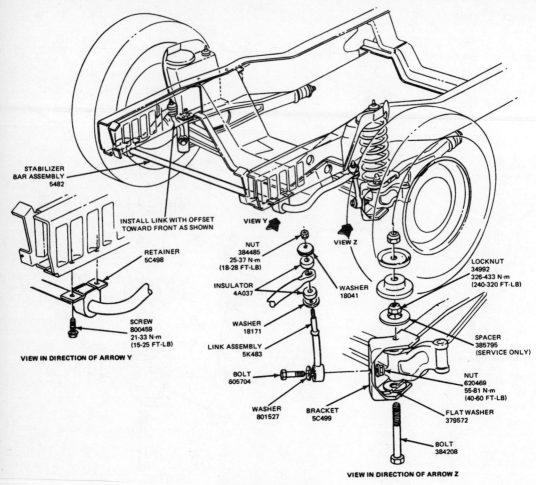

STABILIZER
BAR ASSEMBLY
5482

INSTALL LINK WITH OFFSET
TOWARD FRONT AS SHOWN

VIEW Y

VIEW Z

RETAINER
5C498

NUT
384485
25-37 N·m
(18-28 FT-LB)

LOCKNUT
34992
326-433 N·m
(240-320 FT-LB)

INSULATOR
4A037

WASHER
18041

SCREW
800459
21-33 N·m
(15-25 FT-LB)

WASHER
18171

LINK ASSEMBLY
5K483

SPACER
385795
(SERVICE ONLY)

VIEW IN DIRECTION OF ARROW Y

BOLT
605704

NUT
620469
55-81 N·m
(40-60 FT-LB)

WASHER
801527

BRACKET
5C499

FLAT WASHER
379572

BOLT
384208

VIEW IN DIRECTION OF ARROW Z

1985–88 stabilizer bar

10. Installation is the reverse of removal. Observe the following torques:

- Connecting rod-to-spindle arm nut: 45-55 ft.lb.
- Spindle-to-drag link nut: 45-55 ft.lb.
- Spindle arm-to-spindle nut: 250 ft.lb.

Twin I-Beam Axles

REMOVAL AND INSTALLATION

NOTE: *A torque wrench with a capacity of at least 350 ft.lb. is necessary, along with other special tools, for this procedure.*

1. Raise and support the front end on jackstands.
2. Remove the spindles.
3. Remove the springs.
4. Remove the stabilizer bar.
5. Remove the lower spring seats from the radius arms.
6. Remove the radius arm-to-axle bolts.
7. Remove the axle-to-frame pivot bolts and remove the axles.

To install:

8. Position the axle on the pivot bracket and loosely install the bolt/nut.
9. Position the other end on the radius arm and install the bolt. Torque the bolt to 269-329 ft.lb.
10. Install the spring seats.
11. Install the springs.
12. Torque the axle pivot bolts to 150 ft.lb.
13. Install the spindles.
14. Install the stabilizer bar.

FRONT END ALIGNMENT

Proper alignment of the front wheels must be maintained in order to ensure ease of steering and satisfactory tire life.

The most important factors of front wheel alignment are wheel camber, axle caster, and wheel toe-in.

Wheel toe-in is the distance by which the

wheels are closer together at the front than the rear.

Wheel camber is the amount the top of the wheels incline in or out from the vertical.

From axle caster is the amount in degrees that the top of the steering pivot pins are tilted toward the rear of the vehicle. Positive caster is inclination of the top of the pivot pin toward the rear of the vehicle.

These points should be checked at regulator intervals, particularly when the front axle has been subjected to a heavy impact. When checking wheel alignment, it is important that the wheel bearings and knuckle bearings be in proper adjustment. Loose bearings will affect instrument readings when checking the camber and toe-in.

If you start to notice abnormal tire wear patterns and handling characteristics (steering wheel is hard to return to the straight ahead position after negotiating a turn), then front end misalignment can be suspected. However, toe-in alignment maladjustment, rather than cast or camber, is more likely to be the cause of excessive or uneven tire wear on vehicles with twin I-beam front axles. Seldom is it necessary to correct caster or camber. Hard steering wheel return after turning a corner is, however, a characteristic of improper caster angle. Nevertheless, the toe-in alignment should be

Wheel Alignment Specifications

Years	Models	Caster (deg.) Range	Caster (deg.) Pref.	Camber (deg.) Range	Camber (deg.) Pref.	Toe-in (in.)	Front Wheel Angle (deg.)
1961	All	4¼P–5¾P	5P	⅛P–⅝P	⅜P	1/16–⅛	7½
1962	All	4¼P–5¾P	5P	⅛P–⅝P	⅜P	1/16–⅛	7½
1963	All	4¼P–5¾P	5P	⅛P–⅝P	⅜P	1/16–⅛	7½
1964	All	4¼P–5¾P	5P	⅛P–⅝P	⅜P	1/16–⅛	7½
1965	All	4¼P–5¾P	5P	⅛P–⅝P	⅜P	1/16–⅛	7½
1966	All	4½P–6P	5¼P	⅛P–⅝P	⅜P	1/16–⅛	7½
1967	All	4¼P–5¾P	5P	⅛P–⅝P	⅜P	1/16–⅛	7½
1969	All	4¼P–5¾P	5P	0–1P	½P	1/16–3/16	4
1970	All	½P–5½P	3P	½P–3½P	2P	1/16–3/16	4
1971	E-100	½P–5½P	3P	½P–3½P	2P	1/32–7/32	4
	E-200	½P–5½P	3P	½P–3½P	2P	1/32–7/32	4
	E-300	2½P–7½P	5P	½P–3½P	2P	1/32–7/32	4
1972	E-100	3½P–8½P	6P	½P–3½P	2P	1/32–7/32	4
	E-200	3½P–8½P	6P	½P–3½P	2P	1/32–7/32	4
	E-300	2½P–7½P	5P	½P–3½P	2P	1/32–7/32	4
1973	E-100	3½P–8½P	6P	½P–3½P	2P	1/32–7/32	4
	E-200	3½P–8½P	6P	½P–3½P	2P	1/32–7/32	4
	E-300	2½P–7½P	5P	½P–3½P	2P	1/32–7/32	4
1974	E-100	½P–8½P	4½P	½P–3½P	2P	3/32 out– 5/32 in	4
	E-200	½P–8½P	4½P	½P–3½P	2P	3/32 out– 5/32 in	4
	E-300	2½P–7½P	5P	½P–3½P	2P	3/32 out– 5/32 in	4
1975	E-100	½P–8½P	4½P	½P–3½P	2P	3/32 out– 5/32 in	4
	E-200	½P–8½P	4½P	½P–3½P	2P	3/32 out– 5/32 in	4
	E-300	2½P–7½P	5P	½P–3½P	2P	3/32 out– 5/32 in	4

Wheel Alignment Specifications (cont.)

Years	Models	Caster (deg.) Range	Caster (deg.) Pref.	Camber (deg.) Range	Camber (deg.) Pref.	Toe-in (in.)	Front Wheel Angle (deg.)
1976	E-100	½P–8½P	4½P	½P–3½P	2P	³⁄₃₂ out–⁵⁄₃₂ in	4
	E-200	½P–8½P	4½P	½P–3½P	2P	³⁄₃₂ out–⁵⁄₃₂ in	4
	E-300	2½–7½P	5P	½P–3½P	2P	³⁄₃₂ out–⁵⁄₃₂ in	4
1977	E-100	2P–5¾P	3⅞P	¾N–1¾P	½P	³⁄₃₂ out–⁵⁄₃₂ in	4
	E-150	2P–5¾P	3⅞P	¾N–1¾P	½P	³⁄₃₂ out–⁵⁄₃₂ in	4
	E-250	4P–8¼P	6⅛P	½N–2¼P	⅞P	³⁄₃₂ out–⁵⁄₃₂ in	4
	E-350	4P–8¼P	6⅛P	½N–2¼P	⅞P	³⁄₃₂ out–⁵⁄₃₂ in	4

Beginning in 1973 Ford has stated that no adjustments by bending or any other means may be made to effect changes in the caster or camber of its twin I-beam front axles. Adjustment is by replacement of parts only.
Beginning in 1978 specifications for checking caster and camber are determined by ride height. Use the following charts to determine the proper caster and camber for your vehicle.

Years	Ride Height (inches)	E-100, 150 Caster (deg)	E-100, 150 Camber (deg)	E-250, 350 Caster (deg)	E-250, 350 Camber (deg)
1978	4.00–4.25	3¾P–6½P	¾N–½P	6¼P–9P	1N–¾P
	4.25–4.50	3¼P–5¾P	½N–¾P	5¾P–8¼P	½N–1¼P
	4.50–4.75	2½P–5¼P	0–1¼P	5¼P–7¾P	0–1¾P
	4.75–5.00	2P–4½P	½P–1¾P	4½P–7¼P	½P–2¼P
	5.00–5.25	1¼P–4P	1¼P–2½P	4P–6½P	1P–2¾P
	5.25–5.50	¾P–3¼P	1¾P–3¼P	3¼P–6P	1½P–3¼P
	5.50–5.75	0–2¾P	½P–3¾P	—	—
1979	3.25–3.50	¼P–8P	1¾N–¼N	9P–10½P	1¾N–¼N
	3.50–3.75	5¾P–7¼P	1½N–¼P	8½P–9¾P	1½N–¼P
	3.75–4.00	5P–6¾P	1N–¾P	7⅞P–9P	1N–¾P
	4.00–4.25	4½P–5¾P	½N–1¼P	7⅛P–8½P	½N–1¼P
	4.25–4.50	4P–5¼P	0–1¾P	6½P–7¾P	0–1¾P
	4.50–4.75	3¼P–4½P	½P–2¼P	5¾P–7P	½P–2¼P
	4.75–5.00	2½P–4P	1P–2¾P	5¼P–6½P	1P–2¾P
	5.00–5.25	2P–3¼P	1½P–3¼P	4⅝P–6P	1½P–3¼P
	5.25–5.50	1½P–2¾P	2P–3¾P	4P–5½P	2P–3¾P
1980	3.25–3.50	6¼P–8P	1¾N–¼N	9P–10½P	1¾N–¼N
	3.50–3.75	5¾P–7¼P	1½N–¼P	8½P–9¾P	1½N–¼P
	3.75–4.00	5P–6¾P	1N–¾P	7⅞P–9P	1N–¾P
	4.00–4.25	4½P–5¾P	½N–1¼P	7⅛P–8½P	½N–1¼P
	4.25–4.50	4P–5¼P	0–1¾P	6½P–7¾P	0–1¾P
	4.50–4.75	3¼P–4½P	½P–2¼P	5¾P–7P	½P–2¼P

Wheel Alignment Specifications (cont.)

Years	Ride Height (Inches)	E-100, 150 Caster (deg)	E-100, 150 Camber (deg)	E-250, 350 Caster (deg)	E-250, 350 Camber (deg)
	4.75–5.00	2½P–4P	1P–2¾P	5¼P–6½P	1P–2¾P
	5.00–5.25	2P–3¼P	1½P–3¼P	4⅝P–6P	1½P–3¼P
	5.25–5.50	1½P–2¾P	2P–3¾P	4P–5½P	2P–3¾P
1981	3.25–3.50	6¼P–8P	1¾N–¼N	9P–10½P	1¾N–¼N
	3.50–3.75	5¾P–7¼P	1½N–¼P	8½P–9¾P	1½N–¼P
	3.75–4.00	5P–6¾P	1N–¾P	7⅞P–9P	1N–¾P
	4.00–4.25	4½P–5¾P	½N–1¼P	7⅛P–8½P	½N–1¼P
	4.25–4.50	4P–5¼P	0–1¾P	6½P–7¾P	0–1¾P
	4.50–4.75	3¼P–4½P	½P–2¼P	5¾P–7P	½P–2¼P
	4.75–5.00	2½P–4P	1P–2¾P	5¼P–6½P	1P–2¾P
	5.00–5.25	2P–3¼P	1½P–3¼P	4⅝P–6P	1½P–3¼P
	5.25–5.50	1½P–2¾P	2P–3¾P	4P–5½P	2P–3¾P
1982	3.25–3.50	6¼P–8P	1¾N–¼N	9P–10½P	1¾N–¼N
	3.50–3.75	5¾P–7¼P	1½N–¼P	8½P–9¾P	1½N–¼P
	3.75–4.00	5P–6¾P	1N–¾P	7⅞P–9P	1N–¾P
	4.00–4.25	4½P–5¾P	½N–1¼P	7⅛P–8½P	½N–1¼P
	4.25–4.50	4P–5¼P	0–1¾P	6½P–7¾P	0–1¾P
	4.50–4.75	3¼P–4½P	½P–2¼P	5¾P–7P	½P–2¼P
	4.75–5.00	2½P–4P	1P–2¾P	5¼P–6½P	1P–2¾P
	5.00–5.25	2P–3¼P	1½P–3¼P	4⅝P–6P	1½P–3¼P
	5.25–5.50	1½P–2¾P	2P–3¾P	4P–5½P	2P–3¾P
1983	3.25–3.50	6¼P–8P	1¾N–¼N	9P–10½P	1¾N–¼N
	3.50–3.75	5¾P–7¼P	1½N–¼P	8½P–9¾P	1½N–¼P
	3.75–4.00	5P–6¾P	1N–¾P	7⅞P–9P	1N–¾P
	4.00–4.25	4½P–5¾P	½N–1¼P	7⅛P–8½P	½N–1¼P
	4.25–4.50	4P–5¼P	0–1¾P	6½P–7¾P	0–1¾P
	4.50–4.75	3¼P–4½P	½P–2¼P	5¾P–7P	½P–2¼P
	4.75–5.00	2½P–4P	1P–2¾P	5¼P–6½P	1P–2¾P
	5.00–5.25	2P–3¼P	1½P–3¼P	4⅝P–6P	1½P–3¼P
	5.25–5.50	1½P–2¾P	2P–3¾P	4P–5½P	2P–3¾P
1984	3.25–3.50	6¼P–8P	1¾N–¼N	9P–10½P	1¾N–¼N
	3.50–3.75	5¾P–7¼P	1½N–¼P	8½P–9¾P	1½N–¼P
	3.75–4.00	5P–6¾P	1N–¾P	7⅞P–9P	1N–¾P
	4.00–4.25	4½P–5¾P	½N–1¼P	7⅛P–8½P	½N–1¼P
	4.25–4.50	4P–5¼P	0–1¾P	6½P–7¾P	0–1¾P
	4.50–4.75	3¼P–4½P	½P–2¼P	5¾P–7P	½P–2¼P
	4.75–5.00	2½P–4P	1P–2¾P	5¼P–6½P	1P–2¾P
	5.00–5.25	2P–3¼P	1½P–3¼P	4⅝P–6P	1½P–3¼P
	5.25–5.50	1½P–2¾P	2P–3¾P	4P–5½P	2P–3¾P
1985	3.25–3.50	6¼P–8P	1¾N–¼N	9P–10½P	1¾N–¼N

Wheel Alignment Specifications (cont.)

Years	Ride Height (Inches)	E-100, 150 Caster (deg)	E-100, 150 Camber (deg)	E-250, 350 Caster (deg)	E-250, 350 Camber (deg)
	3.50–3.75	5¾P–7¼P	1½N–¼P	8½P–9¾P	1½N–¼P
	3.75–4.00	5P–6¾P	1N–¾P	7⅞P–9P	1N–¾P
	4.00–4.25	4½P–5¾P	½N–1¼P	7⅛P–8½P	½N–1¼P
	4.25–4.50	4P–5¼P	0–1¾P	6½P–7¾P	0–1¾P
	4.50–4.75	3¼P–4½P	½P–2¼P	5¾P–7P	½P–2¼P
	4.75–5.00	2½P–4P	1P–2¾P	5¼P–6½P	1P–2¾P
	5.00–5.25	2P–3¼P	1½P–3¼P	4⅝P–6P	1½P–3¼P
	5.25–5.50	1½P–2¾P	2P–3¾P	4P–5½P	2P–3¾P
1986	3.75–4.00	4⅝P–6P	¾N–⅝P	7⅝P–9P	¾N–⅝P
	4.00–4.25	4⅞P–5⅞P	¾N–⅝P	6¾P–8¾P	¾N–⅝P
	4.25–4.50	3½P–5½P	¼N–⅞P	6⅞P–8⅞P	¼N–⅞P
	4.50–4.75	2½P–4½P	¼P–1½P	5½P–7½P	¼P–1½P
	4.75–5.00	2P–4P	⅞P–2P	5P–7P	⅞P–2P
	5.00–5.25	1½P–3½P	1¼P–2⅜P	3½P–5½P	1¼P–2⅜P
	5.25–5.50	¾P–2¾P	1⅝P–2¾P	2¾P–4¾P	1⅝P–2¾P
	5.50–5.75	¼P–2¼P	2¼P–3⅜P	2¼P–4¼P	2¼P–3⅜P
	5.75–6.00	0–2P	2¾P–3⅞P	2P–4P	2¾P–3⅞P
1987	3.75–4.00	4⅝P–6P	¾N–⅝P	7⅝P–9P	¾N–⅝P
	4.00–4.25	4⅞P–5⅞P	¾N–⅝P	6¾P–8¾P	¾N–⅝P
	4.25–4.50	3½P–5½P	¼N–⅞P	6⅞P–8⅞P	¼N–⅞P
	4.50–4.75	2½P–4½P	¼P–1½P	5½P–7½P	¼P–1½P
	4.75–5.00	2P–4P	⅞P–2P	5P–7P	⅞P–2P
	5.00–5.25	1½P–3½P	1¼P–2⅜P	3½P–5½P	1¼P–2⅜P
	5.25–5.50	¾P–2¾P	1⅝P–2¾P	2¾P–4¾P	1⅝P–2¾P
	5.50–5.75	¼P–2¼P	2¼P–3⅜P	2¼P–4¼P	2¼P–3⅜P
	5.75–6.00	0–2P	2¾P–3⅞P	2P–4P	2¾P–3⅞P
1988	3.75–4.00	7¾P–9P	¾N–½P	7P–8¾P	¾N–1¼P
	4.00–4.25	6¾P–8¾P	¾N–½P	6¼P–8¼P	¼N–1¼P
	4.25–4.50	6½P–8¼P	¼N–1¼P	5¾P–7¾P	¼P–1½P
	4.50–4.75	5½P–7½P	¼P–1½P	5¼P–7¼P	1P–2¼P
	4.75–5.00	5¼P–7¼P	⅞P–2⅛P	5P–7P	1¼P–2½P
	5.00–5.25	4¼P–6¼P	2P–3¼P	4⅛P–6¼P	2⅛P–3¼P
	5.25–5.50	4P–6P	1¾P–3P	3¾P–5¾P	2¼P–3½P
	5.50–5.75	3½P–5¼P	2¼P–3¼P	3⅛P–5⅛P	2½P–4¼P
	5.75–6.00	3⅛P–5⅛P	2⅝P–4P	—	—

Ride height is the measurement determined between the bottom of the spring tower and the top of the axle immediately below.

1978 toe-in: E-100, 150—0–¼ inch
       E-250, 350—³⁄₃₂ inch out–⁵⁄₃₂ inch in
1979–87 toe-in: all models ¹⁄₃₂ inch in
1988 toe-in: E-150—¹⁄₃₂ inch out
       E-250, 350—¹⁄₃₂ inch in

checked before the caster and camber angles after making the following checks:

1. Check the air pressure in all the tires. Make sure that the pressures agree with those specified for the tires and vehicle model being checked.

2. Raise the front of the vehicle off the ground. Grasp each front tire at the front and rear, and push the wheel inward and outward. If any free-play is noticed between the brake drum and the brake backing plate, adjust the wheel bearings.

NOTE: *There is supposed to be a very, very small amount of free-play present where the wheel bearings are concerned. Replace the bearing if they are worn or damaged.*

3. Check all steering linkage for wear or maladjustment. Adjust and/or replace all worn parts.

4. Check the torque on the steering gear mounting bolts and tighten as necessary.

5. Rotate each front wheel slowly, and observe the amount of lateral or side run-out. If the wheel run-out exceeds ⅛", replace the wheel or install the wheel on the rear.

6. Inspect the radius arms to be sure that they are not bent or damaged. Inspect the bushings at the radius arm-to-axle attachment and radius arm-to-frame attachment points for wear or looseness. Repair or replace parts as required.

Caster

The caster angles are designed into the front axle and cannot be adjusted.

Camber

The camber angles are designed into the front axle and cannot be adjusted.

Toe-in Adjustment

All Models

Toe-in can be measured by either a front end alignment machine or by the following method:

With the front wheels in the straight ahead position, measure the distance between the extreme front and the extreme rear of the front wheels. In other words, measure the distance across the undercarriage of the vehicle between the two front edges and the two rear edges of the two front wheels. Both of these measurements (front and rear of the two wheels) must be taken at an equal distance from the floor and at the approximate centerline of the spindle. The difference between these two distances is the amount that the wheels toe-in or toe-out. The wheels should be always adjusted to toe-in according to specifications.

1. Loosen the clamp bolts at each end of the left tie rod, seen from the front of the vehicle. Rotate the connecting rod tube until the correct toe-in is obtained, then tighten the clamp bolts.

2. Recheck the toe-in to make sure that no changes occurred when the bolts were tightened.

NOTE: *The clamps should be positioned $\frac{3}{16}$" from the end of the rod with the clamp bolts in a vertical position in front of the tube, with the nut down.*

REAR SUSPENSION

Semi-elliptic, leaf type springs are used at the rear axle. The front end of the spring is attached to a spring bracket on the frame side member. The rear end of the spring is attached to the bracket on the frame side member with a shackle. Each spring is attached to the axle with two U-bolts. A spacer is located between the spring and the axle on some applications to obtain a level ride position.

Springs

REMOVAL AND INSTALLATION

1. Raise the vehicle by the frame until the weight is off the rear spring with the tires still on the floor.

2. Remove the nuts from the spring U-bolts and drive the U-bolts from the U-bolt plate. Remove the auxiliary spring and spacer, if so equipped.

3. Remove the spring-to-bracket nut and bolt at the front of the spring.

4. Remove the upper and lower shackle nuts and bolts at the rear of the spring and remove the spring and shackle assembly from the rear shackle bracket.

5. Remove the bushings in the spring or shackle, if they are worn or damaged, and install new ones.

NOTE: *When installing the components, snug down the fasteners. Don't apply final torque to the fasteners until the truck is back on the ground.*

6. Position the spring in the shackle and install the upper shackle-to-spring nut and bolt with the bolt head facing outward.

7. Position the front end of the spring in the bracket and install the nut and bolt.

8. Position the shackle in the rear bracket and install the nut and bolt.

9. Position the spring on top of the axle with the spring center bolts centered in the hole provided in the seat. Install the auxiliary spring and spacer, if so equipped.

10. Install the spring U-bolts, plate and nuts.

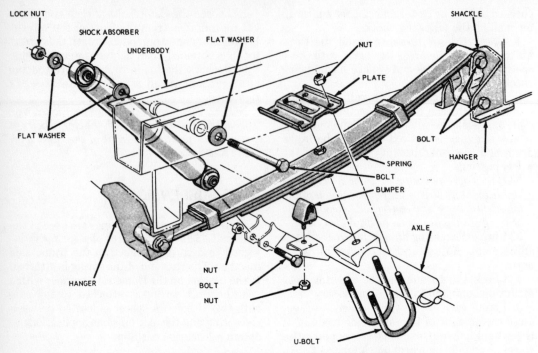

Rear spring installation for 1969–75 E-100/150/200

11. Lower the vehicle to the floor and tighten the attaching hardware as follows:

U-bolts nuts
- 1961-67: 30-40 ft.lb.
- 1969 E-100, 200:
  - ½"-13 — 45-60 ft.lb.
  - ⁹⁄₁₆"-12 — 100-120 ft.lb.
- 1974-76 E-100/150, 200/250:
  - ½"-13 — 45-70 ft.lb.
  - ⁹⁄₁₆"-12 — 85-115 ft.lb.

- 1969-77 E250HD, E-300/350: 150-200 ft.lb.
- 1977 E-100/150: 74-107 ft.lb.
- 1978-81 E-100/150: 85-115 ft.lb.
- 1978-81 E-250/350: 150-200 ft.lb.
- 1982-83 E-100/150: 75-105 ft.lb.
- 1984-88 E-150, 250: 74-107 ft.lb.
- 1982-88 E-250HD, 350: 150-180 ft.lb.

Spring to front spring hanger
- 1961-67: 30-50 ft.lb.

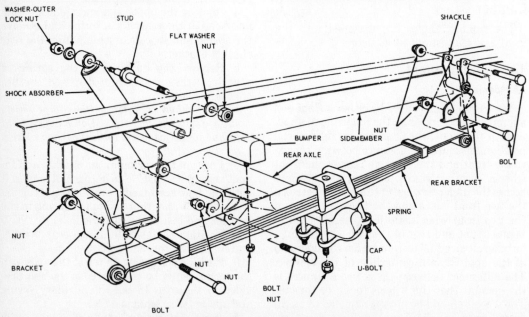

Rear spring installation for 1969–75 E-250/300-350

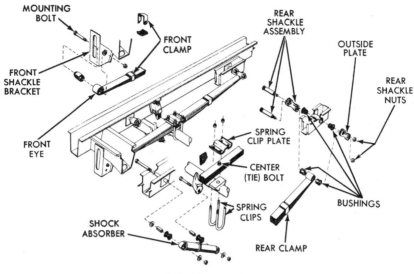

1961–65 rear spring

- 1969: 90-130 ft.lb.
- 1974-75:
    - $^9/_{16}$"-12 — 75-105 ft.lb.
    - $^5/_8$"-11 — 150-190 ft.lb.
- 1976: 150-190 ft.lb.
- 1977: 150-204 ft.lb.
- 1978-79: 110-160 ft.lb.
- 1980-83: 150-200 ft.lb.
- 1984-88: 150-204 ft.lb.

Spring to rear spring hanger
- 1961-64: 20-32 ft.lb.
- 1965-67: 30-40 ft.lb.
- 1969: 55-80 ft.lb.
- 1974-75: 55-90 ft.lb.
- 1976-88: 75-105 ft.lb.

Shock Absorbers

TESTING

Check, inspect and test the rear shock absorbers in the same manner as outlined for the front shock absorbers.

REMOVAL AND INSTALLATION

To replace the rear shock absorber, remove the self-locking nut, steel washer, and rubber bushings at the upper and lower ends and remove the shock absorber.

When a new shock absorber is installed, use new rubber bushings. Position the shock on the

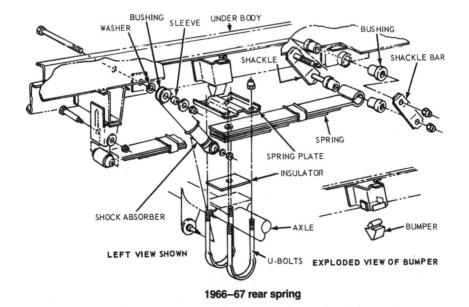

1966–67 rear spring

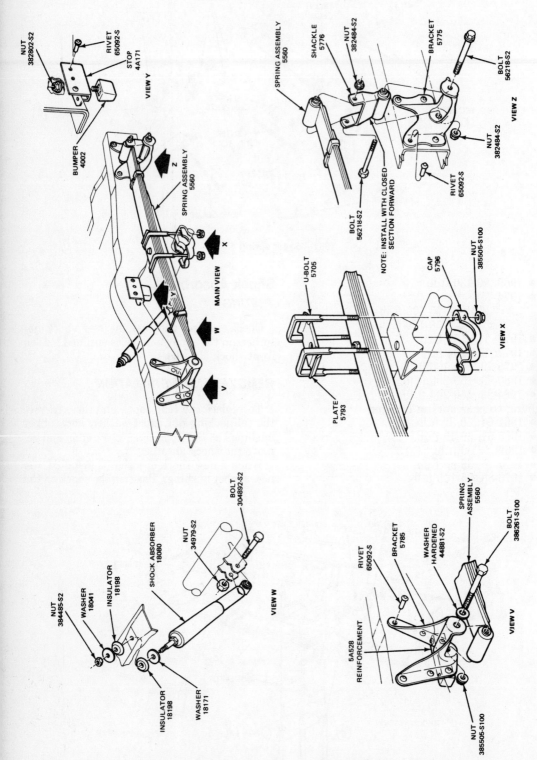

1976—78 E250/350 rear spring

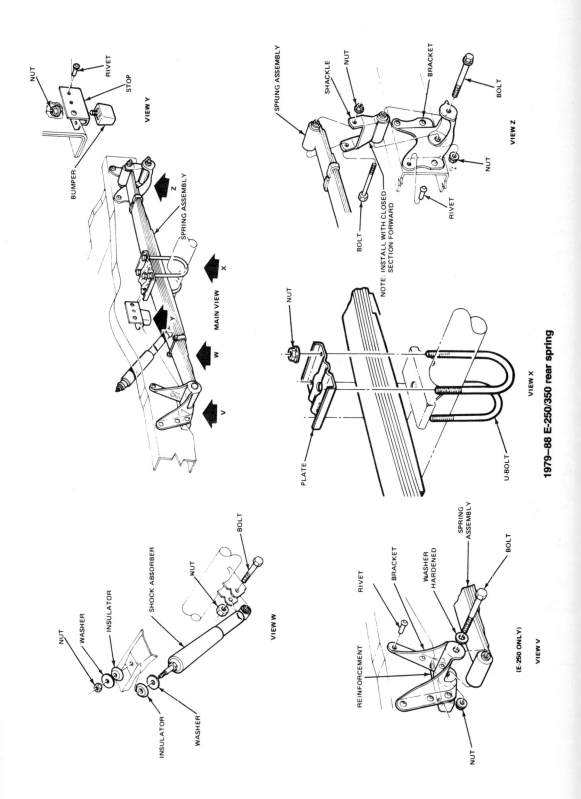

VIEW Y

NUT
RIVET
STOP
BUMPER
SPRING ASSEMBLY
Z
X
MAIN VIEW
Y
W
V

VIEW Z

SPRING ASSEMBLY
SHACKLE
NUT
BRACKET
BOLT
NUT
RIVET
BOLT
NOTE: INSTALL WITH CLOSED
SECTION FORWARD

VIEW X

NUT
PLATE
U-BOLT

1979—88 E-250/350 rear spring

VIEW W

NUT
WASHER
INSULATOR
SHOCK ABSORBER
BOLT
NUT
INSULATOR
WASHER

VIEW V

(E-250 ONLY)

RIVET
BRACKET
WASHER
HARDENED
SPRING
ASSEMBLY
BOLT
REINFORCEMENT
NUT

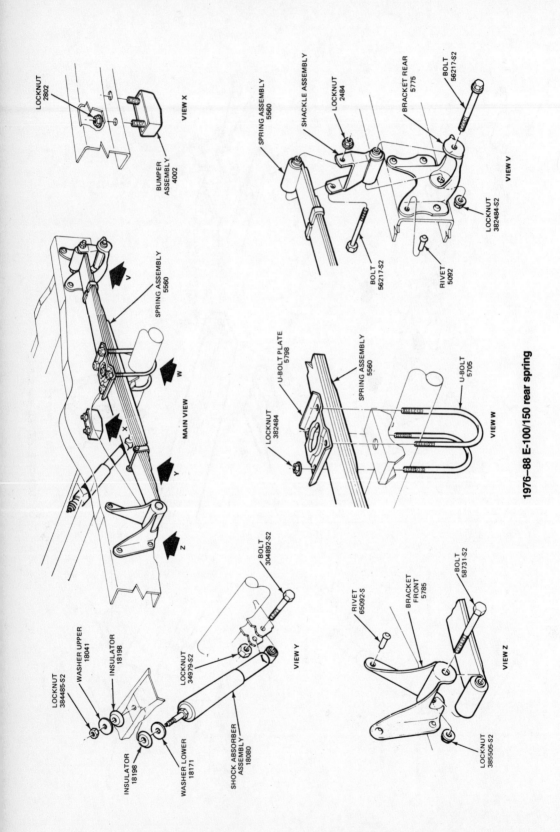

LOCKNUT 2802

BUMPER ASSEMBLY 4002

VIEW X

SPRING ASSEMBLY 5560

SHACKLE ASSEMBLY

LOCKNUT 2484

BRACKET REAR 5775

BOLT 56217-S2

VIEW V

LOCKNUT 382484-S2

BOLT 56217-S2

RIVET 5092

SPRING ASSEMBLY 5560

V

W

X

Y

MAIN VIEW

Z

U-BOLT PLATE 5798

SPRING ASSEMBLY 5560

U-BOLT 5705

LOCKNUT 382484

VIEW W

1976—88 E-100/150 rear spring

BOLT 304892-S2

LOCKNUT 34979-S2

SHOCK ABSORBER ASSEMBLY 18080

VIEW Y

LOCKNUT 384485-S2

WASHER UPPER 18041

INSULATOR 18198

INSULATOR 18198

WASHER LOWER 18171

RIVET 65092-S

BRACKET FRONT 5785

BOLT 58731-S2

VIEW Z

LOCKNUT 385505-S2

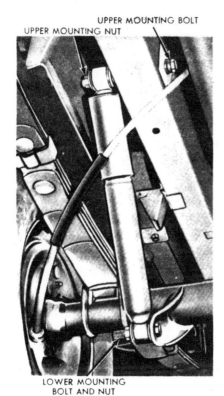

UPPER MOUNTING NUT
UPPER MOUNTING BOLT

LOWER MOUNTING
BOLT AND NUT

Early model rear shock installation

mounting brackets with the large hole at the top.

Install the rubber bushings, steel washer, and self-locking nuts. Tighten the nut until it rests against the shoulder of the stud. Observe the following torques:

Upper
- 1961-67: 30-40 ft.lb.
- 1969-73 E-100, 200: 40-50 ft.lb.
- 1969-73 E-300: 50-75 ft.lb.
- 1974-75: 40-60 ft.lb.
- 1976-77: 18-28 ft.lb.
- 1978-83: 15-25 ft.lb.
- 1984-88: 18-28 ft.lb.

Lower
- 1961-67: 30-40 ft.lb.
- 1969-88: 40-60 ft.lb.

STEERING

Steering Wheel

REMOVAL AND INSTALLATION

1. Set the front wheel in the straight ahead position and make chalk marks on the column and steering wheel hub for alignment purposes during installation.

2. Disconnect the negative battery cable.

3. Remove the one screw from the underside of each steering wheel spoke, and lift the horn switch assembly (steering wheel pad) from the steering wheel. On vehicles equipped with the sport steering wheel option, pry the button cover off with a screwdriver.

4. Disconnect the horn switch wires at the connector and remove the switch assembly. On trucks equipped with speed control, squeeze the J-clip ground wire terminal firmly and pull it out of the hole in the steering wheel. Don't pull the wire out without squeezing the clip.

5. Remove the horn switch assembly.

6. Remove the steering wheel retaining nut and remove the steering wheel with a puller.

WARNING: *Never hammer on the wheel or shaft to remove it! Never use a knock-off type puller.*

7. Install the steering wheel in the reverse order of removal. Tighten the shaft nut to 40 ft.lb.

Turn Signal Switch

REMOVAL AND INSTALLATION

1. Disconnect the battery ground cable.

2. Remove the steering wheel.

3. Remove the turn signal lever by unscrewing it from the steering column.

4. Disconnect the turn signal indicator switch wiring connector plug by lifting up the tabs on the side of the plug and pulling it apart.

5. Remove the switch assembly attaching screws.

6. On trucks with a fixed column, lift the switch out of the column and guide the connector plug through the opening in the shift socket.

7. On trucks with a tilt column, remove the connector plug before removing the switch from the column. The shift socket opening is not large enough for the plug connector to pass through.

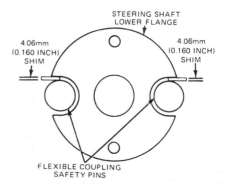

STEERING SHAFT
LOWER FLANGE

4.06mm
(0.160 INCH)
SHIM

4.06mm
(0.160 INCH)
SHIM

FLEXIBLE COUPLING
SAFETY PINS

VIEWED FROM TOP OF
STEERING COLUMN

1982–88 flexible coupling alignment

Troubleshooting the Steering Column

Problem	Cause	Solution
Will not lock	• Lockbolt spring broken or defective	• Replace lock bolt spring
High effort (required to turn ignition key and lock cylinder)	• Lock cylinder defective • Ignition switch defective • Rack preload spring broken or deformed • Burr on lock sector, lock rack, housing, support or remote rod coupling • Bent sector shaft • Defective lock rack • Remote rod bent, deformed • Ignition switch mounting bracket bent • Distorted coupling slot in lock rack (tilt column)	• Replace lock cylinder • Replace ignition switch • Replace preload spring • Remove burr • Replace shaft • Replace lock rack • Replace rod • Straighten or replace • Replace lock rack
Will stick in "start"	• Remote rod deformed • Ignition switch mounting bracket bent	• Straighten or replace • Straighten or replace
Key cannot be removed in "off-lock"	• Ignition switch is not adjusted correctly • Defective lock cylinder	• Adjust switch • Replace lock cylinder
Lock cylinder can be removed without depressing retainer	• Lock cylinder with defective retainer • Burr over retainer slot in housing cover or on cylinder retainer	• Replace lock cylinder • Remove burr
High effort on lock cylinder between "off" and "off-lock"	• Distorted lock rack • Burr on tang of shift gate (automatic column) • Gearshift linkage not adjusted	• Replace lock rack • Remove burr • Adjust linkage
Noise in column	• One click when in "off-lock" position and the steering wheel is moved (all except automatic column) • Coupling bolts not tightened • Lack of grease on bearings or bearing surfaces • Upper shaft bearing worn or broken • Lower shaft bearing worn or broken • Column not correctly aligned • Coupling pulled apart • Broken coupling lower joint • Steering shaft snap ring not seated • Shroud loose on shift bowl. Housing loose on jacket—will be noticed with ignition in "off-lock" and when torque is applied to steering wheel.	• Normal—lock bolt is seating • Tighten pinch bolts • Lubricate with chassis grease • Replace bearing assembly • Replace bearing. Check shaft and replace if scored. • Align column • Replace coupling • Repair or replace joint and align column • Replace ring. Check for proper seating in groove. • Position shroud over lugs on shift bowl. Tighten mounting screws.
High steering shaft effort	• Column misaligned • Defective upper or lower bearing • Tight steering shaft universal joint • Flash on I.D. of shift tube at plastic joint (tilt column only) • Upper or lower bearing seized	• Align column • Replace as required • Repair or replace • Replace shift tube • Replace bearings
Lash in mounted column assembly	• Column mounting bracket bolts loose • Broken weld nuts on column jacket • Column capsule bracket sheared	• Tighten bolts • Replace column jacket • Replace bracket assembly

Troubleshooting the Steering Column (cont.)

Problem	Cause	Solution
Lash in mounted column assembly (cont.)	• Column bracket to column jacket mounting bolts loose	• Tighten to specified torque
	• Loose lock shoes in housing (tilt column only)	• Replace shoes
	• Loose pivot pins (tilt column only)	• Replace pivot pins and support
	• Loose lock shoe pin (tilt column only)	• Replace pin and housing
	• Loose support screws (tilt column only)	• Tighten screws
Housing loose (tilt column only)	• Excessive clearance between holes in support or housing and pivot pin diameters	• Replace pivot pins and support
	• Housing support-screws loose	• Tighten screws
Steering wheel loose—every other tilt position (tilt column only)	• Loose fit between lock shoe and lock shoe pivot pin	• Replace lock shoes and pivot pin
Steering column not locking in any tilt position (tilt column only)	• Lock shoe seized on pivot pin	• Replace lock shoes and pin
	• Lock shoe grooves have burrs or are filled with foreign material	• Clean or replace lock shoes
	• Lock shoe springs weak or broken	• Replace springs
Noise when tilting column (tilt column only)	• Upper tilt bumpers worn	• Replace tilt bumper
	• Tilt spring rubbing in housing	• Lubricate with chassis grease
One click when in "off-lock" position and the steering wheel is moved	• Seating of lock bolt	• None. Click is normal characteristic sound produced by lock bolt as it seats.
High shift effort (automatic and tilt column only)	• Column not correctly aligned	• Align column
	• Lower bearing not aligned correctly	• Assemble correctly
	• Lack of grease on seal or lower bearing areas	• Lubricate with chassis grease
Improper transmission shifting— automatic and tilt column only	• Sheared shift tube joint	• Replace shift tube
	• Improper transmission gearshift linkage adjustment	• Adjust linkage
	• Loose lower shift lever	• Replace shift tube

Troubleshooting the Ignition Switch

Problem	Cause	Solution
Ignition switch electrically inoperative	• Loose or defective switch connector	• Tighten or replace connector
	• Feed wire open (fusible link)	• Repair or replace
	• Defective ignition switch	• Replace ignition switch
Engine will not crank	• Ignition switch not adjusted properly	• Adjust switch
Ignition switch wil not actuate mechanically	• Defective ignition switch	• Replace switch
	• Defective lock sector	• Replace lock sector
	• Defective remote rod	• Replace remote rod
Ignition switch cannot be adjusted correctly	• Remote rod deformed	• Repair, straighten or replace

Troubleshooting the Turn Signal Switch

Problem	Cause	Solution
Turn signal will not cancel	• Loose switch mounting screws	• Tighten screws
	• Switch or anchor bosses broken	• Replace switch
	• Broken, missing or out of position detent, or cancelling spring	• Reposition springs or replace switch as required

Troubleshooting the Turn Signal Switch (cont.)

Problem	Cause	Solution
Turn signal difficult to operate	• Turn signal lever loose • Switch yoke broken or distorted • Loose or misplaced springs • Foreign parts and/or materials in switch • Switch mounted loosely	• Tighten mounting screws • Replace switch • Reposition springs or replace switch • Remove foreign parts and/or material • Tighten mounting screws
Turn signal will not indicate lane change	• Broken lane change pressure pad or spring hanger • Broken, missing or misplaced lane change spring • Jammed wires	• Replace switch • Replace or reposition as required • Loosen mounting screws, reposition wires and retighten screws
Turn signal will not stay in turn position	• Foreign material or loose parts impeding movement of switch yoke • Defective switch	• Remove material and/or parts • Replace switch
Hazard switch cannot be pulled out	• Foreign material between hazard support cancelling leg and yoke	• Remove foreign material. No foreign material impeding function of hazard switch—replace turn signal switch.
No turn signal lights	• Inoperative turn signal flasher • Defective or blown fuse • Loose chassis to column harness connector • Disconnect column to chassis connector. Connect new switch to chassis and operate switch by hand. If vehicle lights now operate normally, signal switch is inoperative • If vehicle lights do not operate, check chassis wiring for opens, grounds, etc.	• Replace turn signal flasher • Replace fuse • Connect securely • Replace signal switch • Repair chassis wiring as required
Instrument panel turn indicator lights on but not flashing	• Burned out or damaged front or rear turn signal bulb • If vehicle lights do not operate, check light sockets for high resistance connections, the chassis wiring for opens, grounds, etc. • Inoperative flasher • Loose chassis to column harness connection • Inoperative turn signal switch • To determine if turn signal switch is defective, substitute new switch into circuit and operate switch by hand. If the vehicle's lights operate normally, signal switch is inoperative.	• Replace bulb • Repair chassis wiring as required • Replace flasher • Connect securely • Replace turn signal switch • Replace turn signal switch
Stop light not on when turn indicated	• Loose column to chassis connection • Disconnect column to chassis connector. Connect new switch into system without removing old. Operate switch by hand. If brake lights work with switch in the turn position, signal switch is defective.	• Connect securely • Replace signal switch

Troubleshooting the Turn Signal Switch (cont.)

Problem	Cause	Solution
Stop light not on when turn indicated (cont.)	• If brake lights do not work, check connector to stop light sockets for grounds, opens, etc.	• Repair connector to stop light circuits using service manual as guide
Turn indicator panel lights not flashing	• Burned out bulbs • High resistance to ground at bulb socket • Opens, ground in wiring harness from front turn signal bulb socket to indicator lights	• Replace bulbs • Replace socket • Locate and repair as required
Turn signal lights flash very slowly	• High resistance ground at light sockets • Incorrect capacity turn signal flasher or bulb • If flashing rate is still extremely slow, check chassis wiring harness from the connector to light sockets for high resistance • Loose chassis to column harness connection • Disconnect column to chassis connector. Connect new switch into system without removing old. Operate switch by hand. If flashing occurs at normal rate, the signal switch is defective.	• Repair high resistance grounds at light sockets • Replace turn signal flasher or bulb • Locate and repair as required • Connect securely • Replace turn signal switch
Hazard signal lights will not flash— turn signal functions normally	• Blow fuse • Inoperative hazard warning flasher • Loose chassis-to-column harness connection • Disconnect column to chassis connector. Connect new switch into system without removing old. Depress the hazard warning lights. If they now work normally, turn signal switch is defective. • If lights do not flash, check wiring harness "K" lead for open between hazard flasher and connector. If open, fuse block is defective	• Replace fuse • Replace hazard warning flasher in fuse panel • Conect securely • Replace turn signal switch • Repair or replace brown wire or connector as required

Troubleshooting the Manual Steering Gear

Problem	Cause	Solution
Hard or erratic steering	• Incorrect tire pressure • Insufficient or incorrect lubrication • Suspension, or steering linkage parts damaged or misaligned • Improper front wheel alignment • Incorrect steering gear adjustment • Sagging springs	• Inflate tires to recommended pressures • Lubricate as required (refer to Maintenance Section) • Repair or replace parts as necessary • Adjust incorrect wheel alignment angles • Adjust steering gear • Replace springs
Play or looseness in steering	• Steering wheel loose • Steering linkage or attaching parts loose or worn	• Inspect shaft spines and repair as necessary. Tighten attaching nut and stake in place. • Tighten, adjust, or replace faulty components

Troubleshooting the Manual Steering Gear (cont.)

Problem	Cause	Solution
Play or looseness in steering (cont.)	• Pitman arm loose	• Inspect shaft splines and repair as necessary. Tighten attaching nut and stake in place
	• Steering gear attaching bolts loose	• Tighten bolts
	• Loose or worn wheel bearings	• Adjust or replace bearings
	• Steering gear adjustment incorrect or parts badly worn	• Adjust gear or replace defective parts
Wheel shimmy or tramp	• Improper tire pressure	• Inflate tires to recommended pressures
	• Wheels, tires, or brake rotors out-of-balance or out-of-round	• Inspect and replace or balance parts
	• Inoperative, worn, or loose shock absorbers or mounting parts	• Repair or replace shocks or mountings
	• Loose or worn steering or suspension parts	• Tighten or replace as necessary
	• Loose or worn wheel bearings	• Adjust or replace bearings
	• Incorrect steering gear adjustments	• Adjust steering gear
	• Incorrect front wheel alignment	• Correct front wheel alignment
Tire wear	• Improper tire pressure	• Inflate tires to recommended pressures
	• Failure to rotate tires	• Rotate tires
	• Brakes grabbing	• Adjust or repair brakes
	• Incorrect front wheel alignment	• Align incorrect angles
	• Broken or damaged steering and suspension parts	• Repair or replace defective parts
	• Wheel runout	• Replace faulty wheel
	• Excessive speed on turns	• Make driver aware of conditions
Vehicle leads to one side	• Improper tire pressures	• Inflate tires to recommended pressures
	• Front tires with uneven tread depth, wear pattern, or different cord design (i.e., one bias ply and one belted or radial tire on front wheels)	• Install tires of same cord construction and reasonably even tread depth, design, and wear pattern
	• Incorrect front wheel alignment	• Align incorrect angles
	• Brakes dragging	• Adjust or repair brakes
	• Pulling due to uneven tire construction	• Replace faulty tire

Troubleshooting the Power Steering Gear

Problem	Cause	Solution
Hissing noise in steering gear	• There is some noise in all power steering systems. One of the most common is a hissing sound most evident at standstill parking. There is no relationship between this noise and performance of the steering. Hiss may be expected when steering wheel is at end of travel or when slowly turning at standstill.	• Slight hiss is normal and in no way affects steering. Do not replace valve unless hiss is extremely objectionable. A replacement valve will also exhibit slight noise and is not always a cure. Investigate clearance around flexible coupling rivets. Be sure steering shaft and gear are aligned so flexible coupling rotates in a flat plane and is not distorted as shaft rotates. Any metal-to-metal contacts through flexible coupling will transmit valve hiss into passenger compartment through the steering column.

Troubleshooting the Power Steering Gear (cont.)

Problem	Cause	Solution
Rattle or chuckle noise in steering gear	• Gear loose on frame	• Check gear-to-frame mounting screws. Tighten screws to 88 N·m (65 foot pounds) torque.
	• Steering linkage looseness	• Check linkage pivot points for wear. Replace if necessary.
	• Pressure hose touching other parts of car	• Adjust hose position. Do not bend tubing by hand.
	• Loose pitman shaft over center adjustment	• Adjust to specifications
	NOTE: A slight rattle may occur on turns because of increased clearance off the "high point." This is normal and clearance must not be reduced below specified limits to eliminate this slight rattle.	
	• Loose pitman arm	• Tighten pitman arm nut to specifications
Squawk noise in steering gear when turning or recovering from a turn	• Damper O-ring on valve spool cut	• Replace damper O-ring
Poor return of steering wheel to center	• Tires not properly inflated	• Inflate to specified pressure
	• Lack of lubrication in linkage and ball joints	• Lube linkage and ball joints
	• Lower coupling flange rubbing against steering gear adjuster plug	• Loosen pinch bolt and assemble properly
	• Steering gear to column misalignment	• Align steering column
	• Improper front wheel alignment	• Check and adjust as necessary
	• Steering linkage binding	• Replace pivots
	• Ball joints binding	• Replace ball joints
	• Steering wheel rubbing against housing	• Align housing
	• Tight or frozen steering shaft bearings	• Replace bearings
	• Sticking or plugged valve spool	• Remove and clean or replace valve
	• Steering gear adjustments over specifications	• Check adjustment with gear out of car. Adjust as required.
	• Kink in return hose	• Replace hose
Car leads to one side or the other (keep in mind road condition and wind. Test car in both directions on flat road)	• Front end misaligned	• Adjust to specifications
	• Unbalanced steering gear valve	• Replace valve
	NOTE: If this is cause, steering effort will be very light in direction of lead and normal or heavier in opposite direction	
Momentary increase in effort when turning wheel fast to right or left	• Low oil level	• Add power steering fluid as required
	• Pump belt slipping	• Tighten or replace belt
	• High internal leakage	• Check pump pressure. (See pressure test)
Steering wheel surges or jerks when turning with engine running especially during parking	• Low oil level	• Fill as required
	• Loose pump belt	• Adjust tension to specification
	• Steering linkage hitting engine oil pan at full turn	• Correct clearance
	• Insufficient pump pressure	• Check pump pressure. (See pressure test). Replace relief valve if defective.
	• Pump flow control valve sticking	• Inspect for varnish or damage, replace if necessary

Troubleshooting the Power Steering Gear (cont.)

Problem	Cause	Solution
Excessive wheel kickback or loose steering	• Air in system	• Add oil to pump reservoir and bleed by operating steering. Check hose connectors for proper torque and adjust as required.
	• Steering gear loose on frame	• Tighten attaching screws to specified torque
	• Steering linkage joints worn enough to be loose	• Replace loose pivots
	• Worn poppet valve	• Replace poppet valve
	• Loose thrust bearing preload adjustment	• Adjust to specification with gear out of vehicle
	• Excessive overcenter lash	• Adjust to specification with gear out of car
Hard steering or lack of assist	• Loose pump belt	• Adjust belt tension to specification
	• Low oil level **NOTE:** Low oil level will also result in excessive pump noise	• Fill to proper level. If excessively low, check all lines and joints for evidence of external leakage. Tighten loose connectors.
	• Steering gear to column misalignment	• Align steering column
	• Lower coupling flange rubbing against steering gear adjuster plug	• Loosen pinch bolt and assemble properly
	• Tires not properly inflated	• Inflate to recommended pressure
Foamy milky power steering fluid, low fluid level and possible low pressure	• Air in the fluid, and loss of fluid due to internal pump leakage causing overflow	• Check for leak and correct. Bleed system. Extremely cold temperatures will cause system aeration should the oil level be low. If oil level is correct and pump still foams, remove pump from vehicle and separate reservoir from housing. Check welsh plug and housing for cracks. If plug is loose or housing is cracked, replace housing.
Low pressure due to steering pump	• Flow control valve stuck or inoperative	• Remove burrs or dirt or replace. Flush system.
	• Pressure plate not flat against cam ring	• Correct
Low pressure due to steering gear	• Pressure loss in cylinder due to worn piston ring or badly worn housing bore	• Remove gear from car for disassembly and inspection of ring and housing bore
	• Leakage at valve rings, valve body-to-worm seal	• Remove gear from car for disassembly and replace seals

Troubleshooting the Power Steering Pump

Problem	Cause	Solution
Chirp noise in steering pump	• Loose belt	• Adjust belt tension to specification
Belt squeal (particularly noticeable at full wheel travel and stand still parking)	• Loose belt	• Adjust belt tension to specification
Growl noise in steering pump	• Excessive back pressure in hoses or steering gear caused by restriction	• Locate restriction and correct. Replace part if necessary.

Troubleshooting the Power Steering Pump (cont.)

Problem	Cause	Solution
Growl noise in steering pump (particularly noticeable at stand still parking)	· Scored pressure plates, thrust plate or rotor · Extreme wear of cam ring	· Replace parts and flush system · Replace parts
Groan noise in steering pump	· Low oil level · Air in the oil. Poor pressure hose connection.	· Fill reservoir to proper level · Tighten connector to specified torque. Bleed system by operating steering from right to left—full turn.
Rattle noise in steering pump	· Vanes not installed properly · Vanes sticking in rotor slots	· Install properly · Free up by removing burrs, varnish, or dirt
Swish noise in steering pump	· Defective flow control valve	· Replace part
Whine noise in steering pump	· Pump shaft bearing scored	· Replace housing and shaft. Flush system.
Hard steering or lack of assist	· Loose pump belt · Low oil level in reservoir **NOTE:** Low oil level will also result in excessive pump noise · Steering gear to column misalignment · Lower coupling flange rubbing against steering gear adjuster plug · Tires not properly inflated	· Adjust belt tension to specification · Fill to proper level. If excessively low, check all lines and joints for evidence of external leakage. Tighten loose connectors. · Align steering column · Loosen pinch bolt and assemble properly · Inflate to recommended pressure
Foaming milky power steering fluid, low fluid level and possible low pressure	· Air in the fluid, and loss of fluid due to internal pump leakage causing overflow	· Check for leaks and correct. Bleed system. Extremely cold temperatures will cause system aeriation should the oil level be low. If oil level is correct and pump still foams, remove pump from vehicle and separate reservoir from body. Check welsh plug and body for cracks. If plug is loose or body is cracked, replace body.
Low pump pressure	· Flow control valve stuck or inoperative · Pressure plate not flat against cam ring	· Remove burrs or dirt or replace. Flush system. · Correct
Momentary increase in effort when turning wheel fast to right or left	· Low oil level in pump · Pump belt slipping · High internal leakage	· Add power steering fluid as required · Tighten or replace belt · Check pump pressure. (See pressure test)
Steering wheel surges or jerks when turning with engine running especially during parking	· Low oil level · Loose pump belt · Steering linkage hitting engine oil pan at full turn · Insufficient pump pressure	· Fill as required · Adjust tension to specification · Correct clearance · Check pump pressure. (See pressure test). Replace flow control valve if defective.
Steering wheel surges or jerks when turning with engine running especially during parking (cont.)	· Sticking flow control valve	· Inspect for varnish or damage, replace if necessary

Troubleshooting the Power Steering Pump (cont.)

Problem	Cause	Solution
Excessive wheel kickback or loose steering	• Air in system	• Add oil to pump reservoir and bleed by operating steering. Check hose connectors for proper torque and adjust as required.
Low pump pressure	• Extreme wear of cam ring • Scored pressure plate, thrust plate, or rotor • Vanes not installed properly • Vanes sticking in rotor slots • Cracked or broken thrust or pressure plate	• Replace parts. Flush system. • Replace parts. Flush system. • Install properly • Freeup by removing burrs, varnish, or dirt • Replace part

8. Install the turn signal switch in the reverse order of removal.

1980-88 Ignition Switch

NOTE: *For 1961-79 switches, see Chapter 6.*

REMOVAL AND INSTALLATION

1. Disconnect the battery ground cable.
2. Remove the steering column shroud and lower the steering column.
3. Disconnect the switch wiring at the multiple plug.

4. Remove the two nuts that retain the switch to the steering column.
5. Lift the switch vertically upward to disengage the actuator rod from the switch and remove the switch.
6. When installing the ignition switch, both the locking mechanism at the top of the column and the switch itself must be in the LOCK position for correct adjustment.

To hold the mechanical parts of the column in the LOCK position, move the shift lever into PARK (with automatic transmissions) or REVERSE (with manual transmissions), turn the

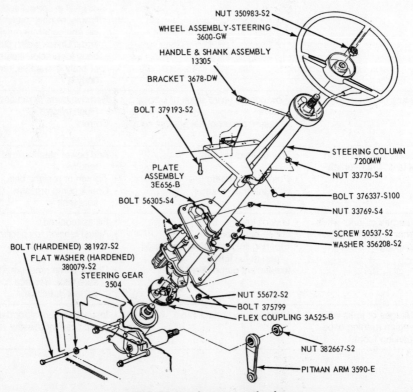

NUT 350983-S2
WHEEL ASSEMBLY-STEERING 3600-GW
HANDLE & SHANK ASSEMBLY 13305
BRACKET 3678-DW
BOLT 379193-S2
STEERING COLUMN 7200MW
NUT 33770-S4
PLATE ASSEMBLY 3E656-B
BOLT 376337-S100
NUT 33769-S4
BOLT 56305-S4
SCREW 50537-S2
WASHER 356208-S2
BOLT (HARDENED) 381927-S2
FLAT WASHER (HARDENED) 380079-S2
STEERING GEAR 3504
NUT 55672-S2
BOLT 375799
FLEX COUPLING 3A525-B
NUT 382667-S2
PITMAN ARM 3590-E

1969–72 steering gear and column

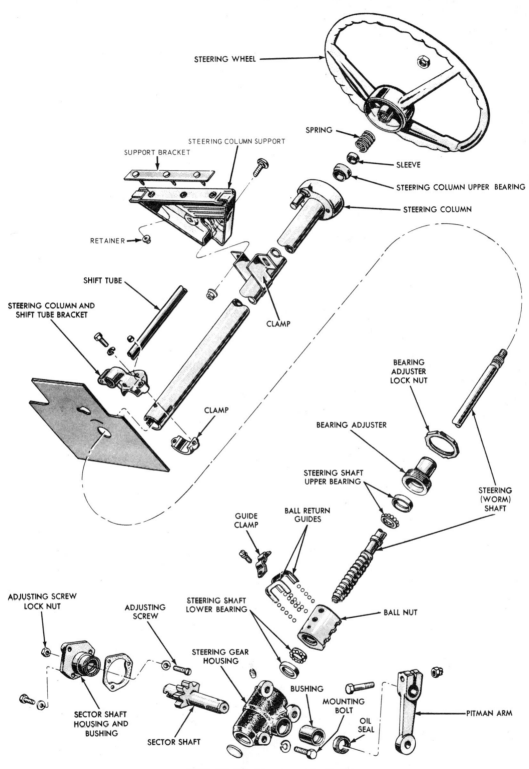

STEERING WHEEL

STEERING COLUMN SUPPORT

SUPPORT BRACKET

SPRING

SLEEVE

STEERING COLUMN UPPER BEARING

STEERING COLUMN

RETAINER

SHIFT TUBE

STEERING COLUMN AND
SHIFT TUBE BRACKET

CLAMP

BEARING
ADJUSTER
LOCK NUT

CLAMP

BEARING ADJUSTER

STEERING SHAFT
UPPER BEARING

STEERING
(WORM)
SHAFT

GUIDE
CLAMP

BALL RETURN
GUIDES

ADJUSTING SCREW
LOCK NUT

ADJUSTING
SCREW

STEERING SHAFT
LOWER BEARING

BALL NUT

STEERING GEAR
HOUSING

BUSHING

SECTOR SHAFT
HOUSING AND
BUSHING

SECTOR SHAFT

MOUNTING
BOLT

OIL
SEAL

PITMAN ARM

1961–67 steering gear and column

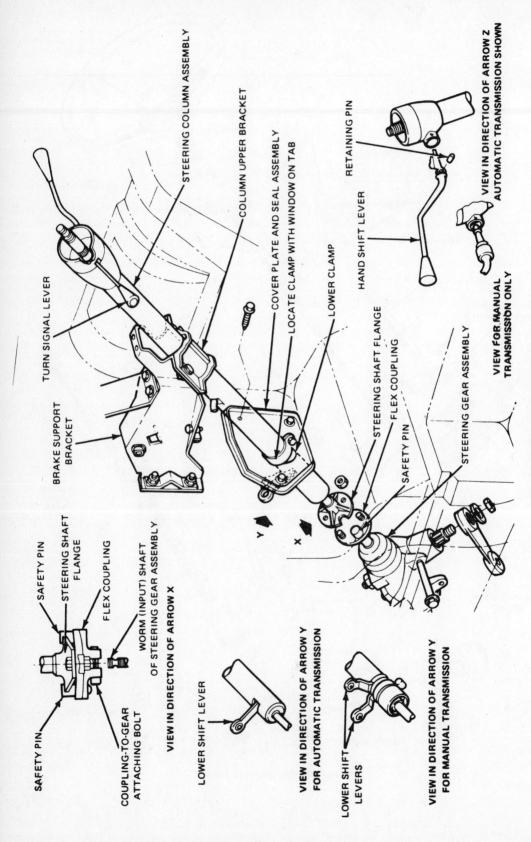

TURN SIGNAL LEVER

STEERING COLUMN ASSEMBLY

COLUMN UPPER BRACKET

COVER PLATE AND SEAL ASSEMBLY

LOCATE CLAMP WITH WINDOW ON TAB

LOWER CLAMP

HAND SHIFT LEVER

RETAINING PIN

VIEW IN DIRECTION OF ARROW Z
AUTOMATIC TRANSMISSION SHOWN

BRAKE SUPPORT BRACKET

STEERING SHAFT FLANGE

FLEX COUPLING

SAFETY PIN

STEERING GEAR ASSEMBLY

VIEW FOR MANUAL TRANSMISSION ONLY

Y

X

1973–79 steering gear and column

SAFETY PIN

STEERING SHAFT FLANGE

FLEX COUPLING

WORM (INPUT) SHAFT OF STEERING GEAR ASSEMBLY

SAFETY PIN

COUPLING-TO-GEAR ATTACHING BOLT

VIEW IN DIRECTION OF ARROW X

LOWER SHIFT LEVER

VIEW IN DIRECTION OF ARROW Y FOR AUTOMATIC TRANSMISSION

LOWER SHIFT LEVERS

VIEW IN DIRECTION OF ARROW Y FOR MANUAL TRANSMISSION

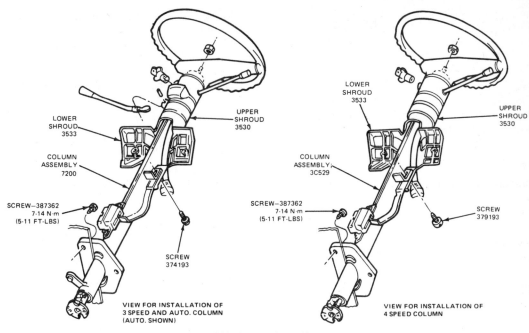

1980–81 steering column

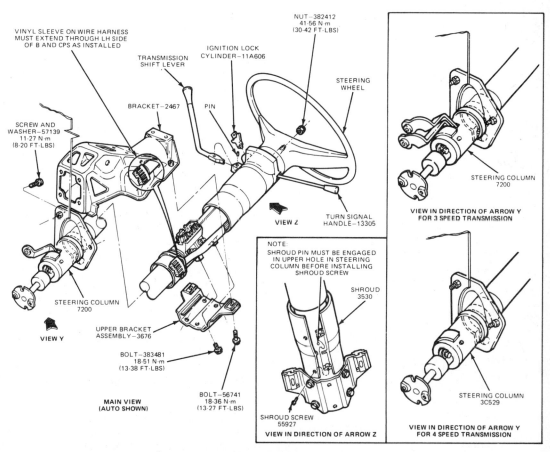

1982–88 steering column

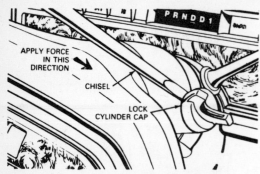

Breaking the cap away from the lock cylinder

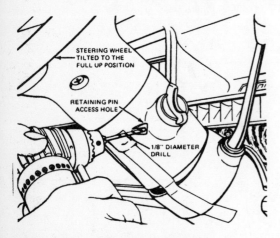

Drilling out the lock cylinder retaining pin

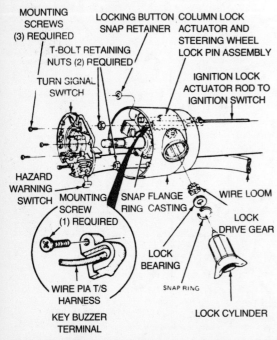

Non-tilting column mechanism

key to the LOCK position, and remove the key. New replacement switches, when received, are already pinned in the LOCK position by a metal shipping pin inserted in a locking hole on the side of the switch.

7. Engage the actuator rod in the switch.

8. Position the switch on the column and install the retaining nuts, but do not tighten them.

9. Move the switch up and down along the column to locate the mid-position of rod lash, and then tighten the retaining nuts.

10. Remove the locking pin, connect the battery cable, and check for proper start in PARK or NEUTRAL.

Also check to make certain that the start circuit cannot be actuated in the DRIVE and REVERSE position.

11. Raise the steering column into position at instrument panel. Install steering column shroud.

1980-88 Ignition Lock Cylinder

NOTE: *For 1961-79 locks, see Chapter 6.*

REMOVAL AND INSTALLATION

With Key

1. Disconnect the battery ground.

2. On tilt columns, remove the upper extension shroud by unsnapping the shroud from the retaining clip at the 9 o'clock position.

3. Remove the trim shroud halves.

4. Unplug the wire connector at the key warning switch.

5. Place the shift lever in **PARK** and turn the key to **ON**.

6. Place a ⅛" wire pin in the hole in the casting surrounding the lock cylinder and depress the retaining pin while pulling out on the cylinder.

7. When installing the cylinder, turn the lock cylinder to the RUN position and depress the retaining pin, then insert the lock cylinder into its housing in the flange casting. Assure that the cylinder is fully seated and aligned in the interlocking washer before turning the key to the OFF position. This will allow the cylinder retaining pin to extend into the cylinder cast housing hole.

8. The remainder of installation is the reverse of removal.

Non-Functioning Cylinder or No Key Available

FIXED COLUMNS

1. Disconnect the battery ground.

2. Remove the steering wheel.

3. Remove the turn signal lever.

4. Remove the column trim shrouds.

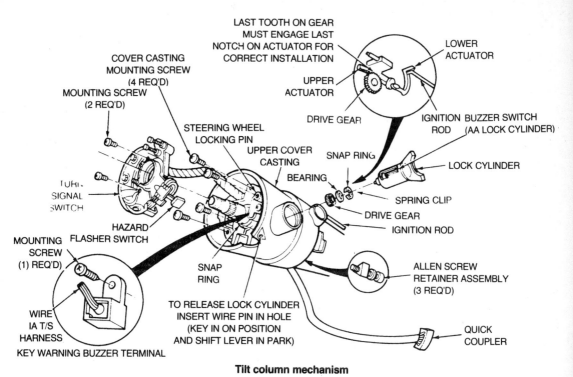

COVER CASTING
MOUNTING SCREW
(4 REQ'D)

LAST TOOTH ON GEAR
MUST ENGAGE LAST
NOTCH ON ACTUATOR FOR
CORRECT INSTALLATION

LOWER
ACTUATOR

MOUNTING SCREW
(2 REQ'D)

UPPER
ACTUATOR

DRIVE GEAR

IGNITION BUZZER SWITCH
ROD   (AA LOCK CYLINDER)

STEERING WHEEL
LOCKING PIN

UPPER COVER
CASTING

SNAP RING

LOCK CYLINDER

TURN
SIGNAL
SWITCH

BEARING

SPRING CLIP

DRIVE GEAR

IGNITION ROD

HAZARD
FLASHER SWITCH

MOUNTING
SCREW
(1) REQ'D)

SNAP
RING

ALLEN SCREW
RETAINER ASSEMBLY
(3 REQ'D)

WIRE
IA T/S
HARNESS

TO RELEASE LOCK CYLINDER
INSERT WIRE PIN IN HOLE
(KEY IN ON POSITION
AND SHIFT LEVER IN PARK)

QUICK
COUPLER

KEY WARNING BUZZER TERMINAL

Tilt column mechanism

5. Unbolt the steering column and lower it carefully.

6. Remove the ignition switch and warning buzzer and pin the switch in the LOCK position.

7. Remove the turn signal switch.

8. Remove the snapring and T-bolt nuts that retain the flange casting to the column outer tube.

9. Remove the flange casting, upper shaft bearing, lock cylinder, ignition switch actuator and the actuator rod by pulling the entire assembly over the end of the steering column shaft.

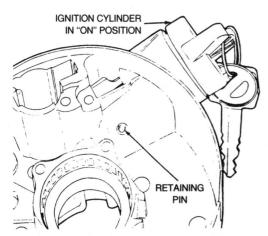

IGNITION CYLINDER
IN "ON" POSITION

RETAINING
PIN

Lock retaining pin access slot on non-tilt columns

10. Remove the lock actuator insert, the T-bolts and the automatic transmission indicator insert, or, with manual transmissions, the key release lever.

11. Upon reassembly, the following parts must be replaced with new parts:
- Flange
- Lock cylinder assembly
- Steering column lock gear
- Steering column lock bearing
- Steering column upper bearing retainer
- Lock actuator assembly

12. Assembly is a reversal of the disassembly procedure. It is best to install a new upper bearing. Check that the truck starts only in PARK and NEUTRAL.

TILT COLUMNS

1. Disconnect the battery ground.

2. Remove the steering column shrouds.

3. Using masking tape, tape the gap between the steering wheel hub and the cover casting. Cover the entire circumference of the casting. Cover the seat and floor area with a drop-cloth.

4. Pull out the hazard switch and tape it in a downward position.

5. The lock cylinder retaining pin is located on the outside of the steering column cover casting adjacent to the hazard flasher button.

6. Tilt the steering column to the full up position and prepunch the lock cylinder retaining pin with a sharp punch.

7. Using a ⅛″ drill bit, mounted in a right an-

gle drive drill adapter, drill out the retaining pin, going no deeper than ½" (12.7mm).

8. Tilt the column to the full down position. Place a chisel at the base of the ignition lock cylinder cap and using a hammer break away the cap from the lock cylinder.

9. Using a ⅜" drill bit, drill down the center of the ignition lock cylinder key slot about 1¾" (44mm), until the lock cylinder breaks loose from the steering column cover casting.

10. Remove the lock cylinder and the drill shavings.

11. Remove the steering wheel.

12. Remove the turn signal lever.

13. Remove the turn signal switch attaching screws.

14. Remove the key buzzer attaching screw.

15. Remove the turn signal switch up and over the end of the column, but don't disconnect the wiring.

16. Remove the 4 attaching screws from the cover casting and lift the casting over the end of the steering shaft, allowing the turn signal switch to pass through the casting. The removal of the casting cover will expose the upper actuator. Remove the upper actuator.

17. Remove the drive gear, snapring and washer from the cover casting along with the upper actuator.

18. Clean all components and replace any that appear damaged or worn.

19. Installation is the reverse of removal.

Steering Column

REMOVAL AND INSTALLATION

1961-67

1. Disconnect the horn and turn signal wires under the instrument panel.

2. Pull up the floor mat and rubber seal and remove the floor pan cover.

3. Loosen the 3 steering column support attaching bolts.

4. Remove the 2 steering column-to-support clamp bolts.

5. Disconnect the transmission shift rods from the shift tube arms.

6. Remove the 3 steering gear mounting bolts.

7. Remove the nut and bolt which clamp the pitman arm to the sector shaft.

8. Using a thin chisel, separate the pitman arm split, move the gear away from the frame and slide the pitman arm from the sector shaft.

9. Lift the steering column, shift tube and gear out through the passenger compartment.

10. Remove the steering wheel.

11. Remove the 2 clamp bolts and the clamp which holds the steering column to the bracket.

12. Slide the column and shift tube out of the gear housing and wormshaft. Catch the wormshaft upper bearing sleeve and spring.

To install:

13. Slide the column and shift tube over the wormshaft so that the boss in the column and shift tube brackets pilots into the hole in the column.

14. Install the column-to-bracket clamp and bolts, but don't tighten the bolts yet.

15. Install the assembly into the van through the floor.

16. With the sector shaft centered and the wheels straight ahead, install the pitman arm onto the sector shaft.

17. Install the steering gear mounting bolts and slide the pitman arm fully onto the shaft. Torque the bolt to 50 ft.lb.

18. Torque the steering gear mounting bolts to 40 ft.lb.

19. Tighten the column support nuts and clamp nuts just enough to permit movement while maintaining position.

20. Center the shift tube over the top of the column tube. The centerline of the shift tube should be 1⁹⁄₁₆" from the steering gear box mounting surface.

21. Adjust the column so that the shaft is centered in the tube and rotates without contacting the column upper bearing with the sleeve removed.

22. Check for free rotation of the steering shaft and torque the support and clamp nuts to 18 ft.lb.

23. The remainder of installation is the reverse of removal.

1969-73

1. Raise the hood and remove the windshield washer reservoir.

2. Disconnect the shift rods from the shift levers.

3. Remove the lower bolt from the steering shaft flexible coupling.

4. Remove the clamp bolt and 5 retaining bolts from the steering column lower retainer.

5. Remove the retainer from the column tube.

6. Disconnect the turn signal and horn wires.

7. Remove the steering wheel.

8. Remove the column upper retainer clamp and lift the column from the van.

To install:

9. Position the column in the van making sure that the flex coupling splines align with the steering shaft.

10. Loosely install the upper column clamp bolts.

11. Slide the column as required to obtain free operating clearance between the column

and shaft, then tighten the flexible coupling bolts and the upper clamp bolts.

12. Connect the wiring.
13. Install the lower clamp and retainer bolts.
14. Install the steering wheel.
15. Connect the shift rods using new clips.
16. Install the reservoir.

1974

1. Disconnect the turn signal, back-up light, and horn wires.
2. Remove the steering wheel.
3. Disconnect the shift rods from the shift levers.
4. Remove the nuts from the steering shaft flexible coupling.
5. Remove the column upper retainer-to-instrument panel clamp.
6. Remove the retaining bolts from the steering column lower retainer.
7. Remove the bolt and nut from the lower clamp.
8. Lift the column from the van

To install:

9. Position the column in the van making sure that the flex coupling fits over the bolt studs.
10. Loosely install the upper column clamp bolts.
11. Slide the column as required to obtain free operating clearance between the column and shaft, then tighten the flexible coupling bolts and the upper clamp bolts to 20 ft.lb..
12. Connect the wiring.
13. Install the lower clamp and retainer bolts.
14. Install the steering wheel.
15. Connect the shift rods using new clips.

1975-79

1. Set the front wheels in the straight-ahead position.
2. Matchmark the steering shaft flange and flexible coupling.

3. Remove the steering wheel.
4. Remove the steering column trim cover from the instrument panel.
5. Disconnect the ignition switch connector and the back-up and neutral start switch wires.
6. Disconnect the shift rods at the column levers.
7. Remove the two flexible coupling nuts.
8. Remove the bolts securing the column opening cover to the floor.
9. Loosen the column lower clamp bolt.
10. Remove the column upper bracket-to-brake support bolts and lift the column from the van.

To install:

11. Position the column in the van.
12. Loosely install the column upper bracket-to-brake support bolts.
13. Position the shaft flange and flexible coupling so that the matchmarks align. Make sure that the coupling pins are centered in their slots. Install the 2 nuts and torque them to 35 ft.lb.
14. Pull the column upward until the flexible coupling is in a position between being flat and concaved upward about $3/32$". With the column in this position, tighten the upper support bolts to 20 ft.lb.
15. Connect the shift lever and rods. Align the rods as described in Chapter 7.
16. Install the lower cover plate. Tighten the bolts to 20 ft.lb.
17. Position the lower clamp against the cover so that the window in the clamp engages the tab on the column. Tighten the bolt to 20 ft.lb.
18. Connect the wiring.
19. Install the trim cover.
20. Install the steering wheel.
21. Road test the van for proper steering shaft operation.
22. Recheck the flexible coupling for proper pin-in-slot centering. If necessary, align the column as follows:

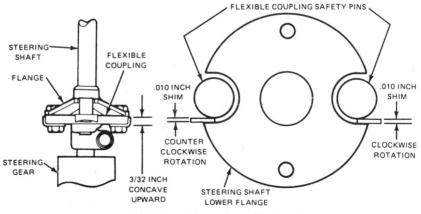

STEERING SHAFT
FLEXIBLE COUPLING
FLANGE
STEERING GEAR
3/32 INCH CONCAVE UPWARD
.010 INCH SHIM
COUNTER CLOCKWISE ROTATION
FLEXIBLE COUPLING SAFETY PINS
.010 INCH SHIM
CLOCKWISE ROTATION
STEERING SHAFT LOWER FLANGE

1975—81 steering column alignment

a. Remove the trim cover.

b. Loosen the upper retaining bracket bolts.

c. Loosen the lower clamp and cover plate bolts.

d. Make sure the flexible coupling nuts are at the proper torque.

e. Place the wheels in the straight-ahead position.

f. Pull the column upward until the flexible coupling is in a position between being flat and concaved upward about $3/32''$. With the column in this position, tighten the upper support bolts to 20 ft.lb.

g. Tighten the lower cover plate bolts to 20 ft.lb.

h. Position the lower clamp against the cover so that the window in the clamp engages the tab on the column. Tighten the bolt to 20 ft.lb.

i. Insert a 0.010″ shim between the flexible coupling right safety pin and the steering column lower flange cut-out, and turn the steering wheel 1 revolution clockwise.

j. If the shim is tight, so that it can't be removed, loosen the cover plate clamp and the cover plate bolts and re-align the column so that the shim remains loose enough to be removed after the steering wheel rotation.

k. Repeat the procedure for the left safety pin, rotating the wheel counterclockwise, in this case.

1980-81

1. Set the parking brake.
2. Disconnect the battery ground cable.
3. Disconnect the flexible coupling from the steering shaft flange.
4. Disconnect the shift linkage rod(s) from the column.
5. Remove the steering wheel.
NOTE: *If you have a tilt column, the steering wheel MUST be in the full UP position when it is removed.*
6. Remove the floor cover screws at the base of the column.
7. Remove the steering column shroud by pulling the shroud tabs out of the clip at the bottom of the column.
8. Remove the instrument cluster column opening cover.
9. Remove the 2 bolts securing the column support bracket to the pedal support bracket.
10. Disconnect the turn signal/hazard warning harness and the ignition switch harness.
11. Lift the column from the truck.
To install:
12. Position the column in the van.
13. Connect the wiring.
14. Insert the column through the floor so that the flange engages the flexible coupling, then, raise the column and loosely install the bracket bolts.
15. Loosely install the flexible coupling nuts and floor plate screws.
16. Install the steering wheel.
17. Adjust the steering column as follows:

a. Tighten the flexible coupling nuts to 35 ft.lb.

b. Place the wheels in the straight-ahead position.

c. Pull the column upward until the flexible coupling is in a position between being flat and concaved upward about $3/32''$. With the column in this position, tighten the upper support bolts to 20 ft.lb.

d. Tighten the lower cover plate bolts to 20 ft.lb.

e. Insert a 0.010″ shim between the flexible coupling right safety pin and the steering column lower flange cut-out, and turn the steering wheel 1 revolution clockwise.

f. If the shim is tight, so that it can't be removed, loosen the cover plate clamp and the cover plate bolts and re-align the column so that the shim remains loose enough to be removed after the steering wheel rotation.

g. Repeat the procedure for the left safety pin, rotating the wheel counterclockwise, in this case.

18. Install the shroud.
19. Connect the battery.
20. Connect the shift linkage.

1982-88

1. Set the parking brake.
2. Disconnect the battery ground cable.
3. Disconnect the flexible coupling from the steering shaft flange.
4. Disconnect the shift linkage rod(s) from the column.
5. Remove the steering wheel.
NOTE: *If you have a tilt column, the steering wheel MUST be in the full UP position when it is removed.*
6. Remove the floor cover screws at the base of the column.
7. Remove the steering column shroud by loosening the bottom screw and placing the shift lever in the No.1 position (on automatics) and pulling the shroud up and away from the column.
8. Remove the instrument cluster column opening cover.
9. Remove the 2 bolts securing the column support bracket to the pedal support bracket.
10. Disconnect the turn signal/hazard warning harness and the ignition switch harness.
11. Lift the column from the truck.
To install:

12. Position the column in the van.

13. Connect the wiring.

14. Insert the column through the floor so that the flange engages the flexible coupling, then, raise the column and loosely install the bracket bolts.

15. Loosely install the flexible coupling nuts and floor plate screws.

16. Install the steering wheel.

17. Adjust the steering column as follows:

   a. Tighten the flexible coupling nuts to 35 ft.lb.

   b. Place the wheels in the straight-ahead position.

   c. Verify the safety pin-to-flange cut-out clearance of 0.160″ with a feeler gauge.

   d. If necessary, loosen the flange nuts to adjust the clearance, then retighten the nuts when clearance is established.

   e. Tighten the column support bracket bolts to 20 ft.lb.

   f. Tighten the cover plate screws to 10 ft.lb.

   g. Tighten the lower clamp bolt to 10 ft.lb.

Pitman Arm

REMOVAL AND INSTALLATION

1961-67

1. Raise and support the front end on jackstands. Place the wheels in a straight-ahead position.

2. Disconnect the clutch pedal return spring, remove the pedal-to-pivot bolt and pull the pedal from the pivot to get it out of the way of pitman arm removal.

3. Remove the cotter pin and nut and disconnect the drag link from the pitman arm using a ball joint puller.

4. Remove the pitman arm-to-sector shaft clamp bolt and nut.

5. Spread the pitman arm with a chisel and slide it from the sector shaft.

6. Installation is the reverse of removal. Torque the nuts to 50 ft.lb.

1969-74

MANUAL STEERING GEAR

1. Raise and support the front end on jackstands.

2. Remove the steering gear from the van.

3. Center the sector shaft — 3 full turns from either lock.

4. Matchmark the pitman arm and gear housing.

5. Remove the pitman arm nut.

6. Using a puller, remove the pitman arm.

7. Installation is the reverse of removal.

Torque the pitman arm nut to 150 ft.lb. on 1969-70 models; 250 ft.lb. on 1971-74 models.

POWER STEERING

1. Raise and support the front end on jackstands.

2. Place the wheels in a straight-ahead position.

3. Disconnect the pitman arm from the control valve link.

4. Disconnect the pitman arm upper end fasteners.

5. Remove the pitman arm.

6. Installation is the reverse of removal. Torque the fasteners to 60 ft.lb. If necessary, advance the castellated nut to align the cotter pin holes. Never loosen the nut to align the holes.

1975-83

1. Raise and support the front end on jackstands.

2. Place the wheels in a straight-ahead position.

3. On models with power steering, place a drain pan under the gear and disconnect the hoses. Plug the hoses and ports.

4. Disconnect the drag link from the pitman arm. A ball joint separator will be necessary for this.

5. Remove the steering gear.

6. Center the sector shaft.

7. Matchmark the pitman arm and gear housing.

8. Remove the pitman arm nut and pull the pitman arm off with a 2-jawed puller.

9. Installation is the reverse of removal. Torque the pitman arm nut to 200 ft.lb.; the drag link stud nut to 75 ft.lb.

1984-88

1. Place the wheels in a straight-ahead position.

2. Disconnect the drag link at the pitman arm. You'll need a puller such as a tie rod end remover.

3. Remove the pitman arm-to-gear nut and washer.

4. Matchmark the pitman arm and gear housing for installation purposes.

5. Using a 2-jawed puller, remove the pitman arm from the gear.

6. Installation is the reverse of removal. Align the matchmarks when installing the pitman arm. Torque the pitman arm nut to 170-230 ft.lb.; torque the drag link ball stud nut to 50-75 ft.lb., advancing the nut to align the cotter pin hole. Never back off the nut to align the hole.

1961-67 Drag Link
REMOVAL AND INSTALLATION

1. Raise and support the front end on jackstands.

2. Place the wheels in a straight-ahead position.

3. Remove the cotter pin and nut and disconnect the drag link from the spindle arm. A tie rod end separator will be necessary.

4. Remove the cotter pin and nut and disconnect the drag link from the pitman arm. A tie rod end separator will be necessary.

5. Installation is the reverse of removal. Never back-off the nuts to align the cotter pin holes; always advance them. Torque both nuts to 45-55 ft.lb.

1969-73 Drag Link
REMOVAL AND INSTALLATION

1. Raise and support the front end on jackstands.

2. Place the wheels in a straight-ahead position.

3. Remove the cotter pin and nut and disconnect the drag link from the idler arm. A tie rod end separator will be necessary.

4. Remove the cotter pin and nut and disconnect the drag link from the pitman arm. A tie rod end separator will be necessary.

5. Installation is the reverse of removal. Never back-off the nuts to align the cotter pin holes; always advance them. Torque both nuts to 45-55 ft.lb.

1974-76 Drag Link
REMOVAL AND INSTALLATION

1. Raise and support the front end on jackstands.

2. Remove the cotter pins and nuts from the drag link, ball studs and from the right connecting rod ball stud.

3. Remove the right connecting rod ball stud from the drag link.

4. Remove the drag link ball studs from the spindle and pitman arm.

5. Installation is the reverse of removal. Torque all nuts to 50-75 ft.lb. Never back-off nuts to align the cotter pin holes; always advance them.

1977 and Later Tie Rod and Link
REMOVAL AND INSTALLATION

Except Rubberized Ball Socket Linkage

1. Place the wheels in a straight-ahead position.

2. Remove the cotter pins and nuts from the drag link and tie rod ball studs.

3. Remove the drag link ball studs from the right hand spindle and pitman arm.

5. Remove the tie rod ball studs from the left hand spindle and drag link.

6. Installation is the reverse of removal. Seat the studs in the tapered hole before tightening the nuts. This will avoid wrap-up of the rubber grommets during tightening of the nuts. Torque the nuts to 70 ft.lb. Always use new cotter pins.

7. Have the front end alignment checked.

Rubberized Ball Socket Linkage

1. Raise and support the front end on jackstands.

2. Place the wheels in the straight-ahead position.

3. Remove the nuts connecting the drag link ball studs to the connecting rod and pitman arm.

4. Disconnect the drag link using a tie rod end remover.

5. Loosen the bolts on the adjuster clamp. Count the number of turns it take to remove the drag link from the adjuster.

6. Installation is the reverse of removal. Install the drag link with the same number of turns it took to remove it. Make certain that the wheels remain in the straight-ahead position during installation. Seat the studs in the tapered hole before tightening the nuts. This will avoid wrap-up of the rubber grommets during tightening of the nuts. Torque the adjuster clamp nuts to 40 ft.lb. Torque the ball stud nuts to 75 ft.lb.

7. Have the front end alignment checked.

Spindle Connecting Rod (Tie Rod)
REMOVAL AND INSTALLATION

1961-74

1. Raise and support the front end on jackstands.

2. Loosen both connecting rod end clamps.

3. Unthread the connecting rod until it drops off both ends. On end is left hand thread; the other, right hand thread.

To install:

4. Lubricate the threads, place the clamps on the new connecting rod and start the rod about one thread on one end.

5. Start the other end and continue to turn the rod until the rod ends have entered the rod about the same distance as the original installation. This will provide an approximate toe-in setting. Position the clamps about $\frac{3}{16}$" from the ends of the rod with the clamp bolts located horizontally below the rod.

6. Have the toe-in checked.

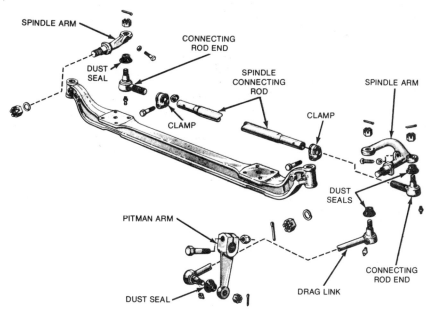

1961–67 steering linkage

1975-88

1. Raise and support the front end on jackstands.

2. Place the wheels in the straight-ahead position.

3. Disconnect the connecting rod from the drag link by removing the nut and separating the two with a tie rod end remover.

4. Loosen the bolts on the adjusting sleeve clamps. Count the number of turns it takes to remove the connecting rod from the adjuster sleeve and remove the rod.

5. Installation is the reverse of removal. Install the connecting rod the exact number of turns noted during removal. Torque the tie rod nuts to 40 ft.lb.; the ball stud nut to 75 ft.lb.

6. Have the front end alignment checked.

Tie (Connecting) Rod Ends
REMOVAL AND INSTALLATION
1961-84
1985-87 Except Rubberized Ball Socket Linkage

1. Raise and support the front end on jackstands.

2. Remove the cotter pin and nut and disconnect the spindle arm fron the connecting rod using a ball joint separator.

3. Loosen the clamp bolt and turn the rod end off of the rod. Count the exact number of turns required to remove the end.

4. Installation is the reverse of removal. Turn the new end on the exact number of turns noted during removal. The clamps should be

position $\frac{3}{16}$" from the end of the rod with the bolt horizontally below the rod on 1961-67 models, or, as shown in the accompanying illustrations for 1969 and later models. Torque the bolt to:

- 1961-67: 25-35 ft.lb.
- 1969-74 E-100, 200: 35-45 ft.lb.
- 1969-74 E-300: 40-60 ft.lb.
- 1975-87: 30-40 ft.lb.

1985-87 Rubberized Ball Socket Linkage
All 1988

1. Raise and support the front end on jackstands.

2. Place the wheels in a straight-ahead position.

3. Remove the ball stud from the pitman arm using a tie rod end remover.

4. Loosen the nuts on the adjusting sleeve clamp. Remove the ball stud from the adjuster, or the adjuster from the tie rod. Count the number of turns it takes to remove the sleeve from the tie rod or ball stud from the sleeve.

5. Install the sleeve on the tie rod, or the ball in the sleeve the same number of turns noted during removal. Make sure that the adjuster clamps are in the correct position, illustrated, and torque the clamp bolts to 40 ft.lb.

6. Keep the wheels straight ahead and install the ball studs. Torque the nuts to 75 ft.lb. Use new cotter pins.

7. Install the drag link and connecting rod.

8. Have the front end alignment checked.

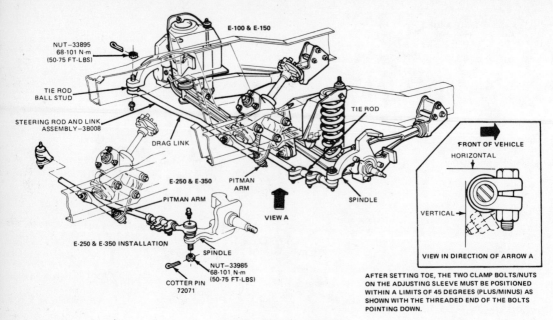

NUT—33895
68-101 N·m
(50-75 FT-LBS)

TIE ROD
BALL STUD

STEERING ROD AND LINK
ASSEMBLY—3B008

DRAG LINK

E-100 & E-150

TIE ROD

E-250 & E-350

PITMAN ARM

PITMAN
ARM

SPINDLE

VIEW A

E-250 & E-350 INSTALLATION

SPINDLE

NUT—33985
68-101 N·m
(50-75 FT-LBS)

COTTER PIN
72071

FRONT OF VEHICLE

HORIZONTAL

VERTICAL

VIEW IN DIRECTION OF ARROW A

AFTER SETTING TOE, THE TWO CLAMP BOLTS/NUTS
ON THE ADJUSTING SLEEVE MUST BE POSITIONED
WITHIN A LIMITS OF 45 DEGREES (PLUS/MINUS) AS
SHOWN WITH THE THREADED END OF THE BOLTS
POINTING DOWN.

1981—88 steering linkage

Manual Steering Gear
ADJUSTMENTS

1961-71

WORM AND SECTOR GEAR ADJUSTMENTS

1. Raise and support the front end on jackstands. Center the front wheels.

2. Remove the floor mat, rubber seal and floor pan cover.

3. Disconnect the drag link from the pitman arm.

4. Remove the steering wheel.

5. Make sure that there is no binding in the steering column bearing and shaft.

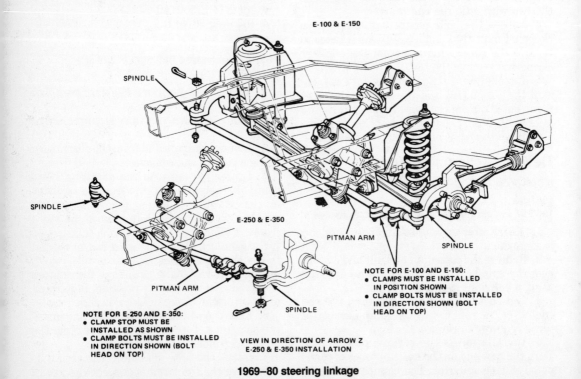

E-100 & E-150

SPINDLE

SPINDLE

E-250 & E-350

PITMAN ARM

PITMAN ARM

SPINDLE

NOTE FOR E-100 AND E-150:
• CLAMPS MUST BE INSTALLED
  IN POSITION SHOWN
• CLAMP BOLTS MUST BE INSTALLED
  IN DIRECTION SHOWN (BOLT
  HEAD ON TOP)

PITMAN ARM

SPINDLE

NOTE FOR E-250 AND E-350:
• CLAMP STOP MUST BE
  INSTALLED AS SHOWN
• CLAMP BOLTS MUST BE INSTALLED
  IN DIRECTION SHOWN (BOLT
  HEAD ON TOP)

VIEW IN DIRECTION OF ARROW Z
E-250 & E-350 INSTALLATION

1969—80 steering linkage

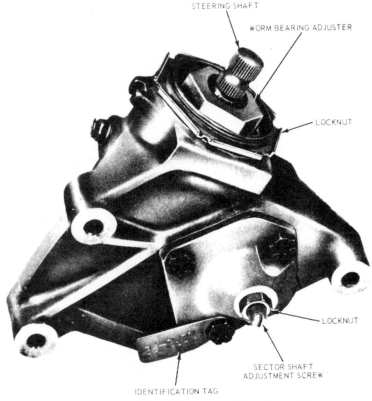

STEERING SHAFT

WORM BEARING ADJUSTER

LOCKNUT

LOCKNUT

SECTOR SHAFT
ADJUSTMENT SCREW

IDENTIFICATION TAG

Recirculating ball steering gear used in early models

6. Woring through the floor pan hole, loosen the sector shaft locknut and turn the screw counterclockwise about 3 full turns.

7. Thread the steering wheel retaining nut back onto the shaft as far as it will go. Using an inch-pound torque wrench on the nut, note the torque necessary to turn the steering shaft 1½ turns to either side of center. If the reading is not with 4-5 in.lb., proceed.

8. Loosen the steering shaft bearing adjuster locknut and turn the adjuster as required to bring the reading within specifications. Tighten the locknut while holding the adjuster and recheck the reading.

9. Install the steering wheel. Turn the steering wheel SLOWLY to either stop, then turn the shaft back 2¼ turns to center the ball nut.

10. Turn the sector adjusting screw clockwise until 9-10 in.lb. is noted when rotating the shaft over center.

11. With the gear centered and the sector shaft held to prevent rotation, check the lash between the ball nut, balls and wormshaft by applying a 15 in.lb. torque on the steering gear input shaft to both the right and left. Total steering wheel rim travel should not exceed 1¼" with 15 in.lb. applied on the steering wheel nut.

12. Tighten the sector shaft adjusting screw locknut while holding the screw and recheck the backlash.

13. Reconnect all parts.

1972-74

WORM AND SECTOR GEAR ADJUSTMENTS

WARNING: *Failure to perform the adjustments in the order given will result in steering gear damage and/or failure!*

1. Make certain that there is no binding within the steering column.

2. Remove the steering gear from the van.

3. Loosen the sector shaft locknut and turn the screw counterclockwise about 3 full turns.

4. Using an inch-pound torque wrench on the input shaft, note the torque necessary to turn the shaft 1½ turns to either side of center. If the reading is not with 4-5 in.lb., proceed.

5. Loosen the worm bearing adjuster locknut and turn the adjuster as required to bring the reading within specifications. Tighten the locknut while holding the adjuster and recheck the reading.

6. Turn the input shaft SLOWLY to either stop, then turn the shaft back 3 turns to center the ball nut.

7. Turn the sector adjusting screw clockwise

until 9-10 in.lb. is noted when rotating the shaft over center.

8. With the gear centered and the sector shaft held to prevent rotation, check the lash between the ball nut, balls and wormshaft by applying a 15 in.lb. torque on the steering gear input shaft to both the right and left. Total wrench travel should not exceed 1¼" with 15 in.lb. applied on the steering shaft.

9. Tighten the sector shaft adjusting screw locknut while holding the screw and recheck the backlash.

10. Install the steering gear.

1975-83

WORM AND SECTOR ADJUSTMENTS

WARNING: *Failure to perform the adjustments in the order given will result in steering gear damage and/or failure!*

1. Make certain that there is no binding within the steering column.

2. Remove the steering gear from the van.

3. Tighten the worm bearing adjuster plug until all endplay is removed, then back it off ¼ turn.

4. Using an ¹¹⁄₁₆" 12-point socket and an inch-pound torque wrench, carefully turn the wormshaft all the way to the right, then back ½ turn.

5. Tighten the adjuster plug until a thrust bearing preload of 5-8 in.lb. is recorded. Hold the plug and tighten the locknut.

6. Turn the wormshaft from stop-to-stop counting the total number of turns. Then center it by turning it back ½ the number of turns from wither stop.

7. Turn the sector shaft adjusting screw clockwise to remove all lash between the ball nut and sector teeth. Tighten the locknut.

8. Turn the gear through center, noting the highest reading over center. Proper over center reading should be 16 in.lb. Adjust it with the sector shaft as necessary. Tighten the locknut and recheck the reading.

9. Install the gear.

1984-87

PRELOAD AND MESHLOAD CHECK

1. Raise and support the front end on jackstands.

2. Disconnect the drag link from the pitman arm.

3. Lubricate the wormshaft seal with a drop of automatic transmission fluid.

4. Remove the horn pad from the steering wheel.

5. Turn the steering wheel slowly to one stop.

6. Using an inch-pound torque wrench on

the steering wheel nut, check the amount of torque needed to rotate the steering wheel through a 1½ turn cycle. The preload should be 5-9 in.lb. If not, proceed with the rest of the steps.

7. Rotate the steering wheel from stop-to-stop, counting the total number of turns. Using that figure, center the steering wheel (½ the total turns).

8. Using the inch-pound torque wrench, rotate the steering wheel 90° to either side of center, noting the highest torque reading over center. The meshload should be 9-14 in.lb., or at least 2 in.lb. more than the preload figure.

PRELOAD AND MESHLOAD ADJUSTMENT

1. Remove the steering gear.

2. Torque the sector cover bolts on the gear to 40 ft.lb.

3. Loosen the preload adjuster nut and tighten the worm bearing adjuster nut until all endplay has been removed. Lubricate the wormshaft seal with a few drops of automatic transmission fluid.

4. Using an ¹¹⁄₁₆", 12 point socket and an inch-pound torque wrench, carefully turn the wormshaft all the way to the right.

5. Turn the shaft back to the left and measure the torque over a 1½ turn cycle. This is the preload reading.

6. Tighten or loosen the adjuster nut to bring the preload into range (7-9 in.lb.).

7. Hold the adjuster nut while torquing the locknut to 187 ft.lb.

8. Rotate the wormshaft stop-to-stop counting the total number of turns and center the shaft (½ the total turns).

9. Using the torque wrench and socket, measure the torque required to turn the shaft 90° to either side of center.

10. Turn the sector shaft adjusting screw as needed to bring the meshload torque within the 12-14 in.lb. range, or at least 4 in.lb. higher than the preload torque.

11. Hold the adjusting screw while tightening the locknut to 25 ft.lb.

12. Install the gear.

REMOVAL AND INSTALLATION

1961-67

1. Disconnect the horn and turn signal wires under the instrument panel.

2. Pull up the floor mat and rubber seal and remove the floor pan cover.

3. Loosen the 3 steering column support attaching bolts.

4. Remove the 2 steering column-to-support clamp bolts.

5. Disconnect the transmission shift rods from the shift tube arms.

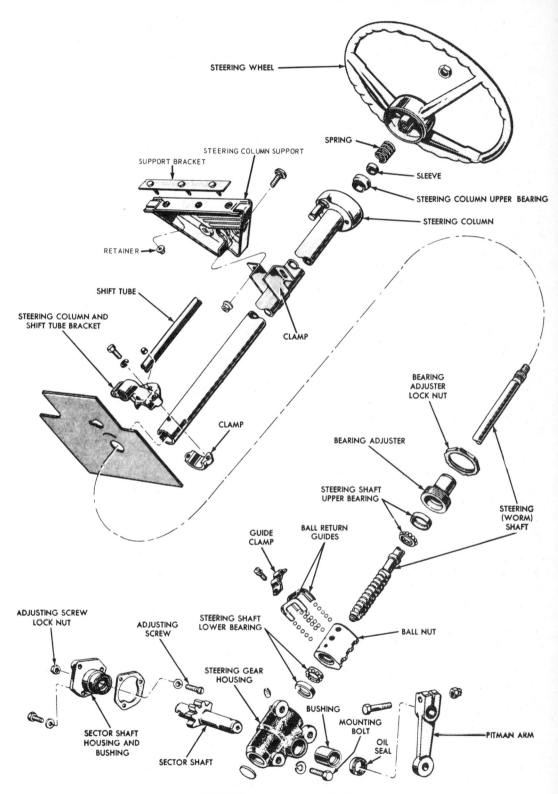

1961–67 steering gear and column

6. Remove the 3 steering gear mounting bolts.

7. Remove the nut and bolt which clamp the pitman arm to the sector shaft.

8. Using a thin chisel, separate the pitman arm split, move the gear away from the frame and slide the pitman arm from the sector shaft.

9. Lift the steering column, shift tube and gear out through the passenger compartment.

10. Remove the steering wheel.

11. Remove the 2 clamp bolts and the clamp which holds the steering column to the bracket.

12. Slide the column and shift tube out of the gear housing and wormshaft. Catch the wormshaft upper bearing sleeve and spring.

To install:

13. Slide the column and shift tube over the wormshaft so that the boss in the column and shift tube brackets pilots into the hole in the column.

14. Install the column-to-bracket clamp and bolts, but don't tighten the bolts yet.

15. Install the assembly into the van through the floor.

16. With the sector shaft centered and the wheels straight ahead, install the pitman arm onto the sector shaft.

17. Install the steering gear mounting bolts and slide the pitman arm fully onto the shaft. Torque the bolt to 50 ft.lb.

18. Torque the steering gear mounting bolts to 40 ft.lb.

19. Tighten the column support nuts and clamp nuts just enough to permit movement while maintaining position.

20. Center the shift tube over the top of the column tube. The centerline of the shift tube should be $1\frac{9}{16}''$ from the steering gear box mounting surface.

21. Adjust the column so that the shaft is centered in the tube and rotates without contacting the column upper bearing with the sleeve removed.

22. Check for free rotation of the steering shaft and torque the support and clamp nuts to 18 ft.lb.

23. The remainder of installation is the reverse of removal.

1969-74

1. Raise and support the front end on jackstands.

2. Remove the bolt from the lower half of the flex coupling.

3. Disconnect the pitman arm from the drag link.

4. Support the gear and remove the 3 mounting bolts. Remove the gear.

5. Place the wheels in a straight-ahead position.

6. Center the steering gear input shaft — about 3 full turns from either stop. The pitman arm should be facing downward.

7. Raise the steering gear into position and engage the input shaft with the flexible coupling.

8. Install the mounting bolts and torque them to 65 ft.lb.

CAUTION: *If you are using new mounting bolts they MUST be grade 9!*

9. Connect the pitman arm and drag link. Torque the nut to 55 ft.lb. on E-100 and 200; 75 ft.lb. on E-300.

10. Install the flexible coupling bolt and torque it to 20 ft.lb.

1975-83

1. Raise and support the front end on jackstands.

2. Disconnect the flex coupling from the steering shaft flange by removing the two attaching nuts.

3. Disconnect the pitman arm from the drag link.

4. Support the gear and remove the 3 mounting bolts. Lower the gear.

5. Remove the bolt from the lower half of the flex coupling and separate the coupling from the gear.

6. Place the wheels in a straight-ahead position.

7. Center the steering gear input shaft — about 3 full turns from either stop. The pitman arm should be facing downward.

7. Install the flexible coupling on the input shaft and install a NEW bolt. Torque it to 20 ft.lb.

8. Raise the steering gear into position and engage the flexible coupling with the flange.

9. Install the mounting bolts and torque them to 75 ft.lb. on 1974-76 models; 65 ft.lb. on 1977-79 models; 70 ft.lb. on 1980-83 models.

CAUTION: *If you are using new mounting bolts they MUST be grade 9!*

10. Connect the pitman arm and drag link. Torque the nut to 75 ft.lb.

11. Install the flexible coupling nuts and torque them to 35 ft.lb. See Steering Column Removal and Installation for proper alignment.

1984-87

1. Raise and support the front end on jackstands.

2. Place the wheels in a straight-ahead position.

3. Disengage the flex coupling shield from the steering gear input shaft shield and slide it up the intermediate shaft.

4. Disconnect the flexible coupling from the steering shaft flange by removing the 2 nuts.

5. Disconnect the drag link from the pitman arm.

6. Matchmark and remove the pitman arm.

7. Support the steering gear and remove the attaching bolts.

8. Remove the coupling-to-gear attaching bolt and remove the coupling from the gear.

To install:

9. Install the flex coupling on the input shaft. Make sure that the flat on the gear is facing upward and aligns with the flat on the coupling. Install a new coupling-to-gear bolt and torque it to 21 ft.lb.

10. Center the input shaft.

11. Place the steering gear into position. Make sure that all bolts and holes align.

12. Install the gear mounting bolts and torque them to 65 ft.lb.

CAUTION: *If you are using new mounting bolts they MUST be grade 9!*

13. Connect the drag link to the pitman arm and hand-tighten the nut.

14. Install the pitman arm on the sector shaft. Torque the sector shaft nut to 230 ft.lb.

15. Make sure that the wheels are still in the straight-ahead position and tighten the drag link stud nut to 70 ft.lb. Install a new cotter pin, advancing the nut to align the hole.

16. Torque the sector shaft-to-flex coupling nuts to 20 ft.lb.

17. Make sure that the steering system moves freely and that the steering wheel is straight with the wheels straight-ahead.

Power Steering Gear

Applications:

1971-74: Thompson Power Cylinder Type
1975-82: Saginaw Integral Type
1983-88: Ford Integral Type

THOMPSON TYPE ADJUSTMENTS

Pitman Arm Stops

1. Loosen the locknut on both pitman arm stops and turn the adjusting screws inwards several turns each.

2. Turn the steering wheel right until the right spindle steering arm contacts the stop.

3. Adjust the forward stop outward until it contacts the pitman arm. Tighten the locknut.

4. Repeat the procedure for the left side.

SAGINAW TYPE ADJUSTMENTS

Mesh Load

1975-78

1. Raise and support the front end on jackstands.

2. Place the wheels in a straight-ahead position.

3. Disconnect the drag link from the pitman arm.

4. Remove the horn pad.

5. Disconnect the fluid return line at the reservoir and cap the port.

6. Place the open end of the return line in a clean container and turn the steering wheel left

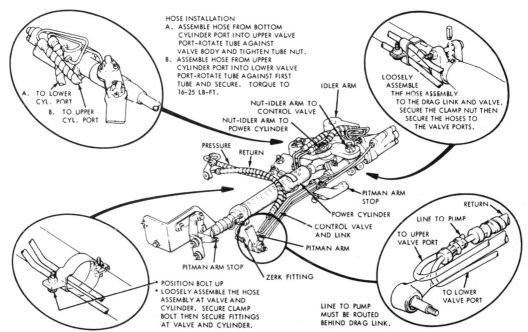

The 1971–74 linkage assist power steering mechanism

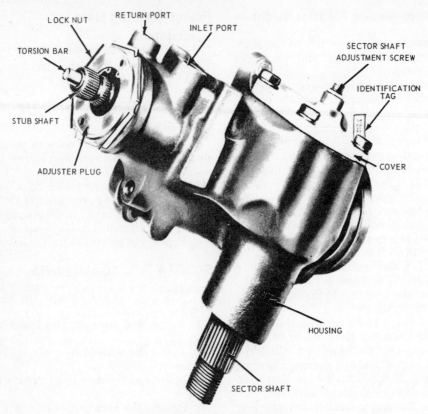

LOCK NUT
RETURN PORT
INLET PORT
TORSION BAR
SECTOR SHAFT
ADJUSTMENT SCREW
IDENTIFICATION
TAG
STUB SHAFT
ADJUSTER PLUG
COVER
HOUSING
SECTOR SHAFT

1975 and later power steering gear

and right several times to discharge the fluid from the gear.

7. Place an inch-pound torque wrench on the steering wheel nut and check the following torques:

- ½ turn from both the left and right stops.
- ½ turn left and right of center.
- 180° arc over-center.

8. The correct over-center meshload is as follows:

- new gear over-center torque should be 4-8 in.lb. greater than the end stop readings, but not to exceed 18 in.lb.
- The used (over 400 miles) gear over-center torque reading should be 4-5 in.lb. greater than the end readings, but not to exceed 14 in.lb.

9. If the over-center reading is not within specifications, loosen the locknut and back the adjusting screw out all the way, then turn it back in ½ turn.

10. Rotate the wheel from lock-to-lock, counting the number of turns, then turn it back ½ the number of turns to center the gear.

11. Turn the wheel ¼ turn off center and rotate it, with the torque wrench, to ¼ turn the other side of center, noting the highest torque reading. Turn the adjusting screw inward until the reading is 3-6 in.lb. higher than the reading

noted in Step 8. The total reading should not exceed 14 in.lb.

12. When the adjustment has been accomplished, hold the adjusting screw and tighten the locknut to 35 ft.lb.

13. Connect the drag link.

14. Connect the fluid line and refill and bleed the reservoir.

1979-82

1. Raise and support the front end on jackstands.

2. Place the wheels in a straight-ahead position.

3. Matchmark the pitman arm and gear housing and disconnect the pitman arm from the sector shaft.

4. Remove the steering wheel hub.

5. Disconnect the fluid return line at the reservoir and cap the port.

6. Place the open end of the return line in a clean container and turn the steering wheel left and right several times to discharge the fluid from the gear.

7. Place an inch-pound torque wrench on the steering wheel nut.

8. Turn the steering wheel ½ turn off of center to either side.

9. Using the torque wrench, determine the torque required to turn the wheel through a 20° arc.

10. Turn the wheel back to center and repeat Steps 8 & 9 to the other side of center.

11. Loosen the adjusting screw locknut and, using a $^7/_{32}"$ allen wrench, turn the adjusting screw inward until the reading is 5 in.lb. greater than that previously recorded.

12. Hold the adjusting screw and tighten the locknut.

13. Recheck the readings.

14. Install the pitman arm.

15. Connect the fluid line and refill and bleed the reservoir.

FORD TYPE ADJUSTMENTS

Meshload

1. Raise and support the front end on jackstands.

2. Matchmark the pitman arm and gear housing.

3. Set the wheels in a straight-ahead position.

4. Disconnect the pitman arm from the sector shaft.

5. Disconnect the fluid RETURN line at the pump reservoir and cap the reservoir nipple.

6. Place the end of the return line in a clean container and turn the steering wheel lock-to-lock a few times to expel the fluid from the gear.

7. Turn the steering wheel all the way to the right stop. Place a small piece of masking tape on the steering wheel rim as a reference and rotate the steering wheel 45° from the right stop.

8. Disconnect the battery ground.

9. Remove the horn pad.

10. Using an inch-pound torque wrench on the steering wheel nut, record the amount of torque needed to turn the steering wheel $^1\!/_8$ turn counterclockwise. The preload reading should be 4-9 in.lb.

11. Center the steering wheel ($^1\!/_2$ the total lock-to-lock turns) and record the torque needed to turn the steering wheel 90° to either side of center. On a truck with fewer than 5,000 miles, the meshload should be 15-25 in.lb. On a truck with 5,000 or more miles, the meshload should be 7 in.lb. more than the preload torque.

On trucks with fewer than 5,000 miles, if the meshload is not within specifications, it should be reset to a figure 14-18 in.lb. greater than the recorded preload torque.

On trucks with 5,000 or more miles, if the meshload is not within specifications, it should be reset to a figure 10-14 in.lb. greater than the recorded preload torque.

12. If an adjustment is required, loosen the adjuster locknut and turn the sector shaft adjuster screw until the necessary torque is achieved.

13. Once adjustment is completed. hold the adjuster screw and tighten the locknut to 45 ft.lb.

14. Recheck the adjustment readings and reset if necessary.

15. Connect the return line and refill the reservoir.

16. Install the pitman arm.

17. Install the horn pad.

THOMPSON TYPE REMOVAL AND INSTALLATION

1. Raise and support the front end on jackstands.

2. Disconnect the control valve and link from the pitman arm.

3. Disconnect the tie rods from the idler arm.

4. Remove the pawl nut, attaching nut, washer and insulator from the end of the power cylinder rod.

5. Disconnect the pressure and return lines from the pump.

6. Remove the bolts securing the idler arm bracket to the crossmember.

7. Remove the control valve and link, power cylinder, hoses, idler arm and bracket as an assembly.

To install:

8. Thread the valve onto the link until the roll pin can be inserted behind the clamp in the notch. Torque the clamp bolt to 15 ft.lb.

9. Connect the fluid lines to the control valve. Torque the $^5/_{16}"$ fittings to 20 ft.lb.; the $^3/_8"$ fittings to 25 ft.lb. DO NOT OVERTIGHTEN!

10. Rest the assembly on the crossmember.

11. Attach the idler arm bracket to the crossmember. If new bolts are being used they must be Grade 9! Install a washer under each bolt head and under each nut. Torque the bolts to 60 ft.lb.

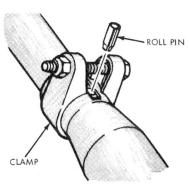

Disconnecting the control valve from the link on Thompson-type steering

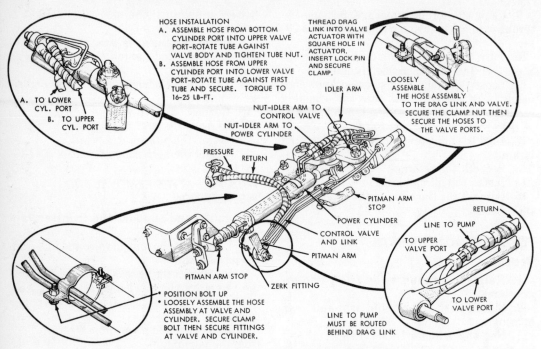

HOSE INSTALLATION
A. ASSEMBLE HOSE FROM BOTTOM CYLINDER PORT INTO UPPER VALVE PORT-ROTATE TUBE AGAINST VALVE BODY AND TIGHTEN TUBE NUT.
B. ASSEMBLE HOSE FROM UPPER CYLINDER PORT INTO LOWER VALVE PORT-ROTATE TUBE AGAINST FIRST TUBE AND SECURE. TORQUE TO 16-25 LB-FT.

THREAD DRAG LINK INTO VALVE ACTUATOR WITH SQUARE HOLE IN ACTUATOR. INSERT LOCK PIN AND SECURE CLAMP.

LOOSELY ASSEMBLE THE HOSE ASSEMBLY TO THE DRAG LINK AND VALVE. SECURE THE CLAMP NUT THEN SECURE THE HOSES TO THE VALVE PORTS.

A. TO LOWER CYL. PORT
B. TO UPPER CYL. PORT

IDLER ARM

NUT-IDLER ARM TO CONTROL VALVE
NUT-IDLER ARM TO POWER CYLINDER

PRESSURE
RETURN

PITMAN ARM STOP

POWER CYLINDER

CONTROL VALVE AND LINK

PITMAN ARM

RETURN
LINE TO PUMP
TO UPPER VALVE PORT

TO LOWER VALVE PORT

PITMAN ARM STOP

ZERK FITTING

• POSITION BOLT UP
• LOOSELY ASSEMBLE THE HOSE ASSEMBLY AT VALVE AND CYLINDER. SECURE CLAMP BOLT THEN SECURE FITTINGS AT VALVE AND CYLINDER.

LINE TO PUMP MUST BE ROUTED BEHIND DRAG LINK

1971–74 Thompson-type power steering linkage

12. Connect the lines to the pump.

13. Attach the power cylinder to the front bracket. Torque the ⅜"-24 nut to 21 ft.lb. and the pawl nut to 45 in.lb.

14. Connect the control valve and link to the pitman arm and the tie rods to the idler arm. Observe the following torques:
- E-100, 200 tie rod — 45 ft.lb.
- E-300 tie rod — 60 ft.lb.
- Pitman arm nuts — 60 ft.lb.

NOTE: *Never back-off a nut to align the cotter pin holes. Always advance the nut.*

15. Fill the reservoir.

16. Start the engine and let it run for at least 2 minutes to warm the fluid.

17. Turn the wheel from lock-to-lock several times and check for leaks.

18. Increase the idle to 1,000 rpm and turn the wheel lock-to-lock several times again. Check for leaks again.

19. Add fluid if necessary.

20. Recheck the level after the first 20 minutes of driving.

SAGINAW TYPE REMOVAL AND INSTALLATION

1. Raise and support the front end on jackstands.

2. Label the fluid lines.

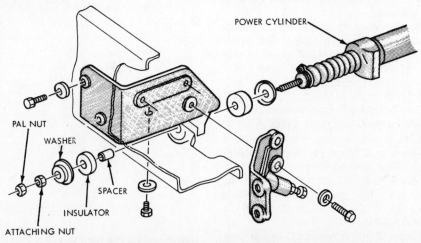

POWER CYLINDER

PAL NUT

WASHER

SPACER

INSULATOR

ATTACHING NUT

1971–74 Thompson-type power cylinder rod bracket attachments

3. Place a drain pan under the gear and disconnect the lines. Plug the lines and ports.

4. Disconnect the drag link from the pitman arm.

5. Remove the flex coupling-to-flange nuts.

6. Support the gear and remove the attaching bolts.

7. Remove the gear.

To install:

8. Center the gear — about 3 turns from either lock.

9. Position the gear on the frame and install the bolts. If new bolts are being used, they must be Grade 9! Torque the bolts to 75 ft.lb.

10. Joint the flex coupling and flange and install the nuts. Torque them to 35 ft.lb.

11. Connect the fluid lines. Torque the fittings to 25 ft.lb.

12. Disconnect the coil lead, fill the reservoir and crank the engine while turning the wheel lock-to-lock several times to bleed off any air.

13. Recheck the fluid level and refill as necessary.

14. Connect the coil wire.

FORD TYPE REMOVAL AND INSTALLATION

1. Raise and support the front end on jackstands.

2. Place the wheels in the straight-ahead position.

3. Place a drain pan under the gear and disconnect the pressure and return lines. Cap the openings.

4. Remove the splash shield from the flex coupling.

5. Disconnect the flex coupling at the gear.

6. Matchmark and remove the pitman arm from the sector shaft.

7. Support the steering gear and remove the mounting bolts.

8. Remove the steering gear. It may be necessary to work it free of the flex coupling.

To install:

9. Place the splash shield on the steering gear lugs.

10. Slide the flex coupling into place on the steering shaft. Make sure the steering wheel spokes are still horizontal.

11. Center the steering gear input shaft with the indexing flat facing downward.

12. Slide the steering gear input shaft into the flex coupling and into place on the frame side rail. Install the flex coupling bolt and torque it to 30 ft.lb.

13. Install the gear mounting bolts and torque them to 65 ft.lb.

14. Make sure that the wheels are still straight ahead and install the pitman arm. Torque the nut to 230 ft.lb.

15. Connect the pressure, then, the return lines. Torque the pressure line to 25 ft.lb.

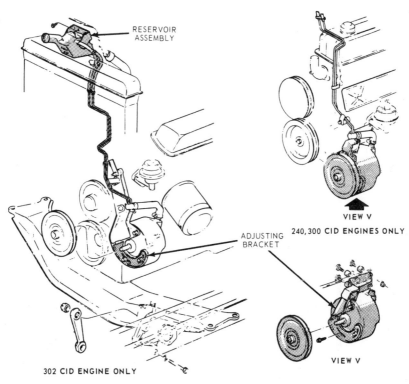

RESERVOIR ASSEMBLY

VIEW V
240,300 CID ENGINES ONLY

ADJUSTING BRACKET

VIEW V

302 CID ENGINE ONLY

Thompson-type power steering pump

16. Snap the flex coupling shield into place.

17. Fill the steering reservoir.

18. Run the engine and turn the steering wheel lock-to-lock several times to expel air. Check for leaks.

Power Steering Pump

REMOVAL AND INSTALLATION

1971-74

1. Raise and support the front end on jackstands.

2. Place a drain pan under the pump and disconnect the pressure and return lines. Cap the lines and ports.

3. On vans with a 6-cylinder engine, lower the van.

4. Loosen the pump retaining bolts, slide the pump inward and remove the belt.

5. Disconnect the reservoir line.

6. On 6-cylinder engines, remove the nuts that hold the pump bracket to the block. Remove the pump and bracket from under the van.

On V8 engines, remove the pump-to-bracket bolts and lay the pump on the cross-member. Loosen the bracket-to-block bolts and nuts, move the bracket forward and remove the pump.

7. Installation is the reverse of removal. Torque the pump-to-bracket bolts to 50 ft.lb.; the bracket-to-block bolts to 15 ft.lb.; the pressure hose nut to 30 ft.lb.

8. Refill the reservoir with power steering fluid and start the engine. Turn the steering wheel from lock-to-lock several times to expel any air. Don't hold the wheel against the stops! Check for leaks.

1975-88

1. Place a drain pan under the pump.

2. Disconnect the pressure and return lines and cap the ports and lines.

3. Remove the belt tension nut.

4. Remove the attaching bolts and take off the belt. Lift out the pump.

5. Installation is the reverse of removal. Adjust the belt. Torque all retainers to 40 ft.lb. Torque the pressure line nut to 25 ft.lb. Refill the pump. Start the engine and turn the wheel from lock-to-lock several times to expel any air. Refill the pump with power steering fluid.

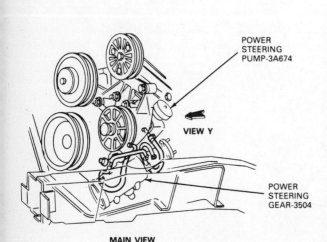

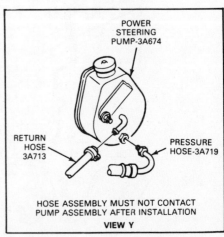

1987–88 8-302 power steering pump installation

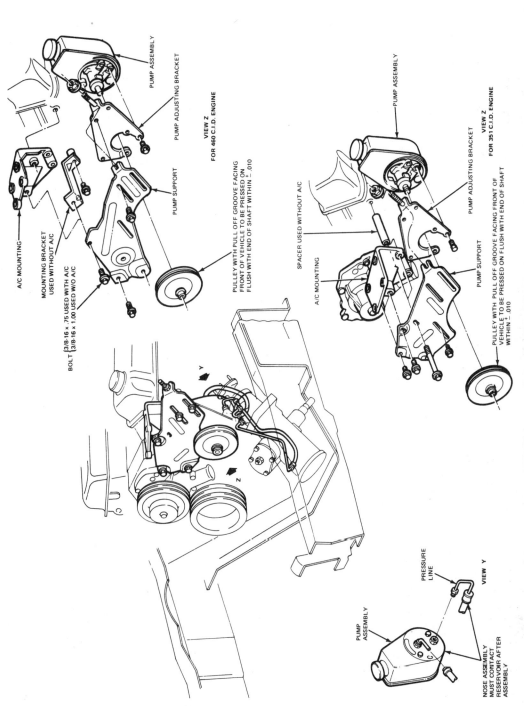

PUMP ASSEMBLY

PUMP ADJUSTING BRACKET

VIEW Z
FOR 460 C.I.D. ENGINE

PUMP SUPPORT

A/C MOUNTING

MOUNTING BRACKET
USED WITHOUT A/C

BOLT 3/8-16 x .75 USED WITH A/C
3/8-16 x 1.00 USED W/O A/C

PULLEY WITH PULL OFF GROOVE FACING
FRONT OF VEHICLE TO BE PRESSED ON
FLUSH WITH END OF SHAFT WITHIN ± .010

PUMP ASSEMBLY

PUMP ADJUSTING BRACKET

VIEW Z
FOR 351 C.I.D. ENGINE

SPACER USED WITHOUT A/C

A/C MOUNTING

PUMP SUPPORT

PULLEY WITH PULL OFF GROOVE FACING FRONT OF
VEHICLE TO BE PRESSED ON FLUSH WITH END OF SHAFT
WITHIN ± .010

PRESSURE
LINE

VIEW Y

PUMP
ASSEMBLY

NOSE ASSEMBLY
MUST CONTACT
RESERVOIR AFTER
ASSEMBLY

1977 V8 power steering pump installation

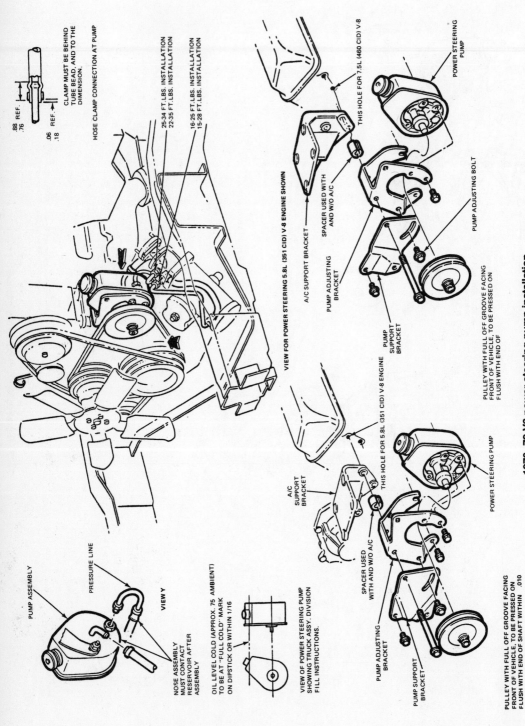

HOSE CLAMP CONNECTION AT PUMP

CLAMP MUST BE BEHIND TUBE BEAD AND TO THE DIMENSION.

.88 REF.
.76 REF.
.06 REF.
.18 REF.

25-34 FT.LBS. INSTALLATION
22-35 FT.LBS. INSTALLATION

16-25 FT.LBS. INSTALLATION
15-28 FT.LBS. INSTALLATION

VIEW FOR POWER STEERING 5.8L (351 CID) V-8 ENGINE SHOWN

THIS HOLE FOR 7.5L (460 CID) V-8

POWER STEERING PUMP

A/C SUPPORT BRACKET

SPACER USED WITH AND W/O A/C

PUMP ADJUSTING BRACKET

PUMP ADJUSTING BOLT

PUMP SUPPORT BRACKET

PULLEY WITH FULL OFF GROOVE FACING FRONT OF VEHICLE, TO BE PRESSED ON FLUSH WITH END OF

1978–79 V8 power steering pump installation

PUMP ASSEMBLY

PRESSURE LINE

VIEW Y

NOSE ASSEMBLY MUST CONTACT RESERVOIR AFTER ASSEMBLY

OIL LEVEL COLD (APPROX. 75 AMBIENT) TO BE AT "FULL COLD" MARK ON DIPSTICK OR WITHIN 1/16

VIEW OF POWER STEERING PUMP SHOWING TRUCK ASSY. DIVISION FILL INSTRUCTIONS.

A/C SUPPORT BRACKET

THIS HOLE FOR 5.8L (351 CID) V-8 ENGINE

POWER STEERING PUMP

SPACER USED WITH AND W/O A/C

POWER STEERING PUMP

PUMP ADJUSTING BRACKET

PUMP SUPPORT BRACKET

PULLEY WITH FULL OFF GROOVE FACING FRONT OF VEHICLE, TO BE PRESSED ON FLUSH WITH END OF SHAFT WITHIN .010

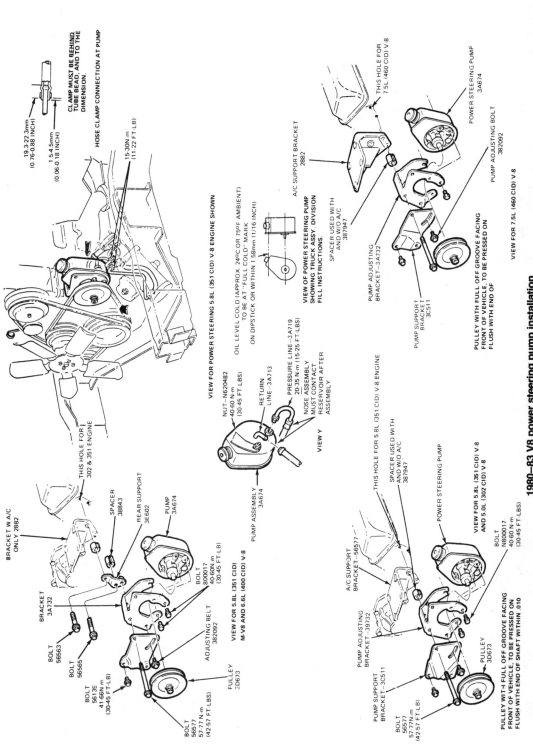

CLAMP MUST BE BEHIND TUBE BEAD, AND TO THE DIMENSION.

19.3-22.3mm (0.76-0.88 INCH)

1.5-4.5mm (0.06-0.18 INCH)

HOSE CLAMP CONNECTION AT PUMP

15-30N·m (11-22 FT·LB)

THIS HOLE FOR 7.5L (460 CID) V-8

POWER STEERING PUMP 3A674

A/C SUPPORT BRACKET 2882

PUMP ADJUSTING BOLT 382092

PUMP ADJUSTING BRACKET—3A732

SPACER USED WITH AND W/O A/C 387947

PUMP SUPPORT BRACKET 3C511

VIEW FOR 7.5L (460 CID) V-8

PULLEY WITH FULL OFF GROOVE FACING FRONT OF VEHICLE, TO BE PRESSED ON FLUSH WITH END OF

VIEW OF POWER STEERING PUMP SHOWING TRUCK ASSY. DIVISION FILL INSTRUCTIONS.

OIL LEVEL COLD (APPROX. 24°C OR 75°F AMBIENT) TO BE AT "FULL COLD" MARK ON DIPSTICK OR WITHIN 1.58mm (1/16 INCH)

VIEW FOR POWER STEERING 5.8L (351 CID) V-8 ENGINE SHOWN

NUT—N620482 40-60 N·m (30-45 FT LBS)

RETURN LINE—3A713

PRESSURE LINE—3A719 20-35 N·m (15-25 FT·LBS)

NOSE ASSEMBLY MUST CONTACT RESERVOIR AFTER ASSEMBLY

VIEW Y

PUMP ASSEMBLY 3A674

THIS HOLE FOR 5.8L (351 CID) V-8 ENGINE

SPACER USED WITH AND W/O A/C 387947

POWER STEERING PUMP

VIEW FOR 5.8L (351 CID) V-8 AND 5.0L (302 CID) V-8

BOLT N800017 40-60 N·m (30-45 FT·LBS)

A/C SUPPORT BRACKET—56577

PUMP ADJUSTING BRACKET—39732

PUMP SUPPORT BRACKET—3C511

BOLT 56577 57-77 N·m (42-57 FT·LB)

PULLEY 3D673

PULLEY WITH FULL OFF GROOVE FACING FRONT OF VEHICLE, TO BE PRESSED ON FLUSH WITH END OF SHAFT WITHIN .010

BRACKET W A/C ONLY 2882

THIS HOLE FOR 302 & 351 ENGINE

SPACER 38843

REAR SUPPORT 3E602

PUMP 3A674

BRACKET 3A732

BOLT 56563

BOLT 56565

BOLT 56135 41-66 N·m (30-45 FT·LB)

BOLT 800017 40-60 N·m (30-45 FT·LB)

ADJUSTING BELT 382092

VIEW FOR 5.8L (351 CID) M-V8 AND 6.6L (400 CID) V-8

FULLEY 3D673

BOLT 56577 57-77 N·m (42-57 FT·LBS)

1980–83 V8 power steering pump installation

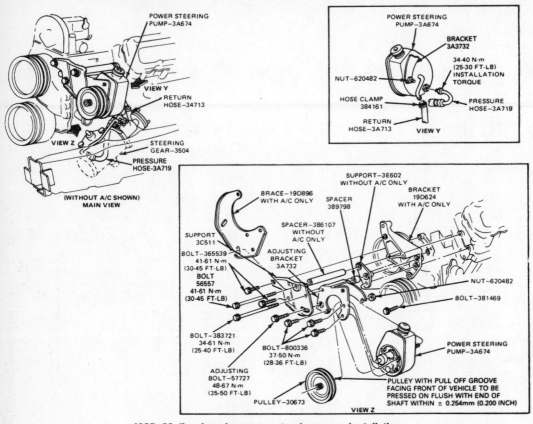

1985–86 diesel engine power steering pump installation

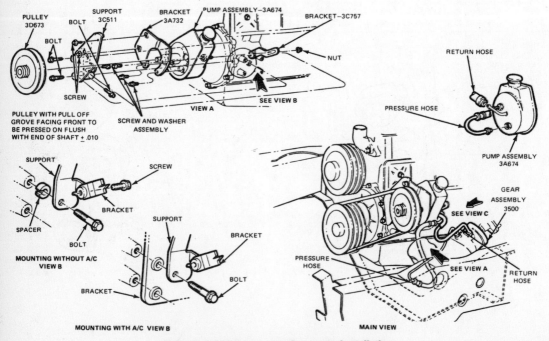

1978–86 6-300 power steering pump installation

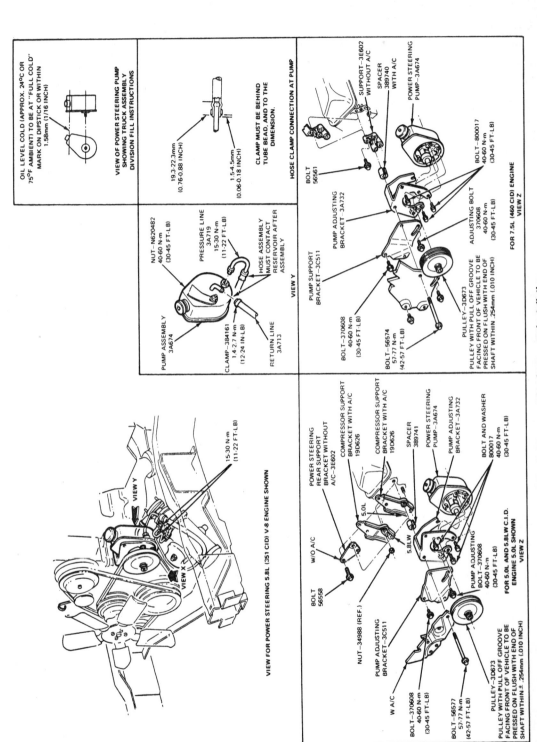

OIL LEVEL COLD (APPROX. 24°C OR 75°F AMBIENT) TO BE AT "FULL COLD" MARK ON DIPSTICK OR WITHIN 1.58mm (1/16 INCH)

VIEW OF POWER STEERING PUMP SHOWING TRUCK ASSEMBLY DIVISION FILL INSTRUCTIONS

19.3-22.3mm (0.76-0.88 INCH)

1.5-4.5mm (0.06-0.18 INCH)

CLAMP MUST BE BEHIND TUBE BEAD, AND TO THE DIMENSION.

HOSE CLAMP CONNECTION AT PUMP

PRESSURE LINE 3A719 15-30 N·m (11-22 FT-LB)

NUT—N620482 40-60 N·m (30-45 FT-LB)

HOSE ASSEMBLY MUST CONTACT RESERVOIR AFTER ASSEMBLY

VIEW Y

PUMP ASSEMBLY 3A674

CLAMP—384161 1.4-2.7 N·m (12-24 IN-LB)

RETURN LINE 3A713

BOLT 56561

SUPPORT—3E602 WITHOUT A/C

SPACER 389740 WITH A/C

POWER STEERING PUMP—3A674

BOLT—800017 40-60 N·m (30-45 FT-LB)

PUMP ADJUSTING BRACKET—3A732

PUMP SUPPORT BRACKET—3C511

BOLT—370608 40-60 N·m (30-45 FT-LB)

BOLT—56574 57-77 N·m (42-57 FT-LB)

PULLEY—3D673 PULLEY WITH PULL OFF GROOVE FACING FRONT OF VEHICLE TO BE PRESSED ON FLUSH WITH END OF SHAFT WITHIN .254mm (.010 INCH)

ADJUSTING BOLT 370608 40-60 N·m (30-45 FT-LB)

FOR 7.5L (460 CID) ENGINE VIEW Z

15-30 N·m (11-22 FT-LB)

VIEW Y

VIEW X

VIEW FOR POWER STEERING 5.8L (351 CID) V-8 ENGINE SHOWN

POWER STEERING REAR SUPPORT BRACKET WITHOUT A/C-3E602

COMPRESSOR SUPPORT BRACKET WITH A/C 19D626

COMPRESSOR SUPPORT BRACKET WITH A/C 19D626

SPACER 389741

POWER STEERING PUMP—3A674

PUMP ADJUSTING BRACKET—3A732

BOLT AND WASHER 800017 40-60 N·m (30-45 FT-LB)

BOLT 56558

W/O A/C

5.0L

5.8LW

NUT—34988 (REF.)

PUMP ADJUSTING BRACKET—3C511

W A/C

PUMP ADJUSTING BOLT—370608 40-60 N·m (30-45 FT-LB)

FOR 5.0L AND 5.8LW C.I.D. ENGINE 5.0L SHOWN VIEW Z

BOLT—370608 40-60 N·m (30-45 FT-LB)

BOLT—56577 57-77 N·m (42-57 FT-LB)

PULLEY—3D673 PULLEY WITH PULL OFF GROOVE FACING FRONT OF VEHICLE TO BE PRESSED ON FLUSH WITH END OF SHAFT WITHIN ± .254mm (.010 INCH)

1984–86 V8 power steering pump installation

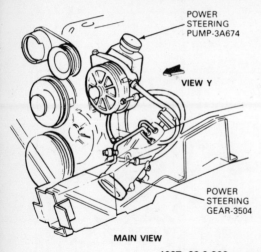

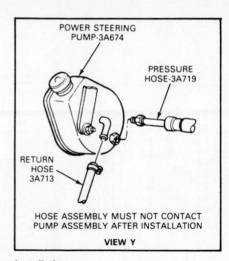

1987–88 6-300 power steering pump installation

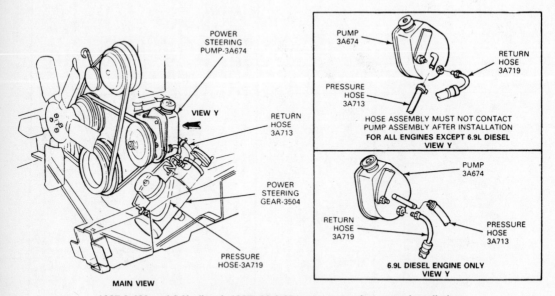

1987 8-460 and 6.9L diesel; 1987–88 8-351 power steering pump installation

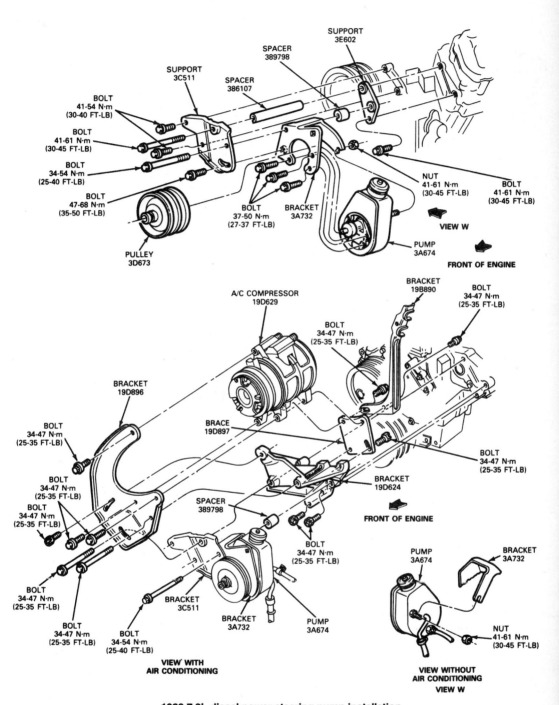

SUPPORT
3E602

SPACER
389798

SUPPORT
3C511

SPACER
386107

BOLT
41-54 N·m
(30-40 FT-LB)

BOLT
41-61 N·m
(30-45 FT-LB)

BOLT
34-54 N·m
(25-40 FT-LB)

BOLT
47-68 N·m
(35-50 FT-LB)

PULLEY
3D673

BOLT
37-50 N·m
(27-37 FT-LB)

BRACKET
3A732

NUT
41-61 N·m
(30-45 FT-LB)

BOLT
41-61 N·m
(30-45 FT-LB)

VIEW W

PUMP
3A674

FRONT OF ENGINE

A/C COMPRESSOR
19D629

BRACKET
19B890

BOLT
34-47 N·m
(25-35 FT-LB)

BOLT
34-47 N·m
(25-35 FT-LB)

BRACKET
19D896

BOLT
34-47 N·m
(25-35 FT-LB)

BRACE
19D897

BOLT
34-47 N·m
(25-35 FT-LB)

BOLT
34-47 N·m
(25-35 FT-LB)

BRACKET
19D624

BOLT
34-47 N·m
(25-35 FT-LB)

FRONT OF ENGINE

BOLT
34-47 N·m
(25-35 FT-LB)

SPACER
389798

PUMP
3A674

BRACKET
3A732

BOLT
34-47 N·m
(25-35 FT-LB)

BOLT
34-47 N·m
(25-35 FT-LB)

BRACKET
3C511

BRACKET
3A732

PUMP
3A674

NUT
41-61 N·m
(30-45 FT-LB)

BOLT
34-47 N·m
(25-35 FT-LB)

BOLT
34-54 N·m
(25-40 FT-LB)

VIEW WITH
AIR CONDITIONING

VIEW WITHOUT
AIR CONDITIONING
VIEW W

1988 7.3L diesel power steering pump installation

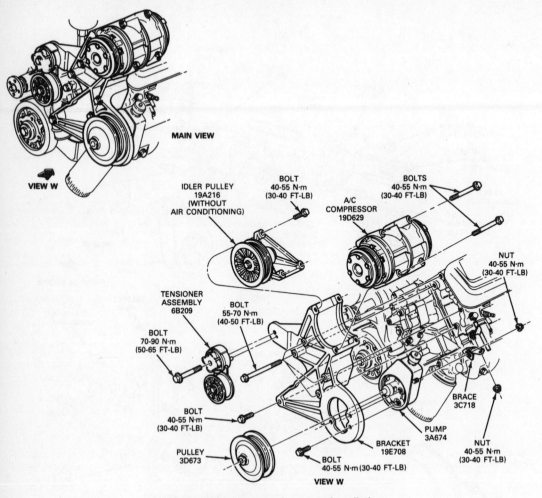

MAIN VIEW

VIEW W

IDLER PULLEY
19A216
(WITHOUT
AIR CONDITIONING)

BOLT
40-55 N·m
(30-40 FT-LB)

A/C
COMPRESSOR
19D629

BOLTS
40-55 N·m
(30-40 FT-LB)

NUT
40-55 N·m
(30-40 FT-LB)

TENSIONER
ASSEMBLY
6B209

BOLT
55-70 N·m
(40-50 FT-LB)

BOLT
70-90 N·m
(50-65 FT-LB)

BRACE
3C718

BOLT
40-55 N·m
(30-40 FT-LB)

PUMP
3A674

PULLEY
3D673

BRACKET
19E708

NUT
40-55 N·m
(30-40 FT-LB)

BOLT
40-55 N·m (30-40 FT-LB)

VIEW W

1988 8-460 power steering pump installation

BASIC OPERATING PRINCIPLES

Hydraulic systems are used to actuate the brakes of all automobiles. The system transports the power required to force the frictional surfaces of the braking system together from the pedal to the individual brake units at each wheel. A hydraulic system is used for two reasons.

First, fluid under pressure can be carried to all parts of an automobile by small pipes and flexible hoses without taking up a significant amount of room or posing routing problems.

Second, a great mechanical advantage can be given to the brake pedal end of the system, and the foot pressure required to actuate the brakes can be reduced by making the surface area of the master cylinder pistons smaller than that of any of the pistons in the wheel cylinders or calipers.

The master cylinder consists of a fluid reservoir and a double cylinder and piston assembly. Double type master cylinders are designed to separate the front and rear braking systems hydraulically in case of a leak.

Steel lines carry the brake fluid to a point on the vehicle's frame near each of the vehicle's wheels. The fluid is then carried to the calipers and wheel cylinders by flexible tubes in order to allow for suspension and steering movements.

In drum brake systems, each wheel cylinder contains two pistons, one at either end, which push outward in opposite directions.

In disc brake systems, the cylinders are part of the calipers. One cylinder in each caliper is used to force the brake pads against the disc.

All pistons employ some type of seal, usually made of rubber, to minimize fluid leakage. A rubber dust boot seals the outer end of the cylinder against dust and dirt. The boot fits around the outer end of the piston on disc brake calipers, and around the brake actuating rod on wheel cylinders.

The hydraulic system operates as follows: When at rest, the entire system, from the piston(s) in the master cylinder to those in the wheel cylinders or calipers, is full of brake fluid. Upon application of the brake pedal, fluid trapped in front of the master cylinder piston(s) is forced through the lines to the wheel cylinders. Here, it forces the pistons outward, in the case of drum brakes, and inward toward the disc, in the case of disc brakes. The motion of the pistons is opposed by return springs mounted outside the cylinders in drum brakes, and by spring seals, in disc brakes.

Upon release of the brake pedal, a spring located inside the master cylinder immediately returns the master cylinder pistons to the normal position. The pistons contain check valves and the master cylinder has compensating ports drilled in it. These are uncovered as the pistons reach their normal position. The piston check valves allow fluid to flow toward the wheel cylinders or calipers as the pistons withdraw. Then, as the return springs force the brake pads or shoes into the released position, the excess fluid reservoir through the compensating ports. It is during the time the pedal is in the released position that any fluid that has leaked out of the system will be replaced through the compensating ports.

Dual circuit master cylinders employ two pistons, located one behind the other, in the same cylinder. The primary piston is actuated directly by mechanical linkage from the brake pedal through the power booster. The secondary piston is actuated by fluid trapped between the two pistons. If a leak develops in front of the secondary piston, it moves forward until it bottoms against the front of the master cylinder, and the fluid trapped between the pistons will operate the rear brakes. If the rear brakes develop a leak, the primary piston will move forward until direct contact with the secondary piston takes place, and it will force the secondary piston to actuate the front brakes. In either case, the brake pedal moves farther when the brakes are applied, and less braking power is available.

All dual circuit systems use a switch to warn the driver when only half of the brake system is operational. This switch is located in a valve body which is mounted on the firewall or the frame below the master cylinder. A hydraulic piston receives pressure from both circuits, each circuit's pressure being applied to one end of the piston. When the pressures are in balance, the piston remains stationary. When one circuit has a leak, however, the greater pressure in that circuit during application of the brakes will push the piston to one side, closing the switch and activating the brake warning light.

In disc brake systems, this valve body also contains a metering valve and, in some cases, a proportioning valve. The metering valve keeps pressure from traveling to the disc brakes on the front wheels until the brake shoes on the rear wheels have contacted the drums, ensuring that the front brakes will never be used alone. The proportioning valve controls the pressure to the rear brakes to lessen the chance of rear wheel lock-up during very hard braking.

Warning lights may be tested by depressing the brake pedal and holding it while opening one of the wheel cylinder bleeder screws. If this does not cause the light to go on, substitute a new lamp, make continuity checks, and, finally, replace the switch as necessary.

The hydraulic system may be checked for leaks by applying pressure to the pedal gradually and steadily. If the pedal sinks very slowly to the floor, the system has a leak. This is not to be confused with a springy or spongy feel due to the compression of air within the lines. If the system leaks, there will be a gradual change in the position of the pedal with a constant pressure.

Check for leaks along all lines and at wheel cylinders. If no external leaks are apparent, the problem is inside the master cylinder.

Disc Brakes
BASIC OPERATING PRINCIPLES

Instead of the traditional expanding brakes that press outward against a circular drum, disc brake systems utilize a disc (rotor) with brake pads positioned on either side of it. Braking effect is achieved in a manner similar to the way you would squeeze a spinning phonograph record between your fingers. The disc (rotor) is a casting with cooling fins between the two braking surfaces. This enables air to circulate between the braking surfaces making them less sensitive to heat buildup and more resistant to fade. Dirt and water do not affect braking action since contaminants are thrown off by the centrifugal action of the rotor or scraped off the by the pads. Also, the equal clamping action of the two brake pads tends to ensure uniform, straight line stops. Disc brakes are inherently self-adjusting.

There are three general types of disc brake:
1. A fixed caliper.
2. A floating caliper.
3. A sliding caliper.

The fixed caliper design uses two pistons mounted on either side of the rotor (in each side of the caliper). The caliper is mounted rigidly and does not move.

The sliding and floating designs are quite similar. In fact, these two types are often lumped together. In both designs, the pad on the inside of the rotor is moved into contact with the rotor by hydraulic force. The caliper, which is not held in a fixed position, moves slightly, bringing the outside pad into contact with the rotor. There are various methods of attaching floating calipers. Some pivot at the bottom or top, and some slide on mounting bolts. In any event, the end result is the same.

All the cars covered in this book employ the sliding caliper design.

Drum Brakes
BASIC OPERATING PRINCIPLES

Drum brakes employ two brake shoes mounted on a stationary backing plate. These shoes are positioned inside a circular drum which rotates with the wheel assembly. The shoes are held in place by springs. This allows them to slide toward the drums (when they are applied) while keeping the linings and drums in alignment. The shoes are actuated by a wheel cylinder which is mounted at the top of the backing plate. When the brakes are applied, hydraulic pressure forces the wheel cylinder's actuating links outward. Since these links bear directly against the top of the brake shoes, the tops of the shoes are then forced against the inner side of the drum. This action forces the bottoms of the two shoes to contact the brake drum by rotating the entire assembly slightly (known as servo action). When pressure within the wheel cylinder is relaxed, return springs pull the shoes back away from the drum.

Most modern drum brakes are designed to self-adjust themselves during application when the vehicle is moving in reverse. This motion causes both shoes to rotate very slightly with the drum, rocking an adjusting lever, thereby causing rotation of the adjusting screw.

Power Boosters

Power brakes operate just as non-power brake systems except in the actuation of the master cylinder pistons. A vacuum diaphragm is located on the front of the master cylinder and assists the driver in applying the brakes, reducing both the effort and travel he must put into moving the brake pedal.

The vacuum diaphragm housing is connected to the intake manifold by a vacuum hose. A check valve is placed at the point where the hose enters the diaphragm housing, so that during periods of low manifold vacuum brake assist vacuum will not be lost.

Depressing the brake pedal closes off the vacuum source and allows atmospheric pressure to enter on one side of the diaphragm. This causes the master cylinder pistons to move and apply the brakes. When the brake pedal is released, vacuum is applied to both sides of the diaphragm, and return springs return the diaphragm and master cylinder pistons to the released position. If the vacuum fails, the brake pedal rod will butt against the end of the master cylinder actuating rod, and direct mechanical application will occur as the pedal is depressed.

The hydraulic and mechanical problems that apply to conventional brake systems also apply to power brakes, and should be checked for if the tests below do not reveal the problem.

Test for a system vacuum leak as described below:

1. Operate the engine at idle without touching the brake pedal for at least one minute.

2. Turn off the engine, and wait one minute.

3. Test for the presence of assist vacuum by depressing the brake pedal and releasing it several times. Light application will produce less and less pedal travel, if vacuum was present. If there is no vacuum, air is leaking into the system somewhere.

Test for system operation as follows:

1. Pump the brake pedal (with engine off) until the supply vacuum is entirely gone.

2. Put a light, steady pressure on the pedal.

3. Start the engine, and operate it at idle. If the system is operating, the brake pedal should fall toward the floor if constant pressure is maintained on the pedal.

Power brake systems may be tested for hydraulic leaks just as ordinary systems are tested.

BRAKE SYSTEM

Single-anchor, internal-expanding, duo-servo, self-adjusting, hydraulic drum brakes with a safety, dual master cylinder are used on the front of Ford vans through 1974 and on the rear of all years.

Disc front brakes are used on 1975 and later models; dual piston on E-250 and 350, single piston on E-100 and 150.

The E-100 and E-150 use a sliding caliper, single piston brake; the 1975 E-250 and E-350 and some 1979-88 use a floating caliper, dual piston brake; and the 1976 and later E-250 and E-350 and some 1979-88 E-100, 150 use a rail sliding caliper, dual piston brake. Both he floating and sliding calipers are allowed to move slightly to align with the disc (rotor). The floating caliper is retained by through-bolts, and the sliding caliper by a key.

The dual, safety-type master cylinder contains a double hydraulic with two fluid reservoirs, two hydraulic pistons (a primary and a secondary), and two residual check valves on all-drum systems, located in the outlet ports. The master cylinder's primary and secondary pistons function simultaneously when both the primary and secondary systems are fully operative.

Failure in either the front or rear brake system does not result in failure of the entire hydraulic brake system. Should hydraulic failure occur in the rear system, the hydraulic pressure from the primary piston (which actuates the front brakes) causes the secondary piston to bottom out in its bore, due to the lack of hydraulic pressure. The primary piston then actuates the front brakes with the continued stroke of the brake pedal.

Clean, high-quality brake fluid is essential to the safe and proper operation of the brake system. You should always buy the highest quality brake fluid that is available. If the brake fluid becomes contaminated, drain and flush the system and fill the master cylinder with new fluid.

NOTE: *Never reuse any brake fluid. Any brake fluid that is removed from the system should be discarded.*

The system has a pressure differential valve that activates a warning light if either hydraulic circuit is losing pressure. On 1975 and later models, the pressure differential valve id combined with a metering valve that restricts flow to the front brakes until the rear brakes overcome their retracting spring to prevent front brake lockup, and a proportioning valve that limits rear brake hydraulic pressure to prevent rear brake lockup.

WARNING: *Clean, high quality brake fluid is essential to the safe and proper operation of the brake system. You should always buy the highest quality brake fluid that is available. If the brake fluid becomes contaminated, drain and flush the system and fill the master cylinder with new fluid.*

Troubleshooting the Brake System

Problem	Cause	Solution
Low brake pedal (excessive pedal travel required for braking action.)	• Excessive clearance between rear linings and drums caused by inoperative automatic adjusters	• Make 10 to 15 alternate forward and reverse brake stops to adjust brakes. If brake pedal does not come up, repair or replace adjuster parts as necessary.
	• Worn rear brakelining	• Inspect and replace lining if worn beyond minimum thickness specification
	• Bent, distorted brakeshoes, front or rear	• Replace brakeshoes in axle sets
	• Air in hydraulic system	• Remove air from system. Refer to Brake Bleeding.
Low brake pedal (pedal may go to floor with steady pressure applied.)	• Fluid leak in hydraulic system	• Fill master cylinder to fill line; have helper apply brakes and check calipers, wheel cylinders, differential valve tubes, hoses and fittings for leaks. Repair or replace as necessary.
	• Air in hydraulic system	• Remove air from system. Refer to Brake Bleeding.
	• Incorrect or non-recommended brake fluid (fluid evaporates at below normal temp).	• Flush hydraulic system with clean brake fluid. Refill with correct-type fluid.
	• Master cylinder piston seals worn, or master cylinder bore is scored, worn or corroded	• Repair or replace master cylinder
Low brake pedal (pedal goes to floor on first application—o.k. on subsequent applications.)	• Disc brake pads sticking on abutment surfaces of anchor plate. Caused by a build-up of dirt, rust, or corrosion on abutment surfaces	• Clean abutment surfaces
Fading brake pedal (pedal height decreases with steady pressure applied.)	• Fluid leak in hydraulic system	• Fill master cylinder reservoirs to fill mark, have helper apply brakes, check calipers, wheel cylinders, differential valve, tubes, hoses, and fittings for fluid leaks. Repair or replace parts as necessary.
	• Master cylinder piston seals worn, or master cylinder bore is scored, worn or corroded	• Repair or replace master cylinder
Decreasing brake pedal travel (pedal travel required for braking action decreases and may be accompanied by a hard pedal.)	• Caliper or wheel cylinder pistons sticking or seized	• Repair or replace the calipers, or wheel cylinders
	• Master cylinder compensator ports blocked (preventing fluid return to reservoirs) or pistons sticking or seized in master cylinder bore	• Repair or replace the master cylinder
	• Power brake unit binding internally	• Test unit according to the following procedure: (a) Shift transmission into neutral and start engine (b) Increase engine speed to 1500 rpm, close throttle and fully depress brake pedal (c) Slow release brake pedal and stop engine (d) Have helper remove vacuum check valve and hose from power unit. Observe for backward movement of brake pedal. (e) If the pedal moves backward, the power unit has an internal bind—replace power unit

Troubleshooting the Brake System (cont.)

Problem	Cause	Solution
Spongy brake pedal (pedal has abnormally soft, springy, spongy feel when depressed.)	• Air in hydraulic system • Brakeshoes bent or distorted • Brakelining not yet seated with drums and rotors • Rear drum brakes not properly adjusted	• Remove air from system. Refer to Brake Bleeding. • Replace brakeshoes • Burnish brakes • Adjust brakes
Hard brake pedal (excessive pedal pressure required to stop vehicle. May be accompanied by brake fade.)	• Loose or leaking power brake unit vacuum hose • Incorrect or poor quality brakelining • Bent, broken, distorted brakeshoes • Calipers binding or dragging on mounting pins. Rear brakeshoes dragging on support plate.	• Tighten connections or replace leaking hose • Replace with lining in axle sets • Replace brakeshoes • Replace mounting pins and bushings. Clean rust or burrs from rear brake support plate ledges and lubricate ledges with molydisulfide grease. **NOTE:** If ledges are deeply grooved or scored, do not attempt to sand or grind them smooth—replace support plate.

	• Caliper, wheel cylinder, or master cylinder pistons sticking or seized
	• Power brake unit vacuum check valve malfunction
		• Repair or replace parts as necessary
		• Test valve according to the following procedure:
		  (a) Start engine, increase engine speed to 1500 rpm, close throttle and immediately stop engine
		  (b) Wait at least 90 seconds then depress brake pedal
		  (c) If brakes are not vacuum assisted for 2 or more applications, check valve is faulty

	• Power brake unit has internal bind	• Test unit according to the following procedure:
		  (a) With engine stopped, apply brakes several times to exhaust all vacuum in system
		  (b) Shift transmission into neutral, depress brake pedal and start engine
		  (c) If pedal height decreases with foot pressure and less pressure is required to hold pedal in applied position, power unit vacuum system is operating normally. Test power unit. If power unit exhibits a bind condition, replace the power unit.

	• Master cylinder compensator ports (at bottom of reservoirs) blocked by dirt, scale, rust, or have small burrs (blocked ports prevent fluid return to reservoirs). • Brake hoses, tubes, fittings clogged or restricted • Brake fluid contaminated with improper fluids (motor oil, transmission fluid, causing rubber components to swell and stick in bores • Low engine vacuum	• Repair or replace master cylinder **CAUTION:** Do not attempt to clean blocked ports with wire, pencils, or similar implements. Use compressed air only. • Use compressed air to check or unclog parts. Replace any damaged parts. • Replace all rubber components, combination valve and hoses. Flush entire brake system with DOT 3 brake fluid or equivalent. • Adjust or repair engine

Troubleshooting the Brake System (cont.)

Problem	Cause	Solution
Grabbing brakes (severe reaction to brake pedal pressure.)	• Brakelining(s) contaminated by grease or brake fluid	• Determine and correct cause of contamination and replace brakeshoes in axle sets
	• Parking brake cables incorrectly adjusted or seized	• Adjust cables. Replace seized cables.
	• Incorrect brakelining or lining loose on brakeshoes	• Replace brakeshoes in axle sets
	• Caliper anchor plate bolts loose	• Tighten bolts
	• Rear brakeshoes binding on support plate ledges	• Clean and lubricate ledges. Replace support plate(s) if ledges are deeply grooved. Do not attempt to smooth ledges by grinding.
	• Incorrect or missing power brake reaction disc	• Install correct disc
	• Rear brake support plates loose	• Tighten mounting bolts
Dragging brakes (slow or incomplete release of brakes)	• Brake pedal binding at pivot	• Loosen and lubricate
	• Power brake unit has internal bind	• Inspect for internal bind. Replace unit if internal bind exists.
	• Parking brake cables incorrrectly adjusted or seized	• Adjust cables. Replace seized cables.
	• Rear brakeshoe return springs weak or broken	• Replace return springs. Replace brakeshoe if necessary in axle sets.
	• Automatic adjusters malfunctioning	• Repair or replace adjuster parts as required
	• Caliper, wheel cylinder or master cylinder pistons sticking or seized	• Repair or replace parts as necessary
	• Master cylinder compensating ports blocked (fluid does not return to reservoirs).	• Use compressed air to clear ports. Do not use wire, pencils, or similar objects to open blocked ports.
Vehicle moves to one side when brakes are applied	• Incorrect front tire pressure	• Inflate to recommended cold (reduced load) inflation pressure
	• Worn or damaged wheel bearings	• Replace worn or damaged bearings
	• Brakelining on one side contaminated	• Determine and correct cause of contamination and replace brakelining in axle sets
	• Brakeshoes on one side bent, distorted, or lining loose on shoe	• Replace brakeshoes in axle sets
	• Support plate bent or loose on one side	• Tighten or replace support plate
	• Brakelining not yet seated with drums or rotors	• Burnish brakelining
	• Caliper anchor plate loose on one side	• Tighten anchor plate bolts
	• Caliper piston sticking or seized	• Repair or replace caliper
	• Brakelinings water soaked	• Drive vehicle with brakes lightly applied to dry linings
	• Loose suspension component attaching or mounting bolts	• Tighten suspension bolts. Replace worn suspension components.
	• Brake combination valve failure	• Replace combination valve
Chatter or shudder when brakes are applied (pedal pulsation and roughness may also occur.)	• Brakeshoes distorted, bent, contaminated, or worn	• Replace brakeshoes in axle sets
	• Caliper anchor plate or support plate loose	• Tighten mounting bolts
	• Excessive thickness variation of rotor(s)	• Refinish or replace rotors in axle sets
Noisy brakes (squealing, clicking, scraping sound when brakes are applied.)	• Bent, broken, distorted brakeshoes	• Replace brakeshoes in axle sets
	• Excessive rust on outer edge of rotor braking surface	• Remove rust

Troubleshooting the Brake System (cont.)

Problem	Cause	Solution
Noisy brakes (squealing, clicking, scraping sound when brakes are applied.) (cont.)	• Brakelining worn out—shoes contacting drum of rotor	• Replace brakeshoes and lining in axle sets. Refinish or replace drums or rotors.
	• Broken or loose holdown or return springs	• Replace parts as necessary
	• Rough or dry drum brake support plate ledges	• Lubricate support plate ledges
	• Cracked, grooved, or scored rotor(s) or drum(s)	• Replace rotor(s) or drum(s). Replace brakeshoes and lining in axle sets if necessary.
	• Incorrect brakelining and/or shoes (front or rear).	• Install specified shoe and lining assemblies
Pulsating brake pedal	• Out of round drums or excessive lateral runout in disc brake rotor(s)	• Refinish or replace drums, re-index rotors or replace

Never reuse any brake fluid. Any brake fluid that is removed from the system should be discarded.

Adjustments
DRUM BRAKES

The drum brakes are self-adjusting and require a manual adjustment only after the brake shoes have been replaced, or when the length of the adjusting screw has been changed while performing some other service operation, as i.e., taking off brake drums.

To adjust the brakes, follow the procedures given below:

Drum Installed

1. Raise and support the rear end on jackstands.

2. Remove the rubber plug from the adjusting slot on the backing plate.

3. Insert a brake adjusting spoon into the slot and engage the lowest possible tooth on the starwheel. Move the end of the brake spoon downward to move the starwheel upward and expand the adjusting screw. Repeat this operation until the brakes lock the wheels.

4. Insert a small screwdriver or piece of firm wire (coat hanger wire) into the adjusting slot and push the automatic adjusting lever out and free of the starwheel on the adjusting screw and hold it there.

5. Engage the topmost tooth possible on the starwheel with the brake adjusting spoon. Move the end of the adjusting spoon upward to move the adjusting screw starwheel downward and contract the adjusting screw. Back off the adjusting screw starwheel until the wheel spins freely with a minimum of drag. Keep track of

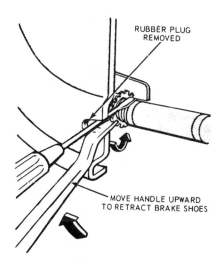

RUBBER PLUG REMOVED

MOVE HANDLE UPWARD TO RETRACT BRAKE SHOES

Positioning and operation of the brake adjusting tools during the adjustment procedure on E-100, E-150, and E-200 models—backing off the brakes

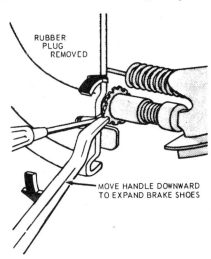

RUBBER PLUG REMOVED

MOVE HANDLE DOWNWARD TO EXPAND BRAKE SHOES

Positioning and operation of the brake adjusting tools during the adjustment procedure on E-250, E-300, and E-350 models—expanding the brakes

the number of turns that the starwheel is backed off, or the number of strokes taken with the brake adjusting spoon.

6. Repeat this operation for the other side. When backing off the brakes on the other side, the starwheel adjuster must be backed off the same number of turns to prevent side-to-side brake pull.

7. When the brakes are adjusted make several stops while backing the vehicle, to equalize the brakes at both of the wheels.

8. Remove the safety stands and lower the vehicle. Road test the vehicle.

Drum Removed

CAUTION: *Brake shoes contain asbestos, which has been determined to be a cancer causing agent. Never clean the brake surfaces with compressed air! Avoid inhaling any dust from any brake surface! When cleaning brake surfaces, use a commercially available brake cleaning fluid.*

1. Make sure that the shoe-to-contact pad areas are clean and properly lubricated.

2. Using and inside caliper check the inside diameter of the drum. Measure across the di-

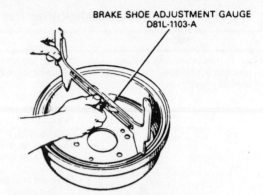

BRAKE SHOE ADJUSTMENT GAUGE
D81L-1103-A

Measuring drum inside diameter

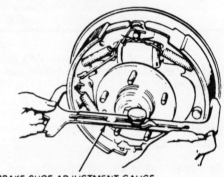

BRAKE SHOE ADJUSTMENT GAUGE
D81L-1103-A

Measuring brake shoe installation

ameter of the assembled brake shoes, at their widest point.

3. Turn the adjusting screw so that the diameter of the shoes is 0.030″ less than the brake drum inner diameter.

4. Install the drum.

Brake Light Switch
REMOVAL AND INSTALLATION
1961-67

1. Remove the floor pan cover.
2. Disconnect the wires at the switch.

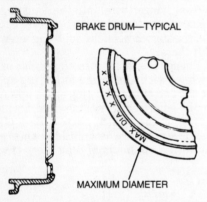

BRAKE DRUM—TYPICAL

MAXIMUM DIAMETER

The maximum inside diameter is stamped on each brake drum

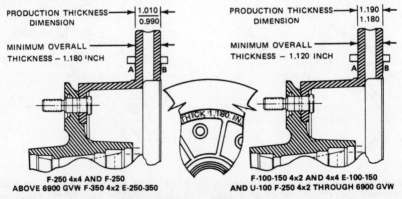

| PRODUCTION THICKNESS DIMENSION | 1.010 0.990 |
| MINIMUM OVERALL THICKNESS – 1.180 INCH | |

| PRODUCTION THICKNESS DIMENSION | 1.190 1.180 |
| MINIMUM OVERALL THICKNESS – 1.120 INCH | |

THICK 1.180 IN

F-250 4x4 AND F-250 ABOVE 6900 GVW F-350 4x2 E-250-350

F-100-150 4x2 AND 4x4 E-100-150 AND U-100 F-250 4x2 THROUGH 6900 GVW

Disc brake rotor service limits

1961–67 brake light switch

3. Unscrew the switch from the master cylinder.

4. Installation is the reverse of removal.

1969-74

1. Carefully disconnect the wires from the switch.

2. Unscrew the switch from the pressure differential valve.

3. Installation is the reverse of removal.

1975-88

1. Lift the locking tab on the switch connector and disconnect the wiring.

2. Remove the hairpin retainer, slide the stoplamp switch, pushrod and nylon washer off of the pedal. Remove the washer, then the switch by sliding it up or down.

NOTE: *On trucks equipped with speed control, the spacer washer is replaced by the dump valve adapter washer.*

3. To install the switch, position it so that the U-shaped side is nearest the pedal and directly over/under the pin.

4. Slide the switch up or down, trapping the master cylinder pushrod and bushing between the switch side plates.

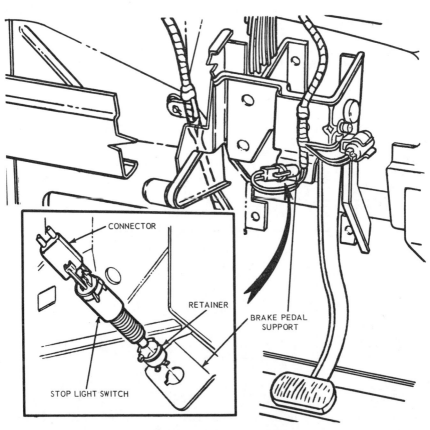

CONNECTOR

RETAINER

BRAKE PEDAL
SUPPORT

STOP LIGHT SWITCH

1969–74 brake light switch

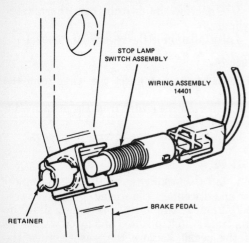

1979 brake light switch

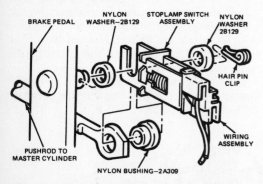

1980–83 brake light switch w/non-power brakes

5. Push the switch and pushrod assembly firmly towards the brake pedal arm. Assemble the outside white plastic washer to the pin and install the hairpin retainer.

CAUTION: *Don't substitute any other type of retainer. Use only the Ford specified hairpin retainer.*

6. Assemble the connector on the switch.
7. Check stoplamp operation.

CAUTION: *Make sure that the stoplamp switch wiring has sufficient travel during a full pedal stroke!*

Master Cylinder

REMOVAL AND INSTALLATION

1961-67

1. Raise and support the front end on jackstands.
2. Unbolt the forward splash shield.
3. Disconnect the pedal return spring.
4. Remove the locknut and eccentric bolt connecting the return spring bracket and mastering cylinder pushrod to the brake pedal bracket.
5. Remove the snapring from the pedal pivot pin.
6. Disconnect the brake lines and the stoplight switch.
7. Remove the mounting bolts and swing the cylinder down. Remove it from the pedal pivot pin bushings.
8. On installation, torque the mounting bolts

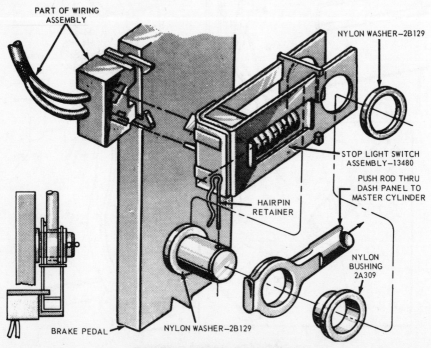

1975–78 and 1980 brake light switch

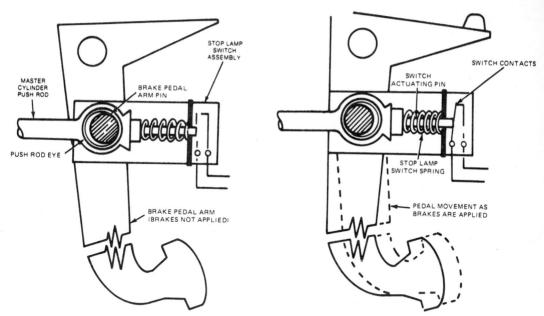

1981–88 brake light switch w/power brakes

to 23-29 ft.lb. Adjust the eccentric bolt so that there is ¼-⁷⁄₁₆″ pedal free-travel. Torque the eccentric bolt to 12-24 ft.lb.

9. Bleed the system of air.

1969-74

1. Disconnect the wires from the stoplight switch.

2. Disconnect the hydraulic system brake lines at the master cylinder.

3. Remove the shoulder bolt and nut retaining the pushrod to the brake pedal. Remove the pushrod bushing.

4. Slide the master cylinder pushrod off the brake pedal pin. Remove the bushings and washers.

5. Remove the master cylinder retaining bolts and remove the master cylinder.

To install the master cylinder:

6. Position the master cylinder assembly on the firewall and install the retaining bolts.

7. Connect the hydraulic brake system lines to the master cylinder.

8. Lubricate the pushrod bushing. Insert the bushing in the pushrod and install the shoulder bolt which secures the pushrod to the brake pedal.

9. Connect the stoplight switch wires to the switch.

10. Bleed the hydraulic brake system.

1975-83 without Power Brakes

1. Disconnect the wires from the brake light switch at the pedal arm.

2. Disconnect the dustboot from the rear of the master cylinder at the firewall.

3. Remove the retaining nut, shoulder bolt, spacers and bushing securing the master cylinder pushrod to the pedal.

4. Remove the brake light switch from the pedal.

5. Remove the boot from the master cylinder pushrod.

6. Disconnect the brake lines at the master cylinder.

7. Support the master cylinder and remove the mounting bolts.

To install:

8. Position the master cylinder on the firewall and install the bolts. Torque them to 25 ft.lb.

9. Loosely connect the brakes lines.

10. Position the boot over the pushrod and secure it to the master cylinder.

11. Lubricate the pushrod bushing with chassis lube and install it on the pushrod.

12. Connect the pushrod to the pedal with the shoulder bolt. Install the self-locking nut.

13. Connect the wiring.

14. Bleed the master cylinder and the entire system.

1975-83 with Power Brakes
1984 All

1. With the engine off, push the pedal down to release the vacuum from the booster. Release the pedal.

2. Disconnect the hydraulic lines.

3. Unbolt the master cylinder from the booster or firewall.

4. Before installing the master cylinder, check the distance from the outer end of the

booster assembly push rod to the front face of the brake booster assembly. Turn the push rod adjusting screw in or out as required to obtain the length shown. Torque the mounting nuts to 25 ft.lb.

5. Bleed the system of air after installation.

1985-86

1. With the engine off, push the pedal down to release the vacuum from the booster. Release the pedal.

2. Disconnect the hydraulic lines.

3. Remove the nuts holding the retainer to the master cylinder.

4. Remove the retainer and clutch master cylinder and position it out of the way so as to avoid spilling the fluid.

NOTE: *The two upper mounting holes are used for E-350 models; the two lower holes for the E-150 and 250.*

5. Remove the master cylinder-to-booster nuts and lift off the master cylinder.

6. Before installing the master cylinder, check the distance from the outer end of the booster assembly push rod to the front face of the brake booster assembly. Turn the push rod adjusting screw in or out as required to obtain the length shown. Torque the mounting nuts to 10-18 ft.lb.

7. Install the clutch master cylinder and retainer. Torque the nuts to 10-18 ft.lb.

8. Loosely install the brake lines. Bleed the master cylinder, then the entire brake system.

1987-88

1. With the engine off, push the pedal down to release the vacuum from the booster. Release the pedal.

2. Disconnect the hydraulic lines and the fluid level indicator wires.

3. Remove the wrap-around clip and attaching nut from the master cylinder mounting stud.

4. Remove the master cylinder mounting nuts and lift off the master cylinder from the booster.

5. Before installing the master cylinder, check the distance from the outer end of the booster assembly push rod to the front face of the brake booster assembly. Turn the push rod adjusting screw in or out as required to obtain the length shown. Torque the mounting nuts to 18-25 ft.lb.

6. Loosely connect the brake lines.

7. Install the wrap-around clip and secure it with the attaching nut.

8. Connect the wiring.

9. Fill and bleed the master cylinder, then the entire system.

OVERHAUL

The most important thing to remember when rebuilding the master cylinder is cleanliness. Work in clean surroundings with clean tools and clean cloths or paper for drying purposes. Have plenty of clean alcohol and brake fluid on

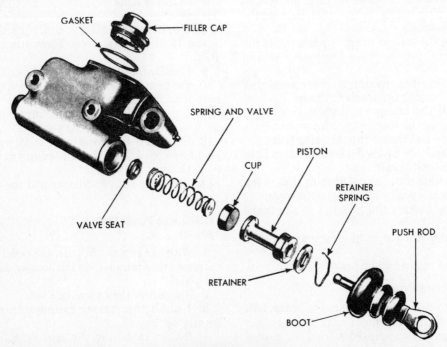

1961–66 master cylinder

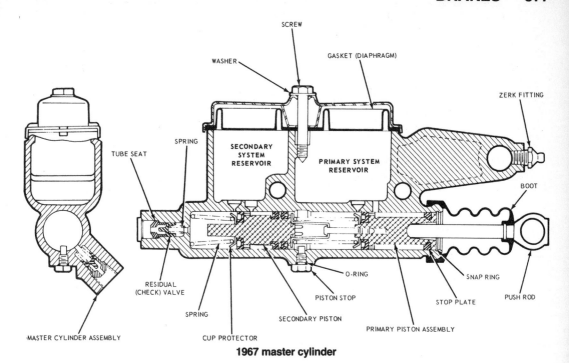

1967 master cylinder

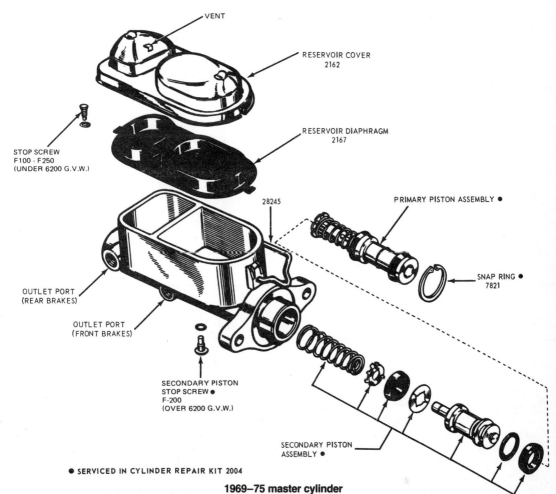

● SERVICED IN CYLINDER REPAIR KIT 2004

1969–75 master cylinder

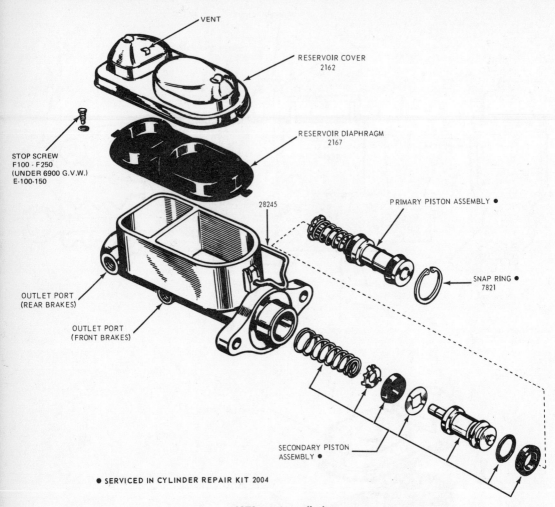

VENT

RESERVOIR COVER
2162

RESERVOIR DIAPHRAGM
2167

STOP SCREW
F100 - F250
(UNDER 6900 G.V.W.)
E-100-150

28245

PRIMARY PISTON ASSEMBLY ●

SNAP RING ●
7821

OUTLET PORT
(REAR BRAKES)

OUTLET PORT
(FRONT BRAKES)

SECONDARY PISTON
ASSEMBLY ●

● SERVICED IN CYLINDER REPAIR KIT 2004

1976 master cylinder

hand to clean and lubricate the internal components. There are service repair kits available for overhauling the master cylinder.

1961-67

1. Clean the outside of the master cylinder and remove the filler cap and gasket. Pour out any fluid that remains in the cylinder reservoir. Do not use any fluids other fluids than brake fluid or alcohol to clean the master cylinder.

2. Remove the rubber boot from the pushrod end.

3. Remove the retaining ring from the pushrod end, then remove the retainer, piston, cup, spring and valve assembly, and valve seat from the bore.

4. Clean and inspect all parts. Any part that appears worn should be replaced. If you have a master cylinder rebuilding kit, use ALL of the parts supplied. Make sure all ports and passages are clean.

5. Inspect the bore for scratches, rust or oth-

er damage. The cylinder bore can be honed, but don't remove more than 0.003″ of material!

6. Prior to assembly, dip all parts in clean brake fluid and install them, depressing the piston to install the retainer.

1969

1. Clean the outside of the master cylinder and remove the filler cap and gasket. Pour out any fluid that remains in the cylinder reservoir. Do not use any fluids other fluids than brake fluid or alcohol to clean the master cylinder.

2. Unscrew the piston stop from the bottom of the cylinder body. Remove the O-ring seal from the piston stop. Discard the seal.

3. Remove the pushrod boot from the groove at the rear of the master cylinder and slide the boot away from the rear of the master cylinder.

4. Remove the snapring which retains the primary and secondary piston assemblies within the cylinder body.

5. Remove the pushrod and primary piston

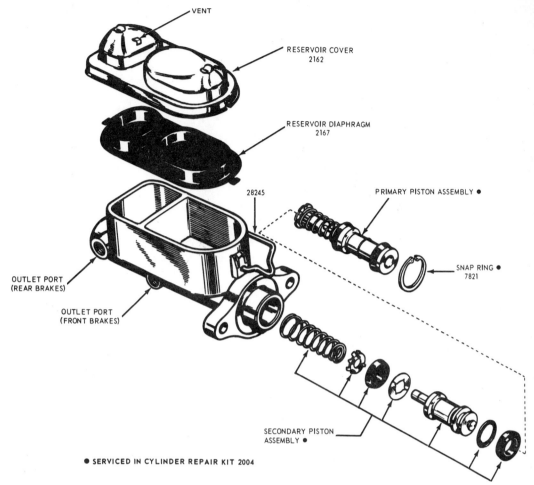

VENT

RESERVOIR COVER
2162

RESERVOIR DIAPHRAGM
2167

28245

PRIMARY PISTON ASSEMBLY ●

SNAP RING ●
7821

OUTLET PORT
(REAR BRAKES)

OUTLET PORT
(FRONT BRAKES)

SECONDARY PISTON
ASSEMBLY ●

● **SERVICED IN CYLINDER REPAIR KIT 2004**

1977–86 master cylinder

assembly from the master cylinder. Discard the piston assembly, including the boot.

6. Invert the cylinder body and tap it lightly to remove the secondary piston.

7. Using a 6-32 self-tapping screw and flat washer, pry the tube seats out of the front and rear outlet bores. Discard the seats and valves.

8. Remove the return spring, spring retainer, cup protector, and cups from the secondary piston. Discard the cup protector and cups.

9. Clean all the remaining parts in clean isopropyl alcohol and inspect the parts for chipping, excessive wear or damage. Replace them as required.

NOTE: *When using a master cylinder repair kit, install all the parts supplied in the kit.*

10. Check all recesses, openings and internal passages to be sure that the are open and free of foreign matter. Used compressed air to blow out remaining dirt and cleaning solvent remaining after the parts have been cleaned in the alcohol. Place all the parts on a clean pan, lint-free cloth, or paper to dry.

11. Dip all the parts, except the cylinder body, in clean brake fluid.

12. Install the new check valve springs, check valves and tube seats. With the use of tube nuts and a wrench, press the tube seats inward until they bottom. Remove the tube nuts.

13. Assemble the new seals and spring and cup protector on the secondary piston.

14. Install the secondary piston assembly in the master cylinder.

15. Install a new O-ring on the piston stop, and start the stop into the cylinder body.

16. Position the retainer clip in the groove in the pushrod. Seat the pushrod in the primary piston assembly.

17. Install the primary piston assembly in the master cylinder. Push the primary piston inward and tighten the secondary piston stop to retain the secondary piston in the bore.

18. Press the pushrod and pistons inward and install the snapring in the cylinder body.

19. Before the master cylinder is installed on the vehicle, the unit must be bled: support the

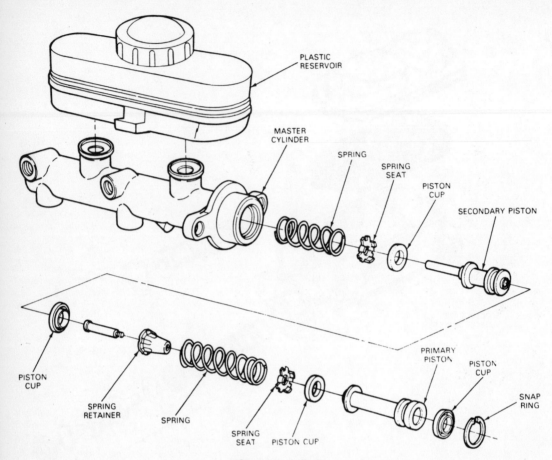

1987 master cylinder

master cylinder body in a vice, and fill both fluid reservoirs with brake fluid.

20. Loosely install plugs in the front and rear brake outlet bores. Depress the primary piston several times until air bubbles cease to appear in the brake fluid.

21. Tighten the plugs and attempt to depress the piston. The piston travel should be restricted after all air is expelled.

22. Remove the plugs. Install the cover and gasket (diaphragm) assembly, and make sure that the cover retainer is tighten securely.

23. Install the master cylinder in the vehicle and bleed the hydraulic system.

1970-73

1. Clean the outside of the master cylinder and remove the filler cap and gasket. Pour out any fluid that remains in the cylinder reservoir. Do not use any fluids other fluids than brake fluid or alcohol to clean the master cylinder.

2. Unscrew the piston stop from the bottom of the cylinder body. Remove the O-ring seal from the piston stop. Discard the seal.

3. Remove the pushrod boot from the groove at the rear of the master cylinder and slide the boot away from the rear of the master cylinder.

4. Remove the snapring which retains the primary and secondary piston assemblies within the cylinder body.

5. Remove the pushrod and primary piston assembly from the master cylinder. Discard the piston assembly, including the boot.

6. Invert the cylinder body and tap it lightly to remove the secondary piston.

7. Using a 6-32 self-tapping screw and flat washer, pry the tube seats out of the front and rear outlet bores. Discard the seats and valves.

8. Remove the return spring, spring retainer, cup protector, and cups from the secondary piston. Discard the cup protector and cups.

9. Clean all the remaining parts in clean isopropyl alcohol and inspect the parts for chipping, excessive wear or damage. Replace them as required.

NOTE: *When using a master cylinder repair kit, install all the parts supplied in the kit.*

10. Check all recesses, openings and internal passages to be sure that the are open and free of foreign matter. Used compressed air to blow

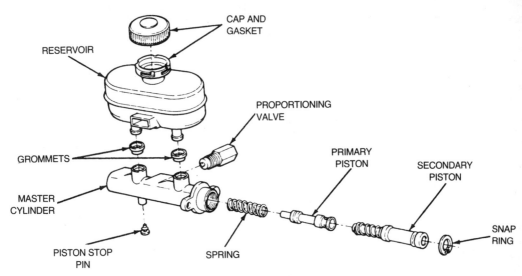

1988 master cylinder

out remaining dirt and cleaning solvent remaining after the parts have been cleaned in the alcohol. Place all the parts on a clean pan, lint-free cloth, or paper to dry.

11. Dip all the parts, except the cylinder body, in clean brake fluid.

12. Install the new check valve springs, check valves and tube seats. With the use of tube nuts and a wrench, press the tube seats inward until they bottom. Remove the tube nuts.

13. Assemble the new cups, back-to-back and spring and cup protector on the secondary piston.

14. Install the secondary piston assembly in the master cylinder.

15. Install a new O-ring on the piston stop, and start the stop into the cylinder body.

16. Position the retainer clip in the groove in the pushrod. Seat the pushrod in the primary piston assembly.

17. Install the primary piston assembly in the master cylinder. Push the primary piston inward and tighten the secondary piston stop to retain the secondary piston in the bore.

18. Press the pushrod and pistons inward and install the snapring in the cylinder body.

19. Before the master cylinder is installed on the vehicle, the unit must be bled: support the master cylinder body in a vice, and fill both fluid reservoirs with brake fluid.

20. Loosely install plugs in the front and rear brake outlet bores. Depress the primary piston several times until air bubbles cease to appear in the brake fluid.

21. Tighten the plugs and attempt to depress the piston. The piston travel should be restricted after all air is expelled.

22. Remove the plugs. Install the cover and

gasket (diaphragm) assembly, and make sure that the cover retainer is tighten securely.

23. Install the master cylinder in the vehicle and bleed the hydraulic system.

1974-75

1. Clean the outside of the master cylinder and remove the filler cap and gasket. Pour out any fluid that remains in the cylinder reservoir. Do not use any fluids other fluids than brake fluid or alcohol to clean the master cylinder.

2. Unscrew the piston stop from the bottom of the cylinder body. Remove the O-ring seal from the piston stop. Discard the seal.

3. Remove the pushrod boot (if equipped) from the groove at the rear of the master cylinder and slide the boot away from the rear of the master cylinder.

4. Remove the snapring which retains the primary and secondary piston assemblies within the cylinder body.

5. Remove the pushrod (if equipped) and primary piston assembly from the master cylinder. Discard the piston assembly, including the boot.

6. Using an air hose at the rear outlet port, carefully force the secondary piston from the bore.

7. Remove the return spring, spring retainer, cup protector, and cups from the secondary piston. Discard the cup protector and cups.

8. Clean all the remaining parts in clean isopropyl alcohol and inspect the parts for chipping, excessive wear or damage. Replace them as required.

NOTE: *When using a master cylinder repair kit, install all the parts supplied in the kit.*

9. Check all recesses, openings and internal

passages to be sure that the are open and free of foreign matter. Used compressed air to blow out remaining dirt and cleaning solvent remaining after the parts have been cleaned in the alcohol. Place all the parts on a clean pan, lint-free cloth, or paper to dry.

10. Dip all the parts, except the cylinder body, in clean brake fluid.

11. Assemble the new cups, back-to-back and spring and cup protector on the secondary piston.

12. Install the secondary piston assembly in the master cylinder.

13. Install a new O-ring on the piston stop, and start the stop into the cylinder body.

14. Position the retainer clip in the groove in the pushrod. Seat the pushrod in the primary piston assembly.

15. Install the primary piston assembly in the master cylinder. Push the primary piston inward and tighten the secondary piston stop to retain the secondary piston in the bore.

16. Press the pushrod and pistons inward and install the snapring in the cylinder body.

17. Before the master cylinder is installed on the vehicle, the unit must be bled: support the master cylinder body in a vice, and fill both fluid reservoirs with brake fluid.

18. Loosely install plugs in the front and rear brake outlet bores. Depress the primary piston several times until air bubbles cease to appear in the brake fluid.

19. Tighten the plugs and attempt to depress the piston. The piston travel should be restricted after all air is expelled.

20. Remove the plugs. Install the cover and gasket (diaphragm) assembly, and make sure that the cover retainer is tighten securely.

21. Install the master cylinder in the vehicle and bleed the hydraulic system.

1976-81

1. Clean the outside of the master cylinder and remove the filler cap and gasket. Pour out any fluid that remains in the cylinder reservoir. Do not use any fluids other fluids than brake fluid or alcohol to clean the master cylinder.

2. Remove the pushrod boot (if equipped) from the groove at the rear of the master cylinder and slide the boot away from the rear of the master cylinder.

3. Remove the snapring which retains the primary and secondary piston assemblies within the cylinder body.

4. Remove the pushrod (if equipped) and primary piston assembly from the master cylinder. Discard the piston assembly, including the boot.

5. Using an air hose at the rear outlet port,

carefully force the secondary piston from the bore.

6. Remove the return spring, spring retainer, cup protector, and cups from the secondary piston. Discard the cup protector and cups.

7. Clean all the remaining parts in clean isopropyl alcohol and inspect the parts for chipping, excessive wear or damage. Replace them as required.

NOTE: *When using a master cylinder repair kit, install all the parts supplied in the kit.*

8. Check all recesses, openings and internal passages to be sure that the are open and free of foreign matter. Used compressed air to blow out remaining dirt and cleaning solvent remaining after the parts have been cleaned in the alcohol. Place all the parts on a clean pan, lint-free cloth, or paper to dry. If the bore shows any signs of damage or excessive wear, replace the master cylinder. DO NOT HONE THE BORE!

9. Dip all the parts, except the cylinder body, in clean brake fluid.

10. Assemble the new cups, back-to-back and spring and cup protector on the secondary piston.

11. Install the secondary piston assembly in the master cylinder.

12. On vans without power brakes, position the boot, snapring and pushrod retainer on the pushrod. **Make sure that the pushrod retainer is seated securely on the ball end of the rod**. Seat the pushrod in the primary piston assembly.

13. Install the primary piston assembly in the master cylinder.

14. On vans with power brakes, position the stop plate and snapring on the primary piston. Depress the primary piston and install the snapring in the cylinder body.

15. On vans without power brakes, push inward on the pushrod and pistons and install the snapring.

16. Before the master cylinder is installed on the vehicle, the unit must be bled: support the master cylinder body in a vice, and fill both fluid reservoirs with brake fluid.

17. Loosely install plugs in the front and rear brake outlet bores. Depress the primary piston several times until air bubbles cease to appear in the brake fluid.

18. Tighten the plugs and attempt to depress the piston. The piston travel should be restricted after all air is expelled.

19. Remove the plugs. Install the cover and gasket (diaphragm) assembly, and make sure that the cover retainer is tighten securely.

20. Install the master cylinder in the vehicle and bleed the hydraulic system.

1982-86

1. Clean the outside of the master cylinder and remove the filler cap and gasket. Pour out any fluid that remains in the cylinder reservoir. Do not use any fluids other fluids than brake fluid or alcohol to clean the master cylinder.

2. Remove the snapring which retains the primary piston assembly within the cylinder body.

3. Remove the primary piston assembly from the master cylinder. Discard the piston assembly, including the boot.

4. Using an air hose at the rear outlet port, carefully force the secondary piston from the bore.

5. Clean all the remaining parts in clean isopropyl alcohol and inspect the parts for chipping, excessive wear or damage. Replace them as required.

NOTE: *When using a master cylinder repair kit, install all the parts supplied in the kit.*

6. Check all recesses, openings and internal passages to be sure that the are open and free of foreign matter. Used compressed air to blow out remaining dirt and cleaning solvent remaining after the parts have been cleaned in the alcohol. Place all the parts on a clean pan, lint-free cloth, or paper to dry. Check the master cylinder bore for wear or damage. If any problems exist, replace the master cylinder. DO NOT HONE THE BORE!

7. Dip all the parts, except the cylinder body, in clean brake fluid.

8. Assemble the new cups, back-to-back and spring and cup protector on the secondary piston.

9. Install the secondary piston assembly in the master cylinder.

10. Install the primary piston assembly in the master cylinder. Depress the piston and install the snapring.

11. On vans without power brakes, install the pushrod retainer onto the pushrod and insert it in the primary piston assembly. Make sure the retainer is seated and holding the pushrod in position.

12. Before the master cylinder is installed on the vehicle, the unit must be bled: support the master cylinder body in a vice, and fill both fluid reservoirs with brake fluid.

13. Loosely install plugs in the front and rear brake outlet bores. Depress the primary piston several times until air bubbles cease to appear in the brake fluid.

14. Tighten the plugs and attempt to depress the piston. The piston travel should be restricted after all air is expelled.

15. Remove the plugs. Install the cover and gasket (diaphragm) assembly, and make sure that the cover retainer is tighten securely.

16. Install the master cylinder in the vehicle and bleed the hydraulic system.

1987-88

1. Remove the plastic cap and gasket.

2. Drain the fluid.

3. Remove the proportioning valve from the cylinder body.

4. Remove the step-bolt from the bottom of the cylinder body.

5. Depress the secondary piston and remove the snapring at the rear of the body.

6. Remove and discard the secondary piston assembly.

7. Direct low pressure compressed air in the outlet port at the blind end of the body while plugging the other port and force out the primary piston. Discard the piston assembly.

8. Clean the body thoroughly with isopropyl alcohol. Inspect the bore carefully. If there are signs of wear or damage of any kind, replace the master cylinder. DO NOT HONE THE BORE! If the bore is not damaged, obtain a rebuilding kit and rebuild the body. Use ALL of the parts contained in the kit.

9. Dip all internal parts in clean brake fluid prior to assembly.

10. Install the complete primary piston in the bore.

11. Install the complete secondary piston in the bore.

12. Depress the secondary piston and install the snapring.

13. Install the step-bolt.

14. Install the proportioning valve.

15. Refill the revservoir.

16. Install the cap and bleed the master cyinder before installing it.

17. Install the unit and bleed the system.

Pressure Differential (Proportioning) Valve

REMOVAL AND INSTALLATION

1967

1. Raise and support the front end on jackstands.

2. Remove the splash shield.

3. Disconnect the wiring at the warning light switch.

4. Disconnect the brake lines at the valve.

5. Unbolt and remove the valve from the frame.

6. Install the new valve and connect the lines and wiring.

7. Bleed the brake system.

8. Install the splash shield.

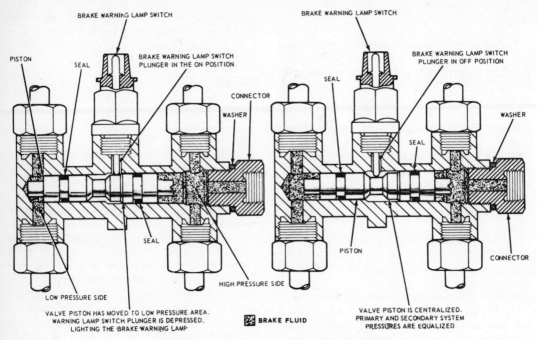

Presssure differential valve used through 1974

1969-86

1. Raise and support the front end on jackstands.

2. Remove the splash shield.

3. Disconnect the wiring at the warning light switch.

4. Disconnect the brake lines at the valve.

5. Unbolt and remove the valve from the frame.

6. Install the new valve and connect the lines and wiring.

7. Bleed the brake system.

8. Install the splash shield.

1987-88

1. Disconnect the electrical leads from the valve.

2. Unscrew the valve from the master cylinder.

3. Install the valve in the reverse order of removal.

4. Bleed the master cylinder.

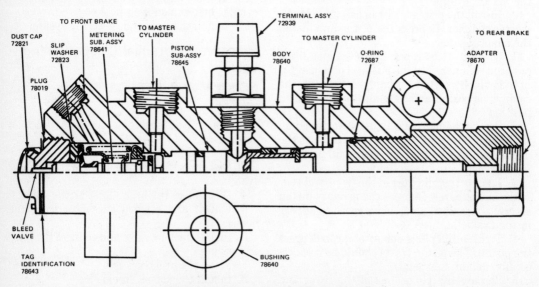

1975—86 E-250/350 pressure differential valve

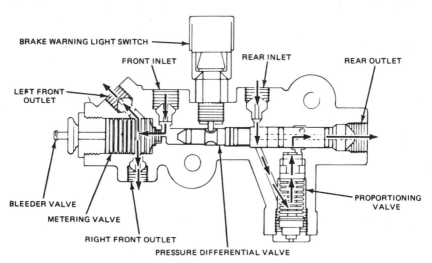

BRAKE WARNING LIGHT SWITCH

FRONT INLET

REAR INLET

REAR OUTLET

LEFT FRONT
OUTLET

BLEEDER VALVE

METERING VALVE

RIGHT FRONT OUTLET

PROPORTIONING
VALVE

PRESSURE DIFFERENTIAL VALVE

1975–86 E-100/150 pressure differential, metering and proportioning valve

CENTERING THE PROPORTIONING VALVE

After the brake system has been opened for any reason the warning light will remain on until the proportioning valve is centralized.

1985-88 valves are self-centering after the brakes are properly bled.

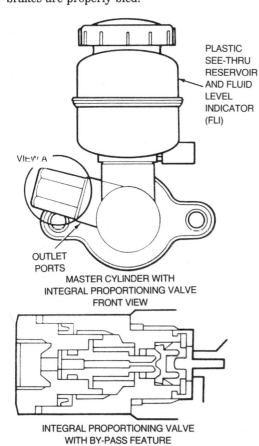

PLASTIC
SEE-THRU
RESERVOIR
AND FLUID
LEVEL
INDICATOR
(FLI)

VIEW A

OUTLET
PORTS

MASTER CYLINDER WITH
INTEGRAL PROPORTIONING VALVE
FRONT VIEW

INTEGRAL PROPORTIONING VALVE
WITH BY-PASS FEATURE
VIEW IN CIRCLE A

1987–88 integral pressure differential valve

1967-73

1. Raise and support the front end on jackstands.
2. Remove the splash shield.
3. Turn the ignition switch to ON.
4. Loosen the brake line at the valve for the part of the system that was not opened, or, if both sides were opened, loosen the line opposite the side that was bled last.
5. Depress the brake pedal slowly until the light goes out. If both sides were opened, it may be necessary to repeat the procedure for another line at the valve.
6. Refill the master cylinder.

1974-84

1. Turn the ignition switch to **ACC** or **ON**.
2. Make sure the master cylinder level is full.
3. Press down slowly on the brake pedal and the valve should center itself.

Height Sensing Proportioning Valve
REMOVAL AND INSTALLATION

1985-88 E-250, 350

1. Raise and support the rear end on jackstands so that the suspension is fully extended.
2. Disconnect the linkage arm from the valve.
3. Disconnect the brake line from the valve.
4. Unbolt and remove the valve from its bracket.
5. Install the valve on its bracket and torque the bolts to 18 ft.lb.
6. Install the brake hose using NEW copper washers. Torque the bolt to 34 ft.lb.
7. Connect the brake line to the valve.

Height sensing brake proportioning valve

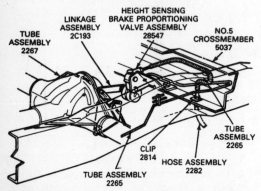

1985 height sensing brake proportioning valve installation

8. Connect the linkage arm to the valve. Torque the nut to 10 ft.lb.

9. Bleed the brakes.

Power Booster

REMOVAL AND INSTALLATION

1971-74

1. Disconnect the brake lines from the master cylinder.

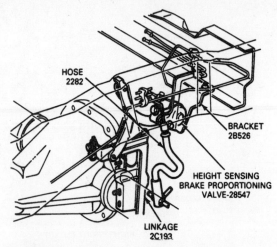

1986 height sensing brake proportioning valve installation

2. Disconnect the booster pushrod from the brake pedal.

3. Unbolt the booster from the firewall.

4. Disconnect the vacuum line from the booster and remove the booster and master cylinder as an assembly.

5. Check and, if necessary, adjust the booster pushrod clearance.

6. Torque the master cylinder-to-booster nuts to 25 ft.lb.

7. Connect the vacuum hose.

8. Install the booster and torque the bolts to 25 ft.lb.

9. Connect the booster pushrod to the brake pedal.

10. Loosely install the brake lines and bleed the master cylinder.

11. Bleed the entire system.

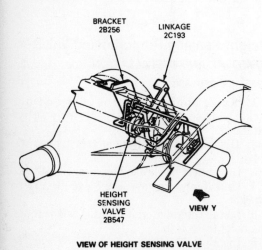

1987–88 height sensing brake proportioning valve installation

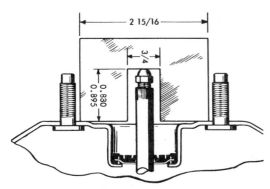

Booster pushrod gauge dimensions and adjustment, through 1976

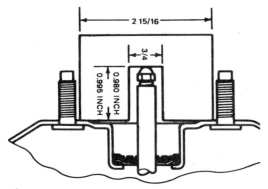

Booster pushrod gauge dimensions and adjustment, 1977–88

1975-76 E-100/150

1. Support the master cylinder from the underside with a prop.

2. Remove the master cylinder-to-booster retaining nuts.

3. Loosen the clamp that secures the manifolds vacuum hose to the booster check valve, and remove the hose.

4. Pull the master cylinder off the booster and leave it supported by the prop, far enough away to allow removal of the booster assembly.

5. From inside the cab on vehicles equipped with push rod mounted stop lamp switch, remove the retaining pin and slide the stop lamp switch, push rod, spacers and bushings off the brake pedal arm.

6. From the engine compartment remove the bolts that attach the booster to the dash panel.

7. Mount the booster assembly on the engine side of the dash panel by sliding the bracket mounting bolts and valve operating rod in through the holes in the dash panel.

NOTE: *Make certain that the booster push rod is positioned on the correct side of the master cylinder to install onto the push pin prior to tightening the booster assembly to the dash.*

8. From inside the cab, install the booster mounting bracket-to-dash panel retaining nuts.

9. Position the master cylinder on the booster assembly, install the retaining nuts, and remove the prop from underneath the master cylinder.

10. Connect the manifold vacuum hose to the booster check valve and secure with the clamp.

11. From inside the cab on vehicles equipped with push rod mounted stop lamp switch, install the bushing and position the switch on the end of the push rod. Then install the switch and rod on the pedal arm, along with spacers on each side, and secure with the retaining pin.

12. Start the engine and check brake operation.

1975-76 E-250/350

1. Disconnect the stop lamp switch wiring to prevent running the battery down.

2. Support the master cylinder from the underside with a prop.

3. Remove the master cylinder-to-booster retaining nuts.

4. Loosen the clamp that secures the manifolds vacuum hose to the booster check valve, and remove the hose. Remove the booster check valve.

5. Pull the master cylinder off the booster and leave it supported by the prop, far enough away to allow removal of the booster assembly.

6. From inside the cab on vehicles equipped with push rod mounted stop lamp switch, remove the retaining pin and slide the stop lamp switch, push rod, spacers and bushings off the brake pedal arm.

7. From the engine compartment remove the bolts that attach the booster to the dash panel.

8. Mount the booster assembly on the engine side of the dash panel by sliding the bracket mounting bolts and valve operating rod in through the holes in the dash panel.

NOTE: *Make certain that the booster push rod is positioned on the correct side of the master cylinder to install onto the push pin prior to tightening the booster assembly to the dash.*

9. From inside the cab, install the booster mounting bracket-to-dash panel retaining nuts.

10. Position the master cylinder on the booster assembly, install the retaining nuts, and remove the prop from underneath the master cylinder.

11. Install the booster check valve. Connect the manifold vacuum hose to the booster check valve and secure with the clamp.

12. From inside the cab on vehicles equipped with push rod mounted stop lamp switch, install the bushing and position the switch on the end of the push rod. Then install the switch and

rod on the pedal arm, along with spacers on each side, and secure with the retaining pin.

13. Connect the stop lamp switch wiring.

14. Start the engine and check brake operation.

1977-84

NOTE: *On the E-100/150/250, make sure that the booster rubber reaction disc is properly installed if the master cylinder push rod is removed or accidentally pulled out. A dislodged disc may cause excessive pedal travel and/or extreme operation sensitivity. The disc is black compared to the silver colored valve plunger that will be exposed after the push rod and front seal is removed. The booster unit is serviced as an assembly and must be replaced if the reaction disc cannot be properly installed and aligned, or if it cannot be located within the unit itself.*

1. Disconnect the stop lamp switch wiring to prevent running the battery down.

2. Support the master cylinder from the underside with a prop.

3. Remove the master cylinder-to-booster retaining nuts.

4. Loosen the clamp that secures the manifolds vacuum hose to the booster check valve, and remove the hose. Remove the booster check valve.

5. Pull the master cylinder off the booster and leave it supported by the prop, far enough away to allow removal of the booster assembly.

6. From inside the cab on vehicles equipped with push rod mounted stop lamp switch, remove the retaining pin and slide the stop lamp switch, push rod, spacers and bushings off the brake pedal arm.

7. From the engine compartment remove the bolts that attach the booster to the dash panel.

8. Mount the booster assembly on the engine side of the dash panel by sliding the bracket mounting bolts and valve operating rod in through the holes in the dash panel.

NOTE: *Make certain that the booster push rod is positioned on the correct side of the master cylinder to install onto the push pin prior to tightening the booster assembly to the dash.*

9. From inside the cab, install the booster mounting bracket-to-dash panel retaining nuts.

10. Position the master cylinder on the booster assembly, install the retaining nuts, and remove the prop from underneath the master cylinder.

11. Install the booster check valve. Connect the manifold vacuum hose to the booster check valve and secure with the clamp.

12. From inside the cab on vehicles equipped with push rod mounted stop lamp switch, in-

stall the bushing and position the switch on the end of the push rod. Then install the switch and rod on the pedal arm, along with spacers on each side, and secure with the retaining pin.

13. Connect the stop lamp switch wiring.

14. Start the engine and check brake operation.

1985-88

NOTE: *On the E-100/150/250, make sure that the booster rubber reaction disc is properly installed if the master cylinder push rod is removed or accidentally pulled out. A dislodged disc may cause excessive pedal travel and/or extreme operation sensitivity. The disc is black compared to the silver colored valve plunger that will be exposed after the push rod and front seal is removed. The booster unit is serviced as an assembly and must be replaced if the reaction disc cannot be properly installed and aligned, or if it cannot be located within the unit itself.*

1. Disconnect the stop lamp switch wiring to prevent running the battery down.

2. Support the master cylinder from the underside with a prop.

3. Loosen the clamp that secures the manifolds vacuum hose to the booster check valve, and remove the hose. Remove the booster check valve.

4. Remove the nuts securing the clutch master cylinder and retainer to the booster. Remove the clutch cylinder and bracket from the booster and position the assembly out of the way so that no fluid spills On E-150/250, the two lower holes are used for installation; on the E-350, the two upper holes are used.

5. Remove the master cylinder mounting nuts.

6. Pull the master cylinder off the booster and leave it supported by the prop, far enough away to allow removal of the booster assembly.

7. From inside the cab, remove the retaining pin and slide the stop lamp switch, push rod, spacers and bushings off the brake pedal arm.

8. From inside the cab remove the nuts that attach the booster to the dash panel.

9. Mount the booster assembly on the engine side of the dash panel by sliding the bracket mounting bolts and valve operating rod in through the holes in the dash panel.

NOTE: *Make certain that the booster push rod is positioned on the correct side of the master cylinder to install onto the push pin prior to tightening the booster assembly to the dash.*

10. From inside the cab, install the booster mounting bracket-to-dash panel retaining nuts. Torque the nuts to 18 ft.lb.

11. Position the master cylinder on the boost-

er assembly, install the retaining nuts, and remove the prop from underneath the master cylinder. Torque the nuts to 18 ft.lb.

12. Install the clutch cylinder and bracket. Torque the nuts to 18 ft.lb.

13. Install the booster check valve. Connect the manifold vacuum hose to the booster check valve and secure with the clamp.

14. From inside the cab on vehicles equipped with push rod mounted stop lamp switch, install the bushing and position the switch on the end of the push rod. Then install the switch and rod on the pedal arm, along with spacers on each side, and secure with the retaining pin.

15. Connect the stop lamp switch wiring.

16. Start the engine and check brake operation.

BRAKE BOOSTER PUSHROD ADJUSTMENT

The pushrod has an adjustment screw to maintain the correct relationship between the booster control valve plunger and the master cylinder piston. If the plunger is too long it will prevent the master cylinder piston from completely releasing hydraulic pressure, causing the brakes to drag. If the plunger is too short it will cause excessive pedal travel and an undesirable clunk in the booster area. Remove the master cylinder for access to the booster pushrod.

To check the alignment of the screw, fabricate a gauge (from cardboard, following the dimensions in the above illustration) and place it

against the master cylinder mounting surface of the booster body. Adjust the pushrod screw by turning it until the end of the screw just touches the inner edge of the slot in the gauge. Install the master cylinder and bleed the system.

Diesel Brake Booster Vacuum Pump

Unlike gasoline engines, diesel engines have little vacuum available to power brake booster systems. The diesel is thus equipped with a vacuum pump, which is driven by a single belt off of the alternator.

Diesels are also equipped with a low vacuum indicator switch which actuates the BRAKE warning lamp when available vacuum is below a certain level. The switch senses vacuum through a fitting in the vacuum manifold that intercepts the vacuum flow from the pump. The low vacuum switch is mounted on the right side of the engine compartment, adjacent to the vacuum pump on E-250 and E-350 models.

NOTE: *The vacuum pump cannot be disassembled. It is only serviced as a unit (the pulley is separate).*

REMOVAL AND INSTALLATION

1. Remove the hose clamp and disconnect the pump from the hose on the manifold vacuum outlet fitting.

2. Loosen the vacuum pump adjustment bolt

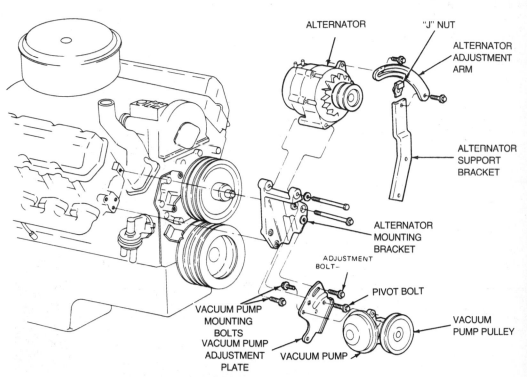

Brake booster vacuum pump installation for all diesel engines

and the pivot bolt. Slide the pump downward and remove the drive belt from the pulley.

3. Remove the pivot and adjustment bolts and the bolts retaining the pump to the adjustment plate. Remove the vacuum pump and adjustment plate.

4. To install, install the pump-to-adjustment plate bolts and tighten to 11-18 ft.lb. Position the pump and plate on the vacuum pump bracket and loosely install the pivot and adjustment bolts.

5. Connect the hose from the manifold vacuum outlet fitting to the pump and install the hose clamp.

6. Install the drive belt on the pulley. Place a ⅜" drive breaker bar or ratchet into the slot on the vacuum pump adjustment plate. Lift up on the assembly until the proper belt tension is obtained. Tighten the pivot and adjustment bolts to 11-18 ft.lb.

7. Start the engine and make sure the brake system functions properly.

NOTE: *The BRAKE light will glow until brake vacuum builds up to the normal level.*

Brake Hoses and Lines
HYDRAULIC BRAKE LINE CHECK

The hydraulic brake lines and brake linings are to be inspected at the recommended intervals in the maintenance schedule. Follow the steel tubing from the master cylinder to the flexible hose fitting at each wheel. If a section of the tubing is found to be damaged, replace the entire section with tubing of the same type (steel, not copper), size, shape, and length. When installing a new section of brake tubing, flush clean brake fluid or denatured alcohol through to remove any dirt or foreign material from the line. Be sure to flare both ends to provide sound, leak-proof connections. When bending the tubing to fit the underbody contours, be careful not to kink or crack the line. Torque all hydraulic connections to 10-15 ft.lb.

Check the flexible brake hoses that connect the steel tubing to each wheel cylinder. Replace the hose if it shows any signs of softening, cracking, or other damage. When installing a new front brake hose, position the hose to avoid contact with other chassis parts. Place a new copper gasket over the hose fitting and thread the hose assembly into the front wheel cylinder. A new rear brake hose must be positioned clear of the exhaust pipe or shock absorber. Thread the hose into the rear brake tube connector. When installing either a new front or rear brake hose, engage the opposite end of the hose to the bracket on the frame. Install the horseshoe type retaining clip and connect the tube to the hose with the tube fitting nut.

Always bleed the system after hose or line replacement. Before bleeding, make sure that the master cylinder is topped up with high temperature, extra heavy duty fluid of at least SAE 70R3 quality.

Bleeding the Brakes

When any part of the hydraulic system has been disconnected for repair or replacement, air may get into the lines and cause spongy pedal action (because air can be compressed and brake fluid cannot). To correct this condition, it is necessary to bleed the hydraulic system after it has been properly connected to be sure that all air is expelled from the brake cylinders and lines.

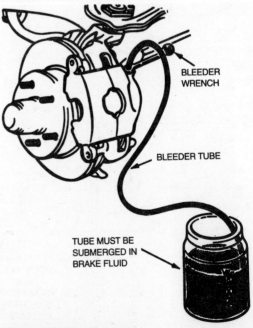

BLEEDER WRENCH

BLEEDER TUBE

TUBE MUST BE SUBMERGED IN BRAKE FLUID

Brake bleeding equipment

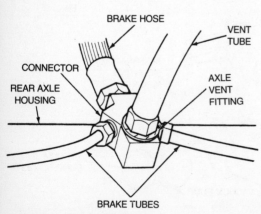

BRAKE HOSE

VENT TUBE

CONNECTOR

REAR AXLE HOUSING

AXLE VENT FITTING

BRAKE TUBES

Rear brake tube connector

When bleeding the brake system, bleed one brake cylinder at a time, beginning at the cylinder with the longest hydraulic line (farthest from the master cylinder) first. Keep the master cylinder reservoir filled with brake fluid during bleeding operation. Never use brake fluid that has been drained from the hydraulic system, no matter how clean it is.

It will be necessary to centralize the pressure differential valve after a brake system failure has been corrected and the hydraulic system has been bled.

The primary and secondary hydraulic brake systems are individual systems and are bled separately. During the entire bleeding operation, do not allow the reservoir to run dry. Keep the master cylinder reservoirs filled with brake fluid.

WHEEL CYLINDERS AND CALIPERS

1. Clean all dirt from around the master cylinder fill cap, remove the cap and fill the master cylinder with brake fluid until the level is within ¼" of the top of the edge of the reservoir.

2. Clean off the bleeder screws at the wheel cylinders and calipers.

3. Attach the length of rubber hose over the nozzle of the bleeder screw at the wheel to be done first. Place the other end of the hose in a glass jar, submerged in brake fluid.

4. Open the bleed screw valve ½-¾ turn.

5. Have an assistant slowly depress the brake pedal. Close the bleeder screw valve and tell your assistant to allow the brake pedal to return slowly. Continue this pumping action to force any air out of the system. When bubbles cease to appear at the end of the bleeder hose, close the bleed valve and remove the hose.

6. Check the master cylinder fluid level and

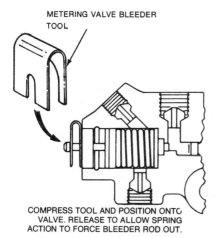

METERING VALVE BLEEDER TOOL

COMPRESS TOOL AND POSITION ONTO VALVE. RELEASE TO ALLOW SPRING ACTION TO FORCE BLEEDER ROD OUT.

A spring clip can be used to hold the pressure differential/metering/proportioning valve's bleeder valve out on E-100 and 150 disc brake systems

add fluid accordingly. Do this after bleeding each wheel.

7. Repeat the bleeding operation at the remaining 3 wheels, ending with the one closest to the master cylinder. Fill the master cylinder reservoir.

MASTER CYLINDER

1. Fill the master cylinder reservoirs.

2. Place absorbent rags under the fluid lines at the master cylinder.

3. Have an assistant depress and hold the brake pedal.

4. With the pedal held down, slowly crack open the hydraulic line fitting, allowing the air to escape. Close the fitting and have the pedal released.

5. Repeat Steps 3 and 4 for each fitting until all the air is released.

DISC BRAKES

CAUTION: *Brake shoes contain asbestos, which has been determined to be a cancer causing agent. Never clean the brake surfaces with compressed air! Avoid inhaling any dust from any brake surface! When cleaning brake surfaces, use a commercially available brake cleaning fluid.*

Application

• 1975 E-250 and E-350: heavy duty, dual piston floating caliper design.

• 1975-88 E-100/150: light duty, single piston sliding caliper

• 1976-88 E-250 and E-350: heavy duty, dual piston sliding caliper

Disc Brake Pads

INSPECTION

Remove the brake pads as described below and measure the thickness of the lining. If the lining at any point on the pad assembly is less 0.0625" ($^1/_{16}$"; 1.5mm) for LD brakes or 0.03125" ($^1/_{32}$"; 0.794mm) for HD brakes, thick (above the backing plate or rivets), or there is evidence of the lining being contaminated by brake fluid or oil, replace the brake pad.

REMOVAL AND INSTALLATION

NOTE: *NEVER REPLACE THE PADS ON ONE SIDE ONLY! ALWAYS REPLACE PADS ON BOTH WHEELS AS A SET!*

1975 E-250 and E-350

1. Remove with discard some of the fluid from the master cylinder without contaminating the contacts to avoid overflow later on.

2. Support the front suspension on jackstands. Remove the wheel.

3. Remove the pad mounting pins, anti-rattle springs, and the pads.

4. Loosen the piston housing to caliper mounting bolts enough to put in the new pads. Do not move the pistons.

5. Install the new pads, mounting pins, and anti-rattle springs. Be sure the spring tangs engage the pad holes. Tighten the pad mounting pins to 17-23 ft.lb.

6. Tighten the piston housing bolts evenly and sparely to reset the pistons in the cylinders. Torque them to 155-185 ft.lb.

7. Replace the wheels and tires and lower the truck to the floor. Fill the master cylinder as specified in Chapter 1. Depress the brake pedal firmly several times to seat the pads on the disc. Don't drive till you get a firm pedal.

1975-85 E-100 and E-150

1. Remove and discard some of the fluid from the master cylinder without contaminating the contents to avoid overflow later on.

2. Support the front suspension on jackstands. Remove the wheels.

3. Put an 8″ C-clamp over the caliper and use it to push the outer pad in and pull the caliper out. This bottoms the caliper piston in its bore.

4. Remove the key retaining screw. Drive the

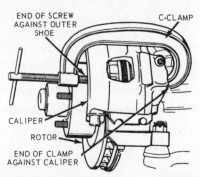

Bottoming the caliper piston on light duty sliding calipers through 1985

caliper support key and spring out toward the outside, using a brass drift.

5. Push the caliper down and rotate the upper end up and out. Support the caliper, so as not to damage the brake hose.

6. Remove the out pad from the caliper. You may have to tap it to loosen it. Remove the inner pad, removing the anti-rattle clip from the lower end of the shoe.

7. Thoroughly clean the sliding contact areas on the caliper and spindle assembly.

8. Put the new anti-rattle clip on the lower end of the new inner pad. Put the pad and clip in the pad abutment with the clip tab against the abutment and the loop-type spring away from the disc. Compress the clip and slide the upper end of the pad into place.

9. If the caliper piston isn't bottomed, bottom it with a C-clamp.

10. The replacement outer pad may differ slightly from the original equipment. Put the outer pad in place and press the tabs into place with your fingers. You can press the tabs in with a C-clamp, but be careful of the lining.

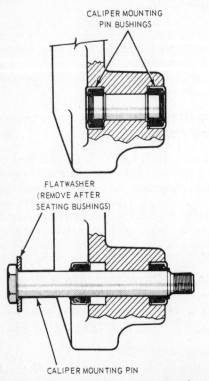

Floating pin caliper mounting pin bushing installation

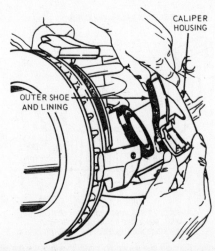

Removing the outer shoe on light duty sliding calipers through 1985

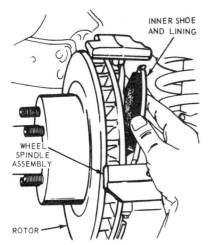

Removing the inner shoe on light duty sliding calipers through 1985

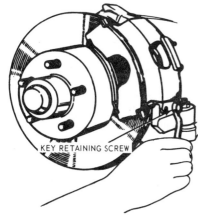

Removing the key retaining screw on light duty sliding calipers through 1985

11. Position the caliper on the spindle assembly by pivoting it around the upper mounting surface. Be careful of the boot.

12. Use a screwdriver to hold the upper machined surface of the caliper against the support assembly. Drive a new key and spring assembly into place with a plastic mallet. Install the retaining screw and tighten to 12-20 ft.lb.

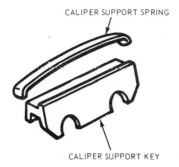

Caliper support spring and key used on light duty sliding calipers through 1985

13. Replace the wheels and tires and lower the truck to the floor. Fill the master cylinder as specified in Chapter 1. Depress the brake pedal firmly several times to seat the pads on the disc. Don't drive until you get a firm pedal.

1976-85 E-250 and E-350

1. Remove and discard some of the fluid from the master cylinder without contaminating the contents to avoid overflow later on.

2. Support the front suspension on jackstands. Remove the wheels.

3. Remove the key retaining screw. Drive the key and spring out toward the inside, using a bass drift.

4. Rotate the key end of the caliper out and away from the disc. Slide the opposite end clear and support the caliper, to prevent brake hose damage.

5. Remove the pad anti-rattle spring and both pads.

6. Thoroughly clean the sliding contact areas on the caliper and support.

7. Put the old inner pad back in place and use a C-clamp to force the pad and pistons back, until the pistons bottom. Make sure the pistons are bottomed.

8. Install the new pads and anti-rattle spring.

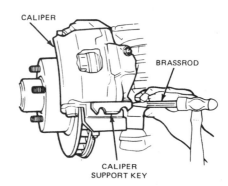

Removing the caliper support spring and key on light duty sliding calipers through 1985

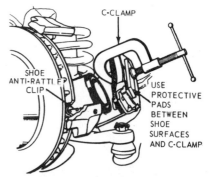

Installing the anti-rattle clip and outer shoe on light duty sliding calipers through 1985

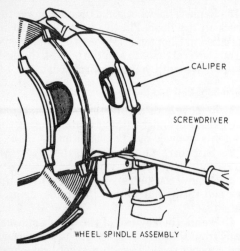

Installing the light duty sliding caliper, through 1985

9. Put the caliper rail into the support slide and rotate the caliper onto the disc.

10. Put the key and spring in place and start them by hand. The spring should be between the key and caliper and the spring ends should overlap the key. If necessary, use a screwdriver to hold the caliper against the support assembly. Drive the key and spring into position, aligning the correct notch with the hole in the support. Install the key retaining screw and tighten to 12-20 ft.lb.

11. Replace the wheels and tires and lower the lower to the floor. Fill the master cylinder as specified in Chapter 1. Depress the brake pedal firmly several times to seat the pads on the disc. Don't drive till you get a firm pedal.

1986-88 E-150

1. Raise and support the front end on jackstands.

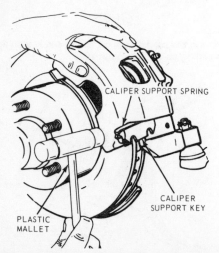

Installing the light duty sliding caliper support spring and key, through 1985

2. Remove the wheels.

3. Remove about half the fluid from the master cylinder reservoir.

4. Place an 8″ C-clamp over the caliper to bottom the piston in its bore.

5. Remove the clamp.

6. Clean the excess dirt from around the caliper pin tabs.

7. Drive the upper caliper pin inward until the tabs on the pin touch the spindle.

8. Insert a small prybar into the slot provided behind the pin tabs on the inboard side of the pin.

9. Using needlenosed pliers, compress the outboard end of the pin while, at the same time, prying with the prybar until the tabs slip into the groove in the spindle.

10. Place the end of a $7/16″$ punch against the end of the caliper pin and drive the pin out of the caliper slide groove.

11. Repeat this procedure for the lower pin.

12. Lift the caliper off of the rotor.

13. Remove the brake pads and anti-rattle spring.

NOTE: *Do not allow the caliper to hand by the brake hose.*

14. Thoroughly clean the areas of the caliper and spindle assembly which contact each other during the sliding action of the caliper.

15. Place a new anti-rattle clip on the lower end of the inboard shoe. Make sure that the tabs on the clip are positioned correctly and the loop-type spring is away from the rotor.

16. Place the lower end of the inner brake pad in the spindle assembly pad abutment, against the anti-rattle clip, and slide the upper end of the pad into position. Be sure that the clip is still in position.

17. Check and make sure that the caliper piston is fully bottomed in the cylinder bore. Use a large C-clamp to bottom the piston, if necessary.

18. Position the outer brake pad on the caliper, and press the pad tabs into place with your fingers. If the pad cannot be pressed into place by hand, use a C-clamp. Be careful not to damage the lining with the clamp. Bend the tabs to prevent rattling.

19. Position the caliper on the spindle assembly. Lightly lubricate the caliper sliding grooves with caliper pin grease.

20. Position the a new upper pin with the retention tabs next to the spindle groove.

NOTE: *Don't use the bolt and nut with the new pin.*

21. Carefully drive the pin, at the outboard end, inward until the tabs contact the spindle face.

22. Repeat the procedure for the lower pin.

WARNING: *Don't drive the pins in too far,*

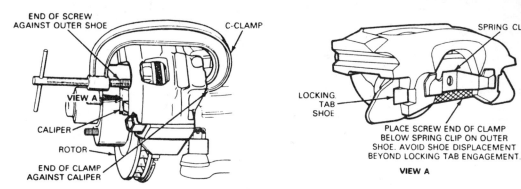

Bottoming the caliper piston on 1986–88 light duty calipers

PLACE SCREW END OF CLAMP
BELOW SPRING CLIP ON OUTER
SHOE. AVOID SHOE DISPLACEMENT
BEYOND LOCKING TAB ENGAGEMENT.

VIEW A

or it will be necessary to drive them back out until the tabs snap into place. The tabs on each end of the pin MUST be free to catch on the spindle sides!

23. Install the wheels.

1986-88 E-250, E-350

1. To avoid overflowing of the master cylinder when the caliper pistons are pressed into the caliper cylinder bores, siphon or dip some brake fluid out of the larger reservoir.
2. Raise and support the front end on jackstands.
3. Jack up the front of the truck and remove the wheels.
4. Place an 8" C-clamp on the caliper and tighten the clamp to bottom the caliper pistons in the cylinder bores. Remove the C-clamp.
5. Clean the excess dirt from around the caliper pin tabs.
6. Drive the upper caliper pin inward until the tabs on the pin touch the spindle.
7. Insert a small prybar into the slot provided behind the pin tabs on the inboard side of the pin.
8. Using needlenosed pliers, compress the outboard end of the pin while, at the same time,

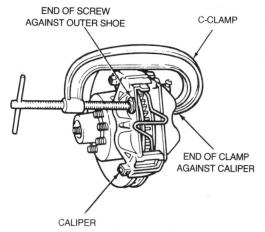

Bottoming the caliper piston on heavy duty calipers

prying with the prybar until the tabs slip into the groove in the spindle.
9. Place the end of a $^7/_{16}$" punch against the end of the caliper pin and drive the pin out of the caliper slide groove.
10. Repeat this procedure for the lower pin.
11. Lift the caliper off of the rotor.
12. Remove the brake pads and anti-rattle spring.

Compressing the pin tabs on 1986–88 light duty calipers

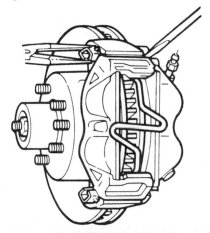

Compressing the pin tabs on heavy duty calipers

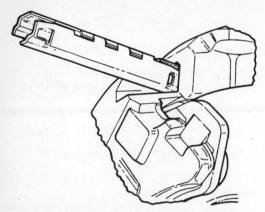

Caliper pin installation on 1986–88 light duty calipers

NOTE: *Do not allow the caliper to hand by the brake hose.*

13. Thoroughly clean the areas of the caliper and spindle assembly which contact each other during the sliding action of the caliper.

14. Place a new anti-rattle clip on the lower end of the inboard shoe. Make sure that the tabs on the clip are positioned correctly and the loop-type spring is away from the rotor.

15. Place the lower end of the inner brake pad in the spindle assembly pad abutment, against the anti-rattle clip, and slide the upper end of the pad into position. Be sure that the clip is still in position.

16. Check and make sure that the caliper piston is fully bottomed in the cylinder bore. Use a large C-clamp to bottom the piston, if necessary.

17. Position the outer brake pad on the caliper, and press the pad tabs into place with your fingers. If the pad cannot be pressed into place by hand, use a C-clamp. Be careful not to damage the lining with the clamp. Bend the tabs to prevent rattling.

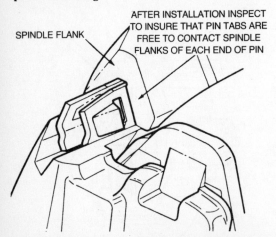

The caliper pin correctly installed on 1986–88 light duty calipers

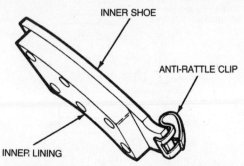

Installing the anti-rattle clip on the inner shoe on light duty calipers

18. Position the caliper on the spindle assembly. Lightly lubricate the caliper sliding grooves with caliper pin grease.

19. Position the a new upper pin with the retention tabs next to the spindle groove.

NOTE: *Don't use the bolt and nut with the new pin.*

20. Carefully drive the pin, at the outboard end, inward until the tabs contact the spindle face.

21. Repeat the procedure for the lower pin.

WARNING: *Don't drive the pins in too far, or it will be necessary to drive them back out until the tabs snap into place. The tabs on each end of the pin MUST be free to catch on the spindle sides!*

22. Install the wheels.

Disc Brake Calipers

REMOVAL AND INSTALLATION

1975 E-250, 350 Floating Caliper

1. Support the front end on jackstands. Remove the wheel and tire.

2. Disconnect the brake hose. Cap the hose and plug the caliper.

3. Remove the pins and nuts holding the caliper to the anchor plate and remove the caliper.

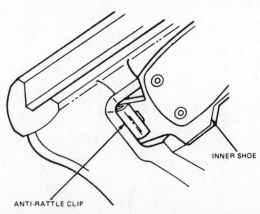

Installing the inner shoe and anti-rattle clip on light duty calipers

4. Grease the pins lightly before installation. Tighten the nuts to 17-23 ft.lb. Use a new brake hose washer.

5. Bleed the system of air.

6. Replace the wheel and tire.

1975-86 All Sliding Caliper

1. Support the front end on jackstands. Remove the wheel and tire.

2. Disconnect the brake hose. Cap the hose and plug the caliper.

3. Remove the key retaining screw and drive the key out with a brass drift.

4. Rotate the key end of the caliper out and slide the other end out.

5. Thoroughly clean the sliding areas.

6. To install, position the caliper rail into the slide on the support and rotate the caliper onto the rotor. Start the key and spring by hand. The spring should be between the key and caliper and the spring ends should overlap the key. If necessary, use a screwdriver to hold the caliper against the support assembly. Drive the key and spring into position, aligning the correct notch with the hole in the support. Install the key retaining screw and tighten to 12-20 ft.lb.

7. Bleed the system of air. Replace the wheel and tire and lower the truck to the floor.

1987-88

1. Raise and support the front end on jackstands.

2. Remove the wheels.

3. Remove the caliper and the brake pads as outlined under Disc Brake Pad Removal and Installation.

4. Disconnect the brake hose from the caliper.

5. When connecting the brake fluid hose to the caliper, it is recommended that a new copper washer be used at the connection of the brake hose and caliper.

6. Bleed the brake system and install the wheels. Lower the truck.

OVERHAUL

1975 Floating Caliper (Dual Piston)

1. Drain the fluid from the cylinder.

2. Place the caliper in a vise.

3. Remove the brake pads.

4. Place a ⅛″ piece of wood between the caliper body and the pistons.

5. Apply low pressure compressed air to the brake line port and force the pistons from the bores. DON'T GET YOUR FINGERS IN THE WAY!

6. Remove the bolts attaching the caliper to the cylinder housing and separate the caliper from the housing.

7. Discard all rubber pieces. Wash all parts in isopropyl alcohol. If the pistons are scored, rusted or worn, replace them. If the cylinders are scored, rusted or worn, replace the housing. DO NOT HONE THE CYLINDER BORES!

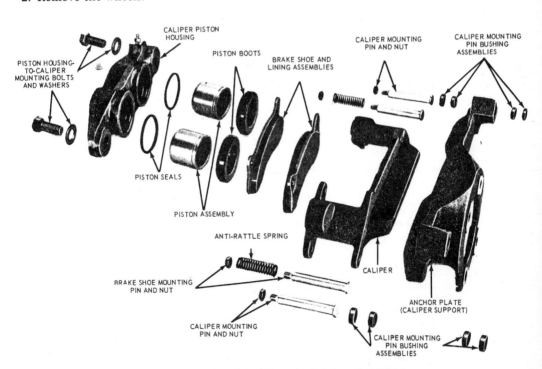

E-250, 350 floating caliper dual piston disc brake

8. Lubricate the new piston seals with clean brake fluid and install them in the bores.

9. Apply a film of clean brake fluid to the bores.

10. Coat the retaining lips of new boots with clean brake fluid and install them in the bores.

11. Apply a flim of clean brake fluid to the pistons and carefully start them into their bores as far as possible by hand. Don't dislodge the seals.

12. Place your wood piece over the pistons and press them into place using a large C-clamp.

13. Install the brake pads.

14. Join the housing and caliper and torque the bolts to 155-185 ft.lb.

LD Sliding Caliper (Single Piston)

1. Clean the outside of the caliper in alcohol after removing it from the vehicle and removing the brake pads.

2. Drain the caliper through the inlet port.

3. Roll some thick shop cloths or rags and place them between the piston and the outer legs of the caliper.

4. Apply compressed air to the caliper inlet port until the piston comes out of the caliper bore. Use low air pressure to avoid having the piston pop out too rapidly and possible causing injury.

5. If the piston becomes cocked in the cylinder bore and will not come out, remove the air pressure and tap the piston with a soft hammer to try and straighten it. Do not use a sharp tool or pry the piston out of the bore. Re-apply the air pressure.

6. Remove the boot from the piston and seal from the caliper cylinder bore.

7. Clean the piston and caliper in alcohol.

8. Lubricate the piston seal with clean brake fluid, and position the seal in the groove in the cylinder bore.

9. Coat the outside of the piston and both of the beads of dust boot with clean brake fluid. Insert the piston through the dust boot until the boot is around the bottom (closed end) of the piston.

10. Hold the piston and dust boot directly above the caliper cylinder bore, and use your fingers to work the bead of dust boot into the groove near the top of the cylinder bore.

11. After the bead is seated in the groove, press straight down on the piston until it bottoms in the bore. Be careful not to cock the piston in the bore. Be careful not to cock the piston in the bore. Use a C-clamp with a block of wood inserted between the clamp and the piston to bottom the piston, if necessary.

12. Install the brake pads and install the caliper. Bleed the brake hydraulic system and recenter the pressure differential valve. Do not drive the vehicle until a firm brake pedal is obtained.

HD Sliding Caliper (Two Piston)

1. Disconnect and plug the flexible brake hose.

2. Remove the front shoe and lining assemblies.

3. Drain the fluid from the cylinders.

4. Secure the caliper in a vise and place a block of wood between the caliper bridge and the cylinders.

5. Apply low pressure air to the brake hose inlet and the pistons will be forced out to the wood block.

6. Remove the block of wood and remove the pistons.

7. Remove the piston seals.

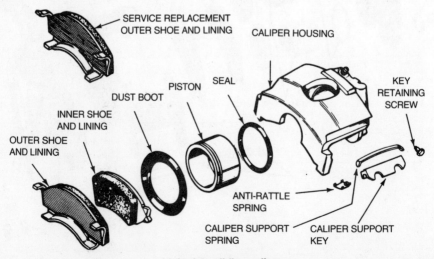

Light duty sliding caliper

SERVICE REPLACEMENT OUTER SHOE AND LINING

CALIPER HOUSING

PISTON   SEAL

DUST BOOT

KEY RETAINING SCREW

INNER SHOE AND LINING

OUTER SHOE AND LINING

ANTI-RATTLE SPRING

CALIPER SUPPORT SPRING

CALIPER SUPPORT KEY

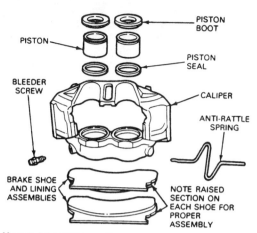

Heavy duty sliding caliper

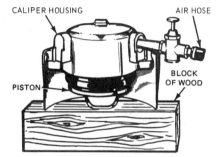

Removing piston using compressed air

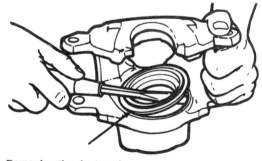

Removing the dust seal

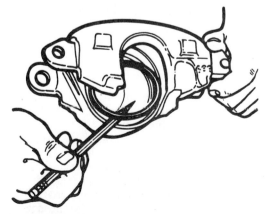

Removing the O-ring

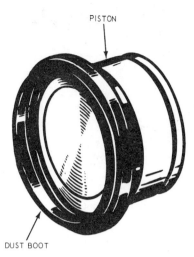

Piston and dust boot

8. Lubricate the new piston seals with clean brake fluid and install them in the seal grooves in the cylinder bores.

9. Lubricate the retaining lips of the dust boots with clean brake fluid and install them in the grooves of the cylinder bores.

10. Apply a film of clean brake fluid to the pistons.

11. Insert the pistons into the dust boots and start them into the cylinders by hand until they are beyond the piston seals. Be careful not to dislodge or damage the piston seals.

12. Place a block of wood over one piston and press the piston into the cylinder. Be careful not to cock the piston in the cylinder bore.

13. Install the second piston in the same manner.

14. Install the brake shoe assemblies and anti-rattle clip in the caliper assembly.

15. Install the brake hose. Torque the fitting to 25 ft.lb.

16. Install the caliper and bleed the system.

Brake Disc (Rotor)

REMOVAL AND INSTALLATION

1. Jack up the front of the truck and support it with jackstands. Remove the front wheel and tire assembly.

2. Remove the caliper assembly and support it to the frame with a piece of wire without disconnecting the brake fluid hose.

3. Remove the hub and rotor assembly as described in Chapter 1.

4. Install the rotor in the reverse order of removal, and adjust the wheel bearing as outlined in Chapter 1.

INSPECTION

If the rotor is deeply scarred or has shallow cracks, it may be refinished on a disc brake ro-

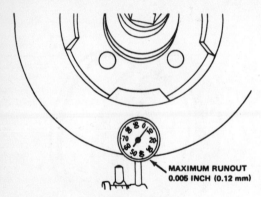

MAXIMUM RUNOUT
0.005 INCH (0.12 mm)

Checking the rotor lateral runout

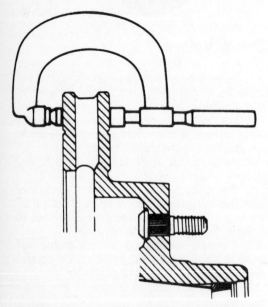

Measuring the rotor thickness with a micrometer

tor lathe. Also, if the lateral run-out exceeds 0.010″ within a 6″ radius when measured with a dial indicator, with the stylus 1″ in from the edge of the rotor, the rotor should be refinished or replaced.

A maximum of 0.020″ of material may be removed equally from each friction surface of the rotor. If the damage cannot be corrected when the rotor has been machined to the minimum thickness shown on the rotor, it should be replaced.

The finished braking surfaces of the rotor must be parallel within 0.007″ and lateral run-out must not be more than 0.003″ on the inboard surface in a 5″ radius.

DRUM BRAKES

CAUTION: *Brake shoes contain asbestos, which has been determined to be a cancer*

causing agent. Never clean the brake surfaces with compressed air! Avoid inhaling any dust from any brake surface! When cleaning brake surfaces, use a commercially available brake cleaning fluid.

Brake Drums
INSPECTION

Check that there are no cracks or chips in the braking surface. Excessive bluing indicates overheating and a replacement drum is needed. The drum can be machined to remove minor damage and to establish a rounded braking surface on a warped drum. Never exceed the maximum oversize of the drum when machining the braking surface. The maximum inside diameter is stamped on the rim of the drum.

REMOVAL AND INSTALLATION
Front

1. Raise the vehicle until the tire clears the floor.
2. Remove the wheel cover or hub cap and the wheel bearing dust cap. Remove the cotter pin, nut lock, nut and washer.
3. Pull the brake drum approximately 2″. out, then push it back into position. Remove the wheel bearing and pull off the brake drum and hub assembly. Back off on the brake adjustment if the brake drum will not slip over the brake shoes.

To install the brake drums:

4. If the hub and drum assembly are to be replaced, remove the protective coating from a new drum with carburetor degreaser. Install new bearings and a new grease seal. Pack the wheel bearings. If the original drum is being used, be sure that the hub is clean and lubricated adequately.
5. Install the drum assembly, outer wheel bearing, washer, and adjusting nut.
6. Adjust the wheel bearing, install the nut lock and cotter pin, and the grease cap.
7. Install the wheel and hub cap. Adjust the brake shoes if they were backed off to remove the drum.

Rear
E-150, AND E-250 LIGHT DUTY

1. Raise the vehicle so that the wheel to be worked on is clear of the floor and install jackstands under the vehicle.
2. Remove the wheel. Remove the three retaining nuts and remove the brake drum. It may be necessary to back off the brake shoe adjustment in order to remove the brake drum. This is because the drum might be grooved or worn from being in service for an extended period of time.

3. Before installing a new brake drum, be sure to remove any protective coating with carburetor degreaser.

4. Install the brake drum in the reverse order of removal and adjust the brakes.

E-250HD, E-350

1. Raise the vehicle and install jackstands.

2. Remove the wheel. Loosen the rear brake shoe adjustment.

3. Remove the rear axle retaining bolts and lockwashers, axle shaft, and gasket.

4. Remove the wheel bearing locknut, lockwasher, and adjusting nut.

5. Remove the hub and drum assembly from the axle.

6. Remove the brake drum-to-hub retaining screws, bolts or bolts and nut. Remove the brake drum from the hub.

7. Place the drum on the hub and attach it to the hub with the attaching nuts and bolts.

8. Place the hub and drum assembly on the axle and start the adjusting nut.

9. Adjust the wheel bearing nut and install the wheel bearing lockwasher and locknut.

10. Install the axle shaft with a new gasket and install the axle retaining bolts and lockwashers.

11. Install the wheel and adjust the brake shoes. Remove the jackstands and lower the vehicle.

Brake Shoes

REMOVAL AND INSTALLATION

E-100, E-150, AND E-200

1. Raise and support the vehicle and remove the wheel and brake drum from the wheel to be worked on.

NOTE: *If you have never replaced brakes before and are not too familiar with the procedures involved, only disassemble and assemble one side at a time, leaving the other side intact as a reference during reassembly.*

2. Install a clamp over the ends of the wheel cylinder to prevent the pistons of the wheel cylinder from coming out, causing loss of fluid and much grief.

3. Contract the brake shoes by pulling away from the starwheel adjustment screw and turn the starwheel up and back until the pivot nut is drawn onto the starwheel as far as it will come.

4. Pull the adjusting lever, cable and automatic adjuster spring down and toward the rear to unhook the pivot hook from the large hole in the secondary shoe web. Do not allow to pry the pivot hook from the hole.

5. Remove the automatic adjuster spring and the adjusting lever.

6. Remove the secondary shoe-to-anchor

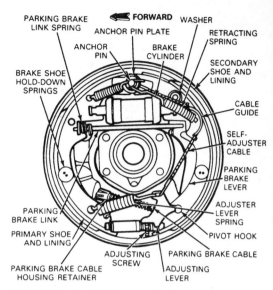

E-100/150 self-adjusting rear brakes

spring with a brake tool. (Brake tools are very common implements and are available at auto parts stores). Remove the primary shoe-to-anchor spring and unhook the cable anchor. Remove the anchor pin plate.

7. Remove the cable guide from the secondary shoe.

8. Remove the shoe hold-down springs, shoes, adjusting screw, pivot nut, and socket. Note the color of each hold-down spring for assembly. To remove the hold-down springs, reach behind the brake backing plate and place one finger on the end of one of the brake hold-down spring mounting pins. Using a pair of pliers, grasp the washer-type retainer on top of the hold-down spring that corresponds to the pin which you are holding. Push down on the pliers and turn them 90 degrees to align the slot in the washer with the head on the spring

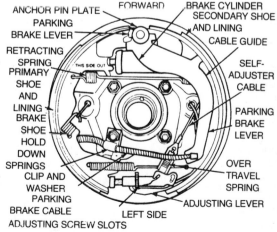

E-250/350 self-adjusting rear brakes

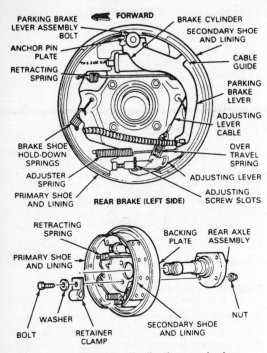

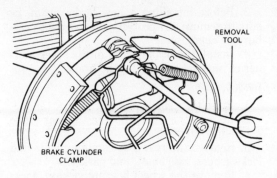

BRAKE CYLINDER CLAMP

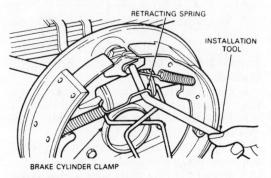

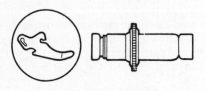

E-250-350 REAR; F-250,F-350

Heavy duty E-250/350 self-adjusting rear brakes

Brake spring replacement

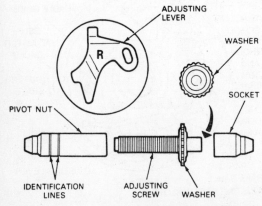

Adjusting screw and lever for self-adjusting brakes

mounting pin. Remove the spring and washer retainer and repeat this operation on the hold-down spring on the other shoe.

9. On rear brakes, remove the parking brake link and spring. Disconnect the parking brake cable from the parking brake lever.

10. After removing the rear brake secondary shoe, disassemble the parking brake lever from the shoe by removing the retaining clip and spring washer.

To assemble and install the brake shoes:

11. On rear brakes, assemble the parking brake lever to the secondary shoe and secure it with the spring washer and retaining clip.

12. Apply a light coating of Lubriplate® at the points where the brake shoes contact the backing plate.

13. Position the brake shoes on the backing plate, and install the hold-down spring pins, springs, and spring washer-type retainers. On the rear brake, install the parking brake link, spring and washer. Connect the parking brake cable to the parking brake lever.

14. Install the anchor pin plate, and place the cable anchor over the anchor pin with the crimped side toward the backing plate.

15. Install the primary shoe-to-anchor spring with the brake tool.

16. Install the cable ground guide on the secondary shoe web with the flanged holes fitted into the hole in the secondary shoe web. Thread the cable around the guide groove.

17. Install the secondary shoe-to-anchor (long) spring. Be sure that the cable end is not cocked or binding on the anchor pin when installed. All of the parts should be flat on the anchor pin. Remove the wheel cylinder piston clamp.

18. Apply Lubriplate® to the threads and the

socket end of the adjusting screw into the adjusting pivot nut to the limit of the threads and then back off ½ turn.

NOTE: *Interchanging the brake shoe adjusting screw assemblies from one side of the vehicle to the other would cause the brake shoes to retract rather than expand each time the automatic adjusting mechanism operated. To prevent this, the socket end of the adjusting screw is stamped with an R or an L for RIGHT or LEFT. The adjusting pivot nuts can be distinguished by the number of lines machined around the body of the nut; one line indicates a left hand nut and two lines indicates a right hand nut.*

19. Place the adjusting socket on the screw and install this assembly between the shoe ends with the adjusting screw nearest to the secondary shoe.

20. Place the cable hook into the hole in the adjusting lever from the backing plate side. The adjusting levers are stamped with and **R** (right) or an **L** (left) to indicate their installation on the right or left-hand brake assembly.

21. Position the hooked end of the adjuster spring in the primary shoe web and connect the loop end of the spring to the adjuster lever hole.

22. Pull the adjuster lever, cable and automatic adjuster spring down toward the rear to engage the pivot hook in the large hole in the secondary shoe web.

23. After installation, check the action of the adjuster by pulling the section of the cable between the cable guide and the adjusting lever toward the secondary shoe web far enough to lift the lever past a tooth on the adjusting screw starwheel. The lever should snap into position behind the next tooth, and release of the cable should cause the adjuster spring to return the lever to its original position. This return action of the lever will turn the adjusting screw starwheel one tooth. The lever should contact the adjusting screw starwheel one tooth above the centerline of the adjusting screw.

If the automatic adjusting mechanism does not perform properly, check the following:

1. Check the cable and fittings. The cable ends should fill or extend slightly beyond the crimped sections of the fittings. If this is not the case, replace the cable.

2. Check the cable guide for damage. The cable groove should be parallel to the shoe web, and the body of the guide should lie flat against the web. Replace the cable guide if this is not so.

3. Check the pivot hook on the lever. The hook surfaces should be square with the body on the lever for proper pivoting. Repair or replace the hook as necessary.

4. Make sure that the adjusting screw starwheel is properly seated in the notch in the shoe web.

E-250, E-300, and E-350

1. Raise and support the vehicle.

2. Remove the wheel and drum.

3. On a front wheel, remove the spring clip retainer fastening the adjustment cable anchor fitting to the brake anchor pin. On a rear wheel, remove the parking brake lever assembly retaining nut from behind the backing plate and remove the parking brake lever assembly.

NOTE: *From this point on, the removal of the front and rear brakes is the same.*

4. Remove the adjusting cable assembly from the anchor pin, cable guide, and adjusting lever.

5. Remove the brake shoe retracting springs.

6. Remove the brake shoe hold-down spring from each shoe.

7. Remove the brake shoe and adjusting screw assembly.

To install the brake shoes:

8. Clean the ledge pads on the backing plate. Apply a light coat of Lubriplate® to the ledge pads (where the brake shoes rub the braking plate).

9. Apply Lubriplate® to the adjusting screw assembly and the hold-down and retracting spring contacts on the brake shoes.

10. Install the upper retracting spring on the primary and secondary shoes and position the shoe assembly on the backing plate with the wheel cylinder pushrods in the shoe slots.

11. Install the brake shoe hold-down springs.

12. Install the brake shoe adjustment screw assembly with the slot in the head of the adjusting screw toward the primary shoe, lower retracting spring, adjusting lever spring, adjusting lever assembly, and connect the adjusting cable to the adjusting lever. Position the cable in the cable guide and install the cable anchor fitting on the anchor pin.

13. Install the adjusting screw assemblies in the same location from which they were removed. Interchanging the brake shoe adjustment screws from one side of the vehicle to the other will cause the brake shoes to retract rather than expand each time the automatic adjusting mechanism is operated. To prevent incorrect installation, the socket end of each adjusting screw is stamped with an **R** or an **L** to indicate their installation on the right or left-side of the vehicle. The adjusting pivot nuts can be distinguished by the number of lines machined around the body of the nut. Two lines indicate a right-hand nut; one line indicates a left-hand nut.

14. On a rear wheel, install the parking brake assembly in the anchor pin and secure with the retaining nut behind the backing plate.

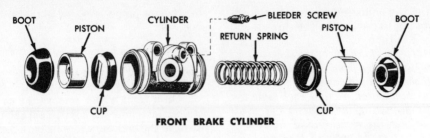

FRONT BRAKE CYLINDER

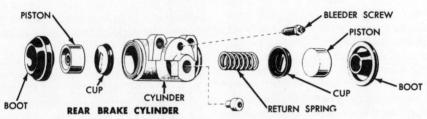

REAR BRAKE CYLINDER

1961–73 front and rear wheel cylinders

15. Adjust the brakes before installing the brake drums and wheels. Install the brake drums and wheels.

16. Lower the vehicle and road test the new brakes. New brakes may pull to one side or the other before they are seated. Continued pulling or erratic braking should not occur.

Wheel Cylinders

CHILTON TIP: *Front brake lining life can be increased on 1969-74 E-200 and E-300 models by decreasing the size of the front wheel cylinders and increasing the size of the rear. Front cylinders are decreased from 1⅛" to 1¹⁄₁₆", E-200 rear cylinders are increased from ¹³⁄₁₆" to ⅞", E-300 rear cylinders are increased from ⅞" to ¹⁵⁄₁₆" The necessary part numbers are given in Ford Technical Service Bulletin No. 86 of March 21, 1975.*

REMOVAL AND INSTALLATION

1. Remove the brake drum.
2. Remove the brake shoes.
3. Loosen the brake line at the wheel cylinder.
4. Remove the wheel cylinder attaching bolt and unscrew the cylinder from the brake line.

5. Installation is the reverse of removal. Torque the nuts to 20 ft.lb. Bleed the brakes.

OVERHAUL

Purchase a brake cylinder repair kit. Remove and disassemble the wheel cylinder. Follow the instructions in the kit. Never repair only one cylinder. Repair both at the same time.

Brake Backing Plate

REMOVAL AND INSTALLATION

1. In order to remove the brake backing plate, the brake assemblies must be removed.
2. Disconnect the hydraulic line from the wheel cylinder and submerge the end of the line in a container of brake fluid to minimize brake fluid loss and bleeding.
3. Remove the wheel cylinder.
4. On rear brakes, remove the parking brake cables.
5. On rear brakes, refer to Chapter 7 under Rear Axle Shaft and Bearing Removal and Installation, and remove the backing plate after the axle shaft has been removed.
6. On the front brake assemblies, remove the

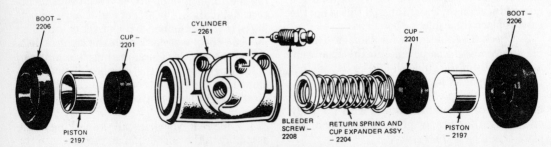

1974–88 wheel cylinder

capscrews which retain the backing plate to the spindle and remove the backing plate.

7. Install the backing plate in the reverse order of removal. Torque the backing plate nuts to 60 ft.lb. on the front; as required in Chapter 7 for the rear.

PARKING BRAKE

ADJUSTMENT

1961-67

1. Make a few stops in reverse to make sure the rear drum brakes are fully adjusted.
2. Raise and support the rear axle.
3. Pull the parking brake handle up one notch from the release position.
4. Loosen the locknut on the cable equalizer (under the truck).
5. Tighten the adjusting nut until a slight drag is felt when turning the rear wheels forward.
6. Tighten the locknut to hold the adjustment.
7. Release the parking brake handle. There should be no drag at the rear wheels.

1969-86

The factory-recommended procedure is to no use a tension gauge on the cables with the handle fully applied (1969-74) or with the pedal pushed down two clicks (1975-88). Tension should be 300 lbs. for 1969-74 E-100 and 200, 225 lbs. for 1969-74 E-300, and 70 lbs. for 1975-88. If the tension gauge is not available, a method similar to that explained for 1961-67 models can be used. The most important point is to make sure the there is no drag when the brake is released and that the brake locks the wheel

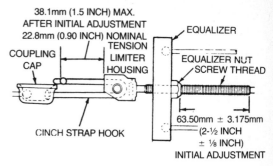

Parking brake cable tension limiter assembly

when fully applied. If there is brake shoe drag after adjustment on E-250, 300, and 350 models, remove the drums and check the clearance between the parking brake operating lever and the cam plate. It should be 0.015″ with the parking brake released.

Cables

REMOVAL AND INSTALLATION

Equalizer-to-Control Cable

1961-77

1. Raise the vehicle on a hoist.
2. Loosen the adjusting nut on the equalizer assembly and remove ball end of the brake control-to-equalizer cable from the equalizer arm. Remove the clip holding the cable housing to the bracket.
3. Lower the vehicle.
4. From the inside of vehicle, disconnect the cable at the parking brake control clevis.

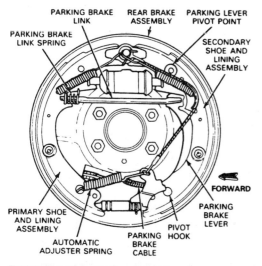

E-100/150 parking brake assembly

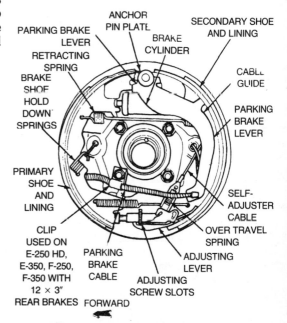

E-250/350 parking brake assembly

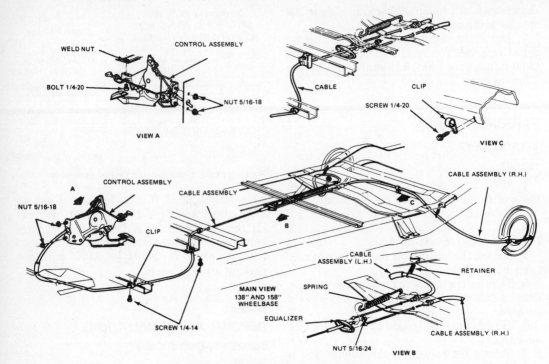

Pedal operated parking brake linkage

5. Raise the vehicle on a hoist.

6. Pull the paring brake control-to-equalizer cable through the hole in the dash panel and remove it from the vehicle.

7. Insert the parking brake control-to-equalizer cable upward through the hole in the dash panel. Place the cable on the mounting bracket.

8. Lower the vehicle.

9. Control the cable to the parking brake control clevis.

10. Raise the vehicle on a hoist.

11. Position the cable housing on the bracket and install the retaining clip.

12. Connect the ball end of cable to the equalizer arm, and install the adjusting nut.

13. Adjust the parking brakes, as described in this chapter.

14. Lower the vehicle. Check brake operation.

1978-79

1. Raise the vehicle on a hoist. Remove the equalizer nut.

2. Remove the parking brake cable from the crossmember and all retaining clips.

3. Lower the vehicle. Remove the forward ball end of the parking brake cable from the control assembly clevis.

4. Remove the cable and hair pin retainer from the control assembly.

5. Using a fishing line or cord attached to the control lever end of the cable, remove the cable from the vehicle.

6. Transfer the fishing line or cord to the new cable. Position the cable in the vehicle, routing the cable through the dash panel. Remove the fish wire and secure the cable to the control with the hair pin retainer.

7. Connect the forward ball end of the brake cable to the clevis of the control assembly and raise the vehicle on a hoist.

8. Route the cable through the crossmember(s) and secure in place with the retaining clip(s).

9. Connect the rod end to the rear cables and equalizer using adjusting nut. Adjust the parking brake cable at the equalizer as described in this chapter.

10. Rotate both rear wheels to be sure that the parking brakes are not dragging.

1980-88

1. Raise the vehicle on a hoist. Back off the equalizer nut and remove slug of front cable from the tension limiter.

2. Remove the parking brake cable from the retaining clips.

3. Lower the vehicle. Remove the forward ball end of the parking brake cable from the control assembly clevis.

4. Remove the cable and hair pin retainer from the control assembly.

5. Using a fish wire or cord attached to the control lever end of the cable, remove the cable from the vehicle.

6. Transfer the fish wire or cord to the new cable. Position the cable in the vehicle, routing the cable through the dash panel. Remove the fish wire and secure the cable to the control with the hair pin retainer.

7. Connect the forward ball end of the brake cable to the clevis of the control assembly and replace the hairpin clip around the conduit end fitting. Raise the vehicle on a hoist.

8. Route the cable and secure in place with retaining clips.

9. Connect the slug of the cable to the tension limiter connector. Adjust the parking brake cable at the equalizer.

10. Rotate both rear wheels to be sure that the parking brakes are not dragging.

Equalizer-to-Rear Wheel Cables

1961-77

1. Raise the vehicle and remove the hub cap, wheel, and brake drum. Loosen the locknut on the equalizer rod and disconnect the cable from the equalizer.

2. Remove the horseshoe-type clip that retains the cable housing to the frame bracket, and pull the cable and housing out of the bracket.

3. Working on the wheel side, compress the prongs on the cable retainer so they can pass through the hole in the carrier plate. Draw the retainer cable out of the hole.

4. With the spring tension off the parking brake lever, lift the cable out of the slot in the lever, and remove the cable through the carrier plate hole.

5. Pull the cable through the housing until the end of the cable is inserted over the slot in the parking brake lever. Pull the excess slack from the cable and insert the cable housing into the carrier plate access hole until the retainer prongs expand.

6. Thread the front end of the cable housing through the frame bracket and install the horseshoe-type retaining clip. Insert the ball end of the cable into the equalizer and slightly tighten the lock nut on the equalizer.

On vehicles with web ledge brakes, check the clearance between the parking brake operating lever and cam plate. The clearance should be 0.015″ when the brakes are fully released.

7. Install the rear brake drum, wheel, and hub cap, and adjust the rear brake shoes.

8. Tighten the lock nut on the equalizer rod until the slack is taken out of the cables.

9. Rotate both rear wheels to be sure that the parking brakes are not dragging.

1978-79

1. Raise the vehicle and remove the hub cap, wheel, and brake drum. Loosen the locknut on

the equalizer rod and disconnect the cable from the equalizer.

2. Compress the prongs that retain the cable housing to the frame bracket, and pull the cable and housing out of the bracket.

3. Working on the wheel side, compress the prongs on the cable retainer so they can pass through the hole in the brake backing plate. Draw the cable retainer out of the hole.

4. With the spring tension off the parking brake lever, lift the cable out of the slot in the lever, and remove the cable through the brake backing plate hole.

5. Pull the cable through the brake backing plate until the end of the cable is inserted over the slot in the parking brake lever. Pull the excess slack from the cable and insert the cable housing into the brake backing plate access hole until the retainer prongs expand.

6. Insert the front end of the cable housing through the frame crossmember bracket until the prong expands. Insert the ball end of the cable into the equalizer and slightly tighten the locknut on the equalizer.

On vehicles with web ledge brakes, check the clearance between the parking brake operating lever and cam plate. The clearance should be 0.015″ when the brakes are fully released.

7. Install the rear brake drum, wheel, and hub cap, and adjust the rear brake shoes.

8. Tighten the locknut on the equalizer rod until the slack is taken out of the cables. Adjust the cable as outlined in this Part.

9. Rotate both rear wheels to be sure that the parking brakes are not dragging.

1980-88

1. Raise the vehicle and remove the hub cap, wheel, tension limiter and brake drum. Remove the locknut on the threaded rod and disconnect the cable from the equalizer.

2. Compress the prongs that retain the cable housing to the frame bracket, and pull the cable and housing out of the bracket.

3. Working on the wheel side, compress the prongs on the cable retainer so they can pass through the hole in the brake backing plate. Draw the cable retainer out of the hole.

4. With the spring tension off the parking brake lever, lift the cable out of the slot in the lever, and remove the cable through the brake backing plate hole.

5. Pull the cable through the brake backing plate until the end of the cable is inserted over the slot in the parking brake lever. Pull the excess slack from the cable and insert the cable housing into the brake backing plate plate access hole until the retainer prongs expand.

6. Insert the front end of the cable housing

through the frame crossmember bracket until the prong expands. Insert the ball end of the cable into the key hole slots on the equalizer, rotate the equalizer 90 degrees and recouple the tension limiter threaded rod to the equalizer.

On vehicles with web ledge brakes, check the clearance between the parking brake oper-

ating lever and cam plate. The clearance should be 0.015″ when the brakes are fully released.

7. Install the rear brake drum, wheel, and hub cap, and adjust the rear brake shoes.

8. Adjust the parking brake tension.

9. Rotate both rear wheels to be sure that the parking brakes are not dragging.

Brake Specifications

All specifications in inches

Years	Models	Master Cyl. Bore	Brake Disc		Brake Drum		Wheel Cyl. or Caliper Bore	
			Minimum Thickness	Maximum Run-out	Orig. Inside Dia.	Max. Wear Limit	Front	Rear
1961	All	1.00	—	—	10.00	10.06	1.125	0.813
1962	All	1.00	—	—	10.00	10.06	1.125	0.813
1963	All	1.00	—	—	10.00	10.06	1.125	0.813
1964	All	1.00	—	—	10.00	10.06	1.125	0.813
1965	All	1.00	—	—	10.00	10.06	1.125	0.813
1966	All	1.00	—	—	10.00	10.06	1.125	0.813
1967–68	All	1.00	—	—	10.00	10.06	1.125	0.813
1969	All	1.00	—	—	10.00	10.06	1.125	0.813
1970	E-100	1.00	—	—	10.00	10.06	1.125	0.813
	E-200	1.00	—	—	10.00	10.06	1.125	0.813
	E-300	1.00	—	—	12.00	12.06	1.125	0.875
1971	E-100	1.00	—	—	10.00	10.06	1.125	0.813
	E-200	1.00	—	—	11.03	11.09	1.125	0.813
	E-300	1.00	—	—	12.00	12.06	1.125	0.875
1972	E-100	1.00	—	—	10.00	10.06	1.125	0.813
	E-200	1.00	—	—	11.03	11.09	1.125	0.813
	E-300	1.00	—	—	12.00	12.06	1.125	0.875
1973	E-100	1.00	—	—	10.00	10.06	1.125	0.813
	E-200	1.00	—	—	11.03	11.09	1.125	0.813
	E-300	1.00	—	—	12.00	12.06	1.125	0.875
1974	E-100	1.00	—	—	10.00	10.06	1.125	0.813
	E-200	1.00	—	—	11.03	11.09	1.125	0.813
	E-300	1.00	—	—	12.00	12.06	1.125	0.875
1975	E-100,150	1.00	0.940	0.003	10.00	10.06	2.875	0.813
	E-250	1.062	1.120	0.003	11.03	11.09	2.180	0.813
	E-350	1.062	1.120	0.003	12.0	12.06	2.180	0.875
1976	E-100,150	1.000	1.120	0.003	11.03	11.06	2.875	0.938
	E-250	1.062	1.180	0.003	12.00	12.06	2.180	1.000
	E-350	1.062	1.180	0.003	12.00	12.06	2.180	1.063

Brake Specifications (cont.)
All specifications in inches

Years	Models	Master Cyl. Bore	Brake Disc		Brake Drum		Wheel Cyl. or Caliper Bore	
			Minimum Thickness	Maximum Run-out	Orig. Inside Dia.	Max. Wear Limit	Front	Rear
1977	E-100,150	1.000	1.120	0.003	11.03	11.09	2.875	0.938
	E-250	1.062	1.180	0.003	12.00	12.06	2.180	1.000
	E-350	1.062	1.180	0.003	12.00	12.03	2.180	1.063
1978	E-100,150	1.000	1.120	0.003	11.03	11.09	2.875	0.938
	E-250	1.062	1.180	0.003	12.00	12.06	2.180	1.000
	E-350	1.062	1.180	0.003	12.00	12.06	2.180	1.063
1979	E-100,150	1.000	1.120	0.003	11.03	11.06	2.875	0.938
	E-250	1.062	1.180	0.003	12.00	12.06	2.180	1.000
	E-350	1.062	1.180	0.003	12.00	12.06	2.180	1.063
1980	E-100,150	1.000	1.120	0.003	11.03	11.06	2.875	0.938
	E-250	1.062	1.180	0.003	12.00	12.06	2.180	1.000
	E-350	1.062	1.180	0.003	12.00	12.06	2.180	1.063
1981	E-100,150	1.000	1.120	0.003	11.03	11.06	2.875	0.938
	E-250	1.062	1.180	0.003	12.00	12.06	2.180	1.000
	E-350	1.062	1.180	0.003	12.00	12.06	2.180	1.063
1982	E-100,150	1.000	1.120	0.003	11.03	11.06	2.875	0.938
	E-250	1.062	1.180	0.003	12.00	12.06	2.180	1.000
	E-350	1.062	1.180	0.003	12.00	12.06	2.180	1.063
1983	E-100,150	1.000	1.120	0.003	11.03	11.09	2.875	1.000
	E-250	1.062	1.180	0.003	12.00	12.06	2.180	1.000
	E-350	1.125	1.180	0.003	12.00	12.06	2.180	1.063
1984	E-100,150	1.000	1.120	0.003	11.03	11.09	2.875	1.000
	E-250	1.062	1.180	0.003	12.00	12.06	2.180	1.000
	E-350	1.125	1.180	0.003	12.00	12.06	2.180	1.063
1985	E-100,150	1.000	1.120	0.003	11.03	11.09	2.875	1.000
	E-250	1.062	1.180	0.003	12.00	12.06	2.180	1.000
	E-350	1.125	1.180	0.003	12.00	12.06	2.180	1.063
1986	E-100,150	1.000	1.120	0.003	11.03	11.09	2.875	1.000
	E-250	1.062	1.180	0.003	12.00	12.06	2.180	1.000
	E-350	1.062	1.180	0.003	12.00	12.06	2.180	1.063
1987	E-100,150	1.000	1.120	0.003	11.03	11.09	2.875	1.000
	E-250	1.062	1.180	0.003	12.00	12.06	2.180	1.000
	E-350	1.125	1.180	0.003	12.00	12.06	2.180	1.063
1988	E-100,150	1.000	1.120	0.003	11.03	11.09	2.875	1.000
	E-250	1.062	1.180	0.003	12.00	12.06	2.180	1.000
	E-350	1.125	1.180	0.003	12.00	12.06	2.180	1.063

Body

10

EXTERIOR

Front Doors

ADJUSTMENT

NOTE: *Loosen the hinge-to-door bolts for lateral adjustment only. Loosen the hinge-to-body bolts for both lateral and vertical adjustment.*

1. Determine which hinge bolts are to be loosened and back them out just enough to allow movement.

2. To move the door safely, use a padded pry bar. When the door is in the proper position, tighten the bolts to 24 ft.lb. and check the door operation. There should be no binding or interference when the door is closed and opened.

3. Door closing adjustment can also be affected by the position of the lock striker plate.

Loosen the striker plate bolts and move the striker plate just enough to permit proper closing and locking of the door.

REMOVAL AND INSTALLATION

NOTE: *On early models, the hinges are riveted to the doors; bolted to the door frames. If the hinges are to be replaced, remove the door and drill out the rivets. On later models, the hinges are bolted to the doors. Before removing the hinges from the doors, in either case, matchmark their location.*

1. Matchmark the hinge-to-body locations. Support the door either on jackstands or have somebody hold it for you.

2. Remove the lower hinge-to-frame bolts.

3. Remove the upper hinge-to-frame bolts and lift the door off of the body.

4. If the hinges are being replaced, drill out

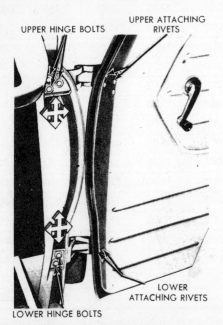

1961–67 front door hinge adjustment

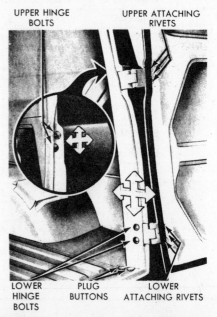

1961–67 rear and side door hinge adjustment

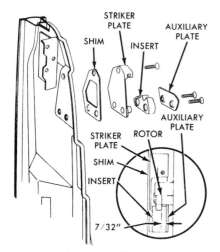

1961–67 door striker plate adjustment

the rivets using a 1" drill bit. New hinges are to be attached to the door with bolts, lockwashers and nuts. Use only hardened bolts of at least Grade 5.

5. Install the door and hinges with the bolts finger tight.

6. Adjust the door and torque the hinge bolts to 24 ft.lb.

Swing-Open Side Doors

ADJUSTMENT

NOTE: *Loosen the hinge-to-door bolts for lateral adjustment only. Loosen the hinge-to-body bolts for both lateral and vertical adjustment.*

1. Determine which hinge bolts are to be loosened and back them out just enough to allow movement.

2. To move the door safely, use a padded pry bar. When the door is in the proper position, tighten the bolts to 24 ft.lb. and check the door operation. There should be no binding or interference when the door is closed and opened.

3. Door closing adjustment can also be affected by the position of the lock striker plate. Loosen the striker plate bolts and move the striker plate just enough to permit proper closing and locking of the door.

REMOVAL AND INSTALLATION

NOTE: *The hinges are riveted to the doors; bolted to the door frames. If the hinges are to be replaced, remove the door and drill out the rivets.*

1. Matchmark the hinge-to-body locations. Support the door either on jackstands or have somebody hold it for you.

2. Remove the lower hinge-to-frame bolts.

3. Remove the upper hinge-to-frame bolts and lift the door off of the body.

4. If the hinges are being replaced, drill out the rivets using a 1" drill bit. New hinges are to be attached to the door with bolts, lockwashers and nuts. Use only hardened bolts of at least Grade 5.

5. Install the door and hinges with the bolts finger tight.

6. Adjust the door and torque the hinge bolts to 24 ft.lb.

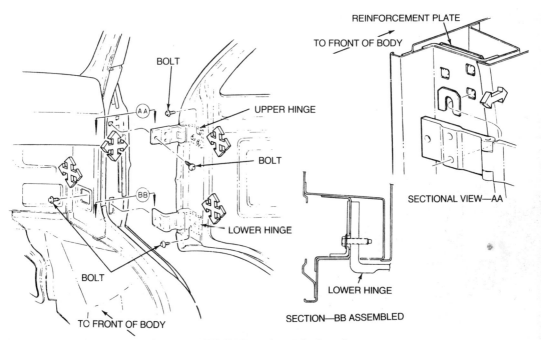

1969–74 front door adjustment

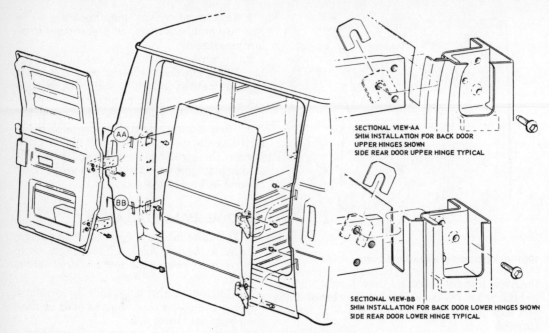

1969–74 cargo door adjustment

Sliding Side Doors

ADJUSTMENT

1972-77

FORE-AFT ADJUSTMENT

1. Remove the interior stationary quarter glass molding.

2. Remove the center track shield nuts from inside the vehicle and the remaining 2 screws holding the center track shield from the outside.

3. Remove the center track shield.

4. Loosen the three bolts at the hinge check.

These bolts must be kept loose when making the fore-aft adjustment.

5. Remove the B-pillar post trim panel.

6. Loosen the 3 striker screws and remove the striker.

7. Fit the door in the opening and adjust the door check so that it is fully engaged with the upper hinge lever and the check bumper is firmly depressed with the hinge casting.

8. Install the front striker assembly and add or remove shims as necessary.

9. Loosen the two screws and push the door so that the lower guide roller is firmly against the over-slam bumper.

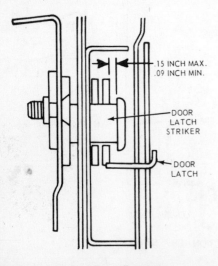

1969–74 door latch striker adjustment

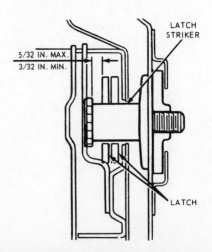

1975–83 door latch striker plate adjustment

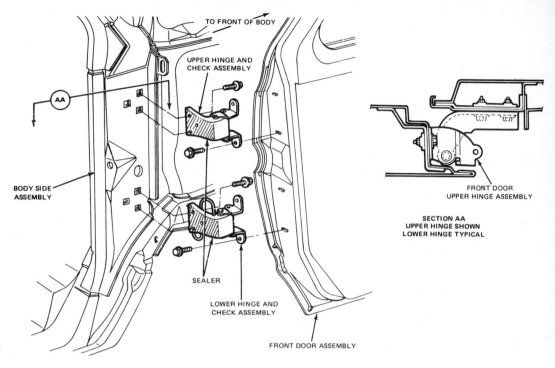

1975—88 front door adjustment

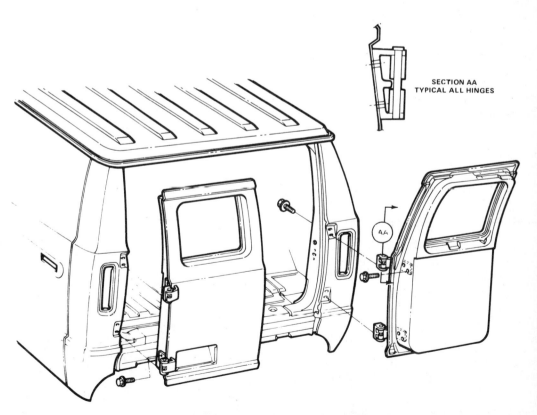

1975—88 cargo and back door adjustment

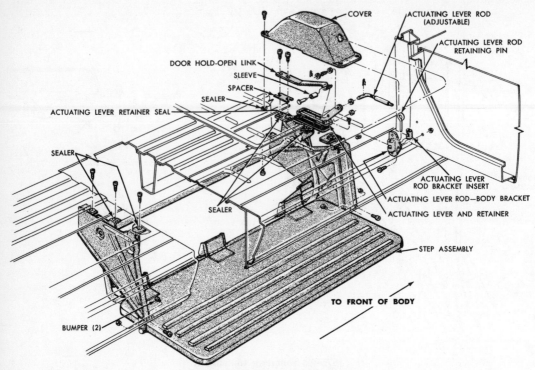

Side door auxiliary step adjustment

10. Adjust the check so that it is engaged with the edge of the hold-open stop and tighten the attaching screws.

11. Remove the sliding door trim panel. The front and rear latch assembly adjustments are made with the rear latch actuating rod assembly. Set the front latch in the latched position and the rear latch in the secondary position. Disconnect the retainer at the rear latch and

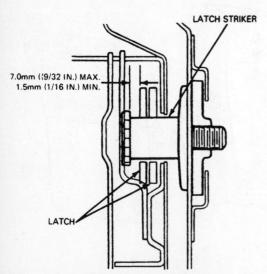

1984–88 door latch striker plate adjustment

adjust the sleeve and actuating rod to match the pivot arm on the latch. Connect the retainer to the rear latch and check the door operation.

1978-81

IN OR OUT

1. Loosen the upper roller retaining nut and move the door in or out as required to obtain a flush fit. Tighten the nut.

2. Support the door so that no up or down movement can occur during the following adjustment:

3. Loosen the retaining screws on the lower guide and move the guide forward to obtain a closer fit to the body, or rearward to move it away from the body at the B-pillar. Tighten the screws.

UP OR DOWN

1. To adjust the front edge of the door:

    a. Loosen the three lower guide attaching screws and rotate the guide at the lower attaching screw to obtain the desired up or down position. Tighten the screws.

    b. Loosen the upper roller bracket screws and adjust the bracket so that the bottom edge of the roller assembly is about $1/16''$ from the bottom flange of the upper track. Tighten the screws.

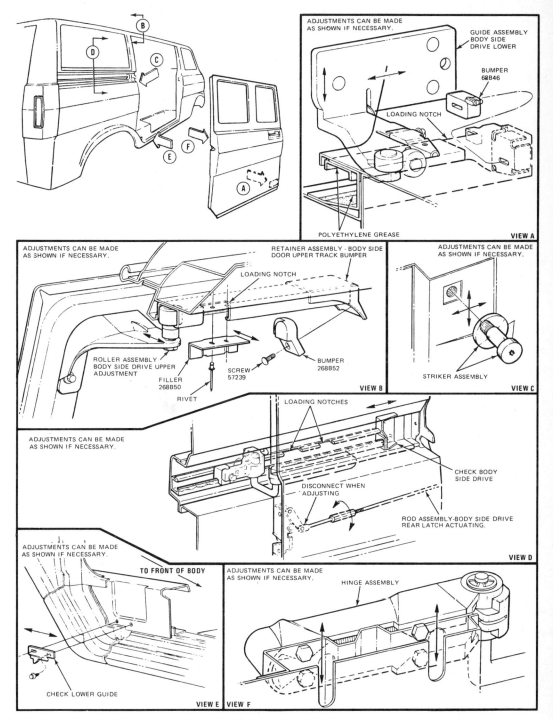

1972–74 sliding door adjustments, part 1

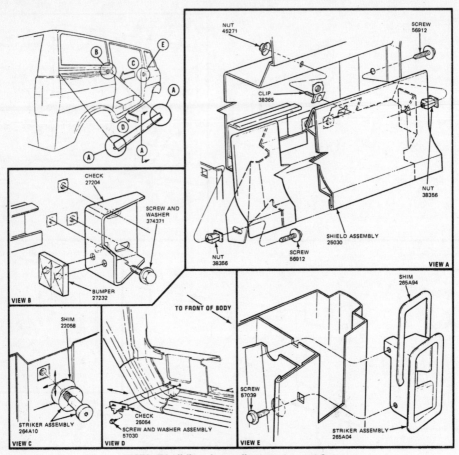

1972–74 sliding door adjustments, part 2

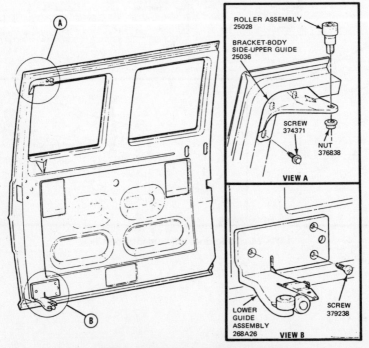

1972–74 sliding door guides and rollers

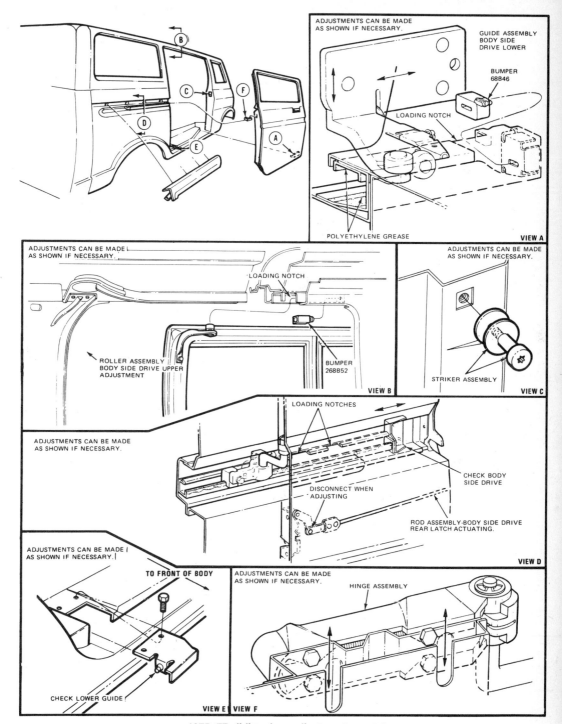

ADJUSTMENTS CAN BE MADE
AS SHOWN IF NECESSARY.

GUIDE ASSEMBLY
BODY SIDE
DRIVE LOWER

BUMPER
68B46

LOADING NOTCH

POLYETHYLENE GREASE

VIEW A

ADJUSTMENTS CAN BE MADE
AS SHOWN IF NECESSARY.

LOADING NOTCH

ROLLER ASSEMBLY
BODY SIDE DRIVE UPPER
ADJUSTMENT

BUMPER
268B52

VIEW B

ADJUSTMENTS CAN BE MADE
AS SHOWN IF NECESSARY.

STRIKER ASSEMBLY

VIEW C

LOADING NOTCHES

ADJUSTMENTS CAN BE MADE
AS SHOWN IF NECESSARY.

CHECK BODY
SIDE DRIVE

DISCONNECT WHEN
ADJUSTING

ROD ASSEMBLY-BODY SIDE DRIVE
REAR LATCH ACTUATING.

VIEW D

ADJUSTMENTS CAN BE MADE
AS SHOWN IF NECESSARY.

TO FRONT OF BODY

ADJUSTMENTS CAN BE MADE
AS SHOWN IF NECESSARY.

HINGE ASSEMBLY

CHECK LOWER GUIDE

VIEW E   VIEW F

1975–77 sliding door adjustments, part 1

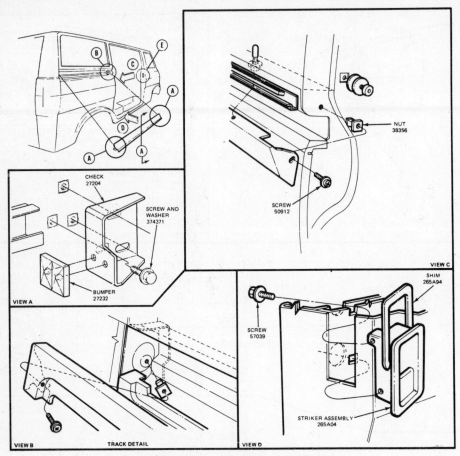

1975–77 sliding door adjustments, part 2

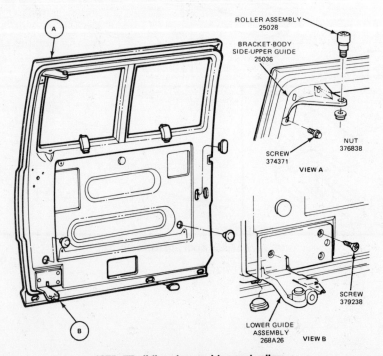

1975–77 sliding door guides and rollers

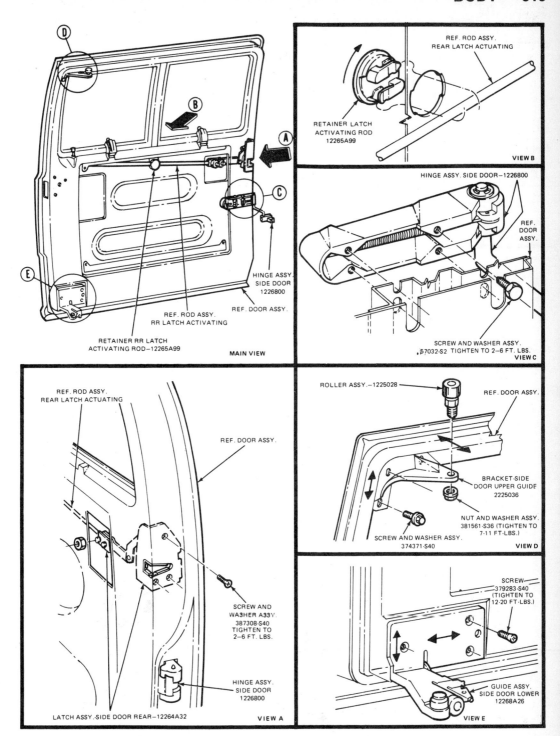

REF. ROD ASSY.
REAR LATCH ACTUATING

RETAINER LATCH
ACTIVATING ROD
12265A99

VIEW B

HINGE ASSY. SIDE DOOR—1226800

REF.
DOOR
ASSY.

SCREW AND WASHER ASSY.
57032-S2 TIGHTEN TO 2–6 FT. LBS.

VIEW C

HINGE ASSY.
SIDE DOOR
1226800

REF. ROD ASSY.
RR LATCH ACTIVATING

REF. DOOR ASSY.

RETAINER RR LATCH
ACTIVATING ROD—12265A99

MAIN VIEW

REF. ROD ASSY.
REAR LATCH ACTUATING

REF. DOOR ASSY.

SCREW AND
WASHER ASSY.
387308-S40
TIGHTEN TO
2–6 FT. LBS.

HINGE ASSY.
SIDE DOOR
1226800

LATCH ASSY. SIDE DOOR REAR—12264A32

VIEW A

ROLLER ASSY.—1225028

REF. DOOR ASSY.

BRACKET-SIDE
DOOR UPPER GUIDE
2225036

NUT AND WASHER ASSY.
381561-S36 (TIGHTEN TO
7-11 FT-LBS.)

SCREW AND WASHER ASSY.
374371-S40

VIEW D

SCREW
379283-S40
(TIGHTEN TO
12-20 FT-LBS.)

GUIDE ASSY.
SIDE DOOR LOWER
12268A26

VIEW E

1978–79 sliding door adjustments: in/out; up/down

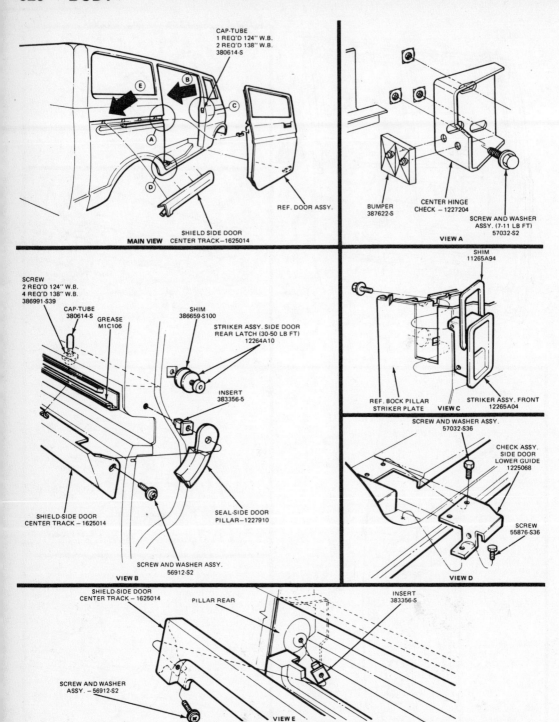

CAP-TUBE
1 REQ'D 124" W.B.
2 REQ'D 138" W.B.
380614-S

E

B

C

A

D

REF. DOOR ASSY.

SHIELD SIDE DOOR
CENTER TRACK—1625014

MAIN VIEW

BUMPER
387622-S

CENTER HINGE
CHECK — 1227204

SCREW AND WASHER
ASSY. (7-11 LB FT)
57032-S2

VIEW A

SCREW
2 REQ'D 124" W.B.
4 REQ'D 138" W.B.
386991-S39

CAP-TUBE
380614-S

GREASE
M1C106

SHIM
386659-S100

STRIKER ASSY. SIDE DOOR
REAR LATCH (30-50 LB FT)
12264A10

INSERT
383356-5

SHIELD-SIDE DOOR
CENTER TRACK — 1625014

SEAL-SIDE DOOR
PILLAR—1227910

SCREW AND WASHER ASSY.
56912-S2

VIEW B

SHIM
11265A94

REF. BOCK PILLAR
STRIKER PLATE

STRIKER ASSY. FRONT
12265A04

VIEW C

SCREW AND WASHER ASSY.
57032-S36

CHECK ASSY.
SIDE DOOR
LOWER GUIDE
1225068

SCREW
55876-S36

VIEW D

SHIELD-SIDE DOOR
CENTER TRACK — 1625014

PILLAR REAR

INSERT
383356-S

SCREW AND WASHER
ASSY. - 56912-S2

VIEW E

1978–79 sliding door adjustments: fore/aft

2. To adjust the rear edge of the door:

a. Remove the door trim panel and/or plug buttons.

b. With the door open, loosen the hinge assembly attaching screws and move the hinge assembly up or down to obtain the desired fit. Tighten the screws.

3. To adjust the rear latch striker:

a. Loosen the striker bolts just enough to move the striker.

b. Move the striker as required to obtain proper fit with the latch.

FORE AND AFT

1. Remove the center track shield nuts from inside the vehicle and the remaining 2 screws holding the center track shield from the outside.

2. Remove the center track shield.

3. Loosen the three bolts at the hinge check. These bolts must be kept loose when making the fore-aft adjustment.

4. Remove the B-pillar post trim panel.

5. Loosen the 2 striker screws and remove the striker.

6. Fit the door in the opening and adjust the door check so that it is fully engaged with the upper hinge lever and the check bumper is firmly depressed with the hinge casting.

7. Install the front striker assembly and add or remove shims as necessary.

1982-88

IN OR OUT

1. Loosen the upper roller retaining nut and move the door in or out as required to obtain a flush fit. Tighten the nut.

2. Support the door so that no up or down movement can occur during the following adjustment:

3. Loosen the retaining screws on the lower guide and move the guide forward to obtain a closer fit to the body, or rearward to move it away from the body at the B-pillar. Tighten the screws.

UP OR DOWN

1. To adjust the front edge of the door:

a. Loosen the three lower guide attaching screws and rotate the guide at the lower attaching screw to obtain the desired up or down position. Tighten the screws.

b. Loosen the upper roller bracket screws and adjust the bracket so that the bottom edge of the roller assembly is about $\frac{1}{16}$" from the bottom flange of the upper track. Tighten the screws.

2. To adjust the rear edge of the door:

a. Remove the rear hinge assembly mounting bolt covers.

b. With the door open, loosen the hinge assembly attaching screws and move the hinge assembly up or down until the hinge pin is

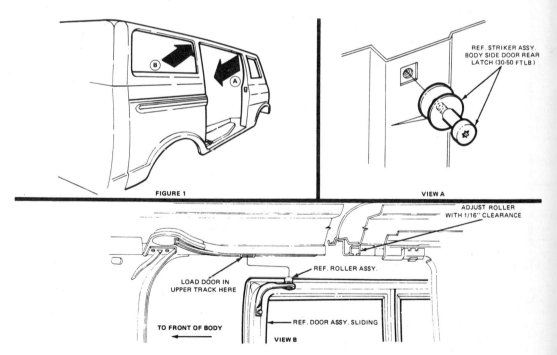

1978–79 sliding door guides and rollers

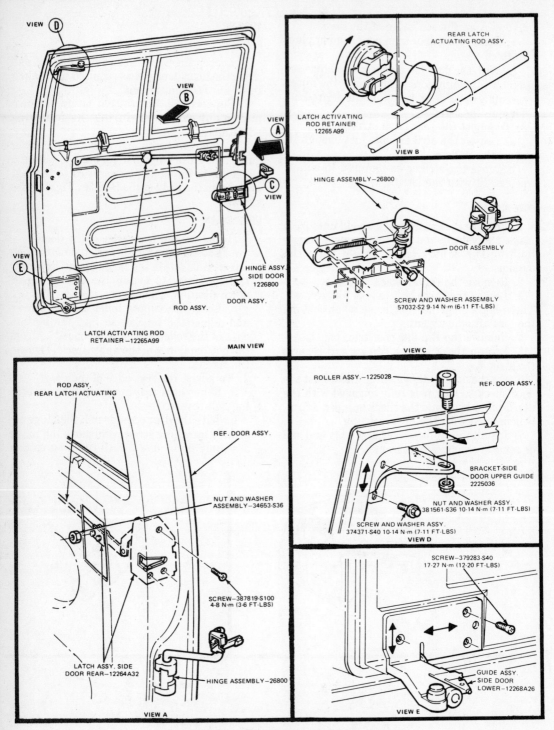

VIEW D

VIEW B

VIEW A

VIEW C

VIEW E

REAR LATCH
ACTUATING ROD ASSY.

LATCH ACTIVATING
ROD RETAINER
12265 A99

VIEW B

HINGE ASSEMBLY—26800

DOOR ASSEMBLY

SCREW AND WASHER ASSEMBLY
57032-S2 9-14 N·m (6-11 FT·LBS)

VIEW C

HINGE ASSY.
SIDE DOOR
1226800

DOOR ASSY.

ROD ASSY.

LATCH ACTIVATING ROD
RETAINER —12265A99

MAIN VIEW

ROD ASSY.
REAR LATCH ACTUATING

REF. DOOR ASSY.

NUT AND WASHER
ASSEMBLY—34653-S36

SCREW—387819-S100
4-8 N·m (3-6 FT·LBS)

LATCH ASSY. SIDE
DOOR REAR—12264A32

HINGE ASSEMBLY—26800

VIEW A

ROLLER ASSY.—1225028

REF. DOOR ASSY.

BRACKET-SIDE
DOOR UPPER GUIDE
2225036

NUT AND WASHER ASSY.
381561-S36 10-14 N·m (7-11 FT·LBS)

SCREW AND WASHER ASSY.
374371-S40 10-14 N·m (7-11 FT·LBS)

VIEW D

SCREW—379283-S40
17-27 N·m (12-20 FT·LBS)

GUIDE ASSY.
SIDE DOOR
LOWER —12268A26

VIEW E

1980–88 sliding door adjustments: in/out; up/down

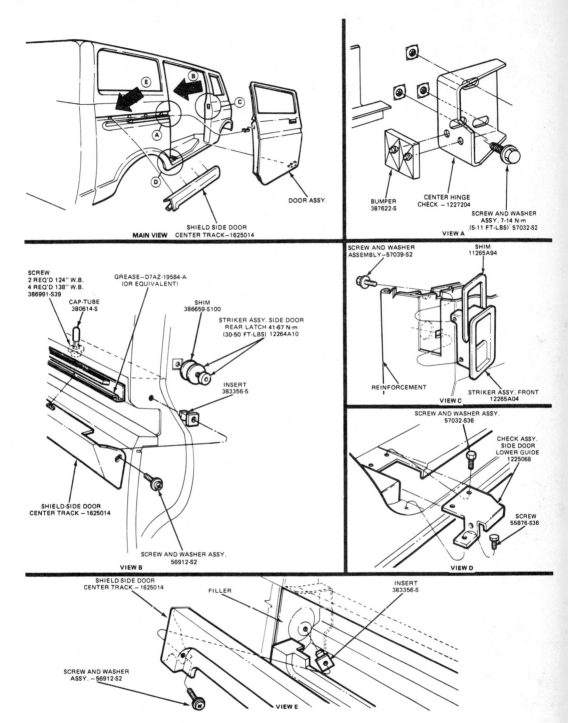

MAIN VIEW
DOOR ASSY.
SHIELD SIDE DOOR CENTER TRACK—1625014

BUMPER 387622-S
CENTER HINGE CHECK — 1227204
SCREW AND WASHER ASSY. 7-14 N·m (5-11 FT-LBS) 57032-S2
VIEW A

SCREW 2 REQ'D 124" W.B. 4 REQ'D 138" W.B. 386991-S39
CAP-TUBE 380614-S
GREASE—D7AZ-19584-A (OR EQUIVALENT)
SHIM 386659-S100
STRIKER ASSY. SIDE DOOR REAR LATCH 41-67 N·m (30-50 FT-LBS) 12264A10
INSERT 383356-5
SHIELD-SIDE DOOR CENTER TRACK — 1625014
SCREW AND WASHER ASSY. 56912-S2
VIEW B

SCREW AND WASHER ASSEMBLY—57039-S2
SHIM 11265A94
REINFORCEMENT
STRIKER ASSY. FRONT 12265A04
VIEW C

SCREW AND WASHER ASSY. 57032-S36
CHECK ASSY. SIDE DOOR LOWER GUIDE 1225068
SCREW 55876-S36
VIEW D

SHIELD-SIDE DOOR CENTER TRACK — 1625014
FILLER
INSERT 383356-S
SCREW AND WASHER ASSY. — 56912-S2
VIEW E

1980–88 sliding door adjustments: fore/aft

horizontal and the roller is seated properly on the center track. Tighten the screws. Adjust the rear latch striker.

3. To adjust the rear latch striker:

a. Loosen the striker bolts just enough to move the striker.

b. Move the striker as required to obtain proper fit with the latch.

FORE AND AFT

1. Remove the center track shield nuts from inside the vehicle and the remaining 2 screws holding the center track shield from the outside. On the short wheelbase models, the rear side marker lamp must be removed to gain access to the rear center track rear attaching screws.

2. Remove the center track shield.

3. Loosen the three bolts at the hinge check. These bolts must be kept loose when making the fore-aft adjustment.

4. Remove the B-pillar post trim panel.

5. Loosen the 2 striker screws and remove the striker.

6. Fit the door in the opening and adjust the door check so that it is fully engaged with the upper hinge lever and the check bumper is firmly depressed with the hinge casting.

7. Install the front striker assembly and add or remove shims as necessary.

REMOVAL AND INSTALLATION

1. Remove the center track shield as described in ADJUSTMENTS, above.

2. Remove the lower guide check screws and remove the check.

3. Open and support the door.

4. Matchmark the upper guide bracket and door.

5. Remove the 3 attaching screws and remove the upper guide bracket.

6. Remove the door from the body.

7. Installation is the reverse of removal.

Rear Doors

ADJUSTMENT

NOTE: *Loosen the hinge-to-door bolts for lateral adjustment only. Loosen the hinge-to-body bolts for both lateral and vertical adjustment.*

1. Determine which hinge bolts are to be loosened and back them out just enough to allow movement.

NOTE: *For access to the upper hinge bolts on passenger van/bus models, remove the side trim panels. Left side trim panel removal requires removal of the rear seat.*

2. To move the door safely, use a padded pry bar. When the door is in the proper position, tighten the bolts to 24 ft.lb. and check the door operation. There should be no binding or interference when the door is closed and opened.

3. Door closing adjustment can also be affected by the position of the lock striker plate. Loosen the striker plate bolts and move the striker plate just enough to permit proper closing and locking of the door.

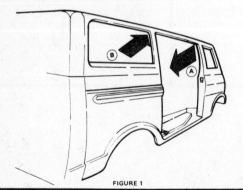

FIGURE 1

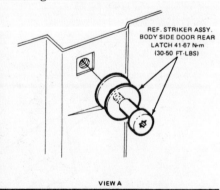

REF. STRIKER ASSY.
BODY SIDE DOOR REAR
LATCH 41-67 N·m
(30-50 FT-LBS)

VIEW A

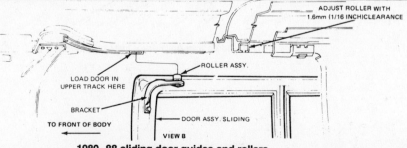

ADJUST ROLLER WITH
1.6mm (1/16 INCH)CLEARANCE

LOAD DOOR IN
UPPER TRACK HERE

ROLLER ASSY.

BRACKET

DOOR ASSY. SLIDING

TO FRONT OF BODY

VIEW B

1980—88 sliding door guides and rollers

REMOVAL AND INSTALLATION

NOTE: *The hinges are riveted to the doors; bolted to the door frames. If the hinges are to be replaced, remove the door and drill out the rivets.*

1. Matchmark the hinge-to-body locations. Support the door either on jackstands or have somebody hold it for you.

2. Remove the lower hinge-to-frame bolts.

NOTE: *For access to the upper hinge bolts on 1961-67 passenger van/bus models, remove the side trim panels. Left side trim panel removal requires removal of the rear seat.*

3. Remove the upper hinge-to-frame bolts and lift the door off of the body.

4. If the hinges are being replaced, drill out the rivets using a 1″ drill bit. New hinges are to be attached to the door with bolts, lockwashers and nuts. Use only hardened bolts of at least Grade 5.

5. Install the door and hinges with the bolts finger tight.

6. Adjust the door and torque the hinge bolts to 24 ft.lb.

Exterior Hood
REMOVAL AND INSTALLATION
1969-76

1. Open and prop up the hood.
2. Remove the bolts from each hinge and lift off the hood.
3. Installation is the reverse of removal.

1977-78

1. Open and prop up the hood.
2. Remove the check cable attaching screw from the hood.
3. Remove the bolts from each hinge and lift off the hood.
4. Installation is the reverse of removal.

1979-88

1. Open and prop up the hood.
2. Remove the bolts from each hinge and lift off the hood.
3. Installation is the reverse of removal.

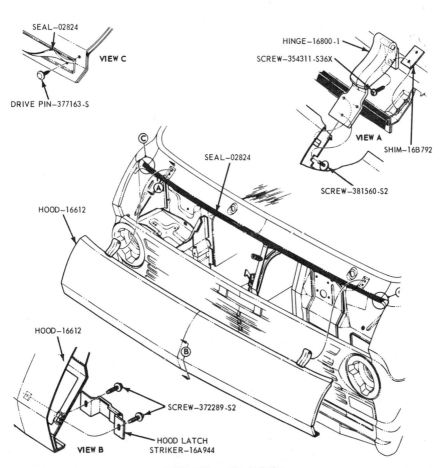

1969–74 hood installation

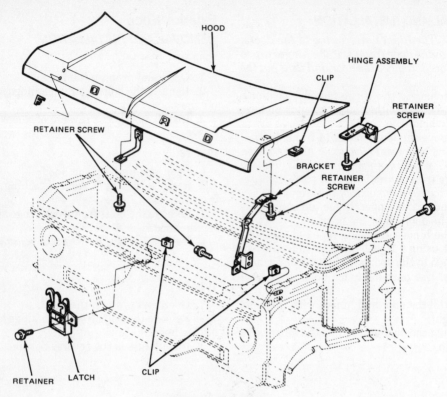

1975 hood installation

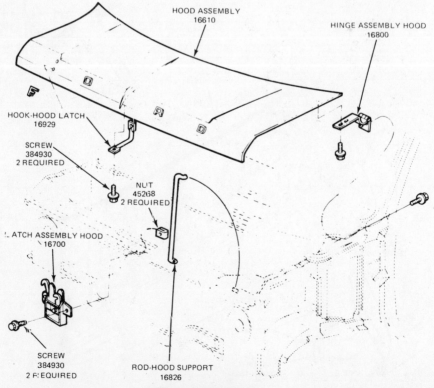

1976 hood installation

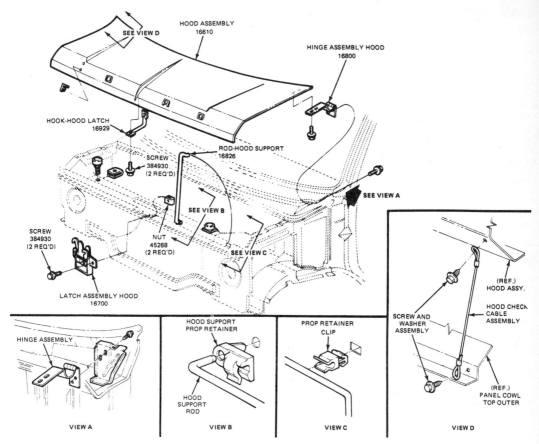

SEE VIEW D

HOOD ASSEMBLY
16610

HINGE ASSEMBLY HOOD
16800

HOOK-HOOD LATCH
16929

SCREW
384930
(2 REQ'D)

ROD-HOOD SUPPORT
16826

SEE VIEW A

SEE VIEW B

SCREW
384930
(2 REQ'D)

NUT
45268
(2 REQ'D)

SEE VIEW C

LATCH ASSEMBLY HOOD
16700

HINGE ASSEMBLY

VIEW A

HOOD SUPPORT
PROP RETAINER

HOOD
SUPPORT
ROD

VIEW B

PROP RETAINER
CLIP

VIEW C

SCREW AND
WASHER
ASSEMBLY

(REF.)
HOOD ASSY.

HOOD CHECK
CABLE
ASSEMBLY

(REF.)
PANEL COWL
TOP OUTER

VIEW D

1977 hood installation

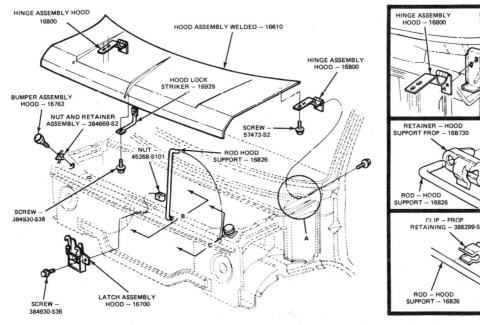

HINGE ASSEMBLY HOOD
16800

HOOD ASSEMBLY WELDED — 16610

HINGE ASSEMBLY
HOOD — 16800

HOOD LOCK
STRIKER — 16929

BUMPER ASSEMBLY
HOOD — 16763

NUT AND RETAINER
ASSEMBLY — 384669-S2

NUT
45268-S101

ROD HOOD
SUPPORT — 16826

SCREW —
57473-S2

SCREW —
384930-S36

SCREW —
384930-S36

LATCH ASSEMBLY
HOOD — 16700

HINGE ASSEMBLY
HOOD — 16800

SCREW —
57473-S2

VIEW A

RETAINER — HOOD
SUPPORT PROP — 16B730

ROD — HOOD
SUPPORT — 16826

VIEW B

CLIP — PROP
RETAINING — 386299-S

ROD — HOOD
SUPPORT — 16826

VIEW C

1978–88 steel hood installation

628   BODY

ALIGNMENT
1969-88
The hood can be adjusted fore-aft and up-and-down to obtain a proper fit.

1. Loosen the hood-to-hinge bolts until the are finger-tight.
2. Reposition the hood as required.
3. Tighten the bolts.

Tailgate
REMOVAL AND INSTALLATION
1961-67
1. Remove the 2 bolts that retain the hinges to the rear lower body panel.
2. Disconnect the support arms and remove the tailgate and hinges.
3. Installation is the reverse of removal.

Bumpers
REMOVAL AND INSTALLATION
1. Support the bumper.
2. Remove the nuts and bolts attaching the bumper to the frame and/or bumper arms.
3. Installation is the reverse of removal. Torque the bracket-to-frame bolts to 100 ft.lb. on models with frame mounted bumpers. On models through 1985 with bracket mounted

front bumpers torque the bolts to 65 ft.lb. on painted bumpers; 40 ft.lb. on chrome bumpers. On 1986-87 models torque the bolts to 30 ft.lb. on painted bumpers; 25 ft.lb. on chrome bumpers. On 1988 models, the torque figure is 65 ft.lb. for all front bumpers. For rear bumpers, the torque figures are 30 ft.lb for painted bumpers; 25 ft.lb. for chrome bumpers.

Grille
REMOVAL AND INSTALLATION
1961-67
1. From inside the van, remove the 4 nuts from the studs in the grille top flange.
2. From outside, remove the 5 lower retaining bolts.
3. Pull the grille out.
4. When installing the grille, first install the 5 lower bolts, but don't tighten them until you install the 4 inside nuts and align the grille.

1969-74
1. Remove the headlights.
2. Remove the 5 bolts from the bottom edge of the grille.
3. Remove the hood latch-to-grille bolt.
4. Disconnect the parking light wires.

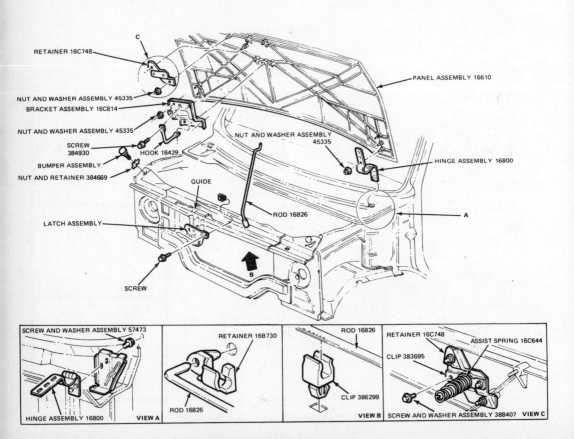

1979–85 fiberglass hood installation

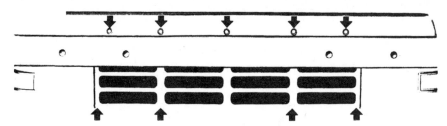

1961–67 grille attaching points

5. Remove the screws at the right and left upper corners and lift out the grille.

6. Installation is the reverse of removal.

1975-77

1. Prop the hood in the open position.

2. Remove the 2 screws which retain the grille center to the radiator grille support.

3. Remove the 6 screw along the bottom of the grille.

4. Remove the 9 upper flange-to-radiator support screws.

NOTE: *There are differences among the 9 screws. DON'T MIX THEM UP!*

5. Pull the grille from the van.

6. Installation is the reverse of removal.

1978-81

1. Prop the hood in the open position.

2. Remove the 2 screws which retain the grille center to the radiator grille support.

3. Remove the 4 screw along the bottom of the grille.

4. Remove the 9 plastic rivets which attach the upper grille flange to the radiator support.

5. Pull the grille from the van.

6. Installation is the reverse of removal. Don't tighten any fasteners until the grille is aligned. Install the plastic rivets last.

1982-88

1. Prop the hood in the open position.

2. Remove the 4 screws which retain the grille center to the radiator grille support.

3. Remove the 4 screw along the bottom of the grille.

4. Remove the 9 plastic rivets which attach the upper grille flange to the radiator support.

5. Pull the grille from the van.

6. Installation is the reverse of removal. Don't tighten any fasteners until the grille is aligned. Install the plastic rivets last.

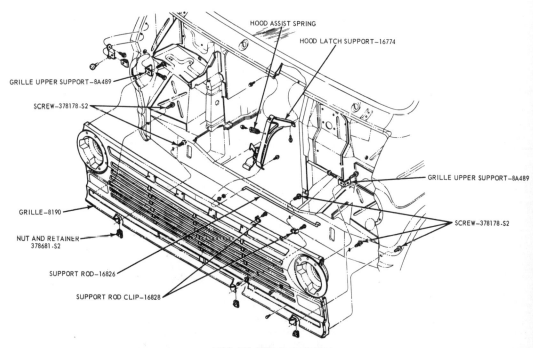

1969–74 grille installation

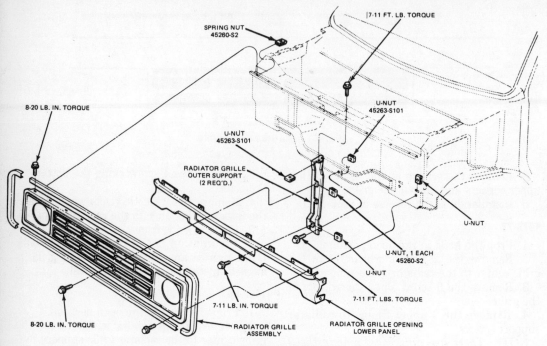

SPRING NUT
45260-S2

7-11 FT. LB. TORQUE

U-NUT
45263-S101

8-20 LB. IN. TORQUE

U-NUT
45263-S101

RADIATOR GRILLE
OUTER SUPPORT
(2 REQ'D.)

U-NUT

U-NUT, 1 EACH
45260-S2

U-NUT

8-20 LB. IN. TORQUE

7-11 LB. IN. TORQUE

RADIATOR GRILLE
ASSEMBLY

7-11 FT. LBS. TORQUE

RADIATOR GRILLE OPENING
LOWER PANEL

1975–77 grille installation

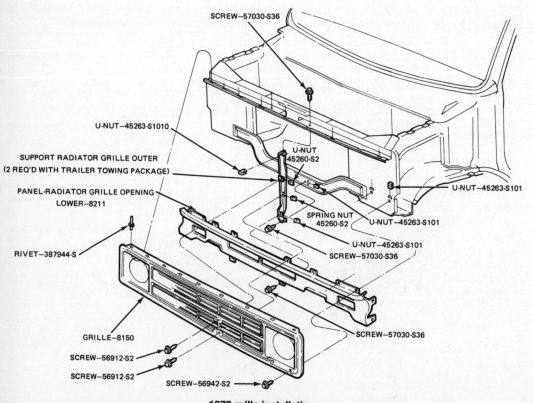

SCREW—57030-S36

U-NUT—45263-S1010

SUPPORT RADIATOR GRILLE OUTER
(2 REQ'D WITH TRAILER TOWING PACKAGE)

PANEL-RADIATOR GRILLE OPENING
LOWER—8211

RIVET—387944-S

GRILLE—8150

SCREW—56912-S2

SCREW—56912-S2

SCREW—56942-S2

U-NUT
45260-S2

U-NUT—45263-S101

SPRING NUT
45260-S2

U-NUT—45263-S101

U-NUT—45263-S101

SCREW—57030-S36

SCREW—57030-S36

1978 grille installation

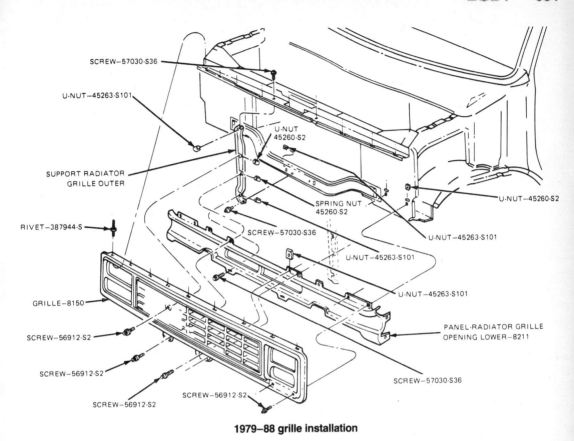

1979–88 grille installation

Outside Mirrors

REMOVAL AND INSTALLATION

All mirrors are remove by removing the mounting screws and lifting off the mirror and gasket.

Antenna

REMOVAL AND INSTALLATION

1961-74

1. Disconnect the antenna cable at the radio by pulling it straight out of the set.
2. Working under the instrument panel, disengage the cable from its retainers.
   NOTE: *On some models, it may be necessary to remove the instrument panel pad to get at the cable.*
3. Remove the mounting nut and star nut and grommet and lift off the antenna, pulling the cable with it, carefully.
4. Installation is the reverse of removal.

1975-88

1. Remove the cowl top grille panel above the radio.
2. Disconnect the antenna lead from the back of the radio.

3. Unsnap the 2 retaining clips from the cable.
4. Unsnap the cap from the base of the antenna.
5. Remove the 4 attaching screws and lift off the antenna, carefully pulling the cable through the opening.
6. Installation is the reverse of removal.

Windshield

REMOVAL AND INSTALLATION

NOTE: *Windshields on 1975 and later models are retained by special sealers and must meet Federal Motor Vehicles Safety Standards for installation quality. Therefore, we recommend that owners of these vehicles have the windshields professionally replaced.*

1961-74

1. Remove the wiper arm and blade assemblies.
2. Have a helper stand outside the windshield and, working from the inside, push the windshield and weatherstripping outward, starting at the upper left corner, working across the top.

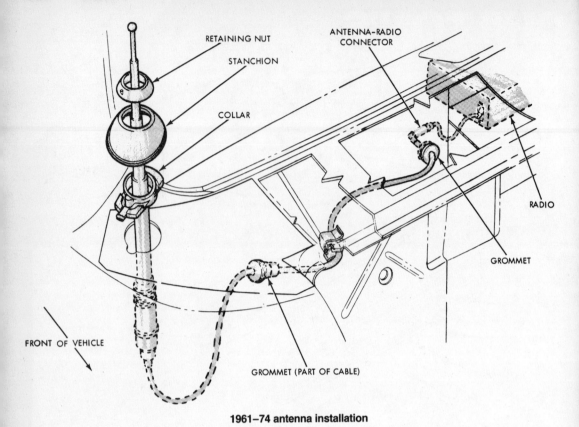

RETAINING NUT

STANCHION

ANTENNA-RADIO
CONNECTOR

COLLAR

RADIO

GROMMET

FRONT OF VEHICLE

GROMMET (PART OF CABLE)

1961–74 antenna installation

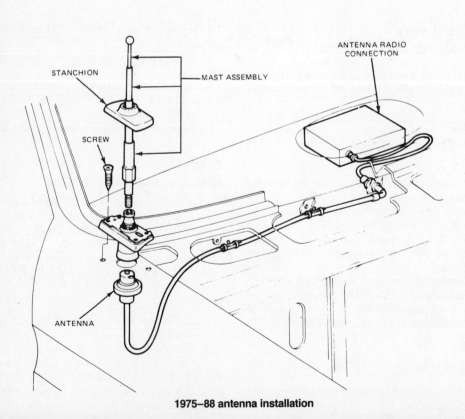

ANTENNA RADIO
CONNECTION

STANCHION

MAST ASSEMBLY

SCREW

ANTENNA

1975–88 antenna installation

CHILTON'S
AUTO BODY REPAIR TIPS

**Tools and Materials • Step-by-Step Illustrated Procedures
How To Repair Dents, Scratches and Rust Holes
Spray Painting and Refinishing Tips**

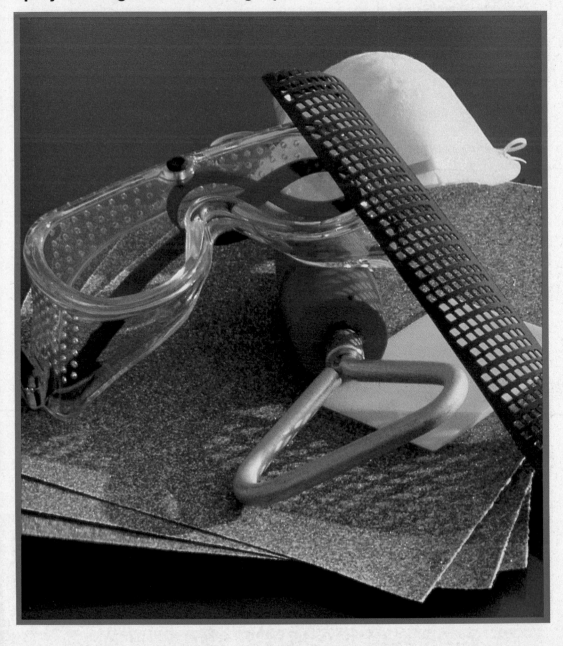

With a little practice, basic body repair procedures can be mastered by any do-it-yourself mechanic. The step-by-step repairs shown here can be applied to almost any type of auto body repair.

TOOLS & MATERIALS

You may already have basic tools, such as hammers and electric drills. Other tools unique to body repair — body hammers, grinding attachments, sanding blocks, dent puller, half-round plastic file and plastic spreaders — are relatively inexpensive and can be obtained wherever auto parts or auto body repair parts are sold. Portable air compressors and paint spray guns can be purchased or rented.

Auto Body Repair Kits

The best and most often used products are available to the do-it-yourselfer in kit form, from major manufacturers of auto body repair products. The same manufacturers also merchandise the individual products for use by pros.

Kits are available to make a wide variety of repairs, including holes, dents and scratches and fiberglass, and offer the advantage of buying the materials you'll need for the job. There is little waste or chance of materials going bad from not being used. Many kits may also contain basic body-working tools such as body files, sanding blocks and spreaders. Check the contents of the kit before buying your tools.

BODY REPAIR TIPS

Safety

Many of the products associated with auto body repair and refinishing contain toxic chemicals. Read all labels before opening containers and store them in a safe place and manner.

• Wear eye protection (safety goggles) when using power tools or when performing any operation that involves the removal of any type of material.

• Wear lung protection (disposable mask or respirator) when grinding, sanding or painting.

Sanding

1 Sand off paint before using a dent puller. When using a non-adhesive sanding disc, cover the back of the disc with an overlapping layer or two of masking tape and trim the edges. The disc will last considerably longer.

2 Use the circular motion of the sanding disc to grind *into* the edge of the repair. Grinding or sanding away from the jagged edge will only tear the sandpaper.

3 Use the palm of your hand flat on the panel to detect high and low spots. Do not use your fingertips. Slide your hand slowly back and forth.

WORKING WITH BODY FILLER

Mixing The Filler

Cleanliness and proper mixing and application are extremely important. Use a clean piece of plastic or glass or a disposable artist's palette to mix body filler.

1 Allow plenty of time and follow directions. No useful purpose will be served by adding more hardener to make it cure (set-up) faster. Less hardener means more curing time, but the mixture dries harder; more hardener means less curing time but a softer mixture.

2 Both the hardener and the filler should be thoroughly kneaded or stirred before mixing. Hardener should be a solid paste and dispense like thin toothpaste. Body filler should be smooth, and free of lumps or thick spots.

Getting the proper amount of hardener in the filler is the trickiest part of preparing the filler. Use the same amount of hardener in cold or warm weather. For contour filler (thick coats), a bead of hardener twice the diameter of the filler is about right. There's about a 15% margin on either side, but, if in doubt use less hardener.

3 Mix the body filler and hardener by wiping across the mixing surface, picking the mixture up and wiping it again. Colder weather requires longer mixing times. Do not mix in a circular motion; this will trap air bubbles which will become holes in the cured filler.

Applying The Filler

1 For best results, filler should not be applied over ¼" thick.

Apply the filler in several coats. Build it up to above the level of the repair surface so that it can be sanded or grated down.

The first coat of filler must be pressed on with a firm wiping motion.

Apply the filler in one direction only. Working the filler back and forth will either pull it off the metal or trap air bubbles.

REPAIRING DENTS

Before you start, take a few minutes to study the damaged area. Try to visualize the shape of the panel before it was damaged. If the damage is on the left fender, look at the right fender and use it as a guide. If there is access to the panel from behind, you can reshape it with a body hammer. If not, you'll have to use a dent puller. Go slowly and work the metal a little at a time. Get the panel as straight as possible before applying filler.

1 This dent is typical of one that can be pulled out or hammered out from behind. Remove the headlight cover, headlight assembly and turn signal housing.

2 Drill a series of holes ½ the size of the end of the dent puller along the stress line. Make some trial pulls and assess the results. If necessary, drill more holes and try again. Do not hurry.

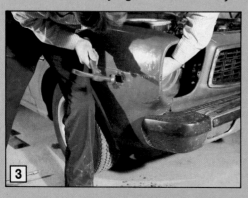

3 If possible, use a body hammer and block to shape the metal back to its original contours. Get the metal back as close to its original shape as possible. Don't depend on body filler to fill dents.

4 Using an 80-grit grinding disc on an electric drill, grind the paint from the surrounding area down to bare metal. Use a new grinding pad to prevent heat buildup that will warp metal.

5 The area should look like this when you're finished grinding. Knock the drill holes in and tape over small openings to keep plastic filler out.

6 Mix the body filler (see Body Repair Tips). Spread the body filler evenly over the entire area (see Body Repair Tips). Be sure to cover the area completely.

7 Let the body filler dry until the surface can just be scratched with your fingernail. Knock the high spots from the body filler with a body file ("Cheesegrater"). Check frequently with the palm of your hand for high and low spots.

8 Check to be sure that trim pieces that will be installed later will fit exactly. Sand the area with 40-grit paper.

9 If you wind up with low spots, you may have to apply another layer of filler.

10 Knock the high spots off with 40-grit paper. When you are satisfied with the contours of the repair, apply a thin coat of filler to cover pin holes and scratches.

11 Block sand the area with 40-grit paper to a smooth finish. Pay particular attention to body lines and ridges that must be well-defined.

12 Sand the area with 400 paper and then finish with a scuff pad. The finished repair is ready for priming and painting (see Painting Tips).

Materials and photos courtesy of Ritt Jones Auto Body, Prospect Park, PA.

REPAIRING RUST HOLES

There are many ways to repair rust holes. The fiberglass cloth kit shown here is one of the most cost efficient for the owner because it provides a strong repair that resists cracking and moisture and is relatively easy to use. It can be used on large and small holes (with or without backing) and can be applied over contoured areas. Remember, however, that short of replacing an entire panel, no repair is a guarantee that the rust will not return.

1 Remove any trim that will be in the way. Clean away all loose debris. Cut away all the rusted metal. But be sure to leave enough metal to retain the contour or body shape.

2 Grind away all traces of rust with a 24-grit grinding disc. Be sure to grind back 3-4 inches from the edge of the hole down to bare metal and be sure all traces of paint, primer and rust are removed.

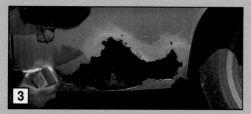

3 Block sand the area with 80 or 100 grit sandpaper to get a clear, shiny surface and feathered paint edge. Tap the edges of the hole inward with a ball peen hammer.

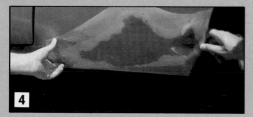

4 If you are going to use release film, cut a piece about 2-3″ larger than the area you have sanded. Place the film over the repair and mark the sanded area on the film. Avoid any unnecessary wrinkling of the film.

5 Cut 2 pieces of fiberglass matte to match the shape of the repair. One piece should be about 1″ smaller than the sanded area and the second piece should be 1″ smaller than the first. Mix enough filler and hardener to saturate the fiberglass material (see Body Repair Tips).

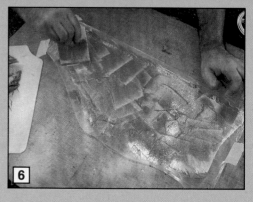

6 Lay the release sheet on a flat surface and spread an even layer of filler, large enough to cover the repair. Lay the smaller piece of fiberglass cloth in the center of the sheet and spread another layer of filler over the fiberglass cloth. Repeat the operation for the larger piece of cloth.

7 Place the repair material over the repair area, with the release film facing outward. Use a spreader and work from the center outward to smooth the material, following the body contours. Be sure to remove all air bubbles.

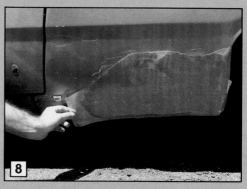

8 Wait until the repair has dried tack-free and peel off the release sheet. The ideal working temperature is 60°-90° F. Cooler or warmer temperatures or high humidity may require additional curing time. Wait longer, if in doubt.

9 Sand and feather-edge the entire area. The initial sanding can be done with a sanding disc on an electric drill if care is used. Finish the sanding with a block sander. Low spots can be filled with body filler; this may require several applications.

10 When the filler can just be scratched with a fingernail, knock the high spots down with a body file and smooth the entire area with 80-grit. Feather the filled areas into the surrounding areas.

11 When the area is sanded smooth, mix some topcoat and hardener and apply it directly with a spreader. This will give a smooth finish and prevent the glass matte from showing through the paint.

12 Block sand the topcoat smooth with finishing sandpaper (200 grit), and 400 grit. The repair is ready for masking, priming and painting (see Painting Tips).

Materials and photos courtesy Marson Corporation, Chelsea, Massachusetts

PAINTING TIPS

Preparation

1 SANDING — Use a 400 or 600 grit wet or dry sandpaper. Wet-sand the area with a ¼ sheet of sandpaper soaked in clean water. Keep the paper wet while sanding. Sand the area until the repaired area tapers into the original finish.

2 CLEANING — Wash the area to be painted thoroughly with water and a clean rag. Rinse it thoroughly and wipe the surface dry until you're sure it's completely free of dirt, dust, fingerprints, wax, detergent or other foreign matter.

3 MASKING — Protect any areas you don't want to overspray by covering them with masking tape and newspaper. Be careful not get fingerprints on the area to be painted.

4 PRIMING — All exposed metal should be primed before painting. Primer protects the metal and provides an excellent surface for paint adhesion. When the primer is dry, wet-sand the area again with 600 grit wet-sandpaper. Clean the area again after sanding.

Painting Techniques

Paint applied from either a spray gun or a spray can (for small areas) will provide good results. Experiment on an old piece of metal to get the right combination before you begin painting.

SPRAYING VISCOSITY (SPRAY GUN ONLY) — Paint should be thinned to spraying viscosity according to the directions on the can. Use only the recommended thinner or reducer and the same amount of reduction regardless of temperature.

AIR PRESSURE (SPRAY GUN ONLY) — This is extremely important. Be sure you are using the proper recommended pressure.

TEMPERATURE — The surface to be painted should be approximately the same temperature as the surrounding air. Applying warm paint to a cold surface, or vice versa, will completely upset the paint characteristics.

THICKNESS — Spray with smooth strokes. In general, the thicker the coat of paint, the longer the drying time. Apply several thin coats about 30 seconds apart. The paint should remain wet long enough to flow out and no longer; heavier coats will only produce sags or wrinkles. Spray a light (fog) coat, followed by heavier color coats.

DISTANCE — The ideal spraying distance is 8″-12″ from the gun or can to the surface. Shorter distances will produce ripples, while greater distances will result in orange peel, dry film and poor color match and loss of material due to overspray.

OVERLAPPING — The gun or can should be kept at right angles to the surface at all times. Work to a wet edge at an even speed, using a 50% overlap and direct the center of the spray at the lower or nearest edge of the previous stroke.

RUBBING OUT (BLENDING) FRESH PAINT — Let the paint dry thoroughly. Runs or imperfections can be sanded out, primed and repainted.

Don't be in too big a hurry to remove the masking. This only produces paint ridges. When the finish has dried for at least a week, apply a small amount of fine grade rubbing compound with a clean, wet cloth. Use lots of water and blend the new paint with the surrounding area.

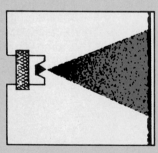

WRONG

Thin coat. Stroke too fast, not enough overlap, gun too far away.

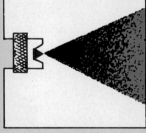

CORRECT

Medium coat. Proper distance, good stroke, proper overlap.

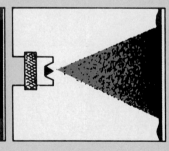

WRONG

Heavy coat. Stroke too slow, too much overlap, gun too close.

3. Remove the weatherstripping from the glass.

To install:

4. Clean the weatherstripping, glass and glass opening with solvent to remove all old sealer.

5. Apply liquid butyl sealer C9AZ-19554-B, or equivalent, in the glass channel of the weatherstripping and install the weatherstripping on the glass.

6. Install the mouldings.

7. Apply a bead of sealer to the opening flange and in the inner flange crevice of the weatherstripping lip.

8. Place a length of strong cord, such as butcher's twine, in the flange crevice of the weatherstripping. The cord should go all the way around the weatherstripping with the ends, about 18″ long each, hanging down together at the bottom center of the window.

9. Apply soapy water to the weatherstripping lip.

10. Have your assistant position the windshield assembly in the channel from the outside, applying firm inward pressure.

11. From inside, you guide the lip of the weatherstripping into place using the cord, working each end alternately, until the window is locked in place.

12. Remove the cord, clean the glass and weatherstripping of excess sealer and leak test the windshield.

Stationary Windows
REMOVAL AND INSTALLATION

NOTE: *You'll need an assistant for this job.*

1. Have your assistant stand outside and support the glass.

2. Working from the inside truck, start at one upper corner and work the weatherstripping across the top of the glass, pulling the weatherstripping down and pushing outward on the glass until your assistant can grab the glass and lift it out.

3. Remove the moldings.

4. Remove the weatherstripping from the glass.

To install:

5. Clean the weatherstripping, glass and glass opening with solvent to remove all old sealer.

6. Apply liquid butyl sealer C9AZ-19554-B, or equivalent, in the glass channel of the weatherstripping and install the weatherstripping on the glass.

7. Install the moldings.

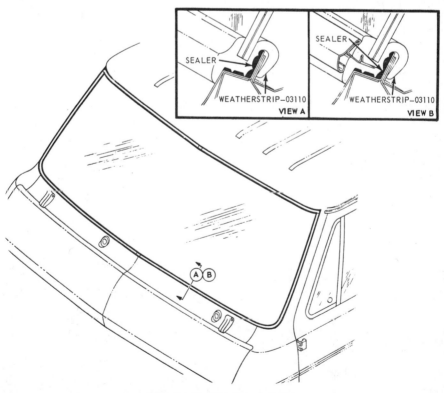

1961–74 windshield installation

8. Apply a bead of sealer to the opening flange and in the inner flange crevice of the weatherstripping lip.

9. Place a length of strong cord, such as butcher's twine, in the flange crevice of the weatherstripping. The cord should go all the way around the weatherstripping with the ends, about 18″ long each, hanging down together at the bottom center of the window.

10. Apply soapy water to the weatherstripping lip.

11. Have your assistant position the window assembly in the channel from the outside, applying firm inward pressure.

12. From inside, you guide the lip of the weatherstripping into place using the cord, working each end alternately, until the window is locked in place.

13. Remove the cord, clean the glass and weatherstripping of excess sealer and leak test the window.

INTERIOR

Door Trim Panels

REMOVAL AND INSTALLATION

1961-67

The door access panel is simply held in place by screws. Remove the screws and lift out the panel.

1969-74

1. Remove the armrest.
2. Remove the door inside shroud (4 screws).
3. Remove the 8 screws retaining the trim panel and lift off the panel.
4. Installation is the reverse of removal

1975-88

FRONT DOORS

1. Remove the armrest.
2. Remove the door handle and trim cup.

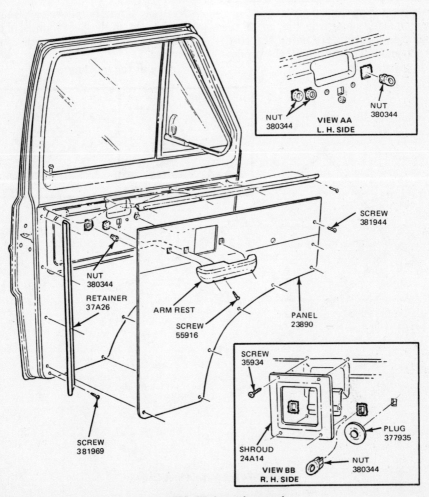

1969–75 door trim panel

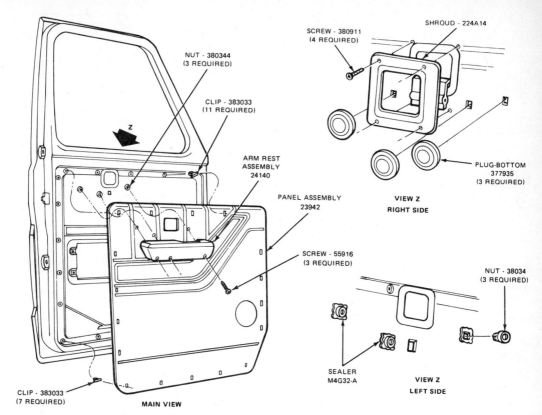

NUT · 380344
(3 REQUIRED)

CLIP · 383033
(11 REQUIRED)

ARM REST
ASSEMBLY
24140

PANEL ASSEMBLY
23942

SCREW · 55916
(3 REQUIRED)

CLIP · 383033
(7 REQUIRED)

MAIN VIEW

SCREW · 380911
(4 REQUIRED)

SHROUD · 224A14

PLUG-BOTTOM
377935
(3 REQUIRED)

VIEW Z
RIGHT SIDE

NUT · 38034
(3 REQUIRED)

SEALER
M4G32-A

VIEW Z
LEFT SIDE

1976–88 door trim panel

3. If the van is equipped with a stereo radio, remove the speaker grille.

4. Remove the setscrew and remove the window crank handle. On models with power windows, remove the window switch trim cup and switch.

5. Using a flat wood spatula, insert it carefully behind the panel and slide it along to find the push-pins. When you encounter a pin, pry the pin outward. Do this until all the pins are out. NEVER PULL ON THE PANEL TO REMOVE THE PINS!

6. Installation is the reverse of removal. Carefully pound the pins into place with the palm of your hand. Be VERY careful to avoid missing the holes and breaking the pins or tearing the panel!

CLUB WAGON SLIDING DOORS

1. Carefully pry the pull-strap endcaps off.

2. Remove the retaining screws and remove the strap.

3. Using a flat wood spatula, insert it carefully behind the panel and slide it along to find the push-pins. When you encounter a pin, pry the pin outward. Do this until all the pins are out. NEVER PULL ON THE PANEL TO REMOVE THE PINS!

4. Installation is the reverse of removal. Carefully pound the pins into place with the palm of your hand. Be VERY careful to avoid missing the holes and breaking the pins or tearing the panel!

Manual Door Locks
REMOVAL AND INSTALLATION

Door Lock Cylinder

1961-88

1. Raise the window all the way.

2. Remove the door trim panel.

3. Disconnect the lock actuating rod from the lock control clip.

4. Remove the lock cylinder retaining clip and pull the lock cylinder from the door. On the side doors, it will be necessary to loosen the inside lock control knob set screw and remove the knob.

5. Installation is the reverse of removal.

Power Door Locks
REMOVAL AND INSTALLATION

Actuator Motor

1. Remove the door trim panel.

2. Disconnect the motor from the door latch.

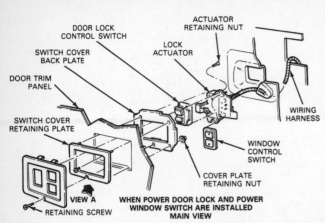

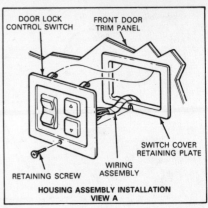

Power door lock control switch

3. Remove the motor and swivel bracket from the door by drilling out the pop rivet.

4. Disconnect the wiring harness.

5. Installation is the reverse of removal. Make sure that the pop rivet is tight.

Control Switch

NOTE: *The switch is an integral part of the pushbutton rod.*

1. Remove the door trim panel.

2. Disconnect the pushbutton rod from the latch.

3. To disengage the wiring connector, insert a thin screwdriver under the tab to exert pressure, then pry the locking tab up from the flange of the connector and pull the halves apart.

4. Installation is the reverse of removal.

Manual Door Glass and Regulator

REMOVAL AND INSTALLATION

1961-67

1. Remove the access panel and watershield.

2. Roll the glass all the way down and discon-nect the regulator arm from the roller by pull-ing the clip from the roller.

3. Loosen the window crank handle setscrew and remove the handle.

4. Remove the 4 regulator retaining screws and remove the regulator.

5. Remove the 5 division bar screws located as follows:

    a. 1 at the lower adjustment bracket.

    b. 1 at the vent frame retainer through the weatherstripping.

    c. 1 at the center below the beltline.

    d. 2 at the top of the door.

6. Carefully pry the upper run down at the first clip rearward of the division bar and re-move the bar.

7. Disconnect both back control links at the door lock.

8. Remove the pushbutton and link from the door.

9. Push the door glass up, position the lock remote control link outboard of the glass and remove the glass downward and out through the access hole.

10. Remove the lower channel from the glass

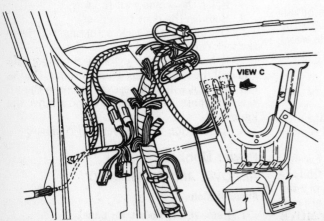

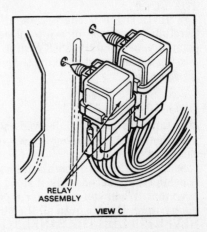

Power door lock relay

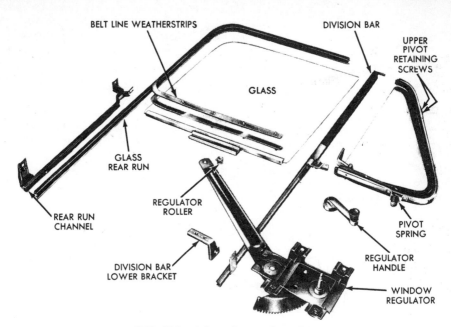

1961–67 front door glass and regulator

if you're replacing the glass. Transfer the channel to the new glass.

To install:

11. Position the glass through the access hole, push it up far enough to position the control link inboard and let the glass rest in the bottom of the door.

12. Connect the control link to the door lock. Install and connect the pushbutton and link.

13. Position the division bar in the door and align it with the glass and door frame. Install the 5 screws loosely.

14. Check the glass sliding effort, adjust the rear glass run and division bar and tighten all screws.

15. Install the regulator.

16. Apply white grease to the glass lower channel, install the roller into the track on the glass channel. Push the regulator arm pin into the roller. Secure the pin to the roller by installing the retaining clip in the groove in the pin.

17. Install the regulator handle and tighten the screw.

18. Install the watershield and access panel.

1969-74

GLASS

1. Remove the access cover from the door.

2. Remove the 3 screws attaching the vent window to the upper leading edge of the door.

3. Remove the screw attaching the vent window to the door at the beltline.

4. Remove the screw attaching the front retainer and division bar bracket to the door.

5. Slide the front run from the retainer and division bar.

6. Disconnect the regulator arm roller from the regulator arm by removing the roller retaining clip and pulling the arm from the roller.

7. Unsnap and remove the beltline weatherstripping from the door.

8. Pull the rear run down and out of the run slot in the door along the top of the glass opening.

9. Tilt the vent window and division bar assembly rearward and separate the vent window from the front run retainer and division bar.

10. Remove the front run retainer and division bar from the door.

11. Remove the glass and channel from the door.

12. If you are installing new glass, transfer the channel.

13. Lubricate the window mechanism.

14. Place the glass assembly in the door.

15. Place the vent window and front retainer and division bar in the door. Insert the front run retainer and division bar in the rear edge of the vent window.

16. Position the glass and channel assembly in the front retainer and division bar and the rear run. Place the vent window assembly into position in the door and install the 3 attaching screws along the upper edge.

17. Install the beltline weatherstripping.

18. Insert the rear run into the slot along the top edge of the window opening.

19. Insert the retaining clip on the regulator

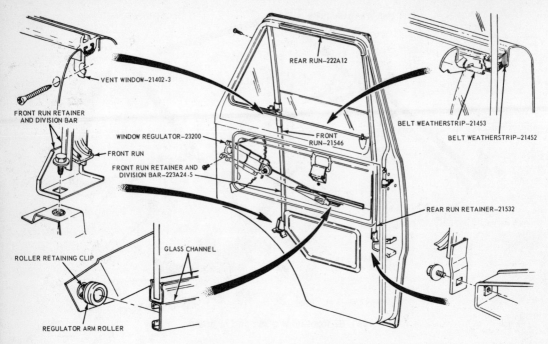

FRONT RUN RETAINER
AND DIVISION BAR

VENT WINDOW—21402-3

REAR RUN—222A12

BELT WEATHERSTRIP—21453

BELT WEATHERSTRIP—21452

WINDOW REGULATOR—23200

FRONT RUN

FRONT RUN RETAINER AND
DIVISION BAR—223A24-5

FRONT
RUN—21546

REAR RUN RETAINER—21532

ROLLER RETAINING CLIP

GLASS CHANNEL

REGULATOR ARM ROLLER

1969–74 front door window mechanism

arm roller and insert the roller in the glass channel.

20. Insert the regulator arm pin in the roller and press it in firmly.

21. Insert the front run in the retainer and division bar.

22. Insert the screw attaching the front retainer and division bar bracket to the door.

23. Install the vent window beltline screw.

24. Adjust the glass as necessary.

25. Install the access cover.

REGULATOR

1. Lower the glass.

2. Remove the window handle setscrew and remove the handle.

3. Remove the door panel access cover.

4. Remove the retaining clip and disconnect the regulator arm roller from the arm.

5. Remove the 4 regulator mounting screws and lift out the regulator.

6. Installation is the reverse of removal.

1975-82

GLASS

1. Remove the trim panel from the door.

2. Remove the 3 screws attaching the vent window to the upper leading edge of the door.

3. Remove the screw attaching the front retainer and division bar bracket to the door.

4. Slide the front run from the retainer and division bar.

5. Unsnap and remove the beltline weatherstripping from the door.

6. Lower the glass and remove the 2 screws that attach the rear run retainer to the door edge. Lower the rear run retainers to the bottom of the door.

7. Tilt the vent window and division bar assembly rearward and separate the vent window from the front run retainer and division bar.

8. Remove the vent window and front run retainer and division bar from the door.

9. Rotate the front of the glass downward and remove the glass and channel from the door, sliding the glass channel off the regulator arm.

10. If you are installing new glass, transfer the channel.

11. Lubricate the window mechanism.

12. Place the glass assembly in the door.

13. Place the vent window and front retainer and division bar in the door. Insert the front run retainer and division bar in the rear edge of the vent window.

14. Install the rear run retainer in the door.

15. Position the glass and channel assembly in the front retainer and division bar and the rear run. Place the vent window assembly into position in the door and install the 3 attaching screws along the upper edge.

16. Install the beltline weatherstripping.

17. Insert the front run in the retainer and division bar.

18. Insert the screw attaching the front retainer and division bar bracket to the door.

19. Adjust the glass as necessary.

20. Install the trim panel.

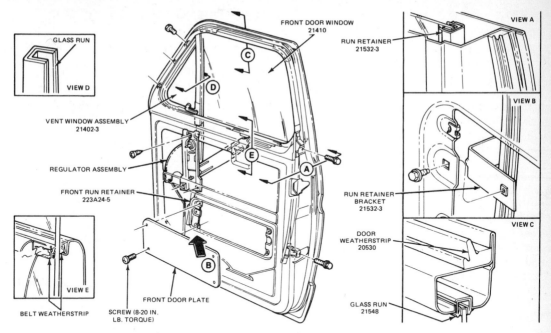

1975–78 front door window mechanism

REGULATOR

1. Lower the glass.
2. Remove the window handle setscrew and remove the handle.
3. Remove the door panel access cover.
4. Support the glass in the full up position.

5. Drill out the regulator attaching rivets with a ¼″ drill bit and punch out the rivets.
6. Disengage the regulator arm from the regulator and lift out the regulator.
7. Installation is the reverse of removal. In place of the rivets you can use ¼″-20 x ½″ bolts and nuts with lockwashers.

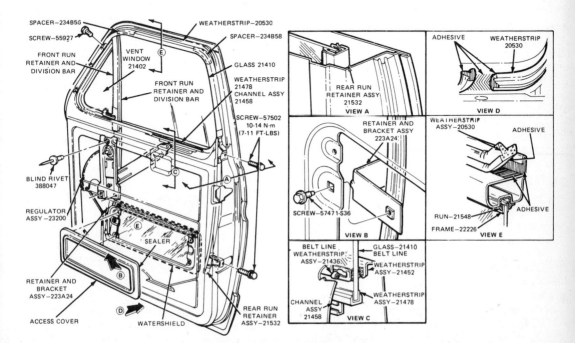

1979–88 front door window mechanism

1983-88

GLASS

1. Remove the trim panel from the door.
2. Remove the 3 screws attaching the vent window to the upper leading edge of the door.
3. Remove the screw attaching the front retainer and division bar bracket to the door.
4. Lower the glass to the full down position.
5. Pull the rear run down and out of the run slot along the top of the glass opening.
6. Tilt the vent window and division bar assembly rearward.
7. Remove the vent window and front run retainer and division bar from the door.
8. Unsnap and remove the beltline weatherstripping.
9. Rotate the front of the glass downward and remove the glass and channel from the door, sliding the glass channel off the regulator arm.
10. If you are installing new glass, transfer the channel. If you are installing new glass, transfer the channel. Remove the glass from the channel using Glass and Channel Removal Tool 2900, made by the Sommer and Mala Glass Machine Co. of Chicago, ILL., or its equivalent.
11. Lubricate the window mechanism.
12. Place the glass assembly in the door inserting the regulator arm roller in the glass channel.
13. Place the vent window and division bar in the door.
14. Install the rear run retainer in the door.
15. Position the glass and channel assembly in the front run retainer and division bar and the rear run. Place the vent window assembly into position in the door and install the 3 attaching screws along the upper edge.
16. Install the front run in the division bar.
17. Install the screw attaching the division bar to the door.
18. Install the beltline weatherstripping.
19. Adjust the glass as necessary.
20. Install the trim panel.

REGULATOR

1. Lower the glass.
2. Remove the window handle setscrew and remove the handle.
3. Remove the door panel access cover.
4. Support the glass in the full up position.
5. Drill out the regulator attaching rivets with a ¼" drill bit and punch out the rivets.
6. Disengage the regulator arm from the regulator and lift out the regulator.
7. Installation is the reverse of removal. In place of the rivets you can use ¼"-20 x ½" bolts and nuts with lockwashers.

Power Door Glass and Regulator Motor

REMOVAL AND INSTALLATION

Glass

1. Remove the trim panel from the door.
2. Remove the 3 screws attaching the vent window to the upper leading edge of the door.
3. Remove the screw attaching the front retainer and division bar bracket to the door.
4. Lower the glass to the full down position.
5. Pull the rear run down and out of the run slot along the top of the glass opening.
6. Tilt the vent window and division bar assembly rearward.
7. Remove the vent window and front run retainer and division bar from the door.
8. Unsnap and remove the beltline weatherstripping.
9. Rotate the front of the glass downward and remove the glass and channel from the door, sliding the glass channel off the regulator arm.
10. If you are installing new glass, transfer the channel. Remove the glass from the channel using Glass and Channel Removal Tool 2900, made by the Sommer and Mala Glass Machine Co. of Chicago, ILL., or its equivalent.
11. Lubricate the window mechanism.
12. Place the glass assembly in the door inserting the regulator arm roller in the glass channel.
13. Place the vent window and division bar in the door.
14. Install the rear run retainer in the door.
15. Position the glass and channel assembly in the front run retainer and division bar and the rear run. Place the vent window assembly into position in the door and install the 3 attaching screws along the upper edge.
16. Install the front run in the division bar.

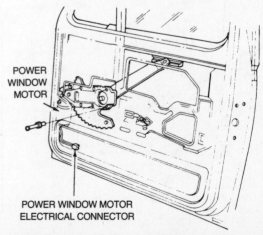

POWER WINDOW MOTOR

POWER WINDOW MOTOR ELECTRICAL CONNECTOR

Power window regulator installation

17. Install the screw attaching the division bar to the door.

18. Install the beltline weatherstripping.

19. Adjust the glass as necessary.

20. Install the trim panel.

Regulator

1. Disconnect the battery ground.

2. Remove the door trim panel.

3. Disconnect the window motor wiring harness.

4. There are 2 dimples in the door panel, opposite the 2 concealed motor retaining bolts. Using a ½" drill bit, drill out these dimples to gain access to the motor bolts. Be careful to avoid damage to the wires.

5. Remove the 3 motor mounting bolts.

6. Push the motor towards the outside of the door to disengage it from the gears. You'll have to support the window glass once the motor is disengaged.

7. Remove the motor from the door.

8. Installation is the reverse of removal. To avoid rusting in the drilled areas, prime and paint the exposed metal, or, cover the holes with waterproof body tape. Torque the motor mounting bolts to 50-85 in.lb. Make sure that the motor works properly before installing the trim panel.

Engine Cover

REMOVAL AND INSTALLATION

1961-67

To remove the cover, raise it, unbolt the support and remove the retaining pins from the hinges.

Inside Rear View Mirror

The mirror is held in place with a single setscrew. Loosen the screw and lift the mirror off.

Repair kit for damaged mirrors are available and most auto parts stores.

Front Seat

REMOVAL AND INSTALLATION

1961-67

1. Remove the 2 bolts that attach the bracket on the outboard side to the wheelhousing.

2. Remove the 2 bolts that attach the tubular support to the floorpan.

3. Remove the seat.

4. Installation is the reverse of removal.

1969-88

Remove the seat track-to-floor nuts and lift out the seat. Installation is the reverse of removal. Torque the nuts to 30 ft.lb. on models through 1975; 60 ft.lb. on 1976-77 models; on 1978-88 models - 15 ft.lb. for bucket seats and 60 ft.lb for folding or captains seats

Center and Rear Seats

REMOVAL AND INSTALLATION

1961-67

To remove either seat, loosen the 4 clamp bolt nuts then turn the bolts to release the T-head from the floor. Lift out the seat.

Installation is the reverse of removal. Torque the nuts to 30 ft.lb.

1969-88

Remove the seat track-to-floor nuts and lift out the seat. Installation is the reverse of removal. Torque the nuts to 30 ft.lb. on models through 1975; 60 ft.lb. on 1976 and later models.

How to Remove Stains from Fabric Interior

For rest results, spots and stains should be removed as soon as possible. Never use gasoline, lacquer thinner, acetone, nail polish remover or bleach. Use a 3' x 3" piece of cheesecloth. Squeeze most of the liquid from the fabric and wipe the stained fabric from the outside of the stain toward the center with a lifting motion. Turn the cheesecloth as soon as one side becomes soiled. When using water to remove a stain, be sure to wash the entire section after the spot has been removed to avoid water stains. Encrusted spots can be broken up with a dull knife and vacuumed before removing the stain.

Type of Stain	How to Remove It
Surface spots	Brush the spots out with a small hand brush or use a commercial preparation such as K2R to lift the stain.
Mildew	Clean around the mildew with warm suds. Rinse in cold water and soak the mildew area in a solution of 1 part table salt and 2 parts water. Wash with upholstery cleaner.

How to Remove Stains from Fabric Interior (cont.)

Type of Stain	How to Remove It
Water stains	Water stains in fabric materials can be removed with a solution made from 1 cup of table salt dissolved in 1 quart of water. Vigorously scrub the solution into the stain and rinse with clear water. Water stains in nylon or other synthetic fabrics should be removed with a commercial type spot remover.
Chewing gum, tar, crayons, shoe polish (greasy stains)	Do not use a cleaner that will soften gum or tar. Harden the deposit with an ice cube and scrape away as much as possible with a dull knife. Moisten the remainder with cleaning fluid and scrub clean.
Ice cream, candy	Most candy has a sugar base and can be removed with a cloth wrung out in warm water. Oily candy, after cleaning with warm water, should be cleaned with upholstery cleaner. Rinse with warm water and clean the remainder with cleaning fluid.
Wine, alcohol, egg, milk, soft drink (non-greasy stains)	Do not use soap. Scrub the stain with a cloth wrung out in warm water. Remove the remainder with cleaning fluid.
Grease, oil, lipstick, butter and related stains	Use a spot remover to avoid leaving a ring. Work from the outisde of the stain to the center and dry with a clean cloth when the spot is gone.
Headliners (cloth)	Mix a solution of warm water and foam upholstery cleaner to give thick suds. Use only foam—liquid may streak or spot. Clean the entire headliner in one operation using a circular motion with a natural sponge.
Headliner (vinyl)	Use a vinyl cleaner with a sponge and wipe clean with a dry cloth.
Seats and door panels	Mix 1 pint upholstery cleaner in 1 gallon of water. Do not soak the fabric around the buttons.
Leather or vinyl fabric	Use a multi-purpose cleaner full strength and a stiff brush. Let stand 2 minutes and scrub thoroughly. Wipe with a clean, soft rag.
Nylon or synthetic fabrics	For normal stains, use the same procedures you would for washing cloth upholstery. If the fabric is extremely dirty, use a multi-purpose cleaner full strength with a stiff scrub brush. Scrub thoroughly in all directions and wipe with a cotton towel or soft rag.

Mechanic's Data

11

1":254mm
TAX
10.16mm
Liter
Parts
Overhaul

General Conversion Table

Multiply By	To Convert	To	
		LENGTH	
2.54	Inches	Centimeters	.3937
25.4	Inches	Millimeters	.03937
30.48	Feet	Centimeters	.0328
.304	Feet	Meters	3.28
.914	Yards	Meters	1.094
1.609	Miles	Kilometers	.621
		VOLUME	
.473	Pints	Liters	2.11
.946	Quarts	Liters	1.06
3.785	Gallons	Liters	.264
.016	Cubic inches	Liters	61.02
16.39	Cubic inches	Cubic cms.	.061
28.3	Cubic feet	Liters	.0353
		MASS (Weight)	
28.35	Ounces	Grams	.035
.4536	Pounds	Kilograms	2.20
—	To obtain	From	Multiply by

Multiply By	To Convert	To	
		AREA	
.645	Square inches	Square cms.	.155
.836	Square yds.	Square meters	1.196
		FORCE	
4.448	Pounds	Newtons	.225
.138	Ft./lbs.	Kilogram/meters	7.23
1.36	Ft./lbs.	Newton-meters	.737
.112	In./lbs.	Newton-meters	8.844
		PRESSURE	
.068	Psi	Atmospheres	14.7
6.89	Psi	Kilopascals	.145
		OTHER	
1.104	Horsepower (DIN)	Horsepower (SAE)	.9861
.746	Horsepower (SAE)	Kilowatts (KW)	1.34
1.60	Mph	Km/h	.625
.425	Mpg	Km/1	2.35
—	To obtain	From	Multiply by

Tap Drill Sizes

National Coarse or U.S.S.

Screw & Tap Size	Threads Per Inch	Use Drill Number
No. 5	40	39
No. 6	32	36
No. 8	32	29
No. 10	24	25
No. 12	24	17
1/4	20	8
5/16	18	F
3/8	16	5/16
7/16	14	U
1/2	13	27/64
9/16	12	31/64
5/8	11	17/32
3/4	10	21/32
7/8	9	49/64

National Coarse or U.S.S.

Screw & Tap Size	Threads Per Inch	Use Drill Number
1	8	7/8
1 1/8	7	63/64
1 1/4	7	1 7/64
1 1/2	6	1 11/32

National Fine or S.A.E.

Screw & Tap Size	Threads Per Inch	Use Drill Number
No. 5	44	37
No. 6	40	33
No. 8	36	29
No. 10	32	21

National Fine or S.A.E.

Screw & Tap Size	Threads Per Inch	Use Drill Number
No. 12	28	15
1/4	28	3
6/16	24	1
3/8	24	Q
7/16	20	W
1/2	20	29/64
9/16	18	33/64
5/8	18	37/64
3/4	16	11/16
7/8	14	13/16
1 1/8	12	1 3/64
1 1/4	12	1 11/64
1 1/2	12	1 27/64

Drill Sizes In Decimal Equivalents

Inch	Decimal	Wire	mm
1/64	.0156		.39
	.0157		.4
	.0160	78	
	.0165		.42
	.0173		.44
	.0177		.45
	.0180	77	
	.0181		.46
	.0189		.48
	.0197		.5
	.0200	76	
	.0210	75	
	.0217		.55
	.0225	74	
	.0236		.6
	.0240	73	
	.0250	72	
	.0256		.65
	.0260	71	
	.0276		.7
	.0280	70	
	.0292	69	
	.0295		.75
	.0310	68	
1/32	.0312		.79
	.0315		.8
	.0320	67	
	.0330	66	
	.0335		.85
	.0350	65	
	.0354		.9
	.0360	64	
	.0370	63	
	.0374		.95
	.0380	62	
	.0390	61	
	.0394		1.0
	.0400	60	
	.0410	59	
	.0413		1.05
	.0420	58	
	.0430	57	
	.0433		1.1
	.0453		1.15
3/64	.0465	56	
	.0469		1.19
	.0472		1.2
	.0492		1.25
	.0512		1.3
	.0520	55	
	.0531		1.35
	.0550	54	
	.0551		1.4
	.0571		1.45
	.0591		1.5
	.0595	53	
	.0610		1.55
1/16	.0625		1.59
	.0630		1.6
	.0635	52	
	.0650		1.65
	.0669		1.7
	.0670	51	
	.0689		1.75
	.0700	50	
	.0709		1.8
	.0728		1.85

Inch	Decimal	Wire	mm
	.0730	49	
	.0748		1.9
	.0760	48	
	.0768		1.95
5/64	.0781		1.98
	.0785	47	
	.0787		2.0
	.0807		2.05
	.0810	46	
	.0820	45	
	.0827		2.1
	.0846		2.15
	.0860	44	
	.0866		2.2
	.0886		2.25
	.0890	43	
	.0906		2.3
	.0925		2.35
	.0935	42	
3/32	.0938		2.38
	.0945		2.4
	.0960	41	
	.0965		2.45
	.0980	40	
	.0981		2.5
	.0995	39	
	.1015	38	
	.1024		2.6
	.1040	37	
	.1063		2.7
	.1065	36	
	.1083		2.75
7/64	.1094		2.77
	.1100	35	
	.1102		2.8
	.1110	34	
	.1130	33	
	.1142		2.9
	.1160	32	
	.1181		3.0
	.1200	31	
	.1220		3.1
1/8	.1250		3.17
	.1260		3.2
	.1280		3.25
	.1285	30	
	.1299		3.3
	.1339		3.4
	.1360	29	
	.1378		3.5
	.1405	28	
9/64	.1406		3.57
	.1417		3.6
	.1440	27	
	.1457		3.7
	.1470	26	
	.1476		3.75
	.1495	25	
	.1496		3.8
	.1520	24	
	.1535		3.9
	.1540	23	
5/32	.1562		3.96
	.1570	22	
	.1575		4.0
	.1590	21	
	.1610	20	

Inch	Decimal	Wire & Letter	mm
	.1614		4.1
	.1654		4.2
	.1660	19	
	.1673		4.25
	.1693		4.3
	.1695	18	
11/64	.1719		4.36
	.1730	17	
	.1732		4.4
	.1770	16	
	.1772		4.5
	.1800	15	
	.1811		4.6
	.1820	14	
	.1850	13	
	.1850		4.7
	.1870		4.75
3/16	.1875		4.76
	.1890		4.8
	.1890	12	
	.1910	11	
	.1929		4.9
	.1935	10	
	.1960	9	
	.1969		5.0
	.1990	8	
	.2008		5.1
	.2010	7	
13/64	.2031		5.16
	.2040	6	
	.2047		5.2
	.2055	5	
	.2067		5.25
	.2087		5.3
	.2090	4	
	.2126		5.4
	.2130	3	
	.2165		5.5
7/32	.2188		5.55
	.2205		5.6
	.2210	2	
	.2244		5.7
	.2264		5.75
	.2280	1	
	.2283		5.8
	.2323		5.9
	.2340	A	
15/64	.2344		5.95
	.2362		6.0
	.2380	B	
	.2402		6.1
	.2420	C	
	.2441		6.2
	.2460	D	
	.2461		6.25
	.2480		6.3
1/4	.2500	E	6.35
	.2520		6.
	.2559		6.5
	.2570	F	
	.2598		6.6
	.2610	G	
	.2638		6.7
17/64	.2656		6.74
	.2657		6.75
	.2660	H	
	.2677		6.8

Inch	Decimal	Letter	mm
	.2717		6.9
	.2720	I	
	.2756		7.0
	.2770	J	
	.2795		7.1
	.2810	K	
9/32	.2812		7.14
	.2835		7.2
	.2854		7.25
	.2874		7.3
	.2900	L	
	.2913		7.4
	.2950	M	
	.2953		7.5
19/64	.2969		7.54
	.2992		7.6
	.3020	N	
	.3031		7.7
	.3051		7.75
	.3071		7.8
	.3110		7.9
5/16	.3125		7.93
	.3150		8.0
	.3160	O	
	.3189		8.1
	.3228		8.2
	.3230	P	
	.3248		8.25
	.3268		8.3
21/64	.3281		8.33
	.3307		8.4
	.3320	Q	
	.3346		8.5
	.3386		8.6
	.3390	R	
	.3425		8.7
11/32	.3438		8.73
	.3445		8.75
	.3465		8.8
	.3480	S	
	.3504		8.9
	.3543		9.0
	.3580	T	
	.3583		9.1
23/64	.3594		9.12
	.3622		9.2
	.3642		9.25
	.3661		9.3
	.3680	U	
	.3701		9.4
	.3740		9.5
3/8	.3750		9.52
	.3770	V	
	.3780		9.6
	.3819		9.7
	.3839		9.75
	.3858		9.8
	.3860	W	
	.3898		9.9
25/64	.3906		9.92
	.3937		10.0
	.3970	X	
	.4040	Y	
13/32	.4062		10.31
	.4130	Z	
	.4134		10.5
27/64	.4219		10.71

Inch	Decimal	mm
	.4331	11.0
7/16	.4375	11.11
	.4528	11.5
29/64	.4531	11.51
15/32	.4688	11.90
	.4724	12.0
31/64	.4844	12.30
	.4921	12.5
1/2	.5000	12.70
	.5118	13.0
33/64	.5156	13.09
17/32	.5312	13.49
	.5315	13.5
35/64	.5469	13.89
	.5512	14.0
9/16	.5625	14.28
	.5709	14.5
37/64	.5781	14.68
	.5906	15.0
19/32	.5938	15.08
39/64	.6094	15.47
	.6102	15.5
5/8	.6250	15.87
	.6299	16.0
41/64	.6406	16.27
	.6496	16.5
21/32	.6562	16.66
	.6693	17.0
43/64	.6719	17.06
11/16	.6875	17.46
	.6890	17.5
45/64	.7031	17.85
	.7087	18.0
23/32	.7188	18.25
	.7283	18.5
47/64	.7344	18.65
	.7480	19.0
3/4	.7500	19.05
49/64	.7656	19.44
	.7677	19.5
25/32	.7812	19.84
	.7874	20.0
51/64	.7969	20.24
	.8071	20.5
13/16	.8125	20.63
	.8268	21.0
53/64	.8281	21.03
27/32	.8438	21.43
	.8465	21.5
55/64	.8594	21.82
	.8661	22.0
7/8	.8750	22.22
	.8858	22.5
57/64	.8906	22.62
	.9055	23.0
29/32	.9062	23.01
59/64	.9219	23.41
	.9252	23.5
15/16	.9375	23.81
	.9449	24.0
61/64	.9531	24.2
	.9646	24.5
31/32	.9688	24.6
	.9843	25.0
63/64	.9844	25.0
1	1.0000	25.4

GLOSSARY OF TERMS

AIR/FUEL RATIO: The ratio of air to gasoline by weight in the fuel mixture drawn into the engine.

AIR INJECTION: One method of reducing harmful exhaust emissions by injecting air into each of the exhaust ports of an engine. The fresh air entering the hot exhaust manifold causes any remaining fuel to be burned before it can exit the tailpipe.

ALTERNATOR: A device used for converting mechanical energy into electrical energy.

AMMETER: An instrument, calibrated in amperes, used to measure the flow of an electrical current in a circuit. Ammeters are always connected in series with the circuit being tested.

AMPERE: The rate of flow of electrical current present when one volt of electrical pressure is applied against one ohm of electrical resistance.

ANALOG COMPUTER: Any microprocessor that uses similar (analogous) electrical signals to make its calculations.

ARMATURE: A laminated, soft iron core wrapped by a wire that converts electrical energy to mechanical energy as in a motor or relay. When rotated in a magnetic field, it changes mechanical energy into electrical energy as in a generator.

ATMOSPHERIC PRESSURE: The pressure on the Earth's surface caused by the weight of the air in the atmosphere. At sea level, this pressure is 14.7 psi at 32°F (101 kPa at 0°C).

ATOMIZATION: The breaking down of a liquid into a fine mist that can be suspended in air.

AXIAL PLAY: Movement parallel to a shaft or bearing bore.

BACKFIRE: The sudden combustion of gases in the intake or exhaust system that results in a loud explosion.

BACKLASH: The clearance or play between two parts, such as meshed gears.

BACKPRESSURE: Restrictions in the exhaust system that slow the exit of exhaust gases from the combustion chamber.

BAKELITE: A heat resistant, plastic insulator material commonly used in printed circuit boards and transistorized components.

BALL BEARING: A bearing made up of hardened inner and outer races between which hardened steel ball roll.

BALLAST RESISTOR: A resistor in the primary ignition circuit that lowers voltage after the engine is started to reduce wear on ignition components.

BEARING: A friction reducing, supportive device usually located between a stationary part and a moving part.

BIMETAL TEMPERATURE SENSOR: Any sensor or switch made of two dissimilar types of metal that bend when heated or cooled due to the different expansion rates of the alloys. These types of sensors usually function as an on/off switch.

BLOWBY: Combustion gases, composed of water vapor and unburned fuel, that leak past the piston rings into the crankcase during normal engine operation. These gases are removed by the PCV system to prevent the build-up of harmful acids in the crankcase.

BRAKE PAD: A brake shoe and lining assembly used with disc brakes.

BRAKE SHOE: The backing for the brake lining. The term is, however, usually applied to the assembly of the brake backing and lining.

BUSHING: A liner, usually removable, for a bearing; an anti-friction liner used in place of a bearing.

BYPASS: System used to bypass ballast resistor during engine cranking to increase voltage supplied to the coil.

CALIPER: A hydraulically activated device in a disc brake system, which is mounted straddling the brake rotor (disc). The caliper contains at least one piston and two brake pads. Hydraulic pressure on the piston(s) forces the pads against the rotor.

CAMSHAFT: A shaft in the engine on which are the lobes (cams) which operate the valves. The camshaft is driven by the crankshaft, via a belt, chain or gears, at one half the crankshaft speed.

CAPACITOR: A device which stores an electrical charge.

CARBON MONOXIDE (CO): a colorless, odorless gas given off as a normal byproduct of combustion. It is poisonous and extremely dangerous in confined areas, building up slowly to toxic levels without warning if adequate ventilation is not available.

CARBURETOR: A device, usually mounted on the intake manifold of an engine, which mixes the air and fuel in the proper proportion to allow even combustion.

CATALYTIC CONVERTER: A device installed in the exhaust system, like a muffler, that converts harmful byproducts of combustion into carbon dioxide and water vapor by means of a heat-producing chemical reaction.

CENTRIFUGAL ADVANCE: A mechanical method of advancing the spark timing by using flyweights in the distributor that react to centrifugal force generated by the distributor shaft rotation.

CHECK VALVE: Any one-way valve installed to permit the flow of air, fuel or vacuum in one direction only.

CHOKE: A device, usually a moveable valve, placed in the intake path of a carburetor to restrict the flow of air.

CIRCUIT: Any unbroken path through which an electrical current can flow. Also used to describe fuel flow in some instances.

CIRCUIT BREAKER: A switch which protects an electrical circuit from overload by opening the circuit when the current flow exceeds a predetermined level. Some circuit breakers must be reset manually, while other reset automatically

COIL (IGNITION): A transformer in the ignition circuit which steps of the voltage provided to the spark plugs.

COMBINATION MANIFOLD: An assembly which includes both the intake and exhaust manifolds in one casting.

COMBINATION VALVE: A device used in some fuel systems that routes fuel vapors to a charcoal storage canister instead of venting them into the atmosphere. The valve relieves fuel tank pressure and allows fresh air into the tank as fuel level drops to prevent a vapor lock situation.

COMPRESSION RATIO: The comparison of the total volume of the cylinder and combustion chamber with the piston at BDC and the piston at TDC.

CONDENSER: 1. An electrical device which acts to store an electrical charge, preventing voltage surges.
2. A radiator-like device in the air conditioning system in which refrigerant gas condenses into a liquid, giving off heat.

CONDUCTOR: Any material through which an electrical current can be transmitted easily.

CONTINUITY: Continuous or complete circuit. Can be checked with an ohmmeter.

COUNTERSHAFT: An intermediate shaft which is rotated by a mainshaft and transmits, in turn, that rotation to a working part.

CRANKCASE: The lower part of an engine in which the crankshaft and related parts operate.

CRANKSHAFT: The main driving shaft of an engine which receives reciprocating motion from the pistons and converts it to rotary motion.

CYLINDER: In an engine, the round hole in the engine block in which the piston(s) ride.

CYLINDER BLOCK: The main structural member of an engine in which is found the cylinders, crankshaft and other principal parts.

CYLINDER HEAD: The detachable portion of the engine, fastened, usually, to the top of the cylinder block, containing all or most of the combustion chambers. On overhead valve engines, it contains the valves and their operating parts. On overhead cam engines, it contains the camshaft as well.

DEAD CENTER: The extreme top or bottom of the piston stroke.

DETONATION: An unwanted explosion of the air fuel mixture in the combustion chamber caused by excess heat and compression, advanced timing, or an overly lean mixture. Also referred to as "ping".

DIAPHRAGM: A thin, flexible wall separating two cavities, such as in a vacuum advance unit.

DIESELING: A condition in which hot spots in the combustion chamber cause the engine to run on after the key is turned off.

DIFFERENTIAL: A geared assembly which allows the transmission of motion between drive axles, giving one axle the ability to turn faster than the other.

DIODE: An electrical device that will allow current to flow in one direction only.

DISC BRAKE: A hydraulic braking assembly consisting of a brake disc, or rotor, mounted on an axle, and a caliper assembly containing, usually two brake pads which are activated by hydraulic pressure. The pads are forced against the sides of the disc, creating friction which slows the vehicle.

DISTRIBUTOR: A mechanically driven device on an engine which is responsible for electrically firing the spark plug at a predetermined point of the piston stroke.

DOWEL PIN: A pin, inserted in mating holes in two different parts allowing those parts to maintain a fixed relationship.

DRUM BRAKE: A braking system which consists of two brake shoes and one or two wheel cylinders, mounted on a fixed backing plate, and a brake drum, mounted on an axle, which revolves around the assembly. Hydraulic action applied to the wheel cylinders forces the shoes outward against the drum, creating friction and slowing the vehicle.

DWELL: The rate, measured in degrees of shaft rotation, at which an electrical circuit cycles on and off.

ELECTRONIC CONTROL UNIT (ECU): Ignition module, module, amplifier or igniter. See Module for definition.

ELECTRONIC IGNITION: A system in which the timing and firing of the spark plugs is controlled by an electronic control unit, usually called a module. These systems have not points or condenser.

ENDPLAY: The measured amount of axial movement in a shaft.

ENGINE: A device that converts heat into mechanical energy.

EXHAUST MANIFOLD: A set of cast passages or pipes which conduct exhaust gases from the engine.

FEELER GAUGE: A blade, usually metal, of precisely predetermined thickness, used to measure the clearance between two parts. These blades usually are available in sets of assorted thicknesses.

F-Head: An engine configuration in which the intake valves are in the cylinder head, while the camshaft and exhaust valves are located in the cylinder block. The camshaft operates the intake valves via lifters and pushrods, while it operates the exhaust valves directly.

FIRING ORDER: The order in which combustion occurs in the cylinders of an engine. Also the order in which spark is distributed to the plugs by the distributor.

FLATHEAD: An engine configuration in which the camshaft and all the valves are located in the cylinder block.

FLOODING: The presence of too much fuel in the intake manifold and combustion chamber which prevents the air/fuel mixture from firing, thereby causing a no-start situation.

FLYWHEEL: A disc shaped part bolted to the rear end of the crankshaft. Around the outer perimeter is affixed the ring gear. The starter drive engages the ring gear, turning the flywheel, which rotates the crankshaft, imparting the initial starting motion to the engine.

FOOT POUND (ft.lb. or sometimes, ft. lbs.): The amount of energy or work needed to raise an item weighing one pound, a distance of one foot.

FUSE: A protective device in a circuit which prevents circuit overload by breaking the circuit when a specific amperage is present. The device is constructed around a strip or wire of a lower amperage rating than the circuit it is designed to protect. When an amperage higher than that stamped on the fuse is present in the circuit, the strip or wire melts, opening the circuit.

GEAR RATIO: The ratio between the number of teeth on meshing gears.

GENERATOR: A device which converts mechanical energy into electrical energy.

HEAT RANGE: The measure of a spark plug's ability to dissipate heat from its firing end. The higher the heat range, the hotter the plug fires.

HUB: The center part of a wheel or gear.

HYDROCARBON (HC): Any chemical compound made up of hydrogen and carbon. A major pollutant formed by the engine as a byproduct of combustion.

HYDROMETER: An instrument used to measure the specific gravity of a solution.

INCH POUND (in.lb. or sometimes, in. lbs.): One twelfth of a foot pound.

INDUCTION: A means of transferring electrical energy in the form of a magnetic field. Principle used in the ignition coil to increase voltage.

INJECTION PUMP: A device, usually mechanically operated, which meters and delivers fuel under pressure to the fuel injector.

INJECTOR: A device which receives metered fuel under relatively low pressure and is activated to inject the fuel into the engine under relatively high pressure at a predetermined time.

INPUT SHAFT: The shaft to which torque is applied, usually carrying the driving gear or gears.

INTAKE MANIFOLD: A casting of passages or pipes used to conduct air or a fuel/air mixture to the cylinders.

JOURNAL: The bearing surface within which a shaft operates.

KEY: A small block usually fitted in a notch between a shaft and a hub to prevent slippage of the two parts.

MANIFOLD: A casting of passages or set of pipes which connect the cylinders to an inlet or outlet source.

MANIFOLD VACUUM: Low pressure in an engine intake manifold formed just below the throttle plates. Manifold vacuum is highest at idle and drops under acceleration.

MASTER CYLINDER: The primary fluid pressurizing device in a hydraulic system. In automotive use, it is found in brake and hydraulic clutch systems and is pedal activated, either directly or, in a power brake system, through the power booster.

MODULE: Electronic control unit, amplifier or igniter of solid state or integrated design which controls the current flow in the ignition primary circuit based on input from the pickup coil. When the module opens the primary circuit, the high secondary voltage is induced in the coil.

NEEDLE BEARING: A bearing which consists of a number (usually a large number) of long, thin rollers.

OHM: (Ω) The unit used to measure the resistance of conductor to electrical flow. One ohm is the amount of resistance that limits current flow to one ampere in a circuit with one volt of pressure.

OHMMETER: An instrument used for measuring the resistance, in ohms, in an electrical circuit.

OUTPUT SHAFT: The shaft which transmits torque from a device, such as a transmission.

OVERDRIVE: A gear assembly which produces more shaft revolutions than that transmitted to it.

OVERHEAD CAMSHAFT (OHC): An engine configuration in which the camshaft is mounted on top of the cylinder head and operates the valve either directly or by means of rocker arms.

OVERHEAD VALVE (OHV): An engine configuration in which all of the valves are located in the cylinder head and the camshaft is located in the cylinder block. The camshaft operates the valves via lifters and pushrods.

OXIDES OF NITROGEN (NOx): Chemical compounds of nitrogen produced as a byproduct of combustion. They combine with hydrocarbons to produce smog.

OXYGEN SENSOR: Used with the feedback system to sense the presence of oxygen in the exhaust gas and signal the computer which can reference the voltage signal to an air/fuel ratio.

PINION: The smaller of two meshing gears.

PISTON RING: An open ended ring which fits into a groove on the outer diameter of the piston. Its chief function is to form a seal between the piston and cylinder wall. Most automotive pistons have three rings: two for compression sealing; one for oil sealing.

PRELOAD: A predetermined load placed on a bearing during assembly or by adjustment.

PRIMARY CIRCUIT: Is the low voltage side of the ignition system which consists of the ignition switch, ballast resistor or resistance wire, bypass, coil, electronic control unit and pick-up coil as well as the connecting wires and harnesses.

PRESS FIT: The mating of two parts under pressure, due to the inner diameter of one being smaller than the outer diameter of the other, or vice versa; an interference fit.

RACE: The surface on the inner or outer ring of a bearing on which the balls, needles or rollers move.

REGULATOR: A device which maintains the amperage and/or voltage levels of a circuit at predetermined values.

RELAY: A switch which automatically opens and/or closes a circuit.

RESISTANCE: The opposition to the flow of current through a circuit or electrical device, and is measured in ohms. Resistance is equal to the voltage divided by the amperage.

RESISTOR: A device, usually made of wire, which offers a preset amount of resistance in an electrical circuit.

RING GEAR: The name given to a ring-shaped gear attached to a differential case, or affixed to a flywheel or as part a planetary gear set.

ROLLER BEARING: A bearing made up of hardened inner and outer races between which hardened steel rollers move.

ROTOR: 1. The disc-shaped part of a disc brake assembly, upon which the brake pads bear; also called, brake disc.
2. The device mounted atop the distributor shaft, which passes current to the distributor cap tower contacts.

SECONDARY CIRCUIT: The high voltage side of the ignition system, usually above 20,000 volts. The secondary includes the ignition coil, coil wire, distributor cap and rotor, spark plug wires and spark plugs.

SENDING UNIT: A mechanical, electrical, hydraulic or electromagnetic device which transmits information to a gauge.

SENSOR: Any device designed to measure engine operating conditions or ambient pressures and temperatures. Usually electronic in nature and designed to send a voltage signal to an on-board computer, some sensors may operate as a simple on/off switch or they may provide a variable voltage signal (like a potentiometer) as conditions or measured parameters change.

SHIM: Spacers of precise, predetermined thickness used between parts to establish a proper working relationship.

SLAVE CYLINDER: In automotive use, a device in the hydraulic clutch system which is activated by hydraulic force, disengaging the clutch.

SOLENOID: A coil used to produce a magnetic field, the effect of which is produce work.

SPARK PLUG: A device screwed into the combustion chamber of a spark ignition engine. The basic construction is a conductive core inside of a ceramic insulator, mounted in an outer conductive base. An electrical charge from the spark plug wire travels along the conductive core and jumps a preset air gap to a grounding point or points at the end of the conductive base. The resultant spark ignites the fuel/air mixture in the combustion chamber.

SPLINES: Ridges machined or cast onto the outer diameter of a shaft or inner diameter of a bore to enable parts to mate without rotation.

TACHOMETER: A device used to measure the rotary speed of an engine, shaft, gear, etc., usually in rotations per minute.

THERMOSTAT: A valve, located in the cooling system of an engine, which is closed when cold and opens gradually in response to engine heating, controlling the temperature of the coolant and rate of coolant flow.

TOP DEAD CENTER (TDC): The point at which the piston reaches the top of its travel on the compression stroke.

TORQUE: The twisting force applied to an object.

TORQUE CONVERTER: A turbine used to transmit power from a driving member to a driven member via hydraulic action, providing changes in drive ratio and torque. In automotive use, it links the driveplate at the rear of the engine to the automatic transmission.

TRANSDUCER: A device used to change a force into an electrical signal.

TRANSISTOR: A semi-conductor component which can be actuated by a small voltage to perform an electrical switching function.

TUNE-UP: A regular maintenance function, usually associated with the replacement and adjustment of parts and components in the electrical and fuel systems of a vehicle for the purpose of attaining optimum performance.

TURBOCHARGER: An exhaust driven pump which compresses intake air and forces it into the combustion chambers at higher than atmospheric pressures. The increased air pressure allows more fuel to be burned and results in increased horsepower being produced.

VACUUM ADVANCE: A device which advances the ignition timing in response to increased engine vacuum.

VACUUM GAUGE: An instrument used to measure the presence of vacuum in a chamber.

VALVE: A device which control the pressure, direction of flow or rate of flow of a liquid or gas.

VALVE CLEARANCE: The measured gap between the end of the valve stem and the rocker arm, cam lobe or follower that activates the valve.

VISCOSITY: The rating of a liquid's internal resistance to flow.

VOLTMETER: An instrument used for measuring electrical force in units called volts. Voltmeters are always connected parallel with the circuit being tested.

WHEEL CYLINDER: Found in the automotive drum brake assembly, it is a device, actuated by hydraulic pressure, which, through internal pistons, pushes the brake shoes outward against the drums.

ABBREVIATIONS AND SYMBOLS

A: Ampere

AC: Alternating current

A/C: Air conditioning

A-h: Ampere hour

AT: Automatic transmission

ATDC: After top dead center

μA: Microampere

bbl: Barrel

BDC: Bottom dead center

bhp: Brake horsepower

BTDC: Before top dead center

BTU: British thermal unit

C: Celsius (Centigrade)

CCA: Cold cranking amps

cd: Candela

cm^2: Square centimeter

cm^3, cc: Cubic centimeter

CO: Carbon monoxide

CO_2: Carbon dioxide

cu.in., in^3: Cubic inch

CV: Constant velocity

Cyl.: Cylinder

DC: Direct current

ECM: Electronic control module

EFE: Early fuel evaporation

EFI: Electronic fuel injection

EGR: Exhaust gas recirculation

Exh.: Exhaust

F: Fahrenheit

F: Farad

pF: Picofarad

μF: Microfarad

FI: Fuel injection

ft.lb., ft. lb., ft. lbs.: foot pound(s)

gal: Gallon

g: Gram

HC: Hydrocarbon

HEI: High energy ignition

HO: High output

hp: Horsepower

Hyd.: Hydraulic

Hz: Hertz

ID: Inside diameter

in.lb.; in. lb.; in. lbs: inch pound(s)

Int.: Intake

K: Kelvin

kg: Kilogram

kHz: Kilohertz

km: Kilometer

km/h: Kilometers per hour

$k\Omega$: Kilohm

kPa: Kilopascal

kV: Kilovolt

kW: Kilowatt

l: Liter

l/s: Liters per second

m: Meter

mA: Milliampere

mg: Milligram

mHz: Megahertz

mm: Millimeter

mm^2: Square millimeter

m^3: Cubic meter

MΩ: Megohm

m/s: Meters per second

MT: Manual transmission

mV: Millivolt

μm: Micrometer

N: Newton

N-m: Newton meter

NOx: Nitrous oxide

OD: Outside diameter

OHC: Over head camshaft

OHV: Over head valve

Ω: Ohm

PCV: Positive crankcase ventilation

psi: Pounds per square inch

pts: Pints

qts: Quarts

rpm: Rotations per minute

rps: Rotations per second

R-12: A refrigerant gas (Freon)

SAE: Society of Automotive Engineers

SO$_2$: Sulfur dioxide

T: Ton

t: Megagram

TBI: Throttle Body Injection

TPS: Throttle Position Sensor

V: 1. Volt; 2. Venturi

μV: Microvolt

W: Watt

∞: Infinity

$<$: Less than

$>$: Greater than

Index

CHILTON'S REPAIR MANUAL MODEL INDEX
Car and truck model names are listed in alphabetical and numerical order

Part No.	Model	Repair Manual Title
6980	Accord	Honda 1973-88
7747	Aerostar	Ford Aerostar 1986-90
7165	Alliance	Renault 1975-85
7199	AMX	AMC 1975-86
7163	Aries	Chrysler Front Wheel Drive 1981-88
7041	Arrow	Champ/Arrow/Sapporo 1978-83
7032	Arrow Pick-Ups	D-50/Arrow Pick-Up 1979-81
6637	Aspen	Aspen/Volare 1976-80
6935	Astre	GM Subcompact 1971-80
7750	Astro	Chevrolet Astro/GMC Safari 1985-90
6934	A100, 200, 300	Dodge/Plymouth Vans 1967-88
5807	Barracuda	Barracuda/Challenger 1965-72
6844	Bavaria	BMW 1970-88
5796	Beetle	Volkswagen 1949-71
6837	Beetle	Volkswagen 1970-81
7135	Bel Air	Chevrolet 1968-88
5821	Belvedere	Roadrunner/Satellite/Belvedere/GTX 1968-73
7849	Beretta	Chevrolet Corsica and Beretta 1988
7317	Berlinetta	Camaro 1982-88
7135	Biscayne	Chevrolet 1968-88
6931	Blazer	Blazer/Jimmy 1969-82
7383	Blazer	Chevy S-10 Blazer/GMC S-15 Jimmy 1982-87
7027	Bobcat	Pinto/Bobcat 1971-80
7308	Bonneville	Buick/Olds/Pontiac 1975-87
6982	BRAT	Subaru 1970-88
7042	Brava	Fiat 1969-81
7140	Bronco	Ford Bronco 1966-86
7829	Bronco	Ford Pick-Ups and Bronco 1987-88
7408	Bronco II	Ford Ranger/Bronco II 1983-88
7135	Brookwood	Chevrolet 1968-88
6326	Brougham 1975-75	Valiant/Duster 1968-76
6934	B100, 150, 200, 250, 300, 350	Dodge/Plymouth Vans 1967-88
7197	B210	Datsun 1200/210/Nissan Sentra 1973-88
7659	B1600, 1800, 2000, 2200, 2600	Mazda Trucks 1971-89
6840	Caballero	Chevrolet Mid-Size 1964-88
7657	Calais	Calais, Grand Am, Skylark, Somerset 1985-86
6735	Camaro	Camaro 1967-81
7317	Camaro	Camaro 1982-88
7740	Camry	Toyota Camry 1983-88
6695	Capri, Capri II	Capri 1970-77
6963	Capri	Mustang/Capri/Merkur 1979-88
7135	Caprice	Chevrolet 1968-88
7482	Caravan	Dodge Caravan/Plymouth Voyager 1984-89
7163	Caravelle	Chrysler Front Wheel Drive 1981-88
7036	Carina	Toyota Corolla/Carina/Tercel/Starlet 1970-87
7308	Catalina	Buick/Olds/Pontiac 1975-90
7059	Cavalier	Cavalier, Skyhawk, Cimarron, 2000 1982-88
7309	Celebrity	Celebrity, Century, Ciera, 6000 1982-88
7043	Celica	Toyota Celica/Supra 1971-87
8058	Celica	Toyota Celica/Supra 1986-90
7309	Century FWD	Celebrity, Century, Ciera, 6000 1982-88
7307	Century RWD	Century/Regal 1975-87
5807	Challenger 1965-72	Barracuda/Challenger 1965-72
7037	Challenger 1977-83	Colt/Challenger/Vista/Conquest 1971-88
7041	Champ	Champ/Arrow/Sapporo 1978-83
6486	Charger	Dodge Charger 1967-70
6845	Charger 2.2	Omni/Horizon/Rampage 1978-88

Part No.	Model	Repair Manual Title
6739	Cherokee 1974-83	Jeep Wagoneer, Commando, Cherokee, Truck 1957-86
7939	Cherokee 1984-89	Jeep Wagoneer, Comanche, Cherokee 1984-89
6840	Chevelle	Chevrolet Mid-Size 1964-88
6836	Chevette	Chevette/T-1000 1976-88
6841	Chevy II	Chevy II/Nova 1962-79
7309	Ciera	Celebrity, Century, Ciera, 6000 1982-88
7059	Cimarron	Cavalier, Skyhawk, Cimarron, 2000 1982-88
7049	Citation	GM X-Body 1980-85
6980	Civic	Honda 1973-88
6817	CJ-2A, 3A, 3B, 5, 6, 7	Jeep 1945-87
8034	CJ-5, 6, 7	Jeep 1971-90
6842	Colony Park	Ford/Mercury/Lincoln 1968-88
7037	Colt	Colt/Challenger/Vista/Conquest 1971-88
6634	Comet	Maverick/Comet 1971-77
7939	Comanche	Jeep Wagoneer, Comanche, Cherokee 1984-89
6739	Commando	Jeep Wagoneer, Commando, Cherokee, Truck 1957-86
6842	Commuter	Ford/Mercury/Lincoln 1968-88
7199	Concord	AMC 1975-86
7037	Conquest	Colt/Challenger/Vista/Conquest 1971-88
6696	Continental 1982-85	Ford/Mercury/Lincoln Mid-Size 1971-85
7814	Continental 1982-87	Thunderbird, Cougar, Continental 1980-87
7830	Continental 1988-89	Taurus/Sable/Continental 1986-89
7583	Cordia	Mitsubishi 1983-89
5795	Corolla 1968-70	Toyota 1966-70
7036	Corolla	Toyota Corolla/Carina/Tercel/Starlet 1970-87
5795	Corona	Toyota 1966-70
7004	Corona	Toyota Corona/Crown/Cressida/Mk.II/Van 1970-87
6962	Corrado	VW Front Wheel Drive 1974-90
7849	Corsica	Chevrolet Corsica and Beretta 1988
6576	Corvette	Corvette 1953-62
6843	Corvette	Corvette 1963-86
6542	Cougar	Mustang/Cougar 1965-73
6696	Cougar	Ford/Mercury/Lincoln Mid-Size 1971-85
7814	Cougar	Thunderbird, Cougar, Continental 1980-87
6842	Country Sedan	Ford/Mercury/Lincoln 1968-88
6842	Country Squire	Ford/Mercury/Lincoln 1968-88
6983	Courier	Ford Courier 1972-82
7004	Cressida	Toyota Corona/Crown/Cressida/Mk.II/Van 1970-87
5795	Crown	Toyota 1966-70
7004	Crown	Toyota Corona/Crown/Cressida/Mk.II/Van 1970-87
6842	Crown Victoria	Ford/Mercury/Lincoln 1968-88
6980	CRX	Honda 1973-88
6842	Custom	Ford/Mercury/Lincoln 1968-88
6326	Custom	Valiant/Duster 1968-76
6842	Custom 500	Ford/Mercury/Lincoln 1968-88
7950	Cutlass FWD	Lumina/Grand Prix/Cutlass/Regal 1988-90
6933	Cutlass RWD	Cutlass 1970-87
7309	Cutlass Ciera	Celebrity, Century, Ciera, 6000 1982-88
6936	C-10, 20, 30	Chevrolet/GMC Pick-Ups & Suburban 1970-87

Chilton's Repair Manuals are available at your local retailer or by mailing a check or money order for **$15.95** per book plus **$3.50** for 1st book and **$.50** for each additional book to cover postage and handling to:

Chilton Book Company
Dept. DM
Radnor, PA 19089

NOTE: When ordering be sure to include your name & address, book part No. & title.

CHILTON'S REPAIR MANUAL MODEL INDEX
Car and truck model names are listed in alphabetical and numerical order

Part No.	Model	Repair Manual Title	Part No.	Model	Repair Manual Title
8055	C-15, 25, 35	Chevrolet/GMC Pick-Ups & Suburban 1988-90	7593	Golf	VW Front Wheel Drive 1974-90
6324	Dart	Dart/Demon 1968-76	7165	Gordini	Renault 1975-85
6962	Dasher	VW Front Wheel Drive 1974-90	6937	Granada	Granada/Monarch 1975-82
5790	Datsun Pickups	Datsun 1961-72	6552	Gran Coupe	Plymouth 1968-76
6816	Datsun Pickups	Datsun Pick-Ups and Pathfinder 1970-89	6552	Gran Fury	Plymouth 1968-76
			6842	Gran Marquis	Ford/Mercury/Lincoln 1968-88
7163	Daytona	Chrysler Front Wheel Drive 1981-88	6552	Gran Sedan	Plymouth 1968-76
6486	Daytona Charger	Dodge Charger 1967-70	6696	Gran Torino	Ford/Mercury/Lincoln Mid-Size 1971-85
6324	Demon	Dart/Demon 1968-76		1972-76	
7462	deVille	Cadillac 1967-89	7346	Grand Am	Pontiac Mid-Size 1974-83
7587	deVille	GM C-Body 1985	7657	Grand Am	Calais, Grand Am, Skylark, Somerset 1985-86
6817	DJ-3B	Jeep 1945-87			
7040	DL	Volvo 1970-88	7346	Grand LeMans	Pontiac Mid-Size 1974-83
6326	Duster	Valiant/Duster 1968-76	7346	Grand Prix	Pontiac Mid-Size 1974-83
7032	D-50	D-50/Arrow Pick-Ups 1979-81	7950	Grand Prix FWD	Lumina/Grand Prix/Cutlass/Regal 1988-90
7459	D100, 150, 200, 250, 300, 350	Dodge/Plymouth Trucks 1967-88	7308	Grand Safari	Buick/Olds/Pontiac 1975-87
7199	Eagle	AMC 1975-86	7308	Grand Ville	Buick/Olds/Pontiac 1975-87
7163	E-Class	Chrysler Front Wheel Drive 1981-88	6739	Grand Wagoneer	Jeep Wagoneer, Commando, Cherokee, Truck 1957-86
6840	El Camino	Chevrolet Mid-Size 1964-88			
7462	Eldorado	Cadillac 1967-89	7199	Gremlin	AMC 1975-86
7308	Electra	Buick/Olds/Pontiac 1975-90	6575	GT	Opel 1971-75
7587	Electra	GM C-Body 1985	7593	GTI	VW Front Wheel Drive 1974-90
6696	Elite	Ford/Mercury/Lincoln Mid-Size 1971-85	5905	GTO	Tempest/GTO/LeMans 1968-73
			7346	GTO 1974	Pontiac Mid-Size 1974-83
7165	Encore	Renault 1975-85	5821	GTX	Roadrunner/Satellite/Belvedere/GTX 1968-73
7055	Escort	Ford/Mercury Front Wheel Drive 1981-87			
			5910	GT6	Triumph 1969-73
7059	Eurosport	Cavalier, Skyhawk, Cimarron, 2000 1982-88	6542	G.T.350, 500	Mustang/Cougar 1965-73
			6930	G-10, 20, 30	Chevy/GMC Vans 1967-86
7760	Excel	Hyundai 1986-90	6930	G-1500, 2500, 3500	Chevy/GMC Vans 1967-86
7163	Executive Sedan	Chrysler Front Wheel Drive 1981-88	8040	G-10, 20, 30	Chevy/GMC Vans 1987-90
7055	EXP	Ford/Mercury Front Wheel Drive 1981-87	8040	G-1500, 2500, 3500	Chevy/GMC Vans 1987-90
			5795	Hi-Lux	Toyota 1966-70
6849	E-100, 150, 200, 250, 300, 350	Ford Vans 1961-88	6845	Horizon	Omni/Horizon/Rampage 1978-88
			7199	Hornet	AMC 1975-86
6320	Fairlane	Fairlane/Torino 1962-75	7135	Impala	Chevrolet 1968-88
6965	Fairmont	Fairmont/Zephyr 1978-83	7317	IROC-Z	Camaro 1982-88
5796	Fastback	Volkswagen 1949-71	6739	Jeepster	Jeep Wagoneer, Commando, Cherokee, Truck 1957-86
6837	Fastback	Volkswagen 1970-81			
6739	FC-150, 170	Jeep Wagoneer, Commando, Cherokee, Truck 1957-86	7593	Jetta	VW Front Wheel Drive 1974-90
			6931	Jimmy	Blazer/Jimmy 1969-82
6982	FF-1	Subaru 1970-88	7383	Jimmy	Chevy S-10 Blazer/GMC S-15 Jimmy 1982-87
7571	Fiero	Pontiac Fiero 1984-88			
6846	Fiesta	Fiesta 1978-80	6739	J-10, 20	Jeep Wagoneer, Commando, Cherokee, Truck 1957-86
5996	Firebird	Firebird 1967-81			
7345	Firebird	Firebird 1982-90	6739	J-100, 200, 300	Jeep Wagoneer, Commando, Cherokee, Truck 1957-86
7059	Firenza	Cavalier, Skyhawk, Cimarron, 2000 1982-88			
			6575	Kadett	Opel 1971-75
7462	Fleetwood	Cadillac 1967-89	7199	Kammback	AMC 1975-86
7587	Fleetwood	GM C-Body 1985	5796	Karmann Ghia	Volkswagen 1949-71
7829	F-Super Duty	Ford Pick-Ups and Bronco 1987-88	6837	Karmann Ghia	Volkswagen 1970-81
7165	Fuego	Renault 1975-85	7135	Kingswood	Chevrolet 1968-88
6552	Fury	Plymouth 1968-76	6931	K-5	Blazer/Jimmy 1969-82
7196	F-10	Datsun/Nissan F-10, 310, Stanza, Pulsar 1976-88	6936	K-10, 20, 30	Chevy/GMC Pick-Ups & Suburban 1970-87
6933	F-85	Cutlass 1970-87	6936	K-1500, 2500, 3500	Chevy/GMC Pick-Ups & Suburban 1970-87
6913	F-100, 150, 200, 250, 300, 350	Ford Pick-Ups 1965-86	8055	K-10, 20, 30	Chevy/GMC Pick-Ups & Suburban 1988-90
7829	F-150, 250, 350	Ford Pick-Ups and Bronco 1987-88	8055	K-1500, 2500, 3500	Chevy/GMC Pick-Ups & Suburban 1988-90
7583	Galant	Mitsubishi 1983-89			
6842	Galaxie	Ford/Mercury/Lincoln 1968-88	6840	Laguna	Chevrolet Mid-Size 1964-88
7040	GL	Volvo 1970-88	7041	Lancer	Champ/Arrow/Sapporo 1977-83
6739	Gladiator	Jeep Wagoneer, Commando, Cherokee, Truck 1962-86	5795	Land Cruiser	Toyota 1966-70
			7035	Land Cruiser	Toyota Trucks 1970-88
6981	GLC	Mazda 1978-89	7163	Laser	Chrysler Front Wheel Drive 1981-88
7040	GLE	Volvo 1970-88	7163	LeBaron	Chrysler Front Wheel Drive 1981-88
7040	GLT	Volvo 1970-88	7165	LeCar	Renault 1975-85

Chilton's Repair Manuals are available at your local retailer or by mailing a check or money order for **$15.95** per book plus **$3.50** for 1st book and **$.50** for each additional book to cover postage and handling to:

Chilton Book Company
Dept. DM
Radnor, PA 19089

NOTE: When ordering be sure to include your name & address, book part No. & title.

CHILTON'S REPAIR MANUAL MODEL INDEX
Car and truck model names are listed in alphabetical and numerical order

Part No.	Model	Repair Manual Title
5905	LeMans	Tempest/GTO/LeMans 1968-73
7346	LeMans	Pontiac Mid-Size 1974-83
7308	LeSabre	Buick/Olds/Pontiac 1975-87
6842	Lincoln	Ford/Mercury/Lincoln 1968-88
7055	LN-7	Ford/Mercury Front Wheel Drive 1981-87
6842	LTD	Ford/Mercury/Lincoln 1968-88
6696	LTD II	Ford/Mercury/Lincoln Mid-Size 1971-85
7950	Lumina	Lumina/Grand Prix/Cutlass/Regal 1988-90
6815	LUV	Chevrolet LUV 1972-81
6575	Luxus	Opel 1971-75
7055	Lynx	Ford/Mercury Front Wheel Drive 1981-87
6844	L6	BMW 1970-88
6344	L7	BMW 1970-88
6542	Mach I	Mustang/Cougar 1965-73
6812	Mach I Ghia	Mustang II 1974-78
6840	Malibu	Chevrolet Mid-Size 1964-88
6575	Manta	Opel 1971-75
6696	Mark IV, V, VI, VII	Ford/Mercury/Lincoln Mid-Size 1971-85
7814	Mark VII	Thunderbird, Cougar, Continental 1980-87
6842	Marquis	Ford/Mercury/Lincoln 1968-88
6696	Marquis	Ford/Mercury/Lincoln Mid-Size 1971-85
7199	Matador	AMC 1975-86
6634	Maverick	Maverick/Comet 1970-77
6817	Maverick	Jeep 1945-87
7170	Maxima	Nissan 200SX, 240SX, 510, 610, 710, 810, Maxima 1973-88
6842	Mercury	Ford/Mercury/Lincoln 1968-88
6963	Merkur	Mustang/Capri/Merkur 1979-88
6780	MGB, MGB-GT, MGC-GT	MG 1961-81
6780	Midget	MG 1961-81
7583	Mighty Max	Mitsubishi 1983-89
7583	Mirage	Mitsubishi 1983-89
5795	Mk.II 1969-70	Toyota 1966-70
7004	Mk.II 1970-76	Toyota Corona/Crown/Cressida/Mk.II/Van 1970-87
6554	Monaco	Dodge 1968-77
6937	Monarch	Granada/Monarch 1975-82
6840	Monte Carlo	Chevrolet Mid-Size 1964-88
6696	Montego	Ford/Mercury/Lincoln Mid-Size 1971-85
6842	Monterey	Ford/Mercury/Lincoln 1968-88
7583	Montero	Mitsubishi 1983-89
6935	Monza 1975-80	GM Subcompact 1971-80
6981	MPV	Mazda 1978-89
6542	Mustang	Mustang/Cougar 1965-73
6963	Mustang	Mustang/Capri/Merkur 1979-88
6812	Mustang II	Mustang II 1974-78
6981	MX6	Mazda 1978-89
6844	M3, M6	BMW 1970-88
7163	New Yorker	Chrysler Front Wheel Drive 1981-88
6841	Nova	Chevy II/Nova 1962-79
7658	Nova	Chevrolet Nova/GEO Prizm 1985-89
7049	Omega	GM X-Body 1980-85
6845	Omni	Omni/Horizon/Rampage 1978-88
6575	Opel	Opel 1971-75
7199	Pacer	AMC 1975-86
7587	Park Avenue	GM C-Body 1985
6842	Park Lane	Ford/Mercury/Lincoln 1968-88
6962	Passat	VW Front Wheel Drive 1974-90
6816	Pathfinder	Datsun/Nissan Pick-Ups and Pathfinder 1970-09
5790	Patrol	Datsun 1961-72
6934	PB100, 150, 200, 250, 300, 350	Dodge/Plymouth Vans 1967-88
5982	Peugeot	Peugeot 1970-74
7049	Phoenix	GM X-Body 1980-85
7027	Pinto	Pinto/Bobcat 1971-80
6554	Polara	Dodge 1968-77
7583	Precis	Mitsubishi 1983-89
6980	Prelude	Honda 1973-88
7658	Prizm	Chevrolet Nova/GEO Prizm 1985-89
8012	Probe	Ford Probe 1989
7660	Pulsar	Datsun/Nissan F-10, 310, Stanza, Pulsar 1976-88
6529	PV-444	Volvo 1956-69
6529	PV-544	Volvo 1956-69
6529	P-1800	Volvo 1956-69
7593	Quantum	VW Front Wheel Drive 1974-87
7593	Rabbit	VW Front Wheel Drive 1974-87
7593	Rabbit Pickup	VW Front Wheel Drive 1974-87
6575	Rallye	Opel 1971-75
7459	Ramcharger	Dodge/Plymouth Trucks 1967-88
6845	Rampage	Omni/Horizon/Rampage 1978-88
6320	Ranchero	Fairlane/Torino 1962-70
6696	Ranchero	Ford/Mercury/Lincoln Mid-Size 1971-85
6842	Ranch Wagon	Ford/Mercury/Lincoln 1968-88
7338	Ranger Pickup	Ford Ranger 1983-88
7307	Regal RWD	Century/Regal 1975-87
7950	Regal FWD 1988-90	Lumina/Grand Prix/Cutlass/Regal 1988-90
7163	Reliant	Chrysler Front Wheel Drive 1981-88
5821	Roadrunner	Roadrunner/Satellite/Belvedere/GTX 1968-73
7659	Rotary Pick-Up	Mazda Trucks 1971-89
6981	RX-7	Mazda 1978-89
7165	R-12, 15, 17, 18, 18i	Renault 1975-85
7830	Sable	Taurus/Sable/Continental 1986-89
7750	Safari	Chevrolet Astro/GMC Safari 1985-90
7041	Sapporo	Champ/Arrow/Sapporo 1978-83
5821	Satellite	Roadrunner/Satellite/Belvedere/GTX 1968-73
6326	Scamp	Valiant/Duster 1968-76
6845	Scamp	Omni/Horizon/Rampage 1978-88
6962	Scirocco	VW Front Wheel Drive 1974-90
6936	Scottsdale	Chevrolet/GMC Pick-Ups & Suburban 1970-87
8055	Scottsdale	Chevrolet/GMC Pick-Ups & Suburban 1988-90
5912	Scout	International Scout 1967-73
8034	Scrambler	Jeep 1971-90
7197	Sentra	Datsun 1200, 210, Nissan Sentra 1973-88
7462	Seville	Cadillac 1967-89
7163	Shadow	Chrysler Front Wheel Drive 1981-88
6936	Siera	Chevrolet/GMC Pick-Ups & Suburban 1970-87
8055	Siera	Chevrolet/GMC Pick-Ups & Suburban 1988-90
7583	Sigma	Mitsubishi 1983-89
6326	Signet	Valiant/Duster 1968-76
6936	Silverado	Chevrolet/GMC Pick-Ups & Suburban 1970-87
8055	Silverado	Chevrolet/GMC Pick-Ups & Suburban 1988-90
6935	Skyhawk	GM Subcompact 1971-80
7059	Skyhawk	Cavalier, Skyhawk, Cimarron, 2000 1982-88
7049	Skylark	GM X-Body 1980-85

Chilton's Repair Manuals are available at your local retailer or by mailing a check or money order for **$15.95** per book plus **$3.50** for 1st book and **$.50** for each additional book to cover postage and handling to:

Chilton Book Company
Dept. DM
Radnor, PA 19089

NOTE: When ordering be sure to include your name & address, book part No. & title.

CHILTON'S REPAIR MANUAL MODEL INDEX
Car and truck model names are listed in alphabetical and numerical order

Part No.	Model	Repair Manual Title	Part No.	Model	Repair Manual Title
7675	Skylark	Calais, Grand Am, Skylark, Somerset 1985-86	7040	Turbo	Volvo 1970-88
7657	Somerset	Calais, Grand Am, Skylark, Somerset 1985-86	5796	Type 1 Sedan 1949-71	Volkswagen 1949-71
7042	Spider 2000	Fiat 1969-81	6837	Type 1 Sedan 1970-80	Volkswagen 1970-81
7199	Spirit	AMC 1975-86	5796	Type 1 Karmann Ghia 1960-71	Volkswagen 1949-71
6552	Sport Fury	Plymouth 1900-76			
7165	Sport Wagon	Renault 1975-85	6837	Type 1 Karmann Ghia 1970-74	Volkswagen 1970-81
5796	Squareback	Volkswagen 1949-71			
6837	Squareback	Volkswagen 1970-81	5796	Type 1 Convertible 1964-71	Volkswagen 1949-71
7196	Stanza	Datsun/Nissan F-10, 310, Stanza, Pulsar 1976-88	6837	Type 1 Convertible 1970-80	Volkswagen 1970-81
6935	Starfire	GM Subcompact 1971-80	5796	Type 1 Super Beetle 1971	Volkswagen 1949-71
7583	Starion	Mitsubishi 1983-89			
7036	Starlet	Toyota Corolla/Carina/Tercel/Starlet 1970-87	6837	Type 1 Super Beetle 1971-75	Volkswagen 1970-81
7059	STE	Cavalier, Skyhawk, Cimarron, 2000 1982-88	5796	Type 2 Bus 1953-71	Volkswagen 1949-71
			6837	Type 2 Bus 1970-80	Volkswagen 1970-81
5795	Stout	Toyota 1966-70	5796	Type 2 Kombi 1954-71	Volkswagen 1949-71
7042	Strada	Fiat 1969-81			
6552	Suburban	Plymouth 1968-76	6837	Type 2 Kombi 1970-73	Volkswagen 1970-81
6936	Suburban	Chevy/GMC Pick-Ups & Suburban 1970-87			
8055	Suburban	Chevy/GMC Pick-Ups & Suburban 1988-90	6837	Type 2 Vanagon 1981	Volkswagen 1970-81
6935	Sunbird	GM Subcompact 1971-80	5796	Type 3 Fastback & Squareback 1961-71	Volkswagen 1949-71
7059	Sunbird	Cavalier, Skyhawk, Cimarron, 2000, 1982-88	7081	Type 3 Fastback & Squareback 1970-73	Volkswagen 1970-70
7163	Sundance	Chrysler Front Wheel Drive 1981-88	5796	Type 4 411 1971	Volkswagen 1949-71
7043	Supra	Toyota Celica/Supra 1971-87	6837	Type 4 411 1971-72	Volkswagen 1970-81
8058	Supra	Toyota Celica/Supra 1986-90	5796	Type 4 412 1971	Volkswagen 1949-71
6837	Super Beetle	Volkswagen 1970-81	6845	Turismo	Omni/Horizon/Rampage 1978-88
7199	SX-4	AMC 1975-86	5905	T-37	Tempest/GTO/LeMans 1968-73
7383	S-10 Blazer	Chevy S-10 Blazer/GMC S-15 Jimmy 1982-87	6836	T-1000	Chevette/T-1000 1976-88
7310	S-10 Pick-Up	Chevy S-10/GMC S-15 Pick-Ups 1982-87	6935	Vega	GM Subcompact 1971-80
			7346	Ventura	Pontiac Mid-Size 1974-83
7383	S-15 Jimmy	Chevy S-10 Blazer/GMC S-15 Jimmy 1982-87	6696	Versailles	Ford/Mercury/Lincoln Mid-Size 1971-85
7310	S-15 Pick-Up	Chevy S-10/GMC S-15 Pick-Ups 1982-87	6552	VIP	Plymouth 1968-76
7830	Taurus	Taurus/Sable/Continental 1986-89	7037	Vista	Colt/Challenger/Vista/Conquest 1971-88
6845	TC-3	Omni/Horizon/Rampage 1978-88	6933	Vista Cruiser	Cutlass 1970-87
5905	Tempest	Tempest/GTO/LeMans 1968-73	6637	Volare	Aspen/Volare 1976-80
7055	Tempo	Ford/Mercury Front Wheel Drive 1981-87	7482	Voyager	Dodge Caravan/Plymouth Voyager 1984-88
7036	Tercel	Toyota Corolla/Carina/Tercel/Starlet 1970-87	6326	V-100	Valiant/Duster 1968-76
			6739	Wagoneer 1962-83	Jeep Wagoneer, Commando, Cherokee, Truck 1957-86
7081	Thing	Volkswagen 1970-81			
6696	Thunderbird	Ford/Mercury/Lincoln Mid-Size 1971-85	7939	Wagoneer 1984-89	Jeep Wagoneer, Comanche, Cherokee 1984-89
7814	Thunderbird	Thunderbird, Cougar, Continental 1980-87	8034	Wrangler	Jeep 1971-90
			7459	W100, 150, 200, 250, 300, 350	Dodge/Plymouth Trucks 1967-88
7055	Topaz	Ford/Mercury Front Wheel Drive 1981-87	7459	WM300	Dodge/Plymouth Trucks 1967-88
6320	Torino	Fairlane/Torino 1962-75	6842	XL	Ford/Mercury/Lincoln 1968-88
6696	Torino	Ford/Mercury/Lincoln Mid-Size 1971-85	6963	XR4Ti	Mustang/Capri/Merkur 1979-88
			6696	XR-7	Ford/Mercury/Lincoln Mid-Size 1971-85
7163	Town & Country	Chrysler Front Wheel Drive 1981-88			
6842	Town Car	Ford/Mercury/Lincoln 1968-88	6982	XT Coupe	Subaru 1970-88
7135	Townsman	Chevrolet 1968-88	7042	X1/9	Fiat 1969-81
5795	Toyota Pickups	Toyota 1966-70	6965	Zephyr	Fairmont/Zephyr 1978-83
7035	Toyota Pickups	Toyota Trucks 1970-88	7059	Z-24	Cavalier, Skyhawk, Cimarron, 2000 1982-88
7004	Toyota Van	Toyota Corona/Crown/Cressida/Mk.II/Van 1970-87	6735	Z-28	Camaro 1967-81
7459	Trail Duster	Dodge/Plymouth Trucks 1967-88	7318	Z-28	Camaro 1982-88
7046	Trans Am	Firebird 1967-81	6845	024	Omni/Horizon/Rampage 1978-88
7345	Trans Am	Firebird 1982-90	6844	3.0S, 3.0Si, 3.0CS	BMW 1970-88
7583	Tredia	Mitsubishi 1983-89	6817	4-63	Jeep 1981-87

Chilton's Repair Manuals are available at your local retailer or by mailing a check or money order for **$15.95** per book plus **$3.50** for 1st book and **$.50** for each additional book to cover postage and handling to:

**Chilton Book Company
Dept. DM
Radnor, PA 19089**

NOTE: When ordering be sure to include your name & address, book part No. & title.

CHILTON'S REPAIR MANUAL MODEL INDEX
Car and truck model names are listed in alphabetical and numerical order

Part No.	Model	Repair Manual Title	Part No.	Model	Repair Manual Title
6817	4×4-63	Jeep 1981-87	6932	300ZX	Datsun Z & ZX 1970-87
6817	4-73	Jeep 1981-87	5982	304	Peugeot 1970-74
6817	4×4-73	Jeep 1981-87	5790	310	Datsun 1961-72
6817	4-75	Jeep 1981-87	7196	310	Datsun/Nissan F-10, 310, Stanza, Pulsar 1977-88
7035	4Runner	Toyota Trucks 1970-88			
6982	4wd Wagon	Subaru 1970-88	5790	311	Datsun 1961-72
6982	4wd Coupe	Subaru 1970-88	6844	318i, 320i	BMW 1970-88
6933	4-4-2 1970-80	Cutlass 1970-87	6981	323	Mazda 1978-89
6817	6-63	Jeep 1981-87	6844	325E, 325ES, 325i, 325iS, 325iX	BMW 1970-88
6809	6.9	Mercedes-Benz 1974-84			
7308	88	Buick/Olds/Pontiac 1975-90	6809	380SEC, 380SEL, 380SL, 380SLC	Mercedes-Benz 1974-84
7308	98	Buick/Olds/Pontiac 1975-90			
7587	98 Regency	GM C-Body 1985	5907	350SL	Mercedes-Benz 1968-73
5902	100LS, 100GL	Audi 1970-73	7163	400	Chrysler Front Wheel Drive 1981-88
6529	122, 122S	Volvo 1956-69	5790	410	Datsun 1961-72
7042	124	Fiat 1969-81	5790	411	Datsun 1961-72
7042	128	Fiat 1969-81	7081	411, 412	Volkswagen 1970-81
7042	131	Fiat 1969-81	6809	450SE, 450SEL, 450 SEL 6.9	Mercedes-Benz 1974-84
6529	142	Volvo 1956-69			
7040	142	Volvo 1970-88	6809	450SL, 450SLC	Mercedes-Benz 1974-84
6529	144	Volvo 1956-69	5907	450SLC	Mercedes-Benz 1968-73
7040	144	Volvo 1970-88	6809	500SEC, 500SEL	Mercedes-Benz 1974-84
6529	145	Volvo 1956-69	5982	504	Peugeot 1970-74
7040	145	Volvo 1970-88	5790	510	Datsun 1961-72
6529	164	Volvo 1956-69	7170	510	Nissan 200SX, 240SX, 510, 610, 710, 810, Maxima 1973-88
7040	164	Volvo 1970-88			
6065	190C	Mercedes-Benz 1959-70	6816	520	Datsun/Nissan Pick-Ups and Pathfinder 1970-89
6809	190D	Mercedes-Benz 1974-84			
6065	190DC	Mercedes-Benz 1959-70	6844	524TD	BMW 1970-88
6809	190E	Mercedes-Benz 1974-84	6844	525i	BMW 1970-88
6065	200, 200D	Mercedes-Benz 1959-70	6844	528e	BMW 1970-88
7170	200SX	Nissan 200SX, 240SX, 510, 610, 710, 810, Maxima 1973-88	6844	528i	BMW 1970-88
			6844	530i	BMW 1970-88
7197	210	Datsun 1200, 210, Nissan Sentra 1971-88	6844	533i	BMW 1970-88
			6844	535i, 535iS	BMW 1970-88
6065	220B, 220D, 220Sb, 220SEb	Mercedes-Benz 1959-70	6980	600	Honda 1973-88
			7163	600	Chrysler Front Wheel Drive 1981-88
5907	220/8 1968-73	Mercedes-Benz 1968-73	7170	610	Nissan 200SX, 240SX, 510, 610, 710, 810, Maxima 1973-88
6809	230 1974-78	Mercedes-Benz 1974-84			
6065	230S, 230SL	Mercedes-Benz 1959-70	6816	620	Datsun/Nissan Pick-Ups and Pathfinder 1970-89
5907	230/8	Mercedes-Benz 1968-73			
6809	240D	Mercedes-Benz 1974-84	6981	626	Mazda 1978-89
7170	240SX	Nissan 200SX, 240SX, 510, 610, 710, 810, Maxima 1973-88	6844	630 CSi	BMW 1970-88
			6844	633 CSi	BMW 1970-88
6932	240Z	Datsun Z & ZX 1970-87	6844	635CSi	BMW 1970-88
7040	242, 244, 245	Volvo 1970-88	7170	710	Nissan 200SX, 240SX, 510, 610, 710, 810, Maxima 1973-88
5907	250C	Mercedes-Benz 1968-73			
6065	250S, 250SE, 250SL	Mercedes-Benz 1959-70	6816	720	Datsun/Nissan Pick-Ups and Pathfinder 1970-89
5907	250/8	Mercedes-Benz 1968-73	6844	733i	BMW 1970-88
6932	260Z	Datsun Z & ZX 1970-87	6844	735i	BMW 1970-88
7040	262, 264, 265	Volvo 1970-88	7040	760, 760GLE	Volvo 1970-88
5907	280	Mercedes-Benz 1968-73	7040	780	Volvo 1970-88
6809	280	Mercedes-Benz 1974-84	6981	808	Mazda 1978-89
5907	280C	Mercedes-Benz 1968-73	7170	810	Nissan 200SX, 240SX, 510, 610, 710, 810, Maxima 1973-88
6809	280C, 280CE, 280E	Mercedes-Benz 1974-84			
6065	280S, 280SE	Mercedes-Benz 1959-70	7042	850	Fiat 1969-81
5907	280SE, 280S/8, 280SE/8	Mercedes-Benz 1968-73	7572	900, 900 Turbo	SAAB 900 1976-85
			7048	924	Porsche 924/928 1976-81
6809	280SEL, 280SEL/8, 280SL	Mercedes-Benz 1974-84	7048	928	Porsche 924/928 1976-81
			6981	929	Mazda 1978-89
6932	280Z, 280ZX	Datsun Z & ZX 1970-87	6836	1000	Chevette/1000 1976-88
6065	300CD, 300D, 300SD, 300SE	Mercedes-Benz 1959-70	6780	1100	MG 1961-81
			5790	1200	Datsun 1961-72
5907	300SEL 3.5, 300SEL 4.5	Mercedes-Benz 1968-73	7197	1200	Datsun 1200, 210, Nissan Sentra 1973-88
5907	300SEL 6.3, 300SEL/8	Mercedes-Benz 1968-73	6982	1400GL, 1400DL, 1400GF	Subaru 1970-88
6809	300TD	Mercedes-Benz 1974-84	5790	1500	Datsun 1961-72

Chilton's Repair Manuals are available at your local retailer or by mailing a check or money order for **$15.95** per book plus **$3.50** for 1st book and **$.50** for each additional book to cover postage and handling to:

**Chilton Book Company
Dept. DM
Radnor, PA 19089**

NOTE: When ordering be sure to include your name & address, book part No. & title.

CHILTON'S REPAIR MANUAL MODEL INDEX
Car and truck model names are listed in alphabetical and numerical order

Part No.	Model	Repair Manual Title	Part No.	Model	Repair Manual Title
6844	1500	DMW 1970-88	6844	2000	BMW 1970-88
6936	1500	Chevy/GMC Pick-Ups & Suburban 1970-87	6844	2002, 2002Ti, 2002Tii	BMW 1970-88
8055	1500	Chevy/GMC Pick-Ups & Suburban 1988-90	6936	2500	Chevy/GMC Pick-Ups & Suburban 1970-87
6844	1600	BMW 1970-88	8055	2500	Chevy/GMC Pick-Ups & Suburban 1988-90
5790	1600	Datsun 1961-72	6844	2500	BMW 1970-88
6982	1600DL, 1600GL, 1600GLF	Subaru 1970-88	6844	2800	BMW 1970-88
6844	1600-2	BMW 1970-88	6936	3500	Chevy/GMC Pick-Ups & Suburban 1970-87
6844	1800	BMW 1970-88	8055	3500	Chevy/GMC Pick-Ups & Suburban 1988-90
6982	1800DL, 1800GL, 1800GLF	Subaru 1970-88			
6529	1800, 1800S	Volvo 1956-69	7028	4000	Audi 4000/5000 1978-81
7040	1800E, 1800ES	Volvo 1970-88	7028	5000	Audi 4000/5000 1978-81
5790	2000	Datsun 1961-72	7309	6000	Celebrity, Century, Ciera, 6000 1982-88
7059	2000	Cavalier, Skyhawk, Cimarron, 2000 1982-88			